THE DOCTRINE OF CREATION

CHURCH DOGMATICS

BY

KARL BARTH

VOLUME III

THE DOCTRINE OF CREATION

PART TWO

EDITORS

REV. PROF. G. W. BROMILEY, PH.D., D.LITT.
REV. PROF. T. F. TORRANCE, D.D., D.THEOL.

EDINBURGH: T. & T. CLARK, 38 GEORGE STREET

THE
DOCTRINE OF CREATION

(Church Dogmatics, Volume III, 2)

BY

KARL BARTH, Dr.Theol., D.D., LL.D.

TRANSLATORS

Rev. HAROLD KNIGHT, M.A., D.Phil.
Rev. Prof. G. W. BROMILEY, Ph.D., D.Litt.
Rev. Prof. J. K. S. REID, M.A., D.D.
Rev. Prof. R. H. FULLER, M.A.

Edinburgh : T. & T. CLARK, 38 George Street

BT
75
B282

Original German Edition
DIE KIRCHLICHE DOGMATIK, III:
Die Lehre von der Schöpfung, 2

Published by
EVANGELISCHER VERLAG A.G.
ZOLLIKON—ZÜRICH

Authorised English Translation © 1960
T. & T. CLARK
EDINBURGH

PRINTED IN GREAT BRITAIN BY
MORRISON AND GIBB LIMITED

FOR

T. & T. CLARK, EDINBURGH
NEW YORK: CHARLES SCRIBNER'S SONS

FIRST PRINTED 1960

EDITORS' PREFACE

Publication of this part-volume in English should finally destroy the charge that Karl Barth has nothing to say about man. Here under the title " The Creature " he has in fact given us the most massive account of the doctrine of man in our times. It is, however, a strictly theological account, starting in the Word of God rather than man himself and controlled by God's revealing and reconciling activity in Jesus Christ rather than by man's independent observations and reflections concerning himself. Acutely aware that the great issues of the day turn on a fundamental decision about man, Barth is the more determined that his exposition be characterised by purity and exactitude in a theological treatment of man as the creature of God, as His dear child and covenant-partner, wholly bounded by His grace and upheld by His faithfulness.

The concern of theological knowledge is not with man generally or in the abstract, but with man in his essential reality and wholeness in relation to God and therefore to fellow-man and the world at large as God's creation. Thus in the doctrine of the creature attention is focused on the one point at the centre of creation where the Creator-creature relationship is revealed in the one creature whose reality and wholeness are directly accessible and comprehensible. On the boundary between heaven and earth, man is in fact the place where God and the creature meet and where the glory of God is thus revealed and is to be praised. Whatever else may be said about creation rests on what is said explicitly about the relationship of God and man.

This means that there can be no ontology of the cosmos, and therefore no Christian cosmology nor biblical or theological *Weltanschauung*. What is given is an ontology of man in relation to God's creative and redemptive work, and only from this standpoint can theology speak of the rest of creation. This does not mean, however, that the natural sciences are to be despised, even in their handling of man. Dealing with man in abstraction from his essential being in relation to God, they cannot do more than present individual features or phenomena of the human. But they can do this, and thus have their proper place when their findings are evaluated by theological knowledge of the essential reality of man as gained from the Word of God.

The presentation of real man is complicated by the fact that man as revealed by God's Word is a sinner and rebel at odds with his own true nature. In other words, real man is impenetrably veiled by distorted and sinful man who cannot be ignored but who also cannot be made the subject of an independent knowledge. The solution is to find real man where the relationship of God and man is perfectly actualised and the full reality of man is thus presented, namely, in Jesus Christ. This means that a theological anthropology is grounded in Christology. It cannot be deduced from it directly. What we read about the man Jesus does not apply *simpliciter* to others whom He is unlike as well as like. Nevertheless, it is from the relation of God to Him that we learn the faithfulness of God the Creator and the unalterable character of human nature as He has created it.

Christologically grounded and guided in this way, the enquiry leads into the four areas of man in relation to God, to his fellows, to his constitution and to time. In each there must be a preparatory consideration of Jesus Himself, namely, as Man for God, Man for other men, Whole Man, and Lord of time. It then emerges that man is God's creature destined to be the covenant-partner of God, and to co-exist with his fellows in an ordered unity of soul and body within the limits of his time yet also in participation in God's gracious decision to share with him His own life and glory. Far from narrowing the field, this exposition has an astonishing breadth in which nothing human is seen to be alien, in which a new turn is given to the discussion between theology and exact science, and in which there is important and illuminating debate with such great thinkers as Fichte, Jaspers, Marx, Nietzsche and Bultmann. The brilliant analysis of Nietzsche and the controversy with Bultmann are particularly valuable features, and the whole section on man in his time is one of the most masterly in the whole *Dogmatics*.

In the translation of this part-volume we are especially indebted to Dr. Knight and Professor Reid for stepping in at a late hour to fill in extensive gaps. Responsibility for § 43 and § 44 (pp. 3–202) has been undertaken by Dr. Harold Knight, for § 45 (pp. 203–324) by Professor G. W. Bromiley, for § 46 (pp. 325–436) by Professor J. K. S. Reid, and for § 47 (pp. 437 to the end) by Professor R. H. Fuller. Invaluable assistance in proof-reading has been given by the Rev. T. H. L. Parker, and the printers have ably and cheerfully handled what was in places a very difficult typescript. Causes beyond our control have unfortunately delayed publication beyond the expected date, but our patient readers may be encouraged to know that III, 3 is already in production and that the whole of III, 4 and most of IV, 3 are already waiting in typescript.

EDINBURGH. *Michaelmas,* 1959.

PREFACE

THIS continuation of the *Church Dogmatics*, and of the " Doctrine of Creation " in particular, has not been able to appear according to plan. The outward cause of delay is that the summer terms of 1946 and 1947—very busy times in other respects—were spent in Bonn, where I could not continue this work. The inward cause is that the theme involved a constant collecting, assessing and shaping of material before I dared publish the results.

The reader will soon realise that at this point the exposition deviates even more widely from dogmatic tradition than in the doctrine of predestination in II, 2. None of the older or more recent fathers known to me was ready to take the way to a theological knowledge of man which I regard as the only possible one. Conversely, I have remained unconvinced that the question of the so-called " soul " ought to dominate this sphere of dogmatics so fully as was the case in the older theologians, or to be handled in its own place as they handled it. In this book, then, few references will be found to their works.

In contrast, I have found it necessary to adduce a very large number of biblical texts to prove my basic points. It may well be argued that in so doing I have strayed out of my true province, especially in the first sub-section of § 47. But I had no real option. In general, there is greater unanimity amongst Protestants to-day than thirty years ago, especially in regard to some of the basic aims of theological work. But the time does not yet seem to have arrived when the dogmatician can accept with a good conscience and confidence the findings of his colleagues in Old and New Testament studies because it is clearly recognised again on both sides that the dogmatician has also an exegetical and the exegete a dogmatic responsibility. So long as so many exegetes have not better learned or practised their part in this common task ; so long as so many still seem to pride themselves on being utterly unconcerned as to the dogmatic presuppositions and consequences of their notions, while unwittingly reading them into the picture, the dogmatician is forced to run the same risk as the non-expert and work out his own proof from Scripture. Yet for all the trouble entailed I personally found particular joy in this part of my task, in which I was only a substitute for others.

Irrespective of details, the attitude to this book will necessarily be determined by whether the reader finally agrees with me that the way of a theological doctrine of man proposed here is not only possible, but the only one possible. In the execution and in detail there are many things which no doubt call for improvement. But it must be remembered even in respect of less satisfactory features that once I had fixed on this new path I had to be a pioneer in many ways. It is a legitimate question, for example, whether in Sections 44–47 I have really covered all the material which ought to be treated in a systematic theological doctrine of man. In a first draft, I had a section on " Man and Humanity," in which I dealt with the individual, societies and society, but I later dropped this because I was not sure enough of the theological approach to this problem and therefore of the right way to treat it. I also think it conceivable that, in spite of the counter-arguments adduced, the limits of the term " creature " may with the necessary boldness and sobriety be more widely drawn than I have dared attempt. At these points, and in relation to other things which may be missed or censured, others may now take up the threads and draw them further. The present volume is again quite thick enough without this. As someone has observed, the Dnieper becomes continually wider the nearer it comes to the Black Sea.

Among those who have reviewed the preceding volumes, and those who have attacked me in various ways without reading them, there are some who have carried things to such a pitch that I contemplated making a very unfriendly reply in this Preface. They ought to be glad that they did not come up against me at an earlier period when I had a greater taste for controversy. I have not yielded even to my less avid taste because in this volume my concern is with the nature of man as God created it good, whereas encounters of this kind (and their objects) belong more to the side of chaos, and would therefore be badly out of place in the Preface to this volume. Those concerned may therefore remain unmolested in respect of their past or present attacks. But I give them warning that in the next volume (amongst other and better things) I shall have a few things to say about demons, so that I may well have occasion to return to them.

I have one great request which is meant in all friendliness and will, I hope, be received in the same spirit. At least those who have had an inner part in the work involved in all these volumes will understand and forgive if I am seldom able to accept the many invitations which I receive to give lectures, to fulfil special tasks, to participate in conferences etc. In many cases I would gladly do so, and sometimes very gladly. But in the last decade I have been in some danger of dispersing my energies in various directions, and if I am to push forward and finish the *Church Dogmatics* I must now concentrate my resources, which do not increase, on this primary task. And I beg the same understanding and forgiveness for the fact that I cannot possibly do justice to invitations in the literary sphere, whether in contributions to papers, the assessments of manuscripts and publications kindly sent to me, and above all, the answering of letters. We must all do what we can. I know what it means to be continually indebted to others. And I should be happy if in this respect I could be granted a kind of general indulgence for past and future omissions in view of the fact that in my own work I have finally addressed myself on a wide front, and *Deo bene volente* shall continue to do so, to my brothers and friends and contemporaries. I have not sworn to devote myself relentlessly to this work, for I know that there is no path from which a man must not allow himself to be summoned if a higher necessity presents itself. This is no less true of the *Church Dogmatics*. My only request is for patience that for the moment I think it right to keep for the most part as firmly as possible to this task unless and until I receive a most urgent summons to the contrary.

My thanks are due to Herr Friedrich Herzog for his services in the compilation of the Indexes and the correction of proofs.

BASEL, *May* 10, 1948.

CONTENTS

CHAPTER X
THE CREATURE

CHAPTER X

THE CREATURE

§ 43

MAN AS A PROBLEM OF DOGMATICS

Because man, living under heaven and on earth, is the creature whose relation to God is revealed to us in the Word of God, he is the central object of the theological doctrine of creation. As the man Jesus is Himself the revealing Word of God, He is the source of our knowledge of the nature of man as created by God.

1. MAN IN THE COSMOS

Even linguistically, the one term " creation " (κτίσις, *creatura*) includes not only the action of the Creator but also its product, the creature; just as the term " work " embraces both the action of the doer and its result. Creator and creation belong together as an integral whole. In the first part of our exposition of the doctrine of creation, it was possible to understand the Creator only in His activity towards His creature. And so when we turn to consider the creature itself as its product, we still have in view the work of the Creator. In the further development of the doctrine of creation we shall be concerned with this special aspect of the matter. For the Creator Himself has turned to His creature not only in general but most particularly. He is concerned about the whole meaning and purpose of His work. In this, which would not be without Him, His will and therefore His own inmost being is manifested. In its existence He responds to and reveals Himself. In creating it, He bound it to Himself. If it pleased the Creator to associate and co-ordinate the creature with Himself, it also pleased Him to associate and co-ordinate Himself with the creature. Creation is the divine distinction of the creature. The doctrine of the creature is the doctrine of that which God distinguished by the very fact that He created it.

But in practice the doctrine of creation means anthropology— the doctrine of man. Hence our first task is to establish this more precise determination.

The God of Holy Scripture and of the Church's confession is, of course, the Creator of heaven and earth. Man is certainly not His only creation. Man is only *a* creature and not *the* creature. The creature of God is the totality, the whole cosmos of the reality posited by Him and distinct from Him, in the plenitude of which man is only a

3

component part, very inconsiderable in some important ways and deeply dependent on creaturely elements and factors which are greatly superior to him. Even the Word of God does not envisage man except in this insignificance. Besides man there are other creatures posited by God and distinct from God, with their own dignity and right, and enveloped in the secret of their own relation to their Creator. Man is a creature in the midst of others which were directly created by God and exist independently of man. The Word of God itself sees man in this context and within these appointed limits. The two creation sagas in the opening chapters of Genesis have made this quite clear. Man is the creature of God as he is placed by God in the world which God has created.

This being the case, it is a serious question whether the theological doctrine of the creature should not be expounded as a doctrine of the totality, of the whole created cosmos. If we confine our considerations to man, our attitude to the wider creation must certainly not be one of blindness, indifference or disparagement. We are concerned with man as set in the cosmos and therefore not with man as alone before God or alone addressed by Him ; not with a cosmos concentrated in man, and perhaps having no independent reality, but being only the phenomenal world, as radical Idealism maintains, of the mind of man. We have to do with the man who in the cosmos is confronted by another reality, and who is the more conscious and sure of its true and genuine reality the more he is conscious and sure of his own humanity and therefore his own reality by the encounter of man with man and of God and man. We do not see man poised in the void, but living under heaven on the earth whose reality is distinct from his own and yet in its otherness of equal dignity with his own. We see him as belonging to heaven and earth, and equally bound and committed to both. We see him in the proximity of angels and animals. If we forget that he must remain loyal to the earth, we shall never truly understand him ; and even less so if we forget that heaven is above him. It has often been missed and has always had to be rediscovered that the Word of God in its ultimate and decisive form in the New Testament has a " cosmic " character to the extent that its message of salvation relates to the man who is rooted in the cosmos, who is lost and ruined with the cosmos, and who is found and renewed by his Creator at the heart of the cosmos. In the present exposition we must not and will not be guilty of any failure to appreciate the significance of the cosmos, of any insulating of man from the realm of the non-human creation. But this does not mean that the task of dogmatics at this point is to outline a cosmology, a so-called world-view. It is noteworthy that even in the past this has only been attempted in certain directions.

The most important of these attempts is found in the fact that right up to the 18th century, and in part even into the 19th, it was customary to preface anthropology by a doctrine of angels, i.e., to introduce the doctrine of the earthly creation, which was considered to reach its climax in man, by a doctrine of the heavenly, whose concrete manifestation was thought to be recognised in angels. But even in this traditional scheme we notice the selectiveness and limitation. If the intention had been to expound a cosmology (and anthropology only within the framework of the latter), why was not the step taken from angelology to far wider considerations about the existence and nature of heaven ? And why was there not encouragement from the curious account of the sixth day of creation (Gen. 1²⁴⁻³¹), or a passage like Mk. 1¹³, to set alongside the doctrine of man at least a doctrine of the animal creation ? Even in the Middle Ages, and especially from the time of the Renaissance, there was sufficiently reliable information (quite apart from the Bible) about heaven and earth, their structure and their inhabitants, to form a basis on which theologians might well have tried to give a higher and deeper account of the created orders surrounding man. But they seem to have been under a material restraint. For the most part they were content merely to touch on those higher and lower spheres in connexion with the Genesis account of the sixth day of creation. They did so with more or less regard to the contemporary state of philosophy and science. But when the doctrine of the creature was in question, they did not in any sense attempt to sketch a world-view, i.e., an even approximately complete exposition of creaturely being as a whole. They were satisfied to speak about angels and then simply to pass on to man. I know of only one exception, viz. the systematic account attempted by Polanus in the fifth volume of his *Syntagma Theol. chr.*, 1609. Here we do in fact find an attempted exposition of the cosmos : beginning with the upper and the lower heavens ; descending to the good and bad angels ; thence to *natura visibilis*, to space and time, fire and light, day and night, the air and meteorological phenomena, the earth and its minerals, plant life and earthquakes ; then upwards again to the sun, moon and stars ; back again to the aquatic sphere, birds and animals ; and then finally and centrally to man, to the anatomy and physiology of his body, to the nature of his soul, to his heavenly and earthly destinies, his divine likeness and his paradisal perfection. Nothing, or very little, seems to have been forgotten, and the skill with which contemporary biblical knowledge, philosophy and science are bound into a whole is remarkable. But why is there no trace of a similar attempt in Polanus' Lutheran contemporary Johann Gerhard, for example ? Why did he have no successor among the dogmatic theologians of the 17th century, some of whom were at least as well informed and enthusiastic as he was ? And why not in the 18th century, which was so interested in the richness of created life ? Indeed, it is not until we reach the Dutch Neo-Calvinists of the 19th century that there seem to be any renewed interest in this line of enquiry. Here we find in Abraham Kuyper's *Dictaten Dogmatiek* (edit. 1910) the sketch : *De Angelis, De creaturis materialibus, De homine*, and in H. Bavinck's *Gereformeerde Dogmatiek* (3rd edit. Vol. II, 1910), as a preface to anthropology, a section on the spiritual world and a second on the material. A similar attempt was clearly made by H. R. Frank of Erlangen, who in his *System der chr. Wahrheit* (2nd edit. 1885, Vol. I, p. 342ff.) prefaced his doctrine of man by a section on " the sub-human material world and the super-human spiritual," though he did not fail to add the explanatory qualification : " in so far as these concern man and the man of God." Otherwise even in the dogmatics of the 19th century we look in vain for anything which might be remotely described as an attempt at a cosmological world-view. Even the work of Arthur Titius, *Natur und Gott* (1926), cannot be claimed as a really comprehensive theological doctrine of creation. This work does, of course, treat of the world as a whole, but to, be precise, it has in view only a harmonisation of theology and science in respect of the world-view of the latter, and there is no attempt at an independent and positive theological view on the basis of this agreement. The same is true of Horst Stephan's *Glaubenslehre* (2nd edit., 1928),

in the third part of which (" The world outlook of the Christian faith ") we are
led to expect a cosmology, but are given what can only be regarded as a formal
account of the Christian attitude to the world as it is understood according to
a very different view. What both the older and the younger theologians were
really interested in, either exclusively or primarily and centrally (and this
applies to Polanus and his few followers), was a view of man rather than of the
world as a whole. The title " Dogmatic Cosmology " is used by Alexander von
Oettingen in his *Lutherische Dogmatik* (Vol. II, 1900, p. 290ff.), but what he means
by this is not a view of the world and the cosmos, but the doctrine of the act
of the divine creation, preservation and governance of the world. Like the older
theologians, he deals ontologically only with man and the world of spirits related
to man (i.e., angels), and in this connexion he coined the phrase " a certain
limitedness " (meaning the necessary anthropological limitation) to describe
the Christian doctrine of the creature. In this respect we may confidently refer
to the overwhelming consensus of dogmatic tradition.

The inner justification of this tradition, and the inner necessity
of following it, are to be found in the fact that by the nature of its
object dogmatics has neither the occasion nor the duty to become a
technical cosmology or a Christian world-view. Were it to do so, it
would be losing its way in a sphere essentially foreign to it. Its true
object is the revealed, written and declared Word of God. Those
who have claimed to have a world-view—it is not for us to say with
what justice—have always derived it from other sources than the
Word of God. Here at the " outset we part company with the exponents
of all world-views. This is imposed upon us negatively by the fact
that the Word of God does not contain any account of the cosmos ;
any ontology of the created totality. The Word of God is concerned
with God and man. It certainly gives us an ontology of man, and we
shall be concerned with this in the doctrine of the creature, i.e., with
the ontology of man living under heaven and on earth. But the Word
of God does not contain any ontology of heaven and earth themselves.
      It is no doubt true that human faith has always expressed itself
in a particular conception, and human witness in a particular presentation, of the Word of God, and in so doing they have attached
themselves to certain cosmologies, assimilating them, understanding
and interpreting them in their own sense, appealing to them to some
extent and allying themselves with them.

Even in the biblical witness to God's revelation, human faith has very simply
and powerfully used the language of more than one oriental world-myth and the
corresponding sciences, and then that of Judaistic speculation and the popular
cosmology of Hellenism. In the centuries which followed, and especially in the
case of some of its most distinguished champions, the Church shared in the great
renewal of Platonism, then very widely in that of Aristotelianism, and later
still, at a time which was particularly decisive for its own formulation, in that
of the ancient Stoics. It followed and expanded almost the entire succession
of ensuing philosophies and their world-views (or rather, the entire cycle of modern
world-views and their accompanying philosophies) by establishing theological
systems corresponding to them. It first took its stand on the original Ptolemaic
system ; then on this system as improved in the Middle Ages ; and then, after
initial hesitation, on the Copernican system perfected by Kant and Laplace, which

it has attempted to follow its most recent physical, chemical and biological interpretations or transformations. In this respect the tireless and fearless way—unfortunately rather too fearless in 1933—in which Karl Heim has pursued the mutations in philosophical method and results during the last fifty years may be taken as an illustration of how faith thinks that it can master every cosmology polemico-irenically, profiting from each in turn and applying the " All things are yours " to the constant changes of philosophical outlook.

The fact that this has continually happened does not mean, however, that the Word of God itself, which is the object of Christian faith and therefore of Church dogmatics, contains a specific cosmology which it is our duty to expound. We justify this assertion by the following considerations.

1. It cannot fail to strike us that the faith which grasps the Word of God and expresses it in its witness, although it has constantly allied itself with cosmologies, has never yet engendered its own distinctive world-view, but in this respect has always made more or less critical use of alien views.

In the Old Testament itself there is no original picture of the world springing solely from the revelation of the God of Israel, but what emerges as such—and it is not even self-consistent—is a special adaptation of the cosmologies current in the Near East of the time. The same is even more true of the New Testament in its relation to the mythical and scientific views of the period. The biblical writers shared by and large the particular views of their environment, and made no attempt as the witnesses to God's self-revelation to oppose to them a specific, i.e., a kind of revealed, understanding. The same thing happened in the ancient, mediæval and modern periods of theological history. The Church and its leaders constantly found themselves in the presence of ways of regarding the world. They shared in the decay of old and the rise of new conceptions of this kind. They took part in these changes either eagerly or reluctantly, but usually without any great interest or concern. In this matter they were usually in touch with their age. But in this matter they were never and nowhere creative. They merely came to an understanding with changing cosmologies, which generally meant that with certain reservations they came to terms with the temporarily predominant view, trying to express the Christian message in the current mode of speech or to adapt it to the current philosophy. But they never betrayed any feeling that they should at all costs hold fast to a particular ontology of the universe as if it were uniquely true and biblical and orthodox, or at all costs reject another as false, unbelieving or impious. Even in the particularly critical period when the 17th century gave way to the 18th the conflict between an ecclesiastical and a scientific view was by no means as sharp and fierce as it has been represented in E. Fueter's *Geschichte der exakten Wissenschaften in der schweizerischen Aufklärung* (1941). Obscurantist tendencies on the part of ecclesiastics and theologians have never proved to be necessary or permanent. The Church has to answer for a few martyrs to learning and science, but not for very many. Martyrdom was by no means the rule even in the critical period just mentioned—and this not merely in consequence of the pusillanimity of the scholars concerned, but also of a lack of persecuting zeal on the part of the Church. Even the Roman Church took care not to perpetuate its long resistance to Copernicus and Descartes by the proclamation of a dogma in support of Ptolemy and Aristotle. How could this be explained if from the standpoint of Christian faith it were necessary to reckon seriously with a kind of revealed cosmology ?

2. The reason why there is no revealed or biblical world-view characteristic of and necessary to the Christian *kerygma* is that faith in the Word of God can never find its theme in the totality of the created world. It believes in God in His relation to the man who lives under heaven and on earth ; but it does not believe in this or that constitution of heaven and earth. If in handling its own proper theme it could not help formulating certain theories about heaven and earth, it always formulated them provisionally. And if in its formulations it used material derived from certain modes of conceiving the world, it could never identify itself with these views in any true or essential sense. It could not make them the true content of its own witness and confession.

We may refer those who assert the contrary to Genesis 1–2. For if these sagas use as a matter of course the language and pictures of the cosmological myths proper to their time and environment, it does not follow that their intention is to expound these myths and cosmologies. Their theme is that Yahweh-Elohim, the God and covenant-Lord of Israel, is also the Creator of heaven and earth and man, and the way in which He is this. The same applies to the New Testament in relation to the cosmology of its time. The biblical texts approach the question of creation with an eclectic and limited interest corresponding to the Word of God which is the real theme of their testimony. They have in view the action of God which takes place in the created world, and thus their concern is with the man who exists in the cosmos and in whose history the divine action is revealed. Preoccupied with this action, and essentially with it alone, they make certain cosmological presuppositions and draw certain cosmological consequences, and in both cases use the leading cosmological concepts of their time. But never and nowhere do these concepts form the true content of their message. And wherever in later times faith remained the faith of the biblical witnesses, its attitude to contemporary world-views was formally just as unconcerned and materially just as aloof. Properly and essentially its concern was and is always with other matters than cosmology ; with the Creator and therefore the created world ; yet not with the total created world as such ; but, corresponding to the visible selection and limitation involved in the revealed divine action, with the particular object of this divine action in the created world ; with man in the cosmos.

3. From the fact that faith, committed to its own special theme, can give only incidental attention to creation as a whole, it follows that its relation to the cosmological presuppositions and consequences of its witness and confession could and can only be supremely non-committal. It never accepts the material of changing world-views for its own sake. Sometimes it uses it at one point only to discard it at another. It can pass from one world-view to another without being untrue to itself, i.e., to its object. It is always free in relation to all such conceptions.

In this respect we might go so far as to say that faith is radically disloyal to them. In the last resort it has never taken them seriously, even though it has fiercely opposed them or intimately allied itself to them. It lives only for a time in the context of these ideas, and it thinks and speaks only transiently in their language. It easily tires of them. It touches them only lightly and if

need be can leave them as easily. It accepts no responsibility for their foundation, structure, validity or propagation. It moves within their territory but
cannot be detained at their frontiers. It treats them eclectically but refuses to
be responsible for the outer or inner maintenance of their content. Thus it is
of no consequence to the redactors of Genesis that they bring together the very
different world-views of the two sources of Genesis 1 and 2. There is no world
outlook which can be described as biblical, or even as Old Testament or New
Testament, or as prophetic or Pauline. There can be a welter of cosmological
elements in the Bible deriving from the most diverse sources, and none of them
is given in its totality, none is expounded as a doctrine, and none is made
obligatory for faith. Of course these elements are necessary and the cosmological
form and the theological content of the biblical witness cannot at any point be
dissociated from the exegetical standpoint. But it has also to be realised that
what we have in this form is only fragments from world-views and not the views
themselves, and that even these fragments cannot be understood from the
standpoint of the cosmologies to which they properly belong, but only from the
standpoint of the new context in which they are set in the biblical texts. In
its free and selective articulation of specific world-views the Bible is not trying
to say what the human originators and exponents of the latter intended to say,
but what in responsibility to the Word of God which is ultimately exclusive it
and it alone can say. And this rule is not merely valid for the understanding of
the Old and New Testaments, but it must also be applied if we are to appreciate
at least the intentions of those who later formulated the faith of the Church.
It is open to question whether this faith, for all that it is so weak and exposed
and vulnerable, has ever succeeded in producing a completely false expression
of itself by succumbing wholly and utterly to this or that world outlook. On
any sober reckoning this did not happen even in 2nd century Gnosticism,
even in the almost hopeless entanglement of Roman Catholicism with Aristotelianism from the Middle Ages onwards, even in the rationalistic writings of the 18th
century, even in Schleiermacher and his followers up to the heresy of the German
Christians. However serious the proposal to substitute for the affirmations of
the Christian Gospel those of the regnant world-views, it always happened in
fact that the latter were adjusted and transformed, the attempt being made
to make them more splendid by additions, more tolerable by subtractions, and
more meaningful by involutions. If thinkers gave themselves to their service
more than was seemly, they too were actually set in the service of a creed alien
to their own genius. If these transient views made a deeper impression on the
exponents of the faith than was compatible with its own inner assurance and the
power of its mission to the world, yet for all their zeal the theologians concerned
were obviously unable to please the philosophers or other priests and adherents
of the dominant philosophy. The way of faith itself never completely disintegrated in spite of all the deviations and confusions of rival creeds. Above
and beyond all the temporary accommodations of its own with alien cosmological
conceptions, it always succeeded in its differentiating itself from the latter.
These accommodations never showed themselves to be basic, necessary or permanent. The confession of faith always showed that it had its own meaning
and function in face of cosmology, and its own continuity in face of cosmological
developments.

4. Even where (in certain types of thought among certain Christians
and movements) we think we detect an absolute union of faith with
this or that world-view, we are not really dealing with faith at all,
but with a partial deviation from faith such as is always possible in
the life of the Church and of individuals. Hence it is not legitimate
to infer from this process that this kind of absolute assimilation of

faith to alien world-views is characteristic of or necessary to Christian faith itself.

It constantly happens that individuals and whole groups, aiming to influence the life of the Church at large and often enough succeeding, entangle themselves in contradiction with their faith because in one respect they have the freedom of faith and in others not, partly exercising it and partly failing to do so. In ancient Israel this self-contradiction lay at the root of the constant threat and frequent actuality of defection to the gods of the Canaanites, Babylonians and Egyptians ; and it is to the same factor that all heresies in the Church owe their origin. But faith itself cannot be made responsible for this self-contradiction on the part of believers. In so far as its confession is pure, it will always be able to make an eclectic and non-committal use of current world-views. If it allows itself to be bound by them, its confession has ceased to be a true confession. It is then limited, conditioned, determined and challenged by the autonomy of the alien body to which it has wantonly fettered itself. Our reference is to a peril to the confession of the faith which has been real at all times. That at least a partial obligation towards dominant world-views is axiomatic, was no less an opinion of the ancient than of the modern Church. But a faith embroiled in this self-contradiction and a partial commitment to a specific world-view cannot be the norm which we must accept in this matter.

5. In so far as faith itself is true to itself, i.e., to its object, and in so far as its confession is pure, its association with this or that world-view will always bear the marks of the contradiction between the underlying confession and the principles of the system with which it is conjoined. If there can be no confession of the faith without a cosmological presupposition or consequence (however tacit its acknowledgment), faith can always guard itself against the autonomy of its alien associate. Thus even in these conjunctions of faith with alien world-views its opposition to the latter will always find expression.

This is perfectly clear in Holy Scripture. Although the creation saga of Genesis seems to make an unconcerned use of the Babylonian creation myth, it actually criticises the latter at every stage. And what became of the Judaistic and Hellenistic systems of ideas when apostolic preaching adapted itself to them apparently so completely ? Plato and Plotinus would have been rather surprised and not very pleased by the way in which their philosophy was deepened and illuminated in the thought of Augustine, and no doubt Aristotle would have felt the same about what Thomas made of him. And from the philosophical standpoint the rise of theological Cartesians, Spinozists, Leibnizians, Kantians and Hegelians was a very dubious matter. Only rarely did the originators of the great philosophical systems have the will or the courage to make plain the possible compatibility of their thought with Christian faith. And when this was attempted, as in the case of Kant and the older Schelling, it was inevitably to the detriment not only of faith but also of the system of ideas. It cannot be overlooked that the shrewd and ardent attempt of Schleiermacher to adapt at a given point the Christology of the Bible and the Church to his own system of the harmony of opposites, of the finite and the infinite, of spirit and nature, can hardly be said to have been successful from the standpoint of this particular philosophical presupposition. Christian faith is an element which, when it is mingled with philosophies, makes itself felt even in the most diluted forms, and that in a way which is disturbing, destructive and threatening to the very foundations of these philosophies. To the extent that it is faith in God's Word, and is even partially true to itself, it cannot become faith in current world-views, but can only resist them.

We have seen that the ultimate reason for this peculiar state of affairs lies in the fact that the Word of God speaks of God Himself and also of man, but does not contain either directly or indirectly any disclosure about an independent being and nature of the cosmos.

Cosmology can arise only in the sterile corner where the Word of God with its special revelation has not yet found, or has lost again, hearing and obedience on the part of man. Only then can the cosmos be a third force between God and man and thus become the object of independent attention and consideration. When knowledge of the created world is divorced from that of the covenant, God the Creator becomes a vague factor which is meaningless in practice and therefore dispensable, and the creature can then emerge as a self-contained totality in which man is simply one among many other component parts. The created world dissociated from its transcendent Creator loses its natural axis. And when this is the case, a need is inevitably felt to explain it artificially in terms of itself, to enquire arbitrarily into its inner principle, constitution and meaning, and no less arbitrarily, i.e., according to the choice of this principle, to refashion it, i.e., to reconstruct it, to impose upon it a corresponding structure. It is in this way that cosmology comes into being. And it does so in the unspiritual sphere where for want of a better word we try to entice from the cosmos its own word and secret, or rather—as if it could and must speak of itself, as if it lay in human power to compel it to do so—to place this word on its lips. When faith makes alliance with philosophies, it moves into this unspiritual sphere. But its confession has no true basis in this sphere. Hence faith cannot have any other relation with philosophies but an external, provisional, non-committal and paradoxical one.

The knowledge communicated by the Word of God is the knowledge of creation in its indissoluble connexion with the covenant and therefore the knowledge of heaven and earth as the cosmos of man in covenant with God. As it is directed to man, and makes man known to himself, the Word of God can only glance at the world surrounding man. But without this glance it could not fulfil its function to the man who is set in this world. It could not make him known to himself. The Word of God has a cosmological border. It illuminates the world. It makes it known—heaven and earth—as the sphere in which God's glory dwells and in which He concerns Himself with man. It understands and explains it as one great parable of this happening. It points to heaven as the sum of the created reality which is invisible, unknown and inaccessible to man, as the upper cosmos which as such reminds us of the divine horizon of human life. And it points to earth as the sum of the created reality which is visible and known

to man and under his control, as the lower cosmos which as such is
the sphere of man. This twofold reference is unmistakeable. Nor is
it a little thing, but a very great, a decisive thing, which is thus stated
about the world. In this its dual structure the world is not unlike
but like what takes place in the covenant between God and man
which is the end and meaning of creation. Heaven corresponds to
the being and action of God. Earth corresponds to the being and
action of man. The conjunction of heaven and earth corresponds to
the covenant in which the divine and human being and action meet.
Hence the created world surrounding man, the totality of created
existence above and below him, is the prototype and pattern of that
for which he is addressed by the Word of God, of his life in communion with his Creator. That the cosmos finds itself in this harmony
with the history enacted in it is what the Word of God declares also
about the cosmos as it addresses man in his existence under heaven
and on earth. This—and nothing more than this. The doctrine of
creation must confine itself within these limits. In so doing, it is not
guilty of any caprice. It keeps to its subject which is also the source
of its knowledge. Its understanding of God's creation is " anthro-
pocentric " to the extent that it follows the orientation prescribed for
it by the Word of God ; the orientation on man. To the extent that
it does this, it will merely glimpse at cosmology, and will always find
itself in the relation of tension we have described towards all so-called
cosmological science.

At this point we find ourselves in basic opposition to philosophy, but we are
all the closer methodologically to the inductive sciences based on observation
and inference. The latter are differentiated from theological science by the fact
that their object and the source of their knowledge are neither identical with
each other nor with the Word of God. The source of their knowledge lies in the
process of observation and inference and therefore not in faith in the Word of
God. And the object with which they are concerned is the abundance of external
phenomena susceptible to the inductive method, and therefore not the creature
of God as such, knowable in the Word of God as the being of the reality distinct
from God.

All the same, genuine science has the following points in common with
genuine theological scholarship. (1) It does not carry with it any world-view.
It is content to observe, classify, investigate, understand and describe phenomena.
It does not unfold any ontology of the cosmos. To the extent that it does so it
becomes an interpretation, and ceases to be exact science. Such a process is
no part of its essential function. There is no scientific world-view. On the
contrary, it must essentially renounce all such interpretation. A misunderstanding is always involved when its exponents think that they can present the sum
of the hypotheses which temporarily mark the bounds of their knowledge as a
world-view, as " *the* view of exact science " ; and when theologians in anxious
dismay think they must regard this view as an interpretation of reality always
entitled to respect. Its exponents could and can also be dispassionate, holding
aloof from all mythologising and philosophising. Exact science dedicated to its
object and its method, working positively and not dreaming and romancing,
is in fact pure knowledge : pure in its differentiation from theology ; but pure
also in its differentiation from all pseudo-theology ; pure in the fact that it

confines itself to the study of phenomena but does not lose itself in the construction of world systems.

(2) Exact science also agrees with the theology of creation in the fact that it too investigates and describes the cosmos only as the cosmos of man, that for it too the cosmos exists only anthropocentrically : not of course from the standpoint of Christian faith in God's Word and therefore not theanthropocentrically ; but from the standpoint of human observation and inference, of which it clearly recognises the limits.

(3) It also agrees materially with theology in the fact that it recognises two fundamentally distinct spheres. It does not call them heaven and earth, but no less than theology it respects the distinction between heaven and earth. It reckons with the sphere which is within the range of human observation and thought, to which it turns and which it investigates and describes ; and it also reckons with the sphere which is inaccessible to man, which as exact science it cannot deny, which it must at least accept to the extent that it forms the border of the first sphere, but before which it will halt, not attempting to trespass, but able only, as exact science, to maintain a respectful silence. It, too, constantly reckons with the co-existence of these two realms.

Exact science can furnish no means of approach to an ontology of the cosmos. Our own task is different from that of the scientist. But it is not the latter that we have to oppose. On the contrary, in its initial stages we have to recognise a significant parallel to our own.

Although dogmatics has no business to broaden out into cosmology, it has the duty to expound a specific doctrine of man. If it did not do so, it would fail in its task of interpreting the Word of God no less than if at the proper point it did not become an explicit doctrine of God. For man is the creature to whom, according to His own Word, God has turned in the work of creation with its centre in the covenant of grace. And it is very man that God Himself has become in the perfect and definitive revelation of this Word of His. Who and what man is, is no less specifically and emphatically declared by the Word of God than who and what God is. The Word of God essentially encloses a specific view of man, an anthropology, an ontology of this particular creature. This being the case, we must accept this view in faith, reflect it in the confession of faith, and develop it as a perception of faith. For this reason the doctrine of man has always been the central element in the dogmatics of the creature. It is not alien to this sphere. It has here its necessary right of domicile. And according to what we said earlier, we may justly state that it alone has this right.

Any one acquainted with the older dogmatics will naturally ask why not also at least a doctrine of angels, and to this we may give a provisional answer. We shall treat of the being and mode of angels when, in exposition of the Word of God, we are led to speak of them by Scripture in the further development of the doctrine of creation, i.e., in the doctrine of the relationship of Creator and creature and of the divine providence and overruling. If we do not speak of them here, we do not mean to imply that they do not belong to the creaturely sphere. But theologians were not true to Scripture when they separated their consideration of the angels from their doctrine of the divine activity in relation to the world and especially to man, ascribing to them independent action, and trying to make them the object of a special ontology alongside that of man, as happened to a great extent first in Dionysius the Areopagite and then supremely in Thomas Aquinas. Angels are among the countless creatures whose existenec and nature we must assume according to the data of Scripture, but whom the Word of God does not require us to consirler independently. Dogmatics will necessarily take into account the fact that angels play such an important part in the events attested by the Bible. But they cannot ignore a fact which caused the older dogmaticians so much anxious pondering, viz. that there is no reference in any part of the Bible, including the most important passages in Genesis 1 and 2, to the creation of angels. Man and not the angels is the partner in the covenant of grace which is the whole basis and aim of creation. The Word of God is not addressed to angels but to man. And in the central event to which the Bible bears witness God did not become an angel but man (Heb. 1⁴ᶠᶠ·). And although angels undoubtedly belong to the created order, they do not belong to the establishment and equipment of the lower cosmos ordained for man, as described in Genesis 1 and 2, but to the sphere of the heavenly world, of the upper cosmos, which is equally God-created and equally real, but concealed from man and not revealed in its existence and nature. They are beings whose function we must fully recognise but concerning whose nature, since they belong to heaven and not to earth, we can have no knowledge even from the Word of God or faith. This is what the older dogmaticians overlooked. We can and must know the nature of man as we listen to the Word of God in faith. But since this cannot be said of angels, there is no doctrine of angels alongside the doctrine of man.

The man with whom we are concerned in dogmatics is man in the cosmos. He is man under heaven, i.e., as delimited by a realm of being which like himself was created by God and is therefore real, but which is basically hidden from and inaccessible to man, which absolutely transcends him and is therefore a realm of being higher than man, corresponding though not equal to the transcendence of God. And he is man on earth, i.e., in a realm of being which like himself was created by God and is therefore real and distinct, which is basically open and knowable and under his control, in which the animal and spiritual mingle, which is a lower sphere, corresponding but not equal to the lowliness of man before God and God's condescension to him. Whatever else man is, he is rooted in this twofold determination. And the converse is also true that, whatever else the cosmos is, it is so as heaven and earth, as the beyond and the present, as that which limits and that which is limited for man. The question of the possibility of a cosmos without man is as pointless as the question of the possibility that it might not be, or might not have been created by God. As created by God, it is the heaven and earth of man ; it is his beyond and present ; it constitutes the twofold determination of this creature. The universe was created for the sake of God's gracious plan. Hence its goal and centre is man ; its reality stands or falls with the fact that there is human reality within it. Yet it is also true that man for his part is possible and actual only as man in the cosmos : under heaven and on earth ; within the lower, this-worldly sphere appropriate to him, and confronted by the higher, transcendent sphere which forms its limit. What we say is that he is under heaven and on earth ; that he is in the cosmos. We do not say more. If we are to hear the Word of God, and to expound the insights it discloses, we cannot share the view that the being of man is constituted by the cosmos, being compounded of a heavenly and earthly part (soul and body), and therefore forming a small cosmos within the greater.

Along the lines of this Aristotelian doctrine of the μικρόκοσμος many fine and at a first glance illuminating things have been said in the Christian Church. *Cum corpus e terra et spiritum possideamus e caelo, ipsi terra et caelum sumus et in utroque, id est in corpore et spiritu, ut Dei voluntas fiat, oramus* (Cyprian, *De dom. orat.* 16). By the divine wisdom man is compounded of a mingling of the sentient (νοητόν) and the spiritual (αἰσθητόν), of the earthly and the heavenly, so that from this one work of grace the same glory should shine forth upon the whole of creation (Gregory of Nyssa, *Or. cat.* 6). God has given man substance in common with minerals, life in common with plants, sensual impulse in common with animals and intellect in common with angels (Augustine, *De civ. Dei,* V, II). Poised between greatness and littleness, the spirit and the flesh, there is, so to speak, a second world, a smaller within the greater cosmos, a worshipper of mingled substance, an eye-witness of the visible creation who can also know the invisible and the spiritual, a lord of the earthly who is himself controlled from above, and is himself both earthly and heavenly (Gregory of Nazianzus, *Or.* 38, II). There is a map on which the *summa totius mundi* can be seen (Bucanus, *Instit. theol.*, 1605, VIII, I) ; an epitome of all other creatures (J. Gerhard, *Loci theol.*, 1609, VIII, 9), *inferioris naturae consummatio et finis et superioris congener,* and therefore *totius compendium et vinculum, quo coelestia terrenis conjunguntur* (*Syn. pur. Theol.*, Leiden, 1624, *Disp.* 13. 2). On the same lines J. A. Dorner (*Syst. d. chr. Glaubenslehre,* Vol. I, 1886, p. 507) thought it possible to maintain, on the basis of Schelling's philosophy of nature, that the corporal organism of man is a kind of focus for the perfections of all other natural organisms, and that the human mind is the consciousness of nature in which the latter comprehends itself.

The mistake of these speculations lies primarily in the fact that they obviously attempt to ascribe to anthropology as such the function and the dignity of cosmology. This attempt is too ambitious to be successful. The cosmos is not without man, as we have just said. It exists as it constitutes the twofold determination of man. But this does not mean that we can go on to assert that man is the cosmos *in nuce,* that the essence of the cosmos is contained within the life of man, as though the cosmos could not exist over and above its special relation to man, in quite other dimensions and in quite another sense. But we do not know these other dimensions or this other sense in the cosmos. We know the cosmos only through its relation to man. Yet this does not justify us in supposing that its life is necessarily exhausted in this relation. Anthropology has to do with man in the cosmos. Hence it has no right to aspire to become cosmology. These speculations are also of doubtful value because, beyond the undeniable integration of man with earth, by an appeal to the spiritual nature of his soul they go on to assert his integration with heaven. But in

biblical language heaven is the horizon which limits man no less than
the rest of earthly creation.   It is the sphere from which God speaks
and acts towards man.   Hence it is not a sphere to which man belongs
by nature, not even in virtue of his soul.   For in the language of the
Bible the soul is simply the earthly life of man, and not at all a divine
or heavenly component of his being.   All that we are justified in saying
with regard to the nature of man as the soul of his body is that in the
unity and distinction of these two elements (which are both earthly)
we can see an analogue to the being of the cosmos.   But with equal
justice the same can be said of animals.   Finally, these speculations
are unacceptable because they understand the constitution of man
from the cosmos (and indeed from a definite and questionable interpretation of the cosmos) instead of from the Creator Himself.   The
determination of man by the cosmos which surrounds him is undeniable.   But theological anthropology cannot purport to be a doctrine
of man as a cosmic being explicable in the light of this determination.
The fact that he is determined by the cosmos, by heaven and earth,
and how this is the case, theology will explain only by reference to his
divine Creator, and therefore to the Word of God, not to the cosmos
or a particular view of the cosmos.

Man is not therefore the world.   He is not even a microcosm.   He
is both less and more than this.   He is less because both in his bodily
and spiritual nature he is wholly of earth and not of heaven.   He is
on earth and *under* heaven, and even on earth he is far too insignificant
to be understood as the measure and epitome of all things.   But he is
also more than the world because, although he is only an earthly
creature, only a small particle of the lower cosmos with many other
and different particles, he is yet something which heaven with all its
secrets and earth with all its disclosures are not.   He is the object
of God's purpose for the cosmos, in which this purpose is revealed.
All things in heaven and earth are the objects of the divine purpose.
But this purpose is not disclosed in all things ; it is disclosed only
in man.   The cosmos surrounding man is not alien to God.   It is not
independent and sovereign in face of Him.   It does not follow an
intrinsic law, but the will and work of its Creator.   It, too, is wholly
at His disposal and in His service.   It, too, reflects the glory of God,
and praises Him as its Master.   Whatever cosmic reality is, it is
conditioned by God, and belongs to God and owes allegiance to God,
whether it is the beyond or the present.   But it is not in the cosmos
that the meaning and purpose of the lordship of the Creator, and of
the praise offered Him by the creature in the surrounding cosmos, are
brought to light.   To be sure, we know that this lordship and praise
are exercised in the universe as a whole.   We know this by the Word
of God which is undoubtedly addressed to man living on earth and
under heaven.   The Word of the almighty God tells man directly
that He who thus speaks is the Creator and Lord of heaven and earth,

and that heaven and earth cannot avoid giving Him glory. But we do not know how the lordship and praise of God are exercised in the cosmos around us. We do not know this even from the Word of God. The Word of God is silent on this point. It tells us how things stand between God and man. But it does not disclose the inner nature of the relation between God and the rest of creation. It does not tell us how God rules and is praised in the cosmos around us. Where it seems to allude to the relation between God and other creatures, what is in question is a reflection of God's lordship over man and an echo of man's praise.

The attempt to penetrate to the inner secrets of the relation between God and the rest of creation, and the consequent attempt to explain and present the latter from the standpoint of this relation, can never be more than exercises in pious surmise or imagination. This does not mean that these attempts are strictly forbidden. But it is to be noted that Holy Scripture does not lead us to make them. And care must be taken that they do not entail the arbitrary errors of philosophical systems. That there are these inner relationships, even exact science cannot deny, and if it is sensible it will not try to do so. But it cannot tell us in what their nature consists. These are secrets which exact science as such does not attempt to fathom. Are there higher, heavenly beings who are able to fathom them? It may be so. But what do we know about the extent and limits of the knowledge of such beings? And what help is it to us as earthly beings if there are heavenly beings who actually know what we do not know? Shall we finally know what we do not know now? It may be so. But how do we know what will then be the extent and limit of our own knowledge? And even supposing we know then, the fact remains that we do not know now. We shall do well to reckon with the fact that perhaps God alone ultimately knows and will know how His lordship is exercised over the non-human creation, and in what the praise consists which the latter brings Him. Perhaps it is eternally for us and all other creatures to worship in face of the fact that there too He rules and is praised. But there is no serious reason to suppose that we shall necessarily fathom and penetrate the nature of these inner relationships.

It is enough for us in fact to know the relationship between God and man. We know this from the Word of God. We know of man— only of man, but of man from the Word of God—that his being on earth and under heaven is wholly determined and created in order that God should speak with him and that he should hear and answer. We know of man—only of man, but of man from the Word of God— the full significance of the depth of God's mercy and goodness towards him; of the seriousness of the interest with which God the Lord has turned to His creature; and the praise and gratitude which He awaits from His creature and which He is ready to receive as His supreme and only honour. We know of man—only of man, but of

man from the Word of God—that God Himself wills to have dealings
with him and to make him His partner in the history between them ;
and that at the climax of this history God Himself willed to become and
did become what man is—the Creator a creature, this creature, not
a stone or plant or animal, but man.   Here in man, then, we see what
we do not see in the cosmos around him.   We see already what perhaps
in all eternity we shall never see with regard to the cosmos.   We see
here in fact the inner mystery of the relationship between God and
His creature.   We see not only the fact but the way in which God
rules over His creature and is praised by it.   At this point the purpose
of God is not concealed but manifest.   That this is the case is man's
peculiar distinction in the whole cosmos, which is itself distinguished
by the fact that God willed to create it.   But what is dark there is
now light.   What is concealed there is now revealed.   And the revelation is that the world is loved by God because it was created by Him,
and that as His creation it may love Him in return.   In this respect
the Word of God is unequivocal.   It is this only in regard to man,
but in this regard it is really unequivocal.   It is in this distinction
that man exists on earth and under heaven.

And inevitably this distinction of man sheds light at least on earth
and heaven and the whole cosmos as well.   Man is not the world ;
not even a reflection of the world ; not even its epitome or compendium.   He is less than this, we said, but we also say that he is
more than this.   He is the point in the cosmos where, in spite of its
very different nature, its relationship to God is illuminated.   That
the purpose of God towards it is revealed here, cannot be without
significance for an understanding of its different nature.   Heaven and
earth, man's beyond and present, were created by the counsel and the
act of God who created man.   To the same end ?   We have no direct
knowledge of heaven and earth to justify us in affirming as much.
And yet we affirm it by the indirect knowledge which we owe to our
knowledge of man as grounded in the Word of God.   He who is the
Creator of man is also the Creator of the cosmos, and His purpose
towards the latter, although hidden as such, is none other than His
revealed purpose for us.   Hence in the disclosed relationship of God
with man there is disclosed also His relationship with the universe.
It is not without significance that in Old and New Testament alike
heaven and earth and their elements and inhabitants are always
described not only as witnesses but as co-workers in the work of God
and that of human praise.   This does not rest on a world-view, but
on a view of man which sees in him the point in the cosmos where the
thoughts of its Creator are disclosed, illuminating man in his totality
and also shedding light on the deepest and ultimate force which moves
the cosmos—the cosmos which has for us no intrinsic light and cannot
reveal the divine plan which governs it.   It is man in covenant with
God who reveals this plan.   He does so representatively for the whole

cosmos. He is not actually alone. He is in the cosmos. He alone sheds light on the cosmos. As he is light, the cosmos is also light. As God's covenant with him is disclosed, the cosmos is shown to be embraced by the same covenant.

Thus we lose nothing and gain everything if we resolutely refuse to make the doctrine of the creature a doctrine of the universe, a cosmology. This is quite unnecessary. For precisely in its concentrated form as a doctrine of man—and quite apart from speculations about man as a microcosm—this doctrine is a doctrine of creation as a whole, of heaven and earth as they were created by the almighty God whose mercy and goodness have been revealed to man and not elsewhere, *in parte pro toto*. It is not therefore arbitrarily, but legitimately, that we concern ourselves with anthropology alone.

2. MAN AS AN OBJECT OF THEOLOGICAL KNOWLEDGE

Man is made an object of theological knowledge by the fact that his relationship to God is revealed to us in the Word of God. We have seen it is this which distinguishes man from the rest of the cosmos. Of all other creatures the Word of God tells us only that they are the creatures of God, subject to His sovereignty, intended for His praise, and the heralds of His glory. How and why this is so is hidden from us. But how and why man is the creature of God is not hidden from us ; it is revealed by the Word of God. As God speaks His Word, He not only establishes the fact but reveals the truth of His relationship to this, the human creature. The description of this relationship, or the account of its history, forms the content of Holy Scripture. This does not give us any description or recount any history of the relationship between God and the rest of the cosmos. God alone and man alone are its theme. This is the distinction of man which makes him the object of theological anthropology.

But anthropology has a special task. It is the task of dogmatics generally to present the revelation of the truth of the relationship between God and man in the light of the biblical witness to its history as a whole. Anthropology confines its enquiry to the human creatureliness presupposed in this relationship and made known by it, i.e., by its revelation and biblical attestation. It asks what kind of a being it is which stands in this relationship with God. Its attention is wholly concentrated on the relationship. Thus it does not try to look beyond it or behind it. It knows that its insights would at once be lost, and the ground cut from beneath it, if it were to turn its attention elsewhere, abstracting from this relationship. Solely in the latter as illuminated by the Word of God is light shed on the creatureliness of man. Thus theological anthropology cleaves to the Word of God and its biblical attestation. But in the revealed relationship between God and man genuine light is thrown, not only on God, but also on man, on the essence of the creature to whom God has turned in this relationship.

The question of Ps. 8[4] : " What is man, that thou art mindful of him ? and the son of man, that thou visitest him ? " is prompted by sheer amazement that man should be distinguished among and before all other creatures : " For thou hast made him a little lower than the angels, and hast crowned him with glory and honour. Thou madest him to have dominion over the works of thine hands ; thou hast put all things under his feet " (vv. 5 f.). The exegesis of this passage given in Heb. 2[5ff.] is correct. The New Testament author identified this " man " with Jesus. He was justified in this because the Psalmist not only saw the exaltation of man over the angels and his dominion over the rest of creation in the fact of the superior dignity of man's creatureliness to that of the rest of the cosmos, but realised and stated that this dignity is to reflect the relationship of God to man and of man to God. " O Lord our Lord, how excellent is thy name in all the earth " (v. 9). The name of God which is here called glorious in view of the dignity conferred on man, means in the Old Testament the manifestation and revelation in the history of Israel of the person of the God who has made a covenant with His people. The astonished question : " What is man ? " gathers its point from the fact that this covenant has been made, that God has been mindful of man and visited him as this has taken place in Israel in this covenant, in the manifestation and revelation of the person of God. The Psalmist's astonishment is at the incomprehensible divine mercy which this action displays. Hence it is not a rhetorical, unanswered question. What is man ? He is the being of whom God is so mindful, when He so visits, that He makes Himself his Covenant-partner, as took place in Israel. The light to which we must keep in this matter is that which falls on the human creature in and with the fact that God is mindful of him and visits him in this way.

Theological anthropology expounds the knowledge of man which is made possible and needful by the fact that man stands in the light of the Word of God. The Word of God is thus its foundation. We hasten to add that for this very reason it expounds the truth about man. As man becomes the object of its knowledge in this way, it does not apprehend or explain an appearance of human essence, but the reality ; not its outward features, but its most inward ; not a part but the whole. It is another matter whether and to what extent, as it uses the material offered, it will do justice to it *in concreto*. Not merely in the doctrine of God, but here too in the doctrine of man, we have always to reckon with the possibility that theology as a human work may and will seriously fail to do justice *in concreto* to its object. The light which falls on this object, and in which it first becomes an object of knowledge, is the divine light. Inevitably, then, theology can give only a dim and blurred reflection. But this does not affect in the least the uniqueness, the height and depth, the richness of the material which it tries to use for better or for worse. As it understands the creatureliness of man from the Word of God addressed to him and illuminating him as no other creature, it draws from the fountain of all truth, and it is enabled to see the depths of the being of man and summoned to utter the true and final word concerning him. This special origin and this special claim mark it off from all the very different attempts at self-knowledge which seem to be its competitors.

Apart from the theological, there are of course other types of anthropology, and a passing glimpse at their very different character and method is indispensable. It might even appear at first as if the field which we now enter as we take up the doctrine of man is one which has been long since occupied, so that what the dogmatics of the Church has to do in this respect is simply to discuss the very different attempts which have always been made. Comprehensively defined, the problem of man is in fact a problem of the universal understanding of being to which, in addition to all kinds of primitive intuitive convictions many serious hypotheses have been given in answer, together with the supposed axioms of generally human, non-theological knowledge, old and new. Indeed, we are forced to say that directly or indirectly, openly or latently, explicitly or implicitly, the problem of man has always been acknowledged as the key-problem of all human reflection.

Anthropology has sometimes disguised itself as cosmology and theology, but it has always experienced dramatic revivals and rediscoveries. And it may seriously be asked whether even in the outstanding forms of myth, philosophy or knowledge, it has ever been less than the real problem of man concerned for an understanding of his relation with God, the world and himself ; whether, for example, the great returns to anthropology which have been so epoch-making in the spiritual history of the West—associated in antiquity with the name of Socrates, in the Middle Ages with that of Augustine, in modern times with that of Descartes and in the 19th century with those of L. Feuerbach, Max Stirner and S. Kierkegaard—were anything but manifestations of the problem which in apparently less anthropologically concerned periods was always the problem of problems : Who am I, who am I now undertaking to give an account of what God and the world mean to me ? The answering of the second and third questions —whenever the Word of God has not directed human reflection onto a different path—has always been decided by the answer to the first. " The proper study of mankind is man " (Alexander Pope). Theology itself has only to be unsure about its foundations and its truth, and this uncertainty has only to mount to a crisis like that which marked the age of Schleiermacher, and it is led at once to the discovery and assertion of L. Feuerbach, that at bottom it too is perhaps nothing but concealed anthropology.

In the non-theological anthropology which apparently dominates the field we do not have a sporadic but a very persistent rival with intentions which are implicitly or explicitly extremely comprehensive. Anthropology, which in the sphere of dogmatics is only one chapter among others, is in non-theological belief, myth, philosophy and science a kind of basic discipline which imposes its criterion on all other knowledge and perhaps claims to embrace it. The question which we have now to decide is whether we can at least orientate ourselves by this anthropology which is independent of theology, i.e., by one of its concrete expressions. In relation to man, can we profit by its methods and results ? An even more radical question is whether we ought deliberately to regard theological anthropology merely as a species, placing it within the framework of a general non-theological anthropology, and establishing and securing it on the basis of the latter. To answer these questions we may recall the two types of non-theological anthropology which usually merge *in concreto*, but which are basically quite distinct, and therefore demand a different attitude in each case.

The first of these types is that of the speculative theory of man. Although there is no compulsion, it may proceed from certain hypotheses put forward by exact science. Alternatively, although there is again no compulsion, it may rest upon a pure self-intuition purporting to be axiomatic. In any event, it goes beyond the hypotheses of exact science, either depriving them of their hypothetical character and treating them as axiomatic principles, or discovering such principles and freely opposing them to the former. Either way, it belongs to the context of a world-view. *De facto*, and probably quite perceptibly, it forms the basic element in such a view, providing the framework which supports and maintains the whole. This speculative theory of man arises in the wide area between myth on the one hand and philosophy on the other. Hence what we have said about world-views as such is applicable to it. It arises in the arid place— unspiritual in the biblical sense of " spirit "—where man has not yet heard the Word of God or hears it no longer. In this place man supposes that he can begin absolutely with himself, i.e., his own judgment, and then legitimately and necessarily push forward until he finally reaches an absolute synthesis, a system of truth exhaustive of reality as a whole. On this assumption he also and primarily thinks that he can know and analyse himself. On this assumption he speculates : whether with or without regard to the hypotheses of exact science ; whether with or without the intuitive discovery of a free basic principle. He thinks that in some way he can know himself. Anthropology on this basis is the doctrine of man in which man is confident that he can be both the teacher and the pupil of truth. Whether teaching of this kind includes or excludes the idea of God, and in what form it may perhaps include it, is unessential. It may well include it, and perhaps even in such a way as to make it of decisive and central importance in the foundation and development of the idea of man. Again, it may develop atheistically, or perhaps sceptic-ally as regards the idea of God. The essential point, however, is not its attitude to this idea, but the fact that this teaching has its origin in that arid corner ; that here at the start of human self-knowledge stands man himself in his unlimited self-confidence either with or without the thought of God, or with this thought or that. It might even assume the form of pure questioning, of the absolute renunciation of all positive theses. The self-confidence characteristic of this speculative type of anthropology then expresses itself in the confidence with which man confines himself to the investigation of himself, thinking it his duty to honour the truth by a perpetual seeking after truth.

This is not the place to grapple with an anthropology of this type. It is obviously an enemy which we can meet only by opposing to it the Christian confession. We need only say that the field which we are entering with our enquiry about man cannot possibly be occupied by an anthropology of this type. What is supposedly or actually achieved by this speculative anthropology is not in any case what we have to achieve. Nor can we achieve what is thought and declared to be achieved by these means. We cannot allow human self-knowledge to begin where this anthropology begins, with that unlimited self-confidence : not primarily because in view of our different understanding of man we consider that self-confidence out of place ; but primarily because—and on this our different understanding of man rests—we are not able to see the essence and nature of man apart from the Word of God. Hence we cannot enter that sterile corner, nor can we argue from it. The Christian Church does not belong to that corner. It would cease to be itself if it wished to do so. This means that we cannot accept the presupposition of all speculative theories about man. Beyond the ground occupied by them we see open territory into which these theorists cannot move because they are not able to make use of our own presuppositions. Legitimately or illegitimately, they are otherwise engaged than we. They are just as incapable of fulfilling our task as we theirs. We cannot orientate ourselves by their attempts. And there can certainly be no question of theological anthropology being constrained or even able to enter the framework of an anthropology which has such a different basis. The different origin of theological anthropology is its frontier against all speculative anthropology. And it goes without saying that it must always guard this frontier.

The second type of non-theological anthropology is that of the exact science of man. Man, too, is an object—one among many, but nevertheless the nearest object—of the physiological and biological, psychological and sociological sciences. With more or less consensus of opinion, these sciences have at their disposal in every period temporarily authoritative formulæ which sum up the results of previous research, and which indicate hypotheses and pointers for future research. It is not difficult in any period to combine and co-ordinate these formulæ to form a picture or system which with due relativity may be advanced as, and may even claim to be, the authoritative doctrine of exact science in the period concerned. A sense of relativity will always be maintained. To the extent that science is exact, it will refrain from consolidating its formulæ and hypotheses as axioms and therefore treating them as revealed dogmas. It will always be conscious that its concern is not with the being of man but the appearance ; not with the inner but the outer ; not with the totality but with the sum of specific and partial phenomena. It will realise that its temporarily valid picture or system can be only a momentary view for to-day which it may have to replace by another to-morrow, for the flux of phenomena is reflected also in the conclusions of science. Its exponents will either abstain from claiming, or will claim only with extreme reserve and with a warning against over-estimation and dogmatism, that their system constitutes the basis and criterion for all other investigation and knowledge. In this their attitude will contrast with that of speculative theorists. To the extent that science is exact its anthropology will necessarily and formally have this very different character. And what it can and will actually achieve corresponds to this character. Strictly speaking, what physiology and biology, psychology and sociology can offer, will not be statements to the effect that man in his physical, psychological and sociological existence is or is not this or that, but statements to the effect that man as a phenomenon is to be seen and understood by man according to this or that standpoint and in this or that aspect of his constitution and development, as determined by current knowledge of these facts accessible to human enquiry. Scientific anthropology gives us precise information and relevant data which can be of service in the wider investigation of the nature of man, and can help to build up a technique for dealing with these questions. Since it is itself a human activity, it presupposes that man is, and what he is, and on this basis shows him as to how he is, in what limits and under what conditions he can exist as the being he is. It is not concerned with his reality, let alone with its philosophical foundation and explanation. But it reveals the plenitude of his possibilities.

This second type obviously requires a different attitude from the first. As such, the exact science of man cannot be the enemy of the Christian confession. It becomes this only when it dogmatises on the basis of its formulæ and hypotheses, becoming the exponent of a philosophy and world-view, and thus ceasing to be exact science. As long as it maintains restraint and openness in face of the reality of man, it belongs, like eating, drinking, sleeping and all other human activities, techniques and achievements, to the range of human actions which in themselves do not prejudice in any way the hearing or non-hearing of the Word of God, which become acts of obedience or disobedience only in so far as they belong to individuals with their special tendencies and purposes, and which even as acts of a disobedient man, and in the context of a wrong purpose, are still good in themselves in so far as they correspond to the creaturehood of man, which as such cannot be changed by his disobedience. Hence the anthropology of science does not necessarily derive from the arid place in which the Word of God has not yet or is no longer heard.

It is not necessarily an unspiritual work, as is unfortunately true of the works of speculative anthropology which as such are to be explained only by the perverse intention of man. To the extent that it remains within its limits, and does not attempt to be more or less than exact science, it is a good work ; as good as man himself as God created him. Hence our differentiation from it need not imply opposition. Opposition is required only if it becomes axiomatic, dogmatic and speculative.

If this is not the case, the differentiation consists simply in the fact that theological anthropology has not to do merely with man as a phenomenon but with man himself ; not merely with his possibilities, but with his reality. It is in this way, in the light of God's Word and therefore in the light of truth, that he is known by it. Hence it may not frame its principles merely as temporarily and relatively valid hypotheses ; as contributions to the wider investigation of the nature of man and the development of a technique for dealing with these questions. It has a responsibility to make the claim of truth. We repeat that this does not mean that it cannot err, that it does not need continually to correct and improve itself. But in virtue of its basis and origin it concerns itself with the real man. It not only comments on him, but denotes and describes him. It gives him his name. Interpreting him, it is concerned with the relation of this creature to God, and therefore with his inner reality and wholeness. This is something which the anthropology of exact science cannot do. How can it understand man as the creature of God ? The fact that he is this does not belong to what is seen of man by exact science, to the external features which it can investigate and present, or to the sum of the parts in which he is present to it. Even the fact that man is the creation of God, standing as such in a special relation to God, is a fact that is not accessible to human thought and perception otherwise than through the Word of God. And this is even more true of the inner essence and character of this relation. It is from within this context that theological anthropology must interpret man. But in so doing it interprets man himself in his inner reality. For what he is as the creature of God, and in his relation to God, is his very being and reality. As theological anthropology concerns itself with this reality, it is fully aware of its own shortcomings, but it raises the claim to truth. Scientific anthropology cannot do this, even when its exponents have occasionally (or not just occasionally) to be taken seriously as obedient hearers of the Word of God ; more seriously perhaps than theologians occupied on the other side. For if they are to fulfil the function of theological anthropology, they must look beyond the phenomenal man who is the object of exact science to the real man perceptible in the light of God's Word. In other words, they must become seekers asking and answering theological questions. And if there is no reason why the scientist who is obedient to God's

Word should not look beyond the phenomenon of man to his inner reality, if it is self-evident that this should be the case and that to this extent he should become more or less basically a theologian, it is still true that what he does as a scientist, a physiologist, psychologist etc., can be no substitute for what theology has to do at this point. Where it is simply a question of man as a phenomenon—and exact science as such can go no further—there can be no perception of man as the creature and covenant-partner of God, and therefore of his true reality and essence, and the task of theological anthropology is thus untouched. Hence we cannot admit that scientific anthropology has already occupied the ground we propose to cover. On this side, too, the way is clear for the enquiry which we must undertake from our own particular standpoint.

But the differentiation of theological anthropology from other types of enquiry into the being of man is simple compared with the problem which now faces us. On our own assumption, what is in fact the theological standpoint from which we are to understand and describe the being and nature of man as created by God ? For the presupposition that man may be known in the light of the Word of God, that in God's revelation man is disclosed as well as God, at once presents a difficulty the overcoming of which will be decisive for the whole course of our further enquiry.

The point is that the revelation of God does not show us man as we wish to see him, in the wholeness of his created being, but in its perversion and corruption. The truth of man's being as revealed in the Word of God and attested generally by Holy Scripture shows us man as a betrayer of himself and a sinner against his creaturely existence. It accuses him of standing in contradiction to God his Creator, but also to himself and the end for which he was created. It presents him as the corrupter of his own nature. It is no doubt true that this does not mean that God ceases to be God for him or that he ceases to stand before God. But his real situation in the sight of God is that he is the one who contradicts the purpose of God and therefore himself, distorting and corrupting his own being. What is sinful and strives against God and himself is not just something in him, qualities or achievements or defects, but his very being. And when he sins, entering into conflict with God and making himself impossible, it is not in virtue of his creation by God, but by his rebellion against it, by his own decisive deed, with which he takes up the history commenced with his creation. This history begins with the fact that at the very moment when God acts with the greatest faithfulness towards man His creature, man in supreme unfaithfulness takes sides against God his Creator. Whatever happens later in the history happens on this presupposition and with the determination that man is in contradiction with himself, thus making himself impossible. Because from the beginning of the history man is at war with himself, in its

further course he can be helped only by the fact that God still takes
his part, irrespective of the attitude of man. For this reason the grace
of God alone can be his salvation.

" The imagination of man's heart is evil from his youth " (Gen. 8²¹). " We
were by nature children of wrath " (Eph. 2³). " This my son was dead, and is
alive again " (Lk. 15²⁴). " By Adam's fall corruption's pall, Has spread o'er
human essence." The poet who wrote this song, Cyriakus Spangenberg, was
one of the religious friends of the Lutheran Matthias Flacius, whose doctrine of
original sin, that after the fall of man sin had become man's very substance, was
not so unreasonable and unacceptable as it was represented by its opponents
and later in many histories of dogma. In any case, Flacius called original sin
only one—the theological—form of human substance. What he rightly rejected
was the idea of the synergists (and later of the *Formula of Concord*) that it was
merely an *accidens*. If this Aristotelian terminology was adopted, sin could
only be called the theological form of man's substance. Man himself is a sinner.
He himself is declared to be such by God, and as such rejected. He has to
confess himself as such, and as such he needs reconciliation with God. This
has been granted him as such with divine freedom in Jesus Christ. A *liberum
arbitrium* as a sort of neutral lever, or *modiculum boni in homine adhuc reliquum*
over and above sinful man, as it was represented by the opponents of Flacius,
is of course excluded by his thesis. That he could be so execrated by his Lutheran
contemporaries because of this thesis shows how little Luther's most important
insights were understood even within his own Church, and how thoroughly
they had been forgotten only two decades after his death.

When man is truly and seriously viewed in the light of the Word
of God, he can be understood only as the sinner who has covered his
own creaturely being with shame, and who cannot therefore stand
before God even though he is the creature of God. And the difficulty
which confronts us is this. In these circumstances how can we possibly
reach a doctrine of man in the sense of a doctrine of his creaturely
essence, of his human nature as such ? For what we recognise to be
human nature is nothing other than the disgrace which covers his
nature ; his inhumanity, perversion and corruption. If we try to
deny this or to tone it down, we have not yet understood the full
import of the truth that for the reconciliation of man with God nothing
more nor less was needed than the death of the Son of God, and for
the manifestation of this reconciliation nothing more nor less than
the resurrection of the Son of Man, Jesus Christ. But if we know man
only in the corruption and distortion of his being, how can we even
begin to answer the question about his creaturely nature ?

We do not forget, of course, that even as the sinner that he is
man is still the creature of God. If his nature is wholly controlled
by the fact that he has fallen away from God and can only be at odds
with himself, yet this nature is not effaced, and he cannot succeed in
destroying it and making himself unreal. The distortion or corruption
of his being is not the same thing as its annihilation. Death itself
does not spell annihilation. We cannot say, therefore, that he has
ceased to exist as the one whom God created. That he still exists

as such is implied in the fact that God still speaks to him. Thus he is still before God. Even as a sinner he is still real ; he is still the creature of God. And therefore the question of his creaturely being, of the nature of man, is still meaningful and necessary in spite of his degeneracy.

This is the point which the *Formula of Concord* (*Sol. decl.* I) rightly emphasised against Flacius. Glory must be given to God by distinguishing His work and the creation of man from the devil's work which has corrupted him. Hence the matter must not be expressed in a way which might suggest that with the fall of man Satan has succeeded in producing a second creation, a *malum substantiale*, or that the result has been the destruction of human nature or its transformation into something quite different. The corrupted nature of man and the sin which corrupts it are two distinct things. It must be taken into account that in so many texts man is described as God's creature and handiwork even after the fall. That he is body and soul, and can think, speak and act and work, is still the work of God. Satan's work is merely that his thoughts, words and works are evil and his nature corrupt. And the Son of God did not assume original sin, but our sinful nature. Not sin, but sinful man, is baptised, sanctified and blessed in the name of the Trinity, and there will one day be a resurrection of the flesh apart from the sin which now taints it. But Flacius himself knew and said all this. As he saw it, original sin is only one form of human substance, i.e., its theological form, by which its original theological form, man's holiness, has been replaced in the sight of God. But human nature has also a physical form, viz. all that which belongs to the natural constitution of man and which has not been lost or even changed as a result of the fall. The older theology was right, therefore, when it refused to give up at the outset the possibility of a knowledge and doctrine of the creaturely essence of man, even though it immediately added the doctrine of sin—and in Protestantism at any rate a very radical doctrine. Zwingli is an exception when at least in his *Comm. de vera et falsa relig.* he compared to the deluding arts of the cuttlefish all attempts at a human self-knowledge not primarily directed by the thought of man's fall from God, and rejected them out of hand. It is no doubt true that in the history of the covenant of grace attested by the Bible man is sinful man from first to last. But we must not forget that when this witness speaks of man it refers to a specific being with determinate qualities—a being which does not cease to be such even as a result of the fact that it is now covered with shame, and stands under the wrath and judgment of God, and has become the prey of death.

On the other hand we have to remember—and this is what makes our problem so difficult—that any tenable distinction between man as created by God and the sinful determination of his being is possible only if his sinful nature, his perversion and corruption, is minimised. But if we consider man truly and seriously in the light of the Word of God, this is just what may not be done. His corruption is radical and total. If there is no sin in which man is not also the creature of God (although in contradiction with God and himself), so also there is no creaturely essence in which man is not seen at strife with God and therefore sinful. Therefore we do not have in any case the direct vision of a sinless being of man fulfilling its original determination. There is no point at which we are not brought up against that corruption and depravity. We must be on our guard against any desire to illuminate the darkness in which the true nature of man is shrouded by taking into account what we suppose we know about man in general and as such from other sources. It must be our aim to view him clearly in the light of the Word of God, and therefore as the sinner which he is in his confrontation with God. If we ask concerning his true nature, we must never lose sight for a moment of his degeneracy.

This is what stands out more plainly in the rigid formula of Flacius that original sin is the *forma substantiae hominis* than in the intrinsically correct refutation of the *Formula of Concord*. We may rightly distinguish between corrupted nature and the sin which corrupts it. But this cannot be a final distinction, unless we are to say that, while this distinction has to be made, it can have no practical value, since we have no knowledge of uncorrupted nature as such on account of the sin which corrupts and in a sense completely conceals it. This is obviously how Zwingli saw it. But the *Formula of Concord* neither said this nor meant it. Its intention was to leave open a sphere for the knowledge and determination of the corrupted (or not yet corrupted) nature of man as such—a sphere which was to be filled from other sources. And the dogmatics of all the older Protestantism, if not the *Formula of Concord* itself, knew how to fill it along these lines. It was thought possible to separate human nature as such from its sinful state, and to view it prior to or apart from this sinfulness. And since the Word of God did not shed any light on this question, this was done on the basis of knowledge derived from other quarters, as in Roman Catholic doctrine. It was done by going to the schools of ancient philosophy for information about the human nature which is to be distinguished from sin. And the inevitable result was that the Semi-Pelagian and Pelagian idea of a neutral *liberum arbitrium*, which the *Formula of Concord* was determined strictly and resolutely to oppose, finally gained an entrance into Protestant theology through the door opened at this point.

We must insist on two points. On the one hand, the realisation of the total and radical corruption of human nature must not be weakened. The shame which covers it is unbroken, and therefore there can be no question of gaining an insight into man as unaffected by sin. On the other hand, the question of human nature as constituted by God is reasonable and necessary. We have no right to be frightened by the difficulty which seems to make the answering of this question almost hopeless. This being the case, our only course is to look to the very point where the riddle seems most impenetrable. It is the Word of God which sets us this problem. For it is this Word which shows us human nature in all its corruption and depravity. But we have reason to believe that it will show us more than this. Therefore we have reason calmly to consider the sin which conceals the creaturely nature of man as this (and in the first instance this alone) is shown us by the Word of God, and to ask whether the very thing which apparently spells darkness and obscurity will not in the light of the same Word be a medium to disclose what it seems to conceal. In the radical depravity of man there is necessarily hidden his true nature ; in his total degeneracy his original form. This cannot be grasped directly. Every supposedly direct apprehension of it turns out to be false.

But, since we have to do with the piercing light of the Word of God, the indirect knowledge communicated by this light might well prove to be true and sound. We shall then be led further at the very point where we seemed to be almost hopelessly blocked. But the greatest caution is demanded. We must not be led further except by the Word of God. And what is primarily shown us by this Word is simply the sin of man. In this event, how can we succeed in distinguishing between the depravity which conceals and the nature which is concealed, between the inhumanity and the humanity of man ? The corruption of man, in which we and our vision and judgment share, is not so relative that we can to some extent survey it from a point of vantage, calmly comparing it with the hidden truth of human nature, distinguishing the former from the latter and comfortably contemplating and explaining both man and his sin. We are not in any position to infer from any residual lineaments in the biblical picture of sinful man the true essence of man as God created him. Nor can we deduce it dialectically by a reversal of concepts. If man is a sinner and not for nothing exposed to the wrath and judgment of God, where is he to find the necessary insight for this process of inference and deduction ? The self-contradiction resulting from our contradiction of God is serious. It really prevents us from understanding ourselves. We are not clear nor transparent to ourselves, nor can we see ourselves from any higher standpoint. We are totally and not just partially incapable of occupying any independent vantage point from the height of which we might penetrate and judge ourselves. The very fact that we stand in rebellion against God and ourselves is something that we do not know as a result of our own insight, but solely from the divine accusation levelled against us, and therefore solely from the Word of God. Who would ever realise and admit, except on the basis of the revealed judgment of God, that he is the enemy and betrayer of God and himself ? Even less by our own insights are we able to know ourselves, our true essence in depravity and nature in degeneracy. The various ways in which we try by our own powers of judgment to distil our true creaturely essence from the disgrace and infamy which now cover us can only be arbitrary and frustrating. It is not self-evident that in spite of the fall our true creaturely being persists even in the shame which covers us, that man really continues as the creature of God. Nor is it self-evident that by the recognition of our fall and shame there is also possible an appreciation of the fact and extent that we are the creatures of God. Yet we are this, and it is still possible for us to recognise this fact. And we do not owe this possibility to the power and skill of our observation and judgment, but solely to the light of God's Word, just as we do not owe the fact itself to our own capacity to escape our self-contradiction, but solely to the grace of the same divine Word according to which it is true that our self-contradiction is not the final truth about us. If there is a necessary connexion between the realisation of our sin and that of our creaturely being, it is not within our power to establish this connexion or to derive the second of these insights from the first. We are capable neither of the one nor of the other, and therefore we cannot connect the two.

But the knowledge of sin and the knowledge of the nature of man are possible both individually and in their inter-connexion within the comprehensive knowledge of the Word of God, i.e., of man as the partner in the covenant which God has made with him, of man as the object of the eternal grace of his Creator and Lord. On the one side, this embracing perception shows us that man is sinful, and indeed totally and radically sinful. But on the other hand the same perception forbids us to stop at this understanding of man and invites and commands us to look further and deeper. If man is the object of divine grace, his self-contradiction may be radical and total, but it is not the last word that has been spoken about him. For with God and from God he has a future which has not been decided by his self-contradiction or the divine judgment which as the sinner guilty of this self-contradiction he must inevitably incur, but which by the faithfulness and mercy of God is definitely decided in a very different way from what he deserves. If he is the object of God's favour, his self-contradiction may be radical and total, but it cannot even be the first word about him. The fact that he became a sinner cannot mean that he has spoken an originally valid word about himself, even in respect of his own origin and beginning. For the fact that he covered his creaturely being with infamy cannot mean that he has annulled or destroyed it. The fact of his fall cannot mean that what he is eternally before God and from God, His Creator and Lord, has been changed. If, as a result of his self-contradiction, he had really ceased to be God's creature and to stand as such before God, how could this very different future, beyond his present contradiction, be disclosed to him by the faithfulness and goodness of God ?

Naturally this is not an insight which man himself can either originate or achieve by his own resources or on his own authority. It springs solely from the fact that he is the object of divine grace. And this truth can only become clear to him by the Word of God in which it is grounded. Only by this Word does he know that while he is a sinner he is not merely a sinner, but that even as sinner he is God's creature and as such real before God. Only in the light of God's Word is his radical and total self-contradiction clear to him, and only in this light may he look beyond this self-contradiction to the creaturely being and essence preserved in spite of it. This does not mean that we lapse into an arbitrary and weakening interpretation of sin, as though we ourselves could see through it into the depths of our sinless creaturehood ; as though it were not so serious a matter that we were not free theoretically at least to release ourselves from its entanglement.

We have not fabricated the pardon of the creature on the truth of which we have stumbled.

But now that we have stumbled on this truth, we cannot escape it. We cannot forget how man is revealed to us in the light of God's Word—that he is a sinner, but that as such and in spite of himself he is also the object of divine grace, the partner in the covenant which God has made with him. Sinful man in himself, without regard to the fact that he is also this covenant-partner and as such still the creature of God, is an abstract concept which must be excluded no less than the abstraction which would create for us a picture of pure creatureliness which takes no account of his sin. Sinful man as such is not the real man. We are not asked to blind ourselves to the fact that he is sinful. The real man is the sinner who participates in the grace of God. Thus the knowledge of the real man depends on the recognition that he shares in divine grace. Even the fact that he is a sinner is true only when seen in connexion with the truth that he is the object of the grace of God. For he sins against the grace of God. As he rebels against this and against God, trying to live, not in dependence on divine grace, but in the power of his own freedom and merits, he entangles himself in self-contradiction. Thus the recognition of his sinfulness is linked up with the recognition that he shares in the divine grace. For only as we realise that the divine grace is offered us can we understand the fact and nature of our sin, and the self-contradiction in which we are involved. The grace of God, the covenant of God with man, is primary. The sin of man is secondary. It is not ultimate, and therefore it is not primary. This excludes the abstraction of man as merely sinful, and implies the pardon of man, who even as a sinner does not cease to be the creature of God.

Of course, the judgment of God which is effective and disclosed in His Word belongs essentially to His action as the gracious God. The judgment of God is not in conflict with His mercy. In all its ineluctable sharpness and severity it is a form of the mercy with which He keeps faith with man. It is a burning fire. Yet it does not burn and consume without reason or for its own sake. The Creator does not retire when He causes this fire to burn. It is the holy fire of His Creator-love consuming and destroying the sin, rebellion and self-contradiction of man. Divine judgment in the biblical sense means that God vindicates Himself against man, but that in so doing He vindicates man against all that is alien and hostile to him. It means that God does what is right for Himself and therefore for man. Hence it is not a No for its own sake, but a No for the sake of the Yes. It repeats and confirms what according to Genesis 1 took place in the act of creation ; the salutary division of light from darkness, of the upper waters from the lower, of earth from sea. It overthrows the usurping tyranny to which the creature yielded in sinning, to the dishonour of his Creator and his own destruction. Thus as an act of divine sovereignty over man it spells his emancipation. It protects man by being so relentless towards him. It secures him by its very sharpness. Thus God's reaction to man's sin—His powerful and effectual opposition which man must bear in consequence of his rebellion against God and betrayal of himself—is the expression of His grace, a corollary of this primary fact. It does not in any way change the will of God as Creator. It confirms this will and contributes to its triumph. For this reason it would be quite wrong even momentarily to consider independently and in isolation the man who stands under the judgment of God. It is certainly not the case that the sin of man has shown God to have miscalculated in some way, as though the sin of man had created a new and second order of creation, a new world, the world of the wrath of God.

Thus the sin of man to which the judgment of God is relevant cannot in any sense be a creative act, an act of primary significance. As an act of enmity to divine grace it is an unpardonable insult to God and a mortal threat to man. It deserves only to be consumed by the fire of God's judgment. It clearly has the character of that which God did not will to create, and therefore separated as darkness from light, excluding it from His creation. From the outset and for ever and in every respect, it stands under the No of God. That is why it is so serious. That is what gives it the stamp of what is irreparable from the standpoint of the sinful creature. When he sins, man chooses what he cannot choose as the creature of God, since God has denied and rejected it. If he does choose it in spite of this, he automatically betrays himself. He causes himself to fall. He as it were wrenches himself away from his true bearings. He delivers himself up to shame and corruption. The calamitous work of Satan begins to be done by him and in him. Given up to Satan by his own choice and decision, he cannot help himself back to the right way. Lost through the choice of what he could not choose as the creature of God, he cannot find himself or rescue himself. He can be found and rescued only by the One to whom he is not lost even by the fact that he is lost to himself. For whatever he has done, and whatever may befall him in consequence, he is not lost to God, and his sin has not brought to birth a new creation, a similar and rival dominion to the lordship of God. He can beat against the fortress of divine faithfulness, but can make no impression upon it. Hence it is not the case that by reason of his sin man has ceased to be the creature of God, and indeed this specific creature man. Though he rebels against God, he cannot escape God. Though he delivers himself up, he is still upheld by God. If he is blind to God, God is not blind to him. If he places himself under the judgment of wrath, even in this way he is still the covenant-partner of God. He has broken the covenant. But he did not make it and he cannot dissolve it. He can sin and make himself impossible. But he cannot even do this outside the covenant. He cannot sin without the grace of God, but only against God. In so doing he brings the divine judgment on himself. Sin is terrible in its reality and consequences just because it takes place within the covenant and is directed against the gracious God, and because man is not abandoned by Him but held firm in the inexorable hand of this supreme Judge. God is alway the Lord and man the partner of the covenant. God does not let man go. Hence he cannot be released from his creaturehood nor from his humanity. He can flee but he cannot escape either God or himself. By the very fact that he would like to escape both God and himself, but cannot do so, he entangles himself in self-contradiction. Yet even in this way he cannot speak a final word against the first word by which he was created and is really man. Because God will not let him go, he is not abandoned nor allowed finally to fall. Because by his sin he cannot achieve anything creative, he remains the object of the merciful will of God as Creator, the object of His grace. And the fact remains that he participates in this grace. The primary and basic orientation of his being persists, which no secondary fact can change. The grace of God necessarily assumes the form of judgment on sinful man. But it does not give him up. Even in this form it does not cease to be grace. It upholds, carries and embraces even the sinful man who stands under its judgment. Thus we must not focus our attention on the sinner, as though by his sin he had founded a new order of things which had an independent meaning. This kingdom of sinful man (the kingdom of Satan) is revealed in the witness of Holy Scripture only to be convicted at once of its meaninglessness and to be put in the shade by the coming kingdom of God. Scripture shows that the only kingdom which abides and has meaning is this coming kingdom of God. Man belongs to God, not to Satan, nor to himself nor any one else. The divine rejection of sinful man does not modify this at all but only confirms its truth. This is the context which even theological anthropology must bear in mind from the outset. If it is really to understand man theologically, i.e., in the light of God's Word, it must derive from this comprehensive perception. That God the Creator is gracious to man His creature is the principle to which it must always return and the presupposition at which it must always start.

On the basis and in the content of this fundamental recognition, it is only too true, in the second instance, that man is also a sinner. At this point, however, we can speak of this only incidentally and allusively.

The doctrine of sin belongs to the context of the doctrine of reconciliation. This is what we must primarily and continually remember when we speak of sin. What should we know of sin if we knew nothing of forgiveness and reconciliation, if the Word of God from which we must derive our awareness of sin, were not decisively and comprehensively the Word of atonement? The meaning of the statement that man is a sinner can only be truly and vividly appreciated when we realise that God is gracious to man : God unflinchingly faithful and man repeatedly unfaithful ; God merciful and man defiant ; God kind and man ungrateful; God eternally powerful for man and man powerless against God; God giving Himself to man and man futilely withdrawing and asserting himself; God wholly concerned about man and man always occupied with other things; God freely bestowing Himself on man and man always wanting to make his own gods; God utterly self-giving and man always turned in upon himself; God always ready to impart Himself and man at bottom never ready to receive; God's self-revealing Word a radiant message of joy and man's response its transformation into a gloomy law which now with tears he tries to obey and now he secretly endeavours to evade. And all this no less against himself than against God. If he is as he is summoned by God, he forgets himself as he forgets God. He persists in choosing what he cannot choose as the creature of God. He makes his life impossible by choosing the impossible. For it is to him that God is gracious. He cannot live if he denies the gratitude which he owes to God. What can be his end, what is to become of him, if he sins against the grace of God? For sin is man's self-alienation from the grace of God from which and in which he has his being. Sin consists in the fact that he neglects the grace of God and therefore his own true interests. Thus it is an offence against the divine majesty and a fatal imperilling of man himself. The dreadful things in which it finds expression against God and in man's own life and in the relationships of man with man are dreadful because this is its incomprehensible nature. It is for this reason that the contradiction which man both effects and suffers is so destructive. It is for this reason that it brings in its train such great and little evils, such problems and sufferings. It is for this reason, finally, that death is the wages of sin. Its infamy lies not only in the fact that it is directed against the Lord of man but that it is turned against this Lord, against the Lord who is man's Friend and Covenant-partner and Helper; that it answers His friendship with hostility. It is rebellion which nothing can justify or excuse. It is treachery of a kind whose odiousness can be extenuated or alleviated by no plea. Thus the grace of God itself is the presupposition of man's sin. Not that it is grace which leads or compels him to sin. Sin resists grace; it affronts it and betrays it. It has no basis in grace. It is in fact so terrible and infamous because it can have no basis in the grace in which God acts as Creator and in which man has his being as His creature. But its inconceivable reality can be grasped only when we see it as rebellion against grace. Thus the one complaint of Old Testament prophecy is that Israel sins to excess and beyond all other peoples in the very position of privilege which it has before all peoples on the basis of its election, in the covenant which God has made and faithfully maintained with it alone; that it has become an adulteress in its marriage with Yahweh. The whole witness of the Bible shows that sin does not originate in the void, as the transgression of a universal law, but in rebellion against the concrete reality which sums up all the divine laws, i.e., that God is gracious to man and that man is the being to whom He is gracious. Sin originates in wanton rebellion against the God who has given Himself to mankind in the person of His son. To this extent it has to be said that sin is impossible without grace; that it has its perverse origin in the grace of God. Man robs the gracious God of His honour, and in so doing he casts into the dust his own honour, the honour of the creature whom this God has created. He would not sin if God were not this God and man were not this creature.

Thus the knowledge of the grace of God is necessary to know that man is a sinner and what this means. This knowledge cannot be obtained in the void or on the basis of general ideas about the majesty of God and the dignity and obligations of man. A knowledge of sin based on such ideas, even though it presumes to be such, can never give us real insight into the absolute impossibility of which man makes himself guilty before God, or into the hopeless situation in which he entangles himself by his own decision and deed. On this basis sin can only seem to be relative, excusable and curable, and serious views and expressions

of human misery will be regarded as pessimistic exaggerations. Where sin is
not measured by the criterion of divine grace, it cannot possibly be realised that
sin is irreparable, that the sinner is in bondage to it, and that he is utterly
dependent on the grace of God. Melancholy resignation, contempt, misanthropy
and even despair are comprehensible on this basis, but not an understanding
of the accusation which man could not escape even by plunging into Mt. Etna.
Only those who taste and see how gracious the Lord is can know their sin. All
others may recognise more or less clearly the preponderance of evil, the faults
in life and attitude of others, also their own shortcomings and perhaps their
inner and outer conflicts. But all these are conceived as so many evil circumstances which can be lived down or at a pinch put right. Their own sin, and
therefore the real sin of real men (as something which cannot be lived down or
in any way put right), is known only by those who have been shown by the
light of divine grace who they are and what they have done and still do. They
know it because they know the grace of God, and in its mirror themselves and
the character of their deeds and decisions. It is because they are held by God
and cannot escape that they see that they are fleeing from Him ; and it is because
they are not let go and finally abandoned that they see that they are held.
Known sin is always forgiven sin, known in the light of forgiveness and the
triumphant grace of God. In the whole of the Bible it is truly known only in
this way. Unforgiven sin, or sin not yet known to be forgiven, is always unrecognised sin. We repent only as we have already found the God of grace and
realised that we are His creatures. Any other penitence moves hopelessly in a
circle. For the knowledge of sin is itself an element in the knowledge of grace.
Otherwise it does not deserve to be called this. For if it does not spring from
grace, it does not lead to grace nor live by grace, and even as the knowledge of
sin it will not be from the heart, or serious and lasting, but only in appearance.
According to the witness of the Bible, the knowledge of sin does not rest on a
universal human possibility, but is one of the privileges of Israel and the Church.
It forms an integral part of the message which the *ecclesia* has to deliver to the
world. It is something new which comes to believers with their recognition of
the love of God in Jesus Christ and which they can pass on to unbelievers only
with this recognition and again as something utterly new for them too. It is
nothing less than the recognition of Jesus as Lord, and as a consequence of this
it is a work of the Holy Spirit which can never be replaced by independent
reflection concerning the being and nature of man.

It is not the case, then, that sin and its recognition shatters or limits the
knowledge of the covenant, forming a kind of second sphere alongside the latter.
On the contrary, it is itself enclosed and embraced by the latter. It stands on
the basis and in the context of the knowledge of the covenant. It is a deeply
significant second factor. But it is only a second factor co-ordinate with the
first and subordinate to it.

In relation to our question, this means that we must remember
that the man whose nature we wish to know may be known only as a
sinner and therefore only in the perversion of his nature. But again,
even in his sin and corruption we are not concerned with an independent
principle, and therefore our knowledge of it is not a knowledge of
first and supreme rank.

We cannot look past it, nor can we look through it. The fact and
knowledge of sin are far too important for us to try to abstract from
it in any way, or to dream of a human nature unaffected by it. To
do so we should have to see human nature very differently from the
way in which it is disclosed to us by the divine revelation. We should

have to remove man from the history of the covenant of grace in which he has his real existence according to the witness of the Bible. We should be freely inventing a man who is very different from real man as he stands in God. This real man is already sinful man.

On the other hand, if we are attentive and loyal to the Word of God, we must not suppose that in describing him as a sinner we have spoken the first and final word about this real man. For it is not the case that because the creaturely being of man may be known by us only in its sinful determination, it is not real and knowable in any other way, as though human nature had been changed into its opposite, and by sinning man had in some sense suffered a mutation into a different kind of creature. For sin itself can arise and take shape only as sin against the grace of God, and it can be known only with the knowledge of grace. And " the grace of God alone remains eternally " —it alone, and therefore not the sin in which man opposes himself to it.

If we cannot relativise sin, looking past it or through it to a pristine purity of human nature which we can isolate and consider independently, it is undoubtedly relativised, and seen past and through, and isolated as secondary, by the grace of God and therefore the will of the Creator. Hence it follows no less undoubtedly for us that, if we do not want to exclude ourselves from the knowledge of grace, we must not absolutise sin, but that, even though we cannot relativise it of ourselves, we must regard it as relativised and secondary from the standpoint of divine grace. It would again be free invention if we tried to elude this necessity, halting at the sinful determination of human nature as though—because we cannot look past it or through it—it were something final, and regarding our corrupted nature as our true nature. The arrogance of all attempts not to take sin as seriously as God Himself takes it is one thing, but its true corrective does not lie in the false humility of a resignation which would take it seriously in a way in which God Himself obviously does not, but in the true humility of faith which is satisfied with, and adapts itself to, the way in which God Himself takes it seriously.

It is true, of course, that sinful man cannot himself forgive, or cancel, or revoke his sin ; that he cannot, therefore, excuse or justify himself, i.e., put himself right ; that he cannot even prepare or equip himself to do this. To be free to justify himself in this way, he would need not to have delivered himself up by opposing himself to the grace of his Creator. If he understands the wrath and the judgment of the gracious God, he will not ascribe this freedom to himself. He certainly does not know that there is a God, or that in Him he has a Saviour, or what sin is, so long as he thinks he has the freedom to justify himself or to begin the process of justification. It is true enough that the doctrine of the *liberum arbitrium* of sinful man is a ridiculous notion which is scattered to the winds once it is touched by the knowledge of the goodness of God. But it is even more true that the God in face of whom he is hopelessly and inexculpably compromised by his sin can do just what he himself cannot do ; that He has the freedom to justify him which he himself must disclaim as soon as he knows this God. The sad truth of our bondage, of our *servum arbitrium*, is far surpassed by the joyful truth that God is free constantly to be the One who created man, the gracious God, i.e., the One who is free to cause man to be unalterably that which he is created, the creature to whom He is gracious.

Again, it is true that man has no power of vision to see through the perversion of his nature to his true nature. His contemplation and apprehension of the gracious God would have to be unclouded if the truth of his own created being were to be in any sense recognisable by him. Again, in his recognition of the wrathful judgment of the gracious God he will be as little inclined to ascribe to himself this self-knowledge as to claim the freedom to justify himself when he has delivered himself up to evil. All this is true. But it is even more true that the God of whom as sinner he knows as little as he does of himself has not ceased to know the truth about him ; to know not merely his perverted nature but also the true nature which it conceals. It is even more true that in this unclouded knowledge of man God is God ; that He knows the mercy in which He created and accepted man, and which He cannot forget. And therefore God knows that, while man may fall, in virtue of this mercy he cannot be allowed to fall, but even in his falling can only continue to be the creature whom He has once-for-all and irrevocably accepted.

What God knows of man beyond his sin, relativising even the sin of man in the freedom of His grace, looking above it and through it, is the real creaturely nature of man which is the subject of our enquiry. And the ground on which we must take our stand is that God knows what we in our guilty blindness do not and can never know. To God we are an open book. He sees not only the degenerate form of our nature, but in this our true nature, the true humanity which for our eyes is thickly concealed by the veneer of our sin. And just because our true nature lies open to God, the degenerate form which alone we can see cannot be for us a final insurmountable factor, and we must neither arrogantly nourish illusions about our own blindness, nor indulge a false humility which would make us forget the sovereign freedom and penetrating vision of the gracious God. Where God is free and has knowledge, there we not only *may* but *must* enquire for what God is free and what He knows. And as He is not only free to chide and judge us, as in His chiding and judgment He is free to be to us the gracious God, as He knows not merely our sin but also the purpose for which He who is gracious has created us, we may and must enquire concerning this and therefore concerning our true nature.

This is a necessary and intelligent question because the freedom and knowledge in which God confronts us are not absolutely closed to us, so that we who are not God have to leave to Him the understanding of our nature and content ourselves with a knowledge of its perversion. Even the realisation that we cannot justify or know ourselves is not an insight that we have gained for ourselves or can control of ourselves. Only as we know the wrath and judgment of God can we know and admit that we cannot save ourselves or know the truth of our nature apart from sin. But the knowledge of the wrath and judgment of God presupposes the knowledge of the grace of God. And because man sins against grace and blinds himself to it, the knowledge of grace presupposes that God has disclosed Himself to man in spite of his blindness, giving sight to the blind and thus making Himself known as the God who is free to forgive sin and to justify the sinner, and who is not prevented by sin from knowing man as His creature and covenant-partner. How could sin be known and taken seriously if it were not God Himself who told man that he is a sinner? And how could this be said to him without his also hearing that God does not refuse but is still prepared to have continual dealings and fellowship with him? How could the judgment of God be seriously known if in it there were not received the declaration of the new and the confirmation of the abiding grace of God? But how could the grace of God itself become even distantly perceptible and comprehensible to sinful man as grace if the perception and comprehension which he has wilfully rejected as a sinner were not imparted afresh by God Himself? Because of this connexion it is impossible for us to say that we have no knowledge of the freedom and truth of God and therefore of the human nature for which God remains free and which He knows in spite of our sin, and therefore that we must be content merely to know our perversity. As we cannot persuade ourselves that we have no knowledge of God and His being, we cannot do so in respect of the knowledge of man and human nature. Even the recognition that God and man are hidden from us is an insight which can only follow from the fact that God has given us information about Himself and us, revealing what is hidden. The man who is not taught by God will never admit that he cannot teach himself; he will much rather suppose that he is very capable of self-knowledge, and in so doing will betray the fact that he is not taught by God. But he who has learned from God that he is incapable of knowing himself will not refuse to accept and recognise the knowledge which God imparts to him on this subject. The realisation that he cannot instruct himself will only be the result, in a sense the negative aspect, of the positive teaching which he has received from God. Even this negative insight would not be genuine if it included an evasion of the positive instruction which it implies. We receive—as certainly as we cannot take. We are justified—as certainly as we cannot forgive ourselves. We know—as certainly as we know nothing of ourselves either about God or about ourselves. But all this is by the revealed Word of God which convinces us of our own ignorance and bondage. Our knowledge of the latter would be more than doubtful if we could suppose that we were not primarily and above all instructed about the former.

If by the Word of God we are denied any capacity of our own to recognise our human nature as such, it is the same Word of God which enables us to know it, in a free demonstration of the free grace of God apart from and against our own capacity. In the Word of God the book is opened for us too. We are told that in spite of our sin God is still free in relation to us because He is the gracious God, and because man is still the creature to whom He is gracious. We are told what God knows in spite of our ignorance as He knows His mercy, which is not only the same but is new every morning. Thus in this apparently indirect but really most direct way of all we are given the clearest information concerning God and His nature and ourselves and ours.

The Word of God reveals a specific attitude of God to man—it is the Word of the acts of God—and in the mirror of this divine attitude we see the human creature to whom the acts of God have reference, his status and endowment. For this divine attitude is not merely determined by what God sees and purposes with regard to the sin of man, but also by the wisdom and will with which He created man to be His covenant-partner. How can this wisdom and will of the Creator be surpassed by what God does in confirmation and execution of His grace as Creator and therefore in the reconciliation of sinful man ? His attitude as revealed in His Word is rather, as it relates to sinful man, following him and thus involving something new after his creation, an expression, intensification and glorification of His wisdom and will as Creator. Positing an inexorable but saving opposition to the being and action of man, as necessitated by his sin, it shows us what kind of a being it is whom God must oppose in the grace of judgment and the judgment of grace. It shows us that God is well aware what He has done in giving this nature to the creature towards whom He now acts in this way, and creating and instituting him His covenant-partner.

For all its newness the behaviour of God to sinful man as revealed in His Word is in continuity with His purpose in creation to the extent that it takes place on the presupposition and in the framework of certain relationships of the being of man which are influenced by sin but not structurally modified by it. His attitude reveals and confirms these relationships in their unchanged and unchangeable character. And the sum of these relationships is what we here understand by the creaturely essence and nature of man. Rightly this has always been taken to mean the invariable being of man as this persists through the antitheses of sin, reconciliation and redemption. It is that which always and in all circumstances belongs to the basic concept and view of man, no less in relation to his status in sin than to his status in the newly demonstrated grace of God and the final status of his eternal perfection. It is the being which according to the biblical witness is common to Jew and Gentile, to the obedient and disobedient, to apostles and Pharisees, to Peter and Judas. The Word of God instructs us concerning it to the extent that God's attitude to man as revealed and knowable in it always refers to and counts on this creaturely essence of man, so that we cannot hear this Word without being instructed concerning this creaturely essence of man as we are instructed concerning the deeds and commands of God, His threats and promises, His judgments and favours. This instruction is formally indirect because it is only incidental, because it is given us only in connexion with a very different instruction. But materially it is very direct because we cannot really receive the true and decisive instruction of the Word of God if we do not accept what it tells us incidentally about our human nature.

We have now reached the point where good reason can be seen for the most important thesis of this section: "As the man Jesus is Himself the revealing Word of God, He is the source of our knowledge of the nature of man as created by God." The attitude of God in which the faithfulness of the Creator and therefore the unchanging relationships of the human being created by Him are revealed and knowable, is quite simply His attitude and relation to the man Jesus: His election of this man; His becoming and remaining one with Him; His self-revelation, action and glorification in Him and through Him; His love addressed to Him and through Him to those who believe in Him and to the whole of creation; His freedom and sovereignty which in this man find their creaturely dwelling and form, their Bearer and Representative. He is God as even in His eternal Godhead He became this man in His human creatureliness. This is God's attitude towards sinful man. He answers or reacts to the sin of man by this relation to the man Jesus. Everything else that the biblical testimony to this divine answer and reaction discloses has at this point its beginning, centre and goal, and receives from it its light and explanation. And our hearing and reception of this testimony are true and right and clear and effective when we allow ourselves to be enlightened and instructed at this point. The Word of God is the Gospel of Jesus Christ. That is, it is the revelation of God's attitude to this man. As it reveals this, it reveals sin in its terrible gravity and judges it with supreme force, showing man that he cannot atone for it, and delivering him by assuring him in his heart that God Himself atones for it, and showing how He does this. In God's attitude to this man the decision is made that the divine grace is primary and the sin of man secondary, and that the primary factor is more powerful than the secondary. Recognising that it is made at this point, we cannot contradict the order which it establishes. We are forbidden to take sin more seriously than grace, or even as seriously as grace. At this point there is disclosed the merciful will of God, who chides and judges but cannot forget man because of his sin, who even in His wrathful judgment on his sin has not ceased to be his Creator, or to be free to justify His creature, knowing him as the being whom He created out of nothing according to His wisdom. At this point it may be seen how God sees man in spite of and through his sin, and therefore how we ourselves are incapable of seeing him. What is impossible with man but possible with God emerges at this point, namely, the vision of nature and essence which can be distorted by sin but not destroyed or transmuted into something different, because even in its sinful distortion it is held in the hand of God, and in spite of its corruption is not allowed to fall.

It would be foolish to expect this vision to be attained in any other way or to be generally accessible.

The attitude of God to sinful man, in which the order of grace and sin is present and revealed, is primarily and originally His attitude to the man Jesus alone. If God has elected any other man to Himself in spite of his sin, He has done so because primarily and originally He eternally elected this man, and in and with Him this other as a member of the body of which Jesus is the Head. If He calls others who are His enemies to fellowship, it is because He does not see and treat their sin as their own but as that of His beloved Son, whose obedience He sees and treats as theirs. If he reveals Himself to these others who have finally forfeited the possibility of knowing Him, it is because He confronts them in this man as the eternal light whose force is more than a match for their blindness. If He acts to and for others, it is in the work of this man which takes place absolutely in their place and favour. If He glorifies Himself in others, it is as this man gives them a part in His own glory. If He loves them, it is in the fact that He loves Him, and them through Him. If the freedom and lordship of His grace, which as sinners they have despised and affronted, is the kingdom in which they too may live, it is because this man, and in and with Him He Himself and therefore His kingdom, are radiantly present in their midst. Always and in every respect it is primarily and originally in this man that we see God's attitude to sinful man to be of such a kind that it maintains and discloses the interrelation of sin and grace. It would be unwise to look elsewhere to discover the interrelation of sin and grace and to become originally and basically certain of it. And it would be unwise not to look back to it continually even though subsequently and by deduction we have become aware and assured of it elsewhere as well. Nowhere but in this man is it primarily and properly established and revealed. In all other connexions, even as a general truth, it can be recognised afresh only on the basis of the special recognition of the attitude of God to this man. He is its disclosure. All other disclosures of it go back to the disclosure in Him. We must look and keep to the man

Jesus when we think we can know and assert that man, even in his sinful corruption, is held in the hand of God and in spite of that corruption is not allowed to fall. Otherwise we do not know what we are saying when we make this statement. We can make it only with a final uncertainty, threatened by the possibility that it might be quite otherwise, or that this perception might again slip from our grasp. It is by faith, and indeed by faith in the Word of God which is the Gospel of Jesus Christ, that we have to say that God is gracious to man and that man is the creature to whom God is gracious. Otherwise this is a mere religious phrase, the sound of which may perhaps for a time refresh us, but by which we cannot live.

The same applies to the view given by this perception of human nature corrupted by sin, but not destroyed nor transmuted into something different. The nature of the man Jesus alone is the key to the problem of human nature. This man is man. As certainly as God's relation to sinful man is properly and primarily His relation to this man alone, and a relation to the rest of mankind only in Him and through Him, He alone is primarily and properly man. If we were referred to a picture of human nature attained or attainable in any other way, we should always have to face the question whether what we think we see and know concerning it is not a delusion, because with our sinful eyes we cannot detect even the corruption of our nature, let alone its intrinsic character, and are therefore condemned to an unceasing confusion of the natural with the unnatural, and *vice versa*. We do not have to rely on these vague ideas, and we are not therefore condemned to this confusion, because true man, the true nature behind our corrupted nature, is not concealed but revealed in the person of Jesus, and in His nature we recognise our own, and that of every man.

But we must really keep to the human nature of Jesus. Thus we may not deviate from it, nor may we on any account rely upon, nor take for granted, what we think we know about man from other sources. We must form and maintain the conviction that the presupposition given us in and with the human nature of Jesus is exhaustive and superior to all other presuppositions, and that all other presuppositions can become possible and useful only in connexion with it.

We have thus to formulate the theological enquiry into the nature of man in the following terms. What is the creaturely nature of man to the extent that, looking to the revealed grace of God and concretely to the man Jesus, we can see in it a continuum unbroken by sin, an essence which even sin does not and cannot change ? It is the special and characteristic task of theological anthropology to consider this question. In so doing, it does not prevent other anthropological discussion. But it cannot be blocked or diverted by any other. Here lies its freedom and objectivity. Even in its investigation of human nature, its enquiries are not based on any creaturely insight into the creature. It places the contemplative and reflective reason of the creature in the service of the Creator's knowledge of the creature revealed by God's own Word. We have seen what this means. Here, too, it asks concerning the revealed grace of God, Jesus Christ, and the treasures of wisdom and knowledge concealed in Him.

But it is as well not to take this as our point of departure without a preliminary understanding of what we are undertaking and not undertaking, and within what limits we have to move as we start from this point. If we rightly consider the special difficulty of a theological anthropology, there can be no question of any other point of departure. But the choice of this point of departure means nothing more nor less than the founding of anthropology on Christology.

In so doing, we leave the traditional way, which was to try first to establish generally what human nature is, and on this basis to interpret the human nature of Jesus Christ in particular. Our whole approach to the relation between human sin and human nature has led us irresistibly in the opposite direction. Human sin excludes us from understanding human nature except by a new disclosure through the perception of divine grace addressed to man and revealing and affirming true humanity in the midst of human sin, i.e., a disclosure which is genuinely new, involving faith in the divine revelation. But if we ask where we may find an authentic revelation in this respect, we are not led to man in general but to man in particular, and in supreme particularity to the one man Jesus. Thus, contrary to the usual procedure, we must first enquire concerning this one man, and then on this basis concerning man in general. In His own person He is God's Word to men, of divine and human essence, man in immediate confrontation and union with God, and therefore true man, and the revelation of the truth about man.

Ecce homo, ἰδοὺ ὁ ἄνθρωπος (Jn. 19⁵). It is exegetically not merely legitimate but imperative to recall at this point the saying of Pilate. We cannot psychologise this as though the reference were to " the closest personal interest of the Roman in the fate of one who had so deeply moved him " (Olshausen) ; or to " his contemptuous pity " (W. Bauer) ; or as though it presented Jesus as one who " was ridiculous to some and to others innocuous " (T. Zahn). It does, of course, depict the reaction of Pilate to the appearance of Jesus in His mock regalia after His scourging : " wearing the crown of thorns, and the purple robe." But the Evangelist does not make him speak of his own unimportant feelings when confronted by this appearance, but of its theological mystery. According to Jn. 19¹⁴, when the same Pilate is finally resolved to deliver up Jesus, he will say in similar terms : ἴδε ὁ βασιλεὺς ὑμῶν. The two sayings, as Bengel has rightly remarked, belong together. Not only according to the Johannine but also according to the Synoptic tradition, Pilate is the unjust human judge who precisely as such must execute the supremely just judgment of God on Jesus. Jn. 19¹¹ : " Thou couldest have no power at all against me, except it were given thee from above " (to have such). Thus in the fine phrase of Hamann he is the *executor Novi Testamenti*. In virtue of this ἐξουσία given him from above, prophetically like Balaam, he utters these two sayings which together constitute a formal definition of the person of the One who is accused before him and condemned by him. He is the man, and He is the king of Israel. But the two phrases are not two different parts of the one definition. Each in its own way, and in explanation of the other, expresses the whole matter. " The man " of v. 5 is indeed the mock king which the soldiers unwittingly but also in a sense prophetically have made of Jesus. And " your king " of v. 11 is indeed, thanks to the unjustly just judgment of Pilate, the man who is now handed over to death. Schlatter rightly interprets the *ecce homo* of v. 5 : " Here in truth was the man who had been crowned by God with the lordship whose power consists in truth."

With what solemn pregnancy the term ἄνθρωπος could be used in other parts of the New Testament as well is shown in 1 Tim. 2⁵, where the word applied to the Mediator between God and man is not θεάνθρωπος but the obviously equivalent ἄνθρωπος Χριστὸς Ἰησοῦς. Hence it is difficult to avoid the view that the term used in Jn. 19⁵ can be anything but equivalent to a phrase which occurs about seventy times in the Synoptists, twelve times in John and sporadically in the rest of the New Testament—the phrase υἱὸς τοῦ ἀνθρώπου in its relationship to υἱὸς τοῦ θεοῦ. Even these two are not mutually exclusive and opposed, but are different aspects of one and the same definition. Both are Messianic titles and describe Jesus as the embodiment of the coming kingdom of God. In the Gospels " the Son of man " is always Jesus' description of Himself. Whether texts in which this name occurs refer to the humiliation of His passion and death or to the glory of His resurrection and future coming makes no difference to its essential meaning. The name as such means the Son of God, namely, the Son of God who as such has become man, and who as man has acted as the Son of God and proved Himself to be such. It undoubtedly goes back to the Old Testament. In the Book of Ezekiel " son of man " is the constant address of God to the prophet. But is it really only the " emphatic expression of the infinite distance between the transcendence of God and the earthly lowliness of the prophet " (H. Schmidt) ? Logically, since this lowly one is honoured by the address and the commission of the Most High, why should it not be also the expression of his extreme distinction ? This is certainly suggested by the well-known passage Dan. 7¹³ff.. " Son of man " means one who as a human son corresponds to his human father, a participant in manhood. In Daniel the Son of Man stands opposed to the animal representatives of the four world kingdoms which precede his own kingdom. But as the Son of Man he comes before the Ancient of Days as the conqueror and judge of these four beasts, and " his dominion is an everlasting dominion, which shall not pass away, and his kingdom that which shall not be destroyed." He Himself rules over the kingdom of God and is its personification. In this connexion we may recall Phil. 2⁷, where Paul says of Jesus Christ that in humbling Himself He was made in the likeness of men (ἐν ὁμοιώματι ἀνθρώπων), and was found in fashion as a man, and became obedient as such, and that therefore God highly exalted Him, and gave Him the name which is above every name. Are we to see in the description in Dan. 7 of the victory and judgment of the Son of Man on the kingdoms of this world an original Old Testament idea arising perhaps out of the complex of an eschatological interpretation of the enthronement festival ? Or do we have here, as passages in Enoch suggest, the influence of the Persian idea of the archetypal man who is to come again as world king ? We need not decide this question. Again, are we to regard the triumphant Son of Man individually as the Messiah of Israel, collectively as the elect people of Israel, or, as is quite possible according to ancient habits of mind, both the individual and collective entities together ? This, too, is a question which need not be decided. On the one hand, whether the figure springs from Persian myth or from within the Old Testament itself, the Son of Man in Daniel is a personage equipped with all the marks of the almighty action of God, embodying the kingdom of God in its victorious advent into a shaken world. " Behold, your king." On the other hand, whether the figure is understood individually or collectively, it is that of a man, not of any man, nor of humanity in general, nor of an ideal man, but a concrete Israelitish figure, similar to other concrete figures of world history, although contrasted as immeasurably superior. It is similar to them because these other figures represent human kingdoms ; those of the Babylonians, the Medes, the Persians and the

Greeks. But it is contrasted as immeasurably superior because in relation to the kingdom of the Israelite man they can be represented only as beast-kingdoms symbolised by the winged lion, the bear, the panther and the leviathan. Of this kingdom it is pregnantly true : " Behold the man."

And it is with this figure—the figure of God and the figure of concrete Israelitish man—that the Jesus of the Gospels continually identified Himself, in respect of His glorification no less than His humiliation. One and the same in both aspects, omnipotent in His impotence and impotent in His omnipotence, God given up for man to human misery, and man taken up by God into divine glory—this is the Son of Man who as such and for this reason is also the Son of God ; this is man. Jesus is man because in Him God stands in man's place, and man is one with God. Hence if we look to the Gospels it cannot possibly be said that it is far-fetched if " the man " or " the son of man " of Ps. 84f., of Paul (1 Cor. 15²⁷) and of the Epistle to the Hebrews (2⁵ff.) is equated with Jesus. How finally are we to resist the assumption that " the man " or " the son of man " of Ps. 8 is to be understood by analogy with the triumphant human figure of Dan. 7 ? In this case, we could readily understand why and in what sense the man in the Psalm is represented as far superior to the rest of creation and in Hebrews as transcending even the angels in heaven. The author of the latter would simply have developed the suggestion implicit in the fact that the Evangelists constantly place in the mouth of Jesus the formula υἱὸς τοῦ ἀνθρώπου. With his equation he has certainly not said anything different from Paul in his comparison of Jesus Christ with Adam as the second man with the first, the heavenly with the earthly, the spiritual with the fleshly (1 Cor. 15²¹⁻²², ⁴⁵⁻⁴⁹ ; Rom. 5¹²⁻²¹). There can be no doubt that everywhere in the Christ-Adam parallel as developed by Paul Christ is the One who actualised the human nature corrupted by Adam. As it fell prey to death in Adam, it was made alive in Christ (1 Cor. 15²¹⁻²²). In Paul, therefore, Christ is man, not in contrast to the fact that elsewhere He is termed the Son of God, but because He is Son of God, and expresses and demonstrates Himself as such in the fact that He is man.

Hence we may say that when the concept " man " is applied to Jesus in the New Testament it includes the concept of " God," namely, of the acting God, and His coming and insurgent kingdom. This man, this man of the people of Israel, this Messiah of Israel, this Jesus of Nazareth, is as such the Lord of lords, the King of kings, who has turned to His creature in mercy in spite of its sin, in order to save it from sin and ensuing death. Only in its application to Jesus has the term this content and scope. I need not show how elsewhere it is contrasted with that of God and has very different implications. But as applied to Jesus it has this content and direction. But if this is its implication here, the fact should not be so consistently overlooked in the discussion of the nature of man as has usually been the case in theological anthropology. We may as little ignore the pointing finger of Pilate in the doctrine of man as that of John the Baptist in the doctrine of reconciliation. His *Ecce homo* demands our full attention. For if in its application to Jesus the concept of " man " has this content and direction, if it stands here in direct relation to the concept of God, this means that in this application it is that of the truth about man ; the true concept of man ; the concept in face of which no other can stand independently or in superiority, but to which all others must be subordinated, and by which they must all be measured. Hence there arises irresistibly the demand that anthropology should be based on Christology and not the reverse. The innovation which we have to decide upon and confess at this point consists quite simply in yielding to this requirement. Hence in our exposition of the doctrine of man we must always look in the first instance at the nature of man as it confronts us in the person of Jesus, and only secondarily—asking and answering from this place of light—at the nature of man as that of every man and all other men.

2. *Man as an Object of Theological Knowledge*

In conclusion, we have to consider the problems involved in grounding anthropology on Christology and to give a first basic and general indication of the way to their solution.

For one thing, it is clear that there can be no question of a direct equation of human nature as we know it in ourselves with the human nature of Jesus, and therefore of a simple deduction of anthropology from Christology. The analysis of individual man, even and especially when undertaken in the light of God's Word, leads us to very different and indeed opposed conclusions. At this point, we can indicate these only in general outline. Human nature as it is and in ourselves is always a debatable quantity ; the human situation as we know and experience it is dialectical. We exist in antitheses which we cannot escape or see beyond. We bear various aspects none of which can be disowned. Our life has no unity. We seek it, as the various theories of man bear witness. But we only seek it. All theories of man are one-sided, and must contradict other theories and be contradicted by them. There is no undisputed and ultimately certain theory of man. At bottom there is only a theoretical search for the real man, as in practice there is only a striving to attain real humanity. The final thing is always unrest : not a genuine, pure and open unrest ; but an unrest which is obscured by a forceful interpretation or dogmatic view of man, by an exculpation and justification of his existence on the basis of this dogma ; or even more simply, an unrest which is made innocuous by conscious resignation or lack of thought. The ultimate fact about our human nature, as we shall constantly see in detail, is the self-contradiction of man, and the conscious or unconscious self-deception in which he refuses to recognise this truth. But the first thing which has to be said about human nature in Jesus is that in Him an effective protest is lodged against our self-contradiction and all the self-deception in which we try to conceal it. It is a protest because the antitheses in which we live are no antitheses in Him, and therefore do not require any attempted solution, so that in Him all illusions about the success of these attempts are quite irrelevant. And it is effective because His human nature shows us the dialectic of our situation and the hopelessness of our illusions by showing them to be the sin which in Him is no longer imputed to us but forgiven, being taken from us and removed and eliminated, like a vicious circle which is ended by Him, so that by right we can no longer move in it. The human nature of Jesus spares and forbids us our own. Thus it is our justification. And because it is this, it is the judgment on our own humanity. It is the revelation of the complete impossibility of explaining, exculpating or justifying it of ourselves, and therefore the revelation of the end of the illusion or the lack of thought in which we might hope to affirm our humanity, and the beginning of the genuine, pure and open unrest about our nature. It is clear from these considerations that when we look in these different directions, at Jesus on the one hand and ourselves and man in general on the other, we at once find ourselves in very different spheres.

But that they are different is not the final thing which is to be said about them. We cannot really look at Jesus without—in a certain sense through Him—seeing ourselves also. In Him are the peace and clarity which are not in ourselves. In Him is the human nature created by God without the self-contradiction which afflicts us and without the self-deception by which we seek to escape from this our shame. In Him is human nature without human sin. For as He the Son of God becomes man, and therefore our nature becomes His, the rent is healed, the impure becomes pure and the enslaved is freed. For although He becomes what we are, He does not do what we do, and so He is not what we are. He is man like ourselves, yet He is not a sinner, but the man who honours His creation and election by God, not breaking but keeping the covenant of grace. The good-pleasure of God rests on Him. And because of this He has power to forgive sin. What God does not find in us He finds abundantly in Him—with sufficient wealth to make up for all that lacks in us. Thus human nature in Jesus is the reason and the just foundation for the mercy in which God has turned to our human nature. Even in His mercy God is not capricious. His holiness, His faithfulness to Himself, to His Creator-will and to the obligations of the covenant of grace, suffer no disruption in the fact that He is gracious to us. He is justified in His own eyes when He justifies us sinful men. For He does this for the sake of Jesus, i.e., in view of human nature as it is in Him. Here God finds human nature blameless. This is the basis of our pardon and of the continuance of the covenant which we have broken. God does not have regard to the fact that we have broken it, but to the fact that Jesus keeps it. And His judgment on us is determined by this. And because it is determined by it, He is to us a gracious—and in His very grace a supremely just—Judge. This does not mean that our sin is overlooked, or unremoved, or unexpiated. The sinlessness, purity and freedom of human nature in Jesus consists precisely in the fact that, laden with the sin which is alien to His own nature, He causes Himself to be condemned and rejected with us. Thus the sin of our human nature is not only covered by Him but rightfully removed and destroyed. But this means that it is truly buried and covered, so that before God and in truth there now remains only the pure and free humanity of Jesus as our own humanity. This is the connexion between those very different and separated spheres. The purity, freedom, peace and clarity of the human nature of Jesus do not remain His privilege alone, but for His sake this privilege becomes ours as well. As God knows Him, He also knows us. As He knows Jesus, He also knows our nature, against which no accusation can stand because He has created it. In virtue of the exoneration from sin validly effected in Jesus, we may count on this nature of ours and its innocence as we could not otherwise do. This judicial pardon gives us the courage and shows us the way to think about man as God created him. It is the true ground of theological anthropology.

There does, of course, remain a true and abiding privilege of Jesus which is exclusive to Him in spite of our justification. We do well not to forget this. It reminds us of the reserve which is incumbent upon us if we are really to venture, on the basis of that judicial pardon, to think about man as created by God. For if our acquittal allows and commands us to recognise in human nature as it is in Jesus our own, we must not fail to appreciate how different are His nature and ours. Human nature in Him is determined by a relation between God and Himself such as has never existed between God and us, and never will exist. He alone is the Son of Man and the Son of God. Our fellowship with God rests upon the fact that He and He alone is one with God. He Himself is the living God. He in His own person is the kingdom of God. He alone is primarily and truly elected as the Head and the Lord of all the elect. If we too are elected, we are only the members of His body. He alone gives grace as well as receives it. We can only receive it. He alone can forgive sins. We can only ask for forgiveness, receiving it as grounded in Him, and imparting it as received from Him. He alone has the Spirit of God directly, as the source of His holy Spirit. We can have it only from His fulness. Thus He alone is in the true sense of the word the Representative, Instrument, Ambassador and Plenipotentiary of God in the creaturely world. He alone is the Revealer, Reconciler and Lord, the Prophet, Priest and King. In these capacities, which devolve on Him alone, we can only follow and serve Him, with no dignity or power which are not His and do not redound to His glory. Hence He alone is the Word of God. We can only hear it. What we say cannot be more than a promise and warning based on this Word. He alone can represent God before men and men before God. We can represent God and men only in so far as He is the true Mediator. It is because He is the foundation that we can build. It is because He has come and died and is risen from the dead and will come again that there is Israel and the Church, and hope for all men and all creation. These are irreversible relationships. In all these things He goes before us once for all ; not in His humanity as such, for in this respect He makes us like unto Himself ; but in the way in which He is a man, i.e., in virtue of His unique relation to God ; and in the fact that we need His humanity in order to be like Him as men. He has it immediately from God to be man in that purity and freedom and peace and clarity. We have it mediately from Him, on the ground of the judicial pardon under which we are placed for His sake. If we may use this privilege and be the servants, friends and children of God, it is for His sake, as His younger brethren, and therefore on the basis of the inequality between Him and us, in the possession and enjoyment of a gift. Without Him we would not be what we are. What we are we must always seek in Him and receive from Him. Our human nature rests upon His grace ; on the divine grace addressed to us in His human nature. It is both His and ours, but it is His in a wholly different way from that in which it is ours.

Our primary emphasis must be upon the fact that on the ground of His unique relation to God it is first His and then and only for this reason ours. It is actualised in Him as the original and in us only as the copy. Jesus is man as God willed and created him. What constitutes true human nature in us depends upon what it is in Him. The fact that natural humanity as God created it was subsequently concealed by our sinful corruption is a lesser mystery than the fact that humanity is originally hidden in Jesus, so that primarily it is His and not ours. What man is, is determined by God's immediate presence and action in this man, by His eternal election and the mighty work of His life and death and resurrection corresponding to this election. There in the eternity of the divine counsel which is the meaning and basis of all creation, and in the work of His life accomplished at the heart of time, the decision was made who and what true man is. There his constitution was fixed and sealed once and for all. For this reason it cannot be different in any other man. No man can elude this prototype. We derive wholly from Jesus not merely our potential and actual relation to God, but even our human nature as such. For it is He who, as the ground and goal of the covenant of grace planned for man, is also the ground and goal of man's creation : man as God willed him to be when He became his Creator ; and as He wills him to be when as the Creator He does not cease to be actively concerned for him. We are partakers of human nature as and because Jesus is first partaker of it. It is for this reason that it is our nature ; that it is ours unchangeably and inalienably ; that while it may be distorted and corrupted by sin, in all its degradation and corruption it cannot be cancelled or annihilated ; that in spite of sin and through the cloak of sin it can and must be recognised as ours. In Jesus both the first and the last word is spoken about us, and the last with all the power of the first. In his relation to God a man may become a sinner and thus distort and corrupt his own nature, but he cannot revoke what was decided in Jesus apart from him concerning the true nature of man. By his fall he can deny his Creator and his own creaturely nature. But he cannot make it a lie. What he is, is decided elsewhere in such a way that he cannot affect the decision. And if Jesus forgives his sins and restores his spoiled relation to God, this means that Jesus again controls what originally belongs to Him ; that again He takes to Himself what was never lost to Him. In so doing, He merely restores in human nature that which originally corresponds to Him, is like Him, and is constituted in Him. He has the freedom and power to do this. He has only to apply them. And

He does just that by making Himself our Saviour. It is with the freedom and power of the Creator that He is also our Saviour. It is His own property, His own house, which He sets in order as such. But to say this is to say that we participate in the true nature of man only because He does so first and that our recognition of this true nature can be effective only in so far as we recognise it in Him, not hearing or accepting as the first word in this matter any other *logos* of supposed humanity, but only Him.

That human nature is one thing in Him and another in us means secondly that in Him it is not distorted by sin and therefore concealed in its reality, but maintained and preserved in its original essence. The second difference to be noted at this point consists, therefore, in the sinlessness of Jesus. This again can be understood only in the light of the unique relationship to God which was His by right. It does not consist, therefore, in any special quality of His humanity by which He is as it were physically incapable of sin. If His relation to God is originally and utterly different from our own, His human nature as such is not different from our own, and does not simply exclude the possibility of the corruption to which it has fallen victim in us. He, too, was tempted as we are. What protects Him and His human nature from temptation is not a particularity of His creatureliness but the particularity of the way in which He is creature. He is so as the Son of God, and therefore as the Creator and Lord. It is the eternal mercy of God which is a human person in Him ; the mercy with which God is so far from abandoning creation to itself that He wills to impart to it nothing less than His own immediate personal presence and action, nothing less than Himself. Again, we are confronted by the basis and goal of the divine covenant of grace which is also the basis and goal of creation. What protects Him from sin, and keeps His human nature from corruption, is the eternal mercy of God which refuses to be limited and suspended, but wills to maintain itself in vulnerable human nature. It is the fact that " God so loved the world, that he gave his only begotten Son," and that Jesus is this Son. Even in Him human nature would not have been capable of this of itself. Even in the person of Jesus it might have become a prey to the corruption which was its fate in us. For even in Him it is still creaturely, not creative and divine, and therefore not precluded from sin, as we should have to say of the creative nature of God itself. It is for this reason that in various places the New Testament speaks very plainly of the liability of Jesus to temptation, and of the temptation which He had actually to face. But He could not succumb, and therefore could not sin, because as the Bearer of humanity He was Himself its Lord, the Creator God active within it. He asserted Himself against temptation with the freedom and power with which God as Creator confronted chaos, separating light from darkness and uttering His Yes to the real and

His definitive No to the unreal. The fact that even and precisely in becoming man God remained true to Himself, true to His mercy to creation, is the secret of the sinlessness of Jesus and therefore of the maintenance of human nature in Him. He delivered it when it could not save itself. There is therefore a deliverance and preservation of human nature as created by God. Hence we cannot in any circumstances understand its distortion and corruption as a natural necessity. Sin is powerless against the faithfulness with which God the Creator is merciful to us. By the fact that He Himself came amongst us, this impossibility was made impossible, as is only right. The same human nature as ours can be sinless on the assumption that God takes up its case. This assumption was realised in the human nature of Jesus. We cannot consider Him without accepting this. Nor, of course, can we accept the assumption without considering Jesus. In our own humanity as such we cannot find any evidence for it. Of this nature we cannot say either that in some hidden depths it is sinless or that it has in some way the power to be sinless. Sinlessness and the power to be sinless are divine qualities. In the creaturely world they are to be seen only in the work which was accomplished in Jesus, and which could be accomplished only in Him, because that assumption was fulfilled in Him, and only in Him.

The third point in which Jesus is the same as us, but very differently in virtue of His unique relationship to God, is simply that in Him human nature is not concealed but revealed in its original and basic form. It is not intrinsic to it to be hidden from us, just as it is not intrinsic to God to be hidden from us. What is real requires no secrecy, and is incapable of it. Essentially, neither the Creator nor the creature is absolutely hidden from us, but strictly speaking only evil, only the darkness which was rejected by God and separated from the light. Divinely created human nature as such is not evil, and therefore essentially it cannot be completely hidden from us. It is the good creature of God, and as such can only be manifest to us. The creature becomes unknowable and unrecognisable only when it is distorted and ruined by sin. In us the real creature is of course unknowable. In us it cannot express itself. Thus of ourselves we do not know what we really are. In respect of self-knowledge we grope no less blindly in the dark than in respect of our knowledge of God. But it is not necessarily so. When God Himself takes the initiative in the creature—and this is what has taken place in Jesus— then the creature also begins to speak ; it becomes manifest to us ; it becomes itself a word. Then the Creator who has become one with His creature speaks of it as well as Himself, and He speaks the truth in both respects. Thus the incarnate Word of God, Jesus Christ, is really the true Word about man as well as God, and about the nature of man. It needed Jesus for the latter to become knowable and known. As it is real in Him first and only then and for this reason in

us, it can only become true for us, i.e., revealed and manifest, through
Him. Through Him ! It is not that we interpret Him, but that He
discloses and explains Himself to us, that through and in Himself
He manifests His nature to us as our own true nature. Hence there
is revelation in this respect also ; the revelation of God which as such
is also the revelation of true man. It is also as such God's own irreplaceable action. This action was performed in Jesus. Here again
we cannot try to stand by His side, nor to anticipate Him, nor to
compete with Him. It is either through Him that we know what we
truly are as men, or we do not know it at all. Our self-knowledge
can only be an act of discipleship. But as an act of discipleship it
can be a true and established and certain knowledge.

These are the limits which theological anthropology cannot exceed.
In its investigation of the nature of man in general, it must first look
away from man in general and concentrate on the one man Jesus, and
only then look back from Him to man in general. If it keeps within
these limits, but also makes use of the possibilities offered within
these limits, it is differentiated from all other forms of human self-
knowledge. In spite of every difference—and this point must be
emphasised again and no less strongly—we share the same nature
with Jesus. If His relation to God is other than our own, and if as a
result human nature is His in a different way from that in which it
is ours, yet it is the same both in Him and us. The threefold fact
that it is first in Him, that in Him it is kept and maintained in
its purity, and that it is manifest in Him, implies a different status
but not a different constitution of His human nature from ours. All
the otherness to be noted here is rooted in the fact that as man He
is also God, and as creature Creator. But this does not mean an
intrinsic otherness of His humanity and creatureliness. Jesus is not
an angel. He is not an intermediate being, a third entity between
God and man. He is both true God and true man. And " true "
does not mean only that He is man as God created him, but also
that He is this as we all are, and that He is therefore accessible and
knowable to us as man, with no special capacities or potentialities,
with no admixture of a quality alien to us, with no supernatural endowment such as must make Him a totally different being from us.
He is man in such a way that He can be the natural Brother of any
other man. And this likeness between Him and us is the other presupposition which is as much actualised and noteworthy in Him as
the presupposition which we have expressed as a threefold dissimilarity.
That Jesus is utterly unlike us as God and utterly like us as man is the
twofold fact which constitutes the whole secret of His person. If
in one respect there were not complete and strict likeness, all that
which on the other side stands only in virtue of His unlikeness to us
would collapse. If the election of Jesus were not the election of true
man even in this sense, how could others realise that they were elected

in Him ?   How could He be the goal and the fulfilment of the covenant
of God with men, the Messiah of a human Israel, the Lord of a human
Church ?   How could the good-pleasure of God for His sake rest on
other men too ?   How could He represent us to God and God to us ?
How could the forgiveness of sins take place in Him and the promise
and law of a new life be established by Him ?   How could men come
to believe in Him, and through belief in Him come to know themselves as the children of God and fellow-recipients of the grace of God
disclosed in Him ?   In this event we could not be the body of which
He is the Head.   We would be creatures of a very different order,
and there could be no communion between Him and us.   It would be
quite impossible to recognise in Him the reality of human nature.
There would be no theological knowledge in this matter—and of
course no knowledge of the relation of God to man—because the
relation between God and man would remain hidden from us, and
therefore finally there would be no theological knowledge at all.
But there is no foundation for this hypothesis.

We should be thinking on Manichean or Marcionite lines in respect of sin,
and docetically in Christology, if we proposed to ascribe to human nature as it
exists in us and in Jesus a difference of constitution.   And perhaps it is because
of a remaining trace of Docetism, which the Church has failed to eliminate in
spite of its formal rejection, that our appreciation of the bearing of the divine
election effected in Jesus Christ, the institution of the covenant fulfilled in Him,
and the reconciliation accomplished in Him, has been so small that it still strikes
us as strange that in Jesus Christ we should have to do not only with the order
and the revelation of the redeeming grace of God the Creator, but also with the
order and revelation of the creature, and therefore of the truth of man.

In this regard the one presupposition is as firm as the other.   The
man Jesus is one nature with us, and we unreservedly with Him.
But this means that we are invited to infer from His human nature
the character of our own, to know ourselves in Him, but in Him
really to know *ourselves*.   When the New Testament speaks of the
Son of God it speaks without any kind of qualification of One who is
a man as we are.   All the extraordinary things that it says of this
man are just as radically meant as said against this background, and
they resist any dilution or distortion into more innocuous statements.
It declares His likeness to all other men no less precisely than it
declares His unlikeness to them all.   Not for a moment shall we lose
sight of His unlikeness to them all.   But this is the very reason why
His likeness to them all is so real, the light in which this likeness is
disclosed.   And we take seriously the likeness between Jesus and
ourselves as grounded and revealed in this way if we now attempt
to press on to an understanding of human nature as such on the
presupposition of the validity of the humanity of Jesus for the question
which mainly concerns us.

§ 44

MAN AS THE CREATURE OF GOD

The being of man is the history which shows how one of God's creatures, elected and called by God, is caught up in personal responsibility before Him and proves itself capable of fulfilling it.

1. JESUS, MAN FOR GOD

In this section we ask concerning the outline and form of our object, its character and limits, and therefore the special characteristics by which it is distinguished from other objects. In this first and comprehensive sense, we ask concerning the whole being and nature of man. Who or what is meant when we speak of man, not referring to God but to a creature of God, yet to this particular creature among all others? Which of the many realities distinct from God are we considering? In the first place, we pose the question from without—on the assumption that besides man there are many other realities distinct from God, many other creatures. To this extent we look back again to the first part of our investigation, to man in the cosmos. Who and what is man within the cosmos? On the basis of the conclusions reached we shall then have to consider and explain his being and nature as it were from within—his inner relation to God as the image of God, and in this relationship his humanity as such, man as the soul of his body, and finally man in his time. It is clear that even at this point we must keep all these later problems in view. For the moment, however, they will not concern us explicitly. Our present concern is with the problem itself which will then be developed in detail in these various problems. We are thus concerned only with the outline or form of man.

Even in this field we must desist from any attempt to give a direct answer to the anthropological question, and apply the christological basis of anthropology.

If in this question of the nature of man we look to the man Jesus as directly or indirectly attested in Holy Scripture, one answer which immediately presents itself is that the nature of man is to be observed and established in its history as determined by Him, in its continuous progress as resolved and executed by Him, through a series of conditions, actions, experiences, in the recurrence and confirmation of its identity through all these active modifications of its being. Who is Jesus? What is His humanity? The statements which Scripture makes concerning Him, the predicates which it applies to Him, the whole significance which it ascribes to Him—all these refer to His being as it is reaffirmed and expressed under specific and changing conditions. According to these statements He is wholly and utterly who and what He is in the continuity of this history.

" He is made unto us wisdom, and righteousness, and sanctification, and redemption," Paul writes of Christ in 1 Cor. 1[30]. On the biblical understanding none of these terms denotes an idea, but they all refer to a history. In the same connexion it is no less significant that in John 14[6] Jesus speaks of Himself primarily and predominantly as the Way : not as the beginning or end of the Way ; but as the Way itself. But even the self-descriptions which follow and explain this point in the same direction, viz. the Truth and the Life. In the Gospel of St. John ἀλήθεια does not mean the truth which is static, but the truth which imparts itself and discloses itself to others ; and ζωή does not mean the life which is self-sufficient but the life which imparts itself and redeems from death. And the other Johannine passages in which Jesus describes Himself as the Light, the Door, the Bread, the Shepherd, the Vine and the resurrection, point to pure process, to a being which is caught up in its products, so that it is impossible to distinguish between this being as such and its products, or to seek and find this being in itself or apart from these products, but only in them. Eduard Schweizer (*Ego Eimi* . . . 1939) has shown that the Johannine Jesus does not simply compare Himself with these things in these so-called metaphorical sayings, but describes Himself as the true and proper object of all these conceptions, as the only legitimate bearer of all these titles, as the real subject of all these predicates, in opposition to the mistaken opinions of the naturally religious man ; that they are all to be understood as pure self-attestations on the part of Jesus. This insight must be taken seriously. When Jesus points to His own person He points to the Way which is as such the Truth and the Life, to the true Light, to the one Door, to the heavenly Bread, to the faithful Shepherd. Hence in all these sentences " I am " means that My being and nature consists in what is suggested by all these words, concepts, titles and names. I am as I exist in the mode thus indicated. What we must note in these statements is first that He alone and no other is the Subject of these predicates; second that in Him alone these predicates rightfully find their full meaning and propriety ; and third (our present concern) that who and what He is, He is in these predicates. Because in all these predicates it is a question of actions, of a history viewed from different angles, He is what He is in these actions, in this history. He is Himself what takes place as described in these predicates. He is the One who is to come, who has come and who will come. From whatever angle He is regarded, He is the One who comes. Hence He does not stand as Subject some where behind or alongside this coming ; He is Subject as this coming takes place. The fact that He is Subject, and what He is as such, can be known only with reference in the light of this coming of His, and can be made known only by reference to it.

Jesus is wholly and utterly the Bearer of an office. Hence He is not first man and then the Bearer of this office, so that it might be possible to conceive of Him apart from this office, or as perhaps the Bearer of a very different office. On the contrary, He is man as He is the Bearer of this office. He is, as He is engaged in the fulfilment of it, in the exercise of its functions, in the claiming of its privileges and in the carrying out of its obligations. There is no neutral humanity in Jesus, which might give Him the choice of not doing what He does, or of doing something different in its place. He is, as He is active in a specific, and always in the same, direction.

He is always at work (ἐργαζόμενος), even on the Sabbath, as He confirms in Jn. 5[17] to the Jews who accuse Him. He must work as long as it is day (Jn. 9[4]). In this respect there is in the New Testament no " not yet," or " not quite," or " no longer." As we know it is almost completely silent about the thirty years or so (Lk. 3[23]) of the life of Jesus before His appearance in Galilee. Even the single exception, the story of Lk. 2[41ff.] about the twelve-year-old boy who remains behind in the temple and is found " in the midst of the doctors, both hearing them and asking them questions " (v. 46), certainly does not mean that He was not yet the Messiah, Prophet, Priest and King, that He had not yet begun His ministry, that He received and entered upon His office only with His baptism in Jordan. His saying about the necessity of His being about His father's business (v. 49) is something which is not understood by His parents (v. 50), and refers already to His mission. And the remark in v. 51 that in Nazareth Jesus was subject to His parents, is certainly not intended to interest readers in the fact that before His public ministry He was a carpenter in Nazareth. This whole incident describes how He grows up into His office, His προκόπτειν (v. 52), but without calling in question what is said at the beginning of the chapter (v. 11), that He was born as Σωτήρ, Χριστὸς and Κύριος. Thus He cannot have become this at the baptism of John. All the three accounts of His baptism speak also of a visible and audible manifestation of His office, but not of His appointment to this office or equipment for it. Again, the descent of the Spirit upon Him like a dove does not mean that He received the Spirit for the first time, but in the words of Jn. 1[33] : " Upon whom thou shalt see the Spirit descending, and remaining on him, the same is he which baptiseth with the Holy Ghost." And at least in Mt. 3[14] it is expressly stated that the Baptist recognised Jesus before His baptism, and on that account would have preferred not to baptise Him ; and in v. 15, that Jesus' subjection of Himself to the baptism of repentance along with the people was intended to be a fulfilment of all righteousness, and thus an anticipation of the baptism (Mt. 20[22f.]) with which He was to be baptised by the giving of His life as a ransom for many. Even less do the Evangelists envisage anything in the nature of a " conversion " of Jesus. All that Jesus might have been outside His office, or apart from its exercise, does not concern them. The remarkable saying of Paul in 2 Cor. 5[16] : " Yea, though we have known Christ after the flesh, yet now henceforth know we him no more," might have been uttered in the name of all four Evangelists. Even in the mouth of Paul it certainly cannot have meant that we are no longer concerned about the fact that Jesus was obviously a man. Even Paul could not have been uninterested in the Christ who according to him too was crucified and rose again as man. But the four Evangelists were not concerned about anything that this man may have been and done apart from His office as the Christ. If they had known this man in this respect (" after the flesh "), they knew Him so no more. They knew Him according to what they could testify of Him in their witness, i.e., only in this very different respect ; only in and not apart from His work. Even when they say of Him that He was hungry and thirsty, that He ate and drank, that He was tired and rested and slept, that he loved and sorrowed, was angry and even wept, they touch upon accompanying circumstances in which we cannot detect a personality with its characteristic concerns and inclinations and affections independently of its work. Nowhere are we invited to compose from these indications a physical picture or even a character study of Jesus. Where necessary, these features accompany the description of His work, and it is always in the latter and never in the former— or in the former only in so far as they bear on the latter—that He Himself is recognisable and is really this man for the Evangelists. And it would be even more arbitrary if from the fact that Jesus was tempted and that He prayed, and that especially in the prayer of Gethsemane He questioned if He also reaffirmed His presupposed obedience to the will of the Father, we were to conclude that the Evangelists were alluding to interruptions of His work which had to be overcome. The Jesus who is tempted and prays is also—precisely and particularly —the Jesus engaged in His office and work. His work does not suffer any interruption. His history is not broken off, as it cannot begin or end anywhere outside. Even the titles Χριστός and Κύριος which the New Testament gives this man, say who He is by telling what He does. The only non-historical element which seems to remain is the proper name Ἰησοῦς. But this corresponds to the Old Testament Joshua, i.e., Yahweh saves. Hence it too tells a story, and it forms a fitting heading to the whole.

It would be extremely foolish to draw from all this docetic consequences, as though this Jesus whose being consists wholly in His work and history were not a real man. There is no doubt that He is a real man. He is born of a human mother ; He lives and works as a man ; He sees and hears as a man ; He speaks in human language ; He suffers and dies as a man. And if the four Evangelists conclude with the account of His resurrection, and if in the light of this all the New Testament witnesses look to Him as the One who sits at the right hand of God and will come again from the heaven to which He has ascended, this does not mean that they have ceased to think of the real man Jesus. But the real man Jesus is the working Jesus. They seem never to have thought of a human being beyond history or prior to history, or hidden from and transcending history, when they thought of the real man Jesus. They always found the real man Jesus in His work and history. It is not the mere fact that He is born as a man, that He speaks and therefore that He can obviously speak and think and perceive as a man, or that He suffers and dies as a man, which makes Him a real man as they see it. It is the fact that He is born as the Saviour, that He speaks words of salvation, and that He has therefore the thoughts of the Saviour and that He suffers death as the Saviour. To be sure, it is as the Son of God that He is empowered to act in all this as the Saviour. But this means that with His saving work He is empowered to be a real man. He is not a real man in spite but because of the fact that He is the Son of God and therefore acts as the Saviour. For this reason He remains a real man even in His resurrection and ascension and session at the right hand of God, and it is as real man that He will come again. No Christian of the apostolic age thought otherwise. Hence He is always to be identified with His history. He is always engaged in His office and work as Prophet, Priest and King, as the Evangelists describe Him. Where can we find any essence or quality in which He is not yet or no longer the Saviour ? What point can we name from which He might equally well be the Saviour or not ? And could such a neutral point indicate the true humanity of the true Son of God ?

The New Testament knows no such neutral point. Whether it looks back to Jesus or upwards to Him or forwards to Him, it knows only the One who was, is and will be the Saviour, and therefore it knows this man only in His work and history. And it is in this capacity that it knows Him as a real man.

The question may be asked whether He was not then a person like other human persons. Was He not a soul and had He not a body like them? Did He not live as a man with other men and with the same humanity as ourselves? Did He not have His time as we do? Even in relation to Him, therefore, do we not have to take account of a universal humanity? Indeed we do, but not a humanity prior to or outside His earthly history in which He was participant in this history under specific limitations and conditions; not a neutral humanity in which He might have had quite a different history; not a humanity which we can seek and analyse in abstraction from or otherwise than in His work. These are conceptions of the humanity of Jesus which the New Testament not only does not encourage but forbids us to entertain. For if it is true that even in Jesus human nature has specific modes and features in which it is also our humanity, yet even more and primarily we must have regard to the fact that it is His nature—the human nature of the Son of God. He is a human person. He is the human soul of a human body. He is a man among men and in humanity. He has a time; His time. It is not the case, however, that He must partake of humanity. On the contrary, humanity must partake of Him. It is not the case, then, that He is subject to these specific determinations and features of humanity. It is not that He is conditioned and limited by them, but in so far as humanity is His it is He who transcends and therefore limits and conditions these features and determinations. As the nature of Jesus, human nature with all its possibilities is not a presupposition which is valid for Him too and controls and explains Him, but His being as a man is as such that which posits and therefore reveals and explains human nature with all its possibilities. But His being as a man is the whole of His action, suffering and achievement. His being as a man is His work. In this His work He has a human nature; He is a person, the soul of a body, man among men and in humanity; He has time. And it is not possible for us to know in advance what all this is and means; it is revealed in Him and therefore in His work. It is real and knowable only in relation to Him. Hence it cannot be known ontically or noetically as a neutral point. It is to be explained by Him, not He by it. It is revealed in His light, and not *vice versa*. The nature of human possibilities rests upon and is knowable by the fact that they are realised in Him. We therefore reckon with the fact that even in Him humanity has specific determinations and features in which it is also ours. But what these determinations and features are, and of what nature they are, is grounded in Him, and therefore in

His work, and must therefore be investigated with reference to Him, and therefore to His work.

But we can clearly grasp this only when we consider the character and content of the history in which the humanity of Jesus is actualised. The formula that Jesus does not merely have a history but is Himself this history, that He not only does but is His work, may sound harsh and repulsive if we do not perceive what are the history and work in question. We have already had to anticipate the decisive definition. The work with which we have to do is the absolutely unique work of the Saviour, resolved and accomplished by Him alone. What Jesus does, and therefore is, is this work, which cannot be interchanged with any other, and can be His work alone. Not any work but this work is the object with which we find the New Testament witnesses exclusively concerned and with which they obviously wish to see their readers and hearers exclusively concerned as well.

Not that something agreeable happens, but that Yahweh saves, is the implication of the name Jesus. The other titles applied to Him point in the same direction. He is the Messiah who delivers Israel, and the Son of Man who triumphs over the beast-kingdoms. The self-designations of Jesus mentioned in John have the same reference. " Great joy shall be to all (the holy) people," is declared to the shepherds in Lk. 2[10] when they are told of the birth of Jesus. " He hath holpen his servant Israel, in remembrance of his mercy ; as he spake to our fathers, to Abraham, and to his seed for ever " (Lk. 1[54ff.]). It is with this particular intention that He was to come, and came and will come again. The statements of Jesus Himself about the purpose of His coming are in this respect particularly illuminating. He has come as a light into the world in order that no one who believes in Him should remain in darkness (Jn. 12[46]). He was born and came into the world to bear witness to the truth (Jn. 18[37]). He came to do so not merely in one but in many places (Mk. 1[38]). He did not come to destroy the Law and the prophets but to fulfil them (Mt. 5[17]). He did not come to be ministered unto, but to minister, and to give His life a ransom for many (Mt. 20[28]). In so doing, and as a further consequence of His coming, He will kindle a fire on the earth (Lk. 12[49]). Fire here undoubtedly means the same as in Mt. 10[34ff.], Lk. 12[51ff.], where we are told that He came not to bring peace but a sword, i.e., διαμερισμός, a certain necessary division even between men who otherwise stand closest together. " For judgment I am come into this world," says Jesus at the climax of the story of the healing and confession of faith of the blind man (Jn. 9[39]). Who stands to the right and the left of the Judge ? The good and the bad ? No, but the unseeing who see on the one side and the seeing who become blind on the other ; sinners as those who are called, and the righteous as those who are not called (Mt. 9[13]). This is the differentiation effected in the presence of Jesus. This is the division made, the fire kindled, when He comes to fulfil the Law and the prophets and to give His life for many. But the real purpose of His coming is not attained with this division. All these texts clearly point only to a temporary though necessary transition. Human roles are radically reversed when He comes. The first shall be last and the last first. But this is not the essential aim of His coming. Hence Jn. 12[47] : " I came not to judge the world, but to save the world." That Jesus comes to bring about the ruin of any man is a thought which is wholly foreign to the New Testament. His coming brings destruction to the demons and only to the demons (Mk. 1[24]). " The Son of man is come to seek and to save that which was lost " (Lk. 19[10]) ; and even more emphatically : " I am come that they

might have life, and that they might have it more abundantly" (Jn. 10¹⁰).
Salvation and life is what Jesus effects by fulfilling the Law and giving His life
for many. It is as He does this that He becomes the Judge ; for His intervention
on behalf of all exalts the lowly and humbles the proud. It is as He does this
that He destroys the demons and becomes the promise of the world. And the
promise which is the meaning of His whole action, is salvation and life. " Unto
you is born this day . . . the Σωτήρ" (Lk. 2¹¹). In the Pauline corpus this title,
which was known at the time in other connexions, is applied to Jesus only in
Phil. 3²⁰, Eph 5²³ and the Pastoral Epistles. It seems on the whole to belong to
the later elements of New Testament witness. But it is easy to see that in a
comprehensive retrospect it necessarily forced itself upon the community of the
apostolic age, since everything that Jesus had done and effected could be
compressed into the terms σώζειν and σωτηρία, and finally into the personal
name Σωτήρ.

Only of this saving work can we say what must be said of Jesus—
that His work itself is one with His active person, and therefore that
He the doer and His deed are indissolubly one. Of Jesus this must
be said. For the work of Jesus is the work of the Saviour. And the
saving work which brings deliverance and life consist materially in the
fact that He gives Himself. We may not and must not understand
by the title Saviour only the death in which He consummates the
self-devotion of His life, but His whole existence. He is the Saviour,
and is born as such, in the fact that He is for the many, for the world.
We will return later to the significance of the fact that He is only as
He lives for the many, for the world. The point which interests us
here is that we cannot separate His person from His work, if only for
the reason that it is in His person, because He gives nothing more
nor less than Himself, that He accomplishes His work. He does not
become the Saviour with something alien to Himself, but with His
person, and not with a part of Himself but through His whole person.
Whatever He is as man He is in this work of His. For this reason
we cannot separate His person from His work—as should now be
clearer. How could He be the Saviour accomplishing this work—
the work of self-sacrifice with which He brings life and salvation to
the world—if He existed otherwise than in His work, or were to be
sought and found elsewhere than in His work ?

It is clear—we may remark in passing—that an important christological
distinction customary in the orthodox dogmatics of the schools is seriously
challenged by this fact. The usual procedure is to treat in two separate chapters
De persona Christi θεανθρώπου and *De officio Christi mediatorio*. The distinction
between *persona* and *officium* (who is He ? and what does He do ?) is logically
correct and apparently unavoidable. But its application to this *persona* and
this *officium* is impossible if it entails a real division rather than one made for
the purposes of exposition. Orthodox dogmatics, however, could only act as if
this were a real distinction. When it spoke of the divine-human person of
Christ, it had to postulate this formally as the presupposition of His work :
θεάνθρωπος *hoc est Deus et homo in una persona esse debuit, ut mediatorem inter
Deum et nos agere possit* (J. Wolleb, *Christ. Theol. Comp*, I, *cap*. 16, 13). And
when it spoke of the work of Christ the Mediator, it had to recognise : *Subiectum*

eius non solum est totus Christus, sed et totum Christi estque mediator secundum utramque naturam, necessarily affirming that it began with His anointing by the Holy Ghost in the womb, and therefore with His incarnation as the beginning of His divine-human existence (J. Wolleb, *ib., cap.* 17, 4 and 6). In fact, this *persona* stands from the very first and wholly in this *officium,* and this *officium* is fulfilled in the mere fact that this *persona* is present. It is in this way—commensurate on both sides with the reality—that the New Testament speaks of Jesus Christ. Where there is a schematic division, however, the necessary consequence is that the mystery of the person of Christ is undervalued because the manner and scope of His work are not perceived directly, and conversely that His work is not understood because the point is missed that it has to be estimated as the work of this person.

But we have not yet touched on the decisive point, which we must now isolate and emphasise in and for itself. As the New Testament witnesses saw it, what conferred on the saving work of the man Jesus the character of an absolutely unique action, resolved and effected by Him alone, was quite simply that, while they did not doubt His true and genuine humanity, they had to regard it directly as God's own work. We cannot say that Jesus did not act in His own right, but in the name of another, namely God. We can describe the work of the prophets and apostles in this way. The position in regard to Jesus is both more complicated and more simple. He acts in the name of God, and therefore in His own name. He is distinguished from the prophets and apostles in the same way as He is distinguished from the most faithful of God's servants, namely, by the fact that He acts in His own cause as He acts in that of God. The saving work of deliverance and life is really the affair of God. Whose else could it be ? What other being could have the mind or presumption or power to do this work ? In what spirit but the Holy Spirit could the will to do so be born ? In what power but the power of God could it be achieved ? Only He who has created it can save that which is lost. When Jesus performs this work, God is revealed in Him. God acts as Jesus acts. The divine work is accomplished in the work of this man. And the work of this man consists in the abandonment of all other work to do the work of God.

The necessary interpretation of the name of Jesus may now be concluded with an emphasising of the Subject. " Jesus " means : " Yahweh saves." No other can render the help that Jesus renders. It is the work of Yahweh alone. For this is total help. It spells deliverance. Thus the scribes in the story of the sick of the palsy are quite right when they say in their hearts (Mk. 2⁷) : " Who can forgive sins but God only ? " Similarly, the man born blind argues rightly when he observes (Jn. 9³³) : " If this man were not of God, he could do nothing " (of what He is doing). Again, the witnesses of the resurrection of the young man of Nain (Lk. 7¹⁶) are on the right track when they—ἔλαβεν δὲ φόβος πάντας —gave God the glory under the impression that a great prophet had arisen among them and that God had visited His people. And the confession of Thomas : ὁ κυριός μου καὶ ὁ θεός μου (Jn. 20²⁸), is not so completely isolated as might at first sight appear. In the Gospel of John we are given a good deal of enlightenment as to how all this is to be interpreted. What does Jesus do ? He can do nothing " of himself " (Jn. 5¹⁹, ³⁰, 12⁴⁹). He cannot speak " of himself " (7¹⁷, 12⁴⁹, 14¹⁰). Never in any event, therefore, does He seek or do His own will (5³⁰, 6³⁸). Why not ? Because there is One who, as we are repeatedly told, has sent Him ; the Father. He is the Son of this Father. And so He says quite expressly : " He is greater than I " (14²⁸). It is because He is the One whom this Father of His has sent, because He has not come of Himself (8⁴²), that He can do nothing of Himself, that He cannot speak of Himself, and that He never in any event seeks or does His own will. There is no " own," no " of Himself," no neutral sphere, from which things might be sought or said or done as from the seat of a will distinct from that of His Father. But what then does He seek, say and do ? He does His works by the command and authority and in the name of His Father (10²⁵). And this is amplified as follows : He sees the Father do something—for the Father also works (5¹⁷)—and what the Father does the Son does in like manner (ὁμοίως, 5¹⁹). And He speaks what He has heard from His Father (8²⁶). What the Father has commanded Him, that He does (14³¹). He keeps the Father's commandments, as it is simply put in 12⁴⁹ and 15¹⁰. Or, He does what pleases the Father (8²⁹). And in all this He acts as the Revealer of the Father who has sent Him. He declares the name of the Father ; the name in which He speaks (17⁶, ²⁶). But as He does this He is not alone (8¹⁶, ²⁹). He does—and more immediate relations emerge at this point—the works which the Father has given Him to accomplish and fulfil (5³⁶, 17⁴). Given ! Thus the similarity of His work with that of the Father must be taken seriously. If it is really parallel to the work of the Father, if He really works ὁμοίως what He sees the Father work, there can be no possible dualism. The works done by the Son are those of the Father Himself, of the One who has sent Him, for the Father has given Him these works to accomplish in the Father's name and for the manifestation of this name (9⁴, 10³⁷). The converse is also true. Because the Father dwells in Him, the Son, it is the Father who performs the works through Him (14¹⁰). Thus the Son is not really alone in His action, but He who sent Him is with Him (8²⁹). Hence He is always one of two : ἐγὼ καὶ ὁ πέμψας με (8¹⁶). The things of the Father are also His, as His things are only those of the Father (16¹⁵, 17¹⁰). He is not alone, but always one of two ? There is more to it than that. He is in the Father, and the Father in Him (10³⁸, 14¹⁰, 20¹⁷, 21²³). This is the penultimate word. But the ultimate word is simply : " I and the Father are one " (10³⁰, 17¹¹, ²²). This finally explains the confession of Thomas. If Jesus is the Son, and as such one with the Father from whom He comes and to whom He goes, then He is, no less than the Father, ὁ κύριος and ὁ θεός. The name ὁ κύριος is then to be interpreted by the concept ὁ θεός. Hence it can be said : " He that hath seen me hath seen the Father " (14⁹, 12⁴⁵) ; " He that honoureth me honoureth the Father " (5²³) ; " He that hateth me hateth my Father also " (15²³) ; " He that believeth on me, believeth not on me, but on him that sent me " (12⁴⁴). And on this ground Jesus did not hesitate to adopt the absolute ἐγώ εἰμι — spoken without predicate—of the Old Testament God (8²⁴, ⁵⁸, 13¹⁹). In the sense of Deut. 32³⁹, and also in the sense of these Johannine texts, the implication is : " I am He who alone can help." He thus described and claimed as His own the δόξα reserved only for God (2¹¹, 9, 16, 11⁴⁰), as is affirmed by the Prologue : " We beheld his glory " (1¹⁴).

The work of this man consists in His doing the work of God to the exclusion of all other works. And to be one with God in the accomplishment of this work is the being of this man to the exclusion of all other being. Hence the doing of the work of God does not mean for Jesus anything alien, anything imposed upon Him from without, anything added later to His own activity and thus limiting and supplanting it. He does not become estranged from Himself by the fact that in doing this work He is one with God, and in this oneness of being with God—to the exclusion of all other being—He has His own being. He would not be accomplishing His own work, but would become alien and unfaithful to Himself, if He were to do any other but the work of God. And it would not be His own but an alien being which did not consist in His oneness of being with God. He is Himself as He does the work of God and in so doing is one with God. Hence the fact that He does the work of God, and in so doing is one with God, does not mean that He Himself—the man as such—is subsumed in the process. On the contrary, it is in this way, in the doing of the work of God, and therefore in His oneness of being with God, that He is Himself, this man. It is in this way that He exists as a creature, which cannot be dissolved in its Creator, which cannot itself be or become the Creator, but which has its own reality and worth in face of the Creator, deriving its own righteousness from the Creator. It is in this way that the man Jesus—not although but because He is the Son of God—is the creature of God which, by fulfilling the will and doing the work of the Creator, and being one with Him, does not lose its existence as a creature. On the contrary, what it means when we say that God is loyal to His creature is revealed by this very fact. Jesus as a creature finds life and nourishment in the fact that He stands in this relation to the Creator. In this way He is a real creature. His glory consists in the fact that He stands so utterly in the service of God, and in this devotion He reveals His own true righteousness, the righteousness with which He is endowed by His Creator. Who and what man is, is manifest in its fullest significance in the fact that the Son of God has become man in Jesus, and that man is placed so wholly at the disposal of God in Him. It is in this that He is real man, and may be known in His reality.

In this respect, too, the Christology of John's Gospel is instructive. No ἐγώ εἰμι affects but each ἐγώ εἰμι confirms the truth that the One who speaks is a real man who as such is a creature not Creator. Because the living Father has sent Him, Jesus Himself also lives by the Father (Jn. 6⁵⁷). And " as the Father hath life in himself ; so hath he given to the Son to have life in himself " (5²⁶). This Son is in no sense a being devoid of will. Even in the Fourth Gospel there are texts which imply the exercise of a very energetic will on the part of Jesus : " The Son quickeneth whom he will " (5²¹) ; " Father, I will that they also, whom thou hast given me, be with me where I am " (17²⁴) ; " If I will that he tarry till I come, what is that to thee ? " (21²²ff.). And so there can be no question of supposing that Jesus is a sort of vacuum, the mere place where God lives and does His work as another and a stranger. When it is said that the Father loves the Son (10¹⁷, 15⁹, 17²³, ²⁴, ²⁶), He is already described as at least an object distinct from the Subject that loves. And that this object is Himself a Subject, and exists independently as such, is implicit in the fact that the Son also loves the Father in doing what the Father gives Him to do (14³¹), and that He abides in His love (15¹⁰) by keeping the Father's commandments. Yes : " Greater love hath no man than this, that a man lay down his life for his friends " (15¹³). Jesus does this work, the work of the Saviour. But He really does it. It is not merely His fate to execute it. It does not simply happen in Him. " No one taketh my life from me, but I lay it down of myself . . . and I have power to take it again." And this laying down of His life is the fulfilment of the commandments which He has received (10[18]). It is because He does this, and does it in this way, that the Father loves Him (10[17]). The same applies to the δόξα of Jesus, the divine glory, in the possession of which He seems to melt into the divine Subject and therefore to disappear as a human Subject. It is true that He does not seek His own glory (7[18]). He does not seek it at all (8[50]). If He honoured Himself, His honour would be nothing (8[54]). Nor does He receive glory from men (5[41]). Those who receive glory from each other cannot even believe (5[44]). How could He belong to them ? In short, the glory which a man may ascribe to himself, or allow others to ascribe to him, has nothing whatever to do with the glory of Jesus. His glory is greater and comes to Him from a very different source. The One who honours and glorifies Him is His Father (8[54], 17[22-23]). The text 17[5] is particularly plain in this regard : " And now, O Father, glorify me with thine own self with the glory which I had with thee before the world was." If He who would neither glorify Himself nor allow others to glorify Him seemed in a sense to disappear as the Subject, He obviously reappears as the object of the divine δοξάζειν. An object lacking in will and energy ? One series of texts (7[39], 11[4], 12[16, 23]) speaks absolutely of His δοξάζεσθαι as if it were a transfiguration or investiture which simply came upon Him. But they are misunderstood if we take them in this sense. In no event which takes place between the Father and the Son is the Son merely an object. The texts about the glorification of the Son by the Father are counterbalanced by others in which the roles are clearly reversed. The glory which Jesus seeks is the glory of the Father who sent Him (7[18]). Hence the Father is to be glorified in the Son (14[13]). To the prayer of 17[5] should be added the prayer of 12[28] : " Father, glorify thy name," with which we must obviously take the words which follow : " Then came there a voice from heaven saying, I have glorified it, and will glorify it again." Here already is a hint that according to some most important passages of the Gospel the two aspects are to be brought into integral connexion with each other : " If God is glorified in him, God shall also glorify him in himself, and shall straightway glorify him " (13[32]). And in the reverse order : " Father . . . glorify thy Son, that thy Son also may glorify thee " (17[1]). " Now is the Son of man glorified, and God is glorified in him " (13[31]). It is clear that in this matter we have to do with a regular circle. It is the circle of the inner life of the Godhead. For the complete explanation of it we should have to return to the perception of the unity and trinity of God—to the Paraclete, too, there is ascribed His own δοξάζειν of the Son (14[16])—and therefore indeed to the most difficult elements in the later dogma, and especially to the fine theologoumenon of the *perichoresis* of the Father, the Son and the Holy Ghost (cf. C.D., I, 1, § 9). It has not yet been possible to give a worthy and acceptable explanation of Johannine Christology without reference to the commentary furnished by the Church's doctrine of the Trinity. But the point which concerns us here is that according to the Fourth Gospel it is not merely the eternal but the incarnate Logos and therefore the man Jesus who is included in this circle. He did not give up His eternal divinity when He concealed it to become man. He is still in the bosom of the Father (ὁ ὢν εἰς τὸν κόλπον τοῦ πατρός, 1[18]) even in His coming to this world. Only on this assumption does Johannine Christology make sense. It is only as Jesus is the eternal Son and Logos who was in the beginning, who was with God, and who was God (1[1]), that He can so fully dispense with all human δόξα, to participate the more fully in the divine δοξάζεσθει, and yet to be no less capable even of the active divine δοξάζειν. It is only as He is a mode of the divine being, and therefore a moment in the circle of the inner life of God, that He can be in the Father and the Father in Him ; that He and the Father can be one ; that the work of the Father assigned to Him can also be His own work and the work performed by Him can be also the Father's work ; that He like the Father can have life in Himself ; that He can love the Father with the same love with which the Father loves Him ; that He can glorify the Father and the Father glorify Him. Undoubtedly all these things describes the inner relations of the Godhead. But oddly enough this mystery of the participation of Jesus in the Godhead is not at all the dissolution but the very foundation of His true humanity. The Johannine Jesus, too, proclaims Himself unequivocally to be man. His history, too, is plainly a human history. Nor is it this only incidentally, as if the Evangelist were making a concession, or relating a myth, or trying to clothe in the form of human history a superhuman, super-historical truth. On the contrary, we might say that the particular concern of the Fourth Gospel, as opposed to contemporary piety and religious philosophy with their superhuman and super-historical deities, and to the related emergence of primitive Christian Docetism, was a desire to show that the eternal divine Logos was this man Jesus, and this man Jesus was in the beginning with God (1^2) ; that the eternal divine Logos cannot be found and known elsewhere than in this man Jesus ; that in relation to Him, in faith or unbelief, in knowledge or ignorance, the door of communion with the divine life, of eternal life, is opened or closed for every man, for the whole world. This man Jesus is the Son of God, and in the Fourth Gospel this identification is not a paradox or contradiction to be accepted in amazed bewilderment by a *sacrificium intellectus*. In this Gospel faith and knowledge are not divided but always mentioned together as the way in which a decision must be made with regard to Jesus. This rests upon the fact that the humanity of Jesus and His participation in the Godhead are not irreconcileable and antithetic, but that it is His very participation in the divine which is the basis of His humanity. The Johannine Jesus is man in and by the very fact that He is the Son of God and that He is included in the circle of the inner life of the Godhead. As by His words and deeds, and finally by His going to the Father, which is also the sacrifice of His life for mankind, He reveals that in this sense He is from above, He is also below, man in the cosmos. He is this in His saving work, which as such can happen only from above but only below, and to which as such He alone can be called and equipped who is in the bosom of the Father but also man. He must be the Saviour of men, of the world. He must be believed and known by other men as the Son of God. He must be able to call them His own and Himself theirs. His history must therefore be a human history within the history of all men. Jesus is both God and man. He is this, not in juxtaposition or in two separate spheres, but in conjunction. He is the Son of God as He is man and man as He is the Son of God. It would take us too far afield to show how in this Gospel the relation of Jesus with His disciples is described in the same categories as the relation between the Father and Himself, so that it is a revelation of the inner life of the Godhead in which Jesus shares. It is in the so-called high-priestly prayer (Jn. 17) that these correspondences are developed with particular fulness. We shall content ourselves with a reference to the decisive point that if the saving work of Jesus consists in His laying down His life for His friends, this is the same thing, only in its aspect as self-revealing work, as is elsewhere (3^{16}) described as God's so loving the world that He gave His only begotten Son. The giving of the Son by the Father indicates a mystery, a hidden movement in the inner life of the Godhead. But in the self-sacrifice of the man Jesus for His friends this intra-divine movement is no longer hidden but revealed. For what the man Jesus does by this action is to lay bare this mystery, to actualise the human and therefore the visible and knowable and apprehensible aspect of this portion of the divine history of this primal moment of divine volition and execution. What would the man Jesus be apart from this mystery, apart from the fact that He is the Revealer of this mystery ? He lives and moves because of this mystery, and as its Revealer, in the necessary decision and achievement here below of what is decided and achieved by God Himself up above—in the place from which He has been sent and has come. It is on this ground that He is real man : " My meat is to do the will of him that sent me, and to finish his work " (4^{34}). This is what Jesus does, and in this action of His we have to recognise Him as man and to apprehend His real humanity.

The particularly important text Jn. 4^{34} is of course only a gloss on the saying with which Jesus answered the tempter's advice in the wilderness that He should make bread out of stones : " Man shall not live by bread alone, but by every word that proceedeth out of the mouth of God " (Mt. 4^4). Yet the Johannine text need not be regarded as a more rigorous form of the Synoptic. It is only apparently the case that the Matthean text says less and is more reserved, as though in the phrase " not by bread alone " Jesus had recognised that man does indeed live by bread too, but that he also needs the words proceeding from the mouth of God. For in this case the trite *applicatio* that man has not only bodily but also spiritual needs is so obvious that the *explicatio* is *a priori* brought under suspicion. The fact is that during the forty days in the wilderness Jesus did not live by bread at all, but according to Mt. 4^2 He was an hungred, and—yet in spite of His hunger He was still alive. Again, His answer to the tempter is a quotation from Deut. 8^3. But in this passage " living by bread " is not one necessity to which " living by every word that proceedeth out of the mouth of God " is added as a second. On the contrary, the reference is to the miracle effected by the Word of the Lord, which consisted in the fact that for forty years God led Israel through the desert, and that where there was no bread, and the people seemed likely to die of hunger, He nevertheless sustained them, namely, by the manna which neither they nor their fathers knew. It was in exactly the same way (except that now there was no question even of manna) that God sustained the hungering Jesus in the desert. For a correct understanding of the text : " Man shall not live by bread alone," we must first note that the reference is not to mankind in general, but that Mt. 4 speaks of Jesus in the wilderness and Deut. 8 of Israel in the desert, so that it is of ἄνθρωπος in this qualified sense that we are told that he does not live by bread alone. And secondly, the text says of this man, not that while he does need bread he must have something else besides bread, but that this man—in one case Israel and in the other Jesus—is not dependent on a supply of bread in order to live, and therefore does not have to procure such a supply, as the tempter suggested to Jesus. No, this man (Israel and Jesus) lives as man solely by the words which God speaks with Him. This divine communication brings it about that He lives and is sustained, nourishing and quickening Him. Even the bread which, if He were not in the wilderness, He might sow, reap, grind and bake, or even purchase or steal, could not give him life as man. This is given Him by the almighty Word of God, whether He has bread or hungers in the wilderness. Hence, in spite of all his cunning, the devil was more stupid than cunning when he proposed to help the hungering Jesus with the advice that He should make bread out of stones. Jesus would not have been this man if He had done so or even if He had been capable of doing so. The allusion to the mighty and wonderful Word of the Lord closes in Deut. 8^5 with the warning : " Thou shalt also consider in thine heart, that, as a man chasteneth his son, so the Lord thy God chasteneth thee " (8^5). The chastening to which Israel was subject consisted in the fact that—as at some future time in the promised land flowing with milk and honey, so now in the wilderness where it must hunger—for good or evil it was wholly and ex-clusively dependent on the providence of God under which alone it should and could live. Israel refused this fatherly discipline. Again and again it rebelled against this providence. Both in the wilderness and later in the promised land it tried to live by bread alone. Jesus, too, was subjected to the same discipline. But He was the Son who heeded the warning. He did not and could not rebel against this providence. For He was really Jesus ; and He commended and entrusted Himself to the providential care of His Father. Obviously, Jesus did not always hunger. He also ate and drank. But hungry or satisfied, He lived as man in the power of the divine providence directed to him through the Word of God. Thus He could both hunger and live. This is what happened in the wilderness. The stupidity of the devil consisted in the fact that he could not see or understand anything of this. He would not have been the devil if he had been able even distantly to see or understand it. And the saying of the disciples (Jn. 4[31]) : " Master, eat," is not altogether unrelated to the stupidity of the devil. There could be only one answer to this, and it was identical with the answer given to the devil in the other passage : " My meat is to do the will of him that sent me, and to finish his work." In this way Jesus is real man.

We shall now attempt to recapitulate. Who and what is man within the cosmos ? is our initial question, and we have posed it first in relation to the man Jesus. Let us assume for a moment that we can say who and what man is, although only in relation to this man. What is the result in terms of the distinctive characteristics of man among other creatures ?

1. If our decisive insights are right, the first and basic answer can only be that among all the creatures man, i.e., this man, is the one in whose identity with himself we must recognise at once the identity of God with Himself. In all other creatures the presence of God is at least problematical, but here it is beyond discussion. It cannot be overlooked ; it is a necessity of thought. It would be impossible to see and think about man, i.e., the man Jesus, if we did not at once see and think about God also. In and through the being of man there immediately meets us at this point the being of God also. In and with the existence of this man we immediately encounter that of God also. This cannot be said of any other creature. In regard to the rest of creation the vision of the Creator in the creature can only be indirect, and therefore the connexion of the concept of the creature with that of the Creator can be made only in the form of subsequent reflection. Here in man, i.e., in this man, the vision and concept of the Creator are both direct and immediate in the creature. In the case of this creature there is no need to reflect about God. God is present and revealed as this creature is present and revealed.

2. This first answer must be made more precise. The presence and revelation of God which distinguish this man do not consist in a quiescent and indifferent relationship between God and this creature. No matter how lofty its other attributes, a being which remained quiescent and indifferent, except that between it and the creature there existed a relationship corresponding to this indifference and quiescence, would not at all be the God present and revealed in man, in this man. The God of man, of this man, is as such (and it belongs to His very nature that this is the case) resolved, energetic and active in a specific direction. He wills and works. And He wills and works in man, in this man, for each and every man. He is the Saviour of men, their eternal and almighty, their unique and total Saviour.

Hence His presence and revelation in man, in this man, is not just a fact but an act. His relationship to him is not a state, but it takes place in an action with a meaning and purpose. And the meaning and purpose are deliverance. That God is in and with this creature means therefore directly and immediately—and here again there is no question of subsequent reflection, discussion or problem—that in and with this man He is the Saviour. His presence in Him means that the history of deliverance is enacted and His revelation in Him means that this history may be known.

3. When God distinguishes this man by willing and working in Him, by becoming the Saviour of each and every man through Him, He does not infringe His own sovereignty. He does not lose Himself in Him by being present and revealed in His existence, and in and with Him addressing Himself as the Saviour to each and every man. His willing and working are always wholly His own. His deliverance is always the act of His freedom. And therefore it is the freedom as well as the love of God which distinguishes His being in man, in this man, and in so doing distinguishes man as His creature. His deliverance is an exercise and demonstration of His sovereignty, of His transcendence and greatness, of His deity. He does not dishonour Himself, but does Himself honour, by being the God of man, of this man. By expressing and declaring Himself in Him as the One who wills and works that none should be lost to Him, but all saved for Him, He confirms Himself and triumphs as the Creator. Hence it is not merely a question of the creature, but also of the Creator's own cause and honour, in this history of His assistance as it is enacted in His presence in man and as it may be known in His revelation in him. And if it is this history of divine help which characterises the creature, then it is a story which must be understood *a priori*, indisputably and axiomatically, as a divine-human history.

4. Since God is sovereign in His presence in and with the existence of the creature, its distinction by this presence means that it exists in the lordship of God. Man, this man, exists as such in the enactment of this history, in the fulfilment of the divine act of lordship which takes place in it. He does not exist outside this act of sovereignty, but within it. He is there as God is there, as He is there in Him, as He is there as the Saviour of each and every man. He is there only as this is the case. The fact that He is a person, that He is the soul of a body, that He has time and so on, does not make Him real man. It merely indicates His possibilities as man. He becomes and is real man, and is there as such as God is there in Him, as the Saviour of each and every man. This man is there in and by the sovereign being of God of which He is born and by which He is sustained and preserved and upheld. Not two juxtaposed realities—a divine and then a human, or even less a human and then a divine—constitute the essence of man, this man, but the one, divine reality, in which as

such the human is posited, contained and included. Man, this man, is the imminent kingdom of God, nothing more and nothing in and for Himself. Similarly, the kingdom of God is utterly and unreservedly this man. He is as He is in the Word of God. And the fact that this is so lifts Him above all other creatures. This is the distinction which is His and His alone.

In this we are repeating in other words the doctrine of the Early Church concerning the *anhypostasia* or *enhypostasia* of the human nature of Christ by which Jn. 1¹⁴ (" the Word became flesh ") was rightly interpreted.: *ut caro illa nullam propriam subsistentiam extra Dei Filium habeat sed ab illo et in eo vere sustentetur et gestetur* (*Syn. pur. Theol. Leiden*, 1624, *Disp.* 25, 4). The correctness of this theologoumenon is seen in the fact that its negative statement is only the delimitation of the positive. Because the man Jesus came into being and is by the Word of God, it is *only* by the Word of God that He came into being and is. Because He is the Son of God, it is only as such that He is real man (cf. C.D. I, 2, pp. 163 ff.).

5. But just because the creature is distinguished at this point by the fact that it lives within the lordship of God, in identity with the divine Subject, it is not neutral in face of the divine action and therefore in its relation to the history of the divine deliverance enacted in it. Its independence is, in fact, that of the God who delivers, eternally and omnipotently, totally and exclusively. How could this be neutrality? Hence the creature is not at this point an object of the divine deliverance. There can be no question of divine grace being imparted to it in the sense that it needs it, but only in the sense that it may itself be the active grace of God. It is not just the locus or sphere of this deliverance. For by the fact that God dwells in it the work of God is already in full operation. The divine deliverance comes as it takes up its dwelling in it. The kingdom of God dawns with the coming of man, of this man. Nor is this creature merely the instrument of the divine aid. The fact that through him God helps each and every man does not mean that He merely uses this creature for this end. No distinction can be made between what this creature is and what it does, between what God does through this creature and what He does in it. For this creature is in the Word of God. It is impossible to look away from it to what it does. " There is no helper beside thee." But again—and this is the point which concerns us here—it is impossible to look away from what it does to itself, to its being and existence in abstraction from its work and office, from what God decides and fulfils in it. As the history of the divine deliverance for each and every man is wholly exclusively He Himself, so He Himself is wholly and exclusively the history of the divine deliverance for each and every man. Hence man, this man, exists as this history takes place. He is Himself this history.

6. To sum up, the distinctiveness of this creature consists in the fact that it is for God. That it is for God means that it is for the

divine deliverance and therefore for God's own glory, for the freedom
of God and therefore for the love of God. Man is the being which is
for God. It is as such that he surpasses all other creatures. At any
rate, we do not know any other creature of which this can be said.
This is what makes man, this man, unique in the whole cosmos. For
how does the creature come to be for God? It belongs essentially
to its general reality, recognisable in other forms, that God should be
for it, that it should owe Him everything. But it is not of the essence
of the creature that it should be for God, that it should have significance
for Him, that He should expect something from it, that it should
have a contribution to make to His being and activity. This reciprocity is the privilege of man, of this man, as we must again add.
Nor does it merely belong to the essence, but it is the essence of this
man, to be for God. He is not a man for nothing, nor for Himself.
He is a man in order that the work of God may take place in Him,
the kingdom of God come, and the Word of God be spoken. Thus
the purpose of the presence and revelation of God actualised in His
life becomes His own purpose. And conversely, the purpose of His
own existence is to serve the purpose of the presence and revelation
of God actualised in Him. The basis of human life is identical with
its *telos*. Deriving from God, man is in God, and therefore for God.
We are not speaking of a predicate which he might have but perhaps
might not have. Man is essentially for God because he is essentially
from God and in God. When we say this we are speaking of the
man Jesus. We cannot say quite the same thing of man generally
and as such. But we cannot speak appropriately about man generally
and as such until we learn that the essence of man as seen in Jesus,
is to be for God.

2. PHENOMENA OF THE HUMAN

On the basis of this initial christological approach we shall attempt
a first definition of the nature of man in general. Our answer to the
question of the nature of the man Jesus could not be more than a
foundation. Anthropology cannot be Christology, nor Christology
anthropology. We remember that between the man Jesus and ourselves as men there stands not only the mystery of our sin, but primarily
and decisively the mystery of His identity with God. It is impossible
to understand Him even as a man except in this identity. But it is
impossible to understand ourselves in this identity. We are here
confronted by the irremovable difference between Him and us. There
can be no question, therefore, of a direct knowledge of the nature of
man in general from that of the man Jesus. But it might well be
possible to know indirectly who and what we are from the fact that

we live in the same world and have the same humanity as this man, so that we are contrasted as men with this very different man. We shall return to this decisive question in the third sub-section.

Already, however, our christological approach has afforded us certain criteria. We need these if we are rightly to pose the question of the nature of man. It is not at all self-evident in which direction we are to look. We might well err even in posing the problem. We might try to find man in general elsewhere than in confrontation with the man Jesus. We might be tempted to explain him in abstractions. What man thinks he can know and say about himself from within himself is something that gives rise to such abstractions. We are faced with a whole host of abstractions of this kind. We shall have to delimit and secure ourselves against them. This will be our task in this second sub-section. It will thus be critical in character. To accomplish this delimitation we need standpoints and standards and criteria. We need to know the minimal requirements essential in all circumstances for a concept of man which can be used theologically. We must know why it is that in our theological enquiry we cannot compromise with those who think they know the nature of man on other grounds than those which are legitimate for us. These minimal requirements or criteria are given us by our christological basis.

We do not call in question the irremovable difference between the man Jesus and ourselves when on the basis already laid we first give as the most general presupposition of our investigation of the nature of man the fact that man must be understood as a being which from the very outset stands in some kind of relationship to God. It will be a different relationship from that which we have found to be characteristic of the man Jesus. But in its different way it will be no less fundamental and radical. We certainly cannot consider man as a self-enclosed reality, or as having a purely general relation *ad extra*, to a part or the whole of the cosmos distinct from God. We must understand him as open and related to God Himself. And we shall have to interpret this relation to God, not as something fortuitous, contingent and temporary, but as a necessary and constant determination of his being, so that from the very outset there can be no question of an understanding of man from which the idea of God is excluded. We can never acknowledge the genuinely godless man to be real man. Otherwise between the man Jesus and ourselves there would be not merely a partial but a total dissimilarity. If in spite of all the dissimilarity there is also something in common, if He is not just man in a different way from ourselves but also a participant in the same human nature as ours, and if the constitutive feature of His humanity is that He is the Son of God and as such man, then the essence of all the minimal requirements for a view and concept of real man is that man cannot be seen or understood apart from God. This means that the knowledge of man as such includes and implies the knowledge of

God ; and again, that the knowledge of man is possible and attainable only from the standpoint of the knowledge of God.

The dual form of this final statement is a repetition of the two theses in which Calvin summarised the content of the introductory chapter of his *Institutio*. The chapter is headed : *Dei notitia et nostri res esse coniunctas, et quomodo inter se cohaereant*. The knowledge of God and the knowledge of man are mutually conditioned and interconnected in such a way that the knowledge of God must precede the knowledge of man. The first thesis runs : *Se nemo aspicere potest, quin ad Dei, in quo vivit et movetur, intuitum sensus suos protinus convertat : quia minime obscurum est, dotes quibus pollemus, nequaquam a nobis esse ; immo ne id quidem ipsum, quod sumus, aliud esse quam in uno Deo subsistentiam* (I, 1, 1). The second is to this effect : *hominem in puram sui notitiam nunquam pervenire constat, nisi prius Dei faciem sit contemplatus atque ex illius intuitu ad seipsum inspiciendum descendat* (I, 1, 2). Calvin's exposition is not intrinsically cogent and satisfying because he does not tell us on what grounds all this is affirmed. Who is the man of whom it may be said that his humanity is explicable only in God, and whose existence can be explained only as a subsisting in God ? And on the other hand, who is the God the knowledge of whom is so unconditionally necessary for the knowledge of man ? We cannot accept the theses of Calvin unless we transplant them from the empty and rather speculative sphere in which they stand in his thinking, and root them once more in the firm ground of the knowledge of Jesus Christ in which they really grew even in Calvin. But they are correct in themselves, and are therefore to be accepted.

On our own basis, however, we are now in a position to define more precisely the criteria which must be used in any attempt to determine the nature of man within this most general presupposition. In the six points in which we summarised our christological investigation we recognise at once the six points which together give us the full and sober limits which we may not in any circumstances transgress in a theological definition of the nature of man.

1. If it is the case in relation to the man Jesus that in His humanity we are confronted immediately and directly with the being of God, then necessarily, assuming that there is similarity between Him and us in spite of all dissimilarity, every man is to be understood, at least mediately and indirectly, to the extent that he is conditioned by the priority of this man, in his relationship with God, i.e., in the light of the fact that he comes from God, and above all that God moves to him.

2. If it is the case in relation to the man Jesus that the presence and revelation of God in Him is the history of the deliverance of each and every man, then necessarily, assuming that there is similarity between Him and us, every man is a being which is conditioned by the fact that this deliverance is for him, that every man as such must exist and have his being in a history which stands in a clear and recognisable relationship to the divine deliverance enacted in the man Jesus.

3. If it is the case in relation to the man Jesus that in the divine action in favour of each and every man in Him it is also a matter of

the freedom, the sovereignty and the glory of God, then necessarily, assuming that there is similarity as well as dissimilarity between Him and us, the being of every man, in so far as this history essentially concerns it, is not an end in itself, but has its true determination in the glory of God (in the very fact that it can participate in that history).

4. If it is the case in relation to the man Jesus that He exists in the lordship, i.e., in the fulfilling of the lordship of God and not otherwise (not outside this occurrence), then necessarily, assuming that there is similarity between Him and us, it must be said of every man that it is essential to him that as he exists God is over him as his Lord and he himself stands under the lordship of God the Lord. Whatever may be the meaning of his freedom, it cannot consist in freedom to escape the lordship of God.

5. If it is the case in relation to the man Jesus that his being consists wholly in the history in which God is active as man's Deliverer, then necessarily, assuming that there is similarity here, the being of every man must consist in this history. Not only his actions but his being will consist in his participation in what God does and means for him. His freedom will be his freedom to decide for God ; for what God wills to do and be for him in this history. The proper action of real man can then be understood only in the light of the fact that it may correspond to the divine action in his favour, doing justice to the grace addressed to him.

6. If the man Jesus is for God, and surpasses all other creatures in the fact that He is only in order that God's work may be done, His kingdom come and His Word be spoken in Him, then necessarily, assuming that there is even the slightest similarity in this respect, the being of no other man can be understood apart from the fact that his existence too, as an active participation in what God does and means for him, is an event in which he renders God service, in which he for his part is for God, because God first willed to bind Himself to man, and in so doing has bound man to Himself.

These are the limits within which we shall always have to move in our search for a theological concept of man.

But we have not yet attained the concept itself. For the latter cannot be deduced so comparatively easily from the nature of this man Jesus. We shall discover it only as we compare man as such, and ourselves, with the man Jesus, asking ourselves what it means for man, for us, that there is the man Jesus apart from all other men and among them.

What we have mentioned are, however, the minimal requirements which we must always bear in mind in face of conceptions of man's nature derived from other sources. They are the criteria by which we must measure the latter, and the light in which alone it will perhaps be possible to estimate them positively. It might indeed be the case that, while we cannot accept the conclusions of these other conceptions as a true account of man's being, yet we may and must perceive phenomena of the human (investigated by us theologically) in the suggestions which we receive from such sources. However this may be, the firm understanding of the nature of the man Jesus which we tried to reach in our preliminary survey gives us also the understanding which we need for a correct appraisal of these other conceptions.

We begin with a general delimitation. No definition of human nature can meet our present need if it is merely an assertion and description of immediately accessible and knowable characteristics of the nature which man thinks he can regard as that of his fellows and therefore of man in general. From the standpoint of all our criteria, human self-knowledge on this basis must be regarded as a vicious circle in which we can never attain to real man. For the point at issue is who is the man who wants to know himself and thinks he can? How does he reach the platform from which he thinks he can see himself? What kind of a platform is it, and what kind of a knowledge will he give himself from it, when for some reason he wants to see himself otherwise than from God, looking at himself and not at God? Who is the man who to know himself first wishes to disregard the fact that he belongs to God, that he exists because he stands in relation to the work of God, that he lives for the glory, under the lordship and in the service of God? Who is the man who thinks he can disregard all this? Real man cannot disregard it. Only a phantom man thinks that of himself he can know himself. But we cannot believe that what this phantom man will come to know will be real man. And in what he declares he knows we can only recognise himself, a phantom man, and not real man. We cannot and will not dispute that he sees and grasps something which perhaps indicates the nature of true man. Why should there not be certain phenomena in the picture of the cosmos in which he who knows real man can see symptoms of real man? But supposing he does not know real man at all? Supposing he cannot know him because from the very outset he has refused to accept the knowledge of God as the presupposition of the knowledge of man, adopting the standpoint that he himself is the measure of the real, and therefore trying to see and understand man in the phenomena of the human which are accessible and transparent to him? In these circumstances he will co-ordinate these phenomena, perhaps combining them to form a system. He will think that in their sum, or in the system which they yield, he can form a picture of real man. But he will not succeed in doing so. And as he does not know the true nature of man, he will also miss the symptoms of the genuinely human—symptoms which he thinks he sees objectively in those phenomena, but which he misuses to cover real man, and is therefore unable to interpret correctly. We have first to see real man if we are to understand his symptoms, and are not to fall into the condemnation of being led astray by such phenomena as are accessible and transparent to us. For these phenomena as such are neutral, relative and ambiguous. They may point in various directions. They may or may not be symptoms of real man. They are so only for those who know him already and can therefore interpret them correctly. In themselves they convey no knowledge of real man. Hence all inadequate answers to our question are characterised in the first instance by the fact that they all refer to a human characteristic which is plain to us but which unfortunately is of no significance for understanding the true nature of man. They all speak in some way or other concerning man, but they are not really speaking about him. They are really speaking about that phantom man, i.e., about certain human characteristics in which each will recognise traits of his own nature, but in which no one will discover himself, or what he truly is. They are speaking only about knives without edges, or handles without pots, or predicates without subjects. It is not merely arbitrary but unrewarding to try even temporarily to set God aside in our search for man, to treat as a *cura posterior*, and therefore to leave open, the question of man's relation to God, and especially that of God's attitude to man, and therefore that of the human history grounded in this divine attitude. For the inevitable judgment on this arbitrary procedure is that real man eludes its grasp, as it were, leaving those who adopt it with mere phenomena which they cannot even interpret correctly, i.e., appraise as his symptoms. We should therefore be ill advised if we were to follow this arbitrary procedure and to seek the nature of man in that circle where man thinks that he can see and understand himself in the light of accessible and transparent characteristics.

We may illustrate the difficulty confronting any one who moves in that circle by a classical example.

Polanus (*Synth. Theol. chr.*, 1609, *col.* 1987) opens his theological anthropology (*Contemplatio theologica hominis*) with the clear-cut Aristotelian definition : *Homo est animal ratione praeditum.* He explains it as follows : " Man belongs to the genus *animal*, i.e., he is a *substantia corpore organico et anima vegetante atque sentente et loco movente constans.* The specific point which differentiates him from other animals is that he is gifted with reason. By this we are to understand the *vis intellectus, qua is* λογίζεται, *ratiocinatur et discurrit, hoc est ex uno aliud vel aliud post aliud ordinat.* Hence the *opus seu officium* of reason consists in *discursus*, i.e., in the swiftness with which his mind moves from one thing to another, from causes to effects, from effects to causes, and therefore to the knowledge of all things. This *vis intellectus* is not given to any other animal, and it is here that there is to be sought the distinction and particularity of man in relation to all other animals and therefore to all other beings in general.

Is it not indisputable that something of the phenomenon of human distinctiveness is correctly perceived and expressed in this definition ? It may indeed be seen and said that man is an animal being, and that as such he consists in the union of an organic body with a living soul, but that in contradistinction to the soul of other animal beings this soul is gifted with reason, which can also be described as *vis intellectus*, as the capacity to think and know, and the exercise of which can also be defined as that *celeritas animae* in its movement from cause to effect and *vice versa*. Indeed, a good deal more might be seen and said along these lines. In particular, the one-sided view of the *vis intellectus* undoubtedly needs to be supplemented. And it is not at all self-evident that the concept *animal* really ought to be the subject of the definition and human *ratio* only a predicate, only a kind of ancillary to the mainly animal being of man. Both the naturalism of this view of the subject and the intellectualism of the understanding of reason could and necessarily did bear evil fruits later. But even if we improved the definition of Polanus, it would still be unacceptable at the decisive point. For what conceivable relationship does it bear to the *contemplatio theologica hominis* which he promised us ? That is the question. Where are now the two basic criteria of Calvin for the knowledge of man ? It is quite obvious that man is now defined as though there were no attitude of God to him, as though he did not live in a history rooted in that attitude, as though all that has to be said of him from this standpoint were really a matter of *cura posterior*. With this definition Polanus did, of course, place himself on a common ground of discussion with the philosophy and science of his day. But in so doing he accepted its limits. Naturally, he thought that he could later widen the ground. Naturally, he did not hesitate to make the *animal ratione praeditum* the object of lofty theological discussions, to define God as its Creator and Lord, and to bring out man's relation to God even in a detailed allegorical explanation of the human body as well as in a description of the soul gifted with reason. Naturally, he did not fail to speak of the determination of man grounded in God and related to Him, and with all seriousness he expounded the doctrine of the divine likeness which underlies it. Yet it is obvious—and in this he was far from alone—that he had to read all this into the *animal ratione praeditum* by way of interpretation. And by adopting this definition he formally encouraged the idea that this theological interpretation could be regarded as an appendix and even ignored. There were others who secretly ignored it in his own day, and many more who later did so openly. If we start with the idea of man as an animal endowed with reason, we are not led by any necessary inference to God, and therefore not to man as a being essentially related to God. If the interpretation is to be valid, the definition must include the truth that man's relation to God is an essential part of his being. Since this is not the case in Polanus, his definition cannot possibly be regarded as having anything to do with real man. In fact it merely points to possibilities. Real man, whether animal or rational, exists in a definite history grounded in God's attitude to him. What he is apart from this history is not real man at all, but a phantom. The fact that he is animal and rational does not make him real man. If this fact is seen in the light of this history, it is indeed a symptom of the human, but if not, it is an indifferent phenomenon, which can be established and observed as such, but which does not shed even the smallest ray of light on the true nature of man. The phenomenon *animal ratione praeditum* can actually be interpreted very differently from the way in which, with the best and sincerest intentions, it was interpreted by Polanus and many others before, with and after him. The *animal ratione praeditum* in itself is a ghost. The purpose of this definition has always been clear. It is to define the most general features of man in order to proceed securely to the particular. But what is overlooked is that it is precisely the most particular thing about man, namely, his existence in a history determined by God's attitude to him, which is the most genuinely universal and decisive feature in which real man may be discerned at once, whereas if we start with a universal obtained by treating man's relation to God as one specific feature with others, and therefore as a *cura posterior*, not to be included in the definition, we shall merely be pointed to the void and never to the face of real man.

The whole difficulty of an arbitrary investigation of the nature of

man, i.e., of one in which we arbitrarily look at man from the standpoint of himself, is fully disclosed when we realise that in this question
we are immediately and necessarily concerned with that which is
specific in man, i.e., with his particularity among other creatures of
the cosmos. The real man whom we are seeking must obviously be
the being which is distinguished as man from all other beings and
which in spite of any affinity or relationship or common features
that it may have with them is always man and only man, and is not
therefore interchangeable with them. Real man cannot merge into
his environment. He cannot surrender to it and be assimilated into
it. If he did, or even if he could, he would cease to be real man. He
is this creature, and as such he is not another, or a mere component
part of a total creaturely reality. Although he belongs to the latter,
he is marked off in specific ways from his fellow-creature.

That this is so is clear at once if from the very outset we view him
in the history which has its basis in God's attitude to him. This does
not require any unbecoming depreciation of any of our fellow-creatures.
We do not know what particular attitude God may have to them,
and therefore what may be their decisive particularity within the
cosmos. We are not in a position either to ascribe or to deny any
such particularity to them. We can and must accept them as our
fellow-creatures with all due regard for the mystery in which God has
veiled them. But we are clearly marked off from them by the history
which has its history in God's attitude to us, to man. Existing in
this history, the being of man is plainly separated and distinguished
from all others.

But supposing that for some reason we temporarily or finally
disregard this in our discussion of the nature of man ? Supposing
that we hope to understand the particularity of man in the cosmos by
again mounting the dubious platform where we think that of ourselves
we see and therefore define—and define means limit—ourselves ?
What we can see of ourselves will again be a specific characteristic
as compared with other creatures, phenomena of the human by whose
greater or less distinctiveness from other phenomena we must and
perhaps will be convinced that they disclose the real man and therefore the difference of his being from other beings. Why should not
such a conclusion be correct ? Why should not these phenomena be
symptoms of the human and therefore reveal this difference ? But
whether or not they are such symptoms obviously depends on whether
we already see and know real man. Only as it is already known to us
can the distinction of man among other beings be indicated and confirmed by these phenomena. In themselves, the phenomena are
silent. They are not yet symptomatic. They are again neutral,
relative and ambiguous. As phenomena, they are indifferent. In
themselves, they may equally well point to the essential unity of
man with surrounding reality as to his difference from it. They can

equally well point away from real man as to him. We are not denying that the study of these phenomena is relevant, interesting, important and legitimate. What is only a phenomenon to one may be a symptom to another. When we think we know the particularity of human nature, how can we help trying to find it reflected on the level of human phenomena ? It is inevitable that this attempt should be made again and again. And it may well be that its results will be significant and even instructive for us. But we cannot expect this attempt to give the initial instruction needed, namely, the real definition of man. And it has never actually yielded the real definition of man, the unambiguous and finally tenable demonstration of his difference from the rest of creation. What can be more or less correctly seen and more or less precisely expressed as a result of the different forms of this attempt is only the relative uniqueness of human nature. This may well be delimited from that of other beings. It may be defended against any attempt to level it down. But this is possible only if a comparison is made with the uniqueness of other beings, and therefore implies some degree of uncertainty whether there can be any real appreciation of the particularity of man along these lines. The autonomy of man disclosed by these means will never be his absolute autonomy among all other creatures—the autonomy which must distinguish him if it is to be a matter of the particularity of real man. In other words, much can be said concerning human particularity, but nothing can really be said about the particularity itself. This can be perceived in its symptoms only when it has already been taken into account in the method of investigating it. What is the man you think you are ? If we think we can ignore this question even temporarily, we shall look in vain for a reliable distinction of the nature of man from that of other beings.

The question of the nature of man in the sense of specifically human as opposed to generally creaturely nature has become a basic question in the so-called apologetics of modern theology. It is worth noting that the various attempts to prove the separate existence of a God distinct from the world had first been abandoned. If only this had been for the real reason ! If only it had resulted from the fact that in view of God's self-demonstration in His words and works no proofs of ours are needed ! If only it had not been that God's self-demonstration was no longer known, and therefore there was no longer any real attempt to believe in God as God, in His existence as distinct from that of the world, and consequently there was no longer any real knowledge of what was to be proved ! Meanwhile, under the vigorous leadership of Schleiermacher, the discovery had been made that the true theme of theology consists in human religion and piety, in its statements concerning itself. Theologians had become accustomed to understand by the word " God " a mere " content " of the pious consciousness of man. Because it was impossible seriously to ascribe to this " God " an existence separate from that of the world—and at bottom this was the only reason—it was quite easy to accept Kant's dissolution of the classical proofs of God's existence. But hardly had this been done, hardly had the effort of apologetics in this respect been allowed to lapse, before apologetic effort was needed in the opposite direction in the second half of the 19th century. What was now doubted and contested as a result of a new emphasis in modern science and the outlook to which it gave birth, was the idea of the special position of man in the universe. And obviously apologetics could not yield at this point. For even in respect of the question of God it had fallen back on the pious self-consciousness of man, and it was sure that in the form of the distinction between the subjective form and the objective content of this consciousness it had a positive answer to this question. But this apparently impregnable fortress was now seen to be under attack. Supposing that, as there was no existence of God as distinct from the world, there was no existence of man as distinct from his environment ? If it had previously had a good reason for not attempting any proof of the existence of God, it would now have had an equally good reason for not attempting to demonstrate the uniqueness of man. It would have realised that in God's self-evidence in His words and works evidence for the uniqueness of man is also implied, and that no further proof need be undertaken by us. But since it had abandoned the former attempt for the wrong reason, modern theology saw no convincing reason at all to abandon the latter. On the contrary, its positive answer to the question of God had taken a form which made further retreat impossible when challenged concerning the special position of man. Cornered by its adversary, it had either to surrender altogether or to make some attempt to furnish the proof required by the so-called scientific outlook. By its very nature, of course, it had no more adopted into its definition of man the attitude of God to man and man's relationship to God than had Polanus before it, but had examined man only from the standpoint of man, trying to interpret what man is, and believing that it could do so, from a consideration of human phenomena, and reserving theological interpretation until later. We shall illustrate its apologetic accomplishments on this presupposition, i.e., its proofs of the unique position of man, by three examples in which we may clearly discern the three historical stages in the development of modern apologetics.

We may begin with some observations from the useful summary of the conservative Greifswald theologian Otto Zöckler in his article " Man " in the *PRE*³. We are in the period when the " descent theory," or more precisely " transmutation theory," founded by Jean-Baptiste Lamarck, Lorenz Oken and Charles Darwin and represented especially by Ernst Haeckel, had reached its height. The theologian was confronted by the theory—alarming because so enthusiastically expounded and supported by such a wealth of illustration— that although man was not the descendant of this or that type of modern ape, an extinct simian race of prehistoric times, closely related to the small-nosed apes of Africa and East India, formed the stem from which the human race sprang under the stimulus of favouring circumstances thousands of years ago. What has theology to say to this ? The reply of Zöckler is as follows.

Certain scientists think quite otherwise. They tell us that between the lowest human types and the highest species of ape there is such a considerable difference in size of skull and weight of brain that the theory of a common origin is confronted with the greatest difficulties. Also in the case of certain pathological phenomena such as microcephaly, idiotism etc., there is no noticeable approximation of man to the ape. Again, the truth of the much lauded " basic law of bio-genetics " is reducible to the fact that the life of the human embryo in its individual phases shows similar reactions to those of certain of the higher animals, and there can certainly be no question of any exact recurrence of the lower animal forms of life. So far the " pithecanthropos " postulated by the exponents of the descent theory has not been discovered either in living form or in a fossil state ; the gap between the minimum skull size of man and the corresponding maximum in the anthropoid ape has not been filled by any of the discoveries so far made ; and no case of definitive transformation from one organic type into another has been conclusively observed. Above all, we cannot overemphasise the psychological gulf which exists between man and the animals. As a spiritual being characterised by freedom and self-consciousness, man represents a stage of being which is absolutely apart from all previous organisms. The capacity for speech especially constitutes an impassable Rubicon between man and the animals. Only an imaginative nature-philosophy can level out the intellectual, moral and spiritual qualities which lift us above the animal kingdom. In brief, man cannot be subsumed in the latter, but forms a natural sphere of his own like that of the mineral, plant and animal kingdoms on the one hand and the world of angels and spirits on the other. This natural sphere always has been and will be a kingdom of the spirit as well, the kingdom of humanity properly so called, whose civilising and ethical tasks have been brought nearer and nearer to fulfilment—" not without saving help from above "—from century to century, and this in " a progression which has recently begun to show signs of a quickening tempo," so that there is no reason to give up " the belief in a final victory of the good in humanity over the retrograde forces of evil," or " to cease to strive for the appointed goal of establishing a supreme stage of cultural development which shall embrace all the inhabitants of the earth."

The apologetics of the rather more critical theology of the early 20th century tried to attain the same end with far greater reserve. For R. Otto (*Naturalistische und religiöse Weltansicht*, 1909, first appeared 1904) it was at least a strong presumption that we must reckon not only with the idea of development as expressed by Aristotle, Leibniz and Kant, Goethe, Schelling and Hegel, but also sooner or later with the descent theory in its most general form, no less self-evidently than with the astronomical theories of Kant-La Place (p. 97). Yet for him, too, " it is a basic requirement of piety, to be retained at all costs, that the human mind is to be regarded as far above the rest of creation, and of quite a different order from that of minerals, plants and animals " (p. 254). Otto first abandons the position still held by Zöckler when he explains that the descent theory, even though it understands evolutionary continuity to be smooth, gradual, uniform and uninterrupted, " can have no detrimental effect on a religious outlook." The latter cannot perhaps welcome but it need not regret the ape-men of Dubois and the chimpanzees of Friedenthal (inoculated with human blood without any disturbing consequences, p. 105). Within the general framework of the descent-theory there is nothing to hinder and a good deal to encourage us in supposing that the final leap from animal life to humanity was so considerable that it signified an incomparably greater expansion and enrichment of the spiritual than anything which had gone before, the latter genuinely coming into its own and revealing all previous forms of life to be only its prelude (p. 102). The continuity between the living and the spiritual is problematic not only in the transition from the animal kingdom to the human race as a whole, but also in the constantly observable emergence from the animal to the human in the development of each individual, in the whole of the intermediate zone between mental health and disease, in all the cases of perversion and arrestation in psychological development, etc., not only in individuals, but even in whole races and epochs (p. 103). And it should also be remembered that the specific originality and newness of the ultimate and highest stage in an evolutionary series is not negated by its continuity with previous stages, nor is the absolute and incomparable worth of this supreme stage diminished but rather established by its emergence from the imperfect (p. 104). On the other hand Otto does not conceal the fact that the religious outlook is bound by a silent sympathy with those exponents of evolution who within the continuity of the process as a whole reckon with the occurrence of leaps and novelties, and suggest the depth and wealth and mystery of nature by their questionings and allusions to the limitations of our knowledge (p. 105). For " if true at all, the limitation of knowledge and the unattainability of the depth and truth of things is true of the knowing mind itself and its secret life " (p. 226). Nowhere is the mental a mere function of the process of physical evolution, but the more it fulfils itself the more its autonomy and independence increases (p. 288 ff.). It is not deducible nor derivative from the physical. It is not related nor subordinate nor secondary to it, but primary. It is not passive in relation to it, but creative (p. 234). And in every act of self-consciousness we do not merely know but we know that we know ; we do not merely think but we also think that we think (p. 241). We combine our ideas in a single and total consciousness (p. 242). And this consciousness is our consciousness, the consciousness of our ego (p. 243). And in this self-consciousness we are not merely media for happenings alien to us, but the authors of what we ourselves do. We are acting and therefore free beings (p. 244). We think and will on the presupposition that there exists a norm of right thinking and willing (p. 247 f.), and we experience ourselves as ego not merely in our reason but in our sense of being individuals who for all that they are conditional cannot just be deduced from what has preceded (p. 251). And in the creative power of artistic, scientific and religious geniuses there seems to emerge something of the essence of mind itself apart from the limitations of spatial and temporal being (p. 253). Does the animal share in all this ? Otto realises that we are completely in the dark about what happens or does not happen in the soul of the animal. Yet he thinks it improbable that elephants, dogs and chimpanzees are capable of forming general ideas, rules and laws, of passing judgments and drawing conclusions, of knowing *a priori*, in short, of thinking. And he sees the decisive difference between man and the animal in the fact that in man and man alone the physical can be developed into the spiritual. " I can *train* a young ape or elephant, and teach it to uncork wine bottles and perform tricks. But I can *educate* the child of the savage, developing in him an intellectual life of similar subtely and depth and energy, and often far greater, than in the case of the average European " (p. 256). " In knowledge and art, in morality and piety, the mind possesses itself, and as such it is a unique and strange guest in this world, absolutely incomparable with everything beneath it and around it " (p. 258). An animal species has no history. It is always the same non-historical product of nature. The animal can only succeed in perfectly developing the natural pattern of its species. But on the natural basis of his membership of the zoological species of *homo sapiens* man can erect in the history of the race and the individual a completely new and characteristic creation : the world and life of the spirit (p. 259). " But as man is fitted for intellectual life and the possession of intellectual gifts, he is able to attain personality." This word includes and denotes everything which expresses the essential dignity of the human being. " Personality is a word which makes us shudder with awe. It expresses what is most proper to us, our true and highest aim and the essential disposition of our innermost being " (p. 260). Personality constitutes the clear and secure distinctiveness of man from the whole world and all other being; it establishes the microcosm over against the macrocosm as a self-enclosed world of its own, free and superior to all other becoming and perishing " (p. 260 f.).

Even more decisively than R. Otto, Arthur Titius (*Natur und Gott*, 1926) takes his stand on the conviction that from the biological point of view man is to be classed with the animals, and specifically with the primates, i.e., with the most highly organised group of mammals as their undoubtedly most highly developed member ; and that the recent type of human, apparently unchanged for many centuries, has grown out of a more animal type proper to the diluvian period. Man is related to the modern ape to the extent that it may reasonably be assumed that the ancestry of the ape and man coincide at an earlier date than in the case of other species (p. 636). The physical development of man is of course superior, as is evident from the special development of his brain, his upright walk and the connected use and formation of his hands. But in these points he clearly approximates to the higher, the so-called anthropoid ape. And according to Titius we cannot exclude from the general process of evolution the emergence of the human psyche. For important psychical functions which form the basis of the higher life of the mind (perception, memory and recollection, the capacity to form associations, the conscious control of impulse through fear and hope, in short the marks of a true even if different kind of intelligence) are not to be denied to the animal (p. 638 ff.). But the comparison of the animal and the human psyche does not lead to the conclusion that the latter has developed from the former. An animal-like ancestor of man is indeed conceivable, " but either he must have been inwardly different from the animals known to us or the development of these animals into man has become possible only through a big leap forward " (p. 640). Even primitive man as compared with the animal, including the anthropoid ape, shows an incomparably greater power of adapta-tion. He dresses. He uses fire. He manufactures tools and weapons. He adorns his clothes and his body with ornaments. He plays with things, and copies them. He has a natural urge for culture and therefore for the unlimited, for that which cannot be confined by natural instinct. (What a pity that none of these apologists considers it worthy of mention that man is apparently the only being accustomed to laugh and smoke !) All this points to the singularity of his mental life, which is distinguished by a superabundance of intellectual energy, a " hypertrophy of the brain." Inevitably, therefore, he follows a different course of development from that of animals (p. 640 f.). He gives names to things. He knows customs, and not merely social instincts (p. 641 f.). Abstractly considered, this mental difference may be only one of degree. Concretely, however, the centre of gravity in man has shifted so much that the result is a new content of life (p. 643). The idea of evolution in itself does not exclude this fact. Organic nature in its tendency towards individualisation and increased organisational complexity has sufficient room for even so peculiar a phenomenon as that of man (p. 644).

In this scientific picture of man Titius has at least indirectly tried to find a place for the " religious idea " and even the Christian concept of man. For him as for so many others there can be no doubt that the divine likeness attested in Gen. 1 has reference to his spiritual or rational endowment including the capacity for free determination, " which is still ascribed to each individual even to-day " (p. 783). And now we come to an interesting Liberal anticipation and parallel to our basing of anthropology on Christology. For Titius goes on to say that the religious ideals of man result only from the supreme religious ideal and therefore from the person of Jesus Christ and His ideals. The original aptitude for the attainment of these ideals must " somehow be found in the general or rational endowment of humanity " (p. 784). He explains this " somehow " more closely as follows.

The first ideal of Jesus is divine sonship as typically realised in Himself. According to the Christian view every normal man is necessarily endowed with an aptitude for this. And he is actually endowed in this way. Both God and the devil are completely beyond the grasp of the animal. But humanity—and this is the enormous but justified optimism of Christianity—carries divine humanity within itself as its determination and therefore its disposition. Not only from the standpoint of religion, but even from that of universal truth, it may be asserted that this ideal is not pitched too high, and that Christianity is thus the religion which springs from and is natural to the essence of humanity. The " idyll of the family," the fountain from which human life renews itself, has become in all its naturalness and directness the symbol of supreme religious inspiration. The transition from the ideal of the father to the Godhead is par-ticularly natural. And finally the feeling of being at home and belonging by right to the father's house widens out to become a feeling of being at home in the world and having the right of citizenship within it. All this is quite congenial to the modern feeling for nature.

The second ideal of Jesus is universal love of humanity, the ideal of religious brotherhood based on communion with the heavenly Father, with which there may easily be connected man's inner participation in the whole cosmos and sympathy with every living creature. Of course, there are certain obstacles to the realisation of this ideal, especially the intensive competition for the means of subsistence in which man is involved with all other creatures and especially his fellow-men. "Nevertheless, it cannot be doubted that man's position in the realm of nature and the constitution of his own being furnish strong indications of the naturalness and inner necessity of these ideals, so that with increasing cultural harmony they usually find general recognition." The aptitude, directly implied in man's highly developed spiritual capacities, to attain to thoughts beyond his own self-interest, to interest himself in every living creature, to be concerned about the well-being of others and thus to enrich himself personally and inwardly, can and must help his striving to reach that ideal—and most certainly so in "the warm atmosphere of religion" (p. 786 f.). Belief in God implies both the impulse to work for the fulfilment of these ideals and the guarantee of the success of these endeavours. In any case, let man do his duty in spite of all hindrances, directing his whole effort to the service of the all-embracing ideal of a divinely willed world-harmony! He will then find himself in the closest harmony with the biological idea of evolution. Work in the service of this ideal as undertaken by man at the peak of the process of evolution, the mastery of nature as a cultural process, is only the continuation of evolution beyond the formation of species to their harmonious integration as a totality.

The third ideal of Jesus is the kingdom of God, i.e., the ideal state in which hindrances are overcome not only in the individual soul but between men and even in nature, and the exclusive rule of divine fellowship and brotherly love is established. At this point it seems that there can be no question of any kind of connexion with our present knowledge of nature. Nevertheless, this metamorphosis, too, presupposes a certain aptitude both in human nature and in nature generally, and it is to be noted that the revolutionary discoveries of recent decades show that nature even as at present constituted may hide unsuspected mysteries and possibilities of further development. "Who would ever have thought that the atom is a luminous soaring world in miniature? And after such a discovery who would presume to dispute the possibility of transmutation from an earthly body into a heavenly body as envisaged by Paul in 1 Cor. 15?" (p. 789 f.). This then, as Titius sees it, is the evidence in favour of an aptitude suggested by the scientific view of man for the religious and Christian determination of man in accordance with an aim and ideal.

Thus in modern theology, when the theologian neither could nor would prove the existence of God, he attempted at least to prove that of man, i.e., his distinctive being of man in the cosmos. As we saw, he was forced to defend the Christian position at this point. And it is certainly relevant to acknowledge that modern theology did defend itself and was not prepared to surrender at this point. There can be no doubt that to the scientific as to every world view the No and Yes of Christian faith, insight and confession had to be plainly spoken. It was essential to oppose the levelling down threatened by this outlook. It was essential to contradict the forgetfulness and denial of the specifically human for which man himself showed a strange capacity and inclination. To-day we are reaping the evil fruits of the seeds partly although not exclusively sown by this world-view. To try to deny man his humanity, and to understand him as the expression of a universal dynamic, was to do something which could only avenge itself, and has done so, and will probably do so further. These Christian apologists of man may have had a foreboding of this coming damage when they opposed to this theory what they thought to be a better. The remarkably optimistic tone so characteristic of their writings might of course be taken to suggest that basically they were as little aware as their adversaries of the danger which threatened. But however that may be, here they made their stand. In this respect they were not prepared to howl with the wolves. They came down on the right side. They made a serious effort to put up the necessary resistance to this view. In so far as theology did this, in this respect at least it did not yield. This is to be noted, however critical may be our attitude to the way in which it tried to do it.

But there is more to be said in favour of these apologists. In their own way they undoubtedly applied themselves seriously and fundamentally to the question of human phenomena. They did so, of course, with a strikingly limited perspective, i.e., within the framework of the biologico-psychological problem which they accepted from their opponents as though it were a matter of course. But within this field (this applies especially to Titius) they were prepared to learn both externally and intensively from the science of their time. Necessarily, therefore, much of what they saw and said about the phenomena of the human was both incontestable and important. To be sure, it may be doubted whether the higher humanity which Zöckler thinks to be engaged in accelerating progress is to be regarded as one of the genuine phenomena of the human. The same doubt occurs with regard to the awe which Otto experienced at the mention of the word personality and in which he thought he should recognise his essential self and therefore the essential mark of the freedom and superiority of mankind in general. Above all, the same question may be asked concerning the assertion of Titius that in the scientific picture of man there may be seen an aptitude for the realisation of religious and Christian ideals, and especially of the ideals of Jesus, the fatherhood of God, the brotherhood of man and the kingdom of God. And curiously enough, these are the very ideas which A. von Harnack (*What is Christianity ?*, 1900, 3rd Lecture) described as the three circles in the preaching of Jesus. Indeed, Harnack himself was probably taking over a scheme drawn up by Hermann Lotze (*Grundzüge der Religionsphilosophie*, 3rd Ed., 1894, § 84) in definition of " the characteristic convictions of any religious outlook." Is it not surprising that in this matter Lotze, Harnack and Titius are so completely in accord ? And is it not almost incredible that at this point Jesus and the most modern scientific knowledge are at one, and that in these three aptitudes of man we are supposed to be dealing with genuine phenomena of the human ? But these detailed objections would be of little avail against the weight of this apologetics if the undertaking as a whole were feasible and successful. What Polanus once advanced as the *differentia specifica* of the human seems very primitive and sketchy as compared with the manifoldness of the points of view from which we are now informed that the phenomena of the human are indeed specific within creaturely being in general. What man is and has, as seen by himself within the framework of his own knowledge, is certainly emphasised and established (with the aforesaid reservation) in a manner deserving of gratitude.

I should like to confirm the positive impression which this mode of viewing man can make by adding to my summaries of these apologetic works some observations of Adolf Portmann in his *Biologische Fragmente zu einer Lehre vom Menschen* (1944).

Unlike the above mentioned essays in apologetics, this book, although it displays no noticeable theological concern, gives evidence from the very outset of an attitude of far greater detachment in respect of the theory of evolution. For Portmann the latter is merely one attempt at explanation, one working principle, one instrument of thought, among others ; it is not a dogma which must be accepted at all costs, an interpretation which must be brought into the sphere of faith (p. 15 ff.). His ultimate objective certainly seems to be the formation of a view of man to which the creative powers of the artistic and above all the religious consciousness must make their contribution (pp. 24 f., 129 f.) But what he offers us is exact knowledge of man ; the singularity of man in his non-human environment. His aim is to emphasise " human particularity by means of biological research " (p. 121) ; no less, but also no more. And it is the problem of the growth of man which especially concerns him. Some of his more important conclusions may be noted. He tells us, for example, that man differs strikingly from all the mammals most closely related to him in the fact that it is only at the end of his first year that he reaches the stage when he really ought to be born according to his constitution, so that every human birth is really a premature birth physiologically (p. 44 f.). Accordingly, his bodily proportions at birth differ far more widely from those of the grown man than is the case with his closest analogies in the animal world (p. 33 f.). Again, in comparison with the latter he is born with three times as great a weight of brain—and, clearly connected with this fact—twice as great a total weight (p. 37 f.). And the construction of his brain reveals the following points of contrast : the less powerful operation of instincts ; the shift of the centres of important functions to the outer covering of the brain ; the quantitative increase in the anatomically perceptible substratum of essentially psychical processes (p. 59 f.). And it is in the unusual premature years of extra-uterine life that there is developed in him with comparative rapidity, by a process of catching up unnecessary in more maturely born mammals, and with the intensive co-operation of his parents, the bearing, movement and speech proper to his kind (p. 47 f.). It is as a result of the special acts of striving, learning and imitation peculiar to this organism—and not by a simple exercise of innate propensities—that his bodily structure achieves its characteristic form. After the mastery of such movements as holding up the head, sitting up and holding the body erect with the help of others, there comes at the end of this momentous premature year the capacity to stand (p. 68 f.). And at the same time there take place other distinctively human processes of growth. From the sixth month of this first year there begins an intensive development of the legs (p. 73), and from the third to the fourth month the exercise of speech as distinct from the mere production of sounds. The spontaneous self-expression of which the higher animals are capable is quite different from the controlled self-expression characteristic of humans (p. 127). Speech is the function " by which, with the help of integrated sound and sign symbols bearing various meanings, we are able to express our perceptions, judgments, wishes etc., and to impart them to others for the purpose of mutual understanding." The tiny human creature now progresses to the stage of babbling, " of genuine babbled monologues in which he produces a real arsenal of sounds, many of which he will never use in speaking his mother tongue, and some of which he will have to reacquire with great effort in the process of learning foreign languages." Eventually he comes to the imitation of individual words in which his observations, wishes and aims find expression, but the psychological content is far richer than what is contained in the sound. " The limit of our present powers of expression proclaims itself already as one of the most important limits of our whole social life and existence as human beings." For the tiny chimpanzee this problem cannot arise because he never imitates in the smallest degree any of the sounds regularly recurring in his environment, neither requiring nor actually acquiring this possibility of controlled self-expression. And while the young chimpanzee does not progress beyond the " aha-experience," the human child in his ninth to tenth month reaches the stage where he begins to note and understand the interconnexions of sense and means of expression, transferring individual solutions to analogous though divergent cases in a movement from subjective to objective apprehension (p. 74 f.). And at the same time he begins to recognise and control his body as his own, each movement being both a use of it and the point of departure for a further movement. At a time when, if he were a genuine mammal, he would have to develop in the darkness of his mother's womb according to purely natural laws, there now take place in his life not only generic processes but innumerable unique and often fateful events, and he thus enters the sphere of the historical (p. 77 f.). And as he does not inherit his social world but must fashion it for himself from his innate tendencies and individual reactions to the outside world, so his mental propensities are not matured by self-differentiation in relation to the slight variations of possible attitude as we know them in the case of animals, but must find a characteristic individual form through contact with their richly varied environment. All this forces us to a conclusion diametrically opposed to " the basic law of bio-genetics," namely, that man must be regarded as adapted already in his mother's womb to the peculiarity of his premature birth and his later acquirement by his own active efforts of the bearing and speech characteristic of his species, and he cannot therefore be placed merely in the same stage of evolution as that of mammals, primates or chimpanzees (p. 81 f.). Looking forward from this premature year we note further that man grows slowly as compared with his animal relations, and at the age of 14 years to 17, i.e., when even the slowest growth among them (e.g., in the case of the orang, the chimpanzee and the elephant) is nearing completion, and puberty is already behind, a period of greater growth begins with the onset of puberty (p. 87 f.). This slowness in his development obviously stands in close relation to man's mode of existence, which unlike that of the animal is open to the world. That his whole organisation should have a long period of youth, capable of rich development, seems to be significantly connected with the special way in which he experiences the world, the plenitude of social connexions and means of communication into which he can enter, and the manifold richness of his environment ; it is the mode of development peculiar to the human manner of existence (p. 102). By way of compensation, human life is distinguished by being about twice as long as that of the anthropoid ape. At the age of 10 the chimpanzee ceases to play and becomes serious. At the age of 30 all mammals are old if not grey-haired. None of them has any hope of achieving the age 80 or 100 of man. But man is obviously too urgently occupied to be able to grow old and die so early. And in his case age need not spell decline but the very opposite. At all events, it implies an increase of individuality, and a higher development of his individual characteristics (p. 115 ff.). In brief, body and soul, development and mode of life, ontogenetic individuality and social relationship, nature and culture appear in man as a unity. And this phenomenon warns us of the reserve necessary in face of a study based merely on man's organic inheritance and evolution, and therefore on his relationship with the animal kingdom. His biological singularity consists in the indissoluble connexion (peculiar to each individual) between his inherited tendencies and development on the one hand and his experience of history on the other (p. 123 f.). I repeat at the conclusion of this account that Portmann did not speak as an apologist, nor was his intention to prove the uniqueness of man. We remember the title of his book, and he expressly tells us in closing : " Life requires from man more than the modest certainty which the fragments of factual research can offer us " (p. 129). It is a pity that the reserve implicit in this whole type of demonstration has not been as plainly observed and indicated by the theological apologists.

From the treasures of the scientific knowledge which they acquired for the occasion, and from a specialist in scientific matters, we have learnt that there are what we have called the phenomena of the human within the field of vision of man as he studies himself and compares himself with other creatures. Man must certainly be viewed in connexion with his environment. The theologians laid almost greater stress on this than the scientist to whom we have appealed. They probably went too far in their basic recognition of the idea of evolution. But no one can doubt that if man is to know himself he must see himself as set in his environment, and therefore primarily, for good or ill, with his animal environment. But again, it is clearly advisable not to remain in this position or to try to see man merely against this background. Otherwise he will not be viewed as a whole. Otherwise we shall not even see correctly what binds him to his environment. We have also to see what is peculiar to man, and if we are really to know him we must see him as a whole from this standpoint. In what does this specific element consist ? The apologists referred to his mind or spirit. The more reserved scientist contented himself with speaking about his openness to the world, his culture, his social conduct, his experience of history. In both cases the reference is roughly to the same phenomena. It would be obstinate to disregard and ungrateful to ignore them. We thus conclude that they must be taken into account.

Above all, however, we maintain that only a modest degree of certainty is possible in this regard. The certainty of the phenomena is obviously that of the competent observer, but this means that it is the certainty of the existing state of biological research. The layman who is unable to participate actively in this research and all that it implies cannot possibly be qualified to demonstrate these phenomena or to check their demonstration. For good or ill he is dependent on specialists who are competent to direct his attention to them. But again, the certainty of these phenomena stands or falls with the certainty of special tendencies within the field of scientific research. It would have been hard for the 19th century to deal with the Darwinians if it had not been for the good fortune that even among scientists there were more or less intelligent and resolute anti-Darwinians to whom the theological apologists could refer. And because—for various reasons—the scientific opposition to Darwinianism was not very successful, even at the beginning of this century it was difficult to make a stand against the arrogant majority of the scientific confraternity. To-day Otto and Titius can perhaps speak with more assurance than formerly, but only because there are indications that there are now more specialists who on the basis of their investigations can again point in a very different way to what is peculiar to man. In relation to this question, we are dependent not merely on specialists but on specialists of this latter type. And they are the very ones who assure us that their fragmentary researches can give us only a modest certainty. They do not oppose another dogma to that of Darwin—the work of Portmann is particularly instructive in this respect. If they fight against it, they do so indirectly rather than directly. They tell us that they see the facts on which this dogma is founded, but that we have also to see certain other facts, not in order to erect a new and opposite dogma, but on the basis of scientific conclusions to do away with the erection of dogmas altogether. The results which they offer us are only indices, and they do not conceal that these indices are only approximate and need to be completed, checked and discussed. The Darwinians once thought that they had discovered true man because they had discovered him to be a near relation of the chimpanzee. But a modern anti-Darwinian, observing that in spite of this close relation there are also remarkable divergences, does not suppose that with this observation he has discovered true man. If he surpasses the Darwinians, it is primarily in modesty. The theologians were unfortunately lacking in modesty in two respects. First, they shared the arrogance of the Darwinians to the extent that they increasingly accepted Darwinian theories as a secure basis for all further progress. And second, they thought it their duty to complete and transcend these theories by opposing to them the further dogma of man as an intellectual and cultural being. But if in regard to the phenomena of the specific-ally human, and especially in regard to positive assertions, modesty is the better part of wisdom, then man's self-knowledge can offer us only modest, i.e., limited, conditioned and relative certainty, and definitely not the certainty which life demands of man. If there is a secure human life, unshakeably sure and conscious of its humanity and therefore of its differentiation from the chimpanzee, it will not be the life which consists in phenomena which even at best can be demons-trated by science with only a modest certainty.

But leaving the question of certainty, we must now ask to what these phenomena really amount. We are no doubt glad to learn, when the case is convincingly put, about our unusual extra-uterine year with all its special characteristics, about our long and obviously for that very reason promising youth, about our longer maturity with all the special possibilities to which it seems to point. Even without this detailed knowledge we are gladly persuaded that our possibilities are undoubtedly very different from those of the chimpanzee, extending to a sphere where the chimpanzee, so far as can be judged, is quite unable to follow us but reaches its limit. Whether we call it psyche, mind, culture or experience of history, there is no doubt that in this direction we are very different from this animal cousin, and that even the points in which we are akin to it can be properly appreciated only when we look beyond the common ground to the differences and then look back again to the affinities. But what have we really seen when we have seen such phenomena? True man? Certainly not, but even at best, i.e., when we already know true man from other sources, something of his aptitudes, capacities and possibilities. Perhaps not even these in their fulness, for how do we know that even human possibilities are fully perceptible to us and are thus to be apprehended in the world of phenomena? But in any case it is only a question of possibilities, of manifold potentialities, of a promise which in comparison with the ape is singularly rich, and which seems to be the portion of true man. Nor is this promise such that it gives us an insight into true man as differentiated from other creatures. If it is clear that human possibilities as compared with those of the animals closest to man are far wider, yet it must also be remembered that not only these higher animals but that others also, which according to the usual scale of values are perhaps much lower in the ladder of creation, have possibilities which put those of man in the shade. And for all we know there may be animal possibilities which do not make us think merely because we do not perceive them, since they are outside the world of phenomena within which we think we can so securely differentiate ourselves from them. And if it is true that psyche, mind, culture and the experience of history are distinctively human phenomena, have we the right for that reason to regard man as not only different but higher and better than those other animals, and to understand him in his real differentiation on the basis of this higher valuation? There can be no doubt at any rate that the value of the distinct phenomena is not itself a phenomenon but the subject of a judgment which has not the slightest connexion with the observation of facts. Supposing that the typically human element of striving were to be regarded with Schopenhauer as the cause of all man's suffering, that the much boasted mind of man were, as L. Klages suggests, his disease and that therefore the usual scale of values were to be completely reversed? On what ground can such theories be contradicted? All that is certain is that the circle of man's supposed self-knowledge is nowhere so visible as in the fact that our real advance upon the animal causes us to regard ourselves as really different from the latter. It is thus to be noted that even from this standpoint our self-knowledge on this basis as that of a distinctive being is limited, conditioned and relative.

We have to know already that we are men, and that as such we are characteristic and different from the animal and all other beings, if we are to recognise ourselves again in these phenomena of the human. Only those who are familiar with a thing can recognise its symptoms. Those who do not, will read them as the letters of a foreign alphabet, persuading themselves that they know what they do not, and inevitably reading wrong words and sentences. The 19th century was one of unparalleled obscurity because it was a time when in the very act of leaping forward to a realisation of his possibilities man became unknown to himself. At no time was it more possible or necessary to see what distinguishes him from the animal than in this age of progress. His capacities as an intelligent and cultured being were far plainer to him then than in all the preceding ages of darkness to which he looked back with pity. And yet this was the very time when he failed to see what distinguishes him from the animal. It was this very century which had to become that of the anthropoid ape and the ape-like man. Darwin did not make it this. But because it could not see real man for all his possibilities it had to have its Darwin, and the scientific and theological anti-Darwinians were necessarily powerless against him. Darwin and his followers had the advantage that the voice of the century spoke through them, and no anti-Darwinian theory could prevail against it. We have seen how even the theologians had to bow to this spirit of the time, and could make their protest only within the framework of a basic acceptance of the Darwinian dogma. If man does not know himself already, long before his attention is directed to these phenomena, he will be blind even though he sees. In face and in spite of these phenomena he will always look on the wrong side. He will always think he should convince himself that his own reality consists in what he has in common with the animal and the rest of creation generally. Thus even from this standpoint the knowledge and interpretation of phenomena of the human is a limited, conditioned and relative knowledge. The knowledge of man himself must precede it, and this has roots in a very different soil.

But perhaps our investigation so far has been too simple. Perhaps we have not so far posed the problem of the phenomena of the human sufficiently seriously, basically and essentially. Perhaps it is for this reason that we have not made more progress in the knowledge of man's essential being, or gained a clear view of real man. Our conception of man's self-knowledge has perhaps been too narrow to permit a more reliable answer to our question. Perhaps we have only to deepen this conception to reach more positive results. Has it not so far been our tacit assumption that the distinctiveness of man is to be sought in certain characteristic phenomena of his organic life within the complexity of other similar phenomena ? Have we not understood this perception of distinctiveness too one-sidedly as a perception based on sensuous experience, and therefore equated man's knowledge of himself too simply with natural scientific knowledge ? Surely man can become an object of self-knowledge in other ways ? Surely he is different in other ways than the form in which he is an object of sensual perception and therefore of natural science ? Surely it is illegitimate to treat the very different form of his being merely as a marginal problem of scientific anthropology, or to bring out this different form only at a point where experimental observation of himself points to certain phenomena which are accessible as such to sensual perception, but not to comprehension, to integration into the total picture of organic life ?

We had occasion to criticise the classical definition of man as *animal ratione praeditum* on the ground that it is naturalistic, far too readily assuming that *animal* is the subject and *ratio* a mere particularisation of this subject. The same naturalism burdens and obscures modern apologetics as well. For it tries to answer the question whether and to what extent man is more than an animal in contradistinction to other animals. It thus makes the fatal mistake of allowing its opponents to determine the form of the question. It assumes with its opponents that man is also and supremely an animal, a higher mammal. Only later in the argument does it go beyond its opponents and see and describe this mammal as something highly distinctive. Only from the common point of departure and *prima veritas* laid down by science does it point to a higher level where in the understanding of man correspondingly higher, non-scientific methods and criteria must be applied. But perhaps we have been guilty of the same one-sidedness, of adopting the same naturalism as a self-evident presupposition. It is in the nature of the case that the kind of scientific anthropology which we have been considering should start with man as a mammal and then in better cases point to what is beyond, recognising its own limits. But we must not allow this fact to mislead us into a canonisation, as it were, of this procedure.

In fact, we constantly see ourselves on other levels than those amenable to natural science. We are constantly aware of ourselves as other than what is perceptible to our senses. And it is not actually the case—only prejudice can affirm as much—that primarily and preferably we are what we perceive ourselves to be sensually and are apprehensible as such. It is not actually the case that our natural being is the main problem, and what lies beyond only the marginal problem, of our self-knowledge. The relationship is in fact reversible, and has often been reversed. Man may first try to see and understand himself from a different angle, and only afterwards examine his natural being. There is no need to decide here whether this reversal is justified and necessary. There is no need to adopt it. But we must certainly reckon with it. If we are to appreciate accurately and fully the phenomena of the human, and to do justice to their possible significance as symptoms of the truth about man, we must certainly take into account this other and resolutely non-scientific method of approach.

To what extent are we constantly very different from what we are to our self-perception, and see ourselves to be such? If there really is here a different approach—and there is, for we do have a continual awareness of ourselves from a very different angle—this can obviously refer only to our willing, conduct and action. This different approach which has to be considered can be only that of our practical reason, of ethics. We can never reach a genuinely different type of self-contemplation if we look only at such knowledge as is founded on our thinking. Our thinking, if it is not empty, is related to our sense perception ; it consists in the ordering and linking of what is sensually perceived. At the moment we are deliberately leaving out of account theological thinking. We are speaking of man's knowledge in so far as it is not founded on God's self-revelation or related to it. Of this, in so far as it is grounded on human thought, we are forced to say that its objects are necessarily those of sense perception. To the extent that it is knowledge, it is scientific knowledge. Knowledge of our knowledge can never lead us beyond a view of ourselves in which we are to ourselves natural phenomena and nothing more. We can no doubt think that we think. We then think of ourselves as thinking beings. But as such, if our thinking is not empty, we are dependent on sense perception. As thinking beings we are to ourselves only what we perceive ourselves to be through our senses. The fact that we think is thus itself a natural phenomenon. In thinking that we think we only see and understand ourselves as a natural phenomenon. We do not move out or become a genuinely different phenomenon. But we do this once we realise that we are not merely thinking creatures. We are not merely directed to think of ourselves as thinking beings. As we think, we also will, behave and act. We do this, of course, as we think, and therefore have scientific knowledge of ourselves, and are what we perceive ourselves to be sensually. Yet all this takes place as we will and do it, in the transcendent act of our existence. The fact that this act takes place, and the way in which it does so in all its individual moments and determinations, is also, of course, a natural phenomenon occurring within the sphere of our perception. But the fact that it is our act and that we are its subject, that we are not the subject of a wholly different act, that it is irreplaceable and integrally connected with our individual selves—this is not a natural phenomenon, and in it we are not the object of any scientific discipline. To contemplate it is to look into the dimension of freedom, to consider our own distinctive being in its absolute and not merely relative differentiation from that of others. And there can be no doubt that we do in fact contemplate it. Even as we think, and think that we think, we are implicitly engaged in the use of our practical reason. And we think truly of ourselves only in so far as we think of ourselves as those who are engaged in the use of practical reason. Nor is it only subordinately and temporarily that we exist in the act of willing, behaving and doing. Where can this process begin or cease so long and so far as we are men? When was our existence merely a sensually perceptible process and not also a free event, our life-act, in which we cannot be studied scientifically but can be perceived ethically? Nor is it only subordinately and temporarily that we can be ethically perceived in this life-act, so that scientific self-knowledge must self-evidently be given the primacy, as has often been the case. That we ourselves behave and act and therefore exist ethically is not something which needs to be present only in the background of our consciousness. Indeed, it might well be asked whether it is not the natural phenomenon of our life which in our existence as men we continually push into the background even though we cannot dissolve it altogether. To " exist " is to " step out," and in relation to man it always means to step out of the sphere in which he is one natural phenomenon among others into the sphere where the phenomenon in question is he himself, not only in what he is, but as the doer of his being, the subject of the act which we call human life. As we know ourselves, we will and conduct ourselves. As we think that we think, we put ourselves into action. What would our thinking, and our thinking that we think, amount to if this action failed, if in it we were not doing? Even as we think we are not neutral. It is as we decide that we think, and the question is an open one whether our decision is an element and expression of our thinking or our thinking only an element and expression of our decision. In any event self-knowledge must also be knowledge of ourselves as those who are caught up in the process of decision ; the knowledge of ourselves as willing, behaving and acting beings ; the knowledge of ourselves in the freedom of our being from its naturalistic determination as disclosed at this point. This, then, is the broadening and deepening of our perspective which is undoubtedly demanded in our investigation of the nature of real man. We could not do justice to the question within the confines of the naturalism in which we have so far moved.

But do we do it sufficient justice by this widening of perspective, by passing from the naturalistic to the idealistic, or more precisely the ethical consideration of man ? Even now, in the phenomenon of human willing, behaving and acting, of human freedom and decision, are we genuinely dealing with real man or his symptoms ?

We must not minimise the step which we have taken. It is necessary. The phenomenon of man as presented by natural science points us beyond itself in this very direction. We might equally well say that it points back to the position from which alone the scientific view of man is possible. But whether we start from this position or go back to it, we find ourselves in another sphere. The man whom previously we thought we should consider (for all the differences in proximity and relationship with the rest of creation) as one of its phenomena, becomes a new and different and specific phenomenon. Whatever the truth of his connexion with the rest of the cosmos, whatever the relationship of his species to other species in the cosmos, we now see him assert himself as a being in his own right. We now see him initiate a process which can of course be explained and described in connexion with the other processes of the cosmos but can never be derived from the latter. We now see him move freely in and out of the world around him, united to it, yet not belonging to it primarily nor ultimately, but only to himself.

If we were to take full account of modern linguistic usage, we might go on to say that we now see him then as a " person," or more solemnly as a " personality," or more obscurely in terms of " personalism." On the other hand, it is hard to see any good reason for regarding this term or these terms as so deeply and even decisively significant. The word *persona* (from *personare* or *perzonare*— to disguise) is etymologically ill-adapted to bear the sense intended. Indeed, we are pointed in a very different direction by its use in classical Latin (the mask or costume of the actor, the character or the part which he represents, the function, rank or significance which accrue to a man in the exercise of his office). And even in its very frequent modern use there has never been any agreement about what is meant by it or by its derivatives. The author of the article " Persönlichkeit " in *RGG²* is quite inclined to see something like personality, but in every type of organism and not just the human. And many questions remain unanswered. Why, for example, should the word " person " denote something weaker and more trivial and the word " personality " something much more lofty ? Can there really be any question of a greater or less in this matter ? Again, is " personality " something that a man is or has ? Is it something

that all men are or have, or only certain individuals ? And why has there
been the more recent coining of terms like " personalist " and " personalism " ?
I see no good cause to build on this group of terms in our present discussion.
Naturally, there can be no objection to their casual use in harmless connexions.
What they seem roughly to suggest in modern speech is the phenomenon of
man in connexion with his environment and yet in freedom from it. But we
are not compelled to use these terms to express this determination.

We might almost say that it is a phenomenon in itself that the
step in this direction is both possible and necessary, that the same
man can and must continually see and understand himself in his
identity in two spheres, passing from the one to the other and back
again. No, we have no reason to depreciate the importance of this
discovery. What is seen here may well be supremely symptomatic.
It may well be significant for the whole further development of our
theological anthropology that according to his own self-knowledge
man exists in these two spheres : in that of being where he thinks
himself and in that of decision in which he realises himself in action ;
in that of relationship to all other being and in that of freedom ;
passing from the one to the other and back, but without ceasing to be
in the one which he seems to have left, and therefore simultaneously
in both. It may well be that in our later consideration of real man we
shall be reminded of this singular result of human self-knowledge.
It may well be that it will prove important to have noted at this
stage that man cannot examine himself without perhaps completing
his naturalistic view of himself by an ethical, or even founding the
former on the latter—the question of priority need not now detain us.

It *may* be. But again we cannot say more. The reference is still
to what is only a human possibility. We have found confirmation
of what was indicated already in our first and scientifically restricted
view—that this possibility is richer and broader than may appear
to thinking which is referred only to sense perception. What formerly
appeared to be merely a very special and marginal case in the sphere of
organic life now emerges as a sphere of its own with its own validity
and value. Man also exists in freedom and decision. His possibility
is as great and comprehensive as this. But does this mean that we
now see his real distinctiveness, the particularity of real man ? Is this
second sphere, and the third which it also implies, man's power of
moving from the one to the other, more than a phenomenon ? In
this sphere, together with the first, do we see real man ? Or are they
at least his symptoms ? The latter has been asserted but the former
has also been maintained with emphasis.

We cannot agree. It is certainly good to have advanced from the
narrowness of naturalism to the breadth of the ethical approach.
But it is not so good that we may think that we have attained to real
man, to his uniqueness in creation. All our six criteria for the discovery of real man forbid this. It is as well to remember at this

important juncture that these are not merely formal but material criteria. If they are right, in relation to real man we have to do with God and man, with God's action towards him, with the glory of God in his existence, with God's lordship over him, with man's action in relation to God, and with the service of God which man must accept in this relation. Even the new human phenomenon which we have just been considering does not satisfy any of these material criteria. Even this new phenomenon fails to tell us whether God even exists. It shows us man, and man alone. But man alone is certainly not real man, the being who as man is finally different from other beings. It shows us man's existence in freedom and decision, but in so doing only a form in which he exists if he really is and is really different from other beings. But his reality and his real difference from other beings does not consist in a mere form. It consists in a specific decision, in a particular, true and exclusive freedom, in the existence which is thus filled with a rich content. The man who could decide otherwise, the man who has another freedom, is not real man, the man who as such is different from other beings. The advance from thinking to action or the reverse is a considerable step compared with the life phenomena of other beings. Yet it is not so considerable that we should be content with it, that we should feel compelled to recognise real man and his distinctive being in the man who is capable of this advance and engaged in it. Even granted the phenomenon of this advance, however clearly it presents itself and can be recognised, the question remains whether in either direction it has anything to do with God, with His action, glory, lordship and service. The phenomenon as such leaves this question open ; it includes both possibilities. As a phenomenon it is neutral and indifferent ; it forbids us to make the decisive statement. No doubt it speaks plainly of a certain possibility. But the possibility of which it speaks is also in the full sense the possibility of the man who fails to make the essential decision and thus forfeits his true nature. It is also the possibility of the sinner, of the man who alienates himself from God. It is not necessarily nor exclusively the freedom of the man who is free in his relation to God. It may also be the freedom of the man who in virtue of his disobedience is enslaved. Hence the ethical view of the phenomena of the human cannot and must not be equated with real man. Hence as far as our crucial question is concerned we must declare ourselves dissatisfied with this broadening of the perspective. Real man must be and must appear to be very different from the man who takes that step. To be sure, he will take it too. He, too, will make use of just the human possibility which we have indicated, of just the practical reason which we have rightly recalled. But we have only seen his shadow when we have seen this form and possibility, when we have seen him as one who is capable of this step. Even though he takes this step, in virtue of his origin and destiny he will have a very different appearance. We have radically deceived ourselves if when we see his shadow we think that we see the man himself. Indeed, when we see his shadow, his ethical singularity, we have not even seen the symptoms of his true self. For the ethical phenomenon alone does not provide these symptoms. Even when we have verified the ethical characteristics of man, we still do not have an unambiguous index of real man. For it is not the shadow which distinguishes real man from the man who has perverted his true nature. The shadow which both the former and the latter cast is precisely the same. The phenomena of the human as such, however accessible and transparent they may be to man's self-knowledge, do not avail to make this difference clear. If they were disclosed to us from another source, namely, from real man, the ethical singularity would also acquire significance. We should discover in the mere form the specific content, in the mere possibility the reality, in the mere shadow the substance, in the mere phenomenon of human progress the indication of man's origin and goal, and therefore in these symptoms real man, the man who is different from all other beings even in the one who has perverted his human reality, in the sinner. But to do so we must first see more than the human phenomenon, even appropriately widened in this way. Only then can we really do justice to this phenomenon, finding man in the particularity which differentiates him from all other beings, not only in the natural but also in the ethical aspect of his being. The phenomenon in itself and as such cannot give us this insight. If, because we have not already understood ourselves, we cannot recognise ourselves in the phenomenon, there is no knowing our human reality at all. No appeal to our ethical nature can change this situation in the slightest.

To test the situation, we may take as an example Johann Gottlieb Fichte : *Die Bestimmung des Menschen*, 1800.

Doubt, knowledge, faith—these are the titles of the three books which make up this work. It is a question of the doubt felt by the human ego about its own reality in face of the external world known by it, of the knowledge that it is the ego itself which as it knows constitutes the reality of even this external world, and of faith as the action in which the ego affirms itself as this sole reality.

It is what we have called the scientific point of view which, as Fichte sees it, plunges man into doubt. Once man has reached the decision worthy of himself, to will to know under all circumstances, then he comes to realise the complete determination of all that is, and the necessity which rules even amid all the changes of being. He knows of a power which determines the origin and the successive modifications of an object : of the multiple powers which determine multiple objects ; and of the one power as the power of all powers by which they are all determined. And he knows that he himself as part of being, of nature, is determined also by this general force of nature. That the condition of man is marked by conscious thought cannot change this at all. " It is the natural destiny of plants to develop according to rule, of animals to move according to purpose, of men to think." The general power of nature, of the cosmos, is also the power to think. Thus even man is only one of the particular determinations or expressions of this universal power. Even the fact that man is self-conscious means only that he is aware of one of the expressions of this universal power. And even the individual and his individual situation is only a representation of the absolutely transcendent capacity and necessity of the one power at a given time and in given circumstances. " All that I am or become, I am and become quite inevitably and it is impossible that I should be anything different." Even the fact that man is self-conscious means only that he is aware of one of the expressions of the one power of nature which moulds man too. To himself he seems to be free, for he thinks ; yet he knows himself to be under necessity. That he is aware of external things means that the universe becomes self-conscious in him, and sees itself from a special standpoint. " The consciousness of all individuals taken together forms the completed consciousness of the universe." And so even the fact that man consciously wills this or that is only the immediate awareness of the efficacy of the one power of nature in one or other of its determinations. Whichever of his inclinations triumphs in his decision triumphs necessarily. The virtue and the vice of each individual is irrevocably determined by the context of the whole. I do not act ; but nature acts in me. Hence I can make myself nothing other than what it has determined me to be. The heart of man protests against this self-contained conception, this dogmatic structure of thought. Man would like to be more than the expression of a power higher than and alien to himself. He would like to be independent. He wills to be free in face of the surrounding world. This freedom is at any rate conceivable as the freedom of a conscious being to the extent that such a being can think out beforehand the purpose of its action, exercising preference and choice between various purposes prior to its execution ; and to the extent that, in thinking concerning its purposes, it is before its own reality. But does not the same apply to this reality, to the action corresponding to its purposive thought ? Here the dispute begins. " Am I free and independent or am I not in myself merely the manifestation of an alien power ? " Neither of these opinions can be proved. The one satisfies, the other slays the human heart. If I decide for my freedom, I do so without reason, only because I love my love, and have interests compelling me in this direction. I must then admit from the other point of view that what I call my love is not indeed mine but the love of an outside power ; the interest of the cosmic force within me to maintain itself as such. What can I object to this ? And if I do not object, how can I fail to be miserable ? Man cannot remain undecided in face of this issue, but neither can he decide that he has no reason to decide one way or the other. This is the meaning of doubt. And he is plunged into this doubt by the best and most courageous decision which he can take—the decision to will to know.

The second book, entitled " Knowledge," gives us an Alexander-like cutting of this Gordian knot. Fichte has given this middle section of his work the form of a dialogue. " A wondrous figure," namely, " mind," seems at midnight to pass before this " poor mortal " and to address him. He is told to take courage, to listen and to answer the questions put to him. The narrative form is paradoxical enough in relation to the conclusions arrived at in the dialogue—that there is in fact no real external world, but what appears as such is only the knowing mind of man and is real only in so far as man is real. How then can a shape pass before man at midnight and address him ? How can there be a dialogue between it and man ? But of course it only appears to pass before him and address him. Hence the dialogue in which the following conclusions are reached is really a monologue. The things perceived by me in all my perceptions are not objects. Directly, and therefore in reality, they are only my feelings, my own conditions, and nothing more. " I feel in myself, and not in the object, for I am myself and not the object : thus I feel only myself and my condition, but not the condition of the object." What as my feelings I could experience only in temporal succession, I imagine in spatial juxtaposition. What I could posit only as a surface I posit as a body. I diffuse my perception in the space which I cannot perceive as such. Thus I transform my feeling into an object of feeling. I know that I am affected. And since I do not find the reason for my affection in myself, I seek and find it outside myself. I thus conceive the object and fashion it according to the mode of my affection, even though I know nothing about it. What I am really conscious of is not, therefore, the object but my consciousness of the object. And this consciousness of the object is the free act of the human mind which we call thought and which is quite other than the sheer spontaneity of feeling. In thought I add to my feeling a ground. And the ground which I conceive as the basis of my feeling is the object which appears to me in perception, even though it may be proved to have no basis in perception. Thus the consciousness which I have is the consciousness of the object, or rather of my own being to the extent that this is a knowing subject. It is my self-consciousness. Who and what am I ? I am subject and object, the identity of both. The only thing is that I cannot grasp this identity ; that it will always appear to me in the separateness of subject and object. But I am both subject and object. *I* look at myself. That is the subject. I look at *myself*, carrying myself out of myself in my looking. That is the object. But I am both my looking and the thing at which I look. As an object, as something external to myself, the thing which I contemplate is only a product of my thought. I fabricate it for myself. And my awareness of it is always in the last resort the awareness of what I fabricate. Thus in the knowledge and contemplation which we call knowledge and contemplation of things, we only contemplate ourselves. In all our consciousness we know only ourselves and our own determinations. Everything external to ourselves, the manifold particulars of the outside world and its inner connexion, arise only through the activity of our thought. The laws by which objects react on each other according to iron necessity and thus form the world system are nothing other than the laws of our own thinking. And so we need not tremble before this iron necessity, nor fear to be enslaved and oppressed by a world of objects alien to ourselves. The necessity of this outer world lies only in our thought. The things of this world and the world itself are our own products. Why should man be afraid of that which is his own creation, and again only himself ? This is the message of freedom which transcendental Idealism opposes to determinism, and the interpretation of human life by means of which it dissolves the antimony developed in the book called " Doubt." The strife between knowledge and will, necessity and freedom, cannot in any event be so hopeless if knowledge and the thing known are identical and if necessity is only the necessity rooted in our own processes of thought. But so far it has not yet been positively shown how far will and freedom exist. It would seem rather that this idealistic interpretation of knowledge throws the greatest doubt on the presupposition of all knowledge and freedom, namely, the reality of the human ego. Hence it is not yet possible to close the book " Knowledge." The dialogue with " mind " becomes dramatic at this point. Is it not the case that I myself become a mere mental concept along with the outer world ? The thinking subject itself merely a product of thought ? If I continue to think on idealistic lines, what I am conscious of is only my actual thinking and willing, but not its subject, not what is capable of thought, and even less a being in which this capacity rests, and which it possesses. I am conscious that I feel, contemplate and think, but I am not conscious that it is I myself who feel, contemplate and think, that I am the real ground producing thought, contemplation and feeling. What I call myself is properly only a certain orientation of consciousness which is called " I " because it is an immediate unprojected awareness which accompanies all my concepts, arising and vanishing with each new concept, but not patient of positive cognition. The supposition that I am continuously self-identical is obviously no less a fabrication of my thought than is the existence of an external world distinct from myself. What is, is only a series of images floating past (but floating past nothing !), meaningless and purposeless (because representing nothing, and relating to nothing), and I myself am only one of these images, or rather a confused picture of these passing images. " All reality is transformed into a strange dream, without a life which is dreamed of or a mind which dreams." My contemplation is the dream and my thought—which I regard as the source of all being and reality—is only the dream of this dream. Yes, this is indeed the case, the midnight spirit assures us. The inference to be drawn is a dangerous one, but it must be drawn. Yet we have not rightly understood the point at issue if we think that the teaching about knowledge which leads to this deduction is the whole truth concerning man. We wanted to learn about human knowledge, and we have done this, with a view to destroying the error concerning human knowledge which consists in supposing that there exists independently of us a world which we perceive and which enslaves us. But we could not do more by this means. All knowledge, and all knowledge of knowledge, is in fact knowledge alone. " A system of knowledge is necessarily a system of mere images, without any reality, meaning or purpose. Did you expect anything else ? Do you wish to change the inner structure of your mind and impute to it the possibility of being more than knowledge ? To know is not reality." We are right in refusing to accept that infamous suggestion. We are rightly concerned about reality. But we cannot possibly see it in our knowledge. If we had no other means of grasping it, we would never actually find it. But we have other means. " Simply enliven and sharpen this power and you will attain perfect satisfaction. I leave you alone with yourself."

And now the third book can and must be opened, the book called " Faith." This entails an advance and penetration into the sphere of ethics. " Your determination does not lie in mere knowledge but in action in accordance with your knowledge : this message rings aloud in my inmost soul as soon as for a moment I collect myself and look into myself. You exist not merely for the purpose of idle self-contemplation or brooding over pious feelings. No, you are there to act ; your action and your action alone decides your worth." That this is the case I know directly as I know myself. For as I know myself I am aware that I have an impulse to realise myself in absolute, independent action. In this impulse, i.e., as I think about what in this respect urges me forward, I ascribe to myself the capacity with complete power and authority to project a definite and purposive idea realisable through my own concrete action, not a reflection of something given, but a foreshadowing of what is to be created. This is just the point on which all awareness of reality is centred. We must not be misled into supposing that we cannot know this reality, that all desire to know must inevitably involve us in a *regressus in infinitum.* For I can believe (and this is the means by which I apprehend reality), i.e., I can voluntarily decide to acquiesce in the view which naturally forces itself upon me in my impulse to affirm myself in action, and in which I see myself to be free. Truth does not stem from knowledge but from conscience and inner disposition ; from the cast of thought which leads me to vindicate that impulse to self-realisation in action in spite of its doubtful theoretical basis ; from my free choice in virtue of which I choose precisely this among the various possibilities of viewing life, because I have concluded that it is the only one suited to my dignity and destiny ; from the innermost spirit of the spirit in which I make this choice, which in the truest sense is produced by myself, and in which I am not subject to an alien power (the antimony of the book called " Doubt " is now completely vanquished) but am my own creation and work. As in this spirit I command and obey myself, I believe. And I believe as I do this, as I relate my thought and knowledge to my action. I believe as I commit myself wholly to that voice of my inmost spirit and accept it as valid without further proof or foundation. Hence I believe as I regard the outer world as the sphere and object of my dutiful action. And because I have direct assurance of the laws of my action, I have indirect assurance of this world surrounding me, the world as the sphere and object of my dutiful action. Here, then, we have the basis and meaning of that projection of objects outside us. I project them as I regard them as the object and sphere of my ethical conduct. And in this way I know them. We do not act because we know ; we know because we are called to act. Practical reason is the basis of all reason. If we renounce it, then inevitably the world and we ourselves sink into absolute nothingness. We then project and know neither the world nor ourselves. If we raise ourselves out of this nothingness and maintain our freedom from it, we do so only by our moral life and to that extent by faith alone. And indeed, as we commit ourselves to the law and command of our action, we apprehend a being which lies in the future, seeing and affirming another and better world realisable by this action. The pledge of its reality lies only in the authority of conscience underlying our action, but this is a secure pledge. If in fact we live in obedience to this law and command, then already in the present we anticipate this new and better world. We cannot accept the fact that the whole structure of the world surrounding us is destined to remain as it is. The ideal of universal humanity becomes our goal and our task. We shall aim at the establishment of a single true and rightly constituted state which will eliminate the temptation to do evil and the possibility of wicked action on rational grounds, and in which there will be no egoistic aims and therefore no conflict other than the common struggle to fulfil the ideals of reason and overcome the opposition of untamed nature. This state is the goal of our earthly life. Reason projects this aim and is the guarantee that it will be infallibly attained. For it is attainable as certainly as there is a world of meaning and within it a humanity which apart from this purpose would be meaningless. It is attainable as certainly as I exist. The reason which projects this purpose and guarantees its fulfilment does not exist for the sake of existence, but existence for the sake of reason. Being is true being to the extent that it satisfies this reason. What constitutes my true dignity is simply that I allow myself to be guided by the law of reason and by the purpose which that law suggests. The will to do this is mine. It is the only thing which is completely mine, which completely depends on me. And because I have it, because I will to obey the law of conscience, I already possess eternal life and live it here and now. Heaven does not lie only beyond the grave. It is diffused about us here, and its light dawns in every pure heart. What is this light of heaven ? It is simply my will determined by the law of reason and constituting true and original action. For the latter alone am I in the strict sense responsible. As regards my individual deeds and the consequences flowing from them in the concrete world, I live always by faith, not by sight. But the present and every future, every possible world in which there are rational beings, can exist only through the obligations arising from the reason that lays upon me the duty of performing the true and original action which has its seat in the good will. Thus man is a member of two orders of life : of a spiritual in which he prevails by the effect of a pure will ; and of a sensual in which he acts through individual deeds. But as he lives in the spiritual world, he is immortal already in spite of the imperfection of his life in the sensual ; as he decides he grasps eternity, putting off the life of the dust and all other sensual lives which might await him, and rising superior to them. All this is on the condition that his will remains pure, that he is himself a first and a last, a will which exists for its own sake and which is itself its purpose to the exclusion of all other purposes. Fulfilling this condition, the will of man is united to the One which eternally is, and shares in its being. He does so principally in the amazing fact that as a free spirit he sees his like and recognises himself in other free spirits. But this is possible and takes place only in virtue of the fact that both he and they flow from a common source. Thus the harmony between our feelings, views and principles of thought, whether obvious or not, derives from the fact that a single eternal will is at work both in ourselves and other men. This will is the eternally existing

One. This is the world Creator who is necessarily reflected in finite reason in our minds, in our inmost selves, through which he continues to shape the world, intervening by the call of duty, and continually sustaining it. Even here Fichte does not utter the name of God. But at this juncture, in what may be called the second paradoxical interlude in his work, he allows himself to be carried away in a sort of lyrical hymn and prayer, in which he addresses this single eternal will as Thou, as the Father who searches the heart. And yet in fact he only says concerning him that he knows that he is united with him, that he regards his own work, knowledge, will and action as that of this Thou, and that in this difference from and unity with himself he is completely incomprehensible, i.e., is a being of a very different kind from that which he can ever think of as a being alone. There can be no doubt that the philosophy of Fichte finally comes to rest in this vision of this one single eternal will which in man is both I and Thou, both subject and object. " I am unmoved in face of whatever may happen in the world, for it happens in thy world." As man knows and loves in the recognition of this eternal will, the highest aim of earth, the one state guaranteeing universal peace, acquires importance not merely as a practical objective but because it is to be brought about by the free will of man and as a great free moral community (an expression of the freedom of the human will). On the other hand, the evil in the world is properly understood as a misuse of the free will, but also as an occasion for new duties and therefore operative in favour of the free will. From this point of view it becomes as clear as daylight that the philosophy of identity developed in the book entitled " Knowledge " is not so infamous as might temporarily appear in that argument. Where the being of man is at home—in the single eternally existing will—his thought is necessarily at home too. " And the truly human and only fitting purpose, that by which man's whole power of thought is expressed, is that by which the sensuous and concrete vanishes into nothing, and becomes for mortal eyes a mere appearance reflecting the invisible which alone is the real." All those who had a great heart and moral instincts, who knew that their citizenship was in heaven, and that here they had no abiding city, but were looking for one to come, all those whose fundamental principle it was to die to the world, and to be born again, did not in fact set the slightest store on sensuous experience, and " were, if I may borrow the expression of the schools, transcendental idealists in practice." But for all others this philosophy can be the power " which enables souls to cast off the caterpillar's skin, to unfold their wings on which they soar aloft above themselves, and, casting one last look at the slough which they have left behind, to live and aspire to higher spheres." From this there derives man's practical attitude in this world : " My spirit is forever closed to all embarrassment and confusion, to all doubt and anxiety, and my heart to grief, repentance and desire. The only thing which remains for me to know is what I am to do, and this I always infallibly know." Man's only legitimate concern is with the progress of reason and morality in the kingdom of rational beings ; and with this only for its own sake, for the sake of this progress. It is a matter of indifference whether it takes place through me or others. The only fact that matters is that it should take place. For " even my total personality has for me long been absorbed in contemplation of the goal." It may be that painful phenomena really serve this progress, and it may be on the other hand that pleasing phenomena really hinder it. Who knows ? " But I do know that I find myself in the world of supreme wisdom and goodness which thoroughly understands its plan and unfailingly carries it out ; and in this conviction I enjoy rest and happiness." " Ought I to be indignant because I see other rational beings striving against the law of reason ? Why should this make me angry ? " Why should it ? My indignation is obviously pointless, for if they are not free, they are not so, but are slaves of blind impassive nature. No doubt I may feel I must treat them as what they are not ; as a responsible member of society I will be capable at times of " noble anger " against them. But the poised, spiritually mature and contemplative man within me will not be angry even in such cases. Similarly, I will feel bodily suffering, pain and illness to be events of nature, but they will affect only the nature with which I am wonderfully connected, and not myself, the being which transcends all nature. Thus they cannot and must not trouble me. Similarly, I cannot and will not die for myself but only for others, for those who survive me. For myself the hour of death can only be the hour of rebirth to a new and more glorious life. " Could my death be anything else, when I am not merely a representation of life but bear within me the original and only true and essential life ? " What is that which is called death but the visible manifestation of a further quickening of life ? The only possible intention of nature, to express and maintain reason, is not yet fulfilled in this world, but when it slays a free independent being it passes solemnly, and in a way which is manifest to reason, beyond this act and the whole sphere which is terminated by it. Thus the phenomenon of death can be to me only the " guide by which I am led to a new life and nature." In short, I live in so far as I see the universe transfigured. " The dead burdensome mass which merely filled space has disappeared, and instead the eternal river of life, energy and act rushes and roars along—the river of original life, of thy life, thou Infinite. . . . I am akin to thee, and what I see around me is akin to myself ; everything is animated and ensouled and looks at me with the translucent eyes of the spirit, and addresses my heart in spiritual harmonies. In manifold division, I see myself reflected in all the figures without, and stream back from them as the morning sunlight, broken up into myriad dew drops, shines back at itself." And conversely the same life which outside me pours out its wealth in trees, plant and grass and which in the animal is expressed in free skipping and dancing, flows through my veins and muscles as a self-creative power, an energy which moves immediately in me in the motions of my own members : in the animal without freedom and in me with freedom. And now this universe is no longer to me a vicious circle, a self-devouring monster constantly engendering itself anew, but " it is now transfigured before my gaze and bears the very mark of the spirit : continuous progress in a straight line towards the perfect which merges into infinity." In all this, however, the transition from an old to a new and a more living life is only beginning, so that the world which I have been admiring may disappear again before my gaze. " This is only the curtain which conceals from me something infinitely more perfect, and the seed from which the latter is to develop. My faith passes beyond the curtain and warms and quickens this seed. . . . Thus I live, and thus I am unshakeable, firm and complete for all eternity ; for this being is not assumed from without but is my own, unified true being."

What does all this amount to, and what are we to say to it ? There is no doubt that it deals in some sense with what we have called the phenomenon of the human from the ethical standpoint. The outlines of this problem are unmistakeable in this exposition of Fichte. That in the act of his will man passes from the sphere of his natural determination to that of his true freedom seems to be the essence of this anthropology. Yet on further consideration the matter is not quite so simple. Fichte himself obviously says more than this. It is our own qualifying and limiting judgment that he is concerned merely with the phenomenon of the human. Fichte guards himself against this criticism. He speaks to us as one who is sovereign in doubt, in knowledge and in faith. He is a doubter who never for one moment thinks of doubting that he himself is called and empowered to know himself. He is so sure of his knowledge that he is capable of declaring its whole content, the objective world in its totality and including the knowing subject, to be a mere appearance. He is so strong and confident a believer that he can transcend this affirmation which he has so strictly attained by knowledge and can convince himself successfully that in his act, in his bold advance into freedom, he can posit and assert himself not only as one but as *the* reality, the ground and truth of the whole world of appearance which surrounds him. What Fichte claims to have understood and seeks to express is undoubtedly more than the phenomenon, more than what we have called symptoms of the human which can be subsequently recognised. On his own view, the ego of Fichte is not just man as seen provisionally or subsequently, but real man really known by himself. Fichte's claim is no less than this. With his doubting, knowing and believing, with his discovery of human freedom in which—in his opinion far too cautiously—we see the quintessence of his train of thought, he thinks he stands at the very goal which we feel has not been reached by this discovery in itself. Seeing in the situation what we also see, and seeming to say in his own way what we also say in ours, he supposes he has seen more and is able to say more than seems legitimate to us on the basis of our own estimate. He thinks that at this point he has found and can give the answer of which we feel convinced no trace can be discovered. And the fascination of the example of Fichte is that it has all the impressive power of something wrong-headed. This is what happens, as we learn from Fichte, when a thinker wants to persuade himself and others that with the discovery of the ethical potentiality of man he has also discovered his reality. The case is a warning to us. We should never equate the first of these discoveries with the second. For the first does not in any sense imply the second. If we think otherwise, making that identification, we really say less than we might on the point. The first discovery is not truly interpreted, and the moral interpretation of the phenomenon of the human darkens more than it illuminates. And this is what has happened in the case of Fichte. What we have called the quintessence of his anthropology has suffered in clarity and cogency from the fact that he tried to speak of much more than of the advance of man into the kingdom of his own freedom.

Fichte was able to see in his insights so much more than we think legitimate, namely, the discovery of true man, because for some reason he was from the outset resolved to understand man in isolation, as a being which is not confronted by any outward reality which might call it in question, from which it must receive instruction, by which man is controlled, and at the disposal of which it must place itself. The man of Fichte is from the very first capable of indefinite expansion. He has from the very first a tendency to be the one and all. The author of this philosophy seems never to have had the slightest interest or even concern about anything else. And so his exposition of man culminates in the triumph of this tendency. Only one thing is lacking to his man : the very thing which he must lack because of this his infinite abundance. He is poor—inconsolably poor—only at the point which constitutes his remarkable wealth. He has no limits. He thus lacks the very thing which is proclaimed in the title of Fichte's work : a determination. How can he have this when there is for him no external reality and therefore no limit ? We are told, of course, that he is self-determinative, but how can there be even self-determination for a being which is limited by no determining power outside itself ? How can there be the law, command, duty and obligation, about which Fichte talks so much in his book on faith, to which man as he sees it must cling, and in the fulfilment of which he is supposed to proceed to action and thus posit as real both himself and with himself the universe ? Again, how can there arise the need and power for decision and action in the strength of which there can be this fulfilment with all its consequences ? Above all how can there be those other worlds in which this being is supposed even after his death to live on, to determine himself and thus continually to affirm his reality ? The Fichtean man has everything, but his creator has denied him a determining limit, a law, a source of the need and strength for action, a true beyond of his life which can also be that of his death. From the very first he has total lack of the other in relation to which he himself can be. For all these things he can always be referred back only to himself.

He can be told only that he himself has to be these things. And he cannot really be told this except by himself. The midnight spirit only " seemed " to pass before him and address him. For how could it really do so ? And what it says, namely, the basic theoretical wisdom of transcendental Idealism concerning the unreality of the external world, betrays plainly enough that it is none other than the creation of man's own mind, that it is again he himself both in his abundance and in the dreadful poverty which accompanies it. Because Fichte has resolved *a priori* to see man in this fundamental insulation, he supposes he sees real man in what he seems to see. This absolutely autarchic being, which for all its expansive potentialities, its tendency to include in itself the one and the all, is self-enclosed, self-sufficient, confined to its own resources and existent only of itself and for itself, seems to Fichte to be the essence of the real and particular. He seems for some reason to think that this autarchic being is especially worthy of man, and therefore he feels that he must ascribe it to man. Because man is endowed with this autarchy, he thinks he can regard and describe him as real, as the most real of all beings, as the only reality. And in consequence he has only apparently seen what at this point, in the ethical consideration of the phenomenon of man, even he could and should have seen, and no doubt to some extent and in some way did see. He has thus obscured rather than illuminated this element in his anthropology.

The teaching of Fichte has been emphatically called the " philosophy of freedom." This is obviously because it really does seem as if its central object is man in his moral aspect and therefore in the light of human freedom. But one cannot say more than that this appears to be the case. For, while the outlines of our problem are indeed recognisable in Fichte's teaching, they can be seen only in confused and distorted form as though reflected in moving water, so that when we think that Fichte is speaking on this subject we cannot avoid the question whether it is really this subject and not another. In other words, we cannot help asking whether at the end of Fichte's train of thought we have really reached anywhere and not just come back to its obscure beginning.

The fact that in the book concerning doubt man's advance into freedom is still invisible because not yet made may at first sight seem to be self-explanatory and in the nature of the case. Man is considered and discussed from the standpoint of his naive and as yet uncritical self-knowledge. He is thus regarded with an unrestricted and inclusive determinism which in the first instance comprehends every *caveat*. But the question arises whether, on a true view of the human phenomenon in its ethical aspect, man may even momentarily, at the point of departure, be legitimately considered in this way, i.e., without any regard to his freedom. If man is in any sense in a valid position fully and consistently to deny himself freedom, as in this initial essay, how can he later come to be in a valid position to attribute it to himself ? He himself, and his authority to consider and declare himself not to be free, ought to have been called in question at the very outset. He himself, with the unproved assertions of which he is guilty, ought to have been doubted. And his freedom ought to have been held out in expectation by presenting him, with his provisional denial of his freedom and interpretation of himself as a mere expression of the general force of nature, as a being known, controlled and supervised from elsewhere, and thus confronted by a superior contradiction and resistance, so that the denial of his freedom is overcome from the very outset. But for obvious reasons there can be no question of this in Fichte's description of doubt. The doubt which is discussed here is only an antinomy within the self-examination of a man who is presented as fully secure and unassailable within himself. That the voice of the heart, of love etc., speaks in favour of indeterminism is indeed maintained, and Fichte returns to it later, advising us to trust this voice with all the power of our will in order by this deliberate resolve to confirm and perceive and know our freedom. But at the outset, and on the first pages of the book, such enthusiastic praise and encouragement is given to the man who wills to know himself by his own efforts, to the proclaimer of determinism, and then in the further course of the description of " Doubt " it is so plainly shown how man's will to know inevitably leads to determinism, and how completely this same enquiry can explain the protest of the heart in a deterministic sense and therefore silence it, that the question cannot be avoided *quo iure* the protest is raised which according to the later argument we must follow so unreservedly—the counter-voice of the same whose voice can here *de iure* proclaim his own slavery. If man is free, and if it is really the phenomenon of the free man which confronts Fichte, how can it fail to be seen that the real theme of doubt is this hesitation of judgment between slavery and freedom, that a relativity of human judgment is implied by this hesitation, and that the justification and reality of human freedom must be declared from some other source than man himself ? According to the logic of Fichte's argument, what this man can declare from within himself is human freedom. And the question obtrudes whether his own critical consideration of the scope of his knowledge can lead to the conclusion that man is free, and is not more calculated to make what follows highly doubtful, i.e., to bring the counter-voice on which so much emphasis is laid under suspicion from the very outset because it proceeds from the same mouth.

Even the second big step in Fichte's sequence of thought, the indication of the way in which human knowledge becomes true critical self-knowledge, cannot mean, according to Fichte's own statement, that the advance into freedom has been made and revealed. What is accomplished is only that the psyche is liberated from its caterpillar's skin, i.e., from its error in supposing that it is determined by an external world, in order that theoretically assured it may achieve its true life and make practical proof of its freedom. But it is open to serious question whether even this is really accomplished. For what does man really know in virtue of what according to Fichte's second book is his true critical knowledge ? Himself ? If Fichte had really seen the phenomenon of the free man the answer would necessarily have been that he knows himself as the subject of his action which leads to freedom. What is the meaning of man's knowledge as that of a free being if it does not at least have this content ? But we are actually told something very different. What we are told is that all that we suppose we know is only an assumption of human knowledge, and that its reality not only stands or falls with the reality of human knowledge but is absolutely identical with it. What man thinks he knows as existing is in truth only in himself, only in his knowledge. As he himself is ? Even his own being is wholly in his knowledge. He knows it, and he knows its reality, only in the same way as other realities, only within the category of the idea which he forms of the event of his knowledge. The fact that he can conceive this event does not in any sense prove that he is its subject and that he himself is. Knowledge is not reality. This applies also to man's knowledge of his knowledge. The obvious result is that even on the higher plane of his critical self-examination man again finds himself included in the same category with all other being. He is one image or concept among many others, and as such he is just as problematical as all other beings. He is known, but by the mere fact that he is known he is as little real as everything else that is known. According to this teaching, he may be withdrawn from the sphere of the cosmic force of nature, from the vicious circle of cause and effect. But he is held all the more surely in the vicious circle of reality and idea, idea and reality, like all other known objects. There is no human freedom in face of this circle. The fact that man is, is not any part of the knowledge which man can attain by his own resources. But, as Fichte sees it, the only question is that of what man can know of himself. And the only answer which he can give to this question is that man can only see and interpret himself like everything else that exists within this circle. We have no option but to ask Fichte himself how it was possible for him to have rightly seen the phenomenon of the human in its ethical aspect, and yet to be in a position to ascribe to man, in respect of the question of his own reality, such a meaningless and empty kind of knowledge. If man is free, and if he is seriously understood and seen to be free, how can he fail at least to know about himself ? How can he be unknown to himself, a mere concept among so many others ? If it is a fact that free man knows about himself, does it not necessarily follow, not that he can know about himself from his own resources, but that he does actually know about himself because it is given him to do so from other sources ? But the question is quite meaningless for Fichte. Man as Fichte understands him has no other source of knowledge. There can be no knowledge from without because there is no " without " anyway. This type of thinking is ended before it has even begun. Hence we can only note that he prefers to speak of a supposedly free man about whom he is nevertheless obliged to report that he knows nothing of himself and can know nothing. But if this is the case, has he really seen the phenomenon at issue ? In view of the third part of his exposition, we can hardly deny that he has done so in some sense. But the way in which he will later say that he has done so is hampered from the very outset by the fact that from the standpoint of an ostensibly critical knowledge he was able to speak of him as though here at least he had not rightly seen the phenomenon in question. At any rate, we can hardly say that this philosophical doctrine of being and its knowledge is quite the most fitting instrument to prepare us for a consideration of the advance to human freedom. How can the being ever be free, and be understood to be free, of which we are now told that it is not even in a position to have a genuine consciousness of itself ?

But we must be just, for it is the glory of faith as described in Fichte's third book that with man's deliberate resolve in face of his naive as well as his critical knowledge, of the vicious circle both of cause and effect and also of reality and idea, there is quite a new beginning, and this time the true beginning of real man, at any rate as Fichte envisages him. If we are to understand Fichte, we must realise that the freedom of man is not compromised by the fact that it could not be anticipated in the teaching concerning his naive and critical knowledge about himself. We confess that we do not feel comfortable about this *metabasis eis allo genos*. We confess that we would be happier if this teaching about man's naive and critical self-knowledge had prepared us for the fact instead of leading us not to expect that the truth lies in what we are now challenged to believe. Are not the doubter, the knower and the believer one and the same person, the one sovereign man who is to be taken equally seriously in all his possible modes of self-contemplation ? Are the doubter and the knower so presented by Fichte that he can now legitimately introduce the same person as a believer in a mode of self-contemplation in which what was formerly invisible is now visible and what formerly seemed unreal suddenly becomes real, and therefore the former mode of self-knowledge is completely shattered and transcended ? How can Fichtean man make this leap when there is nothing outside himself, so that he cannot be induced by any outward cause to make any such radical transformation in his mode of self-contemplation ? Can he really do it ? Has he not shown by his prior self-contemplation that he is far too heavily burdened to do so ? But we will waive this question and concede that he does, that in respect of his practical reason he has the ability in some way to transcend himself, and thus to know that which in respect of his theoretical reason seemed to be completely precluded. We thus take note that now in spite of everything he trusts in the protest of his inner voice in a way which his naive self-knowledge forbids. And to the extent that he decides to do this he takes his existence seriously, as though it were not merely a semblance, or one of many concepts or images—an attitude which his critical self-knowledge forbids. He declares—and this declaration is his faith—that he will not sink into nothingness, but will regard his practical reason as the root of his whole reason. He behaves as he must behave according to the command of his practical reason. And as he considers himself in this action he sees and understands himself as a free being. We are here at the point where it seems beyond dispute that Fichte has before him the phenomenon of the human in its ethical aspect. We might ask : Why not earlier ? Why not from the beginning ? How could the doubter and the knower speak as Fichte makes them speak if his believer must speak in this way ? If what is here said about man is fundamentally and intrinsically valid, how can it fail to have been stated earlier ? How can it be put forward only at this stage of the argument, and only as an article of faith ? But let us waive this point. There can be no doubt that it is stated here, and, if we have an objection, in strict justice it can be only to the way in which it is stated here. And it is in this respect supremely that we do have an objection to make. Our objection is that this man who becomes free through his action, stepping out of the causality of nature into his own sphere of freedom, cannot for one moment be regarded as a valid conception. Hardly has this man posited himself in will and action before he thinks that in so doing he has posited all things, even the whole universe. Hardly does he see himself in action before he sees himself in the strange " peace " which is supposed to rest on the fact that everything which appears to be outside him is really within him, that what is within him forms the epitome of all that is outside him. Hardly has he recognised that in his willing and acting he is free and therefore good before his freedom and goodness becomes the freedom and goodness of the surrounding world in which he says he can find nothing to disturb, arrest, sadden, pain or annihilate him. Simply because he regards himself and all that is in the light of his practical reason, death itself lies at his feet, and this world and all possible future worlds have become transparent to him as a possession which he can enjoy and control. As he steps out into freedom, the whole dead and burdensome mass of his own and all spatial nature is transformed into an eternal stream of life energy and act ; he is already akin to all that is ; he finds everything animated, ensouled and transfigured, his own body no less and no more than tree, plant and animal ; and everything is subsumed in a direct and constant progress to perfection. Already he is eternal, unchangeable, secure and complete. Even though he stands before the veil of eternal life, he can already lift it. Already everything external is within him, and everything within him external. It is the very note of triumph in Fichte's idea of freedom which makes it so dubious and unacceptable as an idea of freedom. There is no doubt that the phenomenon at issue is momentarily glimpsed by him as in a flash of lightning. His description of the event in which man affirms and discovers himself in will and action is exemplary. But Fichte wants to see more than this phenomenon, and so it escapes him again, its outlines are blurred, the picture of man is lost in the abundance of what is outside him, and the controlling theme of the description, instead of being man's conquest of his freedom, is again the one eternal life force which is in all things and there-fore in man. Does not this really bring us back to the point from which the whole essay started, to the vision, as it appears to uncritical knowledge, of the one in the all, of the all in the one, of the great life stream in which man is only a tiny drop ? We do not overlook the fact that everything is now reversed. This is the triumph of Fichtean faith. Man as seen in the light of his practical reason, and therefore understood to be free, is himself the stream in the onward sweep of which all other things are only tiny drops. Man is not, therefore, a slave but free, and not only free but sovereign, the free lord because the creator, the maintainer and the controller of all things. But is this reversal, this transi-tion from bondage to freedom, as important as it seems ? In the last result does it not amount to the same thing whether we see the one which is the all, the all which is the one, from the standpoint of its universal structure or any other part, or from that of man himself ? Is the unique reality of man assured by the fact that he understands himself to be free, to be the centre of all things, to be the morning sun reflected in a myriad dewdrops ? Can this be a final reversal ? Is it proof against a fresh reversal ? May it not be that the wheel which has now turned to the right will turn to the left again ? Supposing that the real morning sun refuses to be broken up like this but insists that it is the role of man to be a tiny dew-drop and therefore its reflector ? In looking back from the book on faith to that on doubt, have we really made any progress when we consider everything from the standpoint of indeterminism rather than determinism, and set it under an optimistic rather than a pessimistic sign ?— everything, i.e., the totality to which in either case man himself belongs. No, we must deny that the phenomenon of man proving his freedom in decision and action has been rightly interpreted even (and supremely) at this point where the concept of human freedom is filled out in this unprecedented fashion. What is really to be seen in this phenomenon is certainly not man in his sovereign unity with the totality which exists apart from him. What is to be seen is something much more modest and therefore much more important, much less and therefore much more. It is man in his uniqueness, the man who is neither a drop in the stream of life nor the stream itself, but simply himself, and therefore something which no other being outside him is. For when man wills and acts, something takes place which neither as an effect nor as a cause takes place in that unity with what is outside him. What takes place is a free and therefore a human event, free whether we look backwards or forwards. And this is what Fichte momentarily glimpsed and then lost again. His anthropology is a naturalistic anthropology even though it culminates in this doctrine of freedom. For even in this doctrine of freedom the picture of man in nature raising himself above nature emerges only for an instant and then fades. And it is obviously at this point that the weakness which from the very outset vitiated Fichte's view of man is avenged, viz., the lack of a limit, the fundamental lack of a counterpart, the absolute subjectivity to which his man was condemned from the very first. Because this unhappy man must be absolutely subjective, and can have no other to limit him, then whether he is viewed deterministically or the reverse, pessimistically or optimistically, as a slave or as the lord of all, he can only be seen in fusion with this all, and in face of it his being cannot be regarded as free. Not even in view of his practical reason ! For at the very point where he is supposed to be seen in his freedom, in his practical reason, he can again (and supremely) be seen only in his unity with the all, and the uniqueness of the phenomenon of man is not brought out. On Fichte's presuppositions it is impossible to make the leap which his believer wants to make. And, looking back from this point, we cannot be surprised that Fichte's teaching about naive and critical knowledge is so negative in relation to this phenomenon.

We have already said several times that Fichte had some reason for trying to work exclusively with this presupposed idea of the autarchy, the absolute subjectivity of man. The reason is quite simple. Fichte was determined to view man apart from God. We must not be deceived by the fact that he gave his third book the title " Faith." For even in this book there is not a single word about faith in God. The god in whom Fichtean man believes is himself, his own mind, the spirit of the protesting voice in which he puts his confidence and in the power of which he knows himself to be free. Nor must we be misled by the passages in this third book where—even in the second person and in a kind of prayer—he speaks of the one single and eternal will. For this Thou is not to be taken any more seriously than the midnight spirit at the beginning of the second book. A Fichtean dialogue can only be an alternative form of monologue— a form which may occasionally be interesting and desirable because Fichtian man is both subject and object, both I and Thou, and because there are con- texts in which this fact must be brought out. A God to whom man belongs as to another ; a God who can act in relation to man and become his Saviour ; a God who has His own glory in which the essential concern of man is to be seen ;

a God who reigns ; a God in relation to whom man gains his freedom and whom he must serve in his freedom ; a God who confronts and limits man and is thus his true determination, is for Fichte non-existent. Fichte's god is Fichte's man, and Fichte's man is Fichte's god. And it is because God is non-existent that Fichte has had to conceive the idea of absolutely autarchic and subjective being, to ascribe this being to man, and to regard the resultant figure as real man. And it is for the same reason that he cannot even see and interpret correctly the phenomenon of the human. It is for this reason that here, too, the contours are all blurred. It is for this reason that his philosophy is particularly unconvincing as a philosophy of freedom. If the aim was to provide a philosophy of freedom, it would have been better not to regard God as non-existent, and therefore to become blind even to the phenomenon of man. This is the warning which we are finally given by this stimulating example.

But our view of the phenomena of the human can and must be deepened further. The ethical understanding of man is at one with the naturalistic in visualising man as a self-contained reality : in the former case, more from the standpoint of his external conditioning and in the latter more from that of his inner freedom ; but in both cases in the wholeness of his self-existent being, as a subject which is an object, and can be seen and understood and controlled as such. This whole presupposition, which is commonly accepted by the naturalistic and ethical, the biological and idealistic views of man for all their differences, can and must be transcended. In its place, it has its indisputable justification and its own special and indispensable function. Man's understanding of himself as the relatively closed natural and ethical reality in which he depicts himself is a definite part of his understanding, and even a basic part from the genetico-psychological standpoint. But this presupposition is not unlimited.

Its limits emerge as soon as the question of man's being is deepened to include the question of his existence, of the distinctive concrete mode in which he exists. This question is raised but not answered by descriptions of his natural and ethical reality. Of course, an answer is prepared, but only prepared, by the transition from a naturalistic to an ethical view. For this entails a widening of perspective from the mode in which he is to that of the way in which he wills to be and thus posits himself, from his natural conditioning to his self-determination in freedom. In this step forward into freedom, a hint is already given of the great fact that he himself exists. He not only knows himself but actualises himself. But does he really see his existence, his true and concrete life, when he recalls his action ? Is the man whom he sees engaged in the advance into freedom really his true self ? Is it himself whom he sees will and therefore move out of nature into freedom ? Is not this view limited by that in which he must always realise that he is a child of nature and as such conditioned ? And is not the equation of freedom of will with existence threatened already by the fact that even in his freedom he still thinks that he can see and understand and master himself, that he can radically perceive and control himself as an object ? The problem

of the existence of man is the problem of the subject which is different
from the object thus seen and understood. If I exist at all, I do so
as this subject, even as a natural and ethical being determined no
less than self-determining. For in my natural and ethical life, to
the extent that I think that I can see and control myself in these
respects, I can only consider and handle myself as an object of this
subject. I myself, existing man in my true and concrete being, am
the subject of this object. And this means that with the raising of
the question of existence the self-contained totality of human reality
as presented in the naturalistic and moral ethical views is radically
shattered. If we ask concerning existence and therefore about man
as subject, we ask concerning something which lies essentially outside
any theory of man and therefore outside all possibilities of understanding and controlling man. We no longer ask concerning the
object but concerning the subject, man. We ask concerning the
source of every concept of man, whether in relation to his nature or
his freedom. If the phrase may be ventured, we ask concerning the
primal phenomenon of man. We ask concerning the one who projects
these concepts. And it is we ourselves who do so. For in so doing
we exist properly and concretely, and not merely as those whom we
see and understand ourselves to be in the light of this or that theory
and therefore as object. And we ask concerning ourselves as such
when we press beyond the question of our nature to that of our existence.

Is there an answer to this question ? There is undoubtedly an
answer. But we have no chance of finding it unless we do not let
ourselves be enticed into seeking it in a given factor which can be seen
and understood as such, and as such has again the character of a
concept and therefore an object. For in this case we should not be
seeking and finding ourselves as those who project the concepts, as
those who exist properly and concretely. If we ask concerning ourselves as such, we must not let our search be deflected for a single
moment or in any way, and the answer can only be that man exists
to the extent that, pressing beyond the question of his nature, and
ignoring every answer to this question, he asks concerning his existence.
His existence is he himself, who in his very subjectivity, in his very
indefinability, is seeking after the mystery of himself, who can certainly
answer the question of his essence, of the " how " of his nature and
freedom, yet who cannot find himself in any of these answers, but
must go beyond all these questions and the answers that may be
given to them, if he is really seeking after himself. Seeking after
himself, he must always transcend himself, going ever beyond the self
which he is able to find. It is always in this act of self-transcendence
that he exists properly and concretely. It is always in this search for
himself that he recognises and affirms himself. And as the being who
transcends himself, and therefore is always in search of himself, he is

the projector of those images and concepts and the subject of himself regarded as object, first seeing and understanding himself as a natural being, then advancing from nature to freedom, and thus seeing and understanding himself as an ethical being. Treading this path, he finds himself on the way which leads him to the limit where there will be no further image or object, but only himself. On this whole path he prepares himself, exercising himself so to speak in symbolic fulfilments, that when he reaches its limit he may transcend and find himself as the subject of all that is still object on this path. And it is as he treads the path which leads to this frontier that he exists. He thus exists in tension, and this tension is on the one hand (subordinately) that between his natural and his moral life, and on the other hand (primarily) the tension between what is merely his nature and himself as the bearer of this nature, the one who exists, and who in relation to everything which constitutes his natural and ethical life, in relation to everything which is the object of his self-recognition and self-mastery, can see and understand himself only as a possibility and never as an actuality. He exists in the historical reality resting on these tensions.

But what is the theme of his asking and the goal of his self-transcending? Is this a valid question? Undoubtedly, for if it were not, if it were illegitimate to ask concerning this theme and goal, we should again be understanding man in search of himself, and therefore transcending himself, as a self-contained and complete reality. And in that case he could and would be an object again. The question of man as subject would then necessarily arise in face of this object. But the self-contained and complete reality of man is really shattered even in this form to the extent that it is set in the light of the genuine question of existence. It is thus the case that the question of man in his existence cannot be avoided for a single moment or in any respect. His existence must be understood as a genuine question. But if it is understood as a genuine question, it is clear that it cannot be self-sufficient, that in its inadequacy as a mere question it calls for an answer, indeed that the indication and proclamation of an answer, whatever it may be, is the reference to a This responding to the What?

Genuine man, properly and concretely existing, is certainly in quest of something. Hence he is not alone, nor does he grope in the void, when he is on the way which leads to that frontier. It is not in vain that he is in quest of himself. Even in his questing he cannot be identified either with God or the world. He exists in tension both from and towards something. He is historical in a history which has a goal. His existence is in relationship, and therefore in a relationship to another being which transcends himself and his natural and ethical life. It is in that transcendent being that he seeks himself. Otherwise he does not seek himself but is ensnared by the delusion that he has found himself and possesses himself. But the legitimate question concerning this other requires a legitimate answer. It is evident, however, that this is not given—the warning with which we began these deliberations is relevant again—if we regard and treat as an object the something for which existent man undoubtedly asks and reaches, namely, the other which is transcendent to his nature. We must not attempt to do this, since it is the subject man which alone we can expect to find even in this other. Being this other, it will undoubtedly elude all objectification, materialisation, or even spiritualisation ; indeed every kind of definition. Strictly speaking, even when we say that it is we say too much or perhaps too little. It can be described only as the origin of being, but in saying this we describe it as unthinkable and inexpressible, as that which we can only miss with all our speaking and thinking.

Is it then unknown to us, and therefore meaningless in practice ? On the contrary, in its very remoteness and inaccessibility it is the content of our existence, which apart from it could only be for us a possibility. For in this remoteness and inaccessibility it continually proclaims itself to us and comes to us, filling our existence with meaning. This happens in the "frontier situations," i.e., in all those paradoxical situations of suffering and death, conflict and guilt, which are not forseen in studies of the natural and ethical nature of man. These are the barriers which continually confront us on our way, and which we can neither avoid nor even explain. Existence is transformed from a mere possibility into a reality (a reality which is actualised by ourselves) in the moments when in these unavoidable and inexplicable situations we have to wrestle with them, or rather with the transcendent which encounters us in them ; when we cannot on any pretext or by any means escape the anguish which they cause us ; when we can answer the true and concrete limit and distress which they impose upon us in these situations only by defiance, which really means enforced surrender, or, overcoming our defiance, by unconditional surrender, in which our anguish is overcome and our resistance made meaningful. Thus, when human existence becomes unavoidable and inexplicable and totally questionable, it acquires value as a question which is worth putting and which, without ceasing to be a question, implies an answer, provided that there is unconditional trust. In it the transcendent other comes to man. To be sure, it will go again. It can never be objectified and defined. But it will not fail to greet man, to set its mark upon him, to make his self-consciousness, which in itself can only be his self-questing, a cypher or symbol of itself, and therefore of the man he seeks. Since for our good we are not spared these frontier incidents, the transcendent other, without which we would not exist (because our existence is a genuine question) can be known and meaningful, and in place of the concept of man as a self-contained and rounded reality there comes the experience of his disruption, and therefore the experience of his openness, his actual relatedness to this transcendent other, and therefore the experience of his real existence.

In this account we have drawn freely on the anthropological teaching of Karl Jaspers (*Philosophie*, I–III, 1932). In the context of our investigation of human phenomena this is important because, in common with other products of modern existentialist philosophy, and unlike Naturalism and Idealism, it emphasises the historical element in human existence and thus breaks through into the dimension to which Sören Kierkegaard formerly pressed in impotent isolation. Without the discovery of this dimension, attempts at human self-understanding which are confined to the question of man's nature may be very suggestive in other respects, but they retain a singularly abstract and remote character and do not escape a final emptiness. In particular, the existentialist philosophy of Jaspers has rightly aroused attention in the most varied quarters because its questions and answers seem to be framed and carried on in characteristic parallelism with those of theology. His doctrine of frontier situations especially seems to approximate at any rate to a genuinely Christian understanding and estimate of man, as, for example, in Luther's account of the relation between election, vocation and temptation. And it seems not impossible to recognise in his interpretation of human existence and its concrete actualisation by means of the idea of man's relatedness to the transcendent, something akin to man's original determination by God, and therefore in this idea of the transcendent God Himself. At any rate, in this circle of ideas there is something reminiscent of K. F. Meyer :

> To Thee I stretch my hand in nights of pain,
> And all unhoped for feel it clasped again.
> What God is, no man can ever know,
> But from His covenant He will never go.

We may certainly say in relation to Jaspers " that in the existentialist philosophy of to-day we find in operation a new and serious philosophical concern with the religious question." (Martin Werner : *Der religiöse Gehalt der Existenzphilosophie*, 1943, pp. 21 ff.) On the other hand, it would have been better if this philosophy had not been accredited with having " unconsciously given new and valid expression to important elements in the Christian tradition," and the detailed attempt had not been made to trace back a connexion beyond G. Keller and K. F. Meyer to the saying in 1 John about the perfect love which casteth out fear. Measured by this criterion, the anthropology of Jaspers is inadequate. We may certainly admit that existentialist philosophy in the form which Jaspers has given it reveals recognisable traces of the proximity of the Christian Church and to that extent of the Christian sphere in which it was planned and projected —and on a sober estimate we can hardly deny as much to G. Keller and K. F. Meyer. It may also be granted that in this case the traces are more relevant and important than those which with a little good will we can also find in the philosophy of Fichte or Hegel. But we cannot say that it gives forceful expression to important elements of the Christian tradition, or that in its own way it says exactly the same thing as 1 John, because it lacks the content which would make its theses Christian. A new human phenomenon is certainly seen in this philosophy : the historicity of man and his relatedness to another. In relation to those previously mentioned, this phenomenon is decisively important. Looking back from real man, we may even claim that it is the most genuine symptom of the human. But we cannot say more of the anthropology of this philosophy than that it has seen a phenomenon of the human. We cannot say that it has shown us real man.

The limit of this anthropology of the frontier is to be found at the point where it has to lay a concrete foundation and give specific support for its programme of demonstrating that human existence is actualised only through its relation to the transcendent. In relation to naturalistic and idealistic anthropology it certainly has the advantage that it can show the being of man dynamically and in its basic openness, as his act in relation to another than himself and in encounter with this other rather than self-grounded, self-resting and self-moving.

According to Jaspers' own definition, existentialist philosophy is the philosophy of human being which leads us beyond man himself (*Die geistige Situation der Zeit*, 1931, p. 134). All mere knowledge of man implies " a particular perspective " which reveals merely the context of his situation but not man himself. And all mere knowledge can be manipulated by the knower. But the knower himself cannot be manipulated in this way. " He himself is to himself the absolutely imperfect and imperfectible, delivered over to another." As he finds that in all knowledge he himself has not been known, " he again breaks through, this time through himself, and so he comes to himself, there is imparted to him what is more than himself, and in transcendence he grasps the being which in the freedom proper to his phenomenal existence he mistook as his own." (*op. cit.*, p. 133 ff.).

But this description of man lacks any concrete assurance with regard to the counterpart of man which underlies this movement and determines its whence and whither ; with regard to the other to which he is so exposed, according to this definition, that he would not exist without it. We have considered the teaching about frontier situations, which in its own way is so striking. Certainly the understanding of the contradictions of life implicit in these situations, and of the negations which they suggest, distinguishes this existentialist anthropology so sharply from that of Naturalism and Idealism that we are tempted to define the former as true and the latter as quite untrue. But what are we to say of the assurance that it is precisely in these situations that the wholly other meets us as that which awakens the deepest anguish and then on the fulfilment of a given condition tranquillises us and fills our being with meaning ? that it is precisely in these situations that we are confronted by transcendence, and therefore by the factor which most radically changes and shapes our life and gives it meaning ? Why in these situations ? What is there to give this assurance credibility ? Certainly not the intrinsic quality of these situations ! Man is always and everywhere involved in suffering and death, conflict and guilt. But it is far from obvious, nor is there any compelling reason to suppose, that it is such crises which really bring man into relation with the wholly other, and lead him to an existence which embodies the meaning of this relation.

It may well be described as one of the most striking and therefore necessary experiences of our own age that this view has not been clearly demonstrated. Millions of our contemporaries have been constantly plunged from one frontier situation (in the most intense sense) to another. But what has it all meant to them in practice ? Has any one encountered the wholly other, and been changed by this encounter, as a result of taking part in the fighting in Russia or Africa or Normandy, of suffering the Hitler terror, of enduring aerial bombardment, hunger and imprisonment, of losing loved ones, of being in extreme danger of death dozens of times, and of having some sense of personal implication in the common guilt ? Humanity is tough. It seems to have been largely capable of dealing with the confrontation of transcendence supposedly implied in these negations of its existence. Surely Jaspers himself noticed that it passed largely unscathed through the first world war, in retrospect of which he wrote his *Philosophie.* And if appearances do not deceive, we have also passed through the second unscathed. If any one has been changed in these years, it is certainly not in virtue of the extraordinary situations into which they have led him. According to the present trend, we may suppose that even on the morning after the Day of Judgment—if such a thing were possible—every cabaret, every night club, every newspaper firm eager for advertisements and subscribers, every nest of political fanatics, every pagan discussion group, indeed, every Christian tea-party and Church synod would resume business to the best of its ability, and with a new sense of opportunity, completely unmoved, quite un-instructed, and in no serious sense different from what it was before. Fire, drought, earthquake, war, pestilence, the darkening of the sun and similar phenomena are not the things to plunge us into real anguish, and therefore to give us real peace. The Lord was not in the storm, the earthquake or the fire (1 Kg. 19$^{11f.}$). He really was not.

It is just not true that specific and particularly negative situations are intrinsically bearers of the mystery of transcendence and therefore of human life. Hence we cannot readily assent to the assurance of existentialist thinkers that in virtue of their inner quality these situations carry a summons to realise the meaning of our life, nor can we admit the authority which this assurance claims.

But what are we to think of the further assertion that that which in these frontier situations confronts us ineluctably and mysteriously like a " wall " is transcendence, the wholly other in relation to which we alone exist and therefore the factor which, in the opinion of Christian interpreters of this anthropology, is no doubt equivalent to God ? Let us admit, and we certainly have reason to do so, that there is a considerable difference between standing in these frontier situations and living in the even tenor of a calm or but little troubled existence, enjoying life in blithe unawareness of the ever present possibility of these situations. Of course there is a difference between sharing or not sharing in certain experiences, between suffering or not suffering, between dying to-day or not dying to-day, between being in the front line of the battle of life or at the base, being more or less guilty in the great web of human guilt (e.g., a notorious war criminal, a foolish collaborator or the honourable member of a resistance movement). Of course there are such things as special experiences, the encounter with specially significant events, special sin and special misery, and perhaps special relations with death. But who can guarantee the assertion that it is transcendence—the genuine transcendence that is itself the guarantee of our existence—which meets us in these special experiences, first judging us and then perhaps, if we fulfil that last condition, saving us ? We should remember that the problem of this transcendence is such that first and last we seek in it ourselves— the answer which it is the business of our existence to find. In these circumstances, could it not equally well be a demon which fools us at that frontier as the ostensible and illusory goal of our search ? The devil as well as God is privileged in his own way to be alien and remote, incapable of objectification or definition. Perhaps it is he who has set us in this final anguish, and then what promise does it hold out ? Perhaps that which beckons us when we have endured the ordeal bravely is only the devil's favour, and what kind of a peace shall we find after the storm if it is only the devil's peace ? And if not the devil himself, how many slighter and less dangerous but not for that reason more profitable deities there are, principalities and powers which in evil as in good, in conflict as in peace, in heavier as in lighter guilt, in the hour of our death as previously, might cloak themselves in remoteness and inaccessibility without really having anything to do with genuine transcendence, with what may also be described as God ! The existential thinker has ascribed too much significance to this point beyond all objects and images, to this power of man to transcend himself, for us to be fobbed off, in relation to this point and what it really implies, with his solemn assurances about the wholly other. In this connexion he has nothing to offer except this solemn assertion. We may gladly admit that in this respect he shows himself to be a religious philosopher. But we cannot admit that he gives us the basis of certainty which he would certainly give us if he were really bringing out elements of the Christian tradition.

And finally what are we to think of the direction which seems to be the real force of the reference in this philosophy to the transcend- ence which meets us in frontier situations ? In itself it does not sound too bad. If we meet the other which comes to us in moments of anguish with unconditional surrender and trust, it will free us from anguish and give itself as perfect peace. But an alternative is possible. We might meet it with a conditional surrender limited by our own defiance. Even then we do in fact give it in our recognition. According to the Christian interpretation, even as defiant deniers of God we confess in involuntary willingness the God whom we have encountered in the frontier situation. In this case, however, we cannot really be freed from anguish or rejoice in the positive revealed in the negative, the peace offered us in the midst of dispeace.

Our first question on this point is how man can choose the second possibility rather than the first. Does not transcendence impose itself upon him in these frontier situations far too seriously and drastically to leave this second alternative open and thus to necessitate a special direction to the former ? Do we not have here a plain in- dication and confirmation that frontier situations as such are not so saturated with transcendence, or that the transcendence which they mediate is not so genuine, as this type of thought suggests ? If the two assertions were true that it is transcendence which meets us precisely in these situations, and that this is genuine transcendence, the wholly other, surely there can be no question of choosing between those two alternatives, and the direction to take the first is superfluous because it presents itself irresistibly and to the exclusion of any other possibility. But since it is admitted that this is not the case even in frontier situations, the main principle of this anthropology, i.e., that human existence is essentially related to transcendence, is necessarily shown to be highly problematical.

But we must ask further whether there is not a third reaction to frontier situations. Is there not a definite and very fatal *via media* between unconditional surrender and defiance, between atheism and faith, and one which we are really far more tempted to adopt when the waters come in upon us, namely, the way of resignation, the unworthy but in its own way very realistic possibility of indifference ?

Here we would add to what we have already said about the signs of our times, that the signature of modern man by many evident tokens seems to consist neither in the happy penetration to peace nor in persistent and titanic rebellion against his fate, but simply and unfortunately in his utter weariness and boredom. It is obvious that man can have such a surfeit of these frontier situations, as has happened to many in our own age, that both the counsel to surrender and the warning against defiance are equally meaningless. The reason is that man is bored with himself. He can no longer work up any interest in himself, or give himself to the stimuli and disillusionments of seeking and self-transcendence. He thus reacts neither positively nor negatively to his experience, however intense. He is no more capable either of the joys of faith or of the fierceness of atheistic defiance. Everything has become a burden to him. He has attained only to the indifference which lets things take their course. To-day this possibility of lethargy seems to be very remote in Russia or America, but it is a pressing reality in Europe, and above all in Germany. And perhaps the last and fateful question for Europe is whether it will succeed in shaking off this lethargy.

Why is existential thought silent about this third possibility ? Perhaps because the religious interpretation of human life obviously reaches its limit at this point. The assertion that human life is related to transcendence presupposes that man is interested in himself, that he is not weary of himself but in search of his true self. " Existence is only in relation to transcendence or not at all," is the magic formula of this philosophy. And there are frontier situations in which this relation necessarily emerges. Hence the direction to adopt an attitude of utter trust and the warning against defiance, although even defiance does in some way reveal this relation. But it is obviously not revealed if alongside the trustful and defiant man we have also to take into account the weary and indifferent man—the very man who not only to-day in Europe but at all times and in all places—not in the foreground but in the dark background and depths of world history—

has formed the vast majority of mankind. The type of thought which claims that human life is related to transcendence cannot take account of this man, or even of approximations to this man, because to do so is to obscure its primary claim. It must describe frontier situations as if the choice lay only between the religious and the anti-religious attitude, as if there could be no question of the choice of an attitude which is purely and simply a-religious. If we make the " wall " which meets us in the frontier situation, and the mystery of transcendence to which it points, the measure of all things, is it fair to take account of the enthusiasm which is able either to affirm or to deny the mystery suggested, but to ignore the lethargy which may also be a reaction in this situation, leaving out of account the tired and indifferent man, as though there could be no place for him too, and for him precisely, in a coherent anthropology ? Is not this unfairness a further indication that it is not quite correct to maintain that the frontier situation is laden with transcendence or that this is genuine transcendence ? Is it not a further indication of the highly problematical nature of the main principle of this philosophy ?

But now we come—and from quite a different angle—to the decisive question which we must put to this philosophy in respect of the direction which plays so important a part in it. Let us suppose that the things which we have found so very questionable are in good order. Let us assume that there are distinctively negative situations in which the mystery of transcendence waits for us or comes to us. And let us assume further that this is genuine transcendence, the wholly other which can be identified with God. We are now told that the battle raging in every man between belief and unbelief may, should and can be decided by his turning in unconditional faith and absolute trust to the other which he encounters in the darkness of his negative experiences. Note that it is a question of man himself fulfilling the condition which he is seriously expected and required to fulfil. And note that it is assumed that man can fulfil this condition. Of course, he can also take up an attitude of defiance, of conditional surrender and suppressed and hampered confidence ; and he is warned against such an attitude. But what interests us at the moment is the assumption that he can trust unconditionally. We gladly accept that as a reward for this fulfilment he is promised participation in the great peace of transcendence. In fact we do not even need to believe it, for it goes without saying that not only is this reward given him but that he already has it in his fulfilment of the condition, indeed, in the very fact that he is a being capable of fulfilling it, capable of unconditional surrender and trust. But consider what this means. It means that the unconditional trust and therefore the transcendence which we supposed him to lack, to have to seek in self-transcendence, or to have to receive from without, is already within him. Is it not then the simplest thing in the world for him to find and obtain it ?

Transcendence was only apparently far away. In reality it was intrinsic to his existence as the possibility of unconditional surrender and faith. What is revealed *in extremis*, in frontier situations, both in the religious man and also in a restricted and conditional form in the anti-religious, is simply that the concept of the relation of existence to transcendence is far too weak and inexact to describe the real truth of the matter. The manner of man as it appears in the fulfilment of that condition is essentially that of transcendence. And the manner of transcendence as it emerges in man's fulfilment of that condition is obviously the most proper manner of man. Thus man does not really need to ask concerning transcendence. Indeed, in the strict sense he cannot. What he can and must do is simply to understand that he himself is the answer to his question. Again transcendence does not need to come to man from without. Indeed, in the strict sense it cannot do so. What can and must happen on its part is simply that it should disclose itself as the transcendence of man. The astonishing thing about the direction which is both the basis and the crown of this philosophy is that its presupposition, namely, that man is capable of this unconditional attitude, means that the other elements in this doctrine are shown to be a solemn, exoteric game, in which a basic unreality characterises the assertion that man's existence consists in the search for it, the statement that he exists constantly in self-transcendence, the tensions in which he lives in consequence, the idea that the other must first come to him or he to it, the fine notions of the openness and the historical nature of his existence, and the idea of the questionableness of existence which we sought to interpret as meaning that human existence is a true and serious and worthy question demanding a no less true and serious and worthy answer. The whole point about this game is that in it there cannot possibly be a true and serious question or answer. For on both sides, within and without, now and then, existence and transcendence are essentially one and the same. This is what is disclosed by the account of the mystery of frontier situations. What is not disclosed is the fact that the rent tearing human existence to its depths is healed and closed in virtue of a historical relation to genuine transcendence. On the contrary, what is disclosed is that at bottom this rent does not exist, that there is no opposition between existence and transcendence, and therefore that there cannot be a historical relation between them, not even in the impressively recollected frontier situations, and particularly not in them. Unmistakeably, even though against the intention and the purpose of this anthropology, we are again confronted by the picture of a self-enclosed human reality beyond which there is nothing to confront it, and which, because it is itself the one and all, cannot be confronted by anything that might be identified with the God who is distinct from man and the world, and superior to both.

According to the express statement of Jaspers himself, the illumination of existence given by this anthropology can lead to no result inasmuch as it is without object, " ungrounded in its objectivity " (*op. cit.*, p. 146). It does, of course, move into a new dimension. But it does not think at all of going beyond the one which for it is the all. It moves only within this one. To be sure, it " attempts " a metaphysics. It is an approach to this. But it does not do more than " conjure up " transcendence (p. 133, 145). And by its very presuppositions this " conjuring up " cannot lead to any goal. For " the creation of the metaphysical world of objects, or the revelation (*sic*) of the origin of being, is nothing when severed from existence. Psychologically considered, it is evoked and consists only in imaginative forms and distinctively fluid thoughts, in the contents of narrative and constructions of being which immediately disappear in the light of penetrating knowledge. In these man attains peace, or the clarity of his dispeace and danger, when the truly real seems to disclose itself to him " (p. 147). There is no point in making the philosopher say more along these lines than what he actually does say according to his explicit statements or can say on the basis of his presuppositions. The door to a being which is not identical with man but confronts him and yet is for man the solution to the conflict of his existence, is certainly aimed at in this anthropology. This is its lasting merit. But we do no injustice to the lofty ethico-religious and sometimes almost prophetic seriousness of Jaspers' philosophy if we maintain that this door is nowhere revealed in it to be an open door.

Accordingly, there is lacking here too a clear view of man himself engaged in the movement towards transcendence. Indeed, it is of a piece with the presuppositions that at the end of all our discussions of existence we shall know no more of him than at the beginning. What could there be to know and to say about him, the pure subject of all objects, under any conceivable circumstances?

" Existentialist philosophy would at once be lost if it thought it knew what man is " (p. 146). It cannot and does not aim to be anthropology any more than psychology or sociology ! " For man who is on the way it is the expression by which he maintains his direction, the means by which his high moments are kept for actualisation in life " (p. 146). " Clearness of consciousness implies a claim but does not bring fulfilment. As those who know, we have to be content with this. For I am not what I know and I do not know what I am. Instead of knowing the truth about my existence, I can only introduce the process of clarification " (p. 147), without having any right to expect that in knowledge I will bring myself to anything but the " suspense of absolute possibility " (p. 133).

And from what we have heard of transcendence and its conjuring up, we cannot expect that this will overcome the difficulty, or yield an illumination in which man's self-understanding will reach a goal and to that extent fulfilment. With the question of transcendence the question of existence, of man himself, must also remain unanswered, because fundamentally it is unanswered. If we speak of the conjuring up of transcendence by an appeal to human freedom, or of the appeal to human freedom made with the conjuring up of transcendence in the event of frontier situations, we say the final and in the last resort the only thing which can be said on this view to describe the proper being of man. And it is not at all clear what is conjured up and by whom, or to what appeal is made and by whom. Indeed, it is doubtful whether there can be any real meaning at all in this talk of conjuring up and appealing, since it all takes place in the sphere of the one human reality.

This means that, while we must accept a certain resemblance between this conception and that of Christian anthropology, we cannot suppose that the two are related or that the latter can be regarded as based on or to be explained by the former. The indisputable resemblance lies in the concepts of the openness and historical character of human existence which are so important in existential anthropology. But it makes a great difference whether these concepts can be taken seriously or whether they remain a mere scheme of thought which it is impossible to carry through on the basis of one's presuppositions. In the latter case, they do not point us to real man but only to the phenomenon of the human. And if we are to see in this a genuine symptom of real humanity, we must first know what true humanity is.

In this sub-section we have spoken of man's attempt to understand himself when he is presumed to be able to do so in his own strength and by his own resources. The naturalistic, ethical and existential views of man are the most important stages on the way of this autonomous self-understanding. But we have not encountered real man in this way. We have not, of course, taken this way without having specific criteria in mind. From the very outset we have not been prepared to recognise real man in a being which is neutral, indefinite or obscure in respect of God's attitude towards it and its own attitude to God. On a very definite ground, that of the view of the man Jesus which is normative for Christian theology, we have postulated that real man must in any event be a being which as such belongs to God, to which God turns as Saviour, the determination of which is God's glory, which exists under the lordship of God and is set in the service of God. We were warned at the outset not to seek real man elsewhere but in this history between God and man, and to recognise as the nature of real man none other than his being in this history. On the basis of this warning, our way through the various stages of self-understanding on the part of autonomous man was necessarily critical, and we could not stop or express ourselves satisfied at any of these stages. We could, of course, maintain, and had to do so, that specific human phenomena are noted with more or less precision and fulness at these stages ; phenomena which can be appraised and interpreted as genuine symptoms of the human if we have a knowledge of real man from other sources. In no case, therefore, have we basically rejected the observations possible at the various levels, naturalistic, idealistic or existentialist. We have not rejected this whole way of human self-examination, this attempt at a progressively more penetrating analysis of the picture in which man can see and understand himself. At the level at which it can be made, we have accepted it. What we have rejected is the idea that more than certain significant human phenomena are visible at any one of the stages or in their sequence and interconnexion, in the coherent system which might be constructed from their detailed conclusions. We frankly confess that more than this cannot be seen on our own presupposition. We can only dispute from the outset the supposition that any understanding of real man can be attained at all by man's autonomous attempt at self-understanding in any of its phases. And in any case we have found this presupposition to be confirmed by the inner incompleteness and obscurity, the self-contradiction, of the portrait of man which has emerged at every stage of this path and in the total result. It became palpably clear to us at the last stage, in face of the existentialist interpretation of man, that everything that can be said and thought about man points beyond or behind himself, like an interesting commentary on a text which must first be known and read for itself if the commentary is to be intelligible and useful. But the same is true of the naturalistic and idealistic interpretations. It is also true of the naively classical definition of man as an *animal ratione praeditum*, to which we referred at the outset. Nor have we merely made a postulate and critique *a priori*. In accordance with the postulate of our theological presupposition we have recognised that the significance of the conclusions about human nature possible on the way of autonomous self-understanding depends on their reference to a reality which does not emerge as such on this way. In other words, their significance consists in the fact that in themselves, as the conclusions of man's own effort at self-understanding, they refer only to phenomena of the human, in which we can see symptoms of the human itself only when the latter is known to us, but which in and of themselves tell us nothing about real man.

But before we take up the question of man himself, real man, on a very different level, it would be as well to consider what is involved in the adoption of another level as opposed to the way of autonomous human self-understanding.

Very generally, the difference consists in the fact that the sovereignty in which man claims to know himself is renounced, or rather that it is regarded as relative rather than absolute. Hence it is seen that, while the conclusions of autonomous human self-understanding are not necessarily false, but in their limits may well be accurate and important, they are all bracketed, and no decisive enlightenment about man is to be expected from within these brackets, but only from a source outside. This source is God. He, the Creator of man, knows who and what man is. For man is His creature, and therefore in the last resort known to Him alone. He must tell man who and what he really is if this is to be known to him. The new level of discussion which we have now to adopt after traversing the way of human self-understanding will be noetically distinguished from the level of this way by the fact that here, if we are to know who and what man is, it is essential that God should have spoken and that we should have listened to His Word. The point is that the man who can teach himself well or badly about the phenomena of the human finds that in respect of his reality he must receive and accept the instruction of God ; that the autonomy of his self-understanding is limited, at the decisive point where phenomena and reality are to be distinguished, by the instruction which is to be received and accepted from God. In general terms again, there stands behind this noetic difference the ontic one that man is not now seen apart from God. As the creature of God, i.e., as a non-divine reality posited by God, he lives only in this relationship to his Creator ; in confrontation and connexion with this absolutely transcendent place and factor. That God is his Creator and he a creature is something which we cannot forget for a single moment when we think of real man, but must always interweave into the very texture of our thoughts. If it is forgotten, if we think of man in isolation from and independence of God, we are no longer thinking about real man. Man exists only in his relation with God. And this relation is not peripheral but central, not incidental but essential to that which makes him a real man, himself. He is to the extent that not he himself but God is His sovereign Lord, and his own sovereignty flows from God.

But this general observation is not precise enough to be adequate. For the instruction concerning himself which man has to receive and accept from God might be thought of as an innate awareness of his relation to God, and his being with God and under His sovereignty as a relation given in and with his being as such. The relation to God would then be a kind of attribute of man. It would in a sense belong to him. It would then be possible, still within the framework of autonomous human self-understanding, to press beyond the conclusions of even existentialist philosophy to the point where man himself can come to realise that his limitation spells a relationship and that he exists in confrontation by a real other. This other, existing with him, would then be noetically and ontically immanent as well as transcendent, and in its immanence as present as man himself is present. A theistic philosophy is conceivable and has been attempted, often more or less clearly as a basis for theology, in which the autonomous self-understanding of man is extended to embrace and enclose his theonomy. The thought of man as not really sealed off from outside, and therefore as only relatively sovereign, is one which is quite conceivable within the framework of autonomous human self-understanding, and so too is that of a wholly other which limits man and determines man absolutely from without. A bolder philosophy than that of the modern West, with its anxious concern for the limits of pure reason, has always dared to think along these lines without reaching either the

Christian idea of God or the Christian idea of man. We shall thus have to consider and express more exactly than we have done what is meant by the instruction which man must receive and accept from God and his being with God and under His sovereignty. Otherwise we might still be moving on the level of understanding which must now be abandoned, and our conclusions might still be hedged in by the reservations which are inevitable on that level. Otherwise we might merely establish another phenomenon of man and not his reality.

We can attain a new insight, however, only if we remember that the noetic and ontic situation with regard to the relation of man does not consist in the mutual co-ordination of two spheres or factors, but in a definite relation or attitude, primarily on the part of God and secondarily on that of man. If we think and speak of God and man in Christian terms, this means according to our criteria, to which we cannot adhere too strictly at this important point of transition, that we think of a history which is enacted between God and man under the transcendent leadership of God, in which decisions are made first by God and then also by man, and in which particular decisions and purposes give rise to action and suffering, speech and hearing, question and answer, on the part of God and then of man—and this in the true sense of these words as terms which denote the filling of time and cannot be taken to refer to timeless and static relationships. What takes place between God and man is both noetically and ontically, both in regard to the instruction which it gives and the being and action which it implies, far more than a mere relationship. It is an attitude, and a very definite attitude, which has its origin, meaning and effectiveness in the initiative of God, and which even as the attitude of man can only be explained by the free and special initiative of God. We pass beyond the limits of autonomous human self-understanding, therefore, to a genuinely different level of thought, only when we realise that the conjunction " God and man " or " God with man " or " man with God " means noetically and ontically that God *acts* towards man, and when we rigidly confine our view to the history which takes place between God and man. It is at this point that the protest is usually lodged against the Christian interpretation of man by the various doctrines of autonomous human self-understanding. It is at this point that offence is usually taken. The theistic notion of God cannot really be incorporated into these doctrines. To be sure, a bolder or humbler conception of the tasks and possibilities of human self-understanding, of the nature of human reason, may very well be prepared to take more or less seriously the idea of a transcendent God distinct from man and the world. It is not, therefore, beyond the bounds of possibility that the concept of man will take a form corresponding to this presupposition. But there is no way from autonomous human self-understanding to awareness of the free action of this transcendent God and therefore to the reality of man established only by this free initiative of God and His temporal and historical dealings with man. This awareness is possible only on the basis of the instruction imparted by this freely acting God to man. If it is to be attained, then the closed circle of man's self-understanding must be broken from without and made accessible to something outside itself. The instruction in question then consists in the recognition that the circle is open, in the acceptance of the instruction which comes to man from without, from God Himself. And the human self understood in this way is the reality concerning which man allows himself to be told from without, by God, that it is his own reality. It necessarily follows that, as the reality of man consists in dealings between God and man initiated by God, so its recognition consists in a concrete, divinely appointed occurrence, in a history of revelation and faith. This means that the recognition necessarily rests upon revelation and is effected in faith in this revelation. In order to become knowledge of real man, human self-understanding must be reversed and refounded, being changed from an autonomous into a theonomous self-understanding.

But we must explain ourselves even more precisely. A type of autonomous human self-understanding is still conceivable, and has in fact been essayed, in which account is taken, not only of the difference and confrontation between man and a wholly other which may be called God, but also of the dynamic character of the relation between them, yet in which the circle of autonomous understanding has not been broken, in which no instruction from without, from God, has actually been received concerning man, and in which therefore the concept of real man has not been attained. For it is not beyond the possibility of autonomous human self-understanding to recognise that the being of man, the being of that other which might be divine, and the relation between them, must be regarded as dynamic rather than static, and that this whole nexus of reality, and within it the reality of man in particular, must be construed in terms of actuality.

That the phenomenon " man " can and must be also regarded quite simply as an organic chemico-physical process taking place in time is easily demonstrated on the level of natural science. On the level of Idealism, emphasis will be laid on the fact that this same phenomenon is to be interpreted in ethical terms, yet even so as a sequence of actions wrought in time. And the whole point of the existential analysis is to understand the distinctive being in man, not as a given natural or intellectual factor, not as a being which is in any sense at rest in itself, but as a striving after being which is to be described as questioning, self-transcendence or anxiety. It is a strange paradox that even the imprisoning of transcendence within human existence, which is, if possible, more characteristic of this final stage of reflection than of those which preceded it, does not prevent it from interpreting existence as pure movement. Thus a philosophy is quite conceivable which bursts the bonds of the monism which prevails at all these stages of reflection, attaining the thought of a wholly other confronting man in clear differentiation and superiority, and to that extent a kind of conception of God, and going on to describe and explain that God and therefore man and the relation between them, in terms of actuality, i.e., on the presupposition of an action taking place between them. We cannot, therefore, say in advance that an anthropology of this type is inconceivable within the bounds of autonomous human self-understanding. In other words, the formation of an actualist anthropology does not necessarily demand divine instruction, or the change from an autonomous understanding of man to a theonomous. Even the form of the actuality of his existence is one of the things about which man is very well able to instruct himself.

He may, for example, learn to know the actuality of his existence as follows. To begin with, he can appreciate the fact that his being, so long as he has it, is an ability to be, a sequence of actions in which he constantly re-posits himself in his conscious or unconscious thinking and willing in relation to another which he may well think of as the wholly other, as God. He thus discovers himself in his freedom ; and especially in our discussion of the second and ethical stage of human self-understanding we have noted how this awareness can be enriched and deepened in detail. Being in the sense of human being is a process of self-enactment. In the light of reason he then discovers that his freedom in its receptive aspect clearly consists in his capacity to assimilate, i.e., in the fact that in relation to the other which may well be God, he can be taught that this other or God can communicate with him, and that he can hear and understand what is said and to that extent make it his own. There can be no being or self-enactment without experience. He is as he learns. It is the manner of his freedom to be " rational " in this sense. He can now see and say that between the two terms, between man and the other which may be God, there is reciprocity, so that human being on its active side can and must always be understood as a reaction to these experiences, as an answer to the communication which comes to him. To be a man is to be responsible. To be a man is to respond to what is said to man. The spontaneity of man consists in the fact that he is capable of this responsibility. In each of the acts in which he constantly re-posits himself man exercises this capacity. His freedom is his freedom to participate in this reciprocal action   And this conception of his freedom can be envisaged in at least three aspects, each of which sheds new light on man.

If his rationality and responsibility are related to the fact that they constitute the freedom of a human subject, his capacity to have experiences of his own, to hear the word addressed to him and to fulfil his own responsibility in answer to it, then by this freedom we may understand what is usually if rather obscurely called the personality of man.

If his rationality and responsibility are understood as the freedom of this human subject to stand in the mutual relationship between that which is without and that which is within, and perhaps therefore in the mutual relationship between man and God, then the freedom of man's being may be brought under the concept of historicity.

If finally his rationality and responsibility are related to the fact that his participation in this mutual relationship both in its receptive and spontaneous aspects in his own concrete choice and act, then his freedom must be understood as his capacity for decision, and his being as an ability to be must be interpreted as the constant seizure of his own possibility.

The idea of the actuality of human existence is undoubtedly possible on these or similar lines ; it has in fact been introduced from the theological standpoint in historical and material connexion with modern existentialist philosophy. But the following points must be remembered. To make this idea possible it is not necessary that there should be divine instruction. Revelation and faith, the change from autonomous to theonomous self-understanding, are not in any sense indispensable. The supposition of any kind of reality distinct from man is sufficient for the purpose. By this reality something like God may be understood. But it is not at all necessary that it should be in relation either to God Himself or to something like Him that the being of man is actual and therefore rational and responsible, and therefore personal, historical and capable of decision. For God there may be substituted a vague summary of everything which from man's point of view confronts him and is superior to him. One interpretation may put in the place of God the impersonal reality of death as the limit of human life ; another the personal reality of his fellows. It is in relation to these that actuality is ascribed to his being. That it is to be described as responsible in relation to the Word of God is a possible but only an optional hypothesis in the formation of this view. The idea of another really distinct from man is a general idea, not necessarily tied to that of God. And even if this other is taken to be God or something like Him, we are not bound to a specific idea of God, as, for example, the Christian. Thus the idea of the actuality of human being which may be attained on these lines is by the very nature of its content a general and neutral idea. If it does not say in relation to whom or what man is responsible and rational, it also does not say in what hearing and answering, in what experience and reaction, the distinctively human is to be found. Necessarily, therefore, it leaves indeterminate the whole idea of human freedom, understanding the freedom which it takes to characterise humanity in purely formal terms as a capacity to seize this or that possibility. It cannot say in relation to what other person the being of man is personal, in connexion with what history it is historical, in what determination it is capable of decision. The answer to all these questions is necessarily related to the other implied when we speak of actuality. If it is uncertain whether this other is God, or if so what is meant by God, the idea of actuality as such will also be uncertain. And there can then result only the general truth that in some way or other man is a reasonable and responsible being, personal, historical and capable of decision.

But if this is the case, it must be pointed out in conclusion that, although the concept speaks of actuality, its true reference is only to potentiality. It presupposes in a general way that there is this other in relation to which man is active, from which he receives something, which he answers, in relation to which he is personal, between which and himself there is a history, and determined by which he decides. Again, it presupposes in a general way that in relation to this other man is active, that in this relation he really receives and answers, that he is really a person, and has a history and decides. But since it does not give any specific account of this other in relation to which man is active, and therefore cannot give any precise account of this action, since in both respects it remains general and formal and must work with vague presuppositions, it does not actually attain the real which it seeks to attain and seems to denote. It would have to speak of a real human action to be able to speak of real human actuality. But it does not do this. It speaks only of possibility. It speaks abstractly of capacity or disposition. It speaks merely of a potentiality and not of the actuality of the human being. To give a true description of the disposition or potentiality of man, it would have to understand the possibility from the reality, referring to a concrete apprehension and not merely to rationality, to a concrete response and not merely to responsibility, to a concrete person and not merely to personality, to the history in which man lives and not merely to his historicity, to his decision itself and not merely to a capacity for decision. As a purely abstract idea of potentiality, it is not the concept of real man, and therefore it too can describe only the phenomena of real man.

Thus even the concept of the actuality of man has not led us any nearer to our goal. We cannot, therefore, support the view that with the formation of this theory we have advanced to a theological idea of man. That this is not the case is clear from the fact that the theory can be developed within the framework of autonomous human self-understanding. And how little it can help us to the desired definition of real man is confirmed by the fact that on this basis we can only make these general and formal observations, attaining nothing more than an empty idea of human possibility.

In making these final observations, I have had in view certain important sections of Emil Brunner's book *Der Mensch im Widerspruch*, 1937 (pp. 45–104, 259–281, 424–479, 554–557, E.T., *Man in Revolt*). If I understand the author rightly, freedom as rationality and responsibility, and therefore as personality, historicity and capacity for decision, is for him the very essence of man. He claims that this is the theological view of the matter, and therefore the concept of real man. In what I have said, am I in agreement with Brunner or in opposition to him ? I should prefer the former, but fear the latter. But the situation is complex and many-sided. We shall thus conclude this study, and our whole investigation of the phenomena of the human, with a question addressed to Brunner.

He says quite explicitly, and has made it clear in relation to the discussions of 1930, that it is his aim to break the closed circle of existentialist " suspense in sheer possibility " by constructing an ontology and theological anthropology in harmony with the Christian faith. The first principle of his anthropology is " that man can be known, not from himself but only from God " (p. 53), which means from the revealed Word of God. " Only an act of cognition . . . in which God gives and we receive, discloses to us the truth about humanity " (p. 54). Man's understanding of himself can take place only in the event of divine self-attestation, i.e., only in Jesus Christ as attested in Holy Scripture " (p. 55 f.). But this Word of God constitutes for man the basis not only of cognition but also being. Man is, lives and subsists in the Word of God (p. 59 ff.). In the triune God who elects him, and in the love of this God, he has an original and counterpart which summons him to a response of love and therefore to responsibility, thus communicating itself to him. This is the ground of his being (p. 63 f.). Human existence is thus something which knows itself to be determined and conditioned by God, and recognises and realises itself as such. It is in the Word of God as it is responsible to God, knowing and determining itself in harmony with the Word of God ; it is " the divinely appointed creaturely counterpart to the divine self-existence, the divinely posited counterpart which can answer God." Man is the being which can echo the primal Word of God, independently reaffirming it, giving to God's " Thou art mine " the reply : " Yes, I am thine." This capacity, rooted in his reason and manifested in his responsibility, is the relation to God which determines the being and nature of man (p. 86 ff.). It makes him a person as distinct from all other creatures (p. 426), and therefore a means adapted to reveal the person of God, and therefore the centre of the cosmos (p. 432). It imparts to his life its character as decision (p. 442). It is the basis of his historicity (p. 451 ff.). And all this, his personality, his character as decision and his historicity, is to be understood Messianically (p. 458) to the extent that its origin and proper locus is not in this or that man as such but in the person of Jesus Christ, in the decision made in Him and the history enacted in Him (p. 456 f.).

We see and admit at once that more is done here to break the closed circle of existentialist thought than we visualised in our own consideration of the possibility. For there is taken into account not merely a frontier situation but a genuine limit with a real that side and this. There is envisaged a real Other, a real Transcendent, a real Opposite to man. Moreover, there is expressly recognised and clearly shown from the very first that this Other is identical with the God of biblical revelation, with His Word and His electing love, and with Jesus Christ as the sum of His Word. The being of man is understood as actuality to the extent that it is defined and described as the capacity to hear this Word and as responsibility towards it. His personality, historicity and capacity for decision are all strictly derived from this Word and related to it. Finally and supremely, there is reference to the Messianic quality of human life. Can the theological character of an anthropology be more plain than is the case here ? Can it be doubted that what is seen and described is not merely phenomena of the human but what on a Christian view can only be called real man ? That we are brought very near to the goal is beyond question. But Brunner thinks that he has reached it. He thinks that in describing man as having his being in the Word of God he has spoken of real man. And since I fail to see this, a serious question must certainly be put to him.

Let us agree that it is so ; that man as the creature of God has his being in the Word of God. The christological content which Brunner so impressively gives to the idea of the Word encourages us to make this assumption It certainly seems as if the concept of human freedom, developed in the ideas of rationality and responsibility, personality and historicity, is a concept filled by the consideration of a certain use of freedom, a certain type of hearing, responsibility, personality, historicity and decision. Occasionally Brunner does actually speak of this filling of the concept. He seems to have in view the act of God's gracious dealings as it takes place between God, i.e., the triune God, God in Christ, the God of Scripture, and man ; he seems to have in view the revelation of God and faith in Him, when he speaks of the actuality of man. But my question is whether we can take it that the actuality in which we recognise real man as God's creature is the actuality, and only the actuality, which he acquires as a partner in the act of God's gracious dealings. Is it, therefore, the possibility or potentiality actualised in the fulfilment of this act ? Is it the disposition and capacity which are imparted to man with its enactment ? Is he free for what God in His freedom does with him and for him in this act ? Is his hearing a real hearing of what God says to him ? Does he come to realise his responsibility by giving to God the answer which is in harmony with His Word ? Is he a person who as such fulfils the demands of this Other, the divine person in which his own being has its origin ? Does the history inaugurated between God and himself reach its goal in his historicity ? Is his capacity for decision his capacity to do justice to the decision of God which is prior to it ? In all this do we have to do with a specific content of his being and not with its mere form, not with a mere possibility, potentiality, disposition and capacity, but with those which are actualised in that act of God's gracious dealings ? Is his freedom, therefore, very different from a neutral freedom in which he might not correspond to the Word of God (as he should do according to Brunner), but might equally well refuse to do so ? Only if this is the case can it be said that he is in the Word of God. If he lives in the Word of God, how can he who corresponds to it oppose it ? Is there in the Word of God, in Jesus Christ, a No as well as a Yes, and therefore a basis for this opposition ? Is there in the Word of God, in Jesus Christ, an indecisiveness which enables man to use his freedom otherwise than in grateful obedience to God's gracious action ? Is the determination of man as God's creature plainly and exclusively his determination to share positively in the history of the covenant of grace which begins with his creation, or can it include also a possibility of withdrawing from this covenant ? Is sin a possibility foreseen and contained in the creaturely being of man ? The unequivocal formula of Brunner that man is in the Word of God, and therefore does not exist apart from it in any way, and his energetic christological interpretation of the term " Word of God," seem to make it necessary for him to understand the being of man as positively determined and filled in relationship to God ; to keep the concept of human freedom, rationality, responsibility, personality, historicity and capacity for decision clear of any confusion occasioned by an implicit neutrality ; to describe man as the creature of God unequivocally as man in covenant with God ; and therefore not to regard the possibility of sin as one of the possibilities given in human creatureliness. If this were the case—and I repeat that it seems to be so according to the introductory thesis and many individual passages (e.g., pp. 266 ff., 468, 474)—I should have no good reason not to agree with him and to recognise that in his anthropology he has attained the concept of real man as the creature of God.

But this is the very thing which is obscure and even contested in his anthropology. At this very point he seems clearly and consciously to veer in another direction. The being of man in the Word of God and in Jesus Christ does not mean, according to Brunner, that in creaturely correspondence to God and as a " Messianic " being he has only one possibility and aim. His rationality, as Brunner sees it, is not conferred on him solely by the fact that he really hears what God has to say to him, so that if he failed to do so he would cease to be a rational being. His responsibility, as Brunner sees it, does not depend on his giving God the answer which corresponds to the divine Word, so that if he failed to do so he would act irresponsibly. That there is also bondage, irrationality, irresponsibility, and therefore apostasy not only from God but also from man's true being, and therefore, not as a possibility but as an impossibility, sin—all this seems to be for Brunner a foreseen possibility within the rationality and responsibility given to man with his creation, and therefore in some sense to have its root in the Word of God in which man has his being. For him personality does not arise solely from the fact that man stands in a positive relation with God, the real and original person, and can exist as a person only in relation to this person, but personality implies that this relationship might also be of a very different and negative kind. His historicity does not mean only that he knows and expresses himself as God's partner in the covenantal dealings which God has opened with him, but also that he can withdraw from this partnership. And his capacity for decision means not only that he is free to elect himself as the one whom God has elected to love God as God loves him, but also that with the same freedom he can choose to be one whom God has rejected, to despise and hate God. In short, the fact that man can sin does not seem to be for Brunner a possibility alien to his true creaturely being, but one which is integral to and foreseen and prepared in it, confronted by the very different positive possibility, but also limiting and challenging it. As Brunner sees it, man seems to be free to realise his being either in loyalty or disloyalty to God, to choose as his master either God, himself or the devil, either to confirm or to deny his creatureliness and therefore his being in the Word of God. This is the strange paradox in the teaching of Brunner. And it is strange because he does not say it incidentally, but seems to think it essential and important to say it consistently, to interpret as a neutral factor the idea of freedom which according to his starting-point and thesis ought to exclude every thought of neutrality. We certainly do not forget the starting-point and thesis of this anthropology, that man is to be known only from God and in the Word of God, because he has his being solely in God and His Word, Jesus Christ. Indeed, it is just because we do not forget it, but remember the stress which Brunner lays on it, that we have to ask why it is that with equal—or perhaps even stronger—emphasis he can interpret in a neutral sense this (for him) very important idea of human rationality and responsibility, personality, historicity and capacity for decision ? If we follow his teaching in the former point, what are we to make of the latter ? And if we follow him in the latter, how can we take seriously the former ?

As I see it, it is impossible to maintain at one and the same time the concept of man constituted by the Word of God and the idea of a neutral capacity in man. If man has his being in the Word of God, he can do only that which corresponds to the Word of God. The actuality in which he has his being is from the very first orientated in this direction. It is the actuality of man caught up in the act of divine self-revelation and human obedience. This is the sense in which I should prefer to be able to understand Brunner, and in which I am encouraged to think that I can understand him when I consider many of his statements. But if I can, I do so only if I overlook an even greater number of statements which it is impossible to reconcile with this view. For if the actuality of man is not dependent on this one particular orientation, if we are to understand human life as a possibility of choice between the right and the left, then it is no longer clear how far his being can subsist in the Word of God, since if the divine Word is the basis of his being this neutrality is excluded. But it is in this sense that I fear I must understand Brunner. His special interest in the idea of man as not yet determined by his direct, concrete and realised relation to divine revelation, and especially his insistence on a type of responsibility and power of decision in which man can freely choose his path, his deliberate attempt to explain both the reality of sin as well as that of faith with reference to this act of free choice—all this suggests that we are to seek his deeper meaning in the latter statements rather than the former. In this case we are forced to take far less seriously than it sounds his assertion that man has his being in the Word of God. And in this case what he says about the identity of this Word of God with historical revelation and with Jesus Christ as attested by Holy

Scripture obviously refers only to the noetic and not the ontic basis of the being of man. The Word of God as the ontic basis of his being is only the universal Logos which is certainly revealed in Jesus Christ but has no intrinsic connexion with the history summed up in and denoted by this name. The Word of God in which man has his being is only the divine original of his capacity and disposition for God—a disposition which is purely formal, in which no decision has yet been taken concerning his being, in which his being has not yet been positively characterised, filled or orientated. Even the love and election of God are for man only an empty counterpart to the extent that, while they suggest the general truth that he belongs to God, they do not imply his positive participation, according to the divine will, in the historical action which God has taken in his favour. Even in the doctrine of the Trinity there seems to be a kind of blind spot to the extent that the eternal Word and the Son of God self-revealed in the flesh seem to be twofold, and the divine decree of our calling, election, sanctification and preservation does not seem to be in force. The Word of God is only the Word of a Creator to be distinguished from the Lord of the covenant, and only of this Word is it ontically valid to say that man has his being in it. Hence the seriousness with which Brunner maintains the thesis that man has his being in the Word of God can be only a seriousness of the second degree. At any rate it is compatible only with the thesis of a mere potentiality of human existence. If it were entertained in full seriousness, this thesis would necessarily be transcended. Since it is not actually transcended, it is at least an open question whether even in Brunner's anthropology we are within the limits within which we can finally know not merely the phenomena of the human but real man himself.

3. REAL MAN

Turning now from the critical to the constructive part of our task, we must try to give a positive answer to the question of the being which within the cosmos constitutes human being, i.e., the question of real man.

The ontological determination of humanity is grounded in the fact that one man among all others is the man Jesus. So long as we select any other starting point for our study, we shall reach only the phenomena of the human. We are condemned to abstractions so long as our attention is riveted as it were on other men, or rather on man in general, as if we could learn about real man from a study of man in general, and in abstraction from the fact that one man among all others is the man Jesus. In this case we miss the one Archimedean point given us beyond humanity, and therefore the one possibility of discovering the ontological determination of man. Theological anthropology has no choice in this matter. It is not yet or no longer theological anthropology if it tries to pose and answer the question of the true being of man from any other angle.

We remember who and what the man Jesus is. As we have seen, He is the one creaturely being in whose existence we have to do immediately and directly with the being of God also. Again, He is the creaturely being in whose existence God's act of deliverance has

taken place for all other men. He is the creaturely being in whom
God as the Saviour of all men also reveals and affirms His own glory
as the Creator. He is the creaturely being who as such embodies the
sovereignty of God, or conversely the sovereignty of God which as
such actualises this creaturely being. He is the creaturely being whose
existence consists in His fulfilment of the will of God. And finally
He is the creaturely being who as such not only exists from God and
in God but absolutely for God instead of for Himself.

From this knowledge of the man Jesus we have derived the criteria
which indicate the limits within which the attempt to attain knowledge
of human existence must always move. We have thus been warned
against confusing the reality of man with mere phenomena of man.
We have been unable to accept those determinations of man in which
his relationship to God, his participation in the history inaugurated
between him and God, and the glory, lordship, purpose and service
of God, are not brought out as the meaning of human life. We have
also had to be critical even where the concept of God seemed to play
a certainly not unimportant role, but where it remained empty to the
extent that there did not emerge anything of His saving action and
the related actuality of the being of man. We have now to show the
fact and extent that the ontological determination of man results
from the fact that one man among all others is this creaturely being,
the man Jesus.

Our first point is that the message of the Bible about this one
man has amongst other things this ontological significance. Speaking
of this one man, it says of all other men—those who were before Him
and those who were after Him, those who knew Him and those who did
not know Him or did so only indirectly, those who accepted Him and
those who rejected Him—at least that they were and are creaturely
beings whom this man is like for all His unlikeness, and in whose
sphere and fellowship and history this one man also existed in likeness
with them. This means that a decision has been made concerning
the being and nature of every man by the mere fact that with him
and among all other men He too has been a man. No matter who or
what or where he may be, he cannot alter the fact that this One is
also man. And because this One is also man, every man in his place
and time is changed, i.e., he is something other than what he would
have been if this One had not been man too. It belongs to his human
essence that Jesus too is man, and that in Him he has a human Neighbour, Companion and Brother. Hence he has no choice in the matter.
The question whether and to what extent he knows this Neighbour,
and what attitude he adopts to Him, is no doubt important, but it is
secondary to that which has already been decided, namely, whether
he can be a man at all without this Neighbour. Once for all this
question has been decided in the negative for every man. We cannot
break free from this Neighbour. He is definitively our Neighbour.

And we as men are those among whom Jesus is also a man, like us for all His unlikeness.

Theological anthropology must not be so timid that it does not firmly insist on this simplest factor in the situation. Nor must it be so distracted that it suggests every possible and impossible foundation for its thesis except the first and simplest of all, namely, that every man as such is the fellow-man of Jesus. The biblical message to which we must keep is neither timid nor distracted in this respect. It dares to be the message of this one man, and with all that it tells us concerning Him, and obviously in the light of it, it makes the massively self-evident ontological presupposition that the existence of this one man concerns every other man as such, and that the fact that He too is a man is the ground on which every other man is to be addressed and to which every other man is to be kept. It is worth noting that the biblical message never addresses man on any other basis. It does not appeal to his rationality or responsibility or human dignity or intrinsic humanity. No other decisive presupposition is made except that every one who bears the name of man is to be addressed as such in the name of Jesus, and therefore that he stands in an indisputable continuity with Him which is quite adequate as a point of contact. The biblical message reckons with a humanity which as such stands in this continuity, and therefore with man as a being whom we immediately expect to respond to the call to order, to his own order, addressed in the name of Jesus. It reckons only with a creatureliness of man constituted by the fact that one man among all others is this man. This is the ontological undertone which we must not miss if we are to understand why as a message about what this One is and does, and as a message about faith in Him, it is so confident and unreserved, and yet not " enthusiastic " but sober. It speaks in fact about the One who not merely *a posteriori* but *a priori*, from the very outset, is the Neighbour, Companion and Brother of every man.

As an ontological determination of man in general, the fact that among many others this One is also man means that we are men as in the person of this One we are confronted by the divine Other. We now adopt this concept. But it is to be noted that we adopt it from the very first as one which has this specific content. Certainly it is a transcendent and divine Other which constitutes man, from which he has his being, and in the light of which alone he can be known as real man. But this divine Other neither dwells in himself nor is it the transcendence of a deity existing abstractly and to be described in abstract terms. On the contrary, this divine Counterpart of every man, of man as such, is concretely this one man in whose creaturely being we have to do with the existence, the saving act, the glory and lordship and the fulfilment of the will of God—with the creaturely being existing for God. That this being Jesus can be the divine Counterpart of every man is implicit in the fact that He is among all other men, that He dwells with them as Himself, a man like others, that He belongs to this fellowship and history. But the same could obviously be said of every other man. Every other man exists as my fellow, and to that extent in the same fellowship and history as myself. But the co-existence of other men does not mean that I am confronted by a divine Other. And this is precisely what the co-existence of this one man, Jesus, does mean. It is not merely that He can be my divine Counterpart. He is this. He is it in all that in which He is unlike other men for all His likeness to them. He is it as the one creaturely being in whom God is present as such in His saving action, in the vindication of His glory, in His lordship and in the fulfilment of His will ; as the creaturely being who does not exist for himself but for God. In this respect Jesus stands above all other creaturely beings, and especially those which are like Him. In this way He confronts them all, and therefore myself. And He does so in a divine manner, in divine existence, action, rule and service. He alone is turned wholly to God. And the ontological determination of all men is that Jesus is present among them as their divine Other, their Neighbour, Companion and Brother. In virtue of His unique relation to God, He stands among them in a way which could be predicated of no other. For although each man as an individual and in his particularity is a relative other for his fellows, yet every man in his relation to God is always comparable to all others, not standing out in this respect or being among them in such a way as to constitute a true and absolute opposite. But the one man Jesus does stand in such a relation to all others, confronting them as a true and absolute Counterpart, because He, this individual, is unique in His particularity and His relation to God : as unique as God Himself is unique in relation to all creatures. It is in fact the singularity and transcendence of God which finds its creaturely correspondence, reflection and representation in this man and therefore among all other men. It is in fact the One who in the full majesty of God is unlike all other men who is like them as this One. In fellowship with Jesus, therefore, to be a man is to be with this correspondence, reflection and representation of the uniqueness and transcendence of God, to be with the One who is unlike us. To be man is thus to be in this the true and absolute Counterpart.

Basically and comprehensively, therefore, to be a man is to be with God. What a man is in this Counterpart is obviously the basic and comprehensive determination of his true being. Whatever else he is, he is on the basis of the fact that he is with Jesus and therefore with God. We shall have to explain and develop this basic determination—that he is with God. But with it we have already reached the point at which the reality of man has its origin, in which the whole creaturely being of man is summed up, behind which we can never go, and from which we can never abstract in considering any specific determination of this being. If it is not indifferent, incidental or subordinate, but ontologically decisive, that one man among all others is the man Jesus ; if to be a man is to dwell with this man who is our true and absolute Counterpart ; if to be a man is to be concretely confronted with this man who is like us for all that He is so unlike in the full majesty of God, then the fact that we are with God is not merely one of many determinations of our being, derivative and mutable, but the basic determination, original and immutable.

Godlessness is not, therefore, a possibility, but an ontological impossibility for man. Man is not without, but with God. This is not to say, of course, that godless men do not exist. Sin is undoubtedly committed and exists. Yet sin itself is not a possibility but an ontological impossibility for man. We are actually with Jesus, i.e., with God. This means that our being does not include but excludes sin. To be in sin, in godlessness, is a mode of being contrary to our humanity. For the man who is with Jesus—and this is man's ontological determination—is with God. If he denies God, he denies himself. He is then something which he cannot be in the Counterpart in which he is. He chooses his own impossibility. And every offence in which godlessness can express itself, e.g., unbelief and idolatry, doubt and indifference to God, is as such, both in its theoretical and practical forms, an offence with which man burdens, obscures and corrupts himself. It is an attack on the continuance of his own creatureliness : not a superficial, temporary or endurable attack, but a radical, central and fatal attack on its very foundation, and therefore its continuance. His very being as man is endangered by every surrender to sin. And conversely, every vindication and restoration of his relation to God is a vindication and restoration of his being as man. For he himself as a man is with Jesus and therefore with God. He himself stands from the very first and inescapably in the order which this fact implies. He himself is thus upheld if he keeps to this order, and he plunges into the void if he falls away from it.

The biblical message necessarily includes the thought of retribution and reward because the necessity and justification of retribution and reward are deeply rooted in this primary ontological basis of man—that he is with God. Since man is from the very first and inescapably bound up with God, in every modification of his being it is a direct question of the affirmation or denial, the destruction or restoration, of his relation to God, and therefore of the fulfilment or frustration of his essential possibilities, of his standing or falling, his being or not being. God can only react to each modification of human being and man can only receive in these modifications what his acts are worth in the sight of the God with whom he is inescapably linked. As he is man, God is necessarily and rightly the One who rewards or punishes. As he is man, in obedience or disobedience, reward or punishment, he can only confirm the order which as the order of his being decides his own possibility or impossibility.

Man is with God because he is with Jesus. And everything that is to be said in explanation and expansion of the fact that he is with God will result from the fact that he is with Jesus. But first we must emphasise that the particularity of man as compared with other creatures is contained in this ontological determination of his being. In a general sense it can and must be said of all other creatures as such that they have their being in the fact that they are with God. God is the Creator of heaven and earth as well as man. And whatever

is, is at its very roots because God is, and by the fact that He is;
that He is the Creator of all creatures, great and small, visible and
invisible; that He has willed and posited their being and nature and
does not cease but continues to do so. All creatures are as God is
with them and they are therefore with God. But not every creature
is with God as man is with God. This does not mean, of course, that
we must rush to the perverse conclusion that the particular thing
which is so basically true of man is not also true of other creatures
in their way, namely, that they are originally and decisively with Jesus,
and in this way with God their Creator, and thus participant in being.

It is impossible to overlook the clear and unequivocal statements of Jn. 1,
Col. 1 and Heb. 1 to the effect that τὰ πάντα, all things in heaven and earth,
were created by God, but by Jesus Christ (δί 'αὐτοῦ), and therefore in such a
way that in their creation God had in mind His only Son, Jesus Christ, and
this Son in His human form and reality, so that this one man was and is and
always will be the meaning and motive of all creation.

We can and must, therefore, say of every creature that it has the
same concrete divine Counterpart as man, and to that extent the same
ontological basis. In respect of all other creatures, we can and must
look confidently to the same ontological basis. But in the case of
non-human creatures we do not know what it means that they have
this basis. We state their (for us) impenetrable secret when, looking
in the same direction as we may and must look in regard to ourselves,
we say of them too that they are with God. We know only that they
are this. We do not know how. For when we say of them, too, that
they are with Jesus and therefore with God, the decisive and distinguishing thing is that the God who is also their God did not become
like them. He was not made an animal, a plant, a stone, a star or
an element of the invisible heavenly world. But He did become
man. It was in this way that in His incomparable majesty He was
made like the creature. It was in this *man* and not in any other creature
that He saw the meaning and motive of His whole creative work.
It is only in the human and not in any other creaturely sphere that the
creaturely correspondence, image and representation of the uniqueness
and transcendence of God has been actualised as an event. Of the
other created spheres we know only that the God who has created all
other men and all other creatures for the sake of this one man confronts
them in majestic dissimilarity. In the other spheres of creation we
see no comparable Representative and Revealer of the majestic
transcendence of God, no creature to reflect and represent the uniqueness and transcendence of God as distinct from other creatures.
This happens only in the human sphere, and it is only as it
happens in this sphere that it is valid and effectual for all other spheres
and for the whole of creation. As in the form of a human creature
the Creator becomes the true and absolute Counterpart of all other

human creatures, He is also the true and absolute Counterpart of all creatures whatsoever. As man is with Jesus and therefore with God, the same is true of all other creatures. We do not know how, but we know that it is the case. And the very significance for all spheres of what happens in the human sphere forbids us to suppose that there is something similar in others, that there might be a kind of identity between the Creator and the creature. God did not need to become an animal, a plant, or a stone because when He became man everything necessary was done for animals, plants and stones to be with Him as their Creator. How and to what extent ? We can give no answer by studying animals, plants and stones. And it is the fact that we cannot do so, that this is concealed from us, which from our standpoint distinguishes them from ourselves. No matter how they are with Jesus and therefore with God, the fact remains that they are, quite irrespective of us or anything without. But we for our part are distinguished from them by the fact that the decisive event of the correspondence, repetition and representation of the uniqueness and transcendence of God does not take place among them but in our human sphere ; that we as men have the divine Counterpart before us in that one man ; and that the implied fellowship with God cannot be for us the mystery which it must be when we consider the rest of creation. As men, and therefore as direct neighbours, companions and brothers of the man Jesus, we do not stand indirectly but immediately and directly in the light of this divine Counterpart. What constitutes the hidden being of all creatures is revealed as human being because Jesus is man. And it is the fact that human being is revealed as being with God which constitutes its particularity. If we affirm and stress this fact, it is not in arrogance towards other creatures, but as an act of humility in face of the secret of God in other spheres and its revelation in our human sphere. It should not be forgotten that in this way the particularity of other creatures is also emphasised. The glory of other creatures lies in the concealment of their being with God, no less than ours in its disclosure. For all we know, their glory may well be the greater. We do not really know that the outer circle of all other creatures exists for the sake of the inner circle of humanity. The very opposite may well be the case. Or perhaps both circles, the outer and the inner, have their own autonomy and dignity, their distinctive form of being with God. What does this difference amount to as against the fact that the man Jesus as a creaturely being is the focal point of both circles ? But when this is said in rebuttal of human pride we must not fail to recognise as such the special grace conferred upon man. Since Jesus as the Bearer of the divine uniqueness and transcendence is like man, God is revealed to man, and in this confrontation with God man is revealed to himself. Knowing himself, and knowing why he can know himself, knowing his being as a being with God and knowing why he can know his being as a being with God, he knows his singularity among all creatures. For he can know his own being as a being with God because the being of the creature with God is not hidden but revealed in the human sphere. In this sphere the Creator has become a creature, making himself a creature for all His unlikeness to other creatures. On the basis of the election of the man Jesus this sphere is singled out from all others.

It is of a piece with the particularity of human being that the problem of godlessness and therefore of sin seems to arise only in the sphere of man. We have noted that godlessness is the ontological impossibility of man ; for man is as he is with God and therefore not without Him. We should have to say the same of other creatures if there were anything resembling godlessness in this sphere too. For as we have seen, all creatures are with Jesus and therefore with God. If there were godlessness in non-human creatures, it would have to be understood as an ontological impossibility. But it would not appear that there can actually be godlessness in non-human spheres. I use this reserved expression intentionally. For since we do not know how non-human creatures are with God, we cannot give a categorical denial. On the other hand, we must remember that these relationships are concealed when we think that we can reply affirmatively and speak about " fallen creation " and so on as though it were something generally known and accepted. If I incline to the contrary opinion and say it would not appear to be the case that we have to reckon with any other kind of godlessness than that of man, I do so because the ontological impossibility of sin is only conceivable where the creature is confronted by its Creator in the immediate and direct manner which is the case with human beings. It is not accidental that Holy Scripture tells us a great deal about the sin of man but does not really say anything at all about sin in any other quarter. Would it not tell us plainly if on the basis of the self-revelation of God which it attests it had something to say about a cosmic fall contemporaneous with the fall of man ? If it does not do so because it cannot refer to any revelation of God and has no real witness to bear on the point, we may well ask whether there is anything at all to say. Is it not obvious that the ontological impossibility of sin can be realised only where God is revealed and therefore known to the creature which is with Him, so that the creature can also be revealed and known to itself in confrontation with God ? This is the case where Jesus as the Bearer of the uniqueness and transcendence of God is like man. This situation is the peculiarity of the human sphere. Since Jesus did not become an animal or a plant or a stone but a man, and since we have not to reckon with a corresponding identity of Creator and creature in other spheres, it does not apply in non-human spheres, where the divine confrontation is always indirect, and in default of the immediate presence of the divine Counterpart the drama which is the meaning and purpose of human life cannot be played out either in its normal or abnormal, its possible or impossible form. And in these circumstances how can the ontological impossibility be seen in actual operation ? Of course even this consideration does not enable us to pronounce a final verdict. But in my view it is a clear indication that a negative answer is at least preferable to a positive.

To be man is to be with God. We have seen that when this definition is concretely understood, as it must be on its christological presupposition, it denotes at once the particularity of man among all other creatures. We shall now proceed to explain and develop the actual content of the definition.

If human being is a being with God, we have to say first and
comprehensively that it is a being which derives from God. It is a
being dependent on God. It is not identical with the being of God.
To say this would be to say both too much and too little. And it
would not then be described as a being with God. It is distinct from
and to that extent independent of the being of God. But in this
distinction and independence it does not exist without but only by
the divine being. It is a being absolutely grounded in the latter
and therefore absolutely determined and conditioned by it. " Absolutely " means that it derives wholly and exclusively from it. It
is, only to the extent that this is the case. It would cease to be if it
did not do so. We shall return more particularly to the exclusiveness
which is calculated to make this clear. For the moment we must
consider the positive assertion as such, namely, that the being of man
as a being with God is also a being from God.

It may be objected that in saying this we have not defined the
concept of man in particular but that of creation in general. To
this we may retort : How can one intelligently and solidly define the
concept of creation in general without having in view man in particular ? We refer to our previous consideration that here in the
human sphere there is revealed and known what is hidden and impenetrable in the non-human, namely, what is implied by a being in
relationship with God. It is not, therefore, by the speculative way of
a general consideration of the relationship between a relative and an
absolute, a dependent and an independent, a conditioned and an
unconditioned being, that we have attained this first explanation of a
being in relationship with God as one which derives from God. If it
were intended in this way it would be valueless even to elucidate
the concept of the creature generally, for the concept of absolute,
independent and unconditioned being cannot form an adequate
description of the Creator Himself, since these negative categories
do not define God but only indicate the limits of our understanding
of the world. When we say that being with God is being which derives
from God, we do not speak speculatively but concretely of man (and
implicitly of creation in general) ; of the man who as such is with
God only in the sense that his being derives from God and is utterly
dependent on God as already described. The concrete form of his
being with God is that he is with Jesus. He belongs to the sphere
of creation to which the man Jesus also belongs. And within this
sphere the man Jesus is the Bearer of the uniqueness and transcendence
of God. In Him therefore, at the heart of this sphere, the lordship
of God is established. It is not merely conceived as an idea, or recognised and proclaimed as a truth, or attested by one who knows it,
but it is lived out and embodied in this man. Man is with God as he
is with the sovereignty of God lived out and embodied in Jesus. He
is with Him as His kingdom comes. He is as man at the point where

God acts, and acts as his Saviour, thus magnifying His own glory.
He is at the point where God makes history. The whole sphere of
man, his whole fellowship and history, is basically determined and
distinguished by the existence of the one man Jesus and the fact that
God makes history and the kingdom of God comes within it. What
does it mean for the being of man that he is in this sphere ? It certainly
does not mean that he is identical with the being of God. The present
and active God confronts him in free and sovereign transcendence
in the one man Jesus who is not at all identical with himself. He
confronts him in this One as the Other indestructibly unlike for all
His likeness. In this sphere the kingdom of God *comes* to man.
What constitutes the being of man in this sphere is not a oneness of
being but a genuine togetherness of being with God. Here too, then,
the being of man is his own being in contrast to that of God. But
here God acts and rules and makes history ; and He does so in the
sovereignty of His omnipotence, in the power of the Creator dealing
with His creature, as the Lord of lords and the King of kings. The
being of man in all its independence and particularity, in all its difference from the being of God, is the being which is acted upon in this
action of God, ruled in this rule of God and drawn into this history
inaugurated and controlled by God. It thus concerns all men and
every man that in the man Jesus God Himself is man, and therefore
acts and rules and makes history. It is to be noted that this fact
concerns man precisely in his independence and particularity, in
his own being as distinct from God. It concerns man himself. For
in the presence of God he cannot retreat into himself and thus remain
inviolate. It is he himself who is affected when God invades his sphere.
Nor can he find shelter from God behind another being outside himself
and connected with himself : his naturalness or rationality, earth
or heaven. He might wish to do so. But in the sphere to which Jesus
as man also belongs he is reached and pierced by God however much
he may wriggle. He is reached and pierced by God even when he
becomes guilty of ontological impossibility, of godlessness.

The well known words of Ps. 139[5-12] may be recalled in this connexion, and
we must remember that they do not speak of the negatively theological phantom
of Indian or Greek philosophy but of the God of Israel who makes history, and
also notice that they do not have the form of an objective statement but the
address of adoration : " Thou hast beset me behind and before, and laid thine
hand upon me. Such knowledge is too wonderful for me ; it is high, I cannot
attain unto it. Whither shall I go from thy spirit ? or whither shall I flee from
thy presence ? If I ascend up into heaven thou art there : if I make my bed in
hell, behold, thou art there. If I take the wings of the morning, and dwell in
the uttermost parts of the sea ; even there shall thy hand lead me, and thy
right hand shall hold me. If I say, Surely the darkness shall cover me ; even
the night shall be light about me. Yea, the darkness hideth not from thee ;
but the night shineth as the day."

What is man from this standpoint ? We answer that he clearly derives from the One who unceasingly comes to the very depths of his being in this way. Only a being which by its constitution is utterly dependent on God can be reached and pierced by God as happens where God acts and rules and makes history and His kingdom comes. Dealing with man in this way God exercises a lordship over him which He does not have to acquire but which belongs to Him in and with the existence of man and from his creation. Thus the human creature, and every creature as seen in man, is the being which is so utterly and inescapably reached and pierced by God because his inmost essence exists only through God, because in that in which he is himself he derives from God, because he can boast of his own most proper being only as he makes his boast in God. This is man as seen in the light of the fact that the human sphere is the sphere in which God is immediately and directly present and acts and rules and makes history in the person of the man Jesus, and in which His kingdom comes in this One. As he dwells in this sphere, man is so with God that he derives solely and exclusively from Him. Again, this does not mean any cancellation of his independence, selfhood and freedom. But it does mean that in his independence, selfhood and freedom, he belongs only to the One who comes to him as Lord. It means that it is only with Him and not without Him or against Him that he can exist, and think and speak, and work and rest, and rejoice and mourn, and live and die. It means that the doing of the will of God is the only realisation of his ontological possibility. It means that in every modification of his being—even in that of sin, in which he tries to realise its impossibility—he is subject to the lordship and judgment of God. It means that his right must be that of God. It means that he can place his trust neither in himself nor in any other being in heaven or earth but only in God. This is the being of man—a being which is related to the being of God with this strict necessity.

We now come to the two material and therefore primary statements in our exposition : that the being of man as a being with Jesus rests upon the election of God ; and that it consists in the hearing of the Word of God.

It rests upon the election of God. This is our first point. The man Jesus, with whom we start, is the man elected by God. Election means a special decision with a special intention in relation to a special object. The existence of Jesus and the meaning of His existence do not depend on His own choice to the extent that He too is a creature. To be sure, it is always by His own choice that He gives Himself to live in fellowship with God and therefore to do the saving work of God, to give God the glory, to establish His lordship, to engage in His service. But He has not elected Himself for this choice. He is elected by God. In all this there is revealed in time an eternal counsel of God, in the created world the will of the Creator, in the self-ordination of this man His divine fore-ordination. Predestination, the divine election of grace, is the basis of the fact that Creator and creature, God and man, are united at this point and the kingdom of God comes. Why is all this true of the man Jesus ? It is true of Him because He is the creature in whom the divine election of grace is already made. Among all other men and all other creatures He is the penetrating spearhead of the will of God their Creator : penetrating because in Him the will of God is already fulfilled and revealed, and the purpose of God for all men and creatures has thus reached its goal ; and the spearhead to the extent that there has still to be a wider fulfilment of the will of God and its final consummation, and obviously this can only follow on what has already been achieved in this man.

What is this will of God ? We may express it most simply as follows. It is the will of God that the Yes which He as the Creator has spoken to His creation should prevail ; that all men and all creatures should be delivered from evil, i.e., from that which God the Creator has rejected, and preserved from its threat and power. There is a whole monstrous kingdom, a deep chaos of nothingness, i.e., of what the Creator has excluded and separated from the sphere of being, of what He did not will and therefore did not create, to which He gave no being, which can exist only as non-being, and which thus forms the menacing frontier of what is according to the will of God. No man, no creature has within himself the power to overcome this threat. Of course, the world created by God is light. Of course, the only ontological possibility of man is the being which his Creator has imparted to him. But it does not lie in the power of the creature to maintain the distinction which God drew when He separated light from darkness and being from non-being. For the maintenance of this distinction established in the created world is a creative and therefore a divine act. And so the will of God for His creation is to preserve it from the nothingness to which it would inevitably succumb apart from the divine initiative, to save the creature from the threat which it cannot overcome of itself. The fact that it cannot overcome it is shown by the wholly irrational and inexplicable fall of man. But sin itself is only man's irrational and inexplicable affirmation of the nothingness which God as Creator has negated. And the saving and preserving will of God is not primarily directed against sin. With a higher and deeper aim, it is directed against the nothingness affirmed in sin. It hastens to help being against non-being in order to destroy the power of the latter, to free the creature by negating its negation, to avert its threat, to constitute a humanity and a world which have nothing more to fear from those frontiers because the abyss of evil has lost its power to attract, and in which God alone is King in His kingdom, as is only meet. To accomplish this can only be the will and work of God. For what power has creaturely being to prevent its own dissolution accompanying and threatening it as the sum of its ontological impossibility ? But the Creator who gave it being can go further and give it a being secure against non-being. And it is the will of God to do this. God created it with the aim of becoming secure. As the Creator, He did not will a threatened and lost creation, but a saved and preserved. And for the fulfilment of this aim He bound Himself to His creation from the very act of creation. As the Creator, He knew its impotence to save and maintain itself. Thus the fall of man, while it formed no part of His intention, was not outside His foresight and plan. From the very first He was determined to be the Preserver of that which He created, of that which He separated as being from non-being. Hence this aim of His will, and His initiative in its realisation, His mercy towards His creatures, was something resolved from the very beginning, even before the foundation of the world.

And if the man Jesus is the penetrating spearhead of this will of God, its realisation and revelation in the creaturely world, His existence is determined from the beginning, before the foundation of the world. This can be said only of Him. For He alone is the man, the creature, in whom the will of God has already been fulfilled and by whom the enemy of being has been slain and the freedom of being attained. He alone is the archetypal man whom all threatened and enslaved men and creatures must follow. He alone is the promise for these many, the Head of a whole body. And because it is grace, grace as free mercy, and not therefore a self-evident compulsion or necessity, which God obeyed when He entertained towards His creation this will to save ; because it is again His free choice to give His saving will this spearhead, to realise and reveal it in this One, it is right and necessary that we should see in this one man Jesus the true and primary object of the divine election of grace. If now in the vast sphere of human fellowship and history we have to do with the man Jesus, it is because His existence was eternally resolved in the sovereign will of God to save us and all creation : resolved before all things, before being was even planned, let alone actualised, before man fell into sin, before light was separated from darkness or being from non-being, and therefore before there was even a potential threat to being, let alone an actual ; resolved as the very first thing which God determined with regard to the reality distinct from Himself ; resolved as the all-embracing content of His predestination of all creaturely being. It is for this reason that the man Jesus is the executive and revelatory spearhead of the will of God fulfilled on behalf of creation. It is for this reason that He is the kingdom of God in person. It is for this reason that as against all other men and the whole world of creation he is the Representative of the uniqueness and transcendence of God. It is for this reason that to be a man is properly and primarily to be with God. For the existence of the man Jesus is not in any sense fortuitous, secondary, or subsequent. It is the true and original object of the divine election of grace. Apart from God Himself there is nothing that was before it. In the decree of God it is the first thing to which everything else is related and which everything else can only follow.

We now return to our main theme—the concept of man in general. The formal definition that the being of man derives from God is given a first material content when we recall the gracious divine election of the man Jesus. To be a man is to be with Jesus, to be like Him. To be a man is thus to be with the One who is the true and primary Elect of God. To be a man is to be in the sphere where the first and merciful will of God towards His creatures, His will to save and keep them from the power of nothingness, is revealed in action. To be a man is to be the witness of this event, and therefore a direct witness of the truth of the basic counsel, the first of all the decrees of God. The general definition that man is with God as he is with Jesus thus acquires a content of almost unfathomable range and significance. Man is brought into direct encounter with the divine election of grace which is as such the beginning, or before the beginning, of all things. He is face to face with the actualisation and revelation of the will to save in which the Creator determined to hasten to the help of His creature even as and before He created it, resolving from the very first to free it from evil and bring it to perfection, and thus sealing His alliance with it from all eternity. As a creature he is like the creature in whose existence this realisation and revelation takes place, and in whom the spearhead of the merciful will of God, which has found its first and proper object in Him, penetrates and illuminates the whole world of creation. To the extent that he is with Jesus and therefore with God, man himself is a creature elected in the divine election of grace, i.e., elected along with or into Jesus. He is elected to the extent that he derives from God, which means concretely that his being rests upon the election of God, namely, the election of the one man Jesus. In this man he is confronted by the majesty of God as the claim of the Lord to whom he already belongs even as and before he is confronted by that claim. He is elected to the extent that as man he is a creature whom the election of the man Jesus (in virtue of the fact that the latter is akin to him) immediately concerns. As man he is the creature who is first struck by the spearhead of the gracious will of God penetrating the world of creation, and first illuminated by the light which streams from it. What it means that God wills to maintain His creation and save it from evil, that He wills to take the initiative for the salvation of the world, applies first to him. The history of conflict and victory as it takes place in the created world on the basis of the eternal divine decree in the man Jesus is enacted first and decisively in his human sphere. Hence he may and must be described as elected along with the man Jesus.

The sphere of human life and history is from the very first sanctified by the fact that the eternal decree of the Creator is executed within it ; that what happens within it is the execution of the eternal decree. Man as such, because he is the fellow of the man Jesus, is from the very first destined to share in the deliverance from evil effected in this one man, to participate in the conflict against the enemy of all creaturely being, to figure in the history of the victory over this enemy, to belong to the body of the Head in whom the triumph of the Creator has been achieved on behalf of the creature.

It is to be noted that here in this grounding of humanity in the election of God is to be found the reason for our affirmation that sin is for man an ontological impossibility. If this were said about man *in abstracto*, the affirmation would be quite untenable and could easily be refuted by the fact of sin. Of man *in abstracto* we should have to say at once that the fall and original sin are an ontological necessity. Man *in abstracto*, i.e., apart from the merciful will of his Creator primarily directed towards him, would be a being hopelessly exposed to the threat of surrounding non-being. In his fall there would take place only something to which he was predestined as a being already abandoned and lost. But when we ascribed to man this ontological impossibility we did not speak of man *in abstracto*. We spoke of the man whose being is a being with God. Yet it is only as we fill out this concept with that of the divine election of grace that we reach solid ground. For man cannot now appeal to his defencelessness, to the natural weakness of all being in face of the overwhelming power of non-being. He cannot bewail and justify himself as a sinner on the ground that he is inevitably delivered up to the forces of evil. He cannot do this because as man he is elected with the man Jesus, and in face of his defencelessness the divine will to pity, help and save is active from the very first. By the very fact that he is man—because as such he has his Head in the man Jesus, and shares in the battle fought and the history of triumph inaugurated by Him—he is from the very first as much preserved and secured as he can be without being himself the man Jesus. The promise which he is given from this source is so weighty and strong that from the very first he can neither bewail nor justify his sin, and therefore his sin can only be understood and described as his ontological impossibility. His election to proximity to the actualised and revealed will to save, which we have seen to be the primary and basic will of God, prevents us from ascribing to his being any possibility in the direction of nothingness. From the very outset God has intervened to separate him from the power of darkness. By the very fact of his creation as man he becomes the covenant-partner and the *protégé* of his Creator, which denies him not only the right but also the possibility of deciding for chaos and darkness. Because from the very outset God stands at his side, his defencelessness is made good by the One who alone can help in this matter, and does in effect do so. It should now be plain that the fall of man is thus set in a light which reveals only the more clearly how serious and dreadful it is. Not only is there nothing in the being of man as created by God to explain why he should decide against his Creator. We cannot even explain this decision by the fact that in himself he is impotent to deliver himself from the power of evil by his decision for his Creator. If man actually decides against God, he does so neither on the basis of a possibility rooted in his own being, nor because he is prevented from choosing his legitimate possibility by the superior power of evil pressing upon him from without. On the contrary, when he chooses evil he grasps that which is made impossible for him and from which he is preserved. And grasping, he falls into the abyss in a twofold sense. He does that for which there is no excuse and which can be justified only by the restoration of a state of right which God alone can effect, i.e., by the divine forgiveness. We cannot now pursue this problem in detail. Our present concern is simply to say that, as the fellow-elect of Jesus, man as the creature of God is predestined to be the victor and not the vanquished in the defence of being against non-being.

Our second point is that the being of man as being with Jesus consists in listening to the Word of God. The man Jesus, and again we start with Him, is the sum of the divine address, the Word of God, to the created cosmos. It is in this way that He is the primary object of God's eternal counsel, of the divine predestination and election. It is in this way that He is the embodiment of the divine will to save. It is in this way that He forms the Counterpart of man, and that it is really true in Him that man is with God, and derives from God and is elected by God. All this is concretely expressed in the fact that the man Jesus is the Word of God; that He is to the created world and therefore *ad extra* what the Son of God as the eternal Logos is within the triune being of God. If the eternal Logos is the Word in which God speaks with Himself, thinks Himself and is conscious of Himself, then in its identity with the man Jesus it is the Word in which God thinks the cosmos, speaks with the cosmos and imparts to the cosmos the consciousness of its God. It is this second meaning of the Word of God which concerns us here. God's will for His creature is at one and the same time—and the two aspects cannot be separated, nor one placed lower or higher than the other—a will which reveals as well as acts, and illuminates as well as quickens. And the object of His election of grace is a creature which not only acts concretely but speaks concretely, acting as it speaks and speaking as it acts, the fountain of light as well as life within the created world. The Creator makes Himself heard and understood and recognised by becoming this creature, the man Jesus, and by acting as the Saviour of the creature in this man. In His action He declares Himself and the purpose of what He does. His action is not, therefore, a mechanical operation in which the creature is simply the material used and has no understanding of what is done. He uses the creature as He speaks with it. The omnipotence of His action is the omnipotence of truth, which refuses to dominate by external means, but is ready to speak for itself, to teach, to convince, to seek and win recognition, and to conquer in this highly individual manner. What we have said about God's sovereign presence in the creaturely world is to be understood in this concrete way. It is not the presence of compelling fate, nor that of a higher power of nature. Nor is it the presence of a dictator and tyrant brutalising the world he controls. It is the presence of the almighty Word of God. It is effective in supreme power, but it operates as it speaks and is heard. It is an almighty address and summons. And this address and summons of God is the person of the man Jesus at the heart of creation. The fact that man is with Jesus and therefore with God means concretely that, because he is with Jesus and in the same sphere, he is in the sphere of the Word which God has spoken and does not cease to speak in and through the existence of this man. The fact that in virtue of the existence of the man Jesus his being derives from God means that he exists because God has spoken and speaks and will continue to speak this Word once and for all, for every past and future. And the fact that in virtue of the man Jesus he is the elect of God means that from the very first he is determined for a being which has its ground in the speaking of God. The man Jesus not only speaks but is Himself the divine speech. He is not merely the Bearer or Instrument of the divine address and summons but is Himself the divine address and summons. And whatever it may mean for man in general that this man too exists among all others, it certainly means concretely that in Him the divine address and summons to each and every man is actualised.

For the sake of clarity we must give a short account of the content of this Word, address and summons. What does the man Jesus say in the midst of the cosmos and all other men ? If we are to put the matter in the simplest terms we must undoubtedly say—Himself. He speaks by the mere fact of his existence. By the very fact that He is, He is the Word of God. And the Word of God at its simplest is to the effect that He, this man Jesus, is. Thus His own existence is the content of the speech of this man. He speaks of the creaturely presence, action and revelation of God actualised in Himself ; of the saving action of God, and therefore of His kingdom, of the doing of His will, of His own creaturely being as wholly dedicated to this purpose, of God's lordship over Him, and therefore of His own freedom for this service. The man Jesus Himself is in fact this act of salvation, His doing of the will of God, this service, this sovereignty of the Creator and freedom of the creature. And He also speaks of it. He declares and shows that the created cosmos, men and each individual man are not without him. He thus declares that what is needed to deliver the creature from the evil of nothingness is about to be done. He declares that the creature is not abandoned by its Creator ; that it is not left to itself and its own defencelessness. He declares that the yawning abyss of non-being will not be allowed to engulf its being. The Creator of all being is beside it in person—He who knew, negated, and rejected non-being as such, and by His wisdom, goodness and power imparted being to His creation, thus judging between light and darkness and separating the one from the other. He makes Himself responsible for the preservation of being, and in so doing He vindicates His own honour as the Creator. If the creature as such is endangered by its own impotence, the kingdom of the Creator comes to it, and the will of the Creator is done in regard to it. The very existence of Jesus tells us this. He is thus the light of the divine election and mercy to the creature. He is the utterance of the promise which the creature is given and under which it can stand from the very outset. He is the expression of the friendliness with which God adopted it in creation. He also declares the righteousness with which God resolved to maintain and order it in creation. Creation is not to be undone or to perish. It belongs to its Creator and to no one else. This is what is declared by the man Jesus within it ; by the man Jesus as the Word of God, and therefore as a Word which is unassailable and irrevocable. And so the world, and in particular the sphere of man, is not without this Word. When we say " man " we have to remember above all that there is one man among many who is this Word, and in respect of the many that it is in their sphere that this Word is to be found—the Word which is for them, which is the Word of their hope, and which in defiance of every threat promises them freedom, security and life.

We now return to the concept of man. Our formal definition that the being of man derives from God has now been given a wider content. To be a man is to be in the particular sphere of the created world in which the Word of God is spoken and sounded. In the wider sense creation as a whole forms this sphere. For the Word of God has certainly been spoken for all creatures as a true and valid promise. But it is in the human kingdom, through the man Jesus among all other men, that the Word has actually been spoken. The election and calling of the people of Israel, the incarnation of the Son of God, the founding and life of the Christian community, this whole pronouncement of the Word of God is an event of human history, the confirmation of the election of man, the fulfilment of his special calling, and therefore a mark of his special creaturely determination. Man is the creaturely being which is addressed, called and summoned by God. He is the being among all others of whom we know that God has directly made Himself known to him, revealing Himself and His will and therefore the meaning and destiny of man's own being. Man *is* the being which is addressed in this way by God. He does not become this being. He does not first have a kind of nature in which he is then addressed by God. He does not have something different and earlier and more intrinsic, a deeper stratum or more original substance of being, in which he is without or prior to the Word of God. He is from the very outset, as we may now say, " in the Word of God." He is a being which is summoned by the Word of God and to that extent historical, grounded in the history inaugurated in this Word. And whatever else his nature may be, it is subordinated to this historicity and explicable only in the light of it.

At this point we may recall, without necessarily endorsing, Michaelangelo's depiction of the creation of Adam. On one side, it shows God approaching the earth like a storm, surrounded by all His angels. And this God speaks. The fact that He also acts is merely indicated by His outstretched arm and finger. There can be no doubt that He does act. He creates as He speaks. For on the other side, lying on the steep incline of a hill, is the newly created Adam, who as he comes or has come into being is also set in movement—although in an incomparably less impressive manner. He has just opened his eyes, and can no longer remain lying, but wishes to stand erect, and—feebly in comparison with the powerful bearing of God, but unmistakeably—he stretches out his hand to meet the arm and finger of his Creator. He, too, from the moment of creation is engaged in action, spontaneously, yet not arbitrarily, but in correspondence with the action of God. He has heard, and as one who has heard he is set in movement in relation to God. The theology of this painting is open to question in many respects. But at one point it is clear and uncontestable. In and with its creation the being of this Adam is an actual and historical being, grounded in and related to the action of God in His Word. It is the unmistakeable answer to a summons in the very act and moment of the divine creating and its own creation, and in such a way that there can be no question of any preceding being.

Summoned because chosen—here we have a first definition of real man. When the reality of human nature is in question, the word " real " is simply equivalent to " summoned." To see the human here is to see our nature and to see it in its entirety. To miss this point is to miss our nature, seeing only the parts and not the whole. If I ask : Who am I ? I do not ask : What belongs to me ? nor : What would I like to be ? nor : What do I pretend to be ? nor : What have I made of myself ?—but if I ask : Who am I myself ? Who am I really ? then if I understand myself in the light of God or His Word, I must answer that I am summoned by this Word, and to that extent I am in this Word. And the same answer is equally true of others. They are men, and may be addressed and seriously regarded as such, because primarily and fundamentally they are summoned by this Word. This is a universal truth. Men are those who are summoned by this Word.

To be summoned means to have heard, to have been awakened, to have to arouse oneself, to be claimed. Our understanding of true and original human nature embraces the whole series of these movements. But there is an immediate obstacle to the systematic development of this view. For automatically and irresistibly we begin to look for a presupposition : Who is thus summoned ? Who and what was he before he was set in motion by this call ? What about the ear which hears, the reason which understands, the will which is active, or the powers which are brought into play ? What about the sleep which seems to be followed by this awakening, the rest by this arousing ? Who and what is the being claimed ? The query seems to be just, but it must be dropped at once. Indeed, it must not be raised. For what precedes human being as a being summoned by the Word of God is simply God and His Word ; God in the existence of the man Jesus. On the level of our own being, of human being as such and in general, if we see and understand it in terms of summons we are on an extreme edge beyond which we cannot look, at a beginning which on the creaturely level has no basis other than the sure basis which the Creator has ordained in the existence of that one man. We are men as God is our Creator, and speaks as such with that one man as His Word. The question of anything preceding our being apart from the divine summons can arise only if we try to explain ourselves by ourselves instead of by our concrete confrontation with God.

The apparent difficulty of recognising this furthest limit of our field of vision because it is the limit of the being which we are given, the apparent embarrassment of having to begin at this point in our thinking about ourselves, and therefore to reject the question of a creaturely beginning of this beginning, is no smaller (although not of course any greater), and the need to accept the appearance of difficulty and embarrassment is formally exactly the same, as that which confronted us in our thinking about the being of God, where we should like to ask concerning a *prius* or basis, but cannot do so because the mere question of a presupposition for the divine being outside God Himself is tantamount to denying God, since God can have only Himself as a presupposition, and can be known to us only in this absence of any other presupposition or not at all. Perhaps the fundamental mistake in all erroneous thinking of man about himself is that he tries to equate himself with God and therefore to proceed on the assumption that he can regard himself as the presupposition of his own being. The presupposition of man is God in His Word. But God in His Word is his only presupposition, and therefore his being is to be understood in terms of a summons which is original and cannot be deduced from anything else. Thus it is only in a denial of man corresponding to the denial of God that we can appeal beyond this summons to another being, asking concerning the man who is not yet summoned, the human ear and reason and will and powers, the preceding condition of sleep and rest, the something which is claimed by the divine address. On this approach we are simply led back to qualities of human nature, or phenomena of the human which can illuminate the truth about real man only to the degree that the fact or extent that he is man is established elsewhere. He is a man as he is summoned, and his endowment merely follows as part of the summons, his constitution being his equipment. God in His Word is the basis of this too, and on the foundation thus laid his being as man is a being summoned.

The very fact that we cannot advance to a systematically developed view, and must not try to do so, compels us to adopt the provisional definition that the being of man is a being summoned which is not preceded by anything apart from God in His Word, but owes its character as being solely to God in His Word. It is not preceded by anything else : by any potentiality which would predispose it for being in this way, or underlie its actuality or historicity ; by any pre-existent material which would be had to according to this pattern. There is nothing prior to it to contribute to what it is, to underlie, condition or prepare what it is, engaging it to gratitude, or subjecting it to its law. For its equipment or endowment rests upon its being, and not *vice versa*. Being summoned, it derives only from God, from His election, and therefore from the Word which reveals this election. It is to this alone that man owes his being. Where there was nothing but the God who in His mercy willed to summon him, and actually did so, on the basis of the divine will and action there now stands man himself confronting God, summoned by Him as the being which is created and has its being in the fact that it is told by God that He adopts it and is its hope and consolation. Man exists in the fact that what he is told by God is the truth. He exists in this truth and not apart from it.

This brings us near to an important aspect of the doctrine of creation in the theology of the Early Church which may best be treated at this point. We refer to the fact that the creation of all things by God was strikingly described as a *creatio ex nihilo*.

Whether the two accounts of creation at the beginning of Genesis can be finally understood without the introduction of this or a similar term is a separate question, but we search them in vain for anything which points specifically in this direction. On the other hand, Job 26⁷ might be thought to express something like it : " He stretcheth out the north over the empty place, and hangeth the earth upon nothing." The formula appears for the first time in 2 Macc. 7²⁸ : οὐκ ἐξ ὄντων ἐποίησεν αὐτὰ ὁ θεός. Hellenistic religious philosophy and the later Gnostic heresies did not think on these lines. In these systems the Creator was only the demiurge and his work consisted in making the κόσμος out of the world which was already supposed to exist as ἀταξία. When Plutarch (*De animae procr.*, 5, 3) writes : οὐ γὰρ ἐκ τοῦ μὴ ὄντος ἡ γένεσις ἀλλ' ἐκ τοῦ μὴ καλῶς μηδ' ἱκανῶς ἔχοντος, it sounds like a direct polemic against this idea, which clearly derives from the context of Israelite thought. On the other hand, Philo (*Som.* 1, 76) says quite plainly that creation is not simply, like the sunrise, the illumination and clarification of an already existent reality, ἀλλὰ καὶ ἃ πρότερον οὐκ ἦν ἐποίησεν, οὐ δημιουργὸς μόνον, ἀλλὰ καὶ κτίστης αὐτὸς ὤν. This opinion seems to have been taken for granted by the New Testament witnesses. For in the New Testament not only are there no expressions with other implications, but

3. *Real Man* 153

in the admittedly difficult text Heb. 11³ we read that by faith we know that the worlds were made through the ῥῆμα θεοῦ, and not therefore in such a way that τὸ βλεπόμενον emerged out of some sort of φαινόμενα. And Romans 4¹⁷ says quite clearly that the God of Abraham is He who quickens the dead, and that He is καλῶν τὰ μὴ ὄντα ὡς ὄντα. Post-apostolic theology followed up this line (obviously in the interests of the struggle against Gnosticism) with complete unanimity and resolution. Thus *creatio ex nihilo* appears right at the beginning of the confession of faith of the *Pastor Hermae* (*Mand.* 1, 1), in Tatian (*Adv. Graec.* 5), in Aristides (*Apol.* 4), in Justin (*Apol.* 10), in Theophilus of Antioch (*Ad. Autol.* 1, 4), in Irenaeus (*fecit ex eo, quod non erat ad hoc ut sint omnia, Adv o. h. I.*, 22, 1, cf. 11, 10, 4), in Tertullian (*Adv. Herm.* 8 and 16, 20–21 ; *Apol.* 17 ; *De praescr. haer.* 13 ; *De carnis resurr.* 11) and also in Origen (*In Joann.* 1, 17, 103) etc., and it later became one of the firmest parts of the general teaching of the Church concerning creation.

Conceptually it was shown to be a necessary truth by the following argument. Admitting that God created all things, the question arises whether He created them out of nothing or out of something. If the latter, the question again arises whether this something was created or uncreated ? If it were something already created, the first question would have to be put again, probably with the threat of a *regressus ad infinitum*. If it were something uncreated, then this would have to be either God Himself or a quantity independently co-existing with God from all eternity. Since this is impossible, there remains only the *creatio ex nihilo* (thus Quenstedt, *Theol. did. pol.*, 1685, 1, *cap.* 10, *sect.* 2, *qu.* 5, *beb.* 5). The exact connotation of the term has of course been plainly worked out only in the course of centuries.

By the *ex nihilo* it was not of course intended to say (1) that the world was created *a nullo*, and therefore that it arose fortuitously or of itself. What was meant was that creation took place *ex nullo alio praeexistente* ; that it took place as the divinely ordained step from *non ens* to *ens* and was thus a creation *ex nihilo* (Quenstedt, *op. cit.*, *sect.* 2, *qu.* 5, *font. sol.* 1). In this sense the term *nihil* had (2) to be expressly contrasted with that of a pre-existent material. *Particula " ex " non designat materiam ex quo, sed excludit. Nihilum . . . non materiae sed termini a quo duntaxat rationem habet* (Quenstedt, *op. cit.*, *sect.* 1, *th.* 13). Before creation there is no reality distinct from God, neither an eternal substance which might compete with God nor one created by God. Creation as the absolutely primary work of God is the beginning of all things. Before it or behind it there is nothing, no ὕλη. In so far as it does not come from God, it does not come from anything. For this reason and to this extent it is *creatio ex nihilo*.

But from an early date the explanation was added (3) that, though all created things did not yet exist in the counsel and being of God before they came into being, yet their archetypes did. *Ante omnia enim Deus erat solus, ipse sibi et mundus et locus et omnia. Solus autem, quia nihil aliud extrinsecus preater illum* (Tertullian, *Adv. Prax.* 5). αὐτὸς (ὁ θεός) δὲ, μόνος ὤν, πολύς ἦν . . . πάντα δὲ ἦν ἐν αὐτῷ, αὐτὸς δὲ ἦν τὸ πᾶν (Hippolytus, *C. haer. Noeti*, 10) ἐποίησεν . . . ὡς ἔμπειρος ὢν τῶν ἐσομένων, πάρεστι γὰρ αὐτῷ καὶ πρόγνωσις (*Philos.* X, 32). It was particularly Augustine who (not without express allusion to the Platonic doctrine of ideas) laid emphasis upon this point. He combined the last words of Jn. 1³ with the first of Jn. 1⁴ to form the sentence : *Quod factum est, in eo vita erat* (*In Joann.* 1, 17), and concluded : *Singula propriis sunt creata rationibus. Has autem rationes ubi arbitrandum est esse, nisi in ipsa mente creatoris ? . . . neque in divina mente quidquam nisi aeterum atque incommutabile potest esse* (*De div. quaest.* 46, 2). Since we cannot suppose that God did not know things before He caused them to be, we must conclude that the *rationes omnium faciendarum rerum* were already previously existent in His wisdom and therefore in His being (*Ad Oros.* 8, 9.) Thus things were before they came to be, *non nihil quantum ad rationem facientis, per quam et secundum quam fierent* (Anselm of Canterbury, *Monol.* 9). And Polanus (*Synt. Theol. chr.*, 1609, *col.* 1718-26) tried to express the matter more precisely in the following way. Before created things as such, and to be fully distinguished from them, there exist as their objective foundations in the being of God Himself *formae praeexistentes et causae effectrices*. Or to put it the other way, before created things there is the being of God Himself to the extent that this wills to reflect an *imitatio* of itself in created things and thus includes from the first the representation (*repraesentatio*) of such things in its eternal being—the being of God as the fulness of divine ideas, of the *exemplaria, archetypa, prototypa, paradigmata, rationes primaevae* of God with reference to the things distinct from God which are to be created. This fulness lies eternally in God in so far as He is the fountain of all life, as the singular number includes all numbers in itself. Hence the act of creation does not take place without a reference back to something preceding it, to the extent that in performing it God proceeds from Himself or from the plenitude of His ideas, and it is the act of *imitatio*. But according to this clarification the doctrine of *creatio ex nihilo* still remains firm, because these ideas are in God. Indeed in the sense indicated they are God Himself, and therefore they have nothing whatever to do with the actual existence of created things as such, so that the latter are not preceded by anything outside the being of God.

On the other hand, it could not fail to be noticed (4) that at various points in the biblical accounts of creation, especially in the account of the creation of man in the second chapter (Gen. 2[7]), reference is incontestably made to a material used by God in the act of creation. And at all times there have been not a few theologians, particularly Augustine, who have taken this to mean that God first created chaos as the *rudis indigestaque moles* and then from this material created the heavens and the earth and all that is. The difficulty was met by distinguishing between the *significatio propria* and the *significatio propriae vicina* of the word *creare* ; or between a *creatio prima et immediata* and a *creatio secunda et mediata*, and correspondingly between a *nihil pure negativum* and a mere *nihil privativum*. Divine creation may well be effected on the assumption that a material already exists, but in this regard it should be noted that (as for example in the chaos of Gen. 1[1], or the dust of the ground of Gen. 2[7]) we are dealing with a *materia inhabilis et indisposita*, so that the *creatio ex aliquo* is at least very near to the *creatio ex nihilo*. If a poor man becomes rich or a sick man healthy, then it is true that he becomes what he was not before (Anselm of Canterbury, *Monol.* 8). And if the material is not to be understood as a divine emanation or as eternally co-existing with God, then there can be no question of describing the presupposed material itself except in terms of the creation *ex nihilo* (Quenstedt, *op. cit.*, sect. 2, qu. 5, ekth. 2–5). *Fecisti mundum de materia informi, quam fecisti de nulla re paene nullam rem* (Augustine, *Conf.* XII, 8, 8).

The problem was finally (5) considered from the standpoint of possibility. Is there a possibility of things prior to their creation ? To this the answer was given that, since things were not real before they were created, there is obviously not, or at least no peculiar possibility. *Sed Deo, in cuius potestate erat, ut fieret* (*mundus*), *possibile erat*. Things exist on the basis of the possibility of God, but on the basis of this possibility alone. Hence even in this respect they are real only through the *creatio ex nihilo* (Anselm of Canterbury, *De Casu Diaboli*, 12).

The importance of this theologoumenon for the whole doctrine of creation is quite unmistakeable. If the Christian doctrine of creation is to be precisely defined over against the two views which stand opposed to it, namely, the doctrine of the world as a part or emanation of the divine being (i.e., monism) and the doctrine of the world as an independent entity eternally co-existing with God (i.e., dualism), then the concept of divine creation must be given this sharp formulation. And whenever these two theses have been kept in view, then (with or without this particular formulation) theology has in fact moved on these lines. But because of the importance of the matter it is as well that we should not be opposing speculation to speculation, but moving on the secure ground of the biblical testimony and therefore of the revealed Word of God. We have indeed seen that in two places the New Testament at any rate points plainly in this direction, and furthermore that the doctrine of the *creatio ex nihilo* has it root in Hebrew and not in Greek thought. But the inner necessity of thinking and teaching as the Church has done in this matter is imposed upon us only in the anthropological context in which we have raised the question.

It could be objected to our definition of man that it is too far reaching in the sense that it characterises not man alone but the creature generally. " To be called into being "—is that not the essence of every creature ? Our answer is that this definition, while it does include the creature generally, has the advantage of incidentally bringing out the inner necessity of this recognition of the *creatio ex nihilo* which is so important and indispensable to the whole idea of creation. Here at least the concept does not remain in the air and cannot be suspected of being an idle speculation. For at this point it expresses the absolutely essential thing which is to be said of the creature of God as such, namely, that it derives from God and no other source, and that it exists through God and not otherwise. Hence it is not itself God or an emanation of God. Nor is it self-engendered and therefore independent of God. It is that which is called into being by Him, with no other or prior rootage, but grounded only in His call. For it is as one called by God that the man exists who is in fellowship with the man Jesus and in whom we are to recognise true man as God created him. In the formula *creatus ex nihilo* we have a fine and clear if negative witness to this man's awareness and confession of the nature of his being. As he is summoned into life by God, he is not God but distinct from God and therefore no part of or emanation from the divine being. And as he is summoned into life by God, he exists through God and not apart from Him or independently of Him. The root common to monism and dualism is here cut off. Here at all events the more exact formulation of the concept of creation is justified. If we think primarily of man, we can even appreciate that all that precision of detail was no idle play of thought, but had in its own place an inward necessity.

(1) The awakened being of man, who apart from God and His Word has nothing behind him—and this point is of importance to-day in its contrast to existentialist philosophy—is not a fortuitous being, self-enclosed, or open only to the yawning abyss of the void. As there stands behind it God and His Word, it is not *ex nihilo* but very much *ex aliquo*.

(2) The awakened being of man, as there is nothing behind it but God and His Word, is not grounded upon nothingness and chaos. Man's origin lies on the other side of all nothingness and chaos. He has no part in the latter. He exists precisely as he turns his back on the void. The void is not his place of origin, but as God elected him it is that which is rejected and neither his origin nor his goal.

(3) But there is a real pre-existence of man as the one who is summoned by God—and we shall lay particular emphasis upon this point in the development of the early doctrine, because it brings us face to face with the positive determination—namely, a pre-existence in the counsel of God, and to that extent, in God Himself, i.e., in the Son of God, in so far as the Son is the uncreated prototype of the humanity which is to be linked with God, man in his unity with God, and therefore " the firstborn of every creature " (Col. 1^{15}). As God Himself is mirrored in this image, He creates man as the one whom He summons into life. He creates him as His eternal Word has this specific content to which He adheres in His action. This eternal Word of God with this specific content is the divine reality apart from which man as summoned by God has nothing behind him.

(4) The creation of man is certainly to be understood also as a *creatio mediata*, and the nothingness which is its background as a mere *nihil privativum*, to the

extent that his being summoned includes and therefore has as a presupposition his constitution, his existence as a natural and spiritual being. But in relation to his being itself, namely, to his awakened being, this presupposition is only a *materia inhabilis et indisposita*. His humanity is not rooted in it and cannot be explained by it, but solely by what God willed to make of him as He ordained it for him. In his humanity as such he is *immediate creatus* : *ex nihilo pure negativo*.

(5) As regards the final question of the possibility of man before God, we may say quite clearly that this certainly cannot be ascribed to him as a possibility from within. The just lives by his faith, and this means that even the potentiality of his being does not lie within but outside himself. His being as one who is summoned has its possibility in the One who summons and in His summons. From this standpoint, too, the being of man confirms the *creatio ex nihilo*.

We may thus say that at all events in its proper anthropological context this theologoumenon is fully justified even in its most subtle conceptual nuances. And we may well ask whether we should not seek here its true setting and material (and perhaps historical) origin, wherever else we may also have to seek them. As the doctrine of the *creatio ex nihilo* makes the same affirmation of all creatures, so biblical man recognises and confesses his own creatureliness. The striking use of the verb καλεῖν in Rom. 4¹⁷ is to be noted, and in the same text the conjunction of καλεῖν τὰ μὴ ὄντα with ζωοποιεῖν τοὺς νεκρούς. The fact that the former comes first shows us that for Paul the idea of the resurrection of the dead was connected with that of the *creatio ex nihilo*. And by the καλεῖν and ζωοποιεῖν Paul wished to denote the God in whom Abraham believed, and believed παρ' ἐλπίδα ἐπ' ἐλπίδι (Rom. 4¹⁸), the God who by His promise alone creates something absolutely new, and who wills to be known, honoured and loved by man as the One who does make all things new. Attention should also be paid to the context in which the matter is expressed in Heb. 11³. Again creation is nothing other than the initiation, heading and sum of all the divine disclosures, promises, intimations and ordinances whose character, so inconceivable to man, serves in this chapter to bring out the no less absolutely miraculous nature of faith. What faith is, is seen from the case of Abraham (Rom. 4) in the form of these divine revelations, in which it is rooted. According to Heb. 11¹, it is " the conviction of things not seen," of things whose truth lies in God alone. Hence the believer who builds his life on such things has God alone and nothing else as His support and basis. This is how man is, how he exists as a believer. He is a new thing in relation to his apparent origin. He has his true origin in the One who is his goal. In this connexion we should think of Heb. 11¹³ᶠ· (which is again related to a direct description of the faith of Abraham and Sarah) : " These all died in faith, not having received the promises, but having seen them afar off, and were persuaded of them, and embraced them, and confessed that they were strangers and pilgrims on the earth. For they that say such things declare plainly that they seek a country. And truly, if they had been mindful of that country from whence they came out, they might have had opportunity to have returned, but now they desire a better country, that is, an heavenly : wherefore God is not ashamed of them to be called their God : for he hath prepared for them a city." This, then, is how it stands with the believer. Why ? Because this God of his is basically (v. 3) the One by whose Word the worlds were created, so that the things that are seen (τὰ βλεπόμενα) are not grounded in anything perceptible (a sort of φαινόμενα) but solely in the Word of God. In harmony with this objective order of being, the believer obviously understands his own existence above all, his fatherland being before and not behind him. He lives according to the rule of Phil. 3¹³ : " Forgetting those things which are behind, and reaching forth unto those things which are before, I press toward the mark for the prize of the high calling of God in Christ Jesus." We are also reminded of Col. 3²ᶠᶠ· : " Set your affection on things above, not on things

on the earth. For ye are dead, and your life is hid with Christ in God." If it is
legitimate and necessary to think of the ontological implications of these texts,
then they show us that the *creatio ex nihilo* is not a speculative construction, but
the most natural expression of man's self-understanding as rooted in God's self-
revelation in the man Jesus. What men are as men, they are through God and
not otherwise.

If this theologoumenon is valid in anthropology because man seen in fellowship
with the man Jesus is true man as God created him, then it is surely right and
sensible to apply this principle not merely to man but—since it is valid for man—
to creation as a whole, the objective order of all things being understood in
accordance with the existence of the believer. The theology of the ancient
Church was agreed that the doctrine of creation should be an article of faith.
And Heb. 11³ begins expressly with the words : " Through faith we understand
that the worlds were framed by the word of God." This obviously means that
what man in faith believes to be the ground of his own creatureliness, the same he
recognises in faith to be the ground of the worlds, of the heavens and the earth,
of all creation. It needs children born, not of blood, nor of the will of the flesh,
nor of the will of man, but of God (Jn. 1¹²ff.), to recognise and confess with Jn 1³ :
" All things were made by him ; and without him was not anything made that
was made." It is these children of God who will unhesitatingly recognise and
confess this. The theology of the ancient Church failed to base the doctrine of
the *creatio ex nihilo* on this biblical insight. Perhaps this is the reason why it
undoubtedly has the savour of scholastic speculation. Once it is understood
on this basis, it loses this savour. Once it is understood in this light, it is no
mere theologoumenon, but what it is intended to be in Heb. 11³ and unquestionably
is in the context of Heb. 11 and Rom. 4, namely, an article of faith which is
necessary in its own place.

We may now recapitulate the insights which we have attained
into the nature of true man. We began by stating that the being of
man is a being with God and that it derives from God. We then
advanced our two main propositions that it rests upon God's election
and consists in hearing His Word. We shall return to this final insight
later. But first we may sum up all that we have said in the statement
that the being of man is a history.

It takes place that the Creator concerns Himself about His creature
by Himself becoming a creature. This is the meaning of the existence
of the man Jesus which we have taken as the point of orientation in
our enquiry into the nature of true humanity and by which theological
anthropology as a whole must be guided. All our previous statements
point in this direction—that the being of man is a history. Yet we
prefer not to deduce this principle from those which immediately
precede, but to go back to the starting-point. It is the existence
of the man Jesus which teaches us that the being of man is a history.
What happens in this existence, i.e., that the Creator shows His
concern for His creation by Himself becoming a creature, is the fulness
and sum of what we mean by talking about history. Here, if anywhere,
the use of the term " primal history " is perhaps appropriate. From
this standpoint alone can we thoroughly realise that the being of man
in general and as such must be regarded as a history.

In contrast to the concept of history is that of a state. There are states that are very much in movement, developing through many changes and varied modes of behaviour. The conception of a stiff and motionless uniformity need not be linked with that of a state. But the idea of a state does involve the idea of something completely insulated within the state in question, the idea of a limitation of its possibilities and therefore of its possible changes and modes of behaviour. It is never capable of more than these particular movements. Even the concept of the most mobile state is not therefore equivalent to that of history.

For example, we do not really know what we are talking about when we speak of the history of a plant or animal, because what we know of plants or animals can appear to us only as fixed circles of changes and modes of behaviour. Nor have we yet realised the meaning of the history of man if we envisage only the plenitude—but limited plenitude—of his characteristic movements in their juxtaposition and sequence, continuity and causal connexion, so that what we have before us is only the nature of man—his nature regarded as the sum total of his possible and actual changes and modes of behaviour.

The concept of history in its true sense as distinct from that of a state is introduced and achieved when something happens to a being in a certain state, i.e., when something new and other than its own nature befalls it. History, therefore, does not occur when the being is involved in changes or different modes of behaviour intrinsic to itself, but when something takes place upon and to the being as it is. The history of a being begins, continues and is completed when something other than itself and transcending its own nature encounters it, approaches it and determines its being in the nature proper to it, so that it is compelled and enabled to transcend itself in response and in relation to this new factor. The history of a being occurs when it is caught up in this movement, change and relation, when its circular movement is broken from without by a movement towards it and the corresponding movement from it, when it is transcended from without so that it must and can transcend itself outwards. It should thus be evident that, if we assume that the history of a being really takes place in this pregnant and deep sense of the term, it is quite inappropriate to say that this being has a history (as though it merely happened to have this history in addition to what it is). If we may and must assume that a history of this being really takes place, this means decisively that it has its being inside and not outside this history, that its being is an element in this history and to this extent is itself this history. It exists, then, in so far as it takes place that that other, that new factor which is foreign to its own nature and the closed circle of its state, encounters it and approaches it, in so far as it moves and is changed in response and in relation to that other. Even then it is still in a state. But it is no longer the sum of its state; it is only in it. Its state is merely the sum of the attributes and modalities of its history. It *is* in the history itself, whereas all the possibilities and realisations of its state only constitute the manner of its true and historical being.

What we have before us with this concept of being as history is the existence of the man Jesus. The history not only of all other beings but of all other men may be interpreted as a state which is in movement. And we must immediately add that in relation to all other beings and men we should be left with no choice but to admit that, no less in respect of men than plants and animals, we are able to understand and apply the concept of history only in an improper sense, what we really mean being only a state which is in movement. We have another choice, and can form and apply the concept of history in the true and pregnant sense, only because in the midst of all other creatures and men we have to reckon also with the fact of the existence of the man Jesus. This forces us, indeed, to form and apply the concept. For what happens here cannot be interpreted as a state. At this point being is not simply movement within itself. It is not confined to the sphere of the specific possibilities characteristic of a specific being. It is both the transcendence and transcending of such a sphere—its transcendence by a new and different factor and its transcending in response and relation to this factor. It is the identity of the Creator and the creature. And the Creator is for the creature the utterly new and other. If it is the case that the man Jesus is Himself the Creator who has become creature, then He exists in a manner which cannot be exhaustively described by any state, but in Him we are faced by the fulfilment of the strict concept of history. For it is really not a state that the Creator and the creature are one. In consideration of the otherness and newness of the Creator in relation to the creature, we can understand it only as history. This creature is what it is as creature in a dynamic movement of the Creator to itself and itself to the Creator. It exists in this movement from another to itself and itself to this other—a movement which, since God the Creator is this Other, it is quite impossible to describe as a movement within itself. And since it represents itself as a being of this kind, it clearly forbids us to seek its essence behind or apart from this movement. It does not " have " a history from which it can itself be distinguished as a substratum. But it " is " in this history, i.e., it is, as it takes place that the Creator is creature and the creature Creator. The fact that as a creature it exists in specific conditions is not its being but only the attribute and modality of its being. Its being as such, the being of the man Jesus, lies in the fact that God is for Him and He for God. And we remember what all this means—that in the existence of this man it takes place that God takes up the cause of His threatened creature. There comes upon the creature the new fact that above and beyond its actual being God gives Himself to it as the Deliverer in order that it may itself be the Deliverer. There comes upon it the fact that it is

elected by God and may therefore elect Him in return. There comes
upon it the fact that in view of the imminent danger of its ruin God
in His eternal mercy pledges Himself to its service, and that it for
its part may serve the eternal righteousness of God. There comes upon
it the fact that God attests and reveals Himself, and that it becomes
itself the witness and revelation of God. The existence of the man
Jesus is this history. It is nothing more. It has nothing behind it
but the eternal will and counsel of God. It has no other foundation.
Thus, apart from the eternal will and counsel of God, Jesus exists
only in this history, i.e., in this history of the covenant and salvation
and revelation inaugurated by God in and with the act of creation.
Jesus is, as this history takes place.

And now let us consider man in general in the light of this truth.
We again ask : What is man ? And we answer : He is the being
whose Kinsman, Neighbour and Brother is the man Jesus, and in
whose sphere therefore this history takes place. He is with God,
confronted and prevented and elected and summoned by Him, in
the fact that this history takes place in his own sphere. This is the
unmistakeable and unforgettable factor with which we have always
to reckon in the interpretation of his being and from which we can
never in any circumstances abstract.

A. Harnack opened his lectures on " What is Christianity ? " (1900) by
recalling the dictum of John Stuart Mill that humanity cannot be reminded
too often of the fact that there was once a man named Socrates ; and he added
a sentence which is worth pondering, that although Mill was right it is even more
important continually to remind humanity that there once stood in its midst
a man named Jesus Christ. We may differ from Harnack as to the way in which
we should remember this man. But we can agree that we cannot be reminded
too often that this man once dwelt in the midst of humanity. In Him we have
the central human factor.

For it is the fact of the existence of the man Jesus which makes it
unavoidable to form a concept of history in contrast with that of a
mere state for the adequate description of the being of man. We
should not be repelled by the fact that Jesus is the only One of whom
it may be said that in Him the Creator is creature and the creature
the Creator. This certainly means that in the original and immediate
sense He alone is the man to whom God has given Himself. He alone
is the man whom God has elected and who elects God in return.
He alone is the man whom the mercy of God has wholly served in
order that He Himself might be entirely at the disposal of the divine
righteousness. He alone is the man who has been divinely kept and
who therefore divinely keeps. He alone is the man to whom God was
revealed that He Himself might reveal God. His history alone is
originally and immediately the history of the covenant of salvation
and revelation inaugurated by God. All this is true. But He alone
is all this on behalf of all those whom He is like as man and who are

like Him as men. The likeness between Him and them means that what He alone is, is valid for them too, that this is the light in which they not only stand outwardly but are inwardly and essentially. Their being consists in the fact that they are now with Him ; their being is wholly determined by the fact that the One who is like them, and whom they are like, as He dwells among them in all His unlikeness, is this divine history in His existence. Their being, too, cannot be fully described as being in a mere state, however active. It cannot be correctly seen and described as such. If we do not know whether or how far the concept of a state may be the ultimate or possibly only the penultimate word in respect of the non-human creation, the fact that the existence of the man Jesus has to be taken into account means that the concept of history is needed for a true description of the human creation. For although the range of possibilities characteristic of man is seen in this fact—there would be no likeness between Jesus and ourselves if the human state as such were simply set aside— yet it is seen to be burst open both from without and outwards. In this fact there encounters us man himself in his state as the being who is transcended from without and is thus able to transcend himself outwards. Hence this fact characterises the being of man even where it is not a question of the being of this one man, but of that of all other men. Confronted by this fact, and related to this one man dwelling at the heart of humanity, they too obviously share in what He is and therefore in the history actualised in Him. This is the truth of God which embraces them too. It is the Word of God which is spoken for them too and therefore applies to them. It is the embodiment of the will of God by which they are affected from the very outset—they who are not Jesus, who cannot reproduce or repeat His existence, and yet who are like Him. This fact lifts them above a mere state. It means that something happens for them too, and that their being thus has the character of history. In their case it is clearly history in a secondary, derivative and indirect sense of the term. There is indeed only one primary, direct and immediate fulfilment of the concept of history. There is only one " primal history." Other men are what they are only in their confrontation and connexion with the fact of this one man. Apart from this relationship their being would obviously not deserve to be described as more than a state. But the fact of this one man is prior to the existence of all other men. It is thus through their relationship to Him that they are what they are. Their being is history only in this relationship, but in this relationship it is really history. Their being is history in or with the history enacted in the existence of the man Jesus. The new and other which God is directly for the man Jesus, Jesus Himself is for all other men, and therefore He is the basis which makes their being history, a being which is transcended in its limitation from without and transcends its limitation outwards. Man is what he is as a creature, as the man Jesus, and in Him God Himself, moves towards him, and as he moves towards the man Jesus and therefore towards God. Man is as he is engaged in this movement in this " to him " from without and " from him " outwards, which, because this fact is his Whence and Whither, cannot be interpreted as a self-centred movement and therefore as a state.

It is obviously true of man in general that his being is not to be sought behind or apart from this movement, as if it were first something in itself which is then caught up in this movement and then participates as such in this movement, having this history in and with the history enacted in the existence of the man Jesus. We have to say of him too that he is as it takes place that he is like the man Jesus and thus participates in the history enacted in Him. He exists in this secondary, derived, indirect history, but a history which takes place *realissime* in its relation to that primal history. Whatever his state may be, he is only *in* this state ; it is not his being but only the attribute and modality of his being. His true being is his being in the history grounded in the man Jesus, in which God wills to be for him and he may be for God. And we must again remember what all this means. The existence of every man as such, through the mediation of the one Jesus, participates in the fact that from the very first, from its very creation, God willed to espouse and did espouse the cause of His threatened creature. To be a man is to be under the sign of the deliverance which comes to the creature from Jesus. To be a man is to be able to look up for the sake of Jesus, and for His sake not to have to fear destruction. To be a man is to be held by the divine mercy, and to adhere to the divine righteousness, for His sake. Man is a being who is kept and keeps through the mediation of Jesus, for as he is guarded it is incumbent on him to guard. As he has himself been helped, he is commissioned to be a helper ; and as he is in the light of revelation, he necessarily becomes in some way a light. This is the history of human existence as such and in general. It is not an independent history. It follows in the wake of the history of the man Jesus. To a certain extent it depends on the latter. But in connexion with it, it too is a part of the history of the covenant, of salvation and of revelation. And in this connexion and therefore in this history man is what he is.

But this gives content to all our earlier statements if they are rightly understood. In formulating them, we were careful to bring out their true implication from the very first. We shall now recapitulate them with new emphases which in the light of what we have just said will rule out any possible misunderstanding.

We defined the being of man as a co-existence with the transcendent God who really confronts him. We must be careful not to understand this co-existence after the mode and analogy of the relationship of two things determined by their states, a finite and relative on the

one side, an infinite and absolute on the other, and the whole process
as their action and reaction. Here there is no play and counterplay.
Here it is not a question of things which apart from what they are in
themselves could still stand in a continually shifting relationship.
What takes place here is history, which means that on either side
there is no being which is not as such an act of God from Himself
to man and therefore a responsive act of man to God. We must see
this act from and to God if we are to see man as the being which is
with God.

We defined the being of man more precisely as a being which
derives from God. But the idea of the dependence of the human being
on the divine which this implies must be cleansed from the notion
that the former is the necessary effect of God as its cause. God is
undoubtedly cause and man effect. But both points are true only
in the reality of encounter and therefore in the reality of the history
in which this encounter takes place. That man is dependent on God,
that he is indeed absolutely dependent, absolutely an effect, is something which he has in common with the rest of creation. What distinguishes him is that he is dependent on God in such a way that God
inaugurates a movement of history between Himself and man, that
precisely in regard to man God takes up the cause of the threatened
creature, that in the midst of creation God guards man and appoints
him a guardian. Thus even when it is more precisely defined as a
being which derives from God, the being of man is identical with the
act or occurrence of this history.

In our first main statement we defined the being of man as a being
which rests on the election of God. If only we keep the idea of election
free from the suggestion of contingency, from this standpoint again
we shall see that history is the essence of his being. Of course election
is not to be understood as a special relationship between God and
man which comes into being by chance or on the basis of an existent
affinity. In our elucidation of the concept, we referred from the
very first to a special counsel with a special intention in relation to a
special object. The special counsel and intention in relation to man
are the inner works of the free God working on His own conscious
initiative. When we say that the being of man rests on the election
of God, we say that it springs from a history which has its prototype
and origin in God Himself. And so from this standpoint again it is
difficult to see how the being of man is to be sought anywhere except
in the occurrence of this history.

And in our second main proposition we defined the being of man
as a being which consists in the hearing of the Word of God. Here
again great caution is needed. At this decisive point we did not
attribute to man a mere potentiality but actuality ; not a mere
capacity to hear but real hearing ; not mere perceptivity but actual
perception ; not merely the formal character of logos but the material

character of a being reached, determined and motivated by the divine Logos. Thus the formula that man is in " the Word of God " does not denote a mere state, but the being of man as history. As he hears the Word of God, there stands over against him, and in contrast with his own inner changes and modes of conduct, the new and other, and he is transcended from without and transcends himself outwards. As he hears the Word of God, he becomes and is among all creatures the specific human creature. It is not the fact that he has ear and reason and the character of logos which makes him this specific creature. The case is rather that he has these qualities only because he is this creature. That he is so, is something which takes place as he hears the Word of God, and therefore in this act, in the history which is peculiarly his. He is man as he is summoned by God.

It is from this second main proposition that we must now proceed. Undoubtedly the most accurate description of the history in which we have to recognise the being of man is to say that this being is determined by the fact that it is called by God. The Word and summons of God to each and every man is the existence of the man Jesus. Every man is man in the fact that Jesus exists for him too, that the call of God embodied in Jesus concerns him too. His being is human as it is called in Jesus.

But the substance of this divine call to every man is, in one word, the grace of God in which He espouses the cause of His creature. The grace of God is the meaning of the existence of the man Jesus, and it is therefore this which in Him is addressed to every other man. The divine grace is the goodness in which God remembers His creature, and His will, determined by this goodness, to keep it from evil by making Himself its Deliverer. The divine grace is the freedom in which God decides thus and not otherwise, and the omnipotence in which He carries out this decision. The divine grace is the mercy and justice of God operative and revealed in this decision. For the compassion in which God refuses to withdraw from His creature, and the zeal with which He will not surrender His right over it, derive from a single source, and they are one as grace. Grace sums up the mind and attitude and work of God towards the creature which confronts Him in its own nature. There is thus good reason to seize on this word which is offered to us by important passages in the New Testament, and which has always been accepted as of central theological importance, especially in Western theology, and to summarise as the Word of grace the Word of God which is spoken and which summons man in the existence of the man Jesus.

The history which constitutes the being of man is primarily that among the many creatures of God there is the one, this creature, to which God addresses this Word in the existence of another creature of its own kind, in the man Jesus. God says to this creature that He is gracious. This is the new and different thing which it does not have intrinsically, which has nothing to do with its own inner changes and modes of conduct, and which cannot therefore be interpreted as its state. This is something which comes to it from without. It is something which transcends the limited sphere of its own possibilities, which constitutes it a creature that is not abandoned to itself and its own arbitrary desires or fate, but stands in a relation to that superior reality without, to God its Creator, so that it is what it is in virtue of this relation. The Word of grace is the breaking through of the Creator to the creature, by which the being of the latter is opened from without and this relation is established. In the Word of grace God its Creator comes to it, gives Himself to it and dwells within it. And in the Word of grace which comes to it, it acquires its own being as man. This is the being of which God has said that He will be gracious to it, that He will remember it in His goodness, that He wills to preserve it from evil, that this is His free and omnipotent decision, the decision of His mercy and righteousness. It is thus the being of real man. And it is obviously at root a historical being. To be what he is, to be real man among all creatures, man needs this event—that God should say that He is gracious to him. He is himself, man, as this is actually said, and therefore in this Word, the Word of the grace of God.

We shall try to pursue this point further. The history of the being of man is set in train by the fact that God says that He is gracious to him. Only now can we fully understand why it is a being summoned. The Word of God is obviously not only a communication but a challenge, not only an indicative but as such an imperative, because it is the Word of His grace. Because grace assures this creature that it is not abandoned but received by God, and promises that it is the will of God to be its Helper and Saviour, this creature cannot be allowed to remain alone. Because this has been said to it, and because its being has been opened by the Word from without, from the side of God, it cannot be confined in the limits of its intrinsic possibility, it cannot remain alone, without realising the truth that these limits have been overcome by God, that God is already with it. This creature cannot exist without being in movement towards the source of its existence. But it is by a Word that it takes its origin in God. It is in the hearing of this Word that it lives. Hence it must be in obedience to this Word that its being and history is continued. Obedience means that this Word claims it. Its being takes its course as it accepts the claim of this Word. It is, as it is called, and it continues to be, as it allows itself to be called. It is thus called historically and not statically. It is not enclosed within the circle of its intrinsic possibilities, but opened towards that other and new reality of God its Creator which has broken through to it in His Word, and in that Word as His promise has come to dwell within it. Man is, as he hears this Word. He is, as he is awakened by this Word. He is, as he raises himself to this Word. He is, as he concentrates on this Word. He is, as, called by this Word, he is ready, and already in the act of transcending himself. All this is possible because he is in the Word of God, in the Word of His grace. To be summoned is to be called out of oneself and beyond oneself. Because it is God who speaks here, what is said has the right and power to enable the creature to transcend itself. Because it is a Word of God, in which God exercises His right and power for this purpose, what the creature experiences is not merely a movement or attraction but a genuine summons outwards. And the fact that it is a Word of grace determines the direction in which the being of man is summoned beyond itself. It is required of him neither to trust in himself nor to despair of himself, but like the ship's anchor cast overboard, to place his trust in God in whom he is grounded, who according to His Word wills to be his Preserver and Keeper, and who acknowledges him in His eternal mercy and righteousness. It is a being summoned because he is required to cast all his trust on his Creator. In this fact and manner his being is in the Word of God. By daring and accomplishing this act of self-committal, it is historical. And in this sense it is, as it is summoned.

But at this point we can and must attempt a more precise and material definition. If the Word of God in which man is, and is therefore historical, is a Word of divine grace, if he is thus summoned to hear and obey this Word, i.e., to be, and to continue to be, in the hearing of this Word, then the being of man can and must be more precisely defined as a being in gratitude. That casting of his faith on God which we have described as the true history and being of man is not so audacious and strange and fantastic as may appear at first sight. Rightly understood, it is in the strictest sense a natural human action. In it the creature remains in full self-possession, and exercises as directly as possible the true being beside which it has no other. It is, as it is told by God that He is gracious to it. In daring to cast itself upon God, it corresponds to the Word without which it would not be this human creature. When we understand the being of man as a correspondence to this Word, we understand it as a being in gratitude. Gratitude is the precise creaturely counterpart to the grace of God. What is by the Word of the grace of God, must be in gratitude ; and man's casting of his trust upon God is nothing other or less, but also nothing more, than the being of man as his act in gratitude.

The term εὐχαριστεῖν or εὐχαριστία, like the objective term χάρις which it reflects, is one of the terms which is only used soteriologically in the New Testament. But in the New Testament the existence of the man Jesus is a soteriological, *the* soteriological reality, and therefore in Jn. 1, Col. 1 and Heb. 1 we can also see its ontological significance. If man as such is not to be understood apart from the existence of the man Jesus, we cannot avoid the term grace and its complement gratitude even in the description of the being

of man as such. As the One who in Jesus meets him as his Saviour, and says that
He is gracious to him, God is already the Creator of man. The creaturely being
of man must as such be understood as a being claimed by this Word, and therefore as a correspondence to the grace of God, and therefore as a being in gratitude.

To be grateful is to recognise a benefit. To be grateful as opposed
to ungrateful is not merely to receive, accept and enjoy a benefit, but to
understand it as such, as a good which one could not take for oneself
but has in fact received, as an action which one could not perform
for oneself but which has nevertheless happened to one. To be grateful
is to recognise and honour as a benefactor the one who has conferred
this good. Gratitude implies obligation towards the benefactor ;
an obligation which will be manifested and proved in a certain attitude
towards the benefactor, but which cannot be exhaustively expressed
in any attitude. If the obligation of thanksgiving could be fully discharged in an attitude towards the benefactor, there would be no
real gratitude, just as a benefit which could be cancelled by an attitude
on the part of the recipient would certainly not have been a benefit.
In such a case both the benefit and the gratitude would simply have
been the two sides of a transaction based on mutual self-interest.
Where a genuine benefit calls for thanks, and where genuine thanks
respond to a benefit, there arises a relationship which, created by one
party, can only be accepted by the other, and not cancelled but continually renewed.

The true Benefactor, however, is God the Creator, and the epitome
of all benefits is His grace ascribed to man, and mediated as it is
ascribed, by the Word and summons with which He calls man into
being. It takes place by the Word of the grace of God, in which He
transcends from the very outset the limits of the human condition and
makes the being of man a history, that the latter becomes what it is,
a being open to God. By this Word God makes for Himself a dwelling
place in man—He his Creator and Saviour, He in His freedom and
omnipotence, His mercy and righteousness, His compassion and zeal,
He as the Guarantor and Protector of human and all creaturely being
against evil, He as his faithful Lord. And so the being of man is on
the basis of this divine grace, not as it first receives it, but in such
a way that, as it is, it is its recipient.

We may thus say that the being of man is a being in gratitude.
His history as constituted by the Word of the grace of God, his being
therefore, continues and must continue in the fact that it is a being
in gratitude. Merely as the promise of the grace of God, it could not
continue, or be the history of man, his own being. This promise is,
like its content, the affair of God and not of man. As it cannot be
gracious to itself, it cannot tell itself that God is gracious to it. This
it can only hear. The Word of grace and therefore grace itself, it can
only receive. But as it does this, as it is content to be what it is by
this Word, as it thus exists by its openness towards God, the question

is decided that it is a being in gratitude. It has not taken the grace of God but the latter has come to it ; it has not opened itself but God has opened it and made it this open being. And it now is what it has been made. But it cannot be without itself actualising this event. It is, as it is under an obligation to the God who has seized the initiative in starting this history ; as it is referred to Him in respect of its whole attitude. It is in the strength of the promise which God makes to it, that He is its Helper and Deliverer. As God comes to it in His Word, it is a being open towards God and self-opening, transcending itself in a Godward direction. Grounded in the Word of divine grace, it is the being which responds and is complementary to that grace. Thus it is a being in gratitude. This means that man is, as he not only receives and accepts as a benefit the promise of God, but also understands that this is a gift which he could not win for himself, a deed which he has not himself wrought, an event to which he has not contributed and which he has not deserved. To see this acceptance as such is to see real man in his own action, not merely as the object but as the subject of the history in which his being consists. For when we see him as the being responsive and complementary to the grace of God, as a being in gratitude, we see him for the first time—and this is the new step which we must take in forming a picture of real man—in his own act. Seen here at its root, and understood as thanksgiving for the grace of God, this is the act in which he accepts the validity of the act which not he but God has wrought. But in this form it is his own act. He is the subject of his history as its divinely posited object. The grace of God demands that it should be accepted as such. It calls for gratitude. The fact that it finds gratitude, that the God who is gracious to His creature is honoured in the world of creation, is the being of man, and this being engaged in its characteristic activity. Hidden in thanksgiving, and therefore in the act of man, grace itself, which came from God in His Word, now returns to God, to its source of origin. Gratitude, the acceptance of grace, can itself be understood only as grace. Man does nothing special, nothing peculiar or arbitrary, when he thanks God. He is permitted to thank God. He has freedom to do so. And yet it is true that the form of grace in this return to its original source is man's action and deed, the being of man as subject, to whom God in its thanksgiving is just as strictly object as it is the object of the Subject God when it receives the divine promise. In this new light we shall later pursue the history which is the being of man to the very end.

Before we turn to this task it is fitting to make clear the meaning of the step which we are now taking by considering the scope of the idea of gratitude in this connexion. We shall formulate the relevant insight in four propositions—two concerning God and two concerning man. All four have formally in common the fact that they imply exclusion, and materially that they suggest that it is in the closed circle of the relationship between divine grace and human gratitude that we have to seek the being of man.

1. Only God deserves the thanks of man. We speak of true and essential gratitude—of the gratitude in which man must accept permanently and unreservedly the benefit he has experienced as the benefit which he simply cannot do without, as the perfect benefit which fulfils all his needs even to the point of overflowing, as a benefit showered upon him in the sovereign freedom of the Benefactor. We thus speak of a gratitude in which acceptance of the blessing has a depth and abandon and constancy corresponding to its character, in which obligation towards the Benefactor is felt to be absolute so that it cannot be fully discharged by any attitude of gratefulness which it may arouse. There are also other and more modest benefits. All the benefits which one creature can be or give towards another belong to this category. We do not underestimate the fact that these other more modest benefits exist, and that they are genuine benefits because first and last God the Creator is their source. Similarly there is also another and more modest type of gratitude—the gratitude which creatures may show one another for reciprocal favour, and which can be genuine because first and last it is to God that they are thankful when they receive genuine benefits. But this also implies that all other thanksgiving is weighed in the scales and placed under the question whether it refers to a genuine benefit of God for which man is giving thanks, and whether it is therefore the true and essential gratitude which is appropriate to this benefit. Our present theme is this true and essential gratitude. The divine benefit demands this. And it alone can do so. It alone is the indispensable, perfect and free blessing poured out upon man. It alone promises the grace which maintains and saves man. It alone spells the salvation which alone can and does help the creature living on the edge of the abyss of destruction. Hence it alone merits thanks in the strictest sense of the term. Because God alone can be and is a Benefactor in this sense, the One in relation to whom man can and will transcend the limits of his intrinsic possibilities (which is what happens when he thanks God), therefore God alone deserves thanks. Thanksgiving is wasted, indeed, it rests on error and can only lead to further error, if it is not directed to the one benefit of this one Benefactor, even in the grateful acceptance of benefits from creaturely benefactors. As thanksgiving which is part of an absolute obligation and is permanently binding, it can be directed to this one benefit alone and therefore to this one Benefactor alone.

2. God can only be thanked by man. We speak of the true and essential thing which is possible and appropriate to man in relation to God, of what is worthy of God in the strict sense, and therefore of the comprehensive thing in which his action towards God must always

consist, of that character of his action which exactly and fully corresponds and does justice to God. We speak of the action in which man confronts the God who promises him His grace and is thus his Benefactor. This action of man towards God may be viewed in many aspects—as obedience, faith, love or trust, and these again in various possible applications and manifestations. Indeed, it will continually find expression in one or other of these aspects, manifestations and applications. But in every conceivable form it will be examined in the light of the criterion whether it is an action which exactly and fully corresponds and is adequate to God's Word of grace. For the fact is that properly and essentially God can only be thanked by man, so that any action of man which is not basically an expression of gratitude is inadequate in the face of God. A god who required and accepted anything else from man, any attitudes and actions otherwise conditioned and grounded, would certainly not be God. For only one attitude can adequately respond to the way in which God meets man with the indispensable and perfect and free gift of His Word of grace, namely, that he should accept this gift as such, that he should recognise and honour the Giver, and that he should realise the binding obligation which this gift lays upon him. With anything more or less or other than this, man could only be grasping in relation to God, and could and would only draw down upon himself wrath and perdition. Obedience without gratitude would be nothing. Love without gratitude would be nothing. The best and most pious works in the service of God, whatever they might be, would be nothing if in their whole root and significance they were not works of gratitude. Whatever man desires and is able to do in his relation to God is tested by the degree to which its meaning is his acceptance of God's gracious Word, of God as the God who reveals and offers Himself to man in this Word. By no other way than that of thanksgiving can man transcend himself. In truth God can only be thanked by man.

3. Only as he thanks God does man fulfil his true being. Our first two propositions were concerned in the main with the position and meaning of God in the matter—that He alone is worthy of man's thanks, and thanks alone are what He requires and accepts from man. We now come to the two more narrowly anthropological aspects of the theme. In the first we shall give concretion to our earlier and more general insight that only in his history is man what he is. His history and therefore his true being has its origin in God with the fact that God tells him that He is gracious to him. As we now consider the way in which this history develops and emerges as a history in which man is not only object but also subject, we have to do with gratitude to God. The fact that God tells man that He is gracious to him, that He reveals to man His grace, His indispensable, pure and perfect benefit, is the objective and receptive aspect of the being of man, and the fact that he gives thanks to God is the subjective and spontan-

eous. We presuppose the former and concentrate attention on the
latter, when we say that only as he gives thanks to God does man
fulfil his true nature. We maintain that among all that man can do
only this is the essential and characteristic action which constitutes
his true being. By doing this and this alone does he distinguish himself as being from non-being. In this action alone does he confirm
the divine separation of light from darkness, and seize his promised
salvation and deliverance. In this action alone is he man. Man
can and does do many things. But only in one way can he confirm
the fact that he is man. He has only the one great possibility of being
man. This is basically opposed only by the one great impossibility,
the actualisation of which can only mean that he is not man and
therefore nothing (for if he were not man, what else could he be ?).
But the realisation of his true possibility, and therefore the fulfilment
of his being, consists in his giving of thanks. In this he gives honour
to the One to whom alone it is due, and the honour which alone is
worthy of Him. In the fact that he does this he responds subjectively
and spontaneously to the objective, receptive foundation of his being
in the Word of God. It is well to recollect at this point that this one
action may assume many forms. But we must also observe that all
these forms are to be tested by the question whether they are first
and last genuine forms of this one action. However man may thank
God, it is only in the fact that he does thank God that he is man,
because it is in this action alone that he does justice to that in which
his being is rooted, to the Word of God which declares that God is
gracious to him. In all action in which this thankfulness does not
find expression, the history in which the being of man alone consists
comes to a halt and breaks off, because it contradicts the Word of
God which is its basis. The scales are strictly accurate in which all
human action and therefore the being of man are weighed. " To be
or not to be ? that is the question," and it is decided by the way in
which we answer the question : To give thanks or not to give thanks ?
The real man is the man who is thankful to God, and he alone. For
the history inaugurated by God, in which he is what he is, can have
on his side only one continuation, i.e., in the thanksgiving which he
owes to God and in which he owes himself to God.

4. To thank God in this way is incumbent on man alone. We
know from our earlier deliberations that we must make this final
exclusion with hesitation and reserve. We cannot penetrate the inner
reality of the relationship between God and other creatures. We
simply do not know the nature of this relationship. We do not know
what grace and thankfulness may mean in this connexion. We speak
of what we know as thankfulness towards God because we are called
to it, because it is required of us, and because our being consists in
offering it. We speak of the thankfulness which arises in connexion
with the Word of grace spoken to man, and which consists in man's

finding himself engaged and committed to the God who shows him this benefit in His Word. We refer to the spirit of thanksgiving by which man is not only the object but the subject of his history and therefore his being. We refer to the gratitude fulfilled in man's responsibility to the Word of God spoken to him. It is this idea of responsibility which we shall have to take up again when we try to explain the implications of the subjectivity and spontaneity of man. We would thus emphasise the phrase " in this way " in our proposition : " To thank God in this way is incumbent on man alone." Man is not the only creature of God. He is on earth under heaven. And as God's Word of grace is spoken to him in his particular sphere, it is also spoken in this greater sphere of heaven and earth and all that therein is. As gratitude is the response to the grace of God required of man, it can have no other response in the depths of earth or heights of heaven. As we must say of man that he is what he is only in gratitude towards God, we shall have to say the same of all other creatures. They too exist as they are preserved by God's Word of grace spoken in their midst, and as they accept the validity of His promise given to them also. They too are threatened, and they too held by the Word of God. As being is for them in some sense the level on which they cannot maintain themselves, but below which they cannot fall because God's Word of grace applies to them too, they belong with us as they too are in their own way thankful to God.

At this point we may recall Luther's explanation of the first article of creed : " I believe that God has created me together with all other creatures . . . out of pure fatherly divine goodness and mercy, without any merit or worth on our part." Luther then continues : " . . . for all this it is my duty to thank and praise Him, to serve and to obey Him." No doubt he was thinking of Ps. 139[14] : " I will praise thee ; for I am fearfully and wonderfully made " ; and of Ps. 103[1ff.] : " Bless the Lord, O my soul : and all that is within me, bless his holy name." But if the " together with all creatures " is true, then the thought will have to be amplified as in Ps. 148, where we find that the angels and all the heavenly hosts, heaven and the waters above the firmament, the dragons and all deeps, fire and hail, snow and vapour and stormy wind, mountains and all hills, fruitful trees and all cedars, beasts and all cattle, creeping things and flying fowl, are all called upon to praise God, and that only in this great chorus are men to praise him, the kings of the earth and all peoples, princes and all judges of the earth, young men and maidens, old men and children : " Let them praise the name of the Lord : for his name alone is excellent ; his glory is above the earth and heaven " (v. 13).

It is not only necessary but salutary to understand the being of all other creatures as a life of thanksgiving towards God, for it compels us to class our human being together with that of all other creatures as a creaturely being. As man thanks God and is man in so doing, he does no more and no less than all other creatures do with their life. He does no less than the sun and Jupiter, but also no more than the sparrow of the lane or indeed the humblest Mayfly. He too may give thanks as a creature and therefore be. He too can only give thanks as a creature. But we must add that in whatever the life of gratitude of other creatures may consist—and we do not know this, because their relationship to God and the way in which His Word of grace applies to them is hidden from us—the form in which thanks are demanded of man is peculiar to man alone. Even the humility in which man, in thanking God, classes himself with the rest of creation, belongs to the essence of *his* gratitude and being, to the character which distinguishes his thinking and action, and which has no analogy in the thanksgiving of the rest of creation. If they too praise the Lord, it is not they who in Ps. 148 call upon man to do so, but man who calls upon them to render this act of worship. It is not they who class themselves with man, but man who classes himself with them. Man's thanksgiving towards God, even as this act of humility, has the character of an act which God's Word of grace requires and he himself performs. The being of man in gratitude towards God has the character of a subjective and spontaneous being. If even man can only do what every creature does, he can do it only in his own act. That God's Word of grace is true and valid is something which may be said in reference to heaven and earth and all creatures. But that the creature itself has to actualise this Word, and to do so by accepting its validity, is something which can be said only of man. At any rate we do not know what we are saying if in brooding thought and fancy we say this of other creatures, and we cannot argue that the Word of God requires us to engage in such speculations. Apart from man we know no other creature on whom it is incumbent to give thanks to God and therefore to fulfil his being in such a way that he himself is made responsible for this fulfilment, and must answer for himself in this fulfilment. It is this being in responsibility for gratitude towards God which isolates the being of man from that of all other creatures even though this can subsist only as a complement to the grace of God and therefore as thanks to God. As the Word of God is addressed to man, it not only wills to be true for him but that he himself should accept its truth. It not only wills to be valid for man but that he himself should allow its validity. It wills not only to be spoken to him as the Word of power but to be accepted and understood by him as the Word of wisdom. It wills to win and hold man freely. As it does this, it marks him off and sets him in this isolation. We said earlier that the Word summons man, i.e., that it lifts him above his mere state. This must now be taken to mean that it calls him out of the chorus of other creatures. These also are. They are in specific states. And their being can only exist in thankfulness. They share this characteristic with us. But that thanksgiving and therefore being are the act and work of the creature itself is attested only by man. His thanks and his thanks alone consist in the fact that he is not only bound and engaged to the divine Benefactor, but that he freely engages himself to this Benefactor, and has in this fact his being. His thanks and his thanks alone consist in the fact that by such self-commitment to his divine Benefactor he transcends himself as a mere state. Being in history is human being alone. We know nothing of the way in which the rest of the creation gives thanks to God and therefore is. It is incumbent on man alone to thank God and therefore to be in this way.

We may now proceed to examine and portray the recurrent meaning of the history in which we have to recognise the being of real man. In the idea of gratitude as the complement to the grace of God, it is clear that the being of man has God as its goal as well as its origin. As thanks, it returns to the grace of God in which it has its source. Deriving from God, it is an object in pure receptivity. And since its place is the circle in which, as it proceeds from God, it can only return to God, it can never cease to be also this object in pure receptivity. But precisely as object of the grace of God in its pure receptivity, it cannot do otherwise than really return to God. Grounded in the Word of divine grace, it becomes the act of thought. It opens itself to God as God first opened it to Himself. It is a being—and now for the first time we see it in its wholeness and humanity—which is doubly opened. And opened to God it is subject in pure spontaneity. This is the second sense in which we have now to see and understand it.

We sum up the being of man as seen and understood in this second sense under the concept of responsibility, which has already emerged unavoidably in our previous discussion. We are now precisely parallel to the point which we earlier described as the Word of grace which realises and reveals the being of man with God, the derivation of his being in God, his being on the basis of the divine election. As man is the hearer of this Word, thanksgiving is the only realisation of what is from the divine and human standpoint man's only possibility ; the realisation by which he is distinguished as man from all other creatures. Being, human thanksgiving, has the character of responsibility.

We note first that it is a question of the act and occurrence of an answer to the Word of God. Here again we must not lose sight of the fact that the being of man is his history. God does not merely make man responsible by His Word, but in speaking His Word He engages man in active responsibility to Himself. " To act responsibly " and " to be a responsible being " are distinguishable as act and potentiality. For this reason we do not take the term responsibility to denote a state of being characterised by a particular potentiality, but an act and occurrence and therefore the being itself.

A responsible being is one to whom it is necessary and possible, and of whom it is characteristic, that he should give an account of himself. We do not deny that the being of man is responsible in this sense. But we are not convinced that the mere reference to this characteristic, possibility and necessity points us to real man, the being of man in itself and as such. The summons of the Word of God to which man owes it and must ever be grateful that he is, and is as man, aims at responsibility realised in action and event. If man's life as gratitude is a complement to the grace of God, if it is a being summoned corresponding to the summons of the divine Word, if it accords with the basic determination which it is given in and with its establishment by the Word of God, then it is the actualisation of responsibility itself and not its mere possibility and necessity. Potential as opposed to actual responsibility is proper to man as the content of the as yet unexpressed and secret counsel of God, of the Word of God awaiting expression and embodiment in the act of creation. Here, before man was, God knows and wills him potentially as the being to whom it is characteristic, possible and necessary to give account of himself. But to the actuality of the expressed creative Word of God there corresponds the actual being of man and therefore the event of his accounting for himself. Thus, although real man is potentially responsible, he is more than this. What makes him real man is that he is engaged in active responsibility to God. He would not be real man if his responsibility were not actualised as history. Basically we always have in view this actuality when we describe him as responsible. We indicate one of the capacities which distinguish him as the subject of this history. We already presuppose his humanity as such. This cannot be described by adjectives, and can be described by substantives only when they do not merely indicate a condition but actual man as he is in his history. It is in this sense that we use the term " responsibility."

If human thanksgiving and therefore human being consists in responsibility, in its own place and manner it is itself a word : different from the Word of God ; in distinction from it a creaturely, human word ; the word of thanks rather than the Word of grace ; rooted in the latter, but not identical with it ; and yet addressed and returning to it, corresponding to it as a word. Thus the being of man is an answer, or more precisely, a being lived in the act of answering the Word of God, a being which in the creaturely sphere and as itself creaturely makes that address and return to God, to the God from whom it flows and in whose Word it is rooted. Called into life by the Word of God, it is not only a reception of His gift, but it fulfils the task of answering Him, and makes that address and return to Him.

To this extent it is an act of responsibility. Man is, and is human, as he performs this act of responsibility, offering Himself as the response to the Word of God, and conducting, shaping and expressing himself as an answer to it. He is, and is man, as he does this.

We shall now develop the concept of real man in this second sense, in relation to man's subjectivity and spontaneity, by attempting briefly to elucidate the inner notes of this act, of his being in responsibility before God. It must be strictly a matter of this act. There is no question of a special state in which man finds himself placed, as every creature is always in some state or other. In his act, as he thanks the God who tells him that He is gracious to him, as he moves to the God from whom he comes, he transcends the limits of his state. We shall return later to the problem of his state. Our present concern is with his being, and therefore his act as such. This act is distinguished by a whole series of inner notes from that which happens elsewhere in the creaturely world. These notes characterise the being of man as history in the strictest sense. We now turn our attention to them.

1. As human life is a being in responsibility before God, it has the character of a knowledge of God.

We have stated that the being of man as responsibility is response, being in the act of response to the Word of God. But if it is as it responds, then it is a being which knows, accepts and affirms the Word of God and therefore God Himself. It responds as it hears the Word of God as such, and receives what it declares. To hear a word as such, and receive what it declares, is to know. Hence to hear and accept the Word of God is to know God. To be man in responsibility before God is to know God. Man knows God because God declares to him His Word, and therefore first knows him. For this reason it takes place as a spontaneous act of gratitude, in which the history inaugurated by God becomes man's own subjective history, that, following on that divine knowledge by the Word as thunder follows lightning, man knows God. Thanksgiving is a readiness to acknowledge. It is a matter of knowing the God who tells man in His Word that He is gracious to him, and therefore of knowing this benefit. But the Benefactor Himself, His own saving and keeping initiative on behalf of mankind, is this benefit, just as His Word in the creaturely mode of existence is again Himself, God the Creator. To know grace as His work is thus to know God Himself as the gracious God. As this takes place, as man does this, he fulfils his responsibility before God and therefore fulfils his own being.

Above all the knowledge of God must not be interpreted as an idle knowledge, survey, examination and understanding of God. We do not have here a relationship between two things of which the one is the knowing subject and the other the known object. Here the known object is the primary and true Subject, on the basis of whose original act the second and knowing subject is summoned to action, being made a subject by this summons of the object. A self-quiescent being would not be the being which knows God and acts in responsibility before God, i.e., it would not be the being of man, any more than a self-quiescent being could possibly be the divine being. The knowledge of God consists in the fact that the man for whom God has decided and whom He has opened to Himself now on his part decides for God and opens himself to Him, thus passing out from himself as through an open door and moving to God as God comes to him. In this movement he is the subject which knows God, and God becomes for him the known object. In this movement it takes place that he finds himself in encounter with the gracious God, and the gracious God in encounter with himself.

As the being of man performs this movement, it fulfils its responsibility before God, responding to the Word of God. For by deciding in relation to God and opening itself and moving towards God, it corresponds to what God does to it. The God who is wholly other than man, alien, high and transcendent, his Creator, tells man that He is gracious to him. His being as a human being is rooted in the fact that God says this. In accordance with this fact, man cannot remain in isolation. He must decide and open himself to see this Other, this alien, high and transcendent God who is his Creator ; to see himself in relation to this God and this God to him ; and to do so in order to go to the One without whom he would not and could not be, but who promises man to be his Saviour and Keeper. As he knows God, as he is the subject who knows God and as God is for him the known object, he both accepts and actualises the truth that the God who is gracious in His majesty and majestic in His grace is his God. He thanks Him. He accepts Him as such. He acknowledges Him as such. He relates himself to Him as He has first related Himself to him. He gives God the glory, the glory which is His due in virtue of His act and revelation. He arises and goes to his Father. The question whether he can do so is pointless. He does so in fact. His being would not be human, but would have lost itself, if he did not do so. He does so as he already comes from the God to whom he now goes. His being is with God, and derives from Him and rests on His election. It consists in hearing the Word of God. He is in the history inaugurated by Him. In virtue of this origin he can do no other. And in virtue of this origin he does just this. He thus fulfils his responsibility before God as he knows God, as God is God for him.

He is really responsible as he knows God. To be responsible is obviously to make oneself a response. As man is responsible before God, he makes himself the response to God's Word, offering himself as this answer just as God offers Himself as the Word which is the foundation of his being. Man is, therefore, wholly and utterly in this relationship to the Word of God. He is, as he is responsible before God, and thus has a share in the Word of God and therefore in God Himself—a creaturely share in a creaturely manner, but nevertheless a real share. Man is the context of this process of knowledge which comes from God and returns to Him ; as the object known, summoned and posited as such by God ; and therefore at the same time as the subject which knows and calls upon God and in so doing posits itself as subject. He is himself in this context, namely, as he is found and known and summoned by God. He posits himself in this context, namely, as he on his part seeks and knows and calls upon God. Thus real man is the being who in this process of knowledge both is himself (in the movement from God) and posits himself (in the movement of return to Him).

And now a final point must be made with regard to human responsibility before God in terms of knowledge. We must see this process of knowledge which comes from God and returns to Him in order to see man himself, real man, in his proper context. Otherwise, apart from this process of knowledge, we do not see man at all, seeing him in a vacuum. We can see him only when we see him with God as the origin and end of this process of knowledge, and therefore in the light of the Word of God as being in responsibility before God. How does man become an object to himself, and aware of himself? This is the great problem of what is called self-knowledge. And we can and must reply that he becomes aware of himself as he sees himself in the context of this process of knowledge. If it is true that in this context man is himself and posits himself, and if it is true that he does so by deciding in relation to God and opening himself and going to Him, then it is also true that in doing this he becomes an object to himself. In proportion as he takes this step, he moves Godwards out of himself, thus detaching himself from himself, and like the God of grace from whom he comes and to whom he goes becoming to himself another. We do not go on to say, as we said of God, that he becomes to himself an alien, high and transcendent being with whom he now finds himself in confrontation. In this act he will find himself only as a relatively other. For this reason we cannot ascribe to human self-knowledge the strict subject-object relationship which is characteristic of the knowledge of God. It can only accompany the knowledge of God as its shadow. Yet it accompanies it necessarily. In the context of that process of knowledge from and to God, in which man distinguishes himself from God, and God as the alien, high and transcendent Other from himself, so that the God of grace becomes object to man, man confronts himself, and is objectively, perceptibly and recognisably conscious of himself as he comes from God and posits himself in return to Him. The simple and pregnant statement : " I am," is now possible and necessary. It is not an independent affirmation. It is not absolutely true. We can dare to affirm it only to the accompaniment and in consequence of the affirmation : " God is." Only so does it have content and meaning. But to the accompaniment and in consequence of this primary statement it must be ventured and it does have content and meaning. For in the context of that prior affirmation it means that I find myself, the being which I am by the Word of God, engaged in the fulfilment of that act of responsibility and therefore in that step. Coming from where I can have nothing behind me but the Word of God, I find myself on the way to God, my Saviour and Keeper, apart from whom I can have nothing before me. There alone do I have the future of my being. There alone do I find myself before myself. But there where I am moving as I seek and know and call upon God, I do really find the future of my being as it must be saved and kept by God. Without God, and without seeking, knowing and calling upon Him, I could find there only my abandonment to nothing, my lostness. And then, moving to my future, I could only be nothing. But I am not without God. On the contrary, I seek and know God, calling upon Him as He has called upon me. I am grateful to Him as He is gracious to me. I am responsible before Him, as I am, through His Word. I am, therefore, as I find myself, knowing myself as I know God, being an object to myself, as God is my object—an object posited in my hope in God. " I am " means, therefore, that I am also present in the Word and work of God, or that I am in the fulfilment of that process of knowledge which proceeds from God and returns to Him. Secondarily, in the creaturely sphere I too am the subject of this process in which I am the object of the divine consideration, and in which I am authorised and invited to have a part in this consideration even of myself. It should now be unmistakeably clear that the statement : " I am," cannot anticipate the affirmation : " God is," let alone render it superfluous, as fools say in their hearts. But we now rejoice in the positive aspect that in due subordination and relativity the statement : " I am," must undoubtedly follow the affirmation : " God is." The being of man as being in responsibility before God includes from the standpoint of knowledge—each in its place and manner—both the knowledge of divine being and also that of human.

2. As the being of man is being in responsibility before God, it has the character of obedience to God.

Our basic discussion has prepared us for the thought that human being is being in hearing the Word of God. Responsibility is the spontaneous and active form of hearing. As hearing becomes the act of the subject, it becomes obedience. Again, our analysis of human responsibility as knowledge has prepared us to see that this kind of knowledge is insight rather than factual or philosophical knowledge. Knowledge itself is an act, an active participation in the process of knowledge which comes from God and returns to Him. It is knowledge in obedience to the law of this process.

If the being of man is a being in responsibility before God, it is determined by the fact that the Word of God is the action of God, that as the Word of His grace it is the Word of the omnipotently active Creator. That God is gracious to man according to His Word is no mere piece of theoretical information which can be written down and learnt. If the being of man is a being in responsibility before God, then it cannot be exhausted in simple acquaintanceship with God, in an insight into His self-revealed being and work, in an understanding of His will, or even in a corresponding disposition of mind and heart. The being of man is all this too. But because it is all this, it is also more than all this. For all this means in fact that it decides for God, that it opens itself to Him, that it rises up and goes to Him. All this means—as would not be the case if it were only a question of acquaintance, insight and disposition—that it cannot remain self-contained and apart from God, but that, summoned by the Word of God, it must move out of itself as God the Creator has come forth

from Himself, coming to man and therefore becoming the very foundation of his being. The omnipotently working Word of God does not
permit the creature to remain self-contained and apart, to be itself
without positing itself. The being of man is as it is claimed and engaged
by this Word. As it is said to man that God is gracious to him, that
He is his Saviour and Keeper, the call goes out to him : " Arise,
and come to Me. Come to be with Me and therefore to be man, to
be saved and kept by Me from chaos. Come to live with Me and by
Me." Man cannot be merely by hearing this call. He can be, fulfilling
his being as knowledge, only as he is obedient to this call.

That he is, and is therefore obedient, means that the statement :
" I am," must be interpreted by the further statement : " I will."
So far we have taken it to mean that I am present in that process of
knowledge which comes from God and returns to Him. But we
must relate it to the statement : " I will," thus emphasising the fact
that the being and presence of man are not merely passive but active.
Man is, of course, purely receptive as regards the movement from God,
but he is also purely spontaneous in the movement to God. He is not
merely a partial function in a dynamic whole. He is not a mere
function at all. In this matter, God is Subject, but over against God
and in relation to Him man is also subject. I imply that I am subject
by saying : " I will." And as I do not merely say this, but really
will, I posit myself as subject. By willing, I recognise the fact that
my being is not simply a gift with which I am endowed but a task
for which I am commissioned. Indeed, I affirm and grasp my being
as my task, and treat it as such. My being as my history does not
merely take place like a drop of water carried along in a river. My
being as history takes place in such a way that I myself see myself
as the one I shall be, as the one it is my task to be.

Am I to see myself as one does in a mirror ? I could only do that if I were a
useless hearer of the Word and not as such a doer of it, if I were like the man
described in Jas. 1 [24] of whom it is said that after looking at himself he goes away
and immediately forgets what manner of man he was, so that his self-knowledge
does not last and was never a knowledge of his true self. Genuine self-knowledge,
according to Jas. 1 [25], is looking into the perfect law of liberty which leads to the
goal—the law in virtue of which I am my true self only in the reality of my own
free will. Genuine self-knowledge is perseverance under this law which forbids
me to be a forgetful hearer and enables me to see myself before myself, positing
as the goal of my desire what I shall be, what it is my task to be.

I am, and I know that I am, as I choose the possibility prescribed
and offered me in my knowledge of God. To will is to obey. I have
only one possibility, and I do not discover this for myself, but it is
prescribed and offered me in my knowledge of God. In it I affirm
and grasp my being in the determination which it has not given itself
but with which it was created. What lies before me is my way to God
from whom I come, and this way has been determined by its origin

and will never abandon the curve which it has begun to describe. What lies before me—before myself as the one who is his own task— is my being as claimed by the Word of God, since any other could only be my non-being. Thus to will is to obey. But to obey is also to will. The drop in the river moves but does not obey ; it moves only as it is impelled. I do not obey if I am merely a drop in the river, if I am merely impelled. The law under which I stand is the law of my free-dom, and therefore the law according to which I have to posit myself as the being whom I shall be, choosing the only possibility prescribed and offered me in my knowledge of God, preferring this to any other, deciding and opening myself for it and for it alone. The being of man as obedience is being in this choice and decision. To obey is to will.

But this must be understood quite literally and precisely. It is a matter of being in this decision. It would not be obedience if it were simply a willing corresponding to the claim laid upon us by the Word of God, our real life to some extent lagging behind, so that there is only a momentary accomplishment and then we again know and possess ourselves apart from this action and without participation in it, our willing itself again being called in question. I do not really will if I have leisure and opportunity for any other kind of being, if I am not what I am in my choice, if as I will I do not begin to do what I will. If I will myself as the one I shall be, I have no leisure or opportunity for any other kind of being alongside this choice. Hence the statement : " I am," requires further explanation. It means : " I do." We are now protected from misunderstanding. Certainly doing as such does not offer this protection. In itself it would not distinguish the being of man from the growth of the plant or the movement of the animal. What makes it the being of man is the fact that this doing is chosen, determined and willed, and that as such it rests upon knowledge of God and knowledge of self. But man's choosing, deciding and willing, his knowledge of God and of self, is only real where it is his action, work or deed. That with my will I posit myself as the one I shall be cannot be a mere matter of desire and planning and contemplation ; it must be embodied in event. However resolutely I chose, however strongly I willed, I should still persist in mere acquaintance, recognition and disposition as regards God, I should still remain in myself when I am called to step out of myself, if, by the mere fact of my choosing and willing it, what I chose and willed did not begin to happen, to be embodied in my action. And however moved I might be by what I have heard as the will of God, I should still not be obedient. When I choose and will in obedience, then not merely my thought and desire, but I myself in the selfhood and totality in which I am claimed, dare to step out into the new sphere of my future, leaving what I was and moving to what I shall be, on the path which was indicated for me by my origin, and on which I can proceed only as active and acting subject.

We have to remember that God not only knows and wills and contemplates but also acts as the source of the history to which we now refer. He acts by speaking His Word. It is in this way that He is the primary Subject of this history, and in this way too, knowing, willing and acting, that the being of man as responsibility before God is its second subject. And as God Himself acts by intervening and giving Himself for man, so man, as the second subject in this history, can do no other than give himself to God, placing himself at the disposal of God as God places Himself at the disposal of man, and therefore in a total commitment. True willing and therefore true human being consists in this action—an action in which, after burning his boats, man would be ruined if he did not conquer because he has pledged himself to this deed. True willing is differentiated from all mere desire, planning and contemplation by the fact that it makes a decision in such a way as to make it impossible to go back. In it the man who wills has his very being in his decision. He no longer knows or possesses himself in any sphere of neutrality such as existed before his decision, and therefore he has neither leisure nor opportunity to raise the question of any other kind of being.

Real man is the man who has decided in this comprehensive sense, who is already committed to action. The being of man would not be being in responsibility before God if it did not have the character of obedience, this active form of hearing God's Word. The drama of human history within the rest of the cosmos has this precise form, whatever may be the case in other spheres. What takes place as the being of man is responsibility before God because man pledges his very self, paying with his very life to be the one he is in virtue of the Word of God—the being to whom God has said that He is gracious. Thus human being is responsibility before God in the fact that man, thankful for this Word and acknowledging its truth and validity, wills what he does and does what he wills. It is responsibility before God because in the creaturely sphere, in all his distinction from God, man realises and fulfils the law which controls the process that originates in God and returns to Him. In so doing, he realises and fulfils his own true being. The obedient man—and properly and in truth only he—knows what he is saying when he says: "I am." He is right when he says that he is, because a being without the character of obedience would not be a being in responsibility, and could not therefore be human.

The stimulus at least to this account of man's responsibility as an act of knowledge and obedience I owe to reflection on the remarkable opening of Calvin's *Catechism* (1542). A short commentary on this text may serve to illuminate the theme.

It has often caused dismay that Calvin should have opened his catechism with a purely anthropological question and answer. The question is: *Quelle est la principale fin de la vie humaine? Fin* means purpose or goal. Human life as a whole and in its single phases and elements runs in a specific direction which is determined by its end. It has, of course, secondary, subordinate and relative aims, but above and beyond and within these it has a *fin principale*, an all-embracing absolute aim. Without the latter it would not be human life. To the question concerning this *fin principale* Calvin returns the answer : *C'est de congnoistre Dieu.*

We may ask in astonishment whether this really describes the goal of human life and not just human life itself as the way to it. But Calvin appears quite certain of what he is about, for way and goal do not seem to be mutually exclusive ideas at this point in his thinking. He continues : *Pourquoy dis-tu cela ?* And the answer is : *Pour-ce qu'il nous a creé et nous a mis au monde pour estre glorifié en nous. Et c'est bien raison, que nous rapportions nostre vie à sa gloire : puisqu'il en est le commencement.* The decisive concept in this answer is obviously that of the divine *gloire* and *glorification*. God wills to glorify Himself. This means that He is not content to be what He is in Himself ; He wills to manifest Himself as such. He wills to be revealed, known and acknowledged as what He is outside the circle of His own being. And for this purpose He has created us men and placed us in this world. In man God is to be glorified. Thus man owes his life to God, and to this particular purpose of God. He has his origin, existence and being as man in the basic divine determination that God should be glorified. Clearly this divine intention provides the answer to the first question concerning the *fin principale* of human life. And it follows that it is only appropriate, reasonable, right and self-evident (*c'est bien raison, aequum est*) that we should devote our lives to the divine glorification. We have no other choice in view of the fact that it is for this that God created us. We should note how in this way the goal of human life, its end and its beginning, is projected back into human life itself ; it is clear that every step on the right way is a step directly towards the goal, a realisation of the divine glorification, so that it is incumbent on us men to orientate our lives wholly to this end. Man lives in this relationship of his life to the glory of God.

And according to Calvin's third question and answer, life as moulded by this determination and direction is *le souverain bien des hommes*—the highest good of man and also the highest good conceivable to him as the end of his striving. At this point Calvin takes up one of the leading concepts of Western theology since the time of Augustine. We should note, of course, how Calvin introduces and employs it. The highest good of man is not that he should be saved by God but that God should be glorified by man. Yet the matter must also be seen from another angle. God is not an egoist when He wills His own glorification in man and through the acts of human life, creating man in order that in and through him His glorification should take place. In this respect Calvin has often been cruelly misunderstood. As he really sees it, in willing His glorification, God has given human life its own most proper aim and thus made it intrinsically purposeful and meaningful. God does not will to be great and glorious apart from man. As God is glorious in His own way, so is man in his. The being of man is thus fulfilled as presence and implication in God's self-glorification. Hence the *c'est bien raison* of the second question is true even and especially from the standpoint of man's own interests. That he should relate his life to the glorification of God is not only the external but also the internal law of his being.

The fourth question and answer of Calvin is again quite noteworthy and instructive : *Pourquoy l'appelles-tu le souverain bien ? Pource que sans cela nostre condition est plus malheureuse que celle des bestes brutes.* And the fifth repeats and emphasises this idea : *par cela donc nous voyons qu'il n'y a nul si grand mal-heur que de ne vivre pas selon Dieu.* In these two questions and answers Calvin emphasises the point intimated in the third, namely, that even from his own point of view man has every reason to live his life in this relationship, *de vivre selon Dieu*, as he now puts it, reproducing a phrase from the oath taken by the citizens of Geneva as early as 1537 in acceptance of the Reformation. But this supplies the answer to the question why participation in the divine glorification is at the same time the *souverain bien*, the highest good which can be ascribed to man. The answer is highly significant not only for the understanding of Calvin but also in itself. The choice which man has can only be that between " the highest good " and the " greatest misery." There is no intermediate stage between a fulfilled and a wasted human life. Hence there are no lesser goods in the attainment of which man could still be human even though he missed this highest good. The highest good is to be called the highest because it is really the only good, because everything else which might also be termed a good can be good and be called good only on condition that at the same time there is the striving for and attainment of this one good. Man as man can stand and walk only in participation in the self-glorification of God. Every step aside from this path is a step into the abyss. Every step aside is the greatest misery in which his position is " more wretched than that of the animals." For the animals do that for which God has created them. They are, and they are that for which they were created, as they fulfil in their own way their particular determination. But if man misses his own quite different determination, he not merely falls to the level of the animals but below it. He cannot become a beast. He has no line of retreat here, and no consolation. He can only be man or nothing. While the animals and all the creatures around him praise the Creator in their manner, by being as God has made them, by remaining true to the law and function of their being, man, if he withdraws from his own determination that God should be glorified in Him, represents a void in the divine creation and is an utter failure in his own sphere. This is that " greatest misery " between which and his " highest good " he must choose. The answer to the first question, that the goal of human life consists in knowing God, has not really been lost to view in all this. For it is now clear that the knowledge of God implies at least the being of man in its relation to the will of God, the fulfilment of which by man is not only the highest but also the only good which can redound to his own salvation.

This is expressed in the sixth question and answer : *Mais quelle est la vraye et droicte congnoissance de Dieu ? Quand on le congnoist, afin de l'honnorer.* There is clearly something which is called knowledge of God but is not really so ; something which cannot be called either true knowledge of God, i.e., founded in, deriving from and related to God, or correct knowledge, i.e., corresponding and moving to Him. It is not real knowledge of God because it does not take place *afin de l'honnorer : ut suus illi ac debitus exhibeatur honor.* Calvin's meaning is not that true and correct knowledge of God leads, or serves as a means, to showing God the honour which is His due (I must correct at this point my interpretation of Calvin in *La confession de foi de l'église*, 1943, p. 9). Otherwise he could hardly have made it, as in the first question, the chief aim of human life. But the meaning of the sentence beginning with *afin* or *ut* is that true and correct knowledge of God is that in which God is honoured, in which therefore what is described in questions 2–5 as the action which is alone possible to man as God's creature is realised. True and correct knowledge of God in itself and as such is the action which is required of man and which alone is salutary for him. Where this knowledge is found, there the honour due from man to God is shown Him. To show honour to another means to give him that which is his due, to estimate him at his true worth, to accept him at his true valuation and to behave towards him accordingly. To each, therefore, the honour that is his due. We can honour no one, and least of all God, if without seeking to know him and therefore the honour due to him, we do something which we think will honour him. To honour God is to meet Him as He gives Himself to us, to be responsible before Him as the One He truly is. But to invent a god according to our own fancy is the source of all error and heathendom.

It cannot therefore surprise us that in the 7th question which closes this introduction Calvin sums up the whole content of the Christian catechism under the heading : *la maniere de bien honnorer Dieu*, or the *ratio rite honorandi Dei*. We are told that this consists in : 1. placing our trust in Him ; 2. serving Him in obedience to His will ; 3. turning to Him with each of our needs end therefore seeking our salvation and all good things in Him ; and 4. worshipping Him with heart and mouth as the One who is the Author of all good. Calvin is plainly alluding to the four main parts of the catechism : the creed, the Ten Commandments, the Lord's Prayer and the sacraments. Again there is much that is noteworthy in this survey. As in definition of the *ratio rite honorandi Dei*, he refers us to the content of the catechism, we can see why in question 1 he places at the head of his whole exposition the concept of the knowledge of God. The learning of the catechism, and therefore quite concretely man's responsibility before the Word of God realised in the form of a definite knowledge of God, seemed to him from the very outset to be the right honouring of God required of man, and therefore man's participation in the divine *glorification*, and therefore his highest good. The *ratio rite honorandi Dei* has the form and character of a specific, of this specific knowledge of God. Why precisely this ? one might ask. The questions 1–6 which led up to it were all of them purely anthropological in nature. Why, then, does he not give a general anthropological answer to the question as to the *maniere de bien honnorer Dieu* ? How does the catechism fit in here with its four main parts ? Has not Calvin made an illegitimate or at least paradoxical leap, a *metabasis eis allo genos* ? Calvin's first and general answer would be that precisely at this point concrete information must undoubtedly be given. And this is what is done in outline in the answer given to the 7th question. What had to be stated here was a divinely given prescription and rule. For the question here was in what manner God is properly (*rite*) to be honoured. God wills to be and must be properly honoured, not in any sort of way, but in the way which is appropriate to Him. But when is He honoured in this appropriate way ? Certainly not when the honour given is prompted by man's own discovery and caprice, but only when it happens according to God's own direction and prescription, and therefore when in its concrete expression it corresponds to this divine direction and prescription. It cannot surprise us that this direction and prescription are stated in the form of the catechism. If Calvin was to deal faithfully with the anthropological problem so far developed, it was essential that at this point he should not merely refer generally to the divine will but specifically to its concrete form and therefore to God's own direction and prescription. And if the *ratio rite honorandi Dei* has the character of a specific insight it must be said what is meant by it. Otherwise questions 1–6 are an illusory bridge leading into the void. But Calvin obviously knew from the very first that he had something to say at this point—the only thing which can be said and can give an answer at this point. What is to be known when God is known, and honoured in the light of this knowledge, is already firmly established, because the divine glorification, to share in which is the goal of human life and the epitome of all good, does not have to wait for man's participation as though it could not be set in motion apart from man. God has already glorified Himself and does so even before man decides to participate in this action. God has already revealed Himself. And it is of the concrete form in which He has done so, in which He has given man direction and prescription to glorify Him and therefore to share in His glorification and thus attain his own highest good ; it is of the form of the Word of God which is already the starting-point of man when he asks how he is rightly to honour God—it is of these concrete things that the Christian catechism concretely speaks in its teaching concerning true faith, true obedience, true prayer and true worship. It is remarkable, and yet not so remarkable, how the catechism here transcends the purely anthropological question of this introduction : remarkable because at first sight it is quite unexpected ; yet not remarkable because Calvin's whole anthropological question would have been a journey into the void if it had not led to this point which was obviously its secret starting-point. The catechism is built on the presence, the lordship and the revelation of God in Jesus Christ. Has this an ontological and anthropological implication with which Calvin has already in some sense reckoned ? The considerations which he advances in *Instit.*, 1, 2–3 concerning man's natural knowledge of God, and which affect us so strangely on every new reading, are explicable only on the assumption that his thought was moving at least along these lines. There can certainly be no doubt that he could not state and therefore could not begin by raising the purely anthropological question of the introduction except on the presupposition that the true knowledge and therefore the true glorifying of God, and therefore man's participation in the divine self-glorification, his absolute and relative good, what constitutes his being as man and therefore his being generally and therefore the purpose for which God created him, are all decided exclusively by the presence, the lordship and the revelation of God in Jesus Christ, so that we are necessarily referred at this point, and can only be referred, to the Christian catechism. Finally we may note the manner in which this is done in the transitional question 7. (Question 8 is intended as a special introduction to the creed and need not detain us.) The reference to the catechism, and therefore to the self-revelation of God, is purely in the form of verbs : *avoir nostre fiance en luy, le servir en obeissant à sa volunté, le requérir, chercher en luy salut et tous biens, reconnaître que tout bien procede de luy seul.* Hence the knowledge which man acquires as instructed by God's revelation—and Calvin must be completely exonerated from the common reproach of intellectualism—is not an idle knowledge or contemplation but a movement and act of the whole man. Even that strange natural knowledge of God at the beginning of the *Institutio* is not described in any other way. Man does not simply believe that in regard to God this or that is true because it stands in the Bible and is elucidated by dogma and dogmatics, but he puts his trust in God as made possible, permitted and commanded by God's self-revelation and as confessed in the creed. He does not submit to the Ten Commandments merely because they are the Ten Commandments, but he serves God in obedience to His will, and therefore according to the Ten Commandments because the divine revelation has shown and opened up the way to this service in the Ten Commandments. He does not say the Lord's Prayer because it is laid down that he should pray this prayer, but he comes to God with all his needs, and he does so in the Lord's Prayer because the Lord has taught us to pray thus and God has revealed to man that He wills to be approached in this way. And his worship as described in the doctrine of the sacraments is not this and no other because this form of worship happens to have been enjoined, but because he cannot avoid thanking God as the Author of all good, and can do no other than thank Him according to His revealed will, and is thus obliged to obey this command. In all these things he arises and goes to his Father, whom he must seek only in the Father's house. This is Calvin's knowledge of God as rooted in and related to the Word of God. This is what it means to learn the catechism, and therefore to glorify God, rightly to contribute to His glorification, and to live the real and fulfilled human life. And as Calvin sees it, all this takes place in movement and act, in the history of responsibility before God, in the realisation of man's being as a being in relation to the Word which God has spoken, speaks and will speak again.

3. As the being of man is a being in responsibility before God, it has the character of an invocation of God.

We must now turn our attention to the special problem of creatureliness, and therefore to the supreme disparity between human being and divine. We have frequently used the image of the circular movement from God and back to God, but we must not let it obscure the fact that on both sides the movement involves a penetration and transcending of the limits of the creature. God comes to man—this is the objective basis of man's being. And man goes to God—this is the subjective basis. But God is the Creator and man is His creature. Hence there is a supreme disparity between the coming of God and the going of man, between the objective and the subjective basis of human being. The grace of God and the gratitude of man, the Word of God and the response of man, the knowledge and act of God and those of man, take place on two very different levels and in two very different ways which even in the content of this history are not the same and are not interchangeable. God transcends the limits of the creature in one way, and man in another.

If God comes to man in His divine Word, He does not do so because He needs man. God does not flee to man for refuge. He is not obliged to be the Creator, nor to be gracious to man. He is glorious in Himself. He could be content with that inner glory. The fact that He is the Creator of man and is gracious to man is a free overflowing of His glory. And so the objective foundation of human being is an act of divine majesty. But for this very reason it is also sure and certain, clear and consistent. It is in no sense a question addressed to man. God does not question man when He calls him into being. He simply does it. Nor does He question him when He is gracious to him. He *is* gracious. What God says and does in His relation to man is an unequivocal Yes to man, rooted only in God Himself and therefore pure, unassailable and immovable. It is thus the power in which man can exist and be human, the law of the freedom in virtue of which he can do no other than arise and go to his Father. As God does not question man, but speaks to him plainly and acts for him, He is the Creator of man. This is how He transcends the limits of the creature.

But we must now consider those limits from below and see how they are transcended by the subject man. If man goes to God in responsibility before Him, he does so because he needs God. Man flees to God for refuge. For God has created him out of nothingness. God alone is his Saviour and Keeper from the powers of darkness. He can do no other but be the creature of God. He lives by the grace of God. He has no glory within himself. He cannot be self-contained and self-content. He lives by the fact that God permits him to share in the divine glory. Thus the subjective foundation of human being cannot be equal in dignity to the objective foundation. It is in no sense an act of majesty. We may say from the very outset that on the contrary it can only be an act of humility. It, too, is certainly the act of a subject. But it is only that of the human and creaturely subject, and has only the measure of freedom and authority accorded to such a subject. The Yes in which man answers the divine Yes, man's knowledge of God and obedience to Him, can never have more than the force and reach of an echo. And if it is true that, when man goes to God in his responsibility, knowledge and act, he too transcends the limits of the creature, yet this does not happen in the same unequivocal, irresistible and unchallengeable way as it does on God's side. If it takes place on man's side too, and perhaps even as his own act and not without a certain definiteness, certainty and joyfulness, it happens with all the difference between what he is enabled and obliged to do as a creature and what God is free and powerful to do as the Creator.

It man really comes to God, if he thus steps out of himself and transcends the limits of the creature, he does that which God summons him to do. He thanks God ; he is responsible before Him. Known by God, he can know Him in return. Since God is his Lord, he may be obedient to Him. And we remember that apart from this he has no other possibility. Apart from non-being he has no choice but the realisation of this being, of being in correspondence with God's Word of grace, of being in decision in the direction indicated by this Word. Deriving from God, he is not asked and he has no leisure or opportunity to ask himself, whether he might exist otherwise than in this fulfilment. He is in this decision or not at all.

But in this decision he is man and not God, the second and not the first subject in the history inaugurated by God. He comes from God and he goes to Him because God has first come to him and not because he has first come to God. Thus he cannot come to God in the way in which God has come to him. He cannot give again to God what God gives to him. He cannot be for God what God is for him. His thankfulness cannot consist in his giving grace for grace, nor his response in repeating with his being the Word which was originally spoken to him. He cannot know God as he is known by Him. He cannot with his obedience take the place of his Lord and the divine law. He can, of course, arise and go to his Father, but he cannot by his being and doing effect his acceptance in the house of his Father. The closing of the circle which has its origin in the will of God, his arriving at the point for which he sets out, is not in his own hands. He can, of course, make for it. He would not be, and he would not be man, if he did not do so. He is created for this, and he is only as he subjects himself to the divine intimation and prescription in his own decision and act to go thither. But his arrival is something which he cannot effect and complete by his own decision and in the power of his own human being. If it happens that he not only goes to God but comes to Him, then his decision and therefore human being at this climax can only have a form in which it surrenders and entrusts itself wholly to the One who is both the first and the last Subject in this history. If man could bring himself to the goal, he would origin-

ally have had to move to God and come to Him in his own strength.
That movement in which he is the second subject would have to be
itself the movement of the divine life. Man would have to be in truth
the first and only subject. And in this case there would be no creaturely
limits. But if we understand man as a creature, and therefore in
relation to God as the second subject of this history, then it is impossible to ascribe to what he effects by his decision the character of
a divine work or to regard his decision as an act of majesty.

What can and does happen in the human decision as such is that
man offers himself to God. He thanks God. He is responsible before
God, i.e., he makes himself a response to the Word of God—no less
but also no more than that. He gives what he has, i.e., what he is,
and therefore himself. No less than this is required of him. Less
than this is not sufficient to constitute true humanity. To offer himself
and place himself at the disposal of God—it is to this that he is summoned and for this that he is strengthened and empowered. Doing
this, he is established as a human subject, and posits himself as such.
Failing to do it, he fails to realise himself as man. For to do this is
his only possibility. Offering and disposing himself to go to God and
to be obedient to the divine call : " Come," he pushes open the gate
and steps out into freedom. As he does so, he is a creature which
transcends the limits of the creature. And in this way he is the human
creature. No less than this is required of him. If he did not do this,
if he decided differently, he would not be man. But also no more is
required of him. It is not required of him that he should make himself
into a gift which necessarily satisfies and pleases God. It is required
of him rather that he should know himself and will himself on the basis
of the fact that he is called by God ; that he should affirm himself
as the being which sets out on its journey to God and is therefore
taking the step to freedom. But it is not required of him that he
should place himself at the side of God, or that his action should
decide or anticipate its justification before God. He can take the first
step, but he cannot ensure that it will successfully lead him to the goal
at which he aims. He cannot give more than he has. It is not within
his power to make himself right and acceptable and well-pleasing to
his Creator, and therefore worthy of being with Him. This is a matter
beyond his control. He cannot impart or attribute it to himself. He
cannot ensure that he will come to God merely by setting out to go to
Him. Hence his going to God, his responsibility before Him, must
be of such a kind as to realise and express his limitation. It must be
a pure self-offering. It must be free from any sort of encroachment.
It must renounce any suggestion that man's decision might anticipate
the decision which only God can take. Man's responsibility before
God must consist in a self-offering to God which is referred to God's
own decision and dependent upon it. Only when it has this character
does it happen that man comes as well as goes to God, so that he

himself transcends the limits of the creature and is thus a human creature, real man.

If man is not merely to set out and go to God but to come to Him, he is dependent upon God's receiving and accepting him. It is not a matter of course that this should happen. God calls him to come. And he is man as he hears and obeys this call. But God calls him to Himself, and He calls him by telling him who and what He Himself is, namely, the God who is gracious to him. Man must not forget that he has to do with the God who is gracious to him. " Gracious to him " means that God has turned to man as Saviour and Keeper. But it means that He has turned to him in freedom and of His own good-pleasure. It means promise, but the promise of mercy. If God is gracious to man, this excludes any idea of man being able to put God under an obligation to him, making himself well-pleasing to God, and thus coming to God and being with God and placing himself at His side. If man is truly obedient to the divine call to come, he is already on his way to the God who owes nothing to man, and he clings to the divine invitation as to a promise that God will receive man and accept him in His mercy. But he will not derive from the promise any ground for asserting rights or making claims. On the contrary, he knows and his conduct reflects the fact that God is always free in fulfilling His promise, and that it rests with Him and Him alone to do so. Hence it will really be the subject man who with his knowledge, will and action follows the divine call and in so doing transcends the limits of the creature. Yet he will not do this in an act of majesty, but in an act of humility, in which he knows and his conduct reflects the fact that it is wholly of God's merciful acceptance that what he does, his knowledge of God and obedience to Him, is right, acceptable and well-pleasing, and thus leads him to the goal and perfects his action. It is God's receiving and acceptance of man in pure mercy which makes him worthy to come to God and be with Him.

We describe the being of man as an act of humility when we say that as responsibility before God it has the character of an invocation of God. God does not need to ask or request when from His side He transcends the limits of the creature and comes to man. But man can only ask and request when he does this. It does not lie in his power, or in the competence of his judgment, to say whether what he does, as gratitude and responsibility, as knowledge and obedience, shall be accepted as righteous and well-pleasing to God. What he can do as man is no less but also no more than the offering of himself. And the offering of himself to God can only mean that he commends himself to the mercy of God. In doing what he does and being what he is, he seeks the divine opinion and judgment, praying for the divine approval and a gracious judgment. He submits himself to God's opinion and judgment. And he does so unreservedly. He really seeks and prays. Hence he cannot anticipate the answer and decision of God. He has nothing to bring before God but what he is and has. He calls upon God as the One who alone can give the final decision in this matter. He knows that God is gracious to him. If he did not know this, he would not have set out to go to God with all that he is and has. If he did not know this he would not be the human being who is summoned of God and challenged to set out on this journey. He is man as he is summoned, and therefore as he knows that God is gracious to him, and as with this knowledge he sets out and goes to God. But again he would not be man if with all that he is and has he did not go to God unreservedly as one who asks and petitions, if he appeared before God otherwise than as one who submits himself to the divine opinion and judgment. God would not be the true and gracious God if in face of Him man did not subject his own decision to this reservation. God must justify it if it is to be right and to reach its goal. To come from God and therefore to go to Him is thus to submit oneself utterly to the judgment of God. There is no way to God which avoids this narrow defile. Man cannot come to God otherwise than by laying himself upon these scales. All gratitude and responsibility, all knowledge and obedience in the fulfilment of human being, if it is genuine and is really related to the true and gracious God, must consist and finally be expressed in the fact that in all these things man appeals to the judgment of the gracious God that he may receive in His Word and pronouncement not only the foundation of his being but also its confirmation and consummation. Hence the whole of man's movement to God would inevitably be futile because aimless if his being on this way did not have the character of such an appeal and invocation. And all that man thinks he achieves and knows as gratitude and responsibility to God, as knowledge of God and obedience to Him, will always have to be tested and revised with reference to the criterion whether it happens with the claim of an act of majesty or with the unreserved humility of an act in which man makes and declares himself ready to receive his justification from the One who alone is capable of justifying him.

If it happens in this way, the being of man transcends itself and the limits of the creature, not only going to God but coming to Him. It is then the being of real man. Taking this step into freedom, it does not lack the definiteness, assurance and joyfulness with which it too in its own place is permitted to realise itself in relationship with God. It realises itself as it asks after God, i.e., as it submits to Him. For in so doing it really offers itself to God, and commends itself to the grace of God, and thus truly comes to God. This is certainly not in virtue of the mere fact that it asks and prays, but because, as it does so, God is God to it, the gracious God who is glorified when His judgment is accepted. The divine judgment is accepted as valid in the world of creation when God is invoked. The limits of the creature are guarded when we understand the being of man as an invocation of

God. Indeed, they are seen in the fact that this alone can be the work of the human subject and the realisation of his being, and that God's hearing alone can decide whether this human work is complete and this human self-realisation has reached its goal. But it may also be seen that they are transcended in the work of the human subject, namely, by the fact that the human subject itself and as such is one long appeal to the divine decision. The only thing is that it must not shrink in fear from this narrow defile where it must abandon every claim to be an act of majesty, and where it must be wholly an act of humility. It must not be afraid of fulfilling itself by allowing God to be its one hope—the gracious and therefore the free God. It has no reason to be afraid of Him because He is so free in His grace and His good-pleasure alone can decide what is really decided in human decision. On the contrary, it has every reason to dare all things with this God, and no reason to expect anything better from its own opinion and judgment concerning itself, its thankfulness and responsibility, its knowledge and obedience, its own decision. The true good of man awaits him only when he is courageous enough to commend and entrust himself to the opinion and judgment of God. Man then places himself wholly in the hands of his Saviour and Keeper. In humbly asking for Him, he is exalted. With his creaturely activity he corresponds to the activity of the Creator. And it spells no obligation but a gracious permission, no deprivation but a possession, no narrowing but the only possible expansion of his creaturely life, indeed of creaturely splendour, that it is concentrated and focused in this act of humility in which it waits for the judgment of God. To wait for the judgment of God is for man, for the second subject in this history, to attain the goal, to come to God. As man invokes God as his Judge and awaits His verdict, the circle is closed. He himself closes it on his side, returning to the God from whose creative Word he has come.

4. As the being of man is a being in responsibility before God, it has the character of the freedom which God imparts to it.

Under this fourth heading we shall summarise all that has been said under the first three, and then break off our attempt to describe real man as the creature of God. Every such account must break off somewhere. Every description of something real, whether of God or Jesus Christ or man, somewhere reaches the point where it must be silent, i.e., where it must leave it to the thing itself to speak. Because it is so comprehensive, the concept of freedom must be the limit beyond which real man can only be seen and no longer defined or described.

The responsibility of man before God is a personal responsibility. This is the element in all that has been said which we now wish to emphasise when we say that the being of man has the character of freedom. The fact that it is a being in responsibility before God precludes any idea of it being a function of God Himself or a function or partial function of the divinely created cosmos. It is man himself who knows and obeys God and seeks God. It is man himself who accepts responsibility before God. It makes no difference that God is man's Saviour and Keeper, and thus makes Himself responsible for man. In the very relationship to this gracious God who sponsors and stands surety for man, the being of man is a being in personal responsibility. In the very relationship to this God who as such is man's Creator, man as a person is called to know and obey and seek God. Man's being is grounded in the fact that it is this God who confronts him—the God who makes Himself responsible for man and is his Saviour and Keeper. The fact that the self-existent God intervenes for man determines his own being as one which on its side too is self-existent. As God tells man that He is gracious to him, He also tells him that he is before Him as his creaturely partner, and in such a way as to answer what God says to him. Hence the being and the work of God in its relation to man does not negate but underlies and discloses the being of man as a being in personal responsibility. And it makes it clear that this character of freedom in the Spirit cannot be taken away from man by the presence and operation of the cosmos around him. However great and violent may be the power of the latter over man, one thing it cannot do. It cannot change the being of man into something quite different. It cannot falsify or silence the divine summons by which man is man. It cannot remove man from his confrontation by God. It cannot free him from the fact that he is as he is responsible before God. It cannot negate the truth that this responsibility is fulfilled in and by man himself. This selfhood of man is the character of his being as freedom.

We would emphasise especially that it is a question of the freedom with which he has been endowed by God. We had necessarily to relate at once the character of his being as knowledge and obedience to his divine Counterpart, and to explain it accordingly. And we saw finally that its character as invocation of God results from the fact that his knowledge and obedience require validation by the judgment of God. Summing all this up, we now affirm that in his knowledge, obedience and invocation man is himself and acts in freedom because God is first free in relation to him, Himself being the ultimate ground of all selfhood and as the Saviour and Keeper of His creature the ultimate ground of all personal responsibility. In the strength and the light of the fact that God freely gives Himself to be known by man, requires man's obedience and pronounces His divine judgment on man, the being towards whom He acts as Creator in this way is a free being. He is free on his side to know God, to obey Him and to call upon Him freely. It may be seen from the divine attitude, which is itself free and indeed that of the being which is originally and properly free, that in the creative counsel of this God man for his part was foreseen and willed and created as a free being.

Freedom is given to man as every other creature is given its peculiar gift by God. It is his creaturely mode. It is adapted and therefore proper to him. If we are to think rightly of human freedom, we must not leave out of our thoughts the God who gives it and His freedom. In the first place God alone is free. Then He alone wills and creates a free being as His creature. As man is this being, he too is free. But this third point is only valid if seen in connexion with the first two. It would be valueless if it related to a freedom which man had gained for himself or had accepted from some other source. He is only in so far as he is willed and created by God. He is himself as God grants him to be himself, as he is given himself by God. This is the unfathomable abyss into which we consciously or unconsciously gaze whenever we say I, Thou, He or She, or use any personal or possessive pronoun. Behind this I, Thou and He, as also behind Mine, Thine and His, there always stands unexpressed but necessarily latent the human self and therefore the human freedom which we cannot acquire for ourselves and which can and actually is given us only by God, because He alone is originally free. This freedom constitutes the being of man and therefore real humanity—the freedom which, in accordance with its origin and responsibility towards it, can be actualised and exercised only in the knowledge of God, in obedience to Him and in asking after Him, whereas in any other freedom man would in some sense be stepping out into the void and could only forfeit and lose himself.

The concept of freedom is thus the decisive definition of what we mean when we describe man as subject. We have seen that he is also object. An object is something posited in its own being by another. Man is the creature of God, and therefore posited by God, known by Him, subjected to His law and judged by Him. Hence man is also object. But he is subject too. A subject is something which freely posits itself in its own being. Man is, as he is responsible before God, as he knows and obeys and seeks after Him, and thus posits himself. Hence he is also subject. Now these are not two mutually inconsistent descriptions of man's being. In the very fact that man is the object of God, he is also human subject. Among all the objects posited by God it is the characteristic mode of this one to posit itself and therefore to be subject. Man is the one creature which God in creating calls to free personal responsibility before Him, and thus treats as a self, a free being. Among all creatures he is the one with which God, in giving it being, also concluded His covenant—the covenant of the free Creator with a free creature, so that man's being bears irrefutably the character of a partner with the divine subject and therefore the character of freedom.

Hence there is no need to disregard the creatureliness of man as willed and posited by God. There is no need to seek his subjectivity and freedom at some level beneath or above his objective being. We should seek it there in vain. It constitutes the very character of his objective being as willed and posited by God. Man is the creature which as such is subject, or he is not in any sense the man of whom we are speaking.

On the other hand, we cannot disregard the subjectivity and freedom of man, nor need we really seek his objective being in some neutral disposition of nature or spirit. In fact we should seek it there in vain. For it is his objective being as such which bears the ineffaceable character of subjectivity and freedom.

If we are to say subject, we must say man. And if we are to say man, we must unquestionably say subject. No amount of misunderstanding or misuse can alter the fact that in speaking of human freedom we are speaking of the most profound and comprehensive aspect of the real man. For whatever we say about man for good or ill, we allude to man in his freedom, to man who is active subject in responsibility before God.

He is active, engaged in movement. This must be stressed again in a final summary. The gift of God which characterises the creatureliness of man, namely, that as His creature he may be himself, is not a gift to be hidden away in a napkin. It is certainly given him to possess, so that he could not be at all unless he found himself in this possession. But freedom cannot be possessed otherwise than by being seized and won. Hence the fact that man is subject is not to be understood in the sense that man is first a passive idler and then becomes active, as though his life were in the first instance a blank sheet on which is later written what he knows, wills and does. The freedom which constitutes man's being is not to be thought of as the mere latent possibility and capacity of man which is then realised in this or that particular use of his freedom. We recall the point that it is not merely a question of man's static but of his active responsibility before God. If his being in this responsibility has the character of freedom, then freedom too means the actualisation of this responsibility —the event of his knowledge of God, his obedience to Him and his asking after Him. The word " freedom " might easily be misunderstood in this connexion, since as an abstract noun it can suggest a passive condition. But it must not be taken in this way. Man is, as he knows God ; he is, as he decides for God ; he is, as he asks after God and moves to His judgment. Thus he is, as he lives. And now we have only to summarise the lessons learned. Who is the man of whom all this had to be said ? We have defined him as the free creature of God ; the subject posited by God for free self-positing ; the recipient of the divine gift, who in his creaturely sphere may be himself no less than God may be Himself in His sphere. What follows, then, in respect of the character of his being ? Obviously that he has no other freedom than that which is exercised in the event or act of human life. We seek this freedom in vain unless we have found it already in the act of man's knowledge, obedience and asking in relation to God. Freedom is not to be found in a background which enables him to live freely. It is the freedom lived out and exercised in the act of responsibility before God, or it is not freedom. And so also there is no other human subject than that which, in accordance with its fundamental positing by God, is engaged in the positing of itself. We shall ask in vain to what extent man may be subject unless we have seen this subject at work in its self-positing. The human subject is not a substance with certain qualities or functions. It is the self-moving and self-moved subject in responsibility before God, or it is not a subject at all. And thus there is no human selfhood created by God except that which actualises itself in the fact that man himself knows, obeys and asks. Man seeks himself in vain unless he knows himself in the act of perception, decision and humble appeal to the divine Judge ; in that act in which no other can intercede for him, but he stands absolutely alone because he stands face to face with the gracious God. Thus the human self is no cave dweller who might one day decide to leave his cave and go hunting and fishing. It is the self which is already summoned, which has already been called out of its cave and is thus active in responsibility towards God. If it is not this, it is not worth while using such weighty terms to describe it. It should now be plain that we were not wide of the mark when in the thesis at the head of the section we defined the being of man as a history in which one of God's creatures is engaged in self-responsibility before Him. The being of man is indeed the history of this self-responsibility. Real man is this history, i.e., he is as this history is enacted, as it really happens that he fulfils his responsibility before God. In this history he is free, a subject, himself : not before or behind it ; not alongside or above it ; but as it takes place and is his own history—which is implied by the concept of freedom.

His own history, but this is the history of his responsibility before God. The final concept of the freedom of the subject, of the human self, must now be illuminated by the material significance of the concept of responsibility. We are not identifying man with a history which is merely fortuitously his own, but with the history which is determined by the concept of responsibility before God. Even the fact that the being of man is marked by freedom must be understood from the standpoint of this determination. We have understood man in his co-existence with God. We have interpreted his being as a being which derives from God, is grounded in the divine choice and consists in the hearing of the divine Word, so that it is a being in responsibility before God. Finally, we have thought of his being in responsibility as knowledge, obedience and asking in relation to God. If now in conclusion we characterise man as free, it is clear that freedom cannot be equated with neutrality but is capable of only the one positive meaning that it is freedom which is exercised in the fulfilment of responsibility before God. Hence it is not merely not inactive. It cannot be active in any sort of way. It is certainly freedom of choice. But as freedom given by God, as freedom in action, it is the freedom of a right choice. The choice is right when it corresponds to the free choice of God. The object of this free choice of God is man as His covenanted partner, as the object of His grace. In the free choice of man which is really made in exercise of the freedom given by God, it is clear that only thanksgiving to the God of grace and the acceptance of responsibility before Him can be chosen. What does the free man choose ? He chooses himself to fulfil this responsibility. He chooses himself as the subject of this knowledge, obedience and asking. Hence he has not to choose between two possibilities, but between his one and only possibility and his own impossibility, and thus between his being and his non-being, between the reality and unreality of his freedom. To choose freely is to choose oneself in one's possibility, being and freedom. Those who think otherwise do not choose freely. Man is subject as he posits and therefore not as he surrenders himself. He posits himself in that positive act of knowledge, obedience and asking. If he were capable of any other action, he would inevitably have surrendered himself already. Hence the freedom of man is never freedom to repudiate his responsibility before God. It is never freedom to sin. When man sins, he has renounced his freedom. Something takes place which does not flow from his creation by God, his creatureliness or his humanity as such, and cannot therefore be explained on these grounds. For if the creature, the human subject, is thrown back upon himself in freedom and exposed to the menace of nothingness for which he is no match, we have to remember that God is not only his Creator but also his covenanted Partner, his Saviour and Keeper and Friend. If man fails in his responsibility towards this God, he cannot be excused on the grounds of his creaturely insignificance and impotence. The freedom of his being in its responsibility before God includes the fact that man is kept from evil ; *potest non peccare* and *non potest peccare*.

In this respect we have nothing other to say about man as subject than what has already been said about him as object. Evil has no place in the creation of God or the creatureliness of man. The affirmation that man is good is correct if applied to real man as God created him and as he exists in the history of his responsibility before Him. In the free fulfilment of this responsibility—and this is his creaturely being—he is indeed good and not evil. Even his sin cannot alter this fact. Sin means that he is lost to himself, but not to his Creator. It does not mean any fresh creation of man in evil. It does not mean that the being of man as such has been changed or replaced by a different being. If real man is concealed from us because he is involved in the incomprehensible chaos of sin which renders his being unintelligible to himself, if we can no longer discover traces of real man in ourselves or others or human history as a whole, nevertheless, as real man is not lost to God, he is not unknown to Him, and in His Word—the selfsame Word which convicts us of sin—He has made known to us too the real man who is not effaced by our sin. We have learned from the Word of God who and what this man is. We have reached our conception of him by thinking about ourselves and others in the light of the fact that one man is the man Jesus. In the light of the same fact, we are forced to conclude our final discussion of human freedom with the statement that man is not evil but good. This is no optimistic assertion. On the contrary, it best expresses at this point the offence of the Gospel. The fact that man in his misdeeds is evil does not change the fact that God in His deeds as Creator is good, and therefore that even man in his creatureliness and hence in what alone can really be called his deeds is always good. He is in the act of his free responsibility before God. His freedom is that which is exercised in this act. Hence it is his freedom for good and for good alone.

We shall conclude by reconsidering our second sub-section on the " Phenomena of the Human." Under this heading we referred to all those aspects of the being of man which are recognisable and knowable elsewhere than in God's Word and revelation, i.e., in other ways than by the confrontation of man with the man Jesus. We have now reached the point in our discussion where a radical reconsideration of these aspects is possible. In our former consideration we did not simply deny or repudiate them. We merely found it necessary to point out repeatedly that in these aspects real man cannot be seen, but only forms which are usually understood and grouped together as phenomena of the unknown real man, without our being able to see or to say to what content they properly belong. We merely asserted that we cannot gather from these forms more than the portrait of a shadow-man. We did not hesitate to admit, however, that there are such forms recognisable to every human eye and to every thinking mind. And now we know the content to which they belong, the reality of which they are appearances. We are now in a position to see them not merely as phenomena but to estimate them as real indications of the human. We can now affirm that all scientific knowledge of man is not objectively empty, but that it has a real object. We can now grant that all human self-knowledge, even though it be autonomous, is justifiable to the extent that, according to what we have learned from the Word and revelation of God, it is not pursuing a will-o'-the-wisp in its investigation of man. Man is. We have seen what and how he is. And as he is, the marks and indices of his being are real symptoms of the human. The being of man cannot be explained from these symptoms. For in order to recognise them as symptoms, we must know the being itself and therefore real man. But these symptoms can be explained from the being of man. On the assumption of a knowledge of real man, of a theological anthropology, one can arrive at a non-theological but genuine knowledge of the phenomena of the human recognisable to every human eye and every thinking mind. It cannot be any part of our purpose to give even an indicatory or encyclopædic exposition of this knowledge. Our only concern with it was critical. Our purpose was simply to refute the claim that it could be a genuine knowledge of a real object independently of a prior knowledge of real man. And in the form of a theological anthropology we had the positive task of indicating this real object of all anthropology. This is what we have attempted and done. Nevertheless we must spare a few words to consider the way in which theological anthropology as a doctrine of real man is open on this side, and of the way in which it forms the presupposition of all other knowledge of man.

We have recognised the true being of man in the divinely initiated history of his self-responsibility before God the Creator. This is " Man as the Creature of God." To this we will simply add that the being of man is the creature which, as it is this history, shows itself capable of being this history. Capacity for this being is the essence of all forms and symptoms of the human. Capacity for this being is the human which is recognisable as such by every human eye and every thinking mind—perhaps only as the essence of human phenomena, perhaps only on the assumption of the existence of a phantom-man, perhaps as the epitome of genuine human symptoms and therefore on the presupposition of a knowledge of real man and thus understood as a capacity for this being, but in any case recognisable. From the standpoint of our knowledge of the being of man, this generally recognisable element in man is his capacity, i.e., his endowment and adaptation as this particular being. We can now take up again the concept which we have so far had to keep in the background. This generally recognisable element is the potentiality of man actualised in his being. As man is the specific being which he is, it is demonstrated *de facto* that he can be this being. What and how he is, i.e., his being in personal responsibility before God, cannot be known except in the light of the Word and revelation of God. Yet the demonstration of his capacity for this being is a generally knowable and known fact, whether or not it is understood in this way. The what and how of his being may be known or unknown, but man is, God has created him, and he thus demonstrates himself as such, i.e., in his capacity to be man. If he does not know himself in his being as man, he knows himself more or less exactly in his capacity to be man. If he does not know himself in his reality, he knows himself more or less comprehensively in his possibility. What and how we are men may be hidden from us, but we are fully aware of our technical capacity to actualise human being. The demonstration of this technical capacity is a fact as man himself is a fact created by God. In its own way this fact speaks for itself and is present as a testimony to real man even where it is not heard and understood. But it may also be present as a testimony which is heard and understood. In the light of God's Word and revelation the true being of man may be knowable and known in that which in itself is visible only as the possibility or technical capacity for the human. Human potentiality may be seen and assessed from the standpoint of the act of real man. The phenomena of the human may be appreciated as symptoms of the human. There can thus be a general knowledge of man which is genuine because it hears and understands this testimony.

From this standpoint we may now take a retrospective glance at the general knowledge of man, genuine and informed or not, with which we were critically concerned in the second sub-section.

What natural science sees and tries to understand and present as man may certainly be a symptom of his true nature. It seeks him in the cosmos, in his interconnexion with other cosmic phenomena, and in his relative distinctiveness within this cosmic structure. And there certainly belongs to the potentiality of real man, to the possibility presupposed in his reality, the fact that among other things his being can occupy space, the space of creatureliness and therefore that of the cosmos, and within this space a particular space, that of the specifically human. As he is man, he has the capacity, and he demonstrates the capacity, to be a creature in this general and particular cosmic space, and therefore to be the creature of God. This capacity is the object of scientific anthropology. If it realises that man cannot be its object except in his capacity to be cosmic both in general and in particular, and therefore to be the creature of God, and if it also realises that this involves a presupposition which is not itself scientific in character, namely, that of the real man who has this capacity, then it is genuine science.

What idealistic ethics sees and tries to understand and present as man may also be a symptom of real man. It sees man in the act of his differentiation within the cosmos. It sees him in his freedom to rise above the organic chemico-biological process into the free field of a history initiated and experienced by himself. It sees him already as the subject of his own life. And there does really belong to the potentiality of real man, to the possibility presupposed in his reality, the fact that his being may be such a history initiated and experienced by himself—a history in which he is not only object but active subject, and can and must posit himself as such. As he is man, he has the capacity, and he demonstrates the capacity, to be such a subject, active in his own history. The object of ethics is this human capacity. If it realises that its object cannot be more than this symptom, this partial symptom, and if it realises that this involves the presupposition of something which does not properly belong to its own field of vision, namely, the reality whose symptoms occupy its attention as ethics, i.e., real man, then it is genuine ethics and its Idealism is genuine Idealism.

Again, man as seen and illumined by existentialist philosophy may also be a symptom of real man. As existentialist philosophy goes beyond natural science and idealistic ethics, it sees man in his openness towards a without which is not merely that of mind against nature, or freedom against a natural process, but the absolute, unfathomable and inaccessible without of true transcendence which proclaims itself only in the fact of the limitation of human existence. It embraces man as seen by science and ethics, but it sees him wholly in or as his relationship to this other, which is not itself another cosmos of nature or mind, but is wholly other in relation to himself and his cosmos. It understands him wholly as history in this relation. It understands him wholly as a being which is questioned by and which quests after this other. And why should there not also belong to the potentiality of real man, to the possibility implied in his reality, the supreme fact that his being can be a relationship in this particular sense (as history, examination and quest), and that he can live his life and express himself as the subject of this relationship? As he is man, he has the capacity, and he demonstrates the capacity, to be in such a relationship. This relationship is the object of existentialist philosophy. If, in what it affirms and denies, it is strictly concerned with this object, and if it realises that this concern presupposes something which as existentialist philosophy it can neither affirm nor deny (namely, real man!), then it too can be a genuinely scientific enterprise.

Finally, what theistic anthropology describes as man can certainly be a symptom of real man. In common with, but going beyond existentialist philosophy, it sees man in relationship to a transcendent God as his origin and goal. From the very outset it understands him as theonomously rather than autonomously determined, the human logos existing through the divine, humanity being the mirror of divinity. It apprehends man as a rational being, able to perceive God, and responsible, able to answer Him, and therefore as a personal being capable of history and decision. Like the other itself, and its confrontation of man, so the being of man which is in this confrontation has concrete form in theistic anthropology, in contrast to the representation of man in existentialist philosophy. We were unable to admit that the task of theological anthropology is thus attained or fulfilled. But we admit without hesitation that a theistic anthropology of this kind can describe in a far-reaching and exhaustive way that which constitutes the potentiality of real man—the possibility, disposition and capacity implied in his reality. To this there undoubtedly belongs in a decisive and comprehensive way the freedom to be both from God and to Him, the endowment and adaptation to be the partner of God, the partner of *God* and not merely of an undefined transcendence, the *partner* of God and therefore not merely the sharer in a transcendence immanent in human existence itself. As man is, he is endowed with reason to perceive God and responsibility to answer Him, he is capable of history and decision, he is therefore—let us accept the term—" personal," and in all these things he is thus able to be the partner of God. And by his very existence he demonstrates that he has this capacity and can live in possession of it. The object of theistic anthropology is this capacity. If it realises that this and this alone is its object, and therefore that whatever it says in explanation of this object presupposes something which cannot be stated in this way, namely, real man, then a theistic anthropology of this kind can also be a genuine and serious concern.

In this way and in this sense, then, a knowledge of man which is non-theological but genuine is not only possible but basically justified and necessary even from the standpoint of theological anthropology. The Word and revelation of God is not the source from which this knowledge, even in the final form, draws its information concerning man. In all its forms it is the general knowledge which man derives from a consideration of himself. But this does not necessarily mean that what it knows of man is false and worthless. As this general knowledge it is not necessarily unenlightened ; it may indeed be enlightened. It cannot, of course, lead us to the knowledge of real man. But it may proceed from or presuppose a knowledge of real man. It may understand and estimate the whole complex of that capacity as the sum of the capacity of real man. It may understand the phenomena of the human as symptoms of the human. It then presupposes that real man is knowable and known in the light of the Word and revelation of God. It then sees and evaluates in this light the human phenomena which are knowable to it in the form of simple human self-understanding. It will then see them more modestly, less metaphysically, but for that very reason so much the more precisely and strictly and completely. Theological anthropology is prepared to welcome all such general knowledge of man.

We have taken up the proper task of theological anthropology by defining and describing as its object the real man who is the creature of God. But we can only begin its genuine task in this way.

MAN IN HIS DETERMINATION AS THE
COVENANT-PARTNER OF GOD

That real man is determined by God for life with God has its inviolable correspondence in the fact that his creaturely being is a being in encounter—between I and Thou, man and woman. It is human in this encounter, and in this humanity it is a likeness of the being of its Creator and a being in hope in Him.

1. JESUS, MAN FOR OTHER MEN

Real man lives with God as His covenant-partner. For God has created him to participate in the history in which God is at work with him and he with God ; to be His partner in this common history of the covenant. He created him as His covenant-partner. Thus real man does not live a godless life—without God. A godless explanation of man, which overlooks the fact that he belongs to God, is from the very outset one which cannot explain real man, man himself. Indeed, it cannot even speak of him. It gropes past him into the void. It grasps only the sin in which he breaks the covenant with God and denies and obscures his true reality. Nor can it really explain or speak of his sin. For to do so it would obviously have to see him first in the light of the fact that he belongs to God, in his determination by the God who created him, and in the grace against which he sins. Real man does not act godlessly, but in the history of the covenant in which he is God's partner by God's election and calling. He thanks God for His grace by knowing Him as God, by obeying Him, by calling on Him as God, by enjoying freedom from Him and to Him. He is responsible before God, i.e., He gives to the Word of God the corresponding answer. That this is the case, that the man determined by God for life with God is real man, is decided by the existence of the man Jesus. Apart from anything else, this is the standard of what his reality is and what it is not. It reveals originally and definitively why God has created man. The man Jesus is man for God. As the Son of God He is this in a unique way. But as He is for God, the reality of each and every other man is decided. God has created man for Himself. And so real man is for God and not the reverse. He is the covenant-partner of God. He is determined by God for life with God. This is the distinctive feature of his being in the cosmos.

But this real man is actually in the cosmos. He is on earth and under heaven, a cosmic being. He belongs to God, but he is still a creature and not God. The one thing does not contradict the other, but explains it. If we are to understand man as the creature of God, we must see first and supremely why God has created him. We must thus regard him from above, from God. We must try to see him as God's covenant-partner, and therein as real man. This is what we have done in the preceding section. But if we are to understand him as God's covenant-partner—which is our present task—we must return to the fact that God has created him and how He has done so, regarding him as a cosmic being, as this particular cosmic being. It is in this distinction from God, in his humanity, that he is ordained to be God's covenant-partner. In this continuation of theological anthropology we now address ourselves to all the problems which might be summed up under the title "The Humanity of Man." Our presupposition is that he is the being determined by God for life with God and existing in the history of the covenant which God has established with him. Only in this way—and we shall not allow ourselves to be jostled off the path which we have found—is he real man, in this being which consists in a specific history. But we must now see and understand this real man as a being distinct from God, as the creature of God, and to that extent as a being here below. It is as he is not divine but cosmic, and therefore from God's standpoint below (with the earth on which and the heaven under which he is), that he is determined by God for life with God. The creation of God, and therefore His positing of a reality distinct from Himself, is the external basis and possibility of the covenant. And the covenant itself is the internal basis and possibility of creation, and therefore of the existence of a reality distinct from God. We must now ask concerning man, the covenant-partner of God, from the cosmic standpoint, in his life here below, in distinction from God, and to that extent in his humanity. If we do not do this, we shall certainly have seen and understood the content of his being, but not the form inseparable from the content.

The question which will occupy us in this section is the necessary transitional question which borders and links the two essential ways of viewing him. Between the determination of man as God's covenant-partner on the one side, and his cosmic and creaturely being on the other, there is obviously an inner relationship, since we have to do with one and the same subject. His humanity can hardly be something which stands in alien remoteness from the fact that in this humanity he is the being which exists in this covenant-history. The man who, seen from above, from God, is the covenant-partner of God and real man as such, can hardly fail to be recognised in what he is below, in his distinction from God. He cannot be radically and totally hidden from himself in this distinction, as though he were a different being altogether. His divine determination and his creaturely form, his humanity, are certainly two very different things, as Creator and creature, God and man, are different. But they cannot contradict each other. They cannot fall apart and confront each other in neutrality, exclusion or even hostility.

To be sure, there may be an actual antithesis. The covenant-partner of God can break the covenant. Real man can deny and obscure his reality. This ability for which there is no reason, the mad and incomprehensible possibility of sin, is a sorry fact. And since man is able to sin, and actually does so, he betrays himself into a destructive contradiction in which he is as it were torn apart. On the one hand there is his reality as God's covenant-partner which he has denied and obscured. And on the other, as something quite different and not recognisably connected with this reality, there is his creaturely form, the humanity which runs amok when it is denied and obscured in this way, and plunges like a meteor into the abyss, into empty space.

In relation to this dreadful possibility and reality even Holy Scripture speaks of two men, a first who is of the earth, earthy, and a second who is the Lord from heaven (1 Cor. 15[47]). The very fact that the one who is really first has become the second, and the one who is really second the first, is an indication of the actual confusion to which there is reference in this passage. There is a similar indication in 2 Cor. 4[16], where in reference to a monstrous contradiction we are told that the outward man perishes, but the inward man is renewed from day to day. And when Col. 3[9f.] tells us that we are to put off the old man and put on the new, we have to remember that what is here called the old is really the new which has illegitimately obtruded itself and which we ought never to have put on, whereas the new is really true and proper man, and to that extent the old and original man which could be put off only in the reckless folly of sin. The confusion indicated in all these apostolic sayings is attested indeed by the very fact that they have to speak of two distinct men in hostile confrontation. It is to be noted, however, that only with relative infrequency does the Bible speak of man in this antithesis.

The good creation of God which now concerns us knows nothing of a radical or absolute dualism in this respect. We cannot blame God the Creator for what sinful man has made of himself. We do despite to Him if in relation to the human creatureliness of His covenant-partner we begin with the actual antithesis, making the contradiction in which he exists a basic principle, and thus overlooking or contesting the fact that he exists originally and properly in an inner connexion and correspondence between his divine determination and his creaturely form, between his being as the covenant-partner of God and his being as man. The fact that of all cosmic beings he belongs so particularly to God necessarily affects him particularly as the cosmic being he is. As the creative operation by which he is brought into being is a special one, so he himself as the one actualised by this work is a special creature, standing in connexion and correspondence with his divinely given determination. If God gives him this determination, whatever else he may be he is obviously one who is determined by it, a being to which this determination is not strange but proper. His humanity cannot, therefore, be alien and opposed to this determination, but the question of a correspondence and similarity between these two sides of his being necessarily arises. Our present question is how far his humanity as his creaturely form corresponds and is similar to his divine determination, his being as the covenant-partner of God.

Presupposing that it does in fact correspond to it, we may say that it does so indissolubly and indestructibly. To be sure, the correspondence and similarity may be covered over and made unrecognisable by the sin of man. It may well be that in consequence of the sin controlling human life we no longer see them at all in ourselves or others or human society, or do so in confused pictures which can be perceived and explained only with the greatest difficulty. It may well be that what we can actually see is so doubtful and equivocal that we despair of finding any solution for the problems involved. This is indeed the case to the extent that man is actually a sinner. We have to reckon with the fact that the similarity is indeed covered over and made unrecognisable. At this point, therefore, we undoubtedly have to do with a mystery of faith which can be disclosed only as we refer to God's revelation. On the other hand, if our creaturely form, humanity, has this similarity to our divine determination, the correspondence and similarity cannot possibly be taken away from it or destroyed. The power of sin is great, but not illimitable. It can efface or devastate many things, but not the being of man as such. It cannot reverse the divine operation, and therefore the divine work, that which is effected by God. Sin is not creative. It cannot replace the creature of God by a different reality. It cannot, therefore, annul the covenant. It cannot lead man to more than a fearful and fatal compromising of his reality, his determination. And so his humanity can be betrayed into the extreme danger of inhumanity. It can become a picture which merely mocks him. But man can as little destroy or alter himself as create himself. If there is a basic form of humanity in which it corresponds and is similar to the divine determination of man, in this correspondence and similarity we have something constant and persistent, an inviolable particularity of his creaturely form which cannot be effaced or lost or changed or made unrecognisable even in sinful man. And the task of theological anthropology is rightly to point to this inviolable and constant factor, so that it is seen as such. Theological anthropology as a doctrine of man as the creature of God has to do with constants of this kind. The being of man as the soul of his body is another unassailable and constant factor of this kind, as is also his being in time. With these anthropological mysteries of faith we shall have to deal in the further course of our exposition. But we must first consider the supreme constant to be found in the mystery of the correspondence and similarity between the determination of man and his humanity.

The practical significance of this question must not be missed.
If the humanity of man genuinely corresponds and is similar to his
divine determination, this means that the mystery of the being and
nature of man does not hover indefinitely over human creatureliness.
It touches and even embraces man below as well. In the form of
this correspondence and similarity it dwells in him too. Even in his
distinction from God, even in his pure humanity, or, as we might say,
in his human nature, man cannot be man without being directed to
and prepared for the fulfilment of his determination, his being in
the grace of God, by his correspondence and similarity to this determination for the covenant with God. Even here below he does not exist
in neutrality, but with a view to the decision and history in which
he is real. Consciously or unconsciously, he is the sign here below of
what he really is as seen from above, from God. And so he is wholly
created with a view to God. It is not, of course, that he is intrinsically
recognisable as this sign. Even in respect of this natural correspondence and similarity of human nature there is no natural knowledge of
God. Even in this matter we are concealed from ourselves, and need
the Word of God to know ourselves. But in this respect too, in our
humanity as such, there is something in ourselves to know. In virtue
of this correspondence and similarity, our humanity too has a real
part in the mystery of faith.

But what is the right way to this mystery ? Everything depends
upon our finding the right way at this critical point in our investigation, and therefore in this transitional question. And here, as in
theology generally, the right way cannot be one which is selected at
random, however illuminating. The arbitrarily selected way would
be one of natural knowledge inevitably leading into an impasse. We
must be shown the right way. And the way which we are shown can
only be the one way. We must continue to base our anthropology on
Christology. We must ask concerning the humanity of the man
Jesus, and only on this basis extend our inquiry to the form and
nature of humanity generally.

That Jesus, who is true man, is also true God, and real man only
in this unity (the unity of the Son with the Father), does not destroy
the difference between divinity and humanity even in Him. And if
in respect of this unity we have to speak of a divinity, i.e., a divine
determination of his humanity too, it is not lacking in genuine humanity. There is a divinity of the man Jesus. It consists in the fact that
God exists immediately and directly in and with Him, this creature.
It consists in the fact that He is the divine Saviour in person, that
the glory of God triumphs in Him, that He alone and exclusively is
man as the living Word of God, that He is in the activity of the grace
of God. It consists, in short, in the fact that He is man for God.
But there is a humanity of the man Jesus as well as a divinity. That
He is one with God, Himself God, does not mean that Godhead has

taken the place of His manhood, that His manhood is as it were swallowed up or extinguished by Godhead, that His human form is a mere appearance, as the Roman Catholic doctrine of transubstantiation maintains of the host supposedly changed into the body of Christ. That he is true God and also in full differentiation true man is the mystery of Jesus Christ. But if He is true man, He has the true creaturely form of a man, and there is thus a humanity of the man Jesus. Therefore, as we turn to the problem of humanity, we do not need to look for any other basis of anthropology than the christological. On the contrary, we have to realise that the existence of the man Jesus is quite instructive enough in this aspect of the question of man in general.

This time we can state the result of our investigation at the very outset. If the divinity of the man Jesus is to be described comprehensively in the statement that He is man for God, His humanity can and must be described no less succinctly in the proposition that He is man for man, for other men, His fellows. We are now considering Jesus here below, within the cosmos. Here He is the Son of God. Here He is distinguished as a man by His divinity. But here He is human, Himself a cosmic being, one creature among others. And what distinguishes Him as a cosmic being, as a creature, as a true and natural man, is that in His existence He is referred to man, to other men, His fellows, and this not merely partially, incidentally or subsequently, but originally, exclusively and totally. When we think of the humanity of Jesus, humanity is to be described unequivocally as fellow-humanity. In the light of the man Jesus, man is the cosmic being which exists absolutely for its fellows.

We must first return to some earlier statements. The man Jesus is, as there is enacted a definite history in which God resolves and acts and He Himself, this man, fulfils a definite office, accomplishing the work of salvation. He does this in the place of God and for His glory. He does it as the One who is sent for this purpose. The Word and grace of God are exclusively at work in Him and by Him. He does it for God. This is again His divinity. But the humanity in which He does that for which He is sent is that He is there in the same totality for man, for other men. In no sense, therefore, is He there for Himself first and then for man, nor for a cause first—for the control and penetration of nature by culture, or the progressive triumph of spirit over matter, or the higher development of man or the cosmos. For all this, for any interest either in His own person or intrinsically possible ideals of this kind, we can find no support whatever in the humanity of Jesus. What interests Him, and does so exclusively, is man, other men as such, who need Him and are referred to Him for help and deliverance. Other men are the object of the saving work in the accomplishment of which He Himself exists. It is for their sake that He takes the place of God in the cosmos. Their deliverance is the defence of the divine glory for which He comes. It is to them that the Word and grace of God apply, and therefore His mission, which is not laid upon Him, or added to His human reality, but to which He exclusively owes His human reality as He breathes and lives —the will of God which it is His meat to do. From the very first, in the fact that He is a man, Jesus is not without His fellow-men, but to them and with them and for them. He is sent and ordained by God to be their Deliverer. Nothing else ? No, really nothing else. For whatever else the humanity of Jesus may be, can be reduced to this denominator and find here its key and explanation. To His divinity there corresponds exactly this form of His humanity—His being as it is directed to His fellows.

We again recall the clear-cut saying in Lk. 2^{11} : " Unto you (men) is born this day in the city of David (the reference is to the son of Mary) a Saviour (i.e., your Deliverer)." He is the Son of Man of Daniel 7, who establishes the right of God on earth and under heaven by helping to his right the man who is vainly interested in himself and all kinds of causes—sinful and therefore lost man. He protects the creation of God from threatened destruction. He gives it (secretly and finally openly) its new form free from every threat. And He does this by liberating man from the threat of the devil and his own sin and the death which is its ineluctable consequence. This is His divine office. And in this office alone, as the New Testament sees it, He is also human and therefore a cosmic being. This being the case, we can readily understand why the New Testament can find no room for a portrayal or even an indication of the private life of the man Jesus. Naturally, it does not deny that He has this. It speaks clearly enough of His birth, of His hunger and thirst, of His family relationships, His temptation, prayer and suffering and death. But it discloses His private life only by showing how it is caught up in His ministry to His fellows which is the concrete form of His service of God. Hence the private life of Jesus can never be an autonomous theme in the New Testament. This is true even of His private life with God. The Johannine discourses contain extensive expositions of the relationship of the Father to the Son and the Son to the Father, but they do not attribute any independent aim to this relationship. In the strict sense, they do not stand alone, but tirelessly aim to show that the man Jesus is for others, near and distant, disciples, Israel and the world, and to show what He is for them, for man. What He is in His relationship as the Son to the Father is not something which He is and has for Himself. He does not experience or enjoy it as a private religious person. He is it as a public person. He manifests it in His relationship to His disciples and through their mediation to the whole world of men. It thus acquires at once the form of a specific action in relation to men and on their behalf. Hence Phil. $2^{6f.}$: " Who, being in the form of God, thought it not a prey to be equal with God : but made himself of no reputation, and took upon him the form of a servant." Or again, 2 Cor. 8^9 : " Though he was rich, yet for your sakes he became poor, that ye through his poverty might be rich." Or again, Heb. 12^2 : " Who for the joy that was set before him endured the cross, despising the shame." Or again, Heb. 2^{14} : " Forasmuch then as the children (of Abraham) are partakers of flesh and blood, he also himself likewise took part of the same ; that through the power of death he might destroy him that had the power of death, that is, the devil ; and deliver them who through fear of death were all their lifetime subject to bondage." Or again, Heb. $2^{17f.}$: " Wherefore in all things it behoved him to be made like unto his brethren, that he might be a merciful and faithful high priest in things pertaining to God. . . . For in that he himself hath suffered being tempted, he is able to succour them that are tempted." Or again, Heb. 4[15] : " For we have not an high priest which cannot be touched (συμπαθῆσαι) with the feeling of our infirmities ; but was in all points tempted like as we are." Or again, the whole sequence of the life of Jesus as recounted by Peter in his address at Cæsarea in Acts 10[38], in which we are told that Jesus of Nazareth was anointed with the Holy Ghost and with power, and went about as a Benefactor (εὐεργετῶν), " healing all that were oppressed of the devil." According to the New Testament, this sympathy, help, deliverance and mercy, this active solidarity with the state and fate of man, is the concrete correlative of His divinity, of His anointing with the Spirit and power, of His equality with God, of His wealth. It is genuinely the correlative of His divinity, so that the latter cannot have any place in the picture of His humanity, as, for example, in the form of His " religious life," but, on the presupposition of His divinity, His humanity consists wholly and exhaustively in the fact that He is for man, in the fulfilment of His saving work. Similarly, His prophetic message and miracles, His life and death, stand under the sign of this relationship. He is wholly the Good Samaritan of Lk. 10[29f.] who had compassion on the man who fell among thieves and thus showed Himself a neighbour to him. And if the parable concludes with the words : " Go, and do thou likewise," this is equivalent to : " Follow thou me," and in this way a crushing answer is given to the question of the scribe : " And who is my neighbour ? " He will find his neighbour if he follows the man Jesus. Our first and general thesis can be summed up in the formula of the second article of the creed of Nicæa-Constantinople : *qui propter nos homines et salutem nostram descendit de coelis et incarnatus est.* The fact that the Son of God became identical with the man Jesus took place *propter nos*, for the sake of His fellow-men, and *propter salutem nostram*, that He might be their Good Samaritan.

In clarification, however, we must dig more deeply and say that in the being of the man Jesus for His fellows we have to do with something ontological. To be sure, the fact that He is a merciful Neighbour and Saviour is indicated and expressed in His words and acts and attitudes, indeed in the whole history of which He is the free Subject. But it is not the case that as this free Subject—for His is the divine freedom—He might have been something very different from the Neighbour and Saviour of His fellows, with a total or partial interest in Himself or a cause. That His divinity has its correlative in this form of His humanity, that it is " human " in this specific sense, i.e., in address to other men, is not arbitrary or accidental. Jesus would not be Jesus at all if we could say anything else concerning Him. He is originally and properly the Word of God to men, and therefore His orientation to others and reciprocal relationship with them are not accidental, external or subsequent, but primary, internal and necessary. It is on the basis of this eternal order that He shows Himself to be the Neighbour and Saviour of men in time.

He was the Head of His community before the existence or creation of all things in Him (Col. 1[17f.]). For God " hath chosen us in him before the foundation of the world " (Eph. 1[4]). " Whom he (God) did foreknow, he also did predestinate to be conformed to the image of his Son, that he might be the first-born among many brethren " (Rom. 8[29]). He was this first-begotten even when He came into the world (Heb. 1[6]). And so an indefinite number of men are " given " Him, to use an expression which frequently recurs in the Fourth

Gospel. They belong to the Father, and He has given them to Jesus (Jn. 17⁶). He will not let them perish (Jn. 6³⁹, 18⁹), nor can any pluck them out of His hand (10²⁹), but they hear His Word (17⁸) and He will be glorified in them (17¹⁰). What has taken place and takes place between Him and them is only as it were the execution of an order which is valid and in force without either His or their co-operation, but both for Him and them. And the same is true of what will take place between Him and them. " I ascend unto my Father, and your Father ; and to my God, and your God " (Jn. 20¹⁷), namely, " to prepare a place for you," and then to return " and receive you unto myself ; that where I am, there ye may be also " (Jn. 14²ᶠ·). And yet that which is resolved concerning Himself and these men is undoubtedly willed by Jesus too : " Father, I will that they also, whom thou hast given me, be with me where I am " (Jn. 17²⁴, cf. 12²⁶).

It is of a piece with this that the solidarity with which Jesus binds Himself to His fellows is wholly real. There is not in Him a kind of deep, inner, secret recess in which He is alone in Himself or with God, existing in stoical calm or mystic rapture apart from His fellows, untouched by their state or fate. He has no such place of rest. He is immediately and directly affected by the existence of His fellows. His relationship to His neighbours and sympathy with them are original and proper to Him and therefore belong to His innermost being. They are not a new duty and virtue which can begin and end, but He Himself is human, and it is for this reason that He acts as He does.

We recall at this point the remarkable verb σπλαγχνίζεσθαι, which in the New Testament is used only of Jesus Himself and three closely related figures in the parables. The word denotes a movement in the " bowels " (in the sense of the innermost or basic parts). " To have mercy," or " to have pity," or " to have compassion," are only approximate translations as this movement is ascribed to the magnanimous king in relation to the hopeless debtor in Mt. 18²⁷, or the Samaritan on the way from Jericho to Jerusalem in Lk. 10³³, or the father of the prodigal son in Lk. 15²⁰, but especially as ascribed to Jesus Himself in face of the leper (Mk. 1⁴¹), the two blind men at Jericho (Mt. 20³⁴), the dead man at Nain and his mother (Lk. 7¹³), the hungry crowd in the wilderness (Mk. 8² and *par.*) and especially the spiritual need of the Galilean masses : " because they fainted, and were scattered abroad, as sheep having no shepherd " (Mt. 9³⁶). The term obviously defies adequate translation. What it means is that the suffering and sin and abandonment and peril of these men not merely went to the heart of Jesus but right into His heart, into Himself, so that their whole plight was now His own, and as such He saw and suffered it far more keenly than they did. ἐσπλαγχνίσθη means that He took their misery upon Himself, taking it away from them and making it His own. There is certainly no suggestion of a passive mood or attitude or the mere feeling of a spectator, as the word " sympathy " might imply. This is made perfectly plain by Mk. 9²² where the father of the epileptic boy says : " If thou canst do anything, βοήθησον ἡμῖν σπλαγχνισθεὶς ἐφ' ἡμᾶς." It is not in vain, but with the immediate consequence of practical assistance, that Jesus undergoes this inner movement and makes the cause of this man His own. He knows at once what to do. And the other stories in which the expression occurs speak similarly of effective help, and the parables of resolute decisions. The verb obviously refers to the action of Jesus, but it tells us that this has an inward source and is the movement of the whole man Jesus.

And this leads us to the further point that if the humanity of Jesus is originally and totally and genuinely fellow-humanity this means that He is man for other men in the most comprehensive and radical sense. He does not merely help His fellows from without, standing alongside, making a contribution and then withdrawing again and leaving them to themselves until further help is perhaps required. This would not be the saving work in the fulfilment of which He has His life. Nor would it serve the glory and right of God, nor help to their right the fellows for whom He is there. For it would not alter their state and fate as sinners fallen victim to death. It would not deal with the root of their misery. The menacing of the cosmos by chaos and the assault on man by the devil are far too serious and basic to be met by external aid, however powerful. And so the being of Jesus for His fellows really means much more. It means that He interposes Himself for them, that He gives Himself to them, that He puts Himself in their place, that He makes their state and fate His own cause, so that it is no longer theirs but His, conducted by Him in His own name and on His own responsibility. And in this respect we have to remember that so long as the cause of men was in their own hands it was a lost cause. Their judgment was just and destruction inevitable, so that anyone taking their place had necessarily to fall under this judgment and suffer this destruction. In His interposition for them the man Jesus had thus to sacrifice Himself in this cause of others. It was not merely a matter of His turning to them with some great gift, but of His giving Himself, His life, for them. It was a matter of dying for them. And if the cause of His fellows was really to be saved and carried through to success, if they were really to be helped, an unparalleled new beginning was demanded, a genuine creation out of nothing, so that the One taking their place had to have the will and the power not merely to improve and alleviate their old life but to help them to a basically new one. Interposing Himself for them, the man Jesus had thus to conquer in this alien cause. He could not merely relieve His fellows of their sin and bear for them its punishment, as though it were enough to set them in this neutral state and wipe the slate clean. He had also to give them the freedom not to sin any more but to be obedient where they had previously been disobedient. To be their Deliverer He had thus to rise again for them to a new life. This is the saving work by which the devilish onslaught on man is repulsed, the menacing of cosmos by chaos overcome and the divine creation inaugurated in a new form in which the glory and right of God are no longer bounded and can no longer be called in question by any adversary. The humanity of Jesus implies that in the execution of His mission as the incarnate Son of God He is for men in this comprehensive and radical sense. It implies that all other men can confidently keep to the fact that this sacrifice was offered once and for all for them, that this victory was won once and for all for them, that the man Jesus died and rose again once and for all for them.

A sum of the whole message of the New Testament may very well be found in the question of Romans 8³¹ : " If God be for us, who can be against us ? " This is quite in harmony with the introductory preaching of Jesus according to the Synoptists (Mk. 1¹⁵ and *par.*) : " The kingdom of God is at hand," i.e., God has acted to establish His right among men and therefore to help men to theirs. But it is to be noted that the reality indicated has the concrete form of the man Jesus. He, as the Son of God, the Messiah, the Son of Man, is the indicated Deliverer. " God for us " in the New Testament is not the general proclamation of the love of God and His readiness to help. For it means that Jesus is for us. The immediate continuation in Rom. 8³² is that He " spared not his own Son, but delivered him up for us all," and so " how shall he not with him also freely give us all things ? " The preposition ὑπέρ *c. Gen.* (less frequently περί and διά, and only once, in Mk. 10⁴⁵ and *par.*, ἀντί) denotes this concrete form of the central declaration of the New Testament. Its meaning " for " signifies for the advantage or in the favour or interests of someone. It can also signify for the sake of a definite cause or goal. It can finally signify in the place or as the representative of someone. In the innumerable passages in the New Testament in which it is said of Jesus Christ that He acted ὑπέρ, the genitive points directly or indirectly to persons. In the majority of cases it is " for us " or " for you," i.e., the men of the community which recognises and confesses Jesus Christ, for His own in this immediate sense. In Eph. 5²⁵ it says expressly for the ἐκκλησία, in Jn. 10¹¹ for the sheep (of the Good Shepherd), in Jn. 15¹³ for His friends, and in Jn. 17¹⁹ for His disciples : " For their sakes I sanctify myself." Only once in the New Testament, as demanded by the context, is it " for me " (Gal. 2²⁰). In these cases the first and third meanings intercross. Jesus acts on behalf of these men, and in their place. The second meaning (of action for a cause or goal) arises where it is explicitly said " for our sins " (Gal. 1⁴, 1 Cor. 15³, 1 Pet. 3¹⁸, 1 Jn. 2²). In these cases what is signified is that He acts because the men referred to are sinners who must be helped, and therefore to expiate and remove their sins as the ground of the impending judgment. Gal. 1⁴ makes the express addition : " That he might deliver us from the present evil aeon, according to the will of God and our Father." And there are some passages where the circle of those to whom this applies still seems to be open outwards. Even in Mk. 10⁴⁵ and *par.* the reference is to the many for whom Jesus will give His life as a ransom, and Calvin himself did not dare to give to this πολλοί the meaning of a restricted number of men. In Jn. 11⁵¹ᶠ. we have the remarkable saying that Jesus was to die for the people " and not for that nation only, but also that he should gather together in one the children of God that were scattered abroad." The same extension is to be found even more plainly in 1 Jn. 2² : " He is the propitiation for our sins : and not for ours only, but also περὶ ὅλου τοῦ κόσμου." And so in 2 Cor. 5¹⁴⁻¹⁵ there is the twofold ὑπὲρ πάντων ἀπέθανεν ; in 1 Tim. 2⁶ we are told that " he gave himself a ransom ὑπὲρ πάντων " ; in Heb. 2⁹ we read " that he by the grace of God should taste death ὑπὲρ παντός " ; and most powerfully of all Jn. 6⁵¹ tells us that " the bread that I will give is my flesh, which I will give ὑπὲρ τῆς τοῦ κόσμου ζωῆς "—a saying which finds an exact parallel in the well-known verse Jn. 3¹⁶, where we read that " God so loved the world, that he gave his only begotten Son." What Jesus is " for us " or " for you " in the narrower circle of the disciples and the community He is obviously, through the ministry of this narrower circle, " for all " or " for the world " in the wider or widest circle. And in the majority of the relevant passages this action of Jesus for others (His disciples, His community, the many, all, the world) is His death and passion. This is the primary reference of the more general expressions which speak of His self-offering for men. But we must see the work in its totality. If it is the one side that He " was delivered for our offences," there is also the other that He " was raised again for our justification " (Rom. 4²⁵). It must not be forgotten that as the New Testament sees it the man Jesus who was given up to death is identical with the Lord now living and reigning in the community, and that this Lord again is the One whose universally visible return is for the community the sum of their future and of that of the world. He has overcome death in suffering it. He has risen again from the dead. And it is in this totality that He is " for men." He removes the sting of sin by taking it to Himself, by being made sin (according to the harsh expression of 2 Cor. 5²¹), by dying for men as though their cause were His. But this delivering-up in our place, in which the traitor Judas is the strange instrument of the will of God, is something which He endures in the omnipotence of the Son of God, executing the divine commission and offering an acceptable sacrifice to God. It is not merely that He suffers Himself to be offered, but He Himself makes the offering, and triumphs in so doing. What is accomplished by Him is the destruction of human sin and the death which is its consequence. And it is done effectively and positively. In His resurrection He reveals Himself as the One He is—the genuine, true and righteous man, the real man, who kept the covenant which all others broke. He kept it in His self-offering, in His death for their sin. The divine and the human fulfilment of the covenant are one and the same in the act of obedience on the part of Jesus, in this final crisis of His saving work. He did this too, and He did it for men, in their favour, for the sake of their cause, and in their place. It was " an offering and a sacrifice to God for a sweetsmelling savour " (εἰς ὀσμὴν εὐωδίας, Eph. 5²) which He offered " for " us. That is to say, He made us possible and acceptable and pleasing to God, representing us in such a way that we are right with Him. Continuing in the passage in Rom. 8 with which we began, we can thus read that there can be no complaint against the elect of God because God justified them, and no condemnation because Jesus Christ died and is risen again, being now at the right hand of the Father and making intercession for us (ὃς καὶ ἐντυγχάνει ὑπὲρ ἡμῶν, Rom. 8³³ᶠ.). But it is the Epistle to the Hebrews which reveals most frequently the positive significance of ὑπέρ. Jesus as πρόδρομος ὑπὲρ ἡμῶν has passed through the veil into the sanctuary (6²⁰). He has appeared ὑπὲρ ἡμῶν, in the presence of God (9²⁴). He ever lives εἰς τὸ ἐντυγχάνειν ὑπὲρ αὐτῶν (7²⁵). It is also to be noted that according to Paul's account the " for " has a place in the blessing of the bread at the institution of the Lord's Supper : τοῦτό μού ἐστιν τὸ σῶμα τὸ ὑπὲρ ὑμῶν (1 Cor. 11²⁴), and it is similarly used in the blessing of the cup according to the Synoptists : τοῦτό μού ἐστιν τὸ αἷμά μου τῆς διαθήκης τὸ ἐκχυννόμενον ὑπὲρ πολλῶν (Mk. 14²⁴ and par.). But if the body and blood ὑπὲρ ὑμῶν or ὑπὲρ πολλῶν undoubtedly refer back to the life of Jesus offered in His death, the decisive event in the Supper is not this recollection as such, but present participation in the fruit of this sacrifice. The offering of My body and blood has for you the effect that as you eat this bread My life is given to you as yours, and that as you drink of this cup you may live with joy and not with sorrow, as innocent and not condemned. As I have given my life for you, it belongs to you. You may live and not die. You may rejoice and not mourn. Do this (" in remembrance of me ") as you eat this bread and drink this cup. Proclaim in this way the Lord's death till He come (1 Cor. 11²⁶), i.e., until His presence, already experienced here and now with this eating and drinking, is revealed to all eyes.

This is the humanity of the man Jesus—the concrete form of His humanity. And the following implications are to be noted.

There is implied first that Jesus has to let His being, Himself, be prescribed and dictated and determined by an alien human being (that of His more near and distant fellows), and by the need and infinite peril of this being. He is not of Himself. He does not live in an original humanity in which He can be far more glorious perhaps in virtue of His divine determination. No, the glory of His humanity is simply to be so fully claimed and clamped by His fellows, by their state and fate, by their lowliness and misery ; to have no other cause but that of the fatal Adam whom He now allows to be really the first, giving him the precedence, ranging Himself wholly with him for his salvation as the second Adam. If there is indeed a powerful I of Jesus, it is only from this Thou, from fallen Adam, from the race which springs from him, from Israel and the sequence of its generations, from a succession of rebels, from a history which is the history of its unfaithfulness. He is pleased to have His life only from His apostles, His community, those whom He called His own and who constantly forsook and forsake Him. He is pleased to be called by them to His own life, to be given the meaning of His life by them. He is pleased to be nothing but the One who is supremely compromised by all these, the Representative and Bearer of all the alien guilt and punishment transferred from them to Him.

There is also implied that His being is wholly with a view to this alien being ; that He is active only in the fact that He makes its deliverance His exclusive task. He moves towards the Thou from which He comes. Disposed by it, He disposes Himself wholly and utterly towards it, in utter disregard of the possibility that another task and activity might better correspond to His divine determination and be more worthy of it. After all, what are these fellow-men ? What are to Him all these representatives of the human race, the more pious and noble and the less ? Why should He not choose and adopt an original work, completely ignoring these pitiable figures in its execution ? Well, He does not do so. He finds it worth His while to live and work for His fellows and their salvation. He does not hold aloof from them. He does not refuse to be like them and with them and in that comprehensive sense for them. He gives Himself freely to them. He has only one goal : to maintain the cause of these men in death and the conquest of death ; to offer up His life for them that they may live and be happy. He therefore serves them, without prospect of reward or repayment, without expecting to receive anything from them which He cannot have far better and more richly without them. He therefore interposes Himself for Adam, for the race, for Israel, for His disciples and community.

" Whosoever of you will be the chiefest, shall be servant of all " (Mk. 10[44]). The man Jesus is the chiefest. He " came not to be ministered unto, but to minister " (v. 45). This is attested by what He said at the institution of the Lord's Supper in the Synoptists and what He did in the foot-washing in John. And He makes no demand upon His own in this respect which He has not first inimitably demonstrated with the act of His own life, thus giving it the character of a demand which can be understood only as the proclamation and offer of the grace of God manifested in Him.

We could hardly see the man Jesus as attested in the New Testament if we closed our eyes to the twofold fact that His being is both from and to His fellows, so that He is with them, and in this way man in His distinctive sovereignty. If we see Him alone, we do not see Him at all. If we see Him, we see with and around Him in ever-widening circles His disciples, the people, His enemies and the countless millions who have not yet heard His name. We see Him as theirs, determined by them and for them, belonging to each and every one of them. It is thus that He is Master, Messiah, King and Lord. " Selfless " is hardly the word to describe this humanity. Jesus is not " selfless." For in this way He is supremely Himself. The theme of the New Testament witness is a kind of incomparable picture of human life and character. What emerges in it is a supreme I wholly determined by and to the Thou. With this twofold definition Jesus is human.

And there is obviously no distance, alienation or neutrality, let alone opposition, between this human definition and the divine. His humanity is not, of course, His divinity. In His divinity He is from and to God. In His humanity He is from and to the cosmos. And God is not the cosmos, nor the cosmos God. But His humanity is in the closest correspondence with His divinity. It mirrors and reflects it. Conversely, His divinity has its correspondence and image in the humanity in which it is mirrored. At this point, therefore, there is similarity. Each is to be recognised in the other. Thus even the life of the man Jesus stands under a twofold determination. But there is harmony between the two. As he is for God, so He is for man ; and as He is for man, so He is for God. There is here a *tertium comparationis* which includes His being for God as well as His being for man, since the will of God is the basis and man the object of the work in which this man is engaged.

For a true understanding, we can and must think of what is popularly called the two-fold law of love—for God and the neighbour (Mk. 12^{29-31} and *par.*). It is no accident that it was Jesus who summed up the Law and the prophets in this particular way. He was speaking primarily and decisively of the law of His own twofold yet not opposed but harmonious orientation. He declared Himself, and therefore the grace of God manifested in Him, to be the sum of the Law. The two commandments do not stand in absolute confrontation. It is clear that Jesus did not regard love for God and love for the neighbour as separate but conjoined. Yet they are not identical. In Mt. 22^{38} the command to love God is expressly called the first and great commandment, and the command to love the neighbour is placed alongside it as the second. God is not the neighbour, nor the neighbour God. Hence love for God cannot be simply and directly love for the neighbour. Yet the command to love the neighbour is not merely an appended, subordinate and derivative command. If it is the second, it is also described as like unto the first in Mt. 22^{39}. A true exposition can only speak of a genuinely twofold, i.e., a distinct but connected sphere and sense of

the one love required of man. It has reference to God, but also to the neighbour. It has the one dimension, but also the other. It finds in the Creator the
One who points it to this creature, fellow-man. And it finds in this creature,
fellow-man, the one who points it to the Creator. Receiving and taking seriously
both these references in their different ways, it is both love for God and love
for the neighbour. Thus the structure of the humanity of Jesus Himself is
revealed in this twofold command. It repeats the unity of His divinity and
humanity as this is achieved without admixture or change, and yet also without
separation or limitation.

We must now take a further step, for it is not only by way of His
utter obedience to God, but because and in the course of it, that He
so fully serves His fellows. The saving work in which He serves His
fellows is not a matter of His own choice or caprice but the task which
He is given by God. Its execution has nothing to do, therefore,
either with the fulfilment of a duty or the exercise of a virtue. For
He exists and lives in His saving work. He would not be the One
He is if He lived in the execution of another work or in any sense for
Himself or a cause alien to this work. He cannot be at all, and therefore for God, without being for men. Hence it is the glory of the One
who has commissioned and sent Him, of God, which is revealed and
proclaimed in the fact that He is for men. In this there is disclosed
the choice and will of God Himself. God first and not the man Jesus
is for men. It is He, God, who from all eternity has established the
covenant of grace between Himself and man, and has pitied and received Him, pitying and receiving this particularly threatened and
needy creature within the threatened cosmos of His creatures and for
its deliverance and preservation. The whole witness and revelation
of the man Jesus in time, the whole point of His life and existence,
is that within the cosmos there should be declared as good news and
operative as saving power the fact that God Himself is for man and
is his Covenant-partner. God interposes Himself for him, sharing his
plight and making Himself responsible for his life and joy and glory.
God Himself is his Deliverer. He wills a free man in a free cosmos—
freed from the threat to which man has culpably exposed himself and
which he is powerless to avert. The God who willed and resolved
this, and acted in this way in His incarnate Son, is the basis of the
saving work of the man Jesus which has man—His fellow-men exactly
as they are—as its object. It is not by accident, then, that Jesus is
for man as He is for God. Between His divinity and His humanity
there is an inner material connexion as well as a formal parallelism.
He could not be for God if He were not on that account for man.
The correspondence and similarity between His divinity and humanity
is not merely a fact, therefore, but has a material basis. The man
Jesus is necessarily for His fellows as He is for God. For God first,
as the One who gives Him His commission, as the Father of this Son,
is for man. This excludes any possibility of the man Jesus not being
for man as He is for God.

Titus 3⁴ gives us the clear-cut description of the incarnation : ὅτεδὲ ἡ χρηστότης καὶ ἡ φιλανθρωπία ἐπεφάνη τοῦ σωτῆρος ἡμῶν θεοῦ. It is to be noted that in company with " kindness " (and in explanation of it) " love " seems here to be almost a quality of God Himself. It is almost integral to His very nature and essence to be our Saviour, ὁ σωτὴρ ἡμῶν θεός. We must be careful to understand this properly. God is not a creature, nor is He necessarily bound to any creature. It is His free decision and act to be " God our Saviour " and the Friend of man. But in this decision and act, in this self-determination to be our Saviour and Friend, we have an eternal presupposition of His creative work and therefore of all creatures. The One who came with the incarnation of His Word could not be other than He was. In His majesty and freedom God willed from all eternity to be for men " God our Saviour." The covenant fulfilled in time is a covenant resolved and established in God Himself before all time. There was no time when God was not the Covenant-partner of man. What appeared, therefore, in the epiphany of the man Jesus was not an accidental manner or disposition of this man, a moral disposition of this creature, but the χρηστότης of the Creator, which is identical with His φιλανθρωπία. This is the inner necessity with which Jesus is at one and the same time both for God and for man.

And now we must take a last and supreme step. There is freedom in God, but no caprice. And the fact that from all eternity God pitied and received man, the grounding of the fellow-humanity of Jesus in the eternal covenant executed in time in His being for man, rests on the freedom of God in which there is nothing arbitrary or accidental but in which God is true to Himself. God for man, participating in and making Himself responsible for him, securing for him fellowship with Himself and therefore His saving help—this whole mystery of the man Jesus is rooted in the mystery of God Himself, which is no mere fact or riddle, but full of meaning and wisdom. And as the mystery of the man Jesus is disclosed to us, we cannot say of the even higher mystery of God Himself that it is simply hidden from us and its meaning and wisdom are unattainable. If " God for man " is the eternal covenant revealed and effective in time in the humanity of Jesus, in this decision of the Creator for the creature there arises a relationship which is not alien to the Creator, to God as God, but we might almost say appropriate and natural to Him. God repeats in this relationship *ad extra* a relationship proper to Himself in His inner divine essence. Entering into this relationship, He makes a copy of Himself. Even in His inner divine being there is relationship. To be sure, God is One in Himself. But He is not alone. There is in Him a co-existence, co-inherence and reciprocity. God in Himself is not just simple, but in the simplicity of His essence He is threefold— the Father, the Son and the Holy Ghost. He posits Himself, is posited by Himself, and confirms Himself in both respects, as His own origin and also as His own goal. He is in Himself the One who loves eternally, the One who is eternally loved, and eternal love ; and in this triunity He is the original and source of every I and Thou, of the I which is eternally from and to the Thou and therefore supremely I. And it is this relationship in the inner divine being which is repeated and reflected in God's eternal covenant with man as revealed and operative in time in the humanity of Jesus.

We now stand before the true and original correspondence and similarity of which we have to take note in this respect. We have seen that there is a factual, a materially necessary, and supremely, as the origin of the factual and materially necessary, an inner divine correspondence and similarity between the being of the man Jesus for God and His being for His fellows. This correspondence and similarity consists in the fact that the man Jesus in His being for man repeats and reflects the inner being or essence of God and this confirms His being for God. We obviously have to do here with the final and decisive basis indicated when we spoke of the ontological character, the reality and the radical nature of the being of Jesus for His fellow-men. It is from this context that these derive their truth and power. The humanity of Jesus is not merely the repetition and reflection of His divinity, or of God's controlling will; it is the repetition and reflection of God Himself, no more and no less. It is the image of God, the *imago Dei*.

The " image "—we must not forget the limitation implicit in this term. If the humanity of Jesus is the image of God, this means that it is only indirectly and not directly identical with God. It belongs intrinsically to the creaturely world, to the cosmos. Hence it does not belong to the inner sphere of the essence, but to the outer sphere of the work of God. It does not present God in Himself and in His relation to Himself, but in His relation to the reality distinct from Himself. In it we have to do with God and man rather than God and God. There is a real difference in this respect. We cannot, therefore, expect more than correspondence and similarity. We cannot maintain identity. Between God and God, the Father and the Son and the Son and the Father, there is unity of essence, the perfect satisfaction of self-grounded reality, and a blessedness eternally self-originated and self-renewed. But there can be no question of this between God and man, and it cannot therefore find expression in the humanity of Jesus, in His fellow-humanity as the image of God. In this case we have a complete disparity between the two aspects. There is total sovereignty and grace on the part of God, but total dependence and need on that of man. Life and blessedness may be had by man wholly in God and only in fellowship with Him, in whom they are to be sought and found. On God's side, therefore, we have a Saviour and Deliverer. And He does not enter into alliance with a second God in His eternal covenant with man as revealed in Jesus Christ. Nor does man become a second God when He takes part in this covenant and is delivered by this Deliverer. The one who enters into this covenant is always the creature, man, who would be absolutely threatened without this help and lost if thrown back upon his own resources. It is in the humanity, the saving work of Jesus Christ that the connexion between

God and man is brought before us. It is in this alone that it takes place and is realised. Hence there is disparity between the relationship of God and man and the prior relationship of the Father to the Son and the Son to the Father, of God to Himself.

But for all the disparity—and this is the positive sense of the term " image "—there is a correspondence and similarity between the two relationships. This is not a correspondence and similarity of being, an *analogia entis*. The being of God cannot be compared with that of man. But it is not a question of this twofold being. It is a question of the relationship within the being of God on the one side and between the being of God and that of man on the other. Between these two relationships as such—and it is in this sense that the second is the image of the first—there is correspondence and similarity. There is an *analogia relationis*. The correspondence and similarity of the two relationships consists in the fact that the freedom in which God posits Himself as the Father, is posited by Himself as the Son and confirms Himself as the Holy Ghost, is the same freedom as that in which He is the Creator of man, in which man may be His creature, and in which the Creator-creature relationship is established by the Creator. We can also put it in this way. The correspondence and similarity of the two relationships consists in the fact that the eternal love in which God as the Father loves the Son, and as the Son loves the Father, and in which God as the Father is loved by the Son and as the Son by the Father, is also the love which is addressed by God to man. The humanity of Jesus, His fellow-humanity, His being for man as the direct correlative of His being for God, indicates, attests and reveals this correspondence and similarity. It is not orientated and constituted as it is in a purely factual and perhaps accidental parallelism, or on the basis of a caparicious divine resolve, but it follows the essence, the inner being of God. It is this inner being which takes this form *ad extra* in the humanity of Jesus, and in this form, for all the disparity of sphere and object, remains true to itself and therefore reflects itself. Hence the factuality, the material necessity of the being of the man Jesus for His fellows, does not really rest on the mystery of an accident or caprice, but on the mystery of the purpose and meaning of God, who can maintain and demonstrate His essence even in His work, and in His relation to this work.

For this final step in our exposition we may refer to a narrow but sharply defined and therefore distinct line in St. John's Gospel. In this Gospel, and most strikingly in chapter 17, it emerges in a number of distinctive expressions which form a special group in the Gospel to the extent that they all indicate that the relationship of Jesus to the disciples is not original, but an exact copy of the relationship in which He stands to the Father and the Father to Him.

This first and original relationship is unmistakeably characterised in these passages, and distinguished from the second, by the fact that it is not within the creaturely world but outside it, before and above the whole history which is played out in the cosmos, and therefore in God Himself. According to Jn. 17[5] there is a glory from which Jesus already comes as man, " which I had with thee before the world was." " I have glorified him," is said by the voice from heaven in 12²⁸, and in 1¹ He is the Word which was in the beginning with God. He is not, then, " of the world " (17¹⁴, ¹⁶). The Father loved him (15⁹, 17²³, ²⁶). But this aorist does not carry a historical reference to what was, but to what is as it was, to what continues as it began in that pre-temporal beginning. Hence Jesus is in the Father (10³⁸, 14¹⁰, ²⁰, 17²¹), the Father is in Him (10³⁸, 14¹⁰, 17²¹, ²³), and He and the Father (" we ") are one (10³⁰, 17¹¹, ²²). And so He is sent by the Father into the world (17³, ⁸, ¹⁸, etc.). This is the original, the relationship within the divine being, the inner divine co-existence, co-inherence and reciprocity.

And in full correspondence and similarity there is the relationship between God and man represented within the creaturely world, as a history played out in the cosmos, in the man Jesus, in His fellow-humanity, in His relationship to His disciples. We remember that the men concerned, in the first instance His disciples, belong properly to the Father, and that it is He who first loved them (14²¹, 16²⁷, 17²³). But they are given by Him to the Son, and therefore to Jesus. Why ? The basic answer is given by the word from heaven in 12²⁸ : " I have both glorified him, and will glorify him again." The point is that the glory proper to Jesus in His relationship as Son to the Father is repeated and reflected on this new level and in this new relationship. " And now, O Father, glorify me . . . with the glory which I had with thee before the world was." " I pray . . . for them which thou hast given me . . . and I am glorified in them." In accordance with the fact that the Son is not of the world, the same can be said of the disciples (17¹⁴, ¹⁶). In accordance with the fact that the Father is in Him, He is in them (17²³). In accordance with the fact that He is in the Father, they are in Him, Jesus (14²⁰). In accordance with the fact that He and the Father are one, they are to be one (17¹¹, ²²), and " no man is able to pluck them out of his hand " (10²⁹). Finally, in accordance with the fact that the Father has sent Him into the world, He sends them (17¹⁸). And if we now read : " Neither pray I for these alone, but for them also which shall believe on me through their word ; that they all may be one ; as thou, Father, art in me, and I in thee, that they also may be one in us : that the world may believe that thou hast sent me " (17²⁰⁻²¹), we are obviously reminded even in this context of the bursting of the inner circle of the community outwards in favour of all men, of the whole world. He who is already glorified by the Father in His relationship to Him is again glorified in them, in His relationship to men. Thus the divine original creates for itself a copy in the creaturely world. The Father and the Son are reflected in the man Jesus. There could be no plainer reference to the *analogia relationis* and therefore the *imago Dei* in the most central, i.e., the christological sense of the term.

Our starting-point was the question of the inner relationship between the determination of man as the covenant-partner of God on the one side and his creaturely and cosmic nature, his humanity, on the other ; of the relationship which is not affected even by the sin of man, and therefore persists even in sinful man. We asked how far man's humanity may in all circumstances be a sign of his divine determination. We asked concerning the mystery of faith of the reference to the grace of God grounded in human nature as such. We have given a first answer to this question in relation to the man Jesus. The answer is that the inner relationship in this man is a relationship of clear agreement because His humanity, in correspondence and similarity with His determination for God and therefore with God Himself, as God's image, consists in the fact that, as He is for God, He is also for man, for His fellows. This gives us a valid basis on which to take up our true question—the anthropological question, directed to all men generally, of this relationship, of the sign given to man in His humanity, of the mystery of faith of the reference to the grace of God in human nature itself.

2. THE BASIC FORM OF HUMANITY

We now turn from the man Jesus to other men—to man in general. Christology is not anthropology. We cannot expect, therefore, to find directly in others the humanity of Jesus, and therefore His fellow-humanity, His being for man, and therefore that final and supreme determination, the image of God. Jesus is man for His fellows, and therefore the image of God, in a way which others cannot even approach, just as they cannot be for God in the sense that He is. He alone is the Son of God, and therefore His humanity alone can be described as the being of an I which is wholly from and to the fellow-human Thou, and therefore a genuine I. In this respect we do not even have to take into account the fact that all other men are sinners and have turned aside from God. This means, of course, that their humanity (in more or less complete antithesis to this description) actually develops from their contradiction of the Thou to fresh opposition, and cannot therefore be a genuine I. But let us assume that there is in every man at least a serious even if hopeless striving in the other direction. The difference between Jesus and ourselves is still indissoluble. It is quite fundamental. For of no other man can we say that from the very outset and in virtue of his existence he is for others. Of no other man can we say that he is the Word of God to men, and therefore that he is directly and inwardly affected by them, or sent, commissioned and empowered to be and act in their place and as their representative, interposing and giving himself for all others, making their life possible and actual in and with his own, and thus being for them, their guarantor, in this radical and universal sense. There can be no repetition of this in anthropology. We are the victims of idealistic illusions if we deck out the humanity of man generally with features exclusive to that of the man Jesus. Man generally may mean and give a great deal to His fellows, but he cannot be their Deliverer or Saviour, not even in a single instance. On the contrary, he is the being on whose behalf the man Jesus is that which is peculiar to Him.

On the other hand, when we ask concerning humanity in general, the fact of the distinctive humanity of Jesus clearly points us in a certain direction and warns us no less clearly against its opposite.

If the humanity of Jesus consists in the fact that He is for other men, this means that for all the disparity between Him and us He affirms these others as beings which are not merely unlike Him in His creaturely existence and therefore His humanity, but also like Him in some basic form. Where one being is for others, there is necessarily a common sphere or form of existence in which the " for " can be possible and effective. If other men were beings whose humanity stood under an absolutely different and even contradictory determination from that of Jesus, it would be idle and confusing to call both Jesus and these others " men." For in the two cases the term would refer to quite different beings which would be better denoted by different terms. It would also be difficult to see how the " man " Jesus could be for and from and to other " men," how He could be inwardly affected by their being, how He could be called and sent to be their Saviour and commissioned and empowered to accomplish their deliverance, how He could interpose Himself with His human life for these other beings, acting and suffering and conquering in their place and as their Representative. The whole distinction of His humanity would thus fall to the ground as quite impossible.

On the other hand, it would also be hard to see how these others could become what Christians are called in Rom. 14[15] and 1 Cor. 8[11] : the beings or brothers for whom Christ died ; those who are helped by the death of Christ, for whose human existence His death can mean deliverance. The creaturely nature of these beings cannot be alien or opposed to that of Christ, for all the disparity.

Where the saving work of the man Jesus is possible and effective in others, where there is this fellowship between Him and others, we have to ask concerning a co-ordination between Himself and others which is not just established by this fellowship but presupposed in the fact that it is made possible and actual. We have thus to ask concerning a basic form of the humanity of other men, of man in general, in which there is given and revealed the presupposition of the fact that the man Jesus can be for them. Is it true that the character of the humanity of the man Jesus as fellow-humanity is not an accident but is grounded in the will of God ? Is it true that in this character of His humanity Jesus is the image of God ? We have seen that this question is to be answered in the affirmative, and on what grounds. But is it not also true that this God is the Creator not merely of the man Jesus but of all men, so that in the form, and especially in the basic form, of the humanity of all men we have to see the creaturely essence which they are given by God ? On these basic assumptions, a theological anthropology is forced to recognise that the question of that presupposition is not merely legitimate but necessary.

We cannot, therefore, stop at the christological assertion that the man Jesus is for others. We have also to ask in respect of others how far as men they are beings which can be represented by the man

Jesus in His suffering and conquering. We have to ask what it is that makes them possible for the covenant which is revealed and operative for them, which God has concluded with them, in this being of Jesus. We have to ask what it is that makes them capable of entering into covenant with God as the creatures of God.

Self-evidently, we do not ask concerning a worth or merit on the basis of which man has a claim to be the covenant-partner of God and to have the man Jesus act on his behalf. There is no claim of this kind ; no claim of the creature against the Creator. It is the inconceivable grace of God that He takes him to Himself, that in the fellow-humanity of Jesus the free choice of the divine will is revealed and exercised as love for man. But since it is revealed and exercised in this way, since this God who is inconceivably gracious to him is the Creator of man, of every man, then the creatureliness of man, his human nature, his humanity, cannot be alien to this grace of God (no matter how inconceivable its address to it) but must necessarily confront it as it were with a certain familiarity.

We must be clear what we mean even when we speak of being capable of entering into covenant. We do not ask concerning an ability on the part of man to take up the relationship to God in covenant with Him, to be His covenant-partner. His creaturely essence has no power to do this. He can do it only as God makes him His partner, as He calls him to take up this relationship, as he exists as the one who is summoned to do so. It is again the inconceivable grace of God that He concludes this covenant with man, that He calls him to it, and sets him in a position to respond. But since He does this— He who is also man's Creator—this is only to say again that man's creaturely essence cannot be alien or opposed to this grace of God, but must confront it with a certain familiarity. If for the restoration and defence of His glory in the cosmos the grace of God has claimed the man Jesus, this shows at least that human creatureliness is not regarded as unsuitable or unserviceable, but as adapted to be employed to this end. We do not ask, then, concerning a capacity to enter into covenant which man himself has to actualise, but concerning that which makes him as the work of His Creator possible, serviceable, adapted and well-pleasing as His covenant-partner before all other creatures, and to that extent capable of entering into covenant.

Here, too, we can and must ask concerning a certain correspondence and similarity. If God had given to man a nature neutral and opposed to His grace and love and therefore to the fellow-humanity of Jesus, alien and antithetical from the very outset to covenant-partnership with Himself, how would He have made him the being marked off for this partnership ? A second creation would have been needed to make this partnership possible and actual. And this second creation, in contrast to the new creation attested in Scripture, would have to be regarded as a contradiction of the first, materially altering and even replacing it. If we are to avoid this conclusion, there has to be a common factor, and therefore a correspondence and similarity, between the determination of man for this covenant-partnership and his creatureliness, between the humanity of Jesus and that of man generally.

Again, we cannot stop at the mere assertion that the man Jesus is the image of God. But in relation to other men we have to ask how far as men they are beings with which Jesus can be ranged as the image of God. If God has in this One, and only in this One, His own image in the cosmos ; if it is the inner essence of God which has its creaturely correspondence and similarity in His fellow-humanity, in His being for men, how can this be denied to those for whom He intervenes, to whom God has turned so seriously and totally in this One ? If this One is their Saviour and Deliverer—He whose humanity is to take their place and give His life for them—and if as such He is the creaturely image of God Himself, how can they be creatures which completely lack this image, which do not at least prefigure and indicate it, when they are creatures of the same God and determined as such for covenant-partnership with Him ? We emphasise again that there can be no question of their being simply and directly that which Jesus alone is. They are not simply and directly the covenant-partners of God as His creatures ; they are destined to become this. And this means concretely that they are destined to participate in the benefits of the fellow-humanity of that One, to be delivered by Him. In their creatureliness they have need of the fact, and they are promised, that He, the One who is the image of God, is for them. What they themselves are in their relationship to God depends on this determination. Its reality, therefore, is not in themselves, but in Him, that One. But this determination, this reality, is genuinely present and is to be taken seriously in Him. From the very first, even in their creatureliness, they stand in the light which is shed by Him. But if they are in His light, they cannot be dark in themselves, but bright with His light. We thus ask concerning their brightness in His light. To that extent we ask concerning the image of God in which every part as such has a share ; concerning the correspondence and similarity with the essence of God peculiar to humanity as such. If it were not wholly proper to it, how could it be compatible with the essence of God to give Himself to solidarity with man as He has done in making the covenant with Himself the meaning and purpose of its creation and therefore the determination of its humanity, in Himself becoming man in Jesus Christ ? For all the disparity, there is here presupposed a common factor, a parity, not merely between Jesus and other men, but, because between Jesus and other men, between God and man generally.

When we ask : What is humanity, human creatureliness ? we must first ask : What is its basic form ? In other words, to what

C.D. III.–II.—8

extent does human essence correspond to the determination of man
to be the covenant-partner of God ?   Our criterion in answering this
question is the humanity of the man Jesus.   If, for all the distance,
there is between His humanity and ours a common factor, a similarity
for all the dissimilarity, now that we turn to ourselves, to man generally, we must first make a great distinction and differentiation in
respect of the human essence presupposed in our question.   We cannot
start with the assumption that there is a known and accepted picture
of man and humanity before which we can pause and from the contours
of which we can read off that which corresponds and is similar in
man to the humanity of Jesus, and therefore supremely his participation in the image of God actualised in the humanity of Jesus.   In
theological anthropology there can be no question of giving a theological meaning to a given text (in this case a picture of man assumed
to be generally known and accepted).   This procedure would merely
arouse the justifiable suspicion that the text itself (the known and
accepted picture of man) is the constant and certain factor, whereas
the theological interpretation is variable and uncertain like any other.
No, in theological anthropology what man is, is decided by the primary
text, i.e., by the humanity of the man Jesus.   And the application of
this criterion means that a whole sphere of supposed humanity is
ruled out as non-human from the very first, and cannot be considered,
because that which in it is regarded and alleged to be human stands
in a contradiction to the humanity of Jesus which denies the essential
similarity between Him and us and therefore excludes the possibility
of the human creature as a covenant-partner of God, thus destroying
the unity of creation and covenant.   It is against any line of anthropological investigation and exposition which results in this denial,
exclusion and destruction that we are warned *a limine* by our christological basis, even though we may seem to have very good reasons
for accepting the picture of man proposed.   We do not have to regard
as human, as the essence of man which God created good, that which
measured by this criterion is non-human, i.e., not yet or no longer
human.   On the contrary, in the application of this criterion we are
free to excise from the proposed picture of man all those features
which are incompatible with the similarity which we presuppose for
all the dissimilarity between the man Jesus and us other men.   That
which is incompatible with this similarity is *ipso facto* non-human.

The excision with which we must begin will be as follows.   It is
not yet or no longer seen what humanity is when there is ascribed to
man an existence which is abstract, i.e., abstracted from the co-
existence of his fellows.   No enriching, deepening or heightening of
the concept of humanity in other directions, even religious, can excuse,
make good or compensate this basic defect.   If we see man in and for
himself, and therefore without his fellows, we do not see him at all.
If we see him in opposition or even neutrality towards his fellows, we

do not see him at all.   If we think that his humanity is only subsequently and secondarily determined, as an incidental enrichment, by
the fact that he is not alone, we do not see him at all.   If we do not
realise and take into account from the very outset, from the first glance
and word, the fact that he has a neighbour, we do not see him at all.
At this point we have no option either to be tolerant or intolerant.
We can only exclude.   If a picture of man does not satisfy this demand,
it has nothing whatever to do with the human essence in question,
and it cannot be brought under discussion.   We ask concerning the
brightness of man in the light of the man Jesus, in the light of the fact
that the man Jesus is for him, and therefore can be for him, because
between the man Jesus and this other man there is similarity as well
as dissimilarity.   A man without his fellows, or radically neutral or
opposed to his fellows, or under the impression that the co-existence
of his fellows has only secondary significance, is a being which *ipso
facto* is fundamentally alien to the man Jesus and cannot have Him
as Deliverer and Saviour.   To be sure, He is the Deliverer and Saviour
of sinful man, and therefore of the man who denies His fellow-humanity,
acting as though he had no God and no neighbour, and therefore
showing himself to be supremely non-human.   But this does not mean
that this sinner has ceased to be a man, or that we are allowed or even
obliged to interpret His inhumanity as his humanity or the work of
sin as the good creation of God.   Even the sinful man who denies
his humanity and in a blatant or more refined way turns his back on
his fellows stands in the light of the humanity of Jesus.   He acts
contrary to his humanity, and he cannot be excused the guilt which
he incurs by projecting a picture of man according to which his inhumanity—his isolation from his fellows, or neutrality or opposition
in relation to them, or the casualness of their significance for him—
belongs to his humanity as a possibility of the nature which he has
been given by his Creator.   No, even as he denies it, his creaturely
nature stands in the light of the humanity of Jesus, and it is bright
in this light, accusing him of sinning in his inhumanity not only
against God and his neighbour but also primarily and finally against
himself, and yet not ceasing to bind him to his Saviour and Deliverer.
To sin is to wander from a path which does not cease to be the definite
and exclusive path of man even though he leaves it.   The fact that
man sins does not mean that God ceases to be God and therefore man
man.   In this context, too, we must say that man does not accomplish
a new creation by sinning.   He cannot achieve any essential alteration
of the human nature which he has been given.   He can only shame
this nature and himself.   He can only bring himself into supreme peril.
But the fact that he has in the man Jesus his Saviour and Deliverer
is the pledge that he has not ceased to be a man, a being ordered in
relation to this Jesus.   The fact that the Good Shepherd has acted
on behalf of His lost sheep shows that He does not give it up for lost

but still numbers it with His flock and deals with it as His own and not an alien possession. This is what makes the idea of a man without his fellows, in any form, quite intolerable. This is what rules it out from the very first. Theological anthropology cannot enter the sphere where this man without his fellows is considered as a serious possibility. It knows man well enough as the man of sin, but not as the man who actualises his creaturely nature in his sin, whom God has created for this actualisation. It cannot blame God for what man has made of himself. And it cannot exculpate man from the permanent reproach of the transgression with which he denies the truth, the truth of his Creator and his own truth. We take sin lightly if we spare sinful man this reproach, giving him the evasion that as a sinner he has forfeited and lost his humanity, or that God has created him in a humanity in which he can choose either to be man or not, and in which inhumanity is more probable than humanity. Every supposed humanity which is not radically and from the very first fellow-humanity is inhumanity. At this point a distinction must be made *a limine*, and humanity must be protected against its decisive and definitive destruction. If we take away fellow-man from the picture of man, and describe the latter as a being which is alien, opposed or casual in relation to him, we have not merely given an inadequate or partially false representation of man, but described a different being altogether. There is nothing else for it. In this respect theological anthropology must be quite pitiless in its opposition to every attempt to seek real man outside the history of his responsibility to God. The very reality of man in his responsibility before God necessarily gives us the negative rule for an understanding of the basic form of his humanity—that in no circumstances may it be sought in that abstraction, in a humanity without the fellow-man.

At this point two marginal observations may be made on the general theological situation, especially at the present time.

1. The last war, with all that led up to it and all its possible consequences, has posed afresh the problem of humanity from the particular angle of the question of the rights, dignity and sanctity of the fellow-man. Humanity stands at the crossroads. In its future development as humanity, will it be for man or against him? Behind the political, social and economic possibilities there stands always with the same urgency, if in different forms, the necessity of this decision. The lot may be cast one way or the other according to the various anthropological views more or less consciously adopted. And it may well be that an anthropology and ethics of compromise is no longer adequate because the dynamic of a resolute humanity without the fellow-man may perhaps steal a march on all mediating positions and finally dominate the field with fatal consequences. Those who cannot approve this development are seriously asked to-day whether they are capable of producing from their own anthropology and ethics an equally and even more dynamic championship of the fellow-man. And the further question then becomes insistent, as it is already, whether any anthropology or ethics is able to do this apart from the Christian. A whole-hearted adoption of this position is possible only where the hostility, neutrality and antithesis between man and man is radically overcome, i.e., in the pre-

supposed concept of humanity, and known and rejected as inhumanity. Where
this is not the case, there can be only half-way teachings, and it is doubtful
whether even a delaying action can be successful against the assault of a humanity
without the fellow-man. The exclusiveness which dares—because it must—to
repudiate this humanity as inhumanity *a limine* and without discussion is not
possible, as far as one can see, except on the basis of a Christian and theological
anthropology and ethics.

2. But all that glitters is not gold, and we cannot accept as genuine Christian
and theological anthropology everything that claims to be such. Where the
claim is justified there will necessarily be ruthlessness at this point, i.e., in the
rejection of all humanity without or against the fellow-man. And this raises
the question of its criterion and its consistent application. If it has a christological basis, then, as we have seen, it has a criterion which will prove to be
divisive from the very first, at the very first sight of the object. A humanity
without the fellow-man will necessarily be abandoned as inhuman at the very
first step. Humanity for man will remain as the only possibility. But in modern
theology it is not the rule to base anthropology on Christology and therefore to
use this criterion from the very outset. The question arises whether the same
radicalness and ruthlessness are really possible on the other paths which are
more customary. Perhaps they only lead again to mediating and therefore
indefensible positions. Perhaps this type of Christian and theological anthropology cannot offer any effective resistance to the onslaught of a humanity
without the fellow-man. And in the light of its lack of radicalness and ruthlessness the question then arises whether it can really claim to be a Christian and
theological anthropology at all.

We have to rule out the possibility of a humanity without the
fellow-man. Hence we must not discuss it. But it will be worth
our while to consider briefly what we are ruling out, what conception
of man we are passing by without discussion. We may begin by
admitting that it is not self-evident that it should be ruled out in this
way, and thus passed by without discussion. In doing this, we follow
the higher right of theological necessity. But on behalf of the rejected
humanity which is either without or against the fellow-man, or pays
him only casual attention, it may be argued that it is not only infinitely
more appealing but even self-evident on a non-theological view. If
we bracket the Christian judgment, does not the word " man "
immediately and at bottom definitively conjure up a being which is
basically and properly for itself, so that although it may be vaguely
recognised in others it can and is seen immediately and directly only
in the self ? According to this constantly victorious conception
humanity consists in the fact that I am, that I am for myself, and
neither from nor to others. In certain circumstances this " I am "
can have a powerful radius. And it is not to be subjected to a moral-
istic judgment and condemnation as limitation or self-seeking. For
after all, it will somewhere embrace others as well. The only trouble
is that basically and properly it is without them or against them or
only secondarily and occasionally with them and for them. " I am "—
this is the forceful assertion which we are all engaged in making and
of which we are convinced that none can surpass it in urgency or
importance ; the assertion of the self in which we can neither be

replaced by any nor restrained by any. " I am " means that I satisfy myself even in the sense that I have to do justice to myself, that I am pressingly claimed by myself. " I am " means that I stand under the irresistible urge to maintain myself, but also to make something of myself, to develop myself, to try out myself, to exercise and prove myself. " I am " means further, however, that in every development and activity outwards I must and will at all costs maintain and assert myself, not dissipating and losing myself, but concentrating even as I expand, and getting even as I give. It means that I must and will acquire and have personality. But the radius is even wider than this. " I am " means that I may and must live ; that I may and must live out my life in the material and spiritual cosmos, enjoying, working, playing, fashioning, possessing, achieving and exercising power ; that I may and must in my own place and within my own limits— and who is to say where these are to be drawn ?—have my share in the goods of the earth, in the fulness of human knowledge and capacity, in the further development of human technique and art and organisa-tion. These are powerful projections of the " I am " outwards into space and time and its truth and poetry, or rather its poetry and truth, its myth and history. And to these projections there certainly belongs the fashioning of a relationship to what is called " heaven " in the Bible and " God," " the gods," or " the divine " elsewhere ; the construction of a positive or negative, believing or sceptical, original or conventional position with reference to the ultimate limits and mystery of life, the incomprehensible which will finally confront all our comprehension. And inevitably in this onward progress of the " I am " the encounter with fellow-men will have its own specific and determinative part ; the burning questions whether this or that person is important or indifferent to me, whether he attracts or repels me, whether he helps and serves or obstructs and harms me, whether he is superior to me or I can master him and am thus superior to him. To these projections there also belong the dealings with him, with all the selection and rejection, the conflict, peace and renewal of conflict, the constant hide-and-seek, the domination and dependence, the morality and immorality which these dealings inevitably involve and without which life would certainly be much easier and simpler but also much poorer and duller. The only thing is that here too we have a projection of the " I am " outwards. Even the many forms of our fellows are ultimately elements in our own myth or history, not found but invented and decked out by us, and merely speaking the words which we put on their lips. There are merely more or less serviceable or unserviceable figures in our own play, drawn into ourselves to the extent that we have in some way transformed them into something that belongs to us. In their genuine otherness and particularity they are without like the rest of the cosmos. Originally and properly within I am still alone by myself : in my freedom in relation to the whole cosmos ; with my poetry and truth ; with the question of my needs and desires and loves and hates ; with my known and sometimes unknown likes and dislikes ; with my capacities and propensities ; as my own doctor, as the sovereign architect, director, general and dictator of the whole, of my own earth and heaven, my cosmos, God and fellow-men ; as the incomparable inventor and sustainer of myself ; in first and final solitude. Within this total conception there is naturally an infinite range of colours and contours, of nuances and emphases, to the final and apparently self-exclusive extremes. It is a unity only in general. In detail the variations are so great as to make the common features almost unrecognisable. It never repeats itself. It constantly takes on new forms not only in the different ages and cultures, not only in the distinction of individuals, but also within their own specific development, in youth and maturity and age, in the changing stations and circumstances of life. But we should not be misled. The " I am " may often be less powerfully at work as the basis and beginning of all things. We may not always see that in everything else we really have projections of this I. Our fellows in their otherness and particularity may often be more forcefully and obstinately and pertinently at work than our depiction suggests. Yet the overwhelming unity of the whole remains—of an attempted humanity in which the fellow-man has no constitutive function. And, if for a moment we suspend our Christian judgment, we at once recognise that it is the most obvious thing in the world to answer the question of humanity with perhaps a more profound and purified and convincing modification of this view. We have to realise what it means that theological anthropology cannot grasp this most obvious of all possibilities, but must reject it *a limine*.

By way of illustration we may refer to Friedrich Nietzsche. We do this for two reasons. He developed this conception of humanity with unequalled logic and perspicacity. And in his refusal to evade its deepest root and supreme consequence, in his enthusiastic acceptance of them, he resolutely and passionately and necessarily rejected, not a caricature of the Christian conception of humanity, but in the form of a caricature the conception itself. He shows us how necessary it is that we for our part must less violently but no less resolutely reject the conception of humanity of which he is a classical exponent.

In 1888 Nietzsche wrote his *Ecce homo*, which was published in 1908. This is an autobiography, of the same genre as Augustine's and Rousseau's *Confessions*, but with no admission of mistakes, and constituting an unequivocal final testimony for the future interpretation of the author. Shortly after writing it, Nietzsche was declared to be afflicted with an incurable mental sickness. It was understandable that Franz Overbeck, one of his closest friends, should at first prevent its publication. But he was not justified on material grounds, for whether Nietzsche was already ill or not when he wrote this book there can be no doubt that in it he rightly perceived and summed up the final intentions of his purposes and work as they had marked him from the very first.

On the first page of *Ecce homo* we read in heavy type the statement : " Hear me, for I am he ; do not at any price mistake me " (Krönersche-Klassiker-Ausgabe, p. 307). And even more menacingly on the final page, again in heavy type: "Am I understood ?—Dionysius against the Crucified . . ." (p. 433). The first saying is a bizarre but genuine form of the first and final proposition of humanity without the fellow-man. Nietzsche liked to see it represented in the form of the ancient Greek god Dionysius. The second is the repudiation of Christianity self-evident on the basis of this humanity.

"Hear me, for I am he ; do not at any price mistake me." We shall first try to see what this means. Goethe too, whom Nietzsche usually although not always mentioned respectfully as a precursor, wanted to be regarded and estimated as "he," with a certain solemnity and joyous reverence making himself and his way and culture and work the theme of special consideration and explanation, and having an obvious consciousness of himself. But Nietzsche was basically and properly self-consciousness and nothing more. His angrily uncertain : "Do not at any price mistake me" and later his eager : "Am I understood ?" would have been quite unthinkable on the lips of Goethe. Goethe was on the same path as Nietzsche, an exponent of the same "I am," but he knew when to stop, and said certain ultimate things about this beginning and end either not at all or very seldom and with great caution. He knew how often and not unjustly he was praised for keeping to the golden mean. He could do so, and necessarily, because his self-consciousness was continually filled with the most attentive and deeply interested world-consciousness. The quiet fulfilment of almost uninterrupted work in the world outside gives to his picture, and his occasional self-portraits, the character of a cheerful sanity in which he could not be tempted by any anxiety lest he should be confused with others, because he was far too worldly wise even to make this a matter of debate. But Nietzsche was the prophet of that humanity without the fellow-man. He did not merely reveal its secret ; he blabbed it out. He was in a non-classical form what Goethe was in a classical. Apollo did not content him ; it had to be Dionysius. Was he no longer sure of himself, as Goethe so obviously was ? He once described himself as a victim of decadence, an example of the decline of the human type which he thought to be perfect and sometimes found to be represented and actualised in certain respects in Goethe. Did he perhaps really speak the final word of this humanity ? At any rate, he had to cry out something which was in Goethe, and to which he occasionally gave expression, but which he wisely preferred to keep to himself—the fact that in a last and deepest isolation he and he alone was the eye and measure and master and even the essence of all things. What Goethe quietly lived out Nietzsche had to speak out continally with the nervous violence of ill-health.

Basically, when he was not engaged in polemics but spoke positively, Nietzsche never spoke except about himself. If we study him, it constantly strikes us how little he deals with material and objective problems. What he himself was not, if it did not repel him and he it, interested him only as a paradigm and symbol, or, to use his own expression, a projection of himself. And even when he repelled, and was repelled, it was only because the object concerned either could not be used as a paradigm of himself (like Christianity), or could no longer be put to this service (like the later Wagner). Nietzsche was originally a Greek philologist, but he no longer needed Greek philology when he had discovered Dionysius as " the one root of all Greek art," as the " philosophising god," and this Dionysius was none other than himself, Friedrich Nietzsche. For a while he devoted himself with fiery energy to natural science under the banner of evolution, but when probably in this sphere he had discovered the " will to power " as the supreme and proper form of human existence—and this, of course, as an unmistakeable but impressive symbol of his own will—the subject did not present him with any further interest or problems. He wrote concerning " Schopenhauer as Educator," but the instructive Schopenhauer was admittedly he himself. And he magnified Wagner so long as he could find and represent in him himself and his own paganism—which was no longer possible after the personal injury done him by Wagner's *Parsifal*, in which he discerned a pilgrimage to Canossa. " Delight in things, it is said, but what is really meant is delight in oneself through the medium of things " (*Menschliches, allzu Menschliches*, p. 366)—this is something which Goethe could never have admitted. Nietzsche did not merely admit it ; he openly championed it as a maxim. In fact, he never really had any other. And so Zarathustra too—and there was little need for the pride with which Nietzsche expressly assures us of the fact— is none other than he himself, and this time the true Nietzsche. Nietzsche admits that by his ophthalmic affliction he had been redeemed from " the book " and had not read for many years—" the greatest benefit which I have ever experienced " (*Ecce homo*, p. 384). For to read as the scholar reads is not to think but simply to answer to an attraction, to react. " I call it criminal that at the crack of dawn, in all the youth and freshness of his powers, the scholar— a decadent — should read a book " (p. 349). There is apparently only one exception : " As I see it, it is one of the most singular distinctions that anyone can evince to take up a book of my own :—I myself will guarantee that he will take off his shoes, not to speak of boots. . . . When Doctor Heinrich von Stein once honestly complained that he could not understand a word of my Zarathustra, I told him that this was quite usual. To have understood, i.e., experienced six sentences of it is to be lifted on to a higher mortal plane than ' modern ' men can reach " (p. 355). Nietzsche was of the opinion that with his Zarathustra he had given humanity a greater gift than any so far given (p. 309). He declared that in comparison with it the rest of human activity was poor and limited ; that a Goethe or a Shakespeare could not last a single moment in this atmosphere of tremendous passion and exaltation ; that face to face with Zarathustra Dante was merely a believer and not one who creates truth, a masterful spirit, a destiny ; that the authors of the *Veda* were priests and unworthy to unloose the shoes of a Zarathustra. And this is only the least to be said concerning it, giving no conception of the distance, the " azure isolation " of the work. " The spirits and qualities of all great souls put together could not produce a single speech of Zarathustra " (p. 400 f.). Naturally this sounds disordered. But it is the position which Nietzsche indicated, and to the representation of which he dedicated his life's work. And what is this position but the " I am " of humanity without the fellow-man, except that this time it is adopted without condition or restraint, in all its nakedness ? I am—in " azure isolation." Nietzsche often thought that he lived in indescribable wealth in this isolation, and these were the moments when he could beseechingly and yet also angrily point to the fact that he had infinite things to give, that infinite things were to be received from him. But then he had to contradict himself, for how could he give wealth and life and joy in this isolation ? On the contrary, " when I have given myself for a moment to my Zarathustra, I walk up and down the room for half an hour, unable to master an unbearable spasm of sobbing " (p. 432).

> " The desert grows : woe to those who fight it,
>   Stone grates on stone, the desert gulps and swallows,
>   And dreadful death looks gleaming brown
>   And cowers—life is a cowering . . .
>   Forget not man, hired out to pleasure,
>   Thou art the stone, the desert, thou art death " (p. 447).

And how is Zarathustra to be anything for others or give anything to them ? If there were others, he would not be Zarathustra. " First give thyself, O Zarathustra " (p. 471). But he cannot do this even if he desired now that it has been and is his necessity and triumph to be " 6,000 feet beyond man and time " (p. 391). " The whole fact of man lies at a dreadful distance below him " (p. 309).

" Alone !
And who would dare
To be a guest,
Thy guest ? . . ." (p. 449).

To whom is he, the superman, the absolute " I am," to give himself ?   And if there is someone, will he thank him for this or any gift ?

" Who can love thee,
The unattainable ?
Thy blessing makes all dry
And poor in love
—a thirsty land . . ." (p. 470).

To this very day Nietzsche has been much admired and honoured and loved. But he had no use for the fact ; he could not love in return. Nothing is more striking than that he had no use at all for women. " They all love me," he could say, but without any satisfaction. He can only ignore them or heap upon them scorn and his choicest invective. And in his very rejection of them he regards himself as " the first psychologist of the eternal-feminine " (p. 363). Yet in addition he cannot repay or be faithful to even the best and most sincere of his male friends. " At an absurdly early age, when I was only seven, I knew that no human word would reach me, but has this ever caused me any obvious concern ? " (p. 353). " An extreme candour towards me is for me a necessary condition of existence ; I cannot live in conditions of insincerity. . . . This means that my intercourse with men constitutes no little problem of patience ; my humanity does not consist in fellow-feeling with men, but in restraint from fellow-feeling. . . . My humanity is a continual self-conquest." It is also to be noted, of course, that Nietzsche described the contempt for man, misanthropy, as his greatest danger, and one from which he thought that he had finally redeemed himself. But how ? By fleeing to a height " where there are no companions to sit at the well " and drink with him.

" On the tree of the future we build our nest ;
Eagles will bring us solitary ones food in their beaks.
Not food which the unclean may eat,
For they would think they were eating fire,
And burn their mouths.

We have no homesteads here for the unclean,
To their bodies and spirits our fortune
Would be an icy cavity,
And we shall live over them like strong winds,
Neighbours of the eagles and the snow and the sun,
Like strong winds " (p. 329 f.).

In this way Zarathustra is lord even of misanthropy. But how ? " Man is for him something unshaped, material, an ugly stone which needs the sculptor." His only impulse towards man is that of the hammer to the stone.

" Oh, ye men, in the stone there sleeps a picture,
The picture of all pictures !
Oh that it must sleep in the hardest and ugliest stone !
My hammer rages furiously against its prison,
And pieces fly from the stone,
But what care I ! " (p. 406 f.).

Has he ever been obviously concerned that man is either unattainable or attainable only in such a way as to cause a repugnance from which he must seek that lofty refuge with the eagles and strong winds ? And yet Zarathustra does frequently seem to be very greatly troubled by this inaccessibility. It is intrinsic to the superman, to Dionysius, to Zarathustra to be almost torn asunder by sorrow at having to be the superman, Dionysius, Zarathustra.

> " The world—a door
> To a thousand deserts silent and cold !
> Who has lost
> What thou lost, can find no rest.
>
> Thou standest pale
> Condemned to winter wandering
> Like smoke
> Always seeking the cold heavens.
>
> Fly, bird, rasping
> Thy song like a wilderness-bird !—
> Conceal, thou fool,
> Thy bleeding heart in ice and disdain !
>
> The crows cry
> In whirring flight to the city.
> —Soon it will snow
> And woe then to him who has no home ! "
> *(Fröhl. Wiss.*, p. 392 f.).

The only thing is that he soon rises up again like the eagle, scorning himself for his weakness, and finding joy and exultation and self-glory in the very thing which pains him :

> " Yea, I know whence I derive !
> Insatiable as the flame,
> I burn and consume myself.
> All I touch is light,
> And what I leave a cinder.
> I am indeed a flame ! "
> *(Fröhl. Wiss.*, p. 30).

Which prevails—the complaint or the rejoicing ? " I know my fate. The memory of something dreadful will be linked with my name, of an unparalleled crisis, of the most profound clash of conscience, of a decision conjured up against everything that has so far been believed and demanded and held sacred. I am no man ; I am dynamite " (*Ecce homo*, p. 422). Is this complaint or rejoicing, or both ? In the same breath Nietzsche can call himself both the incomparable bearer of good news and the " destroyer *par excellence.*" " I am easily the most terrible man there has ever been, but this does not mean that I am not also the greatest benefactor." He promises that only because of him are there renewed hopes. And yet he prophesies : " There will be wars such as never were on earth. Only after me will there be high politics on earth " (p. 412, 423 f.). According to view or inclination, we can be deaf to his true message, rejecting or believing either the one or the other, the *evangelion* or *dysangelion*, but his real place is beyond good and evil, not merely like that of a Hercules choosing between the two, but genuinely as the place of the superman, who conjoins good and evil and evil and good in himself, and is thus, like Voltaire, " a *grandseigneur* of the spirit " (p. 380), " the first true man " (p. 423). It is thus that Nietzsche is he, and declares the fact, proclaiming himself and refusing to be mistaken. " I am the first immoralist " (p. 377, 386, 424). Immoral does not mean non-moral. There is no point in making him a bogeyman in this sense. His immoralism consists in the fact that he has the question of morality behind him, that like God he is without " tables," that he " invents " his own categorical imperative (*Der Antichrist*, p. 216), that he is his own table. With the conclusion of the *Götzendämmerung* in the same year, 1888, there followed indeed a " seventh day ; the stroll of a God along the Po " (*Ecce homo*, p. 413). The one who strolls in this way along the Po is the great " he " whom Nietzsche proclaims and whom he will not have mistaken for any other.

A clever man of our own day has called Nietzsche " the greatest horse-coper of any age." It cannot be questioned that we have here a genuine short circuit, a genuine deception and self-deception. But I should hesitate to accept that severe judgment because it would apply to too many things and people whose last intentions are merely represented with less restraint and we might almost say with greater honesty by Nietzsche. Goethe, Hegel, Kant and Leibniz would come under the same condemnation, and not just a specifically German spirit, but the spirit of all European humanity as fashioned and developed since the 16th century. Outside Germany it has become customary to-day to represent and castigate Nietzsche as one of those who must bear responsibility, and even primary responsibility, for preparing and making possible National Socialism. There is something in this. But it must not be forgotten that Nietzsche directed his most scathing terms against the German nationalism of his age, the age of Bismarck, so that any contribution he made to its development was highly indirect. More positively, dismissing Germany as the " plain " of European culture, he liked to remember that he was half-Polish by descent, and valued no literature or culture more highly than the French. And was he not the man who at the very height of the age of Bismarck expressed the view that it would be worth looking for a time to Switzerland to escape the opportunist outlook prevailing in Germany ? And, like so many others, he praised Italy, and historically the Italian Renaissance, as his true home, perversely maintaining that he found his superman most adequately portrayed in its most notorious representative, Cæsar Borgia. But the Italian Renaissance was the mother and model not merely of Italian but of all European humanity in the modern age. And so Nietzsche-Zarathustra emphatically wished to be understood as a European, as the best and only and final European. If his representation of humanity is " horse-coping," the same is true at root—a hidden and suppressed, but very real root—of a number of others as well. And if Nietzsche prepared the ground for National Socialism, the same may be said with equal justification of other manifestations and expressions of the European spirit during the last centuries. It is thus a very serious and responsible undertaking genuinely to oppose the humanity which he represented. The same consideration holds good in respect of his mental ill-health. If it was only as one who was mentally ill that he was capable of this representation, or conversely, if he became mentally disordered in the course of it, the question who was really deranged amongst them may be seriously asked in relation to many who were perhaps healthy in mind, or seemed to be so, only because they did not or would not see that to be a consistent champion and representative of this humanity is necessarily to be or to become mentally sick. The current affirmation and accusation are so serious that there is every reason to hesitate before making them.

We now turn to the other saying : " Am I understood—Dionysius against the Crucified."

At a first glance, it does not seem as if the book will finally lead to this antithesis, or that Nietzsche all the time wishes it to be taken in the sense of this antithesis. Prior to the last five pages of the *Ecce homo* we are not directly prepared for it even by the occasional flashes which anticipate this conclusion. Its pregnancy and violence do not seem to stand in any real relationship to the polemic of the book or of the life-work of Nietzsche summed up in it. Nietzsche was an indefatigable fighter. Proclaiming that existence on high, he could hardly be otherwise. He was always against what others were for. " I am the anti-donkey *par excellence*, and therefore a monster in world history." The continuation is, of course, as follows : " In Greek, and not only in Greek, I am the Antichrist." And under this title Nietzsche wrote a whole book in 1886. Yet we cannot conclude from the book that this was more than one of the many fronts on which he was active as " anti-donkey." Nietzsche attacked the philosophy, morals, art, science and civilisation of his own and most earlier times, and in none of these spheres did he fail to leave dead and wounded behind him. Often rather sketchily in detail, but always with a sure intuition for essentials, for true correspondence and opposition, he attempted with equal taste and ruthlessness in all these fields a " transvaluation of all values " in the light of the superman and his will to power. It was only natural, therefore, that he should also attack Christianity. But that as " anti-donkey " he should supremely and decisively be " Antichrist," that everything should finally become a formal crusade against the cross, is not immediately apparent, but has to be learned and noted from a reading of Nietzsche. Yet it must be learned and noted if we are to understand him. The strange culmination in the *Ecce homo* is no mere freak. For the book about Antichrist was not just one among many. Nietzsche did not fight on all fronts in all his books. And yet there is not a single one of them, so far as I can see, in which he did not have whole sections or notable individual statements devoted to Christianity and directed in more or less violent polemic against it. And the polemic gained in weight and severity with the passage of time. We might describe this conflict as a swelling base accompanying the others and finally overwhelming and taking them up into itself, until finally there is only the one theme : " Dionysius against the Crucified."

But a second point has also to be learned and noted. The Antichrist has a definite and concrete sense. If he opposes Dionysius to the Crucified, according to the last five pages of the *Ecce homo* this means that he opposes him, or rather himself, to what he calls Christian morality. Already in the sphere of morals as such it might have been said that this was not just one of Nietzsche's foes but like Christianity itself the great enemy which he always had in view when he fought the philosophy, art, science and civilisation of his time. From the very outset Nietzsche was concerned about ethics, and it was for this reason and in this sense that he was an " immoralist." And morality and Christianity finally coalesced for him in a single detestable form, so that wherever he encountered morality he thought that he could see and deplore and attack Christianity. The last five pages of the *Ecce homo* begin with the words : " But in a very different sense as well I have chosen the word immoralist as my banner, my badge of honour ; I am proud to have this word as a mark of distinction from humanity. For no one previously has experienced Christian morality as something beneath him. For this there was required a hardness, a perspective, a hitherto unheard-of psychological depth and radicalness. Christian morality has previously been the Circe of all thinkers—they stood in its service. Who before me has descended to the depths from which there gushes out the poison of this kind of ideal—of world-renunciation ? " (p. 428). And then he continues : " Am I understood ?—What separates and marks me off from the rest of humanity is that I have discovered Christian morality." Discovered it as that which has corrupted humanity ! " Not to have seen this before seems to me to be the greatest stain which humanity has on its conscience . . . an almost criminal counterfeiting *in psychologicis*. Blindness in face of Christianity is the crime *par excellence*, a crime against life itself. . . . Millennia and nations, first and last, philosophers and old wives—apart from five or six moments of history, and myself as the seventh—have all been equally guilty in this respect " (p. 429). And again : " Am I understood ? . . . The discovery of Christian morality is an event without parallel, a veritable catastrophe. Whoever sheds light on it is a *force majeure*, a destiny, breaking the history of humanity into two parts. One either lives before him or after him. . . . The lightning of truth shatters that which formerly stood completely secure. Let him who understands what is destroyed see to it whether he has anything still in his hands " (p. 432). Nietzsche means that which must now be destroyed (it is not yet destroyed) on the basis of this epoch-making discovery. He thus concludes with Voltaire : *Ecrasez l'infame.* And this is what leads him to his final word : " Am I understood ?—Dionysius against the Crucified."

It is not self-evident that Nietzsche's general offensive should finally be against Christianity in this sense and under this sign. Again, in the *Ecce homo* itself and the earlier writings there seems at first to be a certain discrepancy of polemical standpoint. The offence of modern man is primarily at the incredible fact of the past reaching from remote ages into the present in the form of Christianity. " When on a Sunday morning we hear the old bells sounding, we ask ourselves : Is it really possible ? This all has to do with a crucified Jew of two thousand years ago who said that he was the Son of God " (*M. allzu M.*, p. 126). The Greek in him is offended at the " non-Greek element in Christianity " (*ib.*, p. 127). The philologist is offended at the exegetical and historical methods of the apostle Paul : " All these holy epileptics and seers did not possess a thousandth particle of the integrity of self-criticism with which a modern philologist reads a text or tests the truth of a historical event. . . . In comparison with us, they are moral cretins " (*W. z. Macht*, p. 123). He is also incensed at the imprudence, impatience and crudity of modern Christian theologians which drive the philologist in him almost to frenzy (*Antichrist*, p. 280 ; *W. z. Macht*, p. 152). Again, the æsthete in him experiences " a kind of inexpressible aversion at contact with the New Testament " : little, bad-mannered bigots who quite uncalled-for try to speak about the deepest problems ; a quite undistinguished type of man with the swelling claim to have more and indeed all value ; something of *foeda superstitio;* something from which we withdraw our hands in case of defilement (*ib.*, p. 141). " We would no more choose to be ' early Christians ' than Polish Jews. . . . They have a nasty smell. I have looked in vain even for one redeeming feature in the New Testament. It does not contain anything free or generous or open or sincere. Humanity has not even made its first beginning at this point " (*Antichrist*, p. 269). Arguments are also used which show that it was not for nothing that Nietzsche was the friend of F. Overbeck. The greatest witness against Christianity is the pitiable figure of the everyday Christian, whose complacency—he has no thought of seeking his salvation with fear and trembling—is a clear demonstration that the decisive assertions of Christianity are of no importance (*M. allzu M.*, p. 128). It is the Church, which is the very thing against which Jesus preached and taught His disciples to fight, embodying the triumph of that which is anti-Christian no less than the modern state and modern nationalism (*W. zur Macht*, p. 131, 145). It is to be noted that the fact that Nietzsche will have nothing to do with God is so self-evident that it plays no part at all in his arguments against Christianity. In the *Ecce homo* he said that he knew atheism neither as an experience nor as an event, but by instinct. " God is dead "—there is no need for heat or polemics. But is he quite so sure about this ? The Dionysius-dithyrambs of 1888 show that he must have had some misgivings on the point. An " unknown God " obtrudes his obviously dangerous being in the speeches of a curious opponent of Zarathustra, and he is not a complete stranger to Nietzsche himself, this hunter, thief, robber, bandit, this great enemy, this executioner-God etc., who tries to penetrate into his heart, his most secret thoughts (p. 457). But we need not pursue this aspect. Nietzsche's heart was not in contesting the existence of God, or in the other arguments to which we have referred. His central attack, into which he flung himself with all his force, was upon what he called Christian morality. All his other assaults upon Christianity derive their secret strength, and are initiated and directed, from this point. Even in the *Antichrist* this motif has become the *cantus firmus*, suppressing all the others.

But what is the absolutely intolerable and unequivocally perverted element which Nietzsche thinks that he has discovered, and must fight to the death, in Christian morality, and in this as the secret essence of all morality ? Why is it that he must finally act in this matter as if there were no other foe upon earth, and no more urgent task than to vanquish it ? The answer is given by Nietzsche himself with a hundred variations and nuances the complicated pattern of which we cannot follow, but the content of which is perfectly clear. It is because Christianity is not really a faith, and is not really " bound to any of its shameless dogmas," and does not basically need either metaphysics, asceticism, or " Christian " natural science, but is at root a practice, and is always possible as such, and in the strict sense has its " God " in this practice (*Antichrist*, p. 249, *W. z. Macht.* p. 155), that Nietzsche encounters it as the last enemy on his own true field. For he himself is finally concerned about a definite practice ; he is decisively an ethicist. And he encounters it as an enemy because it opposes to Zarathustra or Dionysius, the lonely, noble, strong, proud, natural, healthy, wise, outstanding, splendid man, the superman, a type which is the very reverse, and so far has managed to do this successfully with its blatant claim that the only true man is the man who is little, poor and sick, the man who is weak and not strong, who does not evoke admiration but sympathy, who is not solitary but gregarious—the mass-man. It goes so far as to speak of a crucified God, and therefore to identify God Himself with this human type, and consequently to demand of all men not merely sympathy with others but that they themselves should be those who excite sympathy and not admiration. " The neighbour is transfigured into a God . . . Jesus is the neighbour transposed into divinity, into a cause awakening emotion " (*W. z. Macht*, p. 142). " The absurd residuum of Christianity, its fables, concept-spinning and theology, do not concern us ; they could be a thousand times more absurd, and we should not lift a finger against them. But this ideal we contest " (*ib.*, p. 154). Nietzsche contests it as the greatest misfortune of the human race thus far. For it was the practical victory of a religion and morality of slaves, of failures, of those who go under, of the colourless, the mistaken, the worthless, the under-world, the ghetto, the variegated mass of abjects and rejects, those who creep and crawl on the earth revolting against all that is lofty (*Antichrist*, p. 124, 229, 263, 278 f.). It was " typically Socialist teaching." " What I do not like at all about this Jesus of Nazareth and His apostle Paul is that they put so many things into the heads of little people, as though their modest virtues were of some value. The price was too high ; for they have brought into disrepute the far more valuable qualities of virtue and manhood, opposing a bad conscience to the self-esteem of the excellent soul, and betraying even to self-destruction the noble, generous, bold, excessive inclinations of the strong " (*W. z. Macht*, p. 142 f.). And this pernicious ideal is Christianity both in kernel and in substance right up to the present day. It has been able to insinuate itself into the whole of Western culture, philosophy and morality to their great detriment, namely, at the price of the surrender of their Greek inheritance and their surreptitious and flagrant barbarisation. And apart from six or seven upright figures no one has ever even noticed the fact right up to the present time. " God has chosen what is weak and foolish and ignoble and despised in the eyes of the world, is how the formula ran, and *décadence* conquered *in hoc signo*. God on the cross—do we still not understand the terrible background significance of this symbol ?—Everything that suffers, everything that hangs on the cross, is divine. We all hang on the cross and therefore we are all divine. . . . We alone are divine. . . . Christianity was a victory, and a more excellent way went down before it— Christianity is the greatest misfortune of the human race thus far " (*Antichrist* p. 279).

This was what Nietzsche discovered as Christian morality, and this was his attack against it : the attack in which all his onslaughts on Christianity finally have both their origin and issue ; the attack which finally emerged in *Ecce homo* as the common denominator of his whole Dionysian offensive. What happened to the man that he had finally to burst out in this frenzied way and to give to his whole life-work the stamp of this outburst : Dionysius against the Crucified ?

If we are to understand what took place, we must again draw some comparisons. Goethe, too, had no great time for Christianity. Nor did he merely repudiate the enthusiasm of his friend Lavater and similar contemporary manifestations of Christianity, but there lived and reverberated in him something of the Greek to whom the cross is foolishness, and we may even suspect that he was personally a far more obstinate pagan than Nietzsche. But his repudiation remained cool and good-tempered and mild. For what are the occasional slights which he allowed himself, as in his famous juxtaposition of the four annoyances, " tobacco-smoke, bugs, garlic and † " ? As he was content to be Apollo or preferably Zeus, as he did not think of dramatising himself and his Hellenism in the form of Dionysius (he finally rejected this possibility in his Tasso, who is certainly no Dionysius), so he never even dreamed of compromising himself by explicitly and passionately opposing Christianity as Nietzsche did. And the same is true of the great philosophical Idealists of the time, of Kant, Fichte, Schelling and Hegel. If they could not make much of the Christianity of the New Testament, they were restrained and cautious and sparing in their criticisms, trying to interpret it as positively as possible within the framework of their systems, within the limits of their own understanding. They did not oppose to it any Zarathustra. Among them there was indeed a Herder and a Schleiermacher, with their strange but subjectively quite seriously meant attachment to Christianity and the Church. It is a little different with the heirs and disciples of this classical period. We undoubtedly have to say of a Feuerbach or a Strauss that—more akin to Nietzsche—they suffered all their lives from Christianity, and made it their main task to combat it. But on poor Strauss Nietzsche looked down as from a tower and laughed. He did not even remotely see himself as in the same class. And he was right. What was their critical philosophy and philosophy of religion to him, their biblical and dogmatic criticism, their contesting of Christianity in the name of modern reason and the modern view of things ? Strauss certainly could not have introduced a Dionysius-Zarathustra (any more than Martin Werner in our own day), and certainly not the friend of nature, Feuerbach.

The new thing in Nietzsche was the fact that the development of humanity without the fellow-man, which secretly had been the humanity of the Olympian Goethe and other classical figures as well as the more mediocre, reached in him a much more advanced, explosive, dangerous and yet also vulnerable stage— possibly its last. The new thing in Nietzsche was the man of " azure isolation," six thousand feet above time and man ; the man to whom a fellow-creature drinking at the same well is quite dreadful and insufferable ; the man who is utterly inaccessible to others, having no friends and despising women ; the man who is at home only with the eagles and strong winds ; the man whose only possible environment is desert and wintry landscape ; the man beyond good and evil, who can exist only as a consuming fire. And so the new thing in Nietzsche's relationship to Christianity necessarily consisted in the fact that this pressed and embarrassed him in a way which the others had not seen, or at most had only sensed. On this view Christianity seemed to be so incomparably dreadful and harassing, presenting such a Medusa aspect, that he immediately dropped all the other polemics which he needed to proclaim his Zarathustra in favour of the necessary battle against this newly discovered side of Christianity, and all the other attacks on it, whether in the form of the dignified rejection of Goethe, the speculative reinterpretation of the classical Idealists, or the rational objections of their successors, necessarily seemed to him to be irrelevant, stupid and even—and especially—frivolous. These predecessors had not seen how serious the matter was or how much was at stake. They could not do so, because on the positive side they did not go far enough and were not consistent enough. At bottom, they really knew nothing of the " azure isolation " of the superman. They had been left far, far behind by Zarathustra. They still crept along the ground, having only an inkling of the proximity of the eagles and strong winds in which alone real man can breathe. How could they see the true danger in Christianity ? How could they fail either to reach a frivolous compromise with this enemy, or, if they knew and attacked it as such, to commit the serious error of leaving it intact where it was really dangerous ? Nietzsche, however, was consistent on this positive side. He trod the way of humanity without the fellow-man to the bitter end. And this enabled him, and him alone, to see the true danger at this point.

And the true danger in Christianity, which he alone saw at the climax of that tradition, and on account of which he had to attack it with unprecedented resolution and passion—and with all the greater resolution and passion because he was alone—was that Christianity—what he called Christian morality—confronts real man, the superman, this necessary, supreme and mature fruit of the whole development of true humanity, with a form of man which necessarily questions and disturbs and destroys and kills him at the very root. That is to say, it confronts him with the figure of suffering man. It demands that he should see this man, that he should accept his presence, that he should not be man without him but with him, that he must drink with him at the same source. Christianity places before the superman the Crucified, Jesus, as the Neighbour, and in the person of Jesus a whole host of others who are wholly and utterly ignoble and despised in the eyes of the world (of the world of Zarathustra, the true world of men), the hungry and thirsty and naked and sick and captive, a whole ocean of human meanness and painfulness. Nor does it merely place the Crucified and His host before his eyes. It does not merely will that he see Him and them. It wills that he should recognise in them his neighbours and himself. It aims to bring him down from his height, to put him in the ranks which begin with the Crucified, in the midst of His host. Dionysius-Zarathustra, it says, is not a God but a man, and therefore under the cross of the Crucified and one of His host. Nor can Dionysius-Zarathustra redeem himself, but the Crucified alone can be his Redeemer. Dionysius-Zarathustra is thus called to live for others and not himself. Here are his brothers and sisters who belong to him and to whom he belongs. In this Crucified, and therefore in fellowship with this mean and painful host of His people, he has thus to see his salvation, and his true humanity in the fact that he belongs to Him and therefore to them. This Crucified is God Himself, and therefore God Himself is only for those who belong to His host. They are then the elect of God. And Dionysius-Zarathustra can be an elect of God only if he belongs to them. Away, then, the six thousand feet, the azure, the isolation, the drinking from a lonely well ! Everything is back to disturb and destroy the isolation. The fellow-man has returned whom Zarathustra had escaped or to whom he merely wanted to be a hammer, and he has returned in a form which makes escape impossible (because it embodies something which even Zarathustra cannot escape) and which makes all hammering futile (because in this form of suffering man there is nothing really to hammer).

This was the new thing which Nietzsche saw in Christianity and which he had to combat because he found it so intolerable, wounding and dangerous. It was for this reason that in the last resort his " anti-donkey " meant Antichrist. And it was only perhaps a relic of the frivolity of which he accused others that sometimes he could act as if Christianity were mere donkey-dom and he could meet it with the corresponding attitudes and measures. We might well ask how it was that all their life long even Strauss and Feuerbach found it necessary to keep hammering away at what they declared to be so bankrupt a thing as Christianity, especially in a century when it no longer cut a very imposing figure outwardly, and the battle against it had long since ceased to be a heroic war of liberation. But we have certainly to ask why Nietzsche was guilty of the Donquixotry of acting in the age of Bismarck as if the Christian morality of I Cor. I constituted the great danger by which humanity necessarily found itself most severely imperilled at every turn. Yet the fact remains that Nietzsche, did take up arms against Christianity, and especially the Christianity of I Cor. I, as if it were a serious threat and no mere folly. And he had to do so. We cannot explain this necessity in purely historical terms, which in this context means psychological and psycho-pathological. That Nietzsche became deranged in this attack, or that he was deranged to undertake it, merely throws light on the fact ; it does not alter the necessity. The one who as the heir, disciple and prophet of the Renaissance and its progeny discovered the superman was quite unable—irrespective of historical and psychological circumstances—to overlook the fact that in Western culture, in face of every repudiation, reinterpretation or assault, persisting in spite of every evacuation, there existed at least in the form of the Greek New Testament such a thing as Christianity, so that from the pages of the New Testament he was inevitably confronted by that figure, and could only recognise in that figure the direct opposite of his own ideal and that of the tradition which culminated in him, and was forced to protest and fight against it with the resolution and passion which we find in Nietzsche, not as against asininity, but with the final resolution which is reserved for a mortal threat.

Naturally there is an element of caricature in his depiction. Those who try to fight the Gospel always make caricatures, and they are then forced to fight these caricatures. Nietzsche's caricature consists in his (not very original) historical derivation of Christianity from a revolt on the part of slaves or the proletariat, for which Paul and other mischievous priests provided a metaphysical foundation and super-structure, and which thus became an incubus on the unhappy West. We all grasp at such aids as are available. And the 19th century had tried to bolster up Christianity with historical interpretations of this kind. Nietzsche was undoubtedly conditioned by his age when he thought that he could regard Christianity as typical Socialist teaching and contest it as such ; for there did not lack those who in his own time thought that they should praise and commend it as typical Socialist teaching, or at least find a positive place for it as a transitional stage. At this point Nietzsche was perhaps loyally and sincerely a little class-conditioned. According to the Marxist analysis, he belonged to the middle-class, although in a form worthy of Zarathustra. In this respect he was at one with D. F. Strauss, to whom the moderate Social Democratic teaching of the period was as a red rag to a bull. But this is not really essential. The caricature which he served up was itself an element in his resistance and attack. And of this attack we have to say that it was well aimed, that it centred on the point which was vital for Nietzsche as the most consistent champion and prophet of humanity without the fellow-man. It is another matter, and one that objectively considered is to the praise of Nietzsche, that he thus hurled himself against the strongest and not the weakest point in the opposing front. With his discovery of the Crucified and His host he discovered the Gospel itself in a form which was missed even by the majority of its champions, let alone its opponents, in the 19th century. And by having to attack it in this form, he has done us the good office of bringing before us the fact that we have to keep to this form as unconditionally as he rejected it, in self-evident antithesis not only to him, but to the whole tradition on behalf of which he made this final hopeless sally.

We now know against what orientation of research and representa-

tion of humanity we are warned *a limine* by the humanity of Jesus
Christ, and having secured our rear we can look in the direction to
which we are positively directed by this fact. The humanity of Jesus
consists in His being for man. From the fact that this example is
binding in humanity generally there follows the broad definition that
humanity absolutely, the humanity of each and every man, consists
in the determination of man's being as a being with others, or rather
with the other man. It is not as he is for himself but with others,
not in loneliness but in fellowship, that he is genuinely human, that
he achieves true humanity, that he corresponds to his determination
to be God's covenant-partner, that he is the being for which the man
Jesus is, and therefore real man. If we overlook the fact of his being
in fellowship, and see him for himself, constructing him in terms
of an abstract " I am " in which others are not yet or no longer included, everything collapses, and in respect of the concept of the human
we are betrayed into an obscurity in which it is no longer possible
to make any real distinction between what may be called humanity
and inhumanity. We must avoid this path. We must press straight
on from the fact that the humanity of man consists in the determination of his being as a being with the other.

Before we move on from this point, we must try to clarify three
of the terms employed in this definition.

1. We describe humanity as a determination of human being.
Man is, as he is created by God for God, as this creature of God for
covenant-partnership with God. But this being is a wholly definite
being. It corresponds in its own way to its particular creation and
to the meaning and goal of the particularity of its creation. The
manner of its being is a likeness of its purpose and therefore of the
fact that it is created by God for God. This parabolic determination
of human being, this correspondence and similarity of its nature in
relation to its being as such, is humanity.

2. We describe humanity as a being of man with others. With
this cautious expression we distinguish humanity generally from the
humanity of Jesus. There is also a being for others in the relation of
man to man. But only the humanity of Jesus can be absolutely
exhaustively and exclusively described as a being for man. There
can be no question of a total being for others as the determination of
any other men but Jesus. And to the humanity of other men there
necessarily belongs reciprocity. Others are for them as they are for
others. This reciprocity cannot arise in the humanity of Jesus with
its irreversible " for." We are thus satisfied to describe the humanity
generally with which we are now dealing as a being of the one with
the other, and we shall have to show to what extent this includes a
certain being of the one for the other.

3. We describe humanity as a being of the one man with the
other. Fundamentally we speak on both sides in the singular and

not in the plural. We are not thinking here in terms of individualism. But the basic form of humanity, the determination of humanity, according to its creation, in the light of the humanity of Jesus—and it is of this that we speak—is a being of the one man with the other. And where one is with many, or many with one, or many with many, the humanity consists in the fact that in truth, in the basic form of this occurrence, one is always with another, and this basic form persists. Humanity is not in isolation, and it is in pluralities only when these are constituted by genuine duality, by the singular on both sides.

The singular, not alone but in this duality, is the presupposition without which there can never be humanity in the plural.

We may now move forward, and for the sake of clarity we shall begin with an analysis of the statement " I am," which we have so far understood only as the axiom of humanity without the fellow-man, but which will help us to a true understanding and exposition once we appreciate its true significance. The statement " I am " is ultimately a confession—and perhaps *the* confession—of the man Jesus ; He therefore permits and requires of us an interpretation on which, as at least a corresponding and similar if not an equal confession in the mouth of others, it has a human and not an inhuman form ; an interpretation which does not point us in the direction which we cannot take, but in the opposite and right direction, the being of one man with the other.

What is meant by " I ? " I pronounce the word, and in so doing, even if I only do so mentally or to myself, I make a distinction, but also a connexion. In thinking and speaking this word, I do not remain in isolation. I distinguish myself from another who is not I and yet also not It, not an object, but one who can receive and estimate and understand my declaration " I " because he can make a similar declaration to me. In making this distinction, I presuppose, accept and make, as far as I am able, a connexion with him as one who is like me. Addressing this object as I, I distinguish him not only from myself but from all other objects, from every It, placing myself on the same level or in the same sphere with him, acknowledging that I am not without him in my sphere, that this sphere is not just mine but also his. The mere fact that I say " I " means that I describe and distinguish the object to which I say it as something like myself ; in other words, that with my " I " I also address him as " Thou." By saying " I," I implicitly address and treat him as " Thou." Not, be it noted, as " He " or " She." So long and so far as he is only He or She, he is really It, an object like others, in a different sphere from mine, unlike myself ; and my distinction from him and connexion with him are not yet human. But in this case I do not speak to him ; I speak about him. And the word " I " is meaningful in relation to the one with whom I speak about him. It has no reference to himself. If I speak to him and not about him, he is neither It, He nor She, but Thou. I then make the distinction and connexion in relation to him in the specific form of a demarcation in virtue of which my sphere is no longer my own but his, and he is like me. But there is more to it than this. For when I say " I " and therefore " Thou " to someone else, I empower and invite and summon him to say " Thou " to me in return. The declaration " I " in what I say is the declaration of my expectation that the other being to which I declare myself in this way will respond and treat and describe and distinguish me as something like himself. When he accepts my " I "—and in turning to him I count on it that he is able to do so—he cannot possibly regard me as an It or a mere He or She, but I am distinguished from all other objects for him as he is for me, and distinguished from and connected to me as I am from and to him. And it can only be a matter of fulfilment that he for his part should admit his recognition of this fact by pronouncing the word " Thou " and thus proclaim himself not merely as something like an I but actually as an I. Thus the word " Thou," although it is a very different word, is immanent to " I." It is not a word which is radically alien, but one which belongs to it. The word " I " with which I think and declare my humanity implies as such humanity with and not without the fellow-man. I cannot say " I," even to myself, without also saying " Thou," without making that distinction and connexion in relation to another. And only as I think and say " I " in this way, only as I make this specific distinction and connexion with this word, can I expect to be recognised and acknowledged by others as a " Thou," as something like an " I," and more than that as a real " I," and therefore to be confirmed in the human determination of my being, and regarded, treated and addressed as a human being.

On this basis, what is meant by " I am ? " It certainly means that I posit myself : myself as this being in the cosmos ; myself in all the freedom and necessity of my being ; myself in the totality of the movement of my distinctions and connexions in relation to what is for me the outside world ; myself in my desire and ability to project myself into this world. There can be no objection to this formal description of " I am." But what does all this mean if I cannot say " I " without also saying " Thou," and being a Thou for this " Thou," and only in this way receiving confirmation that I am ? What does " I am " mean on this presupposition ? Who and what am I myself as I confirm my being in this way ? What kind of a being is it in the freedom and necessity of which I posit myself, distinguishing and connecting myself, projecting myself outwards ? One thing at least is certain. A pure, absolute and self-sufficient I is an illusion, for as an I, even as I think and express this I, I am not alone or self-sufficient, but am distinguished from and connected with a Thou in which I find a being like my own, so that there is no place for an interpretation of the " I am " which means isolation and necessarily consists in a description of the sovereign self-positing of an empty subject by eruptions of its pure, absolute and self-sufficient abyss. The I is not pure, absolute or self-sufficient. But this means that it is not empty. It is not an abyss. And so the being of the I cannot consist in the eruption, history and myth of an abyss. On the contrary, as I am—the genuine I—I am in distinction and connexion to the other which in the fact that I am is Thou, my Thou, and for which I am a Thou in return, thus receiving confirmation of my own being, of the " I am." " I am " is not an empty but a filled reality. As I am, the other is like me. I am as I am in a relation. And this means that as I posit myself—I should not be myself if it were otherwise—I at once come up against the fact that there takes place a corresponding self-positing and being on the part of the one whom I must see and treat as Thou as I think and declare myself as I. With this self-positing and being of his he comes towards me, or rather the Thou comes (for that is what he is as I am I in relation to him), and comes in such a way that I cannot evade him, since he is like myself and therefore Thou as surely as I am I, and therefore my sphere is not mine alone but his as well. What I am and posit as myself, I am and posit in relation to his positing and being, in distinction from and connexion with this alien happening which is characterised by the fact that I can see and recognise and accept this alien being and positing as one which corresponds to my own. This alien being and positing does not belong, therefore, to the general mass of happenings in the external world. In face of it I cannot refer back to myself, asserting and developing myself from myself as from a neutral point quite apart from it. The being and positing of this Thou reaches and affects me, for it is not that of an It, but of the Thou without which I should not be I. In its decisive content as a work of the Thou it is not the outside world which I can leave to itself, avoid or control. The work of the Thou cannot be indifferent to me, nor can I evade or master it. I cannot do this because as I do my own work, as I am myself and posit myself, I am necessarily claimed by and occupied with the being and positing of the Thou. My own being and positing takes place in and with the fact that I am claimed by that of the other and occupied with it. That of the other sets limits to my own. It indicates its problems. It poses questions which must be answered. And there are answers for which it asks. I am in encounter with the other who is in the same way as I am. I am under the conditions imposed by this encounter. I am as either well or badly I fulfil the conditions imposed by this encounter. Even if I fulfil them badly, I am as measured by these conditions. I have no being apart from them. I cannot posit myself without coming up against the self-positing of the other. I have no line of retreat to a place where he does not come up against me with his self-positing. If I had, it could only be that of a return to the inhumanity of a being without the being of the other, of the " I am " of an empty subject, of an I which cannot be more than an illusion. And here, too, we must consider the matter from the other side. As I myself am, and posit myself, I confront the other no less than he does me with his being and positing. He is my Thou, and therefore something like myself, in the sphere which is my own. My being and positing is for him more than the external world. Hence he cannot retreat before me into himself, and in this way exist without me. Since I am not an It, but an I and therefore a Thou, he is reached and affected by me no less than I am by him. He, too, is unable to leave aside or to evade or control my work. He, too, is claimed by and occupied with my being and positing. He, too, stands under the conditions which I create for him. I am his encounter as he is mine. In being myself, I cannot help being what I am for him. In this sense, too, there is no line of retreat to a place where I exist neutrally for him, where I do not affect him, where I do not owe him anything, where I with my being and positing do not have to take any account of his. The only line of retreat is again that of a retreat to inhumanity—to the inhumanity of a being without the Thou in relation to which I can be alone, to the " I am " of an empty subject which cannot find fulfilment or really be a human subject, but is always, or always becomes again, an illusion.

" I am "—the true and filled " I am "—may thus be paraphrased : " I am in encounter." Nor am I in encounter before or after, incidentally, secondarily or subsequently, while primarily and properly I am alone in an inner world in which I am not in this encounter, but alongside which there is an outer world in which amongst other things I certainly come up against being, against the being of the Thou, and have to reckon with it, but in such sort that this is not at all essential, since essentially I am always outside this encounter, and can always retreat into this world apart. No, at the very root of my being and from the very first I am in encounter with the being of the Thou, under his claim and with my own being constituting a claim upon him. And the humanity of human being is this total determination as being in encounter with the being of the Thou, as being with the fellow-man, as fellow-humanity. To this extent we must oppose humanity without the fellow-man. This is the reach of the likeness in unlikeness, of the correspondence and similarity between the man Jesus and us other men. The minimal definition of our humanity, of humanity generally, must be that it is the being of man in encounter, and in this sense the determination of man as a being with the other man. We cannot go back on this. We cannot be content with anything less or weaker. We cannot accept any compromise or admixture with the opposite conception which would have it that at bottom—in the far depths of that abyss of an empty subject—man can be a man without the fellow-man, an I without the Thou.

But we must be more precise. Being with means encounter.

Hence being with the other man means encounter with him. Hence humanity is the determination of our being as a being in encounter with the other man. We shall now try to understand the content of this encounter.

The basic formula to describe it must be as follows : " I am as Thou art." Naturally the word " as " does not imply that the " Thou art " is the cause, even the instrumental cause, or the true substance of the " I am." In this respect an excess of zeal in conflict with the idealistic concept of humanity has sometimes led to the emptying out of the baby with the bath-water. Man has been constructed wholly in the light of the fellow-man, and the " I am " has formally disappeared in the " Thou art." The word " as " does not tell us where human being is created—for this we can turn only to God the Creator —but how. It tells us that every " I am " is qualified, marked and determined by the " Thou art." Owing it to God the Creator that I am, I am only as Thou art ; as, created by the same God, Thou art with me. Neither the I am nor the Thou art loses its own meaning and force. I do not become Thou, nor Thou I, in this co-existence. On the contrary, as I and Thou are together, their being acquires the character, the human style, of always being I for the self and Thou for the other. As we are in this encounter we are thus distinguished. On both sides—we shall return to this—the being has its own validity, dignity and self-certainty. Nor is this human being static, but dynamic and active. It is not an *esse* but an *existere*. To say man is to say history. On a false understanding no less than a true we are forced to put the statement " I am " in the form of a little history, describing it as that self-positing. Similarly, the statement " Thou art " denotes a history. Therefore in our formula : " I am as Thou art," we do not describe the relationship between two static complexes of being, but between two which are dynamic, which move out from themselves, which exist, and which meet or encounter each other in their existence. The " I am " and the " Thou art " encounter each other as two histories. It is to be noted that they do not just do this subsequently, as though there were one history here and another there which at a certain point became a common history ; as though there were an " I am " here and a " Thou art " there which in the continuation of their two-sided movement came together and became a partnership. But in and with their creation, and therefore in and with the two-sided beginning of their movement and history, they are in encounter : I am as Thou art, and Thou art as I am. To say man is to say history, and this is to speak of the encounter between I and Thou. Thus the formula : " I am as Thou art," tells us that the encounter between I and Thou is not arbitrary or accidental, that it is not incidentally but essentially proper to the concept of man. It tells us noologically that this concept would at once be empty if the view basic to it were that of a pure subject and not of the subject in this encounter. And it tells us ontologically that we have to do with real man only when his existence takes place in this encounter, only in the form of man with his fellow-man.

On this basis we shall now try to see what are the categories, the constant, decisive and necessary elements in this history or encounter, and to that extent what are the categories of the distinctively human. Great caution is needed at this point. Things which might be said about man without his fellow, qualities and characteristics of that empty subject, are out of place here, because they have no " categorical " significance in the description of humanity, i.e., they tell us nothing about being in encounter and therefore about that which is properly and essentially human. Thus the fact that I am born and die ; that I eat and drink and sleep ; that I develop and maintain myself ; that beyond this I assert myself in face of others, and even physically propagate my species ; that I enjoy and work and play and fashion and possess ; that I acquire and have and exercise powers ; that I take part in all the works of the race either accomplished or in process of accomplishment ; that in all this I satisfy religious needs and can realise religious possibilities ; and that in it all I fulfil my aptitudes as an understanding and thinking, willing and feeling being—all this as such is not my humanity. In it I can be either human or inhuman. In it I am only asked whether I am human or inhuman. In it all I must first answer the question whether I will affirm or deny my humanity. It is only the field on which human being either takes place or does not take place as history, as the encounter of I and Thou ; the field on which it is revealed or obscured that " I am as Thou art." That I exist on this field, and do so in a particular way, does not of itself mean that I am human. But as I exist on this field and in this way, in this restriction or development, poverty or wealth, impotence or intensity, it has to become true and actual that I am human and not inhuman in my existence. There is no reason why in the realisation of my vital, natural and intellectual aptitudes and potentialities, in my life-act as such, and my participation in scholarship and art, politics and economics, civilisation and culture, I should not actualise and reveal that " I am as Thou art." But it may well be that in and with all this I deny it. It may well be that in all this I am only man without my fellow-man, and therefore not really human at all. Nothing of all this is in itself and as such the glory of my humanity.

For example, it is not the case that motherhood or work ennoble as such. It is also not the case that an accomplishment or achievement in any of these spheres ennobles as such. It can all be supremely inhuman. And there can be supreme humanity where it is all absent. Self-evidently, of course, it is equally untrue to try to seek nobility in the absence of distinction on this field, e.g., with a certain perverseness in sickness or poverty or insignificance or the lack of culture. It is rather the case that on this whole field both the positive and the negative only acquire a positive or negative meaning in respect of their relationship to humanity—and have to acquire it in the fulfilment of that history.

The question of the humanity of human being is independent of everything which takes place or does not take place on this field. Or conversely, this whole field with all that takes place or does not take place on it is an empty page on which there has still to be written the answer to the question of the humanity of human being. And this answer is written with the enactment of the history, the realisation of the encounter, in which " I am as Thou art." Hence as the constant, decisive and necessary categories, marks and criteria of humanity we can take into account only the elements which characterise this encounter constantly in all the circumstances which may arise on this field, decisively in face of all circumstances, and necessarily in the midst of all possibilities ; the forms in which there takes place : " I am as Thou art."

Being in encounter is (1) a being in which one man looks the other in the eye. The human significance of the eye is that we see one another eye to eye. It is man who is seen in this way, not things, or the cosmos, but at the heart of things and the cosmos man, and man not after the manner of things or the cosmos, but in his distinction and particularity as man within the cosmos. It is man who is visible to man, and therefore as the other, as the one who is thus distinct from the one who sees him. This one cannot see himself, but he can and must see the other. That this should take place, that the other should be visible to and seen by him as man, is the human significance of the eye and all seeing. Seeing is inhuman if it does not include this seeing, if it is not first and supremely, primarily and conclusively, this seeing—the seeing of the fellow-man. But this is only the one half. When one man looks the other in the eye, it takes place automatically that he lets the other look him in the eye. And it is a necessary part of the human meaning of the eye that man himself should be visible to the other : not an outward form, a something which might be like the rest of the cosmos ; but man himself, the man who as such is particular and distinct within the cosmos. This one is visible in the seeing eye of the one for the other who comes to see him even as he is seen by him. To see the other thus means directly to let oneself be seen by him. If I do not do this, I do not see him. Conversely, as I do it, as I let him look me in the eye, I see him. The two together constitute the full human significance of the eye and its seeing. All seeing is inhuman in which the one who sees hides himself, refusing to be seen by the fellow-man whom he sees. The point is not unimportant that it is always two men, and therefore a real I and Thou, who look themselves in the eye and can thus see one another and be seen by one another. But we may now put the same thing rather more generally and say that being in encounter is a being in the openness of the one to the other with a view to and on behalf of the other.

" I am as Thou art " is basically fulfilled in the fact that I am not closed to thee but open. I am not Thou, and thy being is not mine nor mine thine. But I with all that I am encounter thee with all that Thou art, and similarly Thou dost encounter me, and if this is the encounter of two men and not the collision of two things it means that Thou and what Thou art are not closed to me, and that I for my part do not remain closed to thee and what Thou art. As I am and Thou art we are open to one another. I know thee as a man, as something like myself, and I make it possible for thee to know me in the same way. We give each other something in our duality, and this is that I and Thou are men. We give each other an insight into our being. And as we do this, I am not for myself, but for thee, and Thou for me, so that we have a share and interest in one another. This two-sided openness is the first element of humanity. Where it lacks, and to the extent that it lacks, humanity does not occur. To the extent that we withhold and conceal ourselves, and therefore do not move or move any more out of ourselves to know others and to let ourselves be known by them, our existence is inhuman, even though in all other respects we exist at the highest level of humanity. The isolation in which we try to persist, the lack of participation which we show in relation to others and thus thrust upon others in relation to ourselves, is inhumanity. The expression : " That is no concern of mine," or : " That is no concern of yours," is almost always wrong, because it almost always means that the being of this or that man is nothing to me and my being nothing to him ; that I will neither see him nor let myself be seen by him ; that my eyes are too good for him and I am too good for his eyes ; that my openness reaches its limit in him. But conversely, where openness obtains, humanity begins to occur. To the extent that we move out of ourselves, not refusing to know others or being afraid to be known by them, our existence is human, even though in all other respects we may exist at the very lowest level of humanity. (It is not necessarily the case, but seems to be a fact of experience, that where we think that in other respects we are nearer the depths than the heights of humanity we are generally much more open with and for one another, and to that extent, in spite of all appearances to the contrary, much more human than on the supposed heights.) The duality into which we enter when we encounter one another directly and not indirectly, revealed and not concealed as man with man ; the participation which we grant one another by the very fact that we see and do not not see one another, and let ourselves be seen and not unseen by one another, these are the first and indispensable steps in humanity, without which the later ones cannot be taken, and which cannot be replaced by the exercise of any human capacity or virtue, however highly rated this may rightly or wrongly be. It is a great and solemn and incomparable moment when two men look themselves in the eye and discover one another. This moment, this mutual look, is in some sense the root-formation of all humanity without which the rest is impossible. But it is to be noted again that in the strict sense it can take place only in duality, as I and Thou look one another in the eye. Where a man thinks he sees and knows a group, or a group a man, or one group another group, ambiguity always arises. After all, it might be only a matter of psychology and not the other man, of pedagogics and not the child, of sociological statistics and systematisation and not the individual, of the general and not the particular, which is the only thing that really counts in this respect. This is the dangerous—and usually more than dangerous—limit of all planning and philanthropy, but also of all doctrine and instruction, of all politics, and especially of all socialism. Whether on the one side or the other or both there is maintained or broken a closed and blind existence, thinking and speaking in the group, whether the one concrete man is invisible or visible to the other concrete man, is what decides whether there is humanity in all this or not.

Bureaucracy is the form in which man participates with his fellows when this first step into mutual openness is not taken, and not taken because duality is evaded for the sake of the simplicity of a general consideration and a general programme. Bureaucracy is the encounter of the blind with those whom they treat as blind. A bureau is a place where men are grouped in certain classes and treated, dismissed or doctored according to specified plans, principles and regulations. This may very well have the result that the men themselves, both those who act and those who are acted upon, are invisible to one another. A bureau does not have to be an office. Many a man unwittingly sits and acts all his life in a private bureau from which he considers how to treat and dismiss men according to his private plans, and in the process he may never see the real men and always be invisible to them. Certainly, there can and must be the bureau, both public and private. Bureaucracy does not hold sway in every bureau. But every bureau is situated hard by the frontier beyond which bureaucracy raises its head, and with it inhumanity, even on the presupposition of the most altruistic of intentions. It is not the man who works in a bureau, for to some extent we all have to do this, but the bureaucrat who is always inhuman. In this whole matter we may perhaps refer to the parable of the eye in Mt. 6²²f. : " The light of the body is the eye : if therefore thine eye be single (ἁπλοῦς), thy whole body shall be full of light. But if thine eye be evil (πονηρός), thy whole body shall be full of darkness." With this human picture of the good or bad eye the parable refers to the open or closed relationship of man to the imminent kingdom of God. " If therefore the light that is in thee be darkness, how great is that darkness ! " But it is no accident that this particular picture, that of the clear or clouded eye, is chosen to illustrate this relationship.

Being in encounter consists (2) in the fact that there is mutual speech and hearing. The matter sounds simple, and yet it again consists in a complex action : I and Thou must both speak and hear, and speak with one another and hear one another. No element must be lacking. This is the human significance of speech. At this point we are on a higher level than the first. It is a good thing to see and to be seen. But there is a good deal more to humanity than that.

The openness of encounter is excellent and indeed indispensable as a first step. But encounter is not exhausted in openness. Openness alone is no guarantee that I reach thee and Thou me, that there is thus a real encounter. Openness, seeing and being seen, is always a receptive and not a spontaneous happening. By mere seeing we either do not know one another at all or only imperfectly, for on the plane of mere seeing the one has no opportunity of putting himself before the other, i.e., of interpreting himself, of declaring who and what he is, what his person and being are according to his own understanding of himself. On the plane of mere seeing the one who sees has to form his own picture of the other, understanding the man himself and what he is and does from his own standpoint, and measuring and judging him by his own standards. The other has not contributed anything of his own to make himself knowable. To know him, he is thrown back entirely upon his own resources. And this limitation is a burden to the one who is seen as well. So long as he is known only by sight, he is compelled to exist for the one who sees him in the picture which he has formed of him. He is no more than what he seems to be in his eyes and according to his standards. He has not been able to do anything to give a different and perhaps better and more truthful representation. With his own self-interpretation he still stands impotently before the interpretation which the other has adopted from mere sight, wondering, no doubt, whether he has any real insight into him at all. And if in the encounter of I and Thou there is to be not merely mutual consideration but a mutual contact and intersection of being and activity, if there is to be a field of common life in which the I and Thou not only see themselves but continually have themselves and continually have to take each other into practical account, surely something more is demanded to secure the required intercourse than the pictures mutually formed and the arbitrary notions conceived on both sides ? These pictures in which alone they exist for one another may well hamper instead of helping the intercourse, making it impossible rather than possible. So long as these pictures are normative, it may well be that both parties are only acted upon instead of acting. The extreme case is not excluded that seeing and being seen do not prevent the one or the other or both from entering into this intercourse as a man without his fellow-man, and thus being a genuine and perhaps quite immovable obstacle to true intercourse, leading inevitably to conflict instead of co-operation. What is needed at this point is speech—the human use of the mouth and ears. Humanity as encounter must become the event of speech. And speech means comprehensively reciprocal expression and its reciprocal reception, reciprocal address and its reciprocal reception. All these four elements are vital. Man speaks and hears a good deal. But the line on which he is human in speaking and hearing is a fine one, and there must not be the slightest deviation from it either on the one side or the other.

The I has thus to express itself to the Thou. A word spoken by me is my active self-declaration to the Thou, my spontaneous crossing of the necessary frontier of mere visibility in relation to the other. As I take to words, I testify that I am not leaving the interpretation of myself to the Thou, but am going to help him by at least adding my self-interpretation. As I speak, I set the other in a position to compare his own picture of me with my own, with my own conception of myself. I help him to answer the immediate question whether his picture of me is correct. That I express myself does not mean in the first instance—and from my standpoint it ought not to mean—that I aim to relieve, defend or justify myself against the wrong which I am done or might be done by the picture which the other has of me. My self-expression may later acquire this sense. But this cannot be its primary intention on my part. The real meaning of the fact that I express myself to the other is that I owe him this assistance. Thus my self-expression, if it is genuinely human, has nothing whatever to do with the fear of being misunderstood or the desire to give a better portrait of myself and vindicate myself before him. It is not for nothing that when this intention lurks behind self-expression it usually fails to attain its end. My word as self-declaration is human only when, in seizing the opportunity of making myself clear and understandable, I have before me the necessary concern of the other not only to see but also to understand me, to escape the uncertainty of the view which he has of me, and the embarrassment caused by this uncertainty. I can help him in this respect only as I tell him who I am, what I think of it, what my view is, with whom and what he has to do in me and my whole being according to the insight gained according to the best of my own knowledge and conscience. I can help him in this way with my word. Only when I speak with him with this purpose in view—not for my own sake but for his—do I express myself honestly and genuinely to him. Words are not genuine self-expression when in some respect I keep back myself, not representing or displaying myself. Words are not genuine self-expression when I represent myself in another guise than that in which I know myself to the best of my information and conscience. Nor are they genuine self-expression when they are perhaps a mask—*la parole est donnée à l'homme pour déguiser sa pensée*—by means of which I try to prevent the other from understanding me, and thus do not really intend to express myself at all. How can I take the Thou seriously as a Thou if I express myself to him but do not really intend to express myself at all? How can I then be in true encounter with him? How can my speech be human speech or my mouth a human mouth? To take the Thou seriously is to be concerned for the Thou in self-expression and self-declaration; to have regard in my self-representation for this other who necessarily has to do with me for good or ill; to do my best not to leave him to his own devices in the unavoidable task of making something of me. Only on this presupposition will my self-expression in relation to him be true and not false.

But the I has also to receive the expression of the other. A word heard by me is the active self-declaration of the Thou to me. The other, too, aims to cross the frontier of mere visibility. He, too, does not leave me to the picture which I have formed of him. He, too, tries to represent himself, inviting me to compare my picture of him with what he himself has to contribute. He, too, aims to help me. For this reason and with this intention he speaks with me. To receive or accept him in this sense is to listen to him. I do not hear him if I assume that he is only concerned about himself, either to commend himself to me or to gain my interest, and that he makes himself conspicuous and understandable, forcing himself and his being upon me, only for this reason. When he speaks to me, I must not be affected by the fact that in innumerable instances in which men express themselves to me this might actually be the case or appear to be so. What matters now is the humanity of my hearing, and this is conditioned negatively by the fact that at least I do not hear this other with suspicion, and positively by the fact that I presuppose that he is trying to come to my help with his self-expression and self-declaration. In relation to him I am in the uncertainty and therefore the embarrassment of knowing him only by sight and therefore equivocally ; of knowing him, and with whom or what I have to do in him, only from my own standpoint. This is where the word comes in. He is now trying to fill in or correct my conception of him by his own. He is trying to the best of his ability to help me over the difficulty in which I find myself, giving me by his word the opportunity to verify my view of him. My hearing is human, i.e., I have open ears for the other, only when I listen to him on this presupposition. Only then do I find a place for his self-declaration. If I do not accept the fact that my view is incomplete and needs to be supplemented and corrected, that it may indeed be wholly distorted ; if I do not suffer from the embarrassment caused by the Thou so long as I have to interpret him from myself and his self-declaration is withheld ; if I do not see and deplore the obvious lacuna at this point, there can be no place for the word of the Thou. However loudly it beats against my ear, I cannot hear ; my ear is not in any sense a human ear, and I do not take seriously the Thou of the fellow-man unhesitatingly subordinated to myself. To take the Thou seriously and therefore to have a human ear is to move towards the self-declaration of the other and to welcome it as an event which for my own sake must take place between him and me. It is necessary for me that the other should represent and display himself to me no matter what this may involve or entail. I am not a true I and do not genuinely exist without him. I am only an empty subject if I do not escape that difficulty in relation to him. How can I help thanking him for the favour which he does me by expressing himself ? Whatever he may have in view, whatever he may want of me, however sincere or insincere he may be in what he does, the point at issue, the objective significance of the event of his self-expression to me, is that now at least this supreme favour is done me. Hearing on this presupposition is human hearing of the self-expression of the fellow-man.

But there is another side to the matter. The I is not merely concerned to express itself, but also to address the Thou. The word spoken by me is my impartation to the Thou. Self-declaration to the other cannot be an end in itself. What is the point of crossing that frontier of mere visibility, what inconvenience it may cause the other that I represent myself to him, how little it may genuinely concern him, if the point between us is not that in my self-expression I have something objective to offer and impart for his appropriation ! Why do I necessarily try to make myself clear and explain myself to him ? We have given as our reason the fact that he cannot fulfil the task of knowing me by sight alone. But why does he have to know me at all ? He has to know me, we must now continue, because I am for him the sum of something objective which he needs as a subject but which is in the first instance unattainable, being concealed in me. We remember that I am not Thou, nor Thou I. Hence what the other comes to see in me is something new and strange and different. I am outside for him, an unknown being, near and yet remote. But when he sees and encounters me, I cannot remain strange. Being so near, I cannot continue to be remote. Since there has to be intercourse between us, I cannot be merely external, a self-enclosed object. In this form I am a vital need to him so long as no bridge is built or way found from him to me. His difficulty so long as he knows me only by sight is that he has no way to me ; that he cannot appropriate the new and strange and different thing in me, and therefore cannot have intercourse with me. For this reason he has to know me. And for this reason I have an obligation to make myself known. I have something to say to him, i.e., I have to entrust to him what would remain unknown so long as he knew me only by sight, the new and different thing in me. This is the meaning of the word of address from the one to the other. The word of address is necessary as a kind of penetration from the sphere of the one into the sphere of another being. As I address another, whether in the form of exposition, question, petition or demand, but always with the request to be heard, I ask that he should not remain in isolation but be there for me ; that he should not be concerned only with himself but with me too ; in other words, that he should hear. Address is coming to another with one's being, and knocking and asking to be admitted. As I address him, I allow myself to unsettle and disturb him by drawing attention to the fact that I am there too. In certain cases this may well be a thankless task. For we cannot take it for granted that he is conscious of needing the objective thing which I can offer and impart ; that he wants the new and strange and different thing which I am for him ; that he thinks it a vital matter that there is no bridge or way between him and me and therefore he cannot have intercourse with me ; that he is willing and ready to accept that penetration from my sphere to his, to be told something by me. On the contrary, it is far more likely that the conscious wish of the other will be that I should leave him in peace. But we must not allow this fact to obscure the real point at issue. It merely reminds us that in the genuine address of the I to the Thou we have to do with the imparting of something objective, with the disclosure of a particular side of the great matter of the life to be lived in common by the I and the Thou. The words with which I turn to the other, seeking him out and perhaps reaching him, are human when the new and strange and different thing with which I knock and demand entrance as I address him is directed at himself, when it penetrates to him as a vital element which constrains and is important and indispensable for him. It is thus a human address when in my claim to be heard by the other I have something decisive for himself to give him. Basically, however, there can be no doubt that one man needs another, and particularly in respect of that in which the other is unknown to him ; that one man has something decisive to give another ; that so long as one man does not know another this is a vital need which waits to be satisfied. And because this is the case, nothing can basically compromise the human duty and obligation of addressing the other. We cannot consider the matter merely from the standpoint of the personal need of the one. It is obvious that personal need, when it arises, may just as well constrain to silence as to speech, leading to isolation rather than to fellowship, and therefore not to the addressing of another. What have I to say and offer and impart with my words ? How can I expect that the other will want to listen to me ? Why I cannot be silent but am required to speak is that I necessarily abandon him and leave him to his own devices if I spare myself what is perhaps the thankless venture, and him the unwelcome penetration of his sphere, and withhold from him that which he definitely ought to know, but cannot know until I tell him. I cannot withhold it, because he encounters me as a man, and I should not take him seriously as a man if I did not seriously try to find the way from me to him. No matter what the results, I cannot refrain from knocking. The humanity of the encounter between I and Thou demands that I should not merely make a few tentative efforts in this direction, but do my utmost. Speaking on this presupposition, not for one's own sake but for that of the needy other, is human speaking.

But again the I has to receive the address of the Thou. The words of the Thou heard by me are his impartation to the I. The other has not represented himself to me merely that I should consider him from without. He has not expressed himself to me that he should remain for me a mere object. I have not heard him if the distance between him and me remains. As he speaks with me, his aim is to be known by me, i.e., to seek me out in his own new and strange and different being, and therefore to be seen and grasped from within. This time it is he who comes to me, trying to find a bridge, a way, an open door. It is he who wills to be in me. This is the purpose of his speaking, expounding, questioning and requesting, of his concern, of his claim and the requirement imposed by it. It may appear to me that he wants something from me. In spite of appearance, do I see what is really at stake ? It is really a matter of myself. I cannot be I without accepting this claim of the other, without letting him come to me, and therefore without hearing him. It is a matter of satisfying my vital need, in which I should necessarily sink if I remained alone, if the other and the objective thing with which he knocks on my door and seeks admission were to remain objective, if I did not make it my own. I am in encounter with him, and what is to become of me, how can I be in encounter with him, if he is merely external, an unknown object of consideration, remote even in his proximity ? The question may be raised whether I have any room for him ; whether I can make anything of him ; whether he will really be helped and served by my hearing him and allowing him to come to me. What can it mean for him if I allow this penetration into my sphere, as though he were definitely in good hands with me ? Surely the claim of the fellow-man, however modest, demands far too much for me ever to dream of meeting it. Far too much stands behind the words of others for me ever to hope, even with the best will in the world, to do them justice. Each fellow-man is a whole world, and the request which he makes of me is not merely that I should know this or that about him, but the man himself, and therefore this whole world. It is tempting—and might even seem to be an act of humility in face of too great a task—not to listen too much or too seriously to what is said by the other. Might it not be too presumptuous, and awaken false hopes, to open the door too wide and not just a little ? Is it not too much to demand that I should really and seriously know the man himself ? But the first question is not what we can achieve in this matter, or what it can mean for the other. The first question is what is to become of us if we do not listen to him, if we refuse to allow this penetration into our sphere either as a whole or in part. Whatever may happen to him, whether he is helped or not, or much or little, there he is and there I am : he in his new and strange and different form, so impenetrable and yet so near that I cannot escape him but have to see and have him, speaking to me and expecting to be admitted ; and I in my intolerable isolation (intolerable because it is threatened by his presence), in the seclusion in which I cannot maintain myself now that the encounter with him has taken place, hearing in my ears the words with which he is trying to impart himself to me. Even for my own sake, to save myself like the unjust judge, what option have I but to listen to what the other has to say to me, and therefore to open up myself and receive what he has to give ? So long as I do not stand under this compulsion, so long as I have not grasped that it is not just a matter of the other but of myself, so long as I can think that I can avoid hearing the other without harm to myself, I do not give a human hearing, even though humility may demand a thousand times that I hear only in part or not at all. Human hearing of the other takes place on the presupposition that I am affected myself if I do not hear him, and do so in all seriousness.

Drawing the various aspects together, we again emphasise that the human significance of speech, of the human mouth and human ear, depends absolutely upon the fact that man and his fellow speak to one another and listen to one another ; that the expression and address between I and Thou are reciprocal. As we can look past people, we can also talk past them and hear past them. When this happens, it always means that we are not in encounter and therefore inhuman. But we talk and hear past them when there is no reciprocity. Two men can talk together openly, exhaustively and earnestly. But if their words serve only their own needs, it may well be that as they talk together each is only trying to assure and help himself, so that they do not reach one another or speak to mutual advantage, but merely talk past one another. How can it be otherwise, how can they find each other, when they are not sought by one another, but each is merely speaking for himself and not for the other ? Two monologues do not constitute a dialogue. A dialogue, and therefore the humanity of the encounter of I and Thou, begins only when the spoken word becomes a means to seek and help the other in the difficulty which each entails for the other. On this presupposition the two do not merely speak together, in a commonly produced sound of words, but they genuinely talk with and to one another in human words. The converse is true in hearing. Two men may listen very openly and attentively and tensely to one another, but if there is not in both a genuine need to listen, if they merely listen but not honestly for their own sake, the words mutually spoken will not reach their goal, but their ears will be closed so that they hear past one another. This is inevitable. As hearers, we can find only what we seek. From this standpoint, a dialogue begins only when the hearers are concerned about themselves, about the removal of their own difficulty in respect of the other, so that the words of the other are received and welcomed as a help in this embarrassment. Without this presupposition, hearing is merely a common endurance of a commonly produced sound of words. Only on this presupposition is it mutual hearing, a hearing in which not only the words are human, but also the ears for which they are destined.

No specific proof is required to show that there is much practical justification for suspicion in relation to human words as such. Only words ! Nothing but words ! Empty words ! Words are " sound and fury." There is good cause for the disillusionment expressed in these phrases. Most of the words which we speak and hear obviously have nothing whatever to do with conversation between I and Thou, with the encounter of man and man, with the attempt to speak with one another and listen to one another, and therefore with humanity. Most of our words, spoken or heard, are an inhuman and barbaric affair because we will not speak or listen to one another. We speak them without wanting to seek or help. And we listen to them without letting ourselves be found or helped. This is the case not only in private conversation but in sermons, lectures and discussions, in books and articles. This is how we both hear and read. What we speak and write and hear and read is propaganda. And the result is that our words are emptied and devalued and become mere words. We live in a constant deflation of the word. Yet we have to realise that suspicion and disillusionment are not the way to improve things either here or anywhere. It is not the words that are really empty. It is men themselves when they speak and hear empty words. It is the I which is empty in relation to the Thou, one empty subject confronting another. What is not yet or no longer grasped is that neither I nor Thou can be human in isolation, but only in encounter, and that the word spoken and heard, which leads them both beyond a mere reciprocal view and notion, can be the means in the use of which they can both become human. As we speak with one another and listen to one another, we at least have the possibility for being in encounter, and thus stand on the threshold of humanity. So long as we can speak and hear, there is no compelling force to keep us without, no obstacle to the word spoken and heard finding its fulfilment in a proper use. With suspicion and disillusionment in relation to the word we basically turn our back on humanity. For this reason, although suspicion and disillusionment are no doubt justified in practice, we must not in any circumstances allow them house-room.

Being in encounter consists (3) in the fact that we render mutual assistance in the act of being. We now climb a step higher. There is a being for one another, however limited, even in the relationship of man and man in general. And human being is not human if it does not include this being for one another. As openness between the I and the Thou, their reciprocal visibility, is only a preparatory stage to their mutual expression and address, so the latter cannot be an end, but only the means to something higher, to fellowship in which the one is not only knowable by the other, but is there for him, at his disposal within the necessary limits. Perhaps being in encounter, humanity, is very restricted and broken at the lower levels ; perhaps so little is known in practice about saving openness and therefore real speaking and hearing between one man and another, because even at the lower levels it is a matter of the way to this higher. We see that it is this higher which claims us. We must see and be seen, speak and listen, because to be human we must be prepared to be there for the other, to be at his disposal. We thus hesitate. We are afraid. This is too much to ask. And because this is too much, everything that leads to it is too much : sincere seeing and letting oneself be seen ; sincere speech between man and man. There is indeed a necessary connexion at this point. If I and Thou really see each other and speak with one another and listen to one another, inevitably they mutually summon each other to action. At this higher level it is a matter of the human significance of human activity. If our activity is to be human, this is not guaranteed merely by the fact that it is determined in form by human understanding and volition, art or technique. No degree of perfection which it may have in these respects can ensure that it is not an empty subject which is at work, the man who, because he is without his fellow-man, has not become human, who has not discovered the relationship of I and Thou and therefore himself, who has not become a real I. He may be engaged in the most forceful action both intensively and extensively, and yet he lacks everything for true humanity if he lacks the one thing—that he is not in encounter, and is not therefore human, and has no real part in humanity. Action in encounter is action in correspondence with the summons which the Thou issues to the I when it encounters it, and therefore (for everything is reciprocal in this matter) in correspondence with the summons which the I for its part issues to the Thou in this encounter. The humanity of my activity includes both the fact that I act as one who has received the call of the other and also the fact that I do so as one who has called and must continually call the other. The distinction between human activity and inhuman is not the same as that between altruistic and egoistic. Egoistic activity—for there is a healthy egoism —can be thoroughly human if, without denying itself as such, it is placed at the service of the summons issued by the Thou to the I. And altruistic activity—for there is an unhealthy altruism—can be supremely inhuman if it does not derive from the summons of the one to the other, but the one acts under the illusion that he does not need the other just as much as the other now seems to need him. Action, and therefore being in encounter, and therefore human action, carries with it the twofold correspondence that the other has summoned me and I him ; that he really needs me and I him ; that I act as one who is called but who also calls. This is the higher thing which is decisive beyond mere reciprocal sight and speech and hearing ; the fellowship to which these preliminary stages necessarily lead. It consists in the fact that the one is at the disposal of the other in his activity, and *vice versa*. It is this fellowship—and there is still, of course, a good deal more to be said concerning it—which leads the encounter of I and Thou to its goal and makes human being human. It is actualised concretely in the fact that we render mutual assistance in the act of our being. View and concept are necessarily limited. We cannot replace one another. I cannot be Thou, nor canst Thou live my life. I cannot accept thy responsibility, nor Thou mine. For I and Thou are not inter-changeable. I and Thou are ultimate creaturely reality in their distinction as well as their relationship. If the man Jesus, even though He is Himself, is for us in the strictest sense, living for us, accepting responsibility for us, in this respect, acting as the Son of God in the power of the Creator, He differs from us. This is His prerogative, and no other man can be compared with Him. Correspondence to His being and action consists in the more limited fact that we render mutual assistance. This correspondence is, of course, necessary. Measured by the man Jesus, humanity cannot be less than this for any of us. If our action is human, this means that it is an action in which we give and receive assistance. An action in which assistance is either withheld or rejected is inhuman. For either way it means isolation and persistence in isolation. Only the empty subject can be guilty of such isolation, refusing either to give assistance or to accept it. Only the action of the empty subject and not real man can be autarchic. The more autarchy there is, the more dangerously we skirt the frontier of inhumanity. The more humanity there is, the more the autarchy of our action is pierced. Assistance is actively standing by the other. It is standing so close by him that one's own action means help or support for his. It thus means not to leave him to his own being and action, but in and with one's own to take part in the question and anxiety and burden of his, accepting concern for his life, even though it must always be his and we cannot represent him. Assistance means to live with the other. As we see one another and speak and listen to one another, we call to one another for assistance. As man, as the creature of God, man needs this assistance, and can only call for it. And as man, as the creature of God, he is able and ordained to render assistance to his fellow-man and to receive it from him. God alone, and the man Jesus as the Son of God, has no need of assistance, and is thus able to render far more than assistance to man, namely, to represent him. For us, however, humanity consists in the fact that we need and are capable of mutual assistance. In the very fact that he lives, man calls to his fellow not to leave him alone or to his own devices. He knows well enough that he has to live his own life and bear responsibility for it. But he also knows that he cannot do this if his fellow does not spring to his side and give him his hand and actively stand by him. He cannot be for him in the strict sense. This is possible only for God. But he can be at his disposal. He can be so near to him that his being supports though it does not carry him ; that he gives him comfort and encouragement though not victory and triumph ; that he alleviates though he does not liberate. In the very fact that he lives, man calls for this help that only his fellow-man can give—the being which is in the same position, which can know him, which can enter into his situation and prescribe and offer the help required. No other being can come so near as to offer what is needed in the way of help. No other can know him so well, or see him as he is, or speak with him and listen to him. And so—in so far as he calls for assistance and not for that which God alone can give—he calls to his fellow-man. An action is human in which a man, even as he tries to help himself, also

summons the help of his fellow, reaching out for the support which
he alone can give. His action might seem to be very noble but it is
not human if he really thinks that he can be self-sufficient and refuses
to ask for help. In this very likeness to God he becomes inhuman.
In this apparent nobility he falls into the abyss. Nor is this because
there is no one to help. This might sometimes be the case, and it
only goes to show how much that help is needed. But primarily it is
because he betrays and denies his own being with his pretended self-
sufficiency. Turning his back on the helping Thou he cannot be an I.
He is transformed and dissolved into an empty subject. And he is
thus plunged into misery even though in spite of his perversion a
hundred helping hands are stretched out to him on all sides. If we
will not let ourselves be helped, others cannot help us however much
they would like to do so. My humanity depends upon the fact that I
am always aware, and my action is determined by the awareness,
that I need the assistance of others as a fish needs water. It depends
upon my not being content with what I can do for myself, but calling
for the Thou to give me the benefit of his action as well.

The other aspect of the same situation follows a similar pattern.
In the very fact that he lives a man is summoned by his fellow-man.
The latter does not wish to be left alone or to his own devices in his
action. I cannot represent him. I cannot make his life-task my own.
He cannot expect this from me. He must not confuse me with God.
And he will certainly have no reason to do so. I must try to help
myself, and he will have to do the same. But as he tries to do so, he
has the right to expect that I shall be there for him as well as myself,
that I shall not ignore him but live with him, that my life will be a
support for his, that it will mean comfort, encouragement and alleviation for him. This is what he requests. His whole action is always this
call for my assistance. And as I act for my part, I always stand under
this expectation ; this cry for help always reaches me. Perhaps I
will not look him too straight in the eye, or let him look too straight
into mine ; perhaps I will not speak too sincerely with him, or listen
too sincerely to him, because to look straight and speak sincerely
is at once—and the more sincerely the more compellingly—to accept
this cry for help. I may do so willingly or unwillingly, well or badly,
but the cry goes out and somehow reaches me. I am not a thing, nor
is my fellow. But as a man I have a direct awareness that my fellow—
in the same position as myself—stretches out his hand to me and seeks
my support. I know that he too is not God and cannot therefore be
self-sufficient. And I also know that what he expects of me—namely,
a little support—does not exceed my powers, that this little assistance
is not in any sense a divine but a very human work which may rightly
be expected, that I am able to render it, and under an obligation to
do so. I cannot evade my fellow who asks for it. I must stand by
him and help him. I become inhuman if I resist this awareness or

try to escape the limited but definite service I can render. The humanity of my action is again at stake, and therefore I myself. An action is human when a man who must help himself either well or badly also accepts the call for help issued by another and gives his need a place in the determination of his own action. My action is human when the outstretched hand of the other does not grope in the void but finds in mine the support which is asked. It is inhuman if I am content merely to help myself. It is to be noted that I do not plunge the other but myself into perdition, namely, inhumanity, if I refuse him my support and do not do the modest thing which I could do. If he has called and claimed me, he has done what he can for the humanity of his action. It is I who am affected if I withhold my help. As much as in him lies, he is in encounter. But I am not. I am without the Thou. And therefore I cannot be an I. I transform myself on this side into an empty subject. I am in misery. I am the void in which the other gropes. I am thus a futile being, however perfect may be the help which I give myself, thus satisfying my own needs. If we will not help others, there is no help even in the most perfect self-help. My humanity depends upon the fact that I am always aware, and my action is determined by the awareness, that I need to give my assistance to the Thou as a fish needs water. It depends upon my answering the call of the other, and acting on his behalf, even in and with what I do for myself.

For an understanding of this third step, which is as it were the goal of all that we have so far said, it is to be noted that humanity is not an ideal nor its exercise a virtue. We do not speak of man imagined on the basis of a hypothesis, whose picture we have to fill out, and yet can always escape with the excuse that real man is very different. We are not guilty of idealisation when we say of man that he is created and ordained to receive help from his fellow-man and to give help to his fellow-man. We are speaking of real man. And we are speaking of him realistically, whereas all the descriptions of man in which the presupposition is normative of an empty subject isolated from the fellow-man can only be called idealistic in the wrong sense. For in them, in more or less consistent approximation to Zarathustra, the reference is to a man who does not and cannot exist, but can only be the vision of a maniac. The counterpart of the man Jesus ; the picture of man who, although he is not God, is adopted by God in the man Jesus ; the picture of the man whom God is for as He is for the man Jesus ; the picture of this man is the realistic picture of real man. No optimistic law or lofty aim is given us on this view, but the primitive factuality of our situation as it is—that man is not alone, but with his fellow-man, needing his help and pledged to help him. Is there anything extraordinary in this demand ? Is there any real demand at all ? Can there be any virtue merely in accepting our true situation ? The only extraordinary thing, the only demand, would be the madness and folly of leaving this situation, of ceasing to be human. To be human, and therefore to act accordingly, confessing both the need of assistance and the willingness to render it, is supremely natural and not unnatural. It is the most obvious thing to do, whereas the opposite is by far the most artificial. What is demanded is simply that man should not wander away but be himself in the best sense of the term, keeping to the determination which he has been given as a man. It is to be noted that at the place and in the form in which Christian anthropology sees him man cannot make the favourite excuse that too much is expected of him, that he is given too high and holy a destiny. On the contrary, all that he has to do is simply to see himself in the situation in which he actually finds himself, keeping to this situation, and not trying to adapt himself to any other.

But being in encounter consists (4) in the fact that all the occurrence which we have so far described as the basic form of humanity stands under the sign that it is done on both sides with gladness. We gladly see and are seen ; we gladly speak and listen ; we gladly receive and offer assistance. This can be called the last and final step of humanity. Or, we might equally well say, this is the secret of the whole, and therefore of the three preceding stages. Our description of the three preceding stages still lacks a certain dimension without the underscoring of which we still fall short of the human as such. All that we have so far said about the relationship of I and Thou, and therefore the basic form of humanity, however realistic outwardly the picture of real man, might seem to be no more than the description of a fairly complicated mechanism, or, more organically, of a perfect flower unfortunately detached from its roots. I see the Thou and am pleased to be seen by him. I speak with him and hear as he speaks with me. I need him, and see that he needs me. But all this may take place and be understood and yet leave a great unseen lacuna which must be filled if there is to be true and serious humanity. It may all be merely an inhuman description of the human. It may all lack a decisive, all-animating and motivating dynamic, and therefore the real substance or soul of the human without which all the humanity of our being, however perfect externally, is only external, but internally and properly and essentially is inhuman. In conclusion, therefore, we shall try to incorporate this true and inward element into our picture of real man, of human man, expressly asking concerning the dynamic, the substance or soul of it all, and therefore the secret of humanity.

There must be no confusion. We ask concerning the secret of humanity as such. We presuppose that it is the humanity of the man whose determination is to be the covenant-partner of God. It is the great secret of man that he belongs to God, that God is for him, and for him in the person of the man Jesus. We do not now speak of this great mystery, but of the lesser yet not inconsiderable secret of his humanity, of his human nature, as this is fashioned in correspondence with his determination for covenant-partnership with God. It would not correspond to this determination if it did not contain within itself as such a secret. Because it corresponds to the determination of man, and therefore to the great secret, we must ask concerning its own lesser and in some sense immanent secret. There is no sense in trying to dispute this secret. We do not really honour the great secret of man, which consists in his relationship to God, by ignoring the fact that the man who enters into this relationship to God is fashioned by the same God in such a way that even in his creaturely mode of existence as such, and therefore in his humanity, he is not without mystery, but the bearer, executor and guardian of a secret which is not inconsiderable in its own place and manner.

We cannot solve the mystery as such. That is to say, we can only show that it is a secret by our attempt to describe it. But after all, has not all that we have said concerning humanity been more in the nature of indication than direct description? Has not all that we have finally said concerning the human significance of the eye and mouth and ear and action pointed beyond itself to something decisive which is itself concealed, so that although we can point to it we cannot pinpoint it? If, then, we turn to consider this decisive thing as such, this can only mean that we admit that in our whole description of humanity we can only denote and indicate its final derivation and true essence. With all that we can say we merely point to something inward and hidden which is the meaning and power of its describable exterior. We everywhere point to its secret. And we must now do this expressly, and therefore in the form of a particular discussion, and to that extent in relation to a final and supreme level of the concept of humanity.

The obvious lacuna in our description of humanity consists, however, in the fact that we have not explicitly affirmed that being in encounter, in which we have seen the basic form of humanity, is a being which is gladly actualised by man. I think that this unpretentious word " gladly," while it does not penetrate the secret before which we stand, does at least indicate it correctly as the *conditio sine qua non* of humanity.

The alternative to " gladly " is not " reluctantly " but " neutrally " —which means that I am free to choose between " gladly " and " reluctantly." Do I really have the choice of actualising being in the encounter between I and Thou either gladly or reluctantly? Am I in some sense free to do justice either gladly or reluctantly to the human significance of eyes and mouth and ear and action, and therefore of my whole relationship to the Thou, of which we have been considering the positive content? Can I in some way have both possibilities at my disposal, reserving them both for myself? If we describe the humanity of man in terms such as these, even though we may have had a true perception of the earlier stages, and have portrayed them correctly, we have obviously not taken it seriously as a determination of the true being of man, of man himself. We are still (or again) looking past real man, who is not capable of this reservation and control.

For what would this neutrality between gladly and reluctantly really mean? It would mean that the being of man in encounter is a real fact, the actual situation in which he finds himself and cannot outwardly escape without self-alienation. If he is to do justice to his situation, and therefore to himself, he has thus no option but to keep to the fact, with all that it involves, that the I is ordered in relation to the Thou and the Thou to the I, and that this order must be realised. He thus subjects himself to this order as to an ineluctable law of nature. He actualises the reciprocal openness, the reciprocal self-expression and address, the reciprocal assistance, and therefore the whole concept of humanity to the best of his knowledge and conscience, well aware that he has no real option. But he does have one option, and may leave it open, namely, whether he does it all gladly or reluctantly. In his innermost being, or—to use the popular, and biblical, and very expressive phrase—in his heart, he remains at a point above the gladly or reluctantly, from which he can decide either for the one or the other ; either for or against a spontaneous acceptance of this encounter ; either for or against a willing participation in the Thou ; either for or against an inner Yes as the motive of this participation. The law is thus binding, but only externally. Basically and properly it is not binding. He can affirm and fulfil it as a law which is not his own but an alien law, not established by himself but laid upon him and prescribed for him.

If we accept this view, at the last hour we take a decision which compromises all that we have said and apparently secured. For the unavoidable implication is that the mutual relationship of I and Thou is only an accidental *fact* of human existence, although inescapable and to be respected only as such, but that it does not finally effect the essence of man, man himself, since it is alien to his innermost being. In his essence, his innermost being, his heart, he is only what he is gladly. If we do not speak primarily of what he is gladly, we do not speak of his essence, of himself. If it is an open question whether he is human and engaged in the encounter of I and Thou gladly or reluctantly, this means no more and no less than that it does not belong to his essence as man to be human. He is it in fact, because he has no option in the unavoidable presence of his fellow-man. But in himself he might not be. At bottom, in the innermost recesses of his proper self, he is not. Humanity is alien to him. It is a kind of hat which he can put on and take off. It is not intrinsic to him. It is not the law which he prescribes for himself as a man. It is not the freedom in which he draws his first breath. His first and true freedom is the strange freedom of choice in which he can satisfy the law laid upon him from without either gladly or reluctantly. He breathes first in this freedom, not in the freedom to do justice to his humanity gladly. And this means that, even if he does justice to his humanity, and does it gladly, it is without root, without dynamic, without substance, without soul.

The secret of his humanity, however, is that in his being in the encounter of I and Thou we do not have to do with a determination which is accidental and later imposed from without, but with a self-determination which is free and intrinsic to his essence. He is not a man first, and then has his fellow-man alongside him, and is gladly or reluctantly human, i.e., in encounter with him. He is a man as he is human, and gladly in the sense that there can be no question of a "reluctantly." He is unequivocally and radically human. He follows the voice and impulse of his own heart when he is human, when he looks the other in the eye, when he speaks with him and listens to him, when he receives and offers assistance. There are no secret hiding-places or recesses, no dark forest-depths, where deep down he wills or can will anything else. He himself is human. He himself, in the sense described in those three stages, is not without but with his fellow-man. He would not be a man if he were without and not with his fellow-man. This is the great lacuna in our previous exposition which we must now fill to the best of our ability. This is the dimension which we must now especially and expressly indicate.

That man is not without his fellow-man is not an accident which overtakes him. It is no mere contingent fact. It is not a given factor with which he must arbitrarily wrestle and to which he must somehow adjust himself. From the very outset, as man, he is not without but with his fellow-man. Nor is he one essence with his fellow-man. He is with him in the sense that he is one being and his fellow-man another. We have always had occasion, and have so now, to remember that I am I and Thou Thou ; that Thou art Thou and not I. In humanity it is not a question of the removal and dissolution but the confirmation and exercise of duality as such. At this point, as in the relationship with God, identity-mysticism is not the way to do justice to the facts. Man and fellow-man, I and Thou—this means mutual limitation. But in this relationship, which is not a relationship of things but the very different relationship of people, limitation means mutual determination. And this determination is inward as well as outward. It is not therefore added to his essence, to the man himself, as though it were originally and properly alien to him and he to it, and at some level of his being he were not determined by it. He is not free in relation to it, but as he is determined by it. He is himself in this determination. The externality of the different fellow-man who encounters me has this in common with the very different externality of the God distinct from me—that it is also inward to me ; inward in the sense that this external thing, the other man, is inward and intrinsic to me even in his otherness. Man is not the fellow-man, but he is with him. I am not Thou, but I am with Thee. Humanity is the realisation of this "with." As two men look one another in the eye, and speak with one another and listen to one another, and render mutual assistance, they are together. But everything depends on whether they are not merely together under a law imposed from without, or merely accepting an unavoidable situation. To be sure, there is a law here—the law of the Creator imposed as such on the creature. And there is a situation in which man finds himself—created by the fact that he is not alone, but the fellow-man is present with him. But that law of God is given him as his own law, the law which he himself has set up, the law of his own freedom. Only as such is its validity genuine according to the intention of its Giver. Valid in any other way, it would be obeyed by man, but only as an alien law imposed from without and not as his own law. It would not, therefore, be obeyed gladly. Man would know the other possibility of either not obeying it at all or doing so reluctantly because he himself wills or can will something very different. It would not, then, be valid or known at all. But if he does not really know it, this means that he does not know himself. He is not himself but lost outside himself. For he is himself as he stands under this law as the law of his own freedom. When he is obedient to it in this way, as to the law of his own freedom, he realises that " with "—with the fellow-man, with the Thou—by inner as well as outer necessity, and therefore gladly and spontaneously. Being together thus acquires the character of something absolutely spontaneous. The fellow-man is not merely imposed or thrust upon man, or the Thou upon the I, so that the encounter has almost the instinctive form of a " falling-out," i.e., of a secret or open reversal of encounter, or movement of retreat, in which a hasty greeting is exchanged and then the one seeks safety as quickly as possible from the other, withdrawing into himself for fear of violation and in the interest of self-assertion. On the contrary, the fellow-man belongs to man, the Thou to the I, and is therefore welcome, even in his otherness and particularity. I have waited for Thee. I sought Thee before Thou didst encounter me. I had Thee in view even before I knew Thee. The encounter with Thee is not, therefore, the encounter with something strange which disturbs me, but with a counterpart which I have lacked and without which I would be empty and futile. The situation between man and man is genuinely inescapable, and I do real justice to it, only if it is not subject to my caprice even in the sense that I am not free inwardly to accept or reject it, but can only accept it, knowing that it is only and exclusively in this situation that I am myself, and can act as such. Humanity is the realisation of this togetherness of man and man grounded in human freedom and necessary in this freedom.

We have to safeguard this statement against two misunderstandings. The first in this. Humanity in the highest sense cannot consist in the fact that the one loses himself in the other, surrendering or forgetting or neglecting his own life and task and responsibility, making himself a mere copy of the other, and the life and task and responsibility of the other a framework for his own life. Man is bound to his fellow-man, but he cannot belong to him, i.e., he cannot be his property. This is impossible because if he did he would not see and recognise in him what he is to him, namely, the other. In paying him what seems to be so great an honour, he would pay him too little. In asking what is apparently so complete a self-sacrifice, he would withhold himself. He would encroach too much upon him by changing the encounter with him into a union. He would force himself upon him, and thus become a burden commensurate neither with the dignity nor powers of the other. We cannot subject ourselves to a fellow-man without doing him the deepest injury. For what he can expect of me as another cannot be that I should cease to be his Thou, and therefore to stand before him in my distinction from him. What he gladly and in freedom desires of me is that I should be with him. But I escape him if I lose myself in him, ceasing to be for him a genuine counterpart. He intends and seeks me in my uniqueness and irreplaceability, as a being standing and moving on its own feet. He has no use for a mere adaptation to himself, existing only in dependence on him. I thus escape my fellow-man if I depend on him. He cannot accept this gladly. And the result will be that, unable to use me, he will repulse me, startled by this encounter which is no true encounter, and withdrawing into himself or even turning against me. Make no mistake, there is an excessive relationship to the fellow-man in which the very relationship in which humanity ought to be attained is supremely inhuman because it is not realised that it can arise and persist only in two-sided freedom, and not in the bondage of the one for the sake of the freedom of the other. To belong to another is man's bondage. If I am his property, I am no longer with him gladly. Our being together has become a constraint to which I myself am subject and which I seek to lay on the other. But in this togetherness of mutual constraint I can only at bottom despise myself and cause myself to be despised by the other, having first despised the other by encroaching too much upon him. Humanity is thus the realisation of this togetherness only when I do not lose but maintain myself in it, living my own life with the other, accepting my own task and responsibility, and thus keeping and not overrunning the proper distance between us.

The second misunderstanding is the direct opposite. Humanity in the highest sense cannot consist in the fact that the one only intends and seeks in the other himself, and thus uses the encounter with him to extend and enrich and deepen and confirm and secure his own being. Being in encounter is no more active subjection than passive. It has nothing whatever to do with a campaign of conquest as in cheap love-stories. If I want the other for myself, I do better to stay at home. For there can be no worse self-deception than to desire to be with the other in order to find myself in him. In so doing, do I not forget even my own uniqueness and irreplaceability? I cannot find myself in the other, nor is this what I can intend and seek and strive after gladly and in the necessity of my own freedom. If in the other I seek myself at a higher or deeper level, the Thou is for me merely my extended I. I do not respect it as a being which does not belong to me but must be true to itself and not violated. And in these circumstances I experience something which I can experience only reluctantly, namely, that I am really quite alone even with this

Thou which I have supposedly conquered and appropriated and made my own. Moreover, I have missed the opportunity of experiencing what I might have experienced gladly. In violating the freedom of the other, I have forfeited my own. I have despised him, and in so doing I have basically despised myself. The fellow-man is bound to me only in the sense that he does not belong to me. If I treat him as though he were my own property, he is no longer bound to me. And I need not then be surprised if the supposed and false coming together is really a falling-out, and the encounter between us sooner or later becomes a mutual attack or a mutual withdrawal. Because the relationship has an excessive form, it is wrong from the very first, and the attempt to realise it is bound to end in failure.

The way of humanity, and therefore the way to realise the togetherness of man grounded in human freedom and necessary in this freedom, does not lie between these two misunderstandings but above them. In a togetherness which is accepted gladly and in freedom man is neither a slave nor a tyrant, and the fellow-man is neither a slave nor tyrant, but both are companions, associates, comrades, fellows and helpmates. As such they are indispensable to one another. As such they intend and expect and seek one another. As such they cannot be without one another. As such they look one another in the eye, and speak and listen to one another, and render mutual assistance. All this is impossible if they meet as tyrant and slave. Between tyrant and slave there is no genuine encounter, and even genuine encounter ceases to be genuine to the extent that it is understood and actualised on the one side or the other as the encounter of tyrant and slave. Only in the atmosphere of freedom can it be genuine. Companions are free. So are associates. So are comrades. So are fellows. So are helpmates. Only what takes place between such as these is humanity.

What we indicate in this way is really the *secret* of humanity. For here we have to do with an element in the concept which, in contrast to those previously mentioned, cannot be described or at any rate grounded or deduced from elsewhere, but can only be affirmed as the living centre of the whole. At a pinch we can describe, and have tried to do so, how the encounter takes place between men who meet gladly and in freedom, how they open up themselves to one another, and speak with one another, and listen to one another, and help one another. But in so doing we presuppose as the living centre of the whole the decisive point that they meet gladly and in freedom, not as tyrants and slaves, but as companions, associates, comrades, fellows and helpmates. But how are we to describe this decisive thing? We can say of what takes place between men only something to the following effect—that there is a discovery, the mutual recognition that each is essential to the other. There is thus enacted the paradox that the one is unique and irreplaceable for the other. But this means that there is also an electing and election. Each can affirm the other as the being with which he wants to be and cannot be without. But this leads to mutual joy, each in the existence of the other and both in the fact that they can exist together. For in these circumstances even the co-existence is joy. The fact remains that common existence is still something posited and given, but this givenness is now clear and vital in an active willing of this fellowship, a willing which derives quite simply from the fact that each has received a gift which he necessarily desires to reciprocate to the best of his ability. And if it is asked in what this gift consists, the answer must be that the one has quite simply been given the other, and that what he for his part has to give is again himself. It is in this being given and giving that there consists the electing and election, the mutual acceptance, the common joy, and therefore the freedom of this encounter—the freedom in which there is no room for those misunderstandings, in which both can breathe as they let breathe, in which both keep their distance because they are so close, and are so close because they can keep their distance. But what else is the discovery but the discovery how great and unfathomable and inexpressible is the secret that this may be so. The fact that it may be so, the why and wherefore of it, is never understood. It is simply effected without disclosing itself. It is a pure fact, inward as well as outward. It is the truth of the situation, not only of an outward but also of an inward and mutually recognised or established situation. Thus all words fail at the decisive point. And they fail at the point where we have to describe how and why each man has his own creaturely existence, and is this particular man in fulfilment of it, and continually rediscovers himself as such. Even what is to be discovered at this point is a riddle to which there is no key apart from faith in God the Creator. Nor do we have here two points, two discoveries, two mysteries. For that which cannot be fathomed or expressed, but only established in the fulfilment of our existence, is the one secret of humanity. Man discovers the uniqueness and irreplaceability of the other man in his actuality as the companion, associate, comrade, fellow and helpmate which he is given, and in this way and this way alone, in all the necessity of the presence of this other, he discovers his own uniqueness and irreplaceability, and therefore his own being and actuality as a man. Or conversely, he discovers himself as this particular man existing for himself, and in this way and this way alone, in all the necessity of his own existence, he discovers the other man as the being which is with him and to which he for his part has to give himself as a companion, associate, comrade, fellow and helpmate. Humanity lives and moves and has its being in this freedom to be oneself with the other, and oneself to be with the other.

At this fourth stage we are really speaking of the *conditio sine qua non* of humanity, just because we can only talk around the subject, and cannot describe anything, but only point to something hidden. What we have here is not just an optional addition to the whole, a beautiful crown finally adorning humanity but not indispensable. No, if humanity does not consist first and last in this freedom, it does not exist at all. All true openness, and reciprocal speech and hearing, and mutual assistance, has its basis and stability in this dynamic thing, and all that can be described in this indescribable. If the encounter of I and Thou lacked the secret of this freedom, if its whole realisation were merely external and in some sense hollow, how could it be genuine and effective ? From the very outset we have tried to represent it in its genuineness and force, and not as a mere mechanism or empty form which might have another content than true humanity. We must now expressly add that the presupposition, if we have not described an empty form, is that which we have finally indicated with our reference to freedom as the secret of being in encounter and therefore the secret of humanity. What we have described—openness, and speech and hearing, and mutual assistance—can be real only when there is also this discovery between man and man, and the necessity of this " gladly," this freedom, rules in their seeing and being seen, their speech and hearing, their reciprocal help. This is not merely the crown of humanity, but its root.

But this means that if we are to embrace human nature as such, as created and given by God, then we must grasp as its motivating element the decisive point that man is essentially determined to be with his fellow-man gladly, in the indicated freedom of the heart. By nature he has no possibility or point of departure for any other choice. If we have to maintain that he has this choice in fact, it does not derive from his nature. For we cannot make God his Creator responsible for this fatal possibility. And it is even worse if we praise the Creator for obviously giving man the possibility of a different choice. For this is to praise Him for allowing and enabling man to choose in his heart inhumanity as well as humanity, and therefore to be in his heart inhuman as well as human, or both perhaps alternately. And we then ascribe to human nature the strange distinction of a freedom for its own denial and destruction. We should not call this freedom nature, but sin. And we should not connect it with God the Creator or the creaturely essence of man, but with man's irrational and inexplicable apostasy from God and from himself. It is the man who has fallen away from God and from himself who thinks that he can find his essence in that false freedom and therefore himself in an original isolation from which he emerges either gladly or reluctantly to be with his fellow-man. Real man as God created him is not in the waste of isolation. He does not have this choice. He does not need to emerge from this waste. It is not just subsequently, and therefore not with final seriousness, that he is with his fellow-man. His freedom consists from the very outset in his intending and seeking this other, not to be his tyrant or slave, but his companion, associate, comrade, fellow and helpmate, and that the other may be the same to him. As we call this humanity, and say that everything which belongs to humanity has both its culmination and root in this one thing, we must call this human nature. Human nature is man himself. But man is what he is freely and from the heart. And freely and from the heart he is what he is in the secret of the encounter with his fellow-man in which the latter is welcome and he is with him gladly.

We have now reached a provisional conclusion in our investigation. What we shall have to say in our third sub-section will not add anything material to it. All that we can do is to establish a definite and unequivocal form of being in the encounter of I and Thou, namely, being in the encounter of man and woman. But first, in relation to our present theme, we must fill out what we have said on the fourth and final level of humanity by a critical observation. At this final level of the concept of humanity we have not been speaking about Christian love.

In the light of the Word of God and on the presupposition of the given divine reality of revelation, i.e., of the humanity of the man Jesus, we have been speaking about the creaturely essence of man, human nature. On this basis, we could not say anything other or less of man than that by nature he is determined for his fellow-man, to be with him gladly. It would be inadmissible to describe man as a being to which this determination does not radically belong but is alien. A being to which it was alien would be different by nature from the man Jesus. If man were a being of this kind, we should either have to say that only the man Jesus was real man as God created him, or that Jesus was not a real man at all, but a being of a different order. If, however, there is similarity as well as dissimilarity between him and us, to His being *for* others there must correspond as at least a minimum on our side the fact that our human being is at root a free being *with* others. This is what we have maintained as the secret of humanity.

We do not associate ourselves, therefore, with the common theological practice of depreciating human nature as much as possible in order to oppose to it the more effectively what may be made of man by divine grace. Orientation by the picture of the man Jesus shows us a very definite way from which we must not be frightened by the danger of meeting the false propositions of Roman Catholicism, humanism or natural theology. If we accept this orientation, what we think and say cannot be false. But it may well be so if we arbitrarily try to avoid certain conclusions. That there is a human nature created by God and therefore good and not evil must be accepted as we see man against the background of the man Jesus. It is not by nature, but by its denial and misuse, that man is as alien and opposed to the grace of God as we see him to be in fact. But rightly to appreciate this corruption brought about by man, and therefore the sin of man, we must quietly consider what is corrupted, and calmly maintain that all the corruption of man cannot make evil by nature the good work of God. It is because the secret of humanity remains even when it is shamed by man that sin is always such an inconceivable revolt, and never loses the character of a crime, or becomes a kind of second natural state which is excusable as such. But this enables us to see and understand why the mercy of God to man is not an act of caprice but has its sure basis in the fact that man is not a stranger or lost to his Creator even as a sinner, but in respect of his nature, of the secret of his humanity, still confronts him as he was created. Becoming a sinner, he has not vanished as a man, or changed into a different being, but still stands before God as the being as which he was created, and therefore as the being whose nature consists in that freedom. And as God makes Himself his Deliverer, He merely exercises His faithfulness as the Creator to His creature, which has not become different or been lost to Him by its fall into sin. This does not mean that by ascribing to man this secret of his humanity as an indestructible determination of his nature we concede to him a power to save himself or even to co-operate in his salvation. This is where the false propositions of Roman Catholicism and humanism arise, and we must be on our guard against them. How can it save a man, or what can it contribute to his salvation, that even as a sinner he is a man, and therefore has the manner of a man ? God alone saves and pardons and renews him, and He does so in free mercy. Yet we have still to point to the fact that that secret is proper to man as an indestructible determination of his nature, for to deny this truth would be to deny the continuity of the human subject as a creature, a sinner, and a sinner saved by grace. Our christological starting-point gives us no reason to make this denial. In what we have said, we do not ascribe to man more than belongs to him on this basis. To contest what is proper to him on this basis is hardly to magnify the glory of God and His grace.

But we have not been speaking of Christian love. New Testament ἀγάπη is not a determination of human nature as such. It is the action and attitude of the man who only becomes real and can only be understood in the course of his history with God. Love is the new gratitude of those who have come to know God the Creator as the merciful Deliverer. As such it is the gracious gift of the Holy Ghost shed abroad in the hearts of Christians convicted of sin against God and outrage against themselves, and to that extent lost, but assured of their justification and preservation in faith in Jesus Christ (Rom. 5⁵). In love they respond to the revelation of the covenant fulfilled in Jesus Christ, in which God comes to them as their merciful Father, Lord and Judge, and they see their fellow-men as brothers and sisters, i.e., as those who have sinned with them and found grace with them. It is thus the turning to them of this particular love of God which in Christian love binds and keeps men together in common life and action. Christian love is humility before Him, obedience to Him, hope in Him, the commonly received freedom of those who know that they are born and created anew as His children and are called as His community to the common proclamation of His name. It is another matter that in love that freedom of the human creature and therefore the secret of humanity is also honoured. But the honour which it receives is a completely new one. In it, it is like a brand plucked from the burning. And it is seen in an unexpected and completely new light which has fallen upon it from above, from the God who has dealings with man, when it was previously wrapped in darkness through the sin of man. Christian love is the determination of the man who in the fulfilled covenant of God is snatched from the depth of his guilt and the misery of his consequent isolation from his fellow-man and exalted to life in fellowship with Jesus Christ as his Saviour and therefore to fellowship with his fellow-man. Love itself, and in love man, lives with his fellow-man on the basis of the revelation and knowledge of what God has done for His human creature ; on the basis of the forgiveness declared to and received by him, and his sanctification as it takes place in this justification. But it is not of this Christian love that we have been speaking.

On the contrary, we have been speaking of the nature of the human creature. The same man who in the course of his history with God, in the fulfilment of his fellowship with Jesus Christ, will also participate in and be capable of Christian love for God and his fellow-men as brothers, is as such this creature whose manner is that which we have come to know as humanity. Humanity, even as we finally spoke of it in the secret of that free co-existence of man and man, is not Christian love, but only the natural exercise and actualisation of human nature—something which formally is on the same level as the corresponding vital functions and natural determinations of other beings which are not men. The fact that a stone is a stone involves a definite nexus of chemical, physical and mathematical conditions and determinations. The fact that a plant is a plant involves a specific organic process. The fact that an animal is an animal involves a particular consciousness and spontaneity in this vital process. But the fact that a man is a man involves freedom in the co-existence of man and man in which the one may be, and will be, the companion, associate, comrade, fellow and helpmate of the other. This is human nature, humanity. Down below, in and for himself, the man who is determined from above as the covenant-partner of God is the creature fashioned and determined and existing in this way. For all the differences in detail, he always lives with varying degrees of consistency and perfection the life characterised by this nature. It is to be expressly noted that we do not have here a gracious gift of the Holy Ghost for the possession of which he must be a Christian, or an operation of the Word of God directly proclaimed to man and directly received and believed by him. What we have called humanity can be present and known in varying degrees of perfection or imperfection even where there can be no question of a direct revelation and knowledge of Jesus Christ. This reality of human nature and its recognition are not, therefore, restricted to the Christian community, to the "children" of light, but, as we are told in Lk. 16⁸, the "children of this world" may in this respect be wiser than the children of light, being more human, and knowing more about humanity, than the often very inhuman and therefore foolish Christians. Of course, there is no reason why Christians too should not be human and know about humanity. But this is not what necessarily distinguishes them from other men. In this respect they may be at a disadvantage as compared with other men. At bottom, they are at one with them in this. Hence the totality which we have described as humanity is the determination of human being as such irrespective of what may become of man in the course of his history with God. We cannot, therefore, expect to hear about Christian love when the reference is to humanity in the Christian doctrine of the creature.

"Love never faileth" (1 Cor. 13⁸). It is the life of those who after the fall are restored by the grace of God, and as such a life which cannot be destroyed again, and is not threatened even by death and the end of the world. This is something which cannot be said of humanity and that secret of humanity. Humanity might fail. When man sins, his humanity does not disappear, but it is sick and blurred and perverted and destroyed and unrecognisable. And when man falls victim to death, a term is put even to his life in that freedom. If there were no deliverance from sin and death, if God would not acknowledge the creature in His mercy and keep it from destruction, the end of man would inevitably entail the end of his life in that secret and therefore the extirpation of that freedom. Only as love is shed abroad in our hearts as the love of God can humanity as the nature of man receive new honour and acquire a new stability. As it participates in love, it can and will never fail. We have not, therefore, spoken of that which in itself and as such, as the determination of man, is eternally secure even though man and the world perish. In the history of the covenant between God and man there are two determinations of man which do not belong at all to his creatureliness and therefore to his nature. The one is his determination by the inconceivable act of his own sin, and the other is his determination by the even more inconceivable act of the divine mercy. In his humanity as such there is to be found neither the reality nor even the possibility of his sin, and neither the reality nor even the possibility of divine grace. Hence even in the deepest secret of humanity to which we must continually point there cannot be ascribed to it what may be ascribed only to love.

Yet we must not cease to point to this secret. And it would be highly inappropriate if, to make the distinction between humanity and Christian love even clearer, we adopted a perverse standpoint in defining the concept of humanity, making no use of the Christian judgment, and therefore describing humanity perhaps in the sense of Idealism as humanity without the fellow-man, or as a mere co-existence of man and fellow-man, and therefore excluding from the concept that freedom of the heart in which man and fellow-man are together gladly, as though this freedom could arise only in the sphere of Christian love. To do this is not honest dealing. For how can we fail to see that even outwith the Christian sphere and quite apart from the concept of Christian love humanity is not necessarily present in that perverse and unfounded way, but for all the perverse and unfounded interpretations it is genuinely there, and is to be sought and found in the direction which we have taken. It would fare ill with theological anthropology if it were to fail to keep pace with attempts at something better as they have actually been made outside the sphere of the Church altogether; if in its anxiety not to depreciate grace and Christian love it were to propose a concept of humanity the falsity and untenability of which were immediately apparent even to the decided non-Christian. Surely nothing but the best and most securely grounded is good enough to describe the nature which God Himself has given to man. There is no reason for surprise that in the light of the divine grace shown in the existence of the man Jesus there has to be ascribed to human nature as much as we have actually ascribed to it in the development of our doctrine of humanity. Half-measures are obviously illegitimate at this point, and we are justified least of all by anxiety lest too little will remain for divine grace if we concede too much to human nature. In this respect theological anthropology has to go its own way, and as it pursues it resolutely to the end it is led to statements which are very similar to those in which humanity is described from a very different angle (e.g., by the pagan Confucius, the atheist L. Feuerbach and the Jew M. Buber). But does this constitute any good reason why we should not make them? Of course, if we look carefully, there can be no question of an exact correspondence and coincidence between the Christian statements and these others which rest on very different foundations. We need not be surprised that there are approximations and similarities. Indeed, in this very fact we may even see a certain confirmation of our results—a confirmation which we do not need and which will not cause us any particular excitement, but of which, in view of its occurrence, we shall not be ashamed. Why should there not be confirmations of this kind? In this context we are not speaking of the Christian in particular but of man in general, and therefore of something which has been the object of all kinds of " worldly," i.e., non-Christian wisdom. And surely it need not be, and is not actually, the case, that this worldly wisdom with its very different criteria has always been mistaken, always seeking humanity in the direction of Idealism and finally of Nietzsche, and therefore establishing and describing it as humanity without the fellow-man, the humanity of man in isolation. It would be far more strange if not the slightest trace had ever been found of fellow-humanity, of the humanity of I and Thou. Since we ourselves have reached the conclusion that the nature of man in himself and in general is to be found in this conception of humanity, we shall not take offence, but quietly see an indirect confirmation of our assertion, if we find that a certain knowledge of this conception was and is possible to man in general, even to the pagan, atheist and Jew, and that as *figura* shows it has actually been represented outwith Christian theology. Even with his natural knowledge of himself the natural man is still in the sphere of divine grace ; in the sphere in which Jesus too was man. How, then, can he lack a certain ability to have some better knowledge of himself as well as a good deal worse? But theological anthropology has the advantage over this better knowledge of the natural man that it possesses a criterion—its knowledge of divine grace and the man Jesus—which allows and commands it from the very outset and with final resoluteness and clarity to turn its back on that worse knowledge and ignorance, and from the very first and necessarily and therefore with final consistency to move in the direction of the conception of humanity and therefore of human nature according to which man as such and radically is not without but with the fellow-man, and his humanity at its deepest and highest level consists in the freedom of his heart for the other. As we quietly rejoice in the fact that in the general direction of our investigation and presentation we find ourselves in a certain agreement with the wisest of the wise of this world, we can equally quietly leave it undecided whether and to what extent they for their part follow us even to the final and decisive consequences of this conception, namely, to that " gladly," to that freedom of the heart between man and man as the root and crown of the concept of humanity. If they did not do this, as they surely seem to do in the case of Confucius, Feuerbach and Buber, it would certainly be made clear that *duo cum faciunt idem non est idem.* The difference between a Christian and every other anthropology would then emerge in the fact that even in respect of human nature we finally and decisively reach different conclusions. But we do not insist that this is necessarily so. We should not and do not take offence—" Is thine eye evil, because I am good ? "—if Confucius, Feuerbach and Buber finally had in view this freedom of the heart, and only failed by accident to tread it to its ultimate consequences, and thus to come to this final conclusion. What else can they have meant, or what other goal had in view, once they had taken the right direction of human duality ? At any rate, we have no reason not to welcome the proximity to some of the wiser of the wise of this world in which we in some degree find ourselves in this respect, and therefore we have no reason to allow this proximity to deflect us from the consistent pursuit of our own way.

But this brings me to the real point of this final critical observation. The Christian Church, Christianity, has every reason to take note of the reality which we have discovered in treading our own way of theological anthropology consistently to the end. Properly and at its deepest level, which is also its highest, human nature is not isolated but dual. It does not consist in the freedom of a heart closed to the fellow-man, but in that of a heart open to the fellow-man. It does not consist in the refusal of man to see the fellow-man and to be seen by him, to speak with him and listen to him, to receive his assistance and to render assistance to him. It does not consist in an indifference in which he might just as well be disposed for these things as not. But it consists in an unequivocal inclination for them. Man is human in the fact that he is with his fellow-man gladly. But in Christianity there is an inveterate and tenacious tendency to ignore or not to accept this ; not to know, or not to want to know, this reality of humanity. The reason is obvious, and has been mentioned already. It is thought that the grace of God will be magnified if man is represented as a blotted or best an empty page. But in the light of grace itself, of the connexion between the humanity of Jesus and humanity generally, this representation cannot be sustained. Man cannot be depicted as a blotted or empty page. The fatal consequence of this representation which we have seen to be theologically untenable is that real man as he is and is sometimes known to himself is not known in the Church, but in preaching, instruction and the cure of souls a picture of man is used which does not correspond to the reality, but to an erroneous figment of the imagination. And the consequence of this consequence is that real man cannot normally be reached from the Christian side either with what has to be said to him concerning the grace of God or with what has to be said concerning his own sin, because he simply does not recognise himself in the portrait held up to him on the Christian side. And then in what is said about the grace of God and especially Christian love there will probably be brought in that which was ignored and unrecognised as an attribute of human nature. That is to say, under the title of divine grace and Christian love there will probably be proclaimed the humanity which has to come in somewhere, and which will do so all the more forcefully if it is ignored and suppressed at the point where it ought to be mentioned. And the final result will be that the man addressed will conclude that he does not need the Christian Church and its message to know this, because he can know it of himself, or learn it from some of the wiser of the wise of this world. He will then either not hear at all the new and different thing which he ought to be told as that which is Christian, or he will not receive it as such, and either way he cannot take up the corresponding attitude in relation to it. It is no doubt right and good and even necessary that the Church should call him at least to humanity, but in so doing it does not discharge its real task. And it does not do this because it has failed to see that there is a humanity common to the Christian and non-Christian to which it must relate itself, which it must presuppose, which it must take into account in its message, with which it must contrast its message, and which it must above all know and take seriously as such. And if this humanity is overlooked or denied, when reference is made to sin man is probably accused at a point where he knows that he is fallible and imperfect but cannot honestly see himself as truly and radically evil in the Christian sense of sin. It may then be overlooked that even evil man in the Christian sense, the sinner, is capable of humanity in the sense of that freedom of the heart for others, and in a way which puts many Christians to shame, and that he does not really need to be shown from the Christian pulpit that he finds too little place for this freedom. Or it may happen, as it does, that from the pulpit an attempt is made to blacken even that which is human in him for all his wickedness, and with a more or less clear awareness of the truth he is forced to resist this attack. How can he accept a serious accusation in this respect, as the message of the Christian Church seems to demand ? He will rightly defend himself against what he is told. He will not be convicted of his sin if he is uncharitably—and falsely— addressed concerning his humanity. Just because humanity even at its root and crown is not identical with Christian love, and yet has its own different reality with this root and crown, Christianity has every reason to seek and tread other paths in this respect, and, in order to be able to do so, not to close its eyes any longer to the necessary insights.

I shall try to make this clear by reference to a point which has played a certain role in recent theological discussion and which is of supreme significance in relation to what has here been called the root and crown of humanity, namely, that " gladly," that freedom of the heart between man and man. No inconsiderable literature is now available on the contrast between *eros* and *agape*. The two can easily be played off the one against the other in history. In Greek religion, mysticism and philosophy, and above all in the ancient Greek feeling for life (cf. for what follows the article ἀγαπάω in *TWBzNT*), *eros* was the sum of the human fulfilment and exaltation of life, the experience, depicted and magnified with awe and rapture, of the end and beginning of all choice and volition, of being in transcendence of human being, of that which can take place in sensual or sexual (and thus in the narrower sense erotic) intoxication, but also in an inner spiritual encounter with the suprasensual and suprarational, with the incomprehensible yet present origin of all being and knowledge, in the encounter with the Godhead and union with it. *Eros* is humanity as dæmonism in both the lowest and the highest sense, and as such it is a kind of supreme divinity. According to Euripides it is the τύραννος θεῶν τε κάνθρώπων. According to Aristotle it is the power of attraction by which the original principle of all being is maintained in order and in motion. That is to say, it moves all being as it is itself that which is moved by it, the ἐρώμενον. *Eros* is the " universal love seeking satisfaction now at one point, now at another." It is the indefinite impulse, with no taint of decision or act, for an indefinite object, now one thing and now another. In its purest form it is an impulse from below upwards, from man to what is above him, to the divine. In any case, however, it is not a turning to the other for the other's sake, but the satisfying of the vital hunger of the one who loves, for whom the beloved, whether a thing, a man or the divine, is only as it were consumer goods, the means to an end. It needs little wit to see, or skill to prove, that this *eros* is very different from Christian love. That the realities denoted by the two terms are to be sought at very different levels emerges at once from the fact that the words ἔρως and ἐρᾶν are never used at all in the New Testament. We need not pursue this point in the present context. But because the insight and proof are easy, we are ill-advised to make the contrast a reason for not pressing on to a deeper knowledge of human nature or a more true and valid definition of the essence of humanity. From the fact that *agape* is not to be defined as *eros* it does not follow that humanity, the manner of the natural man, is to be defined as *eros* in this historical sense of the term. This is the conclusion on the basis of which there has been set up on the Christian side a picture of man which has nothing whatever to do with the reality of the natural man, and in which the latter finds it impossible to recognise himself. If Christian love cannot be seen in *eros*, it is also difficult—we naturally have to use a more cautious expression—to see humanity in it. In this *eros* of the Greeks there thrusts unmistakeably into the forefront of the picture Dionysius-Zarathustra, the superman, the man without his fellow-man, the great solitary, who at the peak of his aspiration must inevitably make the mistake of regarding himself as God and thus forfeit his humanity. In him, of course, the supreme freedom of man has already become tyranny and therefore slavery. According to our deliberations, a definition of humanity on the basis of its identification with this *eros* could only be called a bad definition. We make a bad start if we accept this bad definition, equating the being of natural man with this dæmonic form, and in this form contrasting it very rigidly but also very unprofitably with Christian love. Even natural man is not yet the Christian man, the man renewed by love as the gracious gift of the Holy Ghost. But does this mean that he is necessarily the man of this Greek *eros* ? As we have seen, *tertium datur*. The real natural man is the man who in the freedom of his heart is with his fellow-man. It is bad to be fascinated and transfixed as it were by the picture of erotic man in the Greek sense to which the picture of Christian man can be so easily—indeed, far too easily—opposed. The remarkable consequence of this far too simple opposition has been that in whole spheres of Christendom Christian love has been far too unthinkingly accepted merely as an antithesis to Greek *eros* and thus unconsciously depicted and extolled in the contours and colours of the original. At a first glance it is not easy to tell which of the two figures in Titian's famous painting is supposed to be heavenly love and which earthly. For the two sisters are so much alike. And in whole spheres of meditation and speculation on the part of Christian mystics, who have made so liberal a use of Plato and Plotinus, do we not have to ask seriously whether what is called *agape* is not really a spiritualised, idealised, sublimated and pious form of *eros*, an *eros* which was unacceptable in its original form, but from which it was impossible to break free, and which asserted itself all the more strongly ? In face of this repressed eroticism we do well to remember that there is a third factor, something which is neither *agape* nor *eros*, from which there can be a genuine reference to *agape*, and yet in the light of which there can also be done to *eros*, even to the *eros* of the Greeks, the justice which is surely due to so powerful a historical phenomenon, and of which it is not perhaps altogether unworthy, even in substance.

We shall first try to draw an upward line from the concept of humanity discovered and indicated by us, namely, in the direction of Christian *agape*. Humanity as the freedom of the heart for the fellow-man is certainly not Christian love. Man can indeed, not on the basis of a possibility of his nature, but in its inconceivable perversion, fall from God and become sinful man. This does not rob him of his humanity. But what, then, becomes of this humanity, of the freedom of his heart ? What does it mean that even in this state essentially, properly and inwardly he is still undeniably with the other " gladly," and still uses as the vital and indispensable element in his life the mutual vision, speech, hearing and assistance of man and man ? What is man—still and perhaps for the first time genuinely in the freedom of his heart—if his heart, not by nature or divine creation, but in evil factuality, is evil from his youth up ? What does it really mean that he is " gladly " with his fellow-man ? What takes place in this free co-existence ? This state of real man is the one with which we have actually to reckon and in which he really exists in his history with God. He exists against his nature in this state, this state of sin, which is not really a standing but a falling against which he has no safeguard in his nature, but in which his nature develops, so that his nature becomes a fallen nature. He exists under the negative sign of his antithesis to God, and this is also to be said of his humanity. If he is held, upheld in his fall, and thus kept from plunging into the abyss, this is by the fact that God His Creator intervenes for him in Jesus Christ, making his cause His own, and thus being gracious to him afresh. And if his nature, his humanity, now acquires a positive sign and content, if the freedom of his heart for the fellow-man is for himself and the other a saving, upbuilding, beneficial and helpful freedom, if he is together with his fellow-man not just with a formal " gladly," but gladly in the good sense, i.e., in common thankfulness, in praising the divine mercy, this is not due to himself or his human nature, but this fulfilment of the natural is the gracious gift of the Holy Ghost, and Christian love. God as his Saviour from sin and death has said a new Yes to him in his humanity, a Yes which was not spoken in the fact that he was created in his humanity and therefore in that freedom of the heart, and which he, man, could not speak of himself in his humanity. If he lives in Christian love, he lives in the power of this new divine Yes which frees and saves himself and his humanity from sin and death. He owes it to the faithfulness and constancy of the covenant which God made with the creature that his heart is not merely free for this or that togetherness with the other, but free in the peace and joy and holiness and righteousness of a commonly obligatory service to be together with him in the community of those who may live by the forgiveness of sins and therefore for the magnifying of this grace. Hence humanity and Christian love are two very different things. We may thus speak quite calmly of a gulf between them. But even though the gulf cannot be bridged (except by God alone), there is also an unmistakeable connexion. In humanity, even as it falls through human sin and is thus perverted and brought under that negative sign, it is still a matter of the freedom of one man for another. It was in this freedom, even if in its corruption, that the first men sinned. It is in the wickedness of our heart, which as such, as our own true and essential human being, is still determined for this freedom, in an evil use of this freedom which is not instrinsi- cally evil, that we are evil. Even if we mean it wrongly, we still like to be, and are in fact, with the other " gladly." Highly unnaturally and artificially, we pervert the " gladly " into a " reluctantly." And this " reluctantly " is set aside by Christian love, in which human freedom finds its true exercise. This perversion is reversed in Christian love, in the knowledge of the forgiveness of sins, and in the summons to gratitude by the gracious gift of the Holy Ghost. But it must also be said of Christian love that in it and it alone is it a question of the freedom of the one for the other. This is the new co-existence of man and man which is not merely formal but filled out with positive content. In it, then, humanity is not shamed but honoured. The faithfulness and constancy of the covenant, to which man owes wholly and exclusively the gracious gift of the Holy Ghost, is simply the faithfulness and the constancy of God the Creator acknowledging His work by saving it, and by renewing it as its Saviour. It is again a matter of the heart of man, of his true and essential human being, of his own heart, though new in relation to his evil and corrupt heart, even in the Christian love in which man loves God instead of hating Him and may thus love his neighbour instead of hating him (and thus denying his own nature). What would Christian love be if in it there did not become true and actual what man cannot make true and actual of himself even though his nature is determined for it, namely, a co-existence of man and fellow-man " gladly " fulfilled in freedom. What would be the good to the Christian of all his know-ledge of forgiveness and the necessity to be thankful for it, of all the holiness and righteousness of his restored and reconstituted life, of all his praise of God and zeal in His service, if he lacked this element of humanity, and he were not present gladly and in freedom, which means concretely in the freedom of the one man for the other, in the freedom of the heart for the fellow-man ? Where in Christian faith and hope there is no awakening, i.e., no positive fulfilment of humanity, there is no real faith or hope, and certainly no Christian love, how-ever great may be its inward and outward works. And if I am without love I am nothing. For love alone—the love in which there is an awakening and positive fulfilment of humanity, and the Christian is displayed and revealed as real man—is the fulfilment of the Law, because this human and therefore Chris-tian love, the love which includes humanity, is the life of man in the power of the new and saving divine Yes to the creature. This is the connexion between humanity and Christian love.

But now the question seriously arises whether it is not possible and necessary that there should also be a downward connexion in the direction of the world of Greek *eros*, thus enabling us to find a calmer and more objective solution to the dilemma of *eros* and Christian *agape* than that to which Christians far too hastily rush, but without the power to work it out to the extent that it is justified. We perhaps safeguard ourselves better against the danger of slipping back into *eros* (possibly in the most refined of ways), if we refrain from representing it as the one form of sin, and contrasting it as such with *agape*. When we under-stand humanity as a third thing between the two, we can be more perspicacious and just in relation to *eros*. It is obvious enough that in the historical form of this reality we have a form of sin, i.e., of the corruption of man occasioned and conditioned by his fall from God. It is perhaps the greatness of this historical phenomenon that it can be called a classical representation of human sin. It was understandable and right that the early Christians should first turn their backs on the whole world of Greek *eros* with horror and relief. Where man seeks his self-fulfilment in a self-transcending attempt to have the divinity, the fellow-man and all things as consumer goods for himself, where his vital hunger leads him to be himself the one in all things, we have to do unequivocally with the evil which can only have its wages in death. It would have been far better if Christianity had not so often had the idea of interpreting Christian love as the true form of this hunger and fulfilment. As we have already said, Greek *eros* is ill-adapted to be a definition of humanity. But in all this we must not overlook the point that for all its obvious sinfulness, and the obscurity, con-fusion and corruption in which it represents humanity, *eros* contains an element which in its visible form and even in its essence is not evil or reprehensible, but of decisive (and not merely incidental and non-essential) importance for the concept of humanity, and therefore indirectly for that of Christian love. For where else but in the world of ancient Hellenism filled and controlled by this *eros* does there emerge with such vitality and consolation, for all the sinful cor-ruption, that which we have seen and described as the *conditio sine qua non* of humanity, that " gladly," as the true and original motive of human existence, preceding all the choice and volition of man, and limiting and determining all human choice and volition ? Is it a mere accident that the Gospel of Jesus Christ, this seed of Israel, took root in the perishing world of Hellenism ? Has it been a misfortune that this origin has haunted its whole subsequent career ? Is it merely in culpable self-will that we seek in soul the land of the Greeks, and cannot refrain from doing so even to-day, when we see so clearly that the necessary reformation of the Church cannot be the same thing as a renaissance of Greek antiquity ? Is there not here something obligatory, which it is better to see and accept than to ignore and deny, if we are ready and anxious to understand the Gospel of Jesus Christ in the full range of its content ? And is not this factor to be found in the " gladly " which incontestably has a basic significance for the Christian concept of man and his humanity (and therefore indirectly for that of Christian *agape*) ? We see the whole distortion of this " gladly " in Greek eroticism. The freedom of this highly-extolled man-god is only too easily seen and stated to be tyranny. It recognised itself to be such—to be a dæmonism. But there is more to it than that. We cannot ignore it merely because it originally and properly maintains and actualises in a way which is still unmistakeable the tyranny of freedom. It is not finally for nothing that it was in the atmosphere of Greek *eros* that for the first time in the West, and perhaps over the whole earth, human freedom in the co-existence of man and man attained a noteworthy and unforgettable form for every age and place. This does not mean that we can despise the barbarians who knew nothing of this freedom. Paul mentioned them together with the Greeks (Rom. 1^{14}), and declared that he was under a similar obligation to both. But this can hardly mean that as Christians we have to champion the barbarians against the Greeks, or that we should ignore the superiority of the latter to the former. The Early Church certainly did not do this, for all its differentiation of itself from Hellenism. We might almost wish that it had done so more, and that its differentiation had been more radical. But again this cannot mean that we can or should fail to see what is so clearly to be seen. The violence displayed against Hellenism in recent theology is not a good thing, and its continuation can only mean that in a short time we shall again be exposed to the Greek danger. The Greeks with their *eros*—and it was no inconsiderable but a very real achievement—grasped the fact that the being of man is free, radically open, willing, spontaneous, joyful, cheerful and gregarious. The shadow of conflict and suffering, of resignation, pain and death, of tragedy, must and does always fall on them as they can give it only the form of a basically erroneous yearning for an object and a radically capricious and finally disillusioning wandering from one object to another, being unable to realise it except in the dæmonism and hybris of psychical and physical, ideal and only too real intoxication. The imagination which created the Homeric Olympus and its inhabitants is one of the strongest proofs of the fact that the heart of man is evil from his youth. Yet for all that the Greeks were able to reveal the human heart, to show what humanity is in itself and as such even in a state of distortion and corruption, to bring out the enduring factor in humanity which persists in spite of distortion and corruption, in a way which cannot be said of any other ancient people (and especially Israel, the people of God), and which can to some extent be said of the peoples of later Western history only as and because they have learned concerning *eros* from the ancient Greeks. How these Greeks knew how to see themselves as men, to speak with one another, to live together in freedom, as friends, as teachers and scholars, and above all as citizens ! To be sure, even apart from perversion and corruption, they did so only to a certain degree, but in such a way that this emerged so clearly as the secret centre of their reflection and volition, as the measure of all their virtues, and even as the secret of their obvious mistakes and defects and vices, that other peoples which came in contact with them could not forget it, and even the community of Jesus Christ had to see and take note of it. The Greeks with their *eros* could not be for it a fact of salvation or divine revelation. If it let them be this, it soon found itself on bypaths. The Christian love proclaimed by Paul did not come from the school of the Greeks. And the Christian community could not and cannot learn from them even what humanity is. We ourselves have not gained our understanding of the concept from them. But even though we gain our understanding of the concept of humanity elsewhere, from the one true fact of salvation and divine revelation, yet we cannot fail to acknowledge—and this was and is the basis of the legitimate relationship between Christianity and Hellenism—that our understanding finds in the Greek with his *eros* a confirmation which we have every reason to remember and by which we have good cause to orientate ourselves when it is a matter of understanding Christian love as the awakening and fulfilment of humanity, of the distorted and perverted but not forfeited manner of the natural man, i.e., of man as God created him. The theology of Paul and his proclamation of Christian love derives neither from the Greeks nor the barbarians but from Israel. But when he portrays the Christian living in this love he never uses barbarian or Israelitish colours and contours, but he undoubtedly makes use of Greek, thus betraying the fact that he both saw and took note of the Greeks and their *eros*. Otherwise he could not have added quite so directly to the great saying : " The peace of God which passeth all understanding, shall keep your hearts and minds through Christ Jesus," the remarkable verse which follows : " Finally, brethren, whatsoever things are true, whatsoever things are honest (σεμνά), whatsoever things are just, whatsoever things are pure (ἁγνά), whatsoever things are lovely (προσφιλῆ), whatsoever things are of good report (εὔφημα) ; if there be any virtue (ἀρετή), and if there be any praise (ἔπαινος), think on these things " (Phil. 4⁷⁻⁸). Otherwise he could not have written Philippians with its dominating χαίρετε, or even the great hymn to *agape* in 1 Cor. 13. As love itself primarily and from within itself, as the gracious gift of the Holy Ghost, is an open, willing, spontaneous, joyful, cheerful and gregarious being and action, and all this newly awakened and filled, in a good sense and not in a bad, it is obviously ready and willing to recognise itself and its humanity in everything human as in the good gift of God the Creator, even though it may be actual and recognisable only in that distortion and perversion in the man who is without love. Surely we may and must apply to its relationship to the Greek man and his *eros* the unforgettable words of 1 Cor. 13⁴⁻⁶ : " Love suffereth long (μακροθυμεῖ), and is kind (χρηστεύεται) ; love envieth not (οὐ ζηλοῖ) ; love vaunteth not itself (οὐ περπερεύεται), is not puffed up (οὐ φυσιοῦται), doth not behave itself unseemly (οὐκ ἀσχημονεῖ), seeketh not her own, is not easily provoked (οὐ παροξύνεται), thinketh no evil ; rejoiceth not in iniquity, but rejoiceth in the truth (συγχάρει δὲ τῇ ἀληθείᾳ) " ? It would partly do and partly leave undone all the things said of it if there were no way from it to man, even sinful man, refusing to him the humanity which is also its own instead of recognising, welcoming, acknowledging and respecting it, and declaring its solidarity with it, even where it appears in its most alien garb. It could not be the joy referred to in Philippians if it were unable or unwilling to rejoice in the truth even when it encounters it in sinners, and therefore to " rejoice with them that do rejoice " (Rom. 12¹⁵). It says No to the sin of these χαίροντες, but it says Yes to their χαίρειν as such, because it is not as such something inhuman, but that which is human in all their inhumanity. Love is itself a life in the " gladly," in the holy, righteous and pure " gladly " of the gratitude which binds together brothers and sisters in Christ, and therefore of the supreme " gladly." How, then, can it fail to penetrate to the depths of the fellow-man who is not yet awakened to this thankfulness but still held by the intoxication of *eros*, thus being both permitted and commanded to find and accept even in his foolish, confused and evil " gladly " that which is genuinely creaturely and human ? How can the Christian fail to see that in this respect and on this level too, with the natural bond of the " gladly," he is bound to the non-Christian, with whom he knows that he is primarily connected in a very different way by the judgment and grace of God in Jesus Christ ? And let him finally see to it that the non-Christian finds the same in him—humanity, and therefore this " gladly " ! " Let your moderation (ἐπιεικές) be known unto all men " (Phil. 4⁵, cf. Tit. 3²). It is, of course, quite normal that Christian love should seem strange and foolish to those who are without, just as the way in which those who are without live to their *eros* necessarily seems alien and nonsensical from the standpoint of Christian love. But it would be quite abnormal if those who are without did not find in Christian love at least the humanity which is their own ; if they did not perceive in Christians at least that life in the " gladly " ; if this did not speak to them and bind Christians to them. The *agape* of the Christians would perhaps not be all that it professes to be if the Greek man with his *eros* could not see that even in the Christian he has to do with a man and therefore with a being with which he can at least feel and proclaim solidarity in respect of that root of his *eros*. If this were not the case, the love of the supposed Christian would surely be a very loveless love. If it is genuine, in this respect and on this human level at least he will be no less perceptible and understandable to the non-Christian that the non-Christian must be to him. The non-Christian may say No or shake his head in face of what makes the Christian a Christian, but there should be no reason in the Christian why he should not at least say Yes to his χαίρειν as such, because this as such is the human element in him too. This downward connexion of love by way of humanity to the *eros* of the Greeks was obviously present in New Testament times for all the differentiation of the spheres, and it is hard to see why the connexion cannot and should not be seen, respected and used in our own day as well. What we have here is a relationship between the Church and the world without which the Church cannot discharge its function in the world because without it it would not be the Church, the Church of Christian love.

3. HUMANITY AS LIKENESS AND HOPE

In its basic form humanity is fellow-humanity. Everything else which is to be described as human nature and essence stands under this sign to the extent that it is human. If it is not fellow-human, if it is not in some way an approximation to being in the encounter of I and Thou, it is not human. But provision is made that man should not break loose from this human factor. He can forget it. He can misconstrue it. He can despise it. He can scorn and dishonour it. But he cannot slough it off or break free from it. Humanity is not an ideal which he can accept or discard, or a virtue which he can practise or not practise. Humanity is one of the determinations with which we have to do in theological anthropology. It is an inviolable constant of human existence as such. An anthropology which ignored or denied this basic form of humanity would be explicable in terms of the practical corruption and perversion of man. But it would fly in face of a fact which the practical corruption and perversion of man cannot alter, let alone a theoretical judgment based upon it and therefore false. Man is in fact fellow-human. He is in fact in the encounter of I and Thou. This is true even though he may contradict it both in theory and in practice ; even though he may pretend to be man in isolation and produce anthropologies to match. In so doing he merely proves that he is contradicting himself, not that he can divest himself of this basic form of humanity.

He has no choice to be fellow-human or something else. His being has this basic form.

That this is the case it is brought before us by the fact that we cannot say man without having to say male or female and also male and female. Man exists in this differentiation, in this duality. It is to be noted at once that this is the only structural differentiation in which he exists. The so-called races of mankind are only variations of one and the same structure, allowing at any time the practical intermingling of the one with the other and consisting only in fleeting transitions from the one to the other, so that they cannot be fixed and differentiated with any precision but only very approximately, and certainly cannot be compared with the distinct species and sub-species of the animal kingdom. In the distinction of man and woman, however, we have a structural differentiation of human existence. Man has this sexual differentiation in common with animals of all species and sub-species. This is the unavoidable sign and reminder that he exists in proximity to them and therefore within the context of creation as a whole ; within and not above the boundary of the creature. But his creatureliness is to be male or female, male and female, and human in this distinction and connexion. He certainly exists in other essential and non-essential differentiations. He is necessarily a child, and this individual as opposed to others. But these distinctions as such are not structural in character. On the other hand, he does not need to be father or mother, brother or sister, young or old, gifted or not gifted, endowed in this way or that, a man of this or that particular time or sphere or race. Even if he is, it is again not on the basis of structural distinction. In all these essential and non-essential but secondary relationships and distinctions, however, he is primarily male or female, male and female. And the necessity with which he is a child, and a son or daughter, and this or that particular individual, is bound up with the fact that he is male or female, and the one or the other on the basis of structural differentiation. In and with his existence as man, and as this particular man, he is male or female, male and female. And in and with all the other essential and non-essential distinctions and connexions, this is decisive and in a sense exemplary because this alone is structural and runs through all the others, maintaining, expressing and revealing itself in them. In all the common and opposing features of human existence, there is no man in isolation, but only man or woman, man and woman. In the whole reach of human life there is no abstractly human but only concretely masculine or feminine being, feeling, willing, thinking, speaking, conduct and action, and only concretely masculine and feminine co-existence and co-operation in all these things. There is conflict and fellowship, there is encounter between men and therefore human being, only on the presupposition and under the sign and conditions of this one and distinctive differentiation. These things are present only in the encounter of man and woman, but they are present at once, and with particular force, where this takes place as the necessary limitation and determination, whether to the further-ance or the detriment, of the actuality of their co-existence and co-operation. They are present, too, where man encounters man or woman woman, for man remains what he is, and therefore a being which intends and seeks his true partner in woman and not in man, and woman remains what she is, and therefore a being whose true counterpart cannot be found in woman but only in man. And because fundamentally—even though it cannot attain any corresponding form externally, and the counterpart is either absent or unrecognised—human being is a being in encounter, even human being which is temporarily isolated will definitely bear and in some way reveal the character of this one particular distinction and connexion.

Our present concern is not with the physiology and psychology of the sexes, and we shall not attempt to describe their distinctive struc-ture. But we may perhaps be permitted to issue the following warning in respect of the involved psychological question—that it is much better if we avoid such generalised pronouncements as that man's interests are more outward and objective and woman's inward and subjective ; that man is more disposed to freedom and woman to dependence ; that man is more concerned with conquest and con-struction and woman with adornment ; that man is more inclined to wander and woman to stay at home. Statements such as these may sometimes be ventured as hypotheses, but cannot be represented as knowledge or dogma because real man and real woman are far too complex and contradictory to be summed up in portrayals of this nature. It cannot be contested that both physiologically and biblically a certain strength and corresponding precedence are a very general characteristic of man, and a weakness and corresponding subsequence of woman. But in what the strength and precedence consists on the one side, and the weakness and subsequence on the other, what it means that man is the head of woman and not *vice versa*, is some-thing which is better left unresolved in a general statement, and value-judgments must certainly be resisted. Man speaks against him-self if he assesses and treats woman as an inferior being, for without her weakness and subsequence he could not be man. And woman speaks against herself if she envies that which is proper to man, for his strength and precedence are the reality without which she could not be woman. What distinguishes man from woman and woman from man even in this relationship of super- and subordination is more easily discovered, perceived, respected and valued in the encounter between them than it is defined. It is to be constantly experienced in their mutual exchanges and co-existence. Provision is made that it will be experienced here in supreme reality, not in theory, but in the practice of human existence as a being in encounter.

There can be no question that man is to woman and woman to man supremely the other, the fellow-man, to see and to be seen by whom, to speak with and to listen to whom, to receive from and to render assistance to whom is necessarily a supreme human need and problem and fulfilment, so that whatever may take place between man and man and woman and woman is only as it were a preliminary and accompaniment for this true encounter between man and fellow-man, for this true being in fellow-humanity. Why is this the case? Obviously because, however we may describe and represent man and woman phenomenologically, it is only here, where they are structural, that the antitheses between man and man are so great and estranging and yet stimulating that the encounter between them carries with it the possibility of a supreme difficulty otherwise absent, and yet in all these antitheses their relatedness, their power of mutual attraction and their reciprocal reference the one to the other are so great and illuminating and imperative that the possibility also emerges at least of a supreme interest otherwise absent. It is to be noted that the sphere of this special difficulty and interest, of this play and counter-play of the sexes, is much greater than the circle of what is usually understood more narrowly as sexual love in more or less close connexion with the problem of marriage. In the wider circle around the narrower it is to be found in the relationship of fathers and daughters, mothers and sons, brothers and sisters, and in similar relationships it plays its fruitful but perhaps disturbing and even dangerous role in the whole sphere of education and instruction, and the life of churches of all confessions. Indeed, it is the subterranean motive, which has to be taken seriously into account, in all possible forms of fellowship between man and woman, whether in society, industry or life, among which we have to remember, not with malice but with all honour, the innumerable ways in which it finds compensation or sublimation in friendship between man and man or woman and woman. Yet it is obvious that the encounter between man and woman is fully and properly achieved only where there is the special connexion of one man loving this woman and one woman loving this man in free choice and with a view to a full life-partnership; a connexion which is on both sides so clear and strong as to make their marriage both possible and necessary as a unique and definitive attachment. This is naturally the true element of particularity in this intrinsically particular sphere, and constitutes its centre. There takes place here what can only be indicated and prepared in the wider circle, the female becoming to the male, and the male to the female, the other, the fellow-man, which man cannot and will not be without. Here all that we have described as humanity has its proper locus, the home from which it must continually go out and to which it must continually return. Here there is fulfilled first and perfectly the fact that man and man may be companions, associates, comrades, fellows and helpmates.

Here this is all moved and sustained from within by the clear-cut and simple fact that two human beings love each other, and that in small things and great alike they may will and have the same thing, each other. This capacity, the freedom of the heart for the other, and therefore that " gladly," has here its simplest and yet its strongest form. May it not be that this particular place is attended, at least in the so-called civilised nations, by so much interest and curiosity, but also so much reticence and anxiety, so much phantasy, poetry, morality and immorality, and so much empty talk and sighing and sniggering on the part of the inexperienced, because there are so few who realise that they have to do here with the centre of the human, with the basic form of primal humanity ? But whatever we may realise or not realise, in this sphere, with which we gladly reckon the preliminary as well as the inner circle, and therefore the whole field of sexual encounter, we do actually stand before the primary form of all that has occupied us as humanity. To know nothing of this sphere is to know nothing of the I and Thou and their encounter, and therefore of the human. For where else can a man know it if he does not know it here, if he is a man to whom woman as woman (or a woman to whom man as man) is neutral and indifferent, to whom this structurally different counterpart presents neither difficulty nor interest, who does not stand in some relationship to it, however distorted or repressed, clumsy or unfortunate ? Provision is made that no men are excluded from this centre of the human. To be sure, there are only a few who can see clearly and calmly at this point, and therefore live compara- tively clearly and calmly, whether in marriage or outside it. There are innumerable men and women who theoretically and practically are walking blindly in a mist, and never see what they have missed, whether in marriage or outside it. But there is none who can escape the fact that he is man or woman and therefore in some sense man and woman. There is none who can escape this whole sphere. Man cannot escape his existence, and his existence as such stands under this determination. In the light of this we said at the very outset that man is fellow-human, that he is in the encounter of I and Thou, that humanity is not an ideal or virtue but an inviolable constant of human existence. In the fact of the duality of male and female, which cannot be resolved in a higher synthesis, we have this constant so clearly before us that we can only live it out, however well or badly. There can be no question of setting this fact aside, or over- looking it in practice. There is no being of man above the being of male and female.

Is not this fact a subsequent confirmation of the decided and apparently " dogmatic " precaution which we took, at the beginning of the previous sub- section, of taking up the historically important anthropology of man in isolation only in the form of a delimitation from it *a limine*, and therefore of an outright rejection ? We took this path because Christology left us no option, but compelled us to decide for the opposite path. And now we can only add that we were right, and that a little more of the readiness for real life which is so often lacking in the studies of philosophers and theologians would necessarily lead their occupants to the same result. That it has not done so is perhaps due to the fact that for so many centuries the philosophical and theological study of the West was the cloister-cell, from whose distinctive I-speculation in the absence of the Thou it has been difficult to break free even outside the cloister. Nietzsche did not live in a cell. But it is hard to decide where he was most at home, as a prophet of humanity without the fellow-man, in his repudiation of Christianity or in his almost brutal contempt for women (which fortunately was only literary in form). There is a necessary connexion between the two. This ought to have been remembered in the monastic cells where humanity without the fellow-man was not discovered but forcefully advanced and practised. No veneration of Mary or love for God could fill the terrible vacuum in which it was desired to live and a good deal of life was actually lived to the detriment of the Church and the world. But the vacuum is not filled merely by leaving the cloister, just as the external cloister does not necessarily entail the vacuum. It is very possible even for external life in the cloister to be in fact a being in encounter. And it is equally evident that even a flood of love for women such as that which filled the life of Goethe is not strong enough to make impossible a humanity without the fellow-man, or to actualise with certainty a being in encounter. At any rate, it did not prevent Goethe from becoming, if not the prophet, at least the high-priest of this humanity. And when he broke off his deepest and finest love-affair to study Greek antiquity in Italy, there was revealed the fact that his repudiation of humanity was coincident with a repudiation of this nervous centre of humanity, and he gave conclusive proof of an attitude to woman, confirmed rather than altered by his marriage with Christiana Vulpius, which, while it cannot be compared with the scorn of Nietzsche, can only be described as that of the man who is finally emancipated from women. He too, and especially, was finally captured by the secularised cloister. And behind all this there stands the fact that we have here the profoundest symptom of sickness in the world of the Greeks and their *eros* (which only too fully enslaved the West both in real and secularised cloisters). For all the eroticism of theory and practice, it was a man's world in which there was no real place for woman ; and for this reason it was necessarily a world of the I without the Thou, and therefore a world of the I wandering without limit or object, a dæmonic and tyrannical world. It is not surprising, then, that the discovery or the many re-discoveries of the humanity of the free heart present and not absolutely concealed in the Greek world of *eros* were overtaken by such disasters in the narrower and wider Christian sphere, in real and secularised cloisters. The only safeguard against these disasters is Christology, and a little knowledge of life. By a little knowledge of life we mean a placid and cheerful and sure knowledge of the duality of human existence, of the original form of the I and Thou in the continuity of human being as the being of male or female, of male and female. Where Christianity is genuine in the sense that it is not merely theoretical but living wisdom (the biblical ḥokma or σοφία), it unavoidably carries with it a little knowledge of life. This was forgotten in the mediæval cloister, and it has been forgotten in all other studies where its supposedly Christian but inhuman tradition has been continued. But to attain a little knowledge of life Christology must not be despised as has been the case, with equally inhuman results, in secularised, untheological and non-Christian cells, e.g., that of Goethe or Nietzsche. The Christian community, receiving and proclaiming Christian love and Christian theology with its doctrine of man, ought to be secured against those disasters and to be able to pass triumphantly through every cloister, knowing the man Jesus as the man who is for His fellow-man, and therefore knowing man generally, knowing his humanity as fellow-humanity, and this fellow-humanity at the point where it is most concretely and incontestably a fact, in the antithesis and connexion of man and woman. But the test of this twofold and at bottom unitary knowledge is whether it can be ruthless enough to turn its back at once and absolutely on the error of the humanity of man without the fellow-man.

The Old Testament Magna Carta of humanity is the J saga which tells us how God completed the creation of man by giving him woman as a companion (Gen. 2$^{18-25}$). We have already expounded this text in *C.D.* III, 1, p. 288 f., and to establish our present point reference must be made both generally and in detail to this exposition.

The main point may be briefly recapitulated. In Gen. 2 (like Gen. 1), the account of the creation of man as male and female is the climax of the whole history of creation. In both cases it is solemnly emphasised and introduced by the mention of special reflection on the part of the Creator. In this case, the reference is as follows : " It is not good that the man should be alone ; I will make him an help meet for him." In this saying there is a radical rejection of the picture of man in isolation. And the point of the whole text is to say and tell—for it has the form of a story—who and what is the man who is created good by God—good as the partner of God in the history which is the meaning and purpose of creation. This man created good by God must have a partner like himself, and must therefore be a partner to a being like himself ; to a being in which he can recognise himself, and yet not himself but another, seeing it is not only like him but also different from him ; in other words, a " help meet." This helpmeet is woman. With her he is the man created good by God, the complete human creature. He would not be this alone. That he is not alone, but complete in this duality, he owes to the grace of his Creator. But the intention of this grace is as revealed in this completion. And according to the fine declaration of the text its intention is not merely that he should acquire this duality, woman, but, acquiring her from God, recognise and confess her by his own choice and decision as a helpmeet. God the Creator knows and ordains, but He leaves it to man to discover, that only woman and not animals can be this helpmeet. Thus the climax of the history of creation coincides with this first act of human freedom. Man sees all kinds of animals. He exercises his superiority over them by giving them names. But he does not find in them a being like himself, a helpmeet. He is thus alone with them (even in his superiority), and therefore not good, not yet complete as man. In the first instance, then, he exercises his human freedom, his humanity, negatively. He remains free for the being which the Creator will give him as a partner. He waits for woman, and can do so. He must not grasp after a false completion. But who and what is woman ? That man obviously waits for her does not mean that he knows her in advance. She is not his postulate, or ideal, let alone his creation. Like himself, she is the thought and work of God. " And (he) brought her unto the man." She is not merely there to be arbitrarily and accidentally discovered and accepted by man. As God creates both man and woman, He also creates their relationship, and brings them together. But this divinely created relationship—which is not just any kind of relationship, but the distinctive human relationship—has to be recognised and affirmed by man himself. This takes place when he cries triumphantly : " This is now bone of my bones, and flesh of my flesh." Here we have the second and positive step in the act of freedom, in the venture of free thought and speech, of man exercising his humanity in this freedom. At the heart of his humanity he is free in and for the fact that he may recognise and accept the woman whom he himself has not imagined and conjured up by his desire, but whom God has created and brought. With this choice he confirms who and what he is within creation, his own election, the particularity of his creation. He is man in this negative and positive relationship. Human being becomes the being in encounter in which alone it can be good. His last objective assertion concerning another being becomes his subjective confession (as a male) of this other being, this fellow-man, the woman who has her own equal but proper and independent honour and dignity in the fact that she can be his helpmeet, without whose participation in his life he could not be a man, and without whose honour and dignity it would be all up with his own. "Therefore shall a man leave his father and his mother, and shall cleave unto his wife" means that because woman is so utterly from man he must be utterly to her ; because she is so utterly for him he must be utterly for her ; because she can only follow him in order that he should not be alone he must also follow her not to be alone ; because he the first and stronger can only be one and strong in relationship to her he must accept and treat her, the second and weaker, as his first and stronger. It is in this inversion that the possibility of the human, the natural supremacy of the I over the Thou, is developed in reality. It is in this way that the genuinely human declares its possibility. It is in this form that there exists the possibility of man in isolation, but also of all androcracy and gynocracy. "And they were both naked, the man and his wife, and were not ashamed." The human is the male and female in its differentiation but also its connexion. Hence there is no humiliation or shame. The human cannot be a burden or reproach. It is not an occasion for unrest or embarrassment. It does not need to be concealed and hidden. There can be no shame in respect of the human. In the work of God—which is what the human is—there is nothing offensive and therefore no *pudendum*. The work of God is without spot, pure, holy and innocent. Hence man does not need to be ashamed of his humanity, the male of his masculinity or the female of her femininity. There is no need of justification. To be the creature of God is self-justification. Only sin, the fall from God, can shame the human, i.e., the masculine and the feminine, and thus make it an object of shame. And the awful genius of sin is nowhere more plainly revealed than in the fact that it shames man at this centre of his humanity, so that he is necessarily ashamed of his humanity, his masculinity and femininity, before God and men, and every attempt to escape this shame, every self-justification, or concretely every denial and suppression of sexuality can only confirm and increase the shame. It is to be noted carefully that this is the climax of this text, and therefore of the whole biblical history of creation.

The whole of Gen. 2[18f.] points to the man who is fellow-human as such, as the creature of God, in his divinely given nature, and therefore originally and not secondarily. And it speaks of the co-existence of man and woman as the original and proper form of this fellow-humanity. It singles out this among all other possible relationships as the one which belongs to the creation-history preceding all others, and which alone can come into question when it is a matter of describing the nature which man has been given by God. At this point the reference cannot be to parents and children, to brothers and sisters and other relatives, to friends, to Europeans and Asiatics, to Semites and Arians, to old and young, to gifted and ungifted, to rulers and subjects, teachers and scholars, rich and poor, or even the basic distinction of individual and individual. Or rather, this basic distinction, the differentiation and connexion of I and Thou, must be explained as coincident with that of male and female. All other relationships are involved in this as the original relationship. All other humanity is included in this centre. In this connexion, particular attention must be paid to the fact that in Genesis 2 the reference is to man and woman in their relationship as such, and therefore not to fatherhood and motherhood or the establishment of the family. It is true that in the rest of the Old Testament the relationship is seen almost exclusively from the latter aspect, in the light of the question of progeny, and with the main interest in the conception and birth of children, especially the son. But it is equally true that this is not the case in the present passage. No mention is here made of child or family. The relationship of man and woman has its own reality and dignity. As such it is the basic relationship involving all others. At this point the Bible thinks and speaks far more seriously " erotically " than all Hellenism. In the light of this text it cannot be called arbitrary if, having sketched the basic form of humanity in general terms, we make the reference to this particular relationship the climax of our presentation, and without the usual expansion or restriction that when it is a question of man and woman we are inevitably led to father and mother and therefore child as the third thing proceeding from the other two. If the Old Testament is a commentary on the New, and decisive account has to be taken of an important passage like Genesis 2, we can only say that this weakens and obscures the true situation and is thus to be rejected. But this means that the encounter of man and woman as such is being in encounter and therefore the centre of humanity, so that before we proceed to consider the circumference of this centre it is worth pausing at this encounter, since otherwise we shall probably misinterpret all other encounters, even that of parents and children. For it is here first and decisively that we have to see and learn what is meant by freedom of heart for the other, and therefore what constitutes the humanity of all other encounters. Genesis 2 is imperious in this respect. If it is objected that it is isolated in its reference to man and woman, the answer is that creation is isolated in relation to the rest of the creature's history, and the divinely given nature of man in relation to what this became at the hands of man. But our present question concerns creation and the creaturely nature of man, and we have every reason to put this question even to understand the history of the human creature and man in his corruption as a sinner. If we are to find an answer, we must read this passage in Genesis 2 without subtraction or addition, as we have tried to do. And we must therefore learn from it that man is first and unquestionably and generally man and woman, and only then all kinds of other things, including perhaps father and mother.

And in any case Genesis 2 is not absolutely isolated in the Old Testament. We might almost speak of a second Magna Carta of humanity in this connexion when we remember that at a rather curious point in the Old Testament Canon a place is found for the Song of Songs. We should not wish that this book were not in the Canon. We should not treat it as if it were outside. And we should not spiritualise it, as if what is in the Canon can have only a spiritualised significance. As all honest exposition must admit, and as ought to be recognised gladly rather than with hesitation and embarrassment, it is a collection of genuine love-songs in the primitive sense, in which there is no reference to the child, but only to man and woman in their differentiation and connexion, in their being in encounter. At this point the most natural exegesis might well prove to be the most profound.

It is to be noted that in this second text we hear a voice which is lacking in the first. This is the voice of the woman, to whom the man looks and moves with no less pain and joy than she to him, and who finds him with no less freedom —only the " This " of Genesis is lacking—than she is found. Implicitly, of course, this voice is to be heard in Genesis as well. But it now finds expression in words. And what words ! " Set me as a seal upon thine heart, as a seal upon thine arm : for love is strong as death ; jealousy is cruel as the grave : the coals thereof are coals of fire, which hath a most vehement flame. Many waters cannot quench love, neither can the floods drown it : if a man would give all the substance of his house for love, it would utterly be contemned " (8⁶ᶠ·). And so everything is more luminous if not more strong, more direct if not more unequivocal. And all that takes place is sketched and depicted against a background of day and night, of the passing seasons, of the plants and animals of the Palestinian scene. And this is what the Old Testament calls the song of all songs. Again, it is an isolated text, and in its theological assessment we must take the same line as in Genesis 2, except that now we are obviously at the other end of the line, the end and not the beginning. That this song belongs to the so-called Solomonic literature, being attached to Proverbs and Ecclesiastes, reminds us that Solomon the builder of the temple, and his kingdom, glory and wisdom, represent the figure of the King of the last day and His glory. This is how the expected son of David appeared and his kingdom—so powerful, resplendent and wise, and finally so human. And so we must understand eschatologically the songs ascribed to him when we take seriously their very concrete content. On the long line from creation to the last day the Old Testament speaks very differently of man and woman. The dominating question is that of children. The " erotic " notes are few. Everything is controlled by the Law, and especially the danger and prohibition of adultery. In this respect, too, we are in the world of sin and infamy and shame, in which the love-song must always have a rather dubious sound, and the original of the covenant between man and woman, the covenant between Yahweh and Israel, is continually broken on the part of Israel, and has still to be properly constituted. But the beginning and end, the origin and goal, both between Yahweh and Israel and between man and woman, are as depicted in Genesis 2 and the Song of Songs. In retrospect of creation and prospect of the new creation of the last time, we can and may and must speak of man and woman as is done in these texts.

Hence both these passages justify us in speaking of man in this way when we ask concerning his creaturely nature.

In the light of the theological significance of the Song of Songs this is perhaps the point to elucidate an eschatological question which at a first glance might cause considerable difficulty. We read in Gal. 3²⁶ᶠ· : " For ye are all the children of God by faith in Christ Jesus. For as many of you as have been baptised into Christ have put on Christ. There is neither Jew nor Greek, there is neither bond nor free, there is neither male nor female : for ye are all one in Christ Jesus. And if ye be Christ's, then are ye Abraham's seed, and heirs according to the promise." What Paul is saying, and not saying, is quite clear. He is saying that the being of Christians on the basis of the grace of God commonly directed to them and commonly received by them in faith, their being as children of God, the seed of Abraham and heirs according to the promise, their being in correspondence with their baptism, is one which makes impossible any exaltation of the one over the other or hostility of the one to the other, so that in the Christian community there can be no assertion of natural and historical antitheses. For in this community all are one in Christ Jesus in the sense that all live thankfully by the grace which is manifested equally to each of them as mercy. But Paul is not saying that the antitheses are simply set aside and done away by the being of Christians in Christ. *Cest ordre là est inviolable et nostre Seigneur Jésus Christ n'est pas venu au monde pour faire une telle confusion que ce qui est establi de Dieu son Père soit aboli* (Calvin, C.R. 28, 568). Thus the fact that male and female are one in Christ does not mean that they are no longer male and female. Yet it might be asked whether this is the last word. Does it not apply only so long as Christians still share in this present aeon which passes ? In their life which according to Col. 3³ is hidden with Christ in God, and especially in its future manifestation in the resurrection of the dead, will it not perhaps be the case that they are no longer male or female, but a third thing which is higher and better. The question is an obvious one in view of Mk. 12¹⁸⁻²⁷ and *par.*, where in answer to the question of the Sadducees which of the seven brothers should have the woman to wife in the resurrection Jesus said : " For when they shall rise from the dead, they neither marry, nor are given in marriage ; but are as the angels which are in heaven." Does this mean that they will no longer be male and female ? Is A. Oepke right (*TWBzNT*, I, 785) when he says that by proposing for man in the perfected lordship of God a sexless being similar to that of the angels Jesus lifts from woman particularly the curse of her sex and sets her at the side of man as no less justifiably the child of God ? Yet it does not actually say that man and woman will be ἄγγελοι, but ὡς ἄγγελοι (ἰσάγγελοι, Lk. 20³⁶), i.e., those who according to 1 Cor. 13¹² no longer see God, themselves and all things in a glass darkly but face to face, and are thus liberated from the problematical, burdensome and complicated nature of their existence in the form which they now know (through a glass darkly). To this form there belongs marrying and giving in marriage with such implicated questions as that raised by the Sadducees on the basis of Deut. 25⁵ᶠ·, and the overriding concern for children. It is not from the insights of the world of the Song of Songs that the Sadducees ask concerning the solution of such complicated matters in the future aeon, and the stern rebuke which Jesus gives them is fully justified : " Do ye not therefore err, because ye know not the scriptures, neither the power of God ? " This, whole concern for marrying and giving in marriage and the raising up of children, says Jesus, can no longer occupy men in the resurrection when according to Lk. 20³⁶ they cannot " die any more." God is the God of Abraham, Isaac and Jacob, and therefore the God of the living (θεὸς ζώντων) and not the dead ; the God for whom, and before whose eyes which span the centuries, all men (or they all, Lk. 20³⁸) are alive in their time. As such they will be revealed in the resurrection, and with their death the necessary cares which now lie like a cover over their lives will be lifted and left behind. Thus the fact that that woman had belonged to seven successive husbands, and must still belong to them according to the law of marriage, could cast no shadow on her temporal life as disclosed in the resurrection, nor on the life of the seven men. For the fact that she married and was married will then be a past event with many other happenings and finally with the death of those concerned. The only thing that will count is that like Abraham, Isaac and Jacob they have lived in their time for God, the God of the living, and therefore live eternally. To that extent they will be as the angels of heaven, not in heaven, but on the new earth under the new heaven—new because the cosmos will then be revealed in the form in which there will be no more possibility or place for tears and death and sorrow and crying and pain (Rev. 21⁴). They will thus be as the angels of heaven because this is how it is already with the angels. But there is no reference here, and cannot be, to an abolition of the sexes or cessation of the being of man as male and female. It is worth noting that even Augustine, who must have been tempted to this thought, expressly repudiated it (*De civ. Dei*, XXII, 17). He met it in the distinctive variation that from the saying in Rom. 8²⁹ about our being conformed to the image of God's Son, and the saying in Eph. 4¹³ about our coming unto a ἀνὴρ τέλειος, it follows that woman will rise after the fashion of the male and not the female. But as against this Augustine prefers the view of those *qui utrumque sexum resurrecturum esse non dubitant*. What is to be set aside in the resurrection is not nature itself, but the violation of nature. But the female sex belongs in its particularity to nature. And so he maintains the opinion : *qui utrumque sexum instituit, utrumque restituet*. Thus in this Synoptic passage Jesus certainly tells us that there will be no continuation of marriage but not that woman will not be woman in the resurrection. By His very negation He presupposes that men will still be men and women women. It cannot be otherwise. In the *Syn. Theol. Leiden* (1624, *Disp.* 51, 37) it is rightly observed that this is also demanded by the identity of the human subject in the two aeons. The determination as man or woman is not the least important of the *conditiones individuantes* of the human subject, so that if it were to lack in the resurrection the subject would no longer be this subject, and man would no longer be man. And in this case it would no longer be τὸ φθαρτὸν τοῦτο which in the resurrection puts on ἀφθαρσία, nor τὸ θνητὸν τοῦτο which puts on ἀθανασία (1 Cor. 15⁵³ᶠ,). Man would not be man if he were no longer male or female, if his humanity did not consist in this concrete fellow-humanity, in this distinction and connexion. He has lived in no other way in time, and he can live in no other way in eternity. This is something which he cannot lose. For by it there stands or falls his creatureliness. In relation to the goal of our existence in the future aeon we have thus no cause to doubt a statement which we formulated in relation to creation as its beginning. We have no cause not to see together the picture of Genesis 2 and that of the Song of Songs.

Why does it have to be as we have stated on the primary basis of these passages ? Why do Genesis 2 and the Song of Songs give us this particular picture of man and his humanity ? Our statement would seem at least to be rather fortuitous if we simply appealed to this Magna Carta in its twofold form, accepting the fact that this is what is actually written and not something else. Why do we read particularly that man is male or female, male and female ? In fact, there is nothing fortuitous about it. It belongs to the very centre of Holy Scripture. It is necessarily grounded in the decisive content of the Word of God. We can thus see, and if we are to have a proper understanding we must see, that there can be no question of anything but what is actually there, and that we cannot possibly adopt any other view than that which we have actually adopted. We must now try to show why this is the case.

As concerns the Old Testament, we have already sketched our

answer. Behind the relationship of man and woman as we meet it in the picture of Genesis 2 and the Song of Songs there stands the controlling original of the relationship between the God Yahweh-Elohim and His people Israel. Behind these passages there stands Old Testament prophecy. And according to the insight which continually breaks through, the sum of all truth and actuality, which is thus also the beginning and end of all things, the secret of creation and its consummation, is the very different duality merely reflected in the nature of man—that of God and man in their co-existence in the concrete form of the covenant established by God between Himself and His people Israel. This duality, the covenant, is the centre of the Old Testament. And it is the original of which the essence of the human as the being of man and woman can only be the reflection and copy. Man is primarily and properly Yahweh, and woman primarily and properly Israel. That is why it is necessary, and the Old Testament poets of creation and the consummation are compelled to describe the human as they have actually done. That is why what they say belongs as it stands to the Canon of Holy Scripture. That is why we have to do here with God's Word concerning man, so that we cannot deviate on either side from what is said. We note that Old Testament prophecy everywhere presupposes the sin of man, Israel's apostasy and therefore the Law and judgment of God, but also and more particularly the faithfulness of God. It thus speaks in the light of the shattering of the original on the side of man. It speaks of the covenant broken by Israel, and therefore of the unfaithful wife who has forfeited her rights and dignity. But in contrast it also speaks of the kindness and mercy of the Husband whom she has left and injured but who does not abandon her. It thus speaks with reference to the long period between creation and the end. But with this reference it speaks concerning this relationship. And it counts on the fact that in and in spite of its disruption it is not ended but persists. The covenant remains. Yahweh is faithful to Israel. His betrothal and marriage continue. His love also remains. And because everything remains on His side, this means that there is also an indestructible continuity in the being of Israel. Even in its apostasy and the rejection and abandonment which it entails it is still the people which Yahweh has marked out and sought and loved, and with which He has entered into covenant. And the end and goal of its history will prove this continuity which exists from the beginning. The hope of Israel is that its continuation in the covenant (not in virtue of its own goodness, but of that of Yahweh) will finally be revealed. This immutable covenant relationship between Yahweh and Israel, and therefore the centre of the Old Testament witness, stands dominatingly behind Genesis 2 and the Song of Songs. As this original confronts them, shattered in the middle of the line, but also in its totality at the beginning and the end, the poets dare to speak of man and woman as they do. We must be clear that they were not just speaking symbolically or allegorically; they were speaking directly and concretely of man and woman and their relationship. But they could do as they did because they had before them as a model and final basis of the form of humanity of which they wrote the relationship of Yahweh and Israel. It was an unattainable model of humanity because love such as that of Yahweh for Israel is beyond the reach of a human husband in relation to his wife. On the one hand we have a covenant between Creator and creature; on the other only a covenant between creature and creature. But the latter covenant rests on the former. Because even God, God Himself, the Lord and King of the heavenly and earthly space created by Him, did not will to be alone, but to have His concrete counterpart in the people Israel, man was not to be alone, but to have his helpmeet or counterpart in woman. Hence it is not at all impossible to find the outlines of the covenant of grace between Yahweh and Israel even in the details of the story of the creation of man as male and female. Because this is the case, it is not by chance that this story has its present form in the Old Testament, and there is good reason to claim it as the Magna Carta of a concept of humanity in which the basic relationship of man and woman receives due honour.

But the final and decisive step has still to be taken to establish it on a biblical foundation. A last appearance of fortuitousness might still cling to it so long as we move only in the sphere of Old Testament promise and not of New Testament fulfilment.

The Old Testament shows an amazing knowledge in this whole matter. Without a knowledge of the true and final meaning of the relationship of man and woman it would be quite intolerable to see this intra-creaturely relationship in the holy relationship between Yahweh and Israel. Again, without a knowledge of the menacing and shattering of the relationship between man and woman the Old Testament could not have such a terribly plastic view of the devastation of the relationship between Yahweh and Israel. On the other hand, without the hope of the last time with its divine fulfilment of the covenant with Israel it would be impossible to see the covenant of man and woman with the freedom of Genesis 2 and the Song of Songs. Again, without the strictly eschatological character of this hope it would be hard to understand why this view of man and woman is the exception to the normal rule of the Old Testament, which is not to consider man and woman as such, in their mutual relationship of husband and wife, but as father and mother in the light of their destiny to have descendants. Thus the knowledge displayed by the Old Testament is strikingly unanimous and yet strikingly contradictory. Why does it include the primary statements? How does it know the dignity of the relationship of the sexes? And yet how does it also know that it is menaced and shattered? How does it know of the eschatological fulfilment of the covenant of grace with Israel? And how does it know that this fulfilment is not to be sought in the sphere of vision of the Israelite, but beyond his sphere of vision, as an eschatological event? It cannot be contested that the Old Testament does know this. But it is also incontestable that in this respect it rests on a secret which is nowhere revealed and never even takes concrete shape in its own sphere. Thus if we were restricted to this sphere alone we should have to accept that a certain fortuitousness and uncertainty clings to our statement. We could maintain that things are as we have seen them in the Old Testament. But it could not be said or proved that we for our part are forced to see them in this way.

But why should we be restricted to this sphere? The secret on which the unanimous but contradictory knowledge of the Old Testament rests may well be visible and therefore disclosed outwith the witness of the Old Testament if not within it. The witness of the New Testament tells us that this is the case. If we are to take it seriously we are forced to say that the New Testament tells us what the Old for all its knowledge does not know and therefore cannot tell us. It tells us where this Old Testament knowledge of man derives, where it has objectively its origin and basis, and on what grounds things can be only as indicated in the Old Testament. *Vetus testamentum in novo patet.* It is indeed the case that the New Testament reaches back behind the Old, revealing and disclosing the secret presupposed but nowhere revealed or disclosed in the Old, and thus proving what the Old in itself and as such can never prove—that in all its parts it is right and speaks the truth in a way which is normative for us. We can grasp this if we take our previous questions one by one.

How does the Old Testament know the dignity of the relationship between the sexes? How does it have the knowledge which permits and commands it to see this intra-creaturely relationship in the holy relationship between Yahweh and Israel? The New Testament answers that the covenant between Jesus Christ and His community was in the beginning, the first and proper object of the divine will and plan and election, and the internal basis of creation. This covenant is the original of the Old Testament original, the relationship between Yahweh and Israel, and therefore the original of the relationship between man and woman. It is on the basis of this original that the intra-creaturely relationship has its dignity and necessity, and that the Old Testament finds it essential to see this intra-creaturely relationship at the central point in its witness, in the covenant between God and the people.

But again, how does the Old Testament know that the relationship of the sexes is menaced and shattered? How does it have the knowledge which gives to its complaint against Israel its distinctively sharp and drastic quality as an accusation of adultery? The New Testament answers that the covenant between Jesus Christ and His community, which is the secret of creation, is of such a kind that its Lord, Jesus Christ, is the One who for His community—a gathering of sinners who have fallen victim to the wrath of God and their own perdition—gives Himself up to death in order to win it as His own possession. The history of the covenant between Yahweh and Israel must culminate in the crucifixion of the King for the people because it is grounded in this earlier covenant, the covenant of the Holy with the unholy. On the basis of this earlier covenant Israel throughout the history of the covenant between Yahweh and itself has the form of the ungrateful, faithless and adulterous wife. And on this basis the relationship of the sexes is necessarily seen under the shadow which always falls on it in the Old Testament.

How does the Old Testament know of the eschatological fulfilment of the covenant of grace with Israel ? How does it have the knowledge which permits and commands it at least occasionally in these supreme passages to see the relationship of man and woman with this great freedom ? The New Testament answers that in the covenant between Jesus Christ and His community it takes place that man's apostasy from God is finally cancelled and made good, that fidelity and love between God and man are made reciprocal by the gift of the Holy Spirit, and that the accusation against man, and therefore the Law which accuses, drop away. On the basis of this covenant the hope of Israel is ineluctably necessary and sure, as constantly depicted in the Old Testament. And on this basis it is possible and necessary to give to the covenant between man and woman—this intra-creaturely covenant as such, and quite apart from any question of progeny—the dignity and honour which are ascribed to it in Genesis 2 and the Song of Songs.

But how does the Old Testament know that the fulfilment of the covenant of grace with Israel is a strictly eschatological reality, and therefore to be sought outside the sphere of the Israelite ? How does it have the knowledge which compels the Old Testament normally to speak otherwise of man and woman than in Genesis 2 and the Song of Songs, necessarily putting the fatherhood of the man and motherhood of the woman into the forefront of the picture ? The New Testament answers that it is in the covenant between Jesus Christ and His community that the divine will and plan and election have their proper object and thus find their fulfilment. This covenant is the goal even of the covenant between Yahweh and Israel as a promise and preparation. The history of Israel as the history of this covenant has its meaning in the appearance of the Son of God and Son of Man as the Head of a people holy by Him and in Him. And on the basis of this first and proper covenant the Old Testament throughout the middle stretch between creation and the end must display that sober interest in man and woman in their quality as father and mother. This is necessary because in Israel, in the whole sequence of its generations, it is a question only of this promise and preparation, which means finally of the miraculous conception and natural birth of the Son and His people gathered from Jews and Gentiles. Thus the picture of man and woman given in Genesis 2 and the Song of Songs could stand only on the margin of the Old Testament witness, but on this margin it had a place which was not just possible but necessary.

Thus the New Testament witness reaches back behind the Old.

It reveals the source of the knowledge displayed in the Old Testament. It indicates and discloses the secret which does not emerge and is certainly not revealed in the Old Testament. It proves point by point that the Old Testament is right and speaks the truth in a way which is normative for us, and that it does not therefore say fortuitously of humanity that it consists in the co-existence of male and female.

It is only fitting that at this point we should consider the decisive statements of the New Testament independently and in their own context.

We must first remember the general truth that when the New Testament speaks of Jesus Christ and His community it really speaks of the goal (and therefore of the origin and beginning) of all earthly things. Jesus Christ and His community is not an additional promise given to men. The existence and history of Israel in covenant with Yahweh was a promise. The reality of Jesus Christ and His community does not continue this history. It is not a further stage in actualisation of the divine will and plan and election which are the purpose of creation. It concludes this process. It is the complete fulfilment of the promise. It is the goal and end of all the ways of God. It is *the* eschatological reality. It cannot be surpassed, deepened or enriched by anything still to come. It is followed only by its proclamation to all nations and all creation as the task laid upon the community. But the community has not to proclaim a new offer or promise and its law. It has to proclaim the accomplishment of the divine decree as it has already taken place in the appearance of Jesus Christ, in His death and resurrection, and in the outpouring of the Holy Ghost. All that is outstanding is its manifestation as the light of the cosmos which does not yet know it—its manifestation by Jesus Christ Himself. But as the Head of His community He is already the Head of the cosmos (Col. $1^{17f.}$). Hence His return cannot alter or improve anything, let alone introduce anything new. " If any man be in Christ, he *is* a new creature " (2 Cor. 5^{17}). What is to be proclaimed by the ministry of His community, and finally revealed by Himself, is simply the fact that this is the case. He is a new creature. For God has given Jesus Christ to be the κεφαλὴ ὑπὲρ πάντα to the community which is His body and in which He has His own divine fulness and His whole divine fulfilment (Eph. $1^{22f.}$). This completed fact is still to be shown to the cosmos. This completed fact must be revealed as the meaning of the whole cosmos. But it is already a completed fact. There is no salvation which has not already come to the world in the death and resurrection of Jesus Christ and the existence of the community which He has purchased by His blood and has gathered and still gathers by His Holy Spirit.

It was on the basis of this insight that Paul treated his communities, and each of them as *the* community of Jesus Christ. A Christian community is not a religious experiment. It is not a fellowship of faith and hope with a more or less distant and exalted goal to which it is directed and towards which it strives as an ideal. It is this as little as Jesus Christ is a prophet pointing to the future and prophesying something which is not yet real. The people Israel waits for the Son. Its whole history is the history of this expectation. But the community of Jews and Gentiles founded by the apostle derives from the Son. It has its history in the fact that it is in Christ and therefore lives in the fulfilment which has taken place in this Head. It belongs to Him, and what belongs to Him belongs as His gift to it. As the apostle proclaimed to it the Word concerning Him, and it received this Word in faith, as Christians were baptised in the name of Jesus Christ, they were united to Him, and with Him they constitute the eschatological reality and the end of all God's ways, so that they can will only that the glory in which they participate in Him and by Him should

be revealed among them and through them to others, and they can expect only
that Jesus Christ Himself will finally confess them and manifest the glory with
which He has already invested them to their own eyes and those of others, in
order that the whole world may be radiant and full of the glory of God in this
revelation. It is on this basis that Paul addresses the Christian communities,
and always in the light of the fact that the fulfilment has taken place in Jesus
Christ alone, but in Jesus Christ for them. All the instruction, consolation and
admonition which he imparts to them are references back to this completed
fact, to the portion which they have in Jesus Christ and therefore in the fulfilment which has taken place in Him. Any deviation from this line, any return
to the situation of the people Israel, i.e., to that of the unfulfilled promise, any
re-establishment of the Israelitish Law, but also any legalistic demand for faith
and hope, would necessarily mean that Jesus Christ Himself is called in question.
But someone in whom everything is not fulfilled would not be Jesus Christ.
We know how passionately Paul avoided this kind of Christ. And he was not
guilty of any such deviation or compromise. The warfare against sin, error
and disorder which he waged in the Christian community was conducted solely
on the basis of the fact that Jesus Christ and His community in their interconnexion are the reality of the last time beyond which we cannot expect any
other, or any other insights, possibilities or powers, but in which God has reached
with man the end for which He created heaven and earth and all that therein
is. And the whole warfare of the spirit against the flesh, the good fight of faith,
to which Paul summons the community and all its members, can only be the
battle to maintain the position which has already been captured and allotted to
them by the act of God in Jesus Christ, and from which no one and nothing can
ever drive them.

It is on this presupposition that Paul addresses the Corinthians, for example,
when he writes in 2 Cor. 11[2f.] : " For I am jealous over you with godly jealousy :
for I have espoused you to one husband, that I may present you as a chaste
virgin to Christ. But I fear, lest by any means, as the serpent beguiled Eve
through his subtilty, so your minds should be corrupted from sincerity towards
Christ." We do not know in detail against whom or what Paul was jealous.
The only thing which is clear (v. 4) is that an attempt had been made in Corinth
to preach another Jesus than the One whom Paul had preached. But in relation
to the preaching of Paul another Jesus can only be one in whom we can and
must believe without living with him in the fulfilment, or finding consolation in
the fulfilment, or fighting the battles which have still to be fought on the basis
of the fulfilment as it has been accomplished in him. From Paul's standpoint
another Jesus can only be a Jesus who is a mere prophet or the mere bearer of
a further promise. If Paul says that in this matter he is " jealous with a godly
jealousy " for the Corinthians, and the maintenance of fellowship with them,
and the constancy of the faith which he has proclaimed to them, it is obvious
that this is not the jealousy of an Elijah or any other Old Testament figure
for the fidelity of Israel and in face of its infidelity to the promise and the
law of the promise which it has been given. It is the jealousy of God which
Paul must make his own as the apostle of Jesus Christ ; the jealousy of the
God who has brought the history of the covenant to its goal, and who cannot
possibly allow what He has done to be reversed even in the name of another
Jesus, in the very name of the One in whom it has reached its goal. The true
Jesus Himself stands in question. That is why Paul is jealous with a godly
jealousy for the Corinthians. For the true Jesus is not alone. They, too, belong
to Him, the One who has fulfilled the work of God. For the apostolic word has
been heard by them, and received by them in faith. Something irrevocable has
thus taken place for them and to them. The death and resurrection of Jesus
Christ are the reality which not only refers to them (as to the whole world) but
which also embraces them and in which they have their life. To the extent that

they are the Christian community, they are absolutely from Him and to Him, and therefore they are determined in what they are and do and refrain from doing by the fact that there is accomplished in Him that which God intended for man from the very first. He, Paul, is the witness of this. For he has attested to them the real Jesus as their Lord, and even the witness of their faith belongs to him. He thus knows that in this matter he is responsible both to God for them and to them for God. He cannot be content merely with the fact that they are Christians and accept Jesus as a good man in whom they somehow have dealings with God but concerning whose significance they have another view which has to be tolerated side by side with that of Paul. No, says Paul, this is not another view of Jesus. It is another Jesus. And this we cannot in any circumstances or in any sense admit. Between the real Jesus and the Corinthians something has taken place, a decision has been made, which cannot be reversed. And he, Paul, was present when this decision was made. As the messenger of the Gospel he was the man who sought and brought them from afar (as Eliezer brought Rebekah to Isaac in Gen. 24[1f.]). Indeed, we might almost say that as God brought Eve and showed her to Adam, he brought and showed them to the real Jesus as the one Husband, betrothing them to Him as His bride. Between this one Husband Christ and them there is a legal relationship created by His Word and Spirit and therefore solidly established. He, Paul, can testify that everything has been in order in the establishment of this relationship. He has not brought the community to any other husband. The Christ proclaimed by him was the One in whom everything was accomplished for them, for He is the Head over all things, and there cannot possibly be any other. And He has brought them to this Husband as a chaste virgin. He knew that when he brought them to this Husband their past and its sins would not be remembered ; that as the elect and beloved of this One they could come to Him absolutely pure and righteous and holy ; that their faith in this One was genuine and sincere ; and that their baptism was not merely water-baptism but the baptism of the Spirit (so that there could be no question of this One later repulsing them as unworthy). The relationship between the one Husband Christ and His bride is a definitive relationship which no power in heaven or earth can alter, let alone a change of opinion which they have allowed themselves in the meantime. It is to be noted that the distinctness with which Paul speaks of the definitive character of this relationship is not denied even by what follows. He fears for them. He fears that their thoughts might be led away from sincerity towards Christ, and therefore corrupted. He fears that something might happen to them analogous to what took place between the treacherous serpent and Eve who was so terribly deceived. He starts back from the possibility that they might go this ruinous way even in thought ; that even in thought they might try to play the Eve. But he obviously does not believe that he cannot appeal to their sincerity towards Christ as their true position. " Sincerity (ἀπλότης) towards Christ " is the basic knowledge in which, without glancing aside to the right hand or the left, they are content with Christ because all things are given them in Him. He sees the possibility that their thoughts might go astray in spite of this knowledge, as the thoughts of the community of Jesus Christ have often played the Eve in spite of it, and thus been betrayed into error. But even in this danger he still sees it as the community of Jesus Christ which cannot move away from its basis in Jesus Christ, which cannot separate itself from this Head, which cannot be shaken in this basic knowledge. He is not referring to the legal relationship at the establishment of which he was a witness and assistant. He does not question the continuance of this relationship. He would contradict himself if he did. He would be reckoning with another Jesus ; with a Christ whose work could be incomplete or futile like that of so many of the prophets ; with a covenant to which one would rather be unfaithful after entering into it. The Christ with whom Paul reckons is the One who has acted and spoken conclusively in the name of God, and therefore united Himself conclusively with His community, however dangerously its thoughts concerning Him may oscillate, so that even though its fidelity may seem to stand in jeopardy we can always appeal to its sincerity towards Christ, and the threat to its fidelity is most effectively met by this appeal. This appeal can and may and must be made, not because we can trust Christians as those who are united with Him, but because we can be confident that the Lord whose possession they are has not given them His Spirit in vain. We maintain that Paul regarded it as right in elucidation of this thesis to recall the encounter of bridegroom and bride and therefore the primitive form of humanity as being in encounter.

On the same presupposition he declared in Rom. 7[1-6] that Christians are those who in virtue of the death and resurrection of Jesus Christ really have the situation of Israel behind them, who are really liberated from the Law which finally can only accuse and condemn them by confirming that they are sinners. For our present purposes the decisive verses are 3 and 4 : " So then if, while her husband liveth, she shall be married to another man, she shall be called an adulteress : but if her husband be dead she is freed from that law ; so that she is no adulteress, though she be married to another man. Wherefore, my brethren, ye also are become dead to the law by the body (the physical slaying) of Christ ; that ye should be married to another, even to him who is raised from the dead." It is to be noted that in this passage the purity of the bride brought to Christ in 2 Cor. 11[2] is interpreted in the sense in which we understood it in the previous reference. It is not intrinsic but is acquired as she is brought to this Husband. As we are now told explicitly, she had previously belonged to another. This other, her first husband, was none other than the man of the first aeon ; the man of the world standing under the dominion of the sin of Adam and Eve. This man was under the Law which accused and condemned him, which confirmed the fact that he was a sinner, and in this way provoked and quickened his sin, so that the fruit which he produced (v. 5), the reward which he earned (6[23]), could only be death. This man was the first husband of Christians. He was their old man under whose law they had necessarily to stand. So long as he lived ! Only his death could free them from his law and therefore from the fact that they were accused and condemned as sinners. Every attempt made prior to the death of this man to escape his law, to disregard its accusation and condemnation, to act in an arbitrarily gained or imagined freedom in respect of him, to pretend to be elsewhere than on the fatal middle stretch between creation and the consummation, could only make them genuinely guilty and worthy of death. So long as our old man lives, what can we accomplish in this direction but what the Old Testament calls the adultery of Israel against its God, the service of alien gods and the corresponding practical alienation from the true God, the sin which does not drive out sin but merely reveals it in its true colours ? At this point only the intervention of a higher power can save us. Freedom can be legitimately and effectively established only by the death of the old man and the loosing of our connexion with him. And it is on this basis that Christians rest. They no longer belong to the first man because he is no longer alive. He was put to death on Golgotha in the self-offering of the body of Christ. He was crucified and died in and with the slain body of Christ. And with him their sin was also crucified and died (Rom. 6[3f.]). The man of the old aeon was there and then destroyed with his aeon. Thus the law of this man, which was binding so long as he was alive, has lost its validity. He cannot accuse or condemn them any more. He cannot confirm or increase their sin. They are free, not with the illusory and evil freedom of adulterous Israel, but genuinely free. They have not accomplished this themselves. They could have won for themselves only that adulterous freedom. But there and then, in the death of Jesus Christ who alone could do it, they have become genuinely free : free to be the wife of this Other, their Liberator,

Jesus Christ risen from the dead ; and therefore free for life under His law, which according to Rom. 8²ᶠ· is the " Law of the Spirit of Life." " There is therefore now no condemnation to them which are in Christ Jesus " (Rom. 8¹). The community may thus be absolutely pure and righteous and holy as His bride and help meet. It is a creature, but a new creature by His death and resurrection and in the power of His Spirit. Thus man and wife again confront one another as man and fellow-man and need not be ashamed—the original of humanity.

But Paul also spoke on the same presupposition in the passages in which he looked at things from the opposite angle. In 2 Cor. 11²ᶠ· and Rom. 7¹ᶠ· he was obviously considering the relationship between Christ and His community in the light of various aspects of that of the relationship of husband and wife, Jesus Christ being the Bridegroom to whom the community was legally brought as a bride, or the other man by whom and for whom the community is legally free although previously married to another. But there are passages in Paul, understandably better known and more frequently cited, in which he is dealing with some form of the reality of the relationship between husband and wife, and in his interpretation of this reality recalls the relationship between Jesus Christ and the community, explaining the former by the latter. Even and especially in these passages it is obvious that in this relationship, in the act of God which took place on Good Friday, Easter Day and Pentecost, he sees the fulfilment and completion of all things, the dawn of the last time which makes quite impossible any return to the economy of the Old Testament.

In 1 Cor. 6¹²⁻²⁰ we have a clear warning against πορνεία, or sexual intercourse with a πόρνη, i.e., the kind of intercourse in which man turns to woman merely for the satisfaction of his carnal needs and woman is only an occasion and means to provide this satisfaction. The decisive positive statements which serve as the basis of the warning are as follows (vv. 16b–17) : " For two, saith he, shall be one flesh. But he that is joined unto the Lord is one spirit." From what we are told by the second statement, i.e., from the relationship between Jesus Christ and His community, Paul looks back and down on the relationship between man and woman to which the first statement refers. That the Christian is one body with his wife can take place only in correspondence with the fact that he himself is one spirit with the Lord. But in the kind of sexual intercourse referred to there is no such correspondence and therefore it is impossible. It would be wrong to say that it is forbidden. It is not forbidden ; it is intrinsically impossible. The whole purpose of Paul in this passage is to recall to Christians the impossibility. " Know ye not ? " is his insistent question in v. 15, v. 16 and v. 19. It would be wrong to speak of a Pauline prohibition because at the beginning of the passage (v. 12) there stands the impressive and twofold πάντα μοι ἔξεστιν : " I have power over all things." Behind this passage, too, there stands the Pauline message of the liberation of man in Jesus Christ from the law of sin and death, and if we do not understand this we cannot understand his warning. We certainly cannot understand how categorical it is. For it is the freedom created by Jesus Christ and given to His community which has the power of decision of which the Pauline warning speaks. The " know ye not ? " is a reminder of this freedom. It is the freedom to choose that which helps (συμφέρει) the Christian and to repudiate that which would bring him under the domination of an alien power, involving an ἐξουσιάζεσθαι ὑπό τινος, and thus limiting and even destroying his freedom. Not everything is a help to him. Having power over all things, he has the freedom to reject that which does not help him. And many things would bring him under an alien domination. Having power over all things, he has the freedom to reject them. The connexion between freedom and decision is seen in a different light in 1 Cor. 10²³ : πάντα ἔξεστιν, ἀλλ' οὐ πάντα οἰκοδομεῖ. We have to remember here too that the freedom of the Christian is the freedom to play his part in the upbuilding of the community. Who is the Christian ? He is a man who " is joined unto the Lord " (κολλώμενος in v. 17 is the same term as that which the LXX uses in Gen. 2²⁴ᶠ· for the cleaving of a wife to her husband). The Christian is dearly bought (v. 20). At the supreme cost of the self-offering of the Son of God he is freed from the powers which determine a whole world which is now past for him. According to Col. 1¹³ he is translated by God into the kingdom of His dear Son. He has thus become His possession. He shares His lordship over these powers. And his freedom rests in this fact. As he lives in this freedom, he lives in the Spirit. And as he lives in the Spirit, he is one with the Lord. The Christian is thus a man who does not belong to himself but to this Lord (v. 19). He is joined to Him. It is not something abstract which is joined to Him (his soul perhaps), but something very concrete, he himself as the soul of his body. He in his totality, and therefore in his corporeality, does not belong to himself but to the Lord. He is a member of Christ, of His body, of His community (v. 15), and thus participates in His lordship and is free for what is helpful to him as a Christian, free from all alien dominion, and free for the edification of the community. The order under which he stands as this concrete being in his corporeality is, however, that " God hath both raised up the Lord, and will also raise up us by his own power " (v. 14). The Lord took to Himself concrete human being, corporeality. He suffered and died in the body. He accomplished that self-offering in the body. And He was also raised from the dead in the body. In this context the last is the decisive point. As certainly as Christ was raised from the dead in the body the Christian is not subject to death in the body. Jesus Christ has drawn him as His member even in his corporeality after and towards Himself to a new life. In his corporeality he is already determined, disposed and organised for this new life as " the temple of the Holy Ghost, which ye have of God " (v. 19). He is thus summoned to glorify God in his corporeality (v. 20). This is how it stands with the Christian. He is free for what is necessary for him in the light of the resurrection of Jesus Christ ; for what helps him in his being on this basis (as the temple of the Holy Ghost and for the glorifying of God) ; for what confirms and increases his freedom from the powers of the old aeon ; for what edifies the community. He is also free to refrain from the opposite of all these things. He would not be what he is if he had a freedom which could be defined in any other way : the freedom to do the latter and not to do the former ; the freedom to do what does not help him but brings him into captivity and destroys the community. But in this being of the Christian—and Paul thinks it quite impossible that the Corinthians should not know this, or that he should have to do more than give them an interrogative reminder—the decision is already taken what is intrinsically possible and what is intrinsically impossible for the Christian in this matter of sexual intercourse. In the first instance, there is a pre-decision concerning the significance of his action as such. In sexual intercourse it is not merely a question—as some at Corinth obviously seem to have thought (v. 13)—of the satisfaction of a physical and in this case sexual need, which can be met without any particular question of the means, like the need of the stomach by eating. In sexual intercourse we do not move within this kind of physical cycle : " meats for the belly, and the belly for meats " ; a need which cries out for satisfaction, and the satisfaction which answers to the need. Ὁ δὲ θεὸς καὶ ταύτην καὶ ταῦτα καταργήσει. When the time of man is up, God will destroy this physical cycle. It belongs to his corporeality, and therefore to himself. Of course, as Paul himself obviously presupposes a few verses later (7¹ᶠ·), even in sexual intercourse there is a question of this kind of cycle of need and satisfaction belonging to the corporeality of man and therefore to himself. But in sexual intercourse it is also a matter of the body itself and as such, and therefore of man in his corporeality. For sexual intercourse means that at the climax and in the completion of their encounter they become one body, belonging wholly to one another in their corporeality, and mutually attesting and guaranteeing their humanity. In this completion the man no longer belongs to himself, but to the woman ; and the woman no longer belongs to herself, but to the man. In this completion there takes place between them something final and irrevocable. They are both what they became in this completion—a being belonging to this other. This is not, then, a neutral sphere or indifferent occurrence. There is decided here to whom man belongs as in this completion he belongs to another. For the Christian this decision has been made. Belonging to a woman, he cannot contradict but must correspond to the fact that he belongs to Christ. But he would contradict this if he belonged to a harlot and became one body with her. But why is this so total a contradiction ? Why does the " one spirit " with Christ exclude in this way the " one body " with a harlot ? Obviously because Christ is the faithfulness of God in person, whereas the harlot personifies human unfaithfulness against God. He cannot will to become one body with a harlot, or actually become this, in the freedom which is created for and given to him by Christ. In so doing he who is one spirit with the Lord would become something which would not help him, in which he would not be the temple of the Holy Ghost, or glorify God, or edify the community, but merely return to the bondage from which he has been so dearly and definitively ransomed. In sexual intercourse with a harlot there can be only a sorry distortion of the completion between man and woman. For what kind of a completion is it ? The completion of fellowship ? No, it can be only the completion of self-satisfaction, and therefore at the climax of the encounter the denial of any real encounter ; fellowship in the form of the betrayal of fellowship. For in this intercourse man does not seek woman in the totality of her corporeality. He seeks only the sexual being as an occasion and means to the satisfaction of his own corresponding need. He forgets, and wills to forget, that in woman as herself a human being he has to do with the fellow-man ; that as an I he has to do in her with a Thou. He thus denies the humanity of woman, treating her as an It. And the woman does not expect man as a man, or in the totality of his corporeality. He is for her too an It and not a Thou. She does not seek a true and serious and genuine connexion. She merely answers to his sexual impulse, shaming not only her own womanhood but his manhood too. Let there be no mistake—even in this distortion the completion is real enough. There takes place a mutual self-offering. Male and female become one flesh as stated in Gen. 2²⁴. They belong together. Although as betrayers of their humanity, they mutually determine and shame each other. If a Christian seeks intercourse with a harlot, this is not a neutral happening which does not affect the man himself in his being as a Christian. What happens is that he " takes " (ἄρας) his body, i.e., himself in his corporeality, as though it belonged to himself and he could do this with it, and makes it (himself) the member of a harlot (v. 15), thus giving it (himself) a part in that betrayal. His being as a man is thus brought into contradiction with his being as a Christian. He thus sins against his own body (v. 18). That is to say, he does not merely pervert and corrupt something extraneous, but decisively he perverts and corrupts himself. And he perverts and corrupts himself wholly and utterly, and therefore in his relationship to God and his fellow-man. He who in his corporeality is a member of Christ and as such moves forward to the raising of the dead by the power of God pronounces sentence of death upon himself. For if he belongs to a harlot—and this is what intercourse with her means—he can only die totally and with no hope of life. I take it that in the difficult v. 18 Paul is speaking of a sin of which only the Christian is really capable. μὴ γένοιτο, he says to this sin (v. 15), and this is an expression which he usually reserves for the rebuttal of a possibility which is radically excluded. He thinks through this possibility logically and to the bitter end. But he definitely tells the Corinthians that this is a way which cannot be entered. It must be remembered that immediately prior to this passage he had written (6[11]) : " But ye are washed (in baptism), but ye are sanctified, but ye are justified in the name of the Lord Jesus, and by the Spirit of our God." This " ye are " is like a barrier blocking the way. This is what they know according to vv. 15, 16 and 19. This is what Paul has only to remind them in order to say something which is far more powerful than any prohibition. It is the same absolute obstacle to which Jesus Himself referred in Mt. 6[24] : " No man can serve two masters. . . . Ye cannot serve God and mammon." Paul takes the same line. He does not need to present any law or morality. He has only to show what they can and cannot do. They cannot place themselves afresh under forces which they have once and for all escaped as they belong to Christ in their corporeality. Conversely, they cannot escape the service in which they have been placed once and for all as they belong to Christ in their corporeality. They cannot exist in their corporeality as only the victims of death can exist. They have the risen Christ behind them and before. They cannot make the temple of God a den of thieves. They cannot blaspheme God ; they can only glorify Him. They cannot compromise Jesus Christ, with whom they are one spirit, as though He Himself to whom they are joined—in this case they would indeed belong to another Jesus—were one of the powers of the old world and He Himself invited them to do so. They cannot be guilty of that contradiction. For they know perfectly well that that contradiction is itself contradicted, and that it is contradicted victoriously and definitively, so that no option remains. Hence they cannot either seek woman in the form of a harlot, or accept her advances in this form. It is to be noted that this does not merely apply to what is called extramarital intercourse. They cannot make woman a harlot, or accept her as such, either outside marriage or within it. They cannot affirm πορνεία and the πόρνη in any form. They cannot do this because their being excludes this affirmation of the harlot in any form. They can only really do what Paul commands in v. 18 : φεύγετε τὴν πορνείαν. Turn your back on it with the firmness and totality which are the only possibility when we have to do with the impossible. What is intrinsically possible to the man who is one spirit with Christ in the relationship of man and woman and therefore in the completion of this relationship can only be, as an exercise of his freedom and therefore his participation in the lordship of Christ, and in his obedience to " the law of the Spirit of life," the intercourse which beyond all need and its satisfaction is the completion of the encounter of man and fellow-man and the fulfilment of full and serious and genuine fellowship. There is thus possible for him only the becoming " one body " in which there is clearly and unequivocally reflected the full and serious and genuine fellowship of Jesus Christ with His community and each of its individual members. There is possible only the becoming " one body " of which he does not need to be ashamed in face of the fact that he is " one spirit " with Jesus Christ, and in respect of which the man and woman have no cause for mutual shame but for rejoicing as in a reflection of light from above. It is on the basis of this positive recognition that the decision goes against πορνεία. At this critical point, therefore, Paul set the anthropological question as that of man's humanity in the light of Christology, and answered it accordingly. All that remains for us is simply to state that this is what happens in the passage. Paul brings the concrete form of the fellow-humanity of man and woman, and sexual intercourse as its most concrete form, into connexion with the relationship between Jesus Christ and His community, and derives his normative concept of the human—not without express reference to Gen. 2—from this basic norm. The necessary stringency is not lacking. But there is none of the papistical severity which is so often encountered in this sphere. Paul knew how to give a categorical and effective warning on the basis of the whole Gospel, and his warning is far more categorical and effective than that of many who before and after him have tackled the problem purely from the standpoint of the Law.

In 1 Cor. 7^{1-10} and then again in 7^{25-40} Paul took up the question of marriage and celibacy. In 7^{10-17} he dealt with divorce. In 14^{33-38} and 1 Tim. 2^{8-12} he discussed the question of women speaking, or rather being silent, in the ἐκκλησία. We shall not take up these problems here because in these passages (as distinct from 1 Cor. 6^{12-20}) there is no explicit reference to the connexion between man and woman on the one side and Christ and His community on the other. To understand these passages we can hardly avoid making this connexion in their exposition. But our present question is not where it can and must be made, but where it is actually made in the New Testament.

The second passage in which this is indisputably the case is 1 Cor. 11^{1-16}. As a text for this whole section we might well take vv. 11–12 : " Nevertheless neither is the man without the woman, neither the woman without the man, in the Lord. For as the woman is of the man, even so is the man also by the woman ; but all things of God." Man and woman are here considered in relation to a question of liturgical order. It is a small, external and peripheral question. But Paul regards the decision made in its solution as so great, internal and central that he does not hesitate to devote 16 verses to it and to make again the connexion which is our present concern. His aim is to show that because in the Lord and " of God " the woman is not without the man or the man without the woman, a definite course has to be adopted in relation to this peripheral question of order. What was the point at issue ? An enthusiastic attempt was being made to introduce equality where previously the custom had been both at Corinth and in other Christian communities that in their gatherings for worship the men should be uncovered and the women covered. We may well imagine that Gal. 3^{28} (" neither male nor female ") provided either verbally or materially the main argument in favour of abolishing this outward distinction and therefore against Paul, who had given this dictum but now favoured the keeping of the tradition (v. 2). There can be little doubt, as we gather from the earlier chapters of the Epistle, that an attempt of this kind was being made at Corinth, and that it was directed generally against the recognition of the specific authority and office and word of the apostle. Must the freedom won in Christ acquiesce in the irreversibility of the relationship of order and ministry between the apostle and the community ? We learn from 4^8 that the Corinthians were very largely of the opinion that they were full and rich, and had thus attained to a βασιλεύειν independent of the apostle. And it may be gathered from 12^{29} that the slogan " We are all apostles " was only just round the corner. It is certainly no accident that Paul refers briefly to this basic question in vv. 1–2, and even vv. 3–16 with their presentation of the relationship between man and woman (perhaps this is one of the reasons why they are so definite) are to be understood as an indirect elucidation of the relationship between the apostle and the community. The latter is a decisively important derivative of the relationship between Christ and the community. Because it was a matter of the absolute and incomparable authority of the crucified Jesus, Paul as His witness could not yield an inch in the question of his own relative and human authority as an apostle. Without Christ's commission and Spirit there was no apostolic word, but without the apostolic word there was no Christian hearing, no hearing of the Word of Christ, no life in the Holy Spirit. And it was also a question of the relationship between absolute and relative, directly divine and indirectly human order in the problem of man and woman discussed in vv. 3–16. Paul tells us plainly enough in vv. 11–12 that he does not retract anything that he has said in Gal. 3^{28}. In the Lord, " of God," it is just as true that the woman is of the man and the man by the woman. Both are told us by Gen. 2. Woman is taken out of man, but man is man only by the woman taken out of him. Yet only an inattentive enthusiasm could deduce from this that man and woman are absolutely alike, that there can be no question of super-and subordination between them, and that it is both legitimate and obligatory to abolish the distinction between the uncovered and the covered head in divine service. It was the same inattentive enthusiasm which concluded from the fulness of spiritual gifts of which there was evidently no lack in Corinth that there was no further need for the teaching, exhortation and admonition of the apostle. In both cases, as in many other respects, it was forgotten that God (14^{33}) is not a God of ἀκαταστασία but of peace. But there is peace only if distinctions are observed in the fellowship : in the fellowship, so that the antitheses caused by their misunderstanding and misuse are overcome ; but genuinely observed, so that there is true super-and subordination, and it is seen that we are dealing with two different things and not one and the same when we are told by Gen. 2 that woman is from the man and by Gen. 2 again that man is by the woman. The demonstration of this peace, and therefore of these distinctions in the fellowship of man and woman, is the theme of the present passage. Paul is trying to show that the observance of this relative, indirect and human order is necessary because it rests on an absolute, direct and divine order, so that the denial of the one means the denial of the other. The curious saying about the angels in v. 10 is most simply explained as follows. The angels are generally the bearers and representatives of the relative principles necessarily posited with the work of God, and they are specifically the bearers and representatives of the indirect human orders necessarily posited with the divine work of salvation. They cannot, therefore, see these orders violated without sorrow. This is something which should not happen. Hence διὰ τοὺς ἀγγέλους the woman must bear on her head in divine service an ἐξουσία (a sign of her recognition of the ἐξουσία of the man which she does not possess). But what is the connexion between the divine work of salvation and the order in question ? The decisive statement in this regard is undoubtedly to be found in v. 3 : κεφαλὴ δὲ γυναικὸς ὁ ἀνήρ. If this is accepted as a justifiable assertion, we maintain that it proves both the point and even the necessity of the custom. The uncovered head of the man is the sign that in divine service, in his participation in the act of προσεύχεσθαι and προφητεύειν, he has no κεφαλή over him because he is himself κεφαλή. But the covering of the head of the woman is a sign that in the worship of the community, in her participation in the act of προσεύχεσθαι and προφητεύειν, she has a κεφαλή over her and is not therefore herself κεφαλή. The conclusion is drawn in vv. 4–6 that in the light of v. 3b any other practice dishonours both the head of man and that of woman. The particular honour of both demands this custom. Verse 10 underlines this conclusion by referring to the angels, and vv. 12–15 add that it corresponds to natural sensibility. But the whole argument depends on v. 3b and therefore on whether this assertion is justified. What is its basis ? We might refer to the passage in Eph. 5^{22-23}, where this assertion is reversed and explained in v. 23: ἀνήρ ἐστιν κεφαλὴ τῆς γυναικὸς ὡς καὶ ὁ Χριστὸς κεφαλὴ τῆς ἐκκλησίας. On this basis we could argue that the whole point of the statement is that man in his relationship to woman represents Christ in His relationship to the community, and that woman in her relationship to man represents the community in its relationship to Christ, as developed in the Ephesian passage. But in the first instance the assertion in 1 Cor. 11^{3b} should be evaluated in its own context. It is immediately preceded by 3a: παντὸς ἀνδρὸς ἡ κεφαλὴ ὁ Χριστός ἐστιν, and followed by 3c : κεφαλὴ δὲ τοῦ Χριστοῦ ὁ θεός. On the basis of these three statements in their interconnexion Paul then goes on to say : " But I would have you know. . . ." It is to be noted that he does not ask here as in 1 Cor. 6^9 : " Know ye not ? " It is obviously presupposed that they ought to know, but it emerges more plainly at this point that they need the apostle to proclaim and interpret what they might basically know of themselves. Above all, the order of the statements is to be noted. They are not arranged as a demand for perspicuity might suggest : 3c, that God is the Head of Christ ; 3a, that Christ is the Head of man ; and 3b that man is the head of woman. Nor do they take the opposite course—

3b, 3a, 3c. They are necessarily arranged as in the text. They contain neither deduction from above downwards nor induction from below upwards. They are not a scale. They have often been understood in this way, with the absurd result that man is taken to be for woman what Christ is for him and God for Christ, so that it is only indirectly and by way of man that woman is in relationship to Christ and therefore to God. The remarkable position of 3b warns us against this interpretation. Telling us that man is set above woman, it is preceded by the statement that Christ is set above him. And telling us of the subordination of woman, it is followed by a statement which speaks of a subordination of Christ to God. Thus it is grounded and explained in Christ whether it speaks of the superordination of man or the subordination of woman. Both superordination and subordination are primarily and properly in Christ. According to Col. 2¹⁰ He is ἡ κεφαλὴ πάσης ἀρχῆς καὶ ἐξουσίας. According to Eph. 1¹⁰ it was the good-pleasure of God ἀνακεφαλαιώσασθαι τὰ πάντα in Him. "πᾶσα ἐξουσία is given unto me in heaven and in earth" (Mt. 28¹⁸, cf. also Col. 1¹⁶, Eph. 1²⁰ and 1 Pet. 3²²). He, then, is the Head of every man. That is to say, He is the sum of all superordination, and He stands relatively much higher than man behind his majesty. Whatever may be the ἐξουσία of man in relation to woman, it is legitimate and effective only to the extent that primarily and properly it does not belong to him but to Christ, and can therefore only be attested and represented by man. Conversely, Christ is the sum of all humility before God, of all the obedient fulfilment of His will. He is the One who according to Phil. 2⁶ᶠ·, although He was in the form of God, did not count it His prey to be equal with God, but emptied Himself, and took the form of a servant, and made Himself equal to man . . . and humbled Himself. He thus enters on His lordship by becoming the slave of God and man. God has made Him— we must not forget this supreme statement—to be sin for us (2 Cor. 5²¹). Could He stoop any lower before God than this ? He is thus the sum of all subordination, and stands relatively much lower than woman under man. And whatever may be her relationship to the ἐξουσία of man which she lacks, it is sanctified, ennobled and glorified by the fact that her subordination is primarily and properly that of Christ and can only be attested and represented by her. Thus it can really be said between the height and the depth, the lordship and service, the divinity and humanity of Christ : " The head of the woman is the man." So little does this ascribe to man or refer to woman ! So sharply and clearly is it determined and limited on both sides by what is primarily and properly the affair of Christ ! His is the superordination and His the subordination. His is the place of man, and His the place of woman. And what place is there to speak of little or much ? There is assigned to each that which is helpful and right and worthy. If it is no little thing for man to be κεφαλή in relation to woman, i.e., the one who has precedence, initiative and authority, the representative of the order which embraces them both, it is no little thing for woman to take the place which she is assigned in relation to man and therefore not to be κεφαλή but to be led by him, to accept his authority, to recognise the order which claims them both as it is represented by him. In vv. 7–9 Paul refers explicitly to Gen. 2. The determination and limitation of the relationship of man and woman as established in Christ emerge already in the work of creation. Woman is fashioned out of man and for the sake of man. She is not created as he is out of the dust of the earth but (more humanly, we might almost say) out of man himself, in order that he should not be alone but have a helpmeet (vv. 8–9). Thus he is the " image and glory of God," yet not alone or without or against the woman, but together with the woman who is his glory (v. 7). This basic order of the human established by God's creation is not accidental or contingent. It cannot be overlooked or ironed out. We cannot arbitrarily go behind it. It is solidly and necessarily grounded in Christ, with a view to whom heaven and earth and finally man were created. It is so solidly grounded in the lordship and service, the divinity and humanity of Christ that there can be no occasion either for the exaltation of man or the oppression of woman. " If any man be in Christ, he is a new creature." It is the life of this new creature which Paul describes with the saying that the head of the woman is the man. Gal. 3²⁸ is still valid, in spite of shortsighted exegetes, like the Corinthians themselves, who shake their heads and think they can claim a contradiction. The mutuality of the relationship still obtains, as described in vv. 11–12. To that extent there is an equality of man and woman ἐν κυρίῳ in the order in which the one God has with equal directness assigned this place to man and that to woman. Where is there any real knowledge of differentiation and mutuality, and where are the exaltation of man and the oppression of woman radically excluded, except in the community of Jesus Christ, in which His lordship and service are the final word, and the Creator of all things is found and recognised in the baby in the crib, and in the baby in the crib the Creator of all things, no contradiction being seen between majesty and humility, superordination and subordination, lordship and service ? Is not the community of Jesus Christ itself and as such, as adduced in Eph. 5, the model of the woman who has her κεφαλή in the man, and cannot really exist except in subordination to this κεφαλή, but in this way, determined and limited in Him, is exalted above all heavens by His majesty and lowliness, in fellowship with this Head ? It is for this reason that this order cannot be broken in the community ; that the relationship of man and woman established in creation, and the distinctions which it entails, cannot be regarded as transitory and accidental and abolished in Christ, as though Christ were not their meaning and origin. In the community this relationship cannot imperil either man or woman. It can only be their honour and joy and blessing. There is thus no cause to deny or abolish it as though it were a mere convention. On the contrary, dishonour and harm are done both to man and to woman if this clear relationship is abolished. It is quite ridiculous to think that progressiveness should be played off against conservatism in the matter of this relationship. If there is anything which is inwardly necessary and no mere convention, it is this relationship. Progress beyond it can only be regress to the old aeon. It is only in the world of the old aeon that the feminist question can arise. And for this reason the Corinthians should accept the custom. It is a symbolic recognition of the relationship, and therefore of the basis, determination and limitation which it has been given in Christ. This recognition may not be withheld. Self-evidently it might have taken a different form in a different age and place. But in Corinth and all the Christian communities of the time (v. 16) it took this form. And as it was called in question in this form it had to be protected and defended in this form, not for the sake of the form, but for the sake of what was at issue in this form. The fact that it also conformed to natural sensibility, to φύσις (v. 14), was an additional recommendation as Paul saw it. But this statement was only incidental. The decisive point was that the enthusiasm for equality which outran the form was not particularly Christian, but that the custom should be accepted in Christ. We cannot say more than that it should be, for Paul was not arguing from the Law, but centrally from the Gospel. It was not the one who called the Corinthians to order who was thinking legalistically, but the Corinthians themselves, who, armed with a general, liberal, non-christological concept of humanity, thought it their duty to attack this relative and indirectly human order, as though they were all apostles, and as though an apostle were a genius. It was as well for them that they had in Paul a real apostle able to maintain an unruffled front against their impulsive genius ; and they were well-advised to accept his summons to be imitators of him as he himself tried to be of Christ (v. 1).

Our final passage is Eph. 5²²⁻³³, the *locus classicus* for the point at issue. No other passage makes the connexion so emphatically. No other is so primarily concerned to make it. No other is so complete in its exposition of the two

relationships. And no other refers so solemnly to Gen. 2. From it we can
survey the whole landscape which we have traversed : the New Testament
relationship of man and woman in the light of the relationship between Christ
and the community, and conversely the elucidation of the relationship between
Christ and His people by reference to the man-woman relationship ; the Old
Testament marriage between Yahweh and Israel and its reflection in the man
and woman of the Song of Songs ; and finally our starting-point in Genesis 2,
the natural being of man as fellow-humanity, as being in the encounter of I
and Thou. Should we really have the courage or find it necessary to consider
all these things not only in detail but in their manifold relationships if they were
not set before us so authoritatively and perspicuously in Eph. 5 ? But this is
an idle question. This passage does in fact make everything clear. And we
have only to apply ourselves directly to this text in which everything is set
out directly and verbally in an exegetical norm for all other texts. It forms
the introduction to the so-called " house-table " of Ephesians, a list of specific
admonitions to wives, husbands, children, fathers, slaves and masters among
the members of the community, all of which stand under the overriding injunc-
tion : " Be filled with the Spirit ; speaking to yourselves in psalms and hymns
and spiritual songs, singing and making melody in your heart to the Lord ;
giving thanks always for all things in the name of our Lord Jesus Christ ; submitting yourselves one to another in the fear of God " (vv. 18–21). This basic
note must be remembered if we are to understand the ensuing injunctions, and
especially the first and lengthy admonition addressed to husbands and wives.
Be filled with the Spirit, speaking to one another in praise of God, not only
with your lips but in your hearts, not ceasing to give thanks, and subordinating
yourselves to one another as you are engaged in this thanksgiving to God.
Humanity in the New Testament thus derives directly from the practical experience of the Gospel. And we must certainly not forget the negative beginning
to this general exhortation : " Be not drunk with wine." We recall from
1 Cor. 11 that the knowledge of the true relationship between man and wife
established and determined and limited by the knowledge of Jesus Christ stands
in contrast to an enthusiasm for equality which will not accept the fact that
they are both allotted to their distinctive place and way in the peace of God.
Where it is not a matter of this intoxication but of the fulness of the Spirit, not
of the boasting and defiance of man but of the praise of God, not of the establishment of one's own right by one's own might but of constant thanksgiving,
there flows from the Gospel the necessity of the reciprocal subordination in
which each gives to the other that which is proper to him. This is the meaning
of the house-table : *Suum cuique.* It has nothing really to do with patriarchalism,
or with a hierarchy of domestic and civil values and powers. It does not give
one control over the other, or put anyone under the dominion of the other. The
ὑποτασσόμενοι of v. 21 applies equally to all, each in his own place and in
respect of his own way. What it demands is ὑποτασσόμενοι ἀλλήλοις ἐν φόβῳ
Χριστοῦ ; mutual subordination in respect before the Lord. He is the Exalted
but also the Lowly, the Lowly but also the Exalted, who causes each to share
in His glory but also His burden, His sovereignty but also His service. And
here there is only mutual subordination in full reciprocity. In this way order
is created within the creaturely sphere, and humanity established. It is, of
course, no accident that more than half of the table is devoted to the relationship of man and woman, and particularly their relationship in marriage. This
relationship is typical or exemplary for the whole relationship which has to be
estimated in the fear of Christ. In good or evil alike all other relations between
the sexes have their fulfilment and norm in the fact that this man finds this
woman and this woman this man and therefore man the fellow-man to whom
he is referred and with whom he is united. We stated at the outset that expression is given to fellow-humanity as one man looks the other in the eyes and

lets himself be seen by the other. The meaning and promise of marriage is that this should take place between man and woman, that one woman should encounter one man as his, and one man one woman as hers. Where it takes place we have a good marriage ; the marriage which can only be monogamous. It is from this height that the whole field is surveyed. Again, it is no accident that the list of admonitions opens with that to the wife and not to the husband (v. 22). That the participle clause ὑποτασσόμενοι is naturally continued in this way, and general mutual subordination has its first concrete form in the wife, is explained at once in v. 23 by the comparison : " For the husband is the head of the wife (a statement taken from 1 Cor. 11³), even as Christ is the head of the church : and he is the saviour of the body." Because her subordination stands under this comparison, the woman must see to it that it is not broken but maintained. And therefore the subordination of woman to man is the first and most interesting problem which arises in this field. Not man but woman represents the reality which embraces all those who are addressed, whether they be wives or husbands, old or young, slaves or masters, which claims even the apostle himself in his peculiar position, and from which he thinks and speaks and admonishes them to think and act. They are all the community which has in Jesus Christ its Head. They are all set in this place and called and gathered to this community by baptism. For none of them can there be any question of a higher or better place. None of them can ever think of escaping from or trying to climb above it. In the fulness of the Spirit they can only wish to remain at this place, listening, obedient and therefore subordinate to the One from whom and for whose sake the whole community exists, and without whom it could not continue for a single moment or in any respect, since it is the body which is snatched and rescued from the fire of perdition only in virtue of its union with this Head. The advantage of the wife, her birthright, is that it is she and not the man who, in relation to her husband and subordination to him, may reflect, represent and attest this reality of the community. The exhortation specifically addressed to her is simply a particular form of the basic admonition which applies to all. She is subordinated to her husband as the whole community is to Christ. The whole community can only take up the position in relation to Christ which is proper to the wife in relation to her husband. Even husbands and masters must take up the same position in relation to Christ as the wife in relation to her husband. This is what makes the admonition to the wife so urgent and inescapable. And this is what characterises it as a peculiar distinction for the wife. If she does not break but respects the true relationship to her husband, the wife is not less but greater than her husband in the community. She is not the second but the first. In a qualified sense she is the community. The husband has no option but to order himself by the wife as she is subordinate in this way. The curious wish of Schleiermacher that he had been a woman is not so foolish when it is seen against this background. It is striking that the final statement of the whole passage (v. 33b) repeats the admonition to the wife : " And the wife see that she reverence her husband." Whatever is said to the husband stands within the framework of what has to be said to the wife as wife. She and not her husband is the type of the community listening to Christ and the apostolic admonition. She must be mentioned both first and last, for she may first and last take this admonition to heart, all hearing and obedience being represented in her hearing and obedience. On the other hand, the greater part of the passage (vv. 25-33) is devoted to the particular admonition to husbands. This emphasis is significant. What is meant by the mutual subordination in the fear of Christ expected of all (v. 21) is demonstrated in the attitude of the husband, who in his relationship to his wife is the κεφαλή, the superior, the first, the leader, the bearer of primary responsibility. In this respect he is the type of the κεφαλή of the whole, of the Author and Lord of the community, of the Saviour of the body (v. 23). In the being and action of the husband in relation to the wife there is thus decided whether the hearing and obedience of the wife take place in the sense in which they are established ; whether she is really subordinated to him ὡς τῷ κυρίῳ and therefore necessarily and not merely in the sense of an androcracy which might easily become a gynocracy. As men in their being and action towards the wife reflect the being and action of the κεφαλή Christ, the community is the community and not merely seems to be or would like to be. How could it be the body of this Head without this reflection ? And it is the particular calling of husbands to produce this reflection. More has to be said to them than to wives because in respect of the life of the community more has to be said about the being and action of Christ than the being and action of the men concerned. There can be no question of anything more than reflection. Men are not the authors, lords and saviours of women any more than they can be their own authors, lords and saviours. Christ stands equally above both husbands and wives as He stands equally below them. But the reflection of His majesty and lowliness in relation to them and their wives, to the whole community, is the particular responsibility of the men. It consists in the fact that they love their wives. For Christ loved the community—it was in this that He became its Author, Lord and Saviour. He gave Himself for it (v. 25). And in this self-giving He made it His community. It did not make itself His community. It did not even make itself ready to be this. He Himself sanctioned it when it was unholy and purified it when it was unclean. He gives it a part in His own Word and Spirit. He invested it with His own glory, and thus made it the counterpart from which He had taken away every spot of reproach or occasion for blame. He Himself prepared it for Himself. He thus made it His own (vv. 26–27). It owes itself to Him and Him alone. This is the love of Christ for His community. This is the original form of the majesty and humility in which He stands in relation to it, and to both husbands and wives within it. There can be no question of repeating the original of this love of Christ. It is unique and once-for-all. But even less can there be any question of living in the light of this original without accepting the summons to a relative imitation and reflection of this original. This once-for-all and unique light does not shine into the void but into a sphere of men and therefore of males and females, i.e., into the sphere described in Gen. 2, where it is decided that it is not good for man to be alone, where he is to recognise himself in another and another in himself, where humanity relentlessly means fellow-humanity, where the body or existence of woman is the same to man as his own body or existence, where the I is not just unreal but impossible without the Thou, and where all the willing and longing of the I— on the far side of all egoism or altruism—must be the willing and longing of the Thou. This is the humanity of man which in the community is set in the unique and once-for-all light of the love of Christ. What else can this mean but that place is found for this fellow-humanity (which is what is meant by the imitation of that image) ; that man (who is the first to be summoned) takes seriously the " This now " of Gen. 2[23] ; that he loves the woman which God has given him as himself, i.e., that he deals with her as with the fellow-man without whom he could not be himself, in whose person he constantly has to do with himself, in whose person he does good or evil to himself, exalting or abasing himself, and whose existence gives humanity to his own. This is what Paul describes as the particular responsibility of men in vv. 28–29a. They may and should and must precede women by accepting and affirming them in such a way that they do what man did at the climax of his creation in Gen. 2. For, as the decisive passage vv. 29b–32 goes on to tell us, what man did at the climax of his creation ; this humanity as the fellow-humanity of male and female ; the purely creaturely happening that a man leaves his father and mother and cleaves to his wife and they become one flesh—this is not a primary thing, the original, but a secondary, the copy. We have to do here with the great mystery and not just the small

(v. 32). For the creation of man and for this climax, for this form of humanity, the normative pattern, the basic decree and the plan of all the plans of God is " Christ and the community." This stands inaccessibly before and above the copy of man and woman. Thus in the little copy, between man and woman, there can be no question of the self-offering of the one for the other, of the one making the other a worthy counterpart by self-offering, and of the other owing itself and all that it is and has to it. Man cannot be the Creator and Saviour of men, or the man of the woman. On the other hand, it belongs to the very essence of the copy modelled on this pattern that the man should be with the woman, that he should not will to be without her, and that he should therefore love her as himself. And that this may and must take place is the admonition which must be given and heard where the light of this original falls into the human sphere, i.e., in the community created by baptism and the Word of Jesus Christ. And it is to the men first that this admonition must be given, and by them that it must first be heard : " Let every one of you in particular so love his wife even as himself " (v. 33), willing and affirming her existence together with his own, and her honour and welfare with and as his own, willing himself only as he wills her too. Wives must and will hear this also. We remember that this inversion takes place in the Song of Songs. There is a love of the community for Christ as well as a love of Christ for the community. But as the love of Christ precedes the answering love of the community, so the love of the husband precedes that of the wife. In imitation of the attitude of Christ the husband may and should precede at this point as the wife may and should precede him in representing the community in its absolute subordination to Christ. But it is to subordination that the husband himself is summoned. That he should love his wife is his particular part or function in the mutual subordination demanded in v. 21.

" This is a great mystery " (Eph. 5³²). The saying refers to Gen. 2¹⁸ᶠ·. But in Gen. 2¹⁸ᶠ· it is a matter of the creation of man as male and female, and therefore of the basic form of being in the encounter of I and Thou, of humanity as fellow-humanity. In the New Testament a mystery (μυστήριον) is a reality which carries with it a definite message and does so in such a way that it is both concealed and declared. Where the revelation of God does not take place in and with this reality, and in such a way that it evokes the faith of man, and in his faith knowledge, the message is concealed and the mystery undisclosed. It is received, but not revealed. But where in and with it the revelation of God takes place and faith is evoked, it speaks and discloses itself ; it is an open secret. The humanity of man is a reality of this kind. " But I speak," says Paul in Eph. 5³², " concerning Christ and the church." If we read Gen. 2¹⁸ᶠ· in the context of the Old Testament " Yahweh and Israel " is the message contained in this matter and both concealed and declared. The New Testament does not exclude but includes this interpretation. But it reaches above and behind the whole of the Old Testament as such. It sees the same reality, the creation and being of man as male and female, his humanity as fellow-humanity. It also sees the " Yahweh and Israel " contained and both concealed and declared in it. But it sees further and deeper. For it even the " Yahweh and Israel," and the whole Old Testament message grouped around this word of the covenant, is itself a mystery which has still to be disclosed, a prophecy which has still to be fulfilled, a preliminary history which has still to be followed by the true history. The disclosure, the fulfilment, the true history is " Christ and the community." The New Testament knows that before all time, and in the beginning of time posited by the act of creation, and in the perishing time which stands under the sign of the fall and its penalty, and finally in the new time of freedom which has dawned, the resolve and will of God was and is and will be : " Christ and the community." And for this reason it says of the humanity of man that it is *this* mystery ; that it is the concealed and declared content, undisclosed without the Word and the Spirit and faith but disclosed by the Word, in the Spirit and for faith, of the reality " Christ and the community."

This is the biblical confirmation of the presupposition with which we took up this theme at the beginning of the section. We described the humanity of man as a mystery of faith. We had to deal with it accordingly. We had thus to ask first concerning the humanity of the man Jesus. In answer to this question we found that Jesus is the man who is *for* His fellows. We descended from this height to the lower question of humanity generally, and we found that man is the man who is *with* his fellows, the I with the Thou, the male with the female. We could not say more than " with." To say " for " would be to make the false assertion of a general anthropology. It would be to say too much. It can and must be said of the man Jesus, but of Him alone. Yet on the other hand we could not say less. For man without the fellow-man would be a creature which has nothing in common with the man Jesus, and with which the man Jesus has nothing in common. We had to turn our back resolutely on the idea of a man without the fellow-man and the existing anthropology. Setting our aim neither too high nor too low, we had thus to interpret humanity simply as fellow-humanity. And we had finally to realise that in this fellow-humanity we are not dealing with an ideal or law or anything of that kind, but with the normative and natural determination of man. For in the co-existence of man and woman at least we have a difference and fellowship given to man in and with his existence, so that in it he is fellow-human quite apart from his own thought or volition. This I-Thou relationship in its distinctive factuality and necessity is thus characteristic of his whole being, controlling it and giving it its character as fellow-humanity. We also saw that in this fellow-humanity, and at the very point where it emerges unequivocally as a natural fact of creation, i.e., in the co-existence of man and woman, the New Testament finds a great mystery And the New Testament explanation of this mystery is as follows. What is contained and both concealed and declared in this reality, what everyone can receive but not everyone can know because its recognition is conditioned by God's revelation and the obedient faith which it evokes, is " Christ and His community." It is obvious that this brings us back to the starting-point and beginning of our whole investigation and presentation. We have here a confirmation of the fact that to understand what humanity is we had to look first at the man Jesus, the man *for* the fellow-man, and that on this basis we could come to see in man generally only man *with* his fellow-man. According to the main passage in Ephesians 5, but finally in all the relevant New Testament texts, Christ *and* the community means quite unequivocally Christ *for* the community. This dualism stands in clear distinction to that of man and woman and every human I and Thou denoted and controlled by that of man and woman. For the One who takes the place of man—and in this He differs from every other man or I—does not exist and act for Himself or for His own sake, but absolutely for others, for those who are united with Him as His community. He is their Head and Saviour. He is the One who takes away their sins and conquers their death. He is the One who lifts from them the yoke of the corresponding and confirmatory law of their sin and death. He is the One who brings and guarantees their freedom. He is the pledge of the eternal life promised to them. He is wholly for them and not for Himself ; Jesus, the man for His fellows. And the co-existence of man and woman, humanity as fellow-humanity, is a great mystery because it contains and both conceals and discloses this fact that Jesus is the man for His fellows, both hiding and disclosing it, so that it can be received by everyone but not known by everyone. In this reality we have the witness of the creature itself to this truth. The Old Testament plainly attests it with its Yahweh and Israel. In the fact that it does so it is itself a mystery, prophecy and preliminary history, which must speak of man exactly but exclusively in the way in which it actually does in Genesis 2 and the Song of Songs. If, then, humanity as such, as a purely natural and creaturely determination of man, is this mystery, this real witness, disclosed and received or concealed and rejected, to this first and final element in the will and decree of God, it must be seen as we have tried to see it, and we have no option but to resist any idea of man without his fellow-man, and to understand humanity as fellow-humanity. As fellow-humanity, in the form of the co-existence of man and woman, it is this real witness. The general " with " corresponds to the unique " for " of Jesus from which all the plans and ways and works of God proceed and to which they move. If we accept Ephesians 5 and the New Testament view of this matter, we see that the circle closes at this point, that this is the end, and that we could not begin at any other point than that at which we did, or move forward from that point in any other way. Against this background the basic thesis of theological anthropology, that human being is a being in encounter, loses every shred of similarity with a mere hypothetical assertion. It acquires an axiomatic

and dogmatic quality. In the Christian Church we have no option
but to interpret humanity as fellow-humanity. And *si quis dixerit
hominem esse solitarium, anathema sit.* We can now regard this as
secured and demonstrated. And the future history of humanity may
well depend to some extent upon whether the Christian Church can
agree to recognise this as secured and demonstrated, and thereafter
assert that anathema with a stringency for which it has so far lacked
both the perception and the resolution. It is to be noted, however,
that this is possible only on the basis of Ephesians 5.

We have still to draw a concluding line. It is no accident that in
this whole sphere we have had to make such ready use of terms like
image, original, copy, correspondence, analogy, parity, likeness,
similarity, and finally mystery. The title which we have given to the
whole section is : " Man in his Determination as the Covenant-partner
of God." Our starting-point was that man is determined in and with
his creation and existence to be the covenant-partner of God. Our
problem was how far he is this ; how far his creation and existence,
his nature, must correspond to this determination. Our interest has
been focused upon man below, in his reality distinct from God, in his
creaturely nature in relation to that for which he was created, and
may exist, and is summoned to exist from above. We have thus
been concerned with the inner relationship between this being and
his destiny. We have seen that this relationship is not one of contradiction but of correspondence. Man is orientated towards that for
which he is determined. Even when he sins, he can deny and conceal
but he cannot remove or destroy the fact that he is orientated in this
way. Even as a sinner he remains the creature of God and therefore
the being whose orientation is to be the covenant-partner of God.
He can give himself up for lost. But he cannot escape God, or lose
his being as the creature of God, or the nature of this being. He can
trifle with the grace of God, but he cannot make himself wholly
unworthy to be in covenant with God. He does this too. But he
is found and rescued by the free and totally undeserved grace of God
as the creature which even when it gave itself up for lost did not
escape God, but whose being in all its perversion and corruption
remained a being in correspondence with its determination as the
covenant-partner of God. God is faithful. God acknowledges and
confesses Himself the Creator by reconciling the world to Himself
in Christ, in the One for whom and with a view to whom He created
it. He thus proves true that which we contested but which did not
in any way cease to be the truth because we did so, but was always
the truth even in the form of our lie, namely, that our orientation
is to be the covenant-partners of God.

And now we have investigated and described what we are, what
our humanity is, in what way we are orientated to be God's covenant-
partners in spite of our perversion and corruption, in what our

correspondence to this determination consists. Our corresponding being is a being in the encounter of man and fellow-man. In this being we are covenant-partners by nature. This does not mean that we are the covenant-partners of God by nature. This is the determination under which we are created and exist. This is the particular plan and will of God operative and executed in our creation. This is the gracious meaning of our existence and nature. But it is not a human attribute. It does not belong to us in virtue of the fact that as men we are the creatures of God. We are not created the covenant-partners of God, but to be His covenant-partners, to be His partners in the history which is the goal of His creation and in which His work as Creator finds its continuation and fulfilment. That this is achieved, that we fulfil this determination, that this history is in train and moves steadily to its goal, is a matter of the free grace with which God deals in sovereignty with His creature, of the Word and Spirit with which He has intercourse with His creature, of His good-pleasure which we cannot control but must always acknowledge that we do not deserve. Yet the fact remains—and this is something which belongs to us as the creatures of God, which is part of our human essence, which can rightly be called a human and even the typically human attribute—that we are covenant-partners by nature and in our mutual dealings, the man with the fellow-man, the I with the Thou, the man with the woman. This is something which is our own, and is inviolable and indestructible. This constitutes the unbroken continuity of human existence. In this we correspond to our determination, and cannot cease to do so. In this there is a positive relationship between our being and our destiny. In this we ourselves, whether we know and accept the fact or not, are in sheer fact a sign and witness of our determination. We are created as mutual partners. And this leaves open the further possibility that we are created to be the partners of God. The latter statement speaks of the free grace of God in relation to man created with a specific nature. But it does undoubtedly speak of this human nature as such. And the content of the two statements makes it clear that the first is a reflection of the second, its truth being a likeness of that of the second.

It is to be noted that the *tertium comparationis*, the feature common to both likeness and reality, to both copy and original, consists in both cases, between man and his fellow-man on the one hand and God and man on the other, in an indestructible connexion and fellowship between two subjects which are indestructibly distinct. The only point of comparison is that on both sides there is a firm and genuine covenant. A covenant means co-existence for better for worse. It is genuine if it is between two partners who are obviously not identical. And it is sure if there is no question of the dissolution of the relationship between the two partners. More than this cannot be said. For apart from this common feature everything is different.

On the one side we have a union of creature with creature in virtue of
the creaturely nature which they do not owe to themselves but to
their Creator ; on the other we have a union of the Creator and His
creature, in which the Creator is the free Lord of the covenant, and
His mercy is its basis and goal, His wisdom the power of its initiation
and execution, His faithfulness the guarantee of its continuance, and
finally His own person its fulfilment. On the one side we have reciprocity, the giving and receiving of two partners of equal essence and
dignity ; on the other everything is one-sided—the authority, the
rule and the judgment, the plan and the work, being all of God, and
His, too, the gift which makes it possible for the human partner to
have a part in the covenant. On the one side man is with man ; on
the other, God is with man but also for him in a way in which man
can never be for God. On the one side there is an obvious and necessarily two-sided need ; on the other all the need is on the side of man
but on God's side there is the sheer sovereignty of a grace which
knows neither internal nor external compulsion but is wholly free,
its address to man being an overflow of the inconceivable goodness of
God. In our consideration of the man and woman on the one side
and Christ and the community on the other, we have seen how great
are the differences between the two relationships. But we have to
remember that even the autonomy of the two partners is different in
the two cases. In the one case it is only the relative and parallel
autonomy of two creatures, but in the other we have the absolute
autonomy of God on the one side and the relative autonomy of the
creature on the other. And we have to remember that the firmness
of the covenant differs in the two cases. In the one case it is that of
the factuality which man cannot escape because he has this nature
and no other ; but in the other it is that of the constancy of God
which cannot turn from man because it is the free mercy of God
which will not let go of man. It is, therefore, with this disparity that
the being of man corresponds to the fact that man is ordained to be
the covenant-partner of God. And this means that the correspondence of his nature does not give him any right or claim, any power to
decide either to be or not to be the covenant-partner of God. It is
no merit if he is ready to become this. He can only magnify the
grace of God if he may do so. For it is only the grace of God if he is
called and enabled to do so. It thus follows that natural theology
cannot find here a point of contact for the proclamation of the grace
and revelation of God. For if it is true that man in his humanity is
himself a purely factual sign and witness of his determination, this
can only mean that he is himself a mystery, a reality which encloses
the declaration of his ordination to be with God, but only encloses it,
and therefore conceals no less than discloses it, and discloses it only
when it is expressed by the grace and revelation of God, and in the
knowledge of faith thereby awakened. If this does not happen, it is

of no help to man that he is himself a sign and witness. He is dumb even in relation to himself. The declaration of his determination takes place—he is in fact a man with the fellow-man—but he does not receive it. It does not tell him that God is with him and for him ; that he is not merely the covenant-partner of the fellow-man, but of God. This is something which man cannot tell himself. He cannot even prepare himself to receive it. Only the Word and Spirit of God can tell it to him. Only subsequently can the proclamation of the grace and revelation of God draw his attention to the fact that it cannot be anything strange or unnatural for him to be called and set in covenant with God and gathered to the people of God.

And this is the positive thing which results from the fact that for all the dissimilarity there is similarity. This is the firm and genuine covenant in which man finds himself by nature in virtue of the fact that his humanity as such is fellow-humanity—corresponding to the firm and genuine covenant with God to which he, the creature to whom this nature is intrinsic, is summoned by the grace and revelation of God. If this takes place, this calling, this actualisation of his determination, finds him in the deepest sense at home. The Word of God really applies to him, this creature. The Spirit of God really speaks to his spirit. For as God discloses Himself to him, there is also disclosed to him the mystery of his own human reality, the meaning of the fact that he is man with his fellow-man, man with woman. If God comes to man, He comes to His possession which He has already marked as such in creating it. And what man may discover by the Word and Spirit of God as God comes to him is that God has not created him as a being alien to Himself, but as His neighbour and confidant. He has marked his nature, himself in his humanity, with the mark of one who is His neighbour and confidant. Man bears the sign of the firm and genuine covenant in which he may find and have his fellow-man, the I the Thou and man woman. He may recognise and find confirmed in this sign the fact that God really intends and seeks him when He calls him to covenant with Himself, to this covenant which is firm and genuine in a different way because grounded in and maintained by His grace. This sign and likeness, this reality full of declaration, the mystery of his own reality, is no longer dumb but eloquent. His humanity can no longer be a mere fact—a matter of accident or caprice. As the reflection of the light of grace which lay on it even when he did not know it, marking his existence as such, his humanity becomes the task and problem and content of his own action. Now that the meaning of his being is no longer unknown or obscure, he will now will, and will to practise and actualise, what he is by nature. In order that the fact of the human nature of man may be actualised, there is needed the grace and revelation of the covenant which God has concluded with the man created for this purpose. On the side of man there is needed his hearing of the Word of God, his calling by His Spirit, his awakening to faith, his accepting and occupying his place and status as God's partner in this covenant. There is thus needed for the human willing and actualising of humanity the fact that this humanity, which in the first instance is a mere fact and as such a mystery, should be inwardly illumined and made transparent by the free act of God from above. There is needed what takes place in Ephesians 5—that the relationship of husband and wife should be lit up by that of Christ and His community. " In thy light shall we see light." But humanity, the human and natural relationship which is made clear and transparent in this way, itself becomes light. It is the fact of humanity which, giving light and speaking as a sign and mystery, becomes the task and problem and content of human action and therefore, as in Ephesians 5, the theme of Christian admonition. And conversely this fact presupposed in all human action and grounded in the nature of man is as such the sign and witness that as man lives in the human covenant he is obedient to his calling to be the covenant-partner of God and thus participates in this covenant-fellowship. That the covenant between God and man is the original of that between man and man means, therefore, on the one side that the latter covenant may and should be lived out in human action ; and it means on the other side that in its actual existence it is the hope that may also live in covenant with God and live this out too in his own action. This sign given him in and with his own nature tells and assures him that he is the neighbour and confidant of God, that he has not slipped from Him, that marked in this way he has always been regarded by God as His own, and always will be. It tells him that in this nature of his he who stands in this temporal covenant is also called to the eternal, that he may take comfort in and hold to the fact that he is called in this way, and that the Creator is faithful by whom he is called.

It must be pointed out in conclusion that if the being of man in encounter is a being in correspondence to his determination as the covenant-partner of God, the statement is unavoidable that it is a being in correspondence to God Himself, to the being of His Creator. The Initiator, Lord and Sustainer of the covenant between God and man is God Himself, and He alone. If man is ordained to be God's partner in this covenant, and if his nature is a likeness corresponding to this ordination, necessarily it corresponds in this respect to the nature of God Himself. God has created him in this correspondence, as a reflection of Himself. Man is the image of God. This is not an arbitrarily invented statement. In relation to the man Jesus, by whom we are impelled already to this conclusion, it is clear and necessary as a final definition. But in Gen. 1[26f.] the Old Testament also makes it in relation to man generally. I refer to my discussion of this text in *C.D.* III, 1, pp. 191 f., and believe that the present train of thought yields exactly the same results. Man generally, the man with the fellow-man, has indeed a part in the divine likeness of the man Jesus, the man for the fellow-man. As man generally is modelled on the man Jesus and His being for others, and as the man Jesus is modelled on God, it has to be said of man generally that he is created in the image of God. He is in his humanity, and therefore in his fellow-humanity. God created him in His own image in the fact that He did not create him alone but in this connexion and fellowship. For in God's action as the Lord of the covenant, and even further back in His action as the Creator of a reality distinct from Himself, it is proved that God Himself is not solitary, that although He is one in essence He is not alone, but that primarily and properly He is in connexion and fellowship. It is inevitable that we should recall the triune being of God at this point. God exists in relationship and fellowship. As the Father of the Son and the Son of the Father He is Himself I and Thou, confronting Himself and yet always one and the same in the Holy Ghost. God created man in His own image, in correspondence with His own being and essence. He created Him in the image which emerges even in His work as the Creator and Lord of the covenant. Because He is not solitary in Himself, and therefore does not will to be so *ad extra*, it is not good for man to be alone, and God created him in His own image, as male and female. This is what is emphatically said by Gen. I[27], and all other explanations of the *imago Dei* suffer from the fact that they do not do justice to this decisive statement. We need not waste words on the dissimilarity in the similarity of the similitude. Quite obviously we do not have here more than an analogy, i.e., similarity in dissimilarity. We merely repeat that there can be no question of an analogy of being, but of relationship. God is in relationship, and so too is the man created by Him. This is his divine likeness. When we view it in this way, the dispute whether it is lost by sin finds a self-evident solution. It is not lost. But more important is the fact that what man is indestructibly as he is man with the fellow-man, he is in hope of the being and action of the One who is his original in this relationship.

§ 46

MAN AS SOUL AND BODY

Through the Spirit of God, man is the subject, form and life of a substantial organism, the soul of his body—wholly and simultaneously both, in ineffaceable difference, inseparable unity, and indestructible order.

1. JESUS, WHOLE MAN

So far it has been man's being in itself and as such that has occupied us. We have learned to know it as being in covenant with God and in encounter with fellow-men. The anthropology of traditional Christian dogmatics has usually omitted to lay this foundation and addressed itself immediately to the problem to which we turn only now. This is the problem of the constitution of this being, the problem of man's existence and nature. These problems were dealt with in the traditional doctrine of the human soul, which was strongly emphasised, and of the human body, which was almost always emphatically disregarded. Man's being exists, and is therefore soul; and it exists in a certain form, and is therefore body. This is the simplest description of the being of soul and body and their relationship. Man is soul and body—this is in brief the constitution of his being. For this reason, we have now to clarify this being of man in itself and as such. Man's being is being with God and therefore being with fellow-men. With this recognition as our starting point, we too can and must reckon with the fact that this being has an existence and a nature, and therefore with the question concerning body and soul as the constituents of man's being. Thus we have the advantage over the older dogmatics of having firm ground under our feet and of occupying a point of vantage from which the scope of this new problem can really be observed. It is probable that, starting from this point, we shall avoid a certain one-sidedness, exaggeration and vulnerability more easily than could the older dogmatics which did not trouble to lay this foundation.

Advance into the region of new insights and conceptions which we now enter has its own difficulties. For one thing, we come at this point very close to the propositions of all kinds of non-theological studies of mankind, among which one can very easily go astray, especially as they always arouse at this point the burning interest which powerful inner contradictions always bring to light. The danger is all the more acute in view of the fact that the primitive and New Testament witnesses to revelation apparently took no very great interest in the questions here to be answered, but took up their position towards them only incidentally and with a certain carefree inexactness, thus giving the impression that they were to be regarded rather as formal. Hence we must be circumspect if on the one hand we are not to be burdened with the relevant non-theological inquiries and theories, and on the other hand we are to see and think at this point too from an adequately biblical and exegetical ground and thus reach an understanding, and a Christian understanding, in the matter. But we shall affirm that we may still be taught by the revealed Word of God, and that in no circumstances can we interrupt our investigation and presentation at this point. A gap at this point would be intolerable, would have the most fatal consequences, and would give free entrance to the most varied ambiguities and errors.

In this section, we have to prove that man is to be understood as " soul and body," that this constitutes his being ; and we have to show how far this is the case. It will serve to illumine the problem if at the same time we state the other pairs of concepts which more or less exactly express the same truth and might therefore be considered as alternative headings : " Man as spirit and substantial organism," as " rational and sensuous," " inner and outer," " invisible and visible," " inapprehensible and apprehensible," " intelligible and empirical," and even as " heavenly and earthly "—these are certainly not excluded as possible designations of the same thing. What these other pairs of ideas express or indicate must certainly come under discussion under the title " Man as Soul and Body." Of all other possibilities, we choose the latter because they keep us closest to the language of the Bible, and because in their popular simplicity they indicate not only most unpretentiously but also, for all the problems which they involve, most unambiguously, concretely, and comprehensively the questions which are here to be asked and answered.

The presupposition that the constitution of man is to be understood under one of the pairs of ideas that point in this direction, is a theological truth requiring theological foundation and explanation. We cannot, of course, overlook the fact that in themselves the words " soul " and " body," which in combination can be interpreted in so many different ways, indicate a very real problem—or rather a whole complex of problems—concerning man's general understanding of himself. Inevitably in interpretation of this complex of problems we must not only negatively but also positively deal with many an old and new presentation attempted in the course of man's general understanding of himself. But here again we go our own way on our own responsibility. That is, we inquire concerning the nature of man as he is in the Word of God and as he considers and is responsible to himself on the basis of the call of God. By the constitution of this man, the man of whom " thou art mindful " and whom " thou regardest," we understand the true constitution of man. And of the constitution of this man, we say that it is to be understood as soul and body (or at least in terms of one of the pairs of ideas that point in this direction). Thus we do not work with a borrowing from another kind of discipline when we employ these two words and their combination; and we reserve to ourselves the freedom, irrespective of parallel or divergent presentations in other disciplines, to interpret and use them in accordance with the theological inquiry and discipline.

Here too, then, we first go back to the source of understanding which alone can be authentic and normative for the theological doctrine of man's nature. We find our bearings and our instruction as we look to the constitution of the humanity of Jesus. With the clarity and certainty that we gain here, we can then set out the propositions in which the Christian understanding of the constitution of all men generally may be expressed and comprehended.

Rather surprisingly, the first and decisive impression gained when we address our questions to the man Jesus of the New Testament is that the pairs of ideas with which we provisionally designated the problem are insufficient in His case. The differentiation in the constitution of man which they suggest has in His case only a provisional and relative and not an ultimate and absolute meaning. What is there in Him which is only inner and not outer, sensuous and not rational? What does soul or body mean for Him to the extent that either implies an importance and function of its own, different from and opposed to the other?

The Jesus of the New Testament is supremely true man in the very fact that He does not conform to the later definition, and far from existing as the union of two parts or two "substances," He is one whole man, embodied soul and besouled body: the one in the other and never merely beside it; the one never without the other but only with it, and in it present, active and significant; the one with all its attributes always to be taken as seriously as the other. As this one whole man, and therefore as true man, the Jesus of the New Testament is born and lives and suffers and dies and is raised again. Between His death and His resurrection there is a transformation, but no alteration, division or least of all subtraction. The body does not remain behind, nor does the soul depart. As the same whole man, soul and body, He rises as He died, and sits at the right hand of God, and will come again. And He is one whole man in His relation to others, in what He does for them, what He gives them, what He asks of them, what He is for them and for the whole cosmos. He does not fulfil His office and His work from His miraculous annunciation to His fulfilment in such a way that we can separate His outer form from His inner or His inner form from His outer. Everything is the revelation of an inner, invisible, spiritual plane of life. But it is almost more striking and characteristic that everything has an outer, visible, bodily form. There is no logic here which is not as such physics, no cure of souls which is not as such bound up with cure of bodies. The man who is called by Him and who takes part in His way and work as a recipient and fellow-worker does not only receive something to consider and to will and to feel ; he enters into bodily contact and fellowship. The man who comes to hear of the kingdom of God comes also to taste it. He comes to eat and to drink bodily, so that it again becomes apparent that in this bodily eating and drinking he has to do with nothing less than the hidden—in our terminology, " inner " or " spiritual "—savouring and tasting of the heavenly bread and the powers of the world to come. To believe on Him is to be on the way to the same whole manhood which is His own mystery. To serve Him is not only to speak to others, but also to give these others to eat and to drink. And it is again this one whole manhood which is revealed in His person as wide as the future and the hope not only of His community but of the whole cosmos.

This can be illustrated linguistically from the decisive section of the New Testament witness to Christ. In Gal. 1⁴ we read that Jesus Christ gave Himself (ἑαυτόν) up for our sins. The same ἑαυτόν is found in the same expression in Gal. 2²⁰ and Eph. 5², ²⁵. But compare Mt. 20²⁸ and *par.*: the Son of man is come to give His soul (ψυχὴν αὐτοῦ) a ransom for many. Similarly 1 Jn. 3¹⁶ : His ψυχή for us ; Jn. 10¹¹, ¹⁵ : the Good Shepherd gives His ψυχή for His sheep ; Jn. 15¹³ : his ψυχή for his friends. But again compare Lk. 22¹⁹ : This is my body (τὸ σῶμά μου) which is given for you ; Heb. 10¹⁰ : we are sanctified by the sacrifice of the σῶμα ᾿Ιησοῦ Χριστοῦ; Rom. 7⁴ : through the σῶμα τοῦ Χριστοῦ you are dead to the law ; Col. 1²² : He has reconciled you ἐν τῷ σώματι τῆς σαρκὸς αὐτοῦ by His death ; 1 Pet. 2²⁴ : He bore our sins ἐν τῷ σώματι αὐτοῦ on the tree. The action of which all these passages speak is the same, as are also its consequence and significance, its subject, and obviously and above all its object, which is materially identical with the subject. But this object can be designated sometimes as ἑαυτός, sometimes as ψυχὴ αὐτοῦ, sometimes as σῶμα αὐτοῦ. The difference in usage is not, of course, unpremeditated ; yet obviously the one term could always be used in place of the others. Jesus, He Himself, is His soul and His body, and it is this one whole man who died on the cross and thus made our sin inoperative and completed our reconciliation.

That the New Testament really points to this unity is shown by the fact that the passages which especially mention the soul (or even " spirit ") and the body of the man Jesus are comparatively rare in appearance and parsimonious in content. The reader is led to note clearly only the fact that in Jesus we are concerned with the unity of two realms or aspects and thus undoubtedly—and this emphatically prevents all Docetism—with a real man.

In the Fourth Gospel we hear repeatedly of a " troubling " (ταράσσεσθαι) of the soul of Jesus (or of His " spirit,") which in 11³³, ³⁸ (in face of the lamentation over Lazarus) has the character of indignation (ἐνεβριμήσατο τῷ πνεύματι), in 12²⁷ (at the thought of the approaching " hour ") of fright, and in 13²¹ (in face of the traitor Judas) of amazement. According to Lk. 12⁵⁰, He is straitened (συνέχομαι) as He awaits the coming of the baptism with which He is to be baptised. We read in Mk. 8¹² that, at the question : Why does this generation seek after a sign ? Jesus " sighed deeply in his spirit " (ἀναστενάξας τῷ πνεύματι). We read in Mt. 26³⁷ᶠ·, in the description of the scene in Gethsemane : He " began to be sorrowful (λυπεῖσθαι) and very heavy (ἀδημονεῖν). Then saith he unto them, My soul is exceeding sorrowful, even unto death (περίλυπος . . . ἕως θανάτου : the saying is a citation from Ps. 42⁶⁻¹² and 43⁵, where the original has " cast down ") : tarry ye here and watch with me." Relevant, too, is Lk. 22⁴⁴ : " And being in ἀγωνία he prayed more earnestly " ; and also Heb. 5⁷: " Who in the days of his flesh, when he had offered up prayers and supplications, with strong crying and tears unto him that was able to save him from death." From Lk. 19⁴¹, again, we hear how Jesus wept over Jerusalem, and almost more impressive are the sentences in the story of Lazarus in Jn. 11³⁴ᶠᶠ· : He " said, Where have ye laid him ? They said unto him, Lord, come and see. ἐδάκρυσεν ὁ Ἰησοῦς. Then said the Jews, Behold how he loved him ! " According to the context Jesus was called to Bethany : " Lord, behold, he whom thou lovest is sick " (v. 3). And v. 5 (heightening the contrast of the fact that Jesus for two days gave no heed to the summons) records : " Now Jesus loved Martha, and her sister, and Lazarus." That Jesus " loved " individual persons appears else-where in the Fourth Gospel only in the person of the mysterious disciple (ὅν ἠγάπα ὁ Ἰησοῦς, 13²³, 19²⁶, 20², 21⁷, ²⁰), and in the rest of the New Testament only in Mk. 10²¹ where the rich young man is deliberately described in this way. From what is said in Jn. 15¹³⁻¹⁵ the relation of Jesus to His disciples is certainly not to be thought of in terms of what we understand by " friendship." And it is striking that the general expression that Jesus loved His own (Jn. 13¹ ; 15⁹⁻¹² ; Gal. 2²⁰ ; Eph. 5², ²⁵, ²⁸ ; Rev. 1⁵) occurs much more seldom than one would expect. The saying in Lk. 10²¹ is strangely isolated when it tells us that " in the spirit" Jesus breaks into a rapturous cry of jubilation (ἠγαλλιάσατο) in praise of God and of the mystery of the divine election He apprehends in the calling of His disciples to see and hear the revelation which takes place in Him.

What we thus learn of the inner life of Jesus is certainly not little, but it is definitely not very much, and it falls far short of all that we should like to know. Nowhere do we hear of Jesus meditating, deciding, rejoicing or laughing. Of course, we are not told that He did not do these things. There is obviously no attempt at a full portrait or even a characterisation ; and certainly not the exhibition of an inner development. It is customary to take it that Lk. 2⁵², with its reference to the growth (προκόπτειν) of the child Jesus in wisdom and stature and in favour with God and man, is a hint in this direction. Similar hints have also been found in Heb. 5⁸ (ἔμαθεν . . . ὑπακοήν), and of course indirectly in the story of the temptation. But it cannot be overlooked how unfruitful these indications are, if indeed they are indications at all. By all these passages we are only made aware that Jesus had a really human inner life. But we are given no guidance for reflection concerning it, and for forming a picture of this matter we are in fact offered no material at all.

The same indigence characterises the statements about His physical life. It is made unambiguously and emphatically clear that we have to do with a real man. That Jesus is " born of a woman " is the self-evident presupposition of all the New Testament writers ; but its underlining by Paul in Gal. 4⁴ is not gratuitous. All four Gospels speak of Jesus' mother and His brethren. It is, of course, noteworthy that the Second and Fourth Evangelists did not consider it necessary to start with an account of the birth of Jesus or even with a note about it, but begin forthwith *in mediis rebus*. Even Mt. 1²⁵ regards His birth only as a future event, and Mt. 2¹ as a past event. But its reality could not be more powerfully attested than with the ὁ λόγος σὰρξ ἐγένετο (Jn. 1¹⁴) And Luke, the companion of Paul, gives us in 2¹ᶠᶠ· a detailed account, as he also records the saying of that woman of the people (11²⁷) : " Blessed is the womb that bare thee, and the paps which thou hast sucked." The authenticity of the message of the apostles " of the word of life " is expressly based (1 Jn. 1¹) on the fact that they deal not only with what they know and understand, or what they have merely heard and seen and observed with their eyes, but with what " our hands have handled." This physical contact with Jesus is regarded as decisive, not only in the story of the healing of the issue of blood (Mk. 5²⁵ and *par.*), but also in several general reports of His healing works (Mt. 14³⁶ ;

Lk. 6¹⁹). That doubting Thomas (Jn. 20²⁴ᶠ·) wished to see the marks of the nails in the hands of Jesus, and to put his hand in His side, was not really doubt. This was the normal way, the way recognised and even demanded by the risen Jesus, in which as a disciple he should come to believe, and therefore become an apostle. Even the risen Jesus will and must be recognised as true man by His first witnesses through physical sight and bodily apprehension. In Luke's account of the meeting of the eleven with the Resurrected (Lk. 24³⁶ᶠ·), it is expressly said : " Why are ye troubled ? and why do thoughts arise in your hearts ? Behold my hands and feet, ὅτι ἐγώ εἰμι αὐτός : handle me, and see ; for a spirit hath not flesh and bones, as ye see me have." So we read in Mt. 4² of Jesus' hunger in the desert, in Jn. 19²⁸ of His thirst on the cross, in Jn. 4⁶ that He grew tired on the journey, in Lk. 22⁴⁴ that in Gethsemane His sweat was like drops of blood falling to the ground, and in Mt. 8²⁴ that He slept in the ship. In Mt. 11¹⁹ Jesus Himself tells us : " The Son of man came eating and drinking, and they say, Behold a man gluttonous, and a winebibber " ; and in Lk. 15² there is the emphatic accusation : " This man receiveth sinners, and eateth with them." Again, in the story of the resurrection (Lk. 24⁴¹ᶠ·; Jn. 21⁵ᶠ·, cf. also Lk. 24³⁰ᶠ·) we read that Jesus comes to the disciples, that He asks to eat, and that He is recognised by them in His taking a meal with them. On this side, too, we learn more than a little ; and what we are told cannot be ignored. But on this side, again, we are not given a complete, much less a concrete, picture. It is clearly no concern of ours whether Jesus was ever sick. An impenetrable veil of silence lies over the fact that He was a male (Jn. 4²⁷). The noteworthy thing is the absence of both positive and negative information on both points. No attention is paid to the health or to the celibacy of Jesus, nor are these things even mentioned. The fact of His corporeality is crucially important. The substance and nature of this fact, which are so desirable and even necessary to a biographer, remain fundamentally hidden, and can be supplied only by an imagination whose methods have nothing in common with what the New Testament has to say to us.

Clearly, then, the New Testament points consciously and effectively to the one whole man Jesus. On both sides He is seen only in the fact of His wholeness, and this alone is important. To ask concerning the manner, raising questions prompted by biographical curiosity, can only divert attention from what the apostles saw and wanted to attest, obscuring rather than illuminating the oneness and wholeness in which the constitution of man is visible in this man. It is in the palpable poverty of this picture that its richness consists and may be discerned. Its richness is Jesus Himself, in His physical life, as soul and body, both wholly real, and neither in a form of its own nor important only for itself. The soul is real and important only as *His* shocked and grieved and angered but also loving and rejoicing soul ; the body, on the other hand, is real and important only as *His* humiliated but also exalted body. It is always He as both, but in both and also over both the κύριος even and already in this aspect.

We have now to set alongside this another well-known consideration. According to the New Testament authors, and the so-called harmony of the Gospels and Acts, the outline of the life of Jesus is consciously and expressly conceived and presented as a combination or fusion of word and deed, of acts of oral proclamation, of preaching and teaching and of mighty works which are objectively verifiable and effective. " Jesus not only speaks ; He also acts " (K. L. Schmidt, article " Jesus Christus," *RGG*³, III, 142). Neither of these two moments of the New Testament Gospel is dispensable ; neither may be overlooked to the advantage of the other, or regarded as less important than the other. The oneness and wholeness of Jesus' human person is reflected in the works of this person. Against the powerful and too spiritualised conception of the picture of Jesus in the 18th and 19th centuries, it was and is necessary to draw attention to this, especially in relation to the bodily aspect and the whole range of the mighty works of the New Testament. According to the Synoptic and Pauline accounts of the Last Supper, as well as to Jn. 6⁵¹ᶠ·, it is the body (or flesh) and blood of Jesus which in the New Testament is the essence of the fellowship guaranteed by Jesus to the others and of all the gifts to be had from Him in this fellowship. After the crucifixion of Jesus, the burning question concerned (Mt. 27⁵⁸ᶠ· and *par*.; Jn. 2²¹, 19³⁸ᶠ·, 20¹²) the slain body of the Lord, and it is as bodily resurrection that the resurrection on the third day is given as the answer to this question. The community founded on the calling of the twelve apostles and their witness is called the σῶμα τοῦ Χριστοῦ which builds itself up and coheres and lives in its many members in dependence on its Head. Phil. 3²¹ describes the essence of the Christian hope as waiting for the Lord Jesus Christ from heaven, " who shall change our vile bodies " into likeness with σῶμα τῆς δόξης αὐτοῦ. And in Col. 2¹⁷, the irruption of the reality of the kingdom of God (τὰ μέλλοντα) is again compared, in distinction from the shadow world of outward legal observances, with the σῶμα τοῦ Χριστοῦ. In all this, the spirit is not wronged but honoured. But it is clear that, according to the New Testament understanding, the pneumatic characteristically reckons with the somatic, that apart from this it neither has form nor is it active, and that abstracted from it is no longer the pneumatic. From this point of view, we cannot ignore how prominently, even in those communal traditions—cf. Mt. 4²³⁻²⁵ or Mt. 11²ᶠ·—the element of the corporeal and therefore of the acts of Jesus stands in the foreground of the picture of His life and activity which the disciples witnessed and the New Testament offers us. The acts of Jesus do not merely accompany His reported words. It is clear that in the view of the New Testament writers the reported bodily acts of Jesus are to be understood as the decisive indication, declaration and attestation of the speaking Subject and therefore of His words, so that they cannot in any sense be regarded as mere incidentals and accessories. " Another teacher or prophet might also have spoken some or all the words ; but here spoke One equipped with unique authority." And it must be added at once : " Another miracle worker might have done some or all the acts ; but here One operates who stood at the dawn of the kingdom of God actualised in Him and who in virtue of this forgave sins " (K. L. Schmidt, *op. cit.*, 118). But the first contrast is of equal weight with the second : Jesus not only announced the forgiveness of sins but really effected it ; He met the physically sick not only with sympathy and words of comfort, not only as a skilful doctor, but as the One who makes whole. He is the man He is precisely in the unity of His work as it is apprehensible in this second moment. The " Christian science " which isolates the Jesus of this second apprehensible moment, and in the Saviour sees only the Healer, evidently constructs an abstraction as remote from the text and as illegitimate as the Liberal theology which clings only to Jesus the Teacher and at most to His personal life. The person of the Messiah and the ἐξουσία of the Messianic work of the New Testament Jesus, the kingdom or better the kingly rule of God which is operative and evident in this man, comprises these two moments. They are not two parts in Him. They are not two parallels in Him, or two intersecting lines, or two agreeing or concurring functions. They permit no choice. They cannot be considered independently. In and with one another they are the oneness and wholeness of this life.

This oneness and wholeness, then, is the first thing to be noted in consideration of the human nature of Jesus. It is in no sense arbitrary to ask whether there could be any problem of the inner contradictions in human nature if we had to do only with this man. And it may already be seen from afar—since the problem does arise in relation to all other men—in what direction we must look for an answer if in Jesus we have to do with true man.

A second point to be noted is that the oneness and wholeness of this human life is fashioned, structured and determined from within, and therefore necessary and of lasting significance. The interconnexion of the soul and body and Word and act of Jesus is not a chaos but a cosmos, a formed and ordered totality. There is in it a higher and a lower, a first and a second, a dominating and a dominated. But the man Jesus Himself is both. He is not only the higher, the first, the dominating, nor is He both in such a way that the lower, the second, the dominated is associated with him only externally or accidentally. This would again imply the destruction of that oneness and wholeness. He is also the lower, the second, the dominated. He is not only His soul but also His body. But He is both soul and body in an ordered oneness and wholeness. His being is orderly and not disorderly. Nor is He this in such a way that the order is accidental and imposed from without. He is it in an order which derives from Himself. He Himself and from Himself is both the higher and the lower, the first and the second, the dominant and dominated. He Himself is in both cases His own principle. The meaning, plan and intention, the logos of His life is thus not exterior and accidental. It is no foreign law to which He binds Himself but which comes from elsewhere and is established over Him. Rather He is His own law, and He is subject to it in a free obedience arising in Himself and proceeding from Himself. Jesus wills and fulfils Himself. He is His own ground and His own intention. He lives in such a way that command and obedience, ordination and subordination, plan and execution, goal and aim proceed from Himself and thus partake of an equal inward necessity. He lives truly because He does not live secondarily, or in such a way that He as soul and body partakes of a common life which is originally alien to Himself, which is always distinguishable from His own, which must accrue to Him and can be lost again by Him. He lives in sovereignty. His life of soul and body is really His life. He has full authority over it. Thus He can give it and impart it ; He can live it for many others and in many others ; He can make it the life of many others without its ceasing to belong to Him and to be His life, without its being diminished or lost to Him. On the contrary, He can gain it only as He gives and imparts it, living it for many others and in them. He can possess it only by losing it. This is how the New Testament writers describe the oneness and wholeness of this human life.

Our best starting-point in this respect is the decisive statement in which they bring the human person of Jesus into an absolutely unique relation with the Holy Spirit. It is to be noted in advance that this statement is not quite identical with the statement that He is the Messiah of Israel and the Son of God. The latter statement is basic but must be excluded for the sake of clarity.

It is connected with the former to the extent that it is essential for a man who as such really is the Messiah and the Son of God to stand in this unique relationship to the Holy Spirit. But it is not this special relationship to the Holy Spirit which makes this man the Messiah and the Son of God. On the contrary, it is because this man is the Messiah and the Son of God that He stands to the Holy Spirit in this special relationship. We have here to regard this relationship as the particular determination of the human constitution of Jesus.

The New Testament writers see in the existence of the man Jesus the fulfilment of the central prophecy of the coming son of David in Is. 11$^{1f.}$. We read in this passage that " there shall come forth a rod out of the stem of Jesse, and a Branch shall grow out of his roots : And the spirit of the Lord shall rest upon him, the spirit of wisdom and understanding, the spirit of counsel and might, the spirit of knowledge and of the fear of the Lord." In a word, it is the Spirit of the true king that will be the Spirit of this man—of the king that Solomon desired to be according to his prayer (1 K. 3$^{6f.}$), and that according to the continuation of this passage and the rest of the Old Testament tradition he actually was, at least in outline, likeness and prototype. But according to Is. 11, this kingly Spirit is to rest on the Messiah (in contrast to Solomon, to David himself, and to all who in greater or less measure partake of his line). He is to be a man who is pervasively and constantly, intensively and totally filled and governed by this kingly Spirit. Hence Jn. 1^{32} : " And John bare record, saying, I saw the Spirit descending from heaven like a dove, and it abode on him " (καὶ ἔμεινεν ἐπ' αὐτόν) ; Lk. 4^1 : " And Jesus being full of the Holy Ghost (πλήρης πνεύματος ἁγίου) returned from Jordan " ; Mt. 12^{18} (quoting from Is. 42^1) : " I have put my Spirit upon him (θήσω τὸ πνεῦμά μου ἐπ'αὐτον) : he shall bring forth judgment to the Gentiles " ; Lk. 4^{18} (quoting from Is. 61^1) : " The Spirit of the Lord is upon me (πνεῦμα κυρίου ἐπ' ἐμέ), because he hath anointed me " ; Jn. 3^{34} : " For he whom God hath sent speaketh the words of God : for God giveth not the Spirit by measure unto him " (οὐ γὰρ ἐκ μέτρου δίδωσιν τὸ πνεῦμα) ; and Jn. 6^{63} : " The words that I speak unto you, they are spirit, and they are life." Similarly Rom. 1$^{3f.}$ and 1 Pet. 3^{18} tell us that Jesus' resurrection from the dead is grounded on the fact that over against His determination κατὰ σάρκα as the son of David (the determination under which He could be and was slain) stands His determination κατὰ πνεῦμα under which His resurrection from the dead was a divine necessity. Similarly, 2 Cor. 3^{17} can venture the identification : ὁ δὲ κύριος τὸ πνεῦμα ἐστιν ; and 1 Cor. 15^{45} : ἐγένετο . . . ὁ ἔσχατος Ἀδὰμ εἰς πνεῦμα ζωοποιοῦν. The most fundamental New Testament statement concerning this relationship is that concerning the conception of Jesus by the Holy Spirit (cf. *C.D.*, I, 2, p. 172 ff.) as the miraculous sign of the mystery of His Messiahship and divine Sonship. Thus in Lk. 1^{35} we have the annunciation of the angel to Mary : " The Holy Ghost shall come upon thee, and the power of the Highest shall overshadow thee : Therefore also that holy thing which shall be born of thee shall be called the Son of God." Again, we read in Mt. 1^{18} : " When as his mother Mary was espoused to Joseph, before they came together, she was found with child of the Holy Ghost." Again, in Mt. 1^{20} the angel says to Joseph : " Fear not to take unto thee Mary thy wife : for that which is conceived in her is of the Holy Ghost." These passages do not say that the man Jesus is the Son of the Holy Spirit and that the Holy Spirit is thus His Father, but simply that this conception—which is no miracle as conception in the womb of a woman—is nevertheless a pure miracle in so far as this man has no physical father, and that in the event of His conception God deals with His mother as Creator to the exclusion of male volition and action. The relationship of this man to the Holy Spirit is so close and special that He owes no more and no less than His existence itself and as such to the Holy Spirit. But in the Old and New Testaments the Holy Spirit is God Himself in His creative movement to His creation. It is God who breathes specially upon man (Gen. 2^7), thus living for him, allowing him to partake of His own life, and therefore making him on his side a living being. From the standpoint of man, He is thus his possibility of being a "living soul" (Gen. 2⁷, ψυχὴ ζῶσα, 1 Cor. 15⁴⁵), and as such a body. That this Spirit rests on man, is laid on Him and remains over him, that man is full of the Spirit and his being and doing are consequently spiritual, and he himself is spirit because created by the Spirit—these biblical statements are not anthropological but exclusively Messianic. That man in general lives, he owes of course to the Holy Ghost. Hence it can also be said of man in general that the Holy Spirit is given to him, that he receives Him, that he lives by and from the Spirit, that he has the Spirit and is of a spiritual or intellectual nature. But there is this difference. Of man in general, this can be said only in virtue of a special operation of God and of specific events in which God turns towards him and enables him. From the general anthropological standpoint, however, possession of the Spirit is not a human state according to the Bible. In those events, the Spirit is imparted only " by measure " (Jn. 3³⁴). The events can cease. The Holy Spirit does not dwell lastingly in men ; He comes to them. Thus life is given to them from time to time, but if God intermits His gift of the Spirit, if the last of those events lies behind them, they can no longer live but only die. In view of these transitory and partial bestowals of the Spirit, the Bible can speak in general of the spirit (*ruah*, πνεῦμα) of man. In practice, this means nothing else but the soul living through the Spirit (*nephesh*, ψυχή). Occasionally the New Testament speaks of the soul of Jesus in this sense. When Jesus sighs or is moved or angered or troubled in spirit, when He commends His spirit into the hands of God (Lk. 23⁴⁶), and when He gives up the spirit (Mt. 27⁵⁰, Jn. 19³⁰), the word " spirit " is used in a general anthropological sense for the word " soul " and does not refer at all (or only indirectly) to the Holy Spirit. For Jesus does not have the Holy Spirit in the way in which it can be said of any man that he has the Spirit. He does not have Him only in virtue of an occasional, transitory and partial bestowal. He could not be without Him, and would thus be subject to death and corruption. Jesus has the Holy Spirit lastingly and totally. He is the man to whom the creative movement of God has come primarily, originally and therefore definitively, who derives in His existence as soul and body from this movement, and for whom to be the " living soul " of an earthly body and earthly body of a " living soul " is not a mere possibility but a most proper reality. He breathes lastingly and totally in the air of the " life-giving Spirit." He not only has the Spirit, but primarily and basically He is Spirit as He is soul and body. For this reason and in this way He lives. This is His absolutely unique relationship to the Holy Spirit.

In the Holy Spirit, God does of course move towards all His creatures in the fulness of His own life. The fact that they live depends upon this movement. In so far as they live at all, they live by the Spirit. For the manner and measure of their life corresponds to the manner and measure in which this movement of God is of benefit to them. It could be of benefit to man as such in the most perfect manner and measure. But of man as we know him it must be said that in fact it is of only transitory and partial benefit to him. Hence his life is only transitory and partial : transitory, since it comes only to go ; partial, since death and corruption are always near it. But in Jesus the Evangelists and apostles discovered the new man. That is, they rediscovered the true nature of man. They discovered the man upon whom the Spirit not only descends intermittently and partially but on whom He rests, who does not merely live from the Spirit but in the Spirit. They discovered the spirit of man in which life dwells with the fulness with which it is addressed by God to the creature. In other words, they discovered the man who lives in sovereignty, who has power of Himself to live in likeness to God, from whose life they saw life transmitted to themselves and others—a great limitless world of others—while the source remained quite inexhaustible, for it was the fulness of life which they saw poured out in the middle of the creaturely and human world. Correlative to the affirmation about Jesus the perfect Recipient and Bearer of the Holy Spirit, there is a whole series of New Testament statements which are simply intensive or extensive variations of Jn. 1⁴ : " In him (it is the man Jesus to whom the Prologue of the Fourth Gospel also refers) was life." " The life was manifested " (ἐφανερώθη), is how 1 Jn. 1² summarises what the apostles have seen and heard and handled. According to Heb. 7³, Jesus is the prototype of Melchisedec in that He has " neither beginning of days nor end of life " ; and according to Heb. 7¹⁶, He is priest " after the power of an endless life " (ζωῆς ἀκαταλύτου). What Jn. 5²⁶ says is specially important in this connexion : " For as the Father hath life in himself (ἐν ἑαυτῷ) ; so hath he given to the Son to have life in himself " (ἐν ἑαυτῷ). In virtue of this ἐν ἑαυτῷ, we twice have (Jn. 11²⁵ ; 14⁶) the clear-cut declaration : " I am . . . the life." Of Him it is said " that God sent his only begotten Son into the world, that we might live through him " (1 Jn. 4⁹) ; and according to 1 Jn. 5¹², to " have the Son " is equivalent to " have life," and not to have the Son of God is not to have life. For He is the ἀρχηγός of life (Ac. 3¹⁵). " I am the bread of life " (Jn. 6³⁵). " I live and ye shall live also " (Jn. 14¹⁹). It is especially in the Fourth Gospel that this theme is developed : " I am come that they might have life, and that they might have it more abundantly (καὶ περισσόν, Jn. 10¹⁰). But it is also the general declaration of Paul that " we shall be saved by his life " (Rom. 5¹⁰). Again, it is the personal hope of Paul that the life of the Lord Jesus might be manifested in his body (2 Cor. 4¹⁰). And it is Paul who in this matter coins the strongest metaphor : " Your life is hid with Christ in God. When Christ, who is our life shall appear, then shall ye also appear with him in glory " (Col. 3³) ; and again, with supreme directness : " For to me to live is Christ " (Phil. 1²¹), and " Christ liveth in me " (Gal. 2²⁰).

From this can be seen what may be called the meaning, the logic and the rationale of the human existence of Jesus. Since according to the New Testament He is as Messiah and Son of God the perfect Recipient and Bearer of the Spirit, and therefore is and has life in its fulness, His life as soul and body is a personal life, permeated and determined by His I, by Himself. The life which rests on Him is the life which corresponds to that kingly Spirit. It is the life in which the divine βασιλεία itself is present in creaturely form. It is meaningful for this reason. The saying of Jn. 1¹⁴ : " The Word was made flesh, and dwelt among us, and we beheld his glory," must be assessed from this side. What the apostles here found in fulness in a man was significance, meaning, will, purpose, plan and rule. All this in its fulness became flesh. We must not disregard the paradox of this statement on the anthropological side. The word " flesh " is frequently and primarily used in the Bible in the general and neutral sense of human existence or the human mode of being. It can often indicate man or mankind as such. But it undoubtedly has also an evil connotation. It indicates the condition of man in contradiction, in disorder and in consequent sickness, man after Adam's fall, the man who lives a fleeting life in the neighbourhood of death and corruption. Flesh is man, or soul and body, without the Logos. But the New Testament lays weight on the statement that the Logos became flesh. According to 1 Jn. 4¹ᶠ· one recognises the Spirit of God in a Christian and therefore the authenticity of his Christian confession in the very fact that he confesses that Jesus Christ is come " in the flesh," while (cf. 2 Jn. 7) in him who denies this there speaks not only an imperfectly Christian spirit but the spirit of Antichrist. Thus the confessional hymn cited in 1 Tim. 3¹⁶ begins with the words : ὅς ἐφανερώθη ἐν σαρκί. Again, according to Rom. 8³ God sent His Son—the One who brings life because He Himself is and has it— not in another and better human form but in our own familiar human form and therefore in the likeness (ἐν ὁμοιώματι) of sinful flesh (σαρκὸς ἁμαρτίας). Again, according to 1 Pet. 4¹ He suffered in the flesh. Again, according to Col. 1²² He reconciled us " in the body of his flesh " through His death. Again, according to Eph. 2¹⁴ He is in His flesh our peace, who made both one and broke down the middle wall of partition, the natural opposition between Israel and the Gentiles. Again, according to Heb. 10²⁰ He is in His flesh the parted veil to holiness. Again, according to Lk. 24³⁹ He is not a pure spirit even in His resurrection, nor is He merely soul and body, but " flesh and bone " ; and in the remarkable statement of Eph. 5³⁰ we too, as members of His body, are " of his flesh, and of his bones." This is the case, even though according to 1 Cor. 15⁵⁰ flesh and blood cannot inherit the kingdom of God. Again, according to the particularly impressive passage Jn. 6⁵¹ᶠ·, the true food, the bread of life, which Jesus gives, is His flesh. His flesh must be eaten and His blood drunk by those who are to live through and with Him. This is the case even though according to Jn. 6⁶³ it is the Spirit that quickens, while the flesh " profiteth nothing." It is quite evident in all these passages that something happens to the flesh and therefore to the intrinsically more than dubious being of man when the Logos becomes flesh and the human person of Jesus is constituted in this way. Something happens to it here of which otherwise and in itself it is incapable. In the flesh—as He is in the flesh like all of us—something happens for and in the flesh. The flesh, which in itself is disobedient, becomes obedient. The flesh, which in itself profits nothing, becomes a purposeful instrument. The flesh, which in itself is lost, attains a determination and a hope. The flesh, which in itself is illogical and irrational, becomes logical and rational. As the Logos becomes flesh and Jesus is flesh, it is shown that this man has and is spirit and life, and the flesh itself becomes quickening and living and meaningful. In the flesh and for the flesh, words can and must be said and deeds done—words and deeds in which the divine βασιλεία is not only announced but present and effective in the arena of human history : ἐντὸς ὑμῖν (Lk. 17²⁰ᶠ·), so that every pointer in this or that direction (" lo here ! or lo there ! ") is completely superfluous. In the flesh, defiance is made and an end is put to the contingency, diffusion, emptiness and lostness which are otherwise hopelessly characteristic of the flesh. In the flesh, victory is won, or in positive terms the transformation of the fleshly nature achieved. The flesh now becomes the object and subject of saving passion and action. In the flesh the reconciliation of the flesh is completed. This is the triumph of the meaning of the human existence of Jesus.

And from this standpoint it may be seen and understood how this man as soul and body is a whole, shaped and ordered by and of Himself, and therefore not a chaos but a cosmos. The analogy which inevitably suggests itself here is the event of creation. The logicalising and rationalising, and therefore the formation and ordering, which come on the flesh when the Logos becomes flesh and the Spirit rests upon this man, is and creates something quite new in and out of the flesh. The new subject which flesh now becomes suspends its old predicates and demands and supplies new predicates. And this is just the formation and ordering, of the soul and the body of the man Jesus accomplished by and of itself, the passing of the old and the coming into being of a new form in the flesh. The human existence of Jesus is in its totality the event of this formation and ordering and therefore this conquest and renewal of the flesh, its slaying and displacement in the old form and its quickening and coming to life in a new. The totality of the human existence of Jesus is here concerned. The New Testament knows nothing of a part of the person of Jesus which does not take part in this event. Even His soul, whose various affections we have mentioned, does not live outside this event but in the middle of it. Nor does the New Testament know of a time in Jesus' life when this event is not yet, or as yet only partially, in progress, or when it is visible perhaps only on its negative side. In retrospect the Evangelists took care to show that the " breath of the resurrection " (J. A. Bengel) filled and penetrated the life, words and acts of Jesus even before His resurrection, and that from the earliest beginnings the quickening and coming to life of the flesh were in full train. The resurrection of Jesus adds nothing new to what happened from the beginning. It only crowns this event as its disclosure and revelation. According to Lk. 24¹³⁻³⁵, it merely brings the disciples to the point where their sluggish hearts may and must believe and their eyes open upon the totality of the event whose blind witnesses they have hitherto been. It is the totality of the passion and action of which the clarity and glory now overwhelm and are realised by the disciples. This passion and action must be understood in the flesh, as a real event, yet not as a single event or as many single events, but as the totality of the event of the existence of Jesus. It is shown that the Spirit rests upon this man, and that He has and is life in sovereignty, by the fact that through the whole course of His life He is engaged in that passion and action in the flesh. That the Spirit rests upon Him is, of course, His possession and status ; it is proper to Him as the Messiah of Israel and Son of God. But even this implies in practice that His whole being consists in the event in which soul and body come into formation and order, in which chaos is left behind and cosmos is realised, and in which the flesh is slain in its old form and is quickened and comes alive in its new—and all this by and from out of itself. Of the incarnation of the Word of God we may truly say both that in the conception of Jesus by the Holy Spirit and His birth of the Virgin Mary it was a completed and perfect fact, yet also that it was continually worked out in His whole existence and is not therefore exhausted in any sense in the special event of Christmas with which it began. The truth conveyed by the first conception is that the formation and ordering of the flesh in the flesh is represented in the New Testament as a procedure which unfolded itself as it did with a necessity originally imposed upon Jesus. " I have meat to eat that ye know not of. . . . My meat is to do the will of him that sent me, and to finish his work " (Jn. 4³²ᶠ·). " Wist ye not that I must be about my Father's business ? " (Lk. 2⁴⁹). He must work the works of Him that sent Him, while it is day (Jn. 9⁴). He must be lifted up from the earth (Jn. 3¹⁴ ; 12³⁴). He must go to Jerusalem, to suffer many things, and be killed, and rise again, as the Synoptic predictions of the passion repeatedly say. This is the necessity of His action given at the beginning in the person of Jesus—the incarnation as an already completed fact. But alongside this we have to set what is said about His freedom : " Therefore doth my Father love me, because I lay down my life, that I might take it again. No man taketh it from me, but I lay it down of myself (ἀφ᾽ ἐμαυτοῦ). I have power (ἐξουσίαν) to lay it down, and I have power to take it again " (Jn. 10¹⁷ᶠ·). Alongside this we have to set the intentionally revealed and not concealed drama of the temptation at the beginning and Gethsemane at the end of the Synoptic presentation, together with the insufficiently noticed commentary on the latter in Heb. 5⁷ᶠ· : " Who in the days of his flesh, when he had offered up prayers and supplications with strong crying and tears unto him that was able to save him from death, and was heard in that he feared ; though he were a Son (καίπερ ὢν υἱός), yet learned he the obedience by the things which he suffered (ἔμαθεν ἀφ᾽ ὧν ἔπαθεν) ; and being made perfect (τελειωθείς), he became the author of eternal salvation unto all them that obey him." This is clearly the incarnation freely executed. It is to be noted that this aspect is also to be found in the Fourth Gospel, which begins with the ὁ λόγος σὰρξ ἐγένετο, and that it lays upon Jesus, after He has thirsted and drunk of the hyssop, the final word τετέλεσται (Jn. 19³⁰).

We must everywhere reckon with the two dimensions in which this matter is represented in the New Testament. But either way, both in its perfection and its execution, it is a formation accomplished in the flesh and therefore in human nature as it is forfeited and delivered over to death. It is the establishment of an order which is not otherwise proper to this flesh but has been lost in all other men ; of an order opposed to the disorder by which human nature in all other men is degraded to mere "flesh." The fact that the Spirit—that kingly Spirit—rests upon Jesus, that He has and is life and that in Him the Logos became flesh, results in a quite specific relationship of His being as soul and body. The oneness and wholeness of His being is not amorphous, nor is it the victim of arbitrariness and contingency. The meeting of "willing spirit" and "weak flesh" (Mt. 26⁴¹) pursues here a victorious course in favour of the Spirit. And this means that the tempter and his temptation to act as the "flesh" or psycho-physical man without the Logos usually does are vanquished by Jesus (Mt. 4³ᶠ·). His food is to do the will of Him that sent Him. He is supremely assaulted in His psycho-physical humanity and therefore as Bearer of our flesh no less at the end than at the beginning of His way. But his prayer concludes, according to Mt. 26³⁹, with the acknowledgment: "Not as I will, but as thou wilt." In the fidelity of the Son towards the Father and therefore in necessary obedience to His own most proper being and therefore in supreme freedom, He gave up Himself according to the passages already quoted, and therefore He gave up His soul and also His body, giving Himself to the service of the mercy of God towards men, and therefore to the cause of the men to whom God in His mercy wished to make Himself serviceable. It is thus that He is in the flesh. It is thus that He is man as soul and body. But the exaltation of the flesh and of the psycho-physical man which takes place in Him means that in Him there is completed an ordering of the relationship of these two moments of His human existence. These two moments are not in opposition. That the soul is opposed to the body and the body to the soul is due to the flesh, to human nature without the Spirit or lacking the Logos, not only in the case where the body triumphs over the soul but also where the soul successfully —or apparently successfully—resists the body. The New Testament contains not the slightest hint of an emancipation of the bodily life of Jesus from the soul nor of an ascetic conflict of the soul of Jesus against the body. The Spirit resting upon Him clearly makes the one impossible and the other superfluous. The exaltation, the logicalising and rationalising of the flesh, which is the mystery of His humanity, does not permit His body to become the enemy and conqueror of His soul ; nor does it consist in the soul masquerading as the enemy or conqueror of the body. These two possibilities, all too current amongst us, would presuppose something like the parallelism and rivalry of independent substances contingently and unessentially united into a whole. The flesh that is without the Spirit and stranger to the Logos has, of course, only the choice between these two possibilities. But the spiritual man, Jesus who is life, and the Logos becoming and exalting flesh in Him, is not faced by this choice. And the one-ness and wholeness of His humanity forbids us to understand Him from the dualistic standpoint of these alternatives. On the contrary we are confronted by the picture of peace between these two moments of human existence.

This freedom, however, is of such a kind that it contains a first and a second, an upper and a lower, a command and therefore that which controls, an obedience and therefore that which is controlled. The soul is the first and the body the second in this peace—this is the order in this relationship. It presupposes no original separation, and includes not even the most hidden conflict. The superiority of the soul of Jesus is entirely without any flavour of pride, scorn or even hidden apprehension or anxiety concerning the body. Hence the inferiority of His body does not mean that it is subjugated and oppressed and therefore engaged in hidden rebellion in which it is necessarily opposed to His soul. We have here no commanding tyrant nor obeying slave, no triumphing conqueror nor sighing victim. There is super- and subordination, but it is an order of peace in which both moments, each in its own place and function, have equal share in the dignity of the whole, which means the dignity of the one man Jesus and therefore in the fulness of the Spirit that rests upon Him and the glory of the Logos incarnate in Him. Yet as this order of peace, it does include superior and inferior. The equal dignity which soul and body have in this man does not exclude but necessarily includes the inequality of position and function. It is not to be forgotten that before publicly entering upon His Messianic office Jesus fasted forty days and nights in the desert (Mt. 4[1f.]), though it must be added that He obviously did not repeat this fast and that it was after this fast that the tempter met Him, and not at the marriage at Cana or when He ate and drank with publicans and sinners or even with the scribes and Pharisees. This fast from which Jesus comes in His later course shows manifestly that there is here that which controls and that which is controlled, and not a man who first eats and drinks and then has also all kinds of good things to say and do. There is here a man who has something to say and do and who then and for that reason may and will eat and drink. The incident of Mary and Martha (Lk. 10[38f.]), which of course has other dimensions, must be considered here. Mary indeed chose " the good part " because in contrast to Martha she met the real requirement of her guest, not with bodily service, but by sitting listening at His feet. This is the irreversible order within the oneness and wholeness of the man Jesus. His body is the body of His soul, not *vice versa*. His body is in His soul—we have to say this before we can say with right understanding that His soul is in His body. It is thus that He is soul and body. It is thus that He is organised and disposed by the Spirit that rests upon Him. This is life ; the life which God breathed into man here now in its original form and fulness ; and therefore bodily life. In the being of Jesus presented by the New Testament we look in vain for a moment when His corporeality plays a special and independent role. It is never wanting ; it is always present ; it is the companion, helper and servant of all His words and acts. In their depiction it is never hidden, but often enough intentionally displayed. He is not His soul alone ; nor does He speak and act in a medium indifferent and strange. He is also—as is expressly stated in the accounts of the Last Supper—His body, His flesh and His blood. But His body never plays an independent role, nor does the depiction ever direct special attention upon it. It does not occur to the first or even the second generation of the Church to wish to have a bodily picture of Jesus, though the Evangelist Luke is supposed to have been an artist as well as physician and though Paul himself seems to come very near to the thought when he says that he has painted Jesus Christ the Crucified " before the eyes " of the Galatians (3[1]). Jesus spoke and acted and suffered in obedience and omnipotence in and not without His body, so that He was also wholly this body. Yet His action and passion are first, *a parte potiori*, those of His soul, and in that way and on that basis of His body. His body is used and governed by Him for the purpose of a specific and conscious speech and action and suffering. It serves Him in the execution of this purpose. It is impregnated with soul, i.e., a body filled with this consciousness ; but we obviously cannot say that his soul is impregnated with body, i.e., a soul filled by the needs and desires of His bodily life. This is the distinction and inequality to be noted within the oneness and the wholeness. The fulfilment, the willing and the execution and therefore the true movement of this body occurs from above downwards, from soul to body and not *vice versa* ; not in two opposed lines running parallel and of equal originality ; nor in the form of a competitive or even harmonious satisfaction of two different requirements ; nor in a rotation in which each requirement continuously supersedes and takes up the other. The movement of this life is rather of such a kind that the requirement of the soul, of the Spirit resting upon this man, according to His nature can only be first the requirement of the soul, then being made by the soul the requirement of the body as well, and joyfully and willingly accepted by the body. In this way the body, too, acquires its full and undiminished share in the Spirit that rests upon this man, in the life based on this Spirit, in the glory of the Logos in the flesh, in the dignity of the one man Jesus. All this must naturally be applied also to the oneness and wholeness of the work of Jesus and therefore to the relationship between His words and acts. Here too, as we have seen, there is no dualism. The unity of the person of Jesus is reflected intact in the unity of His work also. But here too there is order—superiority and inferiority. The Word leads; the sign follows. The Word affirms; the sign confirms. The Word is the light; the sign its shining. The two cannot be separated; but they are to be seen in this relationship to one another. It was a serious if not perverse thing if people were always wanting a sign before they believed (Mt. 12^{39}; Jn. 4^{48} &c.); yet this is never said of those who wished to hear His word. Similarly, the account of Jesus' stay in Nazareth (Mt. 13^{58}), that He could not do many works there because of their unbelief, has no parallel in a corresponding statement concerning the proclamation of Jesus. It is never said that His mighty works were wholly suspended, but only that on occasion they could retire into the background, and apparently did so frequently. But His proclamation can neither cease nor retire. Jesus spoke even when He was silent before the high-priests (Mt. 26^{63}) and Pilate (Mt. 27^{14}), the high-priests and Pilate themselves involuntarily undertaking the task of expressing the truth. The Word is the proper revealing movement of His work, the act the confirmatory. The act never occurs alone and for itself or for its own sake. It can only be misunderstood, if considered, desired or admired for itself. It is produced by the power of the Word. Indirectly it is itself Word, *verbum visibile*; and it wills to be accepted as such. But one could not say that Jesus' Word is the *signum audibile*. Within the unity of His work, and without breaking the unity, there is a precedence, because it is an ordered unity. It is no chance that He who is at work here is called *a parte potiori* the Logos and not the *dynamis* of God, though there can be no doubt that He is the latter as well. Here, too, the movement is from above to below, from the word to the act, and not *vice versa*. Similarly, the preaching and healing of Jesus are not two activities which, because they are both laudable and excellent, are contingently co-ordinated and harmonised in Him, though in themselves they have different origins and purposes. Here again there is a firm leading and following in which preaching leads and healing —inevitably and as necessary complement—follows, being comprised in the activity of the Prophet and Teacher Jesus, nourished from the origin of this work and serviceable to its purpose. In this order the work as well as the person of Jesus is fashioned into a whole.

Summarising, we may say that Jesus is true man in the sense that He is whole man, a meaningfully ordered unity of soul and body. That His human existence unfolds in these two moments—not in one only, but also in the other—is as visible in Him as it can possibly be. But there is lacking in Him all cleavage between the moments, and to that extent the problem of their relationship is resolved; so much so that one might miss the reality of their difference. Yet it must also be said that their difference is seen particularly in the person of Jesus in the sense that their relationship emerges in Him as a clarified relationship and human existence in these two moments as one which is cosmically fashioned.

All this cannot be stated without looking beyond this human existence as such. Guided by the New Testament, we must think of the Holy Spirit, and more especially of the presence and efficacy of the Holy Spirit, if we would give an account of the special constitution of this man. This immediately reminds us of the supreme particularity that this true man is primarily and at the same time the true God

Himself. It is in this way, this higher unity of His existence with that of God Himself, that He is whole man, a meaningfully ordered unity of soul and body. Can we disregard or fail to note that the constitution of His being as man is a repetition, imitation and correlation of the relationship in which He is primarily and at the same time true God and as such also true man? Soul and body are clearly related to one another in the man Jesus, as His being as Son and Word of God the Creator is related to His creaturely constitution as soul and body of this man. It is with a relationship in absolute totality of these two moments that we have to do primarily and basically in this higher sphere by which the lower is transcended and enveloped. The two moments are indestructibly different even on this higher level, for it is a matter of divinity and humanity. But abstractions and separations are impossible. In the place of man stands the One who is God Himself in man ; and in the place of God stands the same One who is man in Jesus. And in this wholeness and oneness the relationship of God and man, of man and God, in Jesus is itself a meaningfully ordered relation. Here already there manifestly operate superior and inferior, lordship and service, command and obedience, leadership and following—and this in a constant and irreversible relation. We can have no more than an analogy. The soul of Jesus is not His divinity, but only comparable with it in its function within His being as man. And His body is not His humanity, but only comparable with it (in His totality of soul and body) within His humanity. It is only in the same proportions that divinity and humanity confront one another on the higher and the soul and body of Jesus on the lower level. But the power and necessity in which Jesus is whole man are not grounded in themselves but in the fact that He is primarily and at the same time true God and true man. We have seen that they are the power and necessity of the Holy Spirit resting upon Him. It is because He is the Son and Word of God that the Holy Spirit rests upon Him, and that He exists in the fulness of the Holy Spirit, and that He is whole man in a meaningfully ordered unity of soul and body. This foundation, this relationship of Giver and gift, even of Creator and creature, is not reversible. Hence the disparity of the two relationships, and the fact that we cannot have here more than an analogy. But that there is an analogy may be neither overlooked nor denied. It shows us that in this question we do not stand on the periphery but in closest proximity to the theological centre.

We can realise that this is so at a second point of which we are just as immediately reminded by the special constitution of the human being of Jesus. The relationship between soul and body in Jesus is also, and exegetically much more obviously, comparable with the relationship between Him and His community. It is no accident that Paul indicates and describes the community as the " body " of

Jesus and Jesus in His relationship to it as its " Head." If in the relationship between God and man in the person of Jesus we can speak of a comparison upwards, so here we can speak of a comparison downwards. The soul and body of Jesus are here primary, original and basic. Since He exists as man in that ordered wholeness, He anticipates in a measure in His person the relationship in which He is the Lord in the midst of His disciples and those who are called by them. Soul and body are related to one another in Him as He Himself as Prophet, Priest and King is related to the company of those who, in His person reconciled with God, are children of God for His sake, and by faith in Him are aware of this benefit and grateful for it, and have become His witnesses. Between Him and them, too, there is a complete relationship. But it is not accidental, dissoluble, nor amenable to abstractions. Jesus Christ exists in the founding and upbuilding of His community ; His community exists as it is founded and built up by Him. A Christ without His community would be a figment of the imagination, and even more so a community without Christ. The one divine act of election is the election of this head and this body. As Jesus' soul and body are inseparably one, so are He and His people. And as order rules in the one case, so also in the other. The disciples cannot be above their Master, but the Master will be to all eternity above His disciples. The Head is always the Head. The body is always the body. Where Christ does not rule, the body is dead, just as the body without soul can only be dead. But where the body is alive it is obedient to Christ, just as the living body will necessarily serve the soul. Here, too, the relationship is irreversible. Christ is the primary form of this wholeness, Christendom the secondary, and not *vice versa*. Again, we have only an analogy. Perfect similarity is not to be expected between the relationships compared. As Paul named Him the " Head," so in the same fashion He may be regarded as the soul of His community. But this is preceded by the fact that in His own person He is soul and body. And the latter is the original and higher sphere. The one beloved Son of God, in whom men are the object of divine election, is first and foremost the man Jesus for Himself, and only then, through Him and in Him, others. And as the Holy Spirit rests upon Him, He will be directed and poured out upon them also, as the Holy Spirit of the community of the many towards whom God willed to reveal and direct His love in Him and through Him. That He is theirs and they His is primarily and basically effective and necessary in the fact that He is this whole man in the meaningfully ordered unity of His soul and His body. The whole meaning and soundness of the secondary and lower relationship depends on the existence and order of the primary and higher. To this extent there is here not only similarity but also dissimilarity. To this extent there is really only repetition, imitation and correspondence. That this is so here too must not be overlooked or disregarded. We can and must look both upwards and downwards from the structure of the human existence of Jesus—upwards to the mystery of His being with God and downwards to the no less mystery of His being with men. It is no accident that here too, for all the other differences, the proportions are the same.

We refrain from any detailed account of the more distant analogies, some more and some less exact, which might be discerned on this basis. They need only be named. It is not impossible, and even in different degrees promising and fruitful, to ask whether the soul and body of Jesus might not be related to one another like heaven and earth in the totality of creation ; or justification and sanctification in the atoning work of Christ ; or Law and Gospel in the Word of God ; or faith and works in the human response to God ; or preaching and sacrament in the divine service of the community ; or the confessional formula and the corresponding attitude and action in its confession ; or Church and state in the inner articulation of the kingdom of Christ. The mere enumeration may arouse reflection. Since the revealed truth and reality of God and His covenant of grace is single, we cannot wonder if even formally its individual elements obviously stand in a certain connexion, as appears in these analogies. Again, we are certainly not required either to systematise this formal connexion or to discern it everywhere. There are important points of Christian knowledge where we cannot speak of such analogy and where only a combination of lack of taste and direct error would try to discover it. For example, there is no totality in which the Creator and the creature in general, or in which the freedom and initiative of God and of man, are so unified as are the soul and body of Jesus. Similarly, the meaningful order of these two elements in the existence of Jesus has no analogy in the relationship between the grace of God and the sin of man, since we can understand the latter only as the relationship of exclusive opposites. We have good reason, therefore, to refrain from an indiscriminate pursuit of analogies. And even where we may speak of real analogies to the constitution of the humanity of Jesus, in each case we must consider whether and how far the points concerned may be brought into mutual relationship, in cross connexions. At this point no certain conclusions result from logical possibilities alone. For theological truths and relationships of truth have in their own place and way their own worth and fulness, the light of which can be increased but may also be easily diminished when they are set in relation to others. In no case can they be treated as the implications of a single formal principle or brought under a single denominator. We content ourselves, therefore, with the two really close comparisons which we have unfolded. The soul and body of Jesus are mutually related to one another as are God and man in His person, and Himself and His community. These two comparisons are important enough to show us what had to be shown, namely, that with our knowledge of Jesus as the whole man we find ourselves at the centre of all Christian knowledge.

The reason why we have taken trouble over the knowledge of the constitution of the human existence of Jesus is that for all theological knowledge of man as such we must begin with the picture of this man. It is here that the decision must be taken about the true constitution of man. Totality in the meaningful order of his humanity will certainly not be found in man in general and as such. But we do at any rate know in what direction we must look in the general question which occupies us. The only understanding possible for us is one in which this wholeness and its orderliness form the unchangeable standpoint. The picture of the man Jesus demands an understanding of man which is controlled from this standpoint. It protests against an understanding of man which leaves this standpoint out of account or neglected. Thus it is the norm with which we again approach our true task, the anthropological.

2. THE SPIRIT AS BASIS OF SOUL AND BODY

Man exists because he has spirit. That he has spirit means that he is grounded, constituted and maintained by God as the soul of his body. In the briefest formula, this is the basic anthropological insight with which we have to start.

Man is not God. God is the Creator of man. Man is God's creature. It is God's gift to man that he is man and not something else, and that he is and is not not. Man owes it to God that he is man and not something else, and that he is and is not not. This distinction is for man irremovable. For God it is not irremovable. In the existence of the man Jesus, He has in fact removed it. He, the Creator, has become creature. But for man this distinction is irremovable. It is of his essence to be creature—the creature which as such can neither be nor become the Creator. It is of his essence not to be God. We must begin with this negative statement, with the affirmation of this limitation of man, if we are now to establish and describe his constitution.

The very basis of this negative statement compels us at once to formulate in provisionally negative form the supplementary statement that man is not without God. Since he owes it to God that he is and that he is man, how can he be without God who gives him both ? The being of man is from its very origin and basis a being with God, because man is made and determined for covenant with God. But the statement that man is not without God belongs also to the climax of our present description of the constitution of the

being of man. When we say "man" or "soul and body," then
wittingly or unwittingly we have first said "God." From our standpoint, in our attempt at theological anthropology, we have to know
that we have first said God when we say man. There can thus be
no question of revising or reducing our first statement that man is
not God. God does not in any sense belong to the constitution of
man. God is neither a part nor the whole of human nature. He is
identical neither with one of the elements of which in unity and order
we are composed, nor with us ourselves. But the whole which we
are in this unity and order is not without God. In abstraction from
the fact that this being is not without God, we should not really know
ourselves as the being which we thought we knew as a specific unity
and ordering of soul and body, and we should be reckoning with a
fanciful picture which would render us as such unknowable. That
this being is no fanciful picture, that man really is, is ontically and
therefore noetically dependent on the fact that he is not without God.
Man without God is not; he has neither being nor existence. And
man without God is not an object of knowledge. Again, the fact
that he is not without God is not a supplementary, optional or purely
historical determination of his constitution which might well be
lacking according to his decision, or according to his positive or negative formulation of his relation to God, so that provisionally at least
it might be disregarded in describing his constitution. That man is
not without God has nothing to do with the religious convictions or
behaviour in which he in some measure gives or does not give honour
to God. Even the error of a theoretical, practical or methodical
atheism in his self-knowledge can do nothing to alter the fact that
he is not without God. This error can only mean that he unwittingly
regards himself as not being, and therefore renders basically questionable not only his atheistic decision but also his self-knowledge. He
may undertake and do this. Yet even so he is not without God.
Man cannot escape God, because he always derives from Him. This
is the negative form of the basic statement with which we must begin
our description of the constitution of man. Man as soul and body is
in no case so made that he is simply there, as though self-grounded,
self-based, self-constituted and self-maintained. His constitution is
in no case that of a first and last reality; nor is it one which enables
and empowers him to understand himself by himself, or to hold the
criteria of his own perception and thought, however he may define
them, as standards by the help of which he can, secluded in himself,
arrive at the core of the matter. As he is not without God, he cannot
understand himself without God.

It is clear that we must here depart from the way taken by the anthropology
which sets itself the aim of understanding man without God. It is of the essence
of every non-theological anthropology to set itself some such aim. Of course,
it is not essential that this aim be set absolutely and so be intended in the sense

of atheistic dogma. It can be intended only hypothetically. It can deliberately leave open the first and last question concerning the constitution of man. In some circumstances it can even work alongside theology with a more or less concealed or open affinity. But so far as it does not do this, but remains firmly on its own ground, it must seek to understand man primarily without God, as though he were a first and last reality, as though he were in a position to understand himself of himself, as though the criteria of human perception and thought were the standard with whose application alone a knowledge or an adequate knowledge can be founded. It is this " as though " that distinguishes the non-theological from the theological knowledge of man. We have neither to criticise nor to vindicate this non-theological understanding of man here. So far as it conceives its aim atheistically, it rests on a plain error which necessarily involves it in other errors ; but this is a separate question. So far as it conceives it only relatively, it has in its restricted place its own right and responsibility, to which we can only desire that it may attend firmly and therefore, for the sake of assurance, without direct theological ties. But from the point of view of our responsibility we can neither accept this " as though " nor be content with the corresponding inquiry. We cannot try to understand man even hypothetically without God in order to find out whether the last word in the matter is an open question, or a statement borrowed from theology, or perhaps atheistic dogma. On the contrary, we must advance from the starting-point that man is not to be understood without God. If theological anthropology renounced this statement, it would surrender itself along with its object and theme ; and when it later reverted to the question of God it would be of no interest to non-theological science. But in any case, whether we find the others interesting or not, we ourselves must follow our own way in this matter.

The negative formula " not without God " is not of course adequate in itself. We shall now state the same thing positively : Man exists as he is grounded, constituted and maintained by God. God is not, we remember, a higher or highest being with certain personal or impersonal physical and moral attributes and properties appropriate in our estimation and opinion to his eminence. God is He who has revealed Himself in His eternal Word in time as the true and merciful Lord of man. God is the Creator who has maintained and fulfilled His covenant with man by Himself becoming a human creature in Jesus Christ and giving Himself up for us. God is the God of Israel, besides whom is no other, and measured by whom every other is a trivial fabrication. Our first statement concerning the constitution of man is that he is not without this God who is true, not because we regard Him as such, but because He has proved and expressed and manifested Himself as such. And now we make the positive statement that man exists as he is grounded, constituted and maintained by this God. He is, i.e., he is this human being and has existence in this being, as he is from this God. There is no other possibility. This cannot be an open question, for we come from a beginning where the answer is that there are no possibilities. Man cannot even be of and by himself—our starting-point precludes this too. Again, he cannot derive from a high or highest being whose existence must be the basis of ours as we ourselves direct. Our starting-point, the human nature of Jesus, forbids us at this point to look to any kind of a

height selected and adorned by ourselves. Man is from the God whom
the man Jesus called His Father and whose Son He called Himself.
"In him we live, and move, and have our being," and "we are also his off-
spring" (Ac. 17²⁸). In this verse Paul made use of heathen wisdom, but he
immediately gave it a Christian sense and thus in a sense baptised it. He,
whom Paul proclaimed to the Athenians in these words which had once been
heathen, but in his mouth were so no longer, is undoubtedly neither the
classical Zeus nor Hellenistic fate. He is rather the One who has disregarded
the " times of ignorance " as a world of shadows, and who calls men to repentance by causing a day of judgment to dawn, setting a Judge upon the throne,
and demanding faith in Him who is raised from the dead. He is the " unknown
God " to whom in their ignorance they accorded their religious worship. He is
the Creator of the cosmos. He is the Lord of human history, and His object is
that they might " feel after and find " Him on the far side of all man's faith,
heresy, superstition and unbelief. He, this God! This is the missionary message
of Paul (Ac. 17²²ᶠ·). It does not really link up with anything. It immediately
sets up the new in the place of the old. But it sets this new as such immediately
behind and above the man who is imprisoned in the old. It releases him directly
from this imprisonment and places him directly in freedom. It speaks of the
God whom even in his imprisonment man did not and never will escape. It
takes the imprisonment of man seriously only as his impotent attempt to escape
this God, whom he can only confirm as his origin with this attempt.

Just as man is distinguished from the rest of the created world
by the fact that, as the likeness and promise of the divine covenant
of grace, he is called to responsibility before God, so his special constitution corresponding to this calling is determined by the fact that
he owes it to the God who is the Lord of this covenant of grace. This
God as such is also the Creator of man. This God as such gives him
his creatureliness. This God as such establishes him as soul and
body, constituting the unity and order of this being, and maintaining
him in this being in its unity and order. Because He is this God in
the constitution of man we have to do with an unshakeable but also
a saving fact. Since his constitution derives from this God, from
Him who is faithful and does not repent of His goodness, it is therefore unshakeable. It can, of course, be disturbed and perverted by
human sin, but it cannot be destroyed or rendered nugatory. Hence
man remains man even in his deepest fall, even in the last judgment
of death ; and even in death he is still man within the hand and
power of God. In no case, therefore, does He become another being,
a being which is deprived of the promise of the covenant of grace
and cannot even in death and hell appeal to this covenant. And
since the constitution of man is from God, it is a saving fact. For
from its origin from God, like the being of man as man and woman,
it has an inner relation to God's turning towards man and to the
salvation which God intends for him ; for man cannot be what he is,
soul and body in ordered unity, without representing in himself—
long before he understands it, and even when he will not understand
it—the good intention of God towards him, without himself being
guarantor for this good intention of God.

We must look closer at the matter. This God grounds, constitutes and maintains man's constitution. From Him man is, and his being and his existence are. When we say this, we do not describe a property of man. Otherwise the fact that he is from this God would be a kind of element in his constitution as such. But it is not " natural " to him in this sense. What we describe is a transcendental determination of the human constitution, an action and operation of the God who is free in relation to man. That man is from God and is grounded, constituted and maintained by Him, is an event which is willed, decided and effected by God. It is always on the basis of this act of God, and therefore not on the basis of a potency conceded to him by God, nor of a kind of fixed relation of God to him, that man is. He comes to be grounded, constituted and maintained. This must continually take place anew—every morning, every moment. This God is and acts in this way. He does it as the living God. Here, too, it is important not to interchange the God from whom man is with any high or highest being. What value would this have ? For the determination of man by another supposed higher being would be described in the end only as a fixed relation and therefore ultimately only as a human property. But the God of Israel, the Father of Jesus Christ, is the Creator whose mercy is new every morning. That He has made man does not mean that He has ceased to make him. It means rather that God has made him the being who in an ever new act of divine creation is to be again based, again constituted and again maintained—the being over against whom, even when He ceases to do this and therefore in death, there stands the God who is able to do this and from whom such action is to be expected. Man is, as God is in this living way his active basis. And since God is this living and active basis of man, He is and always is the hope of man, even when He will no longer grant him his being. We cannot avoid considering at this point the possibility of human death. The idea of the living God from whom man is, and the idea of His action in which this becomes true, would otherwise be incomplete. This action of God is a free action. This alone distinguishes it from a continuing and fixed relation, and from the operations customarily ascribed to a superior being. God is not obliged to act in this way. It is His gift. It is grace which He shows to man but does not owe to man ; grace by which He binds us but not Himself. This is revealed in human death. He is still the God from whom man is, even when He lets man die. Thus in death and above death, He is still the hope of man. He is the one hope of man, not only in his death—for death only discloses the fact—but in his life. Even in life, man is wholly dependent upon the living God causing His livingness to benefit him, upon this God willing him and thus newly confirming, newly basing, newly constituting, and newly maintaining him in his constitution as soul and body. He must and would perish immediately, hopelessly and eternally, if God ceased to be for him this living God, from whom he may expect that He will continually act on him accordingly.

Man lives and dies in the event of the livingness of God. In this event he is created. In this event he is what he is by nature : soul and body in ordered unity. In this event and not otherwise! He would not be created by and for the grace of God His Creator, if it were otherwise. He is, then, in virtue of the fact that God relates Himself to him in the event of this act. He lives, as the living God lives also and precisely for him, for his benefit and advantage. It is to be noted that we speak now of man's natural condition, of his human existence and of his being in this existence. Of this already, of this creatureliness of his, it must also be laid down that man is, as God is for him. The same thing can and must be said word for word of the historical standing of man in covenant with God which is grounded along with his being and his existence, of his being called by grace to gratitude. He is made for this historical standing. This is man's determination. And it cannot be otherwise than that his creatureliness in its fundamental determination must correspond to this historical standing of his. He will be in this standing only as God is for him. And this is how the matter stands already in the natural condition presupposed in the historical standing. It is of this we now speak. Already in it he is not apart from but by God's grace on the ground of this divine attitude to him. He is determined for this historical standing in his natural condition, and indeed in its determinative ground of his being or non-being. He is determined by the one grace, that of his creation, for the other grace, that of the covenant ; and he is referred by the one to the other. As he is what he is, and as he is and is not not, he is on the way which has only this objective, which as he goes this way he cannot miss. This way is really his way, and this objective really his objective. No other way and no other objective is possible for him. The whence that is most properly his, his creatureliness, permits him no other whither.

We now take a further step. Man is, as he is grounded, constituted and maintained by God as soul of his body. With the expression " soul of his body," we affirm first of all that he is at all events one who also belongs to the visible, outward, earthly world of bodies. Like land and sea and plants and animals, he is also in space. He himself is also an individual being, distinguished from others and isolated in his particular space. He is also a visible form. He is also earthly and therefore material. To be man is not only to be soul in a particular spatial body, but to be soul of one such spatial body, and therefore to be wholly bound to it, to be one with it, and therefore to belong with it to the visible, outward, earthly world of bodies, to be with it in space, to be a being particularly limited in space, a being which with it is visibly shaped and material. He is soul of a material body. But we must be more precise and add at once that he is soul of a physical body. A physical body is also a material body. A physical body is an organic material body, which as such, i.e., to make possible and to realise its organic being and existence, is dependent upon having life. Without life, it can only decay even as material body, necessarily losing its special being and existence over against the other material bodies with their being and their existence which surround it in space. Without life, it cannot begin to enter upon its special being and existence at all. Man is soul of such a material body—one which is organic in its being and exists organically, and is thus dependent upon the reception and possession of life.

To call man " soul " is simply to say in the first place that he is the life which is essentially necessary for his body. This is not to be understood as if first of all he were simply life for itself, which as such had a being and existence beside and outside his body and then entered it as its life, yet all the time continued its own being and existence as well and finally perhaps left it without losing this being and existence. No ; man is the life of this body of his. This body itself is not any body, but his body. If it were not his body, the body whose life he is, it would not be body. It could then at once be only decaying material body ; it could never achieve being and existence even as material body. What this material body is, and the fact that it is, depends on the fact that it is alive. Man is as his material body is *alive* and therefore physical body. The converse must also be viewed and stated—that he is, as his *material body* is alive. He is neither before nor beside nor after his material body. He is the life of his physical body, not a life in itself, and not a life hovering freely over his body or dwelling in it only incidentally. This is what we mean when we describe man as soul. This is all we can mean. The statement that " man is soul " would be without meaning if we did not immediately enlarge and expound it : Soul of one body, i.e., his body. He is soul as he is a body and this is his body. Hence he is not only soul that " has " a body which perhaps it might not have, but he is bodily soul, as he is also besouled body.

Both concepts are analytical. Soul would not be soul, if it were not bodily ; and body would not be body, if it were not besouled. We are not free to make abstractions here, either on one side or the other. When we say that man is the life or soul of his body, this naturally means that he not only belongs to the material world and therefore that he is not only in space and himself spatial, that he not only partakes of earthly material being and an earthly material manner of existence. If he is life or soul—and he would not be body, unless he were life or soul—it is implied that he is essentially and existentially in time as well, that he is not only visible but also invisible, not only outward but also inward, not only earthly but also heavenly. When we use the latter term in this connexion, we remember that as it is used in the Bible " heavenly " does not mean " divine," but merely refers to the higher, upper, inapprehensible side of the whole of created reality. " Soul " is a determination of earthly being. As it can only be the soul of a physical and therefore a material body, from which it cannot be parted, this settles the fact that man belongs to the earth and therefore to the lower side of created reality, but not in such a way that he does not in virtue of his decisive determination—he is *soul* of his body—partake of the invisibility of created reality in the midst of the visibility, and of the being of heaven even as a being which is wholly of earth. Since he is soul of his *body*, he is the earthly representation of that above and below of a world totality. That he is the *soul* of his body decides the fact that he cannot fall victim to his spatiality, visibility and materiality even though he is bound to it, and that the boundary they impose on him is not a prison but a significant and ordered economy. Since he is besouled body and bodily soul and no abstraction is possible, since he lives and partakes of the heavenly side of the cosmos, but also lives bodily and therefore has an indissoluble part in the bodily world, since as soul of his body he is that earthly representation of the whole of created reality, he necessarily stands even as body in clear relation to its higher, invisible and inner side. He could not be living body, or the connexion between body and life could not be indissoluble, if in its unity his body did not also stand in this relation to the upper cosmos—and this without ceasing to be material body. Naturally this could not be said if it were only material body. But in fact it can be material body only in such a way as to have life ; and as physical body, and therefore living material body, it is not merely material body but besouled body. But if it is besouled, to that extent it too, and therefore the whole man, stands in that relation to the upper cosmos and is thus a representation of the whole cosmos.

We must develop and expound in even greater detail the view and concept : " man as soul of his body." And first our attention is claimed by the fact that it is by the free act of God that man is grounded, constituted and maintained as soul of his body. In and of himself he cannot be soul and body and soul of his body. That he is so is based upon God's free creative grace through which he is prepared and equipped for his historical standing in the covenant with Him and in which the grace of the covenant is reflected and announced. That man may be soul of his body, and therefore belong even to space and the material world, is above all God's free act of grace. We say expressly " may." Space and the material world are the outer and substantial and therefore the lower side of the cosmos, but this does not mean that they are a worse side. They do not mean bondage for the soul. It would be real bondage for the soul in the biblical sense to be in a condition in which there is no being in space and the material world, but it is left or becomes bodiless. In its way, earth is no less the Lord's than heaven. That man is soul of his *body* is a divine favour which in its way is no less indispensable for the constitution of man as he is than the fact that he is the *soul* of his body. On this fact that he is soul of his body is dependent nothing less than the reality of his being and existence. If he were not body, he could be only a shadow and less than a shadow. That God has willed it otherwise is not at all to be regarded and construed as a kind of disadvantage or *pudendum* for human existence, for example in contrast to that of the angels. This would be to forget that God has set man high above the angels in the very fact that it is man and not the angels whom He has determined to be His covenant-partner. But in respect of his human constitution, it belongs to his covenant-partnership that man is a representation of the whole of created reality, so that he partakes fully and seriously of the material side, and therefore is not only soul but soul of a body. This is to be understood as God's free unmerited act of grace. He could and can withhold from him that which He bestows with it : He is under no obligation to will to have him and to prepare him as a covenent-partner. He could quite well be content to survey His heavenly and earthly cosmos without choosing and preparing man to represent the whole. No one has any claim to be this wonderful thing, man. And God could and can take back from man what He has given him by willing and making him soul of his body. What is death, if not at least the threat of a bodiless life, a life-negating life ? It is at any rate the impressive reminder that even as body man does not belong to himself. Even as bodily, life is a matter which does not rest in our hands, but in the hand of God. This is applicable not only to material bodiliness, but also to physical bodiliness and therefore to living bodiliness. The benefit of creation consists in the fact that man may be the soul of his body, that as a living material body he is not restricted to space and the world of bodies, but may also be and exist temporally and belong to the invisible upper cosmos. He thus is in the twofold mystery that he lives as a bodily organism, and that his bodily organism is ordained to be the bearer and the expression of his life. He is, as he is material body in this invisible, inner, heavenly relation. Even this he does not assume to himself ; in this too we have the event of a created reality which is every moment wonderful. If it takes place he lives : not merely his bodily organism with its functions, but he himself in and with and yet independent of it and its functions ; he himself as the subject and form of its inner and outer experiences ; he himself as the subject and form of specific apprehensions, thoughts, sensations, feelings, purposes and endeavours which are more or less bound up with these experiences. If that event takes place, then he is in the bodily world and his own material body in such a way that, while identical with it, he also oversees, knows, uses and controls, in short, possesses it, so that he himself is

superior to it and thus far to himself. Life is life of the body, and
while it is this it is more than this. Life is to be subject and form ;
it is freedom, apprehension and control of the body. If man is the
soul of his body, this does not mean that his soul belongs to a body,
but that his body belongs to him, to his soul. As soul of his body,
man is obviously heavenly as he is earthly.

But what do we mean when we say " he is " and " he lives " ?
That he " lives " his life obviously cannot mean that he takes and
gives himself life from somewhere, or that he makes his material
body and therefore himself living and besouled and thus a physical
body, his own body supervised, known, used, controlled and possessed
by him. That he is soul and therefore subject and form of a body,
and thus belongs not only to the lower but also to the upper cosmos,
is something which clearly demands an event over whose occurrence
he has no control. The reality of his being and existence depends upon
this event taking place ; and on it there also depends the call of God and
self-knowledge and response as His creature. In this event it becomes
possible for him to meet the divine person as person, to be a covenant-
partner, if God wills and institutes this covenant. But as this fundamental event of his quickening takes place, and therefore in every
moment of his life before God, and indeed before the free unmerited
act of grace of God the Creator, he is wholly and exclusively dependent
on this act happening to him and on the living God being afresh his
Quickener and dealing with him as such. As he really lives, and is
thus soul of his body, he is always and immediately of God. If he
were not of God, he would not be. And if God were to withdraw
what He alone can and does give in this event, not only would his
body sink back to the status of a purely material body, to rise and
disintegrate even as a material body in the surrounding world of all
other bodies, but he himself would necessarily become a shadow and
less than a shadow, a departed soul which once was but now has been,
an extinct life. He would then no longer be God's covenant-partner,
nor see God's face, nor receive the grace of this covenant. And if
then God should objectively cease to hear or see the one who no
longer sees Him, if He should cease even to be his God, the God of
this man who no longer exists (for it is also possible that He will
not cease to be his God and so his hope), he would not only be lost,
but lost eternally. To live and thus to be soul of his body means on
this side of death to be warned against, and on the other side of
death to be delivered from, this lostness. And it is God Himself
and God alone who can both warn and deliver ; for He alone is the
source of life. His act alone is the event in which the reality of
human being and human existence, the soul of the body, can arise and
remain.

This is the statement with which our description of the constitution of man must begin and which is indispensable for all that follows.

We have not yet expressed it in the form in which it is recognisable as an anthropological statement and therefore useful as a presupposition for other anthropological statements. We repeat and expound all we have hitherto said if we introduce a concept which we earlier saw to be fundamental for an analysis of the human nature of Jesus—the concept of spirit. Man is not without God but by and from God—by and from the God of Israel and His ever new act of grace. In this way alone is he soul of his body. This can and must now be summarised in the single brief statement that man is as he has spirit. This is the form of expression which is now necessary : man *has* spirit. It is, of course, a form which itself requires explanation. We can and must say of man that he is soul ; and from this we go on to say that he is body. But we cannot simply say that he is spirit. This would be to obscure the nature of the spirit as that of man. It would be to miss the very thing which we are trying to say when we describe the constitution of man in terms of spirit.

To call man spirit whether " created " or " ultimate," as modern theology likes to do, especially in the school of Hegel, always involves at least an indirect identification of man with God, or must sooner or later lead to such an identification. That man is spirit could be rightly said only in so far as he is soul and therefore also body in virtue of spirit, a spiritual soul and to that extent also a spiritual body. Man himself cannot be characterised as spirit because in the Bible spirit denotes what God Himself is and does for man, man himself being identified with the fact that he is soul (of his body).

Man has spirit. By putting it in this way we describe the spirit as something that comes to man, something not essentially his own but to be received and actually received by him, something that totally limits his constitution and thus totally determines it. As he is man and soul of his body, he has spirit. We must perhaps be more precise and say that he is, as the spirit has him. Man has spirit, as one who is possessed by it. Although it belongs to the constitution of man, it is not, like soul and body and as a third thing alongside them, a moment of his constitution as such. It belongs to his constitution in so far as it is its superior, determining and limiting basis.

It is to be noted that according to Mt. 27[50] Jesus " yielded up " His spirit ; that according to Lk. 23[46] He commended it into His Father's hands ; and that according to the passages adduced earlier He gives His soul or His body and either way Himself for others, but not His spirit. Here His spirit is not Himself ; nor can it be at His disposal or be given for others. The body can be killed and die ; and the soul can be committed to eternal loss in hell by the One whose right it is to do this, namely, God (Mt. 10[28]) ; it can be " given in exchange " (Mt. 16[26]) ; and it can be lost (Mt. 10[39]). This happens to what man is. But it cannot happen to the spirit which man has as he is man. On the contrary, it is of the very essence of the spirit to prevent this happening to man, so far and so long as man has it. This can happen to man only at the time and with the consequence that he ceases to have spirit. Death is equivalent to absence of spirit. As the spirit makes of man an embodied

soul and a besouled body, so the absence of spirit makes of him a bodiless soul
and a soulless body. The spirit is immortal. For this reason it can be identical
neither with the man nor with a part of the being of man. The spirit is the
basis and the determination of the limit of the whole man ; and in so far it
belongs to his constitution and is thus no third thing in man and no further
moment of his constitution additional to soul and body.

We have thus to consent to the decision which the Early Church took against
the so-called trichotomism espoused by Philo, by Apollinaris of Laodicea in
the christological conflict of the fourth century and by the Arab philosophers
in the Middle Ages. It is another matter that there is no necessary reference
to parts. We could not speak of three sides or moments of the one human reality.
It is soul and it is body, but it is not spirit. Yet it is soul and body as spirit
comes to it, as it receives and has spirit, as spirit has it and will not leave it,
but grounds, determines and limits it. The only biblical passage which can be
regarded as ambiguous in this regard is 1 Thess. 5²³ : " And the very God of
peace sanctify you wholly ; and I pray God your whole spirit and soul and
body be preserved blameless unto the coming of our Lord Jesus Christ." It
must be admitted that this passage sounds difficult, because of the only slightly
differentiated conjunction of the three ideas, and even more because of the
circumstances that Paul seems to describe the spirit as also in need of preservation and therefore as not *per se* completely preserved. Calvin (*Comm. ad loc.,
C.R.* 30, 179) is certainly right when in this connexion he declines to understand
by " soul " the *motus vitalis* (the natural movement of life), and by " spirit "
the *pars hominis renovata* : *atqui tunc absurda esset Pauli precatio*. His own
view is that " spirit " here means the *ratio vel intelligentia*, and " soul " the
voluntas et omnes affectus. This yields good sense : *tunc enim purus et integer est
homo, si nihil mente cogitat, nihil corde appetit, nihil corpore exsequitur, nisi quod
probatur Deo*. But we have to confess that neither in text nor context is there
any support for this meaning. The slight differentiation of " spirit " in relation
to soul and body must be regarded as decisive, for if " spirit " really denotes a
third thing beside soul and body the passage is isolated not only in Paul but in
the rest of the Old and New Testaments. For example, when Lk. 1⁴⁶ᶠ· says of
Mary : " My soul doth magnify the Lord, and my spirit hath rejoiced in God
my Saviour," we do not have a double statement but a *parallelismus mem-
brorum*, in which the subjects, as often happens between " spirit " and " soul "
—we shall come back to this—can be interchanged. And in the passage Heb. 4¹²,
which is often cited in this connexion, it is said that the Word of God is sharper
than a two-edged sword and pierces to the dividing asunder (μερισμός) of soul
and spirit, and that from this point of division, and obviously in such a way
that the spirit comes to stand on God's side and the soul on man's, it becomes
the discerner of the thoughts and intents of the heart. Scripture never says
" soul " where only " spirit " can be meant. But it often says " spirit " where
" soul " is meant ; and there is inner reason for this in the fact that the constitution of man as soul and body cannot be fully and exactly described without
thinking first and foremost of the spirit as its proper basis. We are nowhere
invited to think of three entities. Even Augustine, when he once gave the
almost intolerably harsh formulation : *Tria sunt, quibus homo constat : spiritus,
anima et corpus*, immediately corrected himself : *quae rursus duo dicuntur, quia
saepe anima simul cum spiritu nominatur* (*De fide et symb.* 10, 23). Trichotomism
must necessarily issue in the view and concept of two different souls and therefore in a splitting of man's being. This makes understandable the force with
which it was condemned at the Fourth Council of Constantinople in A.D. 869-70
(*Denz., No.* 338).

We thus understand the statement that man has spirit and is
thereby man as equivalent in content to our first statement, that he

is man, and therefore soul of his body, not without God but by God, i.e., by the ever new act of God. Spirit is, in the most general sense, the operation of God upon His creation, and especially the movement of God towards man. Spirit is thus the principle of man's relation to God, of man's fellowship with Him. This relation and fellowship cannot proceed from man himself, for God is his Creator and he His creature. He himself cannot be its principle. If this is indeed possible for him, and if he on his side realises it as movement from him towards God, this is because the movement of God towards him has preceded and because he may in his movement imitate it. This is what is meant when Scripture says of man that he has spirit or the Spirit, or that he has done this or that in the Spirit or through the Spirit, or has said or done or suffered from the Spirit. This never signifies a capacity or ability of his own nature, but always one originally foreign to his nature which has come to it from God and has thus been specially imparted to it in a special movement of God towards him. It thus describes man as one who on God's initiative stands in relation to and fellowship with God, in order to be what he is in the relation and fellowship, limitation and determination thus based. The Spirit, in so far as He not only comes but proceeds from God Himself, is identical with God.

This is not taken only from the familiar passage Jn. 4^{24}, where πνεῦμα and θεός are expressly equated. It is implicitly stated in the fact that, in some passages in the Old Testament and then emphatically in the New, the Spirit is called the " Holy " Spirit. This has always to be taken into account where He is called the Spirit of God or the " spirit from on high " (Is. 32^{15}), where it is said that He is " from God " or " proceeds " from Him, or that God gives Him, or sends or pours Him forth, or where divine predicates such as omnipresence (Ps. 139^7), sovereignty (Is. $40^{13f.}$), judicial eminence (Is. 34^{16}) and the like, are attributed to Him. So, too, the fundamental meaning of the concepts *ruah* or *neshamah* and πνεῦμα, i.e., wind as breath, leads back of itself to a source in which breath is not to be distinguished from one who breathes. The Church was therefore right when it understood Him as the Holy Ghost, different from all creatures and of one essence with the Father and the Son.

Apart from this origin, we can only say that the question whether the Spirit is God or creature cannot be answered because it is falsely put. Spirit in His being *ab extra* is neither a divine nor a created something, but an action and attitude of the Creator in relation to His creation. We cannot say that Spirit is, but that He takes place as the divine basis of this relation and fellowship. Spirit is precisely the essence of God's operation in relation to His creature. Spirit is thus the powerful and exclusive meeting initiated by God between Creator and creature. It is of this that we have now to think for the understanding of the significance of Spirit for the grounding, constituting and maintaining of man as soul of his body.

After what has been said, it cannot surprise us that we must affirm that by Spirit we have primarily and originally to understand

the movement of God towards man and therefore the principle of
human relation to him and fellowship with Him, in which we do not
have to do with man's natural constitution but in some sense with
his standing in covenant with God. The covenant is the inner basis
of creation. And thus the historical standing of man in covenant
with God, although it seems objectively to follow man's natural constitution, is in fact the original and model to which the natural constitution of man must succeed and correspond. Spirit in His fundamental significance is the element in virtue of which man is actively
and passively introduced as a partner in the covenant of grace, in
which he is installed in his position as God's partner in the particular
stages and decisions of the history of this covenant and in which he
is equipped for his function as such, in order that in this position and
function he himself may begin to speak and act—he himself, not of
himself, but out of the fact that God has first spoken to him and
acted upon him. Hence it is as a recipient of the Spirit, as a charis-
matic, that, neither increased, reduced nor altered, but newly limited
and therefore newly determined in his humanity or as a human subject,
moving therefore in this alien element and placed on this new ground,
he has to answer, to speak certain words, do certain deeds, and manifest
a certain attitude. Whoever is given the Spirit by God becomes, as
the man he is, another man—a man of God, the kind of man whom
God uses, and who as he is used by God begins to live a new life.

To understand biblical anthropology, it is best to start with those passages
and contexts in which the Spirit is described as the power through which certain
human persons are pre-eminently equipped and supplied with their office and
commission in the history of God with men. Passages such as Is. 59[21], where it
is said of the people of Israel as such that the Spirit rests upon it, must be
infrequent in the Old Testament. Even in this passage, the meaning is eschatological, and by Israel is to be understood the converted " remnant." The constant rule confirmed by this exception is that in the reception and possession of
the Spirit the reference is to the election of individuals and not a communal
possession. Only in the New Testament, where the community as the body of
Christ is the object of election, is it otherwise ; and even here individuals specially
endowed with the Spirit are always rising above the common level. To be a
receiver and bearer of the Spirit, a man in the Old Testament must be not only
a member of the people of Israel, but be called Moses (Nu. 11[17, 25, 29]), or
Joshua (Nu. 27[18] ; Deut. 34[9]), or Othniel, Gideon, Jephthah, Samson (Jud. 3[10],
&c.), or Saul (1 Sam. 10[6]), or David (2 Sam. 23[2]), or Elijah (2 K. 2[9, 15]), or
Micah (Mi. 3[8]), or Ezekiel (Ezek. 11[5]). And the bearer of the fulness of the
Spirit, the man on whom the Spirit will rest, is the Messiah (Is. 11[2], 42[1]). The
saying in Neh. 9[30] is to be noted, where the operation of the Spirit and the operation of the prophets are equated. In all these contexts, to have the Spirit is to
have a commission from God and God's authorisation and power for its execution. This commission, authorisation and power can be withdrawn ; the Spirit
can abandon the man who is endowed with Him. This happened in the case of
Samson and Saul. 1 K. 22[24], in the dialogue between the false and the true
prophets, alludes to this. Of course He can be restored in certain circumstances
to the one who is thus deprived, as happens in the case of Samson. God remains
free to give, to take, and to give again. He shows Himself free in the fact that

He can also give an evil spirit to a man—this too is a kind of commission imposed on the man concerned—as again with Saul (1 Sam. 16[14f.], &c.) and in 2 K. 19[7] with the king of Assur; and it can again happen (1 Sam. 16[23]) that this evil spirit too can depart from him. Even the "lying spirit in the mouth of all false prophets" is, as we are told in the remarkable passage in 1 K. 22[21f.], one of the spirits that surround the throne of Yahweh, and it is called and empowered by Yahweh Himself for the infatuation of Ahab. There are other passages (Is. 4[4], 40[7]; Job 4[9]) where the Spirit is the burning blast of the divine judgment, a power of destruction and extermination. Hence we cannot be surprised to hear in Job 20[3] of a spirit "without insight" (Zurich Bible), in Is. 29[24] of an "erring spirit," in Zech. 13[2] of an "unclean spirit"; and even in the New Testament of a "spirit of bondage" (Rom. 8[15]), of "another spirit" which presents another Jesus and another gospel (2 Cor. 11[4]); and further, with a frequency which cannot be disregarded, of evil spirits, unclean spirits and spirits that cause sickness, with all the work of these spirits in and upon men. If God condemns a man and through him other men, He can give him such a spirit. He then falls, not without the active co-operation of God, whose Spirit leaves him, into the power of such an evil spirit. We must keep this before us because it makes it particularly clear that Spirit is God's free encounter with man. The work of the Spirit, according to Jn. 16[7], is twofold, the reproving of the world of sin and of righteousness, and comprehensively of the judgment in which God vindicates His lordship. In such a fulness, He rests upon the Messiah. Similarly (Ac. 2[3f.]) He is poured forth from heaven in the form of tongues of fire upon the New Testament community. Similarly the community is receiver and possessor of the Spirit, first in the apostles and then in its whole membership (1 Cor. 2[12]; Rom. 8[15], &c.). Similarly Christians are "led" by Him (Gal. 5[18]; Rom. 8[14]); they "live" in the Spirit (Gal. 5[25]), and so can be commanded to "walk" in the Spirit (Gal. 5[16]), to undertake the battle of the Spirit against the flesh (Gal. 5[17]), to be "full" of the Spirit (Eph. 5[18]). Similarly the community is constituted by His different gifts (1 Cor. 12[4f.]), and it can and must be asked concerning His fruits (Gal. 5[22f.]). By "Spirit" must always be understood the divine operation of grace in its full scope, as is most clearly comprehended in the idea of the righteous judgment of God. As Israel's Judge, God is already in the Old Testament Israel's Lord and Helper; even in the New the operation of God in the person of His Messiah is to be understood decisively as the act of the helpful, liberating God (Ac. 17[31]). As man receives the Spirit, he comes to deal with God and therefore with his Judge, and he is justly judged by God. It is to be observed how the "new and right" spirit for which Ps. 51[10] prays is in one and the selfsame breath called a joyful (v. 12) and an alarmed spirit (v. 17), and in Is. 66[2] a broken spirit. All this is included in the operation of the Spirit. God's election acts decisively, determining and limiting man; it decides not only this *or* that but this *and* that; so that this decision, no matter from which side it is seen, is to be understood as an event whose subject is God, but also one in which man, as is said of Saul in 1 Sam. 10[6], becomes "another man," or according to Jn. 3[3f.] is born anew from above (ἄνωθεν), being set in relation to God his Judge, subjected to His judgment and therefore in the best sense judged by Him. As such, possessing the Spirit (Rom. 8[23]; 2 Cor. 1[22]), he has the pledge (ἀπαρχή, ἀρραβών) of future glorification in participation of the glory of God, who, as He gave him the Spirit and became his Judge through the Spirit, entered into relationship with him. This is the meaning and function of the Spirit in the historical position which He occupies as a partner in the covenant of grace initiated in the existence of Israel and fulfilled and completed in the existence of the Messiah.

It is from this standpoint that the being and work of the Spirit are to be understood in the narrower anthropological sphere which now concerns us. As the elected and called and to that extent " new " man lives in the covenant by the fact that God gives him His Spirit, the natural man also lives in the same way. The same Spirit, who is there the principle of his renewal, is here the principle of his creaturely reality. Without Spirit, without the absolutely free encounter between God and man initiated by God, and outside the relation and fellowship based on this encounter, there can be no prophet or any other commissioned agent of God, and no living member of the body of Christ. But without the same Spirit man cannot in any sense be man, nor in any sense soul of his body. As he has the Spirit from God, he lives, he becomes and is soul, his material body becomes and is a physical body, and he is soul of this body. If he did not have the Spirit, he would not be able even to begin to live, he would not be soul, nor would his material body become a physical body. If he ceased to have the Spirit, he would no longer live, his soul would become a shadow of itself and his body a purely material body which as such could only dissolve in the world of bodies surrounding it. It is really the Spirit and He alone who quickens man, grounding, constituting and maintaining him as soul of his body. Man has no power over the Spirit ; on the contrary, he is man as the Spirit has power over him. The Spirit belongs to God even as He is given to man. He can have the Spirit only as He is continually given to him. Spirit is the event of the gift of life whose subject is God ; and this event must be continually repeated as God's act if man is to live. In this sense Spirit is the *conditio sine qua non* of the being of man as soul of his body. There is value in reminding ourselves, of course, that the same is also to be said of the beasts. It is only by the Spirit of God the Creator that they also live and are soul of their body. What distinguishes man from beast is the special movement and purpose with which God through the Spirit gives him life ; and, connected with this, the special spirituality of his life, which is determined by the fact that God has not only made him in his constitution as soul of his body, but destined him in this constitution for that position of a partner of the grace of His covenant. We know nothing of such a double determination in respect of the beasts ; and hence we do not understand the manner of their life or of their souls (though we cannot dispute that they have them) and at very best can only intuit. So far as we know, they lack that second determination by the Spirit which is primary and peculiar. Men and beasts can be born, but men alone can be baptised. Yet in the relation Spirit-life and therefore Spirit-life-body as such, there is no difference between men and beasts. The unfathomable free act and attitude of God the Creator is here too the *conditio sine qua non* of the life and therefore the being and existence of His creatures. The Spirit is also Judge of the life and death of man. He is this not only in the historical sense already considered, but also in regard to the natural constitution of man.

In this respect already Spirit means that he may live, and lack of the Spirit that he must die.

The biblical statements about the Spirit as the principle of the existence of man in the covenant of grace are related to those about the Spirit as the principle of his creatureliness in such a way that the former include the latter as presupposition and also as promise : as presupposition, in so far as the latter show and explain how man (together with the beasts) already stands as a creature under the same judgment and what will be his being as partner of the covenant of grace ; as promise, in so far as man has a certain hope in and for his creatureliness—the hope which in the New Testament is described as the resurrection of the dead, the resurrection of the whole man. It follows that the New Testament statements about the Spirit of grace and renewal must always be understood extensively and to the effect that they also refer to man's creatureliness and indirectly explain how it happens that man in the simplest and nearest sense of the word may live and need not die. A saying like Jn. 3[8], which says of the Spirit that " it bloweth where it listeth, and thou hearest the sound thereof, but canst not tell whence it cometh, and whither it goeth," not only can be made of the Spirit that awakens creaturely life, but also, since it refers to the Spirit of renewal, does actually refer to the creative Spirit. He comes—whence ? and goes—whither ? We put these questions if we do not know the ground of our life. For what is real between the two questions, as the mysterious birth by the Spirit that comes and goes, is the life of man, man as soul of his body. So, too, the saying in Jn. 6[63] (cf. also 2 Cor. 3[6]) : " It is the spirit that quickeneth ; the flesh profiteth nothing," while it is meant soteriologically, has an indirectly anthropological significance. We have also anthropological instruction in Rev. 11[11], where of the two dead witnesses it is said that, after three and a half days, " the spirit of life from God " entered into them, " and they stood upon their feet ; and great fear fell upon them which saw them." Reference may also be made to Rom. 8[10-11] : " And if Christ be in you, the body is dead because of sin ; but the Spirit is life because of righteousness. But if the Spirit of him that raised up Jesus from the dead dwell in you, he that raised up Christ from the dead shall also quicken your mortal bodies by his Spirit that dwelleth in you." With its mention of the name of Jesus Christ and the opposition between sin and righteousness which dominates the first sentence, the saying obviously has in view the dispensation of the covenant of grace, the threat of death by sin on the one side and the promise of life by righteousness on the other, with Christ between and looking forward, His back to the one and His face to the other. But the second sentence points beyond the present into the future, and therefore just as clearly includes also the creaturely reality of man. For the Spirit of God, who is also creative Spirit, there is, so long as He dwells in us, a mortal body, but one quickened and again and again maintained alive in its mortality ; and it is this that He will manifest and vindicate in man as the Spirit of Him who raised Jesus from the dead in defiance of sin and death. Or Gal. 4[6] : " And because ye are sons, God hath sent forth the Spirit of his Son into your hearts, crying, Abba, Father " ; and also Rom. 8[26f.] : " Likewise the Spirit also helpeth our infirmities : for we know not what we should pray for as we ought : but the Spirit maketh intercession for us with groanings which cannot be uttered. And he that searcheth the hearts knoweth what is the mind of the Spirit, because he maketh intercession for the saints." Here it is said of the prayer of Christians, and therefore undoubtedly with reference to the dispensation of grace, that it is not in the power of the Christian to be in prayer his own intercessor before God. In fact, when he prays, the Spirit takes his place and effects in his place the invocation of God the Father which is inexpressible for him, which is then heard and accepted by Him as though it were his own prayer. But this tells us implicitly, yet with unsurpassable precision, how it comes about that a man can exercise with supreme reality what he does not have in himself and therefore cannot produce of himself, i.e., his creaturely life, since the same Spirit of God is not only the Advocate and Representative for his prayer as the Spirit of the covenant but also for his life as the creative Spirit, giving him what he cannot take for himself. We might also think of an Old Testament passage like that which describes the restoration of life to the field of dry bones in Ezek. 37$^{1-14}$, for what is the awakening of dead Israel or the regathering of dispersed Israel here mentioned if it is not implicitly the very obvious process by which the living breath of God gives life and sustains it ?

But the Old Testament especially gives us many direct testimonies to this fact. Who is the God of Israel ? Moses and Aaron declare it (Nu. 16^{22}) when, at a moment when the whole community of God is most gravely threatened with annihilating wrath, they cling to this : " O God, the God of the spirits of all flesh, shall one man sin, and wilt thou be wroth with all the congregation ? " The God who is invoked in this way cannot will this. He is and acts (Is. 42^5) as He who " giveth breath unto the people upon (the earth), and spirit to them that walk therein." How He did this at the first is plainly described in Gen. 2^7. He breathed the breath of life into the nostrils of the man formed by Him out of the dust of the earth, and the latter thus became a " living soul." The meaning of this is that by the breathing of God man's own breath is set in motion, and thereby his life is aroused, his soul created, his earthly material body made into an organic body. " The Spirit, entering the form of dust, or earthly organism, creates the soul, which thus carries within itself an essentially indestructible because divine power of life . . . through which it has come into being and consists " (H. Cremer : *PRE*^{3}, Vol. 6, 465). This is poetically illustrated in Prov. 20^{27} : " The spirit of man is the candle of the Lord, searching all the inward parts of the belly." In the Old Testament, therefore, the fact that man lives is directly equated with the fact that he breathes. But he will not breathe without the breath and therefore the Spirit of God who awakened him to his own breathing and therefore to life. As he himself breathes and lives on the basis of the fact that God has breathed into him, he has the Spirit. But that he has the Spirit and therefore breathes and lives demands the continuing work of divine creation. " He giveth to all life, and breath, and all things," as the New Testament has it (Ac. 17^{25}). Hence Job. 33^4 can declare : " The spirit of God hath made me, and the breath of the Almighty hath given me life." Hence also (Ps. 150^6) everything that has breath can be summoned to praise the Lord. To praise God is in fact our natural office.

It should not be overlooked that it is on the basis of God's free operation that man has Spirit and therefore breathes and lives and may be soul of his body ; and further that it is under the judgment of God that, as matters stand, he is placed in his creaturely constitution. This is proclaimed in a fact already mentioned, that he has his breath and life, as well as the Spirit, in common with the beasts. For example, Gen. 1$^{20, 26}$ calls the beasts " living beings " before men ; and Gen. 7^{15} calls them expressly " flesh having the breath of life in them." According to the Old Testament, neither soul nor the Spirit can be simply denied to the beasts. To be sure, their creation is not described as an act of special bestowal such as that which takes place in man according to Gen. 2^7. Yet even so the creative Spirit which awakens man to life is also the life-principle of the beasts (and even of the whole host of heaven according to Ps. 33^6). Eccles. 3$^{19f.}$ develops this insight in a shattering way : " For that which befalleth the sons of men befalleth the beasts ; even one thing befalleth them · as the one dieth, so dieth the other, yea, they have all one breath ; so that a man hath no pre-eminence above a beast : for all is vanity. All go unto one place ; all are of the dust, and all turn to dust again. Who knoweth the spirit of man that goeth upward, and the spirit of the beast that goeth downward to the earth ? " Yes ; who knows ? Man has no right to find in his own favour in this respect. All that he can really know and expect of himself is that his breath and life, like that of the beasts, will end as it began, and that like the beasts he must die. Thus immediately after the fall he is told (Gen. 3¹⁹) : " In the sweat of thy face shalt thou eat bread, till thou return unto the ground ; for out of it wast thou taken : for dust thou art, and unto dust shalt thou return." This is made even more precise in Gen. 6³ : " And the Lord said, My spirit shall not always strive with man (Germ. : dwell in man), for that he also is flesh : yet his days shall be an hundred and twenty years," a span which Ps. 90¹⁰ reduces to the familiar seventy or eighty years. God is not bound to let His Spirit dwell in men always, and when He does so no longer, then it is all up with breath and life, with the being of man as soul of his body ; he must return to the earth from which he was taken, and die. " Thou turnest man to destruction ; and sayest, Return, ye children of men " (Ps. 90³). This is the divine judgment under which man in his creaturely constitution is placed in virtue of the fact that he can have the Spirit only as He is to be had as the free act of God. Since the Spirit can go as He came, it is a precarious thing to be a man " whose breath is in his nostrils " (Is. 2²²). " Verily all that is called man is only a breath " (Ps. 39⁶, Zurich version and versification). " If he set his heart upon man, if he gather unto himself his spirit and his breath ; all flesh shall perish together, and man shall turn again unto dust " (Job. 34¹⁴ᶠ·). Nor is this merely possible, but a fact : " His breath goeth forth, he returneth to his earth ; in that very day his thoughts perish " (Ps. 146⁴). " Then shall the dust return to the earth as it was : and the spirit shall return unto God who gave it " (Eccles. 12⁷). " Thou hidest thy face, they are troubled : thou takest away their breath, they die, and return to their dust. Thou sendest forth thy spirit, they are created : and thou renewest the face of the earth " (Ps. 104²⁹ᶠ·). Observe how in the last passage the relation is reversed, and the withdrawal of the breath of life is succeeded and relativised by a new sending forth. But the seriousness of the withdrawal and therefore of certain death is not thereby diminished. It is certain that there will be this withdrawal ; that there will be a new sending forth is something which we can neither decide nor perceive. In both cases God is at work, and in both He is a free Subject. God is He " in whose hand thy breath is," is the warning given to Belshazzar in Dan. 5²³. If a man breathes and lives and is the soul of his body, since only the breath and Spirit of God can make this possible, he stands inevitably in God's judgment. Man is, as he has Spirit. But this means that it rests with God alone whether he moves to the salvation or loss of his being. It means that in his creaturely constitution man is absolutely dependent upon God's judicial sentence, and therefore upon the fact that the freedom of this Judge is the freedom of His grace.

This leads us to the final question what it means for man to have Spirit. From what has been said, the definition is primarily very simple. To have Spirit means that he may live, and therefore be soul, and therefore be soul of his body. The " may " demands emphasis. It gives rise to a " can " and the " can " to an actualisation. But the " may " is the basis and beginning of everything else. And when Spirit is ascribed to man it means that this " may " is proper to him. What does man " have " ? What he " has " is that he may live and be the soul of his body. This is what is meant when we say that he " has " Spirit. Four delimitations are possible and necessary in the light of this fact.

1. That man has Spirit means that God is there for him. Every

moment that he may breathe and live he has in this very fact a witness that God turns to him in His free grace as Creator, that He has willed him again and again as a living being, and that He has allowed him to become one. It is not that man, having Spirit, is of divine essence even if only in a part or in the core of his being. On the contrary, the creatureliness of the whole man cannot be more evident than in the fact that he stands in need of this " may," of this freedom to live which is not immanent in him but comes to him from without. It would be more possible to ascribe to him a divine nature in virtue of his spiritual or even his corporeal being than in virtue of the Spirit who makes it possible for him to be soul of his body. But since his life rests on this transcendent enabling, we cannot say this even in regard to his soul and body. We must be content that the whole man lives by the fact that God is there for him.

We read in Ovid (*Ars amandi*, III, 549) : *Est Deus in nobis et sunt commercia coeli/Sedibus aetheriis spiritus ille venit.* This conception of an immanent being of God in us is hermetically excluded by the biblical concept of the Spirit, if only because it is the idea of an activity and not of a being. Since we have the Spirit and may therefore live, God is indeed " in us " according to the Bible. But according to the Bible, the Spirit is always a divine work in man, a divine gift to him. And as God's work and gift, it is always free and superior to him. Because He signifies absolutely everything for man, being the *conditio sine qua non* of his fellowship with God and therefore his life, it is impossible that He should be identical with man in any depth of his being and existence, which would involve the transformation of man into a divine being. The relationship between Spirit and man even in its anthropological sense is to be represented on the analogy of expressions used in the soteriological context. He is poured forth upon man, or laid upon him ; but He is not to be thought of as changing human nature into divine nature, against which Paul twice (1 Cor. 15⁴⁵, 2 Cor. 3¹⁷, ¹⁸) ventures the equation $\kappa \acute{\upsilon} \rho \iota o s = \pi \nu \epsilon \hat{\upsilon} \mu a$. These passages tell us that this man, because in His humanity He was also Son of God, accomplished and still accomplishes in His own person the mighty quickening action of God in relation to all other men. Jn. 7³⁸ can also be adduced in this connexion : " Rivers of living water " will flow from the body of those who believe in Him ; but the context (" If any man thirst, let him come unto me, and drink," v. 37) makes it quite clear that this cannot be understood as an identification of human and divine being, but again only as a description of man's being in service of the quickening divine activity.

2. That man has Spirit is the fundamental determination which decisively makes possible his being as soul of his body. The Spirit is in man and belongs to him as the mathematical centre is in and belongs to the circle. The whole man is of the Spirit, since the Spirit is the principle and power of the life of the whole man. Hence he cannot be a third thing beside soul and body. He is rather an augmentation of the stability of man's being. It is the Spirit that brings this into being and stabilises it. He is the " may " on the basis of which the soul is awakened and made soul, and the material body is besouled and thus becomes an organic body and is maintained as such.

The difficulty of 1 Thess. 5²³ would be removed if the terms αὐτὸς ὁ θεός, ὁλοτελεῖς, ὁλόκληρον and τηρηθείη were to be related to one another as in the following paraphrase : " The God of peace sanctify you in the wholeness of your being, and may your spirit (which is the basis and guarantees this wholeness of your being), and with it your soul and body, be preserved without injury until the return of our Lord Jesus Christ." What Paul would then desire for his readers is that the return of Christ and the resurrection of the dead should bring them the renewal and confirmation of that divinely conceded " may," and therefore the freedom to live which He, God alone, has already given them in time, and which He alone can give them again to all eternity. May it bring them the maintenance of their whole being as men by the same Spirit by whom it is already based and constituted. And may this come about through God's sanctifying them in this present being of theirs and thus preparing them for that final salvation and preservation. All other passages which speak of the Spirit of man indicate that the explanation of this saying must be sought along these lines. Whatever else we may be told about the Spirit of man, the reference is always to a centre of his being and existence which is not a third thing beside soul and body but is to be sought in soul and body and at the same time above and beyond them, being understood as the representative of the divine grace of creation over against the whole being and existence of man.

3. Since man has Him, the Spirit is certainly in man—in his soul and through his soul in his body too. It is the nearest, most intimate and most indispensable factor for an understanding of his being and existence. But while He is in man, He is not identical with him. We have seen already that this would imply a transformation of man into God, which is excluded by the fact that Spirit is a conception of activity. The Spirit is not transformed into the soul of man, although He first and supremely creates the soul of man and makes it His own dwelling. Nor does He become corporeal, although as the Spirit of the soul He immediately becomes the Spirit of the body and man is ordained to be not only spiritual soul and besouled body, but also spiritual body. He does not merely become the human subject. He is more than this. He is the principle which makes man into a subject. The human subject is man as soul, and it is this which is created and maintained by the Spirit. But for this very reason the Spirit lives His own superior and alien life over against the soul and the human subject. He is not bound to the life of the human subject. He cannot, therefore, be reached by its death. When the subject dies, He returns to God who gave Him. In distinction from the human subject, He is immortal. Whether or not death is the last word concerning man depends upon whether He is given again and that " may " is renewed.

At this point we must again refer to all the passages in which reference is made to a withdrawal of the Spirit and the death of man which this entails. The sickness of the son of the widow of Sarepta was so grave " that there was no breath left in him " (1 K. 17¹⁷). The Spirit must be " discharged " like a strange guest (Mt. 27⁵⁰), or " given back " like something borrowed into the hands of Him from whom it was received (Lk. 23⁴⁶). The body without Spirit is dead (Jas. 2²⁶). But the Spirit can be saved when a man is delivered to Satan for the destruction of his flesh (1 Cor. 5⁵). Awakening from the dead means that the Spirit returns to the man concerned (Lk. 8⁵⁵), as can sometimes be said in the Old Testament of men who are totally exhausted and apparently dead (Jud. 15¹⁹, 1 Sam. 30¹²). Thus the Spirit, coming and going, lives His own life over against the man. Note must also be taken of 1 Cor. 2¹¹, where an express distinction is made between πνεῦμα τοῦ ἀνθρώπου and man, and it is said o the former that it knows τὰ τοῦ ἀνθρώπου as the Spirit of God knows τὰ τοῦ θεοῦ.

4. The Spirit stands in a special and direct relationship to the soul or soulful element of human reality, but in only an indirect relationship to the body. The soul therefore is the life of the body, and therefore the human life as such which man may not only have but be when he receives the Spirit. He may be soul. Thus it is the besouled body that the Spirit chooses and occupies as His dwelling. It is on and in the soul that the act of God, which is the Spirit, takes place in man ; and on and in the body through the soul. This is the basis of the order of the relationship of soul and body, and of the superiority of the soul over the body. The soul is *a priori* the element in which the turning of God to man and the fellowship of man with God in some way take place. The same is to be said of the body, but only *a posteriori*. It is as the principle of the soul that the Spirit is the principle of the whole man.

Here we stand before the material justification of the possibility of which Scripture makes such frequent use, not speaking of the soul directly, but of that which grounds and maintains the soul as its principle and that of the whole man, namely, the Spirit. Since the Spirit dwells especially in the soul, and therefore the soul especially is spiritual soul, the Spirit participates in the motions and experiences of the soul, and what is said of the former can be said of the latter. In this sense, Gen. 41⁸ can say of Pharaoh that his spirit was uneasy, and 1 K. 21⁵ of Ahab that he became of an ill-humoured spirit. In the same sense Job (6⁴) can complain that his spirit drank the glowing poison of the arrows of the Almighty ; the Psalmist (142⁴, 143⁴) can say that his spirit is cast down in him, or fails him (143⁷), and Is. 57¹⁵ can speak of a contrition and humbling of the spirit. In the same sense, Jesus can be said to sigh in His spirit (Mk. 8¹²), to groan in His spirit (Jn. 11³³), and to be troubled in spirit (Jn. 13²¹). Similarly, 2 Cor. 2¹³ tells us that in certain situations Paul had no rest in his spirit. In the same sense again, it can be said conversely of Jacob that his spirit revived (Gen. 45²⁷) ; and of the king of Assur (1 Chron. 5²⁶), the Philistines (2 Chron. 21¹⁶) and Cyrus (2 Chron. 36²² ; Ezra 1¹) that their spirit was aroused to certain acts and attitudes. We read in Ps. 77⁶ of a spirit which makes diligent search, in Is. 26⁹ of a spirit which desires God, in Is. 38¹⁶ of a spirit which longs for quickening by God, and in Lk. 1⁴⁷ of a rejoicing spirit. In the story of the childhood of John the Baptist (Lk. 1⁸⁰) we read that he grew and waxed strong in spirit. To Daniel (5¹²) there is ascribed an " excellent ' spirit, while Ezek. 13³ charges the false prophets with following their " own " spirit. According to 2 Cor. 7¹, there is a filthiness of the spirit as well as of the flesh, whereas 1 Cor. 6²⁰ tells us that God can be glorified in our body and in our spirit, and 1 Cor. 7³⁴ that Christians can be holy in body and spirit. Eccles 7⁸ compares a " patient " and a " proud " spirit. The Jew Apollos (Ac. 18²⁵) was " fervent in spirit " ; and Prov. 16² can speak of a weighing of spirits. It may be seen how the Spirit stands for soul in this sense from Gal. 6¹⁸, where Paul's desire for his readers is that the grace of Jesus Christ may be with their spirit, or from Rom. 8[16], which speaks of the Spirit of God bearing witness to our spirit. In all these passages we obviously have to do with man as such, and with man in his natural relationship and orientation to God. Even in these passages we cannot of course forget that according to many other clear contexts the Spirit is not man as such, but the divine gift of life which makes him man, and therefore something foreign and superior to the whole man. Yet while this gift does not cease to be a gift, it is really given to man as such and belongs to his very essence. This strange and superior thing is at the same time nearest and most intimate. And this is expressed in the Bible in the fact that man—and therefore man primarily as soul—can be considered and described in terms of that which divinely grounds and maintains him. Note that here again there is no thought of an equation of Spirit and man. Here again the case is different from that of soul. Man " has " the Spirit, but it cannot be said that he is spirit. Yet to have the Spirit is so essential that what he is, and especially his soul, can also be simply described and denoted from the standpoint of this having, and this having, this divine " may," must be understood on all sides as participant in the ebb and flow of the life of his soul and his whole creaturely life. Something of the divine condescension already apparent in the sphere of creation is undoubtedly revealed in the distinctive ambiguity of the biblical terminology at this point. So long as man lives, God has evidently declared Himself in solidarity with him by constantly giving him His Spirit. It is not too trifling a thing for Him to empty Himself and tread with him the different paths of his soul, whether they lead into the heights or the depths. When the Corinthians (1 Cor. 3[16], cf. also 2 Cor. 6[16]) are exhorted by Paul to know that they are the temple of God and that God dwells in them and when the following interpretation is given in 1 Cor. 6[19] : " What ? know ye not that your body is the temple of the Holy Ghost which is in you, which ye have of God, and ye are not your own ? "—the primary reference is of course to Christians as members of the body of Christ, but it has also a more extensive anthropological truth and significance. The Holy Spirit is immediate to the soul, but through the soul He is also mediate to the body, and He is thus the basis and maintenance of the whole Christian and therefore of the man who does not belong to himself. But if by Spirit we understand the creative Spirit, the " may " which goes forth from God and by which man has life, then the relationship of this creative Spirit to the soul and body of the natural man is described in this saying of Paul. As He dwells in man and primarily in his soul, the body as the body of this soul is indirectly the property and sanctuary of God, and even as body man is really withdrawn from his own disposal and power and with his soul made the dwelling of the sovereign Spirit.

3. SOUL AND BODY IN THEIR INTERCONNEXION

We now turn to the question what it is that by God and therefore through the Spirit is grounded, constituted and maintained as human creatureliness. This is the question of the inner structure of this creatureliness. It subdivides into the three questions of its inner unity, its inner differentiation, and its inner order. That is to say, it is a matter of soul and body in their interconnexion, in their particularity, and in their material relationship.

We must first address ourselves to the first of these subsidiary questions—that concerning the inner unity of human creatureliness and therefore soul and body in their interconnexion.

In the preceding sub-section we made it clear that human creatureliness is essentially conditioned by the free action of God the Creator. Man is, as he is from God and through God, i.e., as he has Spirit. This is in some sense the sign which stands before the brackets in which we have to see and understand the being of man. We have now to ask what stands in these brackets and therefore under this sign, taking up the question of the being of man as such. But here we are confronted by the remarkable fact that within these brackets we have to do with a whole, but with a whole in which there is antithesis, and therefore with a duality ; with something resembling at least the distinction between God and the creature in the case of the creature, or Spirit and man in the case of man. Man is twofold. He is soul of his body, as we must put it on the basis of our understanding of the Spirit and the fact that he is conditioned by the action of God. But he is these two things in differentiation : both soul and body.

We may provisionally paraphrase as follows the results of our first proposition. Man is (1) creaturely life—life which by the will and act of the living God is awakened, created and called into temporal existence as the individual life of a body. He is *living* being. And he is (2) creaturely being—being which by the will and act of the same God has a certain spatial form or besouled body. He is living *being*. To put it in another way, he is (1) there, and has existence, and in this respect is soul ; and he is (2) there in a certain manner and has a nature, and in this respect is body. It is obvious that this entails duality, that these determinations and elements of his being are not identical, and that neither of them can be reduced to the other. Soul is not organic body ; for life is not corporeal body, time is not space, and existence is not nature. Similarly, body cannot be soul.

The contrast is so great that the question arises whether in this differentiation within human creatureliness we do not really have a form of the distinction between Creator and creature, Spirit and man. But to ask this question is to answer it. The distinction between Creator and creature is unique and unrepeatable. In expounding our first proposition, we had to emphasise the fact that man neither is nor becomes the Spirit, but that he acquires and has Him, and that the creative turning of God to man, the gift of the Spirit, means that God is for man, but not that man is in any respect or in any part or moment of his natural condition identical with God. God remains God and man man when this turning takes place and the being of man is grounded, constituted and maintained by God. From the very outset, then, the possibility is ruled out that in this inner differentiation within man's being we really have to do with a form of the distinction between Creator and creature, Spirit and man. The being of man in its totality is creaturely being, and, however great and important the inner differentiation, it can never extend to nor include the differentiation in which God confronts human and all created being alike as its Creator. The latter antithesis is absolute and final, the former relative and provisional. The antithesis of soul and body, like that of heaven and earth, is an antithesis within creation and immanent in the world. This does not mean that it is invalid or unworthy of notice. But it does mean that the whole which stands within those brackets, the whole man who is of and through God and is born of the Spirit, must at any rate be seen together as God and man cannot be seen together except in Jesus Christ. Apart from Jesus Christ, God and man are neither one person nor one thing. A master concept including them both can result only in the denial of the existence and being of both. It can only be the concept of a false God or a non-existent man. But the soul and body of man are the one man, as heaven and earth as a whole are one cosmos. The differentiation of soul and body is not denied by this consideration, but set in its proper place. Only in this place can both be seen in their differentiation.

The comparison of the relationship between soul and body with that between Creator and creature does of course contain a *particula veri* which is not suppressed by this consideration. Even the antithesis between heaven and earth is not identical with that between Creator and creature nor equal to it ; yet it is an attestation and reflection of this higher antithesis. But it is incontestable that between heaven and earth on the one hand, and soul and body on the other, there is a similarity ; and while we need not on this account adopt the speculative view that man as soul of his body is the " microcosm," the world in miniature, we must always take this similarity into account. The antithesis between Creator and creature is not in any case an antithesis without relation, for in the person of Jesus Christ it is not only bridged but annulled, and at this point the Creator and His creature are to be seen as one. Hence we need not be surprised if we come across certain traces of this fundamental antithesis even on the side of the creature, finding an analogy and copy, if not the antithesis itself or its equivalent, both in the structure of the cosmos (heaven and earth), and in the being of man (soul and body). The correspondence consists in the fact that in the relation of soul and body too, in irreversible order, there is a higher and a lower, a quickening and a quickened, a factor that controls space and one that is limited by it, an element which is invisible and one which is visible. Does not this inevitably remind us of the relation of Creator and creature as that of heaven and earth with its closer correspondence inevitably reminds us of the basic antithesis ?

It belongs to the creatureliness of all creatures, and therefore to that of man, that even though they cannot reproduce they can copy and attest the differentiation and relation of God towards them in the inner differentiations and relations of their own being. To the absolute antithesis between God and man (with one great exception), there can correspond in man himself only a relative antithesis of two moments which in him are finally and originally bound together and united. The creature is first and last and in all his differentiation *one*, whereas God and His creature in all the relations that exist between them are always and necessarily *two*, even in their unity in Jesus Christ. Thus body and soul belong together otherwise than Creator and creature. In the one case, it is grace that Creator and creature belong together ; but in the case of soul and body, it is nature. In the former case, the interconnexion is grounded in the free creative will of God ; in the latter in the creature itself, of which it is the *ratio essendi* from which it cannot escape without forfeiting its being.

But this negative affirmation has a more important positive side. It is not the case that the creature is deprived of anything by being unable to repeat that original antithesis ; for it could not be good for it to do so. On the contrary, the goodness of its creation is seen in the fact that it is given to be only relatively distinct within itself, to belong together by nature in its inner antithesis, and to have its *ratio essendi* in this interconnexion. The thought of man in his differentiation as soul and body really having to repeat the differentiation between God and the creature is not only an arrogant but a terrifying thought. It would mean—and here perhaps we can first see why it is forbidden—that in every minute of his existence and being man himself must undertake to bridge the chasm which God Himself bridged by calling the creation out of nothing into a reality distinct from Himself. In other words, man would necessarily be placed continually in the position and role of a *creator ex nihilo*. As soul, he would be the absolute lord of his body, absolutely responsible for it, and therefore his own creator ; and as body, he would be the absolute object of his soul, absolutely dependent upon it, and therefore his own creature. He would then have to attempt the hopeless task of being man, and he would have to be equal to God to be able to be true man. He would inevitably be torn asunder by this contradiction even if for a moment he successfully undertook to live in it. It is really for his salvation that the theories about soul and body which directly or indirectly amount to the fact that man as soul is his own creator, and as body his own creature, are merely theories which have never really been put into practice, except in certain experiments or approximations. It is bad enough that sinful man actually finds himself on a way corresponding to one of these theories, and that this usually leads in practice to such dreadful consequences both inward and outward. But it is for man's salvation that he cannot continue this way to the end ; that he cannot be what he is not, his own creator as soul and his own creature as body. He may be creature alone and no more. It is the grace and kindness of the Creator that he may be this. And

therefore in his creatureliness, for all its inner differentiation, he may
be a solid inner unity, a whole. That he is soul and body does not
threaten him with an infinite contradiction which he would have to
meet with an achievement of which only God is capable. That he is
soul does not burden him with the task of being his own creator, nor
that he is body with the fate of being his own creature. However
great and important the antithesis between soul and body, it does
not have this intolerable width. Man is one in his being as soul and
body. He can and may be wholly and simultaneously both in the
peace of his self-united being : soul, without that absolute responsibility for the body ; and body without that absolute dependence
upon the soul. It is not the case that man is his soul alone, his body
being a distinct reality produced and to be controlled by it as such.
This is just what man is graciously spared by the fact that he is
creature and not creator. It is possible to be man. To be man is
not an extravagant task necessarily leading to despair. It appears
as though it were so only in many theories about man and the many
experiments in living corresponding to these theories. Human reality
is neither so powerful nor so powerless. Naturally the perverted will
for life produced by these theories and experiments will avenge itself.
Death is the final and conclusive result of the delusion in which man
wants to be both creator and creature. In death as the unnatural
division of soul and body this sin is paid for. But death, too, makes
it clear that this undertaking is a delusion and nothing else. The
ostensibly all-powerful soul becomes completely impotent in death
because it becomes bodiless. But this does not mean that the body
becomes all-powerful in death. In death, the organic body as such
decays, becoming a mere material body and merging into the surrounding world of material bodies. Even the misery of death is not
so great that the delusion is a reality in its inverted form. Even in
death, the human reality cannot fail to return to the infinite and
intolerable tension between Creator and creature. The difference and
antithesis between soul and body is as great in death as it can possibly
be within the created world. In death man is only the spent soul of
a spent body, and he cannot live at all unless the God who let him
live and then die gives him new life. But the fearful thing which
would befall him if he succeeded in being both creator and creature
cannot befall him even in death. Sin receives its wages in death, but
it does not reach its objective. The difference and antithesis between
soul and body remains relative ; and it is a gracious preservation in
the grounding, constituting and maintaining of man that the difference between soul and body never becomes that basic antithesis but
is always and in all circumstances relative.

But we can and must say something better. The fact that it is
given to man to be only relatively different in himself, to belong
together by nature in his inner antithesis, is the positive benefit of his

creation because by it he is one—an inwardly united and self-enclosed subject. He is not one, of course, in the sense that God is one. The oneness of God is certainly not without its inner differentiation. But there are no different things in God, there are no individual perfections which are not in and for themselves the one totality of His Godhead, the sum of all His perfections. Yet we cannot say of the human soul that it is also the human body, nor of either soul or body that one or other is in itself the whole man. Again, for all the rich differentiation of God, there is no higher and lower in His unity, no prior and posterior in His individual perfections. There is order in God, but no subordination or superordination. The order of man, on the other hand, entails the latter. We speak equivocally when we say that both God and man are one. We may and must say of man that he is one ; just as we may and must say that the cosmos is one, although it is composed of heaven and earth. Man cannot succeed in making an absolute separation of soul from body, nor can this come upon him. Their interconnexion and therefore his inner coherence may be powerfully challenged by himself and then by God, but the God whose creature he is has made them indestructible. Even in death there is only a relative differentiation in man. He can and must die ; but even in death he cannot and must not suffer the destruction of this interconnexion. For even in death God watches over him. And as on either side of death he may live by the gracious will of God, God not only watches over him but awakens him to this interconnexion and then speaks and deals with him as the one who lives in this interconnexion : the God who is one in Himself with the man who is one in himself even in his purely creaturely completeness ; one Subject with the other. It is no more and no less than the being of man before God, his intercourse with Him, which is radically made possible by the fact that for all the differentiation of his being as soul and body it is given to him, not to be two things, but in these two one. This is one of the natural points of contact for the covenant of grace. Indeed, it is the basic one. This is a strange fact, for God is one, a Subject, in a totally different way from man. It really rests upon His creative initiative and action that there may be anything in common between God and man at all. Even the knowledge of this common factor presupposes the covenant of grace and therefore God's revelation to man. Yet for all that it is so strange, it is a real fact. God can be for man and man for God, because in his place and way man is no less one than God. It is not only preservation but the positive blessing of this benefit that man's being and existence as soul and body cannot repeat in itself the absolute opposition of Creator and creature.

We recall that we are required to speak at once not only of the interconnexion but of the unity of soul and body. It is true humanity in the person of Jesus which allows us no other starting-point but bids

us commence at once with this knowledge. And in any case we
should be hard put to it to find a better or more relevant point of
departure. We best keep ourselves from prejudice, abstraction and
one-sidedness if we proceed from the concrete reality in which man
neither lacks the inner differentiation of soul and body, nor is mere
soul or mere body, nor merely a combination and association of the
two, but wholly and simultaneously both soul and body, always and
in every relation soulful, and always and in every relation bodily.
We cannot cease to see both and therefore these two ; for the unity
of soul and body does not consists in their identity, or in the inter-
changeability of soulful and bodily. But again we cannot cease to
see both, and therefore the two together ; for the unity of soul and
body does not consist in the union of two parts which can always be
seen and described separately. It is this double stipulation which
makes difficult our present inquiries and representations, and especially the first in which it is a matter of the unity. On no side may we
evade this difficulty. It would naturally be easier and more agreeable if we could skip the differentiation of soul and body and speak
simply of man as such, as made and willed by God. But then we
should not have man as such before us ; for the concrete reality of
man consists in his being both, and only in both one. Again, it would
be easy and simple if we could speak comfortably of the soul first
and then of the body, and in this succession and combination of man
as such. But we should then miss man as such ; for his concrete
reality consists in his being absolutely one, and only in this way both.
No mitigation is, in fact, possible except at the cost of the thing itself.
And a third stipulation is to be added at the start, which makes the
thing no easier and which is to be observed just as carefully. This is
that in the unity and differentiation of man we do not have a sym-
metrical relation. That he is wholly and simultaneously both soul
and body does not exclude the fact that he is always both in different
ways ; first soul and then body. It would again be easier and more
suitable if instead of this we could reckon with an equal division of
weight and worth between the two moments. But this we may not
do. We should again abandon the concrete reality of man if we did
not reckon from the very outset with the inequality of that which in
man is different and yet one.

We begin then, as is proper, with a statement about man's soul.
We recall our proposition concerning the Spirit, that as the creative
action of God He arouses the soul as the life of man, but that He is
not for that reason identical with it. Applying this statement to the
soul, we must first say concerning it too that it is not identical with
the Spirit. It owes its being and existence to the Spirit. It is spiritual
soul. But it is not a kind of prolongation or continuation of that
divine action. It is the creature grounded by this action, and the
action of this creature.

It is not the effecting of life but life in being (H. Cremer). In the concrete language of the concepts and outlook of the Old Testament, it is not the quickening breath of God but that which lives by it, man's own breath awakened by it. We have already seen how close the connexion is. Since the soul is spiritual soul and entirely from the Spirit, the Old and New Testaments can often speak of the spirit where the wording and context of the passage make it plain that only the soul can be meant. The breath of the creature is never more than the answer to the breathing of the Creator. Occasionally then, though remarkably seldom, the LXX can venture to render *ruaḥ* directly by ψυχή. But the converse is never true that the soul is spoken of where the Spirit is unambiguously meant. The breathing of the Creator cannot be understood as an answer to the breath of the creature, or the work of the Creator as an answer to the work of the creature. There is in fact no case where the LXX translates *nephesh* by πνεῦμα. Even these Alexandrian Jews had a sharp perception that the interchange of the ideas is possible from above downwards but not from below upwards. The condescension of the Spirit has no parallel in the elevation of the soul.

But we cannot complete this delimiting statement about the soul without immediately speaking of the body as well. The soul is not a being for itself, and it cannot exist for itself. Soul can awake and be only as soul of a body. Soul presupposes a body whose soul it is, i.e., a material body which, belonging to soul, becomes an organic body. Soul is inner—how could it be this if it had no outer? Soul is movement in time—how could it be this if it did not have an inalienable spatial complement, if it had no place? Soul fulfils itself in specific perceptions, experiences, excitations, thoughts, feelings and resolutions—how could it do this if it had no means in and through which it could exhibit itself? But all these, outwardness and space and means, it does not have of itself. All these constitute its body. Thus in being soul, it is not without body. It is, only as it is soul of a body. Hence every trivialisation of the body, every removal of the body from the soul, and every abstraction between the two immediately jeopardises the soul. Every denial of the body necessarily implies a denial of the soul. It is in this, when seen from below, that the difference between soul and Spirit consists. The Spirit cannot be said to need a body. It is divine action. It is the free act of grace on the part of the Creator. It needs a body as little as God needs the world. The converse is true that the world needs God, and the body needs the Spirit because it needs the soul. Without the Spirit, it could only be a material body, not the body of a soul, not a quickened and living body, and therefore not an organic body. Man is soul of a body and therefore necessarily both soul and body. This is what distinguishes him from the Spirit, and what distinguishes the act of his existence from the creative act on which his existence is based. Thus the first delimiting definition would be impracticable if it did not also contain the idea of the body.

Soul is " life as it stirs in the individual and quickens the material organism which serves as a means for its activity." Soul is " the inner being of man which on one hand bears the Spirit, and on the other is distinctively determined by the fact that this Spirit is the principle of a corporeal being " (H. Cremer). In the plastic language of the Old Testament, that which according to Gen. 2[7] is created by the breath of God could not enter into being, or would immediately cease to be, if this product of the breath of God were not related to a product of His hands : " And the Lord God formed man of the dust of the ground." Note that this formation, a material body which has not yet become an organic body, is already called " man." He can be called this, only in view of what follows concerning the breath of life which God breathes into the nostrils of this formation. But it is worth noting that this formation is in fact called " man," that the one man can obviously be seen and understood wholly from this bodily side. Man in his totality offers this aspect too. The materialists are quite right : he is wholly this living bodily organism, this corporeal life as well. And this distinguishes his soul from the volitional act of God, from the Spirit, by whom it is awakened and created.

We move on from this delimitation. Soul is life, self-contained life, the independent life of a corporeal being. Life in general means capacity for action, self-movement, self-activity, self-determination. Independent life is present where this self-movement, self-activity, and self-determination are not only the continuation and partial appearance of a general life-process, but where there is a specific living subject. Not every corporeal being is living. Purely elementary corporeal beings are not this. They lack the capacity for action. To ascribe soul to corporeal beings like a stone or a mass of water or a puff of wind or a flame would be an absolute *contradictio in adiecto*. We do not know what we are talking about if we try to do this. Soul is life. What is lifeless is soulless. Again, there are corporeal beings of which there can be no doubt that they are living but real doubt whether their life is independent and not merely the partial appearance of a general life-process. We cannot know whether a specific plant is a subject. We say more than we can answer for if we speak of plant-souls. Independent life, the life of a specific subject, does not emerge except where the capacity for action of a corporeal being is not bound to a specific point in space. The capacity for action of the beast and of man is independent life of this kind. Here again, however, we must make the qualification that, although we recognise the life of the beast as such, we do not know but can only surmise or suspect that it is an independent life, the life of a specific subject. The life of man, and man alone, is for us the object of true and direct knowledge. What we mean when we speak of soul, we can strictly know only when we speak of the human soul. Soul is independent, the life of a particular subject. I know it as such independent life as I know myself. I know life as mine, as the life proper to myself as a subject. With this life of mine I may also be the continuation and partial appearance of a general life-process. But at any rate, as I know myself, I know my life as my own and myself as the subject of my life. Whether the beast is engaged in such self-knowledge or is even capable of it, I cannot know, because the beast cannot tell me anything about it. I myself say to myself that I am engaged in this self-knowledge and therefore capable of it. All the acts of my life consist also at least in the fact that I say this to myself. And my fellow-man tells me—he too with all the acts of his life—that he is engaged in the same self-knowledge and is capable of it. On the basis of this agreement, it is a reasonable hazard to ascribe to him as to myself, and therefore to man as such, independent life and therefore soul.

But this process whereby we become conscious of ourselves, of our independent life and therefore of our soul, is not merely an act of soul, whether in subject or in object. It is indeed true that both in subject and in object it is wholly an act of soul. As I live and am therefore soul I find myself able to become conscious that I am soul. And as I make use of this ability, my life itself and therefore my soul executes a return movement to itself. I come to myself, discover myself and become assured of myself. It belongs to my capacity for action that I continuously do this, that I am continuously engaged in the act of becoming self-conscious and therefore in this return movement. It all takes place in me and therefore in my soul. Yet it cannot be denied that this act in which my soul is at once subject and object is also wholly a corporeal act. The life which I live, and to whose fulfilment this return movement belongs, is in none of its moments other than the independent life of my physical body. I am not this material body of mine ; it is not this material body that lives. But I do not exist without also being this material body. I do not live otherwise than as I live in my body. As certainly as it is a capacity of my soul, this capacity of mine for that return movement is bound up with the fact that I am also a material body, and that as I make use of the capacity, and perform that movement, I necessarily perform also a corporeal act. It would be very hazardous even to affirm that for this return movement I do not need my corporeal senses. Without having some command and making some use of them, I cannot be aware of objects different from myself. And without being aware of objects different from myself, I cannot distinguish myself from others as the object identical with myself, and cannot therefore recognise myself as a subject. In the delimitation and determination of myself as an object of my knowledge, which is decisive for the fulfilment of my self-consciousness and which is necessarily presupposed in my self-knowledge as a subject, I thus have great need even of my corporeal senses. It may well be true that this act of knowledge is not seeing, hearing or smelling or any perception communicated by my physical senses, but an inner experience of myself. Yet it is just as true that this experience, while it is internal and a moment in the history of my soul, is also external and a moment in the history of my material body. Were it not the latter, it would not be the former. If as soul I were not also my material body, I should not be at all. If I did not live as my material body, I should not live at all. Did I not know myself in the common act of my soul and my material body, I should not know myself at all. And if I do in fact know myself, and am engaged in the process of my self-consciousness and therefore come to myself, discover myself and find assurance of myself as happens in every act of my life, the end thus reached, the discovery made and the assurance obtained is certainly my soul, my independent life, I myself as the subject of this life, yet at the same time it is never merely my soul, nor is it my soul alongside or even in my material body (like an oyster in its shell), but it is my soul as the independent life of this material body of mine, and therefore absolutely with this body, and therefore I myself as the subject of my life which is also wholly and utterly a corporeal being. I have not come to myself, discovered myself or received any assurance about myself, if I have not perceived myself as the soul of this material body and therefore my soul as its independent life and myself also as this corporeal being. Thus in both subject and object the act in which we become conscious of ourselves, in which we are known with our soul and therefore with the soul generally, is wholly and at the same time both a soulful and a corporeal act, or, more accurately, a soulful act which directly includes a corporeal. If it is not both, the one within the other, then it does not happen at all. We are not then conscious of ourselves, and we do not know what we are talking about when we speak of soul.

These noetic facts are grounded in ontic. Soul is independent life. But independent life in itself would be an empty and impossible concept. What is life without something quickened and living ? We say nothing at all in the words " life " and " independent," if we do not speak immediately and simultaneously of something quickened and alive. Even when we try to define independent life as the self-movement, self-activity and self-formation fulfilled by a specific subject, we clearly presuppose not only the time but also a place and a material in and on which this movement, activity and formation is accomplished. And when we speak of a subject's independent life, and therefore of soul, we presuppose that there is a spatio-material system of relations which is no less proper to this subject, which is lived and quickened by it, and which by the self-contained life of this subject is alive for its own part, i.e., one in which the self-movement, self-activity and self-formation of this subject fulfils and realises itself, and which thus acquires a share in this life of which in itself it is not participant. This spatio-material system of relations is the material body. Independent life is not for itself ; it is the independent life of a material body. Soul is not for itself ; it is the besouling of a material body. In the material body it has the problem to which it replies, the object in relation to which it is subject, the sphere of action in which it is at work. The material body may be generally defined as a spatio-material system of relations. It is spatial, i.e., it is essential to it to be at its own specific point in space. It is material, i.e., it is essential to it to be distinct from other bodies in virtue of its own specific material mode or composition. It is a system of relations, i.e., it is essential to it to have a specific spatial and material structure, not free in its inner relation, but forming a specific composition. Soul is the besouling of such a body and therefore the principle of its becoming and being alive. Soul is, as it is the soul of such a body, as it is alive in it and for it, thus rendering alive that which as mere material body is not alive. As we have seen, it does not belong to the concept of material body to be alive, and even less to be alive in an independent way and therefore to be besouled. On the contrary, it belongs to the concept of material body, and primarily of every material body, not to be for itself but at best only to be able to become. Again, it does not belong to the concept of any material body that it can be alive and even besouled. It is with the plant that the possibility of a living material body begins, with the beast that of an independent organic body, and with man that of the perceptibility and comprehensibility of an independent organic body. Soul and therefore besouling is in no sense a general determination of the world of bodies, but a matter of selection from among bodies. It thus implies a lack of reflection to speak of a world soul or of all cosmic reality as besouled. All material bodies are spatial and material systems of relations, but not all of them can be alive, let alone alive in an independent manner. This is not even possible for them all. The selection of those that can be has been made and is fixed. A plant will never live in an independent manner ; to do so it would have to be transformed into a very different material body. A stone will never live at all ; to do so it would have to cease to be a stone and adopt the spatiality and corporeality, the system of relations, of a very different material body. On the other hand, the animal body, and distinctly and recognisably the human, will always have at least the possibility of independent life, of being the body of a soul. When a material body is besouled, it does not cease to be material body, but only to be merely material body. As a problem answered, as an object in relation to a subject, as a sphere of action filled and controlled by deed, it becomes organic body. Hence we do not describe real man correctly if we call him soul of his material body, or soul and material body. As man lives, as the material body is his material body and therefore the material body of his soul, the latter is more than material body. It is his organic body, and man must therefore be described as soul of his organic body or as soul and organic body.

It is remarkable and regrettable that the important distinction, material and organic body (*Körper* and *Leib*), cannot be reproduced in Greek, Latin, French or English, and therefore two meanings which in this connexion are fundamentally distinct must be linked with the same word (σῶμα, *corpus*, *corps*, body).

The organic body is distinguished from the purely material body by the fact that as animal or at all events human body—we hardly speak of the organic body of a stone or plant—it is besouled and filled and controlled by independent life. By its selection from among all other material bodies, and without ceasing to be a material body, it can be taken up into unity with a soul and in all respects share its being and willing, though without itself becoming soul. As the organic body of a soul, it is no longer merely an object of its self-movement, self-activity and self-formation ; it is always this of course, but it now moves, activates and develops itself with it. As it may live through and with it, it is no longer for itself—if it were it would not be alive—but is for the soul as the soul is for it. It is and works with the soul. But since the soul is independent and therefore the life of a particular subject, this means that it is not now a mere object—though it is always this—but also a subject. When a living corporeal being says I, this I, as that of its soul, is also that of its body, and not merely of some privileged part of its body, but of its whole body in which there are indeed centres and peripheries, but no parts which are simply excluded from the besouling of the whole. It has also to be considered from the standpoint of the soul that if the body is not organic body but purely material body when it is without soul, so the soul is not soul but only the possibility of soul when it is without body. I may be identical with my soul, but my soul is not for itself, but is the besouling of my body. To this extent I am identical as soul with my body, and my movement, activity and development are never merely soulful, but as such are also bodily. I cannot be without or against but only for my body, as it can only be for me, as it cannot live without me and therefore without my soul, and as it is actually for me, constituting my only possibility of expression without which I could not be even inwardly. I cannot answer for myself without at the same time answering for my body. I cannot express or represent myself without the participation of my body and without its co-responsibility for the manner and genuineness of my expression and representation. In every respect I can only work as this spatio-material system of relations, which as my organic body is my material body, is real, i.e., participant in my work and therefore in my subjectivity. All rejection of this interconnexion, and all attempts to deny it in theory or practice, can only mean a distortion of the nature of man and precipitate it from one disorder into another.

The Old Testament *nephesh* is just as strictly and fully the life of the body as the New Testament ψυχή. This sense does not exhaust the term, but it is always present in all its other uses. The Greek conception of the soul as a second and higher " part," as an imperishable, if possible pre-existent, and in any case immortal spiritual substance of human reality, contrasted with the body as its lower and mortal part—the conception of the soul as a captive in the prison of its body, is quite unbiblical.

The Old Testament sees the soul as the life of the body and therefore in conjunction with it. *Nephesh* like *ruaḥ* means breath,. but now concretely—the breath which comes and goes in a human throat, and which distinguishes the living being from the dead. The word *naphash* must not be forgotten. Where breathing is present or restored, there is soul, but there must also be a body in which it takes place. When someone loses patience (e.g., the people in the desert, Num. 21⁴, or Samson with Delilah, Jud. 16¹⁶), then his breath " is shortened." If someone comes to himself after deathlike weakness (e.g., the son of the widow of Zarephath, 1 K. 17²¹), then his breath returns to him. But breath is only the representative and linguistic cipher for the bodily life as such. Since *nephesh* is bodily life, the soul can " long " and " be satisfied " or " hunger ' and " be filled " (Ps. 107⁹) ; it can also be chastened by fasting (Ps. 69¹⁰) and polluted by forbidden food (Ez. 4¹⁴). Hence " to save his soul " means simply to " go for his life " (like Elijah in 1 K. 19³). Similarly, a man risks his soul, i.e., his life (in a heroic deed, as in 2 Sam. 23¹⁷) ; a word can cost a man his soul, i.e., his life (Adonijah, 1 K. 2²³) ; the soul, i.e., life (A.V. " ghost "), is " breathed out " (Jer. 15⁹) or " poured out " (Lam. 2¹²), or it can " depart " (Gen. 35¹⁸). This just means that the soul dies (Jud. 16³⁰ ; Ez. 13¹⁹). That is, it can die or be " devoured " (Ez. 22²⁵), i.e., be killed (Num. 31¹⁹), as certainly as it is created (Is. 57¹⁶ ; Jer. 38¹⁶) and is the life of the mortal body. The Old Testament is at its most emphatic on this point in Lev. 17¹¹. The soul of the flesh is in the blood, and immediately after (v. 14) there is the rather sententious repetition : " the soul (A.V. " life ") of all flesh is the blood thereof " (cf. Deut. 12²³). Hence all shedding of blood, whether permitted or not, is an act of the highest significance, and the eating of blood is forbidden. Just as *nephesh* as bodily life can always mean the life of an individual corporeal being, so it can always mean the living individual himself. Thus *kol ha'nephesh* in Josh. 10²⁸ denotes the complete human and animal population of a city. Again, in the numbering of the people (e.g., Num. 31³⁵), souls are numbered instead of men. Again, the slaves whom anyone has won can be called " souls " (e.g., Gen. 12⁵). In the long run, " soul " can simply indicate a being or individual, e.g., one who sins (Lev. 4²), and even paradoxically one who is dead (*nephesh met*, Num. 6⁶). Even in the important verse in Gen. 2⁷, where it is said that man became a " living soul " by the *ruaḥ* breathed into him, we have to do with this diluted sense of the concept. And in some emphatic passages *nephesh* can be used for " I myself " or " thou thyself," and therefore as the personal pronoun. The only point to remember is that it is the subjectivity of a corporeal being which is denoted by the term.

We could not claim that the sense and use of ψυχή in the New Testament is essentially different. It is striking that the term is particularly frequent in Acts, and here it obviously bears the Old Testament meanings of life, individual life and individual. But even in the rest of the New Testament there are few passages where there is even the slightest suggestion of the Greek conception of the soul. When the ψυχή is spoken of as loving, finding, preserving, gaining, saving, finding peace and prosperity, forfeiting, losing, perishing, being exterminated and departing, there are no grounds for thinking of anything other than simply the life of man in contrast to his death. Even Mt. 10²⁸ does not say that the soul cannot be killed, but only that no man can kill it, while God has the power to cause both soul and body to pass away and be destroyed in the nether world. Hence we do not have here a doctrine of the immortality of the soul. The difference from the Old Testament consists in the fact that the forfeiture of life to death on the one hand, and the promise and hope of a deliverance of life from death on the other, are now much more strongly bound together. But here, too, the ψυχή is the whole man, the life of his body, he himself as he exists in this bodily life. And the content of the promise and hope given to man is not its immortality but its future deliverance in the resurrection from the dead.

The one man is wholly and simultaneously soul and body. In the light of this fact three delimitations are demanded.

1. We necessarily contradict the abstractly dualistic conception which so far we have summarily called Greek, but which unfortunately must also be described as the traditional Christian view. According to this view, soul and body are indeed connected, even essentially and necessarily united, but only as two " parts " of human nature. Of these, each is to be understood as a special substance, self-contained and qualitatively different in relation to the other. The soul is spiritual, non-spatial, indissoluble, and immortal ; the body material, spatial, dissoluble and mortal. If this is the case, if soul and body are two " parts " of which man is " composed," if these two " parts " are two self-contained substances, if these substances are quite different and even opposed in nature, and if this involves an opposition of the worth of the one (the soul) to the unworthiness of the other (the body), what are we to make of their alleged connexion and unity, and therefore of the unity of man's being ? Is this affirmation of unity more impressive if the unity is called a " mystery " and compared with the unity of the two natures of Christ ? Is it not clear that in these circumstances soul and body neither have nor can have anything in common, but can only be in conflict and finally part from one another ? From the understanding already attained, we may deny that the doctrine of these two shadowy substances is the Christian understanding of man, although for many years it has been self-evidently accepted as such.

" Human nature consists of body and soul " (B. Bartmann : *Lehrbuch der Dogmatik*, 1928, Vol. I, p. 271). Taught by Plato and Aristotle, the fathers, schoolmen and orthodox theologians of older Protestantism all held and taught this view, believing that the anthropology of the Old and New Testaments was to be expounded along these lines. This is the view of man which Roman Catholic dogmatics still represent as the normative Christian understanding. The connexion between soul and body is affirmed by understanding the soul, like Aristotle, as the ἐντελέχεια σώματος, the *forma corporis*, a formula which was raised to the status of a dogma in the *Conc. Viennense* (1311–12, Denz. *No.* 841). The connexion was described as a co-existence of two substances, nor was there any hesitation in saying that the connexion is total, and therefore that the soul, even if not in a local sense, is *tota in toto corpore et tota in qualibet parte corporis* (Voetius, *Disp. theol.*, 1648, p. 767). Mediation was obviously sought between the two spheres by distinguishing within the soul between an *anima vegetativa, sensitiva* and *intellectiva (rationalis)*, the implication being that on the last and highest level the soul of man is distinguished from that of the animals by its *facultas apprehendendi verum et appetendi bonum* (P. v. Mastricht, *Theor. Pract. Theol.*, 1698, III, 9, 6). But in respect of this supreme and distinctively human capacity, it is now described, with Plato, as οὐσία ἀσώματος ἀντοκίνητος as a *substantia talis naturae, quae a corpore etiam separari et subsistere per se posset* (Polanus, *Syn. Theol. chr.*, 1609, *col.* 2060). The central affirmation in this whole anthropology is that of the immortality of this rational thing, the human soul ; and immortality is a property which does not come to it by the special grace of God, but dwells within it by nature, so that it can be proved not only by Holy Scripture but on general rational grounds. Such a proof is given, for example, by P. v. Mastricht (*op. cit.*, III, 9, 17), and it takes the following form : 1. the soul is spiritual, and therefore not material, dissoluble, nor mortal ; 2. the righteousness of God requires the preservation of the soul through death for the purpose of the eternal reward and punishment of man; 3. the wisdom of God cannot permit that the end of man be the same as that of a beast, and his soul must therefore be immortal ; 4. all religion would cease if we were faced with the fact that only the decaying body remained of man and thus his soul too were mortal. *Corpore igitur distracto, discerpto, manet anima substantia, manet cogitans, manet id, quod voce hac " Ego " significatur, nil diminutum, nisi quod integumento suo exuitur* (H. Heidegger, *Corp. theol.*, 1700, VI, 87, quoted by Heppe, p. 181). So strange to one another are soul and body according to this doctrine, that in death they can part from one another in this manner. So little force has the affirmation of the soul as *forma corporis* that the body on the other hand can become the mere *integumentum* of the soul. In this doctrine of the immortality of the soul, an overestimation of the first moment of the human reality betrays and establishes itself which necessarily leads to an almost wholly negative estimation of the second, and to a trivialising or minimising or ignoring of the problem of corporeality. Hence the anthropology of the older dogmatic becomes remarkably sparing of words, and the little it says remarkably gloomy, when it begins to say that which *in thesi* it does not deny but emphasises solemnly as a great mystery, namely, that in the end man is not only a psychical but also a physical being. Polanus is an infrequent exception (*op. cit., col.* 1900 f.) when he accords to the human body as such three whole chapters of his exposition, and even develops an *Anatomia theologica partium humani corporis*, in which he tries to show, in a series of astonishing allegories, that we are instructed by the composition of the human body *de rebus divinis, nempe de Deo, eius essentia, attributis, operibus, beneficiis, iudiciis, etc., de Christo Mediatore, de Angelis, de Ecclesia, de officio nostro, quod debemus cum Deo tum proximo nostro, de aliis denique rebus praeclaris, quibus ad Deum mentes nostrae attolluntur.* A few examples may be taken from the plenitude of his fancies. Thus the form of the human heart, broader above and narrower below, reminds us that while we keep to things below, to that which is earthly, temporal and visible, we should be wide open to higher, heavenly and eternal things. Again, the systole and diastole of the heart remind us of the wisdom of avoiding everything which is superfluous and unhelpful in our worship of God and of zealously making our own that which is necessary for the love of God and our neighbour. Again, the form of the human skull, in contrast to that of the animals, is an imitation of the globe and cosmos. Our forehead reminds us warningly that we may have no connexion with the city of Rome, the whore on whose forehead, according to Rev. 17[5], " Mystery, Babylon the Great " is written. Again, the fact that we have two ears but only one mouth signifies that we should listen more than speak. The ears are more important than the eyes, since it is with the ears and the ears alone that we come to understand doctrine, wisdom, and above all the Word of God. But the mouth is also valuable for proclaiming the Word of God ; nor is it forgotten that it is also of value for breathing and the taking of nourishment. Strict Calvinist that he is, Polanus discourses for two columns about the different kisses that appear in the Bible (from the apostolic *osculum caritatis* to the Old Testament *osculum valedictionis*). It is clear that the existence and activity of the different " spirits of life," with which Polanus deals in accordance with the physiological knowledge of his day, give occasion for significant sidelights on the work of the Holy Spirit. We need not waste time in showing how dubious is this whole line of investigation. I seriously wonder whether my illustrious predecessor did not fall victim occasionally in this chapter to the spirit of the Basel *Fastnacht*, and quite deliberately indulge in pious witticisms. At all events, his work does not form any very useful contribution to an alleviation of the problem. Yet, though we shake our heads at his " theological anatomy," we must remember that the dogmatics of the Early Church did not even accord to the human body this allegorical attention, but treated it only as the boundary of the problem of the soul, which was its only real interest. It will be conceded to Polanus that this stepchild of anthropology, which otherwise was mostly despised, did at all events occupy him in its way, and that he did at least attempt to help it to the honour which was otherwise denied it. In general, the character and result of this anthropology are marked by a separation of soul and body, an exaltation of the soul over the body, a humiliation of the body under the soul, in which both really become not merely abstractions but in fact two " co-existing " figments—a picture in which probably no real man ever recognised himself, and with which one cannot possibly do justice to the biblical view and concept of man. It was disastrous that this picture of man could assert and maintain itself for so long as the Christian picture. We must earnestly protest that this is not the Christian picture.

2. On the other hand, we cannot accept the reactions in which the attempt has been made to set over against the abstract dualism of the Greek and traditional Christian conception a no less abstract monism.

There is first monistic materialism. This is the theory according to which the one substance of man consists in his corporeality, while the soul is treated in practice as at most the boundary of the only real problem, that of the body, and its particular existence is flatly denied. On this view, the real is only what is corporeal, spatial, physical and material. What cannot be brought under this denominator is either mere appearance, imagination, illusion, an irrelevant by-product or " epiphenomenon " of corporeal causes and conditions, or, more mildly conceived and expressed, its subjectively conditioned and necessary phenomenal form. In the true and proper sense, there is in man no soul and nothing spiritual ; he is body only ; besides the causal sequence of material change and other bodily functions, there are only certain processes in the brain and nerves which we are wrong to interpret as actions *suæ originis et sui generis*, as thoughts, decisions, feelings and the like, as an independent being over against that of the body, and for which it is only in enslavement to mythological notions that we feel it necessary to posit a basis in the soul as a genuine element of reality.

This, then, is the materialistic counter-attack. It is historically quite understandable. It does not rest primarily on scientific considerations, but on a certain kind of honesty and sobriety (recognisably antithetical to the Greek and traditional Christian view) in face of the actual course of individual and social life. This is what gives materialism old and new its surprising and confusing power in spite of its theoretical weakness. The Christian Church is forced by this opponent to investigate more seriously the tenability of the abstract dualism of its own conception, since on its side too the connexion of soul and body is continually asserted but cannot really be exhibited within the framework of its conception. Indeed, the contrary thesis cannot be simply or finally denied, for rather disquietingly the biblical picture of man, and especially the resurrection hope of the New Testament, forces us to think along the lines to which materialism now points in one-sided but complementary opposition, but not without right and necessity.

Yet it is obvious that we must also contradict materialism with our statement that man is wholly and simultaneously soul and body. The appropriate philosophical criticism does not interest us here. Our argument against it is simply that its conception does not enable us to see real man. Man is also, and indeed wholly and utterly, body. This is what we must be told by materialism if we have not learned it elsewhere. But there is no sense in trying to seek and find man only in his body and its functions. For if he is really seen as body, he is seen also as soul, that is, as the subject which gives life to his material body, to the spatio-material system of relations which physiology describes, thus distinguishing it as an organic body from a purely material body, and giving it stability even as a material body. Man's material body, its matter and energies, are those of his living organic body. To be sure, man is identical with this living because quickened body in all its organs and with all its functions, actions and passions, but only as the continuously living and quickening subject of his body, only as this body of his continuously becomes identical with him, and he with it. We obviously do not see man if we will not see that, as he is wholly his body, he is also wholly his soul, which is the subject, the life of this body of his. Because materialism will not see this, it is unacceptable, and we have to ask whether it is not even more guilty of the very illusionism with which it charges the Greek and traditional early Christian conception, since the latter does not deny or suppress the problem of corporeality even though it cannot do justice to it, whereas that of the soul is completely eliminated under the hard fists of the materialists. With them, the two figments of the Greek tradition and early Christian conception become one. This is not an advance. They would be right if only they did not want to be exclusively right. But they want to be exclusively right, and therefore they are wrong.

" Materialism " is not a product of modern times alone. As is well known, it played a role in the different phases of ancient philosophy, from Thales and the other Ionians by way of Democritus to Epicureus. Thus it confronted Christian theology not only in the 17th and 18th centuries but long before. For example, at the beginning of the 16th century it confronted it in a form in which it ought to have engaged its attention. In 1516, the same year in which Luther delivered his famous lectures on the Epistle to Romans, there appeared a work by the Italian philosopher Pietro Pomponazzo entitled *De immortalitate animae*, in which the Aristotelian statement, *anima forma corporis* (and therefore the dogma of 1311), was interpreted to mean that the soul belongs to the body, is inseparable from it, cannot persist without it, and therefore, as a mode of its existence, must fade and die with it. The most that Pomponazzo could allow was that, though human knowledge is certainly not a purely immaterial activity, there takes place in it a certain ascent from sensible representations to universal ideas and therefore to eternity, so that the human soul resembles the immaterial and immortal without belonging to it, and thus stands nearer to it than anything else. The sphere of our existence, and of the tasks, duties and hopes in which each and every individual soul is determined, is the here and now, which stands in face of the eternal and hereafter, but is not coincident with it. Pomponazzo did not deny the hereafter. It seems that he did not even deny the resurrection of the dead (as the resurrection of the whole man). But in fact his doctrine of the soul is materialistic. He understood it as only *forma corporis*, and not as a substance independent of the body, different in attributes, immaterial and immortal. Many things would have been different, and many embarrassments would have been avoided in the 18th and 19th centuries, if three years before at the 5th Lateran Council (Denz. *No.* 738) the Roman Church had not dogmatically declared the immortality of the intellective soul, or if Reformation theology at least had girded itself for a new understanding at this point. This philosophical thesis might well have shown it how to apply its Scripture principle seriously in this matter, and thus to institute certain necessary and overdue investigations into the biblical as opposed to the Greek picture of man, especially in relation to biblical eschatology. On such a basis, it would not have needed to accept the materialism of Pomponazzo, but it would have had a better conscience in relation to this and all other materialism both before and after. Failure in this matter was probably a just consequence of the fact that the Reformation had too little time or understanding for biblical eschatology, and therefore saw no occasion to undertake a revision of the traditional anthropology. At all events, even Calvin (*Instit.*, I, 5, 6) identified himself at once with the Roman Catholic rejection of the thesis, his only argument being the platonic rather than biblical consideration that in the reason which encompasses heaven and earth, in its agility in investigating time and space, and in its endowment with free fancy as manifested in dreams and many works of art, we have clear and indestructible signs of the immortality of the human soul. Calvin even wrote expressly : *Certa sunt divinitatis insignia in homine.* Following him, Ursin (*Loci theol.*, 1562, p. 559, quoted by Heppe, p. 179) and the theologians of the 17th century could only deny the thesis *a limine*. In this respect, the Cartesians among them were even more decided than the Aristotelians, and A. Heidan (*Corp. Theol. chr.*, 1686, I, p. 335) could go so far as to say that apart from the denial of the existence of God no thesis was more morally dangerous than this which would put man on the level of the beasts. Christian theology thus dismissed the problem. But with such answers it could not adequately deal with the practical reality of human life in every century, with the contemporary development of speculation about nature, or least of all with the questions arising from the Bible. And so it had to be prepared for the fact that, in virtue of the *particula veri* which cannot be denied, materialism would arise in a new and even more difficult form—as in fact happened.

As an example of the specifically modern form in which it appears as it were in the springtime of its sins, and in which in the middle and the end of last century it evoked as much enthusiastic applause on the one side as anxious shock or angry rejection on the other, we may take the conception in which it was introduced by the Jena zoologist, Ernst Haeckel, in his book *Die Welträthsel*, which first appeared in 1899 and was later very widely publicised. A similar Bible of modern materialism, *Kraft und Stoff*, had already been written in 1855 by a tutor at Tübingen, Ludwig Büchner, who was dismissed because of it. In the same year Karl Vogt (a German exile in Geneva) had published his work *Köhlerglaube und Wissenschaft*, in which there occurs the contemptible sentence that " thoughts are related to the brain in much the same way as gall to the liver and urine to the kidneys." In the middle of the 19th century, Jakob Moleschott, another German tutor, had also emerged as a champion of similar views and was disciplined in consequence. During the forty years between these men and Haeckel, the philosophy of L. Feuerbach was at work on the frontiers of materialism. Man is (*ist*) what he eats (*isst*), was the ingenious formula with which he enriched future discussion. In the work of his old age, *Der alte und der neue Glaube* (1872), D. F. Strauss finally broke with absolute Idealism and crossed over with flags flying into the camp of this very different system. The vote of Haeckel was the last and the most massive and impressive word in the matter. His exposition in chapters 6–11 of his book is as follows. What is called " soul " is a natural phenomenon. Psychology is thus a branch of physiology. The basis of all spiritual events in both man and beast is " psychoplasm," an egg-white carbonic compound. What we call experiences, motions, reflexes, ideas, memories, instincts, conceptions, emotions and decisions, as also what we finally and supremely call self-consciousness, are mere functions of the animal organism alive in virtue of this plasm. Their differences are only steps on a scale rising from the protozoon to man, and they are all subject to the law of the one moved and self-moving material substance. Psyche is only a collective concept for the totality of these functions. The soul comes into being (i.e., the course of these functions begins) in the moment of copulation, in which the male and female cell-kernels come together to form the nucleus of a new body, which is in this sense inherited. With the other vital activities of the organism, this then follows its individual development from the unselfconscious condition of the newly born to the senile decay which hurries on to the dissolution of self-consciousness. Hence man's soul is only the last and supreme form in the history which leads from the soul of the cell by that of a union of cells to the soul of a complete structure, then to the soul of plants and beasts, and in the latter sphere from the soul of primitive animals to that of the higher mammals and finally to man as the highest. Even consciousness, the " central psychological mystery," the " strong citadel of all mystic and dualistic errors, against whose mighty walls all attacks of the best-armed reason are threatened with ruin," is a natural phenomenon, which like all others is subject to the law of substance. It is explained by the fact that in the brain of mammals, in the zone of gray crust which covers the brain, there are not only " sense convolutions " but also four special " thought convolutions " or association centres, of specially developed structure in the case of man, in which the soul has its locus and from which all its phenomena can be explained. Stimulation, numbing and disease of these portions of the brain result in consequential changes in consciousness. Consciousness begins, grows, fails and finally expires in the individual ontogenes. From the consciousness of the amœba to that of the cultured man of the present day, it develops in the universal phylogenes. Hence it follows that this, too, is a physiological function of the brain, and therefore not the immaterial and immortal being of a soul distinct from natural matter. The doctrine of immortality (" athanism ") is an illusory opinion which stands in irresoluble contradiction to the most certain affirmations of modern science, which cannot be justified in face of physiology, histology, pathology, ontogenetics or phylogenetics, and for which finally no serious rational ground can be supplied.

The materialism of the middle and later 19th century was only in a very qualified sense the result of modern natural science, as it was only in a qualified sense that in its earlier form it was connected with a supposedly deeper and more exact knowledge of nature in different fields. There can be no doubt, of course, that the natural science of the 19th century, which was so much more thorough-going than ever before, had a general tendency in this direction, the public being specially aware of it in the bearing of its doctors ; and that conclusions, such as those which Büchner, Vogt, Moleschott and finally Haeckel proposed, found an immense number of exponents and prophets among the *clerus minor* of the world of culture with its contemporary interest in natural science. But it is also true that the leading and famous investigators and teachers in natural science, however much they might be inclined to think along similar lines, displayed strikingly little inclination in general for the conclusions of those who precipitated strife or for the proclamation of a dogmatic materialism. Nor was this because they were hampered by the powers of the state, society and the Church and could not summon up courage, but clearly because of the obvious insight so appropriate to the laboratory that, though these conclusions might seem to be suggested by their science, they could not be drawn by it. The step from affirming that human consciousness is a function of the brain to affirming that it is *only* a function of the brain, from stating that the soul is materially conditioned to stating that it is materially *constituted*, and therefore to materialistic monism, was and still is a μετάβασις εἰς ἄλλο γένος, which, when it is to be carried out, requires another justification than natural science can provide. Haeckel's " psychoplasm " has never actually been seen by mortal eye. Those who noticed that we must here believe, speculate and philosophise if we are to know, did not see a basis for their materialism—if they took this view —in their natural science, but were more likely to find in it a pretext for not committing themselves to materialism or making its proclamation a duty. It is also the case—and Haeckel himself deplored it loudly—that at this time some of those who bore names most prominent in natural science, such as Rudolf Virchow, Emil Dubois-Reymond, Wilhelm Wundt, and also George Romanes, the Englishman whom Haeckel specially prized, held publicly aloof from the systematising and dogmatising of materialism, although in their earlier years they had apparently or genuinely favoured it. The big event in the story of this contradiction was Dubois-Reymond's lecture to the *Naturforscherversammlung* in Leipzig on 14th August 1872, *Über die Grenzen des Naturerkennens*, in which he indicated that the connexion between matter and power, and that between our spiritual activity and its material conditions, constitute the limits beyond which the human spirit cannot go even in the most advanced natural knowledge : *ignoramus—ignorabimus* ! Haeckel declared to Dubois-Reymond and his other colleagues, with firmness and friendliness, that their position was explicable only by a psychological metamorphosis caused by the advancing predominance of age. But when they adopted this position these men had no intention of confessing the spiritualism and dualism of the Early Church, as this had been passed on to them through the decades. Their aim was rather to indicate the reservations which must be made, if science is to be true to itself, against a leap which might perhaps appear to be a close consequence from it, but which can in no case be claimed as what it is usually called a " finding " of science.

But the modern materialism which particularly interests us cannot be dismissed in this way. It had and has the power, not of true science, but of a comprehensive view of the world ; and the emergence and composition of this view rest on the very real " psychoplasm " of very powerful emotions which for their part are related to certain undeniable historical, ethical social and facts. This holds good, not for His Excellency from Weimar, Haeckel, personally, but for the vexatious popular applause which both he and his older spiritual companions found for their poetry. It seems to be a fact that human reality represents itself to the naive consideration of most men of all ages in a form which is far closer to the materialistic picture than to that of Christian dualism. And there can be no doubt that, as the result of rapid social progress since the 17th century, from 1830 at the very latest, a form of life began to distinguish itself which must and did speak with primitive weight in favour of a materialistic anthropology. The general rationalisation of human life in the sense of this progress which had begun in the 18th century, very clearly and decisively involved in the practice of the 19th its subjection to economics, its commercialisation, industrialisation and mechanisation, and therefore its obvious materialisation. At the beginning of the century, the Idealists, e.g., Schleiermacher as a moralist, had still visualised the powerful onslaught and victory of spirit over nature and matter. But the real picture which soon presented itself to all strata of the civilised nations except the dreaming philosophers, poets and unfortunately theologians, was very different. The first railways began to rattle across Europe, the first steamships to cross the Atlantic, the first electric telephones to operate, the first forerunners of the modern photograph to immortalise the physical countenance of man as he is. There began a direction of enormous interest on the part of a noteworthy proportion of the Western intelligentsia towards technics with its promise of substantial rewards. There began the corresponding mass movement of town and country into the factories, forges and mines. The figure of the human robot, who neither asks nor is asked about his soul and therefore cannot ask about that of others, who by an anonymous centre of power is made, moved, regulated, used and then discarded and replaced from an anonymous centre—this materialistic human figure was now arising. Here it had the form of the great industrial and bank magnates, there that of the unperceptive co-operating middle-class townsmen, there in the machine-rooms and under the waterline of the great liners—" For some are in darkness and others in the light ; and one sees those who are in the light but not those who are in darkness "—the new form of the modern proletariat. The real foundation of modern materialism, and the explanation of the validity and expansion which it has enjoyed in and in spite of its scientific weakness, are not to be found in the researches and results of biology and physiology, but in the rise of this form of humanity, in which everyone who lives with open eyes in and with his time must willingly or unwillingly recognise a little of himself. " And so I solve the problem : only he who lives in prosperity lives agreeably " —so thinks the big man contentedly and the little man discontentedly, except that the big man is perhaps seldom honest enough to admit to himself that this is how he thinks. What need is there for biology and physiology to prove to both of them that man must be thought of materialistically ? They do this already. Nor do they do so only in the 19th century but earlier. The 19th century merely brings it to light.

This is where what is called " historical materialism " comes in. For it, what we have hitherto spoken of under the name of materialism is only a necessary weapon and an indispensable apologetic and polemical ally. The doctrine of Karl Marx, which is identical with this historical materialism, is undoubtedly materialism in the sense in which we have used the term, and in practice it stands or falls with the fact that it is so. Yet it is so only *per accidens* and not *per essentiam*. It is certainly one of the historical limits of Marxism that it has bound itself so closely with the dogma of ostensibly scientific materialism. But we quite misunderstand it if we take it to be grounded on this, or adopt the view of older theological polemics that it is one of its evil moral fruits. The very opposite is the case, namely, that ostensibly scientific materialism, at any rate in the 19th century, acquired weight only as it was discovered, appropriated and employed by historical materialism. Over against it, historical materialism is a construction with its own origin.

In face of the modern development of community, historical materialism is 1. the affirmation in which the child at last acquires a name, namely, that the whole history of mankind at its core is the history of human economy or economic history, and that everything else, the achievement of civilisation, science, art, the state, morality and religion, are only phenomenal accompaniments of this one reality, expressions of the current relations of economic forces, attempts to disguise, beautify, justify, and defend them, occasionally perhaps even expressions of its discontent, instruments of its criticism, means of its alteration, but at all events secondary forms or ideologies from which economics is differentiated as true historical reality. The figure of man which arose in the 19th century seemed unambiguously to prove this. At any rate, this is how it was interpreted and understood by Karl Marx.

Historical materialism is 2. a critique of the previous course of human history interpreted in this way. As economic history, it is the history of a struggle between the ruling and ruled strata or classes of the community, i.e., between the economically strong and the economically weak, between the invariable possessors of the earth and all the other means of production and the others who invariably do the work which is economically productive in the true sense. In this struggle, the latter, the workers, have always been the losers, and, under the characteristic modern dominance of anonymous capital striving only for its own increase, they are the losers with an accentuated necessity—the expropriated and exploited. Those ideologies have in fact shown themselves to be only accompanying phenomena which can neither render impossible nor stop the class war which is waged with such unequal weapons, but in different ways can only confirm and further it. How very differently does Karl Marx view what the Idealists only a few decades before had celebrated as the victory of the spirit over nature !

Historical materialism is 3. a prediction concerning the future course of the history of mankind. The dominance of the possessors, which has to-day become the dominance of anonymous capital, will necessarily lead to continually new crises of production and consumption, to warlike developments and revolutionary catastrophes. Thus with an inner necessity, it moves towards a final upheaval. The proletarianisation of the masses becomes sharper and sharper, and encroaches upon greater and greater levels even of the modern middle class. The class of the oppressed, thus increasing, will gradually be automatically compelled to unify itself, and to recognise and seize the power which really lies in its hands, in order finally and conclusively to make political, and if need be forceful, use of it, and to set up its own dictatorship in place of that of the anonymous tyrant. It expropriates those who have so far expropriated. It erects the economic and welfare social state in which there are no more exploiters and therefore no more exploited, in which all other social sicknesses vanish with their common cause, and in which morality, which in the present class-state is possible only in the form of hypocrisy, can become a genuine reality. Again, it will not be ideologies that will lead mankind to this end, but only economic material development as this is rightly understood and therefore directed at the right moment by the right intervention. This was the hope, the eschatology, which Karl Marx gave to his followers as the supreme good and as the appropriate driving motive for socialist action on the way to it.

Historical materialism is 4. a summons. It is not issued to all, and therefore not to the dominant middle class. Historical materialism has nothing to say to the " bourgeois," since *a priori* it does not expect that it will permit itself to have anything said to it or to learn anything, imprisoned as it is in the presuppositions of its economic position, which are stronger than its deepest insights and its best will. There are fortunate exceptions, and these can be put to good tactical use ; but they merely confirm the general rule that there can be no discussion with the middle class as a class. It will have to be reckoned with, and its account finally discharged, but there can be no conversation with it— only dispute. Thus the summons of historical materialism is directed only to the constantly increasing proletariat. It is an appeal to its insight : to openmindedness towards the economic meaning of history in general and the necessity of its critique in the light of the dominating class war ; to faith in its necessarily approaching goal ; and above all to the restoration, by way of trades unions and co-operatives, of the economic and political solidarity of the working class, with the meaning and intention of a more rapid or more gradual advancing of the dissolution of the present class relationship and a more rapid or more gradual preparation of the construction of the new classless community, and all with careful and flexible regard for the contemporary hour and situation and its special economic, political and ideological circumstances. Ideologies, of course, have weight in this practical outworking of historical materialism, yet only as accompanying phenomena which are partly useful and partly useless, partly necessary and partly disruptive, but with no independent significance. It is understandable that to those who stand aloof the doctrine of Karl Marx is usually most impressive and least attractive in this final form as a summons to the warlike solidarity of the working class against them.

It is now clear why the pseudo-scientific materialism of the 19th century, which now concerns us, should acquire so much weight and currency. Marxism as such needed no doctrine of soul and body. For it, speculations along the lines of Feuerbach and Haeckel could only be one middle-class ideology with others. And these middle-class materialists for their part could be notoriously unconcerned with working-class affairs and movements, D. F. Strauss being a fairly bigoted devourer of Socialists. Yet the fact remains that Marxism could use this doctrine of soul and body, even though it was obviously opposed to its own intentions as with the crude materialism of this particular cult. It did in fact make use of it. It allied itself with it to form what began to be called the " Marxist view of the world." Were not body and soul related to each other in the doctrine of these materialists as economic development to the accompanying ideological phenomena in Marxist doctrine ? Did not its doctrine affirm of the human individual and the human race as a whole what was Alpha and Omega to Marxist doctrine in relation to the social structure of its history ? It thus came about that the scientifically inadmissible deduction that the soul is material because materially conditioned became the received dogma of historical materialism. There thus arose the equation, practically sacrosanct even to-day to orthodox socialism, that Marxism is science, i.e., natural science, i.e., the natural philosophy of the cult of Haeckel. There thus arose the mass emotion which first gave to the materialism of the cult of Haeckel its distinctive popularity. It lived and continues to live on the attraction of the class war in the Marxist sense, of which it has proved itself to be a useful and even indispensable ideological instrument. But we must go deeper and say that it lives on that which in historical materialism is not merely a compelling construction but genuinely historical. It lives on the factual existence of that soulless figure of man so forcefully revealed in the 19th century. Marxism with its exclusively economic view of human affairs and all the theoretical and practical consequences, is a violation of history which in its way is no less bad than that which Haeckel and his associates imposed on human nature. Obviously it was and is a congeniality in error which caused Marx to ally himself with this doctrine of human nature. Obviously it is a curse lying on this matter, which will one day avenge itself, that the most determined, consistent and orthodox representatives of the Marxism based on this alliance take on more and more of the spirit, or lack of spirit, of that robot man. But we need not be surprised that this happened when the real life not merely of the Marxist opposition, but of the whole modern community, showed (and still shows) such strong characteristics pointing unmistakeably in this direction. The Christian Church need not be surprised at this, nor that it has come under the fire of Marxist polemic, nor that it must now hear its faith denounced as a " relic of capitalism " in the service of restraint and therefore of reaction. In all the centuries, what has it done positively to prevent the rise of that figure of the soulless man ? Has it not always stood on the side of the " ruling classes " ? At any rate, has it not always been the surest guarantee of the existence and continuance of an order of classes which technically cannot be understood otherwise than as the order of superiority of the economically strong ? And has it not with its doctrine of soul and body at least shown a culpable indifference towards the problem of matter, of bodily life, and therefore of contemporary economics ? Has it not made a point of teaching the immortality of the soul instead of attesting to society, with its proclamation of the resurrection of the dead, that the judgment and promise of

God compass the whole man, and therefore cannot be affirmed and believed apart from material and economic reality, or be denied or pushed aside as ideology in contrast to material and economic reality ? When the masses fell victim first to economic and then to the related pseudo-scientific materialism, as though they had become accustomed to hear from the Church of the day only irrelevant middle-class ideology ; and when the dismayed Christian world could do little more than complain and scold in face of this double defection, was not this the penalty for the fact that quite unthinkingly, and certainly not in obedience but in disobedience to Scripture, it had prescribed that abstract dualism of soul and body, and that even in the time of the Reformation it had not dug very much deeper into this matter ? Against the rise of that materialistic figure of man, it was thus completely impotent. And against the convincing power which both the Marxist doctrine of society and the pseudo-scientific doctrine of soulless man necessarily acquired in the realistic light of this human figure, it had nothing whatever to say from the traditional standpoint. Nor will it have anything to say in the future, but will always have a bad conscience in face of both materialisms and therefore of the so-called " Marxist view of the world," so long as it does not undertake an energetic revision of its anthropology at this point in the light of its eschatology, thus arriving at a very different practical position towards the whole complex. In this sense, it has to be said that even to-day we are by no means done with the materialism of the cult of Haeckel, for all its obvious theoretical weakness. It reminds the Church and theology of debts which they have by no means paid.

3. Reaction against the Greek traditional Christian dualism can, however, come from quite another quarter than materialism. Indeed, monistic materialism past and present obviously calls for the counter-attack of a monistic spiritualism, which takes the opposite view that the soul is the one and only substance of human reality. The advantage which materialism possesses, its greater nearness to the biblical picture of man than abstract dualism, its refusal to allow body and soul to fall apart, its realisation that man is at all events a unity—this advantage belongs also to spiritualism, with of course the difference that whereas for the one the soul is pure appearance and the body the real thing, for the other the body is pure appearance and the soul the real thing. The historical necessity of this reaction is understandable ; and so long as materialism is present and the abstract dualism of the Greek traditional Christian conception is not purified, it will always have a relative justification. The concrete reality of man now demands expression on the other side. Man is not swallowed up as a subject, as obviously happens in materialism. His unity with himself does not go by default, as is the case in the Greek and traditional Christian conception. Here we have to do with a kind of triumph of the distinctive subject, man as posited and known by himself. In contrast to this, the being of the same name which according to materialist doctrine emerges and disappears in the ongoing stream of common organic animal life, is so miserable a being that, given the choice between the two systems, one tends to opt for spiritualism out of regard for man as such. And there may well be the added reason to-day that a quite unexpected ally can be

found for this view in physics, which has undergone so revolutionary a renewal in the last decade. Indeed it may even be supported by a more exact appreciation of the facts as these may be demonstrated without the help of physics.

In this respect, the exposition of Paul Haeberlin (*Der Leib und die Seele,* 1923) demands our attention.

We learn from him that nothing is real but the effective and functioning subject or soul, which I perceive in myself as I identify myself with myself, and which I recognise as the first reality without the co-operation of my corporeality. If I recognise another person, or indeed anything, as real and therefore as a functioning subject, this means that I overcome the boundary set for me by the corporeality concealing his soul. Everything is corporeal only in so far as it remains external to the contemplating subject, not yet perceptible as a real and therefore a functioning subject, and thus surrounded for the contemplating subject by this boundary. Corporeality is only the garment, appearance, expression and symbol of the real, the form which its externality takes. Everything is real, as I am, only in so far as it is spiritual. Thus only the spiritual, the non-spatial, the non-sensible, the immaterial is real, while the spatial, the sensible, the material and therefore the corporeal is not real, and in scientific knowledge must be seen, understood, interpreted or sensed at least as merely the external form of the real. All science, including natural science, is therefore psychology. Only as such can it bring all objects under one denominator, as is proper for science. Only as such is it the synthesis of all real perceptions. If it remains the science of things or bodies and claims to be a synthesis as such, this is only at the cost of strict understanding and therefore of its scientific character. Only as psychology can and will it be true to the task of the understanding in its totality, and therefore real science. Since corporeality does not belong to the character of the real, it is scientifically irrelevant. Body is the essence of the total corporeality of a maximally understood being—of the kind of being which we understand as spiritual and in this way, to the exclusion of its corporeality, as real. Body is thus the purely transparent appearance of a being, whether we actually recognise or merely sense it as such. Thus soul and body are distinguished as the fully understandable and the half understandable parts of man. In reality, man (like all real things) is soul and only soul. As soul, he is fully understandable to himself ; as body, as expression of the soul, he is only half understandable, as experience shows. To be sure, his body must be taken into account both by himself and others. Yet merely as body he is relatively, i.e., spiritually alien to himself and others. Even as body, in fact, he is only his own sensible image which simply requires a right interpretation to be recognised as soul. The body is no objective magnitude. It is only the subjectively determined figure of the human personality as this is still relatively alien to ourselves and others. The body is only the psychological shadow of the spiritual reality of man, as from a different standpoint it is only its expression and representation.

No mention need be made of the many difficulties from which this thesis would free us at a single stroke. Yet we cannot accept it. It is too good to be true. We have to ask how, when man perceives himself and identifies himself with himself, he comes to recognise his soul as the first reality, and to see in it the essence of all that is real, and in his understanding the measure of all that is real. Who or what justifies this basic ontic and noetic assumption ? The real man is naturally soul, subject, he himself.

But he is not this alone. He is not this without conditions or limits. As he is body, yet not body alone but also soul, so he is soul, yet not soul alone but also body. To be sure, he is soul first and then body. He is the soul of his body. But soul of his body, he is no less really his body too. In this respect spiritualism would do well to allow itself to be corrected by materialism. Man himself is also his body. And his body is also himself. As his body, man is certainly more than his material body. Yet it is true that he is also a material body, spatial and sensible. He does not become pure soul in virtue of the fact that he is besouled. He is also that which is quickened and lives, and this as such remains different from the soul as that which quickens. Too much is made of the strict relation of the subject to what is quickened by it, and too little is said of the body, if the latter is regarded only as the expression and representation of the soul, only as its appearance, its external form, its symbol, its psychological shadow. At a pinch we can accept these descriptions. But they cannot signify that the body is fundamentally unreal. They can only signify that the body is these things too in relation to the soul. But they must imply that even as these things the body is real : as real as the soul, which it partly reveals and partly hides ; as real as the man himself who is the soul of his body. He is not the one without the other. And he is the one not only as the reflection of the other. If the body is not without the soul, neither is the soul without the body. The one whole man, to which spiritualism rightly has regard, would not be real, if the body of man, as the revelation and veiling of his soul, as the expression of his inward being, as quickened and living through his life, were not in its own way equally real with his soul.

In sum, if materialism with its denial of the soul makes man subjectless, spiritualism with its denial of the body makes him objectless. Thus both result in a new and fatal division of man, although both are monistic in intention and the declared purpose of both is to demonstrate the unity of the human reality. But this demonstration may not be pursued at the cost of the reality of either of the two elements, reality being found either in body or soul and appearance either in soul or body. A one-sided view of this kind is an act of violence. The Greek and traditional Christian doctrine inevitably leads us to one or other form of this one-sidedness. It is itself fundamentally one-sided, in the direction of spiritualism. It never quite denied the reality of the body, but, with its interest in the immortal and if possible divine soul, it was always on the point of doing so. And when it was attacked by materialism, its lack of understanding for the concern of the latter, and the nervousness with which it reacted against it, showed that it was incapable of providing a really penetrating insight into the whole problem. So long as soul and body are spoken of as two independent and distinct substances, no real insight is possible. Against this abstraction, the concrete reality of the one man must continually and disquietingly call for expression from the one side or the other, and real justice can be done to it only by carrying through the abstraction to its logical but absurd conclusion, i.e., by minimising and if possible juggling away the soul in favour of the body or *vice versa*. What then survives is not alas ! the concrete reality of the one man which was sought, but a substance of soul or body which is rendered spectral by this minimising and juggling. Who could recognise his neighbour, or himself, or any of the great or small figures among the actors of real human history, in man as thus described by materialism or spiritualism ? Over against these opposed abstractions, the Greek and traditional Christian doctrine can always claim a relative justification, since *in thesi* at least it maintains the counter-proposition of the unity of human nature. But we cannot help but see that it gives rise to the two errors. We are, in fact, caught in an endless spiral, so long as the idea of the two substances is not wholly abandoned, and the concrete reality of the one man set up definitively at the start, in the middle and at the end of all consideration, soul and body being understood, not as two parts, but as two moments of the indivisibly one human nature, the soul as that which quickens and the body as that which is quickened and lives. It is to this concrete monism that we found ourselves guided by the biblical view and the biblical concept of the " soul." The abstract dualism of the Greek and traditional Christian doctrine, and the equally abstract materialist and spiritualist monism, are from this standpoint a thoroughgoing and interconnected deviation.

The question how such a deviation was and is possible may be answered as follows. Our statement that man is wholly and at the same time both soul and body presupposes the first statement that man is as he has Spirit. We saw in our second sub-section that it is the Spirit, i.e., the immediate action of God Himself, which grounds, constitutes and maintains man as soul of his body. It is thus the Spirit that unifies him and holds him together as soul and body. If we abstract from the Spirit and therefore from the act of the living Creator, we necessarily abstract between soul and body. If we consider man for himself, i.e., without considering that he is only as God is for him, he is seen as a puzzling duality, his mortal body on the one side and his immortal soul on the other, a totality composed of two parts inadequately glued together, of two obviously different and conflicting substances. And however much we then try to persuade ourselves that this duality is the one man, we stand in the midst of Greek and every other form of heathenism, which sees neither the real God nor real man, and cannot do so, because knowledge of the Spirit is needed for this purpose and this is incompatible with heathenism. Our only relief will then be found in the see-saw movement between ideas and appearance, thinking and speculation and so on, which pervades the history of philosophy in every age. If there is no knowledge of the Spirit, even the practical recollection of the one man can only lead to the materialistic or spiritualist reaction, and therefore to the realm of spectres. What is needed to avoid this whole deviation is simply a refusal to let go of the premise that man is as he has Spirit. Out of this premise arises, in contrast to all abstraction, the conrete and Christian dualism of soul and body. Here human speech is, as often, wiser than human thought. It is a remarkable thing that, in our use of the decisively important personal pronouns, we do not even remotely imagine that our expressions refer to the existence and nature of two substances or merely to one or other of them. On the contrary, we say with equal emphasis and equal right : " I think " and " I see," " I know " and " I have toothache," " I hate " and " I am operated on," " I have sinned " and " I am old." Fundamentally, we know very well—and we cannot dissuade ourselves of it by any synecdochic interpretation, however cunning—that all these things, though some are spiritual and others bodily, concern me myself. They are affairs of the one subject I, which is the soul of its body and for this very reason is wholly and at the same time soul and body. For who, when he speaks, ever thinks of dividing himself or another into soul and body, or of claiming to consider himself or another only as soul or only as body ? At a pinch, therefore, we could give the following prescription for avoiding this deviation—that to be secure against it we must simply hold to the greater wisdom of our speech. Yet the fact remains that we must first know of the Spirit if we are to make illuminating use of this argument.

4. SOUL AND BODY IN THEIR PARTICULARITY

We come to the second subordinate question. It concerns the inner differentiation of human creatureliness, and asks concerning soul and body in their particularity.

The inner unity of human creatureliness and therefore the interconnexion of soul and body consists in the fact that in man the soul is the quickening factor aroused by the Spirit and the body is that which is quickened by it and lives. But this differentiation within the concept of life obviously cannot exhaust our description of the differentiation within human creatureliness and the particularity of the soul and body of man. We could very well halt here if we were merely dealing with an animal. What we perceive in an animal is indeed the connexion of an independent life with that which is quickened and lives by it. The supposition that the animal, too, is soul of a body is tempting at this point. But as we have seen we do not know what we are really saying if we accept this supposition. We do not know the particular element in the independent life of an animal. We do not know how it happens that an animal is self-animating. Nor do we know the particularity in which it is both self-animated and living. Whether and how the animal may be soul and body is hidden from us, since we can neither take the place of the animal and see and appreciate its content from inside, nor can we set up such communication with an animal as would enable it to give us information on the point. But in our own case, and in that of other men, we perceive not only the difference between what animates and what is animated, but also how that which animates and that which is animated are different from one another, what is the peculiarity of each is, and what is therefore the particularity of soul and body. In the case of man, we can clarify what we mean when we speak of soul and body in their differentiation. In the case of man, we must transcend (without forgetting) the unity of soul and body which he has in common with the animal, and give appropriate expression to the differentiation which in the case of the animal is hidden from us but in the case of man is not so hidden. Even the animal has spirit. But we do not know how it has Spirit, i.e., what it means for the animal that through the Spirit it is the soul of a body. We can know, however, what it means for man, and we must make this clear. To do so is the further task which now faces us.

Man has Spirit, and through the Spirit is the soul of his body. This means at least that, by reason of his creaturely being, he is capable of meeting God, of being a person for and in relation to Him, and of being one as God is one. He is capable of being aware of himself as different both from God and from the rest of the created world, yet also bound up with God and with the rest of the created world. He is capable of recognising himself and of being responsible for himself. He exists in the execution of this self-recognition and self-responsibility before his Creator. As far as the animal is concerned, we do not even know whether its being fulfils itself in a corresponding or similar or very different action. Yet we know it of man as certainly as we know His Creator who is not silent to him at least, as certainly as we know the Word of this Creator. Man exists in this Word ; i.e., he is, as over against this Word he is conscious of himself and responsible. We know of this human constitution of ours. But in this knowledge is included the knowledge that we are capable of this activity in which we consist, i.e., that we are qualified, prepared and equipped for it. That we are capable of this is the essence of our human creatureliness. That man has Spirit means, whatever it may mean for the animal, that he is capable of executing this activity. He can recognise himself ; he can be responsible for himself. Whether or how the animal can do this is not apparent to us. It may be that, in a way not apparent to us, it can do so. But we know neither whether nor how it can. In the case of man, on the other hand, there is no question whether he can or cannot. We must replace man by a quite different being if we are to question whether he has this ability. His creatureliness, what he is through the Spirit, is in itself and as such this ability. As he is caught up in this action and continuously involved in self-recognition and self-responsibility, he is man, and he continuously affirms his ability for it, and therefore the particularity of his human creatureliness. If man is the soul of his body—and this we can say of the animal only with the reservation of ignorance—then in his case at least the meaning is that he is qualified, prepared and equipped for this activity. Soul and body, as the essence of human nature, are in any case the presupposition and precondition, the potentiality, which underlies the actuality of his being in the Word of God.

We turn to Gen. 2⁷. When God breathes His breath into the nostrils of man and thus makes him a living being, He seems to be doing materially the same thing as might be said of animals. It is merely a matter of form that it is said specially of man. The material difference emerges only in the fact that the continuation of the story is the history of the covenant and salvation, not between God and animals, but between God and man. The course of events described in Gen. 3 ff. occurs between God and man, not between God and animals. This shows what is involved in the fact that God gave man the Spirit. He gave the Spirit to animals also, but obviously not in the same way. Man is the being between whom and God such events can take place. Only in regard to man is it understandable that in the Old and New Testaments the same word *ruah* and πνεῦμα can denote both the prophetic and the creative Spirit, or that the creaturely soul can be summarily and compendiously described as spirit. The Spirit given to man, and grounding, constituting and maintaining him as soul of his body, has *per se* an affinity to the prophetic Spirit, by whose operation the actuality of his being in covenant with God arises out of the potentiality of his creatureliness. Thus man's soul *per se* has an affinity to the Spirit by whom it is made. And thus it is created *a priori* in this affinity, i.e., for the realisation of a connexion between man and his Creator. This is the factual explanation of these very striking linguistic usages of the Bible. In regard to animals, they would both be inexplicable, because a retrospective consideration of animals, looking from salvation history back to their nature, is impossible for us. In regard to man, both are readily explicable, since we not only can but must understand human nature from the standpoint of salvation history.

We shall now try to see what is to be seen from this standpoint concerning the particularity of man as soul of his body.

Man meets God and stands before Him. God calls him by name and claims his obedience. God takes account of his own decisions, and everything that He does will either be directly revealed in his decisions or will have connexion with them. There will be a correspondence. It will mean that they are confirmed or condemned, rewarded or punished by God. This includes the fact that the independent life of the human creature is the life of a subject to whom God can entrust and from whom He can expect this partnership in intercourse with Him. Man is a subject of his own decision. He forms his own centre and his own periphery. Further, he is aware that he does this. He posits himself as such a centre. He posits himself in connexion with his environment. He posits himself in relation to God. In this way he is the soul of his body. That he is soul means that he is such a centre : the subject of specific engagements, opinions, views and resolves ; a subject which is ordained for action and from which actions are therefore expected. That he is body means that as such a centre he has a periphery, that he can take action appropriate to this determination, that from this centre he can display a specific attitude in the creation around him, that from this point he can take a specific path and thus outwardly represent himself to be a person. It is not that he merely is this, or that it merely happens and occurs to him. Rather, in it all he knows himself and recognises himself to be both centre and periphery. In it all he posits himself wholly and simultaneously both inwardly and outwardly, from within outwards as the person he is and as the representation of this person. To him as a being capable of this existence, it is entrusted and accorded that he should meet God and stand before Him and be His partner. As this being, he may and should be man in the action of self-consciousness and responsibility. In this sense, he, man, is wholly and simultaneously soul, self-animating, and body—self-animated and alive. Human life is independent life. We can and must know that man's life is independent life. We cannot know this of animals. We can and must know it of man, because we know of his confrontation by God, and because in this confrontation with God there is entrusted and accorded to him that he may not only live but live independently. As God gives him soul, making him a soulful being, a besouled body and therefore a true body, man becomes a subject of this kind.

We notice at once that in this peculiar way man is one, a totality. He is independent as he can represent himself independently. His engagements, opinions, views and resolves are displayed in the attitudes and actions in which they are expressed. He lives his life, as he is soul of his body. Conversely, what he represents he is. His attitudes and actions are distinguished from any kind of movements in the realm of nature by the fact that they are the expression of his engagements, opinions, views and resolves. He lives his own specific and independent life as he is soul of his body. Not as soul or as body, but in the unity and totality of the two, it is entrusted and accorded to him to meet God and stand before God. And in their unity and wholeness we have to recognise his creaturely nature.

But we notice—and this is our present concern—that the two moments in this human creaturely nature are differentiated. The centre is not as such the periphery. The person is not as such the representation. The inner is not as such the outer. The soul is not as such the body. That it could not be without it is of course true. But it is not for this reason directly identical with it. It is in the body and the body in it. The soul is with it. It has and uses it. The body serves it, as it is its body. And as this happens, man is the soul of his body. Similarly, the periphery is not as such the centre, but presupposes it. There is no periphery where there is no centre. But in this relation of condition and dependence, the periphery is different from the centre. Similarly, although the person itself cannot be thought away from any of his representations, it is not exhausted in its expression, but remains itself even as it represents and expresses itself, and even though without this it could not be itself. Similarly, the outer is not simply the inner, though the inner needs the outer in order to be the inner. Similarly, the body is not directly the soul. Yet as the body is in the soul and the soul in the body, as the body is used and possessed by the soul and serves it, it takes place that man is the soul of his body and therefore identical with his body too. Man is wholly and simultaneously both soul and body. But the soul and the body are not for this reason identical, in spite of the well-known mathematical rule. On the contrary, they are distinguished from each other as subject and object, as operation and work.

Not without his body, yet not as body but as soul, man is the subject of his own decision. To be this is entrusted to him and expected of him in his relation to God. Not without his body, yet not as body but as soul, he is conscious of what he does and posits himself as such a centre and periphery in relation to his environment and even to God. Not without his body, but as soul and not as body, he fulfils the various engagements, holds the various opinions and forms the various views and resolves in which he lives his personal life. For again it is not without his body, but as soul and not as body, that he is person, and is thus determined and fitted to live his life as an independent life. The body can and must assist him in this. But the body cannot on its own account be the primary factor. It cannot represent the soul or displace it or render it superfluous. It must follow it, and can only follow it.

The same distinction, however, applies also from the other side. Not without his body, but as body and not as soul, man must execute the decisions entrusted to him and expected from him in his relationship to God. He forms not only a centre of his own but also a periphery of his own. This periphery implies not that he is soul but that he is body. Not without his soul, but as body and not as soul, he is able to display a specific attitude corresponding to his self-consciousness, to strike out along a specific path, representing himself outwardly. Not without his soul, but as body and not as soul, he executes the actions in which what he is inwardly attains expression and form. Not without his soul, but as body and not as soul, he lives the independent life for which as soul he is determined and fitted. In all these things the soul, or rather he himself as soul, can only give guidance and direction to his life. But in matters of execution the soul, or rather he himself as soul, cannot displace the body, nor do for it what only the body can do. It can as little dispense with the body as the body with it. It must precede the body, but can only precede it.

This is, in general terms, the differentiation within the unity of soul and body as invisible in animals but visible in man, and very clearly visible in the light of what is entrusted to him and expected from him in his relationship to God. We distinguish within the one man, not two substances, but two moments of his creaturely reality. For within man the animating factor and the animated, the soul and the body, diverge and are distinct from one another in this way. But a more precise exposition is required at this point. As man meets God and stands before Him, two definite presuppositions emerge in regard to his creaturely nature.

1. The first is that man is capable of perceiving the God who meets him and reveals Himself to him ; that he is capable of distinguishing Him from himself and *vice versa* ; that he can recognise His divine being as such, and His Word and His will ; and that he can understand the order which subsists between himself and God. In dealing with man, God appeals to this ability. He presupposes that in man as the subject of a decision of his own, in his existence as his own centre of his own periphery, this ability at least may be appealed to. Without this ability, every appeal would obviously be without object ; and the meeting between God and man, as it took place in the history of the covenant, would obviously be impossible. If God created him to have his being in His Word and as His partner, it is already decided that He created him as a percipient being. As he is ordained and it is given to him to perceive God, he is ordained and it is given to him to perceive generally, to be percipient. To perceive means to receive another as such into one's self-consciousness. To be percipient thus means to be capable of receiving another as such into one's self-consciousness. A being capable only of a purely self-contained self-consciousness would not be a percipient being. Man is not such a self-contained being. He is capable of self-consciousness, but he is also capable of receiving another as such into this self-consciousness of his. Man can not only posit himself. In so doing, he can also posit another, and therefore himself in relation to this other and this other in relation to himself.

He can be aware of another and he can think it. The idea of perception divides into these two functions when applied to man. That man is percipient implies both. We believe that we can see and know that there is awareness in animals. But we do not know whether they think. Not knowing this, we do not really know whether their awareness is not very different from man's. Hence we do not really know whether and in what sense an animal is a percipient being. But we do know that man perceives. That is, we know that this perception always takes place in a compound act of awareness and thought. It is not a pure act of thought, for in a pure act of thought we should not surmount the limits of self-consciousness and so we should be unable to receive and accept another as such into our self-consciousness. Neither is it a pure act of awareness, for when I am merely aware of something and do not think it, it remains external to me and is not received into my self-consciousness. Only the concept of perception can be divided in this way. And it is only for an understanding of the concept that we can allow the division. But the perception proper to man is itself an undivided act, in which awareness makes thinking possible and thinking awareness. The thinking becomes possible and the awareness real as the act of receiving another into the human self-consciousness. As a being capable of such perception, man is claimed in his relation to God, and it is the ability for such perception that has to be ascribed to him through the fact that he is claimed in this way. When we speak of man, to have the Spirit means in the first place to be able to perceive in this sense, to perceive God first and foremost, but because God, therefore and therewith another in general. Existing as man and so as person, man always executes this act of perception. It is thus proper to him to be capable of this act.

Superficially we can recognise the two moments of human nature, body and soul, in the division of the idea of perception into awareness and thought. It is natural and in a certain sense justifiable to say that awareness belongs to the body, i.e., its sense organs, and thought to the soul, so that the act of perception, which is single, has to be understood as an act of the whole man in the sense that one had to understand body and soul in him to be in a kind of distributed co-operation. But the situation is more complicated than this. I am not only my soul; I am my soul only as I am also my body. I am not only my body; I am my body only as I am also my soul. Hence it is certainly not only my body but also my soul which has awareness, and it is certainly not only my soul but also my body which thinks. There can thus be no question of a simple distribution of the two functions in the act of perception to soul and body, or of the simple notion of co-operation between the two. The situation is rather that man as soul of his *body* is empowered for awareness, and as *soul* of his body for thought. Understood thus, the two are different and cannot be interchanged.

Awareness is not only with the body. How could the body or the sense organs have awareness of themselves? What makes man naturally capable of awareness is simply that this body is his body, the body of his soul. Yet he does not execute this act as soul, but as body, by means of his organs; and in these the soul as such has no part, but they must be supplied by the body. That he is body makes it possible for another as such to enter his consciousness, for him to posit another as possible. How could his soul have awareness in and for itself when as such it is inward and not outward ?

Again, thinking is not only with the soul. How could his soul think, if it were not the soul of his brain, his nerves and his whole organism ? Even when he thinks, man lives the life of his body. Even his thought is necessarily disturbed by the disturbance of the life of his body ; and it necessarily ceases if he is deprived of his body. Even his thinking is executed as it is accompanied and assisted in one way or another by the action of his whole body. In thought he brings it about that what comes into his consciousness is received there as his self-consciousness, is posited by this as real, is recognised as another, and is understood in its relation to him. Yet he does this, not as body, but as soul, in the form of an act which certainly has accompanying bodily phenomena and conditions, but which is not for this reason an external and bodily act, but an internal act of the soul. As he thinks, he must necessarily live the life of his soul. How could his body as such, or any of his organs, even the highest, think of itself when as such it is outward and not inward ?

Hence the two functions of perception cannot be distributed as though one were of the soul and the other of the body. But it can be affirmed that a special relation to the body is proper to the one, and a special relation to the soul to the other. Both are functions of both soul and body. We must even say of both that they are primarily of the soul and secondarily of the body, since in both man is the soul of his body and not the body of his soul, the body functioning only as the indispensable participant and the soul as the real bearer of the action of perception.

But a special relation to the body can be ascribed to the act of awareness to the extent that it is in fact the outer and not the inner side of perception. In this act, the other which I perceive comes to me in order that it may then and on this basis come into me. The soul has awareness, but this is possible only in so far as it has in the body its outer form and is thus open to the other of which it is aware. Body is the openness of soul. Body is the capacity in man in virtue of which another can come to him and be for him. Man has awareness, therfore, in so far as he is the soul of his *body*.

So, too, a special relation to the soul can be ascribed to thinking inasmuch as it is in fact the inner and not the outer side of perception. When I think, the other which I perceive comes into me, after it has come to me. The soul does not think without the body, because even thinking can take place only when it is accompanied by the functions of the whole body. It can think only in so far as it is the inner form of the outer, the place in which the other can be received for which it is now open, thanks to the body. The soul is man's self-consciousness taking place in the body. The soul is the capacity in virtue of which he can make another his own, in virtue of which the other can be not only for him but in him.   Man thinks, therefore, in so far as he is the *soul* of his body.

It is the biblical anthropological view of perception which we have before us in these statements, and which compels us to formulate the matter in this and not in another way.

In the Old and New Testaments we look in vain for any abstract interest in the rational nature of man, in his sensible and (in the narrower sense) rational apperceptive capacity.   We look in vain for any abstract doctrine of this object. And if our present concern with the matter is theological, we must take our stand on the fact that abstract attention to the sensible-rational capacity of man as such necessarily means inattention when measured by our task.   The concrete attention demanded of us befits the man who meets his God and stands before his God, the man who finds God and to whom God is present.   What interests the Bible, and therefore ourselves, in dealing with the matter, is that even man's ability to perceive is one of the properties presupposed in his meeting with God, his standing before Him and his finding Him present, which we must thus regard as essential for his creaturely nature.   He is one who perceives in the fact that God, who will deal and treat with him, can be for him and in him, and can approach and enter him.   He should and can perceive God.   For this reason his nature, and he himself as soul of his body, is rational nature.   It is this, and not any autonomous rationality, which marks him off from the animals and the rest of creation.   His rationality is constituted by what he needs, has and employs as the partner of God in His action as the Lord of the covenant between Himself and man.   Hence there is hardly a passage in the Bible which, when it speaks of man's own capacity of awareness and thought, of observation, reflection, recognition and knowledge, does not directly or indirectly mean his capacity to be open to the will and action of God and to give God a place within himself.

Man may sense and think many things, but fundamentally the perceiving man is the God-perceiving man.   It is true, of course, that the other which he perceives is not identical with God, and that he continuously perceives other things as well as God.   But when the Bible speaks of perceiving man, there is nothing else which it is important or necessary for man to perceive.   Man perceives and receives into self-consciousness particular things—the action and inaction of his fellow-men, the relations and events of nature and history, the outward and the inward sides of the created world around him.   But these are important and necessary for man only because God does not usually meet him immediately but mediately in His works, deeds and ordinances, and because the history of God's traffic with him takes place in the sphere of the created world and of the world of objects distinct from God.   Basically, however, it is only in connexion with this history that this world of objects and therefore perception of the reality distinct from God becomes important and necessary for man. First and last and all the time his perception has properly only one object, of which everything else gives positive or negative witness.   Man perceives this witness when he perceives particular things.   He may and must be open to this witness and give it place.   Thus in, behind and over the other things which he perceives by sense and thought there always stands in one way or another the Other who through other things approaches and enters him, who wills to be sensed and thought by him, to be for and in him, not casting him off, not leaving him to himself, willing rather that man should be with Him and that He should be received and enclosed in his self-consciousness.   In order that this may take place, man is percipient.   Thus he does not have an abstract capacity of awareness and thought, but the concrete capacity to sense and think God.   This is the object and content in virtue of which and in relation to which his nature is a rational nature.   This carries with it the fact that he rationalises generally, and that by awareness and thought he can make his own other things beside God. But the general capacity does not come first, so that, among other things, he can make God and the witness to God his own. On the contrary, the general is contained in the particular. The general capacity is given for the sake of the particular, and always first and last in connexion with the particular.

It is thus that the representative men of the Bible perceive. There can be no question of a general rational capacity prescribing the framework and standard and rule for a religious rational capacity. But as they obviously have the special capacity to perceive God and His witnesses, they have also the general capacity, and we see them using it. If there is also in the biblical sphere a purely general perception, i.e., a perception loosed from that particular object and content, if even here men sense and think the creaturely in itself and as such, these are deficiency phenomena, and such perception must be described as improper, as abnormal rather than normal. We have here an awareness and thinking which is basically darkened, false and corrupt. Of course, this exists. Percipient man in the Bible is concretely sinful man, the man who would like to escape perception of God, who contradicts his human nature, and who does not behave wisely and rationally, but for all his ostensible wisdom and pretence of reason behaves as a fool and simpleton. He denies his rational nature. This does not mean, however, that he can alter it. It itself judges and condemns him. It is always directed to God even when he will not have it so and acts as though it were not so. The perception which he then chooses is improper and abnormal, depriving itself of its first and last object and being abstractly directed to other objects. Such a perception can only be deranged and per verted. Neither in the Old Testament nor the New does the Bible recognise such human perception which is estranged from its first and last object and therefore improper and abnormal, but proper and normal in respect of other objects. It knows no reality which is not the creation of God ; and equally it knows no rational activity, knowledge, philosophy or the like which is loosed from the perception of God and yet intrinsically good, useful, valuable and praiseworthy. It certainly gives evidence of knowing that there is in fact a human perception that is loosed from the perception of God. But I know no text or context where it may be taken to recognise and approve this abstraction. On the contrary, it constantly undermines the autarchy of a general human reason loosed from God as its origin and object, and protests against the banishment of the perception of God into a religious corner. Only thought and awareness of God are comprehensive, proper, normal and therefore sound thinking and awareness. This is the first and most important lesson to be learned from biblical anthropology.

But when we have learned it, we can understand to what extent even on the biblical view the act of perception is in fact twofold but not divided, an act of awareness and thought. God wills both to approach and to enter man. He wills to be both known and recognised by man as God. From this angle, this is the meaning of the event of the covenant between God and man for which man is made. What kind of a being is it to which this event can happen ? Clearly the presupposition made on the side of man is that he is capable of letting God approach and enter him. This capability is his capacity of awareness and thought. He is a percipient person in this twofold sense. It is essential that he should be it in this twofold sense.

God is not in him as a matter of course. He would not be creature, but himself the Creator, if God were in him from the very outset, if it belonged to his nature to be master of God, if he did not stand continually in need of God's giving Himself to be his, of God's approaching him from outside and giving Himself to be known by him just because He is not his as a matter of course. That God does this is described in the Bible in the story which tells how God bears witness to Himself before men in the midst of the created world. This witness man does not already have, nor can he give it to himself. It must come to him from outside, as another, in order to enter into him. If he perceives God, then, his perception must be fundamentally an act of outer awareness. He meets God and stands and walks before Him. He sees and hears Him in one of His witnesses. God makes Himself known as One who not only is, but is for him.

But clearly this is inadequate, nor is it the whole of the process concerned even according to the biblical description. Self-evidently man would still be withdrawn into himself if God only approached him and did not enter into him, if He did not make Himself his in such a way that man might recognise Him and know himself claimed and blessed by Him and set in relation to Him. It is in this way that God bestows Himself upon man. Man still remains in need of renewed meeting with Him ; but whatever may be his attitude, he is met and reached by Him. Even if only as Accuser and Judge, God takes up His dwelling in him. In some way, God's witness is powerful in man. If he perceives God, this act must be decisively an inner act, i.e., an act of his thinking. He finds God, and in God's presence finds himself. God is not only for him. He is in him, as he perceives Him.

To be capable of this twofold act of awareness and thought makes him a percipient person. Neither aspect may be lacking. In neither by itself would he be a rational nature. Neither permits replacement by the other. Neither can be interchanged with the other, though each takes place with the other in a single differentiated but not dissociated act. Since this is true of man's perception of God, it is true of his perception in general, and his perception of other things is always twofold, both awareness and thought. It is in the perception of God, in which this order is essential, that man's perception of everything, his reason as such, has its source and rule. Because it is first and last perception of God and as such unfolds in these two moments, it is bound to this development, so far as it is proper and normal perception. And again we have to say of the representative men of the Bible that their perception too stands under this order. They are neither pure empiricists, nor pure thinkers. They live wholly with their eyes and ears, and at the same time in the faith of their hearts. They are always wholly and at the same time engaged in awareness and thought. It is for this reason that they are so seldom of use and of so little value from the standpoint of pure empiricism or pure philosophy. And again it is to be observed that the possibility of living only with eyes and ears, i.e., by awareness, or only in the faith of the heart and therefore by thinking, that every attempt at a diminished perception, can only be a deficiency phenomenon in the sphere of the Bible. Both are possibilities only for sinful man ; both are therefore in the highest degree imminent and common. For man in himself, indeed, they are the only imminent possibilities. Human perception, when displayed as his own act, is indeed a divided capacity. But this division has nothing to do with human nature. It is the consequence of the fact that human perception is accustomed to evade its first and last object and content, i.e., God, and thus becomes improper and abnormal in relation to all its objects and contents. But this does not affect its nature in the very slightest. Man cannot change into a being to whom it is natural to perceive in this divided way. Nor can he prevent intending and missing unity, and reaching out for it, in all his dividedness. Biblical man, the prophet and the apostle, reveal to us something of what natural perception is, for their awareness and thinking obviously take place in a single act.

In the same context we have also to understand the proper relation between awareness and thinking on the one hand, and body and soul on the other. The biblical man ordained for encounter with God is everywhere the whole man. Violence was done to the biblical text when in the last two centuries the salvation history to which it witnesses was construed as a kind of history of piety, when the things recorded as happening to man were reduced to purely religious experiences, when the external was internalised, when it was increasingly forgotten that the Old and New Testaments deal with pure events, which certainly engaged the soul of the man concerned, but for that very reason claimed also his flesh and blood. The biblical men did not so much experience in their relation to God ; it is much truer to say that they simply lived, and no less fully on this side than the God of whom the texts speak on His. But this means that biblical awareness and thinking are always understood as both of soul and body, as both an outer and an inner act. Both the biblical languages are, of course, acquainted with the terms by which the two functions are distinguished as outer and inner, sensuous and mental, physical and psychical. But the meanings of these terms are much closer than appears from Greek thought. And there is no way of denoting the two extremes of pure external observation on the one hand or pure internal reflection on the other. In the strict sense, Hebrew possesses no equivalent for the pure idea of thinking. The only possible term is *binah, sakar* being the concrete consideration and *hashab* the equally concrete contriving or inventing of a matter. In the New Testament, it is only infrequently that the term νοῦς carries a suggestion of its use in this sense in classical Greek. As a rule it does not have a theoretical but a practical meaning, and it is a function of the heart. The term *jada'* is, of course extremely important, but it indicates a knowledge in which our concepts of awareness and thinking are coupled together. Again, the Old and New Testament ideas of " hearing " and " seeing " do not merely denote external, sensuous or bodily perception. We have only to consider what is meant by the context when the biblical " See " is uttered, or what the Old Testament understands by a " seer," or how comprehensive is the biblical " Hear," which certainly speaks of an act of awareness effected by the bodily ear, but in most cases carries the further thought of inner acceptance, of understanding, appropriation and recognition, indicating that something is taken to heart. Where, then, is that which is purely of the soul or purely of the body ? In the Bible percipient man has decisively to do with God, who made him as soul of his body. It cannot well be otherwise than that the one always goes along with the other.

At both points, then, we have to do with the act of man in its totality. But this means that, according to the biblical understanding of this action, we must speak of a primacy of the soul in relation to the two functions of awareness and thinking. The soul—the soul of the body, but still the soul and not the body—is the man himself, the human subject. He not only thinks, but it is he who also senses. He might obviously have eyes and yet not see or ears yet not hear, as is said of the foolish, unperceptive people of Judah (Jer. 5²¹). " He that hath ears to hear, let him hear." This is the call which must particularly go out in the New Testament. Not for nothing man must be continually exhorted to see what is before his eyes. It is evidently not a matter of course that the fulfilment of the outer function immediately implies a fulfilment of the decisively inner function, or that what is sensed by man is also thought by him. Failure to see and hear in spite of the possession of eyes and ears can be an inevitable consequence of divine hardening (Is. 6⁹ᶠ·). The man himself, and therefore his soul, must have awareness if he is to be a real percipient. As he is soul, he stands before God, and it is to his soul, and therefore to himself, that God wills to be present as his blessing, his will, his law and his promise. He himself summons his soul (Ps. 103¹), and therefore himself, to praise of the Lord. This is the normal result of real human perception, although and as this is everywhere a bodily act, just as this praise of the Lord, while it is an act of the soul, must also be a bodily act. From this there follows necessarily what we must describe, not indeed as a distribution of awareness and thought to body and soul, but as a special relation of the former to the body and the latter to the soul. When biblical man perceives, when he properly and normally perceives God in all that he perceives, he is open as whole man ; and again as whole man he is the open place in which God is present in His witnesses and takes up His habitation. His awareness then attains its goal and is itself a thinking. His body stands wholly at the service of his soul. His thinking arises from his awareness, and is itself simply a completed seeing and hearing. His soul is wholly that for which it is determined by the action of his body. Yet it is still the case that in this event he executes two different functions : the one as *what* he is, the function of awareness in which it becomes possible and actual on his side that God should approach him, and give Himself to him for recognition, this being the special function of the body ; the other as *who* he is, the function of thinking (in biblical language, his heart), in which it becomes possible and actual on his side that God should approach him, and become object of his recognition, or perhaps of his non-recognition, but in either case the object with which now he has to come to terms, this being the special function of his soul. He has awareness as he is the soul of his *body* ; he thinks as he is the *soul* of his body. In this differentiation the one act of perception is the act of the whole man, as in the Bible we see him confronted with God.

2. We turn now to the second great presupposition made concerning human nature, and therefore concerning the soul and body of man, by the fact that it is entrusted and accorded to man to be God's partner, to meet God, to stand and walk before Him, to be right in self-reflective responsibility before Him. That he can perceive God is only a first point that calls for consideration in this respect. The second is that, in relation and correspondence to what he perceives of God, he can be active. In His dealings with man, God summons him to this ability. He presupposes from the very outset that even on man's side the fellowship between man and Himself must not be limited to a fellowship of knowledge, but that it can become a fellowship of action. If man is summoned to personal knowledge and responsibility over against his Creator, besides the bare perception of God, which is of course an indispensable and most important presupposition, he is summoned to decisions. And if this does not take place in vain, if it is really possible and not impossible for him to make decisions, to do this or that, and thus to be obedient to the summons which he meets and hears, this means that God has made him an active being. Again it is the case that as he is determined and it is given to him to be active in answer to the summons of God and in encounter with Him, he is determined and it is given to him to be active in general, to be a doer and not a non-doer. To act generally is to set oneself freely in motion in relation to another. A doer is always one who is capable of such free movement in relation to another. A being immovable in relation to another, or capable only of movement that is not free and not self-initiated, is not an active being. Even if capable of being moved, it cannot act. Man can be moved. But he can also take up an attitude towards others which involves action as well as perception. In his co-existence with the other he can desire and will. Thus in the concept of activity as in that of perception, both understood as possibilities given to man, we have to do with two different functions. Desiring and willing characterise man as the distinct subject that he is. In this respect, too, it is instructive to compare him with animals. We think that we see and know that animals desire. But we do

not know for certain whether they will. Since we do not know this, fundamentally we do not know whether animal desire — however often human desire may remind us of it—is not something quite different. Thus we really do not know whether and in what sense animals are active beings. The interpretation which ascribes this to them can be as right or as wrong as that which denies it to them. But we know that man is active, and in what way. That is, we know that this takes place in a single act of desiring and willing of whose occurrence and interconnexion we are well aware.

It does not take place in a pure act of will. Pure volition would take place to some extent in a vacuum, since as such it would have no object, and no other in relation to which to exercise itself. What was purely willed would necessarily be purely internal to us. Pure volition is in fact a movement incapable of execution and can have nothing to do with activity.

Nor is it fulfilled in a pure act of desire. Pure desire would certainly have an object. But it would not as such be our movement in relation to this other. What was purely desired would remain as external to us as something purely sensed. Pure desire, too, is a movement incapable of execution and can have nothing to do with activity.

So again we can quite well divide the concept—but only the concept—of activity into the ideas of desiring and willing. But the activity proper to man is itself the undivided act in which desire makes the willing possible and the willing makes the desiring actual, the possibility and the actuality being the free movement of a man in relation to another. Man in his relation to God is claimed as one capable of such activity. It is the ability for such activity that this engagement ascribes to him and presupposes in him. Therefore when we say of man that he has Spirit, we mean in the second place that he can be active in this sense first and last in relation to God, and for this reason generally in relation to all else. Existing as man and therefore as person, he constantly executes this act, his own action. It is indeed proper to him to be capable not only of perceiving but also of doing, of perceiving as the presupposition of doing, and doing as the end and goal of his capacity for perceiving.

We interject that it is as essential for man to be capable of perceiving as it is of doing, and of doing as perceiving. Between the two presuppositions, there exists the same relation as between sensing and thinking and desiring and willing. The real life-act of real man can and will never consist in pure perception or pure activity. Perception is itself wholly and utterly human activity. Without desiring and willing I cannot sense and think. But again all my activity depends absolutely on the fact that I perceive. Without sensing and thinking I should not desire and will. A perception which had nothing to do with my activity, or stood in contradiction with it, would not be real, or at any rate would be incomplete. If my activity took place without my perception or stood wholly or partly in contradiction to it, then it would reveal that it was either not at all or only incompletely my real activity. All distinction between perception and action, all abstraction to the advantage and disadvantage of one or the other, all action and reaction between *vita contemplativa* and *vita activa*, between "intellectualism" and "voluntaryism"—all these, so far as they succeed, can only lead to all kinds and forms of inhumanity. But the enterprise is impossible on both sides. The really human person is the one who both perceives and acts in each of his life-acts. This reality will always be the refutation of all the distinctions and oppositions which are futilely proposed and championed in this connexion.

In the case of desiring and willing, too, we face the question whether we have to apportion these two characteristic functions of human activity to the soul and the body. The answer can and must be fundamentally the same as in the case of sensing and thinking. There is indeed a special relation of desiring to the bodily nature of man, and of willing to the soul. But there is no partition. On the contrary, we have to understand both desiring and willing as both soulful and bodily, both being primarily of the soul and secondarily of the body.

The case of desiring is as follows. It is intrinsically a bodily process that I desire, wish or long for (or negatively fear, shun or avoid) another, or a certain relation between me and another, or that it arouses my liking (or dislike). In this process, besides the nerves of my brain, those of the most diverse other organs can participate in greater or less measure. A particular sensible experience can let loose in me a particular urge of liking or dislike. This bodily urge as such is in some sense the necessary material of my desiring. To this extent we can and must affirm a special relation between desiring and the body. But the urge as such, the bodily liking or dislike, does not constitute the desire or aversion. If I am to desire or shun, it is necessary that I not only be aware of the urge concerned but that I affirm it, making it my own and committing myself in some sense to it. I can do this. But I can also ignore and disavow it. I am able not to desire (or to shun), though I am urged to it. I can thus accept that material or leave it. That I experience liking or dislike for another is not simply an affair of my nerves. It is this, but it is also my own affair. This constitutes what is obviously the most decisive participation of my soul in my desiring—however true it may be that without my body I am quite unable to desire at all.

The case of willing is as follows. It is a matter of the soul that I allow another to be not merely the object of my desiring (or shunning), but go beyond this to make it an object of my will; that I have a certain intention and come to a resolution with respect to it or to my relation to it; that I set it before me and put myself into the corresponding movement in relation to it. My desiring—which itself has a soulful element, as we have seen—is naturally presupposed. Where I have no desire, I cannot will. But I do not by any means will everything which I desire or for which I admittedly have a liking; nor again do I not will everything for which I have no liking. When I will, I make up my mind. I myself, as soul, make up my own mind as the physico-psychical being provisionally united in like or dislike. I subject the provisional pact between my physical urge and my psychical agreement or rejection to a second proof. I choose, i.e., I determine myself and my activity for the execution or non-execution of my desiring. I prescribe for myself a specific attitude to the desired object. My desiring alone cannot do this. Desiring alone does not lead to any attitude. This is a process of soul. It is also true, of course, that it can be realised only because I am the soul of my body, and that my body too has not only a passive but an active part in my willing. But the activity of the body is at this point purely accessory and dependent. The body itself does not decide or determine, though it offers to me the material for my desiring in the form of an urge. It is I who decide and determine in relation to my desiring, not without parallel physical phenomena and conditions, but in such a way that I elevate myself above myself, above my physico-psychical desiring and therefore above my body, so that I am my own master and the master of my body. If this were not so, I should obviously not yet be willing but only desiring, confronting myself and my desiring in neutrality. I should not then be aware of myself in distinction from my desiring or of my power over it. I am aware of myself only when I realise the distinction between me and my desiring and make use of my power over it. This I do when I will ; for then I abandon my neutrality towards myself and my desiring and take position over against them both. But this abandonment of neutrality and occupation of position is as such my act, the act of my soul, in just the same way as must be said of thinking in relation to awareness.

If we are not to lose touch with biblical anthropology, we must maintain this unity and differentiation of soul and body in respect of the active man as well.

And above all we must again take note of its basis. We observe that in this respect, too, the Bible has no abstract interest in the rational nature of man (and here especially his capacity for action) ; or in a formal antithesis between the sensibility and externality of desire on the one hand and the spirituality and freedom of the will on the other. Here, too, it views man in his concrete wholeness. It does this because it sees him first and foremost in his relation to God, as one who in this relation acts and desires and wills. That he is one who desires and wills is important in the biblical texts because God deals with him, and his own capacity for action is thus presupposed. Man should and can decide for God. God the Other is that Other in relation to which man's desiring and willing is a relevant matter. What distinguishes man from animals and the rest of creation is that he can desire and will in relation to God. The action expected of him is that he acknowledge God. He is man as in and with all he does he stands under the demand that he hear, believe and love God. For this he is claimed by God Himself through His covenant with him. The significance of his nature as active nature is that he can do this. Directly or indirectly, it is always this ability that is concerned when such a nature is ascribed to him. Thus his work has no immanent importance, justification and worth ; it acquires these as in some way it is done in relation to the work of God. Thus the character of his work as good or bad, salutary or destructive, is dependent on no other criterion than what it represents and means in this relation. Of course man also desires and wills in other connexions. Of course the other in relation to which he wills and affirms is always directly this or that component of his natural and historical environment, and therefore of the world of objects distinct from God, over against which he never stands merely in awareness and thought but always in some sense in activity and therefore in desire and volition. But on the biblical view this world of objects distinct from God is itself simply the sphere in which the history of the covenant between God and man unfolds. What meets man in this sphere as the possible object of his desiring and willing does not belong to him (for it is not his creation), any more than it belongs to itself (for it did not create itself). What can meet him in this sphere belongs to God and is His creation. When man is active in relation to it, he is active in relation to God. He acts in one way or another as the partner of God ; and therefore his action is in one way or another measured by what it represents and means in its relation to God. Again, therefore, man has first and fundamentally the ability to be active in relation to God, and only then and for this reason to every other " other." Here, too, the general is contained within the particular, and not *vice versa*.

The idea of a special religious activity is just as strange to the Bible as that of a special religious perception. The people of Israel is not first of all and in general a people which as such unifies, asserts and propagates itself, which seeks a country and a habitation and nourishment in this country, which constructs its order of life, and then in addition to all this has a particular faith, follows a particular worship, and is thus active in a particular sphere in relation to God. On the contrary, the significance of the existence of Israel is that precisely in its general activity, in its unifying and asserting and propagating of itself, its finding of a country and in that country its habitation, nourishment and order of life, it is active in relation to its God, a relation which is expressed in its particular cultic acts, but is materially a total life-relation. This is even more true of the followers of Jesus Christ, the members of His community. They are not first of all and in general men with all kinds of urges and tendencies, and only then representatives and preachers of the Messiah Jesus and faith in Him, and in this particular respect active in relation to God. A Paul acts and lives " in the flesh " and therefore in general ; but this he does in the faith of the Son of God (Gal. 2[20]) ; and whether Christians eat or drink or whatever they do, they do it in all cases under the law of thankfulness and under the determination that everything takes place to the glory of God (1 Cor. 10[31]). There is no place for a general human activity beside what is here done in relation to God. For the sphere of the general is determined and limited by this particular. If Christians also come together in particular, eating and drinking particularly in remembrance of the Resurrected, speaking particularly with one another and with God, it is not this that makes them Christians. In this way they merely confess that they are Christians. They are Christians as in the whole range of their humanity they are active in relation to God in ways determined by Christ. Hence the Bible knows of no general idea of right human conduct loosed from relation to God. Of course it knows that such conduct is continually possible and real, or may become so even in Israel and the Christian community. Of course it knows the constantly recurring attempt of man to withdraw his activity from this fundamental relation and to set up between himself and the world of objects a kind of closed circle in which man's desiring and what he desires, man's willing and what he wills, man's work and its several objects, form among themselves a kind of neutral sphere over against God. Of course it knows that man constantly strives after an intrinsic well-being, a self-grounded fortune and greatness, in the belief that he is commanded, compelled or justified therein, quite apart from the question of his relation to God. And finally of course it knows of the artifice with which man allows himself such an autonomous, self-grounded and self-enclosed desiring and willing and then brings all into a kind of relation to God by also engaging privately or publicly in religious activity. But it is characteristic of the Bible that it inexorably criticises as a deficiency phenomenon any desiring and willing which thus tries to loose itself from relation to God, whatever the necessity from which arises, whatever right it invokes, however morally enlightening the character it bears, and quite irrespective of any religious appendix which it may or may not have. It condemns it as a false and perverted desiring and willing and doing, just as it sees that all sensing and thinking which tries to loose itself from God as its proper object is in all circumstances folly rather than wisdom. It does this because it regards man as actually unable to renounce that fundamental relation of his activity. It sees and affirms that he is of course constantly engaged in the attempt. But even in this attempt, it sees him constantly refuted and judged by his own nature, which he can certainly alienate and violate but cannot alter, and which gives him the lie if he is false to it. It measures him by the fact that in his activity he belongs wholly and utterly to God. For this reason it cannot abandon him to any sphere of neutral righteousness. It cannot concede to him that any action in which he denies that he belongs to God can be a right action. At once and necessarily it sees that such action is evil and pernicious. This explains why it is that neither in the Old Testament nor the New is there any praise of man *in abstracto*, but even where judgment is withheld the references to man's undertakings and performances as such are so cool. Just because it is moved to participate so deeply in the activity of man, it maintains an attitude of great concern for the fundamental relation in which alone it can be right action. It demands desiring and willing that is liberated in this decisive respect. Since it does not meet with, and since it cannot content itself with anything less, it cannot praise man. Here, too, it disturbs his autarchy, the false self-contentment of a general human activity alienated from its proper object. Here, too, it protests against the hypocrisy which on the one side would like to endorse and co-operate in this alienation, but on the other is not prepared to surrender the relation of the active man to God, but justifies human desiring and willing as such, supplementing it by a well-meant but useless religious activity. The biblical texts forbid us to call sound what is sick. The desiring and willing is sick in which man in any respect makes the futile attempt to conduct himself as though in this or that matter he had not to do with God. It is sick because the attempt can never succeed, but can only lead to crippled and convulsive acts unworthy of the name. The proper, normal and sound desiring and willing is that in which the real state of the case, that God first and last constitutes its only object, is conceded, recognised, respected and honoured. The Bible looks to this sound human activity when in so striking a way it looks away from what men do in general.

But this also explains why it is that without division human activity occurs in the twofold function of desiring on the one side and willing on the other. This is true because God, as man is first and last active in relation to Him, wills not only to be willed but first to be desired by man, and not only to be desired but then also willed. To express it in the concrete content of biblical speech, God wills not only to be feared but first to be loved, and not only to be loved but then also to be feared. Man is the being capable of this twofold act in his relation to God and therefore generally. He is in this twofold sense an active person.

In respect of the One who in the Bible is called and is God, man must desire Him wholly, properly, purely, supremely and genuinely, and therefore love Him. This is because, as Calvin strongly emphasises at the very beginning of the *Institutes*, He is the *fons omnium bonorum*, and means not only this and that for man's life but absolutely everything, because man cannot be without Him, because without Him he would be cut off from the source of all that is good for him. That he exists as man and that he stands in need of God, are not two things but one and the same thing. The well-known opening to Augustine's *Confessions* is relevant in this connexion, and it is a correct interpretation of the biblical concept of man : *Quia fecisti nos ad te, et inquietum est cor nostrum, donec requiescat in te (Conf.* I, 1). This need of man for God is not just one—perhaps the deepest—need among others ; nor is it to be explained by any individual need, though it can express itself in every individual need of human life. The " disquiet " of the soul referred to in Pss. 42 and 43 is not a specific disquiet, though it can represent itself in every highest or smallest human disquiet, beginning with bodily hunger and rising to the anxiety of the man who knows that he is hopelessly guilty and lost. Because God is man's Creator, and as such the source of all that is good for him, we have to do here with *the* human need and *the* human disquiet as such—the need which man cannot not have, and the disquiet in which he cannot not find himself. Just because there is nothing human that is more constitutive than man's need for God, his activity must be fundamentally and decisively a desiring of God. That man desires means that he cannot be self-satisfied but needs another for the satisfying of his need. If he could be self-satisfied, he could not and would not desire. Whenever he desires, he begins to notice that he is unable to satisfy himself, and he undertakes the attempt to transcend himself with a view to satisfying himself from elsewhere. But here it becomes evident that genuine and proper desiring can only be desiring of God. It is God the Other and He alone who is the true and complete Other that as such can be the object of genuine desiring. No created thing can be this for man. Fundamentally he does not stand to any created thing in such a relation that his desiring of it cannot again turn out to be the demand for some kind of self-satisfaction, or the fulfilment of his desire for it cannot again complete itself in the form of a kind of self-satisfaction. No created thing, not even the sweet sun itself, stands as an other in such a relation to man that it is wholly and fundamentally withdrawn from his power and his service, or that he does not know how to make it of use in one form or another. In the created world, man with all his neediness is always also the lord and master who knows how to make use of created things. Towards them he is not capable of genuine desiring—or only when he has apprehended that even in his desiring of created things he can first and last desire only their Creator. But in relation to the Creator, there is no self-satisfaction, no utilising, but only genuine desiring, since all human lordship and mastership is here *a priori* and absolutely excluded. Here man is not only accidentally but necessarily needy, i.e., of God. Hence he does not desire accidentally but necessarily. Yet only God can be the object of this genuine, proper and pure desiring. From this there follows the constant presupposition of the Bible, that wherever and however he desires, fundamentally he must necessarily and not just accidentally desire God, that he is caught in the most profound self-misunderstanding in all desiring loosed from the desire for God, and that all other desiring of this kind is only a perverted desiring. Hence when the Decalogue forbids desire for the possession of the wife of another, it does so because such desiring has loosed itself from the desire for God and thus manifested itself as a perverted desiring. If in many passages in the New Testament the word ἐπιθυμία, with or without further specification, signifies evil and sinful desiring ; if lust is described in 1 Jn. 2[15-17] as the form of the passing cosmos in contrast to which only he who does the will of God remains to eternity ; if in Rom. 7[7] and 13[9] the Old Testament command is given a shorter and yet more comprehensive form as οὐκ ἐπιθυμήσεις, the reference is not to desiring as such, but to the human desiring that is loosed from its proper object and has degenerated into a carnal, worldly, irrational, bad and corruptible, in short one's " own " (2 Tim. 4[3] ; 2 Pet. 3[3]) desiring. On the other hand, the Prodigal (Lk. 15[16]) desires to eat of the husks of the swine-trough and Lazarus (Lk. 16[21]) of the crumbs that fell from the rich man's table. Again, Jesus can say : ἐπιθυμίᾳ ἐπεθύμησα to eat this passover with you (Lk. 22[15]), and Paul (1 Thess. 2[17]) that he endeavoured ἐν πολλῇ ἐπιθυμίᾳ to see the community again, or (Ac. 20³³) that he desired the gold or apparel of no one. According to 1 Tim. 3¹, a man can wish for the office of a bishop and in so doing desire a καλὸν ἔργον. All these passages remind us of the natural and by no means pejorative sense of the word. Again, in Mt. 13¹⁷ we read of many prophets and righteous men who desired to see and hear what the disciples see and hear; and in 1 Pet. 1¹² of the angels who desire to look into the things revealed to the Church by the preaching of the Gospel; and again in Lk. 17²² of the disciples, that the days would come when they would desire to see one of the days of the Son of Man. Further, Paul in Phil. 1²³ desires to depart and be with Christ. The writer of Hebrews (6¹¹) desires that everyone in the Church might show the same diligence to the full assurance of hope unto the end. Gal. 5¹⁷ speaks not only of the desire of the flesh against the spirit, but also of the desire of the spirit against the flesh. In these texts we are obviously confronted by the proper, original and comprehensive sense of the term, in which it indicates the desire of man for encounter with God in relation to which evil desiring is not natural but supremely unnatural. Man in the Bible is the being for whom, whether he knows it or not, it is necessary and essential to desire God; and he is the being who by his creation is capable of this. Man can love. The activity of desiring in its genuine, proper and pure form is that he can love, i.e., desire in its otherness another over which he is not lord and master, which he cannot make a means to his own self-satisfaction, but by which he can attain satisfaction and through which he can actually be satisfied. Man can love God. God and God alone—or the witness to God in the created world—is the other which he can desire in its otherness, through which, just because it is always another, he can be satisfied, and which therefore he can really love. It may thus be seen that just because he can desire and love God he can desire and love in general. " In general " does not mean another beside and outside God, but another in God and for the sake of God, God Himself in this other, because this other, God's creation like himself, is God's witness. In practice, he can and will always desire and love God Himself only in such another, in His witnesses, as the God who is active, visible, audible and tangible in His works, as the God who approaches him from outside, entering the sphere of his outer perception. He who in the Bible is called and is God is not a God to be directly experienced, inwardly present to man and possessed by him; He is always the God, strange and mighty, who approaches him from outside. If we think or speak of the matter differently, we must take good care that we have not interchanged God with our own psychical basis and therefore with our self-consciousness and therefore with ourselves, with a suppositional God whom one cannot really desire or really love, to deal with whom is always to be caught again in self-satisfaction and therefore to be worlds away from all real satisfaction. The God of the Bible wills to be perceived, desired and loved in His visible, audible, tangible witnesses. That is why the Bible speaks so anthropomorphically of God's speech and conduct, His coming and going, His action and inaction, His heart and eyes, His arms and hands and feet, as though the reference were to a creature like man. That is why He is described as the Other who can be perceived, desired and known by man (himself only a creature and not the Creator) in the midst of the created world, His creaturely witnesses and demonstrations.

But it is obviously not enough that man can desire Him, just as it is not enough that he can perceive Him. It is only half the matter that man can desire the One who stands over and approaches him as the strange and mighty Creator, even if we understand the term desire in its deepest sense of love. If this were all, we should not have the full idea of an active person. To desire and love God is in itself only his inner activity, and therefore not the complete activity in which God is always present to him purely outwardly—not an activity which can be quite visible in its relationship to God. He who in the Bible is called and is God is the One whom man must also will and therefore fear just as absolutely and supremely as he desires and loves Him. He is responsible to

Him. His willing must consist in surrendering himself to One to whom he belongs. We can again refer at this point to the passage in Calvin already cited, for it is simply an interpretation of the biblical concept of man. Man is *iure creationis addictus et mancipatus* to God. He is under obligation to Him for his life. What he undertakes and does must be positively related to Him if it is to be rightly undertaken and done. He acts in obedience to Him, or else his conduct is perverted. The will of God is his *lex vivendi*. From the standpoint of the biblical concept of man, these are no florid exaggerations, but sober affirmations of the facts of the case. That he wills and that it is in the fear of God that he wills, are not two things, any more than his existence and his need and therefore his desire for God are two things. They are one and the same. He cannot will as such and in general and then also will God, i.e., will what God wills. This is no less true than that he cannot desire as such and in general, and then also desire God among other things. Since he can purely desire God alone, he can purely will God alone. Since he is in truth engaged in this desiring, his decision and his own confession with reference to his desiring can consist only in this willing and can be only the affirmation of this desiring. Wherever the human will recognises and affirms human desiring, man's desiring stands before the question whether it is of such a kind that this may happen, that it may, must and can be endorsed, because it is this pure desiring. And wherever the human will declines and rejects human desiring, it is itself confronted by the question whether it is a pure will, whether it is really an impure and not perhaps a pure desiring which it is in process of rejecting. The question is always posed from both sides. As man wills, he becomes in one way or another responsible for his desiring, for the decision is his. His decision may not merely fall in with his desiring. It depends on whether or not he wills what he desires. But in this decision and resolve he is responsible to God, he lives in or outside the fear of God, and he begins to act, the occurrence of history between God and him being enacted on his side too as his own action. There thus comes into being what he is or is not in his relation to God. Both become possible in his desiring in itself and as such. That he be satisfied is related to his desiring ; that he on his side in return satisfies the God who first satisfies him, is related to his willing. His proper and genuine willing can thus only be the willing bound to God. Man can owe to no creature what he owes to God—himself in his totality. Nothing can claim from him that he serve its satisfaction. When a created thing imposes this demand on man, and when man recognises the demand, we have nothing but the invalid claim of false gods. No created thing can substantiate the Creator's right over man. Thus no created thing can become for him the object of pure willing. He must really will only what he must will in his relation to God. This and this alone can he himself will in freedom. This and this alone is the willing that corresponds and conforms to his nature. On the other hand, everything in his relation to God which is superfluous to it and excluded by it, and everything not demanded by God or contradicting the demand of God, whether in false agreement or in false conflict with his desiring, can be based as such only on the same self-misunderstanding to which his desiring is exposed. Then man in truth does not yet or any longer will genuinely and properly. His will is a corrupted and perverted will, and it is clear that, since he cannot satisfy God with such a will, he is cut off on his side from satisfaction by God ; and what occurs to him in the history between God and himself can only be the painful experience of divine judgment which he cannot escape, so long and so far as he wills something other than God. But man's pure and right will is a will obedient to God. As he is capable of this will, he is capable of will in general. As God made him free for Himself, He made him free in general. The energy of every human decision and every human resolve, the energy of the person deciding and resolving, has its origin and basis in the fact that man first and foremost can fear God, and therefore can purely and rightly will. He does not will this and that, and then perhaps once in a while will the one pure and right thing, namely, God and himself for God. On the contrary, he can will this or that because he can will this one thing first and foremost. He thus makes use of his freedom of will only when in all things, even when he wills this or that, he wills this one thing. He neglects his ability, and denies and forfeits it, when, instead of the one thing, he wills only this and that. But the merely apparent freedom of his thus perverted will, and his energy in evil, bears witness in its very " involuntariness " to the way in which he comes to be able to will, though only apparently, impurely and wrongly. He can will, i.e., he can decide and resolve concerning his desiring, and he is an active person, as he is directly determined to and for God. That is, he can decide and resolve for his desire for God and against his godless desire. As he can do this, he can be man in the biblical sense. God appeals to this ability as He claims him for Himself, calling him and giving him His command and promise. God elects man in order that he may elect Him in return, and therefore on the presupposition that man is capable of this election, not only of desiring (*ḥamad, awah, baqash, araq*, and ἐπιθυμεῖν), but also of willing (*abah, ja'al, ḥapaz*, βούλεσθαι and θέλειν), in which he takes up a positive or negative position to his desiring, " pulling himself together." In this pulling of himself together, he is an active person and therefore a man. He makes decision about himself, as his will and so his election is or is not identical with the fear of God.

This enables us to understand finally the relation of desiring and willing on the one side and body and soul on the other. The biblical man determined for God is the whole man in his activity too. The Old and New Testament terms for man's activity to which we have referred are all closely akin and merge into one another, like those for his perception. Just because they directly or indirectly characterise all the active relation of man to God, his action within the history of the covenant of grace, there is no genuinely neutral zone within their compass.

The man whom God will have for Himself is of course the man who wills and therefore desires ; he is man active in the unity of desiring and willing. Hence the Decalogue speaks not only of stealing and adultery, but also with equal emphasis of the corresponding desire ; and we recall that it is precisely this aspect which is drawn out and emphasised in Jesus' Sermon on the Mount (Mt. 5[27f.]). Man in the whole of the Old Testament is so emphatically made accountable not only for his decisions and resolves, but also for the inclinations and tendencies that precede them, and in the whole Bible it is so emphatically maintained that God will have man for Himself in this sphere too, that it may well be asked whether the relation between soul and body is not reversed, the desiring being understood as the essential and psychical function of active man and willing as the merely incidental outward and physical function. There can be no doubt at least that biblical anthropology completely forbids any abstract understanding of desire as a mere outward and physical function. There can be no doubt that in this sphere, too, we have to do not only with the soul, but with a primacy of the soul. It is not for nothing that there is in the Old Testament a whole series of passages in which *nephesh* is designated as the subject of feeling and affection, joy and sorrow, longing and love, hatred and contempt, aversion and disgust, and yet not only of the animal impulses as one might suppose, but also of the true desire of man for God. In the language of the Bible I can never interpret the fact and object and manner of my desiring as a business of my in some sense independently self-stimulating and self-motivating bodily organs, but only as my very own business, in which I do not merely have a physical part but am myself the one who desires. Here I myself am engaged ; here my soul is revealed before God in its orientation, its nature or degeneration; here I say Yes or No to God ; here I am in one way or another answerable and responsible for the fact that I am this desiring being. That this is the case is exemplified by the fact that in the Bible bodily hunger and thirst as such are not trivialised but always taken seriously, and can thus be applied at once (and not merely as a picture) to the vital need of man for God. The bodily and the soulful together form a coherent sphere in which there is nothing of the body that is not also of the soul. On the biblical view, the body, even in respect of its desiring, has no life of its own apart from the soul It continually has the soul to thank for the fact that it is an organic and not a mere material body, for the functioning of its organs and for the fact that it can desire. That it desires can only mean that it puts into effect the desire of its soul, just as its awareness can only mean that it puts into effect the awareness of its soul. For this, of course, the soul needs a body. But it is the desiring of the soul which is put into effect by the body.

The primacy of the soul does not consist merely in the fact that man decides and resolves concerning his desires in a volitional act which is purely of the soul. For his soul, i.e., he himself, is the subject even of his desiring as this faces the decision of the will. The higher significance of volition as compared with desire is simply that in it the soul comes to a decision concerning itself, undertaking and executing a work corresponding to its tested desire. In this alone consists the differentiation between the element of soul and that of body in the active man. The active man is the man who exercises not only his desire but also his will. He needs soul and body to be able to desire and to will. And he needs both again to exercise his desire and his will. But he needs the body, because it is only as body, i.e., as something, that he can desire and therefore will or not will something else. He needs the body, because he can be induced to desire only in his bodily impulses, only as he lives in them, only through them, i.e., by their agency ; and because he cannot will without being accompanied by these bodily impulses and without using, controlling and guiding them. Again, he needs the soul because he is not merely something but himself, and because his desiring is not alien to him but his own, something that he practises in the fact that in the act of volition he decides and resolves with respect to it, affirming in the willing of a specific act an independence of his desires which is not based upon his body or its impulses, but has its own order for all its interconnexion with these impulses. We can sum up the whole matter in the concluding formula that man desires as the soul of his *body*, and wills as the *soul* of his body.

To summarise, we have asked concerning the inner differentiation of human creatureliness, and we have now seen both the fact and the nature of the distinction between soul and body, between the animating and the animated in man. They are distinguished in the particular way in which he is a percipient and an active being—a way which in the case of the animal is at least not manifest but hidden. The fact that man has Spirit, and that through the Spirit he is the soul of his body, means that he can perceive and be active in this special way. He is the percipient and active soul of the body which puts into effect his perception and action. We have not deduced this from an abstract consideration and assessment of man. We have not given it a basis in scientific or cultural studies, but in theology. The starting-point was that man stands before God, who is his Creator. We brought out the presuppositions which result in respect of his creatureliness. We asked concerning that which is thereby credited to man and expected from him. We tried to understand man's special nature in the light of the fact that at all events it had to be so constituted as to comprise within itself the ability corresponding to his special relationship to God. We then affirmed in general that human life, being wholly and at the same time both of soul and body, is a subjective life with subjective representations, subjective in so far as it is of soul, and with subjective representations in so far as it is of body. Man is capable of standing before God because he can live this kind of life. The rest was merely a development of this basic understanding. As the soul precedes the body, but can only precede and cannot exist as such without the body, so the body follows the soul, but can only follow and cannot exist as such without the soul. The two indissolubly connected moments of human creaturely reality consist in this preceding and following of these two moments. The one never is without the other. Since they are not interchangeable with one another, the one always preceding and the other following, we must accept a differentiation between soul and body, while never speaking of two distinct substances. We have found this to be substantiated in our analysis of the two concrete presuppositions of intercourse between God and man. That is to say, in relation both to human perception and human activity we have encountered a duality exactly corresponding to the dualism of body and soul. In man as he stands before God, we have had to distinguish sensing from thinking, and desiring from willing, in order to construct a complete view and conception of the fact that man is capable of standing before God. However it may be with animals, awareness and thought are different in man, and only when both combine in a single act does human perception take place. And however it may be with animals, desire and volition are different in man, and only when both combine in a single act does human activity take place. We must emphasise in both cases that it is only as they combine in a single act, for we cannot distinguish awareness and desire as an act of the body and thought and volition as an act of the soul. The biblical conception of man is there to warn us that we must also ascribe awareness and desire in their own way to the soul, and thought and volition in their own way to the body. The concrete differentiation is that they must be ascribed in their own distinctive ways which are not the same. The relationship cannot occasionally be reversed. On both sides of the duality we have come upon the primacy of the soul. At no level have we ever found it alone without the body. Nor could we restrict ourselves to the statement that the soul thinks and wills. We had to enlarge it and say that the soul also senses and desires. Only the soul can be meant when we speak of man as an independent subject. The human body cannot be meant, though man is always his body too. But even in the outward fulfilment of his perception and his activity, even in awareness and desire, he is the soul of his body. He expresses himself as such as he goes beyond the outward and thinks and wills, taking up a position in relation to his own awareness and desire, and treating them as his own business and activity. He is not capable of this as body, though for it he stands in need of his bodily life. He does not think without sensing, nor will without desiring. But when he thinks and wills, he stands at a distance from his sensing and desiring. He passes himself under review. He becomes an object to himself. In this freedom to stand at a distance, pass under review and become object, he conducts himself as soul of his body. The body lacks this freedom. It can only participate in it. In and by itself, it does not possess it. But the soul does. The soul is itself the freedom of man, not only to sense and desire, but in thinking and willing to be able to stand at a distance from himself and to live his life as his own. The body on its side is man in so far as it enjoys this primacy of his soul as a corporeal being, being not merely something but the something which is himself. For he could not be himself without this something ; he could not be a real person without this outward form and activity. His body is the organ through which his ability to perceive and do is exercised. It is the bearer and the representation of his thinking and willing. On both sides it is the openness of the soul without which it could not be free. This is its dignity, which in its own way is not less than that of the soul. That man is the soul of his *body* is the secondary fact which is no less indispensable to real man than the first, namely, that he is the *soul* of his body.

5. SOUL AND BODY IN THEIR ORDER

We could not complete the exposition of our third statement without reaching and indeed anticipating the final point which must now claim our specific attention. From the particularity in which man as soul of his body is a perceiving and active being there arises a particular relation between soul and body. From their inner differentiation there arises the inner order of human creatureliness. We cannot analyse the two great presuppositions constitutive of the relation of man to God on the side of man, i.e., that he is a percipient and an active being, without coming upon what we have called the primacy of the soul. In the last analysis we have found the distinction in unity between the two in the fact that the soul *precedes* in its perception, both as awareness and thought, and its activity, both as desire and volition, and that the body follows. But since this matter is decisive for the picture of man as soul and body, we must give it special consideration. We remember the decisive importance of this point, of the phenomenon of order, in the anthropology of Jesus with which we started in our first sub-section. But the formula of the primacy of the soul which is our starting-point can only suggest what we have now to affirm, namely, that the nature of man as soul and body is not an accidental conjunction, a mere juxtaposition, or a hostile *contretemps*, but an intelligibly ordered association of these two moments ; that it is not a chaos but a cosmos, in which there rules a Logos ; that there is control on the one side, i.e., that of the soul, and service on the other, i.e., that of the body. As this takes place man is fully man in the unity and differentiation of his soul and his body. As he is grounded, constituted and maintained by God as soul of his body, and thus receives and has the Spirit, there occurs the rule of the soul and the service of the body. And in this occurrence man is a rational being.

We use this term in a very comprehensive sense. The German word *Vernunft* has something inexact and misleading about it. By linguistic relationship and widespread usage it refers only to the ability to understand (*vernehmen*), which is only one among the many capacities of man. In addition, the term is often one-sidedly used to denote merely the human ability to think. As we use it here, we are giving it the comprehensive sense of the Latin *ratio* and the Greek λόγος. We understand by it a " meaningful order," so that when we say that man is a rational being, what we mean is that it is proper to his nature to be in rational order of the two moments of soul and body, and in this way to be a percipient and active being.

For all its ambiguity, we prefer the term " rational being " (*Vernunftwesen*) to a foreign or a coined word. But we always understand by it a rational or logical being in the true and comprehensive and not a restricted sense of *ratio* and λόγος.

We thus understand man as a rational being with regard not only to his soul but also to his body. For in virtue of his soul, his body also has a full participation in his rationality. It is ruled by the soul and serves the soul. Therefore it, too, is not non-rational but rational, in so far as it finds itself together with the soul in and under that meaningful order. For in its relation to the soul, *ratio* or λόγος is no less proper to it than to the soul, and dwells no less in it. That man is a rational being we also understand as an event, in accordance with the fact that the presupposition of the whole, namely, that he receives and has Spirit, is also an event, a divine action. We speak of a ruling and of a serving, and therefore of an act in which the whole is engaged. We speak of the real man whose existence is his own act and whose being can therefore be revealed and understood only in this act of his. Man lives as man in a meaningful order. He recognises it and subjects himself to it. He himself establishes and observes it. He is man as it is valid ; and he makes use of its validity in human perception and activity. As this happens, i.e., as he himself brings it about, he is a rational being.

At this point we must again remember and maintain that we have no information whether animals are or are not also rational beings in the sense described. We have information about man only as we look at this event and are engaged in it, in the act of human existence, in the fulfilment of that rule and service, in living under and in that meaningful order. If we could and had to observe man too only from outside, it could and would have to be a mere hypothesis for us that man is a rational being. The very thing that we cannot know about animals is whether there is something like that rule and service in their existence. We can know this only as we do it, as we are ourselves engaged in the event, and can thus recognise it in other beings, as is possible and necessary between man and man but not between man and animals. The evidence for this cannot be used for both man *and* animals, nor of course for man *against* animals. It can be used only without reference to animals for man, and for man only as he conducts himself as a rational being. If he does not do so or tries not to do so—and we think sorrowfully of the great number engaged in this attempt—and if he then tries theoretically to contract out of the fact that he always acts as a rational being, attempting to regard himself and his fellow-men from outside as we can only regard animals, then he need not be surprised to discover that the evidence for his rational nature does not apply in his case either. All possible doubts about man's rational nature, and all false or partly false theories about the relation of soul and body, have their basis here. To a terrifying extent man can attempt in practice to act otherwise than as a rational being, and he can then attempt in theory to observe himself and his fellow-men from outside and not first and foremost from inside, in the fact that he and unmistakeably his fellows, as men, act as rational beings. This theoretical attempt is foolish, and far from commendable for all its apparent objectivity and freedom from presuppositions. For in this ostensible objectivity we lose sight of the object which we are supposed to know and discuss, namely, the real man, who even in this observation of himself from outside acts as a rational being. And the ostensible freedom from presupposition involves the very worst presupposition that is possible in this matter, namely, to think it possible the more concretely to see and understand man the more we abstract from the fact that we are ourselves what we wish to see and understand. As man acts as a rational being— and he does so in some measure as he senses and thinks, desires and wills, in contradiction of all practical attempts not to do so and all theoretical attempts to persuade himself that he does not do so—he gives proof of the fact that, however it may be with animals, he is a rational being. He gives it not only by approximating to the ideal of a rational being, to a perfection of that ruling and serving, but also by moving away from or falling far short of it. He gives it even in his omissions and mistakes. He gives it even by caricaturing himself. He gives it even when he appears to exist as a complete denial of his rational nature. Strictly speaking, he never gives it except in a negative form, in the form of all kinds of deficiency phenomena, some

worse, some not so bad, some almost tolerable. Yet he gives it none
the less factually and evidently, whereas we cannot say whether
animals, unknown to us, give it or not. That is to say, man always
exists as the soul of his body, whereas we do not know whether an
animal is also the soul of its body or merely the vegetative body of
its soul. Whether he considers or respects it or experiences it or not,
man is always first of all himself : this subject, who thus or thus rules,
determines, stamps and guides himself and with himself his body ;
who as this person thinks and wills in his willing, pulling himself
together, deciding and resolving who he is and then and on this basis
what he is bodily in the service of himself and his soul, as that which,
used and fashioned by himself and therefore by his soul, represents
himself and his soul. As we ourselves exist, and exist with other
men, we do in fact continually exemplify this distinction and reckon
with this order, superordination and subordination. In fact, the soul
rules and the body serves with whatever incompleteness or confusion.
We see ourselves and other men actually engaged in a relation concerning which we have in the case of animals no information—not of
course the negative information that this relation does not hold good for
them too, but no information at all. But in the case of men, ourselves,
we have this information. We supply it ourselves as we exist as men.

It is to be observed, however, that this information is certain and
convincing, and the proof that man is a rational being is final and
conclusive, only when it is given theologically. We may seriously
ask : Who or what compels man to make this recognition of his own
rational nature, and therefore of the order in which soul and body
stand, however infinitely near it may seem to be ? Who or what
compels him to take himself and his fellow-men really seriously in the
action of their existence, however integrated they may in fact be in
this act ? Who or what compels him really to abstain from that
observation of man from without, in which his own rational nature
must appear as dubious to him as that of an animal ? Who or what
compels him instead resolutely and finally to acknowledge what can
and apparently must be recognised by him as that order, rationality
or logicality of his existence ? Who or what forbids him occasional
vacillation between these two modes of observation as though one
were as possible as the other, or even perhaps the acceptance and
assertion of ambivalence between an inner and an outer picture of
human existence ? Who or what commands him to regard the inner
picture as the truth and the outer resolutely and finally as error ?
We can hardly overlook the fact that it is of some importance for the
cause of humanity whether this last question must be left open, the
only final answer being a " Perhaps, perhaps not," or whether there
is a compulsion, a prohibition and a command binding us to a recognition plausible in itself. No man, and humanity even less, lives as
if it were self-evident to make this recognition, or as if the proof of

our rational nature which we continually give by the mere fact that we are men were sufficient of itself. On the contrary, real human existence, both individually and as a whole, develops in such a way that the proof is obviously given, yet also in such a way that the proof seems not to be taken with final seriousness but is constantly given in vain. The cause of humanity is in fact constantly threatened, and most severely threatened, by the fact that a true compulsion to decide for the inner picture and therefore for the truth, and against the outer picture as a pernicious error, that a strict prohibition and command, does not seem by a long way to be recognised by us. Is there such a decisive prohibition and command? This is the question to which even the most well-meaning non-theological anthropology can give no answer. In the last resort it is simply referred to man himself, and its demonstration of the demonstration will finally consist only in the call and summons that man, to be man, should value and respect the obvious fact of his rational nature and therefore of that order, that in his being and conduct he should take account of this nature of his and therefore of the law of his better self. This imperative, the recognition and observance of which would actually serve the cause of humanity, can obviously be formulated very categorically. But it cannot really become or be categorical, since to the category of the imperative there belong not only a command but supremely one who commands and who has the competence and authority, the will and the voice, to do so. Where the last word in face of that open question can only be the pious wish that man should command himself, taking himself seriously as the rational being as which he acts, we cannot truly speak of a categorical imperative. How is man to be able to ascribe to himself, i.e., to the inner picture of his false existence, the absolute significance which he must have for himself in order to be able to command himself categorically? He must be categorically commanded categorically to command himself if he is to have this ability. To answer that final question, theological anthropology is needed, for this alone knows of a decisive prohibition and command, and of One who commands with competence and authority, at the point where the only other alternative to that interchange and ambivalence of the two ways of consideration is the pious wish that man himself should attempt that command and prohibition, himself making the decision for truth and against error. If we are interested in the statement that in the sense expounded man is a rational being, it is as a theological statement, i.e., in the form in which it is guaranteed in face of that final question, and in which alone it is ultimately well founded.

Man is a rational being because he is addressed as such by God, and because—we must again draw the same conclusion as we have worked with hitherto—it is thus presupposed that he was created as such by God.

The imperative which commands us always to understand and conduct ourselves as rational beings is thus categorical. But it is categorical not in so far as it is the imperative which man imposes on himself, but so far as it is the imperative which God imposes on him. Imposed by man on himself, it would not be really categorical. But it is this as it is imposed on man by God. Thus imposed by the Creator on His creature, it is not a kind of question to which different answers could be given and which could be finally evaded. It is rather the affirmation concerning his being or non-being. For as the imperative of the Creator to His creature, it does not only command, but in so doing contains and reveals a knowledge of the being of the one whom it commands, the one being beside which he has no other. In this one being of his, the Creator claims the creature. If the creature perceives this claim, it has no choice between life and death with respect to the way in which it must understand and conduct itself. What it is in reality lies before it clearly and plainly, unmistakeably and incontestably. And what it is not, what it is only in its own illusion, flees before it like mist before the sun. There thus remains only one truth about man. There is no second truth beside it. Beside it there is only falsehood. Man has thus to choose between truth and falsehood in his knowledge, and between being and non-being in his conduct. The neutrality in which he thinks he can now take himself seriously and now not as a rational creature, being right in both cases and living under both signs, is quite impossible for him when he is claimed by God. The only choice which now remains for him is to take and conduct himself seriously as a rational being, or to fall into complete error in relation both to God and to himself, electing to defy the revelation and will of God and therefore choosing his own nothingness. It can only be the choice between life and death. Since theological anthropology understands man simply from the standpoint that he is called and claimed by God, the possibility of understanding him as a rational being attains the character of an absolutely decisive necessity.

Theological anthropology cannot go behind this necessity because without this recognition it cannot even begin to consider man at all. The proof of his rational nature which man gives by the fact that he exists as a rational being is convincing for it, and all doubt concerning it on the basis of a purely outer consideration of man is dismissed, not because it thinks that man himself can make this decision in virtue and in the light of his own existence, nor because it ascribes an absolute significance to the inner picture in which he distinguishes himself as man from the animal, but because, behind and above the factual existence of man, and behind and above this inner picture, it sees the competence and authority of the commanding person of God the Creator, by whose claim on man the whole question is answered as it is raised. On this basis the command that man take himself seriously in his factual existence becomes a categorical command. On this basis there is a strict prohibition and command. On this basis an irrevocable decision is taken at the absolutely decisive point. For on this basis the internal proof for man's rational nature is *a priori* strong, and the external questioning of this knowledge *a priori* weak. On this basis the pious wishes, which are the last word of even the best non-theological anthropology, that man would be so good as to adhere to that external proof, are superfluous. On this basis the cause of humanity, which depends on the fact that there is here no open question, is *a priori* secured. On this basis there is a barrier to the otherwise unavoidable vacillation between the inner picture and the outer, between humanity and inhumanity.

As God addresses man, he treats him as a being who can rule himself and serve himself. He thus treats him as a rational being. And it is thus evident that he was created a rational being. We shall develop what is to be said about man as rational being under three heads.

1. If man understands himself in his relation to God as ordained not by himself but by God, he cannot in any sense understand himself as purely soul or as purely thinking and willing subject. As he is created by and for God, the fact that he receives and has Spirit, and is thus a being which lives spiritually, a spiritual soul, is a specific activity in a specific sphere. He is not simply soul. Soul is life. Its thinking and willing (together with its sensing and desiring) is simply the human act of living. The sphere, or at least the proximate and specifically allotted sphere of this act of living, in which it always takes place and to which it always refers, is the body of this soul. It is indeed active in general. Its thinking and willing has an object, and can thus become actual as well as purely potential. For it there can be another, God first and then the world. But all this is dependent on the fact that it is not bodiless but the soul of its body. It is this, however, as it is first active in this sphere in a specific manner—a ruling manner. It is in this way, as one who rules himself, that we find man addressed by God and claimed by Him. Before God, he is not an improper but a proper, i.e., a free subject. He is identical with his body, in so far as he is its soul. He thinks and wills and therefore fulfils the human act of living ; and in so doing he treats his sphere, i.e., his body, as his own domain, and controls and uses it, striding ahead of it in precedence. And because in this he is still identical with his body, it may be said that in his relation to his body he goes ahead of himself, preceding himself, giving himself guidance and direction as his own lord and ruler. His soul is his freedom over his body and therefore over himself. As he acts in this freedom, as in thinking and willing he is his own lord and director, he is spiritual soul. For in order to be active in this way, he is given Spirit by God and through the Spirit he is awakened to be a living being. In this

activity, in a specific thinking and willing and so in the specific act
of his living, he is undoubtedly summoned and claimed by the Spirit
of God, as God has dealings with him. He lives as man so long and
so far as he is not only capable of such activity but actually engages
in it. Death, in which the soul is alienated from the body and the
body from the soul, is the end of such activity. Death puts an end
to his freedom, to the lordship of his soul over the body and therefore
to its direction, so that further life-acts are made impossible. Unless,
therefore, there is deliverance from death, it is simply the end of man.
Man is the ruling soul of his body, or he is not man. We know no
being which we must address and can designate as man, to whom
must be denied this ruling soul, For we know no man to whom,
since God calls and claims man, it is not to be ascribed. This is the
first thing which we have to say theologically concerning man as a
rational being.

2. If man understands himself in his relation to God as established
and ordained by God, he can in no case understand himself merely as
body, merely as a sensing and desiring subject. That he receives and
has Spirit distinguishes him *a priori* from a purely material body. It
is what makes him an organic body, which means of course a soulful
body. Even the fact that he is an organic body signifies a specific
activity in a specific sphere. He is not simply body, but that which
is animated and lives by soul. His sensing and desiring (along with
his thinking and willing) is again nothing but the human life-act. Its
sphere—here we must say its sole sphere, the sphere in which alone
the human life-act can take place on its bodily side—is the soul whose
body it is. It is not without the sensing and desiring of the body,
yet not as body but as soul, that man has a sphere wider than himself, and that there is for him another, God and the world. Since the
body is body in and through the soul, receiving its determination
from the soul, we may say that man is identical with it. Man is also
through and through body. This is revealed in the fact that he is
wholly addressed and claimed by God as one who has to serve himself. How could he be a genuine free subject if he could not at the
same time be a genuine obedient object ? This ability—one may and
must describe it as a freedom—is the bodily moment of his being. As
he senses and desires, it is also true that he serves himself in ruling
himself. The same sphere which from the standpoint of the soul is
the domain in which man must rule, is from the standpoint of the
body the domain in which he may be subject to himself and serve.
As body he does not dispose of himself, but stands at his own disposal ; he does not use himself, but is used by himself. As body he
does not go beyond himself, for it is not as body but as soul that he
is immediate to the Spirit and therefore to God. As body, then, he
cannot precede himself, but only follow. He is spiritual soul. That
he is also spiritual body is not apparent to him, and we cannot speak

of it if we speak of his natural condition, since it will be the gift of grace of future revelation. What is now apparent to us is that he is soulful body and therefore limited and determined by the soul, the body of his soul. The body, the whole man, has his value even according to the bodily moment of his being in the fact that he is active as soul of his body. Certainly as God has dealings with him he is called by God's Spirit to this serving activity which is indirect in relation to the Spirit. Certainly he is called to the sensing and desiring of the soul. Man lives, so long and so far as he is bodily capable of such activity and engaged in it. Death, which makes an end of the soul as the life of the body, is also the end of what is animated and alive through it, and therefore of the body. Where there is no more ruling, there is no more serving; and on this side too—unless there is deliverance from death—we are confronted with the end of man. He is the serving body of his soul, or he is not man. For we know no man who is not called and claimed by God in his totality, and therefore in this moment too. This is the second thing which we have to say theologically concerning man as a rational being.

3. If man understands himself in his relation to God as established and ordained by God, in relation to soul and body as the two moments of his being he can in no case understand himself as a dual but only as a single subject, as soul identical with his body and as body identical with his soul. Soul and body are not two factors which merely co-exist, accompany, supplement, sympathise and co-operate with one another, but whose intentions, achievements and sufferings have different origins, ends and meanings. The one man is the soul of his body and therefore both soul and body. In the relation thus determined, in the order, rationality and logicality which obtains at this point, the one man is just as much soul from head to foot as he is body from the most primitive acts of sensing and desiring to the sublimest and most complicated acts of thinking and willing. He and he alone is subject in both the moments of his being. He rules himself, and again he serves himself. He is free to dispose of himself, and he is also free in standing at his disposal. It is he who thinks and wills, but he too who senses and desires. He always does the one as he does the other. As soul of his body, he is neither in a foreign land, nor in a prison, nor even in a vessel, but wholly in his own house and wholly himself. Again, as body of his soul, he is not merely external; he does not cling to it accidentally; he is not merely its accompanist. Again, he has in it that which is his own, and is in it himself. Man does not exist except in his life-act, and this consists in the fact that he animates himself and is therefore soul, and is animated by himself and is therefore body. His life-act consists in this circular movement, and at every point in it he himself is not only soul or body, but soul and body. He is indeed the one for and by the

soul. For example, physical pain is not merely a conceivable but a verifiable consequence of psychical defects, and psychical treatment can be used to cure it. In place of mere parallelism we have to set the notion of a widespread correspondence which may very well be represented in the form of a kind of transformation of energy on the frontiers of the two spheres. From our standpoint, we welcome the attempt obviously made here to speak of an activity of soul and body proceeding not in a puzzling duality alongside one another, but in a certain unity of thrust and counterthrust. But unfortunately, to obtain this, the theory is forced to withdraw or let go of the insight concerning the identity of the human subject which the theory of parallelism maintained at least in the form of its assertion of an X. For now the differentiation and even disparateness of the two series or sides is more sharply emphasised than before, as when it is sometimes said that the plan for the two series in their unity embraces two polar opposites. The purely philosophical objection concerns the nature of this unity and the way in which anything like intercommunication can really be possible and actual in these circumstances. But that is not our business. We have to ask : Who or what operates from one side or the other ? Where is real man in this play of thrust and counterthrust ? Is he on the one side or the other ? Is there a decision on this ? Or is he on both sides ? And if so, how is he the subject of such a criss-cross and competitive activity ? And if no answer is to be given to these questions, what is really meant by intercommunication ? Or does man stand somewhere in the middle between the two interacting series ? And if so, how is he related to their operation ? The theory of intercommunication obviously does not lead us beyond the fatal co-existence of two human activities, an idea behind which there stands concealed the old doctrine of two independent and exclusive substances of soul and body.

Nor is it easy to see what advance is made if we follow the latest attempt (welcomed on the theological side, for example, by A. Titius) to mediate between the theories of parallelism and interaction by combining the idea of two no less homogeneous than heterogeneous activities beginning simultaneously and following a common course, with the idea of a mutual contact and influence between both. Can they really be combined ? Not unjustly, it has been maintained in face of this attempt that we must choose between parallelism and interaction, since the idea of parallelism excludes that of interaction and if the latter is emphasised there is no place for the former. But this must be settled between the advocates of the attempt and their critics. Our question simply concerns the simple human subject ; and this question cannot in any case be answered by this attempt.

We cannot participate in the solving of the riddle which seems to burden and engage the participants in this discussion. In face of the whole discussion we can only declare our fundamental objection that the soul and the body of the man of whom they speak are the soul and body of a ghost and not of real man. To dispute concerning these and to throw light on their co-existence and relationship is necessarily a waste of time and effort. We can only oppose to all these theories that the soul and body of real man are not two real series or sides existing and observable in isolation. They are the two moments of the one human activity, which as such do not merely accompany each other and cannot influence and condition one another as though there were on both sides an active and passive something. We do not have the body here and the soul there, but man himself as soul of his body is subject and object, active and passive—man in the life-act of ruling and serving, as the rational being as which he stands before God and is real as he receives and has the Spirit and is thus grounded, constituted and maintained by God.

To say this is to bring out again the theological presuppositions of the anthropology here presented. Non-theological anthropology lacks this presupposition. In the last resort, there is something tragic in every non-theological anthropology. This finds expression in the fact that such ghostly pictures of the relationship between soul and body are proposed in these theories. It is to be noted that the advocates of the theories just mentioned are distinguished from others by the fact that they profess to be aware of the one-sidedness of both materialistic and spiritualistic views and that they make a real effort to consider and to take seriously both sides of man, doing equal justice to both the physical and psychical series and to their interconnexion. Yet they can only offer parallelism or interaction. They can only present the two accompanying or corresponding forms of real soul and real body, of which we can never know for certain which is merely the shadow of the other. They can only have reference to an X in which the two may be one and the same and therefore real man. They can give no decisive and final information whether man is or is not a rational being. And on that basis, we can think of no better counsel. Inevitably this is how things work out even in the best non-theological anthropology. Where the question of the confrontation of the human creature by his Creator is handled as a *cura posterior*, from whose consideration we must look away in favour of a prefabricated conception of science, there is no need to understand man from the standpoint of Spirit, and therefore as ruling soul of his serving body, and therefore as rational being. The categorical imperative laid upon the investigator to see man *a priori* in this unity drops away, and it cannot be replaced by corresponding pious wishes.

In these circumstances, if we avoid the one-sidedness of materialism and spiritualism, we are left with two things, with soul and body as two series which are real in themselves and finally as two parts which we exert ourselves in vain to reassemble when we think we have taken them apart and considered them separately. From the world of the purely psychical—if there is such a thing, or if such a thing is fancied—there is no bridge to the world of the really physical. If we think that we can see one, we shall finally end up in spiritualism, for which the body is only an appearance and no reality. Conversely, from the world of the purely physical—if there is such a thing, or if we are convinced that it is real and can be considered as such—there is no bridge to the shore of a world of the really psychical. Once we are rashly compromised on this point, we shall logically end up in some form of materialism, for which the mind is only an appearance and no reality. But the advocates of the doctrines of parallelism and interaction do not improve matters by accepting the false assumptions of both those conceptions. They are more far-seeing than the spiritualists and the materialists in their desire to do justice to the twofold aspect of human reality as this is actually given, but they are less far-seeing in their refusal to see that we cannot divide the one human reality into two and then hope to put it together again. They have the same blind spot as spiritualists and materialists, for they do not think that they can begin with an unshakeable conception of the rational nature of the whole man as soul and body, but think it necessary to take as their axiom and starting-point the fact that the rational nature of man is an open question and that its reality has still to be established. But in this question the end must inexorably correspond to the beginning and the result of the investigation to its starting-point. From the supposed reality of the soul we inevitably finish up with the soul as the only reality, and from that of the body with the body as the only reality. And if we begin more critically but less logically somewhere in the middle with the problem of both realities, we can only finish up in face of the same problem. Thus it seems as though we could and really should begin at quite another point—with the obvious reality of the rational being of man himself, with the capacity with which we actually find ourselves possessed as ruling soul and serving body when we raise the question concerning man and therefore concerning ourselves, with the life-act as such in which we are finally engaged even as we undertake and carry through this investigation. Are we soul only in this act ? or body only ? or only two parallel series accompanying or corresponding to each other ? Can we speak of two worlds, one of which calls the reality of the other in question ? Must not our first enquiry be for a bridge from the one to the other ? Are we not equally present to ourselves as soul and body ? Are we anything but the psycho-physical rational being of man which as a unit, though in irreversible superordination and subordination, senses and thinks, desires and wills, is subject and object, active and passive ? It is here that we should begin. It is to this object that we should apply anthropological analysis. Obviously an analysis of this object will necessarily lead us back to the corresponding synthesis, the end again corresponding to the beginning. Why should we not accept this object ? Are we prevented by the scientific requirement that we put this object out of mind in order first to consider the external aspect in which soul and body each appear to form a world of their own ? So it is said. But can it be good science in which we arbitrarily force ourselves to begin with an aspect which even as we select it we must necessarily regard and describe as a mere appearance in relation to the rational nature which we still exercise in our selection ? Who are we to make this outer aspect with its obviously phenomenal character the measure of all things ? Should we not rather relate the obviously incontestable data of this outer aspect—everything which an external consideration of our psychical or physical existence has to teach us—to the reality of our rational existence as such ? Should we not rather explain the data from the latter instead of giving ourselves the fruitless trouble of trying to deduce the latter from the data and thus to erect the one real world out of two obviously phenomenal worlds ? What is there really to prevent us, as real men, from trying to investigate real man as such ?

But we will not labour the point. For it is obvious that non-theological anthropology is not wholly arbitrary in its constant decision not to begin with real man but with one or other outer aspect, nor in its consequent ending up with spectres instead of returning to real man. If we disregard man's relation to God, there is no obligation to accept what is to us the obvious object of anthropological investigation, nor is there the boldness always to begin where the investigator finds himself, namely, in the middle of his life-act as rational being and man, in the middle of the reality of the ruling soul and the serving body. If man will not understand himself as through and through the being confronted by God, it is only natural that he should suspect and question himself as rational being. And the inevitable result is that the outer aspect of the two series in which he appears to exist gains power and might over him. That is, it then presents itself to him as the aspect which, even if only in phenomenal form, contains the mystery of human reality. To get behind the appearance, to get behind this aspect, then seems to be the only possible scientific task, and the only question is then whether we shall decide for a materialistic or spiritualistic solution, or for one of the proposed compromises. If we are not permitted or obliged to take with absolute seriousness the inner aspect in which man actually finds himself as psycho-physical rational being, we have no freedom to begin at this point and to use the data of the outer aspect as contributions to an anthropology proposed from this standpoint instead of making them something for which they are not fitted, namely, an anthropological basis. We then necessarily lose ourselves to that outer aspect. Yet we cannot stand under this obligation or have this freedom if we will not come to terms with the theological presupposition that in his confrontation with God man is claimed as rational being and imperiously commanded to take himself with absolute seriousness as such. In these circumstances we cannot begin at this other place. We may thus agree that apart from this presupposition the only advice we can give is to decide for one of the remaining ways or evasions. But since we ourselves make this theological presupposition, we regard ourselves as absolved from the task of judging which of these ways or evasions is relatively least unsatisfactory.

The phenomena to which those theories refer in detail cannot of course be overlooked or denied. There are undoubtedly correspondences and connexions, agreements and relationships between psychical and physical conditions of sufficiency or lack, health or sickness, strength or weakness, soundness or degeneration, between psychical and physical actions and passions, conditions and experiences, achievements and omissions.   They form a whole field of undeniably genuine human living reality.   It is the business of non-theological science, of psychology, physiology and biology, to establish and evaluate these facts.   From the standpoint of theological anthropology, we have least reason of all to wish that the facts were otherwise, or to want to shut our eyes to them.   On the contrary, we are tempted to suppose that this field is even greater than is now accepted, and that it will be seen to be much more extensive than is the case to-day.   Our own expectation is that in much greater measure and with much greater strictness it will be perceived that the whole of human life both in particular and in general is governed by these correspondences and connexions, and that in no ostensibly psychical phenomenon do we have to do only with the soul, and in no ostensibly physical phenomenon only with the body, but always and at every point with both soul and body.   Whether regarded from this side or from that, only the whole man is the real man.   Lévy-Brühl has reduced the picture of man in what is called " primitive " religion and the " primitive " outlook to the formula that in it nothing is represented as wholly material and nothing as purely spiritual.   If this is correct, we can say that the " primitives " have maintained or anticipated the view which is lost to " higher " religions and outlooks with their different abstractions, but which may be one day taken for granted again when these phenomena are better and more fully understood and have passed into the general consciousness.   We do not really question the data of the outer aspect of human reality, but we regret that they are not seen together in a very different way and applied as contributions to an anthropology based on the inner aspect of this reality.   Thus we do not dissociate ourselves from the facts brought to light by modern science, but only from the one-sided and the mediating interpretations which it has hitherto given them.   Our opinion is that these very facts are susceptible and worthy of a better interpretation.   Our formula that man is the ruling soul of his serving body has admittedly and consciously a theological basis, and can have no other.   But in our view it does better justice to the facts.   It turns attention from the first upon the whole man, and upon this man in his activity, in the life-act in which he is always soul and body, but each in its proper way.   And each in its proper way does not mean each for itself, but always the one in the appropriate relation to the other.   Nor does this relation consist in a mere reciprocal association of two partners unrelated in themselves.   The human existence of the one man is that he stands in this relation, and that he is the soul of his body and then also the body of his soul.   Nor does this relation and therefore human existence consist merely in a mutual acting and suffering of these two partners.   It is the one man who in this relation is both the doer and the sufferer.

Our interpretation of those phenomena, formulated as briefly as possible in four propositions, would be as follows.

1. The soul does not act on the body, but the one man acts.   And he does it in that as soul he animates himself and is acting subject, but always as soul is soul of his body, animated by himself, determined and enabled to act, and engaged in action.

2. Again, the soul does not suffer from the body, but the one man suffers. And this takes place in that as soul (namely, as acting subject) he is fundamentally exposed and susceptible to such hindrances and injuries, but as soul of his body must actually experience them.

3. Again, the body does not act on the soul, but the one man acts.   He acts in that as body he is animated by himself, determined and enabled to act, and engaged in action, but as body of his soul, animating himself and acting subject.

4. And again, the body does not suffer from the soul, but the one man suffers.   When this takes place, it means that as body he really experiences

such hindrances and injuries, but that as body of his soul he must really make them his own.

The one whole man is thus one who both acts through himself and suffers in himself, but always in such a way that he is first soul (ruling, in the subject) and then body (serving, in the object)—always in this inner order, rationality and logicality of his whole nature. This is the interpretation of those phenomena which from the standpoint of our presupposition we must oppose to the doctrines of both spiritualism and materialism, of both the parallelism and the interaction between psychical and physical reality, and which we in any case regard as in closer correspondence to the facts to which these theories relate. It would naturally be the business of an extensive psychological, physiological and biological science, on the recognition of the basic viewpoints indicated, to procure for itself a freedom which it has to-day only to the extent that in spite of its enslavement to those theories it engages in the investigation and presentation of the facts as such.

It is again the biblical view of man which has been our guide and which we must now consider in detail. We remember that we shall search the Old and New Testaments in vain for a true anthropology and therefore for a theory of the relation between soul and body. The biblical texts regard and describe man in the full exercise of his intercourse with God. Their authors have neither the time nor the interest to occupy themselves with man as such, nor to give to themselves or their readers a theoretical account of what is to be understood by the being of man. We have thus to be content with purely incidental and self-evident presuppositions if we seek information from them on this question, and we must not be surprised if this information seem to us to be unsystematic, defective, partial and even contradictory. The fact is that the biblical authors knew very well what they were talking about when they spoke about man, that there was substantial unanimity among them and that everywhere in their statements we have a much more fundamental and truly systematic treatment than appears at first sight.

We may begin with a general historical characterisation. With respect to the relationship between soul and body, their representation of man is on the whole that of primitive man. This representation knows the double-sidedness of the being of man. It knows what we have called the two moments of the human life-act. It reckons with both. But it knows of no division between them. It knows of no bodiless soul and soulless body. It knows only of the one whole man seen from both sides. It thus parts from the Greek picture of man, and therefore from that which was normative for so long in the Christian Church and theology, and which, basically uncontested, has formed the presupposition of modern discussion concerning soul and body. In classing the biblical picture of man with that of primitive man, we cannot see any reflection on its value. From our whole consideration of the matter, it appears that the supposed " primitives " are in this matter more sophisticated than the sophisticated whose approach has so successfully superseded their own in the civilised west and cultures influenced by it. It is no discredit to the Bible but a point in favour of the so-called primitives that the biblical presuppositions concerning soul and body are in considerable material agreement with theirs. The practical result of such a comparison can only be that, if we look away from the Bible, we have more to learn from the so-called primitives in this matter than in the school of Plato and all his followers.

Of course, the biblical picture of man is marked off from that of the primitives by a distinctive quality which is not easily defined but must always be noted. It is of a piece with the basis proper to the general outlook of the Bible. It sees and knows man decisively, and in the last resort exclusively, in his relation to God, to the God of Israel who is absolutely gracious towards man but also makes an absolute claim upon him, not in any kind of neutral activity, constitution or capacity. It sees and knows him in the responsibility which this imposes on him. It understands what he is from the fact that he has the Spirit. In conformity with this, its view of the inner order of his constitution, of the rule of the soul and the service of the body, has a precision in its representation which it cannot have where this presupposition is not accepted. It has a fundamental precision at this point, even where it is not specially emphasised. But this means that the view of the active unity of soul and body is here fundamentally secured. The same cannot be said of the picture of man of the so-called primitives. From the latter it was and is basically possible to slide over into a picture of man like that of the Greeks with its divisions, because the order of soul and body, though perceived by them, is not fundamentally secured. In passing over from the biblical to the Greek picture of man, there occurs not merely a deviating transition, but a fundamental misunderstanding and a lapse from truth into error. This means in practice that in order to win back the true picture of man we must let ourselves be taught not by the primitive but solely by the biblical picture, and ultimately regard the former only as a confirmation and illumination of the latter.

In accordance with what was earlier said about *ruaḥ πνεῦμα* and *nephesh ψυχή*, the basic outline of biblical anthropology to which we must refer again in this final connexion is as follows.

It is obvious that the Bible treats the body and the bodily organs of man not only as the locus but as the object of his capability and activity as soul. As body, he has no proper persistence or significance. That he lives and moves, experiences good and ill, is healthy and sick, and in the end dies, is not at all an affair of his as mere body. Rather in all these things there acts and suffers the human subject, and therefore the soul of man, with his experience, his thinking and willing, his rejoicing and setbacks, his wants, desires and possessions, and in his temporal limitation. When it is seen on this side one might be inclined to call biblical anthropology far too spiritualistic. Is not its only interest in the body the fact that in its totality it is a besouled body?

But the matter must also be seen and described from the opposite side. It is just as obvious that the Bible regards the body as the locus, even the subject, of man's capability and activity as soul. Where is there here a persistence and significance of the soul? That it wants, desires and possesses, grieves and rejoices, is on the right or wrong way, lives and dies, even that it is before and with God, is not its own affair. It is rather the affair of the body and its organs in and through which all this takes place. When it is seen on this side, could not biblical anthropology be claimed with equal right to be far too materialistic? Is not its only interest in the soul the fact that in its totality it is the life of the body?

Both these extremes have to be held in view if we are to see clearly at this point. We have to realise that it can only be a matter of these two extremes. At a pinch biblical anthropology can be called both spiritualistic and materialistic. On the other hand, we look in vain here for any trace of the theories of parallelism and interaction. In reality, of course, the Bible does not think either spiritualistically or materialistically. In contrast to both, and in contrast to all theories deduced from Greek presuppositions, its conception has been called " realistic." This may be allowed, if we give it a systematic name, and if real man must be regarded as a *res*. On the other hand, we must be clear that in making this connexion we still move fundamentally within the schema of Greek thought to the extent that in some measure of actuality and significance, even though repudiated by the realists, a *res* of man always seems to be confronted by an *idea* or *nomen*. The Bible does not think in terms of this opposition. The real man who would have to be a *res* on this view is not a *res* but the human person self-animating and self-animated in the act of existing under the determination of the Spirit. The Bible has to do with this person. Hence its statements concerning man are to be understood as both spiritualistic and materialistic, but as either they can only be misunderstood, since they are concerned with neither the soul nor the body in themselves, but always with man, and with him as the soul of his body. If we want to give a very suitable name to this biblical conception, our best plan is simply to call it "anthropology," and not to attempt any systematic addition.

We shall now present this basic outline in the form of a brief glance at the way in which the Bible actually describes the activity of the body and its organs wholly as that of its soul, or conversely, and in the same terms, the activity of its soul wholly as that of its body.

We may begin with the most striking passages. According to Ps. 84[2], it is the flesh that cries out for the living God, and according to Ps. 63[1] it is again the flesh that longs for Him in a dry and thirsty land without water. In passages like Eccles. 4[5] "flesh" can also designate the human person. According to Ps. 6[2], man's bones can be vexed, and according to Isa. 58[11] they can be strengthened by God. According to Ps. 32[3], they wax old when a man keeps silent about his guilt before God, and according to Ps. 51[8] they rejoice when God satisfies him with joy and gladness. When the prophet sees the destruction of his people drawing near, his bowels are pained, according to Jer. 4[19]. Job (30[27]) complains that his bowels boil without rest within him, and we read in Lam. 1[20]; 2[11] that they are troubled. The word "bowels" appears in passages like Gen. 43[14] as equivalent to compassion, a usage which is continued in the New Testament employment of σπλάγχνα and σπλαγχνίζεσθαι. When the reference is to the innermost element of man, which others cannot fathom but which is open to God, the Bible speaks of reins, e.g., in Jer. 11[20], Ps. 7[9] and Prov. 23[16]. As the seat of life which can be mortally wounded, Prov. 7[23] can also speak of the liver. In all these equations of soul and body, it is futile to ask whether the emphasis is such as to describe the bodily quality of the soul or the soulful quality of the body. Nor is it much help to seek important material nuances behind the different terms. They all have much the same significance. It is always in some way the whole man who is revealed by the fact that reference is made to his body, but as a besouled body, or to his soul, as a bodily soul. To be sure, the language is poetic; but it is not purely figurative. To see mere figures, the bodily as a mere expression of the soul and therefore what is said about the bodily as mere description of what are properly processes of the soul, is to interpret the statements on the basis of a very different understanding of man from that presented in the texts, and therefore to misunderstand them. They must be taken seriously in what is always the double sense of the verbal expression, or they cannot be understood at all.

More frequent, comprehensive and emphatic than all these other terms is the heart. The Bible speaks of the heart when it wants to speak particularly impressively of the active and suffering man. The passages are too numerous for us to discuss them in detail. *Leb* or καρδία, is really much more than is usually indicated in the lexicons and text-books. It is more than merely the "locus" or "centre" of the mental and spiritual powers and possibilities of man, of his excitations, thoughts, inclinations, resolves and plans. It is more, too, than the "place" of his decisions, the crossroads, so to speak, from which his ways in relation to God and man usually part for good or evil. All this is also true. But when we say it we must be careful not to re-introduce a division between the reality of soul and that of body which it is the intention of this idea to exclude. On the one side the biblical "heart" is undoubtedly identical with what is always called this anatomically; and everything that is said about the activity of the heart, its experiences and undertakings, its purity and evil, its fidelity and infidelity, its joy and sorrow, must undoubtedly be related to what we describe physiologically as the activity of the heart. On the other side, in all that is said of the heart, the reference is to the human subject, the subject existing in the activity and suffering of his bodily heart. Thus man does not only have a heart as his locus, place or centre. He really is what man is in his heart. In his heart, because man as body—as ancient and primitive anatomy and physiology already knew quite well—lives by the heart, animating himself in its diastole and being animated in its systole. The heart is, as it were, the body in the body ; and understood in this way, the expression " centre " is justified. But for this reason, if we are true to the biblical texts we must say of the heart that it is *in nuce* the whole man himself, and therefore not only the locus of his activity but its essence. Always, in every beat of his heart, he is ruling soul and serving body, subject and object. " With all thine heart " necessarily means " with all thy soul " and therefore " with all thy might " (Deut. 6⁵). What a man is, or confesses, or does " from the heart " counts before God as done responsibly before him. What a man takes " to heart " he takes to himself. The mouth speaks out of the fulness of the heart (Mt. 12³⁴). When a man hardens his heart, he is rejected by God ; and on the other hand, those who are pure, i.e., open, in heart, will see God (Mt. 5⁸). That there should be a circumcision of the heart (Ez. 36²⁶, Rom. 2²⁹) is the positive content of the proclamation of the coming day of God. Thus the heart is not merely *a* but *the* reality of man, both wholly of soul and wholly of body. Who would want to say from his heart that it is the one more or less than the other or without the other ? Of this term which in the first instance is wholly physical, but is then given in the Bible a content which is wholly of soul, we are forced to say that it speaks with particular plainness of the order in which man is soul and body, of man as a rational being.

MAN IN HIS TIME

Man lives in the allotted span of his present, past and future life. He who was before him and will be after him, and who therefore fixes the boundaries of his being, is the eternal God, his Creator and Covenant-partner. He is the hope in which man may live in his time.

1. JESUS, LORD OF TIME

Man lives in his time. This simple statement denotes the second circle of problems to which we must now turn in our investigation of the constitution of human existence. We first described this constitution by saying that man is the soul of his body as established by God, namely, by the Spirit of God. He is " soul and body totally and simultaneously, in indissoluble differentiation, inseparable unity and indestructible order."

He lives as the soul of his body. But all along, though we have not yet stated it explicitly, this presupposes that he is temporal. If he lives at all, he lives in his time. His life is a series of the acts of his own movement, enterprise and activity. The fact that this is possible both as a whole and in detail presumes that man has the necessary time to accomplish these acts, i.e., that he is in a position to move in a definite way from his own past through his own present to his own future ; to be engaged in the fulfilment of these acts and therefore in change, and yet always to retain his own individual identity. Yet this is not self-evident. It is perfectly possible that there should be no road leading from the past through the present to the future. In this case there would either be no acts and no change, or their fulfilment would necessarily entail the loss of individual identity. But on these terms human life would be quite impossible. If man had no time, if his existence were timeless, he would have no life. Of course, time is not an exhaustive basis of his life. This consists in the fact that it is given him by the Spirit of God to be the soul of his body. But time is the *conditio sine qua non* of his life. If he is to fulfil his being and nature as the soul of his body, he cannot do without time. He must acquire time and possess it. Even the eternal God does not live without time. He is supremely temporal. For His eternity is authentic temporality, and therefore the source of all time. But in His eternity, in the uncreated self-subsistent time which is one of the perfections of His divine nature, present, past and future, yesterday, to-day and to-morrow, are not successive, but simultaneous. It is in this way, in this eternity of His, that God lives to the extent that He

lives His own life. But man, who is not God, who is a creature and
not the Creator, cannot live like this. If he is to live at all, he needs
an inauthentic temporality distinct from eternity. He needs the
time created by God, in which past, present and future follow one
another in succession, in which he can move from his past through
his present to his future, in which these three elements, corresponding
to his life-act as a whole and in detail, form a sequence. We speak of
" created time," but it would be more accurate to say " co-created."
For time is not a something, a creature with other creatures, but a
form of all the reality distinct from God, posited with it, and therefore
a real form of its being and nature.

When God began to create heaven and earth—according to the first creation-
saga of Genesis—then, long before there were any living beings, when this
primal history before all history began, time also began. There was a first week
culminating in a Sabbath . This was not only the day when God rested, but the
first day in the life of the first man. If the created world were also eternal, it
would in fact be a second god. And in that case it would not be a suitable
field for the free, creative acts of God or the corresponding movements of
His creatures. Time is the form of the created world by which the world is
ordained to be the field for the acts of God and for the corresponding reactions
of His creatures, or, in more general terms, for creaturely life.

Man lives as he has time and is in his time. It is his time to the
extent that it is not God's eternity, not the simultaneity of present,
past and future, but their succession. And it is his time to the extent
that it is given him in a fixed span when he is created the soul of his
body to live before God. It is for the sake of this life willed by God,
and as its form, that he has time. He has it, therefore, as his lifetime ;
as the time for each of his individual life-acts and for their connected
sequence, his total lifetime. He has no more and no less time than this,
and no different time. He is in this time, and this time alone. The
constitution of man's being as the soul of his body presupposes his
temporality. We must now ask and state what is meant by this form.
Both question and answer must again be those of a theological
anthropology. The man whose temporality is the subject of our investigation is the creature whose relation to God is revealed to us in
His Word, and whose being is both the history in which, elected and
called by God, he is engaged in responsibility before Him, and also
a corresponding being in encounter with his fellow-men. When we
speak of man in his time we are speaking of the life of this creature
and of the presupposition of the constitution of this creature. Human
life takes place in the reciprocal relation between God and man on
the one hand, and man and his fellow-men on the other. We have
no knowledge of what life means generally or apart from this, as the
life of plants and animals. We can speak of this only loosely and
hypothetically. But we do know what human life means ; that it
takes place in this two-fold relation. We know this because it is

revealed to us in the Word of God. And in this knowledge we shall here concern ourselves with man, and therefore with his temporality. Man needs time, and acquires and possesses it, to live in this two-fold relation. What interests us here is that his being is a being in time. It is obvious that the problem of time, too, is a problem of all anthropology. We cannot, therefore, ignore the attempts and conclusions of other non-theological understandings of being. But this should not debar us from approaching the problem from our own particular standpoint, the theological; and therefore from noting what is revealed to us in this respect by the Word of God. At this point too, therefore, we must take our bearings first and decisively from the man Jesus in His time. This will enable us to press forward to propositions in which the general Christian understanding of man will find expression in the light of the problem of time.

Cf. for what follows: Rudolf Bultmann, *Offenbarung und Heilsgeschehen*, 1941; Werner Georg Kümmel, *Verheissung und Erfüllung*, 1945; Oscar Cullmann, *Christus und die Zeit*, 1946 (Eng. Trans. *Christ and Time*, 1951); Marcus Barth, *Der Augenzeuge*, 1946; and Fritz Buri, *Die Bedeutung der neutestamentlichen Eschatologie für die neuere protestantische Theologie*, 1935.

" Jesus, Lord of time "—the title of this christological and basic sub-section of our investigation indicates the conclusion to which it will lead us. Let me outline it as briefly as possible. Like all other men, the man Jesus is in His time, His lifetime, the time He needs like all other men to be able to live a human life. But in this time of His He lives as the One He is in virtue of His unity with God. That is, He not only lives with God, but *for* Him; not only as His Elect and Called in responsibility before Him, but as His representative to men. And He not only lives with men, but *for* them; not only as a man like themselves in encounter with them, but as their Representative before God. He lives in His time as the Judge by whose Word and work the right of God is vindicated in the sight of men, and therefore that of men is vindicated before God and among themselves; by whom the kingdom of God is thus established among men and His covenant with them fulfilled. It is in this two-fold representation and vindication of right that the man Jesus lives in His time. And it is this content of His life which makes the barrier of His time on every side a gateway. As in His unity with God He lives the life of the supreme Representative and Judge, His life does not belong exclusively to Himself. It is a life lived for God, and therefore for men. And as He lives this life in His time, it ceases to be exclusively His time. His time becomes time for God, and therefore for all men. The question which God addresses to all men, and the question which they address to God, finds its conclusive answer in the life which Jesus lived in the service of God and man. He represents the grace of God, and thus gives man what is right, what is his due. And he represents the gratitude of man, and thus gives God what is right, what is His due. The answer given by the life of Jesus to the questions of God and man makes His time the time which always was when men lived, which always is when they live, and which always will be when they will live. It makes this life at once the centre and the beginning and end of all the times of all the lifetimes of all men. It is the time of man in its whole extent. Wherever men live and have time the decision taken in the life of Jesus holds good ; the content of His life affects and embraces them all because it is the answer to the question which God addresses to all men and which they address to God. The two-fold answer which He gives, to God on the one hand and to men on the other, makes Him the Contemporary of all men, whether they have lived, live or will live. The way in which He is their Contemporary varies according to whether they live with Him, lived before Him or will live after Him. Yet He is the Contemporary of them all because He lives for God and for them all. The man Jesus has therefore His time, but He has more than just His own time. He lives in His time, and while it does not cease to be His time, and the times of other men do not cease to be their times, His time acquires in relation to their times the character of God's time, of eternity, in which present, past and future are simultaneous. Thus Jesus not only lives in His own time, but as He lives in His own time, and as there are many other times both before and after Him, He is the Lord of time. This is the insight which must now be established and expounded.

Let us take the simplest and most obvious consideration first. Like all men, the man Jesus has His lifetime : the time bounded at one end by His birth and at the other by His death ; a fixed span with a particular duration within the duration of created time as a whole ; the time for his being as the soul of His body. The eternal content of His life must not cause us to miss or to forget or to depreciate this form, separating the content from it and discarding the form, as though we could see and have the content without it. For while the content is eternal, it is His human life, the action or series of actions of this human subject, which could not take place unless He had His own particular time. If we abstract Him from His time, we also lose this content of His life. If we retain the content, we must needs retain the form as well, and therefore His temporality. Just because the content is eternal, the presence of God, the unity of Creator and creature, of the life of God with that of man, He has time, the lifetime of this man. Everything we shall say later about the supremely positive and comprehensive relation of fulfilment and promise between His time and the times before and after, rests wholly on the fact that it is always intrinsically and supremely His time. It is as a man of His time, and not otherwise, that He is the Lord of time. We should lose Jesus as the Lord of all time if we ignored Him as a man in His own time. It is in this history—the history which is inseparable from his temporality—that the man Jesus lives and is the eternal salvation of all men in their different times.

The eternal salvation of all men is absolutely dependent on our being able to recount this history : " Once upon a time there was . . ." Note the " once." " Once " means : " In His time." The New Testament ἅπαξ (1 Pet. 3¹⁸, Heb. 9²⁶, ²⁸) or ἐφάπαξ (Rom. 6¹⁰ ; Heb. 7²⁷, 9¹²) certainly means " once for all." But the event thus designated—the death of Jesus as the climax of His life— could not have happened once for all if it had not happened once, in its own time. It is in this history, and therefore in time, that the fulness of time is reached, and only so. The Gospels distinguish the life of Jesus from myths proclaiming timeless truth by underlining, though not overstressing, the temporal limitations to which Jesus was subject. Palestine, Galilee and Jerusalem are the indispensable background to His life, giving him a concrete relationship to His contemporary social environment and a definite place in history (Luke 2¹ᶠ·, 3¹ᶠ·). The inclusion of Pontius Pilate in the creed means, *inter alia*, that the Church wished to pinpoint the death of Jesus as an event in time. And it is worth noting that the Synoptists record the precise time of the events of the passion almost to the minute—the cock-crow (Mk. 14⁶⁸ and *par.*), the morning (Mk. 15¹), the third hour (Mk. 15²⁵), the sixth hour, the ninth (Mk. 15³³ and *par.*) and the evening (Mk. 15⁴² and *par.*). True, the exact year of Jesus' birth cannot be established with any degree of certainty, nor the year of His death, so we cannot be sure exactly how old He was when He died. Yet it would be wrong to boggle at such chronological obscurities. It was enough for the Evangelists to make clear that the history they record was enacted over a particular period of time, and, in the case of the passion, on particular days and at particular hours. To insist on the fact that Jesus Christ " is come in the flesh " (1 Jn. 4²), that the Logos became flesh and " tabernacled " among men (Jn. 1¹⁴), was the best defence against Docetism in its early stages. At bottom Docetism is " the failure to respect the historically unique character of the redemptive deed of Christ " (Cullmann, *Christ and Time*, E.T., p. 127). The New Testament does not teach any " truth " but that which has its substance in the Johaninne 'Εγώ εἰμι. It proclaims salvation history, and therefore the time of salvation. The lifetime of Jesus is this time of salvation.

But the history of the man Jesus, this salvation history, cannot be recounted unless we remember that the New Testament has something more to say of Him, though still in the form of history, at the very point where the history of any other man would inevitably stop. For Jesus has a further history beginning on the third day after His death and therefore after the time of His first history had clearly come to an end. In temporal sequence, it is a second history—or rather, the fragments of a second history—of Jesus. It is the Easter history, the history of the forty days between His resurrection and ascension. The second stage of our investigation, more difficult, but rewarding, leads us inevitably to this point. For unless we wilfully ignore the clear indication of the New Testament sources, we are bound to recognise that this is a key position for our whole understanding of the man Jesus in His time. It shows us as nothing else can, according to the New Testament, that even as a man in His time Jesus is the Lord of all time. The Jesus whose life and time form the subject matter of the New Testament is the One whom at this time His disciples had heard, and seen with their eyes, and looked upon, and their hands had handled (1 Jn. 1¹) ; " that eternal life, which was with the Father, and was manifested unto us " (ἐφανερώθη 1 Jn. 1²). It is impossible to read any text of the New Testament in the sense intended by its authors, by the apostles who stand behind them, or by the first communities, without an awareness that they either explicitly assert or at least tacitly assume that the Jesus of whom they speak and to whom they refer in some way is the One who appeared to His disciples at this particular time as the Resurrected from the dead. All the other things they know of Him, His words and acts, are regarded in the light of this particular event, and are as it were irradiated by its light. Whatever they proclaim in His name, the power of their message, derives from the fact that it was conveyed and entrusted to them by the man Jesus after He was raised from the dead. And to turn to our own particular problem, whatever His being in time means for their being, and for that of all men in their time, derives from the fact that Jesus was among them even in this particular time, the Easter time.

In the first instance, it is essential to grasp that when the New Testament speaks of the event of Easter it really means the Easter history and Easter time. We are here in the sphere of history and time no less than in the case of the words and acts and even the death of Jesus. The event of Easter is as it were their prism through which the apostles and their communities saw the man Jesus in every aspect of His relation to them—as the One who " was, and is, and is to come " (Rev. 4⁸). But this prism itself is not just a timeless idea, a kind of *a priori*, hovering as it were above the relations between Jesus and His followers, above their memory of His life and death, above His presence in their midst or their expectation of His second coming and the final consummation. No, it happened " once upon a time " that He was among them as the Resurrected. This, too, was an event. And it was by this event that the prism was put into their hands. He, the man Jesus, was also in this time, this later time. Not only their faith in Him, or their preaching of Him, but the recollection which concretely created and fashioned this faith and preaching, embraced this time, the time of the forty days. It was by this specific memory, and not by a timeless and non-historical truth, that the apostles and the Churches they founded lived in all the relations between Jesus and them and them and Jesus.

This statement holds good whatever our personal attitude may be to this later history. Its truth does not depend on our own acceptance or rejection of the Easter story, or whether we prefer to accept it differently from the way in which the New Testament describes it, or to interpret it in a different sense. Nor, finally, does it depend on our recognition of its central importance for our own knowledge of Jesus Christ or faith in Him. (We may relegate it to the periphery, or regard it as an incidental and dispensable feature in the story.

But whatever our own personal attitude to the resurrection may be (and there are many alternatives to choose from), we can at least agree on one point. For the New Testament this later history is not just an appendix or afterthought to the main theme. It is not peripheral to the New Testament, but central ; not inessential or dispensable, but essential and indispensable. And it is all this, not in a different sense, but exactly in the sense in which the New Testament takes it.) The Easter history is the starting-point for the Evangelists' portraits of the man Jesus. It is the real word with which they approached the outside world, whether Jewish or pagan, whenever they spoke of this man. It is the axiom which controls all their thinking about this man in His time. It is not just a mere reflection of their memory of Jesus or of their present life in communion with Him or of the hopes they set upon His person. It is the original object which is itself reflected in their entire relationship to this man, past, present and future. To put it sharply, while we could imagine a New Testament containing only the history of Easter and its message, we could not possibly imagine a New Testament without it. For the history and message of Easter contains everything else, while without it everything else would be left in the air as a mere abstraction. Everything else in the New Testament contains and presupposes the resurrection. It is the key to the whole. We can agree about this quite apart from our own personal attitude to the resurrection. And so we can agree finally that the acceptance or rejection of the Gospel of the New Testament, at any rate as understood by the New Testament itself, depends on our acceptance or rejection of the *evangelium quadraginta dierum*. (Either we believe with the New Testament in the risen Jesus Christ, or we do not believe in Him at all.) This is the statement which believers and non-believers alike can surely accept as a fair assessment of the sources.

R. Bultmann " demythologizes " the event of Easter by interpreting it as " the rise of faith in the risen Lord, since it was this faith which led to the apostolic preaching " (*Kerygma and Myth*, E.T., p. 42). This will not do. Faith in the risen Lord springs from His historical manifestation, and from this as such, not from the rise of faith in Him. But Bultmann evidently admits that the New Testament witnesses themselves took a different view. And we must at least give him credit for emphasising the central and indispensable function of the event of Easter for all that is thought and said in the New Testament. On the other hand, it is a matter for surprise that W. G. Kümmel never so much as mentions the resurrection in His otherwise excellent book. Can the subject of promise and fulfilment really be treated without mentioning the resurrection passages ? Can the general thesis be sustained—legitimate and important though it is in itself—that in the Synoptists the kingdom of God is at once present in the person of Jesus and yet still to come ? The same criticism applies to Cullmann's *Christ and Time*, where the resurrection comes in only at the end of the book (*op. cit.*, E.T., p. 231 ff.) and in a special connexion, without any real significance for the author's reconstruction of the New Testament conception of time and history.

We also join issue with Cullmann at another point. It is wrong to suppose that the New Testament authors started with a particular conception of time as an ascending line with a series of æons, and then inserted into this geometrical figure the event of Christ as the centre of this line. Surely it was a particular memory of particular time filled with a particular history, it was the constraint under which this laid their thinking, which formed and initiated their particular conception of time. What shaped and determined their conception of time was the fact that the God who was the Father of Jesus Christ stood before them as the βασιλεύς τῶν αἰώνων (1 Tim. 1[17]), not in the contemplation of a timeless truth, but in the recollection of this particular history. Jesus, revealed in the event of this particular time as the King of the æons, was the first and proper object upon which the gaze of the primitive community rested. It was from this vantage point that it looked upon the æons themselves. That is why it is hazardous to dogmatise about the early Christian conception of time, or to try and fit it into a nice geometrical pattern. Does it have such a pattern at all ? It may not be impossible to discover one, but it would be wrong to accept as the last word on the subject the picture of an ascending line from infinity to infinity.

But another delimitation which is even more important is demanded by Bultmann's proposed reinterpretation of the resurrection already mentioned. (Cf. for what follows, Walter Claas, *Der moderne Mensch in der Theologie Rudolf Bultmanns*, 1947.) As we have seen, the event of Easter is for Bultmann " the rise of faith in the risen Lord "—this, and no more than this. " Can the resurrection," he asks, " . . . be understood simply as an attempt to convey the meaning of the cross ? Does the New Testament, in asserting that Jesus is risen from the dead, mean that His death is not just an ordinary human death, but the judgment and salvation of the world, depriving death of its power " (*ibid.*, p. 38). As the revelation of the meaning of the cross, it is certainly (with this last act of the Christ-event proper) the " act of God " on which the faith and preaching of the Church are founded. Indeed Bultmann can also speak of " the self-manifestation of the risen Lord " and therefore of " the eschatological event of redemption " (p. 42). But the meaning of the cross, as distinct from the cross itself, is not to be sought in time, but beyond it (p. 36). Apart from the cross and resurrection (understood in this sense) the eschatological event includes " the apostolic preaching which originated in the event of Easter Day " (p. 42), the Church " where the preaching of the word is continued and where believers gather as ' saints,' i.e., those who have been transferred to eschatological existence " (p. 43), and above all the " concrete achievements " of believers, their participation in the cross and resurrection of Christ, in which they die unto sin and the world with Him, and live with Him henceforth in " wrestling freedom " (p. 37 f., 40). All these events in time, says Bultmann, are supra-temporal in context and character, both objectively and also subjectively for faith. For by " eschatological " Bultmann means a verifiable event in history and time which also has a supra-temporal significance accessible only to faith. Thus the eschatological event includes the death of Jesus, the faith of the first disciples, their preaching, the Church, the sacraments and the Christian life. But the resurrection, understood as the allegedly objective fact of the restoration of the man Jesus who died on the cross, of His return to life in this world during the forty days (p. 39), is not a part of this eschatological event. It is a " nature-miracle" (p. 8), a " miraculous proof," and as such it must be " demythologized," like so much else in the New Testament. It is a mistaken objectifying of a concept of the Christian understanding of existence which needs be translated back into the reality (p. 10) because it cannot be accepted as an event in time and space and cannot therefore be recognised in its supra-temporal context and character. An " Easter event " in this sense can be regarded only as an objectifying of primitive Christian Easter faith in terms of the mythical world-view of the time, and it is no longer valid for those who have ceased to hold this view. The real Easter event, which belongs to that eschatological occurrence, is the rise of the Easter faith of the first disciples. This was not based on any event in time, but only on the supra-historical, supra-temporal act of God. For the Easter faith of the later Church and for our Easter faith, it has the significance of an " act of God in which the redemptive event of the cross is completed " (p. 42). Here Bultmann is aware that he himself is on the verge of relapsing into mythology, if indeed he has not already done so. But he reassures himself with the thought that this is not " mythology in the traditional sense," since the reference is not to a " miraculous, supernatural event," but to " an historical event wrought out in space and time " (p. 43).

Our first task is to try to see the implications of this view. If Bultmann is right, there are two ways of taking Jn. 1[14], and the even more explicit saying in 1 Jn. 1[1]. Either we must deny that these texts have anything whatever to do with the One who manifested His life during the forty days, or we must dismiss these statements (though both of them are fundamental in this context) from the sphere of the relevant content of primitive Christian faith and its preaching, explaining them as the mythological garb for the process in which the original disciples were brought by a direct divine influence to see the redemptive significance of the death of Jesus after it had taken place. On this view, the Easter history is merely the first chapter in the history of faith, and the Easter time the first period in the age of faith. The recollection of this time and history is a genuine memory of Jesus only to the extent that it was in this history and time that the disciples made up their minds about Him and about His death in particular. In so doing, they drew far too heavily on the mythical world-view of their age, and we cannot accept their particular way of expressing it as either obligatory or practical. The point is that Jesus Himself is at work during that history and time only in the faith of His disciples. The " self-declaration " of the " Resurrected " is staged in the minds of the disciples and nowhere else. Nothing happened between Him and them. There was no new, and in its novelty decisive and fundamental, encounter between Him and them to give rise to their faith. They alone were engaged in this history. He was not. They were quite alone. To be sure, they had their faith, which had come into being through an " act of God," whatever that may " signify." They had the insight into the mystery of the cross, which had suddenly become possible and actual. But they were alone. Their faith had no object distinct from itself, no antecedent basis on which to rest as faith. It stood majestically on its own feet. The " act of God " was identical with their faith. And the fact that it took place, that they believed, is the real content of the Easter history and the Easter time, the real burden of the Christian message, the basis of the existence of the Church and sacraments. Jesus Himself had not risen. In its simple and unqualified sense, this statement is quite untenable.

For our part, we maintain the direct opposite. The statement is valid in its simplest sense, and only in that sense is it the central affirmation of the whole of the New Testament. Jesus Himself did rise again and appear to His disciples. This is the content of the Easter history, the Easter time, the Christian faith and Christian proclamation, both then and at all times. This is the basis of the existence of the Church and its sacraments. This—if we may call it so—is the " eschatological event " in its manifest form which it acquired at Easter. This is the act of God—the act in which He appeared objectively in the glory of His incarnate Word, encountering first their unbelief and then, when this was overcome, their faith. Hence they were not alone with their faith. It was established, awakened and created by God in this objective encounter. Only in a secondary sense was their faith the imitation and reflection of the death and resurrection of Jesus in their lives. Primarily it meant that they were able to regard themselves as men for whom Jesus died and rose again. Jesus Himself for them ! Hence Jesus and His disciples were not identical in the Easter event. He Himself was with them in time, in this time, beyond the time of His earthly life between His birth and death, in this time of revelation. This is what really took place. In our view, we do violence to the texts of the New Testament if we take a different line, as Bultmann does. But having said that, we must try to explain briefly why we do not find Bultmann's argument convincing.

Bultmann is an exegete. But it is impossible to engage him in exegetical discussion. For he is also a systematic theologian of the type which handles texts in such a way that their exegesis is always controlled by a set of dogmatic presuppositions and is thus wholly dependent upon their validity. In what follows I shall try to come to grips with the most important of these dogmatic presuppositions.

1. Is it true that a theological statement is valid only when it can be proved to be a genuine element in the Christian understanding of human existence ? Bultmann rejects the claim that the resurrection of Jesus was an event in time and space on the ground that it does not fulfil this postulate. This, of course,

is true enough. For in the resurrection God appears to act in a manner " inextricably involved in a nature-miracle " (p. 8). None of the major affirmations of the creed fulfils this postulate. True, they have a certain bearing on human existence. They provide the possibility and basis for a Christian understanding of this existence, and suitably adjusted they can serve as definitions of human existence. But this is not what they are in the first instance. Primarily, they define the being and action of the God who is different from man and encounters man ; the Father, the Son and the Holy Ghost. For this reason alone they cannot be reduced to statements about the inner life of man. And for this reason, too, they are full of " nature," of cosmos. This applies equally to the claim that Jesus rose from the dead. The anthropological strait-jacket into which Bultmann forces his systematic theology, and unfortunately his exegetical theology as well, represents a tradition which goes back to W. Herrmann and even further to Ritschl and Schleiermacher. This tradition can just as easily be exploited in the opposite direction, so as to leave no genuine case against the resurrection of Jesus.

2. Is it true that an event alleged to have happened in time can be accepted as historical only if it can be proved to be a " ' historical ' fact " in Bultmann's sense ?—i.e., when it is open to verification by the methods, and above all the tacit assumption, of modern historical scholarship ? This is Bultmann's opinion. It is on this ground that he rejects the account of the forty days. He cannot include its content, in so far as it deals with the living Jesus, and not merely with the disciples who believed in him, among the " ' historical ' facts " in the restricted sense of the term. He is right enough in this, for it is quite impossible. But he jumps to a false conclusion when he insists that for this reason the facts reported could not have occurred. History of this kind may well have happened. We may well accept as history that which good taste prevents us from calling " ' historical ' fact," and which the modern historian will call " saga " or " legend " on the ground that it is beyond the reach of his methods, to say nothing of his unavowed assumptions. It belongs to the nature of the biblical material that although it forms a consecutive historical narrative it is full of this kind of history and contains comparatively little " history " in Bultmann's sense. The creation narratives in Gen. 1–2, for example, are history in this higher sense ; and so too is the Easter story, except for a tiny " historical " margin. Why should it not have happened ? It is sheer superstition to suppose that only things which are open to " historical " verification can have happened in time. There may have been events which happened far more really in time than the kind of things Bultmann's scientific historian can prove. There are good grounds for supposing that the history of the resurrection of Jesus is a pre-eminent instance of such an event. " It is not," he says, " just a phenomenon of secular history, it is a phenomenon of significant history, in the sense that it realized itself in history." He is referring here to the Church (p. 43). And the same is true, *a fortiori*, of the resurrection of Jesus.

3. Is it true that the assertion of the historicity of an event which by its very nature is inaccessible to " historical " verification, of what we may agree to call the history of saga or legend, is merely a blind acceptance of a piece of mythology, an arbitrary act, a descent from faith to works, a dishonest *sacrificium intellectus* ? This is Bultmann's complaint (p. 4), and he expressly appeals to the shade of W. Herrmann against those who accept the resurrection of Jesus as an historical fact. Can we let this pass ? What grounds have we for accepting the view that the message of Christ's resurrection necessarily has the sinister aspect of a law of faith to which we can subject ourselves, if at all, only in a kind of intellectual contortion ? For the New Testament at any rate the resurrection is good news in which we may believe. And this faith, as those who accepted it were gratefully aware, was made possible only by the resurrection itself. They were not able to accept it because the prevailing mythical world-view made it easier to accept then than it is supposed to be to-day. Even in those

days the Easter message seems to be utterly " incredible " (p. 9), not only to the educated Areopagites, but even to the original disciples. Hence there is no real reason why it should not be accepted freely and gladly even to-day. If it is not presented as something to be accepted freely and gladly there is something wrong with the presentation. But this is no excuse for rejecting it as something which intellectual honesty forbids us to accept.

4. Is it true that modern thought is " shaped for good or ill by modern science " ? Is there a modern world-picture which is incompatible with the mythical world-view and superior to it ? Is this modern view so binding as to determine in advance and unconditionally our acceptance or rejection of the biblical message ? We are again up against the well-known Marburg tradition with its absolute lack of any sense of humour and its rigorous insistence on the honesty which does not allow any liberties in this respect. " It is impossible to use electric light and the wireless and to avail ourselves of modern medical and surgical discoveries, and at the same time to believe in the New Testament world of demons and spirits " (p. 5). Who can read this without a shudder ? But what if the modern world-view is not so final as all that ? What if modern thought is not so uniform as our Marburg Kantians would have us believe ? Is there any criticism of the New Testament which is inescapably posed by the " situation of modern man " ? And above all, what if our radio-listeners recognise a duty of honesty which, for all this respect for the discoveries of modern science, is even more compelling than that of accepting without question the promptings of common sense ? What if they felt themselves in a position to give a free and glad and quite factual assent not to a *fides implicita* in a world of spirits and demons but to faith in the resurrection of Jesus Christ from the dead ? What if they have no alternative but to do this ?

5. Is it true that we are compelled to reject a statement simply because this statement, or something like it, was compatible with the mythical world-view of the past ? Is this enough to make it untenable ? Is not Bultmann being a bit too heavy-handed in expecting us to reject this mythical world-view in its entirety ? After all, is it our job as Christians to accept or reject world-views ? Have not Christians always been eclectic in their world-views—and this for very good reasons ? There is absolutely no reason at all why we should really insist on this particular world-view. But we ought not to overlook the fact that this particular world-view contained a number of features which the primitive community used cautiously but quite rightly in its witness to Jesus Christ. But the world-view accepted nowadays has either lost these features, or regrettably allowed them to slip into the background. Consequently we have every reason to make use of " mythical " language in certain connexions. And there is no need for us to have a guilty conscience about it, for if we went to extremes in demythologising, it would be quite impossible to bear witness to Jesus Christ at all. When, for instance, Bultmann (p. 7 f.) dismisses the connexion between sin and death, or the concept of substitution, or the relation between death and resurrection, on the ground that they are particularly offensive and " obsolete " features in this mythical world-view, he is perhaps a warning example of what becomes of a theologian when he all-too-hastily jettisons the mythical world-view lock, stock and barrel. To speak of the " rise of the Easter faith " in the first disciples is a good thing. But we cannot pretend that this is an adequate substitute for what is now rejected as the " mythical " witness to the resurrection of Jesus Christ from the dead.

As I see it, these are the decisive reasons why, in spite of Bultmann, we must still accept the resurrection of Jesus, and His subsequent appearances to His disciples, as genuine history in its own particular time.

This is not the place to develop a complete theology of the resurrection. Let us confine ourselves to one question. What implications has it for the being of Jesus in time that He was in time in this way too, as the Resurrected ? What is the implication of the fact that after He had completed the span from birth to death He had this subsequent time ? The answer is that the particular content of the particular recollection of this particular time of the apostolic community consisted in the fact that in this time the *man* Jesus was manifested among them in the mode of *God*. It is essential to a true understanding that both his humanity and his deity should be kept in view.

The Resurrected is the man Jesus, who now came and went among them as such, whom they saw and touched and heard, who ate and drank with them, and who, as I believe, was still before them as true man, *vere homo*.

We misunderstand the whole matter, and fall into Docetism at the crucial point, if we refuse to see this and even to see it first. Apart from 1 Jn. 1[1], there are two specific texts in which the New Testament emphatically repudiates any docetic interpretation of the resurrection. The first is Lk. 24[36f.], where Jesus appears in the midst of the eleven just as they are about to listen to the story of the disciples on the road to Emmaus. Jesus says : " Why are ye troubled ? and why do thoughts (διαλογισμοί) arise in your hearts ? Behold my hands and my feet: ὅτι ἐγώ εἰμι αὐτός : handle me, and see ; for a spirit hath not flesh and bones, as ye see me have." And the story continues : " And while they yet believed not for joy, and wondered, he said unto them, Have ye here any meat ? And they gave him a piece of a broiled fish. And he took it, and did eat before them." The second is Jn. 20[24f.], the story of " doubting " Thomas. Much injustice has been done to the latter through wrong exegesis. The fact that he wanted to touch Jesus before he came to believe shows only that he had no more doubts than the other disciples had according to the accounts. It is the fact that the risen Christ can be touched which puts it beyond all doubt that He is the man Jesus and no one else. He is not soul or spirit in the abstract, but soul of His body, and therefore body as well. To be an apostle of Jesus Christ means not only to have seen Him with one's eyes and to have heard Him with one's ears, but to have touched Him physically. This is what is meant by Ac. 1[22], where we are told that what makes an apostle is the fact that he is a " witness of the resurrection." By beholding His glory, by seeing, hearing and touching the flesh in which this glory is made manifest, those who consorted with Jesus during this time were brought to believe in Him, and thus authorised and consecrated to proclaim the Gospel. " Blessed are they that have not seen, and yet have believed " (Jn. 20[29]). This is not a criticism of Thomas, but (cf. 1 Pet. 1[8]) the blessing of all those who, though having no part in the seeing of this particular time, will " believe on me through their word," i.e., through the witness of those who did see (Jn. 17[20]). It is impossible to erase the bodily character of the resurrection of Jesus and His existence as the Resurrected. Nor may we gloss over this element in the New Testament record of the forty days, as a false dualism between spirit and body has repeatedly tried to do. For unless Christ's resurrection was a resurrection of the body, we have no guarantee that it was the decisively acting Subject Jesus Himself, the *man* Jesus, who rose from the dead.

But it is equally important to note that the man Jesus appeared to them during these days in the mode of God. During this period they came to see that He had always been present among them in His deity, though hitherto this deity had been veiled. They now recalled these preliminary manifestations of glory which they had already witnessed during His earthly life, but with unseeing eyes, and which now, in the light of what took place in these days, acquired for them the particular import which they had always had in themselves, though hidden from them. Now they actually beheld His glory. During these forty days the presence of God in the presence of the man Jesus was no longer a paradox. The dialectic of seeing and believing may be helpful when we try to describe the Christian life and the justification and sanctification of Christians, or the Church and its preaching and sacraments. But when we come to the resurrection it leads us nowhere. " God was in Christ " (2 Cor. 5^{19})—this was the truth which dawned upon the disciples during the forty days. He was not both veiled and manifest, both manifest and veiled, in Christ. He had been veiled, but He was now wholly and unequivocally and irrevocably manifest. For the disciples this was not a self-evident truth, nor a discovery of their own, but a conviction that went utterly against the grain. This is made abundantly clear in the resurrection narratives, where the disciples begin by doubting and even disbelieving. But their doubts and disbelief are soon dispelled, never to return. They are definitively overcome and removed in the forty days. " Be not faithless, but believing " (John 20$^{27f.}$). This is not just pious exhortation, but a word of power. And to this Thomas gives the appropriate answer : " My Lord and my God." In and with the presence of the man Jesus during this time, in the unique circumstances of the forty days, a decision is taken between the belief and unbelief of His disciples. There takes place for them the total, final, irrevocable and eternal manifestation of God Himself. God Himself, the object and ground of their faith, was present as the man Jesus was present in this way. That this really took place is the specific content of the apostolic recollection of these days.

The fact of faith was created in this history. This faith did not consist in a reassessment and reinterpretation *in meliorem partem* of the picture of the Crucified, but in an objective encounter with the Crucified and Risen, who Himself not only made Himself credible to them, but manifested Himself as the ἀρχηγὸς τῆς σωτηρίας αὐτῶν (Heb. 2^{10}) and therefore the ἀρχηγὸς καὶ τελειωτής of their πιστις (Heb. 12^2). This being the case, He was among them as God Himself. " All power is given unto me in heaven and in earth " (Mt. 28^{18}). The Jesus of the Easter history speaks not only with binding authority, but with effectiveness ; not only with validity, but with power. His declarations are able to overcome the fears, griefs, bewilderment, doubts and disbeliefs of His disciples. And the directions He gives them (especially the " missionary charge " of Mt. 28^{19}) point to an enterprise which will neither depend on the resources or achievements of the disciples themselves nor be thwarted by their inadequacy. " (He) hath begotten us again . . . by the resurrection of Jesus Christ from the dead " (1 Pet. 1^3). This is true quite apart from any inherent capacity of the disciples or any endowments of their own which they bring to the task. But it is also true quite apart from the obstacles which they might put in the way of this event. When the Bible says that He " hath begotten us again," it can only mean a mighty, creative act of God. That is what those who saw and heard this history remember. They remember it as an event which can never be reversed even when it is behind them as an event of their time and can be only an object of memory and retrospect. But it means something else as well. It means that what they look back upon is the presence of God Himself revealed among them. " God is present "—this is not just an intellectual notion of perception, but it is remembered as a real fact which has taken place before them and which cannot be confessed, but has given them their commission to preach the Gospel to all nations. They live by this recollection ; all their thinking and knowledge is grounded in it.

It is this memory which leads them to add the title *Kyrios* to the simple human name of Jesus. It is a token of their recognition that God was manifestly present in this man. Whether its origin is to be sought in the Hellenistic Emperor cult, or whether, as would seem more likely, it is a reproduction of the LXX rendering of Yahweh, it is the name which, according to Phil. 2^9, " is above every name," signifying absolute deity. This, and the transference of this name to the man Jesus, is borne out by the saying of Thomas in Jn. 20^{28}. We do not have here merely an appraisal and interpretation of the existence of Jesus grounded in the depth and intensity of their contrition. Had it been that, it would have been open to question whether they had not exaggerated His status, and whether we for our part should not content ourselves with a more modest assessment. What we have here is a *Deus dixit* spoken in the existence of Jesus during these days. It is a decision which the apostolic Church cannot discuss or revise. For it is He who is responsible for it. He has appeared and acted as *Kyrios* among them. It is not they who have given Him this name, but God. And God has given it by exalting Him above all things ($ὑπερύψωσεν$, Phil. 2^9) out of and after His death on the cross. Hence this name is inseparable from His person, and His person inseparable from this name. Although they had once known Him, as 2 Cor. 5^{16} puts it, " after the flesh," i.e., otherwise than as *Kyrios*, they now know Him so no more, but henceforth, in retrospect of His resurrection, only as *Kyrios*. And in this way, as the only *Kyrios* they know, they thus proclaim Him—for how else could they have done so ?—and in the certainty given by these days that He was *Kyrios* they proceed to interpret and present His life and His words and acts prior to His death. In practice, therefore, the so-called Gospels, if they are taken and read as their authors intended, reveal from start to finish this decision (and therefore indirectly the resurrection of Jesus), and are to be read, understood and accepted or rejected only in face of this decision and therefore in recollection of the resurrection of Jesus. If we try to bypass this decision, concentrating our attention upon a human Jesus who is not the *Kyrios* because He is not risen, we simply show that we have failed to take note of what they really say, and intend to say.

But when we go on to ask how all this happened, how the man Jesus was present among His disciples during these forty days as God, we must give the straightforward answer that the Jesus who three days earlier had been rejected by the Jews and put to death by the Gentiles and buried by His disciples was among them again as a living man. He was thus the concrete demonstration of the gracious God, who in the death of this man on the cross did not will that His own right, and that of man, should go by default, but willed to vindicate them, as He did in great triumph. He was then the concrete demonstration of the God who not only has authority over man's life and death, but also wills to deliver him from death. Moreover—and this is what interests us especially in this connexion—He was the concrete demonstration of the God who has not only a different time from that of man, but whose will and resolve it is to give man a share in this time of His, in His eternity. The concrete demonstration of this God, His appearance, is the meaning of the appearance and appearances of this man Jesus, alive again after His death, in the forty days. It may and must be said, not as a postulate but as a legitimate explanation of the facts, that if the man Jesus was the incarnate Word of this God, if as such he was the Bearer of a hidden glory, of an initially inapprehensible declaration of His nature, and if finally this hidden declaration of His nature was to be effective as well as operative, if it was not to remain hidden but to be disclosed, then everything had to happen as it actually did according to the Easter story in its simple, literal sense. There was no other way. This man, the incarnate Word of God, had not only to be present but to be apprehensible as the triumphant justification of God and man, as the revelation of the divine sovereignty over life and death which delivers man, and finally as the One who exists in the higher, eternal time of God. This, the Revealer of His hidden glory as God's eternal Word incarnate, is what Jesus was in His real and therefore physical resurrection from the dead, in His appearances as the One who was really and therefore physically resurrected. This is the way in which He was " manifested in the mode of God " to His disciples. This is the way in which He was the appearance of God which afterwards formed the object of their particular recollection of this particular time. This is how He was present to their ears and eyes as the Lord, to whom they could not and would not give this title on a spontaneous assessment or interpretation, but were compelled to do so.

Bultmann is splitting hairs when he calls the literal resurrection a " nature-miracle." Far from helping us to understand it, this is merely an attempt to discredit it. It is true enough, for in the appearance of God we necessarily have to do with the whole apprehensible existence of the man Jesus, and therefore nature, i.e., His body, has a part in this event. As a purely mental or psychological event, the appearance would not have been what it was, i.e., that of the Creator of the whole universe and therefore of the whole man. Yet it was not this circumstance, not the fact that the resurrection included nature, and took place as a physical resurrection, which made it what it was. No, it was because God Himself, the Creator, who was first hidden in the lowliness of this creature, in the death of this man, was now manifested in His resurrection, that it was absolutely necessary for this event genuinely and apprehensibly to include nature, and therefore to be physical. This was the mystery before which the apostolic community could adore. It was not interested in any resurrection or actuality of resurrection in general, but in the resurrection of this man, and the resurrection of all men inaugurated by it. In other words, it was interested in something which is beyond the reach of general polemics against the concept of a miracle which embraces nature, and indeed of general apologetics in favour of this concept. The concern of the New Testament was not with this concept but with the contingent fact to which reference is made in the hymn which probably belongs to the most primitive Christian tradition : ὃς ἐφανερώθη ἐν σαρκί, ἐδικαιώθη ἐν πνεύματι, ὤφθη ἀγγέλοις, ἐκηρύχθη ἐν ἔθνεσιν, ἐπιστεύθη ἐν κόσμῳ, ἀνελήμφθη ἐν δόξῃ (1 Tim. 3¹⁶).

When we remember this, we can understand why the evidence for the resurrection can only be fragmentary and contradictory, as is actually the case in the New Testament. Compare, for instance, the Matthean and Lukan accounts, or the Synoptic accounts as a whole, with that of John ; or again, all the Gospel accounts with that in 1 Cor. 15. It is clearly impossible to extract from the various accounts a nucleus of genuine history, quite apart from the intelligibility or otherwise of the resurrection itself. The statement in Ac. 1³ to the effect that the appearances extended over forty days is obviously connected with the forty days of the flood (Gen. 7⁴ ; cf. also Ez. 4⁶ ; Jonah 3⁴), and with the forty days of the temptation at the beginning of Jesus' ministry (Mt. 4² ; Lk. 4²). And they may also have some positive connexion with the forty days spent in Canaan by the spies when they went on ahead of the children of Israel (Num. 13²⁵), and with the forty days and nights it took Elijah to get to Horeb, during which he went in the strength of the meat provided by the angel. These parallels are sufficient to show that the forty days are not to be taken literally but typically. They do not offer precise chronological information as to the duration of the appearances. The topography is just as vague. There is no clear dividing line between one scene and another, as a comparison of the various episodes will show. Nor have we any independent sources from which to check the evidence. Hence the harmonisations to which the older commentators resorted in an attempt to supply the deficiencies and clear up the obscurities, are almost amusingly incongruous. The narratives are not meant to be taken as " history " in our sense of the word. Even 1 Cor. 15³⁻⁸ is treated in a strangely abstract way if it is regarded as a citation of witnesses for the purpose of historical proof. True, these accounts read very differently from myths. The Easter story is differentiated from myth, both formally and materially, by the fact that it is all about a real man of flesh and blood. But the stories are couched in the imaginative, poetic style of historical saga, and are therefore marked by the corresponding obscurity. For they are describing an event beyond the reach of historical research or depiction. Hence we have no right to try to analyse or harmonise them. This is to do violence to the whole character of the event in question. There can be no doubt that all these narratives are about the same event, and that they are agreed in substance, intention and interpretation. None of the authors ever even dreamed, for example, of reducing the event to " the rise of the Easter faith of the first disciples." On the other hand, each of the narratives must be read for its own sake just as it stands. Each is a specific witness to the decisive things God said and did in this event. And we can be glad that there is the possibility of adducing one in explanation of the others. Ἐγενόμην νεκρὸς καὶ ἰδοὺ ζῶν (Rev. 1¹⁸)—it is here that all these very saga-like accounts have their common ground. This, and this alone, is what they have to tell us.

A few words may be said in conclusion about the empty tomb (Mk. 16¹⁻⁸ and *par.*) and the ascension (Lk. 24⁵⁰⁻⁵³ ; Ac. 1⁹⁻¹²). These stories are indispensable if we are to understand what the New Testament seeks to proclaim as the Easter message. Taken together, they mark the limits of the Easter period, at one end the empty tomb, and at the other the ascension. (It is worth noting that the limits are drawn not only backwards and forwards, but also downwards and upwards.) In the later apostolic preaching both events, like the Virgin Birth at the beginning of the Gospel narrative, seem to be presupposed, and are certainly never questioned, but they are only hinted at occasionally here and there, and never referred to explicitly. Even in the Easter narratives the empty tomb and the ascension are alike in the fact that they are both indicated rather than described ; the one as an introduction, the other as a conclusion ; the one a little more definitely, though still in very general terms, the other much more vaguely. Indeed, in the strict sense the ascension occurs only in Ac. 1⁹ᶠ·. It is not mentioned at all in the genuine Marcan ending (though this is obviously incomplete). In Matthew it is merely implied in the reference of

Jesus to the power given Him in heaven and on earth (Mt. 28¹⁸). Luke's Gospel, according to the more probable reading at 24⁵¹, is also very indefinite : διέστη ἀπ 'αὐτῶν, while in John it occurs only in the comprehensive terms ἀναβαίνειν and ὑπάγειν, ὑψωθῆναι and δοξασθῆναι, which are used to embrace the whole ascent to Jerusalem, the crucifixion, the resurrection and the reappearance, and do not refer to the ascension as a concrete event. There are reasons for this. The content of the Easter witness, the Easter event, was not that the disciples found the tomb empty or that they saw Him go up to heaven, but that when they had lost Him through death they were sought and found by Him as the Resurrected. The empty tomb and the ascension are merely signs of the Easter event, just as the Virgin Birth is merely the sign of the nativity, namely, of the human generation and birth of the eternal Son of God. Yet both signs are so important that we can hardly say that they might equally well be omitted.

The function of the empty tomb, with its backward, downward, earthward reference, is to show that the Jesus who died and was buried was delivered from death, and therefore from the grave, by the power of God ; that He, the Living, is not to be sought among the dead (Lk. 24⁵). " He is risen ; he is not here : behold the place where they laid him " (Mk. 16⁶). " He is not here ; for he is risen, even as he said " (Mt. 28⁶ ; Lk. 24⁶). He is not here ! But it is the angels who say this. Since the nativity and temptation the angels have not played any active part. But they now reappear at the tomb. And it is only the angels who say this ; who as it were draw the line behind which there can be no going back. They only point to the empty tomb. The empty tomb was obviously a very ambiguous and contestable fact (Mt. 27⁶²f. ; 28¹¹f.). And what has happened around this sepulchre is a warning against making it a primary focus of attention. The empty tomb is not the same thing as the resurrection. It is not the appearance of the Living ; it is only its presupposition. Hence it is only the sign, although an indispensable sign. Christians do not believe in the empty tomb, but in the living Christ. This does not mean, however, that we can believe in the living Christ without believing in the empty tomb. Is it just a " legend " ? What matter ? It still refers to the phenomenon ensuing the resurrection, to the presupposition of the appearance of Jesus. It is the sign which obviates all possible misunderstanding. It cannot, therefore, but demand our assent, even as a legend. Rejection of the legend of the empty tomb has always been accompanied by rejection of the saga of the living Jesus, and necessarily so. Far better, then, to admit that the empty tomb belongs to the Easter event as its sign.

The same considerations apply to the ascension. It is less directly attested in the New Testament, but unlike the empty tomb it has found a place in the creed, and has its own special feast in the Church Kalendar. In contrast to the first sign it points forwards and upwards, thus serving a positive function. Just as the discovery of the empty tomb by the women marks the beginning of the Easter time and history, its end is marked by the meeting of the disciples on the mountain, which in Mt. 28¹⁶ is located in Galilee, but which Ac. 1¹² identifies with the Mount of Olives. The end consists in their θεᾶσθαι αὐτὸν πορευόμενον εἰς τὸν οὐρανόν (Ac. 1¹¹). As the empty tomb looks downwards, the ascension looks upwards. But again the ascension—Jesus' disappearance into heaven— is the sign of the Resurrected, not the Resurrected Himself. " Heaven " in biblical language is the sum of the inaccessible and incomprehensible side of the created world, so that, although it is not God Himself, it is the throne of God, the creaturely correspondence to his glory, which is veiled from man, and cannot be disclosed except on His initiative. There is no sense in trying to visualise the ascension as a literal event, like going up in a balloon. The achievements of Christian art in this field are amongst its worst perpetrations. But of course this is no reason why they should be used to make the whole thing ridiculous. The point of the story is not that when Jesus left His disciples He visibly embarked upon a wonderful journey into space, but that when He left them He entered the side of the created world which was provisionally inaccessible and incomprehensible, that before their eyes He ceased to be before their eyes. This does not mean, however, that He ceased to be a creature, man. What it does mean is that He showed Himself quite unequivocally to be the creature, the man, who in provisional distinction from all other men lives on the God-ward side of the universe, sharing His throne, existing and acting in the mode of God, and therefore to be remembered as such, to be known once for all as this exalted creature, this exalted man, and henceforth to be accepted as the One who exists in this form to all eternity. The most important verse in the ascension story is the one which runs : " A cloud received him out of their sight " (Ac. 1⁹). In biblical language, the cloud does not signify merely the hiddenness of God, but His hidden presence, and the coming revelation which penetrates this hiddenness. It does not signify merely the heaven which is closed for us, but the heaven which from within, on God's side, will not always be closed. The words of the angels—note how they reappear at this point after playing no part in the Easter story proper—are a commentary on this : " Ye men of Galilee, why stand ye gazing up into heaven ? this same Jesus, which is taken up from you into heaven, shall so come in like manner as ye have seen him go into heaven " (Ac. 1¹¹). Whatever it is, the cloud which takes Him out of their sight is not a cloud of sorrow. And the view that the ascension is Jesus' " farewell " to His disciples must be treated with caution. The mode of this leavetaking is what matters. He reveals Himself to them not only as the One who according to Mt. 28²⁰ will be with them in this heavenly mode of existence all the days, even to the consummation (συντέλεια) of the age, but also as the One who will come again to usher in this consummation. The ascension is the proleptic sign of the *parousia*, pointing to the Son of Man who will finally and visibly emerge from the concealment of His heavenly existence and come on the clouds of heaven (Mt. 24³⁰). This conclusion to the Easter history gives to the whole retrospective memory of the Resurrected this joyous character. It shows that Jesus did not enter and is not to be sought after the Easter history and the Easter time in any kind of hiddenness, but in the hiddenness of God. And finally it describes the hiddenness of God in such a way as to suggest that it burgeons with the conclusive revelation still awaited in the future. As this sign, the ascension is indispensable, and it would be injudicious as well as ungrateful on any grounds to ignore or reject this upward and forward-looking sign.

For these reasons it was impossible for the apostles to record and depict the history of the man Jesus in His time without adding this post-history, the Easter history. For this particular recollection belonged to their recollection of the man Jesus in His time. And it belonged to it decisively as the recollection of the revelation, of the source of knowledge, of the key to the history previously witnessed by them. The Easter history opened their eyes to the nature of this man and His history, to the previously concealed character of this history as salvation history, and therefore to the fact that what had happened had done so once and once for all, and to the way in which the " once " of this event differed absolutely from that of their own history and all history, and indeed from every other " once." God the Creator had not merely been present to them in the man Jesus, but He had actually appeared in this post-history. This is what illuminated and explained the whole history of this man in His time. This was the light in which this whole history—for it was the history of the same man who had now encountered them as alive from the dead—was revealed as the appearance of God and therefore as incomparable salvation history, as the " once " which is absolutely distinguished from each and every other " once."

It was this fact which gave to the ἅπαξ and ἐφάπαξ of the New Testament its specific import, so that it could not be confused with any other, but would only acquire necessarily the sense of "once for all." It was this fact which necessarily made the evangelical narration the inalienable presupposition of apostolic proclamation. And again it was this fact which made the apostolic community quite immune from Docetism, from the possibility of a faith in Christ detached from the existence and knowledge of the man Jesus. The glory of the risen Christ was identical with the glory of the Jesus of Nazareth who went up from Galilee to Jerusalem to be crucified. It was identical with the glory of His human person, his human words and works. That this Jesus was the appearance of God, the salvation of the world, was what the disciples remembered as they looked back upon that post-history, He Himself as the Resurrected having indelibly impressed it upon their minds in the course of that history.

The Easter time is simply the time of the revelation of the mystery of the preceding time of the life and death of the man Jesus. The two times are inseparably linked. They are together the time of the man Jesus to the extent that His person existing in His words and works, His mystery first and then its revelation, constitute its content. But this means that this whole time is the time of the appearance and presence of God. At the heart of all other times, both before and after, it is the time in which God Himself was this man, and therefore had time, a life-time. It is the Creator of all reality distinct from Himself who, taking flesh of our flesh, also took time, at the heart of what we think we know as time. It is the Lord of time who became temporal and had time : His own time at the heart of all the times of the being created by Him ; and this time in the same way as He had it in Himself before all created being, as He does not cease to have it above all created being, and as He will have it with all created being when the time of this being is over. Here, in this creature, in this man, who had His own time of life and death, and beyond this His time of revelation, God, the Creator and Lord, had already had time before His time, eternal time. It is the time which He took to Himself, thus granting it as a gift to the men of all time. It is the time which He willed to have for us in order to inaugurate and establish His covenant. It is the time which is the time of all times because what God does in it is the goal of all creation and therefore of all created time. Since God in His Word had time for us, and at the heart of all other times there was this particular time, the eternal time of God, all other times are now controlled by this time, i.e., dominated, limited and determined by their proximity to it. This means positively that they are shown not to be mere illusions. The many philosophical theories of time which deny its reality and regard it as a mere form or abstraction or figment of the imagination can only be finally abandoned when we consider that God Himself once took time and thus treated it as something real. But it also means critically that there is no such thing as absolute time, no immutable law of time. Not even its irreversibility can be adduced as an inviolable principle in relation to the time which was once real at the heart of time as that of the life and death and revelation of the man Jesus. There is no time in itself, rivalling God and imposing conditions on Him. There is no god called Chronos. And it is better to avoid conceptions of time which might suggest that there is. On the other hand, we need not be surprised if the nature and laws of all other times, and all that we think we know as time, are seen to be illuminated and relativised by this time. Relativised does not mean discarded. Time is real, and will always be so. Even its end—and it will one day come to an end as it once began—will not mean that it is thrown away. Yet even now its meaning does not lie in itself. But as all creation has its goal in what God purposes and will do and does within it for man, for us, so time as its historical form has its meaning in the particular time which God once took for the execution of this purpose, for establishing His covenant with man. This is the hidden meaning of all time, even of all other time. And time in itself has no property, no laws, to preclude the control of all other times by this time, or to prevent this time of *Deus praesens* impressing upon them—in varying degrees and in different ways—the stamp of its own nature and law. The fact that all other times have been placed in proximity to this time means that even in them there may be discerned traces of this eternal time, of the true and proper time in which they necessarily have a share because, even though at a different level, they too are real times.

The time in which God revealed His Word is summarily defined in Tit. 1³ as the καιροὶ ἴδιοι. This means the times which God has adopted for His purpose and therefore made His own. There are types of this in the Old Testament, a major and a minor, and both are so eloquent that they call for notice.

The minor is the sabbatical year and the year of jubilee in Lev. 25¹⁻³⁴. The sabbatical year (v. 1 f.) occurs once every seven years, and while it lasts the land is left fallow. The year of jubilee (v. 8 f.)—the *locus classicus* for theological opponents of the doctrine of free economy—occurs once every fifty years, being the year after a period of seven times seven years. Its dawn is heralded by the sound of a trumpet through the length and breadth of the land. All agricultural labour must be stopped, and there is a general liberation and restitution. All property is restored to those who have mortgaged it during the previous forty-nine years. The purchase price (only the produce could be bought or sold) varies according to the distance from the year of jubilee, a definite sale of the land being excluded. In this year, which is obviously so important even for relationships in the other forty-nine, the author of Is. 61¹ᶠ· sees a type of the " acceptable year of the Lord," of " the day of vengeance of our God," when all that mourn will be comforted, receiving " beauty for ashes, the oil of joy for mourning, the garment of praise for the spirit of heaviness ; that they might be called trees of righteousness, the planting of the Lord, that he might be glorified." I take it that this refers to the Messianic time of redemption. But according to the sermon in the synagogue at Nazareth (Lk. 4[17f.]), this extra-ordinary year is adopted by Jesus as a type of His own time : " The Spirit of the Lord is upon me, because he hath anointed me to preach good tidings to the poor ; he hath sent me to preach deliverance to the captives, and recovering of sight to the blind, to set at liberty them that are bruised, to preach the acceptable year of the Lord " (v. 18 f.). " This day hath this scripture been fulfilled in your ears " (v. 21). Old Testament scholars tell us that the provisions of Lev. 25 were never actually put into practice, at any rate literally. If that is so, it merely serves to underline the prophetic character of this part of the Old Testament Law. Israel may have failed in this as in other respects, but its failure made no difference to the promise which the Law contained. Its years, the years of its people, of rich and poor alike, were not to drag on indefinitely, but to issue in a year of welcome festivity, liberation and restitution. And this perhaps is the time-consciousness of Old Testament man, not the consciousness of indefinite time, but that of the time of an era destined to culminate in another, and therefore the explanation of a coming time, the end and new beginning by which the present time with its limitation is already illuminated and relativised, being drawn and controlled by it as though by a powerful magnet.

The major Old Testament type, whose connexion with Lev. 25 is sufficiently obvious, is of course the institution of the Sabbath, which is so strongly emphasised in the first creation saga in Gen. 2[1-3]. " And the heaven and the earth were finished, and all the host of them. And on the seventh day God finished his work which he had made ; and he rested on the seventh day from all his work which he had made." In other words, after creating man on the sixth day, God looks back on His whole work of creation and sees that it is good, even very good, i.e., pre-eminently suited for His future purpose. But God does not continue His work on the seventh day in an infinite series of creative acts. He sets a limit to His activity, and thus to His creation as well. The object of His further dealings is this and not another world, the world completed with the creation of man. He now, as it were, ascends His throne and assumes sovereignty over His creation. He has now become its God, co-existing with it, and with man in particular as His last and culminating creation. Without ceasing to be God, He has made Himself a worldly, human, temporal God in relation to this work of His. He is now free to act as that kind of God, and as such He now celebrates and rejoices. Without detriment to His eternal glory, His glory will now be a glory in this distinct realm of heaven and earth and all their hosts, and especially in the existence of man. It is as the Lord of creation and the Lord of man, whose Master He has now become, that He now withdraws and rests. According to the saga, this is the content of the seventh day, of the last of the seven first days of time. This was the day to which time was already moving with its creation, when it became the life-time of other living creatures side by side with the living God. Time was intended for this day, the day in which God thus committed Himself to the world and man. Time was intended for this day as the day of the Lord of the world and of man ; as the day of the Lord of the covenant between Himself and His creatures. But the story continues : " And God blessed the seventh day, and hallowed it : because that in it he rested from all his work which God created and made." Here, for the first time, God's sovereignty over His creature is made manifest in the commandment to man to keep holy the seventh day of creation. But it must be remembered that God's seventh day was man's first. Man now has time as well, the time of life. And primarily, and not just conclusively, it is this time, the day of the Lord, and therefore the time to be a witness of God's completion of His work and His rest, sharing in His Sabbath freedom, Sabbath festivity and Sabbath joy ; the special time to be with God, the God who in this special time finishes His work and rests from it, no longer being the God who wills to be without the world and man but to be with him. The time of man begins, therefore, on the basis of the work God has done before his time and not with reference to any work still ahead of him. The time of man begins, therefore, with a day of rest and not a day of work ; with freedom and not with obligation ; with a holiday and not with a task ; with joy and not with labour and toil ; under the Gospel and not under the Law. These other things will all come, but when they do they will be secondary and additional. The first thing in the time of man is that he belongs to His Creator ; just as the last thing in the time of the Creator is that He belongs to His creature.

Basically, then, it was no innovation when the early Christians (1 Cor. 16² ; Ac. 20⁷) adopted the first day of the week as a holiday instead of the seventh and called it the κυριακὴ ἡμέρα (Rev. 1¹⁰). On the contrary it was a discovery and application of the chronology implicit in Gen. 1–2. For they began the week with a holiday instead of ending it with one. What led to the change was of course the fact that the day after the Sabbath, and therefore the first day of the Jewish week, was the day of Christ's resurrection (Mk. 16² and *par.*). The new chronology surely means that the true meaning of the old is brought to light. When He had created man God saw that everything He had planned and made was good. In the completion of His work, He entered into a free and living fellowship with man, and brought man into fellowship with Himself. Only when this had been achieved could man set off into the week. What looks like his first day, i.e., his first working day, is really his second. His real first day is the Lord's day, the day when God rested from His work and devoted Himself to freedom, festivity and joy. Man is privileged to have a share in this day, descending from its heights to the depths of his first working day. By making God's Sabbath, and the invitation to man to share it, the context of a special day, the first creation saga points clearly and unmistakeably to the fact that the created time series is to include a special time of the salvation planned by God for the whole of His creation ; the day of His appearing, His judgment and His mercy, the " great and notable day of the Lord " (Ac. 2²⁰) : " And it shall come to pass, that whosoever shall call on the name of the Lord shall be saved " (Ac. 2²¹). This calling upon the name of the Lord in connexion with the special time of His appearance and presence is made possible by the institution of the recurrent Sabbath which concludes the week but also marks a new beginning. Will this offer be accepted or not ? Will the Sabbath be kept or broken ? Will the Lord's name be invoked or disregarded ? This is the challenge of the Sabbath from its first institution. Will man in his own time " enter into God's rest " (Heb. 4¹⁻¹¹) or spurn it ? But over and above the human decision of obedience or disobedience the power of this institution, the Sabbath itself (observed or desecrated), is the immutable sign, set up in and with the creation of time, of the particular time of God to which all other times move. Old Testament Israel did not see this day of the Lord. All it saw was the recurrent weekly sign of the Sabbath, and the prophets are full of complaints about its constant failure to keep the Sabbath law and to remember the name of the Lord. Or did it really see this day as it saw the sign, even though it flouted it ? However that may be, God remained faithful to Israel and therefore the sign remained. At the end of every week came this seventh day, the only day of the week with a special name (ἄρα ἀπολείπεται σαββατισμὸς τῷ λαῷ τοῦ θεοῦ, Heb. 4⁹). This was Israel's lack in all its time, but also its promise. The apostolic Church, on the other hand, saw not only the sign, but the actual day of the Lord ; and the real dawn of this day ; the true Sabbath observed and celebrated with God the Creator through the one man Jesus, in whose day it broke for them too, so that they too may enter into God's rest. And they have to see and understand time, not only with a forward but also and decisively with a backward reference to this day of rest, and must observe the year of the birth of Jesus as the first year of that era, and the day of His resurrection as the first day of their week.

We may now turn our attention to the important New Testament concept of " the fulness of time."

We naturally begin with Gal. 4¹ᶠ·. In this passage Paul suggests that there was a time when the heir, i.e., man elected and created by God to be His son, was still in the position of a minor. Although the rightful " Lord of all," he was subjected to " tutors and governors," i.e., the apparently autonomous and omnipotent powers of created being (the στοιχεῖα τοῦ κόσμου). Man would thus seem to be no more than a slave among other slaves. " But when the πλήρωμα τοῦ χρόνου was come, God sent forth his Son, made of a woman, born under the law, to redeem them that were under the law, that we might receive the adoption of sons." The Son of God " came " ; He was sent from God, sent to men. Therefore He was Himself " born of a woman, born under the law." He entered the temporality which is that of each and every man. With Him came the " fulness of time." Note the emphasis laid on the final phrase, at first sight almost as if an independent event had made the mission of the Son possible, as if the time were now ripe, the historical situation favourable, for the mission of the Son. But this is not what Paul meant. The mission of the Son actually brings the fulness of time with it, and not *vice versa*. With the mission of the Son, with His entry into the time process, a new era of time has dawned, so far-reaching in its consequences that it may be justly called the fulness of all time. Man has now reached maturity. He has become God's son and heir, the " Lord of all." He has become a free man. This is the event which gives time its fulness. But the term πλήρωμα τοῦ χρόνου has a further meaning. This event does not merely make this particular time fulfilled time. This fulfilled time is before or after all other time. Hence it makes all time, χρόνος as such, in the sequence and succession of which this fulfilment was achieved, fulfilled time. The *raison d'être* of all time, both past and future, is that there should be this fulfilment at this particular time. Time may seem to move into the void but it is actually moving towards this event ; just as it may seem to move out of the void, but it is actually moving from this event. The fulfilment of time has now " come," epitomising all the coming and going of time. Henceforth all time can be regarded only as time fulfilled in this particular time.

Now let us turn to Eph. 1⁹ᶠ·, where we read that " before the foundation of the world " it was the good-pleasure (εὐδοκία) of God to achieve a purpose which He had decided and resolved to execute. This purpose was once a mystery, but now it is no longer so, for it has been revealed and executed in the Gospel. The content of this purpose is ἀνακεφαλαιώσασθαι τὰ πάντα ἐν τῷ Χριστῷ. That is to say, Christ is to become the Head of all creation. He is to rule it and give it meaning. This is God's plan for the world, and it is the execution of this plan which involves the οἰκονομία τοῦ πληρώματος τῶν καιρῶν. Its execution will coincide with the inauguration of the " fulness of time." This is what has happened and has been revealed by the Gospel. For God's plan to sum up all things under Christ as their Head, and therefore the " fulness of time," has actually taken place and may therefore be known by us in terms of this event. Note again how the one depends on the other. The One who wills and accomplishes and reveals the ἀνακεφαλαίωσις also wills and accomplishes and reveals the " fulfilment of the times." It is with the summing up of all created being in Christ as its Head that the καιροί—the individual times of individual created things—are not cancelled or destroyed but fulfilled. None of these times moved into the void. They all moved towards this goal, this event, and therefore this particular time.

These two Pauline texts will help us to understand Mk. 1¹⁴ᶠ·, which is so important in this connexion. It gives us first a comprehensive summary of the activity of Jesus. He had been baptised by John and confirmed by the voice from heaven as the beloved Son of God, the object here too of His εὐδοκία. Then He had been tempted by the devil forty days in the wilderness among the wild beasts, after which angels came and ministered to Him. And now, we are told, He " came " into Galilee, the intermediate territory between Jew and Gentile. He " came," bringing the " glad tidings " of God, saying : " The time is fulfilled, and the kingdom of God is at hand : repent ye, and believe the gospel." We may accept the translation " is at hand," or, " has drawn nigh," for this is the message of John the Baptist in Mt. 3^2, and the disciples are entrusted with the same declaration in Lk. 10^9, [11]. It implies that the irruption of the kingdom into history is imminent. On the other hand, if we adopt the suggestion that ἤγγικεν is simply a restrained expression for " has come," the use of this term is quite in accordance with the esoteric character of the pre-Easter history of the man Jesus, being wholly in line, for instance, with His command to the disciples to tell no one that He is the Messiah (Mt. 17^9). Jesus' Messiahship is His secret, and can be published only when it has been disclosed from within. Similarly, the kingdom of God can be said to have come only when God has revealed it. Until then men must pray for its coming (Mt. 6^{10}). Indeed, they will still have to pray for its coming even after it has been revealed. Until then the restrained ἤγγικεν must be used. Yet all the time there is a secretly implied ἐλήλυθεν. This is brought out plainly in the Beelzebub controversy (see Kümmel, *op. cit.*, p. 63 f.). " If I by the Spirit of God cast out devils, then is the kingdom of God come upon you " (ἔφθασεν ἐφ᾽ ὑμᾶς, Mt. 12^{28}). The strong man has already been bound, and his house can now be plundered (Mt. 12^{29}). And Jesus' reference to His deeds in the reply to John the Baptist (" the blind receive their sight, and the lame walk . . ." Mt. $11^{2f.}$) implies that the eschatological salvation is no longer just a future expectation, but a present reality. Lk. 17^{21} puts it beyond all doubt : " The kingdom of God is in your midst." So, too, does the saying : " But blessed are your eyes, for they see : and your ears, for they hear. For verily I say unto you, That many prophets and righteous men have desired to see those things that ye see, and have not seen them ; and to hear those things that ye hear, and have not heard them " (Mt. $13^{16f.}$)—a saying which is in remarkable contrast with Lk. 17^{22} : " The days will come, when ye shall desire to see one of the days of the son of man, and ye shall not see it (any longer)." We should also notice the reason Jesus gives for the power which even the disciples have over demons : " I beheld Satan as lightning fall from heaven " (Lk. 10^{18}). How could the kingdom be stormed by violent men (Mt. 11^{12}) if it were not already present ? And how could a dividing line be drawn between the time before John the Baptist and the time after him, as is done in the continuation of the saying : " For all the prophets and the law prophesied until John. And if ye are willing to receive it, this is Elijah, which is to come. He that hath ears to hear, let him hear " (Mt. $11^{13f.}$), if the kingdom had not come after the coming and delivering up of this " Elijah " ? And how could Jesus say that He had come to fulfil the law if the kingdom had not already come (Mt. 5^{17}) ? It is not, therefore, surprising to find Mark 1^{15} prefacing the statement that the kingdom had drawn nigh with the observation that " the time is fulfilled." There is an undoubted tension between the two phrases. The latter is not esoteric or restrained in this context. It is tolerable and intelligible only if ἤγγικεν is given an esoteric sense, if it encloses the mystery of an ἐλήλυθεν. For the phrase πεπλήρωται ὁ καιρός is undoubtedly meant to describe an absolutely unique event marking an end and a new beginning in time. An event of the present gives meaning to the time before it and therefore also to the time after it. " The time is fulfilled " is so emphatic a statement that the one which follows would be quite flat and banal if it really meant no more than that the kingdom had drawn nigh, i.e., if in the ἤγγικεν we did not read the concealed ἐλήλυθεν. Indeed, in Gal. 4^4 the parallel to the " fulness of time " is the solemn assertion that God sent His Son into the world, while in Eph. 1^{10} the parallel is the ἀνακεφαλαίωσις of all things in Christ. Moreover, Mk. 1^{15} speaks expressly of a coming in a very real sense : ἦλθεν ὁ Ἰησοῦς εἰς τὴν Γαλιλαίαν κηρύσσων τὸ εὐαγγέλιον τοῦ θεοῦ. This is certainly more than a mere announcement. It is an actual irruption rather than mere imminence. If the kingdom could only be announced prior to its manifestation with the coming of Jesus as the Bearer of God's good news, in and with Him there also came, in hidden but very real form, the kingdom and therefore the fulness of time, just as with the coming of Jesus the Law was fulfilled and its whole meaning disclosed. When Jesus came, all the promises and prophecies of the Old Testament were fulfilled. No more was now needed than that this coming should run its course in time. The " year of grace," the " great and glorious day of the Lord," the true Sabbath of which the weekly Sabbath was only a sign, the Sabbath kept by God and man together, was not only at the doors but had actually dawned. If the good news of God was that the time was fulfilled, nothing less could have happened. Anything less would be inadequate to explain the tremendous cæsura indicated by the expression " fulness of time," whether we think of the conclusion of the time " until John " on the one hand or the dawning on the other of the new time obviously granted solely for the purpose of enabling men to receive the good news of God, to accept God's immediate presence and rule in time, and therefore to repent and believe, clearly in the form of concrete acts in time. Μετάνοια means a complete re-orientation, both inward and outward, of the whole man to the God who in a very real sense has turned to him in time. Πίστις means the unquestioning trust in this God which is the positive side of this re-orientation ; the new life which is the only possible life after this event in the time which follows it. In the language of Gal. 4¹ᶠ·, it means turning right about and acquiring the confidence of a son who becomes " lord of all " on his coming of age ; or, in the language of Eph. 1⁹ᶠ·, it means a complete re-appraisal of the human situation in the light of the ἀνακεφαλαίωσις which has already been achieved. The difference between Mk. 1 and these other passages is that it explicitly calls attention to the consequence of all this for the time which follows. This is of a piece with the fact that it does not speak abstractly about πλήρωμα, but concretely about an event, the event of πληροῦσθαι, the reference being concretely to the coming of Jesus into Galilee, which, unless we are completely mistaken, is identical with His advent, and therefore with the advent of the kingdom. It also explains why the μετανοεῖτε καὶ πιστεύετε has so imperatively concrete a reference to the future, and therefore why the beginning of the new time is explicitly indicated with the ending of the old. Mk. 1 makes it clear beyond all doubt that in the life of Jesus we have to do with a real event in time, but with a particular event and therefore a particular time, the time of the centre which dominates all other times. The fact that in His life all time comes to fruition means that all time before it moved towards it and all time after it moved away from it. In the last resort the only real reason why men had time at all was that—although they did not realise it, apart from the prophets who prophesied " until John "—this day was to come. And the men after Christ have time only in order to orientate their lives in the light of this day which in the series of days has now appeared ἅπαξ and ἐφάπαξ and is proclaimed with an explicit imperative. A similar idea is expressed in Paul's speech on the Areopagus (Ac. 17³⁰ᶠ·) : " The times of this ignorance (χρόνοι τῆς ἀγνοίας) God winked at ; but now commandeth all men every where to repent : because he hath appointed a day (ἔστησεν ἡμέραν), in the which he will judge the world in righteousness by that man whom he hath ordained ; whereof he hath given assurance unto all men, in that he hath raised him from the dead."

But behind the application of the concept of the fulfilment to that of time in Gal. 4, Eph. 1 and Mk. 1 there lies a definite view of time. It is pictured as an empty vessel, not yet filled, but waiting to be filled up at a particular time. As all the commandments, promises and prophecies of the prophets and righteous men of the Old Testament, as all its sayings and types, are without content, apart from the coming of the kingdom in the man Jesus, and therefore defective in themselves, yet, being related to this event, and destined all along for this content, they are not for nothing, so too it is with time in itself and as such. It, too, is empty in both the negative and positive sense : empty of this content and empty for this content. It has both the defect and the advantage of being time which is hastening toward the time of Jesus and is then destined to move away from His time. Standing as it does in this relation to His time, it is in an indirect, though very real sense, His time. Its fulness resides in His time, in the πληροῦσθαι, the πλήρωμα, of the event of His life. In Him, the Son and Head of all things, in the kingdom of God which came to Galilee and was proclaimed in Galilee, all time is brought to an end and begins afresh as full and proper time.

It is important to remember how concrete all this is. The fulfilment of time itself had this particular time which is datable in relation to other times. There is no fulfilment of time without the time of fulfilment. That is why 1 Pet. 1²⁰, speaking of the time of the revelation of the Lamb chosen before the foundation of the world, calls it the " last " time, the ἔσχατος τῶν χρόνων. It is linked with a whole sequence of prevailing times. It forms the term of this sequence, but also marks the beginning of a new sequence of times. It was on the " last " of these days that God, having at sundry times and in divers manners spoken in those days unto the fathers by the prophets, spoke in His Son, whom He had made the heir of all things, and by whom also He created the times (æons, Heb. 1¹ᶠ·.). " But last of all (when He had sent one servant after another) he sent unto them his son " (Mt. 21³⁷). And it is obviously significant that it was on the last and great day of the feast (Jn. 7³⁷) that " Jesus stood and cried, saying, If any man thirst, let him come unto me, and drink." This fulfilment proceeds even during this great day of His until it is completed and lies behind. The day of Jesus lasts, and as long as it lasts He must work the works of Him that sent Him, standing and issuing His summons and invitation. " As long as I am in the world, I am the light of the world " (Jn. 9⁴ᶠ·). This text clearly envisages a real day, with a morning and evening ; a real time with beginning, duration and end. For it says explicitly : " While it is day," and then continues : " The night cometh when no man can work." Thus the fulfilment of time is itself an event which fulfils time, an event which begins, continues and ends. It is for this reason that Jesus justifies His delay at the marriage of Cana of Galilee with the words : " Mine hour is not yet come " (Jn. 2⁴), and His initial absence from the feast at Jerusalem with the words : " My time is not yet fulfilled " (Jn. 7⁸). The assault of His enemies gathers weight before it reaches its climax and contributes to the fulfilment of time, and it must be held in check until the right moment (Lk. 20¹⁹, 22⁵²ᶠ·). Even the climax is marked by development. First we read : " The hour is at hand, and the Son of man is betrayed into the hands of sinners " (Mt. 26⁴⁵), and only then : " The hour is come " (Jn. 17¹) ; " This is your hour and the power of darkness " (Lk. 22⁵³) ; " Father, save me from this hour " (Jn. 12²⁷). Only then can the clock of Good Friday begin to strike until we reach the τετέλεσται which Jesus can say only as He dies on the cross, and which according to Jn. 19³⁰ is His very last word. It is for this reason, too, that when Heb. 5⁷ᶠ· comes to speak of what He did " in the days of his flesh," and of the way in which He brought in the fulness of time, it sums it all up in a reference to the last of His days, the day of the passion. It is as Jesus travels this road to the bitter end that there takes place what the New Testament calls the " fulfilment of time," and His time becomes fulfilled time, and is revealed as such to His disciples in the Easter time.

We have called this time of His at the heart of other times the time of God : eternal time ; the time which God has assumed for us, and thus granted to us, the men of all times ; the time of His covenant ; or, as the Bible sees it, the great Sabbath ; the year of salvation ; fulfilled time. We must now try to assess the material implications of all this for our understanding of this particular time.

Our previous deliberations should have made it clear that in the first instance the time of Jesus is also a time like all other times ; that it occurred once and once for all ; that it had beginning, duration and end ; that it was contemporary for some, future for others, and for others again, e.g., for us, past. Only a docetic attitude to Jesus can deny that His being in time also means what being in time means for us all. Our recognition of His true humanity depends on our acceptance of this proposition. Even the recognition of His true deity, implying as it does the identity between His time and God's, does not rule out this simple meaning of His being in time. On the contrary, it includes it. Of course there is much more to see and say, but it would all be pointless if we ignored or minimised this simple truth.

It is as well to realise how closely the relevant New Testament formulæ support this view. This is the case with the formula which constantly recurs in different forms in the Apocalypse (Rev. 1[4, 8, 17], 4[8], 21[6], 22[13]), in clear reminiscence of Is. 41[4], 44[6], 48[12] : I am he that was, and is, and is to come, the beginning and the ending, the first and the last, the Alpha and Omega. Of course these formulæ are much too solemn to be taken simply as a description of the being of a man in its temporal limits and in its beginning, duration and end in time, and therefore as a being contemporary, future or past to that of others. The formula says much more than this. But it does include this, as a primary truth within its wider implications. The same holds good of Heb. 13[8] : " Jesus Christ the same yesterday, and today, and for ever." This again means more than that the man Jesus lived in a movement from yesterday through to-day to to-morrow. Yet we miss the deeper implications if we overlook the primary and simple meaning of the words.

The three dimensions which play a part in any conception of time are equally important for an understanding of the time of Jesus as the time of God. But there is a further point to be noticed. The time of Jesus is not only a time like all others ; it is also different from them. For all other times are confined to the three dimensions. They begin, they endure, and they come to an end. According to the standpoint of the observer, they are future, contemporary or past.

1. Every other time begins, and therefore from the standpoint of an earlier time it is a future time. This means that it does not yet exist at this earlier time.

2. Every other time has duration, and therefore from the standpoint of the same time it is present. This means that its contemporaneity is limited to its duration, and to that of the contemporary observer.

3. Every other time comes to an end, and therefore from the standpoint of a later time it is already past. This means that it no longer exists at this time.

But these limitations of all other times—the times of all other living creatures—do not apply to the time of the man Jesus.

1. To be sure, the life of the man Jesus has a beginning, and His time was once future. Yet this does not mean that it did not then exist.

2. The life of Jesus has duration, and therefore it was once contemporary. Yet this does not mean that it was present only in its duration, and from the standpoint of contemporaries.

3. The life of Jesus comes to an end and therefore it became past. Yet this does not mean that it then ceased to be.

The removal of the limitations of its yesterday, to-day and to-morrow, of its once, now and then, is the distinctive feature of the time of the man Jesus. For as such, according to its manifestation in Easter-time, it is also the time of God ; eternal time ; the time of the covenant ; the great Sabbath ; the year of salvation ; fulfilled time. What is for all other times, the times of all other living creatures, an absolute barrier, is for Him in His time a gateway. We shall now try to formulate positively what we have so far stated only in the form of delimitation.

1. The life of Jesus begins, and therefore it was once future. But the man Jesus already was even before He was. Hence the time before His time, the time when this was still future, because it hastened forward to His future, was also His time, the time of His being.

2. The life of Jesus has duration, and therefore it was once present. But for all its singularity this present reaches back to His past when His time was still future, and forward to His future when His time will be past. The man Jesus is as He was and will be. Even the time of His present, just because it is the time of His present, is also the time before and after His time, and is thus His time, the time of His being.

3. The life of Jesus comes to an end, and therefore there was a moment when His time became past. But its end is such that it is always present and still future. The man Jesus was as He is and will be. Even the time after His time, the time in which His time is already past time, because it is the time of His past, the time which derives from Him, is the time of His renewed presence, the time of His new coming, and therefore again His time.

This means, however, that from the standpoint of the three dimensions of every conception of time, His time is not only the time of a man, but the time of God, eternal time. Thus, as the title of this sub-section suggests, He not only is in time and has time like other men, but He is also Lord of time.

It is clear that—whether as delimitation or positive formulation—this could not be said, or could be said only in abstraction, if to the being of the man Jesus in time there did not belong His being in Easter time. If Christ were not risen from the dead, our treatment of the whole subject would have no basis whatever in the Word and revelation of God. Every assertion beyond the mere fact that Jesus' time was like all other times in that it had beginning, duration and end, would be mere speculation, a house of cards built on our subjective impression of His life in time, and liable to collapse at the slightest touch of justifiable doubts as to the validity of our subjective impression and therefore our competence. Jesus is the Lord of time in the sense expounded because He is the Son of God, and as such the eternal God in person, the Creator of all time and therefore its sovereign Ruler. Either He is this, or He is not the Lord of time at all. But we insist that He is the Lord of time because He has revealed Himself as such, because in the resurrection His appearance has proved to be that of the eternal God. Otherwise we have no grounds for making this claim, and it is better not to pretend that we have. The apostles and the Church of the New Testament can and must say what is said in the formulæ of the Epistle to the Hebrews and the Apocalypse—we now turn to their true and explicit sense—because they start at the resurrection of Jesus, because in the light of this event they see the real meaning of Jesus' previous existence in time, and because they regard it as axiomatic that all their thinking and speaking about His whole being in time should start at this point.

Of all the relevant passages in the Apocalypse, the clearest is Rev. 1⁸ : " I am the Alpha and the Omega, saith the Lord, which is, and which was, and which is to come, the Almighty " (παντοκράτωρ). The context leaves us in no doubt that the speaker is not God *in abstracto*, but God *in concreto*, God in His identity with the man Jesus. It is equally clear that when the context speaks of His being in time it implies much more that that time has a beginning, duration and end. " I am," says Jesus here, " *the* Alpha and *the* Omega "—ὁ πρῶτος καὶ ὁ ἔσχατος, ἡ ἀρχὴ καὶ τὸ τέλος, as these letters are interpreted in Rev. 22¹³. Not even this part of the formula speaks of timelessness. For although A and O are the first and last letters, they are part of the Greek alphabet, belonging to the series which includes all the other letters. The first and the last are not outside the series but within it. So, too, it is with Jesus when He calls Himself the Alpha and Omega. He ascribes to Himself a being in time. The same truth emerges unmistakeably from the allusion to the three dimensions, the second dimension being significantly placed first in verse 8 : " which is, and which was, and which is to come." His life embraces a present, past and future. Here is no timeless being, but a strictly temporal one, though of course it differs from all other temporal being as that which is divinely temporal. This is made plain, not only by the addition of " the Almighty " at the end of the formula, although this gives verbal support to our title " Lord of Time," but above all by the fact that Ἐγώ εἰμι is put at the head of the formula and that ὁ ὤν is the first predicate. Ἐγώ εἰμι ὁ ὤν is a quotation from Ex. 3¹⁴ : " I AM THAT I AM." This passage speaks of a being in time, but the reference is to the divine being, the being of Yahweh, in time. And the amplification of ὁ ὤν : ὁ ἦν καὶ ὁ ἐρχόμενος, shows how the author of the Apocalypse understood the " I am " in the predicate : I am (in Rev. 1¹⁷ ὁ ὤν is expressly replaced by ὁ ζών) He who has life in Himself. That is to say, I am sovereign over my own being. Even as present I am He who was and will be. All this is applied to the being of the man Jesus in time. The all-inclusive " I am " rules out any notion that the three dimensions, present, past and future, simply follow one another in succession. The very fact that 1⁸ puts the " I am " and the " which is " first is a plain warning. It means : " I am all this simultaneously. I, the same, am ; I was as the same ; and I will come again as the same. My time is always simultaneously present, past and future. That is why I am the Alpha and Omega, the beginning and the ending, the first and the last. Since my present includes the past and future it is both the first and last of all other times. All times have their source and end in my time. Of course, all these other times are real times, for at the heart of them I have time. But other times are previous or subsequent to mine. They are overshadowed, dominated and divided into periods by my time. It is my present that makes them either past or future, for my present includes both. I was, and I am to come, as surely as I am and live. This is how the author of the Apocalypse sees the being of Jesus in time. How he came to adopt this view is indicated by Rev. 1¹⁷⁻¹⁸, where the formula : " the first and the last, he that liveth," is immediately followed by the reference : " I was dead, and, behold, I am alive εἰς τοὺς αἰῶνας τῶν αἰώνων." There is no doubt that all this is meant to be taken in a concrete sense. It is because He rose from the dead that He liveth. As I am in my time, all time is my time, my before or after.

Heb. 13⁸ has a very similar meaning and intent : Ἰησοῦς Χριστὸς ἐχθὲς καὶ σήμερον ὁ αὐτὸς καὶ εἰς τοὺς αἰῶνας. The context shows that this has a quite practical bearing, for in verse 7 the readers are exhorted to remember their "rulers," those who have preached to them the Word of God. They must take note of their ἔκβασις, i.e., the outcome, the result, the successful conclusion, of their manner of life, and imitate their faith. The exploits of their faith in the past are thus brought into connexion with the present in which the readers are now living. The readers' faith is to be an "imitation," a continual reproduction, of the faith of their rulers. Their faith is not to be a new or different faith. Why not ? Because, says verse 8, Jesus Christ, in whom both the readers and their rulers believed, is the same yesterday, to-day and forever. This saying sounds like a slogan, and can hardly have been coined here for the first time. Probably it is a fragment of one of the early Christian hymns of which traces are to be found elsewhere in the Epistles. But in any case it is of basic importance. "Jesus Christ yesterday" is Jesus in the span of His earthly life, including the Easter period. From the standpoint of the New Testament Church, founded as it was on the testimony and preaching of the apostles, the earthly life of Jesus belongs to yesterday, to the past. Jesus Christ is also in this yesterday. But this Jesus Christ yesterday is the same to-day. Although He has a yesterday, a past, this does not mean that to-day He has become a man of yesterday. On the contrary, He as one and the same is both yesterday and to-day. His time is also the time of His community, and the time of His community is His time. Hence in the time of His community faith can only be faith in Him as He demanded it of His own, and found it in them, in His time. There can be no earlier or later in the time of the community to cause or permit an alteration of its faith. That is why the faith of the readers of the Epistle can only be a constant reproduction of the faith of those who proclaimed the Word of God to them. But the text goes on to speak of the third dimension of time. To "yesterday and to-day it adds : καὶ εἰς τοὺς αἰῶνας. This may best be translated : "in every conceivable future." Like to-day, every coming day will be His, and the faith then required by Him will be no different from the faith in Him required and found yesterday, and that which is the one possible faith to-day. The sequel in verse 9 should be noticed. "Be not carried about with divers and strange doctrines. For it is a good thing that the heart be stablished with grace." Thus Heb. 13⁸ leads to the same conclusion as Rev. 1⁸ and *par*. Jesus Christ belongs not only to yesterday, or to-day, or an indefinite future. He belongs to all times simultaneously. He is the same Christ in all of them. There is no time which does not belong to Him. He is really the Lord of time. If we ask the author of Hebrews how he came to attribute to Jesus this extraordinary being in time, the only answer which he can give is to refer to the point indicated a few verses later (Heb. 13²⁰). Who is "our Lord Jesus" ? He is the great Shepherd of the sheep in the blood of the covenant, whom the God of peace "brought again from the dead." He is the great High Priest who "hath passed through the heavens" (4¹⁴) to sit down on the right hand of the Majesty on high, i.e., God (1³ ; 8¹ ; 10¹² ; 12²). Unless we are prepared to understand 13⁸ in the light of these other passages, and therefore of the Easter axiom of this New Testament author too, we shall not understand it at all.

We cannot afford to lose sight of the key to the whole matter in the Easter history as we now proceed to a brief exposition of the Christian view of the man Jesus in His time with specific reference to the three dimensions of the concept of time.

1. After Easter and Pentecost, the primary conviction of the

New Testament community is that the man Jesus is really but transcendentally present, in a way which could not be said of its contemporary members and other men of their age. His past history, His yesterday, cannot be understood or portrayed as a thing of the past, a thing of yesterday. The yesterday of Jesus is also to-day. The fact that He lives at the right hand of God means that even now He is absolutely present temporally. And to His own on their further journey into time, in and with the witness continually to be proclaimed and heard by them, He has given them His Spirit, the Holy Spirit. But where the Spirit is, there is more than a mere tradition or recollection of Jesus. Of course there is tradition and recollection as well. But the message of His past is proclaimed, heard and believed in order that it should no longer be past but present. Life is lived in contemplation of the kingdom already come, in which everything necessary has been done for the full deliverance and preservation of man, for the fulfilment of the divine covenant. Nor does this rest merely on a retrospective vision, nor on an interpretation and assessment of this past history hazarded at some point and in some way by the men concerned, but on the fact that this history, this time, is not merely past but present, overlapping objectively as it were the present time of the apostles and their communities, pushing beyond its own frontiers to those of this other time and beyond. These men do not make or feel or know themselves the contemporaries of Jesus. It is not they who become or are this. It is Jesus who becomes and is their Contemporary. As a result of this, His past life, death and resurrection can and must and actually do have at all times the significance and force of an event which has taken place in time but is decisive for their present existence. Hence they can and must and actually do understand their present existence as a life of direct discipleship; as their " being in Christ "; as a being done to death with Him at Golgotha, renewed in the garden of Joseph of Arimathea, and on the Mount of Olives (or wherever the ascension took place) entering into the concealment of the heavenly world, or rather, into the concealment of God. Thus its continuation and formation here and now can only be a faithful imitation of their " citizenship in heaven " as it is already actualised proleptically in the man Jesus; an act of faithfulness to the constitution under which they are placed already as God's citizens and members of His household. Their life's work can only be to make known to others who do not know it the lordship of Jesus Christ over the world and men and therefore their time as they themselves know it. Note that if there is anything doubtful for Christians here, it is not His presence but their own. And if there is anything axiomatically certain, it is not their presence but His. There is obviously no baptism or Lord's Supper without His real presence as very God and very Man, both body and soul. But this presence cannot be regarded as restricted to what were later called the " sacraments." For these are only a symbolical expression of the fact that in its worship the community is gathered directly around Jesus Himself, and lives by and with Him, but that through faith He rules over the hearts and lives of all even apart from worship. Hence the gifts of prophecy, teaching, leadership and service, and hence also miracles in the community. Hence, too, the royal freedom of the children of God, but hence also in Christ's stead the apostolic word of witness, the word of knowledge, direction and exhortation. All these are possible because " Christians " have the Spirit and are led by Him.

By way of anticipation we may say that the historical distance, the past, in which Jesus confronts them is not abrogated by His presence. His yesterday is not cancelled by His to-day. The Evangelist does not disappear in favour of the apostle. On the contrary, His presence stimulates interest in the past and in the tradition of Jesus, revealing the unfathomable but clear depths of His prior life on earth. Yet He cannot be regarded merely as a figure of the past. A community interested only in a historical Jesus would be an unspiritual community in the New Testament sense, i.e., a community without the guiding Spirit. The fact that the man Jesus was includes the fact that He is ; but the fact that He is excludes that He is no longer.

Again by way of anticipation, the presence of Jesus in His community is full of import for the future. His presence impels and presses to His future, general and definitive revelation, of which there has been a particular and provisional form in the Easter history. Hence even the presence of Jesus in the Spirit, for all its fulness, can only be a pledge or first instalment of what awaits the community as well as the whole universe, His return in glory. But it must never be forgotten that He who comes again in glory, this future Jesus, is identical with the One proclaimed by the history of yesterday and really present to His own to-day. The thorough-going eschatology for which the interim between now and one day necessarily seems to be a time of emptiness, of futility, of lack, of a progressive and barely concealed disillusionment, is not the eschatology of New Testament Christianity. And again it is only an unspiritual community which can tolerate such a view. The fact that the man Jesus will be includes the fact that He is ; but the fact that He is does not exclude that He is " not yet."

We may summarise this in the words of Rev. 1^8, " I am (he that) is." The present in which there is real recollection of the man Jesus and the particular and preliminary revelation accomplished in Him, and real expectation of this man and God's final and general revelation with Him—this present " between the times " is His own time, the time of the man Jesus.

There is such a wealth of exegetical material available on this point that we must confine ourselves to a few concrete indications. " This day," says Jesus in Lk. 4^{21}, " is this scripture fulfilled in your ears." The reference is to all that is written about the "acceptable year of the Lord." This "to-day" with its fulfilment, with its intimate connexion with the name and history of the man Jesus, is the content of the apostolic message and the meaning of the life of the apostolic community. The Church's "to-day" is likewise the acceptable year, the great Sabbath, the fulfilled time of the man Jesus. According to Rev. 1^{10} it is on "the Lord's day" that the New Testament seer found himself "in the spirit" (ἐγενόμην ἐν πνεύματι), and heard behind him the mighty voice : "as of a trumpet," bidding him see and write down what he saw. It is not only right but necessary to recall here the trumpet of the year of jubilee in Lev. 25^9. The apostolic day is the day of the apostles' Lord, His now, His "to-day." And, in a remarkable manner, the event of that yesterday is the vitality of to-day, the new thing whose perception and propagation is the purpose of the present time. "The times of this ignorance God winked at ; but now commandeth all men every where to repent" (Ac. 17^{30}). "And you, that were sometime alien-ated and enemies in your mind by wicked works, yet now hath he reconciled in the body of his flesh through death . . ." (Col. 1$^{21f.}$). "(You) in time past were not a people, but are now the people of God : which had not obtained mercy, but now have obtained mercy" (1 Pet. 2^{10}). "For ye were sometimes darkness, but now are ye light in the Lord" (Eph. 5^8). "The mystery (was once) hid from ages and from generations : but now is made manifest to his saints" (Col. 1^{26}). "Behold, now is the acceptable time ; behold, now is the day of salvation" (2 Cor. 6^2). "To day if ye will hear his voice, harden not your hearts" (Heb. 3^7). "But exhort one another daily, while it is called To day" (Heb. 3^{13}). Why all this emphasis on "to-day"? Because, as Heb. 4$^{1-8}$ explains, the Sabbath day has dawned. Because we now have not only the weekly recurring sign of the seventh day, but the fulfilment of this sign, the reality to which it had pointed so long. The day of rest has arrived for God and His people, and none must neglect to enter into it to-day. The whole of the Old Testament is before them as an awful warning against neglect. This Sabbath has dawned to-day and must be kept, because "this day have I begotten thee" (Heb. 1^5 ; 5^5, quoting Ps. 2^7), and as "a priest for ever after the order of Melchisedec" (Heb. 5^6, 7$^{17, 21}$), as "a priest continually" (Heb. 7^3), have I appointed Thee ; because "unto you is born this day . . . a Saviour" (Lk. 2^{11}) ; because "this day is salvation come to this house" (Lk. 19^9). All this happened yesterday for the sake of to-day—the birth of Jesus, His visit to the house of Zacchaeus, His death on the cross, His burial and resurrection. And as a con-sequence we to-day, in our time, have died and been buried and risen with Him in baptism. We can therefore walk in newness of life, as described in Rom 6$^{1-11}$. The time which Jesus filled up to His death, and revealed in its fulness during the forty days, this last time up to its last day and its last hour, was as such the future day of the apostles and their community. The day of His death was revealed on Easter Day to be the day of their life. And they now stand in the grey twilight before the dawn. They now advance into this day, which will eventually be theirs, but for the moment is only His. All this does not rule out the idea of a recollection or tradition of Jesus. On the contrary, it is εἰς τὴν ἐμὴν ἀνάμνησιν that the bread and cup of the Lord's Supper are to be dis-tributed and received in the community (1 Cor. 11$^{24f.}$; Lk. 22^{19}). And Timothy is expressly charged to remember (μνημονεύειν) Jesus Christ risen from the dead (2 Tim. 2^8). Note, too, the stress laid on remembrance in 2 Pet. 1$^{12-15}$. On this possibility of real recollection and genuine tradition hangs the whole history and temporality of this event, with all that this involves. There is no place for any "Christ-mysticism," or even Christ-ethics of living, dying and rising again in discipleship of Christ, such as would suppress or replace the history of Jesus or render it superfluous. Nor can any spirit which drives men away from the recollection and tradition of Jesus be His Spirit, the Holy and sanctifying Spirit. On the contrary : "the Holy Spirit, whom the Father will send in my name, he shall teach you all things, and bring all things to your remembrance (ὑπομνήσει) whatsoever I have said unto you " (Jn. 14²⁶). " He shall glorify me ; for he shall receive of mine, and shall shew it unto you " (Jn. 16¹⁴). Hence also the parable of the vine : the branches must abide in Him, for apart from Him they can do nothing ; they cannot bring forth fruit, but only wither and decay (Jn. 15¹⁻⁸). What really happens is that the history of Jesus itself becomes history again ; past time becomes the time of His renewed presence. " Heaven and earth shall pass away ; but my words shall not pass away " (Mk. 13³¹). " I will not leave you comfortless ; I will come to you " (Jn. 14¹⁸). " Lo, I am with you alway, even unto the end of the world " (Mt. 28²⁰). " Where two or three are gathered together in my name, there am I in the midst of them " (Mt. 18²⁰). And in Paul we find the converse. What belongs to the past ? Not Jesus, but the life which we have been living to-day in so far as it has not been lived in the Spirit and therefore in Him, but in the flesh as our own independent life (2 Cor. 5¹⁶). Who are Christians ? Those who by baptism into Jesus' death have been buried with Him (Rom. 6⁴) ; who can no longer live unto themselves, but only unto Him who died and rose again for them (2 Cor. 5¹⁵). And who is Paul ? The man who lives, yet lives no longer, because Christ lives in him ; the man who can live his present life in the flesh only in the faith of the Son of God who loved him and gave Himself for him (Gal. 2²⁰). " If any man be in Christ, he is a new creature : old things are passed away ; behold, all things are become new " (2 Cor. 5¹⁷).

This, then, is how matters stand with the One who is the object of recollection and tradition. The fact that He is this certainly cannot mean that He is to be sought among the dead. In no circumstances is He to be found in that company (Lk. 24⁵). He is " awakened " or " raised " or " brought up " ἐκ τῶν νεκρῶν. This means that for a brief space He was one of the great host of those who once lived but have now perished and live no more. But then He was called and taken from this host as ἀπαρχή (1 Cor. 15²⁰) or πρωτότοκος (Col. 1¹⁸). This shows Him to be the effective appearance of God, which is not only unforgettable but makes itself felt again and again. Thus, while there is recollection and tradition from the standpoint of the action of the community, objectively and in fact He Himself is the acting Subject who lifts the barrier of yesterday and moves into to-day, making Himself present, and entering in as the Lord. This is the inner connexion between Easter and Pentecost. The living One, who is no longer to be sought among the dead, who " died once but . . . liveth unto God " (Rom. 6¹⁰), is not only alive Himself, but quickens others too, proffering Himself as the Creator and ground and soul of life. Having risen from the dead, He promises His followers His Spirit who will shortly come down from heaven as depicted in Ac. 1–2. The description in Jn. 20²¹⁻²³ obviously speeds up the time-table, for after the risen Lord has greeted His disciples with peace, and given them the missionary charge : " As my Father hath sent me, even so send I you," there follows immediately : " He breathed on them, and saith unto them, Receive ye the Holy Ghost." And in the remarkable passage 2 Cor. 3¹⁷⁻¹⁸ it seems to be speeded up even more, for here the risen Lord is Himself the Spirit whose presence means liberty. For all the variations, however, it is clear that Pentecost is the result of the resurrection, achieved in the time of the apostles, yet not by the apostles, but in and to them. It is the result of the revelation of the fulfilment of time accomplished in His life and death. It is the bridging of the gulf between His past and their present ; the assumption of their time into His.

The most illuminating comment on this point is provided by the story of the conversion of Paul, and the appointment, commissioning and sending forth of this new apostle who now appears in such remarkable circumstances. His conversion is brought about by an event which, like the transfiguration of Jesus before His resurrection, would appear to belong in essence to the forty days. For it consists of nothing less than an appearance of the exalted Jesus in person. Paul himself is quite explicit about this, for in 1 Cor. 15⁸ he numbers it with the appearances of the forty days. Elsewhere he appeals to his conversion as a proof that " the gospel which was preached of me is not after man. For I neither received it of man, neither was I taught it, but by the revelation of Jesus Christ " (Gal. 1¹¹ᶠ·). It pleased God " to reveal his Son in me, that I might preach him among the heathen " (Gal. 1¹⁶). Again, it is by an account of his conversion that, according to Ac. 22¹⁻²¹, Paul defends himself before the people of Jerusalem, and later before Agrippa (Ac. 26²⁻²³). It is the story of his conversion which evokes from the Jews the cry : " Away with such a fellow from the earth ; for it is not fit that he should live " (Ac. 22²²), and from the Hellenist Agrippa the ingenuous comment : " Paul, thou art beside thyself ; much learning (τὰ πολλὰ γράμματα) doth make thee mad " (Ac. 26²⁴). What is it that makes his conversion so important to Paul himself for his mission to Jews and Gentiles, and so scandalous and strange to his non-Christian hearers ? Clearly the real reason is that even the time after the life and death of Jesus, and after the forty days, is a time when this man is still a Subject capable of and in fact engaged in action. For this personal appearance of Jesus, this event which changes Saul into Paul, the persecutor into the apostle, this " one born out of due time " (1 Cor. 15⁸) into the executor of the commission laid upon all the apostles, this event so strangely late in time, so long after Jesus had lived and manifested Himself— what does it show ? It shows that the Jesus of that earlier time is still at work. The life and work of the apostles is wholly and utterly dependent on His presence. Their whole recollection and tradition concerning Him is not centred on a figure of the past, on a dead man, but on One who even after His earthly time is still an acting Subject, doing new things, creating in history. It is not from within themselves supported by their fragmentary recollection of past days and the corresponding tradition—this would be a real gospel " after man " (Gal. 1¹¹) —that the apostles and the primitive community derive their *raison d'être* and their commission. It is not from within themselves that they derive their consolation and the necessary defiance in face of the rage of the Jews and the contempt of the Greeks ; their faith, hope and love ; the ordering of their common life and direction for the life of individuals. They receive all these things from the Lord who is Himself Spirit, conducting His own cause, and present amongst them in the hiddenness of God but no less really, indeed with supreme reality. It is the first of the two times, that of the life of Jesus, which makes the second, the time of the Church founded upon the apostolic witness, the interim period prior to His general and definitive revelation, not only possible and necessary, but full of meaning and substance.

That is why, in the second time, it is impossible to dismiss the first as merely past and over. We have now to recognise that this view is an incredible error, the product of wilful ignorance and prejudice. The hidden power of the first time, the fact that it is not past but present, is now disclosed. Jesus was not found among the dead, but among the living ; the living One and the Lifegiver. Yet He was the self-same Jesus who had previously gone about with His disciples ; thronged by the multitudes and the devout of Galilee and Jerusalem ; seen, but not really perceived ; heard but not really understood ; touched but not apprehended ; recognised and yet denied ; respected and yet betrayed ; the great Prophet, the Messiah of Israel, and yet rejected and cast out by His own people and crucified by the Gentiles.

The story of the walk to Emmaus in Lk. 24¹³ᶠ· is the passage which shows most clearly what view of the earthly life of Jesus was vanquished and removed by the resurrection and the gift of the Holy Spirit in the second time, the time of the apostles and the apostolic community ; and also how this came about. As they were walking on the road to Emmaus these two disciples were talking about πάντα τὰ συμβεβηκότα ταῦτα. That is to say, they were talking about the enacted life and death of Jesus as though it were a matter of past history. Hence it is not surprising that when Jesus asked them what they were talking about, they ἐστάθησαν σκυθρωπά (v. 17), they stood still, gazing back like Lot's wife, and were gloomy and sullen and sad. The same word occurs in Mt. 6[16], where it is applied to the Pharisees when they fast. " Can the sons of the bride-chamber mourn (and disfigure their faces like the Pharisees) as long as the bridegroom is with them ? but the days will come, when the bridegroom shall be taken from them, and then shall they fast " (Mt. 9[15]). Now that Jesus had died it would seem that the time for fasting had arrived. Jesus is no more than a bit of past history : " τὰ περὶ τοῦ Ἰησοῦ τοῦ Ναζαρηνοῦ, which was a prophet mighty in deed and word before God and all the people : and how the chief priests and our rulers delivered him up to be condemned to death and crucified him." This is how they remember Him now. " But we trusted (ἠλπίζομεν—even that has become past history!) that it had been he which should have redeemed Israel : and beside all this, to-day is the third day since these things were done " (v. 21). Even the beginning of the Easter story had found its way into this sad history, and they tell how the women had found the tomb empty and how the angels appeared to them saying that He was alive. But so far from cheering them, this news had merely plunged them into further despondency (vv. 22–24), while v. 11 even goes so far as to say that " their words seemed to them in their sight as idle tales (λῆρος) ; and they believed them not." " And certain of them which were with us went to the sepulchre and found it even so as the women had said : but him they saw not " (v. 24). Even this does not get them any further. Even the Easter message, or its prelude, the news of the empty tomb, is still the object of mere recollection, and of very dubious recollection at that. Nor was their gloom dispelled when Jesus reproached them (vv. 25–27) for their stubborn incomprehension and rebuked them for refusing to believe not only the tales of the women, but even what the prophets had said. Nor did they abandon their sorrow when He expounded τὰ περὶ αὐτοῦ from the Old Testament, thus proving that it was necessary for Christ to suffer these things and (through this suffering) to enter into His glory. Not until He performed a certain action was this state of affairs changed (" And their eyes were opened, and they knew him," v. 31). That action was not something new and special, but the very action He had performed on the night of His passion when He re-interpreted the passover as a prefigurement of His own passion and death in their saving significance, thus showing that the deliverance of Israel from Egypt had now become a reality. " And it came to pass, as he sat at meat with them, he took bread, and blessed it, and brake, and gave to them." This was what dispelled their gloom. " He was known of them in the breaking of the bread." That was the momentous news they brought back to the eleven and their companions when they returned to Jerusalem. Clearly the meaning is that the full power of the earthly life of Jesus, hitherto veiled from their eyes, was now made manifest. It was the same Jesus who had lived and died and was buried, none other, who had appeared to them, as in the meantime (v. 34) He had appeared to Peter. He, the Bride-groom, on whom they had hitherto looked back in retrospect as men who were σκυθρωποί, had now come to them in a form in which He could never leave them again, in which He could never again be to them a mere figure of the past, in which they could never think of Him as One who was " no longer " with them. The historical Jesus as such had removed the veil of the merely " historical " from their eyes and came to them as the Lord, the same yesterday and to-day. This was the burden of the apostolic account of the resurrection, of their Easter history. The limitation of the past had been burst. The past of Jesus had become a present reality.

It is surely no accident that Luke, the Evangelist who more than any other has the reputation of being a historian, records this story as an indispensable commentary on all the other Easter narratives. If the prologues of the two books addressed to Theophilus (Lk. 1[1-4] and Ac. 1[1-3]) are read in the light of the Emmaus story we shall see how the various elements are interconnected (not without some overlapping, for Luke is no mere pedant) : the history of the words and works of Jesus ; then, as a link in the chain, the history of the proofs that He was alive during the forty days ; and finally the history of the apostles. He does not allow the first history to lose its significance or sink into the mere past in the final history to which he himself belongs. For the latter would be nothing without the former ; it is simply its sequel. And the intervening history of the Easter period is simply a revelation of the first history which dispels the errors, prejudice and blindness of the apostles and the community. Hence the New Testament necessarily took the form of " the Gospel and the apostle," as Marcion later put it (Marcion may have been a heretic in detail, but he was undoubtedly a genius in general apprehension). It was the substance of the words and works, the passion and death of Jesus ; it was Jesus Himself whose life and ministry and self-offering the disciples and their contemporaries had witnessed—it was this Jesus who encountered them in the Easter time, emerging from the past as a figure of the present, alive for evermore, abiding with them, their Lord and Contemporary for all time. It was He and none other, in the form which belonged to the past, who must now be manifested to them as the content of the Gospel. For the word " Gospel " in the New Testament has the concrete meaning of witness to the Jesus of history. There was no need for uniformity in this testimony. The Early Church never felt the need for a uniform, complete and consistent " life of Jesus." It was possible and even necessary, as Lk. 1¹ suggests, for many " to set forth in order a declaration of those things which are most surely believed among us." It makes no difference that there are several different versions of Christ's resurrection appearances, that they are independent of one another or that they vary in detail. Any idea of a harmony of the Gospels is quite foreign to the Early Church. That we should have Gospels " according to St. Matthew," " according to St. Mark," etc., with all their parallels, their overlappings, and contradictions, is supremely in keeping with the theme recorded, with the figure of the past who in the forty days appeared to so many different people in so many different ways. All that matters was that they should all go back directly or indirectly to this source, the revelation of the event of Easter ; that they should be presentations of this theme, of this figure of the past whose abiding presence is guaranteed by the event of Easter. A true Evangelist is one who draws upon this source, and in his own particular way hands on this object. To take up this tradition and proclaim this object is the function of the apostle, who in contrast to the Evangelist looks forwards and not backwards. There is, of course, no reason why one man should not fulfil both functions. Indeed, in the last resort they must be one and the same person. An Evangelist is *ipso facto* an apostle, for the tradition he records is by its very nature the apostolic *kerygma*. Again, since the apostle is a bearer of the *kerygma*, he is an active bearer of the tradition. There is obviously a sense in which the apostle Paul himself is an Evangelist. He is no less the bearer of a definite tradition, part of which is received directly from the Lord. But the function of the apostle is not that of the Evangelist. As an apostle he does not merely relate the facts about Jesus, but proclaims the meaning behind these facts. He proclaims Jesus as the Lord, the Messiah of Israel and the Saviour of the world. He proclaims this figure of yesterday as alive to-day, and reigning to-day in virtue of what He was yesterday. This is the word of a true apostle, and he derives it from the events of the forty days. These are the source of what the New Testament calls the " Word of God." The apostle knows that Jesus reigns to-day only because He has encountered him as the Resurrected. And the fact that he must proclaim this to Jews and Gentiles rests again on the command he received from the Resurrected. But Jesus the Lord whom he proclaims is identical with that figure of the past who has made Himself eternally present as the Lord in the Easter time. That is why the apostle, too, depends on the tradition of this object, and is responsible for this tradition. Thus the apostle and the Evangelist stand back to back. The " Gospel and the apostle," as the two parts of the New Testament, form an indissoluble unity. They look to two different times. But they both come from the Easter time. And in the light of the Easter time the two different times are made one time in which the present is filled by the past of Jesus, because this past has not remained the past but irrupted into the present; because He has made Himself present, and thus made the present His new time.

2. But the being of Jesus is not restricted to the present. It is also a being in the past, a past being; and it must be independently seen and evaluated as such. The temporality of Jesus does not consist merely in the fact that He is, and is again, continually, from day to day and hour to hour. At any rate, this is not how the New Testament saw it after the first Easter, at the beginning of the great intervening time to which we ourselves belong. Jesus not only is; He has also been. As in the preceding discussion, we shall now try to put ourselves in the position of the community at the beginning of this intervening time, looking in this direction, not at random, but self-evidently with reference to the witness of this first community. Our gaze is directed backward from this present (although always in the presence of the man Jesus). What do we see? What is the yesterday of this to-day?

The answer seems at first sight quite simple. What we see is obviously the pre-Easter life of Jesus: His death on the cross; His parting from His disciples; His going up to Jerusalem; His journeys in Galilee; His words and deeds during this time; and a few glimpses of His boyhood and infancy. But if we really see Him in all this from the standpoint of the first community, and therefore as the One He already was in all this in the light of the Easter revelation; if we see Him as He really lived in New Testament recollection, and is really shown us in the Gospel tradition, we are irresistibly impressed by the fulness of this yesterday, of this time which was. How could it be of less importance than the time of the apostolic present? What advantage has the latter except that in it the revelation of what is concealed in the former is attested, believed and presented by the Holy Spirit? But does not the former also have the advantage that in it there flow the underground waters which come to the surface in the Easter time as a spring which swells to a great river in the time of the apostles? Does not the apostolic to-day derive its mystery, power and dignity wholly and utterly from this yesterday. Here in this yesterday it takes place first and properly that the kingdom of God comes and is proclaimed in parable, but also by signs and wonders. Here it is that the reconciliation of the world with God is accomplished on the cross. Here it is that the foundations of the community are laid. Here it is that the great dividing line is secretly but very really drawn which marks off the new age from the old. Here there lives and moves and acts and suffers the Lord who reveals Himself as such at the resurrection, and then in the power of this revelation builds, maintains

ordination in the creation and ordering of reality distinct from Himself. Hence for the apostolic community the yesterday of Jesus extends beyond the prior yesterday of the Old Testament to the primal history and primal time which are beyond the reach of " historical " investigation, not only in practice, but in principle ; to the history and time when being, history and time began as such. Is this just speculation ? But surely if creation and covenant are so integral to one another even in the Old Testament that neither can be considered apart from the other ; if in the Old Testament the covenant is always eschatological and prophetic in character, and is never actually realised ; if finally—and this is the point on which everything else depends— Jesus is the One who was to come as the fulfilled reality of the covenant, is it speculation to say that even the time of creation was His time ? To the extent that it was the time when the Creator began to execute His will, it too was His time ; the time when He was the primary, proper object of this divine will, foreseen and foreordained in the creation of all things.

And there are a few passages in the New Testament which suggest that the apostolic community no less self-evidently regarded a further unprecedented and yet very obvious step as both possible and necessary. As the man Jesus had been in His appearance on the way, in the prefiguration and expectation of the divine covenant with Israel, and in the divine foresight and foreordination in creation, so He had been in the counsel of God before creation and therefore before all time. If the lesson of Easter is true, if the man Jesus was really the manifestation of God, how can we possibly think of an eternity of God which does not also and primarily include His time, His future, His present, but also His past ? How can it be denied that in God's free plan and resolve He was before the beginning of time and all things, and therefore that He was really, supremely and fully, that He divinely was ?

But two delimitations are required. On the one side, because He was really, supremely and fully, after the manner of God, the fact that He was, His historicity, cannot conflict with His being in the present. On the contrary, as the One who never was " not yet " he cannot possibly be " no longer," but is the same yesterday, and to-day. From this past He can and must be seen and understood as the One who is always present.

On the other side, His real and supreme and full and divine past cannot conflict with His being in the future. On the contrary, in all prior time right back to the eternity of God Himself, He is the One who comes : coming in the eternal counsel of the Father ; coming in the work of creation ; coming in the history of the divine covenant with Israel ; and coming finally in the hiddenness of His pre-Easter life. It is as the One who comes in this totality that He was revealed in the forty days. Hence the fact that He is the One who has been divinely and in fulness is the decisive reason why His presence in His community in all its divinity and fulness must always be understood as that of the One who comes, and cannot be understood otherwise.

Again, it is all summed up in Rev. 1⁸ : " I am—which was." The past to which we look back from the present of the man Jesus is, like this present and the future which lies before it, His time, the time of this man Jesus.

In illustration we must again confine ourselves to the most salient passages.
The transfiguration as recorded in Mk. 9²⁻⁸ and *par.* is a good example of how the apostles regarded the pre-Easter life of Jesus from the present to their own time. It might almost be said to anticipate the Easter-history as the latter does the return of the Lord. At a first glance it looks like any other miracle story. But it is really unique, for this time the miracle happens to Jesus Himself, and is not something performed by Him. It comes wholly from out-side. He does not say or do anything to bring it about. Perhaps it is meant to be taken as a preliminary key to all the other miracles. " He was trans-figured before them." Moses and Elijah appear, talking with Jesus (according to Lk. 9³¹, it was about " his decease which he should accomplish at Jerusalem "). A cloud, the symbol both of concealment and revelation, overshadows them. A voice speaks from the cloud : " This is my beloved Son : hear him." Every-thing suggests a theophany. Hence the note in Mk. 9² and Mt. 17¹ : " after six days " (Lk. 9²⁸ says it was eight days), is not to be dismissed as an irrelevant detail. Immediately before the transfiguration comes the famous saying : "Verily I say unto you, that there be some of them that stand here, which shall not taste of death, till they have seen the kingdom of God come with power." The Markan and Matthaean versions are to be read in the light of Luke's express statement that the transfiguration took place eight (six) days " after these sayings." In other words, the transfiguration, for the Evangelists at least, was a first and provisional fulfilment of the promise contained in that saying. But the six (eight) day interval between promise and fulfilment is no doubt intended to suggest that the transfiguration with its fulfilment of the saying marks the dawn of a special Sabbath. We are obviously in close material proximity to the resurrection story. This is further suggested by the location of the episode on a high mountain ; by the statement in Mt. 17⁶ : " (They) were sore afraid" ; by Lk. 9³² (cf. Jn. 1¹⁴) : " They saw his glory " ; and by Peter's curious pro-posal, recorded in all the versions, to erect three tents (again cf. Jn. 1¹⁴). Evi-dently Peter wanted the vision to stay, if only for a short time. Mark's com-ment on this is : " He wist not what to say " (9⁶), which implies that he did not really understand what he was saying. But the vision did not stay, as Peter hoped it would. It vanished as quickly as it had come. Jesus is again seen alone, and no longer transfigured before them. He tells them (Mk. 9⁹) to say nothing about it to anyone until He is risen from the dead. This obviously suggests that the transfiguration is the supreme prefigurement of the resurrec-tion, and that its real meaning will not be perceived until the resurrection has taken place. It is surprising that 2 Pet. 1¹⁶ᶠ·, speaking of the apostles as eye-witnesses and preachers of the " power and coming of our Lord Jesus Christ," says nothing about the resurrection itself, but seems to regard the preceding transfiguration as more important. The obvious post-Easter parallel to the transfiguration is the conversion of Saul. And its purpose in the pre-Easter period is obviously to demonstrate that even in this time, although in con-cealment, He was actually and properly the One He was revealed to be in His resurrection. And even this time was not without transitory indications of His true and proper being. In Jn. 2¹¹ the account of the miracle of Cana

and Galilee closes with the words : " This beginning of miracles did Jesus . . . and manifested forth his glory." This would seem to imply that the miracles of Jesus are to be taken as " signs " in the sense that they point to what He already was, to the hidden presence of the kingdom of God which would later be unveiled during the forty days in an abiding manifestation, in a σκηνοῦν of the Lord in the midst of His disciples—a disclosure which will become definitive and universal at the end of all time in His coming again. That there are such signs, and that in the transfiguration, as in no other miracle, this sign is performed on Himself, shows that the mystery of His being revealed at the resurrection has not been acquired in the meantime but had been present all along and was in fact *revealed* at this later point.

The baptism of Jesus (Mk. 1⁹⁻¹¹ and *par.* ; cf. Jn. 1³²⁻³⁴) belongs to the same cycle of tradition as the transfiguration. We must emphasise the meaning of this event only as it concerns our present context. That it is related to the transfiguration is obvious at a glance, for we have a similar voice from heaven and much the same words : " Thou art my beloved Son, in whom I am well pleased," or in the Lukan version (Lk. 3²²) : " This day have I begotten thee." The opening of heaven indicates that this is no ordinary miracle, but a divine epiphany. Mt. 3¹⁶ further suggests that it was only Jesus Himself who appreciated its divine significance. In Jn. 1³²ᶠ· the Baptist solemnly and explicitly confesses that he is a witness in this matter. The crucial point is that the Holy Spirit visibly came on Jesus " and abode upon him," as Jn. 1³²ᶠ· twice records. This addition is textually uncertain in Mk. 1¹⁰, while Matthew and Luke clearly know nothing of it. All the same, taken together with the voice from heaven, it offers the only conceivable explanation of the καταβαίνειν of the Spirit, which is obviously very different from a mere prophetic calling and illumination. Who is the man who submits to baptism ? Who is it who now becomes the central figure of the Gospel story ? The divine epiphany gives the answer. It calls Him the beloved Son of God, begotten long before, the object of God's good-pleasure from of old. It marks Him out as the One who, secretly or openly, known or unknown, is this in fact, and always will be on the way which lies ahead of Him. It marks Him out as the One He necessarily must be as the Son of God ; the One who is and will always be the Bearer of the Spirit, the immediate Hearer and Preacher of the Word, the accredited Agent of the divine commission. The baptism of Jesus may also be regarded as an anticipation of the resurrection. For like the resurrection it adds nothing to what He already is. He is already the Son of God, the begotten and beloved of God, the object of His good-pleasure. This is what the voice from heaven so clearly shows. And as regards the Holy Spirit, the texts are quite clear that Jesus was not endowed with the Spirit for the first time at the moment of His baptism. Indeed, Mt. 1²⁰ tells us that He was conceived by the Holy Ghost. What happened at the baptism was that on the basis of divine revelation Jesus (and, according to the Fourth Gospel, John the Baptist as well) saw the καταβαίνειν of the Spirit upon Himself ; His communication from the Father to the incarnate Son. The hour of baptism is thus an hour of revelation ; an early, momentary and unrepeated disclosure of the mystery of this man, which has always been and always will be His mystery.

The infancy narratives must be added to this series as a third, or first, link. We shall confine ourselves to the clearest of these in Lk. 2⁸⁻¹⁴, where the angels announce to the shepherds the birth of Jesus at Bethlehem. Once again everything has already happened as fully as possible. " And she brought forth her first-born son, and wrapped him in swaddling clothes, and laid him in a manger, because there was no room for them in the inn." This is supreme reality, though wrapped in supreme obscurity. There can be no adding to or enriching of it by what transpired in the fields where the shepherds were keeping watch over their flocks by night. What does happen is that the event in the inn is revealed to them in the fields. An angel of the Lord appears to them. This reminds us already of the divine epiphany at the resurrection—an impression which is confirmed by what follows : " The glory of the Lord (δοξά κυρίου) shone round about them, and they were sore afraid." As at the transfiguration and in the resurrection appearances, fear is man's first reaction to a mystery surpassing his understanding. But the fear is always temporary, for " perfect love casteth out fear " (1 Jn. 4^{18}). So the angel says : " Fear not : for, behold, I bring you good tidings of great joy, which shall be to all people "—i.e., when it is revealed to the whole people of Israel. Note that this is a real birth, whether known by few or many, or by these sooner or later. But this birth is made known to the shepherds in the field by God's revelation, and immediately and on the spot it causes them " great joy " : " For unto you is born this day in the city of David a Saviour, ὅς ἐστιν Χριστὸς Κύριος." This is the revelation of the reality of this birth in the darkness of the night in the field. The Saviour is there, the Christ is there, the Messiah is there—ἐτέχθη ! And the word of the angel is not left unsupported. A whole choir of revelation joins in, " a multitude of the heavenly host, praising God and saying . . ." ; adoring yet again the reality of this birth ; declaring that in the existence of this babe there is irrevocably accomplished the complete triumph of God above and the complete assistance of the men below who are the objects of His goodness : " Glory to God in the highest, and on earth peace among the men of his good pleasure." It is impossible to exaggerate the importance of the perfect reality of this event if it is to be understood aright. This is what is made known to the shepherds in the field. Things will not continue in this strain even in Luke, though we are obviously meant to gather that this is how they began. In this Gospel, too, darkness around the new-born Child is thick enough, and the revelation of His glory isolated until we reach the Easter story. But at any rate this is how Luke wanted his account of the words and deeds of Jesus to begin—in this stream of light. In Luke, as in Matthew, the effect on the reader is to make him realise that from the very outset he is in the presence of a mystery which embraces and motivates the whole story. And thus the way in which the Gospels look back to this beginning shows the height from which the forward-looking apostolic Church descends. It descends indeed from the mount of transfiguration. It has not created its " Christ of to-day." But as He was the same yesterday, revealed by the angels at His birth, confirmed by a voice from heaven on the banks of Jordan, and transfigured on the mount, He Himself has created the Church.

But the man Jesus belongs not only to yesterday, but as such to the day before. He is the Christ of Israel and of Israel's Scriptures. His being is one which is hidden, yet not only hidden but also revealed, in this time before. A few remarks must suffice to clarify what we said more generally with reference to this second and higher stage of His past. For further details see, for example, *C.D.*, I, 2, pp. 70–101.

It is best to begin with the fact that the earliest Christians, and especially the Evangelists and apostles, always were obviously forced, directly or indirectly, explicitly or implicitly, to connect their accounts and preaching with this time before, i.e., with the history of Israel, in which Jesus had not yet appeared, but was already present as the One prefigured and expected. If we wanted to obliterate these references and to read the New Testament apart from the Old, it would be necessary to delete not only Matthew, the Epistle of James and the Epistle to the Hebrews, but all the New Testament, and especially the Pauline writings. These references may vary in detail, but they agree in substance that the particular time of the man Jesus was as such the fulfilment of this time before, i.e., that what took place in this particular time was the reality to which all the events of this prior time were moving, so that it is only with the final event in this particular time that the events of this prior time form the perfect and meaningful whole which they do in this context. Hence the references to the Old Testament which we find in the New tell us that the history and time of Israel were prophetic, their meaning and perfection consisting in the fact that they moved towards the history and time of the man Jesus. Prefiguring and expecting this history and time of the man Jesus, they belonged to His time. Indeed, no less really than the history and time of the apostles, although inversely, it *was* His time.

That is what the old man Simeon meant when he held the baby Jesus in his arms and said : " Mine eyes have seen thy salvation, which thou hast prepared before the face of all people ; a light to lighten the Gentiles, and the glory of thy people Israel " (Lk. 2³⁰ᶠ·). What Simeon perceives is not a new but the old salvation prophetically prefigured and expected in Israel. That is why he can now " depart in peace." His time has reached its goal ; his history, having attained this point, has not been in vain. In the same sense Paul is conscious of being ordained by " the God of our fathers " to " know his will, and see that Just One " (Ac. 22¹⁴). That is why he lays so much stress on the fact that the death and resurrection of Jesus took place κατὰ τὰς γραφάς (1 Cor. 15³ᶠ·). That is why he begs the Christians to learn from himself and Apollos the rule μὴ ὑπὲρ ἃ γέγραπται. That is why he calls the Old Testament Law " our schoolmaster to bring us unto Christ " (Gal. 3²⁴), and Christ the " end of the law " (Rom. 10⁴), and the purpose of his preaching, not to destroy, but to establish the Law (Rom. 3³¹). That is why he said to Agrippa (Ac. 26²²) : " I continue unto this day, witnessing both to small and great, saying none other things than those which the prophets and Moses did say should come." That is why he went so far as to say that the rock from which the fathers drank in the wilderness was Christ (1 Cor. 10⁴), and that it was only because of the veil over their hearts that the Jews could not understand their own Scriptures (2 Cor. 3¹⁴ᶠ·). The Fourth Evangelist is just as clear about this point, for he attributed to Jesus the saying : " Search the scriptures ; for in them ye think ye have eternal life ; and they are they which testfy of me " (Jn. 5³⁹). He also makes Jesus say of Moses : " He wrote of me " (Jn. 5⁴⁶) ; and of Abraham : " (He) rejoiced to see my day ; and he saw it, and was glad " (Jn. 8⁵⁶). And the Evangelist himself says of Isaiah : " These things said (he), when he saw his glory ,and spake of him " (Jn. 12⁴¹). Similarly, faith in Jesus according to Lk. 24²⁵, is simply a matter of believing " all that the prophets have spoken," as conversely : " This day is this scripture fulfilled in your ears " (Lk. 4²¹). Finally, it is not just fanciful imagery, but a visible confirmation of the Pauline κατὰ τὰς γραφάς, that in Mk. 9⁴ᶠ· and *par.* Moses and Elijah appear with Jesus at the transfiguration. They belong to Him. He belongs to them. They talk with Him, and according to Lk. 9³¹ they talk concretely about His death.

Particularly in the light of this scene, I find it hard to see how the idea of " contemporaneity " between the history of Jesus and the prophetic history of Israel can be flatly rejected (Cullmann, *op. cit.*, E.T., p. 132 f.). Perhaps Cullmann has allowed himself to be too much influenced by the unfortunate precedent of the Epistle of Barnabas, and too much hampered by his conception of " linear time." The truth is that the contemporaneity in question here does not exclude a certain non-contemporaneity as well. After all, Abraham, Moses and the prophets, and all the other figures of the Old Testament, still remain what they are in their own right. They are clearly distinguished from Jesus, and there is no question of their being identical with Him. Unless they all existed in their own right it would be difficult to account for the fact that the Early Church paid particular attention to them and accepted the Old Testament Canon along with the New, or rather the New along with the existing Old. In their relationship to Jesus the fathers have their own word and their own particular time, just as Jesus in turn has His own word and very different time compared with them. Yet it is none the less true that the non-contemporaneity in question does not exclude a certain contemporaneity. Being what they are, the patriarchs point forward to Jesus. In this they resemble John the Baptist, a figure quite distinct from Jesus, in whom the Old Testament seems to be personified at the beginning of the New, and whose special mission is exactly the same, i.e., to point to Jesus. Speaking to their own age, the fathers do in fact speak of Jesus. And what about Israel, the people of the covenant, in whose history Jesus is certainly promised and expected but has not yet come, and yet is not simply absent, since in all its history He is promised and expected ? Was not the time of Israel necessarily another time as the time when He was still far off, but also His own time as the time when He was promised and expected ? Just as the tradition and recollection of Him makes Him the Contemporary of the Church, so in the time of Israel the promise and expectation of His coming makes Him the Contemporary of Israel. In both cases it is a spiritual contemporaneity, perceptible only through Him, and only in faith. Where there is no revelation on His part or faith on ours, even the Church can see only the place where He is no longer present, and accordingly the history of Israel will become a history in which He has not yet come. The line of time, with its obvious differentiation of distance and proximity, then acquires in both cases an absolute significance. But if we may and must count on a genuine self-declaration and awakening of faith (by the resurrection), and therefore on His spiritual presence in both cases, there is no need to reduce His existence in the history of Israel to the bare fact that He is the clue to its meaning and that it is " permissible " for " believers " to " see " in it the " preparation " for the coming of the crucified and risen Jesus (Cullmann, *ibid.*, p. 131–135)—as though this were not an objective fact. If there is a spiritual presence of Jesus the distance of Israel's time on the regressive line of time makes no difference to the fact that its history was His pre-history, and that He was in it before He was, i.e., before this history reached its consummation, so that when He came, it was not only possible but necessary to recognise Him in this pre-history and its record. If His time is the real divine centre of all time, are we not forced to see it as the time which embraces and controls all time before and after Him ? Consider the decisive place occupied by the Old Testament in the early Christian liturgy. Consider the ease with which the Church accepted the Canon of the Synagogue. Above all consider the degree to which the New Testament is impregnated with the Old. Such phenomena cannot be satisfactorily accounted for on secondary motives, or from accidents of history. We have here an intrinsic necessity of the highest order, an insight which the later Church may have done much to obscure, and which may even strike us as strange, but which for the apostles and their communities was a self-evident truth. They were forced to accept it because they looked back to Jesus. It was not a matter of interpretation or construction, but they obviously knew from the very outset that the man Jesus was the fulfilment of the prophetic history of Israel, that its history was the beginning of His, and that its record in the Old Testament was the record of Him. The only way to Him was by reading, understanding and expounding Moses and the prophets, and therefore hearing His Word as the fulfilled and final Word of God, but the Word already proclaimed and attested. His figure had not merely a forward dimension, into their own time in which He was in their midst, but also a backward dimension in which He was in the midst of the fathers. Now that He, the Saviour, the Christ and the Lord, had come and was revealed, now that the crown and climax of Old Testament history had appeared, the crowd of witnesses to this history sounded out again with new life and vigour, and had to be heard again and genuinely understood. And the the apostles and their communities, with their own testimony, could be as it were a choir responding antiphonally to the first choir and confirming the fulfilment of the promise. Conscious though they were of the differences, they could only form a single people with the people of the God of Israel, seeing the time of this people and their own time fused into a single time of Jesus. To live in the presence of Jesus and the past of the Old Testament was for them one and the same thing. They were not introducing an alien element into their tradition

and recollection of Jesus when they set it in relation to the Old Testament.
Nor were they introducing an alien element into the Old Testament when they
related it to Jesus. They knew the true nature of both. Each was intelligible
only in the light of the other. Had they been faced with the familiar question
of our own age, they would probably have answered with the counter-question
whether not only the Old Testament but Jesus Himself is not interpreted " allegorically " if this relation, this connected past of Jesus as He that was to come
and He that did come, is overlooked and neglected.

But the New Testament does not stop here. In the same direction, and in
the name of the same Old Testament witness, it goes further back than the history
of Israel which began with Abraham. It tells us that Jesus, as the Word of
God, was the real basis of creation whose time thus embraces the beginning of
all created time. " In the beginning was the Word," (Jn. 1¹). Hence this word
is " from the beginning " (1 Jn. 1¹). " Ye have known him that is from the
beginning " (1 Jn. 2¹³ᶠ·). He is Himself " the beginning of the creation of God "
(Rev. 3¹⁴), " the firstborn of every creature " (Col. 1¹⁵), the " head of all princi-
pality and power " (Col. 2¹⁰). Indeed, it was by Him that God established all
things (Col. 1¹⁷) : " For by him were all things created, that are in heaven, and
that are in earth, visible and invisible, . . . all things were created by him,
and for him " (Col. 1¹⁶). " Thou, Lord, in the beginning hast laid the foundation of the earth, and the heavens are the works of thine hands " (Heb. 1¹⁰) ;
" Through whom also he made the ages " (Heb. 1², R.V. margin). And it is
put even more concisely in 1 Cor. 8⁶ : δι' οὗ τὰ πάντα. The clause in Jn. 1² :
" The same was in the beginning with God," would be an unnecessary and confusing repetition from v. 1 if it did not indicate the person who was later to be
the subject of the whole Gospel narrative, and of whom we are told in 1¹⁴ that
the Word was made flesh and dwelt among us. The Prologue is not speaking
of an eternal Son or divine Logos *in abstracto*, but of a Son and Logos who is
one with the man Jesus. It is equally impossible to interpret any of the other
passages cited above *in abstracto*, as a study of the context will in each case
show. What the New Testament says about the being of Jesus Christ in and
as the beginning of all being is distinguished from all contemporary speculation
on that subject, which it resembles formally but refutes in substance, by the fact
that in its adoption and development of the Old Testament wisdom teaching
(1) it does not offer any metaphysical explanation of the mutual relation between
God the Father and the man Jesus, or of their co-existence, but simply
shows what is meant by the statement that Jesus Christ is *Kyrios* ; and (2) it
does not speculate about a hierarchy of mediators, but simply bears witness to
God and man in their co-existence, and therefore to Jesus Christ as very God
but also as very man, the meaning and ground of all creation. In other words,
it offers us an ultimate—or penultimate—word about the sense in which the
man Jesus is called Lord, i.e., that He has revealed Himself and is to be accepted
as He was, in the eternal counsel and purpose of the Father, and as its most
specific content, when all things began to be. It also teaches us that the whole
wisdom and power of the Creator at the beginning of all being were concretely
the power and wisdom which appeared and were revealed in the man Jesus : that
He was the purpose and ground of the divine creative action at the beginning
of all times. It was in this way, not abstractly in His Son, but concretely in
the giving of His only begotten Son, in the unity of His Son with the Son of Man
Jesus of Nazareth (Jn. 3¹⁶), that God willed to demonstrate His love to the
world, having already loved it in creating it. *Mundi factor vere Verbum Dei est :
hic autem est Dominus noster, qui in novissimis temporibus homo factus est* (Irenaeus
Adv. Haer. V, 18, 3). Just as from an external point of view the creation makes
possible and provides the basis for God's covenant, its history, its promise and
finally its fulfilment, so from an internal point of view the covenant makes
possible and provides the basis for creation. If the man Jesus, whose incarnation, crucifixion and resurrection took place in the days of Augustus and

Tiberius, is this fulfilment of the covenant and the meaning and purpose of creation, it follows that He was also its ground, and therefore that He was already at the beginning of time as the One who was to come in the plan of God. Time in its beginning was enclosed by His time, and to that extent was itself His time.

But the New Testament takes a further and higher step still. At a few points it has even more to say about "Jesus Christ yesterday." This is obvious at once from the second and third clauses of Jn. 1^1: "The Word was with God, and the Word was God." It would be inadvisable to take the ἦν in these clauses as implying a timeless existence. Nor should we overlook the immediate continuation : "The same was in the beginning with God." The οὗτος here refers to the incarnate Logos. It is He who was "in the beginning." And not only that, but even before this beginning He was with God and was Himself God, participating in the divine being and nature, before created time began, in the eternity of God. This eternity includes not only the present and future, but also the past. God's eternity does not invalidate past, present and future, and therefore time ; it legitimates them. In it they have their origin and true character. In it yesterday, to-day and to-morrow are one, and in their unity genuine and real. The man Jesus is in this genuine and real yesterday of God's eternity, which is anterior to all other yesterdays, including the yesterday of creation. This is the claim made by the Jesus of the Fourth Gospel (Jn. 17^{24}) : "Thou lovedst me before the foundation of the world." We are reminded of the εὐδόκησα and γεγέννηκα of the baptism narrative, and of the designation of Jesus as the "beloved" or "elect" Son of God in this story and in the account of the transfiguration. These terms probably refer to this antecedent past. Again, we read in 1 Pet. 1^{20} that the "lamb without blemish and without spot" was not only "foreordained before the foundation of the world, but was manifest in these last times for you." As the context shows, this means that in human history, and beyond all history, human or otherwise, there is no other or higher law than that of the divine mercy, now revealed, established and applied in the oblation of the Lamb of God. This is no positive law, to be restricted or repealed by another of the same kind. There is no place from which it can be relativised. It is the true "natural law" which necessarily limits and relativises all positive law. For the Lamb of God foreordained before the foundation of the world is the person and work in which this law had been revealed. In similar vein Eph. 1^4 asserts that God chose us in Jesus Christ "before the foundation of the world, that we should be holy and without blame before him." Once again, this means that every choice and decision made in human history, and indeed in the whole course of created time, is subordinated to the choice and decision made in God's eternity before all created being and its time, i.e., that Jesus Christ was elected by God, and we in Him. A similar idea is expressed in Rev. 13^8 which tells us that there is a "book of life of the Lamb slain," to be included in which "from the foundation of the world" signifies the great decision which alone can offer deliverance in the great tribulation caused by the beast from the abyss. In short, we may say that wherever the verbs προορίζειν, προτίθεσθαι, προετιμάζειν, προγινώσκειν and the substantives πρόγνωσις and πρόθεσις occur, there is a reference to this day before yesterday, the pluperfect of God's time, in which the event of the particular time of Jesus, and in and with it the ensuing time of the community, the calling and sanctification of those who belong to Jesus in and with His own history, their justification in judgment, their deliverance from death and their glorification, were all foreseen and resolved, and to that extent had already taken place. It would be a complete misunderstanding if we were to object that the singularity of this event and its eternity as attested in these passages are mutually exclusive. On the contrary, these passages accentuate its absolute singularity by insisting on its predetermination from all eternity. A thing which is resolved from all eternity necessarily has the character of absolute singularity. At this last and highest stage, the pre-existence of the man Jesus coincides with His eternal predestination and election, which includes the election of Israel, of the Church, and of every individual member of His body.

3. The being of Jesus in time is not merely a being in the present or the past. It is also—and this brings us to our third and final point—a being in the future, a coming being. From the standpoint of the apostles and their communities it has also to be said, and with no less reality and truth, that He comes.

With no less reality and truth !—we must lay primary emphasis on this point. There is no difference of degree between the being of Jesus in the three dimensions, whether in substantiality, importance or urgency, in dignity or value. Regarded from the normative standpoint of the time of the apostles, He is as much He who comes as He who has come and is present. Christians live no less in expectation than in recollection or simply in His presence. Hence the Church's proclamation of Him is no less eschatological than soteriological and pneumatological. It is no less proclamation of His future and the approaching end of time than of His past in which time has found its beginning and centre, or of His present in which we move from that beginning and centre to the end of time.

It is no less so, but, as we must add at once, no more. The apostles did not wait for the Lord, or live in hope in Him, in such a way that the Jesus of Nazareth of yesterday, who was promised in the Old Testament, who was at the beginning of all things, and who was in the counsel of God before the beginning of all things, faded into the background and became colourless and unimportant. And even less was this the case with His living presence, lordship and grace among them, His being in the Spirit in the life, upbuilding and mission of His community, their present life in His Spirit. It is not the case that only in the coming of the Lord do we have to do with His proper being, and with an improper in His first coming and presence. There is no justification for trying to systematise the being of Jesus from this standpoint. The New Testament always thinks and speaks eschatologically, but never with full logical consistence. Its only logical consistence is to think and speak on all sides and in all dimensions and relationships christologically. And it is for this reason that with equal emphasis and seriousness it can always think and speak eschatologically as well.

As, in the New Testament sense, the being of Jesus yesterday and to-day can finally be understood and explained only in the light of the resurrection, so it is with His being εἰς τοὺς αἰῶνας, and therefore with His general and definitive manifestation as Judge, Consummator and new Creator as this is promised and therefore expected in the near it indefinite future. Clearly, it would not be inconceivable *rebus aliter stantibus*, i.e., if there had been no resurrection, for our knowledge of Jesus Christ to have been restricted to His past and present, the past somehow prolonged into and determining the present. In this case the apostles and their communities would have contemplated the future in terms of the propagation, intensification and practical realisation of the Christianity which they championed. Hope would then have meant confidence in the power of the Gospel to cleanse and sanctify the individual and to permeate society. The apostles would have looked forward to a progressive immanent development of the new life opened up by the resurrection, and then of the state of human and creaturely things generally, in the direction of an ideal of good and happy humanity corresponding to the beginning, to be attained approximately in this world and perfectly in a better hereafter, and identifiable with the kingdom of God. Indeed, there have been whole periods in the history of the Church when this version of the Christian hope has been regarded as necessary both in theory and in practice. The New Testament does not contain a single shred of evidence to support this view. Compared with what the New Testament calls hope, this Utopian version can only be described as a fabrication, however well-meaning and attractive. The salient feature about it is that in the last resort it can do without Jesus. It may know Him as the Jesus of yesterday and to-day, but it knows nothing of Him as the One who is εἰς τοὺς αἰῶνας, as the One who comes. Its knowledge of the man Jesus and His time obviously lacks this third dimension. And this raises the question whether there is any real understanding of His yesterday and to-day. In the New Testament, neither the inner life of the community nor its missionary proclamation suggests the initial stages of a growth leading to a better future either here or hereafter. Not even the parables of the mustard seed, the leaven and the seed growing secretly really inculcate this doctrine. No, the New Testament looks forward, not merely to a better future, but to a future which sets a term to the whole time process, and in its perfection includes and surpasses absolutely all the contents of time. This future will be a wholly new order, quite independent of all creaturely and even Christian development. Nor is it a distant prospect, but a sure and immediate hope. It is for this reason that according to the New Testament the community purifies and sanctifies itself; and for this reason that it proclaims the Gospel to the world in this last time. Not is this future merely the result of what Jesus Christ was yesterday and is to-day. It is again He Himself, His own person and work, in a new mode and form. The last time which dawned with His appearance, and in which the community has its mission and task; and the conclusion of time, the judgment and the consummation which, corresponding to the time of creation, will form the content of this concluding time and of the ensuing time of the being of all things in God—this time too, as the New Testament sees it, is wholly and utterly His time, the time of Jesus, the time of His being. The New Testament does not look for an amelioration of present conditions or for an ideal state, but for the coming of the Lord—*Maranatha* (1 Cor. 16²²)—in a definitive and general revelation ; and therefore for the justification and redemption of individuals in judgment ; for the end and new beginning of the cosmos ; for the kingdom as the last thing corresponding to the first which was in the counsel of God before all times. We obviously neglect or forget or deny the Easter revelation of the man Jesus, and therefore the substance of the whole witness of the New Testament, if we misunderstand the Christian hope in this way, ignoring so completely the third dimension of the being of Jesus in time. For the Easter revelation was the per-mission and command which placed the apostles and their communities in a position to believe in Him as the One to whom they owed absolutely everything, to love Him as the One in whom they had everything, and to hope in Him as the One from whom they had to expect every-thing. For everything was really to be expected from the risen Jesus. He could not possibly be known only as the One who had come and was present. As the One who had come and was present He had necessarily to be known also as the One who comes. We have to take into account what it meant and means to look back to the fact of the resurrection of Jesus, to come from this fact. We say that this relationship could not consist in a mere recollection, although it was also a relationship of recollection. It could not possibly be the view of the apostles and their community that now that His past had reached its goal and fruition in the event of the forty days a kind of past had begun when the Bridegroom was taken from them, and could now live on only in their hearts and minds, so that they had to do without Him in reality and in truth, managing without His help. To think of the Resurrected, even when He was no longer seen, was to think of the living Lord, not absent but present to-day and every day to His own. It was to live in faith in Him, and therefore in love for Him, and therefore, even when the forty days were over, in His time, fulfilled time. But this living Lord Jesus yesterday and to-day could not be believed and loved as such without being expected in hope as the One who is εἰς τοὺς αἰώνας, as the One who comes.

His glory could still be known only as His own : both backwards from the event of the forty days to His life and passion and death, to His existence as the promised One of Israel, as the Agent of creation and as the object of the eternal counsel of God ; and forwards from this event in His being as the Lord of His community, in His imperishable words, in His Holy Spirit and the gifts of His Spirit, in baptism and the Lord's Supper, in the very fact that He can be the object of faith and love, and that His name can be proclaimed to Jews and Gentiles. But His glory, although it was His own, was also His glory for them ; His glory as the inheritance of eternal life ordained for them ; His glory as the promise of a new heaven and a new earth. This is what encountered the participants in the forty days in His Easter revelation.

This is what they were privileged to see and hear and touch, to behold as well as to believe, during this period. It was in this recollection that Jesus was present to them. They were already witnesses of His full, conclusive, definitive and general revelation. For this revelation is His visibility for and to the creatures as the Saviour of whom He came and was crucified and raised in the whole existence of His own in the community and also in the world of which the community is ordained to be the salt and the light. What the participants in the forty days saw in the Easter revelation in His person was already the great *consummatum est*—in its fulfilment, in its effectiveness in and to His own, and even in and to the lost for whose sin and salvation He died, and for whose enlightenment concerning His death He was raised again. The first disciples received this enlightenment already. They saw that it had all been done for them and for the whole world. They were granted at this point a foretaste of their inheritance and a glimpse of the new creation.

At this point! It is as the witnesses of what happened at this point, as the witnesses of Jesus' resurrection, that they are apostles, the foundation of His community. It is on the basis of their witness, and of the fact to which they bore witness, that there is faith in Jesus and love for Him within the community. All this was resolved and included in what happened at this point, in the resurrection. The forty days, although they became a thing of the past for those who participated in them and especially for the community gathered by their word, were a strong, irrefutable and sure, but isolated promise, which as such formed the beginning and starting point of the whole time which followed. In this promise there was enclosed the glory of Jesus for His own, the inheritance which was to be theirs, the new creation. This promise entitled them to believe and love, but for the time being they could not see or hear or feel anything more. What was now before the eyes and ears of the apostles and their communities was the fact that they not only had faith and love, but that even they too, not to speak of the world outside, were subject to sin and error, sighing and tears, suffering and death. What they now saw and heard and felt was certainly the word of proclamation, the sacraments of baptism and the Lord's Supper, the fellowship and gifts of the Spirit between brothers and sisters, but also the great " not yet," the almost overwhelming difficulties and tasks arising from their witness to Jesus in the world, the convulsions of the Roman Empire moving to its climax and its fall, the frailty of Christian flesh requiring constant exhortation and comfort and warning and punishment, much weakness and tribulation in which even the voice of the Spirit could only be a sigh and a stammering, a cry of yearning.

Yearning for what? This is where the Christian hope comes in : not as a *Deus ex machina* or a piece of wishful thinking ; but as a grasping of the promise which was the basis of the community and which stood firm in the face of all human weakness and tribulation. For the revelation of Easter was the origin of the community and therefore the beginning, actualised already and therefore past, of the full, conclusive, general revelation of the man Jesus, and therefore of His direct and comprehensive visibility for and to all those for whom as the Son of God He became man, the beginning of the visibility of their participation in His glory. Hence it was no mere escape, but the most natural and basic thing in the world, when in the staggering contrast between their faith and love on the one hand, and their experience of the great " not yet " on the other, the apostles and their communities grasped the promise implicit in the origin of their existence, from this beginning living with a view to its continuation and completion. In recollection of the forty days their only option was expectation of this continuation and completion, and therefore of the return of Jesus. If the event of the forty days was only an indication and a promise of the general revelation of glory still to come, as a genuine temporal event it was real beginning of the justification which abolishes sin, of life victorious over death. To look back to this event is necessarily in this recollection to look forward to the same event, which, having begun at this point, could only be interrupted, but is destined to be consummated when this interim period has run its course and the existence and mission of the community have served their purpose. The Christian community has necessarily to be a gathering in this hope. The Christian has necessarily, then, to be the man who seizes this hope and lives in it. There is no other possibility either for the community or for the individual. The origin of both in the resurrection of Jesus makes it necessary that there should be not only faith in Him who was, and love for Him who is, but also hope in Him who comes.

He who comes is the same as He who was and who is. The Resurrected Himself, therefore, is already He who comes, who restricts His coming to the circle of His then followers, and then interrupts it, to resume and complete it at a later point. For what took place in the resurrection of Jesus was already in the concealment and temporal isolation of this event the revelation of the kingdom of God, of the gracious Judge of all men, and of the life of all the dead. Nothing which will be has not already taken place on Easter Day—included and anticipated in the person of the one man Jesus. And so Jesus in His coming is simply the risen Jesus resuming and completing His coming and thus vindicating that beginning and promise. For what will take place at His return is just that the arch of His time which began with the revelation of His first coming, and then vaulted over the interim time of the community, of the Gospel and the Spirit, of faith and love, the time given for the conversion of the world, will then be completed. It vaults over the interim time as well. Jesus is the Lord in this time too, the Lord of the cosmos no less than the

Lord of His community. Hence even this interim time is His time and therefore fulfilled time. But as His time it needs to be completed as it was begun by Him as an interim time, a time of His invisibility. As the One He has shown Himself to be He must again appear in confirmation of the fulfilment of time, in a glory which is no longer particular and transitory, but universal and permanent, embracing the whole of creation both in heaven and earth. The unity of His glory and our glorification already achieved in His resurrection has again become the future, His future, for us. For us, therefore, the resurrection and the *parousia* are two separate events. But for Him they are a single event. The resurrection is the anticipation of His *parousia* as His *parousia* is the completion and fulfilment of the resurrection.

The hope of the apostles and the community could only be hope in Jesus. It could only be a looking to His being in this third dimension. After all that has been said, this hardly needs to be proved in detail. The first community hoped because it owed its existence to the promise vouchsafed in the resurrection of Jesus : " begotten again unto a lively hope by the resurrection of Jesus Christ from the dead " (1 Pet. 1³). Hence it could hope only in Him, in His coming in glory commenced in the resurrection and to be completed in the *parousia*. Even materially it could not expect any future which was not as such the expectation of His coming. The New Testament community does not hope for the attainment merely of abstract blessings, as for example the resurrection of the dead, or justification in the day of judgment, or a life of eternal bliss. Nor does it hope for crowns or palms or white robes or the glory of a new heaven and new earth or any other spiritual, moral or material blessings in a future kingdom of God. Or rather, it hopes for all these things in and with the fact that it hopes for Jesus Himself. All these things are simply the glorification of the creature which is latent and implicit in His glory, initially revealed in His resurrection, and finally to be revealed in His return. These are merely predicates, appendices and concomitant phenomena of His manifestation. He is and was and will be the kingdom, and in Him will be all the restoration, salvation, perfection and joy of the kingdom. Strictly speaking, there are no " last things," i.e., no abstract and autonomous last things apart from and alongside Him, the last One. Consequently there is no diffused hope, but only the one hope concentrated upon Him, and therefore full and perfect. Hope detached from Him, independent longing and desire, would merely be idle dreaming.

Once this is realised, it is easy to see why New Testament hope could only be hope for the imminent coming of the kingdom, and why this expectation could never give way to disillusionment, but only be constantly renewed. The apostles and their communities lived in faith and love ; in the recollection of the Jesus of yesterday and the consciousness of His to-day ; in the remembrance of the Gospel history (and the history of the covenant with Israel, and creation, and the eternal counsel of God), and therefore in the one great remembrance of His past coming, but also in His direct presence as created by the fellowship of the Holy Spirit. This being the case, how could His future be remote ? After all, He Himself as the Resurrected was the sole but convincing ground of their hope, and its exclusive but all-embracing object. He Himself was the Judge, He the resurrection and the life, the kingdom in all its fulness. This being the case, how could He whom they trusted and loved be other than close at hand as He whom they expected ? " Behold, I stand at the door, and knock " (Rev. 3²⁰). Would He be the One who has come, and is already present, and is trusted and loved, if He did not stand immediately at the door and knock as the One who comes and is expected ? If this is the One whom we expect, we cannot expect Him the day after to-morrow, but to-morrow. The termination of His coming cannot be distant, but imminent. And no dawn and progress of a new day without His coming, no continuation of time apart from the events of His new revelation, can alter this expectation in the very slightest, let alone menace or destroy it. That which necessarily gives rise to this hope and makes it an imminent hope also makes it a constant hope, renewing it every day, and protecting it against disappointment, frustration and scepticism. In His past and present form, as the One who rose again from the dead and is now by His Spirit the living Lord, Jesus accompanies His followers even through the interim time with its great " not yet." How then can any further division of time prior to His coming be other than a part of His time, and therefore fulfilled time ? If His yesterday and to-day in their fulness compel us to look forward to His near coming in the future, the fulness of this yesterday and to-day is great enough to make this forward look a patient expectation. Patience does not mean torpor or somnolence or resignation or indifference. Patience in the New Testament sense is perseverance. To persevere is not to give up expecting the Lord, and expecting Him soon. It is to refrain from grumbling and complaining at having continually to expect Him. It is not to wait for someone and something but for Jesus Himself, who yesterday and to-day does not allow us to wait in poverty and despair, but fills each new portion of time with His fulness, so that there is no worse waste of time than to grumble and complain at His absence instead of continually giving thanks for what He was and rejoicing in what He is. To persevere then, means to continue expecting the Lord and expecting Him soon. It is to live in hope, in glad but patient hope, no less surely than to live in faith and love. For the object of hope is identical with that faith and love. It is the man Jesus, the Lord Himself, who is the Lord of all times, who fulfils all times, and who does not leave His followers empty at any time, but in every time makes them rich, and even very rich.

To understand this, we have only to recall the power of the resurrection, which enabled the apostles and their communities to believe and love and therefore hope. We have only to see that their path was a path from grace to grace, from one revelation to another, and therefore from faith to new faith : ἐκ πίστεως εἰς πίστιν. We must disabuse our minds of the notion that the New Testament community has only darkness or twilight behind it and only the brilliant light of the *parousia* before it. It is not floundering in a slough in which its further progress seems impossible as the great light before it seems to recede into the distance, and it grows tired and perplexed, and is tempted to halt and seek a more solid path. Its consciousness of time is no more dominated by the future being of Jesus in time than His past or present. As we must never forget, its gaze is always on Him. It may look backwards to His past even as far as the eternal counsel of God. It may look to His present at the right hand of God, from which He rules to-day by His Spirit. Or it may look to the future and His general and conclusive revelation. But in every case it looks only to Him. And in Him it sees the fulness of everything for which those enlightened by Him are thankful, whether present or expected. Hence we must not range ourselves with those who according to 2 Peter had grown weary of hope even in New Testament days, because they had grown weary of faith and love, and lost their awareness of the yesterday and to-day of the Lord Jesus. Once they did this, it was inevitable that they should regard an imminent expectation as suspect. But surely not expectation and hope as such ? Surely not the resurrection of Jesus ? Surely not the *consummatum est* revealed by the resurrection ? All the same, we should be foolish to range ourselves with such people, or to regard them as honest witnesses to the truth in face of an early Christian hope which has long since proved to be illusory. If we do, we implicate ourselves in questions, anxieties and problems which would never have occurred to the apostles and their communities from which these people were on the point of separating, because they could not arise on the presupposition of their time-consciousness, i.e., of their knowledge of the man Jesus. To argue as these others do is to create very different premises which are in fact negated by the New Testament. It is to take up a different position from that on which the Christian Church can honestly call itself by this name.

It was obviously wrong to try to ignore or weaken or reinterpret the New Testament hope, the looking to the man Jesus in the third dimension, the concrete form of this hope as imminent expectation, and the patient joy and joyful patience of the early Christian attitude. When this third dimension is no longer considered, and the movement towards the day of the Lord, and therefore expectation and holy impatience and holy patience are forgotten, the very worst has happened at these decisive points, and at earlier points too. If we can really be satisfied with a Jesus of yesterday and to-day, and therefore with an ideal and goal visible only at a distance and to be attained in an indefinite future, it is a clear sign that we have already lost the living Jesus of yesterday and to-day. We are understanding His past only in a " historical sense." We are expunging the true Son of God, the Messiah, Saviour and Lord, and therefore the witness of the Old Testament to Christ, to say nothing of the man Jesus pre-existent in creation, and eternally before creation in God. We are understanding His presence only psychologically and sociologically. The Holy Spirit has vanished into thin air. The heavenly session and rule of Jesus have become the mythological and highly exaggerated expression of a value judgment in which we may still confront Him independently. There is no real reason why we should not dispense with Him altogether as a historical and present figure. If we still confess Him, there is no constraining power of knowledge behind the word of confession. There is no telling where the trouble first began. Perhaps faith grew feeble, or love cold, or hope empty. But in any case, the collapse of one means the collapse of all. And our only point at the moment is that everything depends also on hope, on expectation, and indeed on the imminent expectation of the man Jesus which is both fervent and placid, impatient and patient. Christian knowledge, the Christian community, Christian existence itself, as the resurrection and the message of the resurrection show, is this whole which is equally necessarily faith, love and hope, and equally necessarily directed to the beginning, centre and end, the end no less than the beginning and centre, the object of faith, love and hope being necessarily identical with Jesus.

"I am . . . which is to come." The consciousness of time inherent in this whole is to be summed up in this phrase of Rev. 1[8]. The future to which we look forward from the present of the man Jesus is, like this present itself, and the past which lies behind it, His time, the time of the man Jesus.

Here, too, we shall conclude with some detailed references to New Testament texts.

If we are to understand the New Testament consciousness of time in this third component, it is perhaps best to start with the fact that the apostles and their communities always had before them the witness of the Old Testament to Christ, and therefore the coming Jesus, promised and prefigured, but only prefigured, and according to the Word of God to be expected in the near and certain future. According to the Gospel records before them, however, He had already come, and with Him the kingdom. And on the basis of the climax and crown of these records, of the Easter message, they were privileged to live in His presence. Hence their hope was a hope already fulfilled. It was thus radically distinguished from the ordinary hope or longing in which they might well have been disappointed. Yet they still went on waiting, or began to wait as never before, together with the fathers of the old covenant, hoping and living wholly and utterly in Advent. Clearly, there was a genuine tension in their consciousness of time, a tension between the preliminary glory of the resurrection and its consummation in the future *parousia*. It was in this tension that they believed in Him and proclaimed Him as the Deliverer of those " who through fear of death were all their lifetime subject to bondage " (Heb. 2[15]). This, though already accomplished, was not yet realised and experienced even in themselves, let alone in creation as a whole. They walked by faith and not by sight (2 Cor. 5[7]). They were indeed saved, but only in hope (Rom. 8[24]). They had indeed received the Holy Spirit, but only as an ἀπαρχή (2 Cor. 1[22], 5[5]; Eph. 1[14]), i.e., as a first instalment of the final gift. The instalment was of a piece with the final gift and a pledge and guarantee of it, yet it was no more than the deposit on an account, an ἀπαρχή (Rom. 8[23]), i.e., the first fruits consecrated to the Deity, but not yet the full harvest distributed among all the people. They knew of their hidden life with Christ in God, but only when Christ their life was made manifest would they be manifested with Him in glory (Col. 3[3f.]). " Behold, what manner of love the Father hath bestowed upon us, that we should be called (and be) the sons of God . . . Beloved, now are we the sons of God, and it doth not yet appear what we shall be : but we know that, when he shall appear, we shall be like him : for we shall see him as he is " (1 Jn. 3[1f.]). What has still to be realised, as Paul sees it, is the manifestation of the life of Jesus in His body (2 Cor. 4[10]), the general " manifestation of the sons of God " (Rom. 8[19]), the making of their " body of humiliation " conformable to His " body of glory " (Phil. 3[21]), and the liberation of all creatures from the bondage of corruption to the glorious liberty of the children of God (Rom. 8[21]). When Jesus had been obedient even to the death of the cross, He was exalted by God to be the Bearer of the name which as the name of the Lord is above every other name. This was clear to the proclaimers and recipients of the Easter message, and they believed and responded with their confession and a life of love for Him and for the brethren. But they did not yet see the knees of all things in heaven and earth bow to Him as the only Lord, nor did they yet hear the song of praise with which every tongue must willingly or unwillingly confess Him as the Lord (Phil. 2[9f.]). This was the supremely visible and real tension in their consciousness of time between the times. But it must be seen and understood that this tension—with the need and yearning and sighing inevitably entailed—could not have a negative accent, because they saw themselves set in fellowship with the Old Testament fathers, in the time, not to be evaluated negatively, of their expectation of the coming Lord and His salvation ; because they were privileged to stand with these ancient witnesses of truth in Advent.

2 Pet. 1[16-21] is particularly noteworthy in this connexion. The author is talking about his proclamation of the " power and coming of our Lord Jesus Christ." He maintains that it is different from any " cunningly devised fables " (σεσοφισμένοις μύθοις). To begin with, he points out that he had been an eye-witness (ἐπόπτης) of the transfiguration. He then continues in v. 19 : " Hence we have the word of prophecy the more surely (βεβαιότερον) ; whereunto ye do well that ye take heed, as unto light that shineth in a dark place, until the day dawn, and the day star arise in your hearts." According to the Gospel record, Moses and Elijah had actually stood by the side of Jesus when He was transfigured before their eyes, and had spoken with Him. This prophetic word was not therefore outmoded, but acquired genuine relevance for those who had their origin in the appearance of Jesus. It was confirmed in its character as a prophetic word pointing to the future and became an indispensable light on their path. The disciples did not come down from the mount alone, or as eschatological innovators, but in company with the ancient witnesses, accredited by the fulfilment of the long-prepared history of the covenant and salvation. It was in this company that they moved afresh to meet the coming Lord. The visible and palpable unity of prophecy and fulfilment, of fulfilment and prophecy, is what factually distinguishes their proclamation of the " power and coming of our Lord Jesus Christ " from all " cunningly devised fables."

The same line is taken in Peter's second speech in Ac. 3¹⁹ᶠ·. He summons men to repentance and conversion and the remission of sins on the ground that " seasons of refreshing " are coming ; the sending of Jesus, Israel's destined Messiah, " whom the heaven must receive until the times of restoration of all things (ἀποκατάστασις πάντων), which God hath spoken by the mouth of all his holy prophets since the world began." The implication is that the prophets foretold not only the first advent of Christ, but implicitly His second advent as well, to which the Church now looks and the whole world actually moves. Far from being obsolete, the witness of the prophets has acquired a vital relevance and admonitory significance for the people of Israel to whom the apostles in the first instance addressed their message. Whatever happens, Israel must not miss a second time, and to its final judgment, the chance to experience the fulfilment of this message, as it did the first time to its detriment.

Even more illuminating is 1 Pet. 1¹⁰⁻¹², which merits particularly close attention. In 1⁵ the author had stated that those who had been begotten again unto a living hope by the resurrection of Jesus Christ from the dead were being kept by the power of God through faith unto salvation ready to be revealed at the last time. In vv. 6–9 he had spoken of the " joy unspeakable and full of glory " awaiting those who were now suffering persecution. Although these had not seen Jesus they loved Him, and believed on Him without beholding Him. That joy would be theirs in His final revelation. He now continues in v. 10 f. : " Of which salvation the prophets have inquired and searched diligently, who prophesied of the grace that should come unto you : searching what, or what manner of time the Spirit of Christ which was in them did signify, when it testified beforehand the sufferings of Christ, and the glory that should follow. Unto whom it was revealed, that not unto themselves, but unto us they did minister the things, which are now reported unto you by them that have preached the gospel unto you with the Holy Ghost sent down from heaven, which things the angels desire to look into." The meaning of this is that they have been translated into the state of faith, hope and love by the fact that the prophets, taught by the Spirit of Christ, have done and are still doing them the same service as the messengers of the Gospel now do them as they are sent by the same Holy Spirit. The prophets preached and still preach to them the sufferings and glory of Jesus Christ, and in so doing they preach their salvation already accomplished in Jesus Christ but still to be revealed to them. The fulfilment of Old Testament prophecy has become a reality among them, and they have thus come to participate in the resurrection of Christ. They are born again to a living hope. Therefore, in spite of the sufferings of the present time, they have been translated into the state of love and faith in One whom nevertheless they cannot see or behold. We may note in particular that the enquiries and declarations of the prophets belong formally and subjectively to their own time and history. But in this historical particularity they were materially and objectively inspired and moved and impelled by the Spirit of Christ, by the truth of His coming person and history, by His sufferings and glory. What makes their enquiries and declarations prophetic is that objectively and materially they are witnesses of Him who was still to come, i.e., of the grace now vouchsafed to Christians. It is for their sake that Jesus Christ suffered, and for their sake that He is glorified. Thus the prophets can be of service to Christians because they are prophets, and their testimony is a προμαρτύρεσθαι (v. 11). They too, like the messengers of the Gospel (v. 12), are wholly dependent on the Holy Spirit of Jesus Christ. Like them, they are unable to make the object of their proclamation visible or perceptible to their hearers. For them too the salvation wrought in Jesus Christ is a hidden mystery, only to be revealed later. Hence in a way they really minister to Christians " the things which are now reported unto you." But because their testimony takes the form of a προμαρτύρεσθαι, and their existence that of prophets, unlike the evangelists, and perhaps to their advantage, they are witnesses to the truth that what they attest with the evangelists is not just an ordinary event in the flux of history, and that the God proclaimed by the evangelists as the Father of Jesus Christ is not a new God. *Certitudinem salutis confirmat ab ipsius vetustate : quoniam ab initio mundi legitimum a Spiritu sancto testimonium habuerit* (Calvin). Unlike the evangelists, however, and perhaps to their disadvantage, the prophets are witnesses of the Jesus Christ whom they do not yet know as come, and can attest therefore only as One who is still to come. " What or what manner of time " will be His, is all that they can investigate. They cannot bear witness to His actual manifestation. The sufferings and glory of Jesus may form the object of their message objectively and materially, but they cannot be its content subjectively and formally. Since they think and speak only of their own time, the actual occurrence of the event which they foretell can only be for them a matter of research and investigation. Yet this is no fortuitous limitation. Indeed, it is not really a limitation at all. It makes no difference to their testimony or status. As the sufferings and glory of Christ are revealed to the prophets by His Spirit, it is also revealed to them that with the later evangelists, the heralds of the accomplished event of salvation, even in this apparently disadvantageous distinction they have a very real and special service to render to Christians instructed by the latter. The rigorously future orientation of the prophetic message only becomes vital in Christianity. For Christians living in time the enacted salvation has become past. But in its general revelation it is still future. And in this futurity it is the event which leads Christians forward in time, urging them ahead, drawing them on like a magnet, out of the sufferings of the present time, out of the darkness of the present and into the light. The present status of Christians, with its tribulation, is related to that of the future deliverance to which they move as the sufferings of Christ are related to His subsequent glory. The two together, and in this order, are the Messianic reality : the first being subordinate and transitory, the second real and permanent ; the first being the way and the other the goal. In virtue of this order and structure of the one event commonly attested by the prophets and evangelists, the evangelical and apostolic message can be no less prophetic, no less a message of Advent, than that of the prophets. It proclaims not only the Crucified, but also the Resurrected ; not only the faith and love which Christians are to maintain in their present tribulation as they look back to the completed Messianic event, but, as in vv. 3–9, and in agreement with the structure of this event, the future revelation of the deliverance of those who believe and love (corresponding to the glory of Christ), and therefore Christian hope. Christians could not really come from this event if they were not moving towards it again. Thus it is Christianity which first does justice to prophecy even in its particularity, even in the strict futurity of its message. In fact, this passage seems almost to reduce the apostles and evangelists to the level of subordinates. All that they have to do is to take up the Old Testament message of the future and give it the honour which it could not enjoy prior to the events, in its distinctive character as prophecy. The message of the Messiah already come gives a new edge to the message of the coming Messiah, of the salvation which is not only future, but demonstrated to be future. Now that grace and salvation have become present and future and not just future, the ministry of the prophets really begins, as by the word of the apostles and evangelists the Holy Spirit speaks to Christians in this twofold way, making them Christians, and translating them into the state of living hope in which even in the sufferings of time they move towards the glory of the future revelation. Only here, within the Christian community, does the prophetic word come into its own. Christians have to see themselves standing as it were between two choirs singing antiphonally— the apostles on one side and the prophets on the other. And the passage closes at v. 12 with the statement that even the angels are amongst those who look forward to the future revelation of the salvation already accomplished. They, too, desire to see and look into the mystery of the things, the grace and salvation, in the proclamation of which the prophets and apostles have ministered to them and do so still. Like the apostles and prophets, like Christians themselves, the angels wait for the consummation of the process inaugurated by the resurrection—a consummation which according to 1 Pet. 4[7] will also be " the end of all things." The word used to denote the "looking into" of the angels (παρακύψαι) is the same as that which in Jn. 20[5] is used of Peter when he looks into the empty tomb. Thus Christians are surrounded by a cloud of witnesses, some eloquent and others silent, some on earth and others in heaven, but all looking into the future. This is sufficient to warn them to hold fast to the state of salvation to which they have been called. " Wherefore gird up the loins of your mind, be sober, and hope to the end for the grace that is to be brought unto you at the revelation of Jesus Christ " (v. 13).

Remarkably enough therefore, but also instructively, it was primarily the Old Testament background to the New Testament message which gave to the first Christian consciousness of time its forward direction and eschatological orientation, and to Christian life the form of a " looking for and hasting unto the coming of the day of God " (2 Pet. 3[12]). The Gospels would be very different from what they are, i.e., accounts of the historical existence, fulfilled in His crucifixion and revealed in His resurrection, of the man Jesus who was the Lord, Messiah and Saviour, if in telling of Him who was, they were not everywhere full of Advent, of the One who comes and will be in His revelation.

As is well known, the Fourth Gospel takes its own particular line in this matter. In fulfilment of the promise : " I will not leave you comfortless ; I will come to you " (Jn. 14[18]), Easter, Ascension, Pentecost and *parousia* are here seen as a single event, with much the same foreshortening of perspective as when we view the whole range of the Alps from the Jura. This perspective is legitimate and necessary side by side with the other. The Fourth Gospel shows us that it is necessary to understand the event of Easter and that of the *parousia*, with the intervening history of the community under the present power of the Holy Spirit, as different moments of one and the same act. The theses of those who advocate a thoroughgoing eschatology are quite superfluous once this has been realised. There is no need to suppose that there was unforeseen delay in the *parousia*, or that hope in the *parousia* was repeatedly deferred, or that the primitive Church and even Jesus Himself were disillusioned or mistaken on the subject in consequence of an exaggerated enthusiasm—a view which is so clumsy that it is surely condemned from the very outset.

For there is a unity of eschatological outlook even behind and above the different approach which we find in the Synoptists. As we have seen already, the latter start with the initial assumption that the kingdom of God promised in the Old Testament has already entered history as an effective reality in the person and words and acts of the man Jesus. The time is fulfilled as He is present, embarking on a way which will end in His death as the decisive event of salvation, but which is from the very first this way, on the higher stages of which this end is already the meaning not only of the being of Jesus as such, but of all His words and acts. The Synoptists would agree with the view which the Evangelist attributes to John the Baptist in 1[29]—that from the very outset Jesus is " the Lamb of God, which taketh away the sin of the world." But He is still concealed as the One He is and shows Himself to be in His words and acts. At first, it is only the demons who recognise Him with any certainty in this way : " What have we to do with thee, thou Jesus of Nazareth ? art thou come to destroy us ? We know thee who thou art, the Holy One of God " (Mk. 1[24]). The crowds are amazed and dumbfounded, but they only call Him a great prophet (Lk. 7[16]). Their spiritual leaders are offended at His claim to be the coming One, and dismiss it as a piece of arrogant self-assertion. But this only shows how blind and deaf they are, how far they have abandoned the hope of Israel, whose first and most discerning and willing advocates they ought to have been in face of this fulfilment. John the Baptist surmises His true status, but according to Mt. 11² he is not sure whether Jesus is He that should come or whether they should look for another. Indeed, He is hidden even from His disciples apart from preliminary illuminations like Peter's confession and the transfiguration. They will forsake Him and flee when He stands at the end of His way. Peter will even deny Him, and Judas will be the first and decisive agent in Israel's last act of unfaithfulness and disobedience to its promise, initiating the handing over of its Messiah to the Gentiles. As the One He is Jesus is thus both present and not present. The kingdom of God is real but not operative. It has come, but not come. It has still to be prayed for. It is present in reality, but not in revelation. To the extent that the New Testament contains good news, but not yet Easter news, the prophetic history of the Old Testament is continued in the New. The New Testament witness to the Messianic " now " is unmistakeable, yet it is shot through with the " not yet,' with more expectation, as though the Messiah were still only promised. In the very centre of the picture Jesus Himself waits, looking forward to things to come, to His own future.

This is the second reason—the Advent witness of the Old Testament was the first—why the apostolic community would not concentrate exclusively on the past or present, but when it thought of Jesus had to look forward to this future. Throughout the tradition—in the New Testament even more clearly than in the Old—we see at the heart of the actuality of salvation a people always blind and deaf, obstinate and determined enemies of God, a Church which always runs away and denies and even betrays Him, and above all Jesus Himself still waiting and looking forward to His own future. How could anyone who remembered this Jesus do other than follow Him, looking with His eyes and according to His express command to the future, His future ? But to look to His future is to look to the revelation of His actuality, to the irresistible, invincible and triumphant visibility of His kingdom as it has already come.

The reader of the Gospels is bound to look to the future, if only because the Jesus attested by them was not waiting for nothing but positively living and speaking and acting towards His future revelation. For His goal is not just death, although this is the saving event to which His whole life was in the first instance directed. His goal is the subsequent revelation of the meaning of His death, and therefore the putting into effect of the salvation won in Him for men, for the community, for the whole world, for which He had come as the Fulfiller of time. It is the kingdom with the veil removed, manifest, and visible in glory. Everything Jesus said revolved implicitly, and in the parables explicitly, around the coming kingdom in this sense. And the acts of Jesus, His signs and wonders, are in this sense effective anticipations and therefore real indications of the coming kingdom to which Jesus moves through His provisional concealment and finally His passion, crucifixion, death and burial : not of the reality of the kingdom, for the kingdom was already a reality in His person from the very outset and could not be more real than in His self-offering to death, in which the saving event of His whole existence, His Messianic reality is perfected ; but certainly of its revelation, by which the kingdom acquires form and becomes saving and effective for men, for the community, and for the world.

This also explains why New Testament expectation is always characterised as imminent expectation. It is primarily the expectation of the man Jesus Himself (in the subjective sense) : the expectation in which He Himself lived and went to His death ; the expectation of what He saw before Him as the goal of His life and death. It is the expectation of His own resurrection from the dead. All three predictions of the passion in the Synoptics expressly mention this expectation : " On the third day he will rise again." Yet the Gospels obviously rule out the imminent expectation which is expectation of a definite date. Jesus Himself admitted that He shared the human uncertainty understandable in this respect : " That day and that hour knoweth no man, no, not the angels which are in heaven, neither the Son, but the Father " (Mk. 13³²).

Even after the resurrection He can still say : " It is not for you to know the times or the seasons, which the Father hath set in his own power," i.e., which He has appointed for the manifestation of His kingdom (Ac. 1⁷). The revelation of the kingdom is linked with the consummation of the life of Jesus in His death. It is its revelation. And this fulfilment of His life in His death, which will be followed by His revelation, is accomplished by the incarnate Son in obedience to the will of His Father and therefore in acceptance of the right point of time appointed not by Himself but by the Father. What He does know and teach, because His disciples are always to know it too, is that the kingdom of God, the revelation of its hidden reality, will come soon and suddenly like a thief in the night, as He Himself puts it (Mt. 24⁴³), in a simile repeated in 1 Thess. 5² ; 2 Pet. 3¹⁰ ; Rev. 16¹⁵. Its coming will be soon because it is the goal of the limited life in time of Jesus of Nazareth and will follow hard on His death and therefore in the foreseeable future. And it will come suddenly because it is foreordained and foreknown by God alone, and will occur when men are least expecting it, beneficially if terrifyingly upsetting all their expectations and plans, and thus their anxieties and hopes, as actually happened in the first instance with the resurrection of Jesus.

These considerations throw light on Mk. 9¹ : " Verily I say unto you, that there be some of them that stand here, which shall not taste of death, till they have seen (ἕως ἂν ἴδωσιν) the kingdom of God come with power (ἐληλυθυῖαν ἐν δυνάμει)." This passage assumes that the kingdom of God has already come. What has still to happen is that it should be seen. Some of those standing around Jesus are to see it. It follows, therefore, that this " coming of the kingdom," this revelation of the fact that it has come, must occur within the foreseeable future. The context in which the three Synoptists placed the saying shows that they connected it with the transfiguration, which is its immediate sequel. The indefinite τίνες, which is used to indicate those who are to see the kingdom in their lifetime, is probably meant to confirm this. Only " some " (Peter, James and John) witness the transfiguration. But this event is only a proleptic anticipation of the resurrection, as the latter is only a proleptic anticipation of the *parousia*. This being the case, it is best to see the fulfilment of Mk. 9¹ in all three events, transfiguration, resurrection *and parousia*. In the transfiguration they see and know Him already, though only transitively, as the Resurrected. And in His resurrection they finally see the kingdom come with power, and therefore, *in parte pro toto*, as ἀρραβών and ἀπαρχή that which in the *parousia*, as His general revelation, will be comprehensively and conclusively knowable and known as His glory. Not all, but only a few even of His disciples at the transfiguration, and only the disciples at the resurrection, will in their own lifetime see the kingdom of God come in the person of Jesus, and therefore the end of all time. This is the meaning of Mk. 9¹. Calvin's comment is thus correct : *Antequam vobis moriendum sit, regnum illud Dei, a cuius spe vos pendere iubeo, conspicuum erit oculis vestris. . . . Adventum vero regni Dei intellige gloriae coelestis manifestationem, quam a resurrectione auspicatus est Christus et plenius deinde spiritum sanctum mittendo et mirificas edendo virtutes exhibuit ; nam in illis primitiis gustandum suis praebuit coelestis vitae novitatem, quam veris et certis experimentis ipsum ad patris dexteram sedere agnoscerent (C.R.* 45, 483).

In similar vein Jesus says in Mt. 10²³ : " Ye shall not have gone over the cities of Israel, till the Son of man be come." The disciples' mission to Israel will be overtaken by the coming of the Son of Man ; their proclamation of the Messiah among the Messianic people will be forestalled by His own revelation. This saying, which is peculiar to Matthew, occurs in the missionary charge, where it is placed just after the prediction of persecution and sufferings for the disciples in the course of their mission. There are, of course, more encouraging and consoling features in the charge. When the disciples are brought to trial they are not to be anxious what answer to make because the Spirit of the Father will speak in them (v. 19 f.). And then " he that endureth to the end shall be saved " (v. 22). This encouragement and consolation is not relative but absolute. A new and wonderful source of help will become available. God will intervene and rescue them from their tribulation. And then we come to v. 23, which obviously takes up the catchword τέλος (v. 22). Their own τελειοῦν of their task in the cities of Israel, where all that they can really do is to flee from one city to another, will be suddenly cut short by God's τέλος. The Son of Man will come and put a stop to the activities of their persecutors. But it will also mean the end of their own mission. Clearly, this is the supreme form of the promise of help which Jesus gave to His disciples. This is how the special Matthean source means us to take it. He will come in person and judge between them and their persecutors, between the new Israel and the old. The great transition of Jesus Himself, accomplished in His death and according to Mt. 28[16f.] manifested in His resurrection, from His mission to His own people to His mission to the world ; the exaltation of His office as the Christ of Israel to His office as the σωτήρ κόσμου, is reflected in this saying to the disciples and offers the real clue to its meaning. In the words which immediately follow (vv. 24–25), Jesus predicts the same fate for His disciples as for Himself. It is in this transition, in this exaltation, that the Son of Man " comes " and reveals Himself, but also changes completely the mission and office of His disciples. " Go ye therefore, and make disciples of all nations " (Mt. 28[19]). This mission will be both possible and necessary even before they have finished with the cities of Israel. These cities are only the starting-point of the apostolic mission. They are this still. But the apostles cannot wait any longer for their conversion. " Your blood be upon your own heads ; I am clean : from henceforth I will go unto the Gentiles " (Ac. 18[6]). This is what is in store for the disciples according to this saying. They will witness the resurrection of Jesus, which will not only mark the transition and exaltation of Jesus Himself, but their own transition and exaltation to a new and, according to Mt. 24[14], eschatological ministry of proclaiming the Gospel to the ends of the earth. The coming of Jesus is again spoken of as imminent and the saying had the advantage, the practical significance of showing what the promise must have meant for the " little flock " at the pre-Easter period.

There is another saying of Jesus in Mk. 13[30] and *par.* : " Verily I say unto you that this generation shall not pass, until all these things be done." In this case the exegetical situation differs from that of Mk. 9 and Mt. 10. The things which are so imminent that the existing generation will experience them are not identified directly with the coming of the Son of God as the Gospels see it. For they agree in placing it immediately before the parable of the fig tree. When the sap rises, the branches sprout and the leaves grow, it is a sign that summer is nigh at hand. " So, in like manner, when ye shall see these things coming to pass, know that he is nigh, even at the doors." He is at the doors, not yet present, but near, very near. Since the second half of v. 29 asserts this, the ταῦτα of the first half cannot be referred to the days *after* that tribulation, or to the coming of the Son of Man (vv. 25–26), but only to the immediate prelude. And the ταῦτα πάντα of v. 30 must have a similar reference, at any rate as understood by the Evangelists. The present generation will witness the immediate prelude to the coming of the Son of Man. This clearly means that they will actually witness His coming. But the emphasis here is on the fact that they will be witnesses of the three groups of events described in vv. 7–20 as the immediate prelude to His coming : of world-wide disasters (vv.7–8) ; of the tribulation of the Church (vv. 9–12) ; and as a climax, the fall of Jerusalem, which the surviving elect must escape by headlong flight (vv. 14–20). The complex in vv. 7–20 is enframed at either end by warnings against the seductions of false messiahs and prophets with their fictitious claim : Ἐγώ εἰμι (vv. 5–6 and 21–23). But the point of the whole discourse emerges in vv. 24–27 and 33–37. The light of the sun, moon and stars will be extinguished, i.e., the light of the bodies by which, according to Gen. 1[14], created time is measured. And then (v. 26) God will send forth His angels to gather in the elect from the four winds. But, because the tribulation immediately precedes the final event which is also the end of time, it follows that the Church contemporary with the events of the tribulation—perhaps the Church of to-day!—must (vv. 33 f.) watch. Although it does not know—nobody knows according to v. 32—when the καιρός of the great καὶ τότε of vv. 26 and 27 will occur, yet the Lord of the house will suddenly come at an hour chosen by Himself during the night which begins with these events. The whole point and purpose of the existence of the Church in this night is to watch. This is the point and purpose of the existence of the whole generation which will be overtaken by this night: " And what I say unto you I say unto all, Watch " (v. 37). Be ready for the Messiah, who cannot possibly be mistaken for any other. He will come when all this has taken place. While it is taking place, He is " at the doors " (v. 29)—just as summer is nigh when the sap rises in the fig tree and the branches begin to put forth their leaves. The discourse of Mk. 13 is a repetition of the three prophecies of the passion and resurrection of Jesus elevated to a cosmic scale. It must be remembered that the whole discourse is occasioned by the question of the disciples when Jesus predicted the destruction of the temple (v. 2): " Tell us, when shall these things be ? and what shall be the sign when all these things shall be fulfilled ? " As Mk. 14[58] suggests, the Synoptists too know something of a saying of Jesus about the rebuilding of the temple after three days, and they are clearly aware that this whole complex is susceptible of various interpretations. Jn. 2[19-22] is illuminative in this respect. The destruction of the temple is a reflection of the death of Jesus Himself, and its rebuilding a reflection of His resurrection. The prophecy of what the present generation will experience supremely in the destruction of the temple will begin to be fulfilled at once with the story of the passion (Mk. 14[1ff.]) with which the life story of Jesus reaches its climax. All the disasters of world history, all the persecutions and trials of the community, and above all the judgment on Israel which culminates in the destruction of Jerusalem, are only the great shadow of the cross falling on the cosmos, the Messianic woes which not even the cosmos can evade, the participation in the divine judgment, effected in the death of Jesus, to which even the cosmos is subject, though this judgment is to its salvation, to the salvation of Israel, the salvation of the community, the salvation of all men, and indeed of the whole cosmos. In the cosmos in which and for which Jesus will and must be crucified, things can only turn out as predicted in vv. 7–20. Hence Jesus is primarily foretelling His own impending death when He speaks of these imminent events, and His resurrection when to the comprehensive picture of man tormented by war, division, earthquake and famine, of the persecuted and tormented community, of Jerusalem standing under moral threat, He opposes the imminent end of time, the great καὶ τότε, the coming of the Son of Man to gather His elect, and therefore His triumphant life as the Lord of His community. The disciples can and should look vigilantly to this future in the deep shadows lying across the world, in the afflictions by which it is threatened, in the judgments which must fall on it, and primarily in face of the judgment of which all the other judgments are only the accompaniment, the judgment of His passion, now about to commence. When all this has taken place He will come, He who now goes to destruction. He will then be revealed, He who is now shrouded in the deepest obscurity. He will triumph in judgment upon the cosmos, He who is now vanquished by the cosmos. " Heaven and earth shall pass away : but my words shall not pass away " (v. 31). And according to v. 30 even the present generation shall not " pass away " either until all this has come to pass. Even now, as it begins to experience the passion of Jesus, it is about to take part in the opening of the series of events which will be immediately followed by the coming of the Son of Man. Hence the urgency of the demand that it should look forwards, watching and waiting for

Him, and not waiting for any other, nor confounding His coming with that of any other. It thus receives the law which will be normative for every subsequent generation which in its own time and in its own way will witness these events ; the law of hope in the One who has already come and will come again in His glory.

A further case in point is the eschatological saying at the Last Supper recorded by all three Synoptists (Cf. Markus Barth, *Das Abendmahl*, 1945). The clearest version of this is to be found in Mt. 26[29] : " But I say unto you, I will not drink henceforth of this fruit of the vine, until that day when I drink it new with you in my Father's kingdom." The negative form in which this saying is couched recalls the Nazarite vow. Jesus is consecrating Himself to be the sacrificial victim. How he kept this oath will be recorded in Mt. 27[34]. But more important than the negative aspect is the positive—that His next meal, which is the *terminus ad quem* of the oath, will take place in the kingdom of God, and will therefore be the Messianic banquet. This saying is another expression of urgent expectation. In the brief interval in which a man can go without food and drink Jesus will be with His disciples in the kingdom of God. Next time He sits at meat with them they will see and know that the kingdom of God has come. This is exactly what happened according to Lk. 24[31-35]. There is also emphatic mention of a meal of the Resurrected with His disciples in Jn. 21[5, 12, 15]. Jesus' intercourse with His disciples during the forty days is comprehensively described as a συναλίζεσθαι (" to take salt with ") in Ac. 1[4]. And it is said of the apostles in Peter's speech in Ac. 10[41] : " (We) did eat and drink with him after he rose from the dead." This not only proves the reality of the resurrection (Lk. 24[41f.]), but also its tremendous import and far-reaching consequence. No longer, as at the Last Supper, will they sit at meat with Him in anticipation of His sacrifice, but in retrospect of its completion ; not in a re-presentation and repetition, as in the Romanist doctrine of the Mass, but in a simple and full enjoyment of its benefits, of the eternal life won for us in Him, within the revelation of the completion and benefits of this sacrifice, and therefore with open eyes and ears, and even open mouths, within the kingdom of God. For this reason the κυριακὸν δεῖπνον of the primitive Church, formally celebrated in repetition of the pre-Easter passover in " remembrance " of the Lord (1 Cor. 11[20]), is materially a continuation of these festive meals in the personal presence of the Resurrected. While in the Lord's Supper the Church looks back upon the " night in which he was betrayed," it cannot confine the memory to this night. On the contrary, " the death of the Lord " is " proclaimed " (1 Cor. 11[26]) through the action of the community. It is continually made known to the community and the world, on the basis of His self-revelation at Easter as a saving event. Thus the passover meal becomes an Easter meal : not kept in sorrow but in joy (ἐν ἀγαλλιάσει) ; not with complicated arguments as to the precise nature of the bread and wine, but in " singleness of heart " (καὶ ἀφελότητι καρδίας, Ac. 2[46]). Each occasion is the Messianic banquet of the revealed kingdom of God. Each is the most pregnant form of the fellowship of Christians with the Lord now revealed to them. Each is an anticipation of His final and general revelation, inaugurated, but no more, in His resurrection. The resurrection was the ἀρραβών and ἀπαρχή of this final revelation, but the totality is still to come, so that every celebration of the Lord's Supper can only look forward to it. For that reason and to that extent it is celebrated " till he come " (1 Cor. 11[26])—and His own general and visible presence renders the Church's human proclamation of His death superfluous. For that reason and to that extent it is particularly appropriate at the Lord's Supper to use the grace : " Come, Lord Jesus, be our Guest." Hence the Gospel accounts of the Last Supper and the institution of the Lord's Supper are to be numbered with the many passages which in the first instance point to the resurrection, which find in the resurrection their initial yet very real fulfilment, but which in the light of this fulfilment point all ages in imminent expectation to the *parousia* as the last event consummating that of Easter.

Our final example is Jesus' reply to the Sanhedrin when He was asked whether He was the Christ, the Son of God. According to Mt. 26⁶⁴ this is as follows : " Thou hast said : nevertheless I say unto you, Henceforth ye shall see the Son of man sitting on the right hand of power, and coming in the clouds of heaven." The Markan version has (14⁶²) : " I am " (*'Εγώ εἰμι*), but lacks the pregnant " henceforth." The Lukan version (22⁶⁷f.) puts the question with greater reserve : " Art thou the Christ ? tell us," and Jesus first answers : " If I tell you, ye will not believe : and if I ask you, ye will not answer me," and only then adds : " Hereafter shall the Son of man sit on the right hand of the power of God,"—with no mention of the coming on the clouds. Only then is the direct question put by the Sanhedrin : " Art thou then the Son of God ? " and the reply is a combination of the Markan and Matthean versions : " Ye say that I am." All three Gospels agree that Jesus makes a public declaration of His Messiahship just before the end of His life on earth. It is this admission, together with the prediction of His impending exaltation and second coming, that seals His fate in the eyes of His enemies. The high priest rends his clothes. There is no need of further evidence against Him, for this is blasphemy. The death sentence is pronounced forthwith, and the mocking and scourging follow. We will now confine ourselves to the Matthean version. It is at this point that the passion story proper begins. The Messiah is arraigned by the supreme authority on earth—the high court of the Messianic people. For centuries they have been without a king. Political power has been in the hands of the priestly caste. Now their promised King stands before them, accused before the bar of the priestly aristocracy. Until now He has never publicly claimed to be this King. Indeed, He has prevented His disciples from spreading it abroad. According to Jn. 6¹⁵, He withdrew to the mountains when the crowd wanted to make Him a King by force. He deliberately staged His entry into Jerusalem in such a way as to make it clear that, as far as He is concerned, there is no question of any royal claim. True, He is their King, but He must keep this a secret. Now, however, the whole position has changed at a single stroke. He now stands before a body which can rightfully claim to be " anointed." It has a right to ask whether He is the Christ. There is no telling what happy results might flow from the question. Here is Israel's great opportunity. Never before has it had such a chance to affirm and accept its King through the mouth of its supreme representatives. At last the covenant, so faithfully kept on God's side since the days of the patriarchs and now fulfilled, must be ratified by a practical decision on the part of His people. If it is, the kingdom of God will come on earth in all its glory. Thus Jesus' answer : " Thou sayest it," is not to be regarded as ironical. We should remember that Jn. 11⁵¹ expressly ascribes to the high priest in his official capacity the power to speak as a prophet. Jesus nails him to his own saying : *σὺ εἶ ὁ Χριστὸς ὁ υἱὸς τοῦ θεοῦ*, which is identical with Peter's confession at Cæsarea Philippi : (Mt. 16¹⁶), and which might be taken as indicative, and might even have been meant as such. He is, as it were, making a last offer through the high priest to the whole people of Israel : You say yourself who and what I am. What follows—the *sessio ad dexteram* and the *parousia*—can and must in the first instance be seen in connexion with this final offer. The King of Israel who stands before them will " henceforth," i.e., now that Israel has decided its attitude to Him, disclose and reveal Himself. It will now see Him as the One He is, the Son of Man enthroned in the glory of God and coming from His glory. But what will He see in His people when He comes ? Will He find it obedient, ready and willing ? And what will His coming mean for it ? Redemption as a reward for its proven loyalty ? We are at the supreme crisis in salvation history, and world history. Did the high priest really mean what He said ? Jesus at any rate took him at his word, and affirmed in all seriousness that he had spoken the truth. And by way of confirmation He elaborates it further. He promises to the high priest, to the Sanhedrin, and through them to the whole people, what hitherto He has confined

can and should stand at the side of the returning Lord at the end of time, the oil represents something which makes this witness vital and strong not only now but then, something which is essential if it is to render this supreme service in the final revelation, because, if it does not have it, it cannot acquire it, and it will be unable to render this supreme service. The parable asks the community of the interim between the resurrection and the *parousia*, which might stand at any moment before the goal of creation which is the goal of its very existence, whether it will have this absolutely indispensable something. It is a matter of that which will make its witness equal to the revelation of its Lord in this decisive test, even though it may have failed a thousand times in the interval. It is a matter of the harmony in which it must find itself with Him for all its human frailty and perversity if it is to stand at His side in face of the world. What is meant is clearly the self-witness of Jesus by the Holy Spirit apprehended in faith and love. This is what founded the community of the intervening time. That is the content of its witness. This alone can give its witness vitality and strength. That is the only pledge of its hope, constant in all its inconstancy. That is the vital element in virtue of which the community can be equal to its returning Lord for all its lowliness, associating itself with Him and having a place at its side in His final revelation. The parable does not ask the community concerning its witness as such. It presupposes that it will finally be there with its lamps burning and shining. And it asks concerning the oil to furnish these lamps of witness at the decisive moment when its mission reaches its goal ; and therefore, since the goal may be reached any moment, concerning that which makes its witness possible here and now, in the interim period. What is its attitude to the source which alone can preserve it ? What is its attitude to the self-witness of Jesus now given to it by the Holy Spirit ? How about its faith in Him and love to Him ? If it lacks that which is necessary enough now but absolutely indispensable at the end, its hope will prove to be its judgment, its witness will be lacking at the very moment when its hope is on the brink of fulfilment, and it will be incapacitated at the very moment of its supreme service. Let the community see to it that it is wise and not foolish. Let it see to it that its relation to the Jesus Christ who was yesterday and is to-day is such that it can only encounter and serve as His community the One who will live and reign for ever.

The parable of the talents (Mt. 25[14-30]) deals with the same theme, though from rather a different angle. The question is now directed more definitely to the community's present action, for the meaning and results of which it will have to account when the Lord returns. Its Lord has " (gone) into a far country " (v. 14). This is how the interim period is now described. Before His departure, however, He has given His community the care and control of His goods. In this case one is given more and another less : " to every man according to his several ability " (v. 15). But however small or great the amount entrusted, each represents the Lord in the handling of what is no less genuinely His own property and no less valuable. In all its manifold tasks, the Church has the duty of turning this property to profitable use. What is entrusted is His Gospel, and His Spirit. The interval between the resurrection and the *parousia* is the time of Jesus because it is the time of the community and its service. His final revelation will therefore be critical for His community because it will reveal that, entrusted with His Gospel and Spirit, it has really served Him. It will be admitted to the marriage feast only if it has increased in good and loyal service the comparatively few goods entrusted to it. The Word which belongs to it seeks new hearers ; it must not cease to pass it on to others. The Spirit given to it seeks new dwelling-places and new witnesses ; it must so obey the Spirit that its witness makes new dwelling-places and evolves new witnesses. This is the whole purpose of the witnessing time, the time of the Church. It is not a time when it can be content to guard and keep what it has received. Naturally it must do this too. It can hardly render its service if it fritters away its heritage. The New Testament speaks very plainly at other points about the duty of maintaining what is given in relation to the last time : " I come quickly : hold that fast which thou hast, that no man take thy crown " (Rev. 3[11]). But the parable of the talents shows us that this cannot be an end in itself. The servant who buried his talent made it safe, but did not put it to use. His conduct was not merely unprofitable, but positively lazy and wicked. It was not merely a refusal of service, but rebellion against the Lord. Thus the community which in the interim period is not a missionary community, winning others by its witness according to the measure of its power, will be banished, at the return and final revelation of the Lord, into outer darkness, where there can be only weeping and gnashing of teeth instead of the promised banquet. At the end of the time between the community will be justified before the Lord, and will stand and have a share in His glory, only if in the time between it has understood and realised that all its faith and love, all its confession and works, are nothing at all without daring and aggression, without sowing in hope ; only if it has understood and practised its witness as a commission. For the time between is not the time of an empty absence of the Lord, nor is it the time of a bewildering delay in His return, in which it is enough for the community to maintain and help itself as best it can. On the contrary, it is the time of God's patience and purpose, and it is the business of the community to recognise the character of this time, and therefore never to think that it has plenty of time in this time, but to " buy up " this time in relation to those who are " without " (Col. 4[5] ; Eph. 5[16]). It can never have enough time here and now for the fulfilment of its task. For it knows what the world does not know, and it owes it to its Lord to make it known to the world. It has the light which cannot be placed under a bushel (Mt. 5[15]) but must be put in a candlestick. Note that in the series of historical signs listed in Mt. 24[6-14], the last and culminating sign is the work of the community : " And this gospel of the kingdom shall be preached in all the world for a witness unto all nations ; and then shall the end come." Whether this sign is set up or not, is the question of its present existence, addressed to it in this parable in relation to the end of time which will decide concerning it too.

The discourse on the last judgment (Mt. 25[31-46]) presses home the same question in a third form. It is the Son of Man, the Messianic King, who according to v. 31 f. will come in glory with His angels, take His seat upon His throne, gather the nations around Him, and divide them as a shepherd divides the sheep from the goats. In the centre of the picture, among all the nations, stands the community. It is asked concerning its being and conduct in this present age, again in the light of the approaching end. This community hopes for this Judge, and rightly so. As surely as it is His community, and has received His Word and His Spirit, and bears witness to Him, it expects to be identical with the flock on the right hand, and to be invited to enter the kingdom prepared for it from the foundation of the world (v. 34). How else can the community live but in this expectation ? Who but the community can do so ? But what is the community that it may enjoy this expectation ? This has not yet been decided. It will be decided when Jesus comes again : " We must *all* be made manifest before the judgment seat of Christ " (2 Cor. 5[10]). And it is from this future that the parable looks back so strikingly to the present time when Jesus is still hidden. The issue will be decided by the attitude and conduct of the community to Him while He is still hidden. Then it will be known what the community will be which will stand at His right hand in this future. But where is He hidden now ? With God, at the right hand of the Father ? in His Word and sacraments ? in the mystery of His Spirit, which bloweth where it listeth ? All this is true enough, but it is presupposed in this parable, and the further point is made, on which everything depends, that He is no less present, though hidden, in all who are now hungry, thirsty, strangers, naked, sick and in prison. Wherever in this present time between the resurrection and the *parousia* one of these is waiting for help (for food, drink, lodging, clothes, a visit, assistance), Jesus Himself is waiting. Wherever help is granted or denied, it is granted or denied to Jesus Himself. For these are the least of His brethren. They represent the world for which He died and rose again, with which He has made Himself supremely one, and declared Himself in solidarity. It is for them that He sits at the right hand of the Father, so that no one can know Him in His majesty, or honour and love Him as the Son of God, unless he shows concern for these least of His brethren. No one can call God his Father in Christ's name unless he treats these least as his brethren. This is the test which at the last judgment will decide concerning the true community which will inherit the kingdom : whether in this time of God's mercy and patience, this time of its mission, it has been the community which has succoured its Lord by giving unqualified succour to them in this needy world. It will be well with it if it has obviously done this, if it has been affected by the concrete miseries of the world, not passing by on the other side with haughty disdain, but being simply and directly human, with no excuses for the contrary. It will then be shown to be the community devoted to God in the person of Jesus. It will then be found righteous at the last judgment and be able stand on the right hand as the community which participates in the work of its Master. It is to be noted, however, that the righteous and therefore the justified at the last judgment do not know with whom they really have to do when they act with simple humanity (v. 37 f.) : " When saw we thee an hungred, and fed thee . . . ? " They had helped the least of His brethren, they had helped the world in its misery for its own sake. They had no ulterior motive. As the true community of Jesus, they saw the need and did what they could without any further design or after-thoughts. They could not do their duty or fulfil their mission without realising their solidarity with those in affliction and standing at their side. They found themselves referred quite simply to their neighbours in the world and that wholly " secular " affliction. They had no spiritual strategy. They obeyed without explanations. They thus carried their lamps like the wise virgins or the faithful stewards of the other parables. They were not occupied with metaphysical considerations. They were simply concerned with men as men, and therefore treated them as brothers. If they had not done so, they could not have claimed Jesus as their Brother or God as their Father. It is because they knew Jesus as their Brother and God as their Father that they fed the needy, gave them drink, clothed and visited them. But did they do this ? This is what will be revealed when Jesus returns. So will everything they have left undone. The false community will also be revealed and rejected and condemned for its inhumanity. Such is the question addressed to the community of the present by the approaching *parousia*. It is posed to all its members, to its orders and cultus and preaching and theology. What has all this had to do with the afflicted who as such are Jesus' brethren ? Has the community been first and foremost human in all that it has done ? The question may be comforting or disconcerting, but there can be no doubt that it is crucial, and where it is heard it can hardly fail to be incisive and therefore admonitory. This is the *Magna Carta* of Christian humanitarianism and Christian politics, established not only as a promise but as a warning in view of the approaching end—not so much because it will be the end of all things, but because it bears the name of Jesus, who has come, and will come again.

The situation of the community in the time between, as presented in Mt. 25, may be summed up by saying that it is really the community of the last time. That is to say, it has the completion inaugurated with the resurrection of Jesus as a driving force behind it and the consummation in His *parousia* as a drawing force before it. It comes from the revelation of the man Jesus as it moves towards it, and it moves towards it as it comes from it. " This same Jesus, which is taken up from you into heaven, shall so come in like manner as ye have seen him go into heaven " (Ac. 1[11]). This is what determines the whole logic and ethic of the community of the end. If we are to understand what is meant by ἄγεσθαι πνεύματι (Gal. 5^{18} ; Rom. 8^{14}), by περιπατεῖν or στοιχεῖν πνεύματι (2 Cor. 12^{18} ; Gal. 5$^{16, 25}$), it is essential that we keep in mind this double motivation of Christian existence in this intervening time. The Christ who comes again in glory is as near to His community as the Christ of the resurrection. As the risen Christ cannot fall behind it and become merely historical, so the Christ of the *parousia* cannot yield before it, so that it has only a profane and empty future not determined by Him, and its situation between the two comings can only repeat and renew itself at every moment of the continuing interim. The community lives under the lordship of Jesus in the form of the Spirit. In the Spirit that double proximity is actual presence. In the Spirit Jesus at every moment of the interim is not only at the right hand of the Father, but also here on earth. Hence the community at every moment is really His and under His lordship. " Lo, I am with you alway, even unto the completion of time " (ἕως τῆς συντελείας τοῦ αἰῶνος, Mt. 28^{20}). Two opposite but closely connected errors must be noted at this point and avoided.

The first consists in an underestimation of the majesty of Jesus in this intervening time in consequence of an underestimation of the origin of the community in His resurrection, or, as we may also say, of a failure to recognise the consolation of the Holy Spirit in whose work the community may find full satisfaction at every moment in its time of waiting. If this is not perceived, the imminent expectation in which it lives is bound to be an enigma and the " delay," the constant " non-arrival," of the *parousia* an offence. The view is thus adopted that early hopes quickly gave way to disappointment and disillusion ; that a lofty but impractical expectation was replaced by a clever adaptation to realities ; that a new and more subtle interpretation was given of the original attitude. This movement is thought to be the true secret of the New Testament consciousness of the present. And it may be recalled that there were some who thought along these lines even in the New Testament itself : " Where is the promise of his coming ? for since the fathers fell asleep, all things continue as they were from the beginning of the creation " (2 Pet. 3^4). But the adoption of this conclusion entails the hazardous assumption that this opinion, naturally repudiated in 2 Peter, expresses the painful, laboriously suppressed, but clear and objective truth of the witness of the New Testament. If this is so, the whole of the New Testament must be expounded accordingly, as though it were really wrestling at every point with this opinion, or occupied rather feebly with this objective truth. The real witness of the Evangelists and apostles, and in the last resort Jesus Himself, is to the delay of the *parousia*, though they will not admit it. Any exposition of the New Testament running counter to this opinion (or objective truth), from the days of the apostolic fathers right down to the present, must be denounced as a dishonest and unsuccessful evasion. The one question to be asked of New Testament and theological research is whether and how far it has voluntarily or involuntarily helped to support this opinion and further exposed the insincerity of all attempts to deal with the question which are not consistently eschatological. A kind of monomania develops. Everything thought and said and written is demagogic. Pride is found in being to the whole cosmos a great and maliciously ignored source of unsettlement, and the tedium thereby caused to more usefully employed angels, men and animals is not perceived. The mistake in all this is to be found in its failure to take account of the Holy Spirit as the driving and drawing force behind the community in the time between the resurrection and the *parousia*. For through the Spirit the lordship of Jesus is never merely past or merely future. It is always present, but in such a way that we must expect His coming, indeed, His imminent coming, and yet may wait for it with patience. If this eager expectation of the *parousia* is a genuine problem in the New Testament, of crucial importance for the present, the same cannot be said of anxiety over its supposed delay or non-occurence. Regarded in the light of the New Testament teaching about the situation of the community in the last time, this anxiety bears all the marks of a pseudo-problem. The answer given in 2 Pet. 3 is just as true to-day as it was then. It is that the question comes from "mockers with mockery" (ἐν ἐμπαιγμονῇ ἐμπαῖκται v. 3). There will be plenty of them in the "last days." But they are people who do not realise (vv. 5–7) that the created world as we know it is only temporary, as the story of the flood once proved. It is moving, indeed, towards total dissolution—"reserved unto fire." The question is that of those who, for all that they are so critical when it would be better to be uncritical, are far too uncritical about their own existence and existentialist philosophy. And when Christians hear their question, they are not ignorant (v. 8) that "one day is with the Lord as a thousand years, and a thousand years as one day" (Ps. 90⁴). In God's sight—and after all they live in His sight—not only is nearness distance, but distance nearness. What are thousands and thousands of years when it is a matter of the longsuffering of God, giving us time right up to the end of time (v. 9), "not willing that any should perish, but that all should come to repentance"? It is to be noted in passing that in 1 Tim. 2⁴ the existence of the state is attributed to the same divine purpose. For Christians who remember this, can even a single day be wasted in thousands and thousands of years? Is there any cause to complain, then, at the delay of the final denouement? Have they time to worry their fellow creatures with a theology of self-satisfied complacency? No, the objective truth is very different from this theory: "The Lord is not slack concerning his promise, as some count slackness" (v. 9). The theory has to be read *into* the New Testament, for the New Testament itself contradicts it both implicitly and explicitly. Only if it is read in can it have any importance for an understanding of the New Testament awareness of the present. And it needs only little experience of the consolation of the Holy Spirit to make this understanding completely impossible.

The opposite error consists in an exaggerated estimate of the greatness of the community in consequence of an equally exaggerated estimate of its present existence in relation to the *parousia*, or, as we may also say, of a failure to recognise the criticism of the Holy Spirit, whose work keeps the community moving towards its Lord in dissatisfaction with its present condition, preventing it from regarding its condition as absolute. When this is not perceived, the community—or the "Church" as it loves to call itself—forgets that it is on the march, and that though the inauguration of Jesus' revelation of His glory is behind it, the consummation is still to come. It secretly anticipates the change of front foretold in Mt. 25 and 1 Thess., when at the end of time it will stand at the side of its Lord before the world. It is not content to be a handmaid like the virgins at the marriage feast, but obviously behaves as if the *causa Dei* were in its own hands. Instead of bearing witness to the authority of Jesus, it invests itself with His authority, attributing absolute perfection to its order and ministry and cultus and dogma, and interpreting historical evolution as the automatic development of the divine truth incarnate in itself. Thus at each successive stage of its development it acts and speaks as if it were itself permitted and commanded to blow the last trumpet now. Its doctrine at any given moment is the normative voice of Jesus and His apostles. Its tradition perpetuates the original apostolic witness, claiming equal dignity and attention. Its particular interpretation of the original witness is the authentic interpretation. Its divine commission is the basis of a claim made in its own favour. But in these circumstances, what place is there for Christian hope? In what sense are we still in an intervening time, still waiting for the consummated revelation? Has it not been realised already in the being and activity of the Church? Is there any need for the risen Lord to come again? Is there any more embracing form of His presence and power than that taken already by the Church itself? In 1944 the Congregation of the Sacred Office passed a remarkable resolution to the effect that belief in a visible second coming could "not be taught as a certainty"—the very thing which for the New Testament is the greatest certainty of all on the basis of the resurrection. On this view, all we have left to hope for is the golden lining of a future heavenly glory. And even this is under the control and apparently belongs to the sphere of the Church on earth, with its indulgences, its merited assurances and guarantees, its purchased rights, its express beatifications and canonisations. Certainly there can be no place for a Judge who will confront the Church itself in sovereignty and whom it is bound to fear. If He comes at all, it will be to judge the world for persecuting and oppressing the poor Church in time, for resisting and ignoring it. The Church itself will stand triumphant at His right hand, self-evidently before the judgments have even begun. The future at the end of time will simply be the confirmation of its own present and distinctive perfection. The true and divine safeguard against the real threat of Christian arrogance and pride and sloth and obstinacy has been abandoned. The Church on earth, with its power to change bread and wine into the body of Christ, and to effect this in daily sacrifice, with its infallible teaching office, its Virgin Mary already ascended into heaven, is itself already on the throne with the returning Lord. What need is there then for His return ? And how can it take place in this time that judgment begins at the house of God (1 Pet. 4[17]) ? It is obviously treason even to contemplate the mere possibility. The Church has completely forgotten Mt. 25, and the Seven Letters of the Apocalypse. Yet in these Letters it is not just fallible Christian men but the very angels of the churches who are summoned to judgment at the *parousia*. And what about the prophetic word of the Old Testament, which as such, in its reference to the Lord coming to judgment, is addressed with unparalleled severity, not to the world but typically to the elect people of God with its temples and priests and authorised sacrifices ? This is the " de-eschatologising " of Christianity with a vengeance ! This is real obstinacy in face of the critical power of the lordship of Jesus Christ in the form of the Holy Spirit. The Church of Rome is the typical form of this de-eschatologised Christianity. But there are also Protestant, Anglican and other versions. Wherever the Church entertains an exaggerated estimate of itself, the same error is at work in its opposite form. For in both cases it is Jesus Himself who is absent, the Lord of the Church who as such is the Lord of time. In the first case He is absent because there is no recognition of the consoling power of His resurrection for the present life of the community. In the second He is absent because no serious account is taken of His future and its critical power for the present life of the community. And as His future is also denied in the one, His presence is also missed in the other, being identified with that of the community. The one error leads to the other. If the community of the last time is already seated on the throne of Christ, it is high time to say that His return is not to be expected. And if that is not to be expected, it is quite in order to look for a self-sufficient community which can dispense with this expectation. But if we are to follow the New Testament, we must resist both errors with the same determination.

2. GIVEN TIME

The subject of our enquiry is the being of man in his time. In order to see man in his time correctly, we have investigated the being of the man Jesus in His time. To do this, we had to start with the revelation of the being of this man in His resurrection from the dead. This enabled us to see His being as that of the Lord of time, and His time as the fulfilment of all time, which, as His own time, extends backwards and embraces all prior time as its beginning, the beginning of all time, and extends forwards and embraces all subsequent time as its end, the end of all time.

We cannot expect to say the same of man in his time ; of man in himself and in general. For his being in time is certainly not that of the Lord of time, nor is his time the fulfilment of time. This can be said neither of the human species as a whole, nor of any of its social groups, nor of any individual man. Our anthropology can and must be based on Christology, but it cannot be deduced from it directly. What is to be predicated of the being of the man Jesus in time is true because this man is also God. But while He is this for us and for the world, it can be said only of Him. It is because the Word was made flesh, the Eternal entered time, that the man Jesus is the Lord of time, and His time is the fulfilment of time, embracing all time, the first and last time which in every present is His own time. As there can be no repetition of the being of this man, there can be no repetition of this human being in time.

It is immediately apparent how differently man in himself and in general, the man who is not Jesus Christ, is in time, has time and is temporal. What, then, is the significance of our own movement from the past through the present to the future, of the fact that we were yesterday and are to-day and will be to-morrow ? We may begin by sketching the phenomenon as it presents itself to us, i.e., in its contrasts to the picture of the Lord of time which we have just delineated.

For us the past is the time which we leave and are in no longer. It was once ours. We had our life in it years ago or yesterday or even this morning. In it we made our contribution to history. In it we were then ourselves. But we are so no longer. For, with all that filled or did not fill it, it has now eluded us and been taken from us. It has remained behind, never to be restored. With all its achievements, with ourselves as we then were and cannot be again, it may be partially or completely forgotten. It may almost be thought of as though it had never been. And this is what seems to happen to most of our own past, though it was once ours. The past of the individual and the race and the nations and other social groupings is a great flood of forgotten reality which once had its time but now has it no longer, which has now gone as though it has never had it. Of course there is in the ocean of oblivion an island or two of memory. A few names, figures, events and circumstances are not entirely forgotten. Some of them are shadowy and insubstantial. Some are more clearly defined. Given the means and the skill, it may be possible to reconstruct and recall them plastically. As well as forgetting, there is also memory—abiding or fleeting, direct or indirect, weak or vivid, natural or artificial. There is the voluntary or involuntary evocation of the past and its contents. In fact, much of our life is made up of memories. But it is a sign of life drawing to its close, of old age and decay, when individuals, nations and other historical societies begin to be absorbed in memory, to live mainly in the past, to be interested chiefly in history and antiquities. And even at best memory is limited. We can recall only a few scraps of the vanished and forgotten past and its contents, its life and history. And even what we recall soon sinks back to oblivion. And in its limited sphere memory is not the present reality. It is simply the subjective accident or skill by which we conjure up the shades of what was once present but is so no more. Thus in the last resort memory, like oblivion, merely demonstrates the gulf which lies between what was and what is. The past has ceased to belong to us. We are no longer the people we were years ago, yesterday, or even this morning. Of course we should like to cling to what was, but the present and the future are already beckoning us. We must press on. The past is already slipping away, never to return. It is a mere conjecture, and a highly dubious one at that, to suppose that we are still what we were and still have what we had.

Similarly, the future is the time which we do not yet have but perhaps will have. We can at least look back at the past as it slips away—both our own past and that of the world at large. But it may well be pure illusion to suppose that we can look to our own being of the future or the world of the future. We do not even know whether we will have a future. We do not know whether the time to come will be ours at all. But even if it will be, it is not ours now. We are only moving towards it. We do not know and cannot conceive its contents, its nature and happenings. We may anticipate it in expectation, but it is only in expectation that we can anticipate it, filling it with definite conceptions, hopes and fears, desires, intentions and plans. And even this anticipatory filling of the future is very restricted, for only the future itself can teach us what is really desirable or dangerous, necessary or superfluous, possible or impossible. Anticipation is no substitute for the reality anticipated. And the future when it comes may partially or totally confound our expectations. It is almost a law of nature that this should be the case. We are always poor prophets even of what is to happen within the next hour or so, to say nothing of a year or two hence, or centuries to come. The future—if we have one at all, and in whatever form we have it—is even more obscure than the past. In relation to it, even our identity with ourselves is only a guess, and a doubtful one at that.

The real nature of our being in time is most obscure of all, however, at the very point where it ought to be clearest, namely, at the moment which we regard as our present. Here, where midway between the vanished past, which we have largely forgotten or only dimly remember, and the unknown future which awaits us (or perhaps does not await us !), we think we can take our ease and enjoy in impregnable security our being and having, and our identity with ourselves, we find that we are wholly and utterly insecure. For what is our present but a step from darkness to darkness, from the " no longer " to the " not yet," and therefore a continual deprivation of what we were and had in favour of a continual grasping of what we will (perhaps) be and have ? Our past and future do at least have a real if limited content, but the fulness of our present is obviously only the remarkable act of existence itself in which we have already been deprived of our past, but have not yet been able to grasp the future, everything being wholly behind us and everything (or nothing) wholly before us. What are we now ? And what do we have ? The past had at least duration ; the definite duration of our own and all human days and years which, whether remembered or forgotten, did actually come and go in their sequence. Similarly the future, if it comes at all, can at least have duration, consisting in a further sequence of hours and days. But what is Now ? What is the present ? It is the time between the times. And this, strictly speaking and as we actually experience it, is no time at all, no duration, no series of moments, but only the boundary between past and future, a boundary which is never stationary, but always shifts further ahead. It is the moment we can never prevail upon to stay, for always it has already gone or not yet come. In practice, the present can be experienced only in the form of recollections and expectations. Whether it is a matter of our personal present, or present history ecclesiastical or secular, we can pin it down and describe it only in historical retrospect, in descriptions of a situation already created, or in the form of prognostications, hopes and fears, and the corresponding postulates and programmes. We are and live out only what we were in a partly forgotten, partly remembered past and will be (perhaps) in an unknown future, i.e., in all the questionableness of our being in past and future time. In the present in which we think we have it most securely we have no time.

This is our being in time. " Thus we live all our days." Of course it is possible to shut our eyes to all this. But we cannot escape it. We cannot be as men—our reference is to man in himself and in general —except in this way, in this riddle of time. If the being of man in time is interpreted in any other way ; if either as an individual or as a representative of the race man is said to have time now and not just to have had it or to be about to have it, to be in time and not just to have been and (perhaps) to be about to be ; if an attempt is made to interpret positively the temporality of man in its three dimensions, the venture is nurtured either by illusions or by secret borrowings from theology. A human self-understanding genuinely orientated by a general picture of man will be halted by the riddle of human temporality, and will have to be content to assert that we must live our life in the absolute uncertainty given with this riddle because we are not asked whether we would prefer a different possibility.

Whether we realise it or not, we are up against an ultimate truth about the being of man in time, which we can neither evade nor contest. It is a truth which doubtless finds suitable expression in the metaphysical conception of the infinity of time. Infinite is the abyss into which the past and all that it comprises, all that we have been, sinks and disappears before our eyes ; an abyss which is deeper than all the virgin forests of pre-historic times, with the fabulous monsters that inhabited them. Infinite, too, is the future (perhaps even that of nothing) to which everything is bound to hasten, whether it likes it or not. Infinite, above all, is the flight which is also a chase, the chase which is also a flight ; what we call the present ; the succession of moments, or rather of constant shiftings of the boundary, between the darkness there and the darkness here. Infinite is the impossibility of escaping time, of not accepting time, of not being in time. Infinite, also, is the impossibility of escaping its enigma as the enigma of man himself, man who is, and who would like to be in time and have time, who is in point of fact temporal, and whose being in time is of this nature.

The metaphysician is usually silent at this point, and silently enjoins resigna-tion. Hence the last word rests with the seer or poet who can dream of beings very different from ourselves, of beings which are eternal, and thus tell us that our being in time is in its infinity an infinitely tragic destiny, which it is the final task of those to whom the gods give the means to describe in a pious song, yet which eschews all cheap and easy consolation. Perhaps Friedrich Hölderlin has given us one of the best examples in his " Hyperion's Song of Fate " :

> Ye soar above in light,
> Softly borne, blessed spirits !
> Radiant winds divine
> Caress you lightly,
> As artists' fingers
> Playing on holy strings.
>
> Unbound by fate, heavenly beings
> Breathe like the sleeping infant.
> Their spirits bloom eternally,
> Chastely inviolate
> In a modest bud,
> And their happy eyes
> Look out serenely
> In calm, eternal clarity.
>
> But to us poor men
> Is given no place to rest.
> Harried by pain,
> We grope and fall
> Blindly from hour to hour,
> Like water dashed
> From cliff to cliff,
> In lifelong insecurity.

This is what *we* are. This is how we are in time. And now let us recall the beginning and conclusion of our christological investigation.

" I am . . . which is, and which was, and which is to come, the Almighty." This is what the man Jesus is. This is how He is in time.

Yet we cannot be content with this simple contrast, for Jesus is not only God and therefore different from us, but also man and therefore like us. He is not only the Creator, but also a creature among creatures. He is not only eternal, but—in His own particular way—with us in time. To compare our lot with that of " blessed spirits," with very different and purely eternal beings, may produce a gloomy Hymn of Fate, but it gives us the easy evasion that we men in time are so totally different. Our comparison, however, is with the man Jesus. And although as the Son of God He is so utterly different from us, yet as the Son of Man He is wholly like us. Hence we cannot escape the contrast by pleading His absolute dissimilarity.

Nor can the painful contrast between Him and us be the last word on the subject. For it is intolerable to be able to develop the statement that we have time only in the form of the antithesis that we do not have it at any time ; that we no longer have the past, do not yet have the future and certainly do not have the present, because it is only the step from the one darkness to the other. The monstrous nature of this situation may perhaps be overlooked or forgotten, but once seen and remembered, it cannot be denied. Nor can it be explained by invoking the contrast between man and God, creature and Creator, time and eternity. Along these lines, the only possible way of accounting for it is to shift it back into the Godhead which has made man in this way, into the will of the Creator which has created this type of creature, into the eternity of which this temporality is the foil. In this case we should have to resign ourselves to our fate, not hymning it like Hyperion but defying it like Prometheus. But its monstrous character remains. That this is the case, that neither questioning, complaint nor protest can be suppressed, is shown by the innumerable theoretical attempts to reinterpret this disconcerting picture of man's being in time. Perhaps a fulness of time, and a prolongation of human being in time, is sought in a deepening of the recollection of the past by relating man to his origin in a world of immutable being. Perhaps expectation of the future can be understood along similar lines with the help of the idea of endless progress. Perhaps the present as the step from the past into the future may be regarded as a creative, saving, redeeming and liberating act, as a divine or at least a God-like work accomplished in the act of our existence, a work which makes man eternal in every " moment." But it is painfully obvious that these interpretations gloss over the reality. And the reality is so monstrous that it asserts itself against these interpretations, like the original of a picture which has been badly painted over. It is worth noting, however, that it has always been felt necessary to cover up the original. For this shows us with what cares and questions and protests man faces this reality, how hard he finds it to accept his being in time as normal. We all run away from this picture. We would all prefer it otherwise. This comes out even more plainly in the fact that in practice we usually close our eyes to the problems of our being in time, that we try not to see or consider the matter but live as if our past and future were really ours, as if we really had time. For when we prefer not to look or think, trusting that we can find help in a resolute " as if," what is hidden beneath the surface is definitely something abnormal and unnatural : not an inevitability which we can calmly recognise and accept ; but a contradiction in face of which we are powerless, yet which we try to escape by hook or by crook, even by putting it right out of our minds. In other words, the difference which emerges between our general being in time and that of the man Jesus does not seem to be one which is original or natural.

On the contrary, when we make this comparison between Jesus and ourselves—and the presupposition of our whole enquiry is that we have to see and understand man in this comparison—the antithesis between Jesus and ourselves points not merely to the contrast between man and God, creature and Creator, eternity and time, but to God's judgment upon man ; not merely to the nature and order of God and man, but to God's indictment against man, to His sentence and punishment, and to man's existence under His wrath. What we have been describing is *sinful* man in time. The man who lives in that monstrous situation, in that loss of time which cannot be denied, reinterpreted or even forgotten, is the man who is alienated from his Creator and therefore from himself, from his creaturely nature, and who has to pay for his rebellion against God by living in contradiction with himself, in contradiction with his God-given nature. The enigmatic reality of our being in time is a perverted and disturbed reality determined by this twofold contradiction. And the real reason why we cannot accept it calmly, or gloss it over, or forget it, or effectively deny it, is that man is not left to his own devices in this contradiction, but that in the existence of the man Jesus with His very different being in time a divine protest is made against his perverted and disturbed reality. Whether man hears and accepts this protest is quite another matter. The protest has been registered, and registered for all time. It is an effective protest, upsetting all our attempts to call black white. For within humanity and men generally, whose being in time consists in that continual loss of time, the man Jesus exists as the Lord of time. God did not undertake to recognise and accept our monstrous being in time. In the existence of the man Jesus it is decided and revealed that God did not at all create man in that state of falling " from cliff to cliff " ; that it is not at all His will which is manifested in the fact that our being in time is very different from the creaturely nature given by Him ; and that He is determined to vindicate and protect His right as Creator and ours as His creatures in face of the

monstrous perversion and corruption in which we exist. Because
this protest is made, we may look our situation in the face and either
handle it with metaphysical profundity or hymn it as our fate, or
we may refuse to look it in the face, either glossing it over or simply
living on in spite of it, but we cannot escape its monstrous abnormality
or accommodate ourselves to it. We may think we have succeeded in
doing so, but this is sheer illusion. For it stands under the divine
protest. It cannot be our situation as willed, created and recognised
by God. It is one of the exponents of divine judgment, of the indictment, condemnation and punishment under which we now stand,
having placed ourselves in this position, in this sphere of His wrath,
as sinners against Him. But God has vindicated His right and ours.
He has come to our rescue, and therefore to the defence of our true
creaturely nature against the unnatural condition into which it had
fallen. He has come to save us. This divine protest, effective and
revealed in the existence of Jesus Christ, makes it objectively impossible for man to be content with his being in time, to accept the
abnormal as normal or the monstrous as the rule. Man is uneasy at
this point because God is uneasy before him. And God is uneasy
because man, even sinful man, is His creature and even His covenant-
partner whom none can pluck from His hands, to whom neither
the devil nor man himself can give another nature, another being in
time, than that which God has given. God is uneasy because His
grace, His grace towards man as His creature, is not broken or limited
by the fact that man has sinned and thus incurred His wrath. God
is uneasy because He has not ceased to seek and find lost man, even
the man who exists in the loss of his time. This reality of God the
gracious Creator is the power which combats our direct and indirect
attempts to escape, and which does so victoriously, however we may
writhe and turn. And if it is asked whether and how and how far it
really does this, the answer is that this takes place and is revealed in
the existence of the man Jesus as the Lord of time.

But the being of Jesus in time has this power to unmask and
sober man, to recall him to the truth from every height and depth
and reinterpretation and forgetfulness, because the monstrosity of
general human being in time is overcome in Him. Thus the primary
significance of His being is not critical. It is critical only as it actualises
and reveals positively the real being of man in the time really created
by God and given to man. It depicts our general being in time as the
plunge into falsehood against which God protests. It allows us no
rest in this falsehood, because it is itself the truth which confronts it ;
the truth of human nature as God created it ; the truth of our being
in our time. We have already maintained that the existence of the
man Jesus does not mean only that God confronts man, the Creator
the creature, eternity time. If this were all, there would be many
easy or more costly ways of resolving the antithesis. It would then

be possible and necessary to accommodate ourselves somehow or other to the situation. But the existence of the man Jesus means that God became man, the Creator a creature, eternity time. It means, therefore, that God takes and has time for us ; that He Himself is temporal among us as we are. Yet He does this in a manner appropriate to Himself. He is temporal in unity and correspondence with His eternity. But what can this mean but that He is temporal in a way which also corresponds to man as His creature, in the original and natural form of the being of man in time before it was perverted and corrupted ? That Jesus is the Lord of time, He who was and is and is to come, is of course unique to Himself. In this respect He is incomparable. It is the divine determination of His human being alone. But this unique determination includes a being in time which is true and genuine in contrast to the plunge into falsehood. For Jesus, to live in the present does not mean the flight and chase from darkness to darkness, but being which is independently filled and therefore self-resting and lasting. For Him the past has not become being which has gone, which is lost, which is no more, a mere shadow, but being which is also present in the present, filling it and filled by it. Similarly, the future is not just being which comes, which is therefore dark and empty, which has to be filled artificially, which is not yet, but being which is self-filled and therefore fills both present and past. As Jesus is in time in this way, He is the object of the Father's good-pleasure, not only as His unique, eternal Son, but also as man like us, in His likeness to us. And it is because of Him, of His life and death, of His existence, that God does not turn away from us whose being in time is so utterly different from His, but rather turns to us.

God is righteous. He sees that our being in time is condemned to disintegration and extinction. He makes this plain to us as He is merciful to us in this One. But first and foremost He sees this One Himself. He judges us according to His judgment on Him. He finds in Him the fulness which He cannot find in us. He sees this One, and us in Him—not alongside or beyond Him, but in Him. Thus He finds in us all that He finds in Him. In our disintegrating being in a lost time He finds His true and genuine being in the time created by Him and given to man. Because we are the men loved by God from all eternity, He places our being in time in the light and under the promise of the true and genuine being in time actualised in this One. This is the righteousness of God in the mercy in which He encounters us in the man Jesus. For what is revealed by His mercy in this One is His will in the creation of man, and therefore the true nature of man as he was created, the right of the Creator over His creature and also the right of His creature. What is actual and true and revealed in Him is no more and no less than our own natural condition as willed and planned by God and pleasing to Him. If we see this man as He stands before God in our place, we see ourselves in Him in the nature from

which we have fallen by falling away from God, and in which God
has not ceased to know us in spite of our apostasy. The existence
of the man Jesus means that God is not deceived by the two-fold
contradiction in which we have entangled ourselves when He confesses
us as His creatures and covenant-partners. It means that before Him
—and therefore in truth—our true nature has not been destroyed or
invalidated by our corruption ; that our human nature as God willed
and created it has not ceased to be true and actual even in respect
of our being in time. It is still our true and actual nature in the
truth and actuality of the righteousness in which God willed to
turn, and has actually turned, to us in this One from all eternity.
We cannot and will not find it in ourselves. We do not have it in
ourselves. What we find and have in ourselves is our perverted,
corrupt nature, a being in time which is one long loss of time. Yet
we find and have our true and actual nature in the One in whom God
has loved and loves and will love us, and therefore in Him our true
being in time. As He is the pledge of the faithfulness of the Creator,
He is also of the continuity of His creature, of its preservation and
maintenance. Surprising as it is, it is to the free grace of God in Jesus
Christ that we owe the fact that the nature in which we were created,
and from which we have fallen by falling away from God, is not taken
away from us, but is maintained and preserved ; that in spite of the
falsehood in which we have become involved we may be genuinely
in time and have true and genuine time.

To see the truth of this, we have only to cease trying to ignore the free grace
of God in Jesus Christ. We have only to cease trying to make use of " natural "
theology and therefore anthropology. Illusion always results when we seek
light on human nature from any other source than the man Jesus Christ. To
do so is to trifle with the fact of sin. It is to dig leaking wells. It is to entangle
ourselves in conjectures and reinterpretations. It is again to seek final refuge
in oblivion. The profound unrest concerning our corrupted nature and our
forfeiture of time remains unassuaged. The only real way to meet it is the way
which the righteous God, who is merciful in His righteousness, has taken, takes
and will take to all eternity in Jesus Christ. The only genuinely victorious
protest against it is His protest against our contradiction, which is also His
protest against its consequences and therefore against our perishing, against the
possibility that His creature will cease to be His creature. This divine protest
is the rock on which we take our stand when we count on it that there is a human
nature preserved for man in spite of his fall, and therefore a true and genuine
being of man in time. There is no other ground on which we can seriously make
this claim. But on this ground the claim can and must be made seriously.

The anthropological truth with which we are here concerned may
be combined with its christological basis in a first proposition which
must occupy us in this sub-section. It is that the existence of the man
Jesus in time is our guarantee that time as the form of human existence
is in any case willed and created by God, is given by God to man, and
is therefore real.

It is real. We are, therefore, in time. Time is not, therefore, the abyss of our non-being, however perverted and corrupt we may be in it. We have time. Threatened though we may be, we are not in time in such a way that it continually slips away into infinity and is therefore lost forever. Time is. It is the form of man's existence, the form of our existence. To be man is to live in time. Humanity is in time. This is involved in the fact that the being of man is his life, and that his life is reception and action, rule and service. If this life of his is real, so too is his time as the stage on which he lives out his being.

We can say this in the strict sense only of man. We do not know what time means for animals or plants, or for the rest of the universe. We live in constant relationship to the rest of the universe. Therefore, since we ourselves are in time, we may conclude or suspect that time is the form of existence of everything created. At any rate, the mode of existence of the earthly cosmos as observed and conceived by us shows countless analogies to our own to support this view. Even the apparently timeless truths of mathematics may be observed and conceived by us only in the form of temporal acts of consciousness, analyses and syntheses, demonstrations and definitions. Moreover the biblical accounts of creation, especially the first, seem clearly to imply that time was created simultaneously with the universe as its form of existence. Like man, the whole universe is in time as created by God and therefore real. But to the universe there also belongs heaven as the upper cosmos—the inconceivable and inaccessible side of created reality. And we would be making a bold step to say that this has time as its form of existence. Indeed, we do not know what it means for beings in the earthly cosmos to be in time. We have no means of observing or conceiving their temporality. But we can observe and conceive our own. We can and must see and apprehend that we ourselves are in time and only in time ; that—whatever its significance—we are only in the movement from the past to the present and no mere " presupposition " of human reality, as though the positing of it, or the reality as such, were really timeless. Man is, only as he is in his time. Even in eternal life he will still be in his time. For he will then be the one who, when there is no time but only God's eternity, and he is finally hidden in God, will have been in his time. Just as he is the soul of his body, so he exists in his time. We might almost say that he is himself his time in the sequence of his life-acts. He is himself his time fulfilling itself in the sequence of his life-acts. So close is the relation between the real being of man and the real time in which he is.

So close is the relation between them that we may ask (although we cannot give a conclusive answer) what is the exact nature of this movement from the past through the present and into the future. Is it time that moves ? This is how we generally think and speak of it, because the hands of the clock move, and because our external environment is always changing and never stationary. But does time really move before our eyes like a film, or the carriages of a railway train, so that we stand still and look on ? Or is it we who move ? Is time the constant dimension in which we move about like ramblers, riders, drivers or airmen ? Is it a landscape through which humanity as a whole marches on a broad front, the nations and other historical social entities in narrower formations, and the individual on a linear track, his so-called path of life ? Are the times only stages on this journey ? Are they stopping points which have been awaiting our arrival, but which, once reached, will be left behind ? Or are both views equally true ? Are we ourselves on the move, but time also on the move in and with us, only in the opposite direction ? Are we speaking of something external to ourselves when we speak of yesterday, to-day and to-morrow ? Can we speak of ourselves apart from our yesterday, to-day and to-morrow ? This much at least is certain—that it is as difficult to separate time as the form of our existence from ourselves as it is to separate ourselves from time. All such abstractions are as absurd as the separation of body and soul.

Humanity is temporality. Temporality, as far as our observation and understanding go, is humanity. The first of these two statements is clear. However we may interpret it, human life is that movement from the past through the present into the future. Human life means to have been, to be, and to be about to be. Human life means to be temporal. The second statement is not so clear. But at any rate we do not know what we are really saying when we ascribe to " temporality " a different content from " humanity." We cannot espouse with confidence even the more modest statement that the concept of temporality might have other contents.

How intimate is the relation between man and time may be seen from the fact that such decisive relations for human being as that between God and man on the one hand and man and man on the other are purely temporal, i.e., historical relationships ; actions the reality of which consists absolutely in their performance and therefore in the sequence of their initiation, execution and completion. What God and my fellow-man are to me, they are to me in the history of their being and action, and therefore in the time they have for me. And what I am to God and to my fellow-man, I am in the history of my being and acting, and therefore in my time, to the extent that in some way I am in my time for them.

God would not be my God if He were only eternal in Himself, if He had no time for me. That He loves and elects me, that He wills and intends me, that He calls, judges, punishes, accepts, delivers, preserves and rules me, that He is my Light, my Commander, my Succour, my Comfort, and my Hope—all this is history, and has its time, and refers to me in this time of mine, even in God's eternity before I was and when I shall have ceased to be. And that I recognise it or not, that I refuse or accept it, that I am grateful or ungrateful, that I hear His word and in some way respond to it, that I sin against Him but also believe in Him and love Him and hope in Him—all this must take place, and does take place, as I live before Him in my time.

And the same applies to my fellow-man. He does not confront me as an abstract idea, but for good or evil in his historical reality, in the totality of what he was and is and will be, and in this totality as the Thou without whom I could not be a human I. That I see and understand him or not, that I help him or ignore him, this, and anything else my relation with him might involve, has reference to his being in time. Similarly I for my part cannot be for him just an abstract idea. I encounter him in my historical reality. I may be a source of joy or a burden to him, an encouragement or a temptation. But whatever I am, I am in my temporal reality, in the totality of what I was and am and will be.

We have no knowledge of an analogy to our relationship to God and our fellows in the being of plants and animals and the rest of the universe, but in this respect are left in the sphere of inference and conjecture. Hence we do not know whether being in time is as essential and inalienably peculiar to them as it is to us. In the last analysis we do not know what we are saying when we call time the form of their existence too. It may be that this is the point of difference between man and the rest of the universe. It is equally possible that there is no difference in this respect. We do not need to know the answer to this problem. What we must know is that it is essential to us, that it belongs to our nature, to live in time, as is conclusively proved when we recall our relationship to God and to our fellow-man.

It is of a piece with this that the message of the Old and New Testaments, unlike any other religious tradition, and even more so any philosophy, is the concrete message of a history wrought out in time. God's relation to His creatures, as attested in Holy Scripture, is quite unlike anything we find in mythology. It is not a permanent, universal relation (as that between finite and infinite, matter and spirit, good and evil, perfection and imperfection, the sovereign and the dependent, etc.), which develops and differs only in local manifestations, and which only fortuitously and not necessarily is more or less evident at a particular point, in a particular way and in particular individuals. God's attitude to His creatures as attested in the Bible is a necessary action in its concrete particularity. It occurs at this particular place, in this particular way, as a relation to those particular men with definite names in a definite environment, each with his own particular origin, determination, burdens, capabilities, perils and promises, each with his own character, prejudices, experiences and functions. It is in these concrete relations, in His acts, that the God of the Bible is Himself, and always the living God. He is this in the history initiated and continued by His acts and conducted to its particular goals and ultimately its final goal. The history of these acts both individually and in their interconnexion forms the content and time of Holy Scripture. And not merely subjectively and from below, as the manifestation of a totally different being somewhere above it, but from above and objectively it is the individual and interconnected history of these particular men. It is their history before Him and with Him and with their fellow-men. It is the history in which no man in his time is just an instance, a representative figure. None may be confused with any other. Each has his own special part to play, each his own special, divinely given endowment and responsibility. The God of Holy Scripture does not hover motionless above the flux of human history, above the times with their kaleidoscopic variety, above the passage of each individual from yesterday through to-day and into to-morrow. God accompanies them in person. " God is not ashamed to be called their God," says Heb. 11[16] of those who left their native land in faith and wandered about the earth seeking a new country. He calls Himself the " God of Abraham, Isaac and Jacob " (Ex. 3[6]).

The New Testament calls Him " the Father of our Lord Jesus Christ." His eternal will is embodied concretely in the lives of these men, each with his own existence in time. His acts are identical with the history, so trivial compared with His eternity, of the people of Israel and of the Christian community which has its centre in the history of Jesus, to this which His people first look forward and then look back. " To everything there is a season, and a time to every purpose under the heaven " (Eccles. 3¹). This does not have only the restrictive meaning that everything is confined to its own time. This is, of course, true. It is true that no man—no individual in his time, and *a fortiori* in any of the times which go to make up his life as a whole—" can find out the work that God maketh from the beginning to the end " (Eccles. 3¹¹). He has his place and function in the history of the acts of God ; but these acts are not exhausted in his history, still less in any one part of his history, however important. Before him, contemporary with him and after him there are other times than his, while even his own life contains other than these particular times, however full of consequence they may be. Man is not called to know the beginning and end and therefore the totality of the divine work. Yet Eccles. 3¹¹ also, and primarily, tells us that God " made everything beautiful in its time." In the context of His work, God has given every hour a perfection of its own. Again in the context of His work, He has set eternity in the heart of every individual human being, each in his own time and in his different times. He has allowed him to share something of the meaning and content of all created time. and therefore of all times, even those which are not his own. He has made the history of each individual, *in nuce* and *pars pro toto*, the history of His own mighty acts. " I know that, whatsoever God doeth, it shall be for ever : nothing can be put to it, nor anything taken from it : and God doeth it, that men should fear before him " (Eccles. 3¹⁴). In each man's time God is unreservedly with man, for him and against him. Similarly, God's covenant with man is not just an idea, but a connected history in a continuum of time in which individuals share in its initiation and execution, its grace and judgment, having their own particular part in it with their own history in their own time. Hence this covenant can be proclaimed and believed only as the meaning and secret of all human history and time, and all individual histories and times. But this means that it necessarily directs anthropology, the understanding of human nature, to regard temporality, the being of man in time, as something necessary and essential, and not just incidental and fortuitous.

But it is not enough to assert the inextricable unity of man and time. It is equally important to remember that man is in the time given to him. Unless we remember this, we shall fail to realise that time is our real form of existence. We have no control over time and our being in it. We can only have it *de facto*, and the question arises what this fact is. On the basis of what fact do we really have time ? We do not have it in virtue of our being. We cannot create it. We cannot either take it or keep it. Do we really have it at all ? Would it not be better to say that time has us ? However that may be, there can be no doubt that we must have it ; that we cannot escape from it. In relation to its movement past us or over us we have no option but to go with it. And even if it really consists in our own movement, we can only make this movement. We cannot contract out of it. We cannot arrest it. We cannot jump the queue. We cannot accelerate or retard it. Above all, we cannot reverse it, making it move back from the future through the present and into the past.

We can run a film backwards, but not human reality. Allusion may be made to the remarkable phenomenon that in their conscious utterances dying men often seem to survey the whole course of their lives in reverse. Perhaps this is an extreme instance of something which is characteristic of old age generally. A dying man often imagines himself to be getting younger and younger until he reaches his childhood. It would be interesting to know whether the moment he reaches his birth coincides with the moment of his death. If the phenomenon is patient of explanation, we might perhaps say that it is the rebounding of the whole course of life and movement of time against its *terminus ad quem* in death which is proclaimed prophetically in this process with its retrogressions in the direction of the *terminus a quo*. The strange contradiction between this phenomenon and reality would thus seem to confirm our thesis that the life of man and the movement of time proceed steadily in one and the same direction so long as they are not broken off as such.

All this supports the view that time as our form of existence is no less ordained by a higher power than existence itself. Time can and must be seen in the most intimate connexion with ourselves and our being and action. We are and work only in this connexion. We cannot possibly persuade ourselves that it is we who can create or assume this form, or even set and maintain ourselves in this connexion. We can only see that we are actually in this connexion. What we have here is obviously an exact parallel to the other anthropological fact that man is as he has spirit, i.e., as he is established, constituted and maintained by God as the soul of his body. Indeed, it may even be said that the fact that we are in time and have it is simply another aspect of the same fact. What emerges in both is that man is not God, but a needy creature of God. He does not have his existence and nature autonomously, but as they are given by God. He does not have his time as his own possession, achievement, acquisition, or choice. He has it as he acquires it. And he acquires it—we must again add—as and because he is not without God, though not himself God. He would not be in time if he were without God. But he is in time. Hence he is not without God. To say " man " or " time " is first and basically, even if unwillingly and unwittingly, to say " God." For God is for man as He has time for him. It is God who gives him his time.

The presence and gift of God cannot, therefore, be ignored in this matter if we are to think of human nature. For it is in virtue of the presence and gift of God that temporality too belongs to human nature. All man's unbelief, error and superstition cannot alter this original relationship of God to him or its far-reaching implications. Unbelief, error and superstition certainly involve a misuse of the time given by the presence and gift of God. By means of them man may very well compromise himself. His being in time may acquire the character of dissipation and corruption. But it cannot be destroyed. For God Himself, His presence and gift, cannot be abrogated or destroyed. Time as the form of human existence is always in itself and as such a silent but persistent song of praise to God. This is not merely because it is laid upon us, because we cannot escape from it, because we cannot alter its implied conditions, or because we cannot take and keep it of ourselves. All this simply serves to call our attention to the fact that time in itself and as such proclaims the praise of God. It does not do so, however, because it is so powerful and transcendent, but because it is the dimension for the history of the covenant between God and man, thus making possible a history between man and his fellow-men, a history of humanity. If man were not in time there would be no dimension for this history, for the history of the divine covenant and his own salvation, and therefore for the history of humanity. But the time which he has, the hours and days and years which he is given, are as such the declaration of the acts of God's righteousness and mercy, of His wisdom and patience, whose witness and object he is privileged to be in virtue of his existence in time. The time given to man tells him that he is not only the creature of God, but His covenant-partner. It speaks of God's faithfulness to Himself and His creature. That is why it is so inseparable from ourselves. That is why it is so irresistible and immutable in its own way. That is why it is so powerful an ordinance, which we cannot produce of ourselves but can only accept. In all its hiddenness it is the rustling of the Holy Spirit by which, however deaf to it we may be, we are surrounded in virtue of the fact that we are in the movement of time and are obliged to make this movement in and with our own life, so long as we have it. And in the modest garment of time, this mere form of our existence, given in such sovereign freedom, we are actually confronted by the presence and gift of God's grace. If we are to speak of prevenient grace it is difficult to see in what better form it may be better perceived and grasped than in the simple fact that time is given to us men.

Time, then, is willed and created by God as the form at any rate of human existence. A few words of explanation are needed here. Time is not eternity. Eternity itself is not timeless. It is the simultaneity and coinherence of past, present and future. Thus eternity is the dimension of God's own life, the life in which He is self-positing, self-existent and self-sufficient as Father, Son and Holy Ghost. It is this in contrast to time as the dimension of our life—the dimension in which past, present and future follow in succession. Eternity is not created. Eternity is God Himself. For as God is self-existent, He is also His own dimension. But time is willed and created by God as a reality distinct from Himself. It is willed and created as the universe is willed and created, and in the universe man. It is willed and created to be our dimension, corresponding to His. This must obviously mean that God willed and created time as the dimension of the life He ordained for us when we were willed and created, and therefore as the dimension of a life in communion with Himself as the eternal and living God, and also in relationship with our fellow-men, to whom He has given that same dimension for the same life in communion with Himself. Time was in fact willed and created in order that there might take place His dealings in the covenant with man, which finds its counterpart in the relationship between man and his fellows. It is for this reason and in this sense that time is the form of our existence. As our existence is not an end in itself, neither is time as its form. It is our time and we have it only to the extent that we belong to God, i.e., to the God who turned to us even in His eternity. It is ours and we have it only to the extent that as our time it rests in His hands, which from beginning to end are of course at work for us. It is in this sense and to this extent that time is given to us, and this mighty ordinance of time, which we can only accept as such, is as we receive and possess it a hymn of praise to God, a proclamation of His mighty acts, the hidden rustling of the Holy Spirit, the garment and form of the grace in which God wills to meet us. Everything depends upon the fact that God willed and created time for this purpose.

But it is to this extent that time is real, and we are in time and have it. Its secret is the will and act of God—the Creator who will not be thwarted or confused by human sin, but remains faithful to Himself and therefore to us in defiance of sin and its consequences. The dangers to which the reality of our time is exposed may bewilder and terrify us, as indeed they must. But they do not invalidate the truth of His presence and gift. They cannot frustrate His creative will or reverse His creative act. Bearing in mind the ground on which alone all this is possible, we shall now attempt a second and very different analysis of the being of man in time.

1. Let us consider it first in the tense in which its reality is most impressive and palpable, but also most vulnerable—as our being in the present. That man is in time means at its simplest that he always is now, i.e., that he is always crossing the frontier between past and future which one moment is just ahead and the next just behind, only to be ahead again, to have to be recrossed, and again to be behind. If man really is in his time, if he really has time, it is always now, in the crossing of this frontier. Every conception of human being, life and activity (even when ostensibly concerned with the past or future) has to do concretely with this step from the past to the future. It is always now that I am or am not, that I have or have not, that I know or do not know, that I do or leave undone, that I enjoy or eschew, love or hate, am sad or happy. It is always now that my reaction to my environment both human and non-human is positive or negative, critical or neutral. It is always now that decisions are made concerning me, and my own decisions are taken. The reality of all this—for it might, of course, be only a dream or empty show—and my own reality in it, depends upon the fact that I really have time for it, that I am really in time with all my being and life and action. It depends upon the fact that this present moment, which I need for it all, is real.

Is it real ? I am. But is it really true that I am ? The question has a comprehensive reference. Always when I take this step from the past into the future I distinguish between the two. Always when I take this step I engage in recollection and expectation, living my whole life. And I do this in such a way that from this point I recollect the past as a Now like that in which I now cross this frontier, and also expect the future as a Now like the present. If I say " I was," this implies in principle and in certain recollected outlines a present which is now past. And if I say " I shall be," this implies in principle and in certain expected outlines a present which is to come. In other words, from the standpoint of the present I always see and understand my being in time as the totality of the previous and subsequent times now distinguished by me and meeting in my Now ; and I always see and understand my past and my future, and therefore the totality of my being in time, as a present like my actual present. But is this present real ? And if not, what about the reality of my whole being in time ?

It is true, of course, that nothing is more impressive and palpable than our being in the present. How many sceptics have thought they could take refuge in the boast, " I am " ! And what structures of assurance have been erected on the foundation of this boast ! But what does this boast mean on the lips of man and as an expression of his conviction that he really exists in the present and therefore in time ? The insecurity of our being in the present is no less impressive and palpable. For the present is merely the frontier between past and future, and our being in it is merely the crossing of this frontier. The present is without duration or extension. What then do we mean by being in the present ? Where am I, and how, as I am now ? How far am I now in time ? We are sometimes assured that our being in the present is pre-eminently our proper, immediate, absolute being in time. But this is only to make a virtue of necessity. Is it not obvious that in the actual present we have no time ? Schleiermacher's contention that we are eternally in every moment would seem to be nearer the mark. All this boasting about being in the present really amounts to Schleiermacher's contention. But this suffers from two disadvantages. First, by speaking of eternal being it abandons the problem of man's being in time ; and secondly, by claiming for man what can only be postulated of God, it rules out the problem of human being altogether. We cannot evade the question how far man is really in time merely by boasting " I am." So if by " I " we really mean man, and by " am " his being in time, the phrase " I am " simply begs the question. But if we surreptitiously take the " I " for God, and the " am " for His eternal being, we are left with an answer which has nothing whatever to do with the original question.

If we ourselves had to secure and safeguard our being in time, at this crucial point where we are faced by the problem of the present our only alternatives would be either to abandon the attempt to find a solution at all, or to adopt one of the illusory solutions which are possible and have been attempted on the basis of the boasting " I am." But we are not left to our own resources in this matter if we have reason to believe that the will and act of God are the secret of our time, of our being in it, and therefore of our being in the present moment, in each present Now.

It is clear that of all the prophets of " I am," the Christian theologian, Schleiermacher, came nearest the truth. If only, instead of all his exaggerated and confusing talk about our own eternity, he had spoken of the eternity of God, of the eternity of His righteousness and mercy, of His wisdom and patience at every moment of our lives, in each successive Now in which we cross that frontier ! And if only we could interpret in this sense all those who boast about the present ! But since this is out of the question, we must pass them by and proceed as follows.

It is true that we are now, as we cross the frontier and thus distinguish between past and future, so that we are always sure that our past was a similar now and that our future will be. It is thus true that the present seems to be the basic form of our time as a whole. It is true again that the very reality of this basic form, and therefore the reality of our time as a whole, seems to be hopelessly called in question by the fact that our present is without duration or extension, disappearing as soon as it comes. Primarily, however, it is not we who are now but God who is now : God who created us and is in process of rescuing and preserving us ; God who is not dismayed at our sin, and does not cease to be for us, nor reverse our determination to be for Him and in mutual fellowship ; God in all the defiance of our unfaithfulness by His own faithfulness. He is now primarily ; and we secondarily. He is in the height of His majesty ; we in the depths of our creatureliness and sinfulness, which even in conjunction are shallow compared with the depth of His mercy. He is in His wisdom and patience ; we in our folly and anxiety, in the flight and chase to which we referred earlier. He is in His self-existence and self-repose ; we " pass hence, and wander from one year to another." He is now properly ; we improperly in relation to Him. But more important for our present purpose than these differences is the relationship. He, too, is now in His way as we are in ours. He is now as Creator. But this means that there is first a divine stepping from the past to the future. This is His present. We speak of His eternity, in which the past is not " no longer " nor the future " not yet," in which therefore the Now has duration and extension. It is in His eternity that God is now. But we do not speak of God's abstract eternity, but of the eternity of His free love, in which He took and takes and will take time for our sakes, in which He wills to be for us and also wills that we should be for Him and therefore in mutual fellowship. That God is now means that all this is now the meaning of a divine stepping from the past to the future, of a divine Word spoken now, a divine action performed now. And we now continue that there is also—in relationship from the very first to what God is and does—our human stepping from the past to the future. This is our present in our time, in which the past is no more and the future not yet and therefore the Now is that middle point between the two with neither duration nor extension. Yet as we may not speak of God's abstract eternity, we may not speak of our abstract time. For us, to be in time, to be now, is to be under and with God, to be under and with the eternal God, who wills to be, and actually is, not merely for Himself but for us, not merely in the heights but in the depths. That we are in the present means that we are in the present of the gracious, judging, commanding will and action in which He has turned wholly to us, but claims us wholly for Himself, for fellowship with Him, and therefore for human fellowship. It is in doing this that He gives us time, and first of all the present, and what the present is in our time, that moment between the times which is without duration or extension. It is our past on the basis of His, in His and for His. That is why it takes the form it does. That is why it is a stepping from the past to the future. That is why it means a leaving of the past which is " no longer " and a grasping of the future which is " not yet." And finally that is why it is in itself only that frontier and our crossing of that frontier and therefore apparently nothing intrinsically its own. That God is present to us is what fills our present : from the past, for He is not " no longer," into the future, for He is not " not yet " ; and therefore also in the centre, because His movement from the past into the future has the duration and extension which escape our own Now. That I am now—with all the inescapable problems which this involves—means that as I am continually there in movement from my past to my future, I am referred wholly to Him and cast back upon Him, upon His being in time addressed to me. Without Him, without the fact that He is for me, I should have no time and therefore, since I can be only in time, I should not be at all. The very fact that I am now far from giving that boastful certainty of my real being, would then show me only that I am in process of sinking into nothingness. But I really am now because God is, and is first, and is not only for Himself but for me. Because God loves me without cause or merit, I am now. And I can add with confidence, and with a precision of which the prophets of " I am " have not the slightest inkling, that because God loves me I really am now, and really have time as I have it. I do not sink into a void, although I still have that great " no longer " behind me and the great " not yet " in front of me, and although I have only the unstable moment, the ice-floe of the present, beneath my feet. If I have God (or rather, if God has me), I need no more. I have space and therefore time. Time is given me, and with all the certainty and solidity that I could desire because it is given me directly by Him, because, as I am in time in this way, I have to do with Him, and therefore with eternity as the fount and sum and source of all time. His presence as such is the gift of my time. He Himself pledges both its reality and its goodness. I am His creature. All I need to be this is time. Only if I want to be as God can I desire more, and suffer and sigh and complain because I only have time, and my now has the remarkable form of this transition. Only if I had to be a creature without God should I have to regard this transition as my destruction. But I am a creature under God and with Him. I have time. I have my now in the form in which I need it. I am where I may live neither threatened by illusion nor enmeshed in falsehood, i.e., in real time, in the present of God. Tersteegen is right after all : " Content is he, who hath Thee, Whose spirit to Thee cleaveth, Every yearning leaveth."

We next ask concerning the significance of the fact that man is always now. We have seen that all human being, action and experience is either now or else unreal. Even as past and future it can be understood as a totality only in relation to the present, as a past or present now. We are always in this transition. Our own reality depends upon the reality of this transition. And this transition, and therefore the Now in which we are, is real as and because the present of the eternal God as the Creator of time is the secret of our present. What is this transition, then, but the offer, the summons, the invitation, to be with God now, to be present with Him, to make this transition with Him, recognising that He always precedes us, not without us, but for us and on our behalf ? He always does this now. This is what gives our present its distinctive weight, but also its distinctive lightness ; its distinctive seriousness, but also its distinctive radiance. God is primarily and continually present. He is always the same, yet always new, always with a particular offer and summons, always with a particular invitation. In this way, in this particularity, God's present is the secret of our own. It is not merely like the dominant undertone of a painting, or the sustained basic note at the beginning of the St. Matthew Passion. It always has its own particular sound, character and lustre. It is the present of the living God, not of an exalted but static picture of God. And this means that our present is not like the millions of identical oscillations of the clock with which we measure it. It would be like this if we had to live it without God, if our present were lost time, if it were not real but non-existent. The fact that the living God is present makes our present not only real but weighty and therefore important. It encloses the mystery of what God has for us now, of what He has to say to us, to allow, to command us, to give us. It encloses the opportunity which He wills to be realised in and through us now. It encloses, therefore, the mystery of the grateful response we now owe to Him and in consequence to our fellow-men.

Only now can we see how significant it is that every Now, in its particular relation to the past and future, is an opportunity which comes only once and then, perceived and grasped or not, passes never to return. Only now can we see that each Now is indeed a " now or never." Schiller was quite right when he said : " What thou abstractest from the minute can no eternity restore." How do we know that what we now consciously or unconsciously omit is only a paltry thing and not the turning-point which determines our whole being in time both past and future. There are moments like this. Indeed, in the strict sense all moments are like this. At any rate, we have to reckon with each moment because God Himself has particular moments, καιροί, in His being, speech and action in relation to us ; moments which continually come and go. Now is no time for dreaming about past or future. Now is the time to awake, to receive or act, to speak or be silent, to say Yes or No. Now is no time to send as our proxy a recollected or expected picture of ourselves, a ghost or an ideal, to act under our mask. Now we must step out and act as the men we really are. The urgency of the moment demands absolute sincerity and readiness. A general and therefore ungodly view of time and of the present certainly cannot give this weight and promise and claim to our being in the Now. But it is given with supreme clarity and necessity by the concept of the time and present given by God and therefore real. Because we are under God and for Him, as we now are, there is no evading the importance of the Now, and no excuse for missing or misusing it. But there is also no absence of His grace and mercy even in our Now. Our present is indeed joyful, for in it, since God is He who is primarily and properly present, even in our weakness and stupidity, even in our missing or misusing of what is offered, we are not abandoned by Him or left to ourselves, to the power and wisdom of our own decisions, but may always count on the fact that the first and final responsibility for us is in His hands, that He forgives sins, protects erring children and causes tired wayfarers to take their halting steps, that His wisdom exceeds our folly and His goodness our evil, that He is wakeful even though we fall asleep and dream about the past and future when we ought to be buying up the Now which will never come our way again. Even in the particularity of His presence which we have failed to see or use, or perhaps misused, He will not have been present to us in vain. Without us, against us, but finally for us, He will have filled our Now according to His will even though we have not responded to His offer, summons and invitation. When have we ever been a match for Him or done justice to His claim ? Of what past can we think without being driven to seek refuge in His grace and mercy ? What future can we imagine when it will not be our consolation that He will always be much greater with His presence and gifts than our greatest skill and exertion to do justice to the opportunity offered ? This, then, is how the present is filled. It is real. And from this we are entitled to conclude that all our time is real, that we are really in time, that we really have time. God's presence and gift creates, delivers and sustains this reality. This means judgment and grace. This is the mystery of the whole Gospel and the whole Law. But this means that though we are sinners who have forfeited our time, and indeed ourselves, we are not lost, but as we were created, so we are sustained and delivered.

2. Now let us turn to our being in time in the past tense : " I

have been." The juxtaposition of present and perfect—"have" and "been"—raises at once the whole problem we have to solve. In the first place, and positively, it means that I am now the one who has been. As I reach the frontier and cross into the future, I am not a mere cipher, a blank sheet of paper. I am gifted and burdened, freed and enslaved, enriched and impoverished, credited and committed, strengthened and weakened, inclined, directed and determined, by the many earlier transitions I have made in the past and right up to this point. I am what all my past life has made me. It does not matter how insensible I may be to it, how few my clearer recollections. When the hour strikes and registers my present Now, when I embark upon the new transition, I am what my past has made me, formed and moulded by all my previous transitions. Whatever I may be and do and experience now, and whatever I shall be and do and experience after this Now, the prejudices and assumptions which I have brought from the past are in varying degrees significant for this Now and will continue to be so for my future.

Certainly a new page is now turned, a new opportunity is offered, and the whole problem of life is posed afresh. Perhaps it will not merely bring a few or many changes but alter the whole picture of life, revealing it in an entirely new light, and placing it under an entirely new sign. For all I know the present moment may be the most critical turning point in the whole of my life. What I am on the verge of receiving, saying or doing may leave an indelible mark on the whole of my future course. Yet this new page still belongs to the same book as the earlier pages. In some way or other the entries on the earlier pages are connected with the entries which will be made on the pages yet to come. The good and the evil, the achievements and failures of my past are not simply written off ; they belong inalienably to me, whatever changes the future may have in store. I am what my past has made me, even though I may be quite different now from what I was then. I am what I have been.

But is this really so ? What guarantee is there that I am really the same to-day as I was in the past ? What guarantee is there that my past is real ? " I have been "—this juxtaposition of present and perfect may have quite a different meaning which casts a wholly new light (or shadow) on the first. It may mean that I once was—in a present now past—but then something irrevocable happened. That present was followed by another, and my then being became a new and different being which covered over the former and therefore the former present. My being in time was transformed and became a thing of the past. This is what is really meant when we say that we have " been." What we were in the past is past, *passé, vorbei*. A line has been drawn across the page, separating what I was from what I am now. I am what I was, but only underneath this line ; only in the present ; only in so far as this contains my past in a diluted form, as a product or extract ; only to the extent that to-day and in the new form in which I am to-day, I am still the same person that I was yesterday. But what I was yesterday, above that line, has now perished. It is only in the sense that it has been, that the being has been taken out of it. It lives on only as I who lived then still live now, and live as the one who lived then. But I have no more life as the one who lived then because that time has passed. What is marked off from the present by that conclusive event has been put behind me. It has become a " pluperfect." The change it underwent was indeed an absorption to the extent that its then being was deprived of extension and duration, i.e., that its time was irrevocably taken away from it. What was then still exists only as it is to-day. It no longer exists in so far as it was then.

This aspect of the matter is profoundly disquieting. For we know how things stand where the past ought still to exist in that diluted form, in our being to-day, now, in the present. We know that it cannot enjoy duration or extension, and therefore genuinely live on, even here. And this raises the disturbing suspicion that even our present and future are hastening towards the past ; that that fatal line will be drawn again and again ; that our present and all our future being are incontrovertibly condemned to undergo that transformation and therefore to become past being in the sense described, and as such to be no more. From this standpoint again it would seem as if we have no real time. And there are two ways of meeting this disturbing situation : the one by memory ; the other by oblivion. Though diametrically opposed, they both lead to the same result. For they are both equally incapable of remedying the situation. Neither can guarantee that our past being also is as such. Neither can convince us that we really have time. And so both are equally unsatisfactory.

In memory we start with an awareness of the problematical character of our being in the present and therefore in the future as well. But at least it seems certain that we were once : " I once possessed this priceless boon." So we seek refuge from the present and the future in this " once upon a time." Memory is an attempt to restore to the past the duration and extension which it obviously does not have any longer. It is an attempt to recall our then being in time as such. If it were possible to do this, we should have a solid, though limited guarantee of our being in time, a partial assurance of the reality of time and therefore of our own reality. When a man regrets to-day and has no hope for to-morrow, he has recourse to memory. And when the same thing happens to a whole generation, it resorts to historicism, romantically or scientifically investigating what was. The attempt may be partially successful. It is possible to conjure up more or less clear-cut, colourful and animated pictures of the past. This is what happened, and this is how it happened. And in so doing a good deal of light and shade is thrown on the present, for the past lives on in the present, and therefore *historia vitae magistra*—a reconstruction of the past can help to a knowledge of the present. But the real purpose of the study eludes us. Our reconstruction of the past and the past itself are poles apart. The actual past never returns, however vivid and accurate the reconstruction. Indeed, the clearer and more accurate our memory, the more vividly it throws into relief the line which is drawn beneath the past, and its absorption into the present. In its own being it was, and does not return. Its time is up. If ever it was real, it is real no longer. And it is clear that in its initial intention as flight from the present and the future our enterprise is doomed to frustration. Time marches on, with all its problems, even while we are day-dreaming in our memories. We can make this attempt only in our own problematical time, and therefore we fall victim to the very thing which we seek to elude.

In oblivion we start from the opposite end. We know how problematical is our being in the past. It is gone, and memory is powerless to retain or recall it. What is certain is that we are now, and shall be—or at any rate want to be—in the future. So we run away in precisely the opposite direction. We flee from the cathedrals, prisons, inns and catacombs where we were yesterday, into the light of to-day with its promise of even greater light to-morrow. When we try, consciously or unconsciously, to forget the past, we simply let it lie to the extent that it is not absorbed into the present. We do this so as to be free to give all our attention to the solid, though limited, assurance of the being which seems possible now and therefore in all our future Nows. When a man cannot be happy about the past, he seeks happiness in the present and future. And when a whole generation finds it impossible to make sense of the past, it glories all the more readily in the " spirit of the age," that is, of its own age, and succumbs to the belief in progress. This too, as we know, can be partially success-ful. When we are tired of our old letters and diaries we can tear them up and burn them. We can suppress all that we were and experienced and said and did. We can replace it by a picture of what we think we can and should be and ex-perience and say and do now and in the future, finding freedom and beginning life all over again, and this time real life in the admiration and service which it evokes. But again our real intention eludes us. Our being in the present and future is not a secure refuge from the problems of the past. We can paint rosy pictures of our being in the present, but these pictures bear no relation to the reality which is just as problematical as our being in the past. It is as foolish to flee from Scylla to Charybdis as *vice versa*. So far from solving the problem, we are confronted with it in oblivion even more acutely than before. In fact, there is no escaping it. The Scylla of the past haunts us, even though we forget it, in our flight to the Charybdis of the present. It is not merely that a man cannot live down his past or be other than his past has made him. It is not merely that, however cheerfully he may pursue his way, he cannot enter the present and future except *omnia sua secum portans*. The real trouble is that he has behind him the great lacuna of his past being, gone never to return ; that his being in time, even if it had (which it has not) a safe haven in the present and future, has sprung this leak, and would therefore sink even if it were in port. After all, he comes from the past. He is the same person as he was then whether he contrives to forget it or not. And what is he now, what is all his being in time, if his past being in time has gone (as he foolishly seems to confirm by his forgetting), if in the fact that it is now past it is without reality ?

Yet we could only choose memory or oblivion, or possibly a com-bination of the two, if we were dependent on ourselves for assurance of the reality of our being in time, and therefore of our real being even in the past. But we are not dependent on ourselves if we accept the fact that the will and act of God are the meaning and ground of our being in time, and therefore in the time which is behind us. If we really accept this truth, the position is as follows. To be sure, we were. That line has been drawn and will be drawn continually. One day, indeed, it will be drawn for the last time, thus denoting that our whole being in time belongs to the past, and apparently denying it any reality at all. Primarily, however, it is not we who were, but

God. Even then God was our Creator, Deliverer and Preserver. He then continued to be for us in spite of our enmity against Him. He then opposed His faithfulness to our unfaithfulness. He was first in the heights ; then we in the depths. And even then there was not only opposition but relationship between us and Him. Above us, for us and with us, God has also been. For there is a Then, a genuine past, in God's eternity, as surely as it is the eternity of the living God. Of course, no lines are drawn there. The past is not left behind, nor does it fade. The God who was, is now, and ever shall be. It is in the coinherence of past, present and future that His eternity is original, authentic and creative time. And the eternal God was then, in the past, the surety and pledge of the reality of our created time and of our real being in it. Again, of course, we are not concerned here with eternity in the abstract, but with the eternity in which God willed, wills and shall will that we should be His creatures, and therefore that we should not perish and cease to be. We emphasise that God's eternity is the eternity in which He willed this. No line is drawn under this " He willed." It is not subject to any " no longer." It includes the fact that He wills and shall will. And in this " He willed " He was over us, for us and with us when we were in that past reality which now seems to have perished, so that it can only be either remembered or forgotten. More than that, God's eternity is the eternity in which He did what was necessary for our being, for our deliverance and preservation, for securing us against destruction. He was from of old our Creator, Father and Redeemer. He was moved in Himself for us long before He executed this movement, and especially as He did so, and does not cease to do so. In this " He did," which does not come to an end, finally becoming a " no longer," He was over us and with us when we were in our highly problematical being as a past being.

But again we continue that, in relation to what God was and willed and did, there was also at that time our being, experience, volition, action and inaction, the totality of what we were and the way in which we were it. We are invited not to see or understand ourselves abstractly in this our being in the mode of past being. Our time in this dimension is no more to be thought of abstractly than God's eternity. What were we ? We were what we could and should and had to be under and with God, on the basis of His past being. And in what form were we ? We were as those already loved by Him, to whom He willed to give time, and actually gave it. But He gave this time for life, and therefore for continuing life, in the present in which we now live, and the future towards which we move. That we were then and may still be to-day is a proof of the patience of God already shown us then. It is for this reason that our then time could not be permanent or stationary, but could only come and go. It was time which as we had it was marked for dissolution in new time. As our then life-time it

had to become what it is now from the standpoint of the present,
past time. But this does not alter the fact that, because God was then,
it was real and full time. And because God was then, its reality and
fulness cannot be taken away by the fact that it has gone. God does
nothing in vain. What He willed and created cannot disintegrate into
nothingness. It has merely lost its character as our present, which
it once had. But it has not perished as one of the terms of our time.
" Thine eyes did see my substance, yet being unperfect ; and in thy
book all my members were written, which in continuance were
fashioned, when as yet there was none of them " (Ps. 139^{16}). All our
members were in God's book and plan and purpose even before they
were. How then, when they have once been, can they be no more ?
There is a being in the past tense, a past being which is real as such. Our
being in time is real in this tense too. But we can say this only in relation to God. We cannot cling to its then reality nor can we recall it.
Apart from Him, it would be idle and quite inconceivable to maintain
that our being in this tense, our then being, is as real to-day and to-
morrow as it was then. Without God the fact that the past is irrevocably behind us, and that even the present hour and our future days
and years rush irresistibly into the past, would be the leak in virtue
of which we could understand our whole being in time as one which is
condemned to perish. But we are not without God. We can understand this fact in relation to Him. And God, the eternal God, whose
yesterday is also to-day and to-morrow, He loved us even then. And
this means that our then being as the object of His love, which He
will not allow to be taken from Him, has not ceased to be real in His
eyes and therefore in truth. What He has once given He does not take
back again. What was by Him and before Him still is. Nor does
this mean only that our past is included in our present and is present
with it. It has a further, less obvious, but decisive meaning. Our
being in time with its regressive duration and extension not only was
real but is real. It is not lost. It has not escaped us or ceased to be.
It is as genuinely ours as our being in the present and future. We
are in our whole time, in the whole sequence of its parts, and not just
in the one part we call the present. For our time is the dimension of
our whole life. If our whole time is the gift of God, then God also
pledges to maintain its reality as a whole. It is only time. It can
and must be past, and continually pass, and even in the future hasten
towards the past. But again it would be quite wrong for man to try
to be God and therefore eternal instead of being cheerfully and modestly
man and therefore temporal. The passing of our time would only
mean destruction if we had to be men without God, outside the
covenant He has established with us. But this does not correspond
to the reality of man as God has created it. His covenant with man
has stood from the creation of the first man, from the beginning of the
world, from God's eternity. The truth is that we may really have our

time as given by God ; our whole time, even in its character as past and passing time.

But the further question arises what is meant by the fact that we were. That we were is real because primarily, beyond us and for us, God was, in His omnipotent grace and mercy, holiness and righteousness. He loved us in our time then, and because He has not ceased to do so, we are real even in that time. But this means that our past being, which accumulates with each succeeding day and hour, and which we bring behind us, stands wholly under His judgment. In this whole sphere, there is no more divine offer, summons, invitation or opportunity for us. The die has been cast. What we were, we were ; with all that we did and omitted to do, all that we discovered and overlooked, all the good and evil that we did and suffered, all the beauty that we enjoyed or in our stupidity failed to notice, all the joys that we experienced or missed because we were not equal to them. Everything was exactly as it was. Nothing can be taken away from it or added to it, nothing improved upon or made worse. It was all before God, and it is still before Him in all its reality. No recollection is needed, nor can oblivion alter the fact that it is still before God and therefore as real now as it was then. Even our present, the remarkable result of our past, is not needed to establish this. We are really the persons we were in the whole duration and extent of our past, because in it we were before God, to whom we owed everything but were also responsible for everything. He it was who even then gave, withheld and took away. He it was who even then helped and encountered us. He it was who even then rewarded and punished us according to His wisdom and justice. He it was who even then knew us through and through, however much we tried to disguise or conceal ourselves. He it was who even then was greater than our heart, who could use us or find us unserviceable and yet use us otherwise than we perceived. All this past of ours stands under His judgment and sentence. As those we were, in all the unalterability in which we really were it, we are delivered up wholly into His hands, for grace or condemnation. That this is so, that we are simply in His hands and at His disposal, unable to do anything about it ourselves, is what is meant by the fact that we were. It might seem doubtful in the present and especially the future tense. For in the present and especially the future tense our personal plans, decisions and actions might seem to be a secondary and co-operative determination of our existence. But our being in time also has this tense—the past. One day, indeed, it will have only this tense. This does not mean that it is destined to perish. Because God exists, it is real even in this tense. But even the blind is surely compelled to see that in this tense it is in God's hands. If he willed to accept it, it is accepted. If He willed to reject it, it is rejected. And He owed us nothing—we owed Him everything. What was it then ? Exactly what his decision, His judgment, His verdict made

it ; exactly what we shall see it to have been when the book in which
it stood, the book of God, is opened. No more, no less, no different.
" It is God who rules."

In conclusion, this throws a new light on our retrospective view of
the past. If this stands before God and under His judgment in all
its unalterable reality, the possibility both of recollection and oblivion
acquire a new character.

As regards the former, we may say that it would reveal either a
strange ingratitude or a strange timidity to refuse to live in our past,
in the history which is behind us. Why should we ? After all does it
not belong just as really to our being in time as our present and future ?
Is not God alone its Judge ? What reason can we possibly have for
shutting our eyes to the past ? Have we not every reason to look
in this direction as far as we can ? And when we do look carefully,
what else do we discover but traces of God's judgment ? If they are
encouraging, why should we not rejoice ? And if depressing, why
should we not be summoned to humility and modesty ? God does not
need to remember, but we cannot live without memory, even to-day
and to-morrow. A man without an awareness of history, without
definite pictures of what was and the patience to learn from them,
would be an escapist, running away from reality and God, and quite
unreliable in his dealings with his fellow-men. There is no occasion
for this escapism, not merely because it is doomed to disappointment,
but above all because as we look back over the past there is so much
cause for gratitude and shame that no place is left for evasion.

At the same time, however, we must insist just as seriously that
we can never live in the past as if it were our true home and the
present and future an exile. We cannot seek in it a picture of the
life we do not hope to find in the present and future. This flight in
reverse is equally unhealthy. It may take the form of a *laudatio* or a
contemptus temporis acti, but either way it is impossible. For what
matters is not our then being in itself and as such, but the fact that
it was our being under and with God. If it was under and with God,
then it is so to-day and to-morrow. Memory can enable us to live
also but not exclusively in the past. We can live in the past but not
by it. We can be conservative in relation to it, but we cannot be
genuinely reactionary, either by restoring it or even by reacting continuously against a past artificially restored by our own aversion to
the present. In clear and living memory we think to-day and with
a view to to-morrow. There is thus no temptation to falsify it, either
whitewashing or blackening it in our own favour, i.e., for our own
justification. Above all, we realise the limitations of memory. It
can give us pleasant or terrifying glimpses of the past, but it cannot
recall the past itself. As it really was and is, it is before the eyes of
God and not of man—our own but a hidden reality. Because it is safe
in the hands of God, we are freed from any positive or negative paralysis

in relation to it. We do not feel the compulsion of positive or negative historical ideologies. We are delivered, not from living, but from dead and deadening memory. We are delivered for forward-looking life now in quiet contemplation of the past.

We shall also have a different view of oblivion when we remember that what has been is in God's hands, and therefore real. And the first point to notice is that we may forget. God never forgets, any more than He needs to remember. But we need to forget. And we are enabled to do so. If it were otherwise, we should be in a terrible plight. We should never be able to bear the sight of our whole being in time, even in our own pictures of its reality. This is because our past stands under the judgment of God. None of these pictures can justify or save us. And the sight of them all might well overwhelm us. It is a good thing that we are able to forget, that we can pray, *quod vixi tege*. And it is a good thing that God draws this veil over the past even without our asking. In so doing, He allows us to live to-day for to-morrow with just the few memories we need of what was. The deep and salutary meaning and purpose of forgetfulness is that for large stretches we are not compelled to consider our past being in time even in the form of pictures, and therefore that we are not condemned to the constant agitation these pictures cause us. It is enough to have those which actually are before us. Above all, it is enough that our being in time is before the eyes of God in its reality, and stand under His judgment.

It must also be said, however, that we do not have to forget in order to be able to live. If so, we should again be paralysed, for we should have no history. If God is the Judge of our whole life in time, then none of our memories of the past can be a source of regret. Of course, there are things in our past we should prefer to forget but cannot. Since this is the case, God must have ordained that it should be so. There is every reason to think that it is God's good purpose that these fragments of the past should belong to our life in the present and the future, and that it would not be salutary for us if we were able to forget them. Hence nothing could be worse than to try to forget them. No, there is nothing which ought to be torn up and burnt! How much harm comes from the forcible suppression of memories contrary to the will of God : memories which we ought to have, but for some reason or other seek to avoid ; memories which we try to conceal under images of the present and the future, but which God Himself has not concealed ; memories which we cannot really succeed in obliterating, but which merely become the cause of psychological disorders. Enforced oblivion is as bad as enforced recollection. To try to live in oblivion is as bad as to try to live on memory. If we know that God was when we were, we are free in this respect too. In this knowledge we must not and shall not try to forget even what we might otherwise prefer to forget.

3. Finally, let us consider our being in time in the future tense. "I shall be." Here, too, our first reference is to the present and to a distinctive filling of our being in the present. That I shall be has its beginning in the present, and then reaches out beyond the present into the future. We know that the step from the past and the step into the future are not really two steps but one. In popular terms, however, we may think of it as a further step. I am now leaving the Now previously entered, crossing its forward frontier. Like a wayfarer who finds no room in the inn, I am coming out again and continuing my journey in the hope of finding lodging further on. The future is the further side of the present, just as the past is its nearer side. In the present they touch one another. As the past moved towards it, the future moves away from it. I am now awaiting a new present. I am eagerly stepping towards it. I am grasping it. But this eager waiting and stepping and grasping begin now. They immediately cease to be now, but it is worth insisting that they begin now. Hence our Now is always full of the future as well as the past. As we are, we anticipate the future. We project ourselves into the future. We see and will ourselves as we shall be. We act as though our future being had already arrived. To this extent we are determined by it. Our thoughts, feelings, actions and reactions are coloured by specific hopes and fears. All our human activity, but also all our human experience and suffering, hastens towards a *telos*. The farmer's work in springtime is to sow seed for the summer. His work in summer is his harvest for the winter. His work in autumn and winter prepares for next spring's sowing and next summer's harvest. All our present joy is at the decisive point a foretaste of the new and true joy which is still to come. Similarly, every present pain is only a sinister herald of what we fear will be worse pains. And conversely, as we all know from experience, there is always in present joy a foreboding of coming pain, and in present pain a promise of coming joy. Till Eugenspiel was right perhaps to be more anxious in times of ease and more lighthearted in toilsome ascent. At any rate, whether we are conscious of it or not, the present is always openly or secretly pregnant with the future. Coming events cast their shadows before. In the experiences and decisions of to-day, the developments are prepared and proclaimed which we shall have to live through and for which we shall have to answer to-morrow. I am not only what I was, I am already, even if only *in nuce*, what I shall be.

But am I really what I shall be? On that further side of my present, will I be the same person just a stage further on? Is there a forward continuity of my being? Is there still room for my life? "I shall be," I say. But I may not be at all. And in any case, I have not yet reached the place I am aiming at when I say, "I shall be." I am not yet the person I shall be. And it might well be that this undeniable "not yet" threatens my future being no less

inexorably than the " no longer " my past being. The " not yet " is
no sure guarantee of a coming " then " or " one day." It may even
contain a threat, the threat of a " never." For the step in which I
transcend my Now presupposes a place in front of me in which to
plant my feet. But from a distance there is no certainty that I can
do this. That step forward may be a step into the void, into the abyss.
There may be time for others, but not for me. My own time may be
up. The future of which I am full may be a preparation leading to
nothing. It may be an indicator pointing into the void, a presenti-
ment resting on an illusion, a prophecy which will never be fulfilled.
The future of which I am full is not my real future. It is not even a
pledge of it. It proves only that I now live as if I had a real future, a
real being in time in this third tense. As I was and am, I take it for
granted that I shall be. But this is not self-evident. A Now will come
when I can no longer maintain this " as if " or deceive myself with this
assumption. And I never know whether my next Now will not be
the Now of this great illusion which will be followed by the great
disillusionment of the fact that I have no more time. The further
side of my present may turn out to be the further side of my being
generally. This is the possibility of an acute threat ahead of us—a
threat from the very point at which my life aims. Life means time,
but we may find that our time has no more duration and extension,
but is a thing of the past, so that life itself is over, and has only a past
and no future. Can we console ourselves by reflecting that this threat
can be serious, and that the catastrophe can break over us, only once,
and that on every other occasion we shall escape? Or, to put it another
way, is there any comfort in taking a chance that the next moment
will not be that of the great illusion and therefore of the great disillusionment, but that we at least still have time, perhaps quite a bit
of time? There would be some comfort in this if we had a clear view
ahead, and could see the real catastrophe from a distance or even when
it is close at hand, and if that final crisis, which is bound to come
sooner or later, were not the term of all the being in time still ahead
of us, thus impressing its character upon the whole. In fact, however,
the whole space of life before us, beyond the present, is chronically
and therefore continually threatened by this catastrophe. To be sure,
the terrible end can come only once, and it may still be a long way off.
But come it will, and therefore the future which precedes it cannot
be other than unending terror. There is little true consolation in a
prospect like this. But this is in fact the prospect which faces our
being in time in this third tense.

Again there are two ways of facing this prospect. We can shut
our eyes to it, or we can look it straight in the face, and act accordingly.
We can be unreflective and frivolous with regard to the threat which
lies ahead, or reflective and preoccupied. We can be optimists or
pessimists, activists or quietists. These are obviously very different

attitudes, and they are both clear and simple possibilities. They embody the two classical views of life which have always divided men, and will always do so. But they have one point in common—that they both end in a *cul de sac*.

The unreflective way is to stand firmly on the pretence and to assume that it affords solid support, never giving a thought to the fact that our future being in time is enclosed by a great bracket ; that one day—we do not know when— we shall step and fall into the abyss, having a present without a future, en- countering the further side not only of our present moment, but of our whole being in time ; and that with every step we take our being is a being of unending terror under the threat of this catastrophe. It is possible to ignore these un- pleasant facts, to speak and act as though that bracket would be removed. It is possible to persuade ourselves and others that the fear is not so terrible and that we are not really afraid of it at all. This is to posit absolutely the future of which our present is full. It is to treat it as though it were already past and lay behind us. We then speculate as in Jas. 4[13] : " Today or tomorrow we will go into such a city, and continue there a year, and buy and sell, and get gain." We then live by planning, arranging and managing everything. We then live for our programme in the preparation of its execution. We live for the principles and ideas and pictures, both theoretical and practical, which we h ve projected and made for our own personal future, and perhaps for the future of a greater or smaller or perhaps all human society. We fondly imagine that such dreams represent the future as it really will be—in germ, at any rate. As we contemplate them and enjoy a foretaste of the reality, we imagine we are already there. The barrier posed by the question whether everything might not turn out very differently from what we had expected, since there might be no future at all or only a threatened future is triumphantly surmounted by the assertion that the worst has not yet happened ; that we still have a future ; that where there's a will there's a way ; that the future has never failed yet and will not do so on this occasion. This view is superficial, no doubt, but there is something healthy and brave about it. It is certainly a happy thing to gather rosebuds while we may. And we can certainly do so if we are prepared to live without reflection. But this is hardly possible in practice. This is the *cul de sac* to which this kind of outlook leads. When all is said and done, it is not really possible to be careless and unreflective. No one can. We cannot persuade ourselves and others that we are. We can only act as though we are. The facts are stronger than all the healthy assertions and certainties exploited by this outlook. They are stronger than all the cheerful grasping at the future in which we try to put it into practice. It is an illusion to think that we can posit the future absolutely even in the present. We have not the means to do so, and we know very well that we have not. No intention or purpose, plan or programme unless it is that of a madman can fail either consciously or unconsciously to take into account factors unknown as yet, or to be limited by the conditions, needs and demands even of the present itself. No one ever lives exclusively in the future. And in so far as we do, the triumph in which we think we can do so is more like the effect of a self-administered dose of morphia than of genuine, healthy achievement. We are no match for the future which really comes and is so terribly menacing. Our own projected images of the future, now present in us, are not the future itself, or even the germ of it. We do not seize the future ; it seizes us and overpowers us. And at bottom everything always turns out to be very different from what we expected, and in the end totally different A broad shadow of uncertainty lies over all the time we still have. And we know this, and reflect concerning it. We may stifle or suppress this reflection, but we cannot extinguish it. We are terrified even when we maintain that the unending terror to which we move is not so dreadful after all. We should not be men, living in time, if we did not reflect on the hazards to which our being in time is exposed, from the very point to which we must now and continually push forward.

We are thus left with the way of reflection, i.e., reflection avowed and acknowledged and allowed to dominate the scene. Since we cannot stifle our fear of the future, why not bring it out into the open and allow it to be normative and determinative for our whole attitude to life ? Sooner or later we shall step and fall into the void ; we shall have a present without a future ; we shall meet the further side of our being in time. This terrible threat may overwhelm us at any moment, surprising us like an armed man and depriving us of all the consolation we had forged for ourselves against it. Once we are aware of it, it becomes depressingly clear that we have nothing else to look for but unending terror, even before the dreaded prospect actually comes, and we must order our lives accordingly. The way in which we look and step from the present into the future is determined by the fact that we see the whole of the path before us in this shadow. It is always with diffidence and uncertainty, hemmed in and unconcerned, that we now look and move into the future. It is only with broken pinions that we can make the venturesome flight from the present to the future. The present itself now comes to me, to the extent that it is inevitably full of the future as foreseen in this way, as a source of anxiety, a burden to be borne and only to be endured. Here, too, we have a triumph, another victorious way of facing the future. But this time it is to the negative aspect that for some reason we give the preference and dominion. And once finally triumphant, it will quench all hope of a better future, all confidence in ideas and plans, all resolution to put them into effect. We will simply plan and perform the bare essentials, and then just wait in fear and resignation. Here is another view of life, a definite view, if not exactly healthy, brave or cheerful. It is a view which because of its ostensible honesty and realism is often compared favourably with its opposite. Is it not the view of a mature man, of one who has plumbed life to the depths ? Is it not better in the long run to be reflective than unreflective ? Yes, so long as we are really able to be exclusively and totally and definitively reflective. But again we are in a *cul de sac*. No one is a pure pessimist. Even Schopenhauer was so only on paper. Even the suicide is not a pure pessimist, for his very attempt to " make an end " shows that in spite of everything he is looking for a better future. We can only behave as if we were completely reflective. As long as life lasts, we hear the call of a fresh possibility of something to be attained and won. For we cannot help considering that our terrible end may still not be just round the corner ; that the immediate future at any rate is not unending terror, but in spite of all our fear and anxiety it may also offer positive opportunities. No one can manage to live without some plan for the future, however modest. No one is so reflective in his attitude to life as to have no room for a modicum of the unreflective spirit of childhood. Even the reflectiveness of the most reflective is nourished in the last resort on dreams, on dreams of the future fed by his contemplation of the final limit of his being in time, and not on the future itself as it actually comes upon him and overwhelms him. The reflective man, too, forgets that on this side of that final limit everything may turn out very differently from his gloomy prognostications. But he only forgets it. In spite of his forgetting, his future is still open and all he can do is to proceed towards it with a certain openness, which means with a certain unreflective intrepidity. Once again, the conditions under which we have to live in time are stronger than our own view of them. They do not allow even the most unreflective to posit their future absolutely in the form in which they think they know it in the present. So we cannot say without qualification that the reflective are altogether superior to the unreflective.

But we are not left in this dilemma. We do not have to choose between these two equally futile attempts to escape our being in time.

On the contrary, we can count on the fact that the will and act of God are the meaning and ground not only of our being in time generally, but also of our being in the future. True, the future stands at every moment under the question whether it will be our future, our time at all. But in the first instance it is not we who will be in the next moment, to-morrow, or a year hence. It is God, our Creator, Deliverer and Sustainer, who will still be for us and faithful to us. In the first instance it is He in the heights, and then we in our depths. But between Him and us there will be a connexion, for in His eternity—it is the eternity of the living God—there is also a genuine Then. Not, of course, a Then under threat of extinction ! For God there is no " not yet " which might possibly be a threatening " never." But as He was and is He also will be. As He was, is and will be simultaneously without limit or separation, His eternity is original, authentic and creative time. But this eternal God will guarantee the reality of our future too (however long or short it may be), just as He guarantees it even now and has always done so. He will give it to us as the dimension of the life which He has appointed for us. He will do this because His eternity is the eternity of His will which has as its goal that we should live as His creatures and not have to perish, and therefore have our time. This is what God will also will for us in our long or short future. We can know this for a fact because He wills it now, always willed it, and never did not will it. Never did not do it—we must say even more strongly. For He was never not our Creator, Father and Redeemer. He never did not do what had to be done for us to have time for life. He did it as He initiated our particular time, and before He initiated it, as He initiated all time and before He initiated it in His eternal counsel. And with the same definiteness He will do it in our particular future in all the future, and beyond the end of all time in His eternity. Thus He will be over us, for us and with us, as we shall also be in all the uncertainty of our future being.

Furthermore, it is in relation to what God will be and will and do that we too shall be in the short or long time which is our future. And as we are invited to see the eternity of God, not abstractly, but as His eternity for our future, so too we must consider our own future, our being in this tense, not abstractly, but in relation to the eternity in which God is also future to us. What shall we be ? Come what may, we shall be what we shall be under and with God ; what we can and may and must be on the basis of His eternal future, i.e., those who are loved by Him, to whom He will give time to live. It is because it is given for this purpose as the dimension of our life that in the future tense it is the time which we do not yet have, and of which we do not know how long we shall have it. We do not have it yet because we do not need it yet. And we do not know how long we shall have it because we do not know how long we shall need it. But it will be given, and will really be our time, as the time which we need for the life given us by God. We can be sure of this because there is no " not yet " with Him. He always is, even though we are not yet. He is always the Creator and Lord of time, of the time we need for the life which He will also give us. That is why it does not matter that it will end in a catastrophe, and that in view of its approaching end it stands always and inevitably under a threat. If God is taken into account, we have to say that even in the future tense time is a reality which is assured and which assures our life. It is the framework of our being, and its end will not be terror and cannot terrify. This could not be said, of course, without God. The end of our time could then be understood only as a catastrophe, and our whole being in its movement towards this end as a threatened being. But we are not without God. The same God who has loved us and loves us will still love us as surely as He is eternal. And this means that even our future being, as the object of His love which He will not let slip, is real before Him and therefore in truth in all its allotted and salutary compass and to its appointed limit. Come what may, it is genuine space for life. *Amabar, amor,* and therefore *amabor.* We not only have lived and do live, but we shall live. We ourselves cannot guarantee this, but God does. The fact that our time hastens towards its end would be intolerable only if we wanted to be God and therefore eternal instead of real men under and with God, and therefore temporal. And the future tense of our time could terrify us only if we had to be men without God, strangers to His covenant. But there is no natural urge compelling us to be without God and strangers to His covenant. As created by God, human reality has been embraced by God and His covenant from all eternity. It is the case, then, that we may have our time—our whole time, and therefore our time in the future tense as given by God. Its end is not a terrifying end, but the goal which He has set us. And therefore its course is not an unending terror, but the way on which He is always before and over us as well as behind.

From this standpoint we may again ask, as in respect of our present and past, what is really meant when we say that we shall be. Since God will be over us and for us then, in every " then " allotted, including the present in which we shall have no further future, this obviously means that in all our long or short future this side the goal we shall always be under His judgment. We do not yet know—this is the particular nature of our future being—to what this judgment will refer. Even less can we control that which will come under His judgment. As we try to gaze and reach into to-morrow from the vantage point of to-day, this to-morrow comes upon us dark and triumphant : dark because we cannot really see it for all our inklings and hopes and fears ; and triumphant because, although we prepare ourselves to meet it, it cuts right across our preparations, according to its own will and not ours. In spite of our good resolutions we shall make innumerable mistakes both old and new. Our plans and projects will be thwarted by all kinds of obstacles, expected or unexpected. But shall we not also realise positive possibilities which now seem to be dormant in us and of which we are not aware ? Light will come from expected and unexpected quarters. Help will be proffered which is both anticipated and astonishing. And it will all develop and inter-weave so concretely that when it comes we shall be as much surprised by it as a child turning over the pages of a new picture-book. It will all be as it will be. But again, it will all be before God. No reflective-ness or unreflectiveness on our part will alter the fact that it is before God and therefore genuinely real. We shall still have to thank Him for everything, and answer to Him for everything. And if our future gives advance notice of itself in our present in the pictures we make of it, if even now we begin to be what we shall be, we must still remember and insist that even our present is placed anew before God and under Him. No alien fate is laid upon us as a burden to be reduced, borne or rejected. It is not we who have to decide what our future will be as we advance into it. It is not we who have to decide what form it will take. For God has already arranged it, and the point of our stepping into the future, and therefore our present in which we initiate this step, is to look for this arrangement of God.

With this in mind, it is possible and necessary to return to our dilemma, to the question whether it is better and more advisable to take the unreflective or the reflective way in relation to the future.

Surely the unreflective way is right, and it is better and more advisable to step unreflectively from to-day into to-morrow, if we must fix our eyes on God alone. After all, we move towards the more imminent or distant end appointed, and therefore we always move into a future rushing on to this end. If this provokes concern, it is not our concern but God's In other words, we can cast our care on Him, freeing ourselves from the reflectiveness to which it gives rise by realising that it is really His concern, that He cares for us, giving us time and its end, and therefore time which rushes on to this end. Why should this frighten us ? Surely this gives us firm ground on which to set our feet confidently and therefore unreflectively as long as we can. Whatever happens, we shall have God with us and over us. That being so, there is firm ground ahead which will certainly carry us. There is room for us to live and move and have our being. Why should we not proceed with confidence ? And if the judgment of God is already over us, why should we not be allowed and commanded calmly and confidently to show a little interest to-day in the things of to-morrow ? Why should we not plan ahead a little so as to be ready for the forward movement which we are about to make. There is no need to suppose that we are masters of our future, or that we posit it absolutely in the form in which we conceive it. But we are surely free to live to-day responsibly for to-morrow. Is not this the freedom to pray the fourth petition of the Lord's Prayer : " Give us *to-day* our bread for *to-morrow* " ? For to-morrow, even if it be our last, we shall still be under God and with Him. It cannot, therefore, be wrong, or illusory, if to-day—since we unavoidably live to-day for to-morrow— we make the unthinking presupposition that we may and should do this, that it is not arbitrary or presumptuous to do so.

It is certainly not arbitrary or presumptuous to do so. It is not a flight from God into the idea of a beneficent fate or chance as the clue to life's perpetuation. Nor is it a flight from God into the idea of our own mastery as the key to our preservation. An unreflecting consideration and apprehension of the future—limited by all kinds of reflection—is justifiable if it is confidence that the future is that which God gives, and this confidence alone. It is justifiable so long as we remember that in our future we shall be judged and limited by God : not overshadowed by our end, but irradiated by the goal He has set for us. This unreflectiveness which is legitimate and commanded, wholesome and cheerful, has nothing whatever to do with optimism or pessimism. The only thing that we can do with our anxiety for the future is to cast it resolutely upon God. Otherwise all the counter-arguments to this cheerful view are back in full force. It is mere frivolity or even paralysis, day-dreaming or intolerable affliction, and either way an idle and futile pretence, if we expect to maintain ourselves in life even in the near future, even to-morrow. We can only approach this kind of success as a gift. But we can approach it with confidence as a gift actually given, knowing that God will be over and with our future being. So much is undoubtedly said in favour of unreflectiveness, and by way of a summons to it.

But there is also something to be said for the reflective way, even from the same standpoint, and we have to realise that from this standpoint we are summoned to reflectiveness. The being which we approach as future being is not any kind of being, but again our being under God and with Him. It is His judgment which will be pro-nounced over us at the end, and under which we continually stand as we move towards this end. That He constantly gives us life, and the time needed for it, means that we are again and again, and in the end conclusively, challenged to gratitude towards Him and responsi-bility before Him. To be a man is to live before God and therefore in this gratitude and responsibility. There are indeed good reasons for fearing this future. Indeed, if our knowledge of the God who is over and with us banishes all false fears of the future, enabling us to live unreflectively, the very same knowledge evokes and inspires the necessary and serious fear of God Himself. If we are to continue to live within our appointed limits, how can we stand if it is wholly a matter of standing before God ? What are all other anxieties com-pared with the anxiety which must overwhelm us from this quarter ? Are they not all removed in order that we may bear this particular anxiety? It is an indisputable fact that we shall have further time only to live under God and with Him. And at the end we shall be asked whether and how far we have really done this. Indeed, this is the question which is with us all the way. And to-day, coming from the past, we stand in our present before advance into the future, and therefore before this question, as those we now are. All to-day's preparation for to-morrow should correspond to the fact that we shall always have to answer this question of our gratitude and responsibility towards God to-morrow, and that finally the totality of our being in time will have to form a suitable answer to this question. But how can we expect to stand when in relation to our past we can only fall back upon the prayer : *quod vixi tege*? This is not just ordinary pessimism. How insecure our whole position is, and how comical and empty all optimism and activism, emerges in all its frightfulness at the very point where we are summoned so urgently to be unreflective. This is one aspect of the matter which is quite incontrovertible.

But again we must turn the page if we are to see the decisive aspect of the reflectiveness which is also clearly and inexorably required of us. The infinite terror without which we cannot go into the future must be fear of God Himself, and not of an idea of God invented or constructed by ourselves, not even of the idea of a Supreme Judge of absolute holiness and sovereignty. Otherwise it would not be genuine or lasting. Otherwise—for man is astonishingly fickle and powerful in relation to his own ideas—it could be only too easily cast off. But it is fear of God Himself only when we clearly realise that as our Judge, to whose judgment we move every day and conclusively on our last day, He is also the One who from the very outset has intervened and made Himself responsible for us in His almighty mercy. We shall be in the hands of the Lord who from all eternity has been our Covenant-partner and Friend. This will make it impossible for us to escape terror before Him. It will not leave us even the line of retreat which is still left open by any idea of a supreme Judge that we might easily construct for ourselves. It will enable us to stand even under the whole weight of the question addressed to us. Indeed, it does so now. It is this which makes the question serious. The God who is gracious from eternity is the One who calls us even now to gratitude and responsibility, and who will continue to do so to-morrow and every day of our lives. God is not mocked. He is the God who is really to be feared. And it is to Him—the God to whom, looking back over our past, we can only pray for the forgiveness which He does not owe but will not refuse—that we must render an account. It is with Him that we have to do in our genuinely established and unending concern about this future reckoning. That we for our part will be completely unequal to this grace of His is the basis of the only concern about the future which really matters. And in the light of this concern—far surpassing even the religiously most profound pessimism, e.g., of a Schopenhauer—it is right to be reflective concerning our future being. And true reflectiveness on this basis will be distinguished from a false and finally relative one by the fact that it is fruitful and practical. If the gracious God is the Judge to whom we move we cannot be mesmerised before him like a rabbit before a giant snake or a condemned criminal before his executioners. This might be the case if we were dealing with the idea of a supreme Judge, and then at the last moment we might discover that the danger is not so great after all. But this is not so when we have to do with the real God who will judge us in His grace. We cannot escape Him, because all our attempts at evasion cannot alter the fact that He loves us, that we belong to Him, that we are engaged and committed to Him, and must render account to Him. And our terror before Him is not one in which we are transfixed, but the terror of a movement in which we unconditionally acknowledge that He will always be in the right and we in the wrong, yet in which we shall demand that His divine right prevail over our human wrong, His grace over our ingratitude, His word over our poor response ; and that even though we are sinners who have not merited the honour, and are quite incapable of doing so, we may be continually taken into His service. We shall really be terrified before this real God. We shall never fondly imagine that we can stand before Him, or that in the end we are not utterly dependent upon the fact that He is always this gracious God and Judge, even as and though we cannot stand before Him. We cannot escape the fear of Him by trying to forget that with each step into the future we are face to face with Him. The reflectiveness in which we venture this step will always consist practically in the fact that we place ourselves in His hands just as we are, with all the inadequacy and failure which we have no prospect of overcoming, holding ourselves in readiness for Him even as the sinners we are. As we prayed *quod vixi tege* in respect of the past, so we must pray *quod vivam rege* in respect of the future. It is only in this movement that we are really afraid of this real God. However serious our reflectiveness in face of the expected judgment, if it did not take place in this movement it would merely be a new form of the bad old unreflectiveness which is out of the question if we really expect to be under God and with Him in our future. For in this movement, too, we really let Him be our faithful God, who loves us from all eternity and therefore reliably intervenes for us, who genuinely cares and therefore provides for our gratitude and responsibility ; and we therefore enter into the validity and power of that genuine and well-founded unreflectiveness. " Teach me to live according to thy good-pleasure "—with this song of praise in our hearts and on our lips, we are not only genuinely afraid of our future under God and with Him, but we confess a genuine fearlessness in which, in spite of even our future inadequacy and failure, we can find comfort and even joy in relation to the future.

This, then, is how man is in the time given him by God ; this is how he is before God in his present and moving from his past and into his future. The time which we have been considering in these three tenses is the time created by God. We have not been speaking of God's eternity, but of our time as God created it and gave it to us ; yet not of what it must become and be on the presupposition of our alienation from God, but of time as God gave it to man in creation, and as He constantly renews it in allowing him to live ; of the time which as the form of his existence belongs no less to his natural reality than the fact that man is the soul of his body. Always against the background of God's eternity, we have tried step by step to isolate human time—the time created and given by God—from its distorted and obscured manifestation, and to study and present it in and for itself. We began with an analysis of time in the distorted and sinister form we know only too well ; and we found that Hölderlin has the last word on that subject. We then proceeded to analyse time in the reality in which it may be seen as the time given us by God.

In conclusion, however, we do well to remember the presupposition on which alone the second analysis can be meaningful and its result— a view of real time—tenable and secure. We reached this view by taking into account at every stage—starting from the present and looking back from it to the past and forward to the future—the factor which was left out of account in the line of thought which reached its zenith in Hölderlin. We understood time and our being in time as real by considering it as the form of human existence willed and created by God. We thus purged the concept of time from all the abstractions by which it is inevitably confused and darkened when the divine will and action are left out of account and time is not understood as His creation. All the way through we have expressly taken account of God's presence and gift as the open secret of time. We understood man, and therefore his time, as God's creation. Only in this way could we regard it as real. But we must remember how we came to introduce the new factor which enabled us to banish those abstractions and therefore to think and speak of past, present and future as we did. We did not do it merely by introducing the word " God " into the discussion and treating it as an Open Sesame to every problem. If God were merely a word or systematic principle, if we had merely " introduced " Him, or taken Him into account, or made use of Him in our thinking, our second, revised analysis of the concept of time would have been a web of speculation, revealed as such, and scattered, by the first puff of wind. The first and obvious view would then have returned with its absurd infinity (the infinity of its contradictions, impracticability and sterility), and all its emptiness and cheerlessness would have seemed to be more illuminating than the alternative worked out with the help of the idea of God. The mere thought of God as such—even the thought of the living God, to which we have tried to keep as faithfully as possible—is of no avail. No bare concept is adequate to accomplish or even clearly to indicate the inversion depicted.

To recall the clear indication and actual accomplishment of this inversion, we must return to our starting point. We first established that the existence of the man Jesus in time is our assurance that time as the form of human existence is willed and created by God and given to man, and is therefore real. Our whole presentation rests ultimately, not on itself, but on this assurance. We start with the name of Jesus when we introduce the new factor. It is in His light that we can and must see time so very differently, as real time. It is necessary to introduce this new factor because in Jesus it is already present, even in our reflections on the subject. If we leave Him out of the picture only for a moment, our thinking on the subject may have all kinds of other results but it will not enable us to see time as it really is. In Jesus God is not just a word or a systematic principle, but the reality and *prima veritas* which of itself sets itself at the head of all other thoughts and gives them a specific direction and content. In Jesus God is eternal, i.e., eternal in the only way that really matters here—eternal for us. He is this in a twofold sense. First He is not far from us in His eternity, but near us ; not turned away from us, but turned to us ; not indifferent or hostile, but gracious, the One who loves us. And second, He is not just hidden from us in His eternity, but also manifest. The " Lord of Time," as the man Jesus came to be known by us in the first sub-section ; He who is and was and comes, is also the eternal God, who is for us and manifest to us.

This Lord of time stands at the beginning of all our attempted thinking about time, ruling and establishing, illuminating and proving. In Him it is the case, and by Him we may know, that time is real and that we have it. In Him God utters His gracious and saving contradiction of man without God and therefore of a concept of time without God, checking self-perverting and ignorant man and arresting the development of all false and cheerless conceptions of time. In Him who, as the eternal Son of God, is the Lord of time, there is shown to us who are not the eternal children of God, and therefore not lords of time, that time is real, that we are in this real time, and how this is the case. As His time, it is the time created and controlled by God and given to men. And we live on the basis of this reality and think on the basis of the promise which it gives. In Him we see ourselves as God willed and created us ; in the nature in which God has not ceased to see us, and which has not therefore ceased to be our true nature in spite of all the disruption and error caused by sin. Christology gives rise to a definite anthropology in respect of the concept of time too ; the anthropology of the man who is under and with God in his time, not of a second Jesus, but of the man who exists with the one Jesus (as the recipient of the divine promise addressed to him in the man Jesus) in the time created and given him by God. This is the man who is seen and understood in the light of the fact that the contradiction uttered in the man Jesus was not for nothing, that Jesus did not fight and suffer and triumph for all men in vain. The man seen and understood in this light is natural man. But he is more. The man delivered and kept by Jesus, translated into eternal fellowship with God, and one day to be manifested beyond all time, is certainly more than natural man, who as such is exposed to the perils of sin, disintegration and error. If Jesus had not fought and suffered and triumphed for him, man would be a very different creature. But He has in fact fought and suffered and triumphed for him, and therefore even as a natural man he is to be seen and understood in the light of His resurrection. Neither ontological godlessness nor ontological inhumanity is to be ascribed to him—even in respect of the temporality of his existence. It cannot, therefore, be said of him that in himself he is nothing, or that he exists in an empty time and therefore has no real time. It can only be said that he is at least threatened by this peril—for it doth not yet appear what he shall be—and that he would undoubtedly have succumbed to it if it had not been divinely contradicted. But it has been contradicted. Jesus is risen and is the Lord of time. And therefore we can say positively of man that in the true nature in which God sees him he is not destroyed, but has real time and may live in it.

This conclusion, developed in our second analysis, rests on the promise given us in Jesus, on His resurrection and lordship over time. For on this depends the fact that we can relate man's time to God's eternity, and that God's eternity can and must be seen and understood as His eternity for us, God Himself as the Creator and Giver of our time, and therefore our being in time as a reality. All this depends on the reality of the divine being, intervention and work for us as it has taken place in Jesus. All speculation—even that which is based on a perfect idea of God, let alone any other—will inevitably end in a vicious circle. But in theology we are not free to ignore the reality of this divine being, intervention and work, or to start our thinking at any other point. And if we make this our starting point, we shall find it possible and necessary, compelling and illuminating, to break through and invert the concept of time along the lines attempted. Yet we shall not forget that this starting point is not a formula to be adopted and appropriated at will, but an actual encounter with the reality to which theological presentation can only point.

3. ALLOTTED TIME

In the preceding sub-section we have been looking at time as it were from the inside. We have examined the structure, way and movement in which man was and is and will be. We have been occupied with the problem, the riddle, posed by these three forms of time, the question of the reality of time raised at all three points and in their mutual relationship. We have answered this question by understanding time in all its three forms as the time created by God, as the divinely given space for human life.

But this is only one side of the matter. We shall now take it for granted. We shall assume that man has time, that he is really engaged in this movement. To live as a man is to be in time, to be temporal—in relation to God's eternity—because God is eternal, not merely in and for Himself, but as the Creator for His creature, man ; because as the Eternal He is the Giver and Guarantor of his time.

But the fact that it is " his " time, the time of the creature, the time of man, opens up a new aspect of the subject. We shall now consider time as it were from the outside, as the totality of that movement, as the succession of those moments of transition in which we continually come and go, continually leaving ourselves behind us and having ourselves before us. We shall now consider it as the series of moments, and the acts which fill them, in which we are continually present " between the times." In this totality, succession and sequence it is our creaturely, human time. For in this totality, succession and sequence, in its inter-connexion, it is the sphere of human life, of the life of man and men. God gives us time, and we have it, as we need it for life and may actually have it for this purpose—no more and no less. And so this space is not unlimited, but limited. The totality, succession and series have both a beginning and an end. It is the self-enclosed form of human reality which can actually be observed from outside, if only in intellectual perception, just as *mutatis mutandis* man himself, to the extent that he is the soul of his body, can be observed from outside in physical space, and therefore in physical perception. As in the latter sphere he does not have unlimited space, but supremely limited, so it is in respect of the fulfilment of his life. His time is the allotted span, i.e., the limited space, which he needs for this fulfilment and which is given him for this purpose. This span begins at a certain point, lasts for a certain period and finally comes to an end. Man is, therefore, in this span, and not before or after it. It is only in this way, as allotted time, that time is his time. At a certain point this movement began, and it continues and constantly repeats itself until it finally reaches its goal and climax and comes to an end. At this point we have ourselves wholly before us and not at all behind us. Now we have ourselves both behind and before us. One day we shall have ourselves only behind us and no more before us. For at a certain point life began. Now we are somewhere in the middle or before or after the middle. One day it will be over. This is how we are in time. It is our allotted time, and no other.

This raises the new problem to which we must now turn. It is by no means self-evident that human life requires for its development, and therefore acquires and has, only this limited space. Human life demands permanency, or rather duration. Human life would always like to regard itself as an unfathomable, inexhaustible reality. Human life as such will always abhor the suggestion that once it was not and one day it will be no longer, and that it is really to consist in this fulfilment which has a beginning and end, and has duration only between these points. Human life protests against this " only." It protests against the fact that the space for this development is to be that allotted span. And, pending further clarification, we may allow that its demand for duration and protest against the barrier set by the allotting of time are neither mistaken nor presumptuous. Indeed, we must say that it would have no knowledge of itself if it did not know anything of this demand and therefore this protest, if it did not have any question at this point, if it could be readily content with the allotment of the time given it, if it could approve and even welcome it with joy.

As we shall very soon see, it is not simply a matter of accepting this allot-ment of our time, but of welcoming it with gratitude and joy. But we cannot start at this point. It can only be a deduction from an answer which we give to that question. It ought not to suppress the question itself, otherwise we should fail to appreciate the significance of the answer which we are actually given. If it is not a deduction from the answer which we are actually given, if the protest is silenced and transformed into its opposite, the position is far from satisfactory. It is part of the disorder occasioned by the fall if nothing is known of the longing for duration, or the allotment of a set span is not felt to be a threat, or there is a resigned acceptance of the fact that we can only have allotted time. Resignation of this kind is incompatible with the fact that life is created by God. It is an acceptance of sin and its consequent punishment as though they were our original and authentic destiny. It is acquiescence in a condition in which we cannot and should not acquiesce. It casts doubt on the unfathomable and inexhaustible character of our own reality, treating it as if it were a matter of indifference, or even making it appear to be terrifying and unwelcome. The allotment of a set time ceases to be a problem crying out for an answer, and becoming some-thing to be accepted with more or less complacency. But human life is ignorant of its own true nature when it accepts the fall as its original and authentic destiny, and therefore when it is not troubled by the demand for duration and finds no problem in the allotment of its time.

The reason why human life must be conceived as an unfathomable and inexhaustible reality is that from the vertical standpoint it is created by God and for Him, while from the horizontal it is created in relationship to other men. From both standpoints it is human life and remains so even when it falls and denies its true nature in both directions. For man belongs to God. And he belongs to his fellows. Divinity and humanity are his original and authentic determination. In both these directions human life demands no less than perfection. In both it demands duration, for its determination rests upon its creation by God and is therefore enduring. " Enduring " means without limitation or lack. It means inviolably self-subsistent. But surely there is a serious violation, an obvious limitation and a clear lack in the duration of human life, if its only dimension is an allotted span of time. As though in both directions it could be satisfied in practice with something less than perfection! As though it could develop according to its determination, and do itself justice, in either or both directions under this limitation! As though, in view of its determination, it could endure the idea that once it was not and one day it will no longer be! Why not always? What but an unlimited, permanent duration can be adequate for the fulfilment of this determination?

If all this were only an abstract desire for life, life hungering for life and never satisfied, but always beating angrily against the barrier set up by the fact that its time is allotted, that it once began and some day must end—if this were all, it would be easy to dismiss the question as foolish and the protest as unjustified. It would simply be necessary to point out that man has no right to an extension of life, no claim to more than an allotted span, merely for the sake of continuing in life.

It would then be easy to show him that in this world there is no life which lasts for ever. Everything has its time, man included. Instead of demanding an unlimited life, it would be better for him to accept the fact that his life, with all its opportunities, is neither unfathomable nor inexhaustible. It is in no way destined to last for ever. So he had better be modest and cease craving for more than a set span of time, which is to cry for the moon. The craving of sinful man, i.e., of man who considers his life and his desire and hunger for life apart from his determination, his divinity and humanity, is indeed futile. Hence there is no great difficulty in silencing it. But again this does not mean that the problem is removed. It may still come up again in a new form even when silenced in the old.

But human life is more than the satisfying of an abstract craving for life. Man can, of course, pretend and protest that he lives in this abstraction. Indeed, he does this, and in the most dreadful way. But even when it seems to be lived in this abstraction, human life is still primarily and ultimately a fulfilment of the determination given with its divine creation. Even in its wildest perversions and distortions, it is human life, and has the determination to be lived for God and one's fellow-men. To be unfathomable and inexhaustible is proper to it, as its craving for duration is legitimate. It rightly protests against the fact that it has an allotted span of time, for if it is to fulfil its determination it would seem to need unending time. And often the demand for unlimited space may well be most insistent at the very point where man is most estranged from his determination in both directions, where he denies it most emphatically in his life, for in this case he constantly robs himself of the time he actually has, thus showing himself all the more plainly that he has too little time, far too little time, to live his real life. However that may be, when the question is raised on this ground it cannot be so easily suppressed or dismissed. There can, of course, be no question of man's original and authentic determination conferring upon him a right or claim to duration. Where man insists that duration is his by right in virtue of this determination, and where his protest against the allotment of time is directed against his Creator, he is guilty of folly and presumption. The creature can make no demands on the Creator. But supposing that in this demand and question and protest man does not make any demand, but appeals to the promise given with his creation in relationship with God, to the gift and task given him with his creation in relationship to his fellow-men ? Supposing he does not present his own right and claims before God, but simply pleads God's own Word ? Is not God's Word—both as a summons to God Himself and a direction to fellow-men—the real reason why human life must regard itself as an unfathomable and inexhaustible reality ? Does not God's Word provide the real reason why duration must be demanded, why there never seems to be enough time, why the allotment of a particular span is a problem ? Does not the difficulty which confronts us have its source in the fact that our twofold determination by the Word of God is revealed to us, and that we are deaf and disobedient to this Word if it is no problem to us that we have so little time, that we have only this limited span of life ? Of life ? Life under the Word of God demands duration and therefore more than an allotted span. For it never seems as though it can have enough time to fulfil the determination which it is given under the Word of God, and every " only," every limit, can only mean a lack or non-fulfilment. Raised from this standpoint—as it always is at root—it is not a question which we can dismiss by saying that it ought not to be asked. On the contrary, we must try to answer it from the same angle.

The question is undoubtedly right to assume that human life demands duration in the light of the determination given in and with its creation. The demand is not unwarrantable. In fact, it would be an unwarrantable denial of itself not to demand duration. In the light of its determination it has the appearance of, and is indeed, an unfathomable and inexhaustible life. No depth from which it comes is deep enough for it ; no height to which it strives high enough ; no space in which it develops is wide enough. How can it ever be adequately either life for God according to its promise, or life with its fellows according to its gift and task ? In both these directions it may and will and must endure. It has an urge for perfection ; it is impatient with all limitations ; it storms all barriers ; it is by nature the denial of all denials. Man as he really is, man under God and with his fellowmen, cannot accept the fact that once he was not under and therefore for God, and with and therefore for his fellows, and that one day he will be so no longer. Man as he really is, as God created him, stands questioning before those frowning walls of rock which enclose him in the narrow gorge of being, and seem to fling at him the twofold taunt :

Once you were not ! and : One day you will be no more ! But what about his determination then ? And since his life stands wholly under his determination, what about his life ? What will happen when duration is denied it, when the path to perfection is cut off, when it is neither an unfathomable nor inexhaustible life ? How is it to be lived then ? How is it to suffice when in spite of its determination it is only this short—and for other reasons very disturbed and broken— approach to God and one's fellows. The question is justified if at this point it takes account of a demand necessarily inherent and proper to human life, theologically understood.

But it is also right to make the further assumption, viz., that it needs time as its dimension, and that this time is allotted. It has margins. It has a definite measurement, which we may depreciate, which can really be measured very differently from our depreciatory estimate, but which is in any case a definite, limited and fundamentally calculable measure.

1. God also lives in His time. But His time is eternity, which has no fixed span, no margins, no other measure but Himself. Eternity is not time without beginning or end. Time is the mode of existence of the creature. To identify eternity with time without beginning and end would be to attribute to it an idealised form of creaturely existence. This would be wrong ; for to say eternity is to say God. And God does not live in an idealised form of creaturely existence. God Himself is not only the ground and content but also the form of His existence. To the extent that He is His own form of existence He is eternal, and He is in eternity as in His time. When we say this, we say only that He is in Himself. Hence in His eternity He is indeed the Creator of time, but as its Creator He is the One who was, and as such is and will be ; who is, and as such was and will be ; who will be, and as such was and is. In His eternity He is beginning and middle and end. He is not, therefore, apart from all these. If He were, we should have another false definition of eternity. Eternity is not time-lessness. It is beginning, middle and end in fulness, for it is all three simultaneously. It is always the first and second as it is also the third. Thus God is His own dimension. And this dimension underlies, conditions and includes that of His creature, so that that of His creature is always His own, and where His creature is, He is also. But His dimension has no fixed span, no margins, no measure but Himself.

Man on the other hand lives in the time created and given him by God. If he were God and not man, the allotment of his time would not be a problem, for his time would not be allotted. For he would be eternal. But that is a dream, and a bad one at that. Since man is man and not God, and he is not therefore eternal, the dimension which he is left, and over which he has no control (as God has over His, because He is His own dimension), is created time, which in distinction from the eternity of the Creator has a beginning, middle and end which are not simultaneous but separate, distinct and successive, so that it has margins and a measure in its beginning and end, and is thus allotted time, the time between its beginning and end.

But these boundaries are necessarily the boundaries of human life. This brings us to that narrow gorge with precipitous walls on either side. Where does our life come from ? From its beginning, i.e., the beginning of its time, before which it did not exist. Where is it going ? Towards its end, i.e., the end of its time, after which it will be no longer. Why not ? Because it is creaturely life in this its creaturely dimension. Because by acquiring creaturely time it acquires as its time the dimension appropriate to it as a creaturely life. The life of God requires and has a different dimension. For the life of God is not only unfathomable and inexhaustible, but self-grounded and self-creative, welling up from within itself. That is why it is eternal life, and why eternity is its dimension. In clear distinction from His, our life too acquires the dimension it needs, a dimension which fits and suits it like a tailor-made garment. *Suum cuique !* The proper dimension for the life of the creature which is not self-grounded or self-creative, welling up from within itself, but has its basis in the life of God, is the time in which beginning and end are distinct, and therefore constitute its boundaries.

Human life as created by the eternal God has its proper boundaries in respect of which we must speak as the Bible does in relation to man : " They are like grass which groweth up. In the morning it flourisheth, and groweth up ; in the evening it is cut down, and withereth " (Ps. 90⁵ ; cf. Isa. 40⁶ ; Ps. 102¹² ; Job 14²). " Behold, thou hast made my days as an handbreadth ; and mine age is as nothing before thee : verily every man at his best state is altogether vanity. Surely every man walketh in a vain shew " (Ps. 39⁵). " We bring our years to an end as a tale that is told " (Ps. 90⁹ : R.V. Marg : " as a sound or sigh "). " For ye are a vapour, that appeareth for a little time, and then vanisheth away " (Jas. 4¹⁴).

Is not our question already answered when we say that God has His dimension, unallotted eternity, and we ours, allotted time ? Yet the fact is that man stands in relation to God. He has a life with God in virtue of the determination given in and with his creation. Hence he cannot abandon the demand that He should endure and burst the limits of temporality. He cannot possibly acquiesce in a *suum cuique*. That he has with his life in time that promise, gift and task from the eternal God is the cause of the discontent of which we have been speaking, and the reason why it cannot be stilled by a reminder that God is God and man is man. This reminder can only prepare the ground for the answer we require.

2. But we advance a step further if we grasp the following point. Is it really the case that the legitimate demand of human life for limitless duration, its character as a striving after perfection which

can brook no denial, would be genuinely served if unlimited dimension and therefore infinite rather than allotted time were placed at its disposal ? We are now assuming that human life is content to be creaturely and not to be the eternal life of God. We are assuming that it has no desire to leap over this boundary. For if it were divine and eternal life it could not entertain such a desire at all. By the very acknowledgement of this desire it resigns itself to being a life different from the life of God. On this presupposition—and assuming that it is not content with a set span as its dimension—its only option is to want the idealised creaturely dimension which we mentioned above, i.e., an enduring time without beginning or end. We have met the idea of infinite time before. It is the expression of the infinite embarrassment into which man without God is plunged by the question of the reality of his being in the present, past and future. Considering the source, we have no great confidence in the notion. But let us assume for the moment that it has some substance in it. Time is then an unlimited dimension in which human life can develop as an infinite quantity, in the form of a process without beginning or end. It thus has the opportunity to do justice to its determination to live for God and for others.

But would it really do justice to it in this form ? Would it really correspond to man's legitimate craving for duration and fulfilment ? This would obviously be the case only if an infinite quantity of human life could guarantee a duration adequate to its determination and the perfection to which it aspires ; only if it could guarantee that in its relation to God and to others, from the standpoint of its divinity and humanity, it would be the life which it ought to be in correspondence with its determination. It is understandable that it should require and demand time for this purpose, and it receives it. It is understandable that it should require much time rather than little ; that it should rather be a long life than a short ; that in any case it wants a sufficient measure of days and years for its development as the fulfilment of its destiny.

This is the meaning of the " long " life promised to the children of Israel (Deut. 4[40], 25[15]) in the promised land on condition that they remain loyal to the covenant with the God who will bring them into this land. This is what is meant when the bloodthirsty and deceitful men are told that they shall not live out half their days (Ps. 55[23]), and even the righteous complains : " He weakened my strength in the way ; he shortened my days " (Ps. 102[23]), and prays : " O my God, take me not away in the midst of my days " (Ps. 102[24]). It also explains the jubilation in Eccles. 11[7f.] : " Truly the light is sweet, and a pleasant thing it is for the eyes to behold the sun. Yea, if a man live many years, let him rejoice in them all." In particular, it is in this sense that long life is attributed to the king (e.g., Ps. 21[4]), and, in the familiar exaggeration of courtly language (which must not be taken literally), the salutation even goes the length of wishing the king should live for ever (e.g., 1 Kings 1[31]). It is also in the same sense that the Old Testament (Gen. 5[4f.]) recalls the exemplary longevity of the patriarchs from Adam to Noah, Methuselah (v. 27) having reached the astounding age of 969 !

But if even the idea of a "long" life is a doubtful one in relation to its determination—"Because thy lovingkindness is better than life" (Ps. 63³)—"long" life is certainly not life without beginning or end, nor are many years the same as everlasting time. And in any case it is hard to see how everlasting life can guarantee duration and fulfilment in relation to its determination. Short or long time is no guarantee of this duration and fulfilment. Time is only the *conditio sine qua non*, only the indispensable opportunity, both for life itself, and for the realisation of its legitimate craving for duration and fulfilment. And for the latter and decisive factor, for the realization of this craving, even an infinite quantity of human life in a correspondingly infinite time is no guarantee. If life as such, in the light of its determination, is God's good gift to man, the normal man will not only desire but seriously pray that the gift should not be niggardly, that his life should be long and not short. But even length of life, and therefore a great or infinite number of days, cannot guarantee real duration and fulfilment. Long life and an ample measure of time can only mean more opportunities. And an infinite measure of human life can only mean an infinite number of opportunities. But this is not what human life really asks if it has a true understanding of itself. It does not ask merely for the constantly repeated and ultimately infinite possibility of duration and fulfilment, of perfection in accordance with its determination. It does not ask merely for more and ultimately infinite space, although it undoubtedly needs this space and the opportunity to reach out for duration and fulfilment. What it does ask for is the reality of duration and fulfilment, the removal of the restrictions which stand in the way of this realisation, the negation of everything which negates it. No infinity of space or everlasting time can achieve or even guarantee this negation, this removal of restrictions, this realisation, which consists in the perfection of the relationship to God and fellowman to which it aspires. Even if it were in unlimited time, this could only mean the possibility of a constant reaching out to this perfection. In relation to what he really asks for, because he really lacks it, man would still be no better off on the presupposition of the reality of this notion of infinite time than in the allotted span in which he has actually to live. We may thus conclude that no serious renunciation is demanded of him, no resignation in face of a blessing which he may rightly ask and seek, if he accepts the fact that he does not have to live in an everlasting time, which is in any case illusory and invented only in the illusion of a dilemma, but in the real, allotted time created by God and proper to him as the creature of God. He does not lose anything in so doing. In his temporally restricted time he has only opportunities to live up to his determination. But even in a temporally unrestricted life he would still have no more than opportunities.

3. But we must go further. He would actually be worse off rather than better in an unrestricted life. For in a life without beginning

or end he would not only be able but compelled to aspire continually to duration and fulfilment. He would come from an infinite series of opportunities and move towards an infinite series. The actuality of his life before and behind would be a continual reaching for the perfection of the relationship to God and fellow-man. He could only be perpetually *in via*. He could never have reached the goal, and never do so. He would have infinite space before and behind, but only for his creaturely human life, which always seeks satisfaction because full satisfaction, duration, fulfilment and perfection are promised and assigned to him by creation, but which can never attain it because it is not divine. If it were without beginning or end it would always lack and seek this satisfaction, unable to escape its determination or to shake off either its divinity or humanity. Indeed, it would neither come from a beginning of this imperfection and dissatisfaction, nor move towards its end. It would be condemned to perpetual wanting and asking and therefore dissatisfaction. Could there be any better picture of life in hell than enduring life in enduring time ? Do we not have to say that life on this condition—on the assumption of the reality of that notion—would be a life of misery which it would be folly to describe as a good creation and gift of God ? But if this is so, the scales which previously seemed to be equally balanced are tipped against the notion of infinite time and in favour of the allotted time which we actually have. We do not desire a good thing but a bad if we are dissatisfied with the set span God has given us and want unrestricted space. For in it we condemn ourselves to a continuation of the unrest which gives rise to our problem. If it is a restless craving for perfection in our relationship to God and fellow-man, it cannot remain unrest, positing itself absolutely as such and finding pleasure in its perpetuation. If it is genuine unrest, it aspires beyond itself to realisation and therefore to the peace of a permanent life under God and with other men. Life as an endless process, and therefore space for it, is the last thing any one conscious of the humanity of his life can desire. Rather, he will appreciate the fact that the exact opposite, life confined to a set span, is what he has been granted, and that in comparison with that other possibility it is not only equally good but far better.

4. But the real answer to our question has still to be given. Our conclusions thus far are (1) that life in an allotted span is appropriate to man as such in his difference from God ; (2) that it is certainly not to man's disadvantage to live in a definite and not an indefinite span ; (3) that it would be fatal for him if he had to live in an indefinite instead of a definite span. The real answer to our question can be given only as we now try to show that positively as well as in relation to that other possibility it is good and salutary for man to live in allotted time.

Let us first examine what it must mean to be positively good and salutary. It must obviously mean first that the allotment of time, the fact that it begins and ends, has to lose wholly and utterly the character of a restriction and threat to human life in the development corresponding to its determination. The picture of the narrow gorge and its enclosing walls has to cease to be valid. There must be no more occasion for care and anxiety lest the natural craving for duration and perfection should not be satisfied. All our chafing against the limitations of our life must be irrelevant and superfluous. The apparent threat and restriction must be overshadowed by a mighty, beneficent promise. The rock walls must have become the protecting walls of a living-room or workshop. Fear and anxiety must have yielded to confidence and trust, dissatisfaction and complaint to praise and thanksgiving. All this, not in spite of the fact that the time given to man is allotted, but just because of it. The answer must exactly fit the question, and yet the whole prospect alter, so that the question is made meaningful and fruitful by its positive answer. But there is more to it than that. Life in our allotted span must cease to be a series of opportunities with the persistent unsatisfied demand for duration and perfection, and only the possibility of their satisfaction. With the fact that life is a set span an offer must be made which is greater and more powerful than its deepest need or the most urgent question to which it is an answer. In virtue of its beginning and end, and therefore its limits, it must be guaranteed and presented with what is necessarily demanded. The allotment of its time must actually assure it of what its time, whether long or short, or even unending, cannot of itself either achieve or assure. In virtue of its limits, it must be a life which is upheld and sustained, sheltered and provided for, and finally satisfied for all its dissatisfaction. In these limitations it must be engaged in the realisation of its determination, and find full satisfaction in this movement.

All this is true if, as in the previous sub-section, we again have reason and cause to see and set the time in which man is in relationship with God ; with the God from and to whom he may be and live as His creature. Here too, then, we shall have to divest the problem of the being of man in time of the abstraction in which we have had to regard it to see it as a question. It makes all the difference in the world whether we conceive our life as one which is abstractly limited or limited by God ; and whether we have to accept it as a general truth that our time is allotted or realise that God has given it to us in this form. If we regard the matter abstractly and generally, the question of duration and perfection leads us nowhere. It remains a question, and inevitably takes on the character of a complaint and accusation. It is no help to remember that the distinction between Creator and creature rules out any other possibility. Nor is it any good suggesting that things would be just as bad if we lived in unlimited time instead of limited. Nor is it any use convincing ourselves that it might well fare much worse with us if we lived in unlimited time. In itself, this is no reason why our limited time should be the right time for us, or why we should cheerfully and happily and gratefully accept it. It is far more likely that we shall finally and basically shake our heads and bite our lips and simply make the best of the fact that we have no option but to take what we are given—a limited life in an allotted span of time. And this simply brings us back to the starting-point. Does life really have to be like this ? And when we raise this question again we again shake what we think are our prison bars and angrily or anxiously contrast our determination with the conditions under which we are forced to live. And the question itself is still unresolved. We still do not see why things have to be as they are, and not otherwise. The whole picture changes, however, if we are not concerned abstractly and generally with the limitation of our life, but with the God who limits it ; if we are not concerned abstractly and generally with our allotted time, but with the reality of the God who allots it. In both cases, of course, we are concerned with the same thing. But the same thing now becomes quite different. It becomes so different that—if we really count on the reality of God—we are not merely confronted by the convincing and definitive answer to our question, but the question itself is resolved.

Let us assume that we do have good reasons for seeing that the time in which we are stands in direct relationship to God. The relationship consists simply in the fact that He is all round us ; that He is our Neighbour with whom we have to do on the margin of life, at the frontiers of our time. Whether it is our " not yet " or " no longer," our being or not being, He is there behind and before. Therefore the question of our Whence ? and Whither ?, of the duration and perfection of our life, cannot lead into the void, like a broken bridge in a sea of mist, but always to Him. It is not in relation to an indistinct something that we are limited, that we are called in question, with our legitimate demand for life, by the allotment of our time, that we are a vapour, a shade, a sigh, a breath, or grass which flourishes and fades, as the Bible puts it. It is in relation to Him that we are all these things. If we ask concerning the beyond, which undoubtedly compromises and threatens us even in our deepest and most legitimate concern, there is only One either behind or before us, either before our beginning or after our end. He, God, is this beyond. And God is not an " it," a " something," even the negation of a " something." He is absolutely Himself : the One who reveals Himself to us in His Word ; who, according to His own Word, is the Creator and Lord of all the reality distinct from Himself ; whose sovereignty extends even over chaos, the sphere which he purposely excluded from reality ; who, again according to His Word, intervenes and makes Himself responsible for His creature because He loves it ; whose aim, again according to His Word, is to manifest the fellowship which He willed to grant it, and continually does so, as His glory embracing even the creature. God Himself is at the point to which we look in our question how the duration and perfection of our life can be attained in the brief and transitory span which we are allotted in this time of ours. We ask concerning Him when we ask concerning this possibility. We are moved by a concern which always is His concern, and always will be. At this point, if we are not blind, or dazzled by our illusions, we shall see Him, and Him alone.

And we shall see Him indeed as the One in relation to whom our life has its limit and our time is allotted. We shall see Him as the One who has created and wills to have us within this limit and allotted span. The final longing for an unlimited life in unallotted time necessarily falls away once we realise that the limit and set span of our existence is the condition which must be fulfilled in order that He, the eternal God, may be our Counterpart and our Neighbour as described, and that we may be His counterparts and His neighbours. Limit in the creaturely dimension means a clear-cut outline and contour. Man would not be this man, here and now, the concrete subject of this history, if his life did not have this outline and contour, if it did not have these limits and boundaries. A being in unending time would be centrifugal. It would not be that of a concrete subject to whom God can be an equally concrete Counterpart and Neighbour, with whom He can enjoy communication and intercourse.

This shows us again that we are not to think even of the being of God as being in an indefinitely enduring time. If it were, it too would be centrifugal. And it would be quite nonsensical to say that God was, is and will be, that He is beginning, middle and end, because in Him there could then be no beginning or end. God, however, is eternal. That is to say, He is simultaneously and in fulness beginning, middle and end. In this respect He is utterly different from us. But in this respect too, for all the difference, He is a concrete Subject, which can encounter us and be our Neighbour on all sides.

If this is to be the case, however, we as His creatures must not be without limits or boundaries, but must be defined in our life and in our time : not abstractly and generally (in contrast to indefiniteness) ; but by Him and for Him (in contrast to an indefiniteness in which we could be concrete subjects neither by Him nor for Him) ; and therefore genuinely defined. The fact that we are in a set span is thus a benefit, an expression of the divine affirmation under which we stand, for it—and it alone—makes it possible for us to be those whom God encounters in speech and action and who, impelled by the legitimate demand based upon their determination, may look to Him, stand before Him, hear Him and have a part in His action, all their care and anxiety being removed by Him. He really cares for us by giving us an allotted span instead of unending time. For in so doing He sees to it that between Him and us there can be a relationship and fellowship. For this reason, formal if we will, it is wrong to rebel against this limitation or merely to resign ourselves angrily or anxiously to its inevitability. Even for this formal reason gratitude is the only proper response.

5. For a deeper understanding, however, we must first take up again the earlier point that it is the determination given to our life by the same God which makes the craving for duration and perfection a serious, legitimate and weighty craving as distinct from a mere desire for life. This raises the very real question whether our life is not too brief and our time too short to satisfy this demand. In the light of our determination, we are compelled to regard them as unfathomable and inexhaustible. But our determination is given by the God with whom we stand in relationship in our allotted span. And this can mean only that the matter which gives rise to our questions and complaints and protests is not left to us ; that although we have a part in it and responsibility for it, it is not our task to see to its successful accomplishment. The very fact that our life is temporally limited under its God-given determination tells us unmistakeably that with the task which He has laid upon us we are wholly in the hands of God. We are right to ask for duration and perfection in our life ; and to exist in this request. To do this is the task undoubtedly given us with our determination. Our life would not be human, it would not be the life which God has created and given us, if it were not spent in carrying out this task. But we should be wrong if we were to conclude that we ourselves can and must achieve duration and perfection by a power immanent in our life as such, that the fulfilment of our determination consists in this forceful effort and attainment. The fact that our time is allotted is an obvious negative refutation of this view. Its positive refutation is that at the very point where the appointed limit can be clearly discerned at the beginning and end of our lives, there is no prospect of infinite processes of activity and achievement, but we stand quite alone, although genuinely confronted by the eternal God who has given our life its determination, whom we are summoned to obey in our allotted span, who confronts us as the eternal God in a superiority in face of which we can only give up ourselves for lost or surrender in implicit trust. It is in Him, who has determined and limited us in this way, that we have the duration and perfection for which we rightly crave. It is in Him, in His eternal counsel and work, that God and man, and man and man, are brought into the intimate fellowship which we necessarily but disturbingly see to be the goal of our life. We misunderstand ourselves if we think that we can seek and find the object of our legitimate demand elsewhere than in Him. Indeed, we cannot demand it rightly if we do not long for Himself above even the highest good. Apart from anything else, we miss the basic thing—that with our limited life in our allotted span we can stand in confrontation and proximity to the eternal God.

If in our being in time we have to do so concretely with Him, how can we have to do concretely with anyone or anything else when it is a matter of the fulfillment of our determination ? If our determination by Him will not let us go, so that we must anxiously ask concerning its fulfilment, and can never meet its requirements in relation to Him or our fellows, our limitation by Him will not let us go either, so that even if we do all that we are commanded we can never satisfy Him, but must always recognise and confess that we are lost before Him, or rather saved and kept by Him. He is the same God who, as He gives our life its determination, summons us to throw in our lot with Him, and who again, as He sets our life its limits, shows beyond all doubt that the cause we serve is not ours but His. From this standpoint, the fact that our time is allotted is quite in order. And it would not only be rebellious but eminently inadvisable to question this order. What would happen to our legitimate craving for duration and perfection if our discontent did not continually issue in the profound contentment of the knowledge that God Himself undertakes to gratify this craving ? Once this is recognised, so much of its realisation is seen that until its final realisation we can dare to go on living from hour to hour and day to day under the determination which is given our life and which we cannot suppress, but also in the time, our allotted time, which we can receive and have as such as the good gift of God.

6. But a final step has still to be taken if full clarity is to be attained, For again it is not enough merely to bring in the word " God." Here. too, this may well be an empty formula. The contention that it is good and salutary to be restricted and limited by God must be decisively proved. Why should we welcome the fact that at the point where our being and non-being seem to collide so inexorably and so menacingly we have to do with God, with the same God under whose determination our life is human and therefore impelled by that craving for duration and perfection ? We must now bring out into the open something which so far has received only incidental mention. And we must give it such emphasis that all the other associations which the word God has for us will seem trivial when they are measured and illuminated by it, namely, that God is the gracious God. Everything which we have said about the God who restricts and limits us has been leading up to this point. We have been speaking of a God who is not without man or against him, but for him. He is the God who far from thinking it beneath Him made it His glory eternally to elect Himself for man and man for Himself. He is the eternal self-grounded and self-satisfying majesty, but in the full freedom and sovereignty of His work as Creator, Reconciler and Redeemer addressed wholly to another, to man who cannot do anything for it, who cannot merit the divine address, or correspond to it, but can only receive it as a gift, the gift to which he owes everything. This is the free grace of God, which

is not just a benevolent attitude towards man, but the turning to him
of God in person ; of the God who, in inverse ratio to his deserts, enters
into solidarity with him, thus interposing Himself, making the life
of man His concern, the salvation of man His need, the peace of man
the cause for which He fights and wins, so that all human affairs, be
they great or trivial, individual or collective, are first and last His
concern, ordered and solved by Him. That He Himself receives us to
Himself is God's free grace. And this God who is gracious to us in
freedom is the very One who limits our life and bounds our time. He
does not only do this. He bears and sustains our life even with the
span allotted to it. In willing to have it so, He disposes and fashions
that it may always be life, so long as He permits. He protects and
preserves it from the disintegration from which it cannot protect
itself and which would be its inevitable fate if it were to run its course
without Him. He governs it in accordance with the determination
which He has given it—and against the intentions with which we
would like to govern it. He leads it towards His revelation ; the
revelation of His glory which consists in the fact that we may live
under Him and with Him. Yet in doing all this He also limits it.
And thus He is certainly present to us, so long as we have our time and
are privileged to be grateful recipients of His gifts and responsible
executors of His commission in this time of ours as knowing and acting
subjects. There is no part of our time which is not as such also in
His. It is, so to speak, embedded in His eternity. But as we are
thus in God's time, He limits ours. He appoints its beginning before
which we were not, and its end after which we shall be no longer.
And in this He is to us in a particular way the gracious God. This
is shown in the fact that at the very points where we emerge from non-
existence and return to non-existence, we are confronted in a particular way by the gracious God. For at these points we are referred
wholly and absolutely to the fact that He is our gracious God. For
what are we, or were we, or shall we be, if He were not already and
still there as our gracious God even when our own life and being is
not yet or no longer ?

If He is not there for us, who is ? If He is not there for us before
we were and when we shall be no longer, then our only prospect is
annihilation. And if that is not our plight, if we do not sink back into
the void, if our life and being are sustained, it is because—but only
because—He is there for us. To be sure, even during our life and in
our span of time we are utterly dependent on the grace of God. But
during our journey from our beginning to our end this truth may be
veiled from us. During our life and in our span of time it appears—
and the appearance is very strong though it is only an appearance—
that we have to do not only with God, but also with all kinds of elements
and factors which bear us, maintain us, protect, preserve, vivify and
control us, and especially with our own selves, so that we may at

least ask whether man is not his own gracious Lord and God. But in relation to our beginning and our end in time there can be no place either for the appearance or the question. We are faced by the simple alternative. Either the gracious God (and He alone) is for us, or nothingness is the abyss from which we have emerged and to which we shall return. But if we are confronted, not by nothingness, but exclusively, unequivocally, fundamentally and definitively by the gracious God, we are obviously near this God at these two points in a way which cannot be said of our being in the time between, though He is certainly near us there as well. What characterises the nature of man at these frontiers of his being is that, as the God who is wholly and utterly for us, God is wholly and utterly outside us, namely, beyond all our other possibilities. This is generally true as He is near us. But it is clear and essential only at the point where we can cling to no one and nothing but Him who as outside us is for us ; neither to the world nor to chaos, to angel nor devil, nor even our own selves.

Thus the fact that our time is allotted, and allotted by God, simply means the proximity of His free grace in this clarity. In this way, in this clarity of His free grace, He alone being our help, comfort, assurance and hope, His free choice our sole ground and promise, God confronts man from the very first as He gives him a limited life in an allotted span of time. He would obviously not confront him in this way if He gave him an unlimited life in unallotted time. Even then of course—if for the moment we may make the monstrous assumption of man as an infinite subject—it would still be true that man lives solely by the grace of God. But it would not be natural or obvious. He would be blinded by the illusion that he can rely on many other things as well as God, and especially on himself. In the supposed inviolability of an unlimited life in unallotted time in which he is endlessly alone, he might even be tempted by the foolish question whether he himself is not God. The free grace of God would then be relegated to an infinite distance, not in its truth, but in its compelling, exclusive and unequivocal clarity. Even if known, it would be a mere notion without concretion or practical significance. He would then be almost irresistibly invited and enticed to sin, to make idols, to try to justify and save himself. If this is not so, if he is urgently warned against this, it is because the limitation of his life, whether it be long or short, refers him concretely and practically, with supremely unwelcome but supremely valuable proximity and clarity, to the fact that apart from God he has no support, basis or goal, that without Him his existence would merely be a journey from nothingness to nothingness. Thus from this standpoint too his nature does not permit him to sin. If he does so, he cannot blame his nature for it. His nature, as that of a temporally limited being, is a powerful invitation and direction to throw himself upon God's free grace, to give Him alone his trust and full obedience, and in so doing to fulfil his determination and satisfy his craving for duration and perfection. If he fails to do this but falls into sin, he does not conform to his nature but denies it. By his nature, in virtue of its peculiar character as an allotted span, he is referred and bound to the gracious God as the One who is wholly and utterly outside him but wholly and utterly for him. It is now clear how much depends on the fact that our being in time is ordered as it is. From the standpoint of the most basic understanding of man, i.e., in confrontation with the gracious God, we have no reason to reject this order. In fact, we have every reason to recognise it in all its severity as good and wholesome, to accept it as a unique benefit, and to love and praise its Author for it. What greater ground could we have for loving and praising Him than the fact that by nature He has ordered our being as men in time for His free grace, and for this grace in all its clarity?

Here, then, is the basic answer to the problem raised by the fact that we are given only an allotted span. We had to take the successive steps in our analysis to show how it is to be given with increasing definiteness and clarity. Our next task will be to develop it in detail : first, and more briefly, in relation to the fact that our existence and time have a beginning ; and then, more fully, in relation to the more pressing problem presented by the fact that they come to an end. But before we take up these questions, we must remind ourselves of the way in which we have reached this answer. The limitation of our life and restriction of our time is too serious a fact for us to produce a positive answer as it were out of the hat, with no realisation of how we have attained it or on what grounds we may and must hold it. We will therefore recapitulate the various assumptions which we made to come step by step to the point of gratefully and joyfully affirming what at the outset it seemed possible only hopelessly and grimly to deny. We found in the determination of human life for God and our fellow-men the basis of the craving which makes the set span of our life seem so painful at a first glance. We accepted the necessary difference between the eternal existence of God and our temporal existence. We counted generally on the fact that between God and man there is nevertheless encounter and fellowship. And finally and decisively we presupposed that the God with whom we have to do is the God who has turned to us in His grace, who is not only for Himself, but in very truth for us. The conclusive form of our positive answer rested wholly upon this last assumption. But we must now recall that this last assumption (and therefore all the others as well) cannot be taken for granted, but can be adopted only as it is given to us. In our whole assumption that the gracious God is the limit of our time, and our conclusion that it is therefore good and salutary for us to be limited in time in this way, our starting-point has been the man Jesus in His time, but He also as the Lord of time, and it is only in view of this man that we have been able to consider man in the abstract and in general, and therefore his temporality. Was not the life of the man Jesus a limited life in a restricted time ? Yet we saw that that life, with all its limitations, was the life of the eternal Son and Word of God. We saw that His restricted time as such was fulfilled time, filled by the coming of the kingdom of God. We saw that in His resurrection the perfect realisation, based in God Himself, of the true relationship between God and man, and man and his fellows, is revealed as the perfection of this limited temporally restricted life ; and He Himself, this man, is manifested as the One who is in God even before He was and when He was no more, and as the man who will come and reveal the aim and purpose of God in respect of all men. We look at this man, who like us has lived a limited life in its restricted time, when we adopt our understanding of the nature of man in respect of his temporality. We keep to the determination of man revealed in Him when we accept man's craving for life as such. But we also keep to the fundamental difference between God and man also revealed in Him (in His distinction from us) when we acquiesce in the fact that we are temporal and not eternal like God. Again, we keep to the presence of the kingdom in His life in His time when we see the eternal God and temporal man in relation to one another. And again and supremely we accept the scope of His being in God both in His time and before and after it ; we accept the revelation of His lordship over time, inaugurated in His resurrection and to be consummated at His coming again, when we understand the limitation of our time as the clear proximity of God's grace for us. The gracious God of whom we spoke is not an abstraction but the concrete reality of " God in the flesh," the man Jesus, who was in time and the Lord of time. The formulation is bold but not inaccurate that He is the One by whom we are surrounded on all sides. For what time before or after our time is not His as well ?—the time in which and over which, as He is in God and God in Him, He is Lord. " God in the flesh," the man Jesus Himself, is God for us in the whole majesty and condescension of the divine being and action. He Himself is God's free grace. And He is it in the clarity which can enlighten us only from the two frontiers of our life. It is impossible to regard human nature in the light of the existence of this man without realising that it is good and salutary for us to have a limited life in a restricted time because here the grace of God is near and clear to us. But we cannot realise this except as we regard human nature in the light of the existence of this one man. At this point, too, a definite anthropology results from Christology. But this anthropology can be based only on Christology. Here we have the assumption behind all our other assumptions in this matter, and it ought to be clear by now that we can recognise and accept it and count on it and start from it, only as one which has already been made for us. Where for any reason we cannot do this, the answer which we have now given will never have the specific weight which carries conviction, and the question which it is supposed to answer will still be unsolved.

4. BEGINNING TIME

The problem raised by the fact that the time given us is an allotted span has two aspects which we must now consider in detail. Our time begins, and it ends. Attention is usually concentrated on the second aspect—that it ends. There, somewhere ahead of us, lies the term of our life, the frontier of our time, which is firmly drawn at an unknown point, and which we approach with every day and hour. At that point we shall be no longer. But the first aspect is just as real. There is a term and frontier from which we come, a point where we were not yet. The only difference is that we move further and further away from this point with every day and hour, so that the question posed by our beginning seems to decrease in urgency in proportion as the question posed by our end increases. That our being in time will one day come to an end, when our present will never again be followed by a future, appears far more disquieting than the fact that it once began as a present without a past. And it is indeed far more disquieting. For our life, and with it our time, is set irreversibly in this direction, so that what looms before us is the approaching end and not the receding beginning, which we have no urgent or pressing cause to consider, since it is plainly and self-evidently given and lies unquestionably behind us. The two aspects are seen together in an old German proverb : " I come and know not whence . . . I go and know not whither. I marvel that I am still so happy." But it is easy to see why the two aspects are not usually brought together. They do not have equal weight. All the same, the statement : " I come and know not whence," has a weight of its own. The fact that we feel no need to concern ourselves about it does not prove that there is no intrinsic reason to do so. And if we are really troubled by the second aspect : " I go and know not whither," and are surprised that we can still be so happy, this may be connected with the fact that there is a riddle at the point which we do not usually consider because our being in time faces the other direction, but which reveals an ignorance no less complete than in respect of our Whither ? Our beginning is indeed behind us and constantly recedes. It does not attract our attention or arouse our concern. Yet it points to the same fact and confronts us with the same problem as our end : that our being is bordered by our non-being ; that our non-being behind and before is a most terrible threat to our being ; that we are menaced by approaching annihilation ; and that our being thus seems to be a mere illusion and our life irretrievably forfeit. Why are we afraid of our end ? Obviously because, consciously or unconsciously, we carry and bring with us from our beginning a lurking terror which in virtue of the irreversible direction of our life and our time takes the opposite form of fear of our end, but which in both its latent and patent form is essentially one and the same fear of the term set to our life, of the allotment of a fixed span for our time. Since this is so, it is worth spending a few moments in consideration of the first aspect of our problem, and thus realising the scope of our basic answer in this respect too.

Our life once had a beginning. Nor does it make any difference at what point we locate this beginning.

The older theology created difficulties in respect of the soul and its origin which we can spare ourselves because they do not really touch the heart of the problem. Its only theological justification was that unlike ancient and modern Gnosticism, it rejected *a limine* the so-called doctrine of " emanationism." According to this doctrine the human soul is an efflux or emanation of the divine substance. It is not a creature, but of divine essence. This view clearly rules out our problem in advance. It is as pointless to worry about where we were before we were born as to worry about the previous existence of the Deity. Yet it is equally clear that this advantage is purchased at the price of blurring the distinction between divine and human being which is one of the fundamental assumptions of all Christian knowledge and of thus taking up a standpoint from which no theological teaching or discussion is possible. The Early Church and its theology, while rightly insisting on the gulf between Creator and creature, thought that the problem of the origin of the soul, and therefore of human life, could be solved in various ways between which we do not need to choose. Some, following Plato, and within the Church Origen, talked of the pre-existence of created souls. These were either represented as a kingdom of spirits which had to relate themselves to the material bodies allotted to them—the theory of a pre-temporal or at least pre-historical fall, championed in modern times by Julius Müller, might conceivably be adapted to this view—or it was assumed that when God created the first man they were all breathed into him and therefore created with and included in Adam, to be later distributed among his posterity. On both views it was possible to hold the particular doctrine of the migration of souls (metempsychosis or reincarnation), i.e., that the same souls could enter into many associations with different bodies. Partly in opposition to the doctrine of pre-existence, yet inevitably connected with it, and represented particularly by Tertullian in earlier days, and later (surprisingly enough) by Luther and Lutheran theology, was the traducianist doctrine that the soul originates in the act of conception. A soul-seed, distinct from the body-seed, is supposed to be detached from the soul of the parents, thus becoming the independent soul of the child. The doctrine prevailing in the Roman Church, which (again surprisingly) was followed in traditional Reformed theology, is creationism. On this view each individual soul originates in a divine creative act, an immediate *creatio ex nihilo*. This creative act is supposed (cf. F. Diekamp, *Kath. Dogmatik*, Vol. II, 1930, p. 119f.) to take place at the moment of conception when the parents create the requisite physiological conditions for the existence of a human being in this act. The parents are, of course, only *causae secundae*, God Himself being the *causa prima*. And simultaneously God in heaven, this time as the *causa unica*, creates the soul and associates it with this new human body. There is, of course, room for discussion as to the differentiation and unity between the vegetative and sensitive and the properly human or rational soul, and whether the former is progressively shaped to the latter in the period of pregnancy.

According to Thomas Aquinas (*S. Th.* I, *qu.* 118, *art* 2, *ad* 2) the actual creation of the characteristically human *anima intellectualis* would seem to be relegated to a later stage of pregnancy, whereas the dominant view to-day tends to assert that the intellectual life-principle is created and begins to function immediately upon conception, since the human body is apparently antecedently disposed for the reception of this life-principle.

We may have various reasons for refusing to enter into this strange discussion about the date of the inception of human life. In any case, however, none of the various attempted solutions, each of which out-does the other in abstruseness, leads us even the slightest step forward from where we stand, i.e., face to face with the fact that, if we exclude the pantheistic solution, we are bound to reckon with a beginning of human life, and therefore with a time when we were not, which was not yet ours. Before the being of the individual as of the race there was somewhere a non-being. And this non-being from which the individual and the race come is the non-being to which we also move. In the language of traditional theology (which we now find obscure and unacceptable), there was a time when my soul did not exist. In the terms of a more biblical view of man, there was a time when I myself as the soul of my body, I myself as the unity and totality of my psycho-somatic existence, did not yet exist, but I began to be. That this is the case is the occasion of a serious theological concern to which it is possible to give a serious theological answer. For it means—and none of the theories attempted can help us to escape this con-clusion—that even from my origin I am threatened by annihilation, being marked as a being which can only advance towards non-existence. Before a certain point I had no past ; the time before this point was not my time ; I had there no dimension to live in. And even if I associate myself with the whole human race, and regard my soul as an individual member of that kingdom of spirits or as included in the soul of Adam, before the time of Adam there was for him, and before the creation of that world of spirits there was for its individual members and therefore for me, no time, no dimension to live in. This is the shadow which has lain over my being in time ever since it began ; the deficiency which now lies heavily upon me as I pursue life's journey ; the shadow and the deficiency with which I now move towards my future. One day, it will no longer be my future. When I have had my last present, I shall have no more future, but shall only be past and have been. The latter point is not so easily forgotten as the former. But even if I can forget the former, I still live under the shadow and deficiency. I can be only as one who once was not, with all the threat which this entails. I can be only as one who is definitely confronted from behind by his own non-being. Whatever this shadow and deficiency may lack in urgency because it is not before us, it gains in actuality over that which still belongs to the future. For the decision that we were once not yet has already been taken, whereas the decision that one day we shall be no more, for all the certainty with which it awaits us, has still to fall. We still have a present with a little future. We still live. The door to our future non-being is still unopened. But the door through which we came to being from non-being is wide open. It has already been decided that at that time, beyond that door, we had no time. And we must live as those who come from this decision ; as those who are always suspended with all that they were and are and will be. It is as well, therefore, to address ourselves to the further question of our Whence ? so easily forgotten and apparently irrelevant, yet all the more urgent in fact. What are we as those who inexorably come from this point ?

That this question is a relevant one, whether we are aware of it or not, is shown by the phenomenon already touched upon at an earlier point, viz., the general interest and concern to know as much as possible about the past, the phenomenon which we usually call the human interest in history in the narrower sense of the term, namely, the history which lies behind us. That a man can be concerned with his own personal past is understandable, for there, as we have seen, he is concerned with himself, as well as with his present and future. But it is far more difficult, and in fact quite impossible if we ignore this latent question, to understand why man in every age and clime, with varying degrees of zeal and ingenuity, yet with a remarkable unanimity, has always been exercised about what lies beyond his personal recollection and its possibilities, his own life and times ; why he has always wanted to recover and bring within the range of his vision and picture as vividly as possible what happened before his time, and how it happened, in spheres which were not his. Why cannot he let the past remain past ? After all, it was not his past and it has no bearing on his life to-day or to-morrow, as his own personal memories have. How are we to explain the remarkable demand for sagas and legends, for epic poetry or for assured traditions handed on from generation to generation, and finally for the most accurate historical research and presentation ? What do we expect from it all, from these distant figures of the past, from life and times long dead, from the thoughts, words and deeds of men long since departed, from the circumstances under which they lived, the emotions and experiences by which they were actuated, from their achievements, successes and failures ? Why must all these things be called back into this strange second life in the pictures which he forms ? It would be superficial to put it all down to the playful or serious urge of mind or imagination exercised in this as one of many fields. Nor is it sufficient simply to say that man goes to his predecessors to learn about himself and his own present and future, hoping to find in these realms, which were not his, the inspiration, motives, criteria, stimulation, encouragement and warning he needs in order to live a meaningful life in his own sphere. Nor is it the whole story if we point to man's legitimate and serious need of human society—a need which might lead him, and will necessarily do so if he does not find true contemporaries in his own age, to generations long since departed, to the encounter with their needs and hopes, resources and responsibilities, with their particular way of meeting the demands life lays on us all. All this, of course, is perfectly true. Yet at the same time there is a deeper and more powerful force at work. Man is impelled to penetrate beyond his own life and time. He has an urge to carve out for himself living space and therefore time at the point where he was not. He is anxious to dispel the shadow which haunts him from the past, and make good the deficiency under which he suffers from this quarter. He seeks light and fulness there too. He would like to have been and lived at that point. He would like to be " transported " to it—the real aim of every imaginative or scientific attempt at historical reconstruction. He wants to be then as well as now ; to hear and see Bismarck and his opponents ; to be a contemporary of Napoleon I ; to feel and think and hear and smell as people did in the 18th century ; to look over the shoulders of Leibniz and Kant, Luther and Calvin, and countless others as well ; to think with their minds and have direct access to their thought. He finds it intolerable that all this should have happened then, i.e., long before his own day, as though it were no business of his. He cannot bear to think that this dimension of life never belonged to him. Therefore he cannot leave history alone. He cannot accept the fact that he comes from non-being. Therefore he fills the gap by plunging into it with his historical investigations and discoveries. Therefore he must dream and write poetry, preserve monuments and documents, and when he has the tools for it, endeavour scientifically to bring the past within the range of his own experience just as it was. The process is usually stigmatised by its critics as a " flight into history." And there are, of course, certain aspects which justify this criticism. But there are others which give it the appearance of an all-out offensive, a vigorous crusade, a passionate attack on our allotted span of time in which we try to reach out into that field of the past which is so visible and broad that by comparison the expanse ahead which we can exploit for future enterprises and achievements may seem wretchedly obscure and confined. It need hardly be said that this endeavour, which rightly understood is truly titanic, is nevertheless afflicted by a final impotence in all its forms and can never lead to the desired goal. Just as our personal memory is in the last resort confined to recapturing and preserving a few more or less clearly defined and detailed images, so it is, and even more so, when we try to reach out beyond our own time into that of other men of the past. However clear our reproduction, however scientific our research, we can never actually be there ourselves. However hard we try, we can never be in an area where we were not. Of course, pictures of this area can enrich our life, and in this way belong to our life. But our life as such remains within its confines. There can be no backward extension of our being in time. The genuine historian is no stranger to the pathos of the fact—and the more strongly the more clearly he sees it—that even the most vivid pictures can only testify that a recurrence of its reality, or our own return to it, the desired backward extension of our life's dimension, is necessarily an illusion. But the force of the historical impulse in its many different forms does at least show that man is aware of the abyss of non-being which lies behind him, and that he is basically more concerned with the question of his existence in this direction than might at first sight appear, or seem to be demanded by it.

That this problem of the origin of our life, of the beginning of our being in time, is so great, is due supremely to the fact that the theological answer to the problem of allotted time which we have just given has reference to and embraces not only the more obvious problem of our exit, but also the less obvious of our entry. The result of our radical examination—that it is good and salutary for us to be limited because it is the eternal, gracious God who limits us—tells us that we derive from this God. We certainly come from non-being, but we do not come from nothing. We do not come from an abyss which has spewed us out only to swallow us up again. God is not nothing nor chaos. As the Creator of heaven and earth and of man, He is the Victor over chaos, who in His omnipotence has negated and still negates nothing, who intervenes against it for the creature which of itself is no match for it, who protect it against its onslaught, who

rescues it from its most dreadful triumphs, who has made Himself
its Pledge and Helper in all the inviolability of His self-grounded being,
who has always and will always prove Himself to be such. There
was a time when we were not. Nothing can alter this. We should
not be creatures but God if we had been eternally. And we should
not have been concrete creatures, existing as well-defined subjects,
if we had come from an infinite previous time. But the eternal
God was before we were. He was in that past before our present
which our being in time so utterly and painfully lacks. He was
in the " then " which was not yet ours. He was in the unattainable
life-space before ours. We can never regard Him as belonging to the
past like everything before us, as something lost which cannot be
recaptured because only our non-being was before us. He has preceded
us in time, in all the times of our non-being. Indeed, He has preceded
the non-being of all creation, the beginning of all time as its dimension
of life. Where do we come from ? From the being, speaking and
action of the eternal God who has preceded us. This is the particular
answer to this particular question. Before we were, this gracious God
was our gracious God : the God who even when we were not was not
without us but in all that He was Himself was for us ; therefore God for
us ; wisdom and omnipotence for us ; holy and righteous, merciful
and patient for us ; eternal and ineffably glorious for us ; for us the
origin and fulness of all perfection. His inner life as Father, Son and
Holy Spirit, His will and purpose in relation to heaven, earth and
ourselves, His already accomplished and uninterrupted work in
execution of it—this was the content of the time before our time, the
meaning of the pre-history before our history. Hence there is nothing
mysterious or terrifying about the time before we were. It does not
really entail any deficiency or shadow. Our yearning to expand our
being backwards into the past is pointless. Whatever our end may be,
our beginning does not lay us under any threat or curse. Regarded
in the light of its beginning, our life in our allotted time is tolerable
because at this point it does not hang lost and helpless over an abyss
but is reliably held and supported, secured and guaranteed. Indeed,
it stands under a promise. Its progress and even its end are set in
the light of its beginning. From the point where we derive we can
go further, treading to the end the road which begins there. Because
of this beginning, we have no reason to fear that it will be impassable
or lead us finally to catastrophe. On the contrary, we may be confident that the road on which we find ourselves and the goal to which
we are moving will prove good and salutary. For the eternal and
gracious God, who is the boundary of our beginning, will surely
guarantee the whole of our life, the span which we are given, and its
final end. Obviously the theological answer which we have given to
the problem of allotted time is not properly understood if it does not
really have this dimension, if it does not lead us to take seriously the

question of our Whence ?, and give us light and comfort in respect of it. For this reason we cannot just ignore the question.

Nor is Holy Scripture silent in this respect. That Israel was perfectly alive to the problem of our Whence ? is shown by Job 8⁹ : " For we are but of yesterday, and know nothing." And we have a classic expression of the answer given to this question in the prayer attributed to Moses, the man of God, in Ps. 90¹ᶠ· : " Lord, thou hast been our refuge, from one generation to another. Before the mountains were brought forth, or ever the earth and the world were made, thou are God from everlasting, and world without end " (P.B.V.). No violence is done to the text if we then emphasise v. 3 : " *Thou* (who wert our refuge from one generation to another, and God before the world was made) turnest man to destruction ; again thou sayest, Come again ye children of men." But if we are to arrive at a concrete understanding it is essential to give full weight to the first sentence : " Thou hast been our refuge, from one generation to another." According to the Old Testament revelation, when the Israelite contemplates the beginning of his individual existence he is confronted with God Himself and with the history of the people of which he is a member. His thinking is indeed " historical," but under a particular token. For the Israelite God is not a first principle or an idea. It is significant that passages like Ps. 90¹ᶠ·, which at a pinch can be regarded as the expression of a physico-metaphysical world-view, are extremely rare in the Old Testament. And it is clear that even Ps. 90 is not meant to be taken in this way. Yahweh has been the refuge of Israel and of all Israelites from generation to generation. This massive historical reality is the form of the God who was before man was, before ever the earth and the world were made. And the fact that He was Israel's refuge before man was, is not, e.g., subordinated to the earlier point (viz., that He was before the earth and the world were created), as the particular to the general. On the contrary, the general point is included in the particular, and can be stated only in the light of it. The true way to put it is that in the first place Yahweh is Israel's refuge, and only then and as such the God who was before all the world. For Yahweh, the God of Israel, is in an absolute sense the Founder and Inaugurator, the Lord, Legislator and Guarantor of the covenant in which Israel alone can have its historical existence as a people. He is the Lord of this covenant from all eternity. He has proved Himself as such and acted as such from generation to generation. This is His form to which the individual Israelite looks back when he thinks of the time before his time. This past confronts him with the challenge (again attributed to Moses) : " Remember the days of old, consider the years of many generations : ask thy father, and he will shew thee ; thine elders, and they will tell thee. When the Most High gave to the nations their inheritance, when he separated the children of men, he set the bounds of the peoples according to the number of the children of Israel. For the Lord's portion is his people : Jacob is the lot of his inheritance. He found him in a desert land, and in the waste howling wilderness ; he compassed him about, he cared for him, he kept him as the apple of his eye : as an eagle that stirreth up her nest, that fluttereth over her young, he spread abroad his wings, he took them, he bare them on his pinions : the Lord alone did lead him, and there was no strange god with him " (Deut. 32⁷ᶠ·). The same challenge to remember the former days or years is to be found in Deut. 4³², and also in Job 8⁸, Is. 45²¹ᶠ·, 46⁹, as well as in Jer. 6¹⁶ : " Thus saith the Lord, Stand ye in the ways and see, and ask for the old paths, where is the good way, and walk therein, and ye shall find rest for your souls." And how man lived up to this challenge and responded to it is shown in Ps. 77⁵ᶠ· : " I have considered the days of old, the years of ancient times. I call to remembrance my song in the night : I commune with mine own heart ; and my spirit made diligent search. Will the Lord cast off for ever ? And will he be favourable no more ? Is his mercy clean gone for ever ? Doth his promise fail for

the dead, in whom, before they were, everything took place and is revealed for their present and future, and whom they need to continue and complete their own life. What they need for this purpose is simply His Spirit. But this is only to say again that they need Him who was then ; His Word and presence to-day as yesterday ; the faith, hope and love in which He is one with them. As the One who was before them, who was before they were, He upholds and sustains them. He is the gracious God who has already saved them and will not let them fall, either in the further course of their journey, or at its end.

This has to be realised if it is to be seen that, although the whole problem of the backward context of our existence is the same in the New Testament as the Old, it has to be stated differently. When it is not realised, the centre and therefore the periphery of New Testament faith and life cannot be perceived. In the Old Testament sphere it is not only possible but necessary for the individual to look back to the long history of his people and thus to recall with confidence his own origin and beginning in the grace and election of God. The history and the mediation of the divine promise and command accomplished in it have in this case a fundamental significance. The meaning of every single, human life in Israel is to be found in its participation in this history and in the accompanying mediation of the divine promise and command from generation to generation, until the whole process reaches the goal foreseen and implicit in its beginning with the appearance of the expected salvation, the birth of the Messiah and the inauguration of His kingdom. This fundamental significance of the history which transpires between the election and call of Abraham and any given present is both the completeness and the limit of the completeness with which Old Testament man is comforted in respect of his origin. It is impossible to ascribe any similar basic significance in the New Testament sphere to the history which begins with the foundation of the Church. The establishment of the Church, upon which the individual Christian looks back as the origin and beginning of his own existence, is certainly the work of the same gracious and faithful God with whom the Israelite in earlier days sought, found and possessed his refuge. But " God " now means the salvation which has appeared, the Messiah, born, crucified and resurrected, the kingdom which has now come. This is something far greater than the blessing of the name of Abraham and the succession of blessings which followed under his name. It is the God who elected and called Abraham in a human person. Old Simeon (Lk. 2[25f.]) and Anna (Lk. 2[36f.]), who waited for the consolation of Israel and the deliverance of Jerusalem, are now dismissed like faithful sentinels whose duty is done : " Lord, now lettest thou thy servant depart in peace, according to thy word ; for mine eyes have seen thy salvation " (Lk. 2[29f.]). This final word on this side of the turning-point in time becomes with its fulfilment the first and exclusively normative word for the future. " We have found him, of whom Moses in the law, and the prophets, did write, Jesus of Nazareth, the son of Joseph " (Jn. 1[45]). The apostles can only testify to this search and discovery. It is conclusive and final. Those who would relegate this search and discovery to the same level as the promise and command of Israel, as though the latter had not attained their goal in this search and discovery, would be false apostles. The same applies *a fortiori* to those who would supplement and enrich the testimony to this search and discovery with new promises and commands. The Christian man looks back to this search and discovery and nothing else. He lives directly by the beginning made with it. The Gospel story and the apostolic message mediate to him nothing but this beginning. And so the Church, whose life is sustained by the Gospel story and the apostolic message, can only mediate this beginning, testifying to the individual Christian that this beginning, Jesus Christ, is the beginning of his life too. It has, therefore, nothing else to offer to him ; nothing of its own, whether old or new. The historical existence of the Church is legitimate only in so far as it refrains from giving specific weight to its own possibilities, developments and achievements, from interesting its members in these things and therefore in itself instead of pointing simply to that beginning in direct and exclusive proclamation of Jesus Christ. The Christian Church exists only where it attests to its members and the outside world this beginning and nothing but this beginning. Only as it does this is it the " pillar and ground of the truth." It cannot, therefore, build itself on either its antiquity or its renewals. It cannot consolidate its life around its ministry or dogmas, its cultus or orders. It cannot place its confidence on its ministerial succession or on the religious, intellectual and political lustre of the fathers and saints and doctors and leaders with whom it has been blessed, on the certainty of its doctrinal and constitutional tradition, or on the progressive development of its preaching, institutions or activity. Nor can it insert all these things between that beginning and its contemporary present, between Jesus Christ and the men after His time, as though they had a special and independent value and authority and importance by the side of His. It can understand itself and its history in all its forms only as the context of a service which it has to perform. But in this service it is always pointing beyond itself. With all that it is and has and can do, it is always weighed in the balance. Hence it must always be ready to retire gracefully when the higher interests of the beginning to which it owes its existence demand. Only in this way is it the body, the bride, the people of its Lord. It must never forget what it has to proclaim, that the history of Israel and the history of mankind have attained their goal and end in Jesus Christ, and that this goal and this end are now the *prius* for every human life. It has to take seriously the fact that the time in which we live *post Christum* is the final time, the time when the pendulum is swinging for the last time, and there is no more room for the rise and perpetuation of independent human kingdoms alongside and in competition with the kingdom of God which has come, but all such kingdoms can only prove to be fleeting shadows. This being so, how can it try to found such a kingdom in the name of Jesus Christ ? How can it try to present and preserve itself as such ? This attempt can be made only in misunderstanding and error. It can lead only to shipwreck. It must always allow itself to be recalled to order by its beginning, to the true order of its service ; and it must be full of joy and gratitude when this happens. It must always become small and humble again, and in so doing find its true greatness and glory. Only when this takes place does it mediate to men that search and discovery, and therefore comfort in respect of the Whence ? of their existence—the answer that in life and death they may come from the gracious God. It would be an offence not only against God but also against man for it to insert itself between men and this saving beginning of life, as though it were itself the source of comfort.

But if it is not to fall into this sin, it must never forget that, although it is a people, the new Israel, it is not (like the old Israel) a " nation," a natural society linked by race and blood and the sequence of generations, but a people gathered solely by the preaching of the Word and the free election and calling of the Spirit. The first Israel, constituted on the basis of physical descent from Abraham, has fulfilled its mission now that the Saviour of the world has sprung from it and its Messiah has appeared. Its members can only accept this fact with gratitude, and in confirmation of their own deepest election and calling attach themselves to the people of this Saviour, their own King, whose members the Gentiles are now called to be as well. Its mission as a natural community has now run its course and cannot be continued or repeated. For what begins with the rise of the Christian community is not a natural people, a nexus of blood, a succession of generations, a complex of tribes and families and fathers and sons which are as such the bearers and recipients of the promise. Even the individual Israelite is now confronted with a question which is not answered by the mere fact that he is an Israelite, or is circumcised, or has the blessing of the high-priest. Nor is it answered for the proselyte by the mere fact that he has been given proselyte baptism. Even within Israel there is a new election and decision, and the summons to a new calling and personal faith. " He came unto his own, and his own received him not. But as many as received him, to them gave he power to become the sons of God, even to them that believe on his name : which were born, not of blood, nor of the will of the flesh, nor of the will of man, but of God " (Jn. 1[11f.]). It is in this way that the Church is con- stituted and gathered. This is the question which is put before all men. The fact that woman acquires an independent part in this event illustrates the new situation. And it is for this reason that the Church does not equate baptism with circumcision, but (as in Col. 2[11-12]) draws a radical distinction between them. Of course the individual Christian has a father and mother. He, too, is the member of a family, tribe and nation. And it may well be by this natural mediation that he is led to the Church and pointed to his origin and beginning in the grace of God. But this is obviously not necessary. And the fact that he may live in faith and have assurance of faith in the light of that origin and beginning, that he may become a " son of God," is not created for him by his parents, family or nationality. He does not have this privilege either by birth or descent. Indeed, he does not have it through the Church, but from God Himself through the ministry of the Church. In this matter no man can stand proxy for him. No historical nexus can provide or guarantee it. He owes it directly to Jesus Christ Himself. He owes it to the Holy Spirit. His recognition and assurance that he is a " son of God " he owes to his baptism. For through the Holy Spirit, in whom primarily Jesus Christ is active towards him, he comes to faith. And through baptism, in which primarily Jesus Christ is again active towards him, he is given the confirmation and seal that his faith is not arbitrary, but the gift of God's grace, so that it cannot be shaken by any unbelief, super- stition or heresy which may assault him, but he can live by his faith and rejoice, whatever may befall him. We may indeed make bold to suggest that in the New Testament community baptism has actually replaced the Old Testament blessing as regards meaning and content. At any rate, as a human ministration it is related to the work of Jesus Christ in the same way as in the Old Testament the human act of blessing is related to the real word of blessing which has its power only from God, and which can therefore be uttered only by God Himself. However that may be, the birth of the Christian life " of water and of the Spirit " (Jn. 3[5]) signifies a direct relationship of the individual Christian to Jesus. He does not follow father and mother or the line of his ancestors, but, taken out of this succession, or at any rate in independence of it, he follows Jesus. He believes that there is one holy catholic Church, and that he may be a living member of the same. Yet he does not believe in the Church, but in the Holy Spirit, who is consubstantial with the Father and the Son. He does not there- fore honour and accept the Church's tradition and order in becoming a Christian and confessing himself to be such, but he places himself behind and confesses the beginning which all ecclesiastical tradition and order can only serve, and which he can now recognise and receive as his own beginning. He believes, thinks, speaks and acts therefore, not as the member of a so-called " Christian nation," but in gratitude to the Lord that even in his—in no sense Christian— country He has His community, by and to whose ministry among this people he himself is called.

But a fateful confusion has continually afflicted the Church from its earliest days. It quickly regarded and conducted itself as a kind of continuation, renewal or repetition of pre-Christian Israel. It so easily ceased to understand itself as the community of the last time inaugurated with the death and resurrec- tion of its Lord. It forgot that it comes from the goal of all history. Instead, it understood Jesus Christ, and consequently its own foundation, as the beginning of a new epoch in history. It thus tried to establish, consolidate, assert and propagate itself as one kingdom with others. It was unable or unwilling to honour its Lord in the simplicity which is content to leave Him to speak and act for it, to renounce all striving for its own honour and authority, and there- fore to seek nothing for itself. And so it was unable and unwilling to see men in that immediacy or simply to call them to realise that immediacy : " Ye are Christ's ; and Christ is God's " (1 Cor. 3^{23}). Instead, it began to act as if it were a natural community continuing from generation to generation and bound by ties of kith and kin. It identified itself (on the plea of what was later euphemistically described as " Christianisation ") with a whole succession of genuinely natural communities and finally with the whole of the West, which came to be thought of as the " Christian West." The freedom of the Holy Spirit, the freedom of the divine election and calling, the freedom in which Christ awakens faith in Himself and in which the Christian Church alone can be constituted, was no longer respected. Nor was the responsibility of entry into the community, of its desire for baptism as the desire of faith for its divine confirmation and sealing. It was thought to be known in advance who would become Christians, members of the Church and members of the body of Christ, i.e., all children who find themselves within the sphere of the Church and are born of ostensibly " Christian " parents. Were not the male children of the Israelites circumcised on the eighth day and thus separated as participants in the covenant ? Are the children of Christians to be deprived of a privilege enjoyed in Israel ? So the argument ran, forgetting the tiny detail that now that the covenant has been fulfilled by Jesus Christ, it is no longer possible to foresee and arrange and anticipate the divine separation of participants. With the generous inclusion of girls, all children born in a Christian environment were regarded as potential Christians, as though the Church were a natural and historical entity like Israel. And since they could not be asked about their desire for baptism and required to make a profession of faith, they were baptised without making this question and therefore baptism a matter of personal responsibility commensurate with the freedom of the Holy Spirit. They were made Christians by millions in their sleep and over their heads as it were. These millions of baptised could not and cannot now remember their baptism as an event at which they assisted in the responsibility of the personal faith given by Jesus Christ and now confirmed and sealed. For they did not assist at it in this way. This is the fatal outcome in relation to the present discussion. It certainly sounds rather strange, and demands complicated reflection, if in answer to the question of their Whence ? we simply refer men to the fact that they are baptised, and are therefore assured that they have received the gift of the Holy Spirit, and thus come directly from Jesus Christ, from His birth, His baptism in the Jordan, His crucifixion and resurrection, and may therefore live as members of His body in calm and cheerful confidence that while their faith may be assaulted it can never be destroyed. This is what baptism does in fact tell us *post Christum*. *Post Christum* the only answer to our question is in fact to refer to the fact that baptism tells us this. Hence the embarrassment created by our current practice, which if it does not make this reference impossible at least makes it very difficult, curiously emasculating and obscuring what baptism has to tell us. But this questionable practice of infant baptism is in the last resort the expression of a much more deep-seated ignorance that the Christian community of the last time, as distinct from pre-Christian Israel, can upbuild and fashion and maintain itself only under the law of the Spirit, so that while it is not so visibly and tangibly established as the natural and historical nexus of ancient Israel it is grounded directly in God incarnate, and the consolation which the Christian may receive and have in retrospect of the beginning of his existence indicated in baptism is incomparably greater and deeper and surer than it could ever be for the ancient Israelite, although in effect this was the same. But only under the law of the Spirit does this consolation flourish, whereas under the domination of a supposedly Christian law of history competing with the law of the Spirit it can only be distorted. Because of that deep-seated ignorance, we know the consolation to-day almost exclusively in a distorted form. Christian faith in the so-called Christian West is rarely a matter of absolute certainty and triumphant joy. And the only hope of breaking through and destroying that deep-seated ignorance lies in a fuller recognition and appreciation of the power of the New Testament answer to the question of our Whence ? than *rebus sic stantibus* is generally possible to-day.

5. ENDING TIME

Let us now turn our attention to the other aspect of our problem. Time as we are given it is coming to an end. This is the second point settled with the time given to us. We are proceeding towards a point where we shall be no longer. " I go and know not whither." We have already mentioned one reason why the question of our being or non-being as posed by this end of our set span, the question of our Whither ?, is in practice much more disquieting than when seen from the first standpoint. It is because our life runs from beginning to end, and not in the reverse direction. Hence when we look ahead it is our end that we see and contemplate, and indeed our approaching end. Our beginning on the other hand lies behind us, receding ever further into the past. Hence the nearer our end approaches, the less does our beginning seem to claim our attention.

There is, however, a more profound reason, though one connected with the fact that our beginning causes us disquiet, if not inevitably, yet certainly in practice. Life desires life ; it hungers and thirsts for it ; it strives and calls for further life. Life is terrified at every limitation of life. It would fain overcome these limitations, and that as quickly and as thoroughly as possible. Life would fain assert itself against these limitations and renew itself in defiance of them. It is in flight from the non-existence from which it springs. It is constantly reminded of its origin by the limitations it encounters along its path. It reaches its present point from the non-existence in which it originated. It is in a state of transition. It has its present in this transition, but in no present can it find satisfaction. For the present never stays. It can only be passed through, and offers no abiding. Life must therefore repeatedly demand that transition. And being in time, it continually demands a future. And the real disquiet arising from the fact that our existence in time comes to an end consists in the fact that the point will come when, still alive and therefore still involved in that flight from non-existence, still hungering and thirsting after further life, we shall not be able to live any further. For the time we shall then have will be a time with a present (and with our whole past behind us), but with no more future. We shall then have been, and we shall still be. But the transition will now be out of life as it was formerly into life. It will mean that " all is over." The last of the ice-floes on which we placed our feet again and again will no longer support us. Our progress and transition will then be our fall. Though we still are, we shall be no longer ; or more precisely, we shall only have been. We shall again be confronted, though now very differently, after our being and not before, by the absolute edge of our existence. The very same question from which we started will face us again, namely, whether this is the edge of the abyss, the abyss of our negation. From the very beginning our life could never answer this question. And now it will face us again. There will then be no doubt that all through our life it had never been answered, and never could have been. This will be the last grim fact which will stare us in the face. We shall die. This, and nothing else, will be the end awaiting us. Whether it be near or far, it is certainly approaching nearer and nearer. " Time departs and death comes." And since death comes and time departs, our attempted flight, however long it lasts, becomes increasingly hopeless. The chances of life are for ever diminishing, and its limitations loom ever larger. Our hopes, expectations and plans become increasingly relative and limited, and their futility ever more apparent. They hasten and we hasten—whether we are unconscious of it or not makes no difference—towards the point of negation, the same point from which all things, ourselves included, derive. When we die, all things and we ourselves come to an end. This is what makes the finitude of the time given us the more critical and incisive form of its limitation. Because our time is finite, our life in time—irrespective of whether we are conscious of it—is in fact a time fraught with anxiety and care. It is overshadowed by death. There thus arises again and with particular urgency the question of the relation of our existence to our non-existence, i.e., whether our non-existence in time may not mean our negation, or in what sense it has any other meaning.

If we are to hear what Holy Scripture has to say concerning the finitude of human life in time and the nature and reality of our death, our best plan (on the following cf. Christoph Barth, *Die Errettung vom Tode*, 1947) is to start with the most general type of insight which the Bible has to offer us on this subject. When, for example, Deut. 30[19] says : " I have set before you life and death, blessing and cursing," it is clear beyond all doubt that there are certain connexions between blessing and life, cursing and death. But this is no proof that death is intrinsically a curse, nor life a blessing. Death is intrinsically the end and limit of human life. It challenges it remorselessly and in its totality. It confronts man as an incomprehensible, inexplicable and unassailable reality. But this means it has about it something of the character of what the Bible calls " heaven." At any rate it serves as a concrete reminder that this earth and man's life upon it are overshadowed and surrounded by an incomprehensible and intangible reality beyond his control. That is why death in the Bible always appears (to man at least) as a strange and in the most concrete sense of the word " uncanny " reality. If it is not for man an intrinsic evil, the question inevitably arises whether it may not be so in fact for some factual reason, just as life, while it is not intrinsically good, stands generally under the promise and command that it may be so.

The saying in Ps. 90[12] is best translated : " So teach us to number our days, that we may attain a heart of wisdom." To " become clever " (Luther) or to " attain a heart of wisdom," whatever other implications it may have, is connected with the necessity of remembering that our days are limited, not unending.

And this is to number our days. Whatever existence in death may mean, it cannot consist in a continuation of life in time. One day we shall have had our life. Not even death can throw any doubt upon this. We shall one day have been. Death cannot alter this fact either. But then we shall only have had our life in time. What we shall then have and be on the far side of our life in time, is what death calls in question. We shall then only have been. What will then become of our being as such when it is one which has only been ? This is the question which presses upon us as we contemplate the fact of death. Man desires continuation. That is why he resists the notion of an untimely death in the noonday of life, which would make his life an uncompleted fragment. That is why he prays that he may escape such a death (Is. 38¹⁰ ; Ps. 102²⁴ᶠ·). But is not long life in itself merely a fragment which cries out for continuation ? Death at any rate means being deprived of all prospects for the future. It means being deprived of the capacity of living any longer. Death therefore overshadows even a long and full life. We must die, and according to 2 Sam. 14¹⁴ this means that we " are as water spilt on the ground, which cannot be gathered up again." " As the cloud is consumed and vanisheth away : so he that goeth down to Sheol shall come up no more. He shall return no more to his house, neither shall his place know him any more " (Job 7⁹ᶠ·). " When a few years are come, then I shall go the way whence I shall not return " (Job 16²²). To be dead means to be able to live no longer. To be dead means to be deprived of the freedom for true and meaningful action and movement. The Old Testament never questions the possibility of the dead reappearing to the living, and on occasion (e.g., 1 Sam. 28⁷ᶠ·) it is even presupposed. But in no sense does this imply that they are still alive or continue to live. In no sense does it alter the fact that the essential thing about life, i.e., the capacity for movement and action, and the possibility of entering into fellowship with the living, has ceased. It is from this society that the dead is snatched away. He is no longer to be found in the " land of the living " (Job 28¹³). In the land which is now his, he will " not see the Lord, even the Lord in the land of the living " : he will " behold man no more with the inhabitants of the world " (Is. 38¹¹). Yet he is not entirely alone even in this other place. For, in so far as he has died and been buried, in the common phrase of the Old Testament he has been " gathered to his fathers " or " to his people." To this extent he is still in a certain indirect relationship to his descendants who are still alive and who still belong to the same tribe. But there is no living fellowship in which he can bear an active part, no fellowship either of the dead among themselves or between the living and the dead. " For there is no work, nor device, nor knowledge, nor wisdom, in the grave, whither thou goest " (Eccles. 9¹⁰). The dead exist in a state of utter weakness and helplessness. They are, so to speak, always dying (Is. 14¹⁰). This is what is meant when the dead are called *rephaim* (without power). What the living person had and was is now gone ; death has brought it to extinction. Gone is his character as a living person, his being as the soul of his body. For the fact that he is dead means that the spirit, the power of the living breath of God which constituted him an existent subject, has been withdrawn. He exists only as one who has been, who is therefore deprived of the Spirit, who has disintegrated, and who is thus incapable of enjoying the good things of life, wellbeing, fortune, security, prosperity and honour. And at least the fear suggests itself that there he will have the very opposite—misfortune and decay, poverty and deprivation. That death can in any way be conducive to man's well-being is utterly out of the question, death being what it is. Man cannot even take with him anything he has acquired here or retrieve it as it were from the debris. " Naked came I out of my mother's womb, and naked shall I return thither " (Job 1²¹, cf. Eccles. 5¹⁴). The custom of offerings for the dead, although it is known in the Old Testament (e.g., Ez. 32²⁷), is never approved or made the subject of discussion. Because of this state of complete deprivation the dead are sad. And they are so decisively because they are cut off from the help of

Yahweh which is promised and given to the living, namely, to the living people of Israel (Ps. 88⁶), to the whole life of Israel which is ruled and blessed by Yahweh, and in particular to its life as a worshipping community. " For in death there is no remembrance of thee : in the grave who shall give thee thanks ? " (Ps. 6⁵). " Shall the dust praise thee ? shall it declare thy truth ? " (Ps. 30⁹ᵇ). No, " the dead praise not the Lord, neither any that go down into silence " (Ps. 115¹⁷). " For the grave cannot praise thee, death cannot celebrate thee : they that go down into the pit cannot hope for thy truth. The living, the living, he shall praise thee, as I do this day " (Is. 38¹⁸ᶠ·). And conversely : " Shall thy lovingkindness be declared in the grave ? Or thy faithfulness in destruction ? Shall thy wonders be known in the dark ? And the righteousness in the land of forgetfulness ? " (Ps. 88¹¹ᶠ·). If we are to give due weight to all these questions, we must remember that in the Old Testament the world of the living provides the sphere in which Yahweh speaks to His people and deals with them. It is the land occupied and inhabited by Israel in accordance with the promise and as contrasted with the wilderness, and also with Egypt and Babylon. And in particular it is Jerusalem, and most especially the temple, which is the place where God does all this, and therefore where Israel finds the mainspring of life and may thus live. Death has for him, therefore, something of the wilderness about it, something of Egypt and Babylon. This is what makes it all the more sinister. It removes him from that holy place and cuts him off from that mainspring of life. This is what makes the enigma of death so profound. This is why the greatest of all questions is posed to Israel by the fact of death. How is it possible or tolerable ? What will be the result of it, of the fact that even the great assurance : " With thee is the well of life " (Ps. 36⁹ᵃ), is made pointless if not fallacious by it ? The worst feature of death, which has to be borne but which makes it so bitter, is that we are absolutely precluded from discovering what will be the result of it.

For death does not merely confront man with the limitations of life which he has experienced all along. It is not a partner which in part at least can be known and handled. The menacing feature of all the preceding limitations of life is that they presage this latent and more potent force, death as the power which man cannot hope to know, but which is wholly superior to him. Death is not only a place where man will be, but also a power which holds him in thrall (Ps. 49¹⁵). It is a kingdom (Ps. 89⁴⁹). It is, of course, defined and described in topographical terms in accordance with the various world views of antiquity. But here it is to be observed—and this seems to apply not only to the Old Testament, but also the similar metaphysical speculations of all other peoples— that it is not the particular cosmological and topographical notions which are important here, but the conception of the reality and nature of death itself. The fact that the place of death is conceived as a kind of city or house which is sealed up (Jonah 2⁷), or locked with a key (Rev. 1¹⁸, 9¹, 20¹), or as a place where men are bound with cords (Ps. 18⁵, 116³), or again in Ps. 94¹⁷ and 115¹⁷ as the land of silence, or in Is. 26¹⁹ as the house of " dust," or in Ps. 88⁶ etc. as the realm of " darkness," shows that these are simply pictures which reflect the actual view of death which is being entertained. This is even more true of its localisations, and especially of the fact that the place of death and the realm of the dead is always sought somewhere in the depths, and that it is described as an " underworld " (*Sheol*). It often appears in a remarkable combination of antithesis and unity with heaven as the comprehensive term for that which is " above." With this it makes up the sphere of God's sovereignty (Amos 9² ; Is. 7¹¹ ; Job 11⁸ ; Ps. 139⁸). Properly and primarily, however, it is not in relation to heaven but to earth as the sphere of terrestrial life, or to the surface of the earth as the abode of the living, that it is called the " underworld." It has all the characteristics of the " pit." Into it the dead " descend " or " go down " never to return. It can be called quite simply the " grave " or " pit " Ps. 28¹ ; Is. 38¹⁸, etc.). " In entering the visible world of the grave the dead also become the denizens of the realm of the dead and are subject to the conditions of life obtaining there " (J. Pedersen). The underworld is in an unqualified sense the grave, the " primal pit " (J. Pedersen), of which every individual grave is a manifestation, just as " Israel " or " Moab " is the archetypical Israelite or Moabite respectively, acquiring concrete form in each individual Israelite or Moabite. The terms " grave " and " underworld " evidently mean the individual and total aspect of the one reality of death. But death has not only the " form " of the grave. As the end and terminus of life it stands in an ominous relation to chaos. Now in the creation story of Gen. 1 chaos is represented in the world which is created, and therefore separated from its earth by the upper and nether ocean. And since the upper ocean, according to Gen. 1[6ff.], is separated from the nether, and therefore also from our whole sphere, so that it does not come into account, the place of death is sought as a locality beneath the nether firmament. Hence the floods, the waves which break in from every side, the fathomless deeps and the muddy slime which make residence in the underworld so unpleasant according to so many passages in the Old Testament. Hence, too, the affinity between death and Egypt, or the sea monster Rahab (Is. 30[7], etc.). But the comfortless prolongation of life, the loneliness, dereliction and impotence of man in its sphere, also caused them to identify its location with the wilderness surrounding Babylon and Egypt as well as Canaan. Grave, ocean and wilderness—it would be impossible to harmonise these three most important descriptions of the place of death and the dead. And there is certainly no need to postulate various stages in the development of the whole conception. They are the " three non-worlds " (Pedersen). They manifest and represent and attest death and thus the place of the dead as that which ultimately borders and concludes man's living space. The grave, ocean and wilderness show that it is painfully remote from this living space of ours, being alien and opposed to it in every way. Because they do this, the living Israelite regards them as the place of death, to enter which spells unqualified danger and defilement and a mortal threat. That is why he is always so cautious about such places.

But the Old Testament knows more about the realm of the dead than is indicated by these localisations. For death has and retains not only its own allotted place, but its own dynamic, in virtue of which it invades the areas which properly belong to the world of life. That death is not only an irresistible force but comes as such is a common biblical view. Its kingdom is on the offensive. It has a " hand " which reaches out (Ps. 89[48]). The same is true of the underworld (Ps. 49[15]). The underworld " hath enlarged her desire, and opened her mouth without measure : and their glory, and their multitude, and their pomp, and he that rejoiceth with them, descend into it " (Is. 5[14]). " Death . . . cannot be satisfied, but gathereth to (itself) all nations, and heapeth unto (itself) all peoples " (Hab. 2[5], cf. Prov. 27[20]). Just as no country can be sure that it will not some day be flooded by the ocean or become a desert, and nature in its regular course is inevitably exposed to decay, so man, and his house and people, are threatened by the victorious onslaughts of the kingdom of the dead. The darkness of death spreads like a shadow " under the sun " (Eccles. 1[3f.]). Even during his lifetime man may find himself in its clutches. Sick, accursed, imprisoned or lonely, he may find himself on its slippery slope and under its sentence—a grim picture of the denizens of the underworld and the next-door neighbour of its real and permanent inhabitants. We do not have merely the exaggerations of poetic fantasy, but depictions of real states, in such descriptions of extreme misery, unsurpassed both in quality and quantity as we find in Lamentations and some of the Psalms and above all the Book of Job, whether in relation to the people visited by divine judgment and therefore exposed to this offensive of the realm of the dead, or by individuals in a similar situation. " In the midst of life we are in death." The various descriptions of the different kinds of distress in which men cry aloud to God (e.g., in Ps. 107), the afflictions of those lost in the desert, of the sick, of prisoners, of those in peril on the sea— all these frequently coincide. They are all reduced to the same denomination and set in the same lurid light. All this shows that in the theme of all serious human lamentation we are finally concerned with the same supreme trials and tribulations which cannot be exaggerated, because they call man in his totality in question. Behind them all is the fact that already here and now man can find himself exposed to the onslaughts of the invading realm of the dead. Left alone, he is powerless to face them. The entire Book of Job is a description of such an attack successfully directed against man, though not without the permission and control of God. It is really with death itself that living man has to deal. All this death means in terms of weakness, decay, loneliness, in short, loss of life ; all this makes the grave, the ocean and the wilderness places of death as present here and now in full actuality for the sick, the outcast, the persecuted, defeated and oppressed, the prisoner in his prison, the wanderer in the wilderness, the storm-tossed sea-farer. For although they are not yet actually dead, they already experience the full reality of death. To this context belongs the mirror of old age and final death—a mirror which cannot be too highly commended for its brutal frankness—held before the face of youth in Eccles. 12$^{1-8}$: " Remember now thy Creator in the days of thy youth, while the evil days come not, nor the years draw nigh, when thou shalt say, I have no pleasure in them ; while the sun, or the light, or the moon, or the stars, be not darkened, nor the clouds return after the rain : in the day when the keepers of the house shall tremble, and the strong men shall bow themselves, and the grinders cease because they are few, and those that look out of the windows be darkened, and the doors shall be shut in the street, when the sound of the grinding is low, and he shall rise up at the voice of a bird, and all the daughters of music shall be brought low ; also when they shall be afraid of that which is high, and fear shall be in the way, and the almond tree shall flourish, and the grasshopper shall be a burden, and the caperberry shall fail : because man goeth to his long home, and the mourners go about the streets : or ever the silver cord be loosed, or the golden bowl be broken, or the pitcher be broken at the fountain, or the wheel be broken at the cistern ; then shall the dust return to the earth as it was, and the spirit shall return unto God who gave it. Vanity of vanities, saith the preacher ; all is vanity." And last but not least, the worst thing about death, the really deadly thing about it, is true already here and now, namely, that man can no longer see God, or worship Him, or praise and adore Him. Man is no longer present before God and for Him. He is forsaken by God. God is no longer his Comforter, Helper, Avenger and Saviour. All he can do is to cry and sob helplessly. Where is he then ? What has become of God's promises for him as an individual, or for the whole people of God in this present plight ? In this context it hardly seems to make sense to boggle at the so-called imprecatory Psalms of the Old Testament. What is man's enemy but a human witness of death's onslaught upon him ? And what can man do under its onslaught but beseech God to smite and destroy this witness of death ? In close association with man's enemy there are the friends of Job (surprisingly found in other places as well) who misunderstand and desert and turn against him. The whole bitterness of his complaint against the destruction which overtook him in this form is expressed in Ps. 55$^{13f.}$: " It was thou, a man mine equal, my guide and mine acquaintance. We took sweet counsel together, and walked unto the house of God in company." With his eye on such friends as these the same Psalmist says immediately after : " Let death seize upon them, and let them go down quick into hell : for wickedness is in their dwellings, and among them." But will God hear him ? " Where is thy God " (Ps. 42^{10}): The relevant Old Testament passages in this vein are not to be taken as a kind of final and supreme human achievement. Occasionally to be sure, sometimes very powerfully and sometimes marginally and very quietly, there can burst forth from the depths praise and adoration of God. But this does not mean that man has gone on thinking, and that after all his laments and complaints he comes to the opposite conclusion, that God is present, that He is faithful and gracious, that He will help man, and that He is actually helping him already. How could he come to this opposite conclusion when he is already in the sphere of death ? "*Hope* thou in God : for I shall yet praise him," is the final word which the Psalmist can address to his soul, i.e., to himself, even in Ps. 42⁵, ¹¹, 43⁵. What lies beyond is the absolute miracle of salvation out of the midst of death, and the proclamation of this miracle. In death as such man has no ability to speak in this way. He does not have the right and power to say : "Nevertheless I am continually with thee " (Ps. 73²³). In itself, to be dead is to be unable to live, even to live with God. And the meaning of the tribulation of the people and individuals described in the Old Testament is that it is the tribulation of death, translating man into a depth from which he can never emerge because the way down to it is a one-way street. To be sure, a miracle may still happen. He can still complain to God and inquire of him. This is what makes him different from those who are already dead. He is still only in the territory which death has annexed by its victorious onslaught. He is still only in the territory adjacent to the kingdom of the dead. It may still be said of him that " a living dog is better than a dead lion " (Eccles. 9⁴). He still stands as it were on the very edge of the abyss. There are still many different kinds and degrees of tribulation, varying in intensity in proportion to their proximity to the abyss. The true and final victory of death has not yet come. A man in this type of tribulation is still only in an indirect sense a dead man. All these reservations must be made. Yet we cannot overlook or dispute the fact that already here and now he is assailed by death itself, and therefore in mortal tribulation. Indirectly, he is already a dead man. For what matters is not that he has not yet definitely succumbed to death. What really determines his situation is that death is already so near to him. For this means that its power has already attacked him, that his foot is set " in slippery places." He is on a slippery slope, and as far as mortal eye can see, he cannot stop. And as he looks to his inevitable end, he is already here and now a lost man. To this extent he is " partially," and in a very real sense, already in the realm of the dead.

This, then, is how the Old Testament sees the nature and reality of death. We shall not quote individual New Testament passages to elaborate the picture. In the New Testament death stands wholly under the sign of the divine judgment of sinful man fulfilled in it, and even more so under the sign of the setting aside of this judgment and therefore the defeat of death. We shall have to speak later of these special standpoints from which death is also to be seen. But so far as concerns its nature and reality, the finitude of our time and the inherent limitation of our life, we may simply assume that the Old Testament picture as outlined is accepted in every respect by the Evangelists and apostolic writers (who after all were Israelites), and may thus be presupposed in whatever else they have to say on the topic.

The extraordinarily difficult question which has to be answered in this connexion is whether and how far we have to understand the finitude of our allotted time, and death as the termination of human life, as a determination of the divinely created and therefore good nature of man. How do we stand at the moment ? We began with a comprehensive survey of the limitation of our time as such and as a whole. We saw in general terms how right it is to say that our time is bounded and our life correspondingly limited. We then took up the question afresh, paying special attention to the fact that our time has a beginning. This consideration led us to a confirmation of the general positive result. Shall we again find our position confirmed in respect of the end of time? The question of the beginning of our time was serious enough, but not, as we have seen, so urgent. Consequently, we may also say that it was not so very difficult to give it a positive answer. It is quite different with the question which now concerns us. It may at least be asked whether we shall not be left with a certain disquiet even in respect of the positive answer which we gave to the general and all-embracing question. May it not be that the Yes which we worked out there is not quite right after all? What is there there to cause disquiet? Obviously the fact that our answer embraces the second problem as well as the first, and it perhaps seems to be asking too much that we should give this second question a positive answer. An end is set to our time. One day our life will be no more. Death is a reality. But how is this reality compatible with God? How can God be the good Creator of a human nature good in this respect too? Is not this intolerable and from the standpoint of biblical theology untenable? But if so, we must obviously revise and restrict the general result provisionally attained. We must say that our positive answer applied only to the limitation of our time in a backward direction, only to the fact that our life has a beginning. And perhaps even this aspect of our conclusion is shattered and needs to be replaced by a very different one. Perhaps the whole of our previous investigation and presentation hitherto hinges on whether it is possible and right to push forward to a positive answer at this point too, in respect of the end of our time.

But in fact it cannot be disguised that this is just where the shoe pinches. In our attempt to consider the problem of our destiny we cannot avoid certain emphases which do not arise in respect of that of our origin. We have described our being in time as a flight from our non-being from which we come, a flight which is finally destined to be futile if we must ultimately die and again find ourselves confronted by non-being. Is there any other way of seeing and putting it? Obviously this is the only way we know of. But if our life is a flight, and a futile one at that; if it is a story of fear and failure; if it is therefore a twofold terror, how can it be the good creation of God? When we describe it in these terms, do we not speak of something very different from the good creation of God? Have we not spoken of something which on any positive estimation is intolerable and from the standpoint of biblical theology untenable?

Can we accept the Old Testament's designation and description of the nature and reality of death without realising that, above and beyond what may belong to the nature of man, there speaks in it a view of man and judgment on him which are related to the determination of his existence in which he is still under the will of God, but which is not normal, which is definitely abnormal, which was not there originally but is an intrusion from without, which does not square with God's positive will for man but contradicts it, and only so is subject to

Him ? How else could death be so sinister ? How else could it pose to human life such a threat of complete deprivation, even in its relationship to God ? How else could it be an underworld described in purely negative terms ? How else could it have such dynamic power and force ? How else could its kingdom be so overwhelming and tyrannical, overshadowing the whole of human life ?

Is it possible to make a single statement about the finitude of our being in time without bringing to light this negative aspect of the matter ? And is not all that the Bible itself has to say about the nature and reality of death determined by this negative aspect, which is something for which we have no cause to praise and thank God ?

The question is whether it would not be better simply to stop at this negative aspect of the matter. Is not this all that there is to say about it ? Is not the finitude of our time, i.e., death, to be regarded as an evil which for reasons best known to Himself God has suspended over us, and to that extent willed, but which does not spring as such from His good creation or belong to human nature, so that it is quite impossible to give any positive answer at this point, and we must deliberately refrain from doing so ? Is not the end of our being in time as such an unequivocal negative pronounced over our creaturely existence ? Is not this the only way to understand it ? Can we therefore find any real place for it in a doctrine of the creature of God ?

That is the question which obtrudes upon us here as it could not do in regard to the beginning of our life. In that respect it could acquire significance only at very most in the light of this end. The fact that at a particular moment, at the beginning of our time, we emerged from non-being to being is not intrinsically negative or necessarily evil. It is, indeed, the very opposite. It signifies something supremely positive if it is the case, as we have seen, that we come from God. It can be negative and evil only if our end means passing not only into non-being but into the negation of being. If this is what is meant by the death which is the end of our time, it follows as a consequence that we have also emerged from negation. We are then forced to conclude that our beginning is also negative and evil. At first sight there seems to be no reason why we should draw this conclusion about our beginning. But here, in respect of our end, the whole picture is obviously quite different.

For if death is indisputably a return to non-being, and if this can mean only a return to the same God who called us out of non-being to being, our future prospect is to be seen in a very different light, or rather in a gloomy shadow as compared with our beginning. For between the two termini, the beginning and end of our life as already lived and still to be lived, there stands our life which in accordance with its determination and the freedom we enjoy in it may be lived in a positive relation to God and an equally positive relation to our fellows, but which we have not lived and do not and shall not live in this way but very differently. Between our beginning and our end, between our emergence from God and our final confrontation with Him, there stands the fact of the abysmal and irreparable guilt which we have incurred from the beginning of our existence, are still incurring and will increasingly continue to do so until the end : guilt in relation to God and also to our divinely appointed fellows ; guilt of many kinds, great and trivial, gross and refined, blatant and complicated, but always guilt. Guilt means retrogression. And retrogression consists in a failure to use our God-given freedom ; in a failure to be truly human in our relationships with Him and our fellows ; in an inconceivable renunciation of our freedom ; in our incredible, inexplicable and impossible choice of the imprisonment of a being in renunciation on both sides ; in our incomprehensible lapse into a state of ungodliness and inhumanity. That we are guilty in this boundless and quite inexcusable way is what will confront us at the end of our time and stare us in the face when we die. It is in this irreparable state of transgression that we shall be translated from being to non-being and brought face to face with our Creator. With all our life up to this point, with our life as it is now concluded and a thing of the past, we shall meet Him and be wholly dependent upon Him. That we shall be no more will mean concretely that our past will be only one of total guilt and retrogression—one long failure. Can we doubt that for this reason death must inevitably seem to be negative and have only the character of an unqualified evil ? What else can its onset mean but the approach and execution of God's judgment upon us ? What can this judgment mean but our rejection ? And what can its execution mean but the ending and expulsion of our unworthy and degenerate life from before the eyes of the Creator from whom it has already alienated itself by its guilt ? What can it mean but its total destruction, dissolution and abolition in confirmation of what it has made of itself ? What fate can measure up to life's deserts, and what can its goal be, but absolute negation ? Was it not a thing of nought ? What has it to expect from its end but the divine subscription to its nothingness ? As we approach our end, we approach God. And since we are guilty in relation to Him as our Creator, this excludes any other prospect. Not to be any more is to be powerless to alter the fact. To die is to be caught in the toils of this unalterable fact. It is to be at the point to which we fall. And because even now we are powerless to alter it—and the less so the longer we live—our life is already overshadowed by its end. Hence Holy Scripture is right in describing the realm of death not only as an underworld but as an onslaught to which man's life in time is already exposed.

Death, as it actually encounters us men, is the sign of God's judgment on us. We cannot say less than this, but of course we must not try to say more either.

That this judgment is executed as we die, that when our life comes to its end we shall have to pay what it is worth, or not worth, with the fulfilment of our rejection, our plunge into negation and then, if we may use the phrase, our being in negation, in outer darkness, in the eternal torment of a past and non-recurrent opportunity, this cannot be posited as a general truth. For there is a possibility of our being spared this death because Another has suffered it in His death for us. The New Testament assumes that this is in fact the case.

But it can and must be said generally that death as it actually meets us is the sign of this judgment. In other words, it is its supremely real and full proclamation and representation. Limiting our life and thus belonging to it, it bears all the marks of this judgment. Our life as bounded by it is thus necessarily a life marked for this judgment (like a tree marked for felling). It is devoted and delivered to this judgment, like a bracket with a minus before it which changes every plus in the bracket into a minus. The bracket is still there, but the minus stands in front of it cancelling every other prospect but this fatal change. The inevitability of death means that this threat over-shadows and dominates our whole life. It cannot be gainsaid or defied. It might well be, indeed it is necessarily the case, that the ultimate truth about man, which dominates every prior truth, is that he stands under this threat which is not to be gainsaid or defied. Less than this we cannot say. Death, as it meets us, can be understood only as a sign of God's judgment. For when it meets us, as it undoubtedly does, it meets us as sinful and guilty men with whom God cannot finally do anything but whom He can only regret having made. For man has failed as His creature. He has not used the previous freedom in which he was privileged to exist before God. He has squandered it away in the most incredible manner. He can hope for nothing better than to be hewn down and cast into the fire.

Of death as it actually meets us we certainly cannot say that it is an inherent part of human nature as God created it and as it is therefore good. There is no doubt whatever that it is something negative and evil. Yet we have to realise and state that it is an evil ordained by God as a sign of His judgment, and not therefore a fate but an ordinance which proceeds and is to be accepted from God. And because it is our sin and guilt which God encounters with this sign, we have also to realise and state that when we stand under this sign it is our just desert, so that we have no reason to complain or protest. But our standing under this sign is not something intrinsic to our human nature. For God did not create us to exist under this impending threat of being hewn down and cast into the fire. It does not correspond to our determination to have no other prospect but a being in outer darkness and eternal torment.

We cannot talk ourselves out of it, or persuade ourselves that that is not really our plight. It is so, even though we may wish things were different. And we really know this. There has never been a man who was not afraid of death. It is possible to stifle this fear. But in so doing, we only show that we have it none the less. Man lives in fear for his life. But this fear in all its forms, even that of Stoic resignation, is basically the fear of death which we cannot talk ourselves out of.

Again, we cannot persuade ourselves that death as the sign of divine judgment standing over us, the fear of death and a life spent in fear of death, is natural, normal and good in the sense of being a positive ordinance of God. If there is anything natural about it ; if it belongs in any sense to man's divinely appointed creaturely status that his time should have an end ; if death is not intrinsically and essentially a curse and a misery, then its intrinsic and essential quality is for us at any rate unfathomably and inaccessibly concealed beneath the unnatural and even anti-natural guise in which it now comes to us. In any case, there is no question of our being able to change the meaning of the judgment symbolised by death into something different. We should have to forget our sin and guilt if we were to persuade ourselves that death is after all not so dangerous as all that, and even a cheerful and welcome prospect. The man who fears death, even though he contrives to put a somewhat better face on it, is at least nearer to the truth than the man who does not fear it, or rather pretends that there is no reason why he should do so. Since it is the sign of the divine judgment on human sin and guilt, it is very much to be feared. There is no truth in the suggestion that death is our " brother," or in some way our friend, or even our deliverer. Such turns of expression simply fail to face up seriously to the grim reality, and will only vanish like bubbles in the air. The natural being of man resists his end—perhaps not necessarily his end as such, but at any rate the kind of end we have before our eyes as we contemplate our sin and guilt. And he is right, even though his resistence is futile and the shears of death show no mercy. It is never the natural being of man, but always man deceived and doubly deluded who speaks of death's reaper as though it were a kindly angel of light. Since death is the sign of divine judgment, man as he naturally is can face it only with sorrow. If we are to tackle honestly the question of the meaning of the finitude of our time, this is the first thing to see and accept. The whole situation is in fact very different from what it is when we ask concerning the meaning of its beginning.

In biblical demonstration of what has been said, we can first point only to the wholly negative character which the Old Testament gives to its picture of the nature and reality of death. In the perspective of the Old Testament, what is natural to man is his endowment with the life-giving breath of God which constitutes him as the soul of his body, not his subsequent loss of it. What is natural to him is the fact that he is and will be, not that he has been. What is natural to him is his being in the land of the living, not his being in the underworld. What is natural to him is life, not death. Death, on the other hand, is the epitome of what is contrary to nature. It is not, therefore, normal. It is always a kind of culpable extravagance to man when he longs for death, like Elijah under the juniper tree (1 K. 19⁴) or Jonah under the gourd (Jonah 4⁸).

It is only hypothetically that Job protests to God : " So that my soul chooseth strangling, and death rather than my bones. I loathe my life ; I would not live alway " (Job 7$^{15f.}$). In extreme situations a man may curse the day of his birth (Jer. 15^{10} ; 20$^{14f.}$; Job 3$^{3f.}$). But he cannot rejoice at his death, or seriously welcome it. It is an exception which proves the rule when Job 3$^{21f.}$ speaks of those who " long for death, but it cometh not ; and dig for it more than for hid treasures ; which rejoice exceedingly, and are glad, when they find the grave," or when reflection about all the injustice that there is under the sun culminates (Eccles. 4^2) in the statement : " I praised the dead which are already dead more than the living which are yet alive." Hyperbolic statements of this kind do not mean that death is naturalised or neutralised or made into something heroic. When Saul (1 Sam. 31^4) falls upon his own sword, or when in later days Judas (Mt. 27^5) goes and hangs himself, these are deeds of despair which demonstrate their rejection by God and prove that death is the supreme evil of human life.

But it is the New Testament which is most direct and explicit on the point that death is the sign of God's judgment, and therefore the supreme evil. In the Old Testament this interconnexion of sin, guilt and death is asserted only as it were in specific cases, i.e., in relation to the end of particular ungodly men or in prospect of the wholesale destruction threatened against and in large measure fulfilled upon Israel and other nations. There are also particular sins and transgressions whose perpetrators must " die the death " according to the Law or by a special decree. Above all it is worth noting that a direct encounter with Yahweh is regarded as an experience which results in immediate death. " Thou canst not see my face : for there shall no man see me and live " (Ex. 33^{20} ; Jud. 13^{22}). The story of the call of Moses includes the remarkable story of how Yahweh sought to kill him, so that he enters his office only as one who has escaped the ultimate crisis (Ex. 4$^{24f.}$). Intercourse with Yahweh's holiness is at the very least a threat to life, and in certain cases can actually bring death. This is taught in 1 Sam. 5–6 by the story of the fortunes of the ark among the Philistines and its subsequent restoration, and in 2 Sam 6$^{1f.}$ by the account of its removal to Jerusalem. From such passages it would perhaps be possible to draw the general conclusion that death is the immediate result when man is confronted with the holy God before whom he is unclean and unholy and cannot stand upright. This is an encounter which man cannot survive, because the life-giving breath of God can only be taken away from him again now that he has proved unworthy of Him. But this truth is never stated in general terms. The only direct statement which suggests that death is to be understood generally as the effect of the divine curse and as a punishment is in the threat uttered in Paradise (Gen. 2^{17}), and its confirmation in Gen. 3^{19} and 6^3. From the rest of the Old Testament the only general conclusion to be drawn is that, not merely when it actually comes, but in its total significance for a man's preceding life, death is a great woe which God suspends over him, and which he can only bear in submission and sadness. Its character as such emerges very clearly. But the Old Testament gives us only occasional hints as to why it is a woe.

We are shown this very vividly when we turn to the New Testament. Here the line is drawn with unequivocal clarity even in the Gospels. For Jesus, at least during His Galilean ministry, was from the very outset engaged in open combat with suffering and sickness in all its forms. Now that the Messiah has come, the immediate and inevitable result is an onslaught against the invasion of the realm of death in the world of life. Note that for Jesus even sickness is not a natural but an unnatural evil. It is an outbreak and effect of the demonic world, which, while it operates with divine permission, functions exclusively in opposition to God. In other words, the divine permission is only provisional. It would therefore be utterly nonsensical to try to translate the relevant statements on this subject into the relatively harmless language of modern medicine.

When the Gospels discern the work of demons in sickness, this is not merely the expression of contemporary beliefs, but a fact of theological significance. The Messiah is the Representative of the positive will of God who engages the advance posts of the underworld (i.e., demons) in victorious combat. In His environment the blind necessarily see, the lame walk, the deaf hear, the dead are raised, and the Gospel is preached to the poor, i.e., the oppressed of the Old Testament Psalms. Surely this can only mean that the signs of divine grace and assistance are provisionally set up against the sign of divine judgment. All the miracles of Jesus, including the stilling of the storm (the reader will recall the connexion between the ocean and the underworld !) and the feeding of the multitude (which significantly takes place in the wilderness), are counter-signs of this nature. God will not chide for ever. He will not always allow death, which has broken loose, to run its course. This power of death is already unmasked by the countersign of Jesus' miracles as a power which is opposed to God, as God is opposed to it. No wonder it is the demons who first recognise who Jesus is, and address Him as such (Mk. 1²³, 5⁷).

In Jerusalem He performed no such healings. For the Galilean healings and those on the way to Jerusalem were only preliminary skirmishes. In Jerusalem He Himself died—paradoxically enough, as those who mocked Him on the cross (Mk. 15²⁹ᶠ·) quite rightly observed. Yet the dying of Jesus is the decisive event, the climax of the whole drama, of which the miracles are only a pre-liminary announcement. The only point which has now to be stressed about the significance of this event is that by undergoing death in His person Jesus provided a total and conclusive revelation of its character. For He suffered death as the judgment of God. It would be out of place to say here that He did so as the sign of God's judgment. Here, in the person of the Messiah, it is God Himself, His embodied grace and help, who is genuinely and definitively present, both as Judge and Judged. He judges as He created and established between Himself and man the justice which had to fall on man, so that he had to suffer what he had deserved—death as a consuming force, eternal torment and utter darkness. But He is also judged as, knowing neither sin nor guilt, He caused this judgment to fall on Himself in place of the many guilty sinners, so that it availed for them all, and the judgment suffered by Him was fulfilled on them in Him, and their dying no longer has to be this dying, the suffering of punishment which they have deserved, but only its sign. What death is remorselessly as it encounters us is revealed in this act of judgment. At this point we cannot possibly fail to see that it hangs over us like a threat, and what it threatens us with. It is the enemy, the " last enemy " (1 Cor. 15²⁶), of man, whom God, in the death of Jesus, declares to be His enemy as well, and treats as such by placing Himself at the side of man in the verdict there pro-nounced, and snatching man from its jaws by the death of Jesus for him. It remains for us as a sign of the divine judgment. We have no longer to suffer the judgment itself.

But it is still the case that we have to suffer when we die. We have still to do with this sign, and therefore with the threats of the enemy. The New Testa-ment faces up to this insight at its centre and therefore with full seriousness. Our death is intimately connected with our sin and guilt. This can no longer be disregarded when we remember that man's sin is forgiven, that his guilt is cancelled, that the judgment of God has been executed upon it, and that it has thus been removed from us. As man's eternal corruption, but also as its sign, death is not a part of man's nature as God created it. But it entered into the world through sin as an alien lord (Rom. 5¹², ¹⁴, ¹⁷ ; 1 Cor. 15²²). It is the wages of sin (Rom. 6²³), just as sin, conversely, is its " sting," i.e., that which makes the suffering of death so bitter and poisonous, constituting it an evil for man (1 Cor. 15⁵⁶). According to Heb. 2¹⁴ the power over it which gives it its might is that of the διάβολος. It is with his kingdom that we have to reckon in death, and quite directly. Death is the φρόνημα τῆς σαρκός, as Rom. 8⁶ says so fittingly. This means that death is really the objective goal of carnal, i.e., sinful and guilty and therefore lost man, not life as he imagines. What this man thinks and does is futile, and can only issue in futility. " Sin . . . bringeth forth death " (Jas. 1¹⁵). " If ye live after the flesh, ye must die " (Rom. 8¹³). " He that soweth to his flesh shall of the flesh reap φθορά " (Gal. 6⁸). Living according to the deceitful lusts, the old man is *ipso facto* in decay (φθειρόμενος, Eph. 4²²). " Sin revived, and I died " (Rom. 7⁹ᶠ·). " He that loveth not abideth in death " (1 Jn. 3¹⁴). When Lk. 1⁷⁹ describes the men of Israel as those who " sit in darkness and in the shadow of death," and Heb. 2¹⁵ speaks of all men before Christ as those who " through fear of death were all their lifetime subject to bondage," this is still, as it were, Old Testament language, and falls short of the true New Testament insight, which sees that before and apart from what God has done for him in Jesus Christ man is dead even while he lives (Mt. 8²² ; Lk. 15³² ; Eph. 2¹ ; 1 Tim. 5⁶), and that his works are " dead " works (Heb. 9¹⁴). In the light of this new insight Rev. 3¹ can even say of a whole Christian congregation : " Thou hast a name that thou livest, and thou art dead." It is also to be understood as a superimposition of Old Testament thought upon the insight and language of the New Testament when in Ac. 1¹⁷ᶠ· (Judas) and 5¹ᶠ· (Ananias and Sapphira) particular sins are specially punished with death, or when in Rom. 1³² a catalogue of vices closes with a reference to the divine δικαίωμα according to which " they which commit such things are worthy of death," or when in 1 Cor. 11³⁰ certain specific fatal instances of sickness and infirmity in the Corinthian Church are linked with the unworthy reception of the Lord's Supper. The general understanding of death as the fruit of sin naturally involves such particular applications and can lead to occasional emphasis on them. Yet according to the insight and language of the New Testament, as Rom. 5¹² makes particularly clear, the connexion between sin and death is not conditioned by particular sins, but is necessary and general. Every man dies (and lives already) in this involvement. Every man is liable to death and moves towards it. Every man stands under the sign of the merited judgment of God. It is obvious that the estimation of death as a purely natural phenomenon, or as a friendly or at least conceivably neutral fate, is not only conspicuous by its absence, but basically alien. Death is the great mark of the unnatural state in which we exist. And it is this, not because of a chance fate, but because we exist under the thrall of the devil. It is this because we are sinners involved in guilt. It is this because our behaviour makes our life *eo ipso* a forfeited life given over to death. As we said above, it is the centre of the New Testament perception which makes this particular perspective and language necessary. The centre of the New Testament perception is the cross of Jesus Christ. It is not because the apostles and the earliest Christian Church were for some reason more deeply shocked at death than their Israelite and Hellenistic contemporaries, nor is it because for some reason they took sin more seriously than their contemporaries, that they were so unanimously agreed in seeing death and sin in that strict, general and necessary connexion, and so unequivocal in all that they said on the subject. The reason for their unequivocal unanimity is that they could contemplate it only from the point where they saw man's deliverance accomplished, and life, salvation and felicity offered in ineffable fulness. They were not pessimists, whether in their view of the sinful life of man or in that of the nature and reality of death. But they were realists in their view of what had happened in the crucifixion and death of Jesus Christ and its accompanying revelation in respect of the death of all men. For three decisions were openly declared and given universal validity in this event.

The first is that there is no human greatness and grandeur which is not exceeded, overshadowed and fundamentally called in question by death : not even that of the promised and manifested Messiah and Son of Man ; not even that of the incarnate Son of God and the great Servant of God. When the divine Logos became flesh, this meant that in so doing He delivered Himself wholly and utterly to φθορά. "Be it far from thee, Lord : this shall never be unto thee" (Mt. 16²²), is Peter's reaction to the first prediction of the passion. And the Evangelist frankly calls this reaction an ἐπιτιμᾶν. It was indeed strange that immediately after the first Messianic confession and Jesus' joyful acceptance of it there should follow the prediction that Jesus must go to Jerusalem to be killed. It was strange that He who had done so much to save others from death should face and actually come to the situation of being unable to save Himself from death (Mk. 15³¹). It was strange that death should be permitted to achieve this masterstroke by which all the signs erected against the onslaught of the realm of death, and with them the One who had erected them, were to be wholly called in question again. What was meant by the promised constancy of the Church against the "gates of hell" (Mt. 16¹⁸) if He who gave this promise was Himself obliged to submit to this sphere ? The whole terror of this paradox is reflected in the saying of the disciples on the road to Emmaus in Lk. 24²¹ : "We trusted that it had been he which should have redeemed Israel ; and beside all this, to-day is the third day since these things were done." But it was no use complaining or lamenting. It had to happen, and it was right that it should do so. The life of the man Jesus is included in this bracket. His mission as Messiah and Son of Man is fulfilled along the lines of Is. 53. There is no question of His by-passing death and the grave. He has to tread this road to the bitter end. He is as helpless in face of death as any other man. Nor would he be the Son of God—of a God friendly to man—if he were not "obedient even unto death" (Phil. 2⁸). When Peter rebukes him on this point, he has to endure the shame of being called "Satan" and "offence." He does not think in divine but in human terms (Mt. 16²³). Death must show what it can do on Him supremely, as in a masterpiece. No place must be left for foolish dreams, as though everything were bound to come right in the end. Deliverance from death cannot be deliverance from before it but only deliverance from out of it. Even the power and significance of those countersigns depends on His not refusing to drink this cup (Mt. 26³⁹ᶠ·). They would not be countersigns, the preliminary signs of His resurrection and the resurrection of all the dead, but only the unimportant acts of a skilled wonder worker like many others, if Jesus had refused this course. As the One He is, He must submit to being baptised with a baptism from which He shrinks with fear like any other man, or even more so (for a reason to be indicated in a moment, Lk. 12⁵⁰). For the reality to which He pointed with these countersigns would not be real, that counter-offensive against the onslaught of the realm of death would have been powerless, the fire which He came to kindle on earth would have remained unkindled (Lk. 12⁴⁹), if He had shrunk from this baptism and had not defied death in the realm of the dead by submitting to it as a willing victim. But this seals the fact that it is not merely *de facto* but *de jure* and therefore necessarily and universally that death has power over man. Even on the shattering view of the Old Testament it has this power only *de facto*. Men see and know it only as the grave and underworld which awaits us all. It is the New Testament which tells us that this has to be, and it does so by proclaiming Him who was crucified, dead and buried as the Lord of life.

The second decision is that the death to which we all move implies the threat of eternal corruption. As Jesus suffered it, He suffered *eternal* corruption. This is what distinguishes His death from all others. "He was made a curse for us" (Gal. 3¹³). This cannot be said of every one who is hanged or who dies in any other way. But of Him it must be said. It may surprise us that the ideas of man's being in death are not mitigated or even displaced in the New Testament as compared with the Old. We might have expected this now that the "glad tidings" are proclaimed. But in fact they are accentuated as never before. Instead of the negative picture of a shadowy existence of departed "souls," we now have a picture of human existence in "hell." Hell means punishment of a very positive kind. We can only be disappointed if we foolishly

expect the New Testament to be more " human " in this respect than the Old.
It is the New Testament which first gives us a picture like that of Dives, who
in the realm of the dead is in " anguish in this flame " (Lk. 16²⁴ᶠ·). It is in the
New Testament that we first hear of men being cast out into outer darkness
where " there shall be weeping and gnashing of teeth " (Mt. 22¹³). It is here
that we first read of the " worm which dieth not, and the fire which is not
quenched " (Mk. 9⁴⁸). It is here that we first have threats like those of Rev. 14¹¹ :
" And the smoke of their torment ascended up for ever and ever ; and they
have no rest day nor night, who worship the beast and his image." Is not all
this far worse than the imprecatory Psalms which come in for so much censure ?
It is true, of course, that partly under Persian influences the speculations of
later Judaism about life beyond the grave have intensified this picture. But
this does not really answer the question how the Church of Jesus Christ came to
appropriate these intensified conceptions. If this surprising procedure meant
anything at all, it could only mean that, irrespective of detail, in the sphere of
the revelation and experience of the divine kingdom, grace and salvation, they
were precluded from understanding man's existence in death merely as an existence in unwelcome but tolerable neutrality. On the contrary, they had to
understand it positively as intolerable suffering. And they had to do this
because it was only in this way that they could understand the being of Jesus
in death. This was the unique cup which made Jesus shrink back in fear. This
was the unique baptism of which He was afraid. He did not submit to a blind
fate or chance, but to the judgment of God. In dying, He did not merely
surrender Himself to that alienation from God which, as we learn from the
Old Testament, is the climax of what man has to suffer as one whose life is
over. He did this too, of course, as attested by the word on the cross : " My God,
my God, why hast thou forsaken me " (Mk. 15³⁴). It is no accident that this
saying has come down to us in Aramaic and is a direct quotation of Ps. 22¹. But
the last " loud cry " with which Jesus died (Mk. 15³⁷), and above all the representative character proper to this death, His vicarious bearing of the sin of all Israel
and indeed the whole world, points beyond the comfortless but tolerable situation of the righteous man of the Old Testament as alienated from God in *Sheol*.
In this respect the Old Testament comes close to the New only in those passages
which speak of the deadly significance and effect of the direct encounter between
man and the living God. Here is the direct encounter there conceived only
as a remote possibility. Here we see that it is indeed a fearful thing to fall
into the hands of the living God (Heb. 10³¹). Here man—the man who is wholly
and unreservedly for God—has God against him. Here God is wholly and
unreservedly and in full seriousness against man. Here God metes out to man
the kind of treatment he has deserved at His hand. This is how He must deal
with him now in His mercy, which is " righteous " to the extent that in it He
wills to establish His own right and that of man. Here He treats man as a
transgressor with whom He can only deal in His wrath. Here He treats him in
accordance with the enmity which man has merited from Him. Here, namely,
in this One whom He has destined and appointed the Head of all who are
descended from Abraham and indeed from Adam, the realm of the dead loses
the last traces of creaturely naturalness which still cling to it in the Old Testament perspective. Here it becomes " hell." Here the alienation from God
becomes an annihilatingly painful existence in opposition to Him. Here being
in death becomes punishment, torment, outer darkness, the worm, the flame—
all eternal as God Himself, as God Himself in this antithesis, and all positively
painful because the antithesis in which God here acts cannot be a natural confrontation, but must inevitably consist in the fact that infinite suffering is
imposed upon the creature which God created and destined for Himself, when God
reacted against this creature as it deserves. It is, of course, true that this man
is the Son of God. In Him God Himself suffers what guilty man had to suffer
by way of eternal punishment. This alone gives the suffering of this man its

representative power. This is what makes it the power by which the world is reconciled to God. "God was in Christ reconciling the world unto himself" (2 Cor. 5¹⁹). But it is the Son of God, this man, who in His death as the Representative of all men, as the revelation of what was due to them, endured this suffering, and bore this punishment. And it is this character, this quality of human death as eternal punishment, which the Church of Jesus Christ contemplates in His crucifixion. This is why the New Testament thinks and speaks so much more harshly of man's being in death than does the Old.

The third point is that death is the goal which is the appropriate reward for the life of man as it is actually lived. The warning has already been issued that the New Testament does not speak so harshly about man and his desires, so slightingly about his best possibilities and works, so remorselessly about his relation to God and what he may expect from Him, because the men of the New Testament found reason to abandon an optimistic or at least neutral view of life and to arrive at a pessimistic view. Man's estimate of his life usually oscillates between one extreme and the other when it is measured and evaluated by a norm, standard or law, and then thought to be just or unjust as the case may be. The whole issue at stake in the great struggle of Paul in the apostolic age was that the Old Testament Law must *not* play this part in the Church of Jesus Christ and its preaching. It is, of course, one of the most painful enigmas of Church history that the meaning of this struggle was forgotten as early as the 2nd century, and that only relatively seldom has it been rediscovered and put to profitable use. Yet it should have been obvious that this was not just a special concern of Paul's, but the general concern of the New Testament as a whole. It was the genuine Christian insight on the subject. The New Testament judgment upon the sinfulness of human life and its deserving of death reaches its highest accentuation in the Pauline Epistles : " For all have sinned, and come short of the glory of God " (Rom. 3²³). But this is not because Paul and the other New Testament witnesses viewed man from the standpoint of the Israelite *nomos*, placing him under that standard and measuring him by it. We are not to imagine that it was the Law which caused Paul when he was still Saul the persecutor to fall to the ground on the road to Damascus, convincing him that he was on the road to ruin. Nor are we to suppose that when he said : " By the law is the knowledge of sin " (Rom. 3²⁰, cf. 4¹⁵, 7⁷), he was seeking to ascribe to this instrument the inherent capacity to convince man of his perverse and lost condition in the very serious sense in which Paul understood it. Nor are we to suppose that his realisation that Christ is the end of the Law (Rom. 10⁴) is irrelevant when we are trying to put man in his place in relation to Christ. Nor are we to imagine that the saying : " God will judge the world in righteousness by that man whom he hath ordained " (Ac. 17³¹), or the saying that God will judge the hidden things of man by Jesus Christ (Rom. 2¹⁶ ; 1 Cor. 4⁵), or the saying : " We must all appear before the judgment seat of Christ " (2 Cor. 5¹⁰ ; cf. Eph. 6⁸), or the parables in Mt. 25 (in all of which it is Jesus who is the Judge), apply only to the eschatological end and are not yet in force, so that it is now necessary to pronounce judgment upon man according to very different criteria. The truth is that no law, not even the Law of Moses, can judge a man as the New Testament judges him. No law can say that his life is perverted, so perverted, and so devoid of glory in the sight of God, that death is the only reward it deserves. This is just what even the most zealous Pharisees, and Paul in his Pharisaic stage, could not learn from the Law. But in the light of the crucifixion of Jesus Christ this is just what can be learnt, so radical an expression is it, both in intensity and extent, of the New Testament judgment upon man. The crucifixion of Jesus Christ is the revelation of what it cost to restore the right of God and man which man had disrupted. It shows what that disruption implied. It shows how great was the remissness, and what was its inevitable consequence. This restoration, man's salvation, cost no more and no less than the self-oblation of the incarnate Son of God. It cost His death under the wrath of God, with its quality of eternal punishment. Its cost was that the man Jesus, He, the Son of God, He and no other, He who had not deserved it, should die under this determination as the enemy of God. God was merciful in Him in the fact that He assumed this self-oblation and did not shrink from eternal death. This is the standard by which the New Testament judgment on man is made. This is only norm by which we can know what to think about man, namely, about what he does and fails to do, what he is and is not, in disruption of the right of God and man, and therefore as the one who can be helped only by the judgment executed in this self-oblation. The New Testament sees man from a standpoint from which he is helped. That is why the New Testament thinks and speaks of his guilt and punishment in such a radical way. It does not see man in the abstract, in the light of some norm which he ought to have satisfied. It sees him in the person of One who championed his cause and died for him. And in this One it sees both the sin of man which Jesus took upon Himself and for the sake of which He endured the wrath of God, and the death of man which He suffered in his place as the eternal punishment which is the just lot of the enemies of God. It is just because the New Testament sees and understands man in this light that it cannot oscillate between optimistic, neutral and pessimistic opinions about him. It is for this reason that it sees and understands his way and destiny in the severe, remorseless, uncompromising and unsentimental objectivity with which alone it can be seen and understood with mercy. No judgment pronounced in the light of the Law can be merciful. Such judgments give him no real help, whether severe or lenient. On the contrary, such judgments usually harden him, leaving him indifferent or defiant as he was before. Since the New Testament judgment on man derives from the mercy and help already given to him, it is itself *eo ipso* merciful and helpful. It measures man by what God has done for him, by what Jesus Christ has accomplished in his place for his justification and deliverance from this burden, for his peace and salvation. On the basis of the accomplished restoration of the right of God and his own right it tells him that he is in the wrong and therefore under threat of perdition. It accuses him by showing him that all the charges against him have been dropped. It threatens him by showing him that he is out of danger. No Pharisee or moralist can accuse him as soberly and straightforwardly and totally and comprehensively as this. No existentialist with his teaching about the fallenness of human existence, no imaginative poet singing of the temporal and eternal inferno which he deserves, can terrify him as much as this. All such preaching of repentance and judgment lacks the profound Yes of God which underlies the No and which gives it strength and makes it the really powerful No which man must hear in respect of his way and final destiny. The No uttered by preachers of the Law, including Heidegger and Sartre, is always too human a No. The No of the New Testament, which declares that human life deserves death and meets in death its due, is distinguished from every human No which superficially may look very similar, and perhaps even stronger, by the fact that there is no escaping it once it is pronounced and really apprehended.

This, then, is how the New Testament sees human death in the light of its centre. The centre of this insight is God's judgment accomplished in the crucifixion of Jesus Christ. No other man stands at this centre, and therefore no other really stands under the judgment of God. Other men, Christians consciously and the rest unconsciously, find themselves somewhere on the periphery around this centre, and therefore—for we must now take up this concept— under the sign of this judgment. The threat posed by death, the infinite peril which confronts man through death as the wages of his sin, the assault of the undeniable fact that his way is one which can lead only to eternal punishment— all this is the inevitable lot of those who stand on the periphery around this centre. It is to be noted that the Evangelists and apostles spoke not only of the unbelieving Jews and Gentiles, but also to the Christian communities and all their members, under the unvarying assumption that the threat, peril and assault which proceed from the judgment of God are the lot of all men. On the contrary, those who in the New Testament are always exhorted, warned, reproved and challenged with such urgency to remember this sign, to fear death as the judgment of God, are those who have heard and recognised and apprehended the fact that this judgment made at the centre, in Jesus Christ, has already been accomplished for them, and that they are therefore graciously preserved from the execution of that threat, from the actual irruption of that danger, from succumbing to that assault. Those who know that they are preserved cannot forget, but genuinely to be preserved must always keep before their eyes what it is they have been preserved from. But faith in the free grace of God in Jesus Christ consists in holding fast to Him as our Representative, as the Son of God who has given Himself for us (Gal. 2²⁰). This faith is obviously not the end but the beginning of the fear of God. It does not mean going to sleep on comfortable cushions, but always waking and rising up anew. To wake and rise up in the fear of God, however, is to be constantly aware that the man who finds himself on that periphery is freed from the judgment of God only to the extent that the circle has that centre ; only to the extent that in Jesus Christ there has been accomplished for him his necessary justification and remission. If this were not so ; if he could not hold fast to this ; if he could not live as a man sustained by that centre, to what then could he hold ? And what could hold him ? The judgment of God would have to be executed upon him. In himself man is after all a sinner who has deserved wrath, and he will never be anything else. The crucifixion of Christ teaches him that so far as he himself is concerned there is no height to which he can climb or depth to which he can sink where he will not be found by death as eternal and merited punishment. In himself he is not freed at all from the judgment of God. He never can and never will escape it. In himself, according to the New Testament insight, he is irretrievably fallen. But in Jesus Christ and Him alone, not in any depth of being or height of achievement, he is preserved from this execution of judgment on him with the severity with which it was executed at the cross. This is the only refuge to which he can flee to escape this judgment. Otherwise it awaits him in death, and in his life as it moves inexorably to death. And to flee to this, to flee to Calvary, or, as Rom. 6³ᶠ· entitles us to say without qualification, to baptism, is the meaning of this waking and rising in the fear of God. This is what differentiates Christian faith from a dangerous self-complacency. This is what differentiates it decisively from the mask of a trust in God which does not deserve the name.

In the light of these considerations we can understand the peculiar impetus of the mission to Jews and Gentiles which is so characteristic of New Testament Christianity, and particularly of the apostle Paul, and which makes it so different from later versions of Christianity. Just as the New Testament Christians understood and saw that in themselves they were condemned, but justified and released in the crucifixion of Jesus Christ, that in themselves they stood wholly under its threat but were preserved from its execution in Him, that in themselves they were in the storm of irresistible assault—" In the midst of life we are in death ; of whom may we seek for succour, but of thee, O Lord ? "—they naturally applied this all the more to their Jewish and Gentile neighbours who were still blissfully unaware of their plight. They knew all about that centre, and therefore that they stood on its periphery. They knew about the judgment of God executed there, and therefore that they stood under its sign. They knew of the infinite danger and assault in which man lives, and therefore that it is where this danger and assault is acute and manifest that there is also deliverance and preservation. But the others, the foolish and the blind, with or without the Law, did not know this. They saw neither the danger nor the succour. They felt neither the assault nor the comfort. Instead, they went on dreaming dreams, which could only be disappointed, of a kingdom of Israel which they supposed they could bring about by observing the Sabbath and other laws, or of the gods, ideas, or cosmic principles of old and new religions and philosophies. They had no notion that the Judge had already appeared and delivered the verdict against them all, or that this verdict was primarily and supremely pronounced *for* them. They little dreamt that the capital sentence in which it was a matter of their life and death had already been executed once and for all. This contrast between the Church's awareness and the world's terrible ignorance is the motive, and the bridging of the gap between them the problem, of the early Christian mission. The moralist or philosopher may well be a propagator of his theoretical or practical idea, but he does not have to be. He may end up by keeping it to himself and hiding it in his own heart. The apostle of Jesus Christ not only can but must be a missionary. To him this is not a καύχημα but an ἀνάγκη: "Woe is unto me, if I preach not the gospel" (1 Cor. 9[16]). It is not merely the formal necessity of proclaiming the Word of God, nor the humanitarian love which would rather not withhold this Word from others, that forces him to do this. The determining factor is the concrete content of the Word itself. The truth which he knows about Jesus Christ and human life compels him almost as it were automatically to speak wherever it is not yet known. It is like air rushing into a vacuum, or water downhill, or a fire to more fuel. Man and his life stand under the sign of God's judgment. This is not just a religious opinion. It is a universal truth. It applies to all of us. It decides concerning every man as such. It leaps all frontiers. It is more urgent and binding than any human insight, however clear and compelling, or any convictions, however enthusiastically embraced. This truth is the driving power behind the Christian mission. Apart from it, there would be no indication where it should be pursued or not pursued. Where it is recognised it bursts all barriers. The sign of God's judgment seeks recognition. It is objectively given to all men by the fact that they must all die. All attempts to overlook or reinterpret this fact are doomed to failure. No one can persuade himself that he does not live in fear of death or that this life is normal and natural. But this is after all only the indication, the sign of the sign, so to speak. The sign as such is now set up and revealed, and it demands recognition. According to the New Testament, its power rests exclusively upon the fact that the judgment of God is not only indicated but executed in Jesus Christ, and that humanity is thus made the periphery on which, whether it knows it or not, it is placed under this sign, and its dying, whether it knows it or not, is established as this sign.

We have seen that the finitude of human life stands in fact in the shadow of its guilt. What else can death be for sinful man but the sign of God's judgment, and therefore—if man is indeed not created to be a sinner or to suffer God's judgment—not a divinely willed and created determination natural to his being, but an alien intrusion? Yet this cannot be our ultimate or even penultimate word.

What is the justification for this negative aspect of our being? What is the basis of the profound necessity of human fear in face of death? It is obviously to be found in the fact that death is an enemy with its own destructive purpose and power to which we have rightly fallen a prey in virtue of God's right against us, and the wrong which we have done Him. This means, of course, that we are threatened on this frontier of our being by the negation which corresponds to the power and purpose of this enemy. But it also means that in death we are confronted not only with death itself but also with God; with the very God who is in the right against us and against whom we have done wrong. In death He demands that which we still owe Him. He threatens us with the payment which we have deserved. It is not any negation which threatens us in death. It is not a harmless, neutral and finally welcome negation as imagined by Buddha and his kindred. It is the very dangerous and painful negation of our nothingness before God. If this were not so, if death were a tyrant in its own right, we could await it with secret equanimity or even open defiance. But it is not a tyrant in its own right. It rules only but precisely at the point where God is in the right against His creature and His creature is in the wrong against Him. It reigns in the no man's land where God is in conflict with man and man with God. It rules with the authority and power of the Law of God obtaining even in this no man's land. In the rule of death we have to do with the rule of God. It is really our nothingness in His sight which is revealed in the destructive work of death. This is what makes this work so ineluctable, so bitter and so terrible. Our end is not a tolerable evil, but the great and serious and intolerable evil, to the extent that in our opposition to God we draw upon ourselves God's opposition to us. In its perhaps concealed but very real basis our fear of death is the well-grounded fear that we must have of God.

But this is to say that at the point where we shall be at our end, it is not merely death but God Himself who awaits us. Basically and properly it is not that enemy but God who is to be feared. In death we are not to fear death itself but God. That this makes our plight worse is only one of the things to be noted in this connexion. The second is that we have to do here not merely with death but with God, with the God who is angry with us, who punishes us in death. And God and death are not two equal partners of like dignity and power. What is death compared with God ? Its power is simply the power to convince the creature which strives against God, sinful and guilty man, of his nothingness before God. And it cannot do this of itself but only as a servant commissioned by God. It belongs to chaos, to the world which God has neither willed nor created. It stands under God's No. It exists only to the extent that it is denied by God, just as the world which He willed and created exists only to the extent that it is affirmed by Him. If it must acquire form, power and effect in the no man's land of the conflict between God and man ; if we have to do here with an irruption of chaos, occasioned by man's sin and guilt, into the world willed and created by God, this does not alter in the slightest the fact that death is as much under God as any of His creatures, and therefore stands no less under His power and at His disposal. Though it is our last enemy, it cannot do what it likes with us. God has appointed it to its office, but He can also dismiss it. He has armed it, but He can also disarm it. He has given it power, but He can also take this power away again. Thus in death we are not in the company of death alone, nor are we in the kingdom of a second god. For with death the Lord of death is also present. To be sure, He will be present as the Judge and Avenger, as the One who causes us in death to reap what we have sown, as the One whom we must fear even now, and then still more. But He is also the Lord of death. If death has such terrors for us, it is because in death we shall finally fall into the hands of the living God. But we shall fall into *His* hands and not the hands of another. Death will not be the lord in this happening, but a servant and slave. And the will of the One who alone will be the Lord will always be a free will in face of death. Death will be bound to Him, not He to death. Without Him death will not be able to do us the slightest harm. If God wills otherwise, the purpose of death for us will be frustrated. His whole power over us will become impotence. In the midst of death we shall be shielded from death. In the midst of it we shall find happiness. But what if God does not will otherwise ? What if it be His intention to damn us as we have deserved ? If so, it is He who will do so and not death. It is from Him and not death that we shall have to receive the eternal pains of death. Therefore even in hell we shall be in His hands. Even in its torments we shall be shielded with Him. We shall not be alone in death. We shall be with God who is the Lord of death. And this is not in any sense an unimportant factor.

But the God who awaits us in death and as the Lord of death is the gracious God. He is the God who is for man. Other gods who are not gracious and not for man are idols. They are not the true and living God, the One who speaks to us in His eternal Word incarnate in Jesus Christ and crucified and put to death for us. We do not deprive ourselves of anything when we hold fast to this. In so doing, we simply accept Him as He has given Himself to us. We do not make any arrogant attempt to alleviate our own situation. We simply adjust ourselves to the situation which He Himself has created and in which He himself has set us. He is the gracious God, and for us men, even when He places us in death under the sign of His judgment, and in this sign, but only in this sign, is undoubtedly against us. Indeed, it is just as the One who is so palpably against us that He is so much the more mightily for us. If the fire of His wrath scorches us, it is because it is the fire of His wrathful love and not His wrathful hate. Man has always stood up to the hatred of the gods. But God is not one of these gods of hatred. Man cannot stand up to His wrath because it is the wrath of His love. The reason why His curse falls so hard upon us is that it is surrounded by the rainbow of His covenant. It is the dark side of the blessing with which He has blessed us and wills to bless us. Those whom He loves He chastens. Those whom He will find and have for Himself He pursues to the remotest corner where their backs are to the wall and they can no longer escape Him. From those to whom He wills to be all in all, he strips everything else. This is what we must experience in death, under the sign of His judgment. We do not know what and how we shall be when we are no more and have no more time for being in virtue of our death. But it is certain that we shall be convicted of our most secret sin and guilt ; that we shall thus be convicted of our secret nothingness before God ; that we shall look quite foolish, stripped of all our glory, and standing helpless and naked before Him. It is equally certain that we shall not then be able to press even the slightest claim upon God, not even by appealing to His righteousness, which would be to condemn ourselves, nor by appealing to His grace, which would obviously not be grace if we could appeal and have a claim to it. Again, it is certain that God would be no less God, nor less worthy of our praise, but only meting out to us what we deserve, if He allowed death, His servant, to do its worst with us, bringing us to that perilous and wholly painful state of negation to which we hasten in our life. Again, it is certain that even in our death He will in some way be the gracious God and for us. We cannot see or say how or how far He will be gracious to us and therefore for us. We cannot dictate to Him. We can make no dispositions concerning our future when we shall have no more future. We can only cling to the fact, but we can really do so, that even in our death and as its Lord He will be our gracious God, the God who is for us, and that this is the ineffable sum of all goodness, so that everything that happens to us in death will in some way necessarily work together for good. We shall fail to see this only if we take God for an idol instead of our gracious God, and do not see that as such He guarantees with His own existence that no evil can come our way but only good, however unexpected or hidden its form. Is He not the God who has elected Himself for us and us for Him ? Is He not the God who has entered into solidarity with us and made Himself responsible for us ? We hold fast to this existence revealed to us in His word and effective for us in the act of His Son, when in the last resort we do not fear death because we fear God so much. Since God is the Lord of death, He is the One whom we really ought to fear, and how can we fear the gracious God without finding comfort in Him, and the more powerfully the more clearly we realise that apart from His existence we have no other comfort ? But if we find comfort in the One who is the Lord of death, how can we fear that which is only His slave ?

It is really true that we need not fear death, but only God. But we cannot fear God without finding in Him the radical comfort which we cannot have in any other. But this simply means that it is God who is our Helper and Deliverer in the midst of death. If He, the Lord of death, our gracious God, the ineffable sum of all goodness, is present with us even in death, then obviously in the midst of death we are not only in death but already out of its clutches and victorious over it, not of ourselves but of God. We die, but He lives for us. Even in death we are not lost to Him, and therefore we are not really lost.

One day we shall cease to be, but even then He will be for us. Hence our future non-existence cannot be our complete negation. The ineluctable, remorseless and terrible work of death will be executed on us. But whatever else may happen, we cannot cease to be under His sovereignty, His property, the objects of His love. Death's power and work are not so great as to alter that in any way. We are subject to change and decay. We are mortal and transitory. And death is the seal which shows that this is really so. But God is unchangeable. He is not subject to decay. He is not transitory. And this is true of Him as the gracious God, and therefore as the One whom we have to fear and in whom we may find full and radical comfort even in death. For when we die He is still the One He is. Death is subject to His power and control. Even our last enemy can do nothing more to us than it is ordered to do. Death can be dismissed by the One who has appointed it. It can be disarmed by the One who has armed it. It can be deprived of power by the One who has empowered it. Death is our frontier. But our God is the frontier even of our death. For He does not perish with us. He does not die or decay. As our God He is always the same. Even in death He is still our Helper and Deliverer. But if so, we ourselves derive from Him. As He is our hope, even in death we are already out of its clutches and victorious over it. Even as we suffer it, it is already behind and beneath us. We do not boast of an immortality which is ours when we say this. We do not glory in anything of our own. With our death as the sign of God's judgment it is decided that nothing at all belongs to us, not even grace, let alone a righteousness which can only mean our condemnation. We cannot boast of anything before God, not even of His existence as the Lord of death who is our gracious God. Yet we cannot refrain from saying, without any boasting, that according to His own Word He is this, and that as such He is our Helper and Deliverer and therefore our hope. We cannot refrain from speaking of God Himself. And therefore we must see ourselves as those who in the midst of death are already out of its clutches and victorious over it. Imprisoned by it, we are already freed. Enduring its mighty onslaught, we are already victorious. As those who must die, we shall nevertheless live. Death may still be the tyrant, but it is no longer an omnipotent tyrant. We may not be able to escape it, but a limit is set to it. It is a bitter foe, but not a deadly one. It is terrible, but cannot destroy us. It is our frontier, but one which has its own frontier. It can take away from us everything we have. It puts an end to our existence. But it cannot make God cease to be God, our God, our Helper and Deliverer, and therefore our hope. It cannot do this. And since it cannot, we may seriously ask : What can it do ? What is all that it can do compared with what it cannot do ? What is the power of its prison, its assault, its bitterness and its terror ? What is the meaning of what it can and does do to us ? Is not its great darkness into which we enter already outshone by a dazzling light ? This light, however, is not our own, or under our control. It belongs to God alone. It may seem but a tiny ray, almost imperceptible. And yet it is far brighter than all the lights of immortality which we may have under our own control. For it is the one great and true light, the light of our life in and over death. In this light is not death weak and small instead of great and strong ? Is it not behind and under instead of before and above us. The hushed funeral rites, the coffins and urns and last remembrances of the departed with which we mark the end of human being in time, are not the last word on the subject. Can we not already hear the joy of resurrection over all the coffins and urns and hushed memories when the Word from which this light streams, the Word of our God, is proclaimed and received ?

Was not Paul Gerhardt right in his paraphrase of the 73rd Psalm ?

> If Thou alone, O Hero strong,
> Art with me in my woe,
> I need not fear though all the world
> Be shattered at a blow.
> Thou art my heaven, Thy keeping power,
> Shall ever be my strength and tower,
> When I must leave this earth below.

And in the more familiar hymn :

> Mists give way to sun and light,
> Sorrow to joy and sweet delight,
> Surest grief and bitter pain
> To comfort and to strength again.
> Now my soul which heretofore
> Sank right down to hell's dark door,
> To the gate of heaven doth soar.
>
> He whose terror fills the earth
> Gives my soul a second birth ;
> His all-powerful, saving hand
> Frees me from perdition's band.
> All His love and mercy kind
> Overflows my heart and mind ;
> Sweet refreshment there I find.
>
> I will go through pain and tears,
> I will go through mortal fears,
> I will go, and not be sad,
> All my days I shall be glad
> When the Lord of Hosts is nigh,
> When He lifts me up on high,
> I cannot perish finally.

Can we really see or express it in any other way ?

But perhaps to ask this question is already to have said too much and too little. Too much, because it involves treating as a certainty a hope whose certainty is strictly to be sought and found only in the existence of God as such, so that in respect of its fulfilment all inferences, even in the form of questions, may seem to be only rash anticipations of what is really intended for us. And too little, because we perhaps do not treat seriously enough the certainty of this hope as orientated on God and genuinely grounded, so that in respect of its fulfilment our inferences even in the form of questions fall far short of the reality. There are good grounds for this " too much " and " too little " to the extent that we have so far been moving on biblical but formally on Old Testament ground. The God of whom we do not say too much when we view our lives wholly and utterly in the light of His existence as our Helper and Deliverer, and therefore wholly and utterly on the other side of death, and conversely the God of whom we do not say too little when we seek and find our own being out of and above death wholly and utterly and exclusively in Him, is the God of the New Testament revelation and perception. But this God is the same as that of the Old Testament. Hence there is no need to retract or correct anything we have said. But as the same God, as the Lord of death and our gracious God, and therefore as the infinitely saving but exclusive frontier beyond death, He is revealed and perceptible to us according to the New Testament in such a way that all inquiry concerning Him necessarily carries a positive answer, and the positive answer which we grasp in Him necessarily leads us to genuine inquiry concerning Him.

We learn nothing materially new when we formally enter New Testament ground. We are again concerned with our God as the limit of our death : with the One who is the Lord of death and therefore alone is to be feared in death ; with our gracious God and consolation, our Helper and Deliverer in the midst of death, so that in hope in Him death is already behind and under us. But when we take our stand upon the New Testament revelation and perception, the first thing to strike us is that this is undoubtedly not just a question but a strong positive answer given by God Himself. According to the witness of the New Testament it is enacted in the union of God with the man Jesus of Nazareth. It is in Him that He is our gracious God. For in His union with this one man He has shown His love to all and His solidarity with all. In this One He has taken upon Himself the sin and guilt of all, and therefore rescued them all by higher right from the judgment which they had rightly incurred, so that He is really the true consolation of all. In Him He is our Helper and Deliverer in the midst of death. For in the death of this One it has taken place that all we who had incurred death by our sin and guilt have been released from death as He became a Sinner and Debtor in our place, accepting the penalty and paying the debt. In Him God has already acted in this sense as the Lord of our death, as the One who can dethrone and disarm it and strip it of its power. In Him

God has made use of this freedom in our favour. In Him God, the Lord of death, has already put death behind and beneath us. For He did not merely give this One to suffer in our stead and on our behalf. He caused Him, again in our stead and on our behalf, to triumph over death, not merely dying, but also rising again for us, so that we can now contemplate the prospect of death as something which is really behind and beneath us. In Him, in this One, God is therefore in very truth the boundary of the death that bounds us. What is death ? What meaning can it still have ? Certainly not our condemnation, perdition and negation. What have we to fear from it now that God has suffered and overcome it for us all in this One, thus creating order in the no man's land of conflict between Him and man, and thus setting a limit to the irruption of chaos ? In Him, in this One, God Himself has made our death the mere sign of His judgment. In Him God has decided that our own hope in Him who alone is immortal, our hope of our own life out of and over death as grounded on Him, is not only possible and legitimate but necessary and imperative. In relation to this one man Jesus Christ we cannot set our hopes too high in death and beyond it. Nothing is too bold or lofty or all-embracing. We are no longer in the sphere of inference or hypothesis. In Him the eternal God Himself has really turned to us, and acted for us, and indeed become our own. In Him the promise of eternal life—not just an extension of this life in a continuation of time, but a life in communion with the eternal life of God Himself—is really given. In Him the fulness of this life is already poured out upon us. This One, in whom all this is introduced in a concrete, tangible and unmistakeable form, is the new factor in the New Testament revelation and perception of God in His relation to death. From the Old Testament standpoint we cannot really do more than ask concerning all this. But from the New Testament standpoint we cannot ask concerning it without realising that the answer is given us in such a way that it is quite obviously not the solution to a riddle of our own, and may thus be accepted with true and final assurance.

But on the ground of the New Testament revelation and perception it is also the case that the positive answer which God Himself has given in power is necessarily an object of genuine, meaningful and legitimate inquiry. It is not just a general truth that God is the frontier of our death, that He is the Lord of death, that in death He and He alone is to be feared, that He and He alone is our consolation, that He is our gracious God and therefore our Helper and Deliverer in death, that He is our hope that through death we shall pass into life. This cannot be abstracted from the union of God with the man Jesus of Nazareth as this has taken place according to the witness of the New Testament. We cannot suppose that it is true and valid in itself. The Old Testament certainly does not think so, and the New Testament makes it abundantly clear that it is all true in Him, in this One, and

it says nothing of an unconditional reversal of this failure to the extent that this is the final disappearance of life in death. We should, of course, include among these passages Job 19²⁵. This verse may be obscure in detail, but its general import and true significance are clear : " For I know that my redeemer liveth, and that he shall stand at the latter day upon the earth : and though after my skin worms destroy this body, yet out of my flesh shall I see God : whom I shall see for myself, and mine eyes shall behold him, and not as an enemy." This passage says no more than that God is the Advocate and Representative of man " upon the earth." For even the vision of God of which it speaks is confined, as the context suggests, to this life which hastens towards death. It does not look to a continuation of life after death. It is in the moment of dying that Job expects to see God, not as his enemy but " for him " as his Advocate and Representative, as his " witness in heaven " (Job 16¹⁹) and as the champion who enters the lists for him (Job 17³). But even this famous passage does not seem to go further than that. Finally, in Is. 26¹⁹ and the great vision of Ez. 37¹⁻¹⁴ we obviously have pictures of the promised renewal of Israel in history. The fact that these images are selected is not insignificant, but they cannot be regarded as evidence of Israel's concrete hopes for the solution of the problem of death. And the same is perhaps true of the most explicit of all the Old Testament passages on this subject, namely, Dan. 12² : " Many of them that sleep in the dust of the earth shall awake, some to everlasting life, and some to shame and everlasting contempt." For even this passage refers specifically to the people of Israel as such, and possibly has no more general implication. Otherwise we can only say that here on the fringe of the Old Testament Canon we have the exception which proves the rule.

This rule is to accept a rigid contrast between man's temporally limited being in death on the one side and the temporally unlimited being of God on the other as the Lord not only of life but also of death and the underworld. No attempt is made to resolve this sharp contrast, or to prove it to be a salutary one. Of the dead only two things may be said, and they are so unlike as to sound almost contradictory. First, they were once alive and therefore have not simply become nothing but are as those who used to be. Second, even in this state of having been they are still in the divine power and hand of which Israel knows that there is no limit to the miracles which it can do in evocation of the praise of its creatures, in demonstration of its grace and faithfulness, in salvation and self-revelation. " He fainteth not, neither is weary " (Is. 40²⁸) when men become *rephaim*. Even for those whose life is now past He is not past. Even for them He is present to help as the One He was both when they were and before they were. He is not merely the God and the Lord of the covenant for each successive generation of His people, even though the departed generations no longer have any share in the ongoing fulfilment of His covenant with Israel, and clearly cannot accompany it any further even as spectators. For the fact that in their day they had a share in it, and heard His Word and were the objects of His action, is still true even when they pass. To be sure, it is only their relation to God which still remains. Only to this extent have they themselves not passed for Him and before Him. Yet to the extent that God Himself has not ceased to be their God, even after their being in time has come to an end, they have not really passed. To this extent they are still partners of the covenant, and God is still their hope. But what does this mean for them ? What is the radical hope and deliverance of which they are assured in the fact that God is for them and they are still there for Him ? This question is never answered in the Old Testament. Yet it is not a vain or hopeless question. It is not the question of an eternal unsatisfied hunger and thirst. It is a question full of hope and confidence, bearing its non-answer within it. For it is not flung into an empty void but addressed to God. We may tacitly assume that the New Testament explanation of the saying : " He is not the God of the dead, but of the living " (Mk. 12²⁷), and the Lukan addition : " For all live unto him "

(Lk. 20[38]), represent good Old Testament doctrine to the extent that they express the positive content of the Old Testament question, its secret consolation. Yet it is still a question, and a resurrection and continuation of life after death is definitely not its positive content. This simply consists in the fact that those who have been in their own day are as such before God, who is not a God of the dead, but of the living. All man's deliverance, redemption, preservation, and salvation in and out of death is enclosed in God, in His existence in faithfulness. That it is all enclosed in Him and to be expected from Him, is the hope of the Old Testament in relation to death.

The hope of the New Testament is not materially different. But it has now attained a concrete basis and form in which the positive content of the Old Testament question is so illuminated that the answer which it undoubtedly encloses as a question is unmistakeably and compellingly revealed as such. Yet it is to be noted that even in important passages in Paul its character as a question is still or again indisputable : " O wretched man that I am ! who shall deliver me from the body of this death ? " (Rom. 7[24]). The same is true even of such triumphant passages as Rom. 8[31f.] : " If God be for us, who can be against us ? . . . Who shall lay anything to the charge of God's elect ? . . . who is he that condemneth ? . . . Who shall separate us from the love of Christ ? " and 1 Cor. 15[55] : " O death, where is thy sting ? O death, where is thy victory ? " But everywhere the question is immediately confronted by the answer, in the light of which alone it is properly asked : " I thank God through Jesus Christ our Lord " (Rom. 7[25]). " He that spared not his own Son, but delivered him up for us all, how shall he not with him also freely give us all things ? . . . It is Christ that died, yea rather, that is raised again, who is even at the right hand of God, who also maketh intercession for us . . . Nay, in all these things we are more than conquerors through him that loved us. For I am persuaded, that neither death, nor life . . . shall be able to separate us from the love of God, which is in Christ Jesus our Lord " (Rom. 8[32, 34, 37f.]). " Thanks be to God, which giveth us the victory through our Lord Jesus Christ " (1 Cor. 15[57]). At the same time there are Old Testament overtones in passages like 2 Cor. 1[8f.], where Paul, looking back on his tribulations in Asia Minor, writes : " We were pressed out of measure, above strength, insomuch that we despaired even of life : but we had the sentence of death in ourselves, that we should not trust in ourselves, but in God which raiseth the dead : who delivered us out of so great a death, and doth deliver : in whom we trust that he will yet deliver." But this hope has now a solid basis. It is a hope triumphant in the midst of all the serious threats of death and all the doubts and uncertainties to which they give rise. Even the sentence of death which seems to have been already pronounced serves only to drive the Christian as never before to trust and hope in God as the One who raises the dead. The question now is not where God is, but what has become of the victory and power of death (1 Cor. 15[55]). Man can now look back and down, not upon a past life overcome by death, but upon defeated death itself. Hence these two elements, life (incessantly hastening to its end) and death (1 Cor. 3[22] ; Rom. 8[38]) are no longer contrasted as in the Old Testament. They are placed alongside one another as two neutral possibilities and surveyed from a higher standpoint (Rom. 8[38]). They are thus classified with other possibilities like angels, principalities, things present, things to come, powers, height and depth, which all have it in common with life and death that they cannot separate us from the love of God. It is to be noted how death is thus subjected to a certain relativisation. " For whether we live, we live unto the Lord ; and whether we die, we die unto the Lord : whether we live therefore, or die, we are the Lord's " (Rom. 14[8]).

It is not pious optimism, nor a lack of sensitiveness to the problem of death, but the radical change of view brought about with the giving of a solid basis to the Old Testament hope, which is what makes the apostles think and speak in this way, allowing and commanding them to see and express from above, from the divine standpoint, the hope in which the Old Testament righteous lived but saw and expressed only as it were from below, from the human standpoint. Paul does not think or speak from his own standpoint. When he does, he does so (Rom. 7²⁴) as an Old Testament Psalmist might have done, but he then goes on to make an immediate correction. For " in Christ Jesus " it is he himself who is first behind and under him. He lives (Gal. 2²⁰) by the faith of the Son of God. He thus thinks and speaks from His standpoint. To do so is both his privilege and his responsibility. The Fourth Gospel gives us the decisive commentary on this point ; " He that heareth my word, and believeth on him that sent me, hath everlasting life, and shall not come into condemnation, but is passed from death unto life " (Jn. 5²⁴). " If a man keep my saying, he shall never see death " (Jn. 8⁵¹, cf. 11²⁶). And in brief and summary form : " He that believeth on me hath everlasting life " (Jn. 6⁴⁷). Hence also 1 Jn. 3¹⁴ : " We know that we have passed from death unto life." Paul does not put it in this way, but it is from this level that he speaks. He has not attained to it of himself. In himself he stands at exactly the same point as Job and the Psalmists stood, but " Christ Jesus hath abolished death, and hath brought life and incorruption to light through the gospel " (2 Tim. 1¹⁰). And the strong statements of the Fourth Gospel are not general truths, nor mere affirmations transcending the wisdom of the Old Testament in relation to death, but sayings of the man Jesus : " Verily, verily, *I* say unto you." And they do not transcend the wisdom of the Old Testament. Nor do they refute it. On the contrary, they reveal and confirm that in all its severity this is wisdom because it bases man's hope in death so wholly and exclusively on the existence and faithfulness of God. What else does the New Testament attest but the existence and faithfulness of God as they have now become concrete and historical, and therefore are not merely constant but triumphant on our behalf ? In the man Jesus Christ they were made flesh, and where they are seen and believed in Him there takes place the change of view in virtue of which man can now look back and down upon the death which threatens him and therefore go to meet it victoriously from this new place of his. Jesus is the Victor. Because He is this for man, man may and must be victorious too. As he knows Him, follows Him, believes in Him and sets his hope on Him, man is with Him as surely as He, his Fellow and Brother, is not without him but for him and the Victor with him. The reality of this victory is the death of Jesus, for God Himself has entered the lists for man in this Fellow and Brother of every man, taking his sin and guilt, making death irrelevant as its consequence and thus snatching man from its jaws and accomplishing that redemption. And the token and pledge of this victory is God's self-manifestation during the absolutely unique forty days in which Jesus was present again to His disciples after His death in demonstration of His glory and His victory. The New Testament hope derives from this reality and revelation.

Those who believe in Jesus can no longer look at their death as though it were in front of them. It is behind them. For as they believe in Jesus they belong to Him and are elected to κοινωνία, i.e., to a share in His being (1 Cor. 1⁹). And as they belong to Him they have their death actually behind them. There, in the reality of His death, He has suffered for them, and abolished it, making it irrelevant as the consequence of their sin and guilt. There, too, they are with Him. Their old man which had gone so hopelessly astray, has been crucified (Gal. 2²⁰ ; Rom. 6⁶)—the same word which is used of the two thieves in Mk. 15³²—and has died with him (Rom. 6⁸, Col. 2²⁰, 2 Tim. 2¹¹). With Him ? Yes, with Him. For the fact that they belong to Him is ratified and confirmed in baptism as the correspondence to the burial which sealed the death of Jesus, and in their baptism they have Jesus' burial, or Jesus' burial as the original of their baptism, behind them (Rom. 6⁴, Col. 2¹²). It is quite fitting that those who believe in Jesus should as it were be marked by His death, bearing the στίγματα of Jesus on their bodies as Paul puts it in Gal. 6¹⁷, or the νέκρωσις of Jesus in the even stronger expression of 2 Cor. 4¹⁰, which is followed at once by the

statement that they " are alway delivered unto death for Jesus' sake " even
while they live (2 Cor. 4[11]). In Phil. 3[10] Paul can say that he is " conformed "
to the death of Jesus, being set in the κοινωνία of His suffering. In Col. 1[24]
he can use the bold expression that with his suffering he is " filling " up that
which is lacking of the afflictions of Christ, namely, their correspondence in the
life of His body, the ἐκκλησία. Those who have been crucified and are dead
and therefore live with Him (Gal. 2[20]) cannot help bearing the traces of this
event, suffering the aftermath of His woes and living in His shadow. This
correspondence does not in any way diminish the uniqueness of Christ's death.
On the contrary, it confirms it. For the remarkable point about these passages
is Paul's insistence that his sufferings are not his own but Jesus'. They are the
marks stamped upon him to show that he belongs to this Lord.

And this event, the redemption and reconciliation there accomplished, the
overcoming and destroying of death which there took place, and now form the
starting-point for those who believe in Jesus, is for the New Testament no more
and no less than the end of time, the last day, or to be more precise, the midnight hour of the last night when the last day has dawned for each individual
and all humanity. " Old things are passed away ; behold, all things are become
new " (παρῆλθεν, 2 Cor. 5[17]). This is the case because in this event time is
fulfilled. What is to happen in time and as the meaning of the cosmos existing
in time has happened in this event. Those who believe in Jesus know that
they—and not they only but all other men as well, though they are still unaware
of the fact—live in this last day, and no longer have before them any other
time but the time of this last day. Its dawning after the midnight hour is the
resurrection of Jesus and the appearance of the forty days as an indication
that this event has happened, that death has been deprived of its power and
that time is at an end. What can follow this indication is simply the running
out of this last day, and then its end in accordance with its beginning : the
conclusive, general and definitive revelation of this event ; the manifestation of
the Saviour and Victor of Calvary as the One He is, as the Head not only of
His community but of all creation (Eph. 1[10]). The sole purpose for the extension of time after this decisive event is to allow space before the kingdom comes
to repent and believe the Gospel (Mk. 1[15]) on the basis of this event and its
indication. And there can be no other task for those who believe in Jesus (and
who are thus aware that this is the last day, and what it means) than to make
known this event and its indication as quickly and widely as possible. Unwitting
men, and indeed all creatures, must know that the hour has struck. They
themselves, those who believe in Jesus, continue to live in the only possible
way, namely, in the light of this indication and the resurrection of Jesus. And
they do not do this arbitrarily or in their own strength but as those who were
not only with Him in that night but also in the morning, being raised and
quickened with Him (2 Cor. 4[14] ; Col. 3[1] ; Eph. 2[5]) " through the operation of
God who hath raised him from the dead " (Col. 2[12]), " begotten again unto a
lively hope by the resurrection of Jesus Christ from the dead " (1 Pet. 1[3]). And
as they provisionally live in the power of this indication of the resurrection of
Jesus, their life in provisional correspondence to His resurrection life is necessarily orientated on the definitive point of that revelation, the coming of Jesus
Christ again in glory. They, too, must still wait expectantly, as the whole
universe is engaged in waiting, for this last event. The last day which has already
dawned is still running its course. To be sure, they are already called the " sons
of God." But it has not yet appeared what they shall be, so that the world
which does not yet know Jesus cannot recognise them for what they are
(1 Jn. 3[1f.]). Their life is still hid with Christ in God (Col. 3[3]). And it is not
they who can usher in or even foresee the end of this last day and therefore the
revelation of what was indicated in its beginning, and therefore the goal which
they expectantly await, and not they alone but the whole cosmos (Rom. 8[19f.]).
The last event of this revelation, like the first, will be wholly and utterly the

work of Jesus. All they can then do is to be " with Him " (1 Thess. 4¹⁷ ; Phil.
1²³). When He is revealed, when they see Him as He is, they too will be revealed
with Him (Col. 3⁴ ; 1 Jn. 3²), though this will also mean that they will " appear
before the judgment seat of Christ " (2 Cor. 5¹⁰). It is His life which will then
be revealed to them (2 Cor. 4¹⁰), though this will mean their subjection to the
krisis described in 1 Cor. 3¹²ᶠ·, when they will be tested by fire, and what is
built on the foundation of Christ will be disclosed, whether gold, silver and
precious stones, or wood, hay and stubble. They will then live with Him His
own revealed life (1 Thess. 5¹⁰ ; 2 Cor. 7³ ; 13⁴ ; Rom. 6⁸ and 2 Tim. 2¹¹). They
will then be glorified with Him (Rom. 8¹⁷). They will then be conformed to the
image of His glory (Phil. 3²¹). They will then reign with Him (2 Tim. 2¹²). As
Jas. 1¹⁸ says, they are " the first fruits " of God's creation. Surrounded, as
Rom. 8¹⁹ᶠ· says, by the whole creation groaning and travailing together, they
have death behind them and this prospect before them. Their faces will reflect
the glory of the Lord. They will be transformed into His image (2 Cor. 3¹⁸),
ἀπὸ δόξης εἰς δόξαν, from the lower glory of faith to the higher glory of the
vision of the Son, who will then lay down the kingdom of creation, and Himself
as its King, at the feet of the Father.

This, then, is the New Testament hope. To understand it, we must fix our
eyes firmly on three points :

1. the relationship between the crucifixion of Jesus as the event in which
man's sin and guilt and consequent death are abolished and time is fulfilled, and
His resurrection as the preliminary indication of this event establishing faith in
Jesus as the Deliverer from death ;

2. the relationship between the resurrection of Jesus as the preliminary
indication inaugurating the last time and establishing the Church and its mission,
and His return in glory as the conclusive, general and definitive revelation of
this event ;

3. and above all, the being of man with Him which is promised to and
actualised in faith in Jesus, and in virtue of which he has his own death and
the dawn of the last time behind him in the death of Jesus, is born again in
His resurrection to a life in God concealed throughout the last time, and will
be revealed in glory as one who has this life when Jesus returns in glory as the
goal of the last time.

Points 1 and 2 give us the specific form of the hope of deliverance from
death in the New Testament. The name of Yahweh, the only source of consolation and salvation in the Old Testament, is now filled out concretely by the
saving event whose Subject is the man Jesus, His death, resurrection and
coming again. This is why the Old Testament question concerning deliverance
from death is secretly pregnant with a positive answer. For it is Israel's God
who acts in the man Jesus, confirming in Him His covenant with the fathers.
The saints of the Old Testament were not mistaken or disappointed in believing
that the God of Israel was the Lord of the living and the dead, and in regarding
Him even in death as their rock and refuge. This filling out of the name of
Yahweh by the revelation, perception and attestation of this saving event is the
new element in the New Testament.

Yet point 3 shows the New Testament form of this hope is not only not
alien to the Old Testament form but indirectly identical with it. The rigorous
one-sidedness of the Old Testament, which sees all hope solely in the contrast
between the omnipotence of God and the impotence of man, and all help and
deliverance in the person of God Himself, does not disappear in the New Testament, but is concretely disclosed and shown to be meaningful as never before
now that the man Jesus has come as the filling out of the name of Yahweh and
the Subject of that saving event. The salvation in this event, and the whole
hope of the New Testament, are exclusively dependent on Him as this Subject.
It is only with Him that man has a share in it. There is not a single eschatological statement even in the New Testament which allows us to ignore this

One. His death, resurrection and coming again are the basis of absolutely everything that is to be said about man and his future, end and goal in God. If this gives way, everything collapses with it.

But the question seriously arises whether the New Testament form is really distinguished from that of the Old by the fact that its content and contents are to be understood as new beginnings, developments and continuations of human life in the time after death. For in the crucifixion of Jesus is not the end of time, both for the individual and all time, accomplished ? Does not His resurrection usher in the last day, when even the believer in Jesus can only live a life hidden with God in Christ ? Do not His coming again in glory and the consequent revelation of this hidden life mark the end of this last day and time, the handing over of the kingdom of the Son to the Father ? Even in the chapter he devoted so expressly to the resurrection of the dead in its connexion with the resurrection of Jesus, Paul can see beyond this end only one further prospect : ὁ θεὸς πάντα ἐν πᾶσιν (1 Cor. 15²⁸). It is clear enough that the end of the last time is a historical and therefore a temporal event. But as the event of creation took place in a present without a past, so this event is that of a present without a future, in which, as ἐν ἀτόμῳ, ἐν ῥιπῇ ὀφθαλμοῦ, there does not follow any further information or promise of further occurrence but only the sounding of the " last trump " (1 Cor. 15⁵²). In this unique moment of time, when the secret of Calvary will be revealed as indicated in the forty days, there will be raised up in incorruption, glory and power, as this last temporal event, that which was sown in corruption, dishonour and weakness (1 Cor. 15⁴³). At this moment it will be necessary (δεῖ) for this corruptible to put on incorruption and this mortal to put on immortality (1 Cor. 15⁵³). But nothing further will follow this happening, for then " there shall be time no longer " (Rev. 10⁶). There is no question of the continuation into an indefinite future of a somewhat altered life. The New Testament hope for the other side of death is very different from that. What it looks forward to is the " eternalising " of this ending life. This corruptible and mortal life will be divested of its character as " flesh and blood," of the veil of φθορά (1 Cor. 15⁵⁰). It will put on incorruption and immortality. This earthly tabernacle, which is doomed to destruction, will be " clothed upon " with the building prepared by God, with the house in heaven not made with hands. This mortal will be swallowed up in life (2 Cor. 5¹ᶠ·). Our past and limited life, which did not begin before time and does not continue beyond it, our real but only life, will then fully, definitively and manifestly participate in that καινότης ζωῆς (Rom. 6⁴). It will then be eternal life in God and in fellowship with Him. To be sure, the past life of every man in its limited time has a place in this fellowship with God, the Eternal who was and is and is to come. It can only be a matter, therefore, of this past life in its limited time undergoing a transition and transformation (1 Cor. 15⁵¹) and participating in the eternal life of God. This transition and transformation is the unveiling and glorifying of the life which in his time man has already had in Christ. It is the resurrection of the dead, which according to the indication given after the resurrection of Jesus is our participation in His future revelation. This is our hope in the time which we still have.

The Old Testament never said this explicitly, nor could it do so *ante Christum*. It simply refers transitory man to the abiding existence and faithfulness of God. And it does this so emphatically that there can be no doubt as to the positive implication of the reference. But it never makes it openly. It never actually says that transitory man with his temporal life will one day have a share in the eternal life of God. It never says anything about resurrection, about that transition and transformation, about that manifestation of this life of ours in the glory of God. The New Testament speaks of this as and because it speaks of the saving event whose Subject is the man Jesus. Yet it also confirms what the Old Testament says. For it places transitory man as such, his life in his time, his being with its beginning and end, in the light of the promise vouchsafed in the death, the resurrection and the second coming of the man Jesus. It has not abandoned the sober realism of the Old Testament. On the contrary, it has shown how sound it is, and given it its real force. For as it takes the majesty of God not less but more seriously, because concretely, than the Old Testament, so too it takes the littleness of man in his creatureliness and finitude more seriously. It agrees with the Old Testament that this lowly and finite creature, man, in his time is affirmed by the Most High God and that the power of this affirmation is the secret of his beginning and end, his true help and deliverance in and from death. If we wish the New Testament had more to say about this than the Old, it may well be that we are pursuing pagan dreams of a good time after death, and not letting the New Testament say the radically good thing which it has to say with the realism which it has in common with the Old Testament.

We have now reached the point where we can answer the real question facing us in this connexion, namely, whether in the finitude of our time, in the fact that man's being has an allotted span, we really have to do with its nature as willed and created by God, and therefore with His good and immutable determination. This question has been with us at every step, and the answer has surely been given in the biblical quotations adduced in the last *excursus*. But the question must now be emphasised as such, and a direct answer given.

We saw that finitude means mortality. We tried to show clearly that if we have an end this means that we have to die. And from the very outset we have found it hard to see in this any good determination of our being, or even one in whose immutability we can acquiesce. Even when we considered the biblical view of death, we saw no reason to pretend that black was white. On the contrary, the biblical view compelled us to face up to realities without beating about the bush. Mortality means subjection to death, and death means the radical negation of life and therefore of human existence. Death is not only non-existence. It is the seal and fulfilment of man's negation. Death means that our existence as human beings is really and finally a negation. The necessity of death means, therefore, that our life is one which is bounded by the menace of this negation. We are obliged to live in fear of death. This fear is necessary and justified, and cannot be evaded. How can we help fearing the end of our life when it consists in death ? What good can it do, and what reason is there, to acquiesce in this fact which we are powerless to alter ? What is there to give us courage to face this prospect ? That our existence is finite ; that there is a boundary ahead of the time given to us ; and that on the other side of this boundary we shall be no more, is something which we can regard only as an evil, as an abnormal determination of our being, and therefore as unnatural.

All this was only confirmed when we brought our life and death into connexion with God : our life into connexion with Him as the One to whom we are engaged and responsible ; and our death into connexion with Him as the One who summons us to account and judges

our life according to its deserts. When we set it in this light, we saw
how far our life is really negative in character and therefore can only
hasten towards negation. For in this light we saw that its fatal
mortality, its bondage to death, is not just a blind fate which we
might perhaps accept as a brute fact and make the best of it, reconciling
ourselves to the prospect. For when our life is confronted by God, it
is shown to be that of a debtor who absolutely fails to satisfy and even
contradicts the claim which his existence entails. It is shown to be a
sinful achievement which can only lead to destruction. And if at the
end of life man is finally and conclusively confronted with God, this
means that the negation in which it has been spent will be confirmed
by the negation which he has chosen for himself and which God for
His part can only justly affirm. In death we receive the final evil
which our actions deserve. We saw why the Bible does not hold out
any prospect of relief at this juncture. We saw why the New Testament verdict is even sterner in this respect than that of the Old.
We have to fear death because it is God whom we have to fear in death.
It is our relation of our life and death to God which explains why
death is an evil. This relation explains death as the sign of the divine
judgment under which we are placed. But this does not mean that
death is explained as a natural or normal determination of human
existence. On the contrary, what could be more unnatural than that
the end of human life should consist in the fact that God will say No
to us, allowing us to fall into the negation which we ourselves have
chosen ?

We saw, of course, that this was not the end of the story. In
bringing our life and death into relationship with God, we were not
working with an abstract concept of deity which might have allowed
us to stop at the idea of death as a merited judgment or even as an
overhanging destiny. We had before us the fact that God is the
gracious Creator of man and the Lord of the covenant which He
concluded with man in creating him and to which He is faithful even
though man is unfaithful. We had before us the fact that He is the
God who is merciful even in His righteousness, whose mercy is indeed
the true meaning and work of His righteousness. We had before us
the fact that He is God in the flesh, God in the man Jesus Christ, and
that this means that death is only the sign of God's judgment which
can threaten us in our death because God has graciously undertaken
to suffer the judgment of death in the death of this man and thus to
release us from it. We had before us the fact that God has wiped out
men's sin and guilt, and therefore abolished their death, by taking
the place of all others in this one man, so that He has become their
Deliverer from death in this One. We had before us the fact that He
who is to be feared in death is also man's hope in death, and in his
life as it hastens towards death. He is the hope in which man, as he
moves towards death and inevitably succumbs to it, has death behind

him as an enemy already vanquished, not by himself, but by the merciful and righteous omnipotence of God. That is exactly the case. But even on this view death has not become a friend, a normal and natural phenomenon. What the man Jesus, the Son of God, suffered for us at Calvary is not what God planned for man in creating him. It is not life, nor is it a characteristic or determination of life, but death in its irreducible terror—the death which if He had not suffered it would still have to be feared, and which is thus intrinsically fearful and nothing else. In what He has suffered for us death is clearly revealed as the radical negation of human life, its condemnation to hell. It is in the New Testament that this is indisputably attested. The New Testament has to give this witness. We should not know the God who is our Deliverer from death and as such our hope, and who is attested in the concrete reality of His biblical form as such to be also the God of death, the mighty phenomenon of divine wrath and punishment, if we did not know death as an alien intruder, contrary to human nature as God created it.

The conclusion is everywhere suggested that in the finitude of human life, in the fact that a term is set to it, we have to do with the great curse laid upon man, with an alien and inimical threat to human nature. We have not concealed from ourselves the extraordinary difficulty of understanding aright the temporal character of human nature. If we really had to come to that conclusion, we should find it necessary to revise everything that we said about the fact that man's time is limited. Grave doubts would even be thrown on our affirmations concerning the beginning of this time. Such a revision might well lead us to the further conclusion that the limitation of the time given to man can be understood only as an unmitigated evil and overhanging curse, that unlimited time without beginning or end would be more appropriate to man's true nature, and that man's redemption and deliverance from death ought to consist in the renewed possibility of a temporally infinite life on the other side of death. Is such an idea of redemption too absurd to be true ? Is there no real redemption from death at all ? Was it in His wrath that God created man for only a short span of life ? Is our life as such an unmitigated evil ? If we take up the position which is suggested on all sides, the consequences which seem to be unavoidable are by no means negligible.

In spite of everything, however, it would be ill-considered to jump to this conclusion without thorough investigation. And this will show that even what we have said does not constitute a final objection to the fact that the finitude of our being belongs to our God-given nature.

To clarify this question, and give it a legitimate answer, we have to realise that in our whole exposition thus far, and similarly in the brief recapitulation which we have just given, we have made and continually presupposed an equation whose limitation will emerge once we seek to establish it. We have only to see that it is a legitimate but relative truth, and the way is opened for an answer which will turn out to be very different from that which seems to be forced on us from every side. The equation which we have constantly made is that of the temporal end of human life with death, or of death as the boundary of human life with death in the harsher sense which it usually bears in the Bible, i.e., as the negation of human existence, as the curse lying upon man, as the radical threat of negation, as the sign of the divine judgment, and in relation to Jesus Christ even as this judgment itself, as the execution of the punishment which we deserve as guilty sinners. And it is in the light of this equation that we cannot understand the end of human existence, dying or death, as a normal and natural phenomenon, but only as a determination alien to the creaturely nature of human existence, as an unmitigated evil, as the enemy of man. It is not arbitrarily but for good reason that we have made this equation and assumed it to be self-evident. This identity is a simple fact. In the judgment of God man is in fact a sinner and debtor, and therefore by divine sentence subject to death, i.e., to death in the harsher sense, the " second death." And Jesus Christ has actually gone in our place to death, to death in this second sense, in this absolutely negative sense of the term. It is actually the case that we cannot see or describe in any other way but as the second death the end of human existence and what death means for man. In making and constantly presupposing this equation, we have kept to this fact revealed in God's act of judgment and unequivocally in His act of salvation in the death of Christ. We know the end of our temporal existence, our death, only as it overshadowed by His death. Even those who face death with their hope fixed on God, and in the triumphant retrospect of faith know that death is vanquished in virtue of the death which Jesus Christ suffered in our place, know it only in this form. The death which is behind them is an evil, an enemy of man. In the light of this fact there can be no doubt as to the unnatural and discordant character of death.

Yet this fact itself calls for explanation. Impressive though it is, it does not have in itself the character of a final word.

It is both possible and necessary to see this clearly when we see it in the light of its centre, namely, the death of Jesus on the cross. What was it that happened there ? It was that Jesus suffered the end of His life in death as an atonement, not for His own sin and guilt, but for that of others. In His end, therefore, dying actually coincided with death in this negative sense. But in His case at least death in this negative sense is obviously not the inevitable but the freely accepted end of His human existence. It was an alien burden which did not belong originally to His life. As a man like ourselves, He had not deserved this end. His human life was not one of negation. It was not, therefore, subject to death as the seal of its negation. If in His end He took death upon Himself as God's judgment, He did so as the First-born among His brethren and the Head and Deliverer of a world of sinners who were in bondage to death but to whom God willed to be faithful in spite of their unfaithfulness. In this way there was proved the free grace of God operative and revealed in His person. It did not take place, therefore, out of biological necessity. Even if His end had not been the suffering of this judgment, He would not have been any the less true and natural man. Since He was neither sinful nor guilty, the finitude of His life did not stand in advance and as such under this shadow. His human life might have ended in quite a different way. And it is a most difficult paradox that His life did not end in any other way. In His human person there is manifested a human existence whose finitude is not intrinsically identical with bondage to that other death. Therefore in His person, in which there is revealed with incomparable urgency the fact of this simple identity, we obviously have to do with a limitation and relativisation of this fact.

In the light of this centre, again, it is possible and necessary to ask what was and is the objective range of that event. It obviously meant and still means that we for whom Jesus took to Himself the judgment of God in death have been freed from our sin and guilt and therefore released from that sentence of death and delivered from having to suffer that second death. The end of Jesus Christ has made our end simply the *sign* of God's judgment. As we consider this end and move towards it, we are free to look back upon the end of Jesus, upon the death which He suffered on our behalf and which rescues us from death itself, as a terror which can no longer terrify us. But this can mean only that our end and our death in that second and negative sense are obviously identical only in an empirical way and not as a matter of necessity, as though our end could not have any other character. A strict identity of dying and judgment in death is possible only if we ignore the fact that God has acted for us at Calvary. By what He did for us there, by the action of His free grace, death has been relativised at least to the extent that our death, as suffered by Jesus for us, is set at a certain distance from our end and can only be its sign, reminding us of the judgment and at the same time of His mighty act of salvation. We cannot say that that fact has been simply removed. For we still stand under this sign. We must still submit to God's judgment and sentence. As concerns ourselves, we can only say that we are sinful and guilty, and will be to the end, and could only expect that terrifying end, the second death, if it all depended on us. But the fact that we belong to Jesus Christ implies a limitation and relativisation of this fact. We have received the grace of God in Jesus Christ. We have been delivered and redeemed in Him. Therefore our end does not have to be the judgment of death. There can be no question of an anthropological identity between the two even in our case. Even without it we should be none the less true and natural men. It is still a fact—and indeed the only one which we can see and conceive in this matter—but it is no more than this. The finitude of our temporal existence obviously does not necessarily imply that we stand under the wrath of God.

And now it is both possible and necessary, primarily again in relation to the man Jesus, to ask the further question, whether it was not the case that, to be the First-born among many brethren, the Head and Saviour of a sinful world in bondage to death, He had to share our human nature under the determination of finitude. He did not have to stand under the judgment of God or suffer the death of a reprobate. His life did not have to have this end. It was God's free grace, the great love of this man who was His Son for us, that He took upon Himself this end for us. But He had to be able to die. His being in time had to have this finitude in order that He might take this end upon Himself. Infinitude and immortality would obviously have disqualified Him from doing this for us. His life as God's Son had to have an end in its human form. It had to be able to be given over to death, the point at which the life of all men meets its temporal boundary. Only so could He overstep this boundary. Only so could He surrender His divine-human life and thus accomplish that which brought terror to Him but salvation to us. Only so could the brute fact of identity between man's end and his judgment be achieved and our deliverance from this judgment be accomplished. But the finitude of human existence in time has in His person this indispensable function; if it seems to be for Him an anthropological necessity, the determination of His true and natural being as man, how can we maintain that all this has nothing to do with the nature of man as created good by God? And if His dying—in virtue of what it was as His—is the sum total of the good which God has shown to the world, how can we dare to understand man's mortality as something intrinsically negative and evil?

But let us now turn our attention again to ourselves, to the man who in the end of Jesus, by the capital sentence suffered in His end, is delivered from this sentence. There is here an exact correspondence. Is it not the case that our human existence, if it is to be the object, recipient and vessel of the free grace of God which has been at work for us in Jesus, must stand equally under the determination of His finitude? Must we not also be able to die, to go towards death, if what God has done for us in Jesus is not to have been done in vain? It is only as a boundary is set for us to which we can move, which we shall one day pass and beyond which we shall be no longer, that we are in a position to throw ourselves conclusively and definitively and exclusively on God and therefore concretely on Jesus Christ as our Deliverer from the wrathful judgment of the second death? What would become of us if in an endless life we had the constant opportunity to achieve a provisional ordering of our relationship with God and our fellows in the way we know so well, or rather to postpone the ordering of this relationship, accomplishing it at best only in that daily drowning of the old Adam which is always so doubtful a matter because he can unfortunately swim ? This could only mean in fact that we should be able to sin infinitely and even quantitatively multiply our guilt on an infinite scale. What sense would it then make to say that Jesus Christ has reconciled us to God and spared us suffering our merited punishment ? And in what strange light would the merciful righteousness of God be set if our reconciliation with Him were never to take effect ? We have to be finite, to be able to die, for the ἐφ'ἅπαξ of the redemption accomplished in Christ to take effect for us. As we are finite and mortal, we find ourselves on the same ground as He, and can thus allow Him to be our Deliverer in the form in which He became and is our Deliverer. To belong to Him we must be finite and not infinite. Finitude, then, is not intrinsically negative and evil. There is no reason why it should not be an anthropological necessity, a determination of true and natural man, that we shall one day have to die, and therefore merely have been. It belongs to the revelation of His glory in us, to the final proclamation of our justification in the judgment, to the removal of the overhanging sign of divine judgment, to the settled and incontestable factuality of our participation in God's eternal life, that one day we should merely and definitively have been.

We have argued in purely christological and soteriological terms to prove what has to be proved, namely, that in the fact of the identity between our end and our judgment we do not have to do with an absolute but a relative necessity. This particular argument is essential. There are, of course, many lines of approach which seem more obvious. It might be asked whether it does not belong to the nature of every living process, including the human, to be exhausted and end as it once began. It might be asked whether dying as the natural end of human existence is not to be understood as an intrinsic evil but not a punishment. It might be pointed out that death is a relative evil, but in the last resort no more, which all available experience shows to belong to the nature of all living creatures. These considerations are all true, but they are only secondary. They simply illustrate the point, and have no intrinsic significance. The fact that man, standing under the sentence and judgment of God, is shown in his end to be a damned and lost being, is too massive a truth to be accepted merely on the basis of the correct observation that every innocent fly must perish when it reaches the evening of its day. For man is not just an innocent fly, and the fact that he is mortal like a fly is in itself no proof that it is right and proper for him to be mortal. He may console himself with the recollection that he shares his fate with all living creatures. This is what he does in Ecclesiastes 3[19-21], though clearly not without some degree of irritation. But he can do this only when he learns from the fact itself, from the place where death can only confront him in the first instance as something negative and evil, that it is right and necessary for him to have to die. It is not for nothing that we have taken this as our starting-point. We have caused the fact itself even on its own basis to speak of its limitation and relativity.

On the same basis we have seen that a distinction between end and curse, dying and punishment, death and execution, is not only possible and permissible but necessary and imperative. The fact of their identity is indisputable in the sphere of what we can see and conceive. But it is no less incontestable that nature and unnature, good and evil, God's creation and the answer of divine wrath to man's sin and guilt, are identical in this fact. Nature as well as unnature, good as well as evil, God's creation as well as the disastrous collision between the holy God and fallible man, are all present in man's end, in his dying and death. It would be quite perverse to maintain the presence of the latter without the former. It is thus legitimate and imperative for us to insist on the former, although it is only in christological and soteriological terms that we can see the fact of the identity of the two. When the former are actually seen in this light, however, there can be no doubt that we do really have to reckon with them.

This means that it also belongs to human nature, and is determined and ordered by God's good creation and to that extent right and good, that man's being in time should be finite and man himself mortal. The fact that one day we shall have been answers to a law which does not inevitably mean that we are imprisoned, fettered and condemned to negation by its validity. Death is not in itself the judgment. It is not in itself and as such the sign of God's judgment. It is so only *de facto*. Hence it is not to be feared in itself or necessarily, but only *de facto*. Death is secretly the very serious and sinister but not intrinsically dark and menacing form of the frontier where for good or evil man must finally meet his God. And this hidden form is the true and proper form of this frontier, and in this form it belongs to human nature, dying being no less a part of life, as the end which corresponds neutrally to its beginning, than conception and birth. Death is man's step from existence into non-existence, as birth is his step from non-existence into existence. In itself, therefore, it is not unnatural but natural for human life to run its course to this *terminus ad quem*, to ebb and fade, and therefore to have this forward limit.

Man as such, therefore, has no beyond. Nor does he need one, for God is his beyond. Man's beyond is that God as his Creator, Covenant-partner, Judge and Saviour, was and is and will be his true Counterpart in life, and finally and exclusive and totally in death. Man as such, however, belongs to this world. He is thus finite and mortal. One day he will only have been, as once he was not. His divinely given promise and hope and confidence in this confrontation with God is that even as this one who has been he will share the eternal life of God Himself. Its content is not, therefore, his liberation from his this-sidedness, from his end and dying, but positively the glorification by the eternal God of his natural and lawful this-sided, finite and mortal being. He does not look and move towards the fact that this being of his in his time will one day be forgotten and extinguished and left behind, and in some degree replaced by a new, other-sided, infinite and immortal being after his time. More positively, he looks and moves towards the fact that this being of his in his time, and therewith its beginning and end before the eyes of the gracious God, and therefore before his own eyes and those of others, will be revealed in all its merited shame but also its unmerited glory, and may thus be eternal life from and in God. He does not hope for redemption from the this-sidedness, finitude and mortality of His existence. He hopes positively for the revelation of its redemption as completed in Jesus Christ, namely, the redemption of his this-sided, finite and mortal existence. This psycho-physical being in its time is he himself. He himself as this being makes himself guilty of judgment and the curse. He himself as this being is freed by the crucifixion of Jesus from his guilt and thus released from the judgment and curse of death. He himself is here and now concealed and imperceptible and inconceivable in this freedom, and waits for its revelation. But again he himself as this being clings here and now to God as the One who as the Creator has set him these limits and given him this allotted span, and who now in the concrete form of the appearance and work of Jesus Christ is his only full and perfect hope. And he himself as this being knows that already in the totality of his own this-sided existence, above and beyond which there is no other, he is claimed by and belongs and is committed and thankful here and now to the God who as his gracious Judge and therefore his Saviour from death is his true beyond.

This view of human nature, with its frank recognition of the fact that it ends as well as begins, will be most important for our understanding of the divine command and the bearing of Christian ethics, giving to human life an importance as something which will one day be completed and not be continued indefinitely, and therefore to that which is required of it an urgency which would obviously be lacking if we set our hopes on deliverance from the limitation of our time, and therefore on a beyond, instead of on the eternal God Himself.

It lies in the nature of the subject that at this final turn in our presentation we shall have to be content with a narrower compass of biblical demonstration. When the Bible speaks of the end of human life, it generally means the fact of the end of the sinful being of man in conflict with God and apostasy from Him. Because man stands in a perverted relationship with God, he awaits death as an enemy, as an overwhelming judgment, as the threat of negation. To him death is the punishment of apostasy already announced in Paradise (Gen. 2^{17}; $3^{4f.}$). And since it is God who suspends it over him and executes it by taking away the breath of life which He gave him, it is God Himself who encounters him in death as his enemy. " I was at ease, but he hath broken me asunder ; he hath also taken me by my neck, and shaken me to pieces, and set me up for his mark. His archers compass me round about, he cleaveth my reins asunder, and doth not spare ; he poureth out my gall upon the ground. He breaketh me with breach upon breach ; he runneth upon me like a giant " (Job 16$^{12f.}$). The death of the ungodly means that his name is " come to an end for ever " (Ps. 9^5 ; cf. 41^5, 109$^{13f.}$). His death is the δεύτερος θάνατος of which we read in Rev. 20^{14} that it and the realm of the dead are thrown into the lake of fire. This cannot mean the same thing as the triumphant saying in Rev. 21^4 that " death shall be no more," or what is described in 1 Cor. 15^{26} as the καταργεῖσθαι of death as the " last enemy." It denotes rather the act of judgment in which death and the whole realm of the dead will only then acquire this character of the " last enemy." For it is into the lake of fire that those are thrown whose names are not written in the book of life (Rev. 20^{15} ; cf. 21^8). Death in this sense is clearly unnatural. It is, so to speak, the death in death. We see it in Is. 14$^{4f.}$ in the particular curse of death which seems to be laid on the king of Babylon as distinct from the general fate of death affecting all the other inhabitants of *Sheol*, so that when he comes this whole realm breaks out into an uproar and the shades are dispersed and burst into a terrible cry of justified triumph. " The seed of evil doers shall not be named for ever " (Is. 14^{20}). The fact that he must die can mean for man unmitigated woe. It is for liberation from this evil, hostile, threatening, judging, annihilating death and its woes, that biblical man cries out. And it is just this liberation which is promised and assured him by the existence of his God. In both the Old Testament and the New the Bible sees man as one who is corrupt and ungodly, and therefore it usually views death in this second form. This is the form which is absolutely normative for human observation and apprehension. Wherever death assumes a different guise, it always indicates a remarkable change of standpoint connected with a particular and extraordinary intervention on the part of God.

Yet we cannot ignore the fact that this change of standpoint does actually take place. Another form of death is actually to be seen in the Bible. In the biblical presentation, it is not the case that the unnatural aspect of death has simply crowded out or veiled the naturalness of man's end in itself and as such. There is no compelling necessity why death should be for man an unqualified evil. At the very outset we pointed out that even in the Old Testament blessing and life, curse and death, are not identical even though they stand in a clear relation to one another. According to Ps. 90^{12} men acquire wisdom of heart by numbering their days, thus reminding themselves that no matter what happens they must die. " I go the way of all flesh," says David to Solomon on his death-bed (1 K. 2^2). He obviously has no idea that death is a curse, or that things ought to be different. It may be that the dead—the reference is to the kings of the nation—" all of them lie in glory, every one in his own house " (Is. 14^{18}). The memory of the departed may perhaps be perpetually blessed in contrast to the way in which the name of the ungodly shall perish (Prov. 10^7). Indeed, " his name shall endure for ever, and be continued as long as the sun " (Ps. 72^{17}). His gray hairs may come in peace into the realm of the dead (1 K. 2^6 ; cf. Lk. 2^{29}). Balaam's wish can make perfectly good sense : " Let me die the death of the righteous, and let my last end be like his ! " (Num. 23^{10}). Even an Abraham (Gen. 25^8) or an Isaac (Gen. 35^{29}) can " die an old man, and full of years." There is no suggestion here of morose resignation. It is merely accepted that when life has run its course it is fit and proper than a man should die. For the same reason and in the same sense as Jacob he can die gladly (Gen. 46^{30}). On certain assumptions the awful guest may come in quite a different guise from that of the second death, hardly indeed as a friend, but with a neutral and even natural aspect. It never fails to come. And it always retains its awful character. But its enmity and menace can disappear. Hence we read in Rev. 2^{11} and 20^6 that there are some over whom the " second death " has no power. It can do them no harm, although death is still for them a serious matter. It can be that in all their finitude and mortality, and in spite of everything, men are so in the hands of God and under His protection, and stand and walk and continue in such fellowship with Him, that their transition from existence into non-existence, and their final state of having been, does not mean their defeat by the " last enemy," but its overthrow and their perfect and final encounter with God, their eternal confrontation and supremely positive coexistence with Him. It can be that the life of the Creator and Lord secures and brings to perfection what they would otherwise forfeit as His creatures by reason of their finitude and mortality. It can be that it is no longer a cause of doubt that they have no future because God makes Himself their future, the future of their whole life that is past. It can be that human nature, the finitude of human being in the time of the unnature which conceals it, is actually put off by the grace of God. And it can be that it is thus seen to be an act, not of God's wrath and even less of His envy, but of His goodness and preservation, that man was kept by the cherubim with flaming swords from enjoying the fruit of the " tree of life " which was never meant for him, and thus prevented from "living for ever " (Gen. 3²²). It can be that the boundary thus drawn becomes the place where God frees man from the curse which would otherwise have destroyed him on this boundary.

That there is here a positive element as well as the evil of death is recognised in one or two Old Testament passages in which the end and dying of certain men is wrapped in a remarkable obscurity, or set in a supremely distinctive light, and thus totally and unequivocally distinguished from the fate of others in death, from their bondage to death as an evil.

It is expressly stated in Deut. 34⁵ᶠ· that Moses, the servant of the Lord, died in the land of Moab according to the sentence passed upon him (Deut. 32⁵⁰). We are told, however, that God Himself buried him opposite Baal-peor, and that no one knows his grave until this day. We also read that " his eye was not dim, nor his natural force abated " (Deut. 34⁷). The boundary of his life is thus exposed, and at this boundary the judgment of God, the grave and the underworld. Even Moses died. But he died as a man in the fulness of life, and when he overstepped that boundary and ceased to be, God Himself undertook to bury him. In this way, He showed that this boundary was wholly natural. And the grave, which is the most obvious and easily conceived aspect of the whole matter, could not be found. By the act of God peace between this man and his fate was assured by God Himself in a way which could be seen by all Israel.

It is rather different with the death of Enoch briefly described in Gen. 5²⁴. Enoch walked with God, " and he was not, for God took him." The comment of Heb. 11⁵ is as follows : " By faith Enoch was translated (μετετέθη) that he should not see death ; and was not found, because God had translated him : for before his translation he had this testimony, that he pleased God." In this case the penal character of death seems to have wholly disappeared. As the New Testament explains, Enoch did not " see death." He stepped over that boundary almost, as it were, unawares. Even more fully than in the case of Moses, μετάθεσις obviously signifies an exit from life directly effected by God Himself and known only to Him. Because Enoch " walked with God," the problematic character of this exit was concealed from himself as well as from others. He himself did not see the crisis of death, and therefore no one else saw him in its throes. In a moment he was no longer there. He was not even at the place where all other men are found at the end of their life. He was not wrestling with the question of the after-life which this end poses and which man is quite unable to answer. This question was directly answered by God's presence and intervention. It was not death which removed him from this life, but God. To be sure, he was no longer there. He ceased to belong to the society of the living. His being in time was at an end. And therefore we are told in fact, though indirectly, that he died as Moses died. In both cases we learn that this death took place in complete concealment. But it is not denied that his life was over and that he had had only an allotted span of time like others. Enoch is seen and described as an instance in which there is no doubt whatever of the salvation which awaits man on the other side of the frontier of his time.

Another special case is presented by the story of the disappearance of Elijah in 2 K. 2$^{1-18}$. This is the most explicit of all the hints in this direction in the Old Testament. It is also the most difficult. And yet with proper elucidation it could be the most illuminating one. It undoubtedly refers to the temporal end and natural frontier beyond which he ceases to be. The question is what this means and does not mean for his relation as the older prophet to Elisha as the younger. It is the relation of master and pupil, not unlike that between Moses and Joshua. Was the end of Elijah the extinction of his life ? This question is answered in the text by a record which completely obscures the fact that Elijah actually died and takes the form of a revelation to Elisha of the divine mission, authority and power of his master. This means that the life which Elijah the prophet lived before and with God was not extinguished when his end came, but that he now lives it before and with God as never before. For his office, commission, authority and power, now revealed to Elisha, are transferred to this one who is left. Elijah's departure consists in the swallowing up of his mortality in life before the eyes of Elisha. This positive meaning of his end is indicated by the question which the sons of the prophets of Bethel and Jericho put to Elisha : " Knowest thou not that the Lord will take away thy master from thy head to-day ? " But they did not need to tell him this : " Yea, I know it ; hold ye your peace." What will happen is not, of course, in any sense self-evident. The twofold summons that Elisha should remain behind makes this clear. It is also shown by the necessity of Elisha's prayer for a double portion of his master's spirit, i.e., the share of the first-born. It is shown again by Elijah's answer : " Thou hast asked a hard thing : nevertheless, if thou see me when I am taken from thee, it shall be so unto thee ; but if not, it shall not be so." All these retarding elements in the narrative show that it could all have turned out very differently. It is far easier to suppose that it would have done. For it is not in the least self-evident that at the end of human life death should not be seen, but only a life undoubtedly past. It is not at all self-evident that even and particularly a prophet should depart and yet not merely depart. But the sons of the prophets and Elisha were right. It could not be otherwise in the end of the prophet Elijah. Even his last miracle shows this. For Elijah divides the waters of Jordan—the type of death—with his mantle. Master and pupil, predecessor and successor, pass through together dry-shod. Here is a repetition in reverse of the crossing of the people of Israel over the same Jordan into the promised land. And now, prefigured by the miracle, comes the revelation itself : " And it came to pass, as they (i.e., the one who was leaving and the one who was staying behind) went on, and talked (and therefore *ceteris imparibus* like Moses in the action of their interrelation), there appeared a chariot of fire, and horses of fire, and parted them both asunder ; and Elijah went up by a whirlwind into heaven. And Elisha saw it, and he cried, My father, my father, the chariots of Israel and the horsemen thereof. . . . And he then took hold of his own clothes, and rent them in two pieces." The fact that he did this (the well-known sign of mourning), and that the sons of the prophets curiously forgot their own prophecy and engaged in a futile search for the departed prophet with fifty men, is a clear indication that we have to do here with the final departure of Elijah, with his temporal end, with what is usually called death. But this is just the point. What is usually called death, even the very last trace of a judgment connected with the temporal end of man, is in this case completely veiled, concealed, and indeed annulled by the revelation of the true nature of the life here concluded, i.e., of " the chariots of Israel and the horsemen thereof," of

Israel's invincible power, of the gracious God of Israel, with all the force which He has wielded in the human life now completed. If Elijah met his end, and left the " land of the living," he did so without the gloom usually associated with death. For he was fetched in a chariot and horses of fire. Instead of journeying to the underworld, he proceeded heavenwards in a cloud. Yahweh Himself had intervened as the content, goal and end of Elijah's life. Moreover, Elisha shared in this revelation. As the sign of the spirit which had descended on him, of the divine mission, authority and power entrusted to him, he had only to pick up the mantle of Elijah. Elijah no longer needed this. His life in time was over, his work in history done. But Elisha still had to live his life. He was about to begin his real work. And so he came under this sign. Nor was it an empty one, as shown at his return to Jordan. For here, like Elijah, Elisha smote the water with the mantle which was now his own. He still asked : " Where is the Lord God of Elijah ? " But he was answered by what happened : " And when he also had smitten the waters, they parted hither and thither : and Elisha went over." The man Elijah was no longer there. But God had revealed Himself to Elisha as the God of Elijah. Elijah himself had been revealed in his fetching home by God. He was alive to him as the man he had been. For his spirit, office and commission had come upon him by means of this revelation.

Enoch, Moses and Elijah are exceptional cases. All these passages speak of an extraordinary intervention of God without which these men could never have been set in the obscurity or light experienced. And all the other cases in the Old Testament in which men are privileged to die a peaceful death, or the death of the righteous, or to die " full of years " and " gladly," must be understood in close connexion with an extraordinary intervention of God. The fact that these men were naturally capable of dying in this way does not mean that this is a general privilege granted to man. They themselves have no capacity to choose such an end. They are all God's debtors and enemies. Of themselves they can only die an evil death. If they depart in peace and joy, this can only be because God has awakened in them the capacity which they all have by nature but which is as it were suspended and sterilised in the ungodly. It is by God's free grace and the healing of nature that it is possible in any given case. If there is a natural end of existence, which is a real end yet not judgment but communion with God, this may be known by God's extraordinary intervention, by what is recorded in the end of Enoch, Moses and Elijah as deliverance from death. The fact that the gracious God makes Himself the end of man, and that this is not therefore gloom but glory, plainly and definitively confirms that this end as such is not a question of disorder but of order, and that in it we do not have to do with the sphere of chaos but with the good creation of God.

As regards the situation in the New Testament, we have already called attention to the idea of the " second death " which figures so prominently in the Apocalypse. The assumption is that there is a " first " death without the evil, corruptive and unnatural character of the " second." In Heb. 9^{27} the sacrifice of Christ, offered once for all to take away the sins of many, is both formally and materially brought into relation with this notion. We are told in this sense that " it is appointed (ἀπόκειται) unto men once to die, but after this the judgment." From this it would seem that the phrase ἅπαξ ἀποθανεῖν does not of itself signify judgment, but an event which is general and neutral even though in contrast with the sacrificial death of Christ and its uniqueness it also seems to have a higher necessity. Again, the phrase ἄχρι θανάτου in Rev. 2^{10} : " Be thou faithful unto death," and Rev. 12^{11} : " They loved not their lives unto the death," cannot imply that death is the last enemy, but only the *terminus ad quem* of their faithfulness and unselfish devotion coinciding with the boundary of their life. Again it is no less clear that when in 1 Thess. 5^{10}, 1 Cor. 3^{22}, Rom. 8^{38} and $14^{7f.}$ and Phil. 1^{20} life and death are associated under the superior dominion of Christ, death does not signify an armed and powerful foe but the approaching end of human life contrasted with the possibility of its further continuation.

There is a dying which throws no doubt on man's participation in the resurrection and life of Jesus Christ. Death in this sense is not ruled out by man's hope in a resurrection. This is expressly shown by Jn. 11²⁵ : " I am the resurrection, and the life ; he that believeth on me, though he die, yet shall he live." In the New Testament, too, the " death " in death can be abolished. It is never supposed, of course, that this possibility lies in human control. When it happens, it is always the result of God's extraordinary intervention. The concrete form of this is the appearance, death and resurrection of Jesus Christ : " He that heareth my word, and believeth him that sent me, hath everlasting life, and shall not come into condemnation, but is passed from death unto life " (Jn. 5²⁴). In these circumstances the " second death " is abolished and man is freed from unnatural death. But this obviously means that, as he is freed for eternal life, he is also freed for natural death. The New Testament, like the Old, speaks of this natural death.

It is worth noting that the New Testament fully matches the sober realism of the Old in this matter. It is striking, indeed, that it offers no parallels to such hints as we have in the stories of the end of Enoch and Moses or the disappearance of Elijah. The New Testament authors are content to refer to these occasionally without adding similar occurrences from their own historical sphere. These remarkable exceptions were obviously regarded in the New Testament age as types which, once fulfilled in the end of Jesus Christ, in His resurrection and ascension, did not need and were not capable of further multiplication. The Roman Catholic Church definition of the assumption of Mary as a dogma of the faith, quite apart from anything else, is an additional proof of its profound lack of understanding of the basic difference between the situation and order of the New Testament and that of the Old. In the New Testament order the exaltation of the one man Jesus Christ, in which the exaltation of His own is already latently accomplished, is followed by only one assumption of which nothing can be said because it has not yet happened, namely, the assumption of the community to meet its Lord when He comes again at the final revelation in which the exaltation which has already occurred in Jesus Christ will be made manifest. In this assumption the dead will share no less than the living (1 Thess. 4¹⁶ᶠ.) There now are and may be those who have fallen asleep " in Christ " (1 Cor. 15¹⁸) or "in Jesus " (1 Thess. 4¹⁴), or who are even "dead in Christ" (1 Thess. 4¹⁶). They are not lost (1 Thess. 4¹⁵) even though they have not yet been assumed. And no one, not even Mary, can anticipate their assumption with a private one of his own. Death now wears a guise in which we can look it in the face. We can now face it as a natural prospect.

" To fall asleep " (κοιμᾶσθαι) is the characteristic New Testament term for the death which is freed from the " second " death by the death of Jesus Christ and is therefore a wholly natural thing for the Christian. " Our friend Lazarus sleepeth " (Jn. 11¹¹). Some of the witnesses of the resurrection of Jesus " are fallen asleep " (1 Cor. 15⁶). " The fathers (i.e., those who belonged to the first Christian generation) have fallen asleep," say the false teachers in 2 Pet. 3⁴. Similarly, the Corinthian church can look back on not a few of its members who have fallen asleep (1 Cor. 11³⁰). It is noticeable that even David is now said to have fallen asleep (Ac. 13³⁶). Indeed, a violent death like that of Stephen (Ac. 7⁶⁰) is described almost euphemistically in these mild terms. What does this imply ? It relates to the process of dying, or rather to the impression, designated, defined and shaped by faith and love, which the survivors have of what is finally perceptible in the death of a brother or sister. They see him falling asleep. What lies beyond they cannot see. For the Christians of the New Testament Jesus Christ Himself intervenes at once and absolutely on the far side of this event. His death and resurrection avail for those who have now " fallen asleep," as well as for those who survive. The hope in Him is a hope for the former too. The final thing to be said of them (apart from Jesus Christ Himself) is that they have fallen asleep. The expression is deliberately mild. It may be euphemistic, but it conveys an impression of peace. It is a striking expression of the freedom of New Testament Christians—the freedom of their faith and love. As they contemplate the dead they are able to use this peaceful term and keep their memory before their eyes in the form of this peaceful process. The decisive thing is not that they suffered or endured the agony of death. The real conflict with death was fought out long ago. All they had to do was to fall asleep. Even Stephen could simply fall asleep under the hail of stones. The term thus signifies the genuine reality visible in the light of Christian faith and love, of what is finally perceptible to those who remain in the dying of their friends. Their recollection of the dead is rivetted to this term. The deduction that the dead are in a state of sleep is an ancient exaggeration. Κοιμᾶσθαι does not mean to be asleep but to *fall* asleep. Those who have fallen asleep means those whom we saw fall asleep, and whom we now recollect as those who then fell asleep and were therefore delivered from death even in dying. Looking back on them, we really look back on Jesus Christ who, as " the first fruits of them that slept " (1 Cor. 15[20]), robbed their death of its sting and brought life and immortality to light even when they were *in extremis*, so that this death could not be anything but a falling asleep. The deduction that they are now actually asleep may seem to be logical, but it has no material basis. What special revelation did the New Testament Christians enjoy to persuade them that when the departed had fallen asleep their being was one of sleep ? This inference was first drawn when Christians again began to derive their knowledge (in this as in other matters) from sources other than their knowledge of Jesus Christ. The term " fall asleep " shows that the New Testament Christians never asked independently concerning the being or state of man in death, or tried to find an answer in the postulate of an intermediate state. They simply held fast to the confession : " I am the resurrection and the life," and in the light of this hope they came to see in the visible process of dying the last conclusive symptom of a life surrounded by the peace of God.

If hope in Christ is a real liberation for natural death, this rests on the fact that by divine appointment death as such belongs to the life of the creature and is thus necessary to it. Adamic man was created a ψυχὴ ζῶσα (1 Cor. 15[45]), and therefore a being which has only its own span of time. His definitive relationship to God as the end and goal of human life demands that this life itself should be defined and therefore limited. On this limit there is made in its favour the divine decision which is the substance of the New Testament message of salvation. On this limit it was made in the life of the man Jesus. He had to die, to submit to the judgment of God and thus restore the right of God and that of man. " Except a corn of wheat fall into the ground and die, it abideth alone ; but if it die, it bringeth forth much fruit " (Jn. 12[24]). We cannot try to love and maintain finally and absolutely our life in this time ; otherwise we shall lose it. We must give it up in order to save it (Mt. 16[25]). In the harsh terms of Jn. 12[25] we must actually " hate " our " life in the world " in order to preserve it to eternal life. That is why Paul can also say : " Thou fool, that which thou sowest is not quickened, except it die " (1 Cor. 15[36]). If we did not have to do with the definitive end of human life, we should not have to do with its resurrection and definitive co-existence with that of God. Anxious defiance of one's end could only mean the forfeiture of one's destiny. Since Jesus did not love His life and thus rescued our life from destruction, we are invited to accept the limit of the life which He has rescued, and therefore to acquiesce in the fact that we must have an end, and to set our hope wholly and utterly in Him.

In conclusion, however, it is worth noting that, while the New Testament reminds us of the necessity of death and exhorts us not to love our life or seek to save it, it never suggests that we ought to yearn for death or rejoice in it, even in the case of martyrdom, as often happened later. Death is never idealised or made into something heroic. That he should lose his life for Christ's sake is a possibility for which the New Testament Christian is always doubly prepared, but which he never desires or seeks, merely accepting it as a reality when it comes, as Stephen did. Like life itself, the loss of it is in itself a possibility qualified only by the fact that it takes place " in the Lord." In 2 Cor. 5^{1-10} Paul contrasts our present life in a perishable tent with the divinely prepared and eternal house with which we shall be clothed ; our pilgrimage in time with our being at home in the Lord. He makes no attempt to conceal his longing and sighing for the latter. Yet he finds only a relative and not an absolute place for this desire. And from this train of thought he draws the conclusion : " Wherefore we labour, that, whether present or absent, we may be accepted of him. For we must all appear before the judgment seat of Christ ; that every one may receive the things done in his body, according to that he hath done, whether it be good or bad." Again, what he says in Philippians $1^{20f.}$ is similar. That Christ should be glorified in his body, whether by life or death, is the prospect which elates him ($\pi\alpha\rho\rho\eta\sigma\iota\alpha$). He again makes no secret of the fact that it is better for him to die. He has " a desire to depart, and to be with Christ." This is preferable. But he again qualifies his desire. For him to live is Christ. And this, as he puts it bluntly in v. 22, is " fruit " ($\kappa\alpha\rho\pi\grave{o}\varsigma$ $\check{\epsilon}\rho\gamma o\upsilon$) in His service. Though dissolution would be preferable, his " abiding in the flesh " is thus more necessary for the sake of his communities (v. 24). Faced by this dilemma, with pressing arguments on both sides, he decides in this most important passage for life rather than death. The New Testament Christian does not fear death. But he never hopes for it. He hopes for the One who has delivered him from death. It is because he hopes for Him, and expects to be with Him when he dies, that he is willing to die " gladly " like Jacob. Death is the preferable alternative. But he does not will it. He wills the life bounded by it as the sphere of the decisions in which he moves towards Christ as his Judge. He wills it as the opportunity to serve the One who will be his only hope in his end. And it is because he can already serve in his life the One who even in death will be his Lord that he rejoices in this perfect form of His lordship, in the prospect of being definitely with Him. He does not rejoice in the prospect of being freed from His service, of having his time behind him. On the contrary, the definitive prospect in which he rejoices is for him an authorisation and command to serve God in his allotted span with all the preliminary joy without which his joy in his end and new beginning with Him would be purely imaginary. He affirms Jesus Christ as his beyond. And it is for this reason that he understands his life here and now as one which is affirmed by his beyond.

INDEXES

I. SCRIPTURE REFERENCES

II. NAMES

III. SUBJECTS

Adam, 150.
Agape, 275 f., 285.
  cf. *Eros*; Freedom; God; Humanity;
    Jesus Christ.
Analogia entis, 220, 244.
  v. Theology/natural.
Analogia relationis, 220 f., 323 f.
Angel, 46, 171, 352, 511, 569.
Angelology, 5, 13.
Animal, 81 f., 183 f., 276, 286, 291, 359,
  374, 394 f., 407, 417, 521, 523.
Anthropology—
  biological, 76 f., 108, 125 f.
  ethical, 93 f., 125 f., 277.
  existentialist, 113, 125 f.
  idealistic, 93 f., 125 f., 277.
  naturalistic, 76 f., 108, 125 f.
  philosophical, 21.
  scientific, 23.
  theistic, 201 f.
Anthropology, Theological, 4, 12 f.,
  15, 228 f., 276 f., 346, 423,
  434 f., 438, 511 f.
  Christian basis, 55 f., 207, 228 f.,
    289 f., 308 f., 571 f., 631 f.
  criteria, 73 f.
  cf. Word of God.
Antichrist, 236 f.
Apostle, 470 f., 493 f., 582.
  cf. Evangelist.

Baptism, 303, 359, 585 f., 606, 621.
Biology—
  cf. Anthropology/biological; Man/
    phenomena, biological.
Blessing, 580, 634.
Buddhism, 608.

Chaos, 52, 143, 212, 569, 576, 608, 615.
  cf. Nothing.
Christianity, 237, 284, 290.
  Christian West, 585 f.
  cf. Church History; Greek An-
    tiquity.
Christology—
  cf. Anthropology, Theological; Crea-
    tion; God; Jesus Christ.
Church, 278 f., 285, 444.
  cf. Christianity; Community;
    Israel; State.
Church History—
  v. History.
Circumcision, 584 f.
Command, 184 f., 216 f., 579.

Community, 210 f., 213 f., 275, 283 f.,
  300, 341 f., 410, 427, 466, 475,
  489, 504 f., 582, 638 f.
  body of Jesus Christ, 9, 54, 145 f.
  cf. Church.
Cosmology, 5, 11, 13.
Cosmos, *v.* Man.
Covenant, 18, 144 f., 194, 217 f., 223,
  243, 271, 281, 294, 297 f., 321 f.,
  357, 372 f., 439, 467, 476, 526,
  546, 578, 616, 624.
  basis, 50.
  cf. Jesus Christ.
  covenant-partner, *v.* Man.
  history, *v.* History.
  knowledge of, 11 f.
  cf. Community; Creation; God;
    Israel; Jesus Christ; Man.
Creation, 3, 136 f., 152 f., 204, 293 f.,
  352, 438, 457, 476, 595, 631
  articulus fidei, 157.
  basis, 299, 483
  creatio ex nihilo, 152 f., 157
  new, 488
  second, 33, 224 f.
  cf. Death; Jesus Christ; Man; Sin.
Creationism, *v.* Man/soul.
Creator, *v.* God.
Creature and Creator, 3, 8, 10 f., 16 f.,
  53 f., 139, 177, 216 f., 219 f.,
  223, 247 f., 269, 297 f., 319 f.,
  343 f., 366 f., 414, 422 f., 440,
  517, 519, 554, 557
  neutrality? 131.
  cf. God/Creator.

Death, 102, 112, 127, 209, 276, 295,
  318, 348, 353, 370, 427 f., 588.
  deliverance from, 610 f., 617, 627,
    629.
  dynamic, 591.
  enemy? 600, 608, 628, 634.
  final sleep, 638 f.
  idealisation? 639 f.
  judgment, cf. God/judgment.
  limit, cf. Man/limit.
  limitation, 629
  natural, 639.
  negation, cf. nothing.
  power, 599, 616 f.
  punishment, 599 f., 633 f.
  realms of, 590 f., 617.
  second god? 608, 616 f.
  sign, 597, 614, 625, 634, 637.